T0134770

Lecture Notes in Computer Science   11215

Commenced Publication in 1973
Founding and Former Series Editors:
Gerhard Goos, Juris Hartmanis, and Jan van Leeuwen

More information about this series at http://www.springer.com/series/7412

Vittorio Ferrari · Martial Hebert
Cristian Sminchisescu · Yair Weiss (Eds.)

Computer Vision – ECCV 2018

15th European Conference
Munich, Germany, September 8–14, 2018
Proceedings, Part XI

 Springer

Editors
Vittorio Ferrari
Google Research
Zurich
Switzerland

Martial Hebert
Carnegie Mellon University
Pittsburgh, PA
USA

Cristian Sminchisescu
Google Research
Zurich
Switzerland

Yair Weiss
Hebrew University of Jerusalem
Jerusalem
Israel

ISSN 0302-9743   ISSN 1611-3349   (electronic)
Lecture Notes in Computer Science
ISBN 978-3-030-01251-9   ISBN 978-3-030-01252-6   (eBook)
https://doi.org/10.1007/978-3-030-01252-6

Library of Congress Control Number: 2018955489

LNCS Sublibrary: SL6 – Image Processing, Computer Vision, Pattern Recognition, and Graphics

This Springer imprint is published by the registered company Springer Nature Switzerland AG
The registered company address is: Gewerbestrasse 11, 6330 Cham, Switzerland

Foreword

It was our great pleasure to host the European Conference on Computer Vision 2018 in Munich, Germany. This constituted by far the largest ECCV event ever. With close to 2,900 registered participants and another 600 on the waiting list one month before the conference, participation more than doubled since the last ECCV in Amsterdam. We believe that this is due to a dramatic growth of the computer vision community combined with the popularity of Munich as a major European hub of culture, science, and industry. The conference took place in the heart of Munich in the concert hall Gasteig with workshops and tutorials held at the downtown campus of the Technical University of Munich.

One of the major innovations for ECCV 2018 was the free perpetual availability of all conference and workshop papers, which is often referred to as open access. We note that this is not precisely the same use of the term as in the Budapest declaration. Since 2013, CVPR and ICCV have had their papers hosted by the Computer Vision Foundation (CVF), in parallel with the IEEE Xplore version. This has proved highly beneficial to the computer vision community.

We are delighted to announce that for ECCV 2018 a very similar arrangement was put in place with the cooperation of Springer. In particular, the author's final version will be freely available in perpetuity on a CVF page, while SpringerLink will continue to host a version with further improvements, such as activating reference links and including video. We believe that this will give readers the best of both worlds; researchers who are focused on the technical content will have a freely available version in an easily accessible place, while subscribers to SpringerLink will continue to have the additional benefits that this provides. We thank Alfred Hofmann from Springer for helping to negotiate this agreement, which we expect will continue for future versions of ECCV.

September 2018

Horst Bischof
Daniel Cremers
Bernt Schiele
Ramin Zabih

Preface

Welcome to the proceedings of the 2018 European Conference on Computer Vision (ECCV 2018) held in Munich, Germany. We are delighted to present this volume reflecting a strong and exciting program, the result of an extensive review process. In total, we received 2,439 valid paper submissions. Of these, 776 were accepted (31.8%): 717 as posters (29.4%) and 59 as oral presentations (2.4%). All oral presentations were presented as posters as well. The program selection process was complicated this year by the large increase in the number of submitted papers, +65% over ECCV 2016, and the use of CMT3 for the first time for a computer vision conference. The program selection process was supported by four program co-chairs (PCs), 126 area chairs (ACs), and 1,199 reviewers with reviews assigned.

We were primarily responsible for the design and execution of the review process. Beyond administrative rejections, we were involved in acceptance decisions only in the very few cases where the ACs were not able to agree on a decision. As PCs, and as is customary in the field, we were not allowed to co-author a submission. General co-chairs and other co-organizers who played no role in the review process were permitted to submit papers, and were treated as any other author is.

Acceptance decisions were made by two independent ACs. The ACs also made a joint recommendation for promoting papers to oral status. We decided on the final selection of oral presentations based on the ACs' recommendations. There were 126 ACs, selected according to their technical expertise, experience, and geographical diversity (63 from European, nine from Asian/Australian, and 54 from North American institutions). Indeed, 126 ACs is a substantial increase in the number of ACs due to the natural increase in the number of papers and to our desire to maintain the number of papers assigned to each AC to a manageable number so as to ensure quality. The ACs were aided by the 1,199 reviewers to whom papers were assigned for reviewing. The Program Committee was selected from committees of previous ECCV, ICCV, and CVPR conferences and was extended on the basis of suggestions from the ACs. Having a large pool of Program Committee members for reviewing allowed us to match expertise while reducing reviewer loads. No more than eight papers were assigned to a reviewer, maintaining the reviewers' load at the same level as ECCV 2016 despite the increase in the number of submitted papers.

Conflicts of interest between ACs, Program Committee members, and papers were identified based on the home institutions, and on previous collaborations of all researchers involved. To find institutional conflicts, all authors, Program Committee members, and ACs were asked to list the Internet domains of their current institutions. We assigned on average approximately 18 papers to each AC. The papers were assigned using the affinity scores from the Toronto Paper Matching System (TPMS) and additional data from the OpenReview system, managed by a UMass group. OpenReview used additional information from ACs' and authors' records to identify collaborations and to generate matches. OpenReview was invaluable in refining conflict definitions and in generating quality matches. The only glitch is that, once the matches were generated, a small percentage of papers were unassigned because of discrepancies between the OpenReview conflicts and the conflicts entered in CMT3. We manually assigned these papers. This glitch is revealing of the challenge of using multiple systems at once (CMT3 and OpenReview in this case), which needs to be addressed in future.

After assignment of papers to ACs, the ACs suggested seven reviewers per paper from the Program Committee pool. The selection and rank ordering were facilitated by the TPMS affinity scores visible to the ACs for each paper/reviewer pair. The final assignment of papers to reviewers was generated again through OpenReview in order to account for refined conflict definitions. This required new features in the OpenReview matching system to accommodate the ECCV workflow, in particular to incorporate selection ranking, and maximum reviewer load. Very few papers received fewer than three reviewers after matching and were handled through manual assignment. Reviewers were then asked to comment on the merit of each paper and to make an initial recommendation ranging from definitely reject to definitely accept, including a borderline rating. The reviewers were also asked to suggest explicit questions they wanted to see answered in the authors' rebuttal. The initial review period was five weeks. Because of the delay in getting all the reviews in, we had to delay the final release of the reviews by four days. However, because of the slack included at the tail end of the schedule, we were able to maintain the decision target date with sufficient time for all the phases. We reassigned over 100 reviews from 40 reviewers during the review period. Unfortunately, the main reason for these reassignments was reviewers declining to review, after having accepted to do so. Other reasons included technical relevance and occasional unidentified conflicts. We express our thanks to the emergency reviewers who generously accepted to perform these reviews under short notice. In addition, a substantial number of manual corrections had to do with reviewers using a different email address than the one that was used at the time of the reviewer invitation. This is revealing of a broader issue with identifying users by email addresses that change frequently enough to cause significant problems during the timespan of the conference process.

The authors were then given the opportunity to rebut the reviews, to identify factual errors, and to address the specific questions raised by the reviewers over a seven-day rebuttal period. The exact format of the rebuttal was the object of considerable debate among the organizers, as well as with prior organizers. At issue is to balance giving the author the opportunity to respond completely and precisely to the reviewers, e.g., by including graphs of experiments, while avoiding requests for completely new material or experimental results not included in the original paper. In the end, we decided on the two-page PDF document in conference format. Following this rebuttal period, reviewers and ACs discussed papers at length, after which reviewers finalized their evaluation and gave a final recommendation to the ACs. A significant percentage of the reviewers did enter their final recommendation if it did not differ from their initial recommendation. Given the tight schedule, we did not wait until all were entered.

After this discussion period, each paper was assigned to a second AC. The AC/paper matching was again run through OpenReview. Again, the OpenReview team worked quickly to implement the features specific to this process, in this case accounting for the existing AC assignment, as well as minimizing the fragmentation across ACs, so that each AC had on average only 5.5 buddy ACs to communicate with. The largest number was 11. Given the complexity of the conflicts, this was a very efficient set of assignments from OpenReview. Each paper was then evaluated by its assigned pair of ACs. For each paper, we required each of the two ACs assigned to certify both the final recommendation and the metareview (aka consolidation report). In all cases, after extensive discussions, the two ACs arrived at a common acceptance decision. We maintained these decisions, with the caveat that we did evaluate, sometimes going back to the ACs, a few papers for which the final acceptance decision substantially deviated from the consensus from the reviewers, amending three decisions in the process.

We want to thank everyone involved in making ECCV 2018 possible. The success of ECCV 2018 depended on the quality of papers submitted by the authors, and on the very hard work of the ACs and the Program Committee members. We are particularly grateful to the OpenReview team (Melisa Bok, Ari Kobren, Andrew McCallum, Michael Spector) for their support, in particular their willingness to implement new features, often on a tight schedule, to Laurent Charlin for the use of the Toronto Paper Matching System, to the CMT3 team, in particular in dealing with all the issues that arise when using a new system, to Friedrich Fraundorfer and Quirin Lohr for maintaining the online version of the program, and to the CMU staff (Keyla Cook, Lynnetta Miller, Ashley Song, Nora Kazour) for assisting with data entry/editing in CMT3. Finally, the preparation of these proceedings would not have been possible without the diligent effort of the publication chairs, Albert Ali Salah and Hamdi Dibeklioğlu, and of Anna Kramer and Alfred Hofmann from Springer.

September 2018

Vittorio Ferrari
Martial Hebert
Cristian Sminchisescu
Yair Weiss

Organization

General Chairs

Horst Bischof   Graz University of Technology, Austria
Daniel Cremers   Technical University of Munich, Germany
Bernt Schiele   Saarland University, Max Planck Institute for Informatics, Germany
Ramin Zabih   CornellNYCTech, USA

Program Committee Co-chairs

Vittorio Ferrari   University of Edinburgh, UK
Martial Hebert   Carnegie Mellon University, USA
Cristian Sminchisescu   Lund University, Sweden
Yair Weiss   Hebrew University, Israel

Local Arrangements Chairs

Björn Menze   Technical University of Munich, Germany
Matthias Niessner   Technical University of Munich, Germany

Workshop Chairs

Stefan Roth   TU Darmstadt, Germany
Laura Leal-Taixé   Technical University of Munich, Germany

Tutorial Chairs

Michael Bronstein   Università della Svizzera Italiana, Switzerland
Laura Leal-Taixé   Technical University of Munich, Germany

Website Chair

Friedrich Fraundorfer   Graz University of Technology, Austria

Demo Chairs

Federico Tombari   Technical University of Munich, Germany
Joerg Stueckler   Technical University of Munich, Germany

Publicity Chair

Giovanni Maria   University of Catania, Italy
   Farinella

Industrial Liaison Chairs

Florent Perronnin   Naver Labs, France
Yunchao Gong   Snap, USA
Helmut Grabner   Logitech, Switzerland

Finance Chair

Gerard Medioni   Amazon, University of Southern California, USA

Publication Chairs

Albert Ali Salah   Boğaziçi University, Turkey
Hamdi Dibeklioğlu   Bilkent University, Turkey

Area Chairs

Kalle Åström   Lund University, Sweden
Zeynep Akata   University of Amsterdam, The Netherlands
Joao Barreto   University of Coimbra, Portugal
Ronen Basri   Weizmann Institute of Science, Israel
Dhruv Batra   Georgia Tech and Facebook AI Research, USA
Serge Belongie   Cornell University, USA
Rodrigo Benenson   Google, Switzerland
Hakan Bilen   University of Edinburgh, UK
Matthew Blaschko   KU Leuven, Belgium
Edmond Boyer   Inria, France
Gabriel Brostow   University College London, UK
Thomas Brox   University of Freiburg, Germany
Marcus Brubaker   York University, Canada
Barbara Caputo   Politecnico di Torino and the Italian Institute
                           of Technology, Italy
Tim Cootes   University of Manchester, UK
Trevor Darrell   University of California, Berkeley, USA
Larry Davis   University of Maryland at College Park, USA
Andrew Davison   Imperial College London, UK
Fernando de la Torre   Carnegie Mellon University, USA
Irfan Essa   GeorgiaTech, USA
Ali Farhadi   University of Washington, USA
Paolo Favaro   University of Bern, Switzerland
Michael Felsberg   Linköping University, Sweden

Sanja Fidler	University of Toronto, Canada
Andrew Fitzgibbon	Microsoft, Cambridge, UK
David Forsyth	University of Illinois at Urbana-Champaign, USA
Charless Fowlkes	University of California, Irvine, USA
Bill Freeman	MIT, USA
Mario Fritz	MPII, Germany
Jürgen Gall	University of Bonn, Germany
Dariu Gavrila	TU Delft, The Netherlands
Andreas Geiger	MPI-IS and University of Tübingen, Germany
Theo Gevers	University of Amsterdam, The Netherlands
Ross Girshick	Facebook AI Research, USA
Kristen Grauman	Facebook AI Research and UT Austin, USA
Abhinav Gupta	Carnegie Mellon University, USA
Kaiming He	Facebook AI Research, USA
Martial Hebert	Carnegie Mellon University, USA
Anders Heyden	Lund University, Sweden
Timothy Hospedales	University of Edinburgh, UK
Michal Irani	Weizmann Institute of Science, Israel
Phillip Isola	University of California, Berkeley, USA
Hervé Jégou	Facebook AI Research, France
David Jacobs	University of Maryland, College Park, USA
Allan Jepson	University of Toronto, Canada
Jiaya Jia	Chinese University of Hong Kong, SAR China
Fredrik Kahl	Chalmers University, USA
Hedvig Kjellström	KTH Royal Institute of Technology, Sweden
Iasonas Kokkinos	University College London and Facebook, UK
Vladlen Koltun	Intel Labs, USA
Philipp Krähenbühl	UT Austin, USA
M. Pawan Kumar	University of Oxford, UK
Kyros Kutulakos	University of Toronto, Canada
In Kweon	KAIST, South Korea
Ivan Laptev	Inria, France
Svetlana Lazebnik	University of Illinois at Urbana-Champaign, USA
Laura Leal-Taixé	Technical University of Munich, Germany
Erik Learned-Miller	University of Massachusetts, Amherst, USA
Kyoung Mu Lee	Seoul National University, South Korea
Bastian Leibe	RWTH Aachen University, Germany
Aleš Leonardis	University of Birmingham, UK
Vincent Lepetit	University of Bordeaux, France and Graz University of Technology, Austria
Fuxin Li	Oregon State University, USA
Dahua Lin	Chinese University of Hong Kong, SAR China
Jim Little	University of British Columbia, Canada
Ce Liu	Google, USA
Chen Change Loy	Nanyang Technological University, Singapore
Jiri Matas	Czech Technical University in Prague, Czechia

Tinne Tuytelaars	KU Leuven, Belgium
Jasper Uijlings	Google, Switzerland
Joost van de Weijer	Computer Vision Center, Spain
Nuno Vasconcelos	University of California, San Diego, USA
Andrea Vedaldi	University of Oxford, UK
Olga Veksler	University of Western Ontario, Canada
Jakob Verbeek	Inria, France
Rene Vidal	Johns Hopkins University, USA
Daphna Weinshall	Hebrew University, Israel
Chris Williams	University of Edinburgh, UK
Lior Wolf	Tel Aviv University, Israel
Ming-Hsuan Yang	University of California at Merced, USA
Todd Zickler	Harvard University, USA
Andrew Zisserman	University of Oxford, UK

Technical Program Committee

Hassan Abu Alhaija
Radhakrishna Achanta
Hanno Ackermann
Ehsan Adeli
Lourdes Agapito
Aishwarya Agrawal
Antonio Agudo
Eirikur Agustsson
Karim Ahmed
Byeongjoo Ahn
Unaiza Ahsan
Emre Akbaş
Eren Aksoy
Yağız Aksoy
Alexandre Alahi
Jean-Baptiste Alayrac
Samuel Albanie
Cenek Albl
Saad Ali
Rahaf Aljundi
Jose M. Alvarez
Humam Alwassel
Toshiyuki Amano
Mitsuru Ambai
Mohamed Amer
Senjian An
Cosmin Ancuti

Peter Anderson
Juan Andrade-Cetto
Mykhaylo Andriluka
Anelia Angelova
Michel Antunes
Pablo Arbelaez
Vasileios Argyriou
Chetan Arora
Federica Arrigoni
Vassilis Athitsos
Mathieu Aubry
Shai Avidan
Yannis Avrithis
Samaneh Azadi
Hossein Azizpour
Artem Babenko
Timur Bagautdinov
Andrew Bagdanov
Hessam Bagherinezhad
Yuval Bahat
Min Bai
Qinxun Bai
Song Bai
Xiang Bai
Peter Bajcsy
Amr Bakry
Kavita Bala

Arunava Banerjee
Atsuhiko Banno
Aayush Bansal
Yingze Bao
Md Jawadul Bappy
Pierre Baqué
Dániel Baráth
Adrian Barbu
Kobus Barnard
Nick Barnes
Francisco Barranco
Adrien Bartoli
E. Bayro-Corrochano
Paul Beardlsey
Vasileios Belagiannis
Sean Bell
Ismail Ben
Boulbaba Ben Amor
Gil Ben-Artzi
Ohad Ben-Shahar
Abhijit Bendale
Rodrigo Benenson
Fabian Benitez-Quiroz
Fethallah Benmansour
Ryad Benosman
Filippo Bergamasco
David Bermudez

Jesus Bermudez-Cameo
Leonard Berrada
Gedas Bertasius
Ross Beveridge
Lucas Beyer
Bir Bhanu
S. Bhattacharya
Binod Bhattarai
Arnav Bhavsar
Simone Bianco
Adel Bibi
Pia Bideau
Josef Bigun
Arijit Biswas
Soma Biswas
Marten Bjoerkman
Volker Blanz
Vishnu Boddeti
Piotr Bojanowski
Terrance Boult
Yuri Boykov
Hakan Boyraz
Eric Brachmann
Samarth Brahmbhatt
Mathieu Bredif
Francois Bremond
Michael Brown
Luc Brun
Shyamal Buch
Pradeep Buddharaju
Aurelie Bugeau
Rudy Bunel
Xavier Burgos Artizzu
Darius Burschka
Andrei Bursuc
Zoya Bylinskii
Fabian Caba
Daniel Cabrini Hauagge
Cesar Cadena Lerma
Holger Caesar
Jianfei Cai
Junjie Cai
Zhaowei Cai
Simone Calderara
Neill Campbell
Octavia Camps

Xun Cao
Yanshuai Cao
Joao Carreira
Dan Casas
Daniel Castro
Jan Cech
M. Emre Celebi
Duygu Ceylan
Menglei Chai
Ayan Chakrabarti
Rudrasis Chakraborty
Shayok Chakraborty
Tat-Jen Cham
Antonin Chambolle
Antoni Chan
Sharat Chandran
Hyun Sung Chang
Ju Yong Chang
Xiaojun Chang
Soravit Changpinyo
Wei-Lun Chao
Yu-Wei Chao
Visesh Chari
Rizwan Chaudhry
Siddhartha Chaudhuri
Rama Chellappa
Chao Chen
Chen Chen
Cheng Chen
Chu-Song Chen
Guang Chen
Hsin-I Chen
Hwann-Tzong Chen
Kai Chen
Kan Chen
Kevin Chen
Liang-Chieh Chen
Lin Chen
Qifeng Chen
Ting Chen
Wei Chen
Xi Chen
Xilin Chen
Xinlei Chen
Yingcong Chen
Yixin Chen

Erkang Cheng
Jingchun Cheng
Ming-Ming Cheng
Wen-Huang Cheng
Yuan Cheng
Anoop Cherian
Liang-Tien Chia
Naoki Chiba
Shao-Yi Chien
Han-Pang Chiu
Wei-Chen Chiu
Nam Ik Cho
Sunghyun Cho
TaeEun Choe
Jongmoo Choi
Christopher Choy
Wen-Sheng Chu
Yung-Yu Chuang
Ondrej Chum
Joon Son Chung
Gökberk Cinbis
James Clark
Andrea Cohen
Forrester Cole
Toby Collins
John Collomosse
Camille Couprie
David Crandall
Marco Cristani
Canton Cristian
James Crowley
Yin Cui
Zhaopeng Cui
Bo Dai
Jifeng Dai
Qieyun Dai
Shengyang Dai
Yuchao Dai
Carlo Dal Mutto
Dima Damen
Zachary Daniels
Kostas Daniilidis
Donald Dansereau
Mohamed Daoudi
Abhishek Das
Samyak Datta

Achal Dave
Shalini De Mello
Teofilo deCampos
Joseph DeGol
Koichiro Deguchi
Alessio Del Bue
Stefanie Demirci
Jia Deng
Zhiwei Deng
Joachim Denzler
Konstantinos Derpanis
Aditya Deshpande
Alban Desmaison
Frédéric Devernay
Abhinav Dhall
Michel Dhome
Hamdi Dibeklioğlu
Mert Dikmen
Cosimo Distante
Ajay Divakaran
Mandar Dixit
Carl Doersch
Piotr Dollar
Bo Dong
Chao Dong
Huang Dong
Jian Dong
Jiangxin Dong
Weisheng Dong
Simon Donné
Gianfranco Doretto
Alexey Dosovitskiy
Matthijs Douze
Bruce Draper
Bertram Drost
Liang Du
Shichuan Du
Gregory Dudek
Zoran Duric
Pınar Duygulu
Hazım Ekenel
Tarek El-Gaaly
Ehsan Elhamifar
Mohamed Elhoseiny
Sabu Emmanuel
Ian Endres

Aykut Erdem
Erkut Erdem
Hugo Jair Escalante
Sergio Escalera
Victor Escorcia
Francisco Estrada
Davide Eynard
Bin Fan
Jialue Fan
Quanfu Fan
Chen Fang
Tian Fang
Yi Fang
Hany Farid
Giovanni Farinella
Ryan Farrell
Alireza Fathi
Christoph Feichtenhofer
Wenxin Feng
Martin Fergie
Cornelia Fermuller
Basura Fernando
Michael Firman
Bob Fisher
John Fisher
Mathew Fisher
Boris Flach
Matt Flagg
Francois Fleuret
David Fofi
Ruth Fong
Gian Luca Foresti
Per-Erik Forssén
David Fouhey
Katerina Fragkiadaki
Victor Fragoso
Jan-Michael Frahm
Jean-Sebastien Franco
Ohad Fried
Simone Frintrop
Huazhu Fu
Yun Fu
Olac Fuentes
Christopher Funk
Thomas Funkhouser
Brian Funt

Ryo Furukawa
Yasutaka Furukawa
Andrea Fusiello
Fatma Güney
Raghudeep Gadde
Silvano Galliani
Orazio Gallo
Chuang Gan
Bin-Bin Gao
Jin Gao
Junbin Gao
Ruohan Gao
Shenghua Gao
Animesh Garg
Ravi Garg
Erik Gartner
Simone Gasparin
Jochen Gast
Leon A. Gatys
Stratis Gavves
Liuhao Ge
Timnit Gebru
James Gee
Peter Gehler
Xin Geng
Guido Gerig
David Geronimo
Bernard Ghanem
Michael Gharbi
Golnaz Ghiasi
Spyros Gidaris
Andrew Gilbert
Rohit Girdhar
Ioannis Gkioulekas
Georgia Gkioxari
Guy Godin
Roland Goecke
Michael Goesele
Nuno Goncalves
Boqing Gong
Minglun Gong
Yunchao Gong
Abel Gonzalez-Garcia
Daniel Gordon
Paulo Gotardo
Stephen Gould

Venu Govindu
Helmut Grabner
Petr Gronat
Steve Gu
Josechu Guerrero
Anupam Guha
Jean-Yves Guillemaut
Alp Güler
Erhan Gündoğdu
Guodong Guo
Xinqing Guo
Ankush Gupta
Mohit Gupta
Saurabh Gupta
Tanmay Gupta
Abner Guzman Rivera
Timo Hackel
Sunil Hadap
Christian Haene
Ralf Haeusler
Levente Hajder
David Hall
Peter Hall
Stefan Haller
Ghassan Hamarneh
Fred Hamprecht
Onur Hamsici
Bohyung Han
Junwei Han
Xufeng Han
Yahong Han
Ankur Handa
Albert Haque
Tatsuya Harada
Mehrtash Harandi
Bharath Hariharan
Mahmudul Hasan
Tal Hassner
Kenji Hata
Soren Hauberg
Michal Havlena
Zeeshan Hayder
Junfeng He
Lei He
Varsha Hedau
Felix Heide

Wolfgang Heidrich
Janne Heikkila
Jared Heinly
Mattias Heinrich
Lisa Anne Hendricks
Dan Hendrycks
Stephane Herbin
Alexander Hermans
Luis Herranz
Aaron Hertzmann
Adrian Hilton
Michael Hirsch
Steven Hoi
Seunghoon Hong
Wei Hong
Anthony Hoogs
Radu Horaud
Yedid Hoshen
Omid Hosseini Jafari
Kuang-Jui Hsu
Winston Hsu
Yinlin Hu
Zhe Hu
Gang Hua
Chen Huang
De-An Huang
Dong Huang
Gary Huang
Heng Huang
Jia-Bin Huang
Qixing Huang
Rui Huang
Sheng Huang
Weilin Huang
Xiaolei Huang
Xinyu Huang
Zhiwu Huang
Tak-Wai Hui
Wei-Chih Hung
Junhwa Hur
Mohamed Hussein
Wonjun Hwang
Anders Hyden
Satoshi Ikehata
Nazlı Ikizler-Cinbis
Viorela Ila

Evren Imre
Eldar Insafutdinov
Go Irie
Hossam Isack
Ahmet Işcen
Daisuke Iwai
Hamid Izadinia
Nathan Jacobs
Suyog Jain
Varun Jampani
C. V. Jawahar
Dinesh Jayaraman
Sadeep Jayasumana
Laszlo Jeni
Hueihan Jhuang
Dinghuang Ji
Hui Ji
Qiang Ji
Fan Jia
Kui Jia
Xu Jia
Huaizu Jiang
Jiayan Jiang
Nianjuan Jiang
Tingting Jiang
Xiaoyi Jiang
Yu-Gang Jiang
Long Jin
Suo Jinli
Justin Johnson
Nebojsa Jojic
Michael Jones
Hanbyul Joo
Jungseock Joo
Ajjen Joshi
Amin Jourabloo
Frederic Jurie
Achuta Kadambi
Samuel Kadoury
Ioannis Kakadiaris
Zdenek Kalal
Yannis Kalantidis
Sinan Kalkan
Vicky Kalogeiton
Sunkavalli Kalyan
J.-K. Kamarainen

Martin Kampel
Kenichi Kanatani
Angjoo Kanazawa
Melih Kandemir
Sing Bing Kang
Zhuoliang Kang
Mohan Kankanhalli
Juho Kannala
Abhishek Kar
Amlan Kar
Svebor Karaman
Leonid Karlinsky
Zoltan Kato
Parneet Kaur
Hiroshi Kawasaki
Misha Kazhdan
Margret Keuper
Sameh Khamis
Naeemullah Khan
Salman Khan
Hadi Kiapour
Joe Kileel
Chanho Kim
Gunhee Kim
Hansung Kim
Junmo Kim
Junsik Kim
Kihwan Kim
Minyoung Kim
Tae Hyun Kim
Tae-Kyun Kim
Akisato Kimura
Zsolt Kira
Alexander Kirillov
Kris Kitani
Maria Klodt
Patrick Knöbelreiter
Jan Knopp
Reinhard Koch
Alexander Kolesnikov
Chen Kong
Naejin Kong
Shu Kong
Piotr Koniusz
Simon Korman
Andreas Koschan

Dimitrios Kosmopoulos
Satwik Kottur
Balazs Kovacs
Adarsh Kowdle
Mike Krainin
Gregory Kramida
Ranjay Krishna
Ravi Krishnan
Matej Kristan
Pavel Krsek
Volker Krueger
Alexander Krull
Hilde Kuehne
Andreas Kuhn
Arjan Kuijper
Zuzana Kukelova
Kuldeep Kulkarni
Shiro Kumano
Avinash Kumar
Vijay Kumar
Abhijit Kundu
Sebastian Kurtek
Junseok Kwon
Jan Kybic
Alexander Ladikos
Shang-Hong Lai
Wei-Sheng Lai
Jean-Francois Lalonde
John Lambert
Zhenzhong Lan
Charis Lanaras
Oswald Lanz
Dong Lao
Longin Jan Latecki
Justin Lazarow
Huu Le
Chen-Yu Lee
Gim Hee Lee
Honglak Lee
Hsin-Ying Lee
Joon-Young Lee
Seungyong Lee
Stefan Lee
Yong Jae Lee
Zhen Lei
Ido Leichter

Victor Lempitsky
Spyridon Leonardos
Marius Leordeanu
Matt Leotta
Thomas Leung
Stefan Leutenegger
Gil Levi
Aviad Levis
Jose Lezama
Ang Li
Dingzeyu Li
Dong Li
Haoxiang Li
Hongdong Li
Hongsheng Li
Hongyang Li
Jianguo Li
Kai Li
Ruiyu Li
Wei Li
Wen Li
Xi Li
Xiaoxiao Li
Xin Li
Xirong Li
Xuelong Li
Xueting Li
Yeqing Li
Yijun Li
Yin Li
Yingwei Li
Yining Li
Yongjie Li
Yu-Feng Li
Zechao Li
Zhengqi Li
Zhenyang Li
Zhizhong Li
Xiaodan Liang
Renjie Liao
Zicheng Liao
Bee Lim
Jongwoo Lim
Joseph Lim
Ser-Nam Lim
Chen-Hsuan Lin

Shih-Yao Lin
Tsung-Yi Lin
Weiyao Lin
Yen-Yu Lin
Haibin Ling
Or Litany
Roee Litman
Anan Liu
Changsong Liu
Chen Liu
Ding Liu
Dong Liu
Feng Liu
Guangcan Liu
Luoqi Liu
Miaomiao Liu
Nian Liu
Risheng Liu
Shu Liu
Shuaicheng Liu
Sifei Liu
Tyng-Luh Liu
Wanquan Liu
Weiwei Liu
Xialei Liu
Xiaoming Liu
Yebin Liu
Yiming Liu
Ziwei Liu
Zongyi Liu
Liliana Lo Presti
Edgar Lobaton
Chengjiang Long
Mingsheng Long
Roberto Lopez-Sastre
Amy Loufti
Brian Lovell
Canyi Lu
Cewu Lu
Feng Lu
Huchuan Lu
Jiajun Lu
Jiasen Lu
Jiwen Lu
Yang Lu
Yujuan Lu

Simon Lucey
Jian-Hao Luo
Jiebo Luo
Pablo Márquez-Neila
Matthias Müller
Chao Ma
Chih-Yao Ma
Lin Ma
Shugao Ma
Wei-Chiu Ma
Zhanyu Ma
Oisin Mac Aodha
Will Maddern
Ludovic Magerand
Marcus Magnor
Vijay Mahadevan
Mohammad Mahoor
Michael Maire
Subhransu Maji
Ameesh Makadia
Atsuto Maki
Yasushi Makihara
Mateusz Malinowski
Tomasz Malisiewicz
Arun Mallya
Roberto Manduchi
Junhua Mao
Dmitrii Marin
Joe Marino
Kenneth Marino
Elisabeta Marinoiu
Ricardo Martin
Aleix Martinez
Julieta Martinez
Aaron Maschinot
Jonathan Masci
Bogdan Matei
Diana Mateus
Stefan Mathe
Kevin Matzen
Bruce Maxwell
Steve Maybank
Walterio Mayol-Cuevas
Mason McGill
Stephen Mckenna
Roey Mechrez

Christopher Mei
Heydi Mendez-Vazquez
Deyu Meng
Thomas Mensink
Bjoern Menze
Domingo Mery
Qiguang Miao
Tomer Michaeli
Antoine Miech
Ondrej Miksik
Anton Milan
Gregor Miller
Cai Minjie
Majid Mirmehdi
Ishan Misra
Niloy Mitra
Anurag Mittal
Nirbhay Modhe
Davide Modolo
Pritish Mohapatra
Pascal Monasse
Mathew Monfort
Taesup Moon
Sandino Morales
Vlad Morariu
Philippos Mordohai
Francesc Moreno
Henrique Morimitsu
Yael Moses
Ben-Ezra Moshe
Roozbeh Mottaghi
Yadong Mu
Lopamudra Mukherjee
Mario Munich
Ana Murillo
Damien Muselet
Armin Mustafa
Siva Karthik Mustikovela
Moin Nabi
Sobhan Naderi
Hajime Nagahara
Varun Nagaraja
Tushar Nagarajan
Arsha Nagrani
Nikhil Naik
Atsushi Nakazawa

P. J. Narayanan
Charlie Nash
Lakshmanan Nataraj
Fabian Nater
Lukáš Neumann
Natalia Neverova
Alejandro Newell
Phuc Nguyen
Xiaohan Nie
David Nilsson
Ko Nishino
Zhenxing Niu
Shohei Nobuhara
Klas Nordberg
Mohammed Norouzi
David Novotny
Ifeoma Nwogu
Matthew O'Toole
Guillaume Obozinski
Jean-Marc Odobez
Eyal Ofek
Ferda Ofli
Tae-Hyun Oh
Iason Oikonomidis
Takeshi Oishi
Takahiro Okabe
Takayuki Okatani
Vlad Olaru
Michael Opitz
Jose Oramas
Vicente Ordonez
Ivan Oseledets
Aljosa Osep
Magnus Oskarsson
Martin R. Oswald
Wanli Ouyang
Andrew Owens
Mustafa Özuysal
Jinshan Pan
Xingang Pan
Rameswar Panda
Sharath Pankanti
Julien Pansiot
Nicolas Papadakis
George Papandreou
N. Papanikolopoulos

Hyun Soo Park
In Kyu Park
Jaesik Park
Omkar Parkhi
Alvaro Parra Bustos
C. Alejandro Parraga
Vishal Patel
Deepak Pathak
Ioannis Patras
Viorica Patraucean
Genevieve Patterson
Kim Pedersen
Robert Peharz
Selen Pehlivan
Xi Peng
Bojan Pepik
Talita Perciano
Federico Pernici
Adrian Peter
Stavros Petridis
Vladimir Petrovic
Henning Petzka
Tomas Pfister
Trung Pham
Justus Piater
Massimo Piccardi
Sudeep Pillai
Pedro Pinheiro
Lerrel Pinto
Bernardo Pires
Aleksis Pirinen
Fiora Pirri
Leonid Pischulin
Tobias Ploetz
Bryan Plummer
Yair Poleg
Jean Ponce
Gerard Pons-Moll
Jordi Pont-Tuset
Alin Popa
Fatih Porikli
Horst Possegger
Viraj Prabhu
Andrea Prati
Maria Priisalu
Véronique Prinet

Victor Prisacariu
Jan Prokaj
Nicolas Pugeault
Luis Puig
Ali Punjani
Senthil Purushwalkam
Guido Pusiol
Guo-Jun Qi
Xiaojuan Qi
Hongwei Qin
Shi Qiu
Faisal Qureshi
Matthias Rüther
Petia Radeva
Umer Rafi
Rahul Raguram
Swaminathan Rahul
Varun Ramakrishna
Kandan Ramakrishnan
Ravi Ramamoorthi
Vignesh Ramanathan
Vasili Ramanishka
R. Ramasamy Selvaraju
Rene Ranftl
Carolina Raposo
Nikhil Rasiwasia
Nalini Ratha
Sai Ravela
Avinash Ravichandran
Ramin Raziperchikolaei
Sylvestre-Alvise Rebuffi
Adria Recasens
Joe Redmon
Timo Rehfeld
Michal Reinstein
Konstantinos Rematas
Haibing Ren
Shaoqing Ren
Wenqi Ren
Zhile Ren
Hamid Rezatofighi
Nicholas Rhinehart
Helge Rhodin
Elisa Ricci
Eitan Richardson
Stephan Richter

Gernot Riegler	Torsten Sattler	Tianmin Shu
Hayko Riemenschneider	Bogdan Savchynskyy	Zhixin Shu
Tammy Riklin Raviv	Johannes Schönberger	Kaleem Siddiqi
Ergys Ristani	Hanno Scharr	Gunnar Sigurdsson
Tobias Ritschel	Walter Scheirer	Nathan Silberman
Mariano Rivera	Bernt Schiele	Tomas Simon
Samuel Rivera	Frank Schmidt	Abhishek Singh
Antonio Robles-Kelly	Tanner Schmidt	Gautam Singh
Ignacio Rocco	Dirk Schnieders	Maneesh Singh
Jason Rock	Samuel Schulter	Praveer Singh
Emanuele Rodola	William Schwartz	Richa Singh
Mikel Rodriguez	Alexander Schwing	Saurabh Singh
Gregory Rogez	Ozan Sener	Sudipta Sinha
Marcus Rohrbach	Soumyadip Sengupta	Vladimir Smutny
Gemma Roig	Laura Sevilla-Lara	Noah Snavely
Javier Romero	Mubarak Shah	Cees Snoek
Olaf Ronneberger	Shishir Shah	Kihyuk Sohn
Amir Rosenfeld	Fahad Shahbaz Khan	Eric Sommerlade
Bodo Rosenhahn	Amir Shahroudy	Sanghyun Son
Guy Rosman	Jing Shao	Bi Song
Arun Ross	Xiaowei Shao	Shiyu Song
Samuel Rota Bulò	Roman Shapovalov	Shuran Song
Peter Roth	Nataliya Shapovalova	Xuan Song
Constantin Rothkopf	Ali Sharif Razavian	Yale Song
Sebastien Roy	Gaurav Sharma	Yang Song
Amit Roy-Chowdhury	Mohit Sharma	Yibing Song
Ognjen Rudovic	Pramod Sharma	Lorenzo Sorgi
Adria Ruiz	Viktoriia Sharmanska	Humberto Sossa
Javier Ruiz-del-Solar	Eli Shechtman	Pratul Srinivasan
Christian Rupprecht	Mark Sheinin	Michael Stark
Olga Russakovsky	Evan Shelhamer	Bjorn Stenger
Chris Russell	Chunhua Shen	Rainer Stiefelhagen
Alexandre Sablayrolles	Li Shen	Joerg Stueckler
Fereshteh Sadeghi	Wei Shen	Jan Stuehmer
Ryusuke Sagawa	Xiaohui Shen	Hang Su
Hideo Saito	Xiaoyong Shen	Hao Su
Elham Sakhaee	Ziyi Shen	Shuochen Su
Albert Ali Salah	Lu Sheng	R. Subramanian
Conrad Sanderson	Baoguang Shi	Yusuke Sugano
Koppal Sanjeev	Boxin Shi	Akihiro Sugimoto
Aswin Sankaranarayanan	Kevin Shih	Baochen Sun
Elham Saraee	Hyunjung Shim	Chen Sun
Jason Saragih	Ilan Shimshoni	Jian Sun
Sudeep Sarkar	Young Min Shin	Jin Sun
Imari Sato	Koichi Shinoda	Lin Sun
Shin'ichi Satoh	Matthew Shreve	Min Sun

Qing Sun
Zhaohui Sun
David Suter
Eran Swears
Raza Syed Hussain
T. Syeda-Mahmood
Christian Szegedy
Duy-Nguyen Ta
Tolga Taşdizen
Hemant Tagare
Yuichi Taguchi
Ying Tai
Yu-Wing Tai
Jun Takamatsu
Hugues Talbot
Toru Tamak
Robert Tamburo
Chaowei Tan
Meng Tang
Peng Tang
Siyu Tang
Wei Tang
Junli Tao
Ran Tao
Xin Tao
Makarand Tapaswi
Jean-Philippe Tarel
Maxim Tatarchenko
Bugra Tekin
Demetri Terzopoulos
Christian Theobalt
Diego Thomas
Rajat Thomas
Qi Tian
Xinmei Tian
YingLi Tian
Yonghong Tian
Yonglong Tian
Joseph Tighe
Radu Timofte
Massimo Tistarelli
Sinisa Todorovic
Pavel Tokmakov
Giorgos Tolias
Federico Tombari
Tatiana Tommasi

Chetan Tonde
Xin Tong
Akihiko Torii
Andrea Torsello
Florian Trammer
Du Tran
Quoc-Huy Tran
Rudolph Triebel
Alejandro Troccoli
Leonardo Trujillo
Tomasz Trzcinski
Sam Tsai
Yi-Hsuan Tsai
Hung-Yu Tseng
Vagia Tsiminaki
Aggeliki Tsoli
Wei-Chih Tu
Shubham Tulsiani
Fred Tung
Tony Tung
Matt Turek
Oncel Tuzel
Georgios Tzimiropoulos
Ilkay Ulusoy
Osman Ulusoy
Dmitry Ulyanov
Paul Upchurch
Ben Usman
Evgeniya Ustinova
Himanshu Vajaria
Alexander Vakhitov
Jack Valmadre
Ernest Valveny
Jan van Gemert
Grant Van Horn
Jagannadan Varadarajan
Gul Varol
Sebastiano Vascon
Francisco Vasconcelos
Mayank Vatsa
Javier Vazquez-Corral
Ramakrishna Vedantam
Ashok Veeraraghavan
Andreas Veit
Raviteja Vemulapalli
Jonathan Ventura

Matthias Vestner
Minh Vo
Christoph Vogel
Michele Volpi
Carl Vondrick
Sven Wachsmuth
Toshikazu Wada
Michael Waechter
Catherine Wah
Jacob Walker
Jun Wan
Boyu Wang
Chen Wang
Chunyu Wang
De Wang
Fang Wang
Hongxing Wang
Hua Wang
Jiang Wang
Jingdong Wang
Jinglu Wang
Jue Wang
Le Wang
Lei Wang
Lezi Wang
Liang Wang
Lichao Wang
Lijun Wang
Limin Wang
Liwei Wang
Naiyan Wang
Oliver Wang
Qi Wang
Ruiping Wang
Shenlong Wang
Shu Wang
Song Wang
Tao Wang
Xiaofang Wang
Xiaolong Wang
Xinchao Wang
Xinggang Wang
Xintao Wang
Yang Wang
Yu-Chiang Frank Wang
Yu-Xiong Wang

Zhaowen Wang
Zhe Wang
Anne Wannenwetsch
Simon Warfield
Scott Wehrwein
Donglai Wei
Ping Wei
Shih-En Wei
Xiu-Shen Wei
Yichen Wei
Xie Weidi
Philippe Weinzaepfel
Longyin Wen
Eric Wengrowski
Tomas Werner
Michael Wilber
Rick Wildes
Olivia Wiles
Kyle Wilson
David Wipf
Kwan-Yee Wong
Daniel Worrall
John Wright
Baoyuan Wu
Chao-Yuan Wu
Jiajun Wu
Jianxin Wu
Tianfu Wu
Xiaodong Wu
Xiaohe Wu
Xinxiao Wu
Yang Wu
Yi Wu
Ying Wu
Yuxin Wu
Zheng Wu
Stefanie Wuhrer
Yin Xia
Tao Xiang
Yu Xiang
Lei Xiao
Tong Xiao
Yang Xiao
Cihang Xie
Dan Xie
Jianwen Xie

Jin Xie
Lingxi Xie
Pengtao Xie
Saining Xie
Wenxuan Xie
Yuchen Xie
Bo Xin
Junliang Xing
Peng Xingchao
Bo Xiong
Fei Xiong
Xuehan Xiong
Yuanjun Xiong
Chenliang Xu
Danfei Xu
Huijuan Xu
Jia Xu
Weipeng Xu
Xiangyu Xu
Yan Xu
Yuanlu Xu
Jia Xue
Tianfan Xue
Erdem Yörük
Abhay Yadav
Deshraj Yadav
Payman Yadollahpour
Yasushi Yagi
Toshihiko Yamasaki
Fei Yan
Hang Yan
Junchi Yan
Junjie Yan
Sijie Yan
Keiji Yanai
Bin Yang
Chih-Yuan Yang
Dong Yang
Herb Yang
Jianchao Yang
Jianwei Yang
Jiaolong Yang
Jie Yang
Jimei Yang
Jufeng Yang
Linjie Yang

Michael Ying Yang
Ming Yang
Ruiduo Yang
Ruigang Yang
Shuo Yang
Wei Yang
Xiaodong Yang
Yanchao Yang
Yi Yang
Angela Yao
Bangpeng Yao
Cong Yao
Jian Yao
Ting Yao
Julian Yarkony
Mark Yatskar
Jinwei Ye
Mao Ye
Mei-Chen Yeh
Raymond Yeh
Serena Yeung
Kwang Moo Yi
Shuai Yi
Alper Yılmaz
Lijun Yin
Xi Yin
Zhaozheng Yin
Xianghua Ying
Ryo Yonetani
Donghyun Yoo
Ju Hong Yoon
Kuk-Jin Yoon
Chong You
Shaodi You
Aron Yu
Fisher Yu
Gang Yu
Jingyi Yu
Ke Yu
Licheng Yu
Pei Yu
Qian Yu
Rong Yu
Shoou-I Yu
Stella Yu
Xiang Yu

Yang Yu
Zhiding Yu
Ganzhao Yuan
Jing Yuan
Junsong Yuan
Lu Yuan
Stefanos Zafeiriou
Sergey Zagoruyko
Amir Zamir
K. Zampogiannis
Andrei Zanfir
Mihai Zanfir
Pablo Zegers
Eyasu Zemene
Andy Zeng
Xingyu Zeng
Yun Zeng
De-Chuan Zhan
Cheng Zhang
Dong Zhang
Guofeng Zhang
Han Zhang
Hang Zhang
Hanwang Zhang
Jian Zhang
Jianguo Zhang
Jianming Zhang
Jiawei Zhang
Junping Zhang
Lei Zhang
Linguang Zhang
Ning Zhang
Qing Zhang

Quanshi Zhang
Richard Zhang
Runze Zhang
Shanshan Zhang
Shiliang Zhang
Shu Zhang
Ting Zhang
Xiangyu Zhang
Xiaofan Zhang
Xu Zhang
Yimin Zhang
Yinda Zhang
Yongqiang Zhang
Yuting Zhang
Zhanpeng Zhang
Ziyu Zhang
Bin Zhao
Chen Zhao
Hang Zhao
Hengshuang Zhao
Qijun Zhao
Rui Zhao
Yue Zhao
Enliang Zheng
Liang Zheng
Stephan Zheng
Wei-Shi Zheng
Wenming Zheng
Yin Zheng
Yinqiang Zheng
Yuanjie Zheng
Guangyu Zhong
Bolei Zhou

Guang-Tong Zhou
Huiyu Zhou
Jiahuan Zhou
S. Kevin Zhou
Tinghui Zhou
Wengang Zhou
Xiaowei Zhou
Xingyi Zhou
Yin Zhou
Zihan Zhou
Fan Zhu
Guangming Zhu
Ji Zhu
Jiejie Zhu
Jun-Yan Zhu
Shizhan Zhu
Siyu Zhu
Xiangxin Zhu
Xiatian Zhu
Yan Zhu
Yingying Zhu
Yixin Zhu
Yuke Zhu
Zhenyao Zhu
Liansheng Zhuang
Zeeshan Zia
Karel Zimmermann
Daniel Zoran
Danping Zou
Qi Zou
Silvia Zuffi
Wangmeng Zuo
Xinxin Zuo

Contents – Part XI

Poster Session

Deep Boosting for Image Denoising

Chang Chen, Zhiwei Xiong$^{(\boxtimes)}$, Xinmei Tian, and Feng Wu

University of Science and Technology of China, Hefei, China
changc@mail.ustc.edu.cn, {zwxiong,xinmei,fengwu}@ustc.edu.cn

Abstract. Boosting is a classic algorithm which has been successfully applied to diverse computer vision tasks. In the scenario of image denoising, however, the existing boosting algorithms are surpassed by the emerging learning-based models. In this paper, we propose a novel deep boosting framework (DBF) for denoising, which integrates several convolutional networks in a feed-forward fashion. Along with the integrated networks, however, the depth of the boosting framework is substantially increased, which brings difficulty to training. To solve this problem, we introduce the concept of dense connection that overcomes the vanishing of gradients during training. Furthermore, we propose a path-widening fusion scheme cooperated with the dilated convolution to derive a lightweight yet efficient convolutional network as the boosting unit, named Dilated Dense Fusion Network (DDFN). Comprehensive experiments demonstrate that our DBF outperforms existing methods on widely used benchmarks, in terms of different denoising tasks.

1 Introduction

Image denoising is a typical problem in low-level computer vision. Observed a contaminated image with a certain kind of noise (e.g., additive white Gaussian noise), plenty of methods have been investigated to restore the original signal. Among them, modeling image priors for restoration is a prominent approach, such as nonlocal similarity based models [1–3] and sparsity based models [4–6]. Specifically, BM3D [7], CSF [8], and WNNM [9] are several representative methods for image denoising.

Recently, with the rapid advancement of GPU-based parallel computing frameworks, increasingly more learning-based denoising models [10–13] began to adopt the paradigm of end-to-end training based on a convolutional neural network (CNN). These learning-based models have achieved competitive or even better performance than previous methods. On the other hand, several traditional models [14–16] based on the boosting algorithm studied the denoising problem in a unique perspective. By extracting the residual signal or eliminating the noise leftover, these methods boost the restoration quality iteratively. Beyond them, Romano and Elad proposed a notable variant of the boosting algorithm, named Strengthen-Operate-Subtract (SOS) [17]. By combining the denoised image with the original input, it increased the signal-to-noise ratio iteratively and achieved promising improvements.

© Springer Nature Switzerland AG 2018
V. Ferrari et al. (Eds.): ECCV 2018, LNCS 11215, pp. 3–19, 2018.
https://doi.org/10.1007/978-3-030-01252-6_1

Nevertheless, the existing boosting algorithms still have performance gaps compared with the learning-based models. In this paper, we embed the deep learning technique into the boosting algorithm and significantly boost its performance in the scenario of image denoising. Specifically, we construct a Deep Boosting Framework (DBF) that integrates several CNNs in a feed-forward fashion, where each network serves as a boosting unit. To the best of our knowledge, this is the first time that deep learning and boosting are jointly investigated for image restoration. Although this paper mainly focuses on denoising, the proposed DBF can be readily generalized to other image restoration tasks.

Theoretically, the boosting unit in the DBF can be any type of networks. In practice, however, we find that not all structures are suitable to be employed as the boosting unit. The reason is that, along with the integrated networks for boosting, the depth of the DBF is substantially increased. It thus causes the difficulty of convergence during training. To fully exploit the potential of the DBF, we further propose a Dilated Dense Fusion Network (DDFN), which is highly optimized to serve as the boosting unit.

We reform the plainly connected network structure in three steps to obtain the DDFN. First, to overcome the vanishing of gradients during training, we introduce the dense connection [18] to construct the boosting unit, which also improves the re-usage of features and thus guarantees the efficiency. Second, to obtain better performance based on the densely connected structure, we adopt the dilated convolution [19] for widening the receptive field without additive parameters, which maintains the lightweight structure of the boosting unit. Last but not least, we further propose a path-widening fusion scheme cooperated with the dilated convolution to make the boosting unit more efficient.

The contributions of this paper are summarized as follows:

(1) We propose a novel boosting framework for image denoising by introducing deep learning into the boosting algorithm, named DBF. It not only outperforms existing boosting algorithms by a large margin but also performs better than extensive learning-based models.

(2) We optimize a lightweight yet efficient convolutional network as the boosting unit, named DDFN. With the dense connection, we address the difficulty of convergence in DBF. Cooperating with the dilated convolution, we propose a path-widening fusion scheme to expand the capacity of each boosting unit.

(3) Our DDFN-based DBF has a clear advantage over existing methods on widely used benchmarks when trained at a specific noise level. If trained for blind Gaussian denoising, it achieves a new state-of-the-art performance within a wide range of noise levels. Also, the proposed method is demonstrated effective when generalized to the image deblocking task.

2   Related Work

CNN-Based Image Denoising. Research along this direction focuses on the exploration of the network structure. Advanced design of architecture yields better restoration quality. For instance, Burger et al. [10] trained a multi-layer perceptrons (MLPs) with a large image database, which achieved comparable results with BM3D [7]. Chen et al. [11] proposed a stage-wise model (i.e., TNRD) which introduced the well-designed convolutional layers into the non-linear diffusion model to derive a flexible framework. And Zhang et al. [12] composed the deep DnCNN model by utilizing batch normalization (BN) [20] and residual connection [21]. Essentially, DnCNN can be viewed as the generalization of one-stage TNRD. Besides, a recently proposed model [13] combined image denoising with semantic classification using CNNs, which bridged the gap between these two different tasks and improved the restoration quality. Following the successful paradigm of end-to-end training, we also adopt the CNN for image denoising. Different from its common usages, however, the employed CNN is just a component of our denoising model. Specifically, it is integrated as a boosting unit in the DBF. Experimental results demonstrate the superior performance of our boosting framework compared with a single CNN model.

Boosting Algorithm. Boosting is a widely used algorithm to improve the performance of diverse tasks by cascading several steerable sub-models. A plenty of models based on the boosting algorithm have been investigated for image denoising in literature [14–16,22]. Generally, the detailed implementation can be divided into 3 classes: (a) re-utilizing the residual [14], (b) re-enhancing the denoised signal [15], and (c) strengthening the SNR iteratively [17]. However, these boosting algorithms with classic models are surpassed by the emerging learning-based models. Contrastively, our proposed DBF inherits both advantages of boosting and CNN and achieves a new state-of-the-art performance for image denoising. Note that, boosting and CNN have been combined for image classification tasks before, e.g., IB-CNN [23] and BoostCNN [24], yet our proposed DBF is the first deep boosting framework in the field of image restoration.

3   Deep Boosting Framework

3.1   Boosting Perspective of Denoising

The fundamental image denoising problem is the recovery of an image $x \in \mathbb{R}^{N \times M}$ from a contaminated measurement $y \in \mathbb{R}^{N \times M}$, which can be formulated as

$$y = x + v, \tag{1}$$

where v stands for the additive noise that is generally modeled as zero-mean white Gaussian noise with a standard deviation σ. The denoising process can be represented as

$$\hat{x} = \mathcal{S}(y) = \mathcal{S}(x + v), \tag{2}$$

where the operator $\mathcal{S}(\cdot)$ stands for a general denoising method and $\hat{x}$ stands for an approximation of x.

However, the image $\hat{x}$ recovered by any algorithm cannot ideally equal to x, and the gap between them can be denoted as

$$u = \hat{x} - x = v_r - x_r, \tag{3}$$

where x_r represents the unrecovered signal and v_r stands for the leftover noise in $\hat{x}$. In other words, by adding x_r and subtracting v_r, we then obtain the clean image x from $\hat{x}$.

A straightforward idea to apply the boosting algorithm to image denoising is that we iteratively extract the unrecovered signal x_r from the residual and add it back to $\hat{x}$

$$\hat{x}^{n+1} = \hat{x}^n + \mathcal{H}(y - \hat{x}^n), \tag{4}$$

where $\mathcal{H}(\cdot)$ is an operator for the iterative extraction and we set $\hat{x}^0 = 0$. Note that, however, the residual $y - \hat{x}$ contains not only the unrecovered signal x_r but also a part of noise

$$
\begin{aligned}
y - \hat{x} &= (x + v) - (x + u) \\
&= (x + v) - (x + v_r - x_r) \\
&= x_r + (v - v_r).
\end{aligned}
\tag{5}
$$

Another native idea is that we remove the leftover noise v_r by filtering the denoised image $\hat{x}$ iteratively

$$\hat{x}^{n+1} = \mathcal{F}(\hat{x}^n), \tag{6}$$

where $\mathcal{F}(\cdot)$ stands for a certain denoising model. However, it could lead to over-smoothing since it neglects x_r which contains most high frequency information.

To further improve the performance of the boosting framework, Romano and Elad proposed a novel SOS algorithm. The denoising target in each iteration step is the "strengthened" image $y + \hat{x}^n$, instead of the residual $y - \hat{x}^n$ or the denoised image $\hat{x}^n$, which improves the signal-to-noise ratio (SNR) [17]. To guarantee the iterability of SOS, however, it has to "subtract" the identical $\hat{x}^n$ in each step as

$$\hat{x}^{n+1} = \mathcal{G}(y + \hat{x}^n) - \hat{x}^n, \tag{7}$$

where $\mathcal{G}(\cdot)$ is a certain denoising model imposed on the strengthened image. To better clarify the insight of the SOS algorithm, we decompose $y + \hat{x}$ as

$$
\begin{aligned}
y + \hat{x} &= (x + v) + (x + u) \\
&= 2x + (v + u).
\end{aligned}
\tag{8}
$$

Assuming that $||u|| = \delta ||v||$, where $\delta \ll 1$. Then we have $SNR(y + \hat{x}) > SNR(y)$ according to the Cauchy-Schwarz inequality [17]. All we need to achieve so is a general denoising method even if it is a "weak" one.

3.2   CNN-Based Boosting

Inspired by SOS [17], we propose a new boosting framework by leveraging deep learning. Specifically, we introduce a CNN to learn the denoising model in each stage. Following Eq. (7), we have

$$\hat{x}^{n+1} = \mathcal{G}_\theta(y + \hat{x}^n) - \hat{x}^n, \tag{9}$$

where θ denotes the trainable parameter set of the CNN.

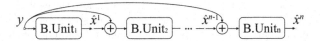

Fig. 1. CNN-based deep boosting framework. The B.Unit$_n$ denotes the nth boosting unit (i.e., $\mathcal{G}_{\theta_n}$) in the framework. The investigation of B.Unit is detailed in Sect. 4

The subtraction of identical $\hat{x}^n$ inherited from Eq. (7) aims to guarantee the iterability of the SOS algorithm. Such constraint in Eq. (9) is no longer needed since we can learn different denoising models in each stage. In other words, our deep boosting framework can adjust its parameters without the constraint of identical subtraction, which actually yields a better performance as will be demonstrated in Sect. 5.3. The output of the final stage can be represented as

$$\hat{x}^n = \mathcal{G}_{\theta_n}\{y + \mathcal{G}_{\theta_{n-1}}[y + \cdots \mathcal{G}_{\theta_2}(y + \mathcal{G}_{\theta_1}(y))\cdots]\}, \tag{10}$$

where n stands for the serial number of each stage. Figure 1 illustrates a flowchart for Eq. (10) for a better understanding.

The loss function for training the parameters $\Theta = \{\theta_1, \theta_2, ..., \theta_n\}$ is the mean square error (MSE) between the final output $\hat{x}^n$ and the ground truth x

$$\mathcal{L}_\Theta(\hat{x}^n, x) = \frac{1}{2B} \sum_{i=1}^{B} ||\hat{x}_i^n - x_i||_2^2, \tag{11}$$

where B denotes the size of mini-batch for the stochastic gradient descent. Such training scheme is called joint training which optimizes the parameters in all stages simultaneously. We also consider a greedy training scheme, for which the parameters are firstly optimized stage-wise and then fine-tuned among all stages. Related experimental results will be described in Sect. 5.3.

3.3 Relationship to TNRD

The TNRD model proposed in [11] is also a stage-wise model trained jointly, which can be formulated as

$$\hat{x}^n - \hat{x}^{n-1} = -\mathcal{D}(\hat{x}^{n-1}) - \mathcal{R}(\hat{x}^{n-1}, y), \tag{12}$$

where $\mathcal{D}(\cdot)$ stands for the diffusion term which is implemented using a CNN with two layers and $\mathcal{R}(\cdot)$ denotes the reaction term as $\mathcal{R}(\hat{x}^{n-1}, y) = \gamma(\hat{x}^{n-1} - y)$, where γ is a factor which denotes the strength of the reaction term.

Actually, TNRD can be interpreted as a special case of the boosting algorithm. Combining Eqs. (4) and (6), we have

$$\hat{x}^n = \hat{x}^{n-1} + \mathcal{H}(y - \hat{x}^{n-1}) + \mathcal{F}(\hat{x}^{n-1}). \tag{13}$$

Providing $\mathcal{F}(\cdot) = -\mathcal{D}(\cdot)$ and $\mathcal{H}(\cdot) = -\gamma(\cdot)$, we then obtain the basic equation of the TNRD model.

Table 1. From the plain structure to the dilated dense fusion: the evolution of structure for the boosting unit. Part 1 is the feature extraction stage, part 2 is the feature integration stage, and part 3 is the reconstruction stage. $C(\cdot)$ stands for the convolution with (kernel size × kernel size × number of filters) and $D(\cdot)$ denotes the corresponding parameters of dilated convolution. $[\cdot] \times$ or $\{\cdot\} \times$ stands for an operator of concatenation with certain blocks (the ×1 is omitted). And the symbol "/" denotes the path-widening fusion. Detail structures are illustrated in Fig. 2 for a better understanding

Parts	PN	DN	DDN	DDFN
1	$C(3 \times 3 \times 24)$	$C(3 \times 3 \times 32)$	$\begin{bmatrix} C(3 \times 3 \times 16) \\ D(3 \times 3 \times 16) \end{bmatrix}$	$\begin{bmatrix} C(3 \times 3 \times 8/6) \\ D(3 \times 3 \times 8/6) \end{bmatrix}$
2	$C(3 \times 3 \times 24) \times 8$	$\begin{bmatrix} C(1 \times 1 \times 32) \\ C(3 \times 3 \times 8) \end{bmatrix} \times 8$	$\begin{bmatrix} C(1 \times 1 \times 32) \\ D(3 \times 3 \times 8) \end{bmatrix} \times 8$	$\begin{Bmatrix} C(1 \times 1 \times 24) \\ C(3 \times 3 \times 6/3) \\ D(3 \times 3 \times 6/3) \\ C(1 \times 1 \times 8) \end{Bmatrix} \times 8$
3	$C(3 \times 3 \times 1)$	$C(1 \times 1 \times 1)$	$C(1 \times 1 \times 1)$	$C(1 \times 1 \times 1)$

However, by further decomposing Eq. (12), we demonstrate the fundamentally different insights between TNRD and DBF as follows. Without loss of generality, let $\hat{x}^{n-1} = x + u$ and we discuss a special case when $\gamma = 1$. Considering Eqs. (1) and (3), we have

$$\begin{aligned} \mathcal{R}(\hat{x}^{n-1}, y) &= \hat{x}^{n-1} - y \\ &= (x + u) - (x + v) \\ &= u - v. \end{aligned} \tag{14}$$

Substituting Eq. (14) into Eq. (12), we then have

$$\begin{aligned} \hat{x}^n &= \hat{x}^{n-1} - \mathcal{D}(\hat{x}^{n-1}) - \mathcal{R}(\hat{x}^{n-1}, y) \\ &= (x + u) - \mathcal{D}(\hat{x}^{n-1}) - (u - v) \\ &= x - \mathcal{D}(\hat{x}^{n-1}) + v. \end{aligned} \tag{15}$$

The target of TNRD is to let $\hat{x}^n \to x$, i.e., $\mathcal{D}(\hat{x}^{n-1}) \to v$. Thus, the diffusion term is actually trained for fitting the white Gaussian noise v. In contrast, our proposed DBF is trained for directly restoring the original signal x, leveraging on the availability of denoised images and the growth of SNR. Intuitively, it may be more difficult to find correlations between training examples when fitting the irregular noise. Moreover, from the perspective of SNR, it is more difficult to predict the "weaker" noise when the input image has a lower noise level. These are the advantages of our DBF in comparison with TNRD.

4   Dilated Dense Fusion Network

An efficient boosting unit is desired to fully exploit the potential of the proposed DBF. Theoretically, the function $\mathcal{G}_\theta(\cdot)$ in Eq. (10) has no restriction on

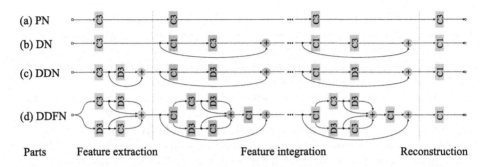

Fig. 2. Details of the evolution for the boosting unit. "C" and "D" with a rectangular block denote the convolution and its dilated variant, respectively. The following "1" and "3" denote the kernel size. "+" with a circular block denotes the concatenation. Each layer in DDFN (except the last one) adopts ReLU [25] as the activation function, which is omitted here for simplifying the illustration

the detailed implementation of the boosting unit. Thus, we have a wide choice of diverse network structures. We start our investigation from a simple structure which is the simplified DnCNN [12] without batch normalization and residual connection, i.e., the plain network (PN), as shown in Table 1 and Fig. 2(a). We find in experiments that, given the same number of parameters, deepening a network properly contributes to the efficiency (as detailed in Sect. 5.2). However, when we introduce the PN into our DBF to derive a 2-stage boosting framework, this benefit tends to vanish as the network depth continues to increase, probably due to the vanishing of gradient during the back propagation.

4.1 Dense Connection

To overcome the propagation problem of gradient during training, we introduce the dense connection to derive the dense network (DN), as shown in Table 1 and Fig. 2(b), which is inspired by the successful model for image recognition [18]. The dense connection enables the lth layer to receive the features of all preceding layers (i.e., $f_0, ..., f_{l-1}$) as input

$$f_l = g_l([f_0, f_1, ..., f_{l-1}]), \tag{16}$$

where $g_l(\cdot)$ denotes the lth layer in $\mathcal{G}_\theta$ and $[f_0, f_1, ..., f_{l-1}]$ stands for the concatenation of the features output from preceding layers. We demonstrate in experiments that the dense connection can address the propagation issue of gradient during training (as detailed in Sect. 5.2).

4.2 Dilated Convolution

Widening the receptive field of the CNN is a well-known strategy for enhancing the performance in both image classification [26] and restoration [27] tasks. The convolution with a larger kernel size can widen the receptive field, however, it increases the number of parameters at the same time. Another strategy is stacking multiple convolutional layers with a 3×3 kernel size to obtain a large receptive field equivalently. However, it causes difficulty of convergence due to the increasing of the network depth.

Recently, a notable alternative called dilated convolution has been investigated in semantic segmentation [19] and image classification [28]. The dilated convolution can widen the receptive field without additive parameters and it also prevents the increasing of depth. Inspired by that, we introduce the dilated convolution to derive the dilated dense network (DDN) based on the DN, as shown in Table 1 and Fig. 2(c). By widening the receptive field efficiently, a better denoising performance can be achieved (as detailed in Sect. 5.2).

4.3 Path-Widening Fusion

We further propose a path-widening fusion scheme to make the boosting unit more efficient. As shown in Table 1 and Fig. 2(d), we expand the number of forward paths to derive the DDFN from the DDN. Specifically, in a certain block, the order between the dilated convolutions (Dconv for short) and the normal convolutions (Conv for short) is exchanged in different branches. It is very likely that the Conv-ReLU-Dconv and Dconv-ReLU-Conv branches can learn different feature representations. The proposed path-widening fusion exploits the potential of these two orders at the same time, and thus promotes the possibility to learn better representations. Experimental results demonstrate that the denoising performance can be further improved in this way (as detailed in Sect. 5.2). Note that, we restrict the parameter number of DDFN not greater than DDN (i.e., about 4×10^4) to eliminate the influence of additional parameters due to path-widening fusion, and thus the efficiency of DDFN is also justified.

5   Experimental Results

5.1   Datasets and Settings

We adopt 400 images at a 180×180 resolution for training our models following TNRD [11] and DnCNN [12]. The images are partitioned into sub-image patches with a size of 50×50, and the mini-batch number is set to 64 for the stochastic gradient decent. Two widely-used datasets, "Set12" and "BSD68" [29] are employed as the benchmarks for image denoising. Moreover, to compare with the SOS algorithm [17], the "Set5" dataset is adopted following [17].

Besides grey-level image denoising, we also apply our method to two additional tasks, i.e., color image denoising and JPEG image deblocking, following the setting of DnCNN [12]. The color version of "BSD68" is adopted for the color image denoising task. And the "Classic5" and "LIVE1" datasets are adopted for evaluating the deblocking task as in [30].

We use TensorFlow and the "Adam" [31] solver for optimization with the momentum factor set as 0.9 and the coefficient of weight decay (L_2-Norm) as

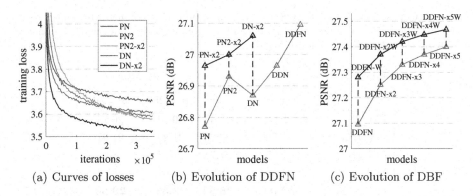

(a) Curves of losses   (b) Evolution of DDFN   (c) Evolution of DBF

Fig. 3. Illustrations of the ablation experiments. (a) The curves show the advantage of dense connection over plain structure in terms of convergence. (b) The evolution from plainly connected structure to DDFN. (c) Performance comparisons between DBF and its variants. The symbol "W" means wide and all of these models are tested on the "Set12" dataset at $\sigma = 50$

0.0001. The learning rate is decayed exponentially from 0.001 to 0.0001. We stop training when no notable decay of training loss is observed after 3.6×10^5 iterations. The algorithm proposed in [32] is adopted for initializing the weights except the last layer. Specifically, the last layer for reconstruction is initialized by the random weights drawn from Gaussian distributions with $\sigma = 0.001$. And we set zeros for initializing the biases in each convolutional layer.

5.2   Ablation Experiments of DDFN

The proposed DDFN integrates three concepts: dense connection, dilated convolution, and path-widening fusion, deriving a fundamentally different structure compared with existing models. In this section, we design extensive ablation experiments to evaluate them respectively.

Investigation of Depth (PN). We described the structure of PN in Sect. 4. To investigate the effect of depth to the boosting unit, we construct a variant of PN (named PN2) with a deeper yet thinner structure, which has the same number of parameters compared with PN. Specifically, it contains more layers (i.e., 18) in the feature integration part and less filter numbers (i.e., 16) in each layer than PN. Meanwhile, we keep the other hyper-parameters and the training procedure of PN2 the same as PN. As shown in Fig. 3(b), the deeper and thinner PN2 outperforms PN. This observation suggests that deepening the framework gives a better performance. However, when we introduce PN2 into DBF to derive PN2-x2, the advantage of plainly connected deeper structure tends to vanish.

Dense Connection (DN). We then introduce the dense connection to address the propagation issue of gradient during training. As shown in Fig. 3(a), DN converges faster than PN2. While maintaining a quicker convergence, the derived DN-x2 shows a clear advantage over PN2-x2 for a 2-stage DBF, as shown in

Table 2. Comparisons with the SOS boosting algorithm [17] combined with four classic models. DDFN-x5W is employed as a representative of our DBF. We evaluate the mean PSNR on the "Set5" dataset following [17]

Models	Original		Boosting	
	$\sigma = 25$	$\sigma = 50$	$\sigma = 25$	$\sigma = 50$
NLM [2]	29.93	26.43	30.34	26.73
K-SVD [5]	31.02	27.20	31.28	27.97
EPLL [1]	30.97	27.74	31.23	28.04
BM3D [7]	31.58	28.51	31.61	28.58
DDFN (Ours)	**32.04**	**28.93**	**32.38**	**29.50**

Fig. 3(b). Note that, the parameters of DN are 15% less than PN2, yet DN-x2 still outperforms PN2-x2.

Dilated Convolution (DDN). Based on DN, we adopt the dilated convolution to widen the receptive field. Specifically, we introduce it into two places of the network: the feature extraction part and each dense block, as shown in Fig. 2(c). The ratio of dilation is fixed to 2 for each dilated convolution layer. Experimental results demonstrate that further improvements of the boosting unit can be achieved, i.e., DDN as shown in Fig. 3(b).

Path-Widening Fusion (DDFN). As described in Sect. 4, we further propose the path-widening fusion which aggregates the concatenated features of preceding layers using a 1×1 convolution in the dense block, as shown in Fig. 2(d). This fusion can further promote the denoising performance, i.e., DDFN as shown in Fig. 3(b).

5.3 Investigation of Framework

Ablation of Subtraction and Training Scheme. As described in Sect. 3.2, the proposed DBF no longer needs an subtraction of $\hat{x}^n$ as in SOS to guarantee the iterability. We design an ablation experiment based on a 3-stage DBF. Experimental results demonstrate a better performance (+0.12 dB) without the subtraction. As for the training scheme, we consider both joint and greedy training as described in Sect. 3.2. Evaluated on a 3-stage DBF, we find joint training and greedy training give competitive performance.

Boosting - The Deeper, the Better. We investigate the performance by increasing the stage number of DBF. Experimental results demonstrate the capacity of our DBF in term of the extension in depth, as can be observed from Fig. 3(c). Specifically, a 5-stage DBF brings 0.30 dB gain compared with a single stage one.

DDFN - The Wider, the Better. Besides the exploration of depth, we also investigate the contribution of width by doubling the number of filters in each

Table 3. Comparisons of mean PSNR (dB) between our DBF and seven representative learning-based models. We evaluate the results on two widely used benchmarks (i.e., "Set12" and "BSD68"). Best results reported in the corresponding papers are presented

Dataset	σ	MLP [10]	CSF [8]	GCRF [33]	TNRD [11]	NLNet [34]	DeepAM [35]	DnCNN [12]	DDFN/-x5W
Set12	15	-	32.32	-	32.50	-	-	32.86	32.73 **32.98**
	25	30.03	29.84	-	30.06	-	30.40	30.44	30.33 **30.60**
	50	26.78	-	-	26.81	-	-	27.18	27.10 **27.46**
BSD68	15	-	31.24	31.43	31.42	31.52	31.68	31.73	31.66 **31.83**
	25	28.96	28.74	28.89	28.92	29.03	29.21	29.23	29.16 **29.35**
	50	26.03	-	-	25.97	26.07	26.24	26.23	26.19 **26.42**

(a) Original   (b) Noisy   (c) KSVD/25.87 dB   (d) NCSR/26.60 dB

(e) BM3D/26.72 dB   (f) TNRD/26.81 dB   (g) DnCNN/27.18 dB   (h) Ours/27.46 dB

Fig. 4. Visual comparisons of the image "Couple" from the "Set12" dataset at $\sigma = 50$

layer of DDFN (deriving models with the symbol "W"). Experimental results in Fig. 3(c) demonstrate that widening can further enhance the performance.

5.4 Comparison with State-of-the-Art Methods

Comparison with the SOS Algorithm. We adopt four classical models [1, 2,5,7] and their corresponding SOS [17] variants for comparison. As shown in Table 2, our boosting unit DDFN has a clear advantage over these classic models, e.g., +0.46 dB when $\sigma = 25$ and +0.42 dB when $\sigma = 50$ than BM3D [7]) on the "Set5" dataset. With the proposed DBF, our DDFN-x5W achieves notable improvements over BM3D-SOS [17], i.e., +0.77 dB ($\sigma = 25$) and +0.92 dB ($\sigma = 50$).

Table 4. Comparisons for the blind Gaussian denoising (grey-level). We evaluate the mean PSNR (dB) on the "Set12" dataset

Models / σ	5	10	15	20	25	30	35	40	45	50
BM3D [7]	38.03	34.38	32.37	31.01	29.97	29.13	28.40	27.65	27.19	26.72
DnCNN-B [12]	37.70	34.53	32.68	31.38	30.36	29.53	28.83	28.22	27.69	27.21
DDFN-B	37.31	34.30	32.45	31.15	30.13	29.30	28.60	27.98	27.44	26.96
DDFN-x5W-B	**38.14**	**34.76**	**32.86**	**31.55**	**30.54**	**29.71**	**29.02**	**28.41**	**27.87**	**27.44**

Table 5. Comparisons for the blind color image denoising. We evaluate the mean PSNR (dB) on the color version of "BSD68" dataset. A color variant of DDFN-x3W is adopted as the representative to compared with CBM3D [36] and DnCNN-B [12]

Models / σ	5	10	15	20	25	30	35	40	45	50
CBM3D [36]	40.24	35.91	33.52	31.91	30.71	29.73	28.89	28.09	27.84	27.38
DnCNN-B [12]	40.10	36.12	33.89	32.37	31.23	30.32	29.58	28.95	28.40	27.92
DDFN-x3W-B	**40.47**	**36.42**	**34.17**	**32.65**	**31.52**	**30.62**	**29.88**	**29.26**	**28.72**	**28.26**

(a) Original   (b) Noisy   (c) CBM3D/28.86 dB   (d) CDnCNN/29.46 dB   (e) Ours/29.92 dB

Fig. 5. Visual comparisons of an image from the "BSD68" dataset at $\sigma = 35$

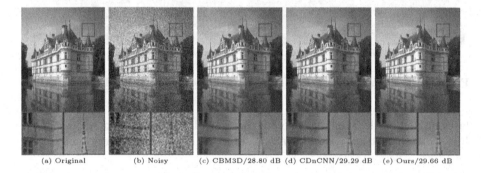

(a) Original   (b) Noisy   (c) CBM3D/28.80 dB   (d) CDnCNN/29.29 dB   (e) Ours/29.66 dB

Fig. 6. Visual comparisons of an image from the "BSD68" dataset at $\sigma = 45$

Comparison with Other Learning-Based Models. We adopt seven representative models for comparison: MLP [10], CSF [8], GCRF [33], TNRD [11], NLNet [34], DeepAM [35] and DnCNN [12]. The restoration results of our DDFN and DDFN-x5W are listed in Table 3 to compare with them. Specifically, DDFN-

Table 6. Compression of the JPEG image deblocking. We evaluate the mean PSNR (dB) and SSIM on the "Classic5" and "LIVE1" datasets in terms of four quality factors (QF). All methods are implemented using officially available codes

Dataset	QF	AR-CNN [30]	TNRD [11]	DnCNN [12]	DDFN-x3W
		PSNR / SSIM	PSNR / SSIM	PSNR / SSIM	PSNR / SSIM
Classic5	10	29.03 / 0.7929	29.28 / 0.7992	29.40 / 0.8026	**29.55 / 0.8086**
	20	31.15 / 0.8517	31.47 / 0.8576	31.63 / 0.8610	**31.70 / 0.8636**
	30	32.51 / 0.8806	32.78 / 0.8837	32.91 / 0.8861	**33.03 / 0.8881**
	40	33.34 / 0.8953	-	33.77 / 0.9003	**33.90 / 0.9023**
LIVE1	10	28.96 / 0.8076	29.15 / 0.8111	29.19 / 0.8123	**29.39 / 0.8186**
	20	31.29 / 0.8733	31.46 / 0.8769	31.59 / 0.8802	**31.76 / 0.8839**
	30	32.67 / 0.9043	32.84 / 0.9059	32.98 / 0.9090	**33.19 / 0.9117**
	40	33.63 / 0.9198	-	33.96 / 0.9247	**34.20 / 0.9273**

(a) JPEG   (b) AR-CNN/29.63 dB   (c) TNRD/29.75 dB   (d) DnCNN/29.82 dB   (e) Ours/30.12 dB

Fig. 7. Visual comparisons of an image from the "LIVE1" dataset at QF = 10

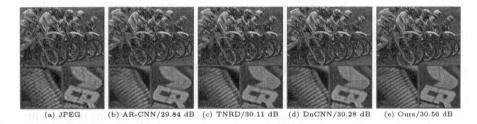

(a) JPEG   (b) AR-CNN/29.84 dB   (c) TNRD/30.11 dB   (d) DnCNN/30.28 dB   (e) Ours/30.56 dB

Fig. 8. Visual comparisons of an image from the "LIVE1" dataset at QF = 20

x5W achieves a superior performance than TNRD [11] (+0.65 dB) and DnCNN [12] (+0.28 dB) on the "Set12" dataset when $\sigma = 50$.

Comparison for Blind Gaussian Denoising. Following the settings of training proposed in [12], we re-train our models to derive the DDFN-B and DDFN-x5W-B for blind Gaussian denoising. We adopt the BM3D [7] and the variant of DnCNN (i.e., DnCNN-B [12]) for comparison. Experimental results listed in

Table 7. Comparison of runtime (s) for Gaussian image denoising on the "Set12" dataset with respect to different resolutions. All methods are implemented using officially available codes

Resolution	K-SVD	EPLL	BM3D	MLP	CSF	TNRD	DnCNN	Ours
256×256	71.886	19.352	0.369	1.211	1.006	1.125	0.061	**0.051**
512×512	56.689	90.184	1.561	3.486	2.491	2.238	0.212	**0.156**

Table 4 demonstrate the superiority of our model within a wide range of noise levels. Specifically, when the noise level is small (i.e., $\sigma = 5$), our proposed DDFN-x5W-B has a clear advantage (+0.44 dB) over DnCNN-B. We also evaluate the performance on the task of blind color image denoising. Experimental results listed in Table 5 demonstrate the advantage of our proposed DBF.

Comparison for JPEG Image Deblocking. We also evaluate our model on the task of image deblocking. Three representative models: AR-CNN [30], TNRD [11], and DnCNN [12] are adopted for comparison. Experimental results listed in Table 6 demonstrate the superiority of our model over existing ones.

Running Time. Although the cascaded structure of our proposed DBF involves more computation than a single stage one (which is the inevitable cost of boosting), it is still quite efficient. Detailed results are listed in Table 7.

Visual Comparison. To evaluate the perceptual quality of restoration, we show a few examples including grey-level denoising (Fig. 4), blind color image denoising (Figs. 5 and 6), and image deblocking (Figs. 7 and 8). As can be seen, our model performs better than the competitors in both the smooth and edge regions.

6   Conclusions

In this paper, we propose the DBF which first integrates the boosting algorithm with deep learning for image denoising. To fully exploit the potential of this framework, we elaborate the lightweight yet efficient DDFN as the boosting unit. By introducing the dense connection, we address the vanishing of gradients during training. Based on the densely connected structure, we further propose the path-widening fusion cooperated with the dilated convolution to optimize the DDFN for efficiency. Compared with the existing models, our DDFN-based DBF achieves the state-of-the-art performance in both non-blind and blind image denoising on widely used benchmarks.

Besides the scenario of image denoising, the proposed DBF can be readily generalized to other image restoration tasks, e.g., image deblocking, as demonstrated in this paper. Also, the idea of path-widening fusion is demonstrated to be useful in the task of spectral reconstruction from RGB images [37]. We believe the proposed method could inspire even more low-level vision applications.

Acknowledgements. We acknowledge funding from National Key R&D Program of China under Grant 2017YFA0700800, and Natural Science Foundation of China under Grants 61671419 and 61425026.

References

1. Zoran, D., Weiss, Y.: From learning models of natural image patches to whole image restoration. In: IEEE International Conference on Computer Vision (ICCV), pp. 479–486 (2011)
2. Buades, A., Coll, B., Morel, J.M.: A non-local algorithm for image denoising. In: IEEE Conference on Computer Vision and Pattern Recognition (CVPR), vol. 2, pp. 60–65, June 2005
3. Buades, A., Coll, B., Morel, J.: Nonlocal image and movie denoising. Int. J. Comput. Vis. (IJCV) **76**(2), 123–139 (2008)
4. Mairal, J., Bach, F., Ponce, J., Sapiro, G., Zisserman, A.: Non-local sparse models for image restoration. In: IEEE International Conference on Computer Vision (ICCV), pp. 2272–2279 (2009)
5. Elad, M., Aharon, M.: Image denoising via sparse and redundant representations over learned dictionaries. IEEE Trans. Image Process. **15**(12), 3736–3745 (2006)
6. Dong, W., Zhang, L., Shi, G., Li, X.: Nonlocally centralized sparse representation for image restoration. IEEE Trans. Image Process. **22**(4), 1620–1630 (2013)
7. Dabov, K., Foi, A., Katkovnik, V., Egiazarian, K.: Image denoising by sparse 3-D transform-domain collaborative filtering. IEEE Trans. Image Process. **16**(8), 2080–2095 (2007)
8. Schmidt, U., Roth, S.: Shrinkage fields for effective image restoration. In: IEEE Conference on Computer Vision and Pattern Recognition (CVPR), pp. 2774–2781, June 2014
9. Gu, S., Zhang, L., Zuo, W., Feng, X.: Weighted nuclear norm minimization with application to image denoising. In: IEEE Conference on Computer Vision and Pattern Recognition (CVPR), pp. 2862–2869, June 2014
10. Burger, H.C., Schuler, C.J., Harmeling, S.: Image denoising: can plain neural networks compete with BM3D? In: IEEE Conference on Computer Vision and Pattern Recognition (CVPR), pp. 2392–2399, June 2012
11. Chen, Y., Pock, T.: Trainable nonlinear reaction diffusion: a flexible framework for fast and effective image restoration. IEEE Trans. Patt. Anal. Mach. Intell. **39**(6), 1256 (2017)
12. Zhang, K., Zuo, W., Chen, Y., Meng, D., Zhang, L.: Beyond a gaussian denoiser: residual learning of deep CNN for image denoising. IEEE Trans. Image Process. **26**(7), 3142–3155 (2017)
13. Remez, T., Litany, O., Giryes, R., Bronstein, A.M.: Deep class-aware image denoising. In: International Conference on Sampling Theory and Applications (SampTA), pp. 138–142, July 2017
14. Charest, M.R., Elad, M., Milanfar, P.: A general iterative regularization framework for image denoising. In: Conference on Information Sciences and Systems, pp. 452–457, March 2006
15. Milanfar, P.: A tour of modern image filtering: new insights and methods, both practical and theoretical. IEEE Sig. Process. Mag. **30**(1), 106–128 (2013)
16. Talebi, H., Zhu, X., Milanfar, P.: How to SAIF-ly boost denoising performance. IEEE Trans. Image Process. **22**(4), 1470–1485 (2013)

17. Romano, Y., Elad, M.: Boosting of image denoising algorithms. SIAM J. Imaging Sci. **8**(2), 1187–1219 (2015)
18. Huang, G., Liu, Z., van der Maaten, L., Weinberger, K.Q.: Densely connected convolutional networks. In: IEEE Conference on Computer Vision and Pattern Recognition (CVPR), pp. 2261–2269, July 2017
19. Yu, F., Koltun, V.: Multi-scale context aggregation by dilated convolutions. In: International Conference on Learning Representations (ICLR) (2016)
20. Ioffe, S., Szegedy, C.: Batch normalization: accelerating deep network training by reducing internal covariate shift. In: International Conference on Machine Learning (ICML), pp. 448–456 (2015)
21. He, K., Zhang, X., Ren, S., Sun, J.: Deep residual learning for image recognition. In: IEEE Conference on Computer Vision and Pattern Recognition (CVPR), pp. 770–778, June 2016
22. Buades, A., Coll, B., Morel, J.M.: A review of image denoising algorithms, with a new one. SIAM J. Multiscale Model. Simul. **4**(2), 490–530 (2005)
23. Han, S., Meng, Z., Khan, A.S., Tong, Y.: Incremental boosting convolutional neural network for facial action unit recognition. In: Lee, D.D., Sugiyama, M., Luxburg, U.V., Guyon, I., Garnett, R. (eds.) Advances in Neural Information Processing Systems (NIPS), pp. 109–117. Curran Associates, Inc. (2016)
24. Moghimi, M., Saberian, M., Yang, J., Li, L.J., Vasconcelos, N., Belongie, S.: Boosted convolutional neural networks. In: British Machine Vision Conference (BMVC), pp. 24.1–24.13 (2016)
25. Nair, V., Hinton, G.E.: Rectified linear units improve restricted Boltzmann machines. In: International Conference on Machine Learning (ICML), pp. 807–814 (2010)
26. Szegedy, C., Vanhoucke, V., Ioffe, S., Shlens, J., Wojna, Z.: Rethinking the inception architecture for computer vision. In: IEEE Conference on Computer Vision and Pattern Recognition (CVPR), pp. 2818–2826, June 2016
27. Kim, J., Lee, J.K., Lee, K.M.: Accurate image super-resolution using very deep convolutional networks. In: IEEE Conference on Computer Vision and Pattern Recognition (CVPR), pp. 1646–1654, June 2016
28. Yu, F., Koltun, V., Funkhouser, T.: Dilated residual networks. In: IEEE Conference on Computer Vision and Pattern Recognition (CVPR), pp. 636–644, July 2017
29. Roth, S., Black, M.J.: Fields of experts: a framework for learning image priors. In: IEEE Conference on Computer Vision and Pattern Recognition (CVPR), vol. 2, pp. 860–867, June 2005
30. Dong, C., Deng, Y., Loy, C.C., Tang, X.: Compression artifacts reduction by a deep convolutional network. In: IEEE International Conference on Computer Vision (ICCV), pp. 576–584, December 2015
31. Kingma, D., Ba, J.: Adam: a method for stochastic optimization. In: International Conference on Learning Representations (ICLR), vol. 5 (2015)
32. He, K., Zhang, X., Ren, S., Sun, J.: Delving deep into rectifiers: surpassing human-level performance on ImageNet classification. In: IEEE International Conference on Computer Vision (ICCV), pp. 1026–1034, December 2015
33. Vemulapalli, R., Tuzel, O., Liu, M.Y.: Deep Gaussian conditional random field network: a model-based deep network for discriminative denoising. In: IEEE Conference on Computer Vision and Pattern Recognition (CVPR), pp. 4801–4809, June 2016
34. Lefkimmiatis, S.: Non-local color image denoising with convolutional neural networks. In: IEEE Conference on Computer Vision and Pattern Recognition (CVPR), pp. 5882–5891, July 2017

35. Kim, Y., Jung, H., Min, D., Sohn, K.: Deeply aggregated alternating minimization for image restoration. In: IEEE Conference on Computer Vision and Pattern Recognition (CVPR), pp. 284–292, July 2017
36. Dabov, K., Foi, A., Katkovnik, V., Egiazarian, K.: Color image denoising via sparse 3D collaborative filtering with grouping constraint in luminance-chrominance space. In: IEEE International Conference on Image Processing (ICIP), vol. 1, I-313–I-316, September 2007
37. Shi, Z., Chen, C., Xiong, Z., Liu, D., Wu, F.: HSCNN+: advanced CNN-based hyperspectral recovery from RGB images. In: IEEE Conference on Computer Vision and Pattern Recognition (CVPR) Workshops, June 2018

Self-Supervised Relative Depth Learning for Urban Scene Understanding

Huaizu Jiang[1]($\boxtimes$), Gustav Larsson[2], Michael Maire[2,3], Greg Shakhnarovich[3], and Erik Learned-Miller[1]

[1] UMass Amherst, Amherst, USA
{hzjiang,elm}@cs.umass.edu
[2] University of Chicago, Chicago, USA
{larsson,mmaire}@cs.uchicago.edu
[3] TTI-Chicago, Chicago, USA
gregory@ttic.edu

Abstract. As an agent moves through the world, the apparent motion of scene elements is (usually) inversely proportional to their depth (Strictly speaking, this statement is true only after one has compensated for camera rotation, individual object motion, and image position. We address these issues in the paper). It is natural for a learning agent to associate image patterns with the magnitude of their displacement over time: as the agent moves, faraway mountains don't move much; nearby trees move a lot. This natural relationship between the appearance of objects and their motion is a rich source of information about the world. In this work, we start by training a deep network, using fully automatic supervision, to predict relative scene depth from *single images*. The relative depth training images are automatically derived from simple videos of cars moving through a scene, using recent motion segmentation techniques, and no human-provided labels. The *proxy* task of predicting relative depth from a single image induces features in the network that result in large improvements in a set of downstream tasks including semantic segmentation, joint road segmentation and car detection, and monocular (absolute) depth estimation, over a network trained from scratch. The improvement on the semantic segmentation task is greater than that produced by any other automatically supervised methods. Moreover, for monocular depth estimation, our unsupervised pre-training method even outperforms supervised pre-training with ImageNet. In addition, we demonstrate benefits from learning to predict (again, completely unsupervised) relative depth in the specific videos associated with various downstream tasks (*e.g.*, KITTI). We adapt to the specific scenes in those tasks in an unsupervised manner to improve performance. In summary, for semantic segmentation, we present state-of-the-art results among methods that do not use supervised pre-training, and we even exceed the performance of supervised ImageNet pre-trained models for monocular depth estimation, achieving results that are comparable with state-of-the-art methods.

Electronic supplementary material The online version of this chapter (https://doi.org/10.1007/978-3-030-01252-6_2) contains supplementary material, which is available to authorized users.

Keywords: Self-supervised learning · Unsupervised domain adaptation · Urban scene understanding · Semantic segmentation Monocular depth estimation

1 Introduction

How does a newborn agent learn about the world? When an animal (or robot) moves, its visual system is exposed to a shower of information. Usually, the speed with which something moves in the image is inversely proportional to its depth.[1] As an agent continues to experience visual stimuli under its own motion, it is natural for it to form associations between the appearance of objects and their relative motion in the image. For example, an agent may learn that objects that look like mountains typically don't move in the image (or change appearance much) as the agent moves. Objects like nearby buildings and bushes, however, appear to move rapidly in the image as the agent changes position relative to them. This continuous pairing of images with motion acts as a kind of automatic supervision that could eventually allow an agent both to understand the depth of objects and to group pixels into objects by this predicted depth. Thus, by moving through the world, an agent may learn to predict properties (such as depth) of *static* scenes.

A flurry of recent work has shown that *proxy tasks* (also known as *pretext* or *surrogate tasks*) such as colorization [3,4], jigsaw puzzles [5], and others [6–13], can induce features in a neural network that provide strong pre-training for subsequent tasks. In this paper, we introduce a new proxy task: estimation of relative depth from a single image. We show that a network that has been pre-trained, without human supervision, to predict relative scene depth provides a powerful starting point from which to fine-tune models for a variety of urban

(a)   (b)   (c)   (d)   (e)

Fig. 1. Sample frames from collected videos and their corresponding relative depth maps, where brightness encodes relative depth (the brighter the farther). From top to bottom: input image, relative depth image computed using Eq. (3), and predicted (relative) depth maps using our trained VGG16 FCN8s [1,2]. There is often a black blob around the center of the image, a singularity in depth estimation caused by the focus of expansion. (a) (b) (c): images from the CityDriving dataset, (d): images from the KITTI dataset, and (e): images from the CityScapes dataset.

scene understanding tasks. Not only does this automatically supervised start-ing point outperform all other proxy task pre-training methods. For monocular depth understanding, it even performs better than the heavily supervised Ima-geNet pre-training, yielding results that are comparable with state-of-the-art methods.

To estimate relative scene depths without human supervision, we use a recent motion segmentation technique [14] to estimate relative depth from geometric constraints between a scene's motion field and the camera motion. We apply it to simple, publicly available YouTube videos taken from moving cars. Since this technique estimates depth *up to an unknown scale factor*, we compute *relative depth* of the scene during the pre-training phase, where each pixel's value is in the range of $[0, 1]$ denoting its depth percentile over the entire image.[1]

Unlike work that analyzes video paired with additional information about direction of motion [15], our agent learns from "raw egomotion" video recorded from cars moving through the world. Unlike methods that require videos of mov-ing objects [8], we neither depend on, nor are disrupted by, moving objects in the video. Once we have relative depth estimates for these video images, we train a deep network to predict the relative depth of each pixel from a *single image, i.e.,* to predict the relative depth *without* the benefit of motion. One might expect such a network to learn that an image patch that looks like a house and spans 20 pixels of an image (about 100 m away) is significantly farther away than a pedestrian that spans 100 image pixels (perhaps 10 m away). Figure 1 illustrates this prediction task and shows sample results obtained using a standard convolu-tional neural network (CNN) in this setting. For example, in the leftmost image of Fig. 1, an otherwise unremarkable traffic-light pole is clearly highlighted by its relative depth profile, which stands out from the background. Our hypothesis is that to excel at relative depth estimation, the CNN will benefit by learning to recognize such structures.

The goal of our work is to show that pre-training a network to do relative depth prediction is a powerful proxy task for learning visual representations. In particular, we show that a network pre-trained for relative depth prediction (from automatically generated training data) improves training for downstream tasks including semantic segmentation, joint semantic reasoning of road segmen-tation and car detection, and monocular (absolute) depth estimation. We obtain significant performance gains on urban scene understanding benchmarks such as KITTI [16,17] and CityScapes [18], compared to training a segmentation model from scratch. Compared to nine other proxy tasks for pre-training, our proxy task consistently provides the highest gains when used for pre-training. In fact, our performance on semantic segmentation and joint semantic reasoning tasks comes close to that of equivalent architectures pre-trained with ImageNet [19], a massive labeled dataset. Finally, for the monocular (absolute) depth estimation, *our pre-trained model achieves better performance than an ImageNet pre-trained model,* using both VGG16 [1] and ResNet50 [20] architectures.

---

[1] Later, we will fine-tune networks to produce absolute depths.

As a final application, we show how our proxy task can be used for *domain adaptation*. One might assume that the more similar the domain of unlabeled visual data used for the proxy task (here, three urban scene understanding tasks) is to the domain in which the eventual semantic task is defined (here, semantic segmentation), the better the representation learned by pre-training. This observation allows us to go beyond simple pre-training, and effectively provide a domain adaptation mechanism. By adapting (fine-tuning) a relative depth prediction model to targets obtained from unlabeled data in a novel domain (say, driving in a new city) we can improve the underlying representation, priming it for better performance on a semantic task (*e.g.*, segmentation) trained with a small labeled dataset from this new domain. In experiments, we show that pre-training on unlabeled videos from a target city, absent any labeled data from that city, consistently improves all urban scene understanding tasks.

In total, our work advances two pathways for integrating unlabeled data with visual learning.

- We propose a novel proxy task for self-supervised learning of visual representations; it is based on learning to predict relative depth, inferred from unlabeled videos. This unsupervised pre-training leads to better results over all other proxy tasks on the semantic segmentation task, and even outperforms supervised ImageNet pre-training for absolute depth estimation.
- We show that our task can be used to drive domain adaptation. Experiments demonstrate its utility in scene understanding tasks for street scenes in a novel city. Our adapted model achieves results that are competitive with state-of-the-art methods (including those that use *large supervised pre-training*) on the KITTI depth estimation benchmark.

Such methods of extracting knowledge from unlabeled data are likely to be increasingly important as computer vision scales to real-world applications; here massive dataset size can outpace herculean annotation efforts.

2   Related Work

Self-supervised Learning. The idea of formulating supervised prediction tasks on unlabeled data has been leveraged for both images and videos. The idea, often called self-supervision, is most typically realized by removing part of the input and then training a network to predict it. This can take the form of deleting a spatial region and trying to inpaint it [10], draining an image of color and trying to colorize it [3,4,21], or removing the final frame in a sequence and trying to hallucinate it [22–27]. Generative Adversarial Networks, used for inpainting and several future frame prediction methods, can also be used to generate realistic-looking samples from scratch. This has found secondary utility for unsupervised representation learning [28–30]. Another strategy is to extract patches and try to predict their spatial or temporal relationship. In images, this has been done for pairs of patches [31] or for 3-by-3 jigsaw puzzles [5]. In videos, it can be done by predicting the temporal ordering of frames [9,13]. The correlation of frames in video is also a rich source of self-supervised learning signals. The assumption that close-by frames are more similar than far apart frames can be used to train embeddings on pairs [32–34] or triplets [6] of frames. A related idea that the representation of interesting objects should change slowly through time dates back to Slow Feature Analysis [35].

The works most closely related to ours may be [7,8,15], which aim to learn useful visual representations from unlabeled videos as well. Jayaraman & Grauman [15] learn a representation equivariant to ego-motion transformations, using ideas from metric learning. Agrawal *et al.* [7] concurrently developed a similar method that uses the ego-motion directly as the prediction target as opposed to as input to an equivariant transformation. Both of these works assume knowledge of the agent's own motor actions, which limits their evaluation in sample size due to lack of publicly available data. In our work, the ego-motion is inferred through optical flow, which means we can leverage large sources of crowd-sourced data, such as YouTube videos. Pathak *et al.* [8] use optical flow and a graph-based algorithm to produce unsupervised segmentation maps. A network is then trained to approximate these maps, driving representation learning. The reliance on moving objects, as opposed to a moving agent, could make it harder to collect good data. Using a method based on ego-motion, the agent can promote its own representation, learning simply by moving, instead of having to find objects that move.

There is also work on using multi-modal sensory input as a source of supervision. Owens *et al.* [12] predict statistics of ambient sounds in videos. Beyond studying a single source of self-supervision, combining multiple self-supervision sources is increasingly popular. In [36], a set of self-supervision tasks are integrated via a multi-task setting. Wang *et al.* [37] propose to combine instance-level as well as category-level self-supervision. Both [36,37] achieve better performance than a single model.

Unsupervised Learning of Monocular Depth Estimation. A single-image depth predictor can be trained from raw stereo images, by warping the right image with a depth map predicted from the left and training it to reconstruct the left image [38,39]. This idea was extended in recent work to support fully self-supervised training on regular video, by predicting both depth and camera pose difference for pairs of nearby frames [40,41].

Although [40,41] are closely related to our work in the sense of unsupervised (or self-supervised) learning of depth and ego-motion from unlabeled videos, our work differs from them in two ways. First, neither of these two works emphasizes more general-purpose feature learning. Second, neither of them demonstrates their scalability to large-scale YouTube videos. [40] requires intrinsic camera parameters that are not available for most YouTube videos; our approach relies on optical flow only. [41] only reports experimental results on standard benchmark datasets, whose scale is an order of magnitude smaller than videos we use. It is unclear whether the heuristics (*e.g.*, the manually set camera intrinsic parameters, number of motion clusters) are robust to YouTube videos in the wild.

3   Inducing Features by Learning to Estimate Relative Depth

As a proxy task, our goal is to induce a feature representation $f(I)$ of an RGB image $I(x, y)$ by predicting its depth image $z(x, y)$, where the representation $f(I)$ could be transferred to other downstream tasks (*e.g.*, semantic segmentation) with fine-tuning. In Sect. 3.1, we introduce technical details of gathering images and corresponding depth maps. In Sect. 3.2, we provide details of training CNNs to learn the feature representation $f(I)$.

3.1   Self-Supervised Relative Depth

As described above, we automatically produce depth images for video frames by analyzing the motion of pre-existing videos. In our experiments, we used three sets of videos: YouTube videos, videos from the KITTI database [16,17], and videos from the CityScapes database [18]. The YouTube videos consist of 135 videos taken from moving cars in major U.S. cities.[2] We call this dataset City-Driving. The stability of the camera in these videos makes them relatively easy for the depth estimation procedure. Some of the videos are extremely long, lasting several hours. The CityDriving dataset features a large number of man-made structures, pedestrians and cars. Following [42], we only keep two consecutive frames if they have moderate motion (*i.e.*, neither too slow nor too fast). To eliminate near duplicate frames, two consecutive depth maps must be at least 2 frames apart. We keep only the first one of two consecutive frames and the computed depth image. In total, we gathered 1.1M pairs of RGB images and their corresponding depth maps, where the typical resolution is 640 × 360. Similarly, we collect 30 K and 24 K pairs of RGB images and their relative depth maps for CityScapes and KITTI, respectively.

Denote the instantaneous coordinates of a point P in the environment by $(X, Y, Z)^T$, and the translational velocity of the camera in the environment by $(U, V, W)^T$. Let the motion field component (idealized optical flow) of the point P (in the image plane) be (u, v), corresponding to the horizontal and vertical image motion, respectively. The motion field can be written as the sum of translation and rotation components[3]

$$u = u_t + u_r, \quad v = v_t + v_r, \tag{1}$$

where the subscript t and r denote translation and rotation, respectively. According to the geometry of perspective projection [43], the following equations hold if the motion of the camera is purely translational,

$$u_t = \frac{-U + xW}{Z}, \quad v_t = \frac{-V + yW}{Z}, \tag{2}$$

---

[2] They are crawled from a YouTube playlist, taking less than an hour.

[3] Any motion in the image is due to the relative motion of a world point and the camera. This addresses motion of the object, the camera, or both.

where x and y are the coordinates of the point P in the image plane (the origin is at the image center).

Note that the depth Z can be estimated from either one of these equations. However, the estimate can be unstable if either u_t or v_t is small. To obtain a more robust estimate of Z, we square the two equations above and add them:

$$Z = \sqrt{\frac{(-U + xW)^2 + (-V + yW)^2}{u_t^2 + v_t^2}}. \tag{3}$$

Because we can only recover $(U, V, W)^T$ up to scale (see below), we can only compute the depth map of an image up to scale. To induce feature representations, we use depth orderings of pixels in an image. We compute the relative depth $z \in [0, 1]$ of the pixel P as its depth percentile (divided by 100) across all estimated depth values for the image. Since these percentiles are invariant to the velocity's unknown scale, we do not need to recover the absolute scale of velocity. Examples of these automatically obtained depth maps are given in Figs. 1 and 2.

To compute the optical flow, we use the state-of-the-art unsupervised method [44]. It first computes sparse pixel matchings between two video frames. It then interpolates to get dense pixelwise optical flow fields from sparse matchings, where we replace the supervised edge detector [45] with its unsupervised version [42]. Based on the optical flow, we use the method proposed in [14] to recover the image motion of each pixel due to translational motion only (u_t, v_t), and also, the global camera motion $(U, V, W)^T$ up to an unknown scale factor. Specifically, the rotation of the camera can be estimated by finding the rotation such that the remaining motion, by removing the rotational component from the motion field, can be well-explained by angle fields, which are the angle part of the motion field. This procedure produces a translational optical flow field (u_t, v_t),

Fig. 2. Samples of image pairs and computed translational optical flow that we use to recover the relative depth. From left to right: first images, second images, translational optical flow between input two images, and relative depth of the first images.

and a set of regions in the image corresponding to the background and different object motions, along with the motion directions (U, V, W) of those regions. We refer readers to [14] for more technical details.

In summary, to obtain the depth map of each frame from a video, we:

- compute the optical flow (u, v) between a pair of frames [44];
- estimate the translational component (u_t, v_t) of the optical flow and the direction of camera translation (U, V, W) from the optical flow, using the method of [14];
- estimate the scene depth Z using Eq. 3, up to an unknown scale factor, from the translational component of the optical flow and the camera direction estimate and convert it to relative depth $z \in [0, 1]$.

3.2 Predicting Relative Depth from a Single Image

While a CNN for predicting depth from a single image is a core component of our system, we are primarily interested in relative depth prediction as a proxy task, rather than an end in itself. We therefore select standard CNN architectures and focus on quantifying the power of the depth task for pre-training and domain adaptation, compared to using the same networks with labeled data. Specifically, we work with variants of the standard AlexNet [46], VGG16 [1], and ResNet50 [20] architectures.

Given an RGB image I, we need pixelwise predictions in the form of a depth image z, so we modify both AlexNet, VGG16, and ResNet50 to produce outputs with the same spatial resolution as the input image. In particular, we consider Fully Convolutional Networks (FCNs) [2] and an encoder-decoder with skip connections [39, 40]. Detailed discussions can be found in the experiment section.

Since the relative depth (*i.e.*, the depth percentile) is estimated over the entire image, it is essential to feed the entire image to the CNN to make a prediction. For CityDriving and KITTI, we simply resize the input image to 224 × 416 and 352 × 1212. For CityScapes, we discard the bottom 20% portion or so of each video frame containing mainly the hood of a car, which remains static over all videos and makes the relative depth estimation inaccurate (recall our relative depth estimation is mainly based on motion information). The cropped input image is then resized to 384 × 992. During training, we employ horizontal flipping and color jittering for data augmentation. Since relative depth serves as a proxy, rather than an end task, even though the relative depth estimation is not always correct, the network is able to tolerate some degree of noise as shown in [8]; we can then repurpose the network's learned representation.

In all experiments, we use L_1 loss for each pixel when training for depth prediction, *i.e.*, we train networks to regress the relative depth values. All AlexNet, VGG16, and ResNet50 variants are trained for 30 epochs using the Adam optimizer [47] with momentum of $\beta_1 = 0.9, \beta_2 = 0.999$, and weight decay of 0.0005. The learning rate is 0.0001 and is held constant during the pre-training stage.

4   Experiments

We consider three urban scene understanding tasks: semantic segmentation, joint semantic reasoning consisting of road segmentation and object detection [48], and monocular absolute depth estimation.

4.1   Semantic Segmentation

We consider three datasets commonly used for evaluating semantic segmentation. Their main characteristics are summarized below:

KITTI [49]: 100 training images, 46 testing images, spatial dimensions of 370×1226, 11 classes.

CamVid [50,51]: 367 training images, 101 validation images, 233 testing images, spatial dimensions of 720×960, 11 classes.

CityScapes [18]: 2975 training images, 500 validation images, 1525 testing images, spatial dimensions of 1024×2048, 19 classes. We conduct experiments on images at half resolution.

The first two datasets are much too small to provide sufficient data for "from scratch" training of a deep model; CityScapes is larger, but we show below that all three datasets benefit from pre-training. We use the curated annotations of the CamVid dataset released by [53]. As a classical CNN-based model for semantic segmentation, we report results of different variants of the Fully Convolutional Network (FCN) [2].

We compare our results to those obtained with other self-supervision strategies surveyed in Sect. 2. Since only AlexNet pre-trained models are available for

Table 1. Comparisons of mean IoU scores of AlexNet FCN32s for semantic segmentation using different self-supervised models. CS = CityScapes, K = KITTI, CV = CamVid

Pre-training method	Supervision source	CS	K	CV
Supervised	ImageNet labels	**48.1**	**46.2**	**57.4**
None	-	40.7	39.6	44.0
Tracking [6]	Motion	41.9	42.1	50.5
Moving [7]	Ego-motion	41.3	40.9	49.7
Watch-move [8]	Motion seg.	41.5	40.8	51.7
Frame-order [9]	Motion	41.5	39.7	49.6
Context [10]	Appearance	39.7	-[a]	37.8
Object-centric [11]	Appearance	39.6	39.1	48.0
Colorization [3,21]	Appearance (color)	42.9	35.8	53.2
Cross-channel [52]	Misc	36.8	40.8	46.3
Audio [12]	Video soundtrack	39.6	40.7	51.5
Ours	Depth	**45.4**	**42.6**	**53.4**

[a] We were unable to get meaningful results of [10] on KITTI.

most of the previous self-supervised methods, we also train an AlexNet. During training, the inputs are random crops of 352×352 for KITTI and 704×704 for CamVid. Each FCN32s using different pre-training models is trained for 600 epochs with a batch size of 16 using 4 GPUs. For CityScapes, the inputs to the network are random crops of 512×512. Each FCN32s is trained for 400 epochs with a batch size of 16. In addition to the random crops, random horizontal flips and color jittering are also performed. The CNNs at this stage (learning segmentation) are trained or fine-tuned using the Adam optimizer, where weight decay is 0.0005. For the learning rate, we use 0.0001 and decrease it by a factor of 10 at the 400th epoch (300th epoch for CityScapes).

Quantitative comparisons can be found in Table 1.[4] Our pre-trained model performs significantly better than the model learned from scratch on all three datasets, validating the effectiveness of our pre-training. Moreover, we obtain new state-of-the-art results on all three urban scene segmentation datasets among methods that use self-supervised pre-training. In particular, our model outperforms all other self-supervised models with motion cues (the first four self-supervised models in Table 1).

4.2   Ablation Studies

We perform ablation studies using VGG16 FCN32s on the semantic segmentation datasets. Specifically, we study the following aspects.

Number of Pre-training Images. Figure 3(a) demonstrates that the performance of our depth pre-trained model scales linearly with the log of the number of pre-training images on CamVid, which is similar to the conclusion of [8].

On KITTI, our pre-trained model initially has a big performance boost when the number of pre-training images increases from 1 K to 10K. With enough data (more than 10K), the performance also scales linearly with the log of the number of pre-training images.

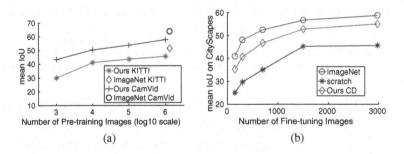

(a)   (b)

Fig. 3. Ablation studies of performance by (a) varying number of pre-training images on KITTI and CamVid, (b) varying number of fine-tuning images of CityScapes.

---

[4] We were unable to get meaningful results with [10] on KITTI and with [15] on all three segmentation datasets.

Number of Fine-Tuning Images. Figure 3(b) shows that every model (ImageNet, scratch, our depth pre-trained model) benefits from more fine-tuning data on the CityScapes dataset. For both ImageNet and our depth pre-trained models, it suggests that more fine-tuning data is also beneficial for transferring the previously learned representations to a new task.

4.3   Domain Adaptation by Pre-Training

In the experiments described above, the two stages (pre-training on self-supervised depth prediction, followed by supervised training for segmentation) rely on data that come from significantly different domains. The self-supervised learning uses videos obtained from moving through North American cities. In contrast, none of the target dataset images were collected in the same geographic locations. For instance, CityScapes includes data from driving in German cities. Thus, in addition to a shift in task, the fine-tuning of the network for segmentation must also deal with a *domain shift* in the input.

CityScapes [18] and KITTI [16] make available video sequences that give temporal context to every image in the dataset. None of these extra frames are labeled, but we can leverage them in the following way. Before training the network on segmentation, we fine-tune it, using the same self-supervised relative depth prediction task described in Sect. 3.1, on these videos. Our intuition is that this may induce some of the modifications in the network that reflect the changing distribution of the input. Then, we proceed as before to train the fine-tuned representation on the semantic segmentation data. Specifically, we fine-tune different FCNs variants based on VGG16 sequentially, *i.e.*, from FCN32s to FCN16s, and finally to FCN8s. For FCN32s, the training procedure is identical to AlexNet FCN32s described earlier. FCN16s and FCN8s are trained for the same number of epochs as FCN32s, where the learning rate is set to 0.00002 and 0.00001, respectively, and kept constant during training.

The effectiveness of our unsupervised domain adaptation for semantic segmentation can be found in Table 2. The last two rows of demonstrate that such fine-tuning can consistently improve the performance of a self-supervised model

Table 2. Mean IoU scores of semantic segmentation using different architectures on different datasets. CD = CityDriving, CS = CityScapes, CV = CamVid, and K = KITTI.

Pre-training	FCN32s			FCN16s			FCN8s		
	CS	CV	K	CS	CV	K	CS	CV	K
ImageNet	**58.7**	**63.7**	**51.5**	**62.9**	**65.9**	**55.3**	63.4	67.0	56.4
Scratch	45.4	41.0	32.4	51.3	44.1	33.1	51.6	44.3	34.2
Ours CD	55.0	57.8	45.6	57.6	**59.0**	47.7	59.8	**60.3**	48.6
Ours CD+K	56.0	**58.5**	46.0	56.9	58.8	**48.2**	58.9	60.1	49.0
Ours CD+CS	**56.2**	**58.5**	**47.4**	**58.5**	58.8	47.8	**60.5**	59.9	**49.6**

Fig. 4. Qualitative semantic segmentation results on CityScapes. From top to bottom: input images, predictions of FCN8s with no pre-training, our FCN8s pre-trained on CityDriving, our FCN8s pre-trained on CityDriving adapted to CityScapes, ImageNet FCN8s, and ground-truth annotations. The difference between the 2nd and 3rd rows shows a clear benefit of pre-training with relative depth prediction. The difference between 3rd rows and 4th rows shows the benefit our unsupervised domain adaptation using pre-training.

over all FCN variants on both CityScapes and KITTI, validating its effectiveness as a domain adaptation approach. Interestingly, we can see that while fine-tuning is helpful for FCN32s on CamVid initially, it does not help much for FCN16s and FCN8s. Perhaps this is due to the domain gap between CamVid and CityScapes/KITTI. Qualitative semantic segmentation results can be found in Fig. 4.

4.4 Joint Semantic Reasoning

Joint semantic reasoning is important for urban scene understanding, especially with respect to tasks such as autonomous driving [48]. We investigate the effectiveness of our pre-trained model and the unsupervised strategy of domain adaptation using the MultiNet architecture [48] for joint road segmentation and car

Table 3. Results of joint semantic reasoning, including road segmentation and car detection.

Pre-training	Road segmentation		Car detection (AP)		
	F_1	AP	Easy	Medium	Hard
ImageNet	**96.33**	**92.26**	**95.59**	**86.43**	**72.28**
Scratch	93.78	91.37	89.37	79.93	66.02
Ours CD	94.74	92.13	92.84	84.73	69.47
Ours CD+K	**95.66**	92.14	**94.31**	**85.72**	**70.50**

detection.[5] MultiNet consists of a single encoder, using the VGG16 as backbone, and two sibling decoders for each task. For road segmentation, the decoder contains three upsampling layers, forming an FCN8s. The car detection decoder directly regresses the coordinates of objects. Following [48], the entire network is jointly trained using the Adam optimizer, using a learning rate of 0.00005 and weight decay of 0.0005 for 200 K steps. We refer readers to [48] for more technical details.

We replace the ImageNet-trained VGG16 network with a randomly initialized one and our own VGG16 pre-trained on CityDriving using relative depth. For the road segmentation task, there are 241 training and 48 validation images. For car detection, there are 7 K training images 481 validation images. Detailed comparisons on the validation set can be found in Table 3. We use the F_1 measure and Average Precision (AP) scores for road segmentation evaluation and AP scores for car detection. AP scores for different car categories are reported separately. We can clearly see that our pre-trained model (Ours CD) consistently outperforms the randomly initialized model (scratch in Table 3). Furthermore, by using the domain adaptation strategy via fine-tuning on the KITTI raw videos (Ours CD+K), we can further close the gap between an ImageNet pre-trained model. Remarkably, after fine-tuning, the F_1 score of road segmentation and AP scores for easy and medium categories of our pre-trained model are pretty close to the ImageNet counterpart's. (See last row of Table 3.)

4.5   Monocular Absolute Depth Estimation

For the monocular absolute depth estimation, we adopt the U-Net architecture [54] similar to [39,40], which consists of a fully convolutional encoder and another fully convolutional decoder with skip connections. In order to use an ImageNet pre-trained model, we replace the encoder with the VGG16 and ResNet50 architectures. We use the training and validation set of [39], containing 22.6 K and 888 images, respectively. We evaluate our model on the Eigen split [39,55], consisting of 697 images, where ground-truth absolute depth values

---

[5] We use the author's released code https://github.com/MarvinTeichmann/MultiNet. As the scene classification data is not publicly available, we only study road segmentation and car detection here.

Table 4. Monocular depth estimation on the KITTI dataset using the split of Eigen *et al.* [55] (range of 0–80 m). For model details, Arch. = Architecture, A = AlexNet, V = VGG16, and R = ResNet50. For training data, Class. = classification, I = ImageNet, CD = CityDriving, K = KITTI, CS = CityScapes. **pp** indicates test-time augmentation by horizontally flipping the input image.

Method	Arch.	Training data				Error metrics				Accuracy metrics		
		Class.	Stereo	Video	GT	Abs Rel	Sq Rel	RMSE	RMSE log	$\delta < 1.25$	$\delta < 1.25^2$	$\delta < 1.25^3$
[55]	A	I	-	-	K	0.203	1.548	6.307	0.282	0.702	0.890	0.958
[56]	A	I	-	-	K	0.202	1.614	6.523	0.275	0.678	0.895	0.965
[39]+pp	R	-	CS+K	-	-	0.114	0.898	4.935	0.206	0.861	0.949	0.976
[40]	V	-	-	CS+K	-	0.198	1.836	6.565	0.275	0.718	0.901	0.960
[57]	R	I	K	-	K	**0.113**	**0.741**	**4.621**	**0.189**	**0.862**	**0.960**	**0.986**
Ours	V	I	-	-	K	0.157	1.115	5.546	0.233	0.768	0.922	0.974
Ours	V	-	-	-	K	0.163	1.241	5.649	0.238	0.765	0.918	0.970
Ours	V	-	-	CD	K	0.154	1.117	5.499	0.228	0.775	0.928	0.976
Ours	V	-	-	CD+K	K	**0.148**	**1.056**	**5.317**	**0.221**	**0.791**	**0.932**	**0.977**
Ours	R	I	-	-	K	0.128	0.933	5.073	0.203	0.827	0.945	0.980
Ours	R	-	-	-	K	0.131	0.937	5.032	0.203	0.827	0.946	0.981
Ours	R	-	-	CD	K	0.128	0.901	**4.898**	0.198	0.834	0.948	0.983
Ours	R	-	-	CD+K	K	**0.125**	**0.881**	4.903	**0.195**	**0.840**	**0.951**	**0.983**

are captured using LiDAR at sparse pixels. Unlike [39], which uses stereo image pairs as supervision to train the network, or [40], which uses neighboring video frames as supervision to train the network (*yet camera intrinsic parameters are required*), we use the absolute sparse LiDAR depth values to fine-tune our network. The entire network (either VGG16 or ResNet50 version) is trained for 300 epochs using the Adam optimizer with a weight decay of 0.0005. The initial learning rate is 0.0001 and decreased by factor of 10 at the 200th epoch.

Detailed comparisons can be found in Table 4. We can observe that our pre-trained models consistently outperforms ImageNet counterparts, as well as randomly initialized models, using either VGG16 or ResNet50 architectures. It is worth noting, however, that converting relative depth to absolute depth is non-trivial. Computing relative depth (*i.e.*, percentile from absolute depth) is a non-linear mapping. The inverse transformation from relative depth to absolute depth is not unique. Following [40], we multiply our relative depth by a factor as the ratio between relative depth and absolute depth, we get pretty bad results (RMSE of 11.08 vs 4.903), showing this task is non-trivial.

Moreover, pre-training as domain adaptation also improves the performance of our pre-trained model. After fine-tuning our pre-trained model using KITTI's raw videos (Ours CD+K), our ResNet50 model achieves better results than most of the previous methods [39,40,55,56]. The results are also on par with the state-of-the-art method [57].

5   Conclusions and Discussions

We have proposed a new proxy task for self-supervised learning of visual representations. It requires only access to unlabeled videos taken by a moving camera.

Representations are learned by optimizing prediction of relative depth, recovered from estimated motion flow, from individual (single) frames. We show this task to be a powerful proxy task, which is competitive with recently proposed alternatives as a means of pre-training representations on unlabeled data. We also demonstrate a novel application of such pre-training, aimed at domain adaptation. When given videos taken by cars driven in cities, self-supervised pre-training primes the downstream urban scene understanding networks, leading to improved accuracy after fine-tuning on a small amount of manually labeled data.

Our work offers novel insights about one of the most important questions in vision today: how can we leverage unlabeled data, and in particular massive amounts of unlabeled video, to improve recognition systems. While a comprehensive picture of self-supervision methods and the role they play in this pursuit is yet to emerge, our results suggest that learning to predict relative depth is an important piece of this picture.

While the gap of the performance between self-supervised methods and their ImageNet counterparts is quickly shrinking, none of current self-supervised methods performs better than ImageNet pre-trained models on tasks involving semantics (*e.g.*, semantic segmentation and object detection). This makes pre-training on ImageNet still practically critical for many computer vision tasks. Despite this fact, this does not mean self-supervised methods are unimportant or unnecessary. The value of self-supervised methods lies in the fact that the training data can easily be scaled up without tedious and expensive human effort.

On other tasks, better performance of self-supervised methods than ImageNet counterparts has been achieved, including our monocular depth estimation and surface normal prediction [37]. Moreover, it has been shown that combining different self-supervised methods can lead to better performance [36,37]. All of these make it very promising that representations learned using self-supervised methods may surpass what ImageNet provides us today.

Acknowledgements. The experiments were performed using equipment obtained under a grant from the Collaborative R&D Fund managed by the Massachusetts Tech Collaborative. GS was also supported by AFOSR award FA9550-18-1-0166. This material is based on research sponsored by the Air Force Research Laboratory and DARPA under agreement number FA8750-18-2-0126. The U.S. Government is authorized to reproduce and distribute reprints for Governmental purposes notwithstanding any copyright notation thereon. The views and conclusions contained herein are those of the authors and should not be interpreted as necessarily representing the official policies or endorsements, either expressed or implied, of the Air Force Research Laboratory and DARPA or the U.S. Government.

References

1. Simonyan, K., Zisserman, A.: Very deep convolutional networks for large-scale image recognition. CoRR abs/1409.1556 (2014)
2. Shelhamer, E., Long, J., Darrell, T.: Fully convolutional networks for semantic segmentation. TPAMI **39**, 640–651 (2017)

3. Larsson, G., Maire, M., Shakhnarovich, G.: Colorization as a proxy task for visual understanding. In: CVPR (2017)
4. Zhang, R., Isola, P., Efros, A.A.: Colorful image colorization. In: Leibe, B., Matas, J., Sebe, N., Welling, M. (eds.) ECCV 2016. LNCS, vol. 9907, pp. 649–666. Springer, Cham (2016). https://doi.org/10.1007/978-3-319-46487-9_40
5. Noroozi, M., Favaro, P.: Unsupervised learning of visual representations by solving jigsaw puzzles. In: Leibe, B., Matas, J., Sebe, N., Welling, M. (eds.) ECCV 2016. LNCS, vol. 9910, pp. 69–84. Springer, Cham (2016). https://doi.org/10.1007/978-3-319-46466-4_5
6. Wang, X., Gupta, A.: Unsupervised learning of visual representations using videos. In: ICCV (2015)
7. Agrawal, P., Carreira, J., Malik, J.: Learning to see by moving. In: CVPR (2015)
8. Pathak, D., Girshick, R.B., Dollár, P., Darrell, T., Hariharan, B.: Learning features by watching objects move. In: CVPR (2017)
9. Misra, I., Zitnick, C.L., Hebert, M.: Unsupervised learning using sequential verification for action recognition. In: ECCV (2016)
10. Pathak, D., Krähenbühl, P., Donahue, J., Darrell, T., Efros, A.: Context encoders: feature learning by inpainting. In: CVPR (2016)
11. Gao, R., Jayaraman, D., Grauman, K.: Object-centric representation learning from unlabeled videos. In: Lai, S.-H., Lepetit, V., Nishino, K., Sato, Y. (eds.) ACCV 2016. LNCS, vol. 10115, pp. 248–263. Springer, Cham (2017). https://doi.org/10.1007/978-3-319-54193-8_16
12. Owens, A., Wu, J., McDermott, J.H., Freeman, W.T., Torralba, A.: Ambient sound provides supervision for visual learning. In: Leibe, B., Matas, J., Sebe, N., Welling, M. (eds.) ECCV 2016. LNCS, vol. 9905, pp. 801–816. Springer, Cham (2016). https://doi.org/10.1007/978-3-319-46448-0_48
13. Lee, H., Huang, J., Singh, M., Yang, M.: Unsupervised representation learning by sorting sequences. In: ICCV (2017)
14. Bideau, P., Learned-Miller, E.: It's moving! a probabilistic model for causal motion segmentation in moving camera videos. In: Leibe, B., Matas, J., Sebe, N., Welling, M. (eds.) ECCV 2016. LNCS, vol. 9912, pp. 433–449. Springer, Cham (2016). https://doi.org/10.1007/978-3-319-46484-8_26
15. Jayaraman, D., Grauman, K.: Learning image representations tied to ego-motion. In: ICCV, pp. 1413–1421 (2015)
16. Geiger, A., Lenz, P., Urtasun, R.: Are we ready for autonomous driving? the KITTI vision benchmark suite. In: CVPR (2012)
17. Geiger, A., Lenz, P., Stiller, C., Urtasun, R.: Vision meets robotics: the KITTI dataset. Int. J. Robot. Res. (IJRR) **32**, 1231–1237 (2013)
18. Cordts, M., et al.: The cityscapes dataset for semantic urban scene understanding. In: CVPR (2016)
19. Deng, J., Dong, W., Socher, R., Li, L.J., Li, K., Fei-Fei, L.: ImageNet: a large-scale hierarchical image database. In: CVPR (2009)
20. He, K., Zhang, X., Ren, S., Sun, J.: Deep residual learning for image recognition. In: CVPR (2016)
21. Larsson, G., Maire, M., Shakhnarovich, G.: Learning representations for automatic colorization. In: Leibe, B., Matas, J., Sebe, N., Welling, M. (eds.) ECCV 2016. LNCS, vol. 9908, pp. 577–593. Springer, Cham (2016). https://doi.org/10.1007/978-3-319-46493-0_35
22. Ranzato, M., Szlam, A., Bruna, J., Mathieu, M., Collobert, R., Chopra, S.: Video (language) modeling: a baseline for generative models of natural videos. arXiv preprint arXiv:1412.6604 (2014)

23. Srivastava, N., Mansimov, E., Salakhutdinov, R.: Unsupervised learning of video representations using LSTMs. In: ICML (2015)
24. Mathieu, M., Couprie, C., LeCun, Y.: Deep multi-scale video prediction beyond mean square error. arXiv preprint arXiv:1511.05440 (2015)
25. Vondrick, C., Pirsiavash, H., Torralba, A.: Generating videos with scene dynamics. In: NIPS (2016)
26. Xue, T., Wu, J., Bouman, K., Freeman, B.: Visual dynamics: probabilistic future frame synthesis via cross convolutional networks. In: NIPS (2016)
27. Lotter, W., Kreiman, G., Cox, D.: Deep predictive coding networks for video prediction and unsupervised learning. In: ICLR (2017)
28. Radford, A., Metz, L., Chintala, S.: Unsupervised representation learning with deep convolutional generative adversarial networks (2016)
29. Springenberg, J.T.: Unsupervised and semi-supervised learning with categorical generative adversarial networks. In: ICLR (2016)
30. Donahue, J., Krähenbühl, P., Darrell, T.: Adversarial feature learning. In: ICLR (2017)
31. Doersch, C., Gupta, A., Efros, A.A.: Unsupervised visual representation learning by context prediction. In: ICCV (2015)
32. Mobahi, H., Collobert, R., Weston, J.: Deep learning from temporal coherence in video. In: ICML (2009)
33. Isola, P., Zoran, D., Krishnan, D., Adelson, E.H.: Learning visual groups from co-occurrences in space and time. arXiv preprint arXiv:1511.06811 (2015)
34. Jayaraman, D., Grauman, K.: Slow and steady feature analysis: higher order temporal coherence in video. In: CVPR (2016)
35. Wiskott, L., Sejnowski, T.J.: Slow feature analysis: unsupervised learning of invariances. Neural Comput. 14(4), 715–770 (2002)
36. Doersch, C., Zisserman, A.: Multi-task self-supervised visual learning. In: ICCV (2017)
37. Wang, X., He, K., Gupta, A.: Transitive invariance for self-supervised visual representation learning. In: ICCV (2017)
38. Garg, R., B.G., V.K., Carneiro, G., Reid, I.: Unsupervised CNN for single view depth estimation: geometry to the rescue. In: Leibe, B., Matas, J., Sebe, N., Welling, M. (eds.) ECCV 2016. LNCS, vol. 9912, pp. 740–756. Springer, Cham (2016). https://doi.org/10.1007/978-3-319-46484-8_45
39. Godard, C., Mac Aodha, O., Brostow, G.J.: Unsupervised monocular depth estimation with left-right consistency. In: CVPR (2017)
40. Zhou, T., Brown, M., Snavely, N., Lowe, D.G.: Unsupervised learning of depth and ego-motion from video. In: CVPR (2017)
41. Vijayanarasimhan, S., Ricco, S., Schmid, C., Sukthankar, R., Fragkiadaki, K.: Sfm-Net: learning of structure and motion from video. arXiv (2017)
42. Li, Y., Paluri, M., Rehg, J.M., Dollár, P.: Unsupervised learning of edges. In: CVPR, pp. 1619–1627 (2016)
43. Horn, B.K.P.: Robot Vision. MIT Press, Cambridge (1986)
44. Hu, Y., Li, Y., Song, R.: Robust interpolation of correspondences for large displacement optical flow. In: CVPR (2017)
45. Dollár, P., Zitnick, C.L.: Fast edge detection using structured forests. IEEE Trans. Patt. Anal. Mach. Intell. 37(8), 1558–1570 (2015)
46. Krizhevsky, A., Sutskever, I., Hinton, G.E.: ImageNet classification with deep convolutional neural networks. In: NIPS, pp. 1106–1114 (2012)
47. Kingma, D.P., Ba, J.: Adam: a method for stochastic optimization. In: ICLR (2015)

48. Teichmann, M., Weber, M., Zöllner, J.M., Cipolla, R., Urtasun, R.: MultiNet: real-time joint semantic reasoning for autonomous driving. In: CVPR (2016)
49. Ros, G., Ramos, S., Granados, M., Bakhtiary, A., Vázquez, D., López, A.M.: Vision-based offline-online perception paradigm for autonomous driving. In: WACV (2015)
50. Brostow, G.J., Shotton, J., Fauqueur, J., Cipolla, R.: Segmentation and recognition using structure from motion point clouds. In: Forsyth, D., Torr, P., Zisserman, A. (eds.) ECCV 2008. LNCS, vol. 5302, pp. 44–57. Springer, Heidelberg (2008). https://doi.org/10.1007/978-3-540-88682-2_5
51. Brostow, G.J., Fauqueur, J., Cipolla, R.: Semantic object classes in video: a high-definition ground truth database. Patt. Recogn. Lett. **30**, 88–97 (2008)
52. Zhang, R., Isola, P., Efros, A.A.: Split-brain autoencoders: unsupervised learning by cross-channel prediction. In: CVPR (2017)
53. Kundu, A., Vineet, V., Koltun, V.: Feature space optimization for semantic video segmentation. In: CVPR (2016)
54. Ronneberger, O., Fischer, P., Brox, T.: U-Net: convolutional networks for biomedical image segmentation. In: Navab, N., Hornegger, J., Wells, W., Frangi, A. (eds.) Medical Image Computing and Computer-Assisted Intervention – MICCAI 2015. MICCAI 2015. Lecture Notes in Computer Science, vol. 9351, pp. 234–241. Springer, Cham (2015). https://doi.org/10.1007/978-3-319-24574-4_28
55. Eigen, D., Puhrsch, C., Fergus, R.: Depth map prediction from a single image using a multi-scale deep network. In: NIPS (2014)
56. Liu, F., Shen, C., Lin, G., Reid, I.D.: Learning depth from single monocular images using deep convolutional neural fields. IEEE TPAMI **38**(10), 2024–2039 (2016)
57. Kuznietsov, Y., Stückler, J., Leibe, B.: Semi-supervised deep learning for monocular depth map prediction. In: CVPR (2017)

K-convexity Shape Priors for Segmentation

Hossam Isack[1(✉)], Lena Gorelick[1], Karin Ng[2], Olga Veksler[1], and Yuri Boykov[1]

[1] University of Waterloo, Waterloo, Canada
hisack@uwaterloo.ca
[2] University of Western Ontario, London, Canada
kng263@uwo.ca

Abstract. This work extends popular star-convexity and other more general forms of convexity priors. We represent an object as a union of "convex" overlappable subsets. Since an arbitrary shape can always be divided into convex parts, our regularization model restricts the number of such parts. Previous k-part shape priors are limited to disjoint parts. For example, one approach segments an object via optimizing its k coverage by disjoint convex parts, which we show is highly sensitive to local minima. In contrast, our shape model allows the convex parts to overlap, which both relaxes and simplifies the coverage problem, e.g. fewer parts are needed to represent any object. As shown in the paper, for many forms of convexity our regularization model is significantly more descriptive for any given k. Our shape prior is useful in practice, e.g. biomedical applications, and its optimization is robust to local minima.

1 Introduction

Regularization is common in computer vision problems/applications such as photo or video editing, biomedical image analysis, weakly-supervised training of semantic CNN segmentation, etc. Typical regularization techniques often correspond to imposing various priors, e.g. smoothness [1–3], shape [4–8], hierarchical [9–11], volumetric [12], or other priors. This work proposes a particularly simple, yet sufficiently discriminant and efficient model of a general shape prior based on the geometric concept of convexity. While our main ideas could be expressed in either discrete or continuous settings, for simplicity we focus on the former and propose a combinatorial optimization technique based on graph-cuts [2,6].

Convexity is a powerful regularization concept for segmentation [4,8,13,14]. However, in practical applications it is rare that objects are strictly convex. Our premise is that an object of interest can be represented as a union of a small number of convex parts. We propose a form of multi-convexity shape prior, namely k-convexity, to regularize the problem of segmenting such objects. Our definition of k-convexity is a generalization of k-stars in computational geometry literature [15], but it differs from how k-convexity is used in [16]. Our general k-convexity approach can be based on different forms of convexity, e.g. star [4], geodesic-star [13], hedgehog [14], or regular convexity [8]. In segmentation, the concept of k-convexity was first discussed by [13] in the context of stars [4], but citing **NP**-hardness they focused on an easier-to-optimize multi-star prior with a predefined region for each star, see k-regions versus k-convexity in Table 1.

© Springer Nature Switzerland AG 2018
V. Ferrari et al. (Eds.): ECCV 2018, LNCS 11215, pp. 38–54, 2018.
https://doi.org/10.1007/978-3-030-01252-6_3

Predefined regions for object parts [13] could be avoided by segmenting these parts as independent objects with appropriate convexity priors a la [14]. This is a viable alternative to k-convexity, see k-disjoint in Table 1, but we found that representing an object via disjoint convex parts leads to local minima. Moreover, compared to overlapping convex parts in k-convexity, a larger number of disjoint convex parts may be needed to represent the same shape, see Table 1.

Similar to [4,6], our shape prior methodology is presented within graph-cut optimization framework, but other optimization techniques are possible. Besides multi-part object modeling, our approach easily adapts to segmenting independent overlapping objects, e.g. cells, addressed earlier by other priors in active contours [7,17], level-sets [18] and graph cuts [19].

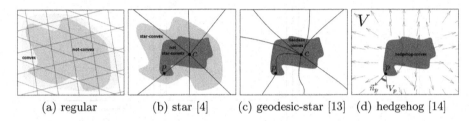

(a) regular   (b) star [4]   (c) geodesic-star [13]   (d) hedgehog [14]

Fig. 1. *Different types of convexity*: (a) regular convexity; yellow shape is convex and green is not. (b) star-convexity; green shape is star-convex w.r.t. center c while red is not. (c) shows geodesic paths to c for which the red shape is geodesic-star-convex. (d) shows vector field V for which the red shape is hedgehog-convex. Lines, rays and vector fields in (a–d) are used to define convexity constraints, see text for details.

Types of Convexity: there is more than one way to define convexity. A shape S is considered to be convex in the regular sense if it forms a convex set, i.e. if $p, q \in S$ then line pq also lies in S. In practice regular convexity is usually approximated by enforcing convexity constraints only along a predefined number of orientations [8] as shown in Fig. 1(a). Furthermore, even when segmenting a single convex object the resulting function is non-submodular [8], i.e. **NP**-Hard. Alternatively easier-to-optimize types of convexity are used in practice, e.g. star-convexity [4].

A shape S is considered star-convex w.r.t. a center c if for any pixel $p \in S$ the line cp lies in S, see Fig. 1(b). Star-convexity was first used as a shape prior in [4]. Later on [13] proposed geodesic-star-convexity, which imposes the same constraints as star-convexity but along a geodesic path between c and p, see Fig. 1(c). The paths are computed using image color information and the distance between c and p. Both [4,13] encode their shape priors as local pairwise pixels constraints which requires ray or path tracing.

Table 1. *Different types of multi-convexity based on* (1): the additional constraints corresponding to each type of multi-convexity are shown in the second row. The last two rows show examples for k = 2. Shape S is shown in solid red, while internal boundaries between parts $\{S_i\}$ are shown in dotted red. The additional constraints limit k-regions and k-disjoint shape representational power, e.g. they require more than two parts to describe the top example of k-convexity.

	k-regions	**k-disjoint**	**k-convexity** (ours)
additional constraints	$R_i \cap R_j = \phi$ $\forall i \neq j \in [1,\dots k]$ $S_i \in R_i \ \forall i \in [1,\dots k]$	$S_i \cap S_j = \phi$ $\forall i \neq j \in [1,\dots k]$	None
example 1			
example 2			

Recently [14] proposed hedgehog-convexity that gives the user more control over the shape space and, unlike [4,13], does not require ray or path tracing. Instead, hedgehog-convexity requires some vector field V to constrain the shape normals $\{\vec{n}_p \,|\, p \in \partial S\}$ to be within a certain tolerance θ, i.e. $\angle \vec{n}_p V_p \leq \theta$, see Fig. 1(d). Hedgehog-convexity is more general than star and geodesic-star convexity [4,13]. For example, it reduces to star-convexity for radial vector field V centered at c and $\theta = \frac{\pi}{2}$. Furthermore, if $\theta = 0$ in the aforementioned case then shape S must be a circle centered at c, as in the examples shown in Fig. 2.

As mentioned earlier, in practice objects of interest are rarely convex but any arbitrary object can always be divided into convex parts. Multi-convexity is a regularization model where an object of interest is assumed to be the union of convex parts. Different forms of multi-convexity where introduced in [13,14] in the context of geodesic-star and hedgehog convexity, respectively.

Multi-Convexity: without lost of generality we will review multi-convexity in the context of regular convexity but our arguments are general and apply to all types of convexity covered earlier. In multi-convexity the final segmentation S is the union of k parts

$$S = \bigcup_{i=1}^{k} S_i \tag{1}$$

where each part S_i is convex. Note that multi-convexity does not guarantee connectivity of S, i.e. S could contain more than one connected component. This could be addressed by adding a connectivity prior but such priors are **NP**-hard [20]. Shape connectivity is beyond the scope of this paper.

Previous forms of multi-convexity enforce additional constraints that either simplify optimization [13] or inherently appear in a different context, e.g. segmentation of independent objects [14]. We observe that such constraints unnecessarily limit the descriptiveness of the multi-convexity shape prior in the context of multi-part object segmentation.

In [13] the image domain is split into k disjoint predefined regions, e.g. Voronoi cells of the star-centers in the context of star-convexity. In addition, each S_i is constrained to be convex and restricted to be within its corresponding region. In the case of star, geodesic-star or hedgehog convexity tying each part to a predefined region results in a submodular energy, i.e. could be solved optimally in polynomial time. We refer to this approach by k-**regions** [13], see Table 1.

Unlike [13], [14] does not tie an object part to a predefined region. However, [14] enforces mutual exclusion between parts. Mutual exclusion was a reasonable assumption in [14] as the authors introduced multi-convexity in the context of multi-object segmentation not multi-part. Nonetheless, [14] could be applied to segmenting multi-part objects but in practice it is very sensitive to local minima. We refer to [14] multi-convexity approach by k-**disjoint**, see Table 1.

Our main contribution is a novel multi-convexity shape prior, k-**convexity**. Unlike [13,14], our approach does not impose any additional constraints on parts besides convexity. Table 1 juxtaposes k-convexity with the previous multi-convexity approaches. Figure 2 demonstrates k-regions and k-disjoint practical drawbacks. Although k-regions could be solved optimally, it is clear that its shape representational power is limited, see Fig. 2(b). While k-disjoint removes the restriction of parts to predefined regions, it is sensitive to initialization and prone to local minima, see Fig. 2(c). Our k-convexity overcomes these drawbacks by relaxing the solution space, i.e. allowing the parts to overlap, see Fig. 2(d).

Our k-convexity prior can also be motivated by shape reconstruction via *medial axis transform* (MAT) [21], which is the union of overlapping skeleton-centered circles with given radii. As discussed earlier, circle can be seen as a particularly tight form of convexity shape prior. Thus, segmentation with our k-convexity shape prior could be seen as a relaxation of MAT shape reconstruction: instead of the union of circles we compute the union of convex parts, we do not assume fixed radii or scales, and we use partial skeletons, e.g. user-scribbles, instead of full skeletons. Note that segmentation with k-convexity shape prior estimates the scale of each part based on image data (e.g. object color model), while MAT reconstruction assumes known circle radii. These differences are illustrated in Fig. 3.

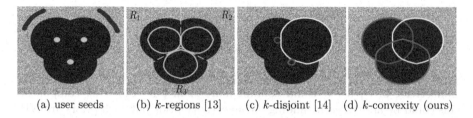

(a) user seeds	(b) k-regions [13]	(c) k-disjoint [14]	(d) k-convexity (ours)

Fig. 2. *Limitations of multi-convexity approaches*: to emphasize them, this synthetic example uses a tight form of convexity shape prior (hedgehogs with $\theta \approx 0$ and radial vector field) enforcing near-circularity for each part. In fact, circularity priors are useful in practice, e.g. cell segmentation [7,17], see Fig. 7. In (b) regions shown in dotted cyan.

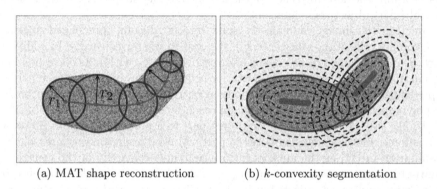

(a) MAT shape reconstruction	(b) k-convexity segmentation

Fig. 3. Illustrates shape reconstruction from skeleton/partial-skeleton (red). The reconstructed shape is the union of the blue parts. (a) reconstruction using a skeleton and radial function. (b) reconstruction using partial skeleton, color cues, and k-convexity with k = 2 and hedgehog-convexity [14] where $\theta \approx 0$. Note, for hedgehog-convexity using the gradient of the scribble's distance map as V and $\theta \approx 0$, limits the set of allowed shapes to the level-sets (black dashed contours) of the distance map.

Our list of contributions are summarized below:

- a novel multi-convexity shape prior for multi-part object or overlapping objects segmentation, namely k-convexity.
- a graph-cuts optimization framework for k-convexity based on [2,6].
- experimental results comparing our k-convexity shape prior to existing multi-convexity approaches [13,14]. We also show k-convexity results for different types of convexity.
- for completeness, a proof that our general formulation of k-convexity is **NP**-Hard.

The paper is organized as follows. In Sect. 2 we formulate k-convexity as multi-labeling energy that permits labels to overlap. We show how to optimize k-convexity in Sect. 3. We compare and validate our approach in the context of biomedical segmentation in Sect. 4, and apply k-convexity to different types of convexity. Finally, Sect. 5 concludes and discusses future work.

2   Energy

Let Ω be the set of all image pixels, and $\mathcal{L} = \{1, \ldots, k\}$ be the set of indices of k overlappable foreground parts, i.e. labels. Also, let $\mathbf{f} = \{f_p \mid \forall p \in \Omega\}$ be a labelling of Ω where f_p is a pixel labelling such that $f_p = \{f_p^i \in \{0,1\} \mid \forall i \in \mathcal{L}\}$. A pixel p belongs to label i if $f_p^i = 1$ and 0 otherwise. Furthermore, a pixel is considered a background pixel if it is not assigned to any foreground label. For notational simplicity in identifying background pixels we will use an indicator function $\phi(f_p)$

$$\phi(f_p) = \begin{cases} 1 & \text{if } f_p^i = 0 \ \forall i \in \mathcal{L} \\ 0 & \text{otherwise.} \end{cases} \tag{2}$$

Our k-convexity multi-part segmentation energy is

$$E(\mathbf{f}) = \overbrace{\sum_{p \in \Omega} D_p(\phi(f_p))}^{\text{data}} + \lambda \overbrace{\sum_{p,q \in \mathcal{N}} V(f_p, f_q)}^{\text{smoothness}} + \overbrace{\sum_{i \in \mathcal{L}} C_i(\mathbf{f}, \theta)}^{\text{convexity}}, \tag{3}$$

where λ is a normalization constant, $\mathcal{N}$ is the pixels' neighborhood system, and the energy terms are described in more details below.

In our *data* term, $D_p(\phi(f_p))$ measures how well a pixel fits the background (Bg) or foreground (Fg) color model depending on in its current labeling. One of the most commonly used data terms is the negative log likelihood

$$D_p(\phi(f_p)) = \begin{cases} -\ln \Pr(I_p \mid Bg) & \phi(f_p) = 1 \\ -\ln \Pr(I_p \mid Fg) & \phi(f_p) = 0 \end{cases} \tag{4}$$

where I_p is the image intensity at pixel p. Since we are segmenting a single object as a multiple convex parts, we assume that the foreground parts have the same color model. Nonetheless, the color models of foreground parts could different if needed, similar to [6].

The *smoothness* term is a regularizer that discourages labeling discontinuities between neighboring pixels $p, q \in \mathcal{N}$. A discontinuity occurs whenever a pixel is assigned to background while its neighbor is assigned to at least one foreground[1]. The simplest form of pairwise discontinuity is,

$$V(f_p, f_q) = w_{pq}[\phi(f_p) \neq \phi(f_q)] \tag{5}$$

where $[\,]$ is the Iverson bracket and w_{pq} is a non-increasing function of I_p and I_q. Note that our energy only penalizes the outside boundary of the union of the foreground parts.

---

[1] Discontinuities between foreground labels could be penalized, as in cell segmentation.

The *convexity* term is used to forbid (or penalize) solutions with non-convex parts. In (3) $C_i(\mathbf{f}, \theta)$ encodes the convexity prior of label i, while θ is a prior specific parameter(s). It is possible to enforce any of the following convexity priors; star [4], geodesic-star [13], hedgehog [14], or regular [8] convexity. For instance, to enforce hedgehog convexity [14] we define C_i as follows

$$C_i(\mathbf{f}, \theta) = w_\infty \sum_{(p,q) \in \mathcal{E}_i(\theta)} [f_p^i = 1, f_q^i = 0], \qquad (6)$$

where w_∞ is a very large constant, θ is the shape tightness parameter, and $\mathcal{E}_i(\theta)$ is, as defined in [14] eq (3), the set of pairwise directed edges used to approximate the hedgehog shape prior for label i given θ. From now on we will adhere to hedgehog-convexity as a show case.

3   Optimization

In Appendix A we prove that (3) is **NP**-hard. To find an approximate solution we follow in the foot steps of [2,6]. They maintain a current labeling $\hat{\mathbf{f}}$ and iteratively try to decrease the energy by switching from $\hat{\mathbf{f}}$ to a near by labeling. Similar to [6], at each iteration in our approach, Algorithm 1, a label $\alpha \in \mathcal{L}$ is randomly chosen and its support region is allowed to simultaneously expand and contract without affecting other foreground parts' support regions. We refer to the aforementioned move by Expansion-Contraction Move (EC-Move), and it is a binary submodular move, see Fig. 4. The algorithm stops when it cannot find an α-EC-Move that decreases the energy anymore.

Algorithm 1: ALPHA-EXPANSION-CONTRACTION

---

1 $\hat{\mathbf{f}} :=$ initial labeling
2 **repeat**
3   **for each** $\alpha \in \mathcal{L}$
4          $\mathbf{f}^\alpha := \arg\min_{\mathbf{f}} E(\mathbf{f})$ where $\mathbf{f}$ is an α-expansion-contration of $\hat{\mathbf{f}}$
5   **if** $E(\mathbf{f}^\alpha) < E(\hat{\mathbf{f}})$
6              $\hat{\mathbf{f}} := \mathbf{f}^\alpha$
7 **until** converged

3.1   Expansion-Contraction Move (EC-Move)

An α-EC-Move allows α to gain or lose pixel support, which is a binary move. We only apply EC-Moves to foreground labels, because an EC-Move on the background label is a non-submodular multi-label move, since a background pixel has more than one foreground label to choose from when contracting. However, it is possible to only allow the background to expand as in [14].

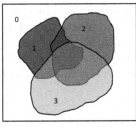 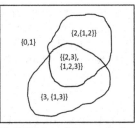 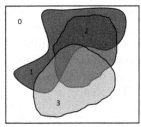

(a) current labeling   (b) EC-Move binary choices   (c) feasible EC-Move

Fig. 4. *EC-Move illustration*: (a) shows a current labeling for a 3-part object. (b) shows the binary choices for each pixel when applying EC-Move for $\alpha = 1$. As you can see in (c) any pixel is allowed to gain or lose α, while other foreground parts remain intact. During an α-EC-Move only the convexity prior of α is taken into account.

Given current labeling $\hat{\mathbf{f}}$ an EC-Move on $\alpha \in \mathcal{L}$ can be formulated as a binary energy as follows:

$$E^\alpha(\mathbf{x}) = \sum_{p \in \Omega} D_p^\alpha(x_p) + \lambda \sum_{p,q \in \mathcal{N}} w_{pq} V^\alpha(x_p, x_q) + C^\alpha(\mathbf{x}, \theta), \qquad (7)$$

where $\mathbf{x} = \{x_p \in \{0,1\} \mid \forall p \in \Omega\}$ such that $x_p = 1$ means that p adds α to its current set of labels $\hat{f}_p$ while $x_p = 0$ means removing α, and functions D^α, V^α and C^α are discussed below.

The *data* term in (7) is defined as

$$D_p^\alpha(x_p) = \begin{cases} D_p(0) & x_p = 1 \\ D_p(\phi(\hat{f}_p)) & x_p = 0, \end{cases} \qquad (8)$$

the *smoothness* term is defined as

$$V^\alpha(x_p, x_q) = \begin{cases} [\phi(\hat{f}_p) \neq \phi(\hat{f}_q)] & x_p = 0, x_q = 0 \\ [\phi(\hat{f}_p) \neq 0] & x_p = 0, x_q = 1 \\ [\phi(\hat{f}_q) \neq 0] & x_p = 1, x_q = 0 \\ 0 & x_p = 1, x_q = 1, \end{cases} \qquad (9)$$

and the *convexity* term is defined as

$$C^\alpha(\mathbf{x}, \theta) = w_\infty \sum_{(p,q) \in \mathcal{E}_\alpha(\theta)} [x_p = 1, x_q = 0]. \qquad (10)$$

Submodularity: as shown in [22], any first-order binary function could be exactly optimized if its pairwise terms are submodular. A binary function h of two variables is submodular if $h(0,0) + h(1,1) \leq h(1,0) + h(0,1)$. Our energy (7) is submodular as it could be written as the sum of submodular pairwise binary energies over all possible pairs of p and q. We prove that V^α is a submodular by showing that

$$V^\alpha(0,0) + V^\alpha(1,1) \leq V^\alpha(0,1) + V^\alpha(1,0) \tag{11}$$

$$[\phi(\hat{f}_p) \neq \phi(\hat{f}_q)] + 0 \leq [\phi(\hat{f}_p) \neq 0] + [\phi(\hat{f}_q) \neq 0] \tag{12}$$

holds for any $\phi(\hat{f}_p)$ and $\phi(\hat{f}_q)$

if $\phi(\hat{f}_p) = 0$, $\phi(\hat{f}_q) = 0$ **then** (12) reduces to $0 + 0 \leq 0 + 0$

if $\phi(\hat{f}_p) = 0$, $\phi(\hat{f}_q) = 1$ **then** (12) reduces to $1 + 0 \leq 0 + 1$

if $\phi(\hat{f}_p) = 1$, $\phi(\hat{f}_q) = 0$ **then** (12) reduces to $1 + 0 \leq 1 + 0$

if $\phi(\hat{f}_p) = 1$, $\phi(\hat{f}_q) = 1$ **then** (12) reduces to $0 + 0 \leq 1 + 1$.

Finally, the hedgehog-convexity constraint $h(x_p, x_q) = [x_p = 1, x_q = 0]$ is submodular

$$h(0,0) + h(1,1) \leq h(1,0) + h(0,1) \tag{13}$$

$$0 + 0 \leq 1 + 0. \tag{14}$$

Optimal EC-Move: the authors in [22] showed how to find the global optimal solution of a submodular energy such as (7) by computing the min-cut of a graph that encodes the submodular energy. It should be noted that not all convexity priors lead to a submodular EC-Move, e.g. [4,13,14] are submodular while [8] is non-submodular which renders the EC-Move **NP**-hard.

4   Experiments

In this section k refers to the number of object seeds provided by the user. We applied k-convexity to liver and overlapping cells segmentation. When applicable we compared our approach to other forms of multi-convexity, i.e. k-regions [13] and k-disjoint [14]. Furthermore, we tested k-convexity on submodular [14] and non-submoudlar [8] convexity priors. Unless stated otherwise parts' convexity prior is assume to be hedgehog-convexity for all multi-convexity approaches. Also, user-seeds were used to compute color models and convexity constraints. In all of our experiments, spatial discontinuity costs, i.e. w_{pq}, were non-negative weights computed using a non-increasing function of the difference in p and q intensities, similar to [23].

4.1   Liver Segmentation

As shown in Fig. 5 column 2, k-regions usually resulted in k disjoint regions. For tight θ, using k-regions often lead to conflicting shape constraints between those regions. In those cases, there was no single contour that would satisfy the conflicting constraints, thus the liver was over segmented as k independent contours. As shown in column 3, k-disjoint was prone to local minima and sensitive to the order in which the foreground parts expanded. Unlike k-regions, our approach was more likely to result in liver segmentation with one connected-component, because each part/label shape constraints were enforced independently. Furthermore, our approach was more robust towards local minima compared to k-disjoint because of its relaxed solution space that allow parts to overlap.

Table 2 shows the average F_1 score of 3D liver segmentation over 12 different subjects. It is clear that our approach is more robust towards the selected θ in comparison to k-regions and k-disjoint. Table 3 shows the average number of connected-components of the segmentation results. In contrast to k-regions and k-disjoint, our approach was more likely to result in a liver segmentation with one connected-component. Note that none of the three methods guarantee connectivity of the shape parts, unless the user provided a single seed. Figure 6 shows a sample of 3D liver segmentation for three different subjects.

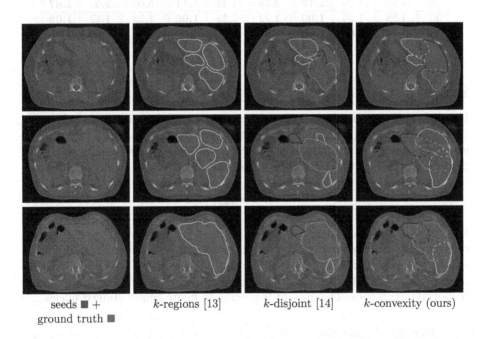

seeds ■ + k-regions [13] k-disjoint [14] k-convexity (ours)
ground truth ■

Fig. 5. Shows 2D liver segmentation of three different subjects. Different object parts are shown in different colors, their union is the liver segmentation (solid multi-colored contour). Also, 0 cost internal boundaries between parts are shown as dotted lines. k-regions was less likely to result in a single connected-component, especially for tight θ. k-disjoint was prone to local minima. Our approach out performed k-regions and k-disjoint. Results are shown for $\theta = 20°$, $\lambda = 1$ and $\mathcal{N}$ was the 8-neighborhood.

Table 2. Shows the average F_1 scores of 3D liver segmentation results for various smoothness λ and shape tightness θ. The three methods behave consistently over different values of λ. Unlike k-regions [13] and k-disjoint [14], our method is more robust towards θ. For $45° < \theta < 70°$ k-regions and our results were comparable. For $\theta \geq 70°$ all methods suffered from hedgehog discretization artifacts, i.e. under-constraining [24]

θ	$\lambda = 0.1$			$\lambda = 0.5$			$\lambda = 1$		
	k-reg.	k-dis.	ours	k-reg.	k-dis.	ours	k-reg.	k-dis.	ours
10°	0.07	0.39	**0.57**	0.06	0.38	**0.56**	0.06	0.29	**0.49**
20°	0.36	0.60	**0.79**	0.33	0.59	**0.79**	0.24	0.50	**0.73**
30°	0.82	0.63	**0.87**	0.83	0.61	**0.87**	0.83	0.61	**0.88**
45°	**0.84**	0.74	0.83	**0.86**	0.75	**0.86**	**0.87**	0.74	**0.87**

Table 3. Shows the average number of connected-components of 3D liver segmentation results. Ideally, the number of connected components should be 1. Our method was the most likely method to result in small number of connected-components, if not one.

θ	$\lambda = 0.1$			$\lambda = 0.5$			$\lambda = 1$		
	k-reg.	k-dis.	ours	k-reg.	k-dis.	ours	k-reg.	k-dis.	ours
10°	5.83	2.50	**1.92**	5.83	2.75	**2.00**	5.83	3.75	**2.67**
20°	4.58	1.25	**1.17**	4.58	1.42	**1.17**	5.00	2.00	**1.67**
30°	1.58	1.25	**1.00**	1.42	1.33	**1.00**	1.58	1.42	**1.08**
45°	1.08	**1.00**	**1.00**	1.08	**1.00**	**1.00**	1.08	**1.00**	1.08

4.2 Cells

Penalizing discontinuities between foreground parts is the main difference between segmenting overlapping objects, e.g. cells, and a multi-part object, e.g. liver. Unlike multi-part object segmentation, when segmenting cells we penalized the discontinuities between the foreground parts, i.e. cells, as follows

$$V(f_p, f_q) = w_{pq} \sum_{i \in \mathcal{L}} [f_p^i \neq f_q^i]. \tag{15}$$

Figure 7 shows various cell segmentation results. Figure 8 compares our approach to a specialized fluorescently stained cell nuclei segmentation approach [17]. In contrast to our approach, [17] used a more complex unary potential that took into consideration that overlapping regions are expected to be brighter than non-overlapping ones. This insight is specific to fluorescently stained nuclei.

4.3 Regular Convexity

Regular convexity is usually approximated by enforcing convexity constraints only along a predefined number of orientations [8] as illustrated in Fig. 1(a). In this section we will refer to regular convexity and its approximation [8] by regular convexity.

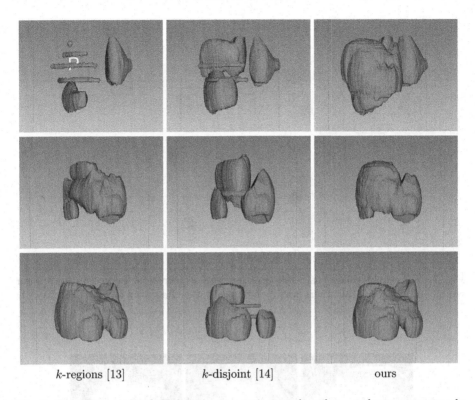

k-regions [13] k-disjoint [14]   ours

Fig. 6. Shows a sample of 3D liver segmentation results where each row corresponds to a different test subject. For most test cases, k-regions was sensitive to the selected θ while k-disjoint usually converged to a poor local minima. In contrast, our approach showed robustness towards the selected θ and k-disjoint local minima. These results were generated using $\theta = 20°$, $\lambda = 0.5$ and $\mathcal{N}$ was the 26-neighborhood system.

Enforcing regular convexity [8] renders energy (3) harder to optimize, since a single EC-move becomes non-submodular and therefore **NP**-hard. To address this problem we optimize each EC-Move with Trust Region based optimization proposed in [8], modifying it to account for the overlap between convex parts. We enforced convexity in an annealing fashion by gradually increasing the convexity term weight.

Figure 9 shows a proof of concept example for k- convexity when using regular convexity [8]. Based on our experience, employing regular convexity prior usually resulted in final segmentation with minimal overlap between parts. However, allowing labels to overlap helped during the optimization intermediate steps.

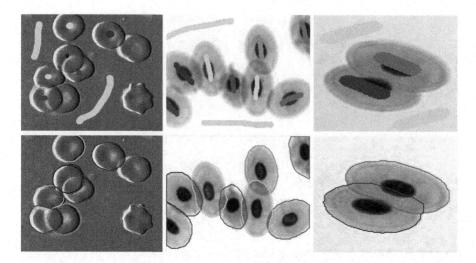

Fig. 7. (Top) shows user seeds, while (Bottom) shows our results. Left column is human red blood cells, while the others are frog blood cells. Results shown for $\theta = 5°$ and $\lambda = 1$.

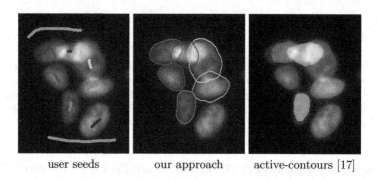

user seeds   our approach   active-contours [17]

Fig. 8. Shows segmentation of fluorescently stained nuclei using k-convexity (with hedgehog-convexity) and [17]. Active-contours result copied from [17]. Note that [17] uses a different unary potential than ours, they assume overlapping regions are brighter.

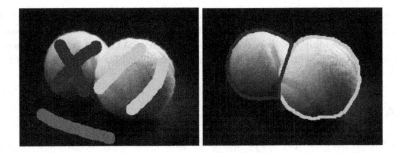

Fig. 9. (Left) shows user-seeds and (Right) shows our results when using regular (non-submodular) convexity [8]. Allowing the labels to overlap helped during the optimization intermediate steps by avoiding local minima. This result was generated using $\lambda = 0.01$ and w_∞ annealing schedule was $[0.002, 0.003, 0.005, 0.01, 0.1]$.

5   Conclusion

Our novel multi-convexity shape prior, i.e. k-convexity, regularizes an object segmentation under the assumption that it consists of k overlappable convex parts. We showed that k-convexity has higher shape representational power compared to existing multi-convexity priors [13,14]. In contrast to our approach, [13,14] use additional constraints that negatively impacts their shape representational power either to simplify the optimization problem [13] or to target a specific problem [14], i.e. multiple independent object segmentation. In addition, we empirically showed that k-convexity is more robust towards local minima and shape prior parameters compared to [13,14], respectively.

Our k-convexity approach is not tied to a specific type of convexity and could be used to enforce a multitude of convexity priors, e.g. star [4], geodesic-star [13], hedgehog [14], and regular convexity [8]. In addition, we illustrated the practicality of k-convexity when using hedgehog-convexity [14] in biomedical applications such as liver and overlapping cells segmentation.

Automating cell segmentation, i.e. dropping the user-seeds requirement, could be achieved by generating a large set of cell proposals, e.g. using Hough Transform for circles, and adding a sparsity prior [25] on top of k-convexity. By adding sparsity prior solutions that use fewer number of convex parts, i.e. cells, will become more favorable. The sparsity prior would not affect the EC-Move submodularity. However, in that case EC-Moves are expected to be prone to weak local minima. Thus, a more powerful move which would allow the removal of multiple parts simultaneously should be considered (a non-submodular move), we leave this as future work.

As discussed earlier multi-convexity priors do not impose parts connectivity. However, we empirically showed that k-convexity is more likely to result in a smaller number of connected components, if not one, compared to other multi-convexity approaches. In general, parts connectivity could be enforced by extending existing connectivity priors [26] to handle overlapping labels, but this will cause α-EC-Move to be non-submodular.

Acknowledgement. This work was supported by NIH grants R01-EB004640, P50-CA174521, R01-CA167632 and U01-CA140206. We thank Drs. S. O'Dorisio and Y. Menda for providing the liver data NIH grant U01-CA140206. This work was also supported by NSERC Discovery and RTI grants (Canada) for Y. Boykov and O. Veksler.

A   A NP-Hardness Proof

Optimization problem (3) is **NP**-hard. To prove this we will reduce a Set Cover problem instance to (3) in polynomial time. In Set Cover problem we are given a universe $U = \{u_1, u_2, \dots u_n\}$, and a set of m subsets $S = \{S_i \subseteq U \mid \forall i \in [1, m]\}$. The Set Cover objective is to find the least number of subsets in S such that their union covers U. Given a Set Cover problem we can construct its corresponding k-convexity (3) instance as follows:

Label Set: $\mathcal{L} := \{i \mid \forall i \in [1, m]\}$ where label i corresponds to subset S_i.

Pixel Set: $\Omega := \{U \cup A\}$ where $A = \{a_i \mid \forall i \in [1, m]\}$. A is a set of auxiliary pixels/nodes. In this section we refer to pixels as nodes. For each set S_i, we introduce an auxiliary node a_i that will be used as an indicator of whether S_i is one of the selected sets to cover U or not.

Data Term: we define the data term as follows

$$
D_p(i) = \begin{cases} 0 & p \in U, \ p \in S_i & (16) \\ \infty & p \in U, \ p \notin S_i & (17) \\ 1 & p \in A, \ p = a_i & (18) \\ 0 & p \in A, \ p \neq a_i & (19) \end{cases}
$$

Equations (16) and (17) prohibit a node $u \notin S_i$ to gain label i. Equations (18) and (19) ensure that our energy increases by 1 if a_i is assigned to label i.

Neighbour System: in Set Cover there is no notion of neighborhood between the nodes, thus $\mathcal{N} := \phi$.

Shape Constraints: for a given set S_i we define the corresponding shape constraints as a set of pairwise edges $\mathcal{E}_i$ as follows:

$$\mathcal{E}_i := \mathcal{C}_i \cup \mathcal{I}_i,$$

where the set of *connectedness* edges is $\mathcal{C}_i := \{(u, v) \mid \forall u, v \in S_i, u \neq v\}$ and the set of *indicator* edges is $\mathcal{I}_i := \{(u, a_i) \mid \forall u \in S_i, a_i \in A\}$. The edges in $\mathcal{C}_i$ ensure that if a node $u \in S_i$ gained label i then every other node in the set S_i will also gain label i. The edges in $\mathcal{I}_i$ ensures that if any node $u \in S_i$ gains label i then the corresponding auxiliary node a_i of S_i gains label i as well.

Objective: the reduced Set Cover problem (3) objective counts the number of selected subsets to cover U. Notice that if a node $u \in S_i$ decides to gain label i then a_i will also gain label i. And, since $D_{a_i}(i) = 1$ by definition then we can conclude that our energy counts the number of subsets used in the final solution.

References

1. Caselles, V., Kimmel, R., Sapiro, G.: Geodesic active contours. Int. J. Comput. Vis. **22**(1), 61–79 (1997)
2. Boykov, Y., Veksler, O., Zabih, R.: Fast approximate energy minimization via graph cuts. IEEE Trans. Patt. Anal. Mach. Intell. **23**(11), 1222–1239 (2001)
3. Pock, T., Cremers, D., Bischof, H., Chambolle, A.: An algorithm for minimizing the Mumford-Shah functional. In: 2009 IEEE 12th International Conference on Computer Vision, pp. 1133–1140. IEEE (2009)
4. Veksler, O.: Star shape prior for graph-cut image segmentation. In: Forsyth, D., Torr, P., Zisserman, A. (eds.) ECCV 2008. LNCS, vol. 5304, pp. 454–467. Springer, Heidelberg (2008). https://doi.org/10.1007/978-3-540-88690-7_34
5. Boykov, Y., Kolmogorov, V., Cremers, D., Delong, A.: An integral solution to surface evolution PDEs via geo-cuts. In: Leonardis, A., Bischof, H., Pinz, A. (eds.) ECCV 2006. LNCS, vol. 3953, pp. 409–422. Springer, Heidelberg (2006). https://doi.org/10.1007/11744078_32
6. Vu, N., Manjunath, B.: Shape prior segmentation of multiple objects with graph cuts. In: 2008 IEEE Conference on Computer Vision and Pattern Recognition, CVPR 2008. pp 1–8. IEEE (2008)
7. Horváth, P., Jermyn, I., Zerubia, J., Kato, Z.: A higher-order active contour model for tree detection. In: 2006 18th International Conference on Pattern Recognition, ICPR 2006, vol. 2, pp. 130–133. IEEE (2006)
8. Gorelick, L., Veksler, O., Boykov, Y., Nieuwenhuis, C.: Convexity shape prior for binary segmentation. IEEE Trans. Patt. Anal. Mach. Intell. **39**(2), 258–271 (2017)
9. Isack, H., Veksler, O., Oguz, I., Sonka, M., Boykov, Y.: Efficient optimization for hierarchically-structured interacting segments (HINTS). In: IEEE Conference on Computer Vision and Pattern Recognition (2017)
10. Delong, A., Boykov, Y.: Globally optimal segmentation of multi-region objects. In: International Conference on Computer Vision (ICCV) (2009)
11. Yin, Y., Zhang, X., Williams, R., Wu, X., Anderson, D.D., Sonka, M.: Logismos-layered optimal graph image segmentation of multiple objects and surfaces: cartilage segmentation in the knee joint. IEEE Trans. Med. Imaging **29**(12), 2023–2037 (2010)
12. Boykov, Y., Isack, H., Olsson, C., Ben Ayed, I.: Volumetric bias in segmentation and reconstruction: secrets and solutions. In: The IEEE International Conference on Computer Vision (ICCV), December 2015
13. Gulshan, V., Rother, C., Criminisi, A., Blake, A., Zisserman, A.: Geodesic star convexity for interactive image segmentation. In: 2010 IEEE Conference on CVPR, pp. 3129–3136. IEEE (2010)
14. Isack, H., Veksler, O., Sonka, M., Boykov, Y.: Hedgehog shape priors for multi-object segmentation. In: The IEEE Conference on Computer Vision and Pattern Recognition (CVPR), June 2016
15. Toranzos, F.A., Cunto, A.F.: Sets expressible as finite unions of starshaped sets. J. Geom. **79**(1–2), 190–195 (2004)
16. Aichholzer, O., Aurenhammer, F., Demaine, E.D., Hurtado, F., Ramos, P., Urrutia, J.: On k-convex polygons. Comput. Geom. **45**(3), 73–87 (2012)
17. Molnar, C., et al.: Accurate morphology preserving segmentation of overlapping cells based on active contours. Nat. Sci. Rep. **6**, 32412 (2016)
18. Qi, X., Xing, F., Foran, D.J., Yang, L.: Robust segmentation of overlapping cells in histopathology specimens using parallel seed detection and repulsive level set. IEEE Trans. Biomed. Eng. **59**(3), 754–765 (2012)

19. Lee, H., Kim, J.: Segmentation of overlapping cervical cells in microscopic images with superpixel partitioning and cell-wise contour refinement. In: Proceedings of the IEEE Conference on Computer Vision and Pattern Recognition Workshops, pp. 63–69 (2016)
20. Vicente, S., Kolmogorov, V., Rother, C.: Graph cut based image segmentation with connectivity priors. In: 2008 IEEE conference on Computer Vision and Pattern Recognition, CVPR 2008, pp. 1–8. IEEE (2008)
21. Siddiqi, K., Pizer, S.: Medial Representations: Mathematics, Algorithms and Applications, vol. 37. Springer, New York (2008)
22. Kolmogorov, V., Zabih, R.: What energy functions can be minimized via graph cuts. IEEE Trans. Patt. Anal. Mach. Intell. 26(2), 147–159 (2004)
23. Boykov, Y., Funka-Lea, G.: Graph cuts and efficient N-D image segmentation. Int. J. Comput. Vis. (IJCV) 70(2), 109–131 (2006)
24. Isack, H., Boykov, Y., Veksler, O.: A-expansion for multiple "hedgehog" shapes. Technical report (2016)
25. Delong, A., Osokin, A., Isack, H., Boykov, Y.: Fast approximate energy minization with label costs. Int. J. Comput. Vis. (IJCV) 96(1), 1–27 (2012)
26. Vicente, S., Kolmogorov, V., Rother, C.: Graph cut based image segmentation with connectivity priors. In: IEEE conference on Computer Vision and Pattern Recognition (CVPR) (2008)

Pixel2Mesh: Generating 3D Mesh Models from Single RGB Images

Nanyang Wang[1], Yinda Zhang[2], Zhuwen Li[3], Yanwei Fu[4], Wei Liu[5], and Yu-Gang Jiang[1](✉)

[1] Shanghai Key Lab of Intelligent Information Processing, School of Computer Science, Fudan University, Shanghai, China
{nywang16,ygj}@fudan.edu.cn
[2] Princeton University, Princeton, USA
yindaz@cs.princeton.edu
[3] Intel Labs, Santa Clara, USA
lzhuwen@gmail.com
[4] School of Data Science, Fudan University, Shanghai, China
yanweifu@fudan.edu.cn
[5] Tencent AI Lab, Bellevue, USA
wl2223@columbia.edu

Abstract. We propose an end-to-end deep learning architecture that produces a 3D shape in triangular mesh from a single color image. Limited by the nature of deep neural network, previous methods usually represent a 3D shape in volume or point cloud, and it is non-trivial to convert them to the more ready-to-use mesh model. Unlike the existing methods, our network represents 3D mesh in a graph-based convolutional neural network and produces correct geometry by progressively deforming an ellipsoid, leveraging perceptual features extracted from the input image. We adopt a coarse-to-fine strategy to make the whole deformation procedure stable, and define various of mesh related losses to capture properties of different levels to guarantee visually appealing and physically accurate 3D geometry. Extensive experiments show that our method not only qualitatively produces mesh model with better details, but also achieves higher 3D shape estimation accuracy compared to the state-of-the-art.

Keywords: 3D shape generation
Graph convolutional neural network · Mesh reconstruction
Coarse-to-fine · End-to-end framework

N. Wang, Y. Zhang and Z. Li—Equal contributions.

Electronic supplementary material The online version of this chapter (https://doi.org/10.1007/978-3-030-01252-6_4) contains supplementary material, which is available to authorized users.

© Springer Nature Switzerland AG 2018
V. Ferrari et al. (Eds.): ECCV 2018, LNCS 11215, pp. 55–71, 2018.
https://doi.org/10.1007/978-3-030-01252-6_4

1 Introduction

Inferring 3D shape from a single perspective is a fundamental human vision functionality but is extremely challenging for computer vision. Recently, great success has been achieved for 3d shape generation from a single color image using deep learning techniques [6,9]. Taking advantage of convolutional layers on regular grids or multi-layer perception, the estimated 3D shape, as the output of the neural network, is represented as either a volume [6] or point cloud [9]. However, both representations lose important surface details, and is non-trivial to reconstruct a surface model (Fig. 1), i.e. a mesh, which is more desirable for many real applications since it is lightweight, capable of modelling shape details, easy to deform for animation, to name a few.

In this paper, we push along the direction of single image reconstruction, and propose an algorithm to extract a 3D triangular mesh from a single color image. Rather than directly synthesizing, our model learns to deform a mesh from a mean shape to the target geometry. This benefits us from several aspects. First, deep network is better at predicting residual, e.g. a spatial deformation, rather than structured output, e.g. a graph. Second, a series of deformations can be added up together, which allows shape to be gradually refined in detail. It also enables the control of the trade-off between the complexity of the deep learning model and the quality of the result. Lastly, it provides the chance to encode any prior knowledge to the initial mesh, e.g. topology. As a pioneer study, in this work, we specifically work on objects that can be approximated using 3D mesh with genus 0 by deforming an ellipsoid with a fixed size. In practice, we found most of the commonly seen categories can be handled well under this setting, e.g. car, plane, table, etc. To achieve this goal, there are several inherent challenges.

The first challenge is how to represent a mesh model, which is essentially an irregular graph, in a neural network and still be capable of extracting shape details effectively from a given color image represented in a 2D regular grid. It requires the integration of the knowledge learned from two data modalities. On the 3D geometry side, we directly build a graph based fully convolutional network (GCN) [3,8,18] on the mesh model, where the vertices and edges in the mesh are directly represented as nodes and connections in a graph. Network feature encoding information for 3D shape is saved on each vertex. Through

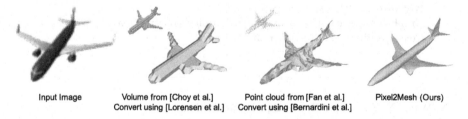

Input Image   Volume from [Choy et al.]   Point cloud from [Fan et al.]   Pixel2Mesh (Ours)
               Convert using [Lorensen et al.] Convert using [Bernardini et al.]

Fig. 1. Given a single color image and an initial mesh, our method can produce a high-quality mesh that contains details from the example.

forward propagation, the convolutional layers enable feature exchanging across neighboring nodes, and eventually regress the 3D location for each vertex. On the 2D image side, we use a VGG-16 like architecture to extract features as it has been demonstrated to be successful for many tasks [10,20]. To bridge these two, we design a perceptual feature pooling layer which allows each node in the GCN to pool image features from its 2D projection on the image, which can be readily obtained by assuming known camera intrinsic matrix. The perceptual feature pooling is enabled once after several convolutions (i.e. a deformation block described in Sect. 3.4) using updated 3D locations, and hence the image features from correct locations can be effectively integrated with 3D shapes.

Given the graph representation, the next challenge is how to update the vertex location effectively towards ground truth. In practice, we observe that network trained to directly predict mesh with a large number of vertices is likely to make mistake in the beginning and hard to fix later. One reason is that a vertex cannot effectively retrieve features from other vertices with a number of edges away, i.e. the limited receptive field. To solve this problem, we design a graph unpooling layer, which allows the network to initiate with a smaller number of vertices and increase during the forward propagation. With fewer vertices at the beginning stages, the network learns to distribute the vertices around to the most representative location, and then add local details as the number of vertices increases later. Besides the graph unpooling layer, we use a deep GCN enhanced by shortcut connections [13] as the backbone of our architecture, which enables large receptive fields for global context and more steps of movements.

Representing the shape in graph also benefits the learning procedure. The known connectivity allows us to define higher order loss functions across neighboring nodes, which are important to regularize 3D shapes. Specifically, we define a surface normal loss to favor smooth surface; an edge loss to encourage uniform distribution of mesh vertices for high recall; and a laplacian loss to prevent mesh faces from intersecting each other. All of these losses are essential to generate quality appealing mesh model, and none of them can be trivially defined without the graph representation.

The contributions of this paper are mainly in three aspects. First, we propose a novel end-to-end neural network architecture that generates a 3D mesh model from a single RGB image. Second, we design a projection layer which incorporates perceptual image features into the 3D geometry represented by GCN. Third, our network predict 3D geometry in a coarse to fine fashion, which is more reliable and easy to learn.

2   Related Work

3D reconstruction has been well studied based on the multi-view geometry (MVG) [12] in the literature. The major research directions include structure from motion (SfM) [27] for large-scale high-quality reconstruction and simultaneous localization and mapping (SLAM) [4] for navigation. Though they are very successful in these scenarios, they are restricted by (1) the coverage that the multiple views can give and (2) the appearance of the object that wants to reconstruct. The former restriction means MVG cannot reconstruct unseen parts of the object, and thus it usually takes a long time to get enough views for a good reconstruction; the latter restriction means MVG cannot reconstruct non-lambertian (e.g. reflective or transparent) or textureless objects. These restrictions lead to the trend of resorting to learning based approaches.

Learning based approaches usually consider single or few images, as it largely relies on the shape priors that it can learn from data. Early works can be traced back to Hoiem et al. [14] and Saxena et al. [25]. Most recently, with the success of deep learning architectures and the release of large-scale 3D shape datasets such as ShapeNet [5], learning based approaches have achieved great progress. Huang et al. [15] and Su et al. [29] retrieve shape components from a large dataset, assemble them and deform the assembled shape to fit the observed image. However, shape retrieval from images itself is an ill-posed problem. To avoid this problem, Kar et al. [16] learns a 3D deformable model for each object category and capture the shape variations in different images. However, the reconstruction is limited to the popular categories and its reconstruction result is usually lack of details. Another line of research is to directly learn 3D shapes from single images. Restricted by the prevalent grid-based deep learning architectures, most works [6,11] outputs 3D voxels, which are usually with low resolutions due to the memory constraint on a modern GPU. Most recently, Tatarchenko et al. [30] have proposed an octree representation, which allows to reconstructing higher resolution outputs with a limited memory budget. However, a 3D voxel is still not a popular shape representation in game and movie industries. To avoid drawbacks of the voxel representation, Fan et al. [9] propose to generate point clouds from single images. The point cloud representation has no local connections between points, and thus the point positions have a very large degree of freedom. Consequently, the generated point cloud is usually not close to a surface and cannot be used to recover a 3D mesh directly. Besides these typical 3D representations, there is an interesting work [28] which uses a so-called "geometry image" to represent a 3D shape. Thus, their network is a 2D convolutional neural network which conducts an image to image mapping. Our works are mostly related to the two recent works [17,24]. However, the former adopts simple silhouette supervision, and hence does not perform well for complicated objects such as car, lamp, etc.; the latter needs a large model repository to generate a combined model.

Our base network is a graph neural network [26]; this architecture has been adopted for shape analysis [31]. In the meanwhile, there are charting-based methods which directly apply convolutions on surface manifolds [2,22,23] for shape analysis. As far as we know, these architectures have never been adopted for 3D reconstruction from single images, though graph and surface manifold are natural representations for meshed objects. For a comprehensive understanding of the graph neural network, the charting-based methods and their applications, please refer to this survey [3].

3   Method

3.1   Preliminary: Graph-Based Convolution

We first provide some background about graph based convolution; more detailed introduction can be found in [3]. A 3D mesh is a collection of vertices, edges and faces that defines the shape of a 3D object; it can be represented by a graph $\mathcal{M} = (\mathcal{V}, \mathcal{E}, \mathbf{F})$, where $\mathcal{V} = \{v_i\}_{i=1}^N$ is the set of N vertices in the mesh, $\mathcal{E} = \{e_i\}_{i=1}^E$ is the set of E edges with each connecting two vertices, and $\mathbf{F} = \{f_i\}_{i=1}^N$ are the feature vectors attached on vertices. A graph based convolutional layer is defined on irregular graph as:

$$f_p^{l+1} = w_0 f_p^l + \sum_{q \in \mathcal{N}(p)} w_1 f_q^l \tag{1}$$

where $f_p^l \in \mathbb{R}^{d_l}$, $f_p^{l+1} \in \mathbb{R}^{d_{l+1}}$ are the feature vectors on vertex p before and after the convolution, and $\mathcal{N}(p)$ is the neighboring vertices of p; w_0 and w_1 are the learnable parameter matrices of $d_l \times d_{l+1}$ that are applied to all vertices. Note that w_1 is shared for all edges, and thus (1) works on nodes with different vertex degrees. In our case, the attached feature vector f_p is the concatenation of the 3D vertex coordinate, feature encoding 3D shape, and feature learned from the input color image (if they exist). Running convolutions updates the features, which is equivalent as applying a deformation.

3.2   System Overview

Our model is an end-to-end deep learning framework that takes a single color image as input and produces a 3D mesh model in camera coordinate. The overview of our framework is illustrated in Fig. 2. The whole network consists an image feature network and a cascaded mesh deformation network. The image feature network is a 2D CNN that extract perceptual feature from the input image, which is leveraged by the mesh deformation network to progressively deform an ellipsoid mesh into the desired 3D model. The cascaded mesh deformation network is a graph-based convolution network (GCN), which contains three deformation blocks intersected by two graph unpooling layers. Each deformation block takes an input graph representing the current mesh model with the 3D shape feature attached on vertices, and produces new vertices locations and features. Whereas the graph unpooling layers increase the number of vertices to increase the capacity of handling details, while still maintain the triangular mesh topology. Starting from a smaller number of vertices, our model learns to gradually deform and add details to the mesh model in a coarse-to-fine fashion. In order to train the network to produce stable deformation and generate an accurate mesh, we extend the Chamfer Distance loss used by Fan *et al.* [9] with three other mesh specific loss – Surface normal loss, Laplacian regularization loss, and Edge length loss. The remaining part of this section describes details of these components.

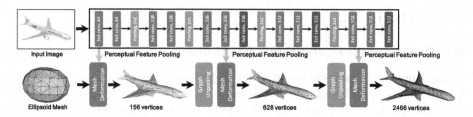

Fig. 2. The cascaded mesh deformation network. Our full model contains three mesh deformation blocks in a row. Each block increases mesh resolution and estimates vertex locations, which are then used to extract perceptual image features from the 2D CNN for the next block.

3.3   Initial Ellipsoid

Our model does not require any prior knowledge of the 3D shape, and always deform from an initial ellipsoid with average size placed at the common location in the camera coordinate. The ellipsoid is centered at 0.8 m in front of the camera with 0.2 m, 0.2 m, 0.4 m as the radius of three axis. The mesh model is generated by implicit surface algorithm in Meshlab [7] and contains 156 vertices. We use this ellipsoid to initialize our input graph, where the initial feature contains only the 3D coordinate of each vertex.

3.4   Mesh Deformation Block

The architecture of mesh deformation block is shown in Fig. 3(a). In order to generate 3D mesh model that is consistent with the object shown in the input image, the deformation block need to pool feature ($\mathbf{P}$) from the input image. This is done in conjunction with the image feature network and a perceptual feature pooling layer given the location of vertex ($\mathbf{C}_{i-1}$) in the current mesh model. The pooled perceptual feature is then concatenated with the 3D shape feature attached on the vertex from the input graph ($\mathbf{F}_{i-1}$) and fed into a series of graph based ResNet (G-ResNet). The G-ResNet produces, also as the output of the mesh deformation block, the new coordinates ($\mathbf{C}_i$) and 3d shape feature ($\mathbf{F}_i$) for each vertex.

Perceptual Feature Pooling Layer. We use a VGG-16 architecture up to layer conv5_3 as the image feature network as it has been widely used. Given the 3D coordinate of a vertex, we calculate its 2D projection on input image plane using camera intrinsics, and then pool the feature from four nearby pixels using bilinear interpolation. In particular, we concatenate feature extracted from layer 'conv3_3', 'conv4_3', and 'conv5_3', which results in a total dimension of 1280. This perceptual feature is then concatenated with the 128-dim 3D feature from the input mesh, which results in a total dimension of 1408. This is illustrated in Fig. 3(b). Note that in the first block, the perceptual feature is concatenated with the 3-dim feature (coordinate) since there is no learnt shape feature at the beginning.

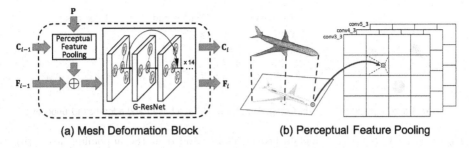

Fig. 3. (a) The vertex locations C_i are used to extract image features, which are then combined with vertex features F_i and fed into G-ResNet. $\oplus$ means a concatenation of the features. (b) The 3D vertices are projected to the image plane using camera intrinsics, and perceptual feature is pooled from the 2D-CNN layers using bilinear interpolation.

G-ResNet. After obtaining 1408-dim feature for each vertex representing both 3D shape and 2D image information, we design a graph based convolutional neural network to predict new location and 3D shape feature for each vertex. This requires efficient exchange of the information between vertices. However, as defined in (1), each convolution only enables the feature exchanging between neighboring pixels, which severely impairs the efficiency of information exchanging. This is equivalent as the small receptive field issue on 2D CNN.

To solve this issue, we make a very deep network with shortcut connections [13] and denote it as G-ResNet (Fig. 3(a)). In this work, the G-ResNet in all blocks has the same structure, which consists of 14 graph residual convolutional layers with 128 channels. The serial of G-ResNet block produces a new 128-dim 3D feature. In addition to the feature output, there is a branch which applies an extra graph convolutional layer to the last layer features and outputs the 3D coordinates of the vertex.

3.5 Graph Unpooling Layer

The goal of unpooling layer is to increase the number of vertex in the GCNN. It allows us to start from a mesh with fewer vertices and add more only when necessary, which reduces memory costs and produces better results. A straight-forward approach is to add one vertex in the center of each triangle and connect it with the three vertices of the triangle (Fig. 4(b) Face-based). However, this causes imbalanced vertex degrees, i.e. number of edges on vertex. Inspired by the vertex adding strategy of the mesh subdivision algorithm prevalent in computer graphics, we add a vertex at the center of each edge and connect it with the two end-point of this edge (Fig. 4(a)). The 3D feature for newly added vertex is set as the average of its two neighbors. We also connect three vertices if they are added on the same triangle (dashed line.) Consequently, we create 4 new triangles for each triangle in the original mesh, and the number of vertex is increased by

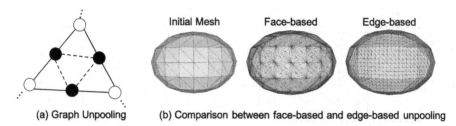

(a) Graph Unpooling   (b) Comparison between face-based and edge-based unpooling

Fig. 4. (a) Black vertices and dashed edges are added in the unpooling layer. (b) The face based unpooling leads to imbalanced vertex degrees, while the edge-based unpooling remains regular.

the number of edges in the original mesh. This edge-based unpooling uniformly upsamples the vertices as shown in Fig. 4(b) Edge-based.

3.6 Losses

We define four kinds of losses to constrain the property of the output shape and the deformation procedure to guarantee appealing results. We adopt the Chamfer loss [9] to constrain the location of mesh vertices, a normal loss to enforce the consistency of surface normal, a laplacian regularization to maintain relative location between neighboring vertices during deformation, and an edge length regularization to prevent outliers. These losses are applied with equal weight on both the intermediate and final mesh.

Unless otherwise stated, we use p for a vertex in the predicted mesh, q for a vertex in the ground truth mesh, $\mathcal{N}(p)$ for the neighboring pixel of p, till the end of this section.

Chamfer Loss. The Chamfer distance measures the distance of each point to the other set: $l_c = \sum_p \min_q \|p - q\|_2^2 + \sum_q \min_p \|p - q\|_2^2$. It is reasonably good to regress the vertices close to its correct position, however is not sufficient to produce nice 3D mesh (see the result of Fan et al. [9] in Fig. 1).

Normal Loss. We further define loss on surface normal to characterize high order properties: $l_n = \sum_p \sum_{q=\arg\min_q(\|p-q\|_2^2)} \|\langle p-k, \mathbf{n}_q \rangle\|_2^2$, s.t. $k \in \mathcal{N}(p)$ where q is the closest vertex for p that is found when calculating the chamfer loss, k is the neighboring pixel of p, $\langle \cdot, \cdot \rangle$ is the inner product of two vectors, and $\mathbf{n}_q$ is the observed surface normal from ground truth.

Essentially, this loss requires the edge between a vertex with its neighbors to perpendicular to the observation from the ground truth. One may find that this loss does not equal to zero unless on a planar surface. However, optimizing this loss is equivalent as forcing the normal of a locally fitted tangent plane to be consistent with the observation, which works practically well in our experiment. Moreover, this normal loss is fully differentiable and easy to optimize.

Regularization. Even with the Chamfer loss and Normal loss, the optimization is easily stucked in some local minimum. More specifically, the network may generate some super large deformation to favor some local consistency, which is especially harmful at the beginning when the estimation is far from ground truth, and causes flying vertices (Fig. 5).

Laplacian Regularization. To handle these problem, we first propose a Laplacian term to prevent the vertices from moving too freely, which potentially avoids mesh self-intersection. The laplaician term serves as a local detail preserving operator, that encourages neighboring vertices to have the same movement. In the first deformation block, it acts like a surface smoothness term since the input to this block is a smooth-everywhere ellipsoid; starting from the second block, it prevents the 3D mesh model from deforming too much, so that only fine-grained details are added to the mesh model. To calculate this loss, we first define a laplacian coordinate for each vertex p as $\delta_p = p - \sum_{k \in \mathcal{N}(p)} \frac{1}{\|\mathcal{N}(p)\|} k$, and the laplacian regularization is defined as: $l_{lap} = \sum_p \|\delta_p' - \delta_p\|_2^2$, where δ_p' and δ_p are the laplacian coordinate of a vertex after and before a deformation block.

Edge Length Regularization. To penalize flying vertices, which ususally cause long edge, we add an edge length regularization loss: $l_{loc} = \sum_p \sum_{k \in \mathcal{N}(p)} \|p - k\|_2^2$.

   The overall loss is a weighted sum of all four losses, $l_{all} = l_c + \lambda_1 l_n + \lambda_2 l_{lap} + \lambda_3 l_{loc}$, where $\lambda_1 = 1.6e - 4$, $\lambda_2 = 0.3$ and $\lambda_3 = 0.1$ are the hyperparameters which balance the losses and fixed for all the experiments.

4   Experiment

In this section, we perform an extensive evaluation on our model. In addition to comparing with previous 3D shape generation works for evaluating the reconstruction accuracy, we also analyse the importance of each component in our model. Qualitative results on both synthetic and real-world images further show that our model produces triangular meshes with smooth surfaces and still maintains details depicted in the input images.

4.1   Experimental Setup

Data. We use the dataset provided by Choy et al. [6]. The dataset contains rendering images of 50k models belonging to 13 object categories from ShapeNet [5], which is a collection of 3D CAD models that are organized according to the WordNet hierarchy. A model is rendered from various camera viewpoints, and camera intrinsic and extrinsic matrices are recorded. For fair comparison, we use the same training/testing split as in Choy et al. [6].

Evaluation Metric. We adopt the standard 3D reconstruction metric. We first uniformly sample points from our result and ground truth. We calculate precision and recall by checking the percentage of points in prediction or ground truth that can find a nearest neighbor from the other within certain threshold τ. A F-score [19] as the harmonic mean of precision and recall is then calculated. Following Fan et al. [9], we also report the Chamfer Distance (CD) and Earth Mover's Distance (EMD). For F-Score, larger is better. For CD and EMD, smaller is better.

On the other hand, we realize that the commonly used evaluation metrics for shape generation may not thoroughly reflect the shape quality. They often capture occupancy or point-wise distance rather than surface properties, such as continuity, smoothness, high-order details, for which a standard evaluation metric is barely missing in literature. Thus, we recommend to pay attention on qualitative results for better understanding of these aspects.

Baselines. We compare the presented approach to the most recent single image reconstruction approaches. Specifically, we compare with two state-of-the-art methods - Choy et al. [6] (3D-R2N2) producing 3D volume, and Fan et al. [9] (PSG) producing point cloud. Since the metrics are defined on point cloud, we can evaluate PSG directly on its output, our method by uniformly sampling point on surface, and 3D-R2N2 by uniformly sampling point from mesh created using the Marching Cube [21] method.

We also compare to Neural 3D Mesh Renderer (N3MR) [17] which is so far the only deep learning based mesh generation model with code public available. For fair comparison, the models are trained with the same data using the same amount of time.

Training and Runtime. Our network receives input images of size 224×224, and initial ellipsoid with 156 vertices and 462 edges. The network is implemented in Tensorflow and optimized using Adam with weight decay 1e–5. The batch size is 1; the total number of training epoch is 50; the learning rate is initialized as 3e–5 and drops to 1e–5 after 40 epochs. The total training time is 72 h on a Nvidia Titan X. During testing, our model takes 15.58 ms to generate a mesh with 2466 vertices.

4.2   Comparison to State of the Art

Table 1 shows the F-score with different thresholds of different methods. Our approach outperforms the other methods in all categories except watercraft. Notably, our results are significantly better than the others in all categories under a smaller threshold τ, showing at least 10% F-score improvement. N3MR does not perform well, and its result is about 50% worse than ours, probably because their model only learns from limited silhouette signal in images and lacks of explicit handling of the 3D mesh.

Table 1. F-score (%) on the ShapeNet test set at different thresholds, where $\tau = 10^{-4}$. Larger is better. Best results under each threshold are bolded.

Threshold	τ				2τ			
Category	3D-R2N2	PSG	N3MR	Ours	3D-R2N2	PSG	N3MR	Ours
plane	41.46	68.20	62.10	**71.12**	63.23	81.22	77.15	**81.38**
bench	34.09	49.29	35.84	**57.57**	48.89	69.17	49.58	**71.86**
cabinet	49.88	39.93	21.04	**60.39**	64.83	67.03	35.16	**77.19**
car	37.80	50.70	36.66	**67.86**	54.84	77.79	53.93	**84.15**
chair	40.22	41.60	30.25	**54.38**	55.20	63.70	44.59	**70.42**
monitor	34.38	40.53	28.77	**51.39**	48.23	63.64	42.76	**67.01**
lamp	32.35	41.40	27.97	**48.15**	44.37	58.84	39.41	**61.50**
speaker	45.30	32.61	19.46	**48.84**	57.86	56.79	32.20	**65.61**
firearm	28.34	69.96	52.22	**73.20**	46.87	82.65	63.28	**83.47**
couch	40.01	36.59	25.04	**51.90**	53.42	62.95	39.90	**69.83**
table	43.79	53.44	28.40	**66.30**	59.49	73.10	41.73	**79.20**
cellphone	42.31	55.95	27.96	**70.24**	60.88	79.63	41.83	**82.86**
watercraft	37.10	51.28	43.71	**55.12**	52.19	**70.63**	58.85	69.99
Mean	39.01	48.58	33.80	**59.72**	54.62	69.78	47.72	**74.19**

Table 2. CD and EMD on the ShapeNet test set. Smaller is better. Best results under each threshold are bolded.

Category	CD				EMD			
	3D-R2N2	PSG	N3MR	Ours	3D-R2N2	PSG	N3MR	Ours
plane	0.895	**0.430**	0.450	0.477	0.606	**0.396**	7.498	0.579
bench	1.891	0.629	2.268	**0.624**	1.136	1.113	11.766	**0.965**
cabinet	0.735	0.439	2.555	**0.381**	**2.520**	2.986	17.062	2.563
car	0.845	0.333	2.298	**0.268**	1.670	1.747	11.641	**1.297**
chair	1.432	0.645	2.084	**0.610**	1.466	1.946	11.809	**1.399**
monitor	1.707	**0.722**	3.111	0.755	1.667	1.891	14.097	**1.536**
lamp	4.009	**1.193**	3.013	1.295	1.424	1.222	14.741	**1.314**
speaker	1.507	0.756	3.343	**0.739**	**2.732**	3.490	16.720	2.951
firearm	0.993	**0.423**	2.641	0.453	0.688	**0.397**	11.889	0.667
couch	1.135	0.549	3.512	**0.490**	2.114	2.207	14.876	**1.642**
table	1.116	0.517	2.383	**0.498**	1.641	2.121	12.842	**1.480**
cellphone	1.137	0.438	4.366	**0.421**	0.912	1.019	17.649	**0.724**
watercraft	1.215	**0.633**	2.154	0.670	0.935	0.945	11.425	**0.814**
Mean	1.445	0.593	2.629	**0.591**	1.501	1.653	13.386	**1.380**

We also show the CD and EMD for all categories in Table 2. Our approach outperforms the other methods in most categories and achieves the best mean score. The major competitor is PSG, which produces a point cloud and has the most freedom; this freedom leads to smaller CD and EMD, however does not necessarily leads to a better mesh model without proper regularization. To demonstrate this, we show the qualitative results to analyze why our approach outperforms the others. Figure 8 shows the visual results. To compare the quality of mesh model, we convert volumetric and point cloud to mesh using standard approaches [1,21]. As we can see, the 3D volume results produced by 3D-R2N2 lack of details due to the low resolution, e.g., the legs are missing in the chair example as shown in the 4-th row of Fig. 8. We tried octree based solution [30] to increase the volume resolution, but found it still hard to recover surface level details as much as our model. PSG produces sparse 3D point clouds, and it is non-trivial to recover meshes from them. This is due to the applied Chamfer loss acting like a regression loss which gives too much degree of freedom to the point cloud. N3MR produces very rough shape, which might be sufficient for some rendering tasks, however cannot recover complicated objects such as chairs and tables. In contrast, our model does not suffer from these issues by leveraging a mesh representation, integration of perceptual feature, and carefully defined losses during the training. Our result is not restricted by the resolution due to the limited memory budget and contains both smooth continuous surface and local details.

4.3   Ablation Study

Now we conduct controlled experiments to analyse the importance of each component in our model. Table 3 reports the performance of each model by removing one component from the full model. Again, we argue that these commonly used evaluation metrics does not necessarily reflect the quality of the recovered 3D geometry. For example, the model with no edge length regularization achieves the best performance across all, however, in fact produces the worst mesh (Fig. 5, the last 2nd column). As such, we use qualitative result Fig. 5 to show the contribution of each component in our system.

Table 3. Ablation study that evaluates the contribution of different ideas to the performance of the presented model. The table reports all 4 measurements. For F-score, larger is better. For CD and EMD, small is better.

Category	-ResNet	-Laplacian	-Unpooling	-Normal	-Edge length	Full model
F (τ)↑	55.308	60.801	60.222	58.668	60.101	59.728
F (2τ)↑	71.567	75.202	76.231	74.276	76.053	74.191
CD↓	0.644	0.596	0.561	0.598	0.552	0.591
EMD↓	1.583	1.350	1.656	1.445	1.479	1.380

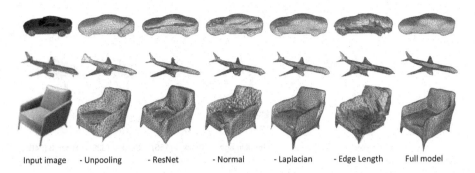

Input image   - Unpooling   - ResNet   - Normal   - Laplacian   - Edge Length   Full model

Fig. 5. Qualitative results for ablation study. This figure truly reflects the contribution of each components especially for the regularization ones.

Graph Unpooling. We first remove the graph unpooling layers, and thus each block has the same number of vertices as in the last block of our full model. It is observed that the deformation makes mistake easier at beginning, which cannot be fixed later on. Consequently, there are some obvious artifacts in some parts of the objects.

G-ResNet. We then remove the shortcut connections in G-ResNet, and make it regular GCN. As can be seen from Table 3, there is a huge performance gap in all four measurement metrics, which means the failure of optimizing Chamfer distance. The main reason is the degradation problem observed in the very deep 2D convolutional neural network. Such problem leads to a higher training error (and thus higher testing error) when adding more layers to a suitably deep model [13]. Essentially, our network has 42 graph convolutional layers. Thus, this phenomenon has also been observed in our very deep graph neural network experiment.

Loss Terms. We evaluate the function of each additional terms besides the Chamfer loss. As can be seen in Fig. 5, removing normal loss severely impairs the surface smoothness and local details, e.g. seat back; removing Laplacian term causes intersecting geometry because the local topology changes, e.g. the hand held of the chair; removing edge length term causes flying vertices and surfaces, which completely ruins the surface characteristics. These results demonstrate that all the components presented in this work contribute to the final performance.

Number of Deformation Blocks. We now analyze the effects of the number of blocks. Figure Fig. 6 (left) shows the mean F-score(τ) and CD with regard to the number of blocks. The results indicate that increasing the number of blocks helps, but the benefit is getting saturated with more blocks, e.g. from 3 to 4. In our experiment, we found that 4 blocks results in too many vertices

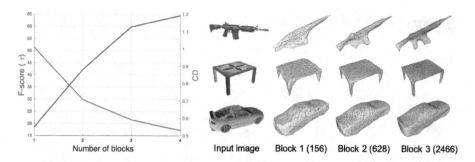

Fig. 6. Left: Effect of number of blocks. Each curve shows the mean F-score (τ) and CD for different number of blocks. Right: Sample examples showing the output after each block.

and edges, which slow down our approach dramatically even though it provides better accuracy on evaluation metrics. Therefore, we use 3 blocks in all our experiment for the best balance of performance and efficiency. Figure 6 (right) shows the output of our model after each deformation block. Notice how mesh is densified with more vertices and new details are added.

4.4 Reconstructing Real-World Images

Following Choy et al. [6], we test our network on the Online Products dataset and Internet images for qualitative evaluation on real images. We use the model trained from ShapeNet dataset and directly run on real images without finetuning, and show results in Fig. 7. As can be seen, our model trained on synthetic data generalizes well to the real-world images across various categories.

Fig. 7. Qualitative results of real-world images from the Online Products dataset and Internet.

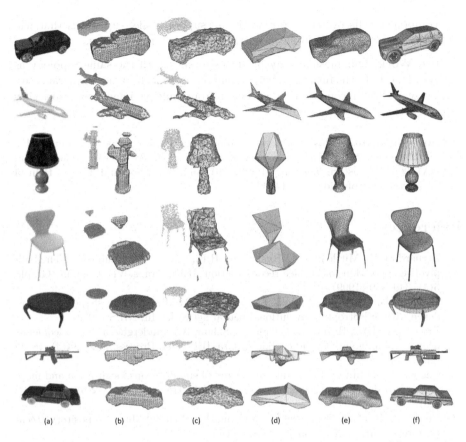

Fig. 8. Qualitative results. (a) Input image; (b) Volume from 3D-R2N2 [6], converted using Marching Cube [21]; (c) Point cloud from PSG [9], converted using ball pivoting [1]; (d) N3MR [17]; (e) Ours; (f) Ground truth.

5   Conclusion

We have presented an approach to extract 3D triangular meshes from singe images. We exploit the key advantages the mesh presentation can bring to us, and the key issues required to solve for success. The former includes surface normal constraints and information propagation along edges; the latter includes perceptual features extracted from images as a guidance. We carefully design our network structure and propose a very deep cascaded graph convolutional neural network with "shortcut" connections. Meshes are progressively refined by our network trained end-to-end with the chamfer loss and normal loss. Our results are significantly better than the previous state-of-the-art using other shape representations such as 3D volume or 3D point cloud. Thus, we believe mesh representation is the next big thing in this direction, and we hope that the key components discovered in our work can support follow-up works that will further advance direct 3D mesh reconstruction from single images.

Future Work. Our method only produces meshes with the same topology as the initial mesh. In the future, we will extend our approach to more general cases, such as scene level reconstruction, and learn from multiple images for multi-view reconstruction.

Acknowledgements. This work was supported by two projects from NSFC (#61622204 and #61572134), two projects from STCSM (#16JC1420401 and #16QA1400500), Eastern Scholar (TP2017006), and The Thousand Talents Plan of China (for young professionals, D1410009).

References

1. Bernardini, F., Mittleman, J., Rushmeier, H.E., Silva, C.T., Taubin, G.: The ball-pivoting algorithm for surface reconstruction. IEEE Trans. Vis. Comput. Graph. 5(4), 349–359 (1999)
2. Boscaini, D., Masci, J., Rodolà, E., Bronstein, M.M.: Learning shape correspondence with anisotropic convolutional neural networks. In: NIPS (2016)
3. Bronstein, M.M., Bruna, J., LeCun, Y., Szlam, A., Vandergheynst, P.: Geometric deep learning: going beyond euclidean data. IEEE Sig. Process. Mag. 34(4), 18–42 (2017)
4. Cadena, C., et al.: Past, present, and future of simultaneous localization and mapping: towards the robust-perception age. IEEE Trans. Robot. 32(6), 1309–1332 (2016)
5. Chang, A.X., et al.: ShapeNet: An Information-Rich 3D Model Repository. Technical report arXiv:1512.03012 [cs.GR] (2015)
6. Choy, C.B., Xu, D., Gwak, J.Y., Chen, K., Savarese, S.: 3D-R2N2: a unified approach for single and multi-view 3D object reconstruction. In: Leibe, B., Matas, J., Sebe, N., Welling, M. (eds.) ECCV 2016. LNCS, vol. 9912, pp. 628–644. Springer, Cham (2016). https://doi.org/10.1007/978-3-319-46484-8_38
7. Cignoni, P., Callieri, M., Corsini, M., Dellepiane, M., Ganovelli, F., Ranzuglia, G.: MeshLAB: an open-source mesh processing tool. In: Eurographics Italian Chapter Conference (2008)
8. Defferrard, M., Bresson, X., Vandergheynst, P.: Convolutional neural networks on graphs with fast localized spectral filtering. In: NIPS, pp. 3837–3845 (2016)
9. Fan, H., Su, H., Guibas, L.J.: A point set generation network for 3D object reconstruction from a single image. In: CVPR (2017)
10. Gatys, L.A., Ecker, A.S., Bethge, M.: Image style transfer using convolutional neural networks. In: CVPR (2016)
11. Girdhar, R., Fouhey, D.F., Rodriguez, M., Gupta, A.: Learning a predictable and generative vector representation for objects. In: Leibe, B., Matas, J., Sebe, N., Welling, M. (eds.) ECCV 2016. LNCS, vol. 9910, pp. 484–499. Springer, Cham (2016). https://doi.org/10.1007/978-3-319-46466-4_29
12. Hartley, R., Zisserman, A.: Multiple View Geometry in Computer Vision. Cambridge University Press, New York (2004)
13. He, K., Zhang, X., Ren, S., Sun, J.: Deep residual learning for image recognition. In: CVPR, pp. 770–778 (2016)

14. Hoiem, D., Efros, A.A., Hebert, M.: Recovering surface layout from an image. Int. J. Comput. Vis. **75**(1), 151–172 (2007)
15. Huang, Q., Wang, H., Koltun, V.: Single-view reconstruction via joint analysis of image and shape collections. ACM Trans. Graph. **34**(4), 87:1–87:10 (2015)
16. Kar, A., Tulsiani, S., Carreira, J., Malik, J.: Category-specific object reconstruction from a single image. In: CVPR (2015)
17. Kato, H., Ushiku, Y., Harada, T.: Neural 3D mesh renderer. In: CVPR (2018)
18. Kipf, T.N., Welling, M.: Semi-supervised classification with graph convolutional networks. In: ICLR (2016)
19. Knapitsch, A., Park, J., Zhou, Q., Koltun, V.: Tanks and temples: benchmarking large-scale scene reconstruction. ACM Trans. Graph. **36**(4), 78:1–78:13 (2017)
20. Li, Z., Chen, Q., Koltun, V.: Interactive image segmentation with latent diversity. In: CVPR (2018)
21. Lorensen, W.E., Cline, H.E.: Marching cubes: a high resolution 3D surface construction algorithm. In: SIGGRAPH (1987)
22. Masci, J., Boscaini, D., Bronstein, M.M., Vandergheynst, P.: Geodesic convolutional neural networks on riemannian manifolds. In: ICCV Workshop (2015)
23. Monti, F., Boscaini, D., Masci, J., Rodolà, E., Svoboda, J., Bronstein, M.M.: Geometric deep learning on graphs and manifolds using mixture model CNNs. In: CVPR (2017)
24. Pontes, J.K., Kong, C., Sridharan, S., Lucey, S., Eriksson, A., Fookes, C.: Image2mesh: a learning framework for single image 3D reconstruction. Technical report arXiv:1711.10669 [cs.CV] (2017)
25. Saxena, A., Sun, M., Ng, A.Y.: Make3D: learning 3D scene structure from a single still image. IEEE Trans. Patt. Anal. Mach. Intell. **31**(5), 824–840 (2009)
26. Scarselli, F., Gori, M., Tsoi, A.C., Hagenbuchner, M., Monfardini, G.: The graph neural network model. IEEE Trans. Neural Netw. **20**(1), 61–80 (2009)
27. Schönberger, J.L., Frahm, J.: Structure-from-motion revisited. In: CVPR (2016)
28. Sinha, A., Unmesh, A., Huang, Q., Ramani, K.: SurfNet: generating 3D shape surfaces using deep residual networks. In: CVPR (2017)
29. Su, H., Huang, Q., Mitra, N.J., Li, Y., Guibas, L.J.: Estimating image depth using shape collections. ACM Trans. Graph. **33**(4), 37:1–37:11 (2014)
30. Tatarchenko, M., Dosovitskiy, A., Brox, T.: Octree generating networks: efficient convolutional architectures for high-resolution 3D outputs. In: ICCV (2017)
31. Yi, L., Su, H., Guo, X., Guibas, L.J.: SyncSpecCNN: synchronized spectral CNN for 3D shape segmentation. In: CVPR (2017)

Boosted Attention: Leveraging Human Attention for Image Captioning

Shi Chen[iD] and Qi Zhao[✉][iD]

Department of Computer Science and Engineering, University of Minnesota,
Minneapolis, USA
{chen4595,qzhao}@umn.edu

Abstract. Visual attention has shown usefulness in image captioning, with the goal of enabling a caption model to selectively focus on regions of interest. Existing models typically rely on top-down language information and learn attention implicitly by optimizing the captioning objectives. While somewhat effective, the learned top-down attention can fail to focus on correct regions of interest without direct supervision of attention. Inspired by the human visual system which is driven by not only the task-specific top-down signals but also the visual stimuli, we in this work propose to use both types of attention for image captioning. In particular, we highlight the complementary nature of the two types of attention and develop a model (Boosted Attention) to integrate them for image captioning. We validate the proposed approach with state-of-the-art performance across various evaluation metrics.

Keywords: Image captioning · Visual attention · Human attention

1 Introduction

Image captioning aims at generating fluent language descriptions on a given image. Inspired by the human visual system, in the past few years, visual attention has been incorporated in various image captioning models [21,26,32,33]. Attention mechanisms encourage models to selectively focus on specific regions while generating captions instead of scanning through the whole image, avoiding information overflow as well as highlighting visual regions related to the task.

Following the success made in [32], visual attention in most conventional image captioning models is developed in a top-down fashion on a word basis. That is, visual attention is computed for each generated word based on visual information from the image and the partially generated natural language description. While such mechanism (*i.e.*, top-down attention) aims at connecting natural language and visual content, without prior knowledge on the visual content

---

Electronic supplementary material The online version of this chapter (https://doi.org/10.1007/978-3-030-01252-6_5) contains supplementary material, which is available to authorized users.

V. Ferrari et al. (Eds.): ECCV 2018, LNCS 11215, pp. 72–88, 2018.
https://doi.org/10.1007/978-3-030-01252-6_5

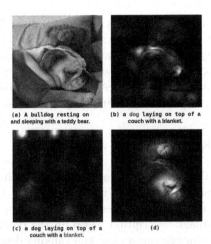

Fig. 1. Top-down attention may fail to focus on objects of interest. (a): original image with human-generated caption, (b–c) two top-down attention maps and their corresponding model-generated captions, and (d) stimulus-based attention map for the image. Words related to the top-down attention maps are colored in red. (Color figure online)

in terms of salient regions (*i.e.*, stimulus-based attention), the computed visual attention can fail to concentrate on objects of interest and attend to irrelevant regions. As shown in Fig. 1, a model with only top-down attention focuses on non-salient regions in the background (Fig. 1(c)) and does not capture salient objects in the image, *i.e.*, *bulldog* and *teddy bear* according to the human-generated caption.

Human attention is driven by both task-specific top-down signals and task-independent visual stimuli. For visual tasks such as image captioning, humans would naturally deploy their gaze based on both top-down and stimulus-based information during the exploration. As a result, the objects being mentioned in the same image by different people are largely consistent and correlated with the objects highlighted by the stimulus-based attention [35]. Therefore, we propose that the visual stimuli can be a reasonable source for locating salient regions in image captioning, which can also complement top-down attention that relates to specific tasks. In Fig. 1(d), we see that stimulus-based attention successfully attends to regions corresponding to objects of interest as mentioned in the human-generated caption.

In this work, we conduct qualitative analyses to understand the role of human stimulus-based attention in image captioning. We then present a Boosted Attention method that leverages stimulus-based attention for image captioning. More specifically, we combine the stimulus-based attention with top-down captioning attention to construct a novel attention mechanism that encourages models to attend to visual features based on task-specific top-down signals from natural language while at the same time focusing on salient regions highlighted by task-independent stimulus. Quantitative results on the Microsoft COCO [19] (MSCOCO) and Flickr30K [24] datasets show that incorporating stimulus-based attention is able to significantly improve the model performance across various evaluation metrics. We also visualize the results to qualitatively illustrate the complementary role of the two types of attention in image captioning. Our method is general and works with various image captioning models.

2   Related Works

Image Captioning. Generating natural language description based on a still image has gained increasing interest in the recent years. To generate captions, [4,14,17] first extract a set of attributes related to elements within an image and then generate language description based on the detected attributes. Several works [6,9,22] view image captioning as a ranking description problem and tackle the problem by conducting a query to retrieve descriptions lies close to an image on embedding space. With the successes of Deep Neural Networks (DNNs), a number of works [2,5,12,20,25,31,32] have developed neural network based methods to generate image captions. Typically, these methods use Convolutional Neural Networks (CNNs) as visual encoder to extract visual features and generate captions with Recurrent Neural Networks (RNNs) such as Long Short Term Memory (LSTM) [8].

Top-down Attention in Captioning. Top-down visual attention has been widely used on various image captioning models in order to allow models to selectively concentrate on objects of interest. Xu et al. [32] combine the memory vector of LSTM with visual features from CNN and feed the fused features to an attention network to compute the weights for features at different spatial locations. Yang et al. [33] propose a reviewer module that applies the visual attention mechanism for multiple times during generating the next word. In [21], an adaptive mechanism is proposed that assigns weights not only to visual features but also to a feature vector obtained based on the memory state of LSTM, since it is unnecessary to attend to the visual features for generating specific words such as 'the' and 'a'. Besides applying the attention mechanism on the spatial domain, Chen et al. [2] introduce channel-wise attention which is operated on different filters within a convolutional layer. Most of these models generate visual attention in a top-down fashion using the original visual features and top-down language information from the partially generated caption. Without direct supervision or prior knowledge with stimulus-based attention from the images, however, the computed top-down attention can fail to concentrate on the correct objects of interest and attend to irrelevant background.

Stimulus-Based Attention in Captioning. To boost the performance of image captioning models, a few works attempt to use human stimulus-based attention. Sugano et al. [28] utilize ground truth human gaze to split top-down attention for gazed and non-gazed regions. Cornia et al. [3] integrate human attention in a captioning model similar as [28] but replace the human gaze with predicted saliency maps. In [29], Tavakoli *et al.* analyze the effects on stimulus-based attention in captioning by substituting the top-down attention with stimulus-based attention. While these models suggest that human attention can have positive effects on image captioning, they either incorporate only stimulus-based attention or use stimulus-based attention to separate the top-down attention at different locations, resulting in relatively marginal improvement over corresponding baselines.

In this work, we propose a Boosted Attention method that incorporates stimulus-based human attention with existing top-down visual attention. While also using human attention, our method differs from the aforementioned works in the following aspects: (1) Different from [29] which solely relies on stimulus-based attention, we emphasize that it is necessary to integrate stimulus-based attention with top-down attention. (2) Unlike [3,28] which utilize stimulus-based attention to split top-down attention and extract features from regions either attended by both attention (gazed) or not attended by stimulus-based attention (non-gazed), our method extracts features from regions attended by either attention so both contribute directly with an equal role, naturally enabling the two types of attention to complement each other. Experimental results validate the complementary nature of them, which contributes to the significant boost in captioning performance. (3) Instead of using the spatial map for encoding stimulus-based attention like [3,28,29], we integrate the attention via attentional CNN features. Compared to spatial map, our features encode more abundant information and introduce channel-wise attention in addition to spatial attention.

3   The Role of Stimulus-Based Attention in Image Captioning

Though human-generated captions are relatively free-form, and with considerable inter-subject variance in descriptions, there exists a large degree of agreement in what people describe (*i.e.*, mentioned words in the captions) and what people look (*i.e.*, fixated objects with stimulus-based attention). In this section, we explore the role of stimulus-based attention in image captioning. Specifically, we show the correlations between stimulus-based attention and captioning attention by comparing them on the SALICON [11] dataset under different evaluation metrics. Note that to provide insights on how stimulus-based attention could contribute to the captioning task, the captioning attention we use here is derived from ground truth labels from MSCOCO and seen as ground truth attention for generating the captions.

Similar to [29], we generate captioning attention using visual object category to sentence's noun (VOS) mapping (please refer to the supplementary materials for details). The evaluation metrics used in the comparison include Coefficient Correlation (CC), Spearman's Rank Correlation (Spearman) and Similarity (SIM) [16]. Additionally, we also compute the probability of objects being described given that they are fixated by stimulus-based attention, *i.e.*, $P(d|f)$.

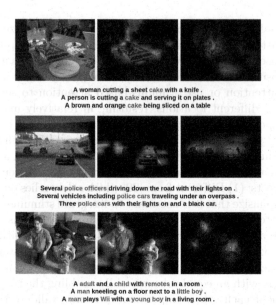

A woman cutting a sheet cake with a knife .
A person is cutting a cake and serving it on plates .
A brown and orange cake being sliced on a table

Several police officers driving down the road with their lights on .
Several vehicles including police cars traveling under an overpass .
Three police cars with their lights on and a black car.

A adult and a child with remotes in a room .
A man kneeling on a floor next to a little boy .
A man plays Wii with a young boy in a living room .

Fig. 2. Visualization for image captioning attention and stimulus-based attention. From left to right: original images, ground truth image captioning attention maps, stimulus-based attention maps. Captions are shown at the bottom of the images with objects of interest mentioned in multiple captions highlighted by red color. (Color figure online)

To compute this probability, we first set up a small threshold (*i.e.*, 0.1) to filter out the false positive introduced during map re-scaling, then traverse all saliency fixations within the captioning attention map. For each fixation, if the attention value is above the predefined threshold, we consider at that fixation the corresponding object is mentioned in the captions.

Quantitative evaluations show that the objects described in the captions are likely to be fixated by stimulus-based attention with the probability $P(d|f) = 0.465$. According to [29], the probability of an object being mentioned given that it exists (*i.e.* $P(d|e)$) is around 0.2, thus stimulus-based attention increases the probability of selecting objects of interest by more than 2, providing reasonably good prior knowledge of the objects of interest for image captioning. However, note that since stimulus-based attention commonly attends to only parts of the salient objects instead of covering all or sometimes even majority of the pixels in the objects, the correlations between stimulus-based attention and captioning attention are not high, with $CC = 0.222$, $SIM = 0.353$ and $Spearman = 0.324$. Thus, even though stimulus-based attention is capable of partially capturing objects of interest for image captioning, solely relying on stimulus-based attention may not be sufficient for an image captioning model. Figure 2 shows examples of captioning attention and corresponding stimulus-based attention. We see that stimulus-based attention, while correctly locating objects of interest (*i.e., cake, police car, man, remote* and *boy*), it typically covers part of the salient regions displayed in the captioning attention maps.

4   Boosted Attention Method

As mentioned in Sect. 3, on the one hand, objects of interest in stimulus-based attention are reasonably consistent with objects of interest in image captioning, suggesting that stimulus-based attention can be used to provide prior knowledge for image captioning. On the other hand, however, with certain level of discrepancy, in both location and coverage, stimulus-based attention alone could lead to loss of visual information and thus decreasing the quality of generated captions.

We therefore propose a Boosted Attention method for image captioning that incorporates stimulus-based attention into the conventional top-down attention framework of a captioning model. The stimulus-based attention is combined with top-down attention to construct a new attention mechanism called Boosted Attention, which encourages the model to focus on certain visual features based on top-down language signals while at the same time attending to the salient regions highlighted by the stimulus-based attention. In all of our experiments, the stimulus-based attention is obtained from a pre-trained saliency prediction network and details about the network can be found in Sect. 5.

Figure 3 illustrates the high-level architecture of our method. The model first takes a single raw image as input and encodes it with a CNN Visual Encoder to obtain the visual features. The encoded features are then passed through a Top-down Attention Module and our Stimulus-based Attention Module in parallel, computing the top-down attention and integrating stimulus-based attention. The proposed Stimulus-based Attention Module mainly consists of three parts, a convolutional layer W_{sal} pre-trained on saliency prediction for producing the stimulus-based attention features (attentional CNN features, Sect. 4.1), a convolutional layer W_v that further encodes the visual features, and an integration

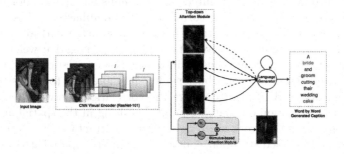

Fig. 3. An illustration of architecture design for proposed Boosted Attention method. Top-down attention maps and their corresponding words are highlighted in purple, blue, green color, while stimulus-based attention map is shown in the red frame. (Color figure online)

module ⊙ that combines stimulus-based attention and visual features. After processing with both the Top-down Attention Module and Stimulus-based Attention Module, visual features integrated with two attention are fed into the Language Generator to sequentially produce the caption.

Note that the proposed method is general and works with different top-down attention and language generation algorithms (*i.e.*, the Top-down Attention Module and the Language Generator in Fig. 3). Details about the modules depend on a selected baseline model and the ones used in this work are described in Sect. 5.

4.1 Attentional CNN Features

Instead of using the final output of the saliency prediction network (*i.e.*, the saliency map), we propose to make use of features from intermediate layers of the network which could encode richer information about stimulus-based attention. In this section, we formulate and provide intuitions behind using the attentional CNN features to encode stimulus-based attention.

Considering a fully-convolutional saliency prediction network, we denote it as the equation below (for simplicity we only take the last two layers into considerations):

$$S = softmax(W_m \; \delta(W_{sal}I)) \tag{1}$$

where I is the output of previous layers with ReLU activation, W_{sal} and W_m represent weight parameters in the layer that is used to produce attentional CNN features and output saliency map respectively, δ denotes the ReLU activation and S is the saliency map. The kernel size of both convolutional layers is 1, which enables the model to better capture cross-filter correlations as discussed in [10].

As shown in Eq. 1, W_{sal} here constructs both channel-wise attention and spatial attention. Specifically, with the use of ReLU activation ensures non-negativity, to highlight salient regions in the saliency map W_{sal} needs to construct the correlations between filters and stimulus-based attention (*i.e.* suppressing filters that have negative correlations and emphasizing those have positive correlations). These correlations (channel-wise attention) are determined by the signs and magnitude of weights in W_m, *e.g.*, negative weights lead to decrease of activation in S and thus indicate negative correlations, larger weights emphasize more significant contributions. Furthermore, due to the use of spatial softmax activation, W_{sal} also considers the correlations between features and stimulus-based attention on spatial domain, resulting in the spatial attention.

Therefore, we in this work use W_{sal} to produce attentional CNN features for encoding stimulus-based attention, constructing not only spatial attention widely used in various captioning models but also channel-wise (filter-wise) attention [2] that recently found beneficial for image captioning. In Fig. 4 we visualize attention maps computed with the CNN features, the results demonstrate that attentional CNN features utilized by our model are capable of highlighting various regions of interest.

4.2 Integrating Stimulus-Based Attention

This section discusses our integration method for introducing stimulus-based attention. We first integrate stimulus-based attention with visual features using an asymmetric function as follows:

$$I' = W_v I \circ log(W_{sal}I + \epsilon) \tag{2}$$

where I and I' are the visual features before and after integrating stimulus-based attention, W_v represents weights in an additional convolutional layer that further encodes the visual features and W_{sal} is the same as in Eq. 1, $\circ$ denotes hadamard product, and ϵ is a hyper-parameter. Note that $\odot$ in Fig. 3 denotes the whole integration process of Eq. 2.

The intuitions behind this integration method are three-fold: First, W_v further encodes visual features, allowing them to adapt to the cross-filter correlations with stimulus-based attention that are stored in W_{sal}. Second, by introducing logarithm, we aim at alleviating the effects of co-adaptation between W_v, W_{sal} and smoothing the contributions of stimulus-based attentional features. Third, with the hyper-parameter ϵ we form a residual mechanism, preserving the original information in visual features and thus preventing potential information loss caused by applying stimulus-based attention. This mechanism is crucial in the proposed integration method, because stimulus-based attention alone may fail to attend to all regions of interest and it is reasonable to allow the model to extract features attended by either one of the attention (stimulus-based or top-down). In our experiments, we define ϵ as a mathematical constant e to preserve the identity of the original visual features. Additional discussion on selecting the hyper-parameter is provided in the supplementary materials.

After obtaining the visual features attended by the stimulus-based attention (i.e. I'), we apply top-down attention on them via hadamard product, enabling two attention to complement to each other. That is, when stimulus-based attention fails to attend to some regions of interest, top-down attention can attend to those regions via assigning larger weights, and vice versa. We further study the corporation between the two types of attention in Sect. 5.3.

5 Experiments

Dataset and Evaluation. We evaluate our method on two popular datasets: (1) Microsoft COCO [19], where most images contain multiple objects in complex natural scenes with abundant context information. The dataset includes 82783, 40504, 40775 images for training, validation and online evaluation, each has 5 corresponding captions. We use the publicly available Karapthy's split [12] for both training and offline evaluation. (2) Flickr30K [24], where most images depict human performing various activities. It has a total of 31000 images from Flickr, each has 5 corresponding captions. Due to the lack of official split, in order to compare with other works we follow split from [12]. Four automatic metrics are used for evaluation, including BLEU [23], ROUGEL [18], METEOR [15] and CIDEr [30].

Saliency Prediction Network. In order to integrate stimulus-based attention, we construct a saliency prediction network with 2 convolutional layers (note that features from the last convolutional layer of a ResNet-101 are viewed as inputs). The first convolutional layer has 2048 filters while the second layer projects the CNN features to spatial saliency map using a single filter. The kernel size for both layers is set as 1 and the whole saliency network can be represented as Eq. 1. We optimize the model on SALICON dataset with cross-entropy loss and SGD optimizer using learning rate 2.5×10^{-4}. Batch size is set to 1. Weights from the first layer of saliency prediction network is utilized to initialize the stimulus-based attention module in the proposed method (*i.e.* W_{sal} in Eq. 2).

Baseline Model. To demonstrate the effectiveness of our method and the advantages of integrating stimulus-based attention, we apply the proposed method on our baseline model constructed based on Soft Attention [32] and several recent tips [2, 26] to enhance performance: we replace the VGG [27] based visual encoder with a more powerful ResNet-101 [7] based one. Instead of fine-tuning the encoder, we directly adopt visual features from the last convolutional layer of the visual encoder as input. When extracting the features, no cropping or re-scaling is applied to the original images, instead, an adaptive spatial average pooling layer is utilized to produce features with a fixed size of $2048 \times 14 \times 14$. Unlike [32] which trains the model solely on cross-entropy loss, we use the optimization method proposed in [26] which contains both supervised learning and reinforcement learning. The LSTM hidden size, word and attention dimensions are set as 512 in our baseline. The other settings remain the same as the original Soft Attention model.

Training. We train our models following the same settings from [26]: we use ADAM [13] optimizer for training all of the models and batch size is set as 50. Models are first trained on cross-entropy loss under supervised learning framework, with initial learning learning rate 5×10^{-4} and Scheduled Sampling [1] feedback probability being 0. During supervised learning, the learning rate is decayed by a factor of 0.8 every 3 epochs and feedback probability increased by 0.05 every 5 epochs. After 25 epochs of supervised learning, we further optimize the models under reinforcement learning framework on the CIDEr metric as [26]. The initial learning rate for reinforcement learning is set as 5×10^{-5} and also decayed by 0.8 every 3 epochs. In supervised learning we fix the weights for stimulus-based attention (W_{sal} in Eq. 2) to establish correlations between filters within parallel layers (W_{sal} and W_v in Eq. 2), while later on in reinforcement learning we fine-tune stimulus-based attention since the filter correlations have already been established.

5.1   Quantitative Results

In this section, we report quantitative results to demonstrate the effectiveness of the proposed method. We perform inter-model comparisons of the proposed method and 8 state-of-the-art models including Soft Attention [32], ATT [34], SCA-CNN [2], SCN-LSTM [5], RLE [25], AdaATT [21], Att2all [26] and PG-BCMR [20]. We also conduct intra-model comparisons on results with and without the proposed approach (*i.e.*, integrating the stimulus-based attention) and whether using pre-trained stimulus-attention for integration. During evaluation, beam search is utilized for generating the captions and the beam size is set as 3. Tables 1 and 2 show the result comparison on Flickr30K and MSCOCO (Karpathy's test split [12] and online testing platform).

According to the comparative results, the proposed Boosted Attention method leads to significant performance increase across all evaluation metrics compared to the original baselines without stimulus-based attention. On Flickr30K, using our method results in 2.6%, 5.6%, 2.3% and 12% of relative improvements on BLEU-4, ROUGE-L, METEOR and CIDEr, while on MSCOCO the improvements are 5.7%, 2.0%, 2.7% and 5.6% for corresponding evaluation metrics. Moreover, boosted by the stimulus-based attention, our models are capable of achieving state-of-the-art performance on both datasets.

To further study the contributions of stimulus-based attention, we conduct experiments using a model with the same architecture as the proposed model but not initialized on pre-trained weights for stimulus-based attention. In this case, the stimulus-based attention W_{sal} is trained end-to-end and not fixed during supervised learning. As shown in Table 1, models with pre-trained stimulus-

Table 1. Performance comparison with the state-of-the-art on Flickr30K and MSCOCO (test split in [12]). Baseline is our augmented baseline model without stimulus-based attention, BAM indicates the proposed Boosted Attention model and BAM* denotes the model without using pre-trained stimulus-based attention but with the same architecture as BAM. Reported scores are BLEU-4 (B@4), METEOR (MT), ROUGE-L (RG) and CIDEr (CD). The relative improvement by using the proposed method over its baseline is shown in percentage.

Model	Flickr30K				MSCOCO			
	B@4	MT	RG	CD	B@4	MT	RG	CD
Soft attention [32]	0.191	0.185	-	-	0.243	0.239	-	-
ATT [34]	0.230	0.189	-	-	0.304	0.243	-	-
SCA-CNN [2]	0.223	0.195	0.449	0.447	0.311	0.250	0.531	0.952
SCN-LSTM [5]	0.265	0.218	-	-	0.330	0.257	-	1.012
RLE [25]	-	-	-	-	0.304	0.251	0.525	0.937
AdaATT [21]	0.251	0.204	0.467	0.531	0.332	0.266	0.549	1.085
Att2all [26]	-	-	-	-	0.342	0.267	0.557	1.140
ours-Baseline	0.267	0.197	0.471	0.523	0.335	0.258	0.551	1.062
ours-BAM*	0.270	0.204	0.477	0.571	0.350	0.262	0.559	1.111
ours-BAM	0.274	0.208	0.482	0.586	0.354	0.265	0.562	1.122
Improvement (%)	2.6%	5.6%	2.3%	12.0%	5.7%	2.7%	2.0%	5.6%

Table 2. Online results (C5) on the MSCOCO evaluation platform, † indicates ensemble of models. Our result is obtained from an ensemble of 4 models trained under different random seeds.

	BLEU-1	BLEU-2	BLEU-3	BLEU-4	ROUGEL	METEOR	CIDEr
ATT† [34]	0.731	0.565	0.424	0.316	0.535	0.250	0.953
SCA-CNN [2]	0.712	0.542	0.404	0.302	0.524	0.244	0.912
SCN-LSTM† [5]	0.740	0.575	0.436	0.331	0.543	0.257	1.003
PG-BCMR [20]	0.754	0.591	0.445	0.332	0.550	0.257	1.013
AdaATT† [21]	0.748	0.584	0.444	0.336	0.550	0.264	1.042
Att2all† [26]	0.781	0.619	0.470	0.352	0.563	0.270	1.147
ours-BAM†	0.794	0.622	0.470	0.349	0.560	0.264	1.083

based attention (BAM) are able to consistently outperform models without stimulus-based attention (BAM*), indicating that stimulus-based attention plays an essential role on boosting the performance and the improvement of our method is not merely due to advantages of modifications on architecture.

5.2   Qualitative Results

In addition to quantitative evaluations, in this section we further demonstrate the effectiveness of proposed method via comparing qualitative results computed by models with and without using our method. Figure 4 shows the captions generated based the two models, together with the corresponding stimulus-based attention maps computed by models using the Boosted Attention method. Stimulus-based attention maps are generated by normalizing the average activation within the CNN features at different spatial locations.

According to the results, introducing stimulus-based attention helps the model efficiently locate the objects of interest within the visual scenarios and generate better captions. For example, in the top two images, the model using Boosted Attention successfully focuses on the *street signs* similar as humans do (as shown in the attention maps as well as the captions in red) while the model without incorporating stimulus-based attention gets lost in the background objects such as the *palm trees* and *bus* (see the captions in black). Furthermore, the results also indicate that the model with the proposed Boosted Attention method is capable of capturing multiple salient objects within images. For example, for the bottom three images, by incorporating stimulus-based attention, the model is able to concentrate on objects including the *bird, mountain* and *laptop* (see the attention maps and captions in red). These objects are missing in the captions generated by the model without using Boosted Attention (captions in black) but mentioned in multiple human generated captions (captions in blue).

Fig. 4. Qualitative results for models with and without using the Boosted Attention method. From left to right: original images, stimulus-based attention map, and captions corresponding to the images. Captions generated by models with and without using Boosted Attention method are colored in red and black respectively, while the ground-truth human generated captions are colored in blue. (Color figure online)

5.3   Attention Corporation in Image Captioning

To explore how the two types of attention, *i.e.*, stimulus-based attention and top-down model attention, corporate with each other during the caption generation process, we first evaluate the correlations between the attention maps from the two types of attention. The stimulus-based attention map is extracted using the same method described in Sect. 5.2. Since top-down attention maps are generated for each corresponding word within a caption, we compute the average correlations between stimulus-based attention map and top-down attention maps for different words.

We compute the correlations on the 5000 images from Karpathy's test split [12]. Two evaluation metrics commonly used for estimating correlations between spatial maps, *i.e.* Coefficient Correlation (CC) and Spearman's Rank Correlation (Spearman), are utilized for analysis. According to the experimental results, CC and Spearman scores are negative ($CC = -0.256, Spearman = -0.369$), indicating that stimulus-based attention tends to focus on regions different from top-down attention thus the two can potentially complement each other.

Next, we show qualitative results to demonstrate that two attention corporate in a complementary manner. Figure 5 compares top-down attention and its corresponding stimulus-based attention, three typical scenarios for the corporation between attention are summarized as follows:

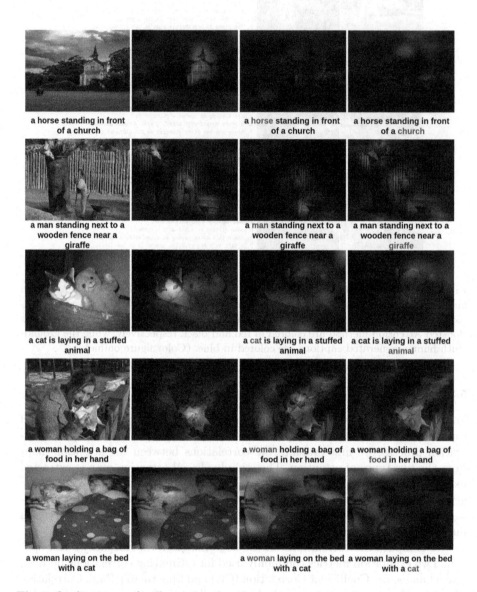

Fig. 5. Qualitative results illustrating that the two types of attention complement each other in various situations. From left to right: original images with generated captions, stimulus-based attention maps, top-down model attention maps for different words within the captions. The word associated with a specific top-down attention map is highlighted in red color. (Color figure online)

Scenario I: Stimulus-based attention has successfully captured all of the objects of interest corresponding to generated caption. In this case, top-down attention tends to play a minor role on discriminating the salient regions related to the task. As shown in the first two images, since stimulus-based attention has already concentrated on the objects of interest mentioned in the captions (*i.e.*, *horse* and *church* in the first image, *man* and *giraffe* in the second image), when generating the words corresponding to the objects, top-down attention either does not have a clear focused region (the 1st image) or attends to similar regions as stimulus-based attention (the 2nd image).

Scenario II: Stimulus-based attention concentrates on only part of an object but not covering the entire object (*e.g.*, the 3rd image), or it covers some but not all objects of interest (*e.g.*, the 4th image). Under these situations, top-down attention will focus on the missing regions to enhance the objects of interest and complement stimulus-based attention. In the 3rd image, stimulus-based attention highlights the *cat* but only the bottom part of the *stuffed animal*, therefore in order to collect enough visual information when generating the word *'animal'*, top-down attention is placed on the upper part of the *stuffed animal*. Furthermore, in the 4th image we can see that since stimulus-based attention does not quite focus on the *woman*, during generating the word *'woman'* top-attention significantly emphasizes the face of the *woman* and reveals the lost visual information.

Scenario III: Stimulus-based attention fails to distinguish salient objects with irrelevant background. In this case, top-down attention will play a major role in extracting regions corresponding to the objects of interest. As shown in the 5th image, due to the complexity of the visual scenario, stimulus-based attention confuses the objects of interest (*i.e. woman* and *cat* according to the caption) with background objects such as bed and blanket. As a result, the model relies on top-down attention to filter out the irrelevant information and concentrate on regions related to the word being generated.

6   Conclusion

In this work, we propose a Boosted Attention method that leverages human stimulus-based attention to improve the performance of image captioning models. Stimulus-based attention provides prior knowledge on salient regions within the visual scenarios and plays a complementary role to the top-down attention computed by the image captioning models. Experimental results on the MSCOCO and Flickr30K datasets show that the proposed method leads to significant improvements in captioning performance across various evaluation metrics and achieves state-of-the-art results. The proposed method is also general and compatible with various image captioning models using top-down visual attention.

Acknowledgements. This work is supported by NSF Grant 1763761 and University of Minnesota Department of Computer Science and Engineering Start-up Fund (QZ).

References

1. Bengio, S., Vinyals, O., Jaitly, N., Shazeer, N.: Scheduled sampling for sequence prediction with recurrent neural networks. In: Proceedings of the 28th International Conference on Neural Information Processing Systems, NIPS 2015, vol. 1, pp. 1171–1179. MIT Press, Cambridge (2015). http://dl.acm.org/citation.cfm?id=2969239.2969370

2. Chen, L., et al.: SCA-CNN: spatial and channel-wise attention in convolutional networks for image captioning. In: 2017 IEEE Conference on Computer Vision and Pattern Recognition (CVPR), pp. 6298–6306 (2017). https://doi.org/10.1109/CVPR.2017.667

3. Cornia, M., Baraldi, L., Serra, G., Cucchiara, R.: Visual saliency for image captioning in new multimedia services. In: 2017 IEEE International Conference on Multimedia Expo Workshops (ICMEW), pp. 309–314 (2017). https://doi.org/10.1109/ICMEW.2017.8026277

4. Farhadi, A.: Every picture tells a story: generating sentences from images. In: Daniilidis, K., Maragos, P., Paragios, N. (eds.) ECCV 2010. LNCS, vol. 6314, pp. 15–29. Springer, Heidelberg (2010). https://doi.org/10.1007/978-3-642-15561-1_2

5. Gan, Z., et al.: Semantic compositional networks for visual captioning. In: 2017 IEEE Conference on Computer Vision and Pattern Recognition (CVPR), pp. 1141–1150 (2017). https://doi.org/10.1109/CVPR.2017.127

6. Gong, Y., Wang, L., Hodosh, M., Hockenmaier, J., Lazebnik, S.: Improving image-sentence embeddings using large weakly annotated photo collections. In: Fleet, D., Pajdla, T., Schiele, B., Tuytelaars, T. (eds.) ECCV 2014. LNCS, vol. 8692, pp. 529–545. Springer, Cham (2014). https://doi.org/10.1007/978-3-319-10593-2_35

7. He, K., Zhang, X., Ren, S., Sun, J.: Deep residual learning for image recognition. CoRR abs/1512.03385 (2015)

8. Hochreiter, S., Schmidhuber, J.: Long short-term memory. Neural Comput. 9(8), 1735–1780 (1997). https://doi.org/10.1162/neco.1997.9.8.1735

9. Hodosh, M., Young, P., Hockenmaier, J.: Framing image description as a ranking task: data, models and evaluation metrics. J. Artif. Int. Res. 47(1), 853–899 (2013). http://dl.acm.org/citation.cfm?id=2566972.2566993

10. Hu, J., Shen, L., Sun, G.: Squeeze-and-excitation networks. CoRR abs/1709.01507 (2017). http://arxiv.org/abs/1709.01507

11. Jiang, M., Huang, S., Duan, J., Zhao, Q.: SALICON: saliency in context. In: 2015 IEEE Conference on Computer Vision and Pattern Recognition (CVPR), pp. 1072–1080 (2015). https://doi.org/10.1109/CVPR.2015.7298710

12. Karpathy, A., Fei-Fei, L.: Deep visual-semantic alignments for generating image descriptions. In: 2015 IEEE Conference on Computer Vision and Pattern Recognition (CVPR), pp. 3128–3137 (2015). https://doi.org/10.1109/CVPR.2015.7298932

13. Kingma, D.P., Ba, J.: Adam: A method for stochastic optimization. CoRR abs/1412.6980 (2014). http://arxiv.org/abs/1412.6980

14. Kulkarni, G., et al.: Baby talk: understanding and generating image descriptions. In: Proceedings of the 24th CVPR (2011)

15. Lavie, A., Agarwal, A.: METEOR: an automatic metric for MT evaluation with high levels of correlation with human judgments. In: Proceedings of the Second Workshop on Statistical Machine Translation, StatMT 2007, pp. 228–231. Association for Computational Linguistics, Stroudsburg (2007). http://dl.acm.org/citation.cfm?id=1626355.1626389

16. Li, J., Xia, C., Song, Y., Fang, S., Chen, X.: A data-driven metric for comprehensive evaluation of saliency models. In: 2015 IEEE International Conference on Computer Vision (ICCV), pp. 190–198 (2015). https://doi.org/10.1109/ICCV.2015.30

17. Li, S., Kulkarni, G., Berg, T.L., Berg, A.C., Choi, Y.: Composing simple image descriptions using web-scale N-grams. In: Proceedings of the Fifteenth Conference on Computational Natural Language Learning, CoNLL 2011, pp. 220–228. Association for Computational Linguistics, Stroudsburg (2011). http://dl.acm.org/citation.cfm?id=2018936.2018962

18. Lin, C.Y.: ROUGE: a package for automatic evaluation of summaries. In: Proceedings of the Workshop on Text Summarization Branches Out (WAS 2004) (2004)

19. Lin, T.Y., et al.: Microsoft COCO: common objects in context. In: Fleet, D., Pajdla, T., Schiele, B., Tuytelaars, T. (eds.) ECCV 2014. LNCS, vol. 8693, pp. 740–755. Springer, Cham (2014). https://doi.org/10.1007/978-3-319-10602-1_48

20. Liu, S., Zhu, Z., Ye, N., Guadarrama, S., Murphy, K.: Improved image captioning via policy gradient optimization of spider. In: 2017 IEEE International Conference on Computer Vision (ICCV), pp. 873–881 (2017). https://doi.org/10.1109/ICCV.2017.100

21. Lu, J., Xiong, C., Parikh, D., Socher, R.: Knowing when to look: adaptive attention via a visual sentinel for image captioning. In: The IEEE Conference on Computer Vision and Pattern Recognition (CVPR) (2017)

22. Ordonez, V., Kulkarni, G., Berg, T.L.: Im2Text: describing images using 1 million captioned photographs. In: Neural Information Processing Systems (NIPS) (2011)

23. Papineni, K., Roukos, S., Ward, T., Zhu, W.J.: BLEU: a method for automatic evaluation of machine translation. In: Proceedings of the 40th Annual Meeting on Association for Computational Linguistics, ACL 2002, pp. 311–318. Association for Computational Linguistics, Stroudsburg (2002). https://doi.org/10.3115/1073083.1073135

24. Plummer, B.A., Wang, L., Cervantes, C.M., Caicedo, J.C., Hockenmaier, J., Lazebnik, S.: Flickr30k entities: collecting region-to-phrase correspondences for richer image-to-sentence models. In: 2015 IEEE International Conference on Computer Vision (ICCV), pp. 2641–2649 (2015). https://doi.org/10.1109/ICCV.2015.303

25. Ren, Z., Wang, X., Zhang, N., Lv, X., Li, L.J.: Deep reinforcement learning-based image captioning with embedding reward. In: 2017 IEEE Conference on Computer Vision and Pattern Recognition (CVPR), pp. 1151–1159 (2017). https://doi.org/10.1109/CVPR.2017.128

26. Rennie, S.J., Marcheret, E., Mroueh, Y., Ross, J., Goel, V.: Self-critical sequence training for image captioning. In: The IEEE Conference on Computer Vision and Pattern Recognition (CVPR) (2017)

27. Simonyan, K., Zisserman, A.: Very deep convolutional networks for large-scale image recognition. CoRR abs/1409.1556 (2014). http://arxiv.org/abs/1409.1556

28. Sugano, Y., Bulling, A.: Seeing with humans: Gaze-assisted neural image captioning. CoRR abs/1608.05203 (2016). http://arxiv.org/abs/1608.05203

29. Tavakoliy, H.R., Shetty, R., Borji, A., Laaksonen, J.: Paying attention to descriptions generated by image captioning models. In: 2017 IEEE International Conference on Computer Vision (ICCV), pp. 2506–2515 (2017). https://doi.org/10.1109/ICCV.2017.272

30. Vedantam, R., Zitnick, C.L., Parikh, D.: CIDEr: consensus-based image description evaluation. In: IEEE Conference on Computer Vision and Pattern Recognition, CVPR 2015, Boston, MA, USA, 7–12 June 2015, pp. 4566–4575. IEEE Computer Society (2015). https://doi.org/10.1109/CVPR.2015.7299087

31. Vinyals, O., Toshev, A., Bengio, S., Erhan, D.: Show and tell: a neural image caption generator. In: CVPR, pp. 3156–3164. IEEE Computer Society (2015)
32. Xu, K., et al.: Show, attend and tell: neural image caption generation with visual attention. In: Blei, D., Bach, F. (eds.) Proceedings of the 32nd International Conference on Machine Learning (ICML 2015), JMLR Workshop and Conference Proceedings, pp. 2048–2057 (2015). http://jmlr.org/proceedings/papers/v37/xuc15.pdf
33. Yang, Z., Yuan, Y., Wu, Y., Cohen, W.W., Salakhutdinov, R.R.: Review networks for caption generation. In: Lee, D.D., Sugiyama, M., Luxburg, U.V., Guyon, I., Garnett, R. (eds.) Advances in Neural Information Processing Systems 29, pp. 2361–2369. Curran Associates, Inc. (2016). http://papers.nips.cc/paper/6167-review-networks-for-caption-generation.pdf
34. You, Q., Jin, H., Wang, Z., Fang, C., Luo, J.: Image captioning with semantic attention. In: 2016 IEEE Conference on Computer Vision and Pattern Recognition (CVPR), pp. 4651–4659 (2016). https://doi.org/10.1109/CVPR.2016.503
35. Yun, K., Peng, Y., Samaras, D., Zelinsky, G.J., Berg, T.L.: Studying relationships between human gaze, description, and computer vision. In: 2013 IEEE Computer Society Conference on Computer Vision and Pattern Recognition (CVPR). IEEE (2013)

Image Inpainting for Irregular Holes Using Partial Convolutions

Guilin Liu[✉], Fitsum A. Reda, Kevin J. Shih, Ting-Chun Wang, Andrew Tao, and Bryan Catanzaro

NVIDIA Corporation, Santa Clara, USA
guilinl@nvidia.com

Abstract. Existing deep learning based image inpainting methods use a standard convolutional network over the corrupted image, using convolutional filter responses conditioned on both valid pixels as well as the substitute values in the masked holes (typically the mean value). This often leads to artifacts such as color discrepancy and blurriness. Post-processing is usually used to reduce such artifacts, but are expensive and may fail. We propose the use of partial convolutions, where the convolution is masked and renormalized to be conditioned on only valid pixels. We further include a mechanism to automatically generate an updated mask for the next layer as part of the forward pass. Our model outperforms other methods for irregular masks. We show qualitative and quantitative comparisons with other methods to validate our approach.

Keywords: Partial convolution · Image inpainting

1 Introduction

Image inpainting, the task of filling in holes in an image, can be used in many applications. For example, it can be used in image editing to remove unwanted image content, while filling in the resulting space with plausible imagery. Previous deep learning approaches have focused on rectangular regions located around the center of the image, and often rely on expensive post-processing. The goal of this work is to propose a model for image inpainting that operates robustly on irregular hole patterns (see Fig. 1), and produces semantically meaningful predictions that incorporate smoothly with the rest of the image without the need for any additional post-processing or blending operation.

Recent image inpainting approaches that do not use deep learning use image statistics of the remaining image to fill in the hole. PatchMatch [2], one of the state-of-the-art methods, iteratively searches for the best fitting patches to fill

Electronic supplementary material The online version of this chapter (https://doi.org/10.1007/978-3-030-01252-6_6) contains supplementary material, which is available to authorized users.

© Springer Nature Switzerland AG 2018
V. Ferrari et al. (Eds.): ECCV 2018, LNCS 11215, pp. 89–105, 2018.
https://doi.org/10.1007/978-3-030-01252-6_6

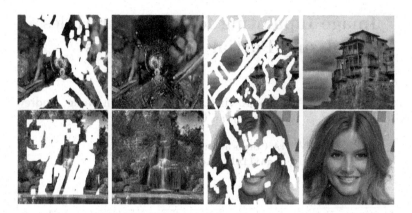

Fig. 1. Masked images and corresponding inpainted results using our partial-convolution based network.

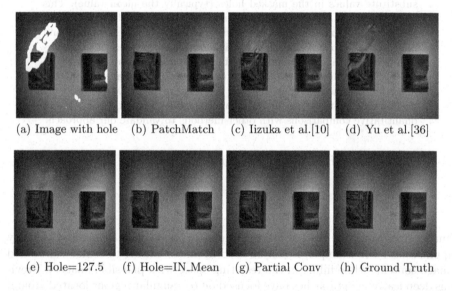

(a) Image with hole   (b) PatchMatch   (c) Iizuka et al.[10]   (d) Yu et al.[36]

(e) Hole=127.5   (f) Hole=IN_Mean   (g) Partial Conv   (h) Ground Truth

Fig. 2. From left to right, top to bottom: Fig. 2(a): image with hole. Fig. 2(b): inpainted result of PatchMatch [2]. Fig. 2(c): inpainted result of Iizuka et al. [10]. Fig. 2(d): Yu et al. [36]. Fig. 2(e) and (f) are using the same network architecture as Sect. 3.2 but using typical convolutional network, Fig. 2(e) uses the pixel value 127.5 to initialize the holes. Fig. 2(f) uses the mean ImageNet pixel value. Fig. 2(g): our *partial convolution* based results which are agnostic to hole values.

in the holes. While this approach generally produces smooth results, it is limited by the available image statistics and has no concept of visual semantics. For example, in Fig. 2(b), PatchMatch was able to smoothly fill in the missing components of the painting using image patches from the surrounding shadow and wall, but a semantically-aware approach would make use of patches from the painting instead.

Deep neural networks learn semantic priors and meaningful hidden representations in an end-to-end fashion, which have been used for recent image inpainting efforts. These networks employ convolutional filters on images, replacing the removed content with a fixed value. As a result, these approaches suffer from dependence on the initial hole values, which often manifests itself as lack of texture in the hole regions, obvious color contrasts, or artificial edge responses surrounding the hole. Examples using a U-Net architecture with typical convolutional layers with various hole value initialization can be seen in Fig. 2(e) and (f). (For both, the training and testing share the same initialization scheme).

Conditioning the output on the hole values ultimately results in various types of visual artifacts that necessitate expensive post-processing. For example, Iizuka et al. [10] uses fast marching [30] and Poisson image blending [21], while Yu et al. [36] employ a following-up refinement network to refine their raw network predictions. However, these refinement cannot resolve all the artifacts shown as Fig. 2(c) and (d). Our work aims to achieve well-incorporated hole predictions independent of the hole initialization values and without any additional post-processing.

Another limitation of many recent approaches is the focus on rectangular shaped holes, often assumed to be center in the image. We find these limitations may lead to overfitting to the rectangular holes, and ultimately limit the utility of these models in application. Pathak et al. [20] and Yang et al. [34] assume 64×64 square holes at the center of a 128×128 image. Iizuka et al. [10] and Yu et al. [36] remove the centered hole assumption and can handle irregular shaped holes, but do not perform an extensive quantitative analysis on a large number of images with irregular masks (51 test images in [8]). In order to focus on the more practical irregular hole use case, we collect a large benchmark of images with irregular masks of varying sizes. In our analysis, we look at the effects of not just the size of the hole, but also whether the holes are in contact with the image border.

To properly handle irregular masks, we propose the use of a *Partial Convolutional Layer*, comprising a masked and re-normalized convolution operation followed by a mask-update step. The concept of a masked and re-normalized convolution is also referred to as segmentation-aware convolutions in [7] for the image segmentation task, however they did not make modifications to the input mask. Our use of partial convolutions is such that given a binary mask our convolutional results depend only on the non-hole regions at every layer. Our main extension is the automatic mask update step, which removes any masking where the partial convolution was able to operate on an unmasked value. Given sufficient layers of successive updates, even the largest masked holes will eventually shrink away, leaving only valid responses in the feature map. The partial convolutional layer ultimately makes our model agnostic to placeholder hole values.

In summary, we make the following contributions:

- we propose the use of *partial convolutions* with an *automatic mask update step* for achieving state-of-the-art on image inpainting.
- while previous works fail to achieve good inpainting results with skip links in a U-Net [32] with typical convolutions, we demonstrate that substituting convolutional layers with partial convolutions and mask updates can achieve state-of-the-art inpainting results.
- to the best of our knowledge, we are the first to demonstrate the efficacy of training image-inpainting models on irregularly shaped holes.
- we propose a large irregular mask dataset, which will be released to public to facilitate future efforts in training and evaluating inpainting models.

2   Related Work

Non-learning approaches to image inpainting rely on propagating appearance information from neighboring pixels to the target region using some mechanisms like distance field [1,3,30]. However, these methods can only handle narrow holes, where the color and texture variance is small. Big holes may result in over-smoothing or artifacts resembling Voronoi regions such as in [30]. Patch-based methods such as [5,15] operate by searching for relevant patches from the image's non-hole regions or other source images in an iterative fashion. However, these steps often come at a large computation cost such as in [26]. PatchMatch [2] speeds it up by proposing a faster similar patch searching algorithm. However, these approaches are still not fast enough for real-time applications and cannot make semantically aware patch selections.

Deep learning based methods typically initialize the holes with some constant placeholder values e.g. the mean pixel value of ImageNet [24], which is then passed through a convolutional network. Due to the resulting artifacts, post-processing is often used to ameliorate the effects of conditioning on the placeholder values. Content Encoders [20] first embed the 128×128 image with 64×64 center hole into low dimensional feature space and then decode the feature to a 64×64 image. Yang et al. [34] takes the result from Content Encoders as input and then propagates the texture information from non-hole regions to fill the hole regions as postprocessing. Song et al. [28] uses a refinement network in which a blurry initial hole-filling result is used as the input, then iteratively replaced with patches from the closest non-hole regions in the feature space. Li et al. [16] and Iizuka et al. [10] extended Content Encoders by defining both global and local discriminators; then Iizuka et al. [10] apply Poisson blending as a post-process. Following [10], Yu et al. [36] replaced the post-processing with a refinement network powered by the contextual attention layers.

Amongst the deep learning approaches, several other efforts also ignore the mask placeholder values. In Yeh et al. [35], searches for the closest encoding to the corrupted image in a latent space, which is then used to condition the output of a hole-filling generator. Ulyanov et al. [32] further found that the network needs no external dataset training and can rely on the structure of the generative network itself to complete the corrupted image. However, this approach can require a different set of hyper parameters for every image, and applies several iterations to achieve good results. Moreover, their design [32] is not able to use skip links, which are known to produce detailed output. With standard convolutional layers, the raw features of noise or wrong hole initialization values in the encoder stage will propagate to the decoder stage. Our work also does not depend on placeholder values in the hole regions, but we also aim to achieve good results in a single feedforward pass and enable the use of skip links to create detailed predictions.

Our work makes extensive use of a masked or reweighted convolution operation, which allows us to condition output only on valid inputs. Harley et al. [7] recently made use of this approach with a soft attention mask for semantic segmentation. It has also been used for full-image generation in PixelCNN [18], to condition the next pixel only on previously synthesized pixels. Uhrig et al. [31] proposed sparsity invariant CNNs with reweighted convolution and max pooling based mask updating mechanism for depth completion. For image inpainting, Ren et al. [22] proposed shepard convolution layer where the same kernel is applied for both feature and mask convolutions. The mask convolution result acts as both the reweighting denominator and updated mask, which does not guarantee the hole to evolve during updating due to the kernel's possible negative entries. It cannot handle big holes properly either. Discussions of other CNN variants like [4] are beyond the scope of this work.

3   Approach

Our proposed model uses stacked partial convolution operations and mask updating steps to perform image inpainting. We first define our convolution and mask update mechanism, then discuss model architecture and loss functions.

3.1   Partial Convolutional Layer

We refer to our partial convolution operation and mask update function jointly as the *Partial Convolutional Layer*. Let $\mathbf{W}$ be the convolution filter weights for the convolution filter and b its the corresponding bias. $\mathbf{X}$ are the feature values (pixels values) for the current convolution (sliding) window and $\mathbf{M}$ is the corresponding binary mask. The partial convolution at every location, similarly defined in [7], is expressed as:

$$x' = \begin{cases} \mathbf{W}^T(\mathbf{X} \odot \mathbf{M})\frac{\text{sum}(\mathbf{1})}{\text{sum}(\mathbf{M})} + b, & \text{if sum}(\mathbf{M}) > 0 \\ 0, & \text{otherwise} \end{cases} \quad (1)$$

where $\odot$ denotes element-wise multiplication, and $\mathbf{1}$ has same shape as M but with all the elements being 1. As can be seen, output values depend only on the unmasked inputs. The scaling factor $\text{sum}(\mathbf{1})/\text{sum}(\mathbf{M})$ applies appropriate scaling to adjust for the varying amount of valid (unmasked) inputs.

After each partial convolution operation, we then update our mask as follows: if the convolution was able to condition its output on at least one valid input value, then we mark that location to be valid. This is expressed as:

$$m' = \begin{cases} 1, & \text{if sum}(\mathbf{M}) > 0 \\ 0, & \text{otherwise} \end{cases} \tag{2}$$

and can easily be implemented in any deep learning framework as part of the forward pass. With sufficient successive applications of the partial convolution layer, any mask will eventually be all ones, if the input contained any valid pixels.

3.2   Network Architecture and Implementation

Implementation. Partial convolution layer is implemented by extending existing standard PyTorch [19], although it can be improved both in time and space using custom layers. The straightforward implementation is to define binary masks of size C × H × W, the same size with their associated images/features, and then to implement mask updating is implemented using a fixed convolution layer, with the same kernel size as the partial convolution operation, but with weights identically set to 1 and no bias. The entire network inference on a 512 × 512 image takes 0.029 s on a single NVIDIA V100 GPU, regardless of the hole size.

Network Design. We design a UNet-like architecture [23] similar to the one used in [11], replacing all convolutional layers with partial convolutional layers and using nearest neighbor up-sampling in the decoding stage. The skip links will concatenate two feature maps and two masks respectively, acting as the feature and mask inputs for the next partial convolution layer. The last partial convolution layer's input will contain the concatenation of the original input image with hole and original mask, making it possible for the model to copy non-hole pixels. Network details are found in the supplementary file.

Partial Convolution as Padding. We use the partial convolution with appropriate masking at image boundaries in lieu of typical padding. This ensures that the inpainted content at the image border will not be affected by invalid values outside of the image – which can be interpreted as another hole.

3.3   Loss Functions

Our loss functions target both per-pixel reconstruction accuracy as well as composition, i.e. how smoothly the predicted hole values transition into their surrounding context.

Given input image with hole $\mathbf{I}_{in}$, initial binary mask $\mathbf{M}$ (0 for holes), the network prediction $\mathbf{I}_{out}$, and the ground truth image $\mathbf{I}_{gt}$, we first define our per-pixel losses $\mathcal{L}_{hole} = \|(1 - M) \odot (I_{out} - I_{gt})\|_1$ and $\mathcal{L}_{valid} = \|M \odot (I_{out} - I_{gt})\|_1$. These are the L^1 losses on the network output for the hole and the non-hole pixels respectively.

Next, we define the perceptual loss, introduced by Gatys at al. [6]:

$$\mathcal{L}_{perceptual} = \sum_{n=0}^{N-1} \|\Psi_n(\mathbf{I}_{out}) - \Psi_n(\mathbf{I}_{gt})\|_1 + \sum_{n=0}^{N-1} \|\Psi_n(\mathbf{I}_{comp}) - \Psi_n(\mathbf{I}_{gt})\|_1 \quad (3)$$

Here, $\mathbf{I}_{comp}$ is the raw output image $\mathbf{I}_{out}$, but with the non-hole pixels directly set to ground truth. The perceptual loss computes the L^1 distances between both $\mathbf{I}_{out}$ and $\mathbf{I}_{comp}$ and the ground truth, but after projecting these images into higher level feature spaces using an ImageNet-pretrained VGG-16 [27]. Ψ_n is the activation map of the nth selected layer. We use layers $pool1$, $pool2$ and $pool3$ for our loss.

We further include the style-loss term, which is similar to the perceptual loss [6], but we first perform an autocorrelation (Gram matrix) on each feature map before applying the L^1.

$$\mathcal{L}_{style_{out}} = \sum_{n=0}^{N-1} \left\| K_n \left((\Psi_n(\mathbf{I}_{out}))^\mathsf{T} (\Psi_n(\mathbf{I}_{out})) - (\Psi_n(\mathbf{I}_{gt}))^\mathsf{T} (\Psi_n(\mathbf{I}_{gt})) \right) \right\|_1 (4)$$

$$\mathcal{L}_{style_{comp}} = \sum_{n=0}^{N-1} \left\| K_n \left((\Psi_n(\mathbf{I}_{comp}))^\mathsf{T} (\Psi_n(\mathbf{I}_{comp})) - (\Psi_n(\mathbf{I}_{gt}))^\mathsf{T} (\Psi_n(\mathbf{I}_{gt})) \right) \right\|_1 (5)$$

Here, we note that the matrix operations assume that the high level features $\Psi(x)_n$ is of shape $(H_n W_n) \times C_n$, resulting in a $C_n \times C_n$ Gram matrix, and K_n is the normalization factor $1/C_n H_n K_n$ for the nth selected layer. Again, we include loss terms for both raw output and composited output.

Our final loss term is the total variation (TV) loss $\mathcal{L}_{tv}$: which is the smoothing penalty [12] on P, where P is the region of 1-pixel dilation of the hole region.

$$\mathcal{L}_{tv} = \sum_{(i,j)\in P,(i,j+1)\in P} \|\mathbf{I}_{comp}^{i,j+1} - \mathbf{I}_{comp}^{i,j}\|_1 + \sum_{(i,j)\in P,(i+1,j)\in P} \|\mathbf{I}_{comp}^{i+1,j} - \mathbf{I}_{comp}^{i,j}\|_1 \quad (6)$$

The total loss $\mathcal{L}_{total}$ is the combination of all the above loss functions.

$$\mathcal{L}_{total} = \mathcal{L}_{valid} + 6\mathcal{L}_{hole} + 0.05\mathcal{L}_{perceptual} + 120(\mathcal{L}_{style_{out}} + \mathcal{L}_{style_{comp}}) + 0.1\mathcal{L}_{tv} \quad (7)$$

The loss term weights were determined by performing a hyperparameter search on 100 validation images.

Ablation Study of Different Loss Terms. Perceptual loss [12] is known to generate *checkerboard artifacts*. Johnson et al. [12] suggests to ameliorate the problem by using the total variation (TV) loss. We found this not to be the case for our model. Figure 3(b) shows the result of the model trained by removing $\mathcal{L}_{style_{out}}$ and $\mathcal{L}_{style_{comp}}$ from $\mathcal{L}_{total}$. For our model, the additional style loss term is necessary. However, not all the loss weighting schemes for the style loss will generate plausible results. Figure 3(f) shows the result of the model trained with a small style loss weight. Compared to the result of the model trained with full $\mathcal{L}_{total}$ in Fig. 3(g), it has many *fish scale artifacts*. However, perceptual loss is

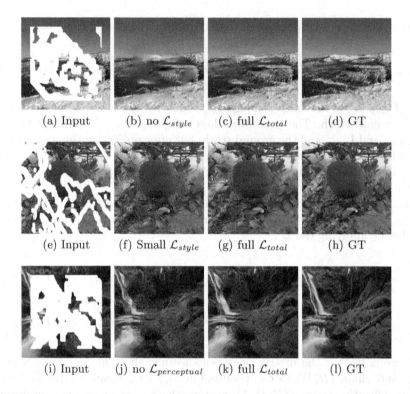

Fig. 3. In top row, from left to right: input image with hole, result without style loss, result using full $\mathcal{L}_{total}$, and ground truth. In middle row, from left to right: input image with hole, result using small style loss weight, result using full $\mathcal{L}_{total}$, and ground truth. In bottom row, from left to right: input image with hole, result without perceptual loss, result using full $\mathcal{L}_{total}$, and ground truth. (a) Input. (b) no $\mathcal{L}_{style}$. (c) full. (d) GT. (e) Input. (f) Small $\mathcal{L}_{style}$. (g) full $\mathcal{L}_{total}$. (h) GT. (i) Input. (j) no $\mathcal{L}_{perceptual}$. (k) full $\mathcal{L}_{total}$. (l) GT.

also important; grid-shaped artifacts are less prominent in the results with full $\mathcal{L}_{total}$ (Fig. 3(k)) than the results without perceptual loss (Fig. 3(j)). We hope this discussion will be useful to readers interested in employing VGG-based high level losses.

4 Experiments

4.1 Irregular Mask Dataset

Previous works generate holes in their datasets by randomly removing rectangular regions within their image. We consider this insufficient in creating the diverse hole shapes and sizes that we need. As such, we begin by collecting masks of random streaks and holes of arbitrary shapes. We found the results of occlusion/dis-occlusion mask estimation method between two consecutive frames

Fig. 4. Some test masks for each hole-to-image area ratio category. 1, 3 and 5 are shown using their examples with border constraint; 2, 4 and 6 are shown using their examples without border constraint.

for videos described in [29] to be a good source of such patterns. We generate 55,116 masks for the training and 24,866 masks for testing. During training, we augment the mask dataset by randomly sampling a mask from 55,116 masks and later perform random dilation, rotation and cropping. All the masks and images for training and testing are with the size of 512×512.

We create a test set by starting with the 24,866 raw masks and adding random dilation, rotation and cropping. Many previous methods such as [10] have degraded performance at holes near the image borders. As such, we divide the test set into two: masks with and without holes close to border. The split that has holes distant from the border ensures a distance of at least 50 pixels from the border.

We also further categorize our masks by hole size. Specifically, we generate 6 categories of masks with different hole-to-image area ratios: (0.01, 0.1], (0.1, 0.2], (0.2, 0.3], (0.3, 0.4], (0.4, 0.5], (0.5, 0.6]. Each category contains 1000 masks with and without border constraints. In total, we have created $6 \times 2 \times 1000 = 12,000$ masks. Some examples of each category's masks can be found in Fig. 4.

4.2 Training Process

Training Data. We use 3 separate image datasets for training and testing: ImageNet dataset [24], Places2 dataset [37] and CelebA-HQ [13,17]. We use the original train, test, and val splits for ImageNet and Places2. For CelebA-HQ, we randomly partition into 27 K images for training and 3 K images for testing.

Training Procedure. We initialize the weights using the initialization method described in [9] and use Adam [14] for optimization. We train on a single NVIDIA V100 GPU (16GB) with a batch size of 6.

Initial Training and Fine-Tuning. Holes present a problem for Batch Normalization because the mean and variance will be computed for hole pixels, and so it would make sense to disregard them at masked locations. However, holes are gradually filled with each application and usually completely gone by the decoder stage.

In order to use Batch Normalization in the presence of holes, we first turn on Batch Normalization for the initial training using a learning rate of 0.0002. Then, we fine-tune using a learning rate of 0.00005 and freeze the Batch Normalization parameters in the encoder part of the network. We keep Batch Normalization enabled in the decoder. This not only avoids the incorrect mean and variance issues, but also helps us to achieve faster convergence. ImageNet and Places2 models train for 10 days, whereas CelebA-HQ trains in 3 days. All fine-tuning is performed in one day.

4.3   Comparisons

We compare with 4 methods:

- **PM:** PatchMatch [2], the state-of-the-art non-learning based approach
- **GL:** Method proposed by Iizuka et al. [10]
- **GntIpt:** Method proposed by Yu et al. [36]
- **Conv:** Same network structure as our method but using typical convolutional layers. Loss weights were re-determined via hyperparameter search.

Our method is denoted as **PConv**. A fair comparison with GL and GntIpt would require retraining their models on our data. However, the training of both approaches use local discriminators assuming availability of the local bounding boxes of the holes, which would not make sense for the shape of our masks.

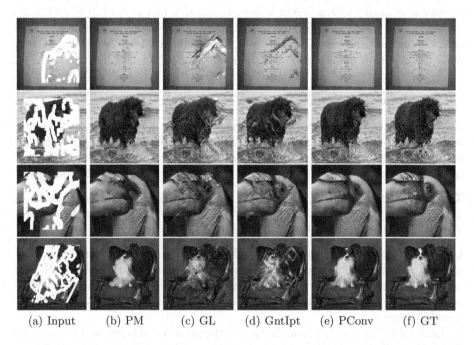

(a) Input   (b) PM   (c) GL   (d) GntIpt   (e) PConv   (f) GT

Fig. 5. Comparisons of test results on ImageNet. (a) Input. (b) PM. (c) GL. (d) GntIpt. (e) PConv. (f) GT.

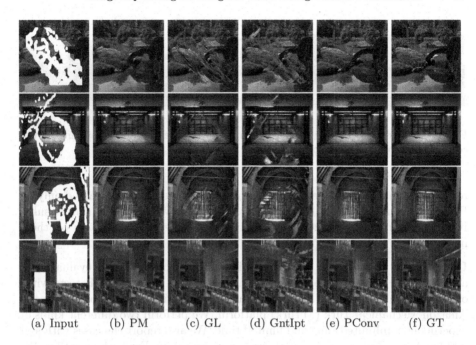

(a) Input   (b) PM   (c) GL   (d) GntIpt   (e) PConv   (f) GT

Fig. 6. Comparison of test results on Places2 images. (a) Input. (b) PM. (c) GL. (d) GntIpt. (e) PConv. (f) GT.

As such, we directly use their released pre-trained models[1]. For PatchMatch, we used a third-party implementation[2]. As we do not know their train-test splits, our own splits will likely differ from theirs. We evaluate on 12,000 images randomly assigning our masks to images without replacement.

Qualitative Comparisons. Figures 5 and 6 shows the comparisons on ImageNet and Places2 respectively. GT represents the ground truth. We compare with GntIpt [36] on CelebA-HQ in Fig. 9. GntIpt tested CelebA-HQ on 256 × 256 so we downsample the images to be 256 × 256 before feeding into their model. It can be seen that PM may copy semantically incorrect patches to fill holes, while GL and GntIpt sometimes fail to achieve plausible results through post-processing or refinement network. Figure 7 shows the results of Conv, which are with the distinct artifacts from conditioning on hole placeholder values.

Quantitative Comparisons. As mentioned in [36], there is no good numerical metric to evaluate image inpainting results due to the existence of many possible solutions. Nevertheless we follow the previous image inpainting works [34,36] by reporting ℓ_1 error, PSNR, SSIM [33], and the inception score [25]. ℓ_1 error, PSNR and SSIM are reported on Places2, whereas the Inception score (IScore) is

---

[1] https://github.com/satoshiiizuka/siggraph2017_inpainting,
https://github.com/JiahuiYu/generative_inpainting.
[2] https://github.com/younesse-cv/patchmatch.

Input	Conv	PConv	Input	Conv	PConv

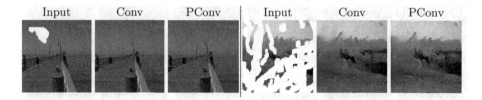

Fig. 7. Comparison between typical convolution layer based results (Conv) and partial convolution layer based results (PConv).

reported on ImageNet. Note that the released model for [10] was trained only on Places2, which we use for all evaluations. Table 1 shows the comparison results. It can be seen that our method outperforms all the other methods on these measurements on irregular masks.

User Study. In addition to quantitative comparisons, we also evaluate our algorithm via a human subjective study. We perform pairwise A/B tests without showing hole positions or original input image with holes, deployed on the Amazon Mechanical Turk (MTurk) platform. We perform two different kinds of experiments: unlimited time and limited time. We also report the cases with and without holes close to the image boundaries separately. For each situation, We randomly select 300 images for each method, where each image is compared 10 times.

Table 1. Comparisons with various methods. Columns represent different hole-to-image area ratios. N = no border, B = border

	[0.01,0.1]		(0.1,0.2]		(0.2,0.3]		(0.3,0.4]		(0.4,0.5]		(0.5,0.6]	
	N	B	N	B	N	B	N	B	N	B	N	B
ℓ_1(PM)(%)	**0.45**	**0.42**	1.25	1.16	2.28	2.07	3.52	3.17	4.77	4.27	6.98	6.34
ℓ_1(GL)(%)	1.39	1.53	3.01	3.22	4.51	5.00	6.05	6.77	7.34	8.20	8.60	9.78
ℓ_1(GnIpt)(%)	0.78	0.88	1.98	2.09	3.34	3.72	4.98	5.50	6.51	7.13	8.33	9.19
ℓ_1(Conv)(%)	0.52	0.50	1.26	1.17	2.20	2.01	3.37	3.03	4.58	4.10	6.66	6.01
ℓ_1(PConv)(%)	0.49	0.47	**1.18**	**1.09**	**2.07**	**1.88**	**3.19**	**2.84**	**4.37**	**3.85**	**6.45**	**5.72**
PSNR(PM)	32.97	33.68	26.87	27.51	23.70	24.35	21.27	22.05	19.70	20.58	17.60	18.22
PSNR(GL)	30.17	29.74	23.87	23.83	20.92	20.73	18.80	18.61	17.60	17.38	16.90	16.37
PSNR(GnIpt)	29.07	28.38	23.20	22.86	20.58	19.86	18.53	17.85	17.31	16.68	16.24	15.52
PSNR(Conv)	33.21	33.79	27.30	27.89	24.23	24.90	21.79	22.60	20.20	21.13	**18.24**	18.94
PSNR(PConv)	**33.75**	**34.34**	**27.71**	**28.32**	**24.54**	**25.25**	**22.01**	**22.89**	**20.34**	**21.38**	18.21	**19.04**
SSIM(PM)	**0.946**	**0.947**	0.861	0.865	0.763	0.768	0.666	0.675	0.568	0.579	0.459	0.472
SSIM(GL)	0.929	0.923	0.831	0.829	0.732	0.721	0.638	0.627	0.543	0.533	0.446	0.440
SSIM(GnIpt)	0.940	0.938	0.855	0.855	0.760	0.758	0.666	0.666	0.569	0.570	0.465	0.470
SSIM(Conv)	0.943	0.943	0.862	0.865	0.769	0.772	0.674	0.682	0.576	0.587	0.463	0.478
SSIM(PConv)	**0.946**	0.945	**0.867**	**0.870**	**0.775**	**0.779**	**0.681**	**0.689**	**0.583**	**0.595**	**0.468**	**0.484**
IScore(PM)	0.090	0.058	0.307	0.204	0.766	0.465	1.551	0.921	2.724	1.422	4.075	2.226
IScore(GL)	0.183	0.112	0.619	0.464	1.607	1.046	2.774	1.941	3.920	2.825	4.877	3.362
IScore(GnIpt)	0.127	0.088	0.396	0.307	0.978	0.621	1.757	1.126	2.759	1.801	3.967	2.525
IScore(Conv)	0.068	0.041	0.228	0.149	0.603	0.366	1.264	0.731	2.368	1.189	4.162	2.224
IScore(PConv)	**0.051**	**0.032**	**0.163**	**0.109**	**0.446**	**0.270**	**0.954**	**0.565**	**1.881**	**0.838**	**3.603**	**1.588**

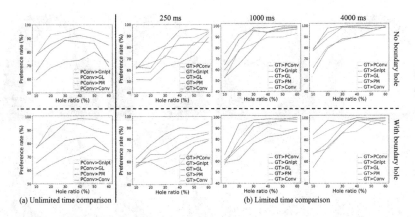

Fig. 8. User study results. We perform two kinds of experiments: unlimited time and limited time. (a) In the unlimited time setting, we compare our result with the result generated by another method. The rate where our result is preferred is graphed. 50% means two methods are equal. In the first row, the holes are not allowed to touch the image boundary, while in the second row it is allowed. (b) In the limited time setting, we compare all methods to the ground truth. The subject is given some limited time (250 ms, 1000 ms or 4000 ms) to select which image is more realistic. The rate where ground truth is preferred over the other method is reported. The lower the curve, the better.

For the unlimited time setting, the workers are given two images at once: each generated by a different method. The workers are then given unlimited time to select which image looks more realistic. We also shuffle the image order to ensure unbiased comparisons. The results across all different hole-to-image area ratios are summarized in Fig. 8(a). The first row shows the results where the holes are at least 50 pixels away from the image border, while the second row shows the case where the holes may be close to or touch image border. As can be seen, our method performs significantly better than all the other methods (50% means two methods perform equally well) in both cases.

For the limited time setting, we compare all methods (including ours) to the ground truth. In each comparison, the result of one method is chosen and shown to the workers along with the ground truth for a limited amount of time. The workers are then asked to select which image looks more natural. This evaluates how quickly the difference between the images can be perceived. The comparison results for different time intervals are shown in Fig. 8(b). Again, the first row shows the case where the holes do not touch the image boundary while the second row allows that. Our method outperforms the other methods in most cases across different time periods and hole-to-image area ratios.

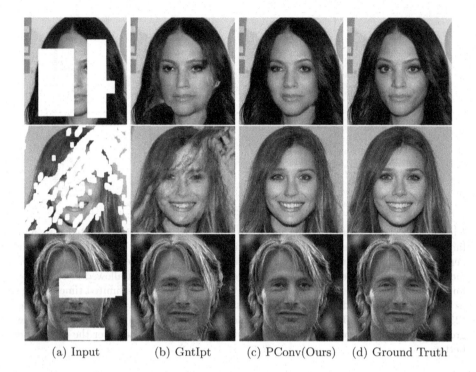

  (a) Input   (b) GntIpt   (c) PConv(Ours)   (d) Ground Truth

Fig. 9. Test results on CelebA-HQ. (a) Input. (b) GntIpt. (c) PConv (Ours). (d) Ground Truth.

5   Discussion and Extension

5.1   Discussion

We propose the use of a partial convolution layer with an automatic mask updating mechanism and achieve state-of-the-art image inpainting results. Our model can robustly handle holes of any shape, size location, or distance from the image borders. Further, our performance does not deteriorate catastrophically as holes increase in size, as seen in Fig. 10. However, one limitation of our method is that it fails for some sparsely structured images such as the bars on the door in Fig. 11, and, like most methods, struggles on the largest of holes.

Fig. 10. Inpainting results with various dilation of the hole region from left to right: 0, 5, 15, 35, 55, and 95 pixels dilation respectively. Top row: input; bottom row: corresponding inpainted results.

Fig. 11. Failure cases. Each group is ordered as input, our result and ground truth.

Acknowledgement. We would like to thank Jonah Alben, Rafael Valle Costa, Karan Sapra, Chao Yang, Raul Puri, Brandon Rowlett and other NVIDIA colleagues for valuable discussions, and Chris Hebert for technical support.

References

1. Ballester, C., Bertalmio, M., Caselles, V., Sapiro, G., Verdera, J.: Filling-in by joint interpolation of vector fields and gray levels. IEEE Trans. Image Process. **10**(8), 1200–1211 (2001)
2. Barnes, C., Shechtman, E., Finkelstein, A., Goldman, D.B.: PatchMatch: a randomized correspondence algorithm for structural image editing. ACM Trans. Graph. TOG **28**(3), 24 (2009)
3. Bertalmio, M., Sapiro, G., Caselles, V., Ballester, C.: Image inpainting. In: Proceedings of the 27th Annual Conference on Computer Graphics and Interactive Techniques, pp. 417–424. ACM Press/Addison-Wesley Publishing Co. (2000)
4. Dai, J., et al.: Deformable convolutional networks. CoRR, abs/1703.06211 **1**(2), 3 (2017)
5. Efros, A.A., Freeman, W.T.: Image quilting for texture synthesis and transfer. In: Proceedings of the 28th Annual Conference on Computer Graphics and Interactive Techniques, pp. 341–346. ACM (2001)
6. Gatys, L.A., Ecker, A.S., Bethge, M.: A neural algorithm of artistic style. arXiv preprint arXiv:1508.06576 (2015)
7. Harley, A.W., Derpanis, K.G., Kokkinos, I.: Segmentation-aware convolutional networks using local attention masks. In: IEEE International Conference on Computer Vision (ICCV), vol. 2, p. 7 (2017)

8. Hays, J., Efros, A.A.: Scene completion using millions of photographs. In: ACM Transactions on Graphics (TOG), vol. 26, p. 4. ACM (2007)

9. He, K., Zhang, X., Ren, S., Sun, J.: Delving deep into rectifiers: surpassing human-level performance on imagenet classification. In: Proceedings of the IEEE International Conference on Computer Vision, pp. 1026–1034 (2015)

10. Iizuka, S., Simo-Serra, E., Ishikawa, H.: Globally and locally consistent image completion. ACM Trans. Graph. (TOG) 36(4), 107 (2017)

11. Isola, P., Zhu, J.Y., Zhou, T., Efros, A.A.: Image-to-image translation with conditional adversarial networks. arXiv preprint (2017)

12. Johnson, J., Alahi, A., Fei-Fei, L.: Perceptual losses for real-time style transfer and super-resolution. In: Leibe, B., Matas, J., Sebe, N., Welling, M. (eds.) ECCV 2016. LNCS, vol. 9906, pp. 694–711. Springer, Cham (2016). https://doi.org/10.1007/978-3-319-46475-6_43

13. Karras, T., Aila, T., Laine, S., Lehtinen, J.: Progressive growing of GANs for improved quality, stability, and variation. arXiv preprint arXiv:1710.10196 (2017)

14. Kingma, D.P., Ba, J.: Adam: a method for stochastic optimization. arXiv preprint arXiv:1412.6980 (2014)

15. Kwatra, V., Essa, I., Bobick, A., Kwatra, N.: Texture optimization for example-based synthesis. In: ACM Transactions on Graphics (ToG), vol. 24, pp. 795–802. ACM (2005)

16. Li, Y., Liu, S., Yang, J., Yang, M.H.: Generative face completion. In: The IEEE Conference on Computer Vision and Pattern Recognition (CVPR), vol. 1, p. 3 (2017)

17. Liu, Z., Luo, P., Wang, X., Tang, X.: Deep learning face attributes in the wild. In: Proceedings of International Conference on Computer Vision (ICCV), December 2015

18. van den Oord, A., Kalchbrenner, N., Espeholt, L., Vinyals, O., Graves, A., et al.: Conditional image generation with PixelCNN decoders. In: Advances in Neural Information Processing Systems, pp. 4790–4798 (2016)

19. Paszke, A., et al.: Automatic differentiation in PyTorch (2017)

20. Pathak, D., Krahenbuhl, P., Donahue, J., Darrell, T., Efros, A.A.: Context encoders: feature learning by inpainting. In: Proceedings of the IEEE Conference on Computer Vision and Pattern Recognition, pp. 2536–2544 (2016)

21. Pérez, P., Gangnet, M., Blake, A.: Poisson image editing. ACM Trans. Graph. (TOG) 22(3), 313–318 (2003)

22. Ren, J.S., Xu, L., Yan, Q., Sun, W.: Shepard convolutional neural networks. In: Advances in Neural Information Processing Systems, pp. 901–909 (2015)

23. Ronneberger, O., Fischer, P., Brox, T.: U-Net: convolutional networks for biomedical image segmentation. In: Navab, N., Hornegger, J., Wells, W.M., Frangi, A.F. (eds.) MICCAI 2015. LNCS, vol. 9351, pp. 234–241. Springer, Cham (2015). https://doi.org/10.1007/978-3-319-24574-4_28

24. Russakovsky, O., et al.: ImageNet large scale visual recognition challenge. Int. J. Comput. Vis. (IJCV) 115(3), 211–252 (2015). https://doi.org/10.1007/s11263-015-0816-y

25. Salimans, T., Goodfellow, I., Zaremba, W., Cheung, V., Radford, A., Chen, X.: Improved techniques for training GANs. In: Advances in Neural Information Processing Systems, pp. 2234–2242 (2016)

26. Simakov, D., Caspi, Y., Shechtman, E., Irani, M.: Summarizing visual data using bidirectional similarity. In: 2008 IEEE Conference on Computer Vision and Pattern Recognition, CVPR 2008, pp. 1–8. IEEE (2008)

27. Simonyan, K., Zisserman, A.: Very deep convolutional networks for large-scale image recognition. arXiv preprint arXiv:1409.1556 (2014)
28. Song, Y., Yang, C., Lin, Z., Li, H., Huang, Q., Kuo, C.C.J.: Image inpainting using multi-scale feature image translation. arXiv preprint arXiv:1711.08590 (2017)
29. Sundaram, N., Brox, T., Keutzer, K.: Dense point trajectories by GPU-accelerated large displacement optical flow. In: Daniilidis, K., Maragos, P., Paragios, N. (eds.) ECCV 2010. LNCS, vol. 6311, pp. 438–451. Springer, Heidelberg (2010). https:// doi.org/10.1007/978-3-642-15549-9_32
30. Telea, A.: An image inpainting technique based on the fast marching method. J. Graph. Tools **9**(1), 23–34 (2004)
31. Uhrig, J., Schneider, N., Schneider, L., Franke, U., Brox, T., Geiger, A.: Sparsity invariant CNNs. arXiv preprint arXiv:1708.06500 (2017)
32. Ulyanov, D., Vedaldi, A., Lempitsky, V.: Deep image prior. arXiv preprint arXiv:1711.10925 (2017)
33. Wang, Z., Bovik, A.C., Sheikh, H.R., Simoncelli, E.P.: Image quality assessment: from error visibility to structural similarity. IEEE Trans. Image Process. **13**(4), 600–612 (2004)
34. Yang, C., Lu, X., Lin, Z., Shechtman, E., Wang, O., Li, H.: High-resolution image inpainting using multi-scale neural patch synthesis. In: The IEEE Conference on Computer Vision and Pattern Recognition (CVPR), vol. 1, p. 3 (2017)
35. Yeh, R., Chen, C., Lim, T.Y., Hasegawa-Johnson, M., Do, M.N.: Semantic image inpainting with perceptual and contextual losses. arXiv preprint arXiv:1607.07539 (2016)
36. Yu, J., Lin, Z., Yang, J., Shen, X., Lu, X., Huang, T.S.: Generative image inpainting with contextual attention. arXiv preprint arXiv:1801.07892 (2018)
37. Zhou, B., Lapedriza, A., Khosla, A., Oliva, A., Torralba, A.: Places: a 10 million image database for scene recognition. IEEE Trans. Patt. Anal. Mach. Intell. **40**, 1452–1464 (2017)

Fighting Fake News: Image Splice Detection via Learned Self-Consistency

Minyoung Huh[1,2], Andrew Liu[1(✉)], Andrew Owens[1], and Alexei A. Efros[1]

[1] UC Berkeley, Berkeley, USA
ahliu@berkeley.edu
[2] Carnegie Mellon University, Pittsburgh, USA

Abstract. Advances in photo editing and manipulation tools have made it significantly easier to create fake imagery. Learning to detect such manipulations, however, remains a challenging problem due to the lack of sufficient amounts of manipulated training data. In this paper, we propose a learning algorithm for detecting visual image manipulations that is trained only using a large dataset of real photographs. The algorithm uses the automatically recorded photo EXIF metadata as supervisory signal for training a model to determine whether an image is *self-consistent* — that is, whether its content could have been produced by a single imaging pipeline. We apply this self-consistency model to the task of detecting and localizing image splices. The proposed method obtains state-of-the-art performance on several image forensics benchmarks, despite never seeing any manipulated images at training. That said, it is merely a step in the long quest for a truly general purpose visual forensics tool.

Keywords: Visual forensics · Image splicing
Self-supervised learning · EXIF

1 Introduction

Malicious image manipulation, long the domain of dictators [2] and spy agencies, has now become accessible to legions of common Internet trolls and Facebook con-men [3]. With only rudimentary editing skills, it is now possible to create realistic image composites [4,5], fill in large image regions [1,6,7], generate plausible video from speech [8,9], etc. One might have hoped that these new methods for creating synthetic visual content would be met with commensurately powerful techniques for detecting fakes, but this has not been the case so far (Fig. 1).

One problem is that standard supervised learning approaches, which have been very successful for many types of detection problems, are not well-suited

---

M. Huh and A. Liu—equal contribution.

Code and additional results can be found on our website

Electronic supplementary material The online version of this chapter (https://doi.org/10.1007/978-3-030-01252-6_7) contains supplementary material, which is available to authorized users.

© Springer Nature Switzerland AG 2018
V. Ferrari et al. (Eds.): ECCV 2018, LNCS 11215, pp. 106–124, 2018.
https://doi.org/10.1007/978-3-030-01252-6_7

Input   Predicted Splice   Ground Truth Mask   Ground Truth Source Images
                    Mask

Fig. 1. Our algorithm learns to detect and localize image manipulations (splices), despite being trained only on unmanipulated images. The two input images above might look plausible, but our model correctly determined that they have been manipulated because they lack self-consistency: the visual information within the predicted splice region was found to be inconsistent with the rest of the image. IMAGE CREDITS: automatically created splice from Hays and Efros [1] (top), manual splice from *Reddit* user */u/Name-Albert_Einstein* (bottom).

for image forensics. This is because the space of manipulated images is so vast and diverse, that it is rather unlikely we will ever have enough manipulated training data for a supervised method to fully succeed. Indeed, detecting visual manipulation can be thought of as an anomaly detection problem — we want to flag anything that is "out of the ordinary," even though we might not have a good model of what that might be. In other words, we would like a method that does not require any manipulated training data at all, but can work in an unsupervised/self-supervised regime.

In this work, we turn to a vast and previously underutilized source of data, image EXIF metadata. EXIF tags are camera specifications that are digitally engraved into an image file at the moment of capture and are ubiquitously available. Consider the photo shown in Fig. 2. While at first glance it might seem authentic, we see on closer inspection that a car has been inserted into the scene. The content for this spliced region came from a different photo, shown on the right. Such a manipulation is called an *image splice*, and it is one of the most common ways of creating visual fakes. If we had access to the two source photographs, we would see from their EXIF metadata that there are a number of differences in the imaging pipelines: one photo was taken with an *Nikon* camera, the other with a *Kodak* camera; they were shot using different focal lengths, and saved with different JPEG quality settings, etc. Our insight is that one might be able to detect spliced images because they are composed of regions that were captured with different imaging pipelines. Of course, in forensics applications, we do not have access to the original source images nor, in general, the fraudulent photo's metadata.

Fig. 2. Anatomy of a splice: One of the most common ways of creative fake images is splicing together content from two different real source images. The insight explored in this paper is that patches from a spliced image are typically produced by different imaging pipelines, as indicated by the EXIF meta-data of the two source images. The problem is that in practice, we never have access to these source images at test time. (Photo credits: NIMBLE dataset [10] and *Flickr* user James Stave.)

Instead, in this paper, we propose to use the EXIF metadata as a *supervisory signal* for training a classification model to determine whether an image is *self-consistent* – that is, whether different parts of the same image could have been produced by a single imaging pipeline. The model is self-supervised in that only real photographs and their EXIF meta-data are used for training. A consistency classifier is learned for each EXIF tag separately using pairs of photographs, and the resulting classifiers are combined together to estimate self-consistency of pairs of patches in a novel input image. We validate our approach using several datasets and show that the model performs better than the state-of-the-art — despite never having seen annotated splices or using handcrafted detection cues.

The main contributions of this paper are: (1) posing image forensics as a problem of detecting violations in learned self-consistency (a kind of anomaly detection), (2) proposing photographic metadata as a free and plentiful supervisory signal for learning self-consistency, (3) applying our self-consistency model to detecting and localizing splices. We also introduce a new dataset of image splices obtained from the internet, and experimentally evaluate which photographic metadata is predictable from images.

2   Related Work

Over the years, researchers have proposed a variety of visual forensics methods for identifying various manipulations [3]. The earliest and most thoroughly studied approach is to use domain knowledge to isolate physical cues within an image. Drawing upon techniques from signal processing, previous methods focused on cues such as misaligned JPEG blocks [11], compression quantization artifacts [12], resampling artifacts [13], color filtering array discrepancies [14], and camera-hardware "fingerprints" [15]. We take particular inspiration from recent work by Agarwal and Farid [16], which exploits a seemingly insignificant difference between imaging pipelines to detect spliced image regions — namely, the way that different cameras truncate numbers during JPEG quantization. While these domain-specific approaches have proven to be useful due to their easy interpretability, we believe that the use of machine learning will open the door to discovering many more useful cues while also producing more adaptable algorithms.

Indeed, recent work has moved away from using a priori knowledge and toward applying end-to-end learning methods for solving specific forensics tasks using labeled training data. For example, Salloum et al. [17] propose learning to detect splices by training a fully convolutional network on labeled training data. These learning methods have also been applied to the problem of detecting specific tampering cues, such as double-JPEG compression [18,19] and contrast enhancement [20]. The most closely related of these methods to ours is perhaps Bondi et al. [21,22]. This work recognizes camera models from image patches, and proposes to use inconsistencies in camera predictions to detect tampering. Another common forensics strategy is to train models on a small class of automatically simulated manipulations, like face-swapping [23] or splicing with COCO segmentation masks [24]. In addition, [23] propose identifying face swaps by measuring image inconsistencies introduced from splicing and blurring. In concurrent work, Mayer [25] proposed using a Siamese network to predict whether pairs of image patches have the same camera model — a special case of our metadata consistency model (they also propose using this model for splice detection; while promising, these results are very preliminary). There has also been work that estimates whether a photo's semantic content (e.g., weather) matches its metadata [26] (Fig. 3).

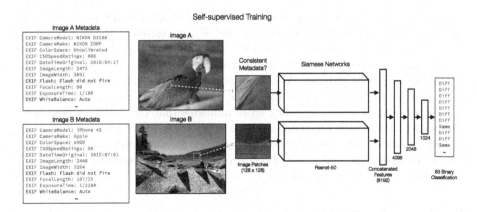

Fig. 3. Self-supervised training: Our model takes two random patches from different images and predicts whether they have consistent meta-data. Each attribute is used as a consistency metric during training and testing.

In our work, we seek to further reduce the amount of information we provide to the algorithm by having it learn to detect manipulations without ground-truth annotations. For this, we take inspiration from recent works in self-supervision [27–32] which train models by solving tasks solely defined using unlabeled data. Of these, the most closely related approach is that of Doersch et al. [28], in which they trained a model to predict the relative position of pairs of patches within an image. Surprisingly, the authors found that their method learned to utilize very subtle artifacts like chromatic lens aberration as a short-cut for learning the task. While imaging noise was a nuisance in their work, it is a useful signal for us — our self-supervised algorithm is designed to learn about properties of the imaging pipeline while ignoring semantics. Our technical approach is also similar to [33], which trains a segmentation model using self-supervision to predict whether pairs of patches co-occur in space or time.

Individual image metadata tags, such as focal length, GPS, hashtags, etc. have long been employed in computer vision as free supervisory signal. A particularly creative use of EXIF metadata was demonstrated by Kuthirummal et al. [34], who used the `CameraModel` tag of a very large image collection to compute per-camera priors such as their non-linear response functions.

Our work is also related to the anomaly detection problem. Unlike traditional visual anomaly detection work, which is largely concerned with detecting unusual semantic events like the presence of rare objects and actions [35,36], our work needs to find anomalies in photos whose content is designed to be plausible enough to fool humans. Therefore the anomalous cues we search for should be imperceptible to humans and invariant to the semantics of the scene.

3   Learning Photographic Self-consistency

Our model works by predicting whether a pair of image patches are consistent with each other. Given two patches, $\mathcal{P}_i$ and $\mathcal{P}_j$, we estimate the probabilities $x_1, x_2, ..., x_n$ that they share the same value for each of n metadata attributes. We then estimate the patches' overall consistency, c_{ij}, by combining our n observations of metadata consistency. At evaluation time, our model takes a potentially manipulated test image and measures the consistency between many different pairs of patches. A low consistency score indicates that the patches were likely produced by two distinct imaging systems, suggesting that they originate from different images. Although the consistency score for any single pair of patches will be noisy, aggregating many observations provides a reasonably stable estimate of overall image self-consistency.

3.1   Predicting EXIF Attribute Consistency

We use a Siamese network to predict the probability that a pair of 128×128 image patches shares the same value for each EXIF metadata attribute. We train this network with image patches randomly sampled from $400,000$ *Flickr* photos, making predictions on all EXIF attributes that appear in more than $50,000$

photos ($n = 80$, the full list of attributes can be found in supplementary files). For a given EXIF attribute, we discard EXIF values that occur less than 100 times. The Siamese network uses shared ResNet-50 [37] sub-networks which each produce 4096-dim. feature vectors. These vectors are concatenated and passed through four-layer MLP with 4096, 2048, 1024 units, followed by the final output layer. The network predicts the probability that the images share the same value for each of the n metadata attributes.

We found that training with random sampling is challenging because: (1) there are some rare EXIF values that are very difficult to learn, and (2) randomly selected pairs of images are unlikely to have consistent EXIF values by chance. Therefore, we introduce two types of re-balancing: unary and pairwise. For unary re-balancing, we oversample rare EXIF attribute values (e.g. rare camera models). When constructing a mini-batch, we first choose an EXIF attribute and uniformly sample an EXIF value from all possible values of this attribute. For pairwise re-balancing, we make sure that pairs of training images within a mini-batch are selected such that for a given EXIF attribute, half the batch share that value and half do not.

Analysis. Although we train on all common EXIF attributes, we expect the model to excel at distinguishing ones that directly correlate to properties of the imaging pipeline such as `LensMake` [21,28]. In contrast, arbitrary attributes such as the exact date an image was taken (`DateTimeOriginal`) leave no informative cues in an image. In order to identify predictive metadata, we evaluated our EXIF-consistency model on a dataset of 50 K held-out photos and report the individual EXIF attribute accuracy in Fig. 4 (chance is 50% due to rebalancing).

Our model obtains high accuracy when predicting the consistency of attributes closely associated with the image formation process such as `LensMake`, which contains values such as *Apple* and *FUJIFILM*. But more surprisingly, we found that the most predictable attribute is `UserComment`. Upon further inspection, we found that `UserComment` is a generic field that can be populated with arbitrary data, and that its most frequent values were either binary strings embedded by camera manufacturers or logs left by image processing software. For example, one of its common values, *Processed with VSCOcam*, is added by a popular photo-filtering application. Please see the supplementary material for a full list of EXIF attributes and their definitions.

3.2 Post-processing Consistency

Many image manipulations are performed with the intent of making the resulting image look plausible to the human eye: spliced regions are resized, edge artifacts are smoothed, and the resulting image is re-JPEGed. If our network could predict whether two patches are post-processed differently, then this would be compelling evidence for photographic inconsistency. To model post-processing consistency, we add three augmentation operations during training: re-JPEGing, Gaussian blur, and image resizing. Half of the time, we apply the same operations to both patches; the other half of the time, we apply different operations. The parameters of each operation are randomly chosen from an evenly discretized set of

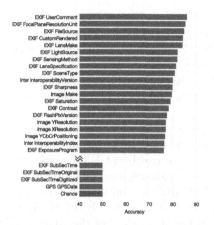

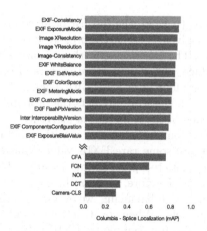

Fig. 4. EXIF Accuracy: How predictable are EXIF attributes? For each attribute, we compute pairwise-consistency accuracy on *Flickr* images using our self-consistency model.

Fig. 5. EXIF Splice Localization: How useful are EXIF attributes for localizing splices? We compute individual localization scores on the *Columbia* dataset.

numbers. We introduce three additional classification tasks (one per augmentation type) that are used to train the model to predict whether a pair of patches received the same parameterized augmentation. This increases the number of binary attributes we predict from 80 to 83. Since the order of the post-processing operations matters, we apply them in a random order each time. We note that this form of inconsistency is orthogonal to EXIF consistency. For example, in the (unlikely) event that a spliced region had exactly the same metadata as the image it was inserted into, the splice could still be detected by observing differences in post-processing.

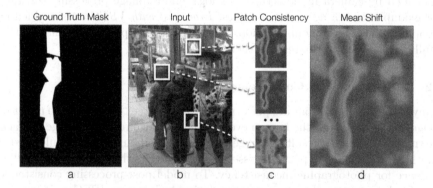

Fig. 6. Test Time: Our model samples patches in a grid from an input image (b) and estimates consistency for every pair of patches. (c) For a given patch, we get a consistency map by comparing it to all other patches in the image. (d) We use Mean Shift to aggregate the consistency maps into a final prediction.

3.3   Combining Consistency Predictions

Once we have predicted the consistency of a pair of patches for each of our EXIF (plus post-processing) attributes, we would like to estimate the pairs' *overall* consistency c_{ij}. If we were solving a supervised task, then a natural choice would be to use spliced regions as supervision to predict, from the n EXIF-consistency predictions, the probability that the two patches belong to different regions. Unfortunately, we do not have spliced images to train on. Instead, we use a self-supervised proxy task: we train a simple classifier to predict, from the EXIF consistency predictions, whether the patches come from the same image.

More specifically, consider the 83-dimensional vector **x** of EXIF consistency predictions for a pair of patches i and j. We estimate the overall consistency between the patches as $c_{ij} = p_\theta(y \mid \mathbf{x})$ where p_θ is a two-layer MLP with 512 hidden units. The network is trained to predict whether i and j come from the same training image (i.e. $y = 1$ if they're the same; $y = 0$ if they're different). This has the effect of calibrating the different EXIF predictions while modeling correlations between them.

3.4   Directly Predicting Image Consistency

An alternative to using EXIF metadata as a proxy for determining consistency between two image patches is to directly predict whether the two patches come from the same image or not. Such a model could be easily trained with pairs of patches randomly sampled from the same or different images. In principle, such a model should work at least as well as the EXIF one, and perhaps better, since it could pick up on differences between images not captured by any of the EXIF tags. In practice, however, such a model would need to be trained on vast

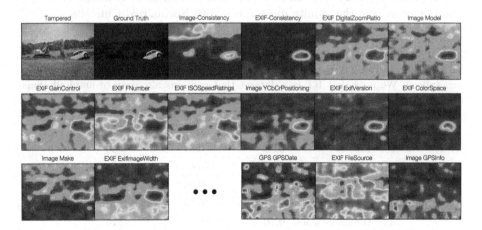

Fig. 7. Consistency map from different EXIF tags: We compute consistency maps for each metadata attribute independently (response maps sorted by localization accuracy). The merged consistency map accurately localizes the spliced car.

amounts of data, because most random patches coming from different images will be easy to detect with trivial cues. For example, the network might simply learn to compare patch color histograms, which is a surprisingly powerful cue for same/different image classification task [33,38]. To evaluate the performance of this model in practice, we trained a Siamese network, similar in structure to the EXIF-consistency model (Sect. 3.1), to solve the task of same-or-different image consistency (see *Image-Consistency* in the Results section).

3.5   From Patch Consistency to Image Self-Consistency

So far we have introduced models that can measure some form of consistency between pairs of patches. In order to transform this into something usable for detecting splices, we need to aggregate these pairwise consistency probabilities into a global self-consistency score for the entire image.

Given an image, we sample patches in a grid, using a stride such that the number of patches sampled along the longest image dimension is 25. This results in at most 625 patches (for the common 4:3 aspect ratio, we sample $25 \times 18 = 450$ patches). For a given patch, we can visualize a response map corresponding to its consistency with every other patch in the image. To increase the spatial resolution of each response map, we average the predictions of overlapping patches. If there is a splice, then the majority of patches from the untampered portion of the image will ideally have low consistency with patches from the tampered region (Fig. 6c).

To produce a single response map for an input image, we want to find the most consistent mode among all patch response maps. We do this mode-seeking using Mean Shift [39]. The resulting response map naturally segments the image into consistent and inconsistent regions (Fig. 6d). We call the merged response map a *consistency map*. We can also qualitatively visualize the tampered image region by clustering the affinity matrix, e.g. with Normalized Cuts [40].

Table 1. Splice Detection: We compare our splice detection accuracy on 3 datasets. We measure the mean average precision (mAP) of detecting whether an image has been spliced. We note that RT is a dataset that contains a variety of manipulations (not just splicing).

Dataset	Columbia [41]	Carvalho [42]	RT [43]
CFA [45]	0.83	0.64	0.54
DCT [46]	0.58	0.63	0.52
NOI [47]	0.73	0.66	0.52
Supervised FCN	0.57	0.56	**0.56**
Camera classification	0.70	0.73	0.15
Image-Consistency	0.97	0.75	0.58
EXIF-Consistency	**0.98**	**0.87**	0.55

To help understand how different EXIF attributes vary in their consistency predictions, we created response maps for each tag for an example image (Fig. 7). While the individual tags provide a noisy consistency signal, the merged response map accurately localizes the spliced region.

4 Results

We evaluate our models on two closely related tasks: splice detection and splice localization. In the former, our goal is to classify images as being spliced *vs.* authentic. In the latter, the goal is to localize the spliced regions within an image.

4.1 Benchmarks

We evaluate our method on five different datasets. This includes three existing datasets: the widely used *Columbia* dataset [41], which consists of 180 relatively simple splices, and two more challenging datasets, *Carvalho* et al. [42] (94 images) and *Realistic Tampering* [43] (220 images), which combine splicing with post-processing operations. The latter also includes other tampering operations, such as copy-move.

One potential shortcoming of these existing datasets is that they were created by a small number of artists and may not be representative of the variety of forgeries encountered online. To address this issue, we introduce a new *In-the-Wild* forensics dataset that consists of 201 images scraped from THE ONION, a parody news website (i.e. fake news), and REDDIT PHOTOSHOP BATTLES, an online community of users who create and share manipulated images (which has been used in other recent forensics work [44]). Since ground truth labels are not available for internet splices, we annotated the images by hand to obtain approximate ground truth (using the unmodified source images as reference when they were available).

Finally, we also want to evaluate our method on automatically-generated splices. For this, we used the scene completion data from Hays and Efros [1], which comes with inpainting results, masks, and source images for a total of 55 images. We note that the ground-truth masks are only approximate, since the scene completion algorithm may alter a small region of pixels outside the mask in order to produce seamless splices.

4.2 Comparisons

We compared our model with three methods that use image processing techniques to detect specific imaging artifacts: Color Filter Array (CFA) [45] detects artifacts in color pattern interpolation; JPEG DCT [46] detects inconsistencies over JPEG coefficients; and Noise Variance (NOI) [47] detects anomalous noise patterns using wavelets. We used implementations of these algorithms provided by Zampoglou et al. [48].

Table 2. Splice Localization: We evaluate our model on 5 datasets using mean average precision (mAP, permuted-mAP) over pixels and class-balanced IOU (cIOU) selecting the optimal threshold per image.

Dataset	Columbia [41]			Carvalho [42]			RT [43]			In-the-Wild			Hays [1]		
Metric	mAP	p-mAP	cIOU	mAP	p-mAP	cIOU	mAP	p-mAP	cIOU	mAP	p-mAP	cIOU	mAP	p-mAP	cIOU
CFA [45]	0.76	0.76	0.75	0.18	0.24	0.46	**0.40**	**0.40**	**0.63**	0.23	0.27	0.45	0.11	0.22	0.45
DCT [46]	0.33	0.43	0.41	0.25	0.32	0.51	0.11	0.12	0.50	0.35	0.41	0.51	0.16	0.21	0.47
NOI [47]	0.43	0.56	0.47	0.23	0.38	0.50	0.12	0.19	0.50	0.35	0.42	0.52	0.15	0.27	0.47
Supervised FCN	0.60	0.61	0.58	0.18	0.22	0.47	0.09	0.10	0.49	0.25	0.26	0.46	0.15	0.17	0.46
Camera classification	0.29	0.65	0.41	0.11	0.29	0.44	0.07	0.10	0.48	0.20	0.31	0.44	0.15	0.31	0.47
Image-Consistency	0.87	0.90	0.80	0.36	0.41	0.55	0.21	0.21	0.54	0.47	**0.53**	**0.59**	0.21	0.37	0.54
EXIF-Consistency	**0.91**	**0.94**	**0.85**	**0.51**	**0.52**	**0.63**	0.20	0.20	0.54	**0.48**	0.49	0.58	**0.48**	**0.52**	**0.65**

Since we also wanted to compare our unsupervised method with approaches that were trained on labeled data, we report results from a learning-based method: E-MFCN [17]. Given a dataset of spliced images and masks as training data, they use a supervised fully convolutional network (FCN) [49] to predict splice masks and boundaries in test images. To test on our new datasets, we implemented a simplified version of their model (a standard FCN trained to recognize spliced pixels) that was trained with a training split of the *Columbia, Carvalho,* and *Realistic Tampering* datasets. We split every dataset in half to construct train/test sets.

Finally, we present two variations of self-consistency models. The first, *Camera-Classification,* was trained to directly predict which camera model produced a given image patch. We evaluate the output of the camera classification model by sampling image patches from a test image and assigning the most frequently predicted camera as the natural image and everything else as the spliced region. We consider an image to be untampered when every patch's predicted camera model is consistent.

The second model, *Image-Consistency,* is a network that directly predicts whether two patches are sampled from the same image (Sect. 3.4). An image is considered likely to have been tampered if its constituent patches are predicted to have come from different images. The evaluations of these models are performed the same way as our full *EXIF-Consistency* model.

We trained our models, including the variations, using a ResNet50 [37] pre-trained on ImageNet [50]. We used a batch size of 128 and optimized our objective using Adam [51] with a learning rate of 10^{-4}. We report our results after training for 1 million iterations. The 2-layer MLP used to compute patch consistency on top of the *EXIF-Consistency* model predictions was trained for 10,000 iterations.

Table 3. Comparison with Salloum et al.: We compare against numbers reported by [17] for splice localization.

Dataset	Columbia [41]		Carvalho [42]	
Metric	MCC	F1	MCC	F1
CFA [45]	0.23	0.47	0.16	0.29
DCT [46]	0.33	0.52	0.19	0.31
NOI [47]	0.41	0.57	0.25	0.34
E-MFCN [17]	0.48	0.61	0.41	0.48
Camera classification	0.30	0.50	0.13	0.26
Image-Consistency	0.77	0.85	0.33	0.43
EXIF-Consistency	**0.80**	**0.88**	**0.42**	**0.52**

4.3 Splice Detection

We evaluate splice detection using the three datasets that contain both untampered and manipulated images: *Columbia, Carvalho,* and *Realistic Tampering.* For each algorithm, we extract the localization map and obtain an overall score by spatially averaging the responses. The images are ranked based on their overall scores, and we compute the mean average precision (mAP) for the whole dataset.

Table 1 shows the mAP for detecting manipulated images. Our *Consistency* models achieves state-of-the-art performance on *Columbia* and *Carvalho* and Realistic Tampering, beating supervised methods like *FCN*.

4.4 Splice Localization

Having seen that our model can distinguish spliced and authentic images, we next ask whether it can also localize spliced regions within images. For each image, our algorithm produces an unnormalized probability that each pixel is part of a splice.

Because our consistency predictions are relative, it is ambiguous which of the two segments is spliced. We therefore identify the spliced region using a simple heuristic: we say that the smaller of the two consistent regions is the splice. We also consider an alternative evaluation metric that flips (i.e. negates) the consistency predictions if this permutation results in higher accuracy. This measures a model's ability to segment the two regions, rather than its ability to say which is which. In both cases, we evaluate the quality of the localization using mean average precision (mAP).

We also propose using a per-class intersection over union (cIOU) which averages the IOU of spliced and non-spliced regions after optimal thresholding.

Fig. 8. Detecting Fakes: *EXIF-Consistency* successfully localizes manipulations across many different datasets. We show qualitative results on images from *Carvalho*, *In-the-Wild*, *Hays* and *Realistic Tampering*.

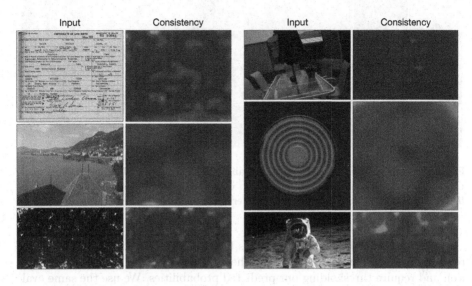

Fig. 9. Response on Untampered Images: Our algorithm's response map contains fewer inconsistencies when given an untampered images.

Fig. 10. Failure Cases: We present typical failure modes of our model. As we can see with outdoor images, overexposure frequently leads to false positives in the sky. In addition some splices are too small that we cannot effectively locate them using consistency. Finally, the flower example produces a partially incorrect result when using the *EXIF Consistency* model. Since the manipulation was a copy-move, the manipulation is only detectable via post-processing consistency cues (and not EXIF-consistency cues).

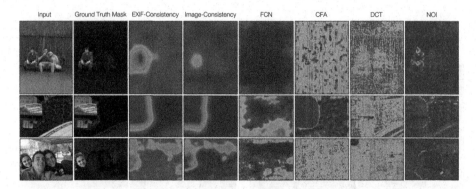

Fig. 11. Comparing Methods: We visualize the qualitative difference between *Self-Consistency* and baselines. Our model can correctly localizes image splices from *In-the-Wild*, *Columbia* and *Carvalho* that other methods make mistakes on.

In order to compare against previous benchmarks [17], we also evaluate our results using MCC and F1 measures[1]. These metrics evaluate a binary segmentation and require thresholding our predicted probabilities. We use the same evaluation procedure and pick the best threshold per splice localization prediction. Since [17] reported their numbers on the full *Columbia* and *Carvalho* datasets (rather than our test split), we evaluated our methods on the full dataset and report the comparison in Table 3.

The quantitative results on Table 2 show that our *EXIF-Consistency* model achieves the best performance across all datasets with the exception of the *Realistic Tampering (RT)* dataset. Notably, the model generally outperformed the supervised baselines, which were trained with actual manipulated images, despite the fact that our model never saw a tampered image during training. The supervised models' poor performance may be due to the small number of artists and manipulations represented in the training data. In Fig. 5, we show the model's performance on the Columbia dataset when using individual EXIF attributes (rather than the learned "overall" consistency).

As expected, *EXIF-Consistency* outperformed *Image-Consistency* on most of our evaluations. But, interestingly, we observed that the gap between the models narrowed as training progressed, suggesting that *Image-Consistency* may eventually become competitive with additional training.

It is also instructive to look at the qualitative results of our method, which we show in Fig. 8. We see that our method can localize manipulations on a wide range of different splices. Furthermore, in Fig. 9, we show that our method produces highly consistent predictions when tested on real images. We can also look at the qualitative differences between our method and the baselines in Fig. 11.

---

[1] F1 score is defined as $\frac{2TP}{2TP+FN+FP}$ and MCC as $\frac{(TP \times TN)-(FP \times FN)}{\sqrt{(TP+FP)(TP+FN)(TN+FP)(TN+FN)}}$.

Finally, we ask which EXIF tags were useful for performing the splice local-ization task. To study this, we computed a response map for individual tags on the Columbia dataset, which we show in Fig. 7. We see that the most successful tags correspond to imaging parameters that induce photographic changes to the final image like `EXIF DigitalZoomRatio` and `EXIF GainControl`.

Failure cases In Fig. 10 we show some common failure cases. Our performance on *Realistic Tampering* illustrates some shortcomings with *EXIF-Consistency*. First, our model is not well-suited to finding very small splices, such as the ones that appear in *RT*. When spliced regions are small, the model's large stride may skip over spliced regions, mistakenly suggesting that no manipulations exist. Second, over- and under-exposed regions are sometimes flagged by our model to be inconsistent because they lack any meta-data signal (e.g. because they are nearly uniformly black or white). Finally, *RT* contains a significant number of additional manipulations, such as copy-move, that cannot be consistently detected via meta-data consistency since the manipulated content comes from exactly the same photo.

Training and running times Training the *EXIF-Consistency* and *Image-Consistency* networks took approximately 4 weeks on 4 GPUs. Running the full self-consistency model took approximately 16 s per image (e.g. Fig. 11).

5   Discussion

In this paper, we have proposed a self-supervised method for detecting image manipulations. Our experiments show that the proposed method obtains state-of-the-art results on several datasets, even though it does not use labeled data during training. Our work also raises a number of questions. In contrast to physically motivated forensics methods [3], our model's results are not easily interpretable, and in particular, it is not clear which visual cues it uses to solve the task. It also remains an open question how best to fuse consistency measure-ments across an image for localizing manipulations. Finally, while our model is trained without any human annotations, it is still affected in complex ways by design decisions that went into the self-supervision task, such as the ways that EXIF tags were balanced during training.

Self-supervised approaches to visual forensics hold the promise of generalizing to a wide range of manipulations — potentially beyond those that can feasibly be learned through supervised training. However, for a forensics algorithm to be truly general, it must also model the actions of intelligent forgers that adapt to the detection algorithms. Work in adversarial machine learning [52,53] suggests that having a self-learning forger in the loop will make the forgery detection problem much more difficult to solve, and will require new technical advances.

As new advances in computer vision and image-editing emerge, there is an increasingly urgent need for effective visual forensics methods. We see our approach, which successfully detects manipulations without seeing examples of manipulated images, as being an initial step toward building general-purpose forensics tools.

Acknowledgements. This work was supported, in part, by DARPA MediFor program and UC Berkeley Center for Long-Term Cybersecurity. We thank Hany Farid and Shruti Agarwal for their advice, assistance, and inspiration in building this project, David Fouhey, Saurabh Gupta, and Allan Jabri for helping with the editing, Peng Zhou for helping with experiments, and Abhinav Gupta for letting us use his GPUs. Finally, we thank the many *Reddit* and *Onion* artists who unknowingly contributed to our dataset.

References

1. Hays, J., Efros, A.A.: Scene completion using millions of photographs. ACM Trans. Graph. (TOG) **26**, 4 (2007)
2. King, D., Cohen, S.F.: The Commissar Vanishes: The Falsification of Photographs and Art in Stalin's Russia. Canongate, Edinburgh (1997)
3. Farid, H.: Photo Forensics. MIT Press, Cambridge (2016)
4. Zhu, J.Y., Krahenbuhl, P., Shechtman, E., Efros, A.A.: Learning a discriminative model for the perception of realism in composite images. In: The IEEE International Conference on Computer Vision (ICCV), December 2015
5. Tsai, Y.H., Shen, X., Lin, Z., Sunkavalli, K., Lu, X., Yang, M.H.: Deep image harmonization. In: CVPR (2017)
6. Barnes, C., Shechtman, E., Finkelstein, A., Goldman, D.B.: Patchmatch: a randomized correspondence algorithm for structural image editing. ACM Trans. Graph. **28**(3), 1–24 (2009)
7. Pathak, D., Krahenbuhl, P., Donahue, J., Darrell, T., Efros, A.A.: Context encoders: feature learning by inpainting. In: The IEEE Conference on Computer Vision and Pattern Recognition (CVPR), June 2016
8. Suwajanakorn, S., Seitz, S.M., Kemelmacher-Shlizerman, I.: Synthesizing obama: learning lip sync from audio. ACM Trans. Graph. (TOG) **36**(4), 95 (2017)
9. Chung, J.S., Jamaludin, A., Zisserman, A.: You said that? arXiv preprint arXiv:1705.02966 (2017)
10. National Institute of Standards and Technology: The 2017 nimble challenge evaluation datasets. https://www.nist.gov/itl/iad/mig/nimble-challenge
11. Liu, Q.: Detection of misaligned cropping and recompression with the same quantization matrix and relevant forgery (2011)
12. Luo, W., Huang, J., Qiu, G.: JPEG error analysis and its applications to digital image forensics. IEEE Trans. Inf. Forensics Secur. **5**(3), 480–491 (2010)
13. Huang, F., Huang, J., Shi, Y.Q.: Detecting double JPEG compression with the same quantization matrix. IEEE Trans. Inf. Forensics Secur. **5**(4), 848–856 (2010)
14. Popescu, A.C., Farid, H.: Exposing digital forgeries by detecting traces of resampling. IEEE Trans. Signal Process. **53**(2), 758–767 (2005)
15. Swaminathan, A., Wu, M., Liu, K.R.: Digital image forensics via intrinsic fingerprints. IEEE Trans. Inf. Forensics Secur. **3**(1), 101–117 (2008)
16. Agarwal, S., Farid, H.: Photo forensics from JPEG dimples. In: Workshop on Image Forensics and Security (2017)
17. Salloum, R., Ren, Y., Kuo, C.J.: Image splicing localization using a multi-task fully convolutional network (MFCN). CoRR abs/1709.02016 (2017)
18. Barni, M., et al.: Aligned and non-aligned double JPEG detection using convolutional neural networks. CoRR abs/1708.00930 (2017)

19. Amerini, I., Uricchio, T., Ballan, L., Caldelli, R.: Localization of JPEG double compression through multi-domain convolutional neural networks. In: Proceedings of IEEE CVPR Workshop on Media Forensics (2017)

20. Wen, L., Qi, H., Lyu, S.: Contrast enhancement estimation for digital image forensics. arXiv preprint arXiv:1706.03875 (2017)

21. Bondi, L., Baroffio, L., Gera, D., Bestagini, P., Delp, E.J., Tubaro, S.: First steps toward camera model identification with convolutional neural networks. IEEE Signal Process. Lett. 24(3), 259–263 (2017)

22. Bondi, L., Lameri, S., Güera, D., Bestagini, P., Delp, E.J., Tubaro, S.: Tampering detection and localization through clustering of camera-based CNN features. In: Proceedings of the IEEE Conference on Computer Vision and Pattern Recognition Workshops, pp. 1855–1864 (2017)

23. Zhou, P., Han, X., Morariu, V.I., Davis, L.S.: Two-stream neural networks for tampered face detection. In: The IEEE Conference on Computer Vision and Pattern Recognition (CVPR) Workshops, July 2017

24. Zhou, P., Han, X., Morariu, V.I., Davis, L.S.: Learning rich features for image manipulation detection. In: The IEEE Conference on Computer Vision and Pattern Recognition (CVPR), June 2018

25. Mayer, O., Stamm, M.C.: Learned forensic source similarity for unknown camera models. In: IEEE International Conference on Acoustics, Speech and Signal Processing (2018)

26. Chen, B.C., Ghosh, P., Morariu, V.I., Davis., L.S.: Detection of metadata tampering through discrepancy between image content and metadata using multi-task deep learning. In: IEEE Conference on Computer Vision and Pattern Recognition Workshops (CVPRW) (2017)

27. de Sa, V.: Learning classification with unlabeled data. In: Neural Information Processing Systems (1994)

28. Doersch, C., Gupta, A., Efros, A.A.: Unsupervised visual representation learning by context prediction. In: ICCV (2015)

29. Jayaraman, D., Grauman, K.: Learning image representations tied to ego-motion. In: ICCV, December 2015

30. Agrawal, P., Carreira, J., Malik, J.: Learning to see by moving. In: ICCV (2015)

31. Owens, A., Wu, J., McDermott, J.H., Freeman, W.T., Torralba, A.: Ambient sound provides supervision for visual learning. In: Leibe, B., Matas, J., Sebe, N., Welling, M. (eds.) ECCV 2016. LNCS, vol. 9905, pp. 801–816. Springer, Cham (2016). https://doi.org/10.1007/978-3-319-46448-0_48

32. Zhang, R., Isola, P., Efros, A.A.: Split-brain autoencoders: unsupervised learning by cross-channel prediction (2017)

33. Isola, P., Zoran, D., Krishnan, D., Adelson, E.H.: Learning visual groups from co-occurrences in space and time (2016)

34. Kuthirummal, S., Agarwala, A., Goldman, D.B., Nayar, S.K.: Priors for large photo collections and what they reveal about cameras. In: Forsyth, D., Torr, P., Zisserman, A. (eds.) ECCV 2008. LNCS, vol. 5305, pp. 74–87. Springer, Heidelberg (2008). https://doi.org/10.1007/978-3-540-88693-8_6

35. Hoai, M., De la Torre, F.: Max-margin early event detectors. Int. J. Comput. Vis. 107(2), 191–202 (2014)

36. Mahadevan, V., Li, W., Bhalodia, V., Vasconcelos, N.: Anomaly detection in crowded scenes. In: 2010 IEEE Conference on Computer Vision and Pattern Recognition (CVPR), pp. 1975–1981. IEEE (2010)

37. He, K., Zhang, X., Ren, S., Sun, J.: Deep residual learning for image recognition. In: Proceedings of the IEEE Conference on Computer Vision and Pattern Recognition, pp. 770–778 (2016)
38. Lalonde, J.F., Efros, A.A.: Using color compatibility for assessing image realism. In: IEEE 11th International Conference on Computer Vision, ICCV 2007, pp. 1–8. IEEE (2007)
39. Cheng, Y.: Mean shift, mode seeking, and clustering. IEEE Trans. Pattern Anal. Mach. Intell. **17**(8), 790–799 (1995)
40. Shi, J., Malik, J.: Normalized cuts and image segmentation. IEEE Trans. Pattern Anal. Mach. Intell. **22**(8), 888–905 (2000)
41. Ng, T.T., Chang, S.F.: A data set of authentic and spliced image blocks (2004)
42. de Carvalho, T.J., Riess, C., Angelopoulou, E., Pedrini, H., de Rezende Rocha, A.: Exposing digital image forgeries by illumination color classification. IEEE Trans. Inf. Forensics Secur. **8**(7), 1182–1194 (2013)
43. Korus, P., Huang, J.: Evaluation of random field models in multi-modal unsupervised tampering localization. In: Proceedings of IEEE International Workshop on Information Forensics and Security (2016)
44. Moreira, D., et al.: Image provenance analysis at scale. arXiv preprint arXiv:1801.06510 (2018)
45. Ferrara, P., Bianchi, T., Rosa, A.D., Piva, A.: Image forgery localization via fine-grained analysis of cfa artifacts. IEEE Trans. Inf. Forensics Secur. **7**(5), 1566–1577 (2012)
46. Ye, S., Sun, Q., Chang, E.C.: Detecting digital image forgeries by measuring inconsistencies of blocking artifact. In: ICME 2007 (2017)
47. Mahdian, B., Saic, S.: Using noise inconsistencies for blind image forensics. In: IVC 2009 (2009)
48. Zampoglou, M., Papadopoulos, S., Kompatsiaris, Y., Bouwmeester, R., Spangenberg, J.: Web and social media image forensics for news professionals. In: Social Media In the NewsRoom, SMNews16@CWSM, Tenth International AAAI Conference on Web and Social Media workshops (2016)
49. Shelhamer, E., Long, J., Darrell, T.: Fully convolutional networks for semantic segmentation. CoRR abs/1605.06211 (2016)
50. Deng, J., Dong, W., Socher, R., Li, L.J., Li, K., Fei-Fei, L.: ImageNet: a large-scale hierarchical image database. In: CVPR 2009 (2009)
51. Kingma, D.P., Ba, J.: Adam: a method for stochastic optimization. CoRR abs/1412.6980 (2014)
52. Ian, J., Goodfellow, Y.B.: Generative adversarial networks. arXiv preprint arXiv:1406.2661 (2014)
53. Szegedy, C., et al.: Intriguing properties of neural networks. arXiv preprint arXiv:1312.6199 (2013)

Hand Pose Estimation via Latent 2.5D Heatmap Regression

Umar Iqbal[1,2($\boxtimes$)], Pavlo Molchanov[1], Thomas Breuel[1], Juergen Gall[2], and Jan Kautz[1]

[1] NVIDIA, Santa Clara, USA
uiqbal@iai.uni-bonn.de
[2] University of Bonn, Bonn, Germany

Abstract. Estimating the 3D pose of a hand is an essential part of human-computer interaction. Estimating 3D pose using depth or multi-view sensors has become easier with recent advances in computer vision, however, regressing pose from a single RGB image is much less straightforward. The main difficulty arises from the fact that 3D pose requires some form of depth estimates, which are ambiguous given only an RGB image. In this paper we propose a new method for 3D hand pose estimation from a monocular image through a novel 2.5D pose representation. Our new representation estimates pose up to a scaling factor, which can be estimated additionally if a prior of the hand size is given. We implicitly learn depth maps and heatmap distributions with a novel CNN architecture. Our system achieves state-of-the-art accuracy for 2D and 3D hand pose estimation on several challenging datasets in presence of severe occlusions.

Keywords: Hand pose · 2D to 3D · 3D reconstruction 2.5D heatmaps

1 Introduction

Hand pose estimation from touch-less sensors enables advanced human machine interaction to increase comfort and safety. Estimating the pose accurately is a difficult task due to the large amounts of appearance variation, self occlusions and complexity of the articulated hand poses. 3D hand pose estimation escalates the difficulties even further since the depth of the hand keypoints also has to be estimated. To alleviate these challenges, many proposed solutions simplify the problem by using calibrated multi-view camera systems [1–9], depth sensors [10–24], or color markers/gloves [25]. These approaches are, however, not very desirable due to their inapplicability in unconstrained environments. Therefore, in this work, we address the problem of 3D hand pose estimation from RGB images taken from the wild.

Electronic supplementary material The online version of this chapter (https:// doi.org/10.1007/978-3-030-01252-6_8) contains supplementary material, which is available to authorized users.

Given an RGB image of the hand, our goal is to estimate the 3D coordinates of hand keypoints relative to the camera. Estimating the 3D pose from a monocular hand image is an ill-posed problem due to scale and depth ambiguities. Attempting to do so will either not work at all, or results in over-fitting to a very specific environment and subjects. We address these challenges by decomposing the problem into two subproblems both of which can be solved with less ambiguities. To this end, we propose a novel 2.5D pose representation and then provide a solution to reconstruct the 3D pose from 2.5D. The proposed 2.5D representation is scale and translation invariant and can be easier estimated from RGB images. It consists of 2D coordinates of the hand keypoints in the input image and scale normalized depth for each keypoint relative to the root (palm). We perform scale normalization of the depth values such that one of the bones always has a fixed length in 3D space. Such a constrained normalization allows us to directly reconstruct the scale normalized absolute 3D pose with less ambiguity compared to full depth recovery from the image crop. Our solution is still ill-posed because of relative normalized depth estimation, but it is better defined compared to relative or absolute depth estimation.

As a second contribution, we propose a novel CNN architecture to estimate the 2.5D pose from images. In the literature, there exists two main learning paradigms, namely heatmap regression [26,27] and holistic pose regression [28,29]. Heatmap regression is now a standard approach for 2D pose estimation since it allows to accurately localize the keypoints in the image via per-pixel predictions. Creating volumetric heatmaps for 3D pose estimation [30], however, results in very high computational overhead. Therefore, holistic regression is a standard approach for 3D pose estimation, but it suffers from accurate 2D keypoint localization. Since the 2.5D pose representation requires the prediction of both the 2D pose and depth values, we propose a new heatmap representation that we refer to as 2.5D heatmaps. It consists of 2D heatmaps for 2D keypoint localization and a depth map for each keypoint for depth prediction. We design the proposed CNN architecture such that the 2.5D heatmaps do not have to be designed by hand, but are learned in a latent way. We do this by a softargmax operation which converts the 2.5D heatmaps to 2.5D coordinates in a differentiable manner. The obtained 2.5D heatmaps are compact, invariant to scale and translation, and have the potential to localize keypoints with sub-pixel accuracy.

We evaluate our approach on five challenging datasets with severe occlusions, hand object interactions and in-the-wild images. We demonstrate its effectiveness for both 2D and 3D hand pose estimation. The proposed approach outperforms state-of-the-art approaches by a large margin.

2   Related Work

Very few works in the literature have addressed the problem of 3D hand pose estimation from a single 2D image. The problem, however, shares several properties with human body pose estimation and many approaches proposed for the human body can be easily adapted for hand pose estimation. Hence, in the following, we discuss the related works for 3D articulated pose estimation in general.

Model-Based Methods. These methods represent the articulated 3D pose using a deformable 3D shape model. This is often formulated as an optimization problem, whose objective is to find the model's deformation parameters such that its projection is in correspondence with the observed image data [31–37].

Search-Based Methods. These methods follow a non-parametric approach and formulate 3D pose estimation as a nearest neighbor search problem in large databases of 3D poses, where the matching is performed based on some low [38, 39] or high [40,41] level features extracted from the image.

From 2D Pose to 3D. Earlier methods in this direction learn probabilistic 3D pose models from MoCap data and recover 3D pose by lifting the 2D keypoints [42–45]. More recent approaches, on the other hand, use deep neural networks to learn a mapping from 2D pose to 3D [46–48]. Instead of 2D keypoint locations, [48,49] use 2D heatmaps [26,27] as input and learn convolutional neural networks for 3D pose regression.

The aforementioned methods have the advantage that they do not necessarily require images with ground-truth 3D pose annotations for training, but their major drawback is that they cannot handle re-projection ambiguities *i.e.*, a joint with positive or negative depth will have the same 2D projections. Moreover, they are sensitive to errors in 2D image measurements and the required optimization methods are often prone to local minima due to incorrect initializations.

3D Pose from Images. These approaches aim to learn a direct mapping from RGB images to 3D pose [50–53]. While these methods can better handle 2D projection ambiguities, their main downside is that they are prone to over-fitting to the views only present in training data. Thus, they require a large amount of training data with accurate 3D pose annotations. Collecting large amounts of training data in unconstrained environments is, however, infeasible. To this end, [52] proposes to use Generative Adversarial Networks [54] to convert synthetically generated hand images to look realistic. Other approaches formulate the problem in a multi-task setup to jointly estimate both 2D keypoint locations and 3D pose [29,30,55–58]. Our method also follows this paradigm. The closest work to ours are the approaches of [29,30,56,58] in that they also perform 2.5D coordinate regression. While the approach in [29] performs holistic pose regression with a fully connected output layer, [56] follows a hybrid approach and combines heatmap regression with holistic regression. Holistic regressions is shown to perform well for human body but fails in cases where very precise localization is required, *e.g.*, fingertips in case of hands. In order to deal with this, the approach in [30] performs dense volumetric regression. This, however, substantially increases the model size, which in turn forces to work at a lower spatial resolution.

Our approach, on the other hand, retains the input spatial resolution and allows one to localize hand keypoints with sub-pixel accuracy. It enjoys the differentiability and compactness of holistic regression-based methods, translation invariance of volumetric representations, while also providing high spatial output resolution. Moreover, in contrast to existing methods such as VNect [58], it does not require hand-designed target heatmaps, which can arguably be sub-optimal for a particular problem, but rather implicitly learns a latent 2.5D heatmap representation and converts them to 2.5D coordinates in a differentiable way.

Finally, note that given the 2.5D coordinates, the 3D pose has to be recovered. The existing approaches either make very strong assumptions such as the ground-truth location of the root [29] and the global scale of the hand in 3D is known [56], or resort to an approximate solution [30]. The approach [57] tries to directly regress the absolute depth from the cropped and scaled image regions which is a very ambiguous task. The approach VNect [58] regresses both 2D and 3D coordinates simultaneously which is ill-posed without explicit modeling of the camera parameters matrix and requires training a specific network for all unique camera matrices. In contrast, our approach does not make any assumptions. Instead, we propose a scale and translation invariant 2.5D pose representation, which can be easily obtained using CNNs, and then provide an exact solution to obtain the absolute 3D pose up to a scaling factor and only approximate the global scale of the hand.

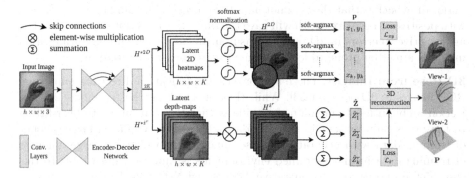

Fig. 1. Overview of the proposed approach. Given an image of a hand, the proposed CNN architecture produces latent 2.5D heatmaps containing the latent 2D heatmaps H^{*2D} and latent depth maps $H^{*\hat{z}}$. The latent 2D heatmaps are converted to probability maps H^{2D} using softmax normalization. The depth maps $H^{\hat{z}}$ are obtained by multiplying the latent depth maps $H^{*\hat{z}}$ with the 2D heatmaps. The 2D pose $\mathbf{p}$ is obtained by applying spatial soft-argmax on the 2D heatmaps, whereas the normalized depth values $\hat{\mathbf{Z}}^r$ are obtained by the summation of depth maps. The final 3D pose is then estimated by the proposed approach for reconstructing 3D pose from 2.5D.

3   Hand Pose Estimation

An overview of the proposed approach can be seen in Fig. 1. Given an RGB image **I** of a hand, our goal is to estimate the 2D and 3D positions of all the $K = 21$ keypoints of the hand. We define the 2D hand pose as $\mathbf{p} = \{p_k\}_{k \in K}$ and 3D pose as $\mathbf{P} = \{P_k\}_{k \in K}$, where $p_k = (x_k, y_k) \in \mathbb{R}^2$ represents the 2D pixel coordinates of the keypoint k in image **I** and $P_k = (X_k, Y_k, Z_k) \in \mathbb{R}^3$ denotes the location of the keypoint in the 3D camera coordinate frame measured in millimeters.

The Z-axis corresponds to the optical axis. Given the intrinsic camera parameters $\mathcal{K}$, the relationship between the 3D location P_k and corresponding 2D projection p_k can be written as follows under a perspective projection:

$$
Z_k \begin{pmatrix} x_k \\ y_k \\ 1 \end{pmatrix} = \mathcal{K} \begin{pmatrix} X_k \\ Y_k \\ Z_k \\ 1 \end{pmatrix} = \mathcal{K} \begin{pmatrix} X_k \\ Y_k \\ Z_{root} + Z_k^r \\ 1 \end{pmatrix} \quad k \in 1, \ldots K \qquad (1)
$$

where $k \in 1, \ldots K$, Z_{root} is the depth of the root keypoint, and $Z_k^r = Z_k - Z_{root}$ corresponds to the depth of the kth keypoint relative to the root. In this work we use the palm of the hand as the root keypoint.

3.1 2.5D Pose Representation

Given an image $\mathbf{I}$, we need to have a function $\mathcal{F}$, such that $\mathcal{F} : \mathbf{I} \to \mathbf{P}$, and the estimated 3D hand pose $\mathbf{P}$ can be projected to 2D with the camera parameters $\mathcal{K}$. However, predicting the absolute 3D hand pose in camera coordinates is infeasible due to irreversible geometry and scale ambiguities. We, therefore, choose a 2.5D pose representation, which is much easier to be recovered from a 2D image, and provide a solution to recover the 3D pose from the 2.5D representation. We define the 2.5D pose as $\mathbf{P}_k^{2.5D} = \{P_k^{2.5D}\}_{k \in K}$, where $P_k^{2.5D} = (x_k, y_k, Z_k^r)$. The coordinates x_k and y_k are the image pixel coordinates of the kth keypoint and Z_k^r is its metric depth relative to the root keypoint. Moreover, in order to remove the scale ambiguities, we scale-normalize the 3D pose as follows:

$$
\hat{\mathbf{P}} = \frac{C}{s} \cdot \mathbf{P}, \qquad (2)
$$

where $s = \|P_n - P_{parent(n)}\|_2$ is computed for each 3D pose independently. This results in a normalized 3D pose $\hat{\mathbf{P}}$ with a constant distance C between a specific pair of keypoints $(n, parent(n))$. Subsequently, our normalized 2.5D representation for keypoint k becomes $\hat{P}_k^{2.5D} = (x_k, y_k, \hat{Z}_k^r)$. Note that the 2D pose does not change due to the normalization, since the projection of the 3D pose remains the same. Such a normalized 2.5D representation has several advantages: it allows to effectively exploit image information; it enables dense pixel-wise prediction (Sect. 4); it allows us to perform multi-task learning so that multiple sources of training data can be used; and finally it allows us to devise an approach to exactly recover the absolute 3D pose up to a scaling factor. We describe the proposed solution to obtain the function $\mathcal{F}$ in Sect. 4, while the 3D pose reconstruction from 2.5D pose is explained in the next section.

3.2 3D Pose Reconstruction from 2.5D

Given a 2.5D pose $\hat{\mathbf{P}}^{2.5D} = \mathcal{F}(\mathbf{I})$, we need to find the depth $\hat{Z}_{root}$ of the root keypoint to reconstruct the scale normalized 3D pose $\hat{\mathbf{P}}$ using Eq. (1). While there exist many 3D poses that can have the same 2D projection, given the

2.5D pose and intrinsic camera parameters, there exists a unique 3D pose that satisfies

$$(\hat{X}_n - \hat{X}_m)^2 + (\hat{Y}_n - \hat{Y}_m)^2 + (\hat{Z}_n - \hat{Z}_m)^2 = C^2, \tag{3}$$

where $(n,\ m = parent(n))$ is the pair of keypoints used for normalization in Eq. (2). The equation above can be rewritten in terms of the 2D projections (x_n, y_n) and (x_m, y_m) as follows:

$$(x_n\hat{Z}_n - x_m\hat{Z}_m)^2 + (y_n\hat{Z}_n - y_m\hat{Z}_m)^2 + (\hat{Z}_n - \hat{Z}_m)^2 = C^2. \tag{4}$$

Subsequently, replacing $\hat{Z}_n$ and $\hat{Z}_m$ with $(\hat{Z}_{root} + \hat{Z}_n^r)$ and $(\hat{Z}_{root} + \hat{Z}_m^r)$, respectively, yields:

$$(x_n(\hat{Z}_{root} + \hat{Z}_n^r) - x_m(\hat{Z}_{root} + \hat{Z}_m^r))^2 + (y_n(\hat{Z}_{root} + \hat{Z}_n^r) - y_m(\hat{Z}_{root} + \hat{Z}_m^r))^2$$
$$+ ((\hat{Z}_{root} + \hat{Z}_n^r) - (\hat{Z}_{root} + \hat{Z}_m^r))^2 = C^2. \tag{5}$$

Given the 2.5D coordinates of both keypoints n and m, Z_{root} is the only unknown in the equation above. Simplifying the equation further leads to a quadratic equation with the following coefficients

$$a = (x_n - x_m)^2 + (y_n - y_m)^2$$
$$b = \hat{Z}_n^r(x_n^2 + y_n^2 - x_nx_m - y_ny_m) + \hat{Z}_m^r(x_m^2 + y_m^2 - x_nx_m - y_ny_m)$$
$$c = (x_n\hat{Z}_n^r - x_m\hat{Z}_m^r)^2 + (y_n\hat{Z}_n^r - y_m\hat{Z}_m^r)^2 + (\hat{Z}_n^r - \hat{Z}_m^r)^2 - C^2. \tag{6}$$

This results in two values for the unknown variable Z_{root}, one in front of the camera and one behind the camera. We choose the solution in front of the camera i.e., $\hat{Z}_{root} = 0.5(-b + \sqrt{b^2 - 4ac})/a$. Given the value of Z_{root}, $\hat{P}^{2.5D}$, and the intrinsic camera parameters $\mathcal{K}$, the scale normalized 3D pose can be reconstructed by back-projecting the 2D pose $\mathbf{p}$ using Eq. (1). In this paper, we use $C = 1$, and use the distance between the first joint (metacarpophalangeal - MCP) of the index finger and the palm (root) to calculate the scaling factor s. We choose these keypoints since they are the most stable in terms of 2D pose estimation.

3.3   Scale Recovery

Up to this point, we have obtained the 2D and scale normalized 3D pose $\hat{P}$ of the hand. In order to recover the absolute 3D pose $\mathbf{P}$, we need to know the global scale of the hand. In many scenarios this can be known a priori, however, in case it is not available, we estimate the scale $\hat{s}$ by

$$\hat{s} = \underset{s}{\text{argmin}} \sum_{k,l \in \mathcal{E}} (s \cdot \|\hat{P}_k - \hat{P}_l\| - \mu_{kl})^2, \tag{7}$$

where μ_{kl} is the mean length of the bone between keypoints k and l in the training data, and $\mathcal{E}$ defines the kinematic structure of the hand.

4   2.5D Pose Regression

In order to regress the 2.5D pose $\hat{\mathbf{P}}^{2.5D}$ from an RGB image of the hand, we learn the function $\mathcal{F}$ using a CNN. In this section, we first describe an alternative formulation of the CNN (Sect. 4.1) and then describe our proposed solution for regressing latent 2.5D heatmaps in Sect. 4.2. In all formulations, we train the CNNs using a loss function $\mathcal{L}$ which consists of two parts $\mathcal{L}_{xy}$ and $\mathcal{L}_{\hat{Z}^r}$, each responsible for the regression of 2D pose and root-relative depths for the hand keypoints, respectively. Formally, the loss can be written as follows:

$$\mathcal{L}(\hat{\mathbf{P}}^{2.5D}) = \mathcal{L}_{xy}(\mathbf{p}, \mathbf{p}_{gt}) + \alpha \mathcal{L}_{\hat{Z}^r}(\hat{\mathbf{Z}}^r, \hat{\mathbf{Z}}^{r,gt}), \tag{8}$$

where $\hat{\mathbf{Z}}^r = \{\hat{Z}_k^r\}_{r \in K}$ and $\hat{\mathbf{Z}}^{r,gt} = \{\hat{Z}_k^{r,gt}\}_{r \in K}$ and gt refers to ground-truth annotations. This loss function has the advantage that it allows to utilize multiple sources of training, i.e., in-the-wild images with only 2D pose annotations and constrained or synthetic images with accurate 3D pose annotations. While $\mathcal{L}_{xy}$ is valid for all training samples, $\mathcal{L}_{\hat{Z}^r}$ is enforced only when the 3D pose annotations are available, otherwise it is not considered.

4.1   Direct 2.5D Heatmap Regression

Heatmap regression is the de-facto approach for 2D pose estimation [26,27,59, 60]. In contrast to holistic regression, heatmaps have the advantage of providing higher output resolution, which helps in accurately localizing the keypoints. However, they are scarcely used for 3D pose estimation since a 3D volumetric heatmap representation [30] results in a high computational and storage cost.

We, thus, propose a novel and compact heatmap representation, which we refer to as 2.5D heatmaps. It consists of 2D heatmaps H^{2D} for keypoint localization and depth maps $H^{\hat{z}^r}$ for depth predictions. While the 2D heatmap H_k^{2D} represents the likelihood of the kth keypoint at each pixel location, the depth map $H_k^{\hat{z}^r}$ provides the scale normalized and root-relative depth prediction for the corresponding pixels. This representation of depth maps is scale and translation invariant and remains consistent across similar hand poses, therefore, it is significantly easier to be learned using CNNs. The CNN provides a $2K$ channel output with K channels for 2D localization heatmaps H^{2D} and K channels for depth maps $H^{\hat{z}^r}$. The target heatmap $H_k^{2D,gt}$ for the kth keypoint is defined as

$$H_k^{2D,gt}(p) = \exp\left(-\frac{\|p - p_k^{gt}\|}{\sigma^2}\right), \quad p \in \Omega \tag{9}$$

where p_k^{gt} is the ground-truth location of the kth keypoint, σ controls the standard deviation of the heatmaps and Ω is the set of all pixel locations in image $\mathbf{I}$. Since the ground-truth depth maps are not available, we define them by

$$H_k^{\hat{z}^r} = \hat{Z}_k^{r,gt} \cdot H_k^{2D,gt} \tag{10}$$

where $\hat{Z}_k^{r,gt}$ is the ground-truth normalized root-relative depth value of the kth keypoint. During inference, the 2D keypoint position is obtained as the pixel with the maximum likelihood

$$p_k = \underset{p}{\arg\max}\ H_k^{2D}(p), \tag{11}$$

and the corresponding depth value is obtained as,

$$\hat{Z}_k^r = H_k^{\hat{z}^r}(p_k). \tag{12}$$

4.2   Latent 2.5D Heatmap Regression

The 2.5D heatmap representation as described in the previous section is, arguably, not the most optimal representation. First, the ground-truth heatmaps are hand designed and are not ideal, $i.e.$, σ remains fixed for all keypoints and cannot be learned due to indifferentiability of Eq. (11). Ideally, it should be adapted for each keypoint, $e.g.$, heatmaps should be very peaky for fingertips while relatively wide for the palm. Secondly, the Gaussian distribution is a natural choice for 2D keypoint localization, but it is not very intuitive for depth prediction, $i.e.$, the depth stays roughly the same throughout the palm but is modeled as Gaussians. Therefore, we alleviate these problems by proposing a latent representation of 2.5D heatmaps, $i.e.$, the CNN learns the optimal representation by minimizing a loss function in a differentiable way.

To this end, we consider the $2K$ channel output of the CNN as latent variables H_k^{*2D} and $H_k^{*\hat{z}^r}$ for 2D heatmaps and depth maps, respectively. We then apply spatial softmax normalization to the 2D heatmap H_k^{*2D} of each keypoint k to convert it to a probability map

$$H_k^{2D}(p) = \frac{\exp(\beta_k H_k^{*2D}(p))}{\sum_{p' \in \Omega} \exp(\beta_k H_k^{*2D}(p'))}, \tag{13}$$

where Ω is the set of all pixel locations in the input map H_k^{*2D}, and β_k is the learnable parameter that controls the spread of the output heatmaps H^{2D}. Finally, the 2D keypoint position of the kth keypoint is obtained as the weighted average of the 2D pixel coordinates as,

$$p_k = \sum_{p \in \Omega} H_k^{2D}(p) \cdot p, \tag{14}$$

while the corresponding depth value is obtained as the summation of the Hadamard product of $H_k^{2D}(p)$ and $H_k^{*\hat{z}^r}(p)$ as follows

$$\hat{Z}_k^r = \sum_{p \in \Omega} H_k^{2D}(p) \circ H_k^{*\hat{z}^r}(p). \tag{15}$$

A pictorial representation of this process can be seen in Fig. 1. The operation in Eq. (14) is known as soft-argmax in the literature [61]. Note that the computation of both the 2D keypoint location and the corresponding depth value is fully differentiable. Hence the network can be trained end-to-end, while generating a latent 2.5D heatmap representation. In contrast to the heatmaps with fixed standard deviation in Sect. 4.1, the spread of the latent heatmaps can be adapted for each keypoint by learning the parameter β_k, while the depth maps are also learned implicitly without any ad-hoc design choices. A comparison between heatmaps obtained by direct heatmap regression and the ones implicitly learned by latent heatmap regression can be seen in Fig. 2.

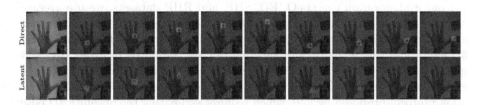

Fig. 2. Comparison between the heatmaps obtained using direct heatmap regression (Sect. 4.1) and the proposed latent heatmap regression approach (Sect. 4.2). We can see how the proposed method automatically learns the spread separately for each keypoint, *i.e.*, very peaky for fingertips while a bit wider for the palm.

5   Experiments

In this section, we evaluate the performance of the proposed approach in detail and also compare it with the state-of-the-art. For this, we use five challenging datasets as follows.

The **Dexter+Object (D+O)** dataset [22] provides 6 test video sequences (3145 frames) recorded using a static camera with a single hand interacting with an object. The dataset provides annotations for the fingertips only.

The **EgoDexter (ED)** dataset [62] consists of 4 test sequences (3190 frames) recorded with a body-mounted camera from egocentric viewpoints and contains cluttered backgrounds, fast camera motion, and complex interactions with various objects. In addition, [62] also provides the so called "SynthHands" dataset of synthetic images of hands from ego-centric views. The images are provided with chroma-keyed background, that we replace with random backgrounds [63] and use them as additional training data for testing on the ED dataset.

The **Stereo Hand Pose (SHP)** dataset [64] provides 3D pose annotations of 21 keypoints for 6 pairs of stereo sequences (18000 frame pairs) recording a person while performing various gestures.

The **Rendered Hand Pose (RHP)** dataset [48] provides 41258 and 2728 synthetic images for training and testing, respectively. The dataset contains 20 different characters performing 39 actions in different settings.

The **MPII+NZSL** [60] dataset provides 2D hand pose annotations for 2800 in-the-wild images split into 2000 and 800 images for training and testing, respectively. In addition, [60] also provides additional training data that contains 14261 synthetic images and 14817 real images. The annotations for real images are generated automatically using multi-view bootstrapping. We refer to these images as MVBS in the rest of this paper.

5.1   Evaluation Metrics

For our evaluation on the D+O, ED, SHP, and RHP datasets, we use average End-Point-Error (EPE) and the Area Under the Curve (AUC) on the Percentage of Correct Keypoints (PCK). We report the performance for both 2D and 3D hand pose where the performance metrics are computed in pixels (px) and millimeters (mm), respectively. We use the publicly available implementation of evaluation metrics from [48]. For the D+O and ED datasets, we follow the evaluation protocol proposed by [52], which requires estimating the absolute 3D pose with global scale. For SHP and RHP, we follow the protocol proposed by [48], where the root keypoints of the ground-truth and estimated poses are aligned before calculating the metrics. For the MPII+NZSL dataset, we follow [60] and report head-normalized PCK (PCKh) in our evaluation.

5.2   Implementation Details

For 2.5D heatmap regression we use an Encoder-Decoder network architecture with skip connections [27,65] and fixed number of channels (256) in each convolutional layer. The input to our model is a 128×128 image, which produces 2.5D heatmaps as output with the same resolution as the input image. Further details about the network architecture and training can be found in the appendix. For all the video datasets, *i.e.*, D+O, ED, SHP we use the YOLO detector [66] to detect the hand in the first frame of the video, and generate the bounding box in the subsequent frames using the estimated pose of the previous frame. We trained the hand detector using the training sets of all aforementioned datasets.

5.3   Ablation Studies

We evaluate the proposed method under different settings to better understand the impact of different design choices. We chose the D+O dataset for all ablation studies, mainly because it does not have any training data. Thus, it allows us to evaluate the generalizability of the proposed method. Finally, since the palm (root) joint is not annotated, it makes it compulsory to estimate the absolute 3D pose in contrast to the commonly used root-relative 3D pose. We use Eq. (7) to estimate the global scale of each 3D pose using the mean bone lengths from the SHP dataset.

  The ablative studies are summarized in Table 1. We first examine the impact of different choices of CNN architectures for 2.5D pose regression. For holistic

Table 1. Ablation studies. The arrows specify whether a higher or lower value for each metric is better. The first block compares the proposed approach of latent 2.5D heatmap regression with two baseline approaches. The second block shows the impact of different training data and the last block shows the impact due to differences in the annotations.

Method	2D pose estimation			3D pose estimation		
	AUC ↑	EPE (px)		AUC ↑	EPE (mm)	
		median ↓	mean ↓		median ↓	mean ↓
Comparison with baselines						
Holistic 2.5D reg.	0.41	17.34	22.21	0.54	42.76	47.80
Direct 2.5D heatmap reg.	0.57	10.33	21.63	0.55	36.97	52.33
Latent 2.5D heatmap reg. (Ours)	0.59	9.91	16.67	0.57	39.62	45.54
Impact of training data						
Latent 2.5D heatmap regression trained with						
SHP [64] + RHP [48]	0.59	9.91	16.67	0.57	39.62	45.54
+ MPII + NZSL [60]	0.67	9.07	10.65	0.68	28.11	32.78
+ MVBS [60]	0.68	8.84	10.45	0.68	27.27	32.75
Comparisons with the baselines with additional training data trained with						
SHP+RHP (3D pose) and MPII+NZSL+MVBS (2d pose) datasets						
Holistic reg.	0.53	12.98	16.17	0.66	31.71	34.86
Direct heatmap reg.	0.65	9.60	12.06	0.68	25.92	35.56
Latent heatmap reg.	0.68	8.84	10.45	0.68	27.27	32.75
Performance after removing labeling discrepancy						
Holistic regression	0.59	10.66	14.10	0.67	30.69	33.80
Direct heatmap reg.	0.72	7.05	9.66	0.68	25.37	34.88
Latent heatmap reg.	0.76	5.95	7.97	0.69	26.56	31.86
Latent heatmap reg. - fast	0.71	6.44	10.67	0.68	28.08	33.35

2.5D pose regression, we use the commonly adopted [29] ResNet-50 [67] model. The details can be found in the appendix. We use the SHP and RHP datasets to train the models. Using a holistic regression approach results in an AUC of 0.41 and 0.54 for 2D and 3D pose, respectively. Directly regressing the 2.5D heatmaps significantly improves the performance of 2D pose estimation (0.41 vs. 0.57), while also raising the 3D pose estimation accuracy from 0.54 AUC to 0.55. Using latent heatmap regression improves the performance even further to 0.59 AUC and 0.57 AUC for 2D and 3D pose estimation, respectively. While the holistic regression approach achieves a competitive accuracy for 3D pose estimation, the accuracy for 2D pose estimation is inferior to the heatmap regression due to its limited spatial output resolution.

We also evaluate the impact of training the network in a multi-task setup. For this, we train the model with additional training data from [60] which provides annotations for 2D keypoints only. First, we only use the 2000 manually annotated real images from the training set of the MPII+NZSL dataset. Using additional 2D pose annotations significantly improves the performance. Adding additional 15,000 annotations of real images from the MVBS dataset [60] improves the performance only slightly. Hence, only 2000 real images are sufficient to generalize the model trained on synthetic data to a realistic scenario. We also evaluate the impact of additional training data on all CNN architectures for 2.5D regression. We can see that the performance improves for all architectures, but importantly, the ordering in terms of performance stays the same.

The annotations of the fingertips in the D+O dataset are slightly different than in the other datasets *i.e.*, they are annotated at the middle of the tips whereas other datasets annotate them at the edge of the nails. To remove this discrepancy, we shorten the last bone of the fingertip by 0.9. Fixing the annotation differences results in further improvements, revealing the true performance of the proposed approach.

We also evaluate the runtime of the used models on an NVIDIA TitanX Pascal GPU. While the holistic 2.5D regression model runs at 145 FPS, direct and latent 2.5D heatmap regression networks run at 20 FPS. We trained a smaller 1-stage model with 128 feature maps (base layers) and replaced 7×7 convolutions in the last 3 layers with 1×1, 3×3 and 1×1 convolutions. The simplifications resulted in 150 FPS and parameter reduction by 3.8x while remaining competitive to direct heatmap regression with the full model. This model is marked with label "fast" in Table 1.

Finally, we also evaluate the impact of using multiple stages in the network, where each stage produces latent 2.5D heatmaps as output. The complete 2-stage network is trained from scratch with no weight-sharing. While the first stage only uses the features extracted from the input image using the initial block of convolutional layers, each subsequent stage also utilizes the output of the preceding stage as input. This provides additional contextual information to the subsequent stages and helps in incrementally refining the predictions. Similar to [26,27] we provide local supervision to the network by enforcing the loss at the output of each stage (see appendix for more details). Adding one extra stage to the network increases the 3D pose estimation accuracy from AUC 0.69 to 0.71, but decreases the 2D pose estimation accuracy from AUC 0.76 to 0.74. The decrease in 2D pose estimation accuracy is most likely due to over-fitting to the training datasets. Remember that we do not use any training data from the D+O dataset. In the rest of this paper, we always use networks with two stages unless stated otherwise.

5.4   Comparison to State-of-the-Art

We provide a comparison of the proposed approach with state-of-the-art methods on all aforementioned datasets. Note that different approaches use different training data. We thus replicate the training setup of the corresponding approaches for a fair comparison.

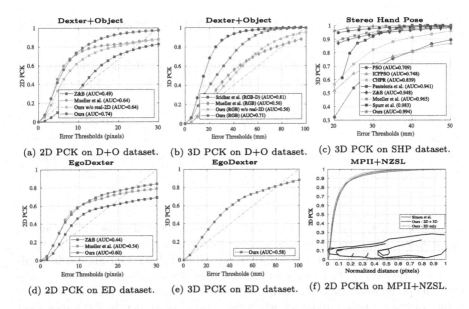

(a) 2D PCK on D+O dataset. (b) 3D PCK on D+O dataset. (c) 3D PCK on SHP dataset.

(d) 2D PCK on ED dataset. (e) 3D PCK on ED dataset. (f) 2D PCKh on MPII+NZSL.

Fig. 3. Comparison with the state-of-the-art on the DO, ED, SHP and MPII+NZSL datasets.

Figure 3a and b compare the proposed approach with other methods on the D+O dataset for 2D and 3D pose estimation, respectively. In particular, we compare with the state-of-the-art approaches by Zimmerman and Brox (Z&B) [48] and Mueller et al. [52]. We use the same training data (SHP+RHP) for comparison with [48] (AUC 0.64 vs 0.49), and only use additional 2D pose annotations (MPII+NZSL+MVBS) provided by [60] for comparison with [52](AUC 0.74 vs 0.64). For the 3D pose estimation accuracy (Fig. 3b), the approach [48] is not included since it only estimates scale normalized root-relative 3D pose. Our approach clearly outperforms the state-of-the-art RGB based method by Mueller et al. [52] by a large margin. The approach [52] utilizes the video information to perform temporal smoothening and also performs subject specific adaptation under the assumption that the users hold their hand parallel to the camera image plane. In contrast, we only perform frame-wise predictions without temporal filtering or user assumptions. Additionally, we report the results of the depth based approach by Sridhar et al. [22], which are obtained from [52]. While the RGB-D sensor based approach [22] still works better, our approach takes a giant leap forward as compared to the existing RGB based approaches.

Figure 3c compares the proposed method with existing approaches on the SHP dataset. We use the same training data (SHP+RHP) as in [48] and outperform all existing methods despite the already saturated accuracy on the dataset and the additional training data and temporal information used in [52].

Figure 3d compares the 2D pose estimation accuracy on the EgoDexter dataset. While we outperform all existing methods for 2D pose estimation, none

Table 2. Comparison with the state-of-the-art on the RHP dataset. *uses noisy ground-truth 2D poses for 3D pose estimation.

Method	2D pose estimation			3D pose estimation		
	AUC ↑	EPE (px)		AUC ↑	EPE (mm)	
		median ↓	mean ↓		median ↓	mean ↓
Z & B [48]	0.72	5.00	9.14	-	18.8*	-
Spurr *et al.* [53]	-	-	-	0.85	19.73	-
Ours	0.89	2.20	3.57	0.91	13.82	15.77
Ours w. GT $\hat{Z}_{root}$ and $\hat{s}$	0.89	2.20	3.57	0.94	11.33	13.41

of the existing approaches report their performance for 3D pose estimation on this dataset. We, however, also report our performance in Fig. 3e.

The results on the RHP dataset are reported in Table 2. Our approach significantly outperforms state-of-the-art approaches [48,53]. Since the dataset provides 3D pose annotations for complete hand skeleton, we also report the performance of the proposed approach when the ground-truth depth of the root joint and the global scale of the hand is known (w. GT $\hat{Z}_{root}$ and $\hat{s}$). We can see that our approach of 3D pose reconstruction and scale recovery is very close to the ground-truth.

Finally, for completeness, in Fig. 3f we compare our approach with [60] which is a state-of-the-art approach for 2D pose estimation. The evaluation is performed on the test set of the MPII+NZSL dataset. We follow [60] and use the provided center location of the hand and the size of the head of the person to obtain the hand bounding box. We define a square bounding box with height and width equal to $0.7 \times head\text{-}length$. We report two variants of our method; (1) the model trained for both 2D and 3D pose estimation using the datasets for both tasks, and (2) a model trained for only 2D pose estimation using the same training data as in [60]. In both cases we use the models trained with 2-stages. Our approach performs similar or better than [60], even though we use a smaller backbone network as compared to the 6-stage Convolutional Pose Machines (CPM) network [26] used in [60]. The CPM model with 6-stages has $51M$ parameters, while our 1 and 2-stage models have only $17M$ and $35M$ parameters, respectively. Additionally, our approach also infers the 3D hand pose.

Some qualitative results for 3D hand pose estimation for in-the-wild images can be seen in Fig. 4.

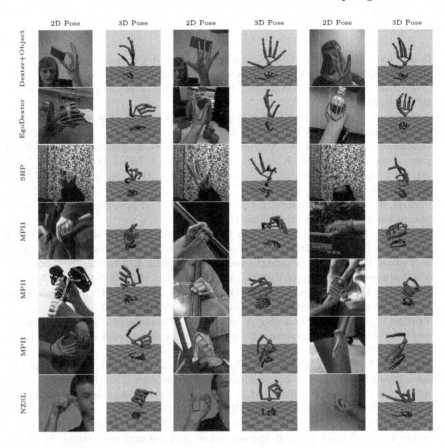

Fig. 4. Qualitative Results. The proposed approach can handle severe occlusions, complex hand articulations, and unconstrained images taken from the wild.

6   Conclusion

We have presented a method for 3D hand pose estimation from a single RGB image. We demonstrated that the absolute 3D hand pose can be reconstructed efficiently from a single image up to a scaling factor. We presented a novel 2.5D pose representation which can be recovered easily from RGB images since it is invariant to absolute depth and scale ambiguities. It can be represented as 2.5D heatmaps, therefore, allows keypoint localization with sub-pixel accuracy. We also proposed a CNN architecture to learn 2.5D heatmaps in a latent way using a differentiable loss function. Finally, we proposed an approach to reconstruct the 3D hand pose from 2.5D pose representation. The proposed approach demonstrated state-of-the-art results on five challenging datasets with severe occlusions, object interactions and images taken from the wild.

Acknowledgements. JG was supported by the ERC Starting Grant ARCA.

References

1. Rehg, J.M., Kanade, T.: Visual tracking of high DOF articulated structures: an application to human hand tracking. In: Eklundh, J.-O. (ed.) ECCV 1994. LNCS, vol. 801, pp. 35–46. Springer, Heidelberg (1994). https://doi.org/10.1007/BFb0028333
2. de Campos, T.E., Murray, D.W.: Regression-based hand pose estimation from multiple cameras. In: CVPR (2006)
3. Oikonomidis, I., Kyriazis, N., Argyros, A.A.: Markerless and efficient 26-DOF hand pose recovery. In: Kimmel, R., Klette, R., Sugimoto, A. (eds.) ACCV 2010. LNCS, vol. 6494, pp. 744–757. Springer, Heidelberg (2011). https://doi.org/10.1007/978-3-642-19318-7_58
4. Rosales, R., Athitsos, V., Sigal, L., Sclaroff, S.: 3D hand pose reconstruction using specialized mappings. In: ICCV (2001)
5. Ballan, L., Taneja, A., Gall, J., Van Gool, L., Pollefeys, M.: Motion capture of hands in action using discriminative salient points. In: Fitzgibbon, A., Lazebnik, S., Perona, P., Sato, Y., Schmid, C. (eds.) ECCV 2012. LNCS, vol. 7577, pp. 640–653. Springer, Heidelberg (2012). https://doi.org/10.1007/978-3-642-33783-3_46
6. Sridhar, S., Rhodin, H., Seidel, H.P., Oulasvirta, A., Theobalt, C.: Real-time hand tracking using a sum of anisotropic Gaussians model. In: 3DV (2014)
7. Tzionas, D., Ballan, L., Srikantha, A., Aponte, P., Pollefeys, M., Gall, J.: Capturing hands in action using discriminative salient points and physics simulation. IJCV 118, 172–193 (2016)
8. Panteleris, P., Argyros, A.: Back to RGB: 3D tracking of hands and hand-object interactions based on short-baseline stereo. arXiv preprint arXiv:1705.05301 (2017)
9. Romero, J., Tzionas, D., Black, M.J.: Embodied hands: Modeling and capturing hands and bodies together. In: SIGGRAPH Asia (2017)
10. Oikonomidis, I., Kyriazis, N., Argyros, A.A.: Full DOF tracking of a hand interacting with an object by modeling occlusions and physical constraints. In: ICCV (2011)
11. Xu, C., Cheng, L.: Efficient hand pose estimation from a single depth image. In: ICCV (2013)
12. Qian, C., Sun, X., Wei, Y., Tang, X., Sun, J.: Realtime and robust hand tracking from depth. In: CVPR (2014)
13. Taylor, J., et al.: User-specific hand modeling from monocular depth sequences. In: CVPR (2014)
14. Tang, D., Chang, H.J., Tejani, A., Kim, T.K.: Latent regression forest: structured estimation of 3D articulated hand posture. In: CVPR (2014)
15. Tompson, J., Stein, M., Lecun, Y., Perlin, K.: Real-time continuous pose recovery of human hands using convolutional networks. ToG 33, 169 (2014)
16. Tang, D., Taylor, J., Kohli, P., Keskin, C., Kim, T.K., Shotton, J.: Opening the black box: hierarchical sampling optimization for estimating human hand pose. In: ICCV 2015)
17. Makris, A., Kyriazis, N., Argyros, A.A.: Hierarchical particle filtering for 3D hand tracking. In: CVPR (2015)
18. Sridhar, S., Mueller, F., Oulasvirta, A., Theobalt, C.: Fast and robust hand tracking using detection-guided optimization. In: CVPR (2015)
19. Sun, X., Wei, Y., Liang, S., Tang, X., Sun, J.: Cascaded hand pose regression. In: CVPR (2015)

20. Oberweger, M., Wohlhart, P., Lepetit, V.: Training a feedback loop for hand pose estimation. In: ICCV (2015)
21. Oberweger, M., Riegler, G., Wohlhart, P., Lepetit, V.: Efficiently creating 3D training data for fine hand pose estimation. In: CVPR (2016)
22. Sridhar, S., Mueller, F., Zollhöfer, M., Casas, D., Oulasvirta, A., Theobalt, C.: Real-time joint tracking of a hand manipulating an object from RGB-D input. In: Leibe, B., Matas, J., Sebe, N., Welling, M. (eds.) ECCV 2016. LNCS, vol. 9906, pp. 294–310. Springer, Cham (2016). https://doi.org/10.1007/978-3-319-46475-6_19
23. Yuan, S., et al.: Depth-based 3d hand pose estimation: from current achievements to future goals. In: IEEE CVPR (2018)
24. Oikonomidis, I., Kyriazis, N., Argyros, A.A.: Efficient model-based 3d tracking of hand articulations using kinect. In: BMVC, vol. 1, p. 3 (2011)
25. Wang, R.Y., Popović, J.: Real-time hand-tracking with a color glove. ToG **28**, 63 (2009)
26. Wei, S.E., Ramakrishna, V., Kanade, T., Sheikh, Y.: Convolutional pose machines. In: CVPR (2016)
27. Newell, A., Yang, K., Deng, J.: Stacked hourglass networks for human pose estimation. In: Leibe, B., Matas, J., Sebe, N., Welling, M. (eds.) ECCV 2016. LNCS, vol. 9912, pp. 483–499. Springer, Cham (2016). https://doi.org/10.1007/978-3-319-46484-8_29
28. Toshev, A., Szegedy, C.: Deeppose: human pose estimation via deep neural networks. In: CVPR (2014)
29. Sun, X., Shang, J., Liang, S., Wei, Y.: Compositional human pose regression. In: ICCV (2017)
30. Pavlakos, G., Zhou, X., Derpanis, K.G., Daniilidis, K.: Coarse-to-fine volumetric prediction for single-image 3D human pose. In: CVPR (2017)
31. Heap, T., Hogg, D.: Towards 3D hand tracking using a deformable model. In: FG (1996)
32. Wu, Y., Lin, J.Y., Huang, T.S.: Capturing natural hand articulation. In: ICCV (2001)
33. Sigal, L., Balan, A.O., Black, M.J.: HumanEva: synchronized video and motion capture dataset and baseline algorithm for evaluation of articulated human motion. IJCV **87**(1), 4–27 (2010)
34. de La Gorce, M., Fleet, D.J., Paragios, N.: Model-based 3D hand pose estimation from monocular video. TPAMI **33**, 1793–1805 (2011)
35. Lu, S., Metaxas, D., Samaras, D., Oliensis, J.: Using multiple cues for hand tracking and model refinement. In: CVPR (2003)
36. Bogo, F., Kanazawa, A., Lassner, C., Gehler, P., Romero, J., Black, M.J.: Keep It SMPL: automatic estimation of 3D human pose and shape from a single image. In: Leibe, B., Matas, J., Sebe, N., Welling, M. (eds.) ECCV 2016. LNCS, vol. 9909, pp. 561–578. Springer, Cham (2016). https://doi.org/10.1007/978-3-319-46454-1_34
37. Panteleris, P., Oikonomidis, I., Argyros, A.: Using a single RGB frame for real time 3D hand pose estimation in the wild. In: WACV (2018)
38. Athitsos, V., Sclaroff, S.: Estimating 3D hand pose from a cluttered image. In: CVPR (2003)
39. Romero, J., Kjellström, H., Kragic, D.: Hands in action: real-time 3D reconstruction of hands in interaction with objects. In: ICRA (2010)
40. Chen, C., Ramanan, D.: 3D human pose estimation = 2D pose estimation + matching. In: CVPR (2017)
41. Iqbal, U., Doering, A., Yasin, H., Krüger, B., Weber, A., Gall, J.: A dual-source approach for 3D pose estimation in single images. CVIU (2018, in Press)

42. Ramakrishna, V., Kanade, T., Sheikh, Y.: Reconstructing 3D human pose from 2D image landmarks. In: Fitzgibbon, A., Lazebnik, S., Perona, P., Sato, Y., Schmid, C. (eds.) ECCV 2012. LNCS, vol. 7575, pp. 573–586. Springer, Heidelberg (2012). https://doi.org/10.1007/978-3-642-33765-9_41

43. Simo-Serra, E., Quattoni, A., Torras, C., Moreno-Noguer, F.: A joint model for 2D and 3D pose estimation from a single image. In: CVPR (2013)

44. Akhter, I., Black, M.J.: Pose-conditioned joint angle limits for 3D human pose reconstruction. In: CVPR (2015)

45. Tome, D., Russell, C., Agapito, L.: Lifting from the deep: convolutional 3D pose estimation from a single image. In: CVPR (2017)

46. Moreno-Noguer, F.: 3D human pose estimation from a single image via distance matrix regression. In: CVPR (2017)

47. Martinez, J., Hossain, R., Romero, J., Little, J.J.: A simple yet effective baseline for 3D human pose estimation. In: ICCV (2017)

48. Zimmermann, C., Brox, T.: Learning to estimate 3D hand pose from single RGB images. In: ICCV (2017)

49. Tekin, B., Marquez-Neila, P., Salzmann, M., Fua, P.: Learning to fuse 2D and 3D image cues for monocular body pose estimation. In: ICCV (2017)

50. Li, S., Chan, A.B.: 3D human pose estimation from monocular images with deep convolutional neural network. In: Cremers, D., Reid, I., Saito, H., Yang, M.-H. (eds.) ACCV 2014. LNCS, vol. 9004, pp. 332–347. Springer, Cham (2015). https://doi.org/10.1007/978-3-319-16808-1_23

51. Zhou, X., Sun, X., Zhang, W., Liang, S., Wei, Y.: Deep kinematic pose regression. In: Hua, G., Jégou, H. (eds.) ECCV 2016. LNCS, vol. 9915, pp. 186–201. Springer, Cham (2016). https://doi.org/10.1007/978-3-319-49409-8_17

52. Mueller, F., et al.: GANerated hands for real-time 3D hand tracking from monocular RGB. In: CVPR (2018)

53. Spurr, A., Song, J., Park, S., Hilliges, O.: Cross-modal deep variational hand pose estimation. In: CVPR (2018)

54. Goodfellow, I., et al.: Generative adversarial nets. In: NIPS (2014)

55. Popa, A., Zanfir, M., Sminchisescu, C.: Deep multitask architecture for integrated 2D and 3D human sensing. In: CVPR (2017)

56. Zhou, X., Huang, Q., Sun, X., Xue, X., Wei, Y.: Weakly-supervised transfer for 3D human pose estimation in the wild. In: ICCV (2017)

57. Nie, B.X., Wei, P., Zhu, S.C.: Monocular 3D human pose estimation by predicting depth on joints. In: ICCV (2017)

58. Mehta, D., et al.: VNect: real-time 3D human pose estimation with a single RGB camera. In: SIGGRAPH (2017)

59. Tompson, J., Goroshin, R., Jain, A., LeCun, Y., Bregler, C.: Efficient object localization using convolutional networks. In: CVPR (2015)

60. Simon, T., Joo, H., Matthews, I., Sheikh, Y.: Hand keypoint detection in single images using multiview bootstrapping. In: CVPR (2017)

61. Chapelle, O., Wu, M.: Gradient descent optimization of smoothed information retrieval metrics. Inf. Retr. 13, 216–235 (2010)

62. Mueller, F., Mehta, D., Sotnychenko, O., Sridhar, S., Casas, D., Theobalt, C.: Real-time hand tracking under occlusion from an egocentric RGB-D sensor. In: ICCV (2017)

63. Silberman, N., Hoiem, D., Kohli, P., Fergus, R.: Indoor segmentation and support inference from RGBD images. In: Fitzgibbon, A., Lazebnik, S., Perona, P., Sato, Y., Schmid, C. (eds.) ECCV 2012. LNCS, vol. 7576, pp. 746–760. Springer, Heidelberg (2012). https://doi.org/10.1007/978-3-642-33715-4_54

64. Zhang, J., Jiao, J., Chen, M., Qu, L., Xu, X., Yang, Q.: 3D hand pose tracking and estimation using stereo matching. arXiv preprint arXiv:1610.07214 (2016)
65. Ronneberger, O., Fischer, P., Brox, T.: U-Net: convolutional networks for biomedical image segmentation. In: Navab, N., Hornegger, J., Wells, W.M., Frangi, A.F. (eds.) MICCAI 2015. LNCS, vol. 9351, pp. 234–241. Springer, Cham (2015). https://doi.org/10.1007/978-3-319-24574-4_28
66. Redmon, J., Farhadi, A.: YOLO9000: better, faster, stronger. In: CVPR (2017)
67. He, K., Zhang, X., Ren, S., Sun, J.: Deep residual learning for image recognition. In: CVPR (2016)

Depth-Aware CNN for RGB-D Segmentation

Weiyue Wang$^{(\boxtimes)}$ and Ulrich Neumann

University of Southern California, Los Angeles, CA, USA
{weiyuewa,uneumann}@usc.edu

Abstract. Convolutional neural networks (CNN) are limited by the lack of capability to handle geometric information due to the fixed grid kernel structure. The availability of depth data enables progress in RGB-D semantic segmentation with CNNs. State-of-the-art methods either use depth as additional images or process spatial information in 3D volumes or point clouds. These methods suffer from high computation and memory cost. To address these issues, we present Depth-aware CNN by introducing two intuitive, flexible and effective operations: depth-aware convolution and depth-aware average pooling. By leveraging depth similarity between pixels in the process of information propagation, geometry is seamlessly incorporated into CNN. Without introducing any additional parameters, both operators can be easily integrated into existing CNNs. Extensive experiments and ablation studies on challenging RGB-D semantic segmentation benchmarks validate the effectiveness and flexibility of our approach.

Keywords: Geometry in CNN · RGB-D semantic segmentation

1 Introduction

Recent advances [4,28,36] in CNN have achieved significant success in scene understanding. With the help of range sensors (such as Kinect, LiDAR etc.), depth images are applicable along with RGB images. Taking advantages of the two complementary modalities with CNN is able to improve the performance of scene understanding. However, CNN is limited to model geometric variance due to the fixed grid computation structure. Incorporating the geometric information from depth images into CNN is important yet challenging.

Extensive studies [5,6,17,22,26,27,34] have been carried out on this task. FCN [28] and its successors treat depth as another input image and construct two CNNs to process RGB and depth separately. This doubles the number of network parameters and computation cost. In addition, the two-stream network architecture still suffers from the fixed geometric structures of CNN. Even if

Electronic supplementary material The online version of this chapter (https://doi.org/10.1007/978-3-030-01252-6_9) contains supplementary material, which is available to authorized users.

© Springer Nature Switzerland AG 2018
V. Ferrari et al. (Eds.): ECCV 2018, LNCS 11215, pp. 144–161, 2018.
https://doi.org/10.1007/978-3-030-01252-6_9

the geometric relations of two pixels are given, this relation cannot be used in information propagation of CNN. An alternative is to leverage 3D networks [26, 31,33] to handle geometry. Nevertheless, both volumetric CNNs [31] and 3D point cloud graph networks [26] are computationally more expensive than 2D CNN. Despite the encouraging results of these progresses, we need to seek a more flexible and efficient way to exploit 3D geometric information in 2D CNN.

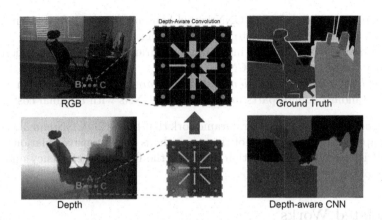

Fig. 1. Illustration of Depth-aware CNN. A and C are labeled as table and B is labeled as chair. They all have similar visual features in the RGB image, while they are separable in depth. Depth-aware CNN incorporate the geometric relations of pixels in both convolution and pooling. When A is the center of the receptive field, C then has more contribution to the output unit than B. Figures in the rightmost column shows the RGB-D semantic segmentation result of Depth-aware CNN.

To address the aforementioned problems, in this paper, we present an end-to-end network, Depth-aware CNN (D-CNN), for RGB-D segmentation. Two new operators are introduced: *depth-aware convolution* and *depth-aware average pooling*. *Depth-aware convolution* augments the standard convolution with a depth similarity term. We force pixels with similar depths with the center of the kernel to have more contribution to the output than others. This simple depth similarity term efficiently incorporates geometry in a convolution kernel and helps build a depth-aware receptive field, where convolution is not constrained to the fixed grid geometric structure.

The second introduced operator is *depth-ware average pooling*. Similarly, when a filter is applied on a local region of the feature map, the pairwise relations in depth between neighboring pixels are considered in computing mean of the local region. Visual features are able to propagate along with the geometric structure given in depth images. Such geometry-aware operation enables the localization of object boundaries with depth images.

Both operators are based on the intuition that pixels with the same semantic label and similar depths should have more impact on each other. We observe that two pixels with the same semantic labels have similar depths. As illustrated in Fig. 1, pixel A and pixel C should be more correlated with each other than pixel A and pixel B. This correlation difference is obvious in depth image while it is not captured in RGB image. By encoding the depth correlation in CNN, pixel C has more contribution to the output unit than pixel B in the process of information propagation.

The main advantages of depth-aware CNN are summarized as follows:

– By exploiting the nature of CNN kernel handling spatial information, geometry in depth image is able to be integrated into CNN seamlessly.
– Depth-aware CNN does not introduce any parameters and computation complexity to the conventional CNN.
– Both *depth-aware convolution* and *depth-ware average pooling* can replace their standard counterparts in conventional CNNs with minimal cost.

Depth-aware CNN is a general framework that bonds 2D CNN and 3D geometry. Comparison with the state-of-the-art methods and extensive ablation studies on RGB-D semantic segmentation illustrate the flexibility, efficiency and effectiveness of our approach.

2   Related Works

2.1   RGB-D Semantic Segmentation

With the help of CNNs, semantic segmentation on 2D images have achieved promising results [4,14,28,36]. These advances in 2D CNN and the availability of depth sensors enables progresses in RGB-D segmentation. Compared to the RGB settings, RGB-D segmentation is able to integrate geometry into scene understanding. In [8,10,21,32], depth is simply treated as additional channels and directly fed into CNN. Several works [9,10,18,23,28] encode depth to HHA image, which has three channels: horizontal disparity, height above ground, and norm angle. RGB image and HHA image are fed into two separate networks, and the two predictions are summed up in the last layer. The two-stream network doubles the number of parameters and forward time compared to the conventional 2D network. Moreover, CNNs per se are limited in their ability to model geometric transformations due to their fixed grid computation. Cheng et al. [5] propose a locality-sensitive deconvolution network with gated fusion. They build a feature affinity matrix to perform weighted average pooling and unpooling. Lin et al. [19] discretize depth and build different branches for different discrete depth value. He et al. [12] use spatio-temporal correspondences across frames to aggregate information over space and time. This requires heavy pre and post-processing such as optical flow and superpixel computation.

Alternatively, many works [30,31] attempt to solve the problem with 3D CNNs. However, the volumetric representation prevents scaling up due to high memory and computation cost. Recently, deep learning frameworks [13,24–26,35] on point cloud are introduced to address the limitations of 3D volume.

Qi et al. [26] built a 3D k-nearest neighbor (kNN) graph neural network on a point cloud with extracted features from a CNN and achieved the state-of-the-art on RGB-D segmentation. Although their method is more efficient than 3D CNNs, the kNN operation suffers from high computation complexity and lack of flexibility. Instead of using 3D representations, we use the raw depth input and integrate 3D geometry into 2D CNN in a more efficient and flexible fashion.

2.2   Spatial Transformations in CNN

Standard CNNs are limited to model geometric transformations due to the fixed structure of convolution kernels. Recently, many works are focused on dealing with this issue. Dilated convolutions [4,36] increases the receptive field size with keeping the same complexity in parameters. This operator achieves better performance on vision tasks such as semantic segmentation. Spatial transform networks [15] warps feature maps with a learned global spatial transformation. Deformable CNN [7] learns kernel offsets to augment the spatial sampling locations. These methods have shown geometric transformations enable performance boost on different vision tasks.

With the advances in 3D sensors, depth is applicable at low cost. The geometric information that resides in depth is highly correlated with the spatial transformation in CNN. Bilateral filters [2,3] is widely used in computer graphics for image smoothness with edge preserving. They use a Gaussian term to weight neighboring pixels. Similarly as bilateral filter, our method integrates the geometric relation of pixels into basic operations of CNN, i.e. convolution and pooling, where we use a weighted kernel and force every neuron to have different contributions to the output. This weighted kernel is defined by depth and is able to incorporate geometric relationships without introducing any parameter.

3   Depth-Aware CNN

In this section, we introduce two depth-aware operations: depth-aware convolution and depth-aware average pooling. They are both simple and intuitive. Both operations require two inputs: the input feature map $\mathbf{x} \in \mathbb{R}^{c_i \times h \times w}$ and the depth image $\mathbf{D} \in \mathbb{R}^{h \times w}$, where c_i is the number of input feature channels, h is the height and w is the width. The output feature map is denoted as $\mathbf{y} \in \mathbb{R}^{c_o \times h \times w}$, where c_o is the number of output feature channels. Although $\mathbf{x}$ and $\mathbf{y}$ are both 3D tensors, the operations are explained in 2D spatial domain for notation clarity and they remain the same across different channels.

3.1   Depth-Aware Convolution

A standard 2D convolution operation is the weighted sum of a local grid. For each pixel location $\mathbf{p_0}$ on $\mathbf{y}$, the output of standard 2D convolution is

$$\mathbf{y}(\mathbf{p_0}) = \sum_{\mathbf{p_n} \in \mathcal{R}} \mathbf{w}(\mathbf{p_n}) \cdot \mathbf{x}(\mathbf{p_0} + \mathbf{p_n}), \tag{1}$$

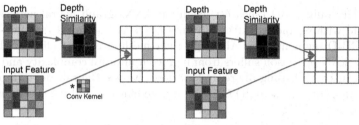

(a) Depth-aware Convolution   (b) Depth-aware Average Pooling

Fig. 2. Illustration of information propagation in Depth-aware CNN. Without loss of generality, we only show one filter window with kernel size 3×3. In depth similarity shown in figure, darker color indicates higher similarity while lighter color represents that two pixels are less similar in depth. In (a), the output activation of depth-aware convolution is the multiplication of depth similarity window and the convolved window on input feature map. Similarly in (b), the output of depth-aware average pooling is the average value of the input window weighted by the depth similarity. (Color figure online)

where $\mathcal{R}$ is the local grid around $\boldsymbol{p_0}$ in $\mathbf{x}$ and $\mathbf{w}$ is the convolution kernel. $\mathcal{R}$ can be a regular grid defined by kernel size and dilation [36], and it can also be a non-regular grid [7].

As is shown in Fig. 1, pixel A and pixel B have different semantic labels and different depths while they are not separable in RGB space. On the other hand, pixel A and pixel C have the same labels and similar depths. To exploit the depth correlation between pixels, depth-aware convolution simply adds a depth similarity term, resulting in two sets of weights in convolution: (1) the learnable convolution kernel $\mathbf{w}$; (2) depth similarity $F_{\mathbf{D}}$ between two pixels. Consequently, Eq. 1 becomes

$$y(\mathbf{p_0}) = \sum_{\mathbf{p_n} \in \mathcal{R}} \mathbf{w}(\mathbf{p_n}) \cdot F_{\mathbf{D}}(\mathbf{p_0}, \mathbf{p_0} + \mathbf{p_n}) \cdot \mathbf{x}(\mathbf{p_0} + \mathbf{p_n}). \qquad (2)$$

And $F_{\mathbf{D}}(\mathbf{p}_i, \mathbf{p}_j)$ is defined as

$$F_{\mathbf{D}}(\mathbf{p}_i, \mathbf{p}_j) = \exp(-\alpha |\mathbf{D}(\mathbf{p}_i) - \mathbf{D}(\mathbf{p}_j)|), \qquad (3)$$

where α is a constant. The selection of $F_{\mathbf{D}}$ is based on the intuition that pixels with similar depths should have more impact on each other. We will study the effect of different α and different $F_{\mathbf{D}}$ in Sect. 4.2.

The gradients for $\mathbf{x}$ and $\mathbf{w}$ are simply multiplied by $F_{\mathbf{D}}$. Note that the $F_{\mathbf{D}}$ part does not require gradient during back-propagation, therefore, Eq. 2 does not integrate any parameters by the depth similarity term.

Figure 2(a) illustrates this process. Pixels which have similar depths with the convolving center will have more impact on the output during convolution.

3.2   Depth-Aware Average Pooling

The conventional average pooling computes the mean of a grid $\mathcal{R}$ over $\mathbf{x}$. It is defined as

$$\mathbf{y}(\mathbf{p}_0) = \frac{1}{|\mathcal{R}|} \sum_{\mathbf{p}_n \in \mathcal{R}} \mathbf{x}(\mathbf{p}_0 + \mathbf{p}_n). \tag{4}$$

It treats every pixel equally and will make the object boundary blurry. Geometric information is useful to address this issue.

Similar to as in depth-aware convolution, we take advantage of the depth similarity F_D to force pixels with more consistent geometry to make more contribution on the corresponding output. For each pixel location $\mathbf{p}_0$, the depth-aware average pooling operation then becomes

$$\mathbf{y}(\mathbf{p}_0) = \frac{1}{\sum_{\mathbf{p}_n \in \mathcal{R}} F_D(\mathbf{p}_0, \mathbf{p}_0 + \mathbf{p}_n)} \sum_{\mathbf{p}_n \in \mathcal{R}} F_D(\mathbf{p}_0, \mathbf{p}_0 + \mathbf{p}_n) \cdot \mathbf{x}(\mathbf{p}_0 + \mathbf{p}_n). \tag{5}$$

The gradient should be multiplied by $\frac{F_D}{\sum_{\mathbf{p}_n \in \mathcal{R}} F_D(\mathbf{p}_0, \mathbf{p}_0 + \mathbf{p}_n)}$ during back propagation. As illustrated in Fig. 2(b), this operation prevent suffering from the fixed geometric structure of standard pooling.

3.3   Understanding Depth-Aware CNN

A major advantage of CNN is its capability of using GPU to perform parallel computing and accelerate the computation. This acceleration mainly stems from unrolling convolution operation with the grid computation structure. However, this limits the ability of CNN to model geometric variations. Researchers in 3D deep learning have focused on modeling geometry in deep neural networks in the last few years. As the volumetric representation [30,31] is of high memory and computation cost, point clouds are considered as a more proper representation. However, deep learning frameworks [25,26] on point cloud are based on building kNN. This not only suffers from high computation complexity, but also breaks the pixel-wise correspondence between RGB and depth, which makes the framework is not able to leverage the efficiency of CNN's grid computation structure. Instead of operating on 3D data, we exploit the raw depth input. By augmenting the convolution kernel with a depth similarity term, depth-aware CNN captures geometry with transformable receptive field.

Many works have studied spatial transformable receptive field of CNN. Dilated convolution [4,36] has demonstrated that increasing receptive field boost the performance of networks. In deformable CNN [7], Dai et al. demonstrate that learning receptive field adaptively can help CNN achieve better results. They also show

Table 1. Mean depth variance of different categories on NYUv2 dataset. "All" denotes the mean variance of all categories. For every image, pixelwise variance of depth for each category is calculated. Averaged variance is then computed over all images. For "All", all pixels in a image are considered to calculate the depth variance. Mean variance over all images is further computed.

	Wall	Floor	Bed	Chair	Table	All
Variance	0.57	0.65	0.12	0.23	0.34	1.20

that pixels within the same object in a receptive field contribute more to the output unit than pixels with different labels. We observe that semantic labels and depths have high correlations. Table 1 reports the statistics of pixel depth variance within the same class and across different classes on NYUv2 [22] dataset. Even the pixel depth variances of large objects such as wall and floor are much smaller than the variance of a whole scene. This indicates that pixels with the same semantic labels tend to have similar depths. This pattern is integrated in Eqs. 2 and 5 with F_D. Without introducing any parameter, depth-aware convolution and depth-aware average pooling are able to enhance the localization ability of CNN. We evaluate the impact on performance of different depth similarity functions F_D in Sect. 4.2.

(a)   (b)   (c)   (d)

Fig. 3. Illustration of effective receptive field of Depth-aware CNN. (a) is the input RGB images. (b), (c) and (d) are depth images. For (b), (c) and (d), we show the sampling locations (red dots) in three levels of 3×3 depth-aware convolutions for the activation unit (green dot). (Color figure online)

To get a better understanding of how depth-aware CNN captures geometry with depth, Fig. 3 shows the effective receptive field of the given input neuron. In conventional CNN, the receptive fields and sampling locations are fixed across feature map. With the depth-aware term incorporated, they are adjusted by the geometric variance. For example, in the second row of Fig. 3(d), the green point is labeled as chair and the effective receptive field of the green point are essentially chair points. This indicates that the effective receptive field mostly have the same semantic label as the center. This pattern increases CNN's performance on semantic segmentation.

3.4 Depth-Aware CNN for RGB-D Semantic Segmentation

In this paper, we focus on RGB-D semantic segmentation with depth-aware CNN. Given an RGB image along with depth, our goal is to produce a semantic mask indicating the label of each pixel. Both depth-aware convolution and average pooling easily replace their counterpart in standard CNN.

Table 2. Network architecture. DeepLab is our baseline with a modified version of VGG-16 as the encoder. The convolution layer parameters are denoted as "C[kernel size]-[number of channels]-[dilation]". "DC" and "Davgpool" represent depth-aware convolution and depth-aware average pooling respectively.

Layer name	conv1_x	conv2_x	conv3_x	conv4_x	conv5_x	conv6 & conv7
Baseline DeepLab	C3-64-1	C3-128-1	C3-256-1	C3-512-1	C3-512-2	C3-1024-12
	C3-64-1	C3-128-1	C3-256-1	C3-512-1	C3-512-2	C1-1024-0
	maxpool	Maxpool	C3-256-1	C3-512-1	C3-512-2	globalpool+concat
			maxpool	maxpool	Avgpool	
D-CNN	DC3-64-1	DC3-128-1	DC3-256-1	DC3-512-1	DC3-512-2	DC3-1024-12
	C3-64-1	C3-128-1	C3-256-1	C3-512-1	C3-512-2	C1-1024-0
	maxpool	maxpool	C3-256-1	C3-512-1	C3-512-2	globalpool+concat
			maxpool	maxpool	Davgpool	

DeepLab [4] is a state-of-the-art method for semantic segmentation. We adopt DeepLab as our baseline for semantic segmentation and a modified VGG-16 network is used as the encoder. We replace layers in this network with depth-aware operations. The network configurations of the baseline and depth-aware CNN are outlined in Table 2. Suppose conv7 has C channels. Following [26], global pooling is used to compute a C-dim vector from conv7. This vector is then appended to all spatial positions and results in a $2C$-channel feature map. This feature map is followed by a 1×1 conv layer and produce the segmentation probability map.

4 Experiments

Evaluation is performed on three popular RGB-D datasets:

– NYUv2 [22]: NYUv2 contains of $1,449$ RGB-D images with pixel-wise labels. We follow the 40-class settings and the standard split with 795 training images and 654 testing images.
– SUN-RGBD [16,29]: This dataset have 37 categories of objects and consists of $10,335$ RGB-D images, with $5,285$ as training and 5050 as testing.

– Stanford Indoor Dataset (SID) [1]: SID contains $70,496$ RGB-D images with 13 object categories. We use Area $1,2,3,4$ and 6 as training, and Area 5 as testing.

Four common metrics are used for evaluation: pixel accuracy (Acc), mean pixel accuracy of different categories (mAcc), mean Intersection-over-Union of different categories (mIoU), and frequency-weighted IoU (fwIoU). Suppose n_{ij} is the number of pixels with ground truth class i and predicted as class j, n_C is the number of classes and s_i is the number of pixels with ground truth class i, the total number of all pixels is $s = \sum_i s_i$. The four metrics are defined as follows: $\text{Acc} = \sum_i \frac{n_{ii}}{s}$, $\text{mAcc} = \frac{1}{n_C} \sum_i \frac{n_{ii}}{s_i}$, $\text{mIoU} = \frac{1}{n_C} \sum_i \frac{n_{ii}}{s_i + \sum_j n_{ji} - n_{ii}}$, fwIoU $= \frac{1}{s} \sum_i s_i \frac{n_{ii}}{s_i + \sum_j n_{ji} - n_{ii}}$.

Implementation Details. For most experiments, DeepLab with a modified VGG-16 encoder (c.f. Table 2) is the baseline. Depth-aware CNN based on DeepLab outlined in Table 2 is evaluated to validate the effectiveness of our approach and this is referred as "D-CNN" in the paper. We also conduct experiments with combining HHA encoding [9]. Following [8, 26, 28], two baseline networks consume RGB and HHA images separately and the predictions of both networks are summed up in the last layer. This two-stream network is dubbed as "HHA". To make fair comparison, we also build depth-aware CNN with this two-stream fashion and denote this as "D-CNN+HHA". In ablation study, we further replace VGG-16 with ResNet-50 [11] as the encoder to have a better understanding of the functionality of depth-aware operations.

We use SGD optimizer with initial learning rate 0.001, momentum 0.9 and batch size 1. The learning rate is multiplied by $(1 - \frac{iter}{max\_iter})^{0.9}$ for every 10 iterarions. α is set to 8.3. (The impact of α is studied in Sect. 4.2.) The dataset is augmented by randomly scaling, cropping, and color jittering. We use PyTorch deep learning framework. Both depth-aware convolution and depth-aware average pooling operators are implemented with CUDA acceleration. Code is available at github.com/laughtervv/DepthAwareCNN.

4.1 Main Results

Depth-aware CNN is compared with both its baseline and the state-of-the-art methods on NYUv2 and SUN-RGBD dataset. It is also compared with the baseline on SID dataset.

NYUv2. Table 3 shows quantitative comparison results between D-CNNs and baseline models. Since D-CNN and its baseline are in different function space, all networks are trained from scratch to make fair comparison in this experiment. Without introducing any parameters, D-CNN outperforms the baseline by incorporating geometric information in convolution operation. Moreover, the performance of D-CNN also exceeds "HHA" network by using only half of its parameters. This effectively validate the superior capability of D-CNN on handling geometry over "HHA".

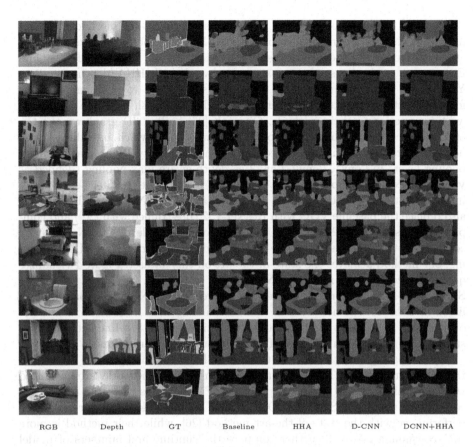

RGB   Depth   GT   Baseline   HHA   D-CNN   DCNN+HHA

Fig. 4. Segmentation results on NYUv2 test dataset. "GT" denotes ground truth. The white regions in "GT" are the ignoring category. Networks are trained from pre-trained models.

Table 3. Comparison with baseline CNNs on NYUv2 test set. Networks are trained from scratch.

	Baseline	HHA	D-CNN	D-CNN+HHA
Acc (%)	50.1	59.1	60.3	**61.4**
mAcc (%)	23.9	30.8	**39.3**	35.6
mIoU (%)	15.9	21.9	**27.8**	26.2
fwIoU (%)	34.2	43.0	44.9	**45.7**

Table 4. Comparison with the state-of-the-arts on NYUv2 test set. Networks are trained from pre-trained models.

	[28]	[8]	[12]	[26]	HHA	D-CNN	D-CNN+HHA	DM-CNN+HHA	[20]	D-ResNet-152
mAcc (%)	46.1	45.1	53.8	55.2	51.1	53.6	56.3	**58.4**	58.9	**61.1**
mIoU (%)	34.0	34.1	40.1	42.0	40.4	41.0	43.9	**44.7**	46.5	**48.4**

We also compare our results with the state-of-the-art methods. Table 4 illustrates the good performance of D-CNN. In this experiment, the networks are initialized with the pre-trained parameters in [4]. Long et al. [28] and Eigen et al. [8] both use the two-stream network with HHA/depth encoding. Yang et al. [12] compute optical flows and superpixels to augment the performance with spatial-temporal information. D-CNN with only one VGG network is superior to their methods. Qi et al. [26] built a 3D graph on the top of VGG encoder and use RNN to update the graph, which introduces more network parameters and higher computation complexity. By replacing max-pooling layers in Conv1, Conv2, Conv3 as depth-aware max-pooling (defined as $\mathbf{y}(\mathbf{p}_0) = \max_{\mathbf{p}_n \in \mathcal{R}} F_{\mathbf{D}}(\mathbf{p}_0, \mathbf{p}_0 + \mathbf{p}_n) \cdot \mathbf{x}(\mathbf{p}_0 + \mathbf{p}_n))$, we can get further performance improvement, and this experiment is referred as DM-CNN-HHA in Table 4. We also replace the baseline VGG with ResNet-152 (pre-trained with [20]) and compare with its baseline [20] in Table 4. As is shown in Table 4, D-CNN is already comparable with these state-of-the-art methods. By incorporating HHA encoding, our method achieves the state-of-the-art on this dataset. Figure 4 visualizes qualitative comparison results on NYUv2 test set.

SUN-RGBD. The comparison results between D-CNN and its baseline are listed in Table 5. The networks in this table are trained from scratch. D-CNN outperforms baseline by a large margin. Substituting the baseline with the two-stream "HHA" network is able to further improve the performance.

By comparing with the state-of-the-art methods in Table 6, we can further see the effectiveness of D-CNN. Similarly as in NYUv2, the networks are initialized with pre-trained model in this experiment. Figure 5 illustrates the qualitative comparison results on SUN-RGBD test set. Our network achieves comparable performance with the state-of-the-art method [26], while their method is more time-consuming. We will further compare the runtime and numbers of model parameters in Sect. 4.3.

Table 5. Comparison with baseline CNNs on SUN-RGBD test set. Networks are trained from scratch.

	Baseline	HHA	D-CNN	D-CNN+HHA
Acc (%)	66.6	72.6	72.4	**72.9**
mAcc (%)	31.5	37.9	38.6	**41.2**
mIoU (%)	22.8	28.8	29.7	**31.3**
fwIoU (%)	51.4	58.5	58.2	**59.3**

Table 6. Comparison with the state-of-the-arts on SUN-RGBD test set. Networks are trained from pre-trained models.

	[18]	[26]	HHA	D-CNN	D-CNN+HHA
mAcc (%)	48.1	**55.2**	50.5	51.2	53.5
mIoU (%)	-	**42.0**	40.2	41.5	**42.0**

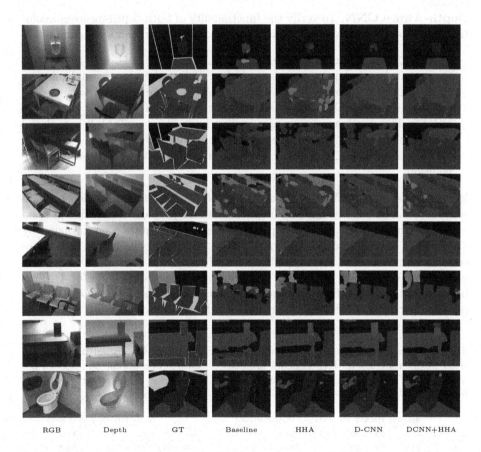

RGB   Depth   GT   Baseline   HHA   D-CNN   DCNN+HHA

Fig. 5. Segmentation results on SUN-RGBD test dataset. "GT" denotes ground truth. The white regions in "GT" are the ignoring category. Networks are trained from pre-trained models.

SID. The comparison results on SID between D-CNN with its baseline are reported in Table 7. Networks are trained from scratch. Using depth images, D-CNN is able to achieve 4% IoU over CNN while preserving the same number of parameters and computation complexity.

Table 7. Comparison with baseline CNNs on SID Area 5. Networks are trained from scratch.

	Baseline	D-CNN
Acc (%)	64.3	**65.4**
mAcc (%)	46.7	**55.5**
mIoU (%)	35.5	**39.5**
fwIoU (%)	48.5	**49.9**

4.2 Ablation Study

In this section, we conduct ablation studies on NYUv2 dataset to validate efficiency and efficacy of our approach. Testing results on NYUv2 test set are reported.

Depth-Aware CNN. To verify the functionality of both depth-aware convolution and depth-aware average pooling, the following experiments are conducted.

- VGG-1: Conv1_1, Conv2_1, Conv3_1, Conv4_1, Conv5_1 and Conv6 in VGG-16 are replaced with depth-aware convolution. This is the same as in Table 2.
- VGG-2: Conv4_1, Conv5_1 and Conv6 in VGG-16 are replaced with depth-aware convolution. Other layers remain the same as in Table 2.
- VGG-3: The depth-aware average pooling layer listed in Table 2 is replaced with regular pooling. Other layers remain the same as in Table 2.
- VGG-4: Only Conv1_1, Conv2_1, Conv3_1 are replaced with depth-aware convolution.

Results are shown in Table 8. Compared to VGG-2, VGG-1 adds depth-aware convolution in bottom layers. This helps the network propagate more fine-grained features with geometric relationships and increase segmentation performance by 6% in IoU. VGG-1 also outperforms VGG-4. Top layers conv4, 5 have more contextual information, and applying D-CNN on these layers still benefits the prediction. As is shown in [24], not all contextual information is useful. D-CNN helps to capture more effective contextual information. The depth-aware average pooling operation is able to further promote the accuracy.

Table 8. Results of using depth-aware operations in different layers. Experiments are conducted on NYUv2 test set. Networks are trained from scratch.

	Baseline	HHA	VGG-1	VGG-2	VGG-3	VGG-4
Acc (%)	50.1	59.1	**60.3**	56.0	59.3	59.5
mAcc (%)	23.9	30.8	**39.3**	32.2	39.2	37.3
mIoU (%)	15.9	21.9	**27.8**	22.4	27.4	26.6
fwIoU (%)	34.2	43.0	**44.9**	40.2	44.0	43.8

Table 9. Results of using depth-aware operations in ResNet-50. Networks are trained from pre-trained models.

	VGG-1	ResNet-50	D-ResNet-50
Acc (%)	69.4	68.9	**69.6**
mAcc (%)	**53.6**	50.2	53.3
mIoU (%)	41.0	38.8	**41.5**
fwIoU (%)	**54.5**	54.4	54.4

We also replace VGG-16 to ResNet as the encoder. We test depth-aware operations on ResNet. The Conv3_1, Conv4_1, and Conv5_1 in ResNet-50 are replaced with depth-aware convolution. ResNet-50 is initialized with parameters pre-trained on ADE20K [37]. Detailed architecture and training details for ResNet can be found in Supplementary Materials. Results are listed in Table 9.

Depth Similarity Function. We modify α and F_D to further validate the effect of different choices of depth similarity function on performance. We conduct the following experiments:

- $\alpha_{8.3}$: α is set to 8.3. The network architecture is the same as Table 2.
- α_{20}: α is set to 20. The network architecture is the same as Table 2.
- $\alpha_{2.5}$: α is set to 2.5. The network architecture is the same as Table 2.
- clipF_D: The network architecture is the same as Table 2. F_D is defined as

$$F_D(\mathbf{p}_i, \mathbf{p}_j) = \begin{cases} 0, & |\mathbf{D}(\mathbf{p}_i) - \mathbf{D}(\mathbf{p}_j)| \geq 1 \\ 1, & \text{otherwise} \end{cases} \tag{6}$$

Table 10 reports the test performances with different depth similarity functions. Though the performance varies with different α, they are all superior to baseline and even "HHA". The result of clipF_D is also comparable with "HHA". This validate that the effectiveness of using a depth-sensitive term to weight the contributions of neurons.

Table 10. Results of using different α and F_D. Experiments are conducted on NYUv2 test set. Networks are trained from scratch.

	Baseline	HHA	$\alpha_{8.3}$	α_{20}	$\alpha_{2.5}$	clipF_D
Acc (%)	50.1	59.1	**60.3**	58.5	58.5	53.0
mAcc (%)	23.9	30.8	**39.3**	35.2	35.9	29.8
mIoU (%)	15.9	21.9	**27.8**	24.9	25.3	20.1
fwIoU (%)	34.2	43.0	**44.9**	42.6	42.9	37.5

Performance Analysis. To have a better understanding of how depth-aware CNN outperforms the baseline, we visualize the improvement of IoU for each semantic class in Fig. 6(a). The statics shows that D-CNN outperform baseline on most object categories, especially these large objects such as ceilings and curtain. Moreover, we observe depth-aware CNN has a faster convergence than baseline, especially trained from scratch. Figure 6(b) shows the training loss evolution with respect to training steps. Our network gains lower loss values than baseline. Depth similarity helps preserving edge details, however, when depth values vary in a single object, depth-aware CNN may lose contextual information. Some failure cases can be found in supplemental material.

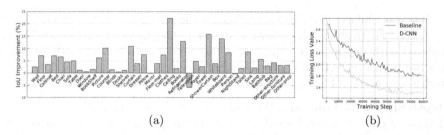

(a)   (b)

Fig. 6. Performance Analysis. (a) Per-class IoU improvement of D-CNN over baseline on NYUv2 test dataset. (b) Evolution of training loss on NYUv2 train dataset. Networks are trained from scratch.

4.3   Model Complexity and Runtime Analysis

Table 11 reports the model complexity and runtime of D-CNN and the state-of-the-art method [26]. In their method, kNN takes $O(kN)$ runtime at least, where N is the number of pixels. We leverage the grid structure of raw depth input. As is shown in Table 11, depth-aware operations do not incorporate any new parameters. The network forward time is only slightly greater than its baseline. Without increasing any model parameters, D-CNN is able to incorporate geometric information in CNN efficiently.

Table 11. Model complexity and runtime comparison. Runtime is tested on Nvidia 1080Ti, with input image size $425 \times 560 \times 3$.

	Baseline	HHA	[26]	D-CNN	D-CNN-HHA
net. forward (ms)	32.5	64.2	214	39.3	79.7
# of params	47.0M	92.0M	47.25M	47.0M	92.0M

5   Conclusion

We present a novel depth-aware CNN by introducing two operations: depth-aware convolution and depth-aware average pooling. Depth-aware CNN augments conventional CNN with a depth similarity term and encode geometric variance into basic convolution and pooling operations. By adapting effective receptive field, these depth-aware operations are able to incorporate geometry into CNN while preserving CNN's efficiency. Without introducing any parameters and computational complexity, this method is able to improve the performance on RGB-D segmentation over baseline by a large margin. Moreover, depth-aware CNN is flexible and easily replaces its plain counterpart in standard CNNs. Comparison with the state-of-the-art methods and extensive ablation studies on RGB-D semantic segmentation demonstrate the effectiveness and efficiency of depth-aware CNN.

Depth-aware CNN provides a general framework for vision tasks with RGB-D input. Moreover, depth-aware CNN takes the raw depth image as input and bridges the gap between 2D CNN and 3D geometry. In future works, we will apply depth-aware CNN on various tasks such as 3D detection, instance segmentation and we will perform depth-aware CNN on more challenging dataset. Apart from depth input, we will exploit more geometric input such as normal map.

Acknowledgements. We thank Ronald Yu, Yi Zhou and Qiangui Huang for the discussion and proofread. This research is supported by the Intelligence Advanced Research Projects Activity (IARPA) via Department of Interior/ Interior Business Center (DOI/IBC) contract number D17PC00288. The U.S. Government is authorized to reproduce and distribute reprints for Governmental purposes notwithstanding any copyright annotation thereon. Disclaimer: The views and conclusions contained herein are those of the authors and should not be interpreted as necessarily representing the official policies or endorsements, either expressed or implied, of IARPA, DOI/IBC, or the U.S. Government.

References

1. Armeni, I., Sax, A., Zamir, A.R., Savarese, S.: Joint 2D–3D-semantic data for indoor scene understanding. ArXiv e-prints (2017)
2. Barron, J.T., Poole, B.: The fast bilateral solver. In: Leibe, B., Matas, J., Sebe, N., Welling, M. (eds.) ECCV 2016. LNCS, vol. 9907, pp. 617–632. Springer, Cham (2016). https://doi.org/10.1007/978-3-319-46487-9_38
3. Chen, J., Paris, S., Durand, F.: Real-time edge-aware image processing with the bilateral grid. ACM Trans. Graph. (TOG) **26**, 103 (2007)
4. Chen, L.C., Papandreou, G., Kokkinos, I., Murphy, K., Yuille, A.L.: Semantic image segmentation with deep convolutional nets and fully connected CRFs. In: ICLR (2015)
5. Cheng, Y., Cai, R., Li, Z., Zhao, X., Huang, K.: Locality-sensitive deconvolution networks with gated fusion for RGB-D indoor semantic segmentation. In: CVPR (2017)
6. Couprie, C., Farabet, C., Najman, L., Lecun, Y.: Indoor semantic segmentation using depth information. In: ICLR (2013)
7. Dai, J., et al.: Deformable convolutional networks. In: ICCV (2017)
8. Eigen, D., Fergus, R.: Predicting depth, surface normals and semantic labels with a common multi-scale convolutional architecture. In: ICCV (2015)
9. Gupta, S., Girshick, R., Arbeláez, P., Malik, J.: Learning rich features from RGB-D images for object detection and segmentation. In: Fleet, D., Pajdla, T., Schiele, B., Tuytelaars, T. (eds.) ECCV 2014. LNCS, vol. 8695, pp. 345–360. Springer, Cham (2014). https://doi.org/10.1007/978-3-319-10584-0_23
10. Hazirbas, C., Ma, L., Domokos, C., Cremers, D.: FuseNet: incorporating depth into semantic segmentation via fusion-based CNN architecture. In: Lai, S.-H., Lepetit, V., Nishino, K., Sato, Y. (eds.) ACCV 2016. LNCS, vol. 10111, pp. 213–228. Springer, Cham (2017). https://doi.org/10.1007/978-3-319-54181-5_14
11. He, K., Zhang, X., Ren, S., Sun, J.: Deep residual learning for image recognition. In: CVPR (2016)

12. He, Y., Chiu, W.C., Keuper, M., Fritz, M.: STD2P: RGBD semantic segmentation using spatio-temporal data-driven pooling. In: CVPR (2017)
13. Huang, Q., Wang, W., Neumann, U.: Recurrent slice networks for 3D segmentation on point clouds. In: CVPR (2018)
14. Huang, Q., Wang, W., Zhou, K., You, S., Neumann, U.: Scene labeling using gated recurrent units with explicit long range conditioning. arXiv preprint arXiv:1611.07485 (2016)
15. Jaderberg, M., Simonyan, K., Zisserman, A., kavukcuoglu, k.: Spatial transformer networks. In: NIPS (2015)
16. Janoch, A., et al.: A category-level 3-d object dataset: Putting the kinect to work. In: ICCV workshop (2011)
17. Khan, S.H., Bennamoun, M., Sohel, F., Togneri, R.: Geometry driven semantic labeling of indoor scenes. In: Fleet, D., Pajdla, T., Schiele, B., Tuytelaars, T. (eds.) ECCV 2014. LNCS, vol. 8689, pp. 679–694. Springer, Cham (2014). https://doi.org/10.1007/978-3-319-10590-1_44
18. Li, Z., Gan, Y., Liang, X., Yu, Y., Cheng, H., Lin, L.: LSTM-CF: unifying context modeling and fusion with LSTMs for RGB-D scene labeling. In: Leibe, B., Matas, J., Sebe, N., Welling, M. (eds.) ECCV 2016. LNCS, vol. 9906, pp. 541–557. Springer, Cham (2016). https://doi.org/10.1007/978-3-319-46475-6_34
19. Lin, D., Chen, G., Cohen-Or, D., Heng, P.A., Huang, H.: Cascaded feature network for semantic segmentation of RGB-D images. In: ICCV (2017)
20. Lin, G., Milan, A., Shen, C., Reid, I.: RefineNet: multi-path refinement networks for high-resolution semantic segmentation. In: CVPR (2017)
21. Ma, L., Stueckler, J., Kerl, C., Cremers, D.: Multi-view deep learning for consistent semantic mapping with RGB-D cameras. In: IROS (2017)
22. Silberman, N., Hoiem, D., Kohli, P., Fergus, R.: Indoor segmentation and support inference from RGBD images. In: Fitzgibbon, A., Lazebnik, S., Perona, P., Sato, Y., Schmid, C. (eds.) ECCV 2012. LNCS, vol. 7576, pp. 746–760. Springer, Heidelberg (2012). https://doi.org/10.1007/978-3-642-33715-4_54
23. Park, S.J., Hong, K.S., Lee, S.: RDFNet: RGB-D multi-level residual feature fusion for indoor semantic segmentation. In: ICCV (2017)
24. Qi, C.R., Su, H., Mo, K., Guibas, L.J.: Pointnet: deep learning on point sets for 3d classification and segmentation. In: CVPR (2017)
25. Qi, C.R., Yi, L., Su, H., Guibas, L.J.: Pointnet++: deep hierarchical feature learning on point sets in a metric space. In: NIPS (2017)
26. Qi, X., Liao, R., Jia, J., Fidler, S., Urtasun, R.: 3d graph neural networks for RGBD semantic segmentation. In: ICCV (2017)
27. Ren, X., Bo, L., Fox, D.: RGB-(D) scene labeling: features and algorithms. In: CVPR (2012)
28. Shelhamer, E., Long, J., Darrell, T.: Fully convolutional networks for semantic segmentation. In: PAMI (2016)
29. Song, S., Lichtenberg, S.P., Xiao, J.: SUN RGB-D: A RGB-D scene understanding benchmark suite. In: CVPR (2015)
30. Song, S., Xiao, J.: Deep sliding shapes for amodal 3D object detection in RGB-D images. In: CVPR (2016)
31. Song, S., Yu, F., Zeng, A., Chang, A.X., Savva, M., Funkhouser, T.: Semantic scene completion from a single depth image. In: CVPR (2017)
32. Wang, J., Wang, Z., Tao, D., See, S., Wang, G.: Learning common and specific features for RGB-D semantic segmentation with deconvolutional networks. In: Leibe, B., Matas, J., Sebe, N., Welling, M. (eds.) ECCV 2016. LNCS, vol. 9909, pp. 664–679. Springer, Cham (2016). https://doi.org/10.1007/978-3-319-46454-1_40

33. Wang, W., Huang, Q., You, S., Yang, C., Neumann, U.: Shape inpainting using 3d generative adversarial network and recurrent convolutional networks. In: ICCV (2017)
34. Wang, W., Wang, N., Wu, X., You, S., Yang, C., Neumann, U.: Self-paced cross-modality transfer learning for efficient road segmentation. In: ICRA (2017)
35. Wang, W., Yu, R., Huang, Q., Neumann, U.: SGPN: similarity group proposal network for 3d point cloud instance segmentation. In: CVPR (2018)
36. Yu, F., Koltun, V.: Multi-scale context aggregation by dilated convolutions. In: ICLR (2016)
37. Zhou, B., Zhao, H., Puig, X., Fidler, S., Barriuso, A., Torralba, A.: Scene parsing through ADE20K dataset. In: CVPR (2017)

CAR-Net: Clairvoyant Attentive Recurrent Network

Amir Sadeghian[1](✉), Ferdinand Legros[1], Maxime Voisin[1], Ricky Vesel[2], Alexandre Alahi[3], and Silvio Savarese[1]

[1] Stanford University, Stanford, USA
{amirabs,flegros,maxime.voisin,ssilvio}@stanford.edu
[2] Race Optimal, Cleveland, USA
vesel.rw@gmail.com
[3] Ecole Polytechnique Federale de Lausanne (EPFL), Lausanne, Switzerland
alexandre.alahi@epfl.ch

Abstract. We present an interpretable framework for path prediction that leverages dependencies between agents' behaviors and their spatial navigation environment. We exploit two sources of information: the past motion trajectory of the agent of interest and a wide top-view image of the navigation scene. We propose a Clairvoyant Attentive Recurrent Network (CAR-Net) that learns where to look in a large image of the scene when solving the path prediction task. Our method can attend to any area, or combination of areas, within the raw image (*e.g.*, road intersections) when predicting the trajectory of the agent. This allows us to visualize fine-grained semantic elements of navigation scenes that influence the prediction of trajectories. To study the impact of space on agents' trajectories, we build a new dataset made of top-view images of hundreds of scenes (Formula One racing tracks) where agents' behaviors are heavily influenced by known areas in the images (*e.g.*, upcoming turns). CAR-Net successfully attends to these salient regions. Additionally, CAR-Net reaches state-of-the-art accuracy on the standard trajectory forecasting benchmark, Stanford Drone Dataset (SDD). Finally, we show CAR-Net's ability to generalize to unseen scenes.

1 Introduction

Path prediction consists in predicting the future positions of agents (*e.g.*, humans or vehicles) within an environment. It applies to a wide range of domains from autonomous driving vehicles [1] and social robot navigation [2–4], to abnormal behavior detection in surveillance [5–10]. Observable cues relevant to path prediction can be grouped into dynamic and static information. The former captures the previous motion of all agents within the scene (past trajectories). The latter consists of the static scene surrounding agents [11–13]. In this work, we want to leverage the static scene context to perform path prediction. The task is formulated as follows: given the past trajectory of an agent (x-y coordinates of

---

F. Legros and M. Voisin—Equally contributed.

© Springer Nature Switzerland AG 2018
V. Ferrari et al. (Eds.): ECCV 2018, LNCS 11215, pp. 162–180, 2018.
https://doi.org/10.1007/978-3-030-01252-6_10

past few seconds) and a large visual image of the environment (top-view of the scene), we want to forecast the trajectory of the agent over the next few seconds. Our model should learn where to look within a large visual input to enhance its prediction performance (see Fig. 1).

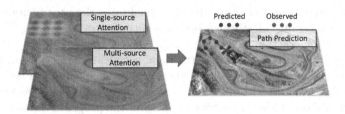

Fig. 1. CAR-Net is a deep attention-based model that combines two attention mechanisms for path prediction.

Predicting agents' trajectories while taking into account the static scene context is a challenging problem. It requires understanding complex interactions between agents and space, and encoding these interactions into the path prediction model. Moreover, scene-specific cues are often sparse and small within the visual input, *e.g.*, a traffic sign within the scene. Finally, these cues might be far from the agent of interest.

Recent research in computer vision has successfully addressed some of the challenges in path prediction. Kitani et al. [14] have demonstrated that the semantic segmentation of the environment (*e.g.*, location of sidewalks and grass areas) helps to predict pedestrian trajectories. Ballan *et al.* [15] modeled human-space interactions using navigation maps that encode previously observed scene-specific motion patterns. These methods rely on scene semantic information collected in advance. Instead, our method relies on raw images, which are easier to obtain, and our method has the potential to infer finer-grained scene semantics and functional properties of the environment. To this end, Lee *et al.* [16] have used raw images to predict agents' trajectories. However, their method does not provide a way to understand what visual information within the scene is "used" by the model to predict future trajectories.

We address the limitations of previous path prediction methods by proposing a visual attention model that leverages agent-space interactions and enhances prediction accuracy. Inspired by the recent use of attention models and neural networks in image captioning [17], machine translation [18], knowledge bases [19,20], and object recognition [21,22], we introduce the first visual attention model that can predict the future trajectory of an agent while attending to the salient regions of the scene. Our method is able to attend to any region, or collection of regions, in the image. Attention based models can be broadly categorized into single and multi-source attention models. Single source attention models (*e.g.*, DRAW [21,23]) attend to features extracted from a single area of the image, while multi-source attention models (*e.g.*, soft attention from [17]) use a combination of features from all areas of the image. In this paper, we propose CAR-Net, a deep neural network architecture which predicts future trajectories - hence being *Clairvoyant* - by processing raw top-view images with a visual *Attentive Recurrent* component. Our attention model combines both single-source and multi-source attention mechanisms. By leveraging both attention mechanisms, our prediction framework makes use of a wider spectrum of agent-space dependencies. Moreover, CAR-Net is simple to implement and train. Hence, it facilitates the use of trajectory prediction in a wide range of other vision tasks such as object tracking [5], activity forecasting [24] and action localization [25].

To study if our proposed architecture is able to learn observable agent-space correlations, we build a new dataset where agents' behaviors are largely influenced by known regions within a scene (*e.g.*, a curve in the road). As opposed to other popular datasets for trajectory prediction, the proposed dataset allows to understand the effect of the environment on agents' future trajectories. Because the dataset is composed of static scenes, future trajectories are not affected by confounding factors such as the behavior of other agents. This disentangles the contributions of scene semantic information and of other agents' interactions, in the task of path prediction. To build this new dataset, we have collected more than two hundred real-world Formula One racing tracks and computed the vehicles' optimal paths given the tracks' curvatures using equations in [26]. In this context, the geometry of the road causes the vehicle to speed up or down, and steer. Our attention mechanism succeeds at leveraging elements of the tracks, and effectively predicts the optimal paths of vehicles on these tracks. As part of our contributions, this new dataset for path prediction and learning agent-space correlations will be released publicly. We further show that the accuracy of our method outperforms previous approaches on the Stanford Drone Dataset (SDD), a publicly available trajectory forecasting benchmark where multiple classes of agents (*e.g.*, humans, bicyclists, or buses) navigate outdoor scenes. CAR-Net is an intuitive and simple model that achieves state-of-the-art results for path prediction, while enabling the visualization of semantic elements that influenced prediction thanks to attention mechanisms.

2   Related Work

Trajectory Forecasting. Path prediction given the dynamic content of a scene has been extensively studied with approaches such as Kalman filters [27], linear regressions [28], or non-linear Gaussian Processes [2,29–31]. Pioneering work from Helbing and Molnar [32–34] presented a pedestrian motion model with attractive and repulsive forces referred to as the Social Force model. All these prior works have difficulty in modeling complex interactions. Following the recent success of Recurrent Neural Networks (RNN) for sequence prediction tasks, Alahi *et al.* [35,36] proposed a model which learns human movement from data to predict future trajectories. Recently, Robicquet *et al.* [37,38] proposed the concept of social sensitivity with a social force based model to improve path forecasting.

Such models suffice for scenarios with few agent-agent interactions, but they do not consider agent-space interactions. In contrast, our method can handle more complex environments where agents' behaviors are severely influenced by scene context (*e.g.*, drivable road vs trees and grass).

Recent works have studied how to effectively leverage static scenes in the path prediction task. Kitani *et al.* [14] used semantic knowledge of the scene to forecast plausible paths for a pedestrian using inverse optimal control (IOC). Walker *et al.* [1] predicted the behavior of generic agents (*e.g.*, vehicles) in a scene given a large collection of videos, but in a limited number of scenarios. Ballan *et al.* [15] learned scene-specific motion patterns and applied them to novel scenes with an image-based similarity function. Unfortunately, none of these methods can provide predictions using raw images of scenes. Recently, Lee *et al.* [16] proposed a method for path prediction given the scene context using raw images. However, all these methods have limited interpretability. Our method is instead designed for this specific purpose: providing an intuition as to why certain paths are predicted given the context of the scene.

Visual Attention. Related work from Xu and Gregor [17,23] introduces attention based models that learn to attend the salient objects related to the task of interest. Xu et al. [17], present soft and hard attention mechanisms that attend to the entire image. Soft attention applies a mask of weights to the image's feature maps. Since the associated training operation is differentiable, it has been applied to a wide range of tasks. The hard attention mechanism is not differentiable and it must be trained by Reinforcement Learning. The non-differentiability of this method has led to scarce applications.

Other attention models apply dimensionality reduction to the image. Their goal is to accumulate information over a sequence of partial glimpses of the image. The recurrent attention model introduced in [21] attends to a sequence of crops of the image. It has been used in many tasks such as digit classification and person identification [23,39,40]. Visual attention models have also been widely applied to many other applications such as image classification [41], image captioning [17,42], and video classification [43]. Inspired by these works, we hereby use visual attention mechanisms in our model to perform trajectory prediction.

3   CAR-Net

Scene context is necessary to predict the future behavior of agents. For instance, a cyclist approaching a roundabout changes his path to avoid collision. Such deviations in trajectories cannot be predicted by only observing the agent's past positions. This motivates us to build a model that can leverage observable scene context while predicting an agent's future path. We introduce CAR-Net, a deep attention-based model for path prediction. It performs trajectory prediction using raw top-view images of scenes and past trajectories of agents. CAR-Net is able to attend to the most relevant parts of the input image. In this section we first describe the overall architecture of our model. Then, we explain our visual attention module.

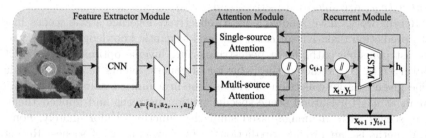

Fig. 2. Overview of CAR-Net architecture. Note that "//" block is concatenation operation.

3.1   Overall Architecture

The objective of our model is to predict the future path of an agent given its past trajectory and a top-view image of the scene. Our model uses a *feature extractor* to derive feature vectors from the raw image (Fig. 2). Then, a *visual attention module* computes a context vector c_t representing the salient areas of the image to attend at time t. Finally, in the *recurrent module*, a long short-term memory (LSTM) network [44] generates the future position of the agent (x_{t+1}, y_{t+1}) at every time step, conditioned on the context vector c_t, on the previous hidden state h_t, and on the previously generated position of the agent (x_t, y_t). Our model is able to capture agent-space interactions by combining both the scene context vector and the past trajectory of the agent.

3.2   Feature Extractor Module

We extract feature maps from static top-view images using a Convolutional Neural Network (CNN). We use VGGnet-19 [45] pre-trained on ImageNet [46] and fine-tuned on the task of scene segmentation as described in [47]. Fine-tuning VGG on scene segmentation enables the CNN to extract image features that can identify obstacles, roads, sidewalks, and other scene semantics that are essential for trajectory prediction. We use the output of the 5th convolutional layer as image features. The CNN outputs $L = N \times N$ feature vectors, $A = \{a_1, ..., a_L\}$, of dimension D, where N and D are the size and the number of feature maps outputted by the 5th convolutional layer, respectively. Each feature vector corresponds to a certain region of the image. Figure 2 depicts the feature extractor module.

3.3   Visual Attention Module

Given a high-dimensional input image of a scene, we want our model to focus on smaller, discriminative regions of this input image. Using a visual attention method, the most relevant areas of the image are extracted while irrelevant parts are ignored. The general attention process works as follows. A layer ϕ within the attention mechanism takes as input the previous hidden state h_t of the LSTM and outputs a vector $\phi(h_t)$ that is used by the attention mechanism to predict the important areas of the image. The vector $\phi(h_t)$ is then applied to feature vectors A (through a function f_{att}), resulting in a context vector c_{t+1} that contains the salient image features at time step $t + 1$:

$$c_{t+1} = f_{att}(A, \phi(h_t)). \tag{1}$$

Our visual attention module can be substituted with any differentiable attention mechanism. Moreover, it can use a combination of several attention methods. Provided that f_{att} and ϕ are differentiable, the whole architecture is trainable by standard back-propagation. We propose three variants for the differentiable attention module that are easily trainable. The first method extracts visual information from multiple areas of the image with a soft attention mechanism. The second method extracts local visual information from a single cropped area of the image with an attention mechanism inspired by [23]. We refer to the first and second methods as *multi-source* and *single-source* attention mechanisms, respectively. Finally, the attention module of CAR-Net combines both attention mechanisms, allowing our prediction framework to learn a wider spectrum of scene dependencies.

CAR-Net Attention. Learning agent-space interactions, and encoding them into the path prediction model is a challenging task. The scene-specific cues are sometimes sparse and spread throughout the entire image far away from the agent, or small within a specific area of the image. Single and multi-source attention mechanisms attend respectively to localized and scattered visual cues in the scene. When the relevant visual cues are scattered all over the input image, a multi-source attention method can successfully extract a combination of features from multiple key areas of the image. In contrast, when the relevant visual information is localized in one particular area of the image, single-source attention methods are a good fit to attend to that specific region. Note that multi-source attention does not necessarily reduce to single-source attention and they complement each other.

To leverage both local and scattered visual cues in path prediction, the core attention module in CAR-Net combines the two context vectors obtained from single and multi-source attention mechanisms. The combination is done by concatenating the context vectors from single-source c_t^{ss} and multi-source c_t^{ms} attention mechanisms, $c_t = [c_t^{ss}, c_t^{ms}]$. The attention module in Fig. 2 depicts the process. More technical details about multi and single-source attention mechanisms can be found in Sec. 3.3. CAR-Net outperforms both single and multi-source attention mechanisms, proving its ability to leverage the strengths of the two attention mechanisms.

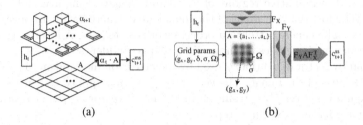

(a)   (b)

Fig. 3. Our multi and single-source attention mechanism

Multi-source Attention. The multi-source attention mechanism applies weights to all spatial areas of the scene based on their importance, and outputs a context vector containing relevant scene context from multiple regions of the image. First, the weights matrix α_{t+1} is calculated by passing the hidden state h_t through a fully connected layer ϕ with weight W_{ms} and bias b_{ms}. Later, the context vector c_{t+1}^{ms} is calculated by element-wise product of the weight matrix α_{t+1} and the feature maps A. Figure 3(a) and Eq. 2 show the entire process:

$$c_{t+1}^{ms} = f_{att}(A, \phi(h_t))$$
$$= a \cdot \phi(h_t) = A \cdot \alpha_{t+1}$$
$$\alpha_{t+1} = softmax(W_{ms}h_t + b_{ms}). \tag{2}$$

The soft (multi-source) attention mechanism described in [17] calculates the weight matrix α_{t+1} conditioned on both the previous hidden vector and the features of the image. However, our α_{t+1} relies only on the previous hidden vector. The distinction is important because for path prediction tasks, we do not have the future images of a scene. Moreover, it reduces the computation cost without impacting the performance of the model.

Single-Source Attention. The single-source attention mechanism illustrated in Fig. 3(b) attends to a single local area in the image. To do so, we adapt the DRAW attention mechanism - which was initially designed for the unsupervised setting of digit generation [23] - to the supervised learning setting of path prediction. The single-source attention mechanism attends to the region of the image defined by a local grid of N Gaussians. The center (g_X, g_Y) of the grid, the stride δ of the grid, and the variance σ of all N Gaussians, are predicted by the model at each time step $t + 1$ by mapping linearly the hidden state h_t to attention parameters $(g_X, g_Y, \delta, \sigma)$. The stride of the grid controls the "zoom" of the local area attended by the model. As the stride gets larger, the grid of

Gaussians covers a larger area of the original image. The exact position (ν_x^i, ν_y^i) of each Gaussian i on the grid is found using the center and the stride of the grid as in Eq. 3.

$$\nu_X^i = g_X + (i - N/2 - 0.5)\delta$$
$$\nu_Y^i = g_Y + (i - N/2 - 0.5)\delta \tag{3}$$

The resulting grid of Gaussians defines two filter-bank matrices F_X and F_Y, using Eq. 4. Using these filter-bank matrices, the single-source attention mechanism is able to attend the region of the image defined by the local grid of Gaussian: F_X and F_Y are convoluted with the feature maps A of the image, as in Eq. 5. The resulting context vector c_{t+1}^{ss} contains scene context from to the single local area of the image corresponding to the grid of Gaussians.

$$F_X[i, a] = \frac{1}{Z_X} exp\left(-\frac{(a - \nu_X^i)^2}{2\sigma^2} \right)$$

$$F_Y[j, b] = \frac{1}{Z_Y} exp\left(-\frac{(b - \nu_Y^j)^2}{2\sigma^2} \right). \tag{4}$$

$$c_{t+1}^{ss} = f_{att}(A, \phi(h_t)) = F_X(h_t)^T A F_Y(h_t). \tag{5}$$

Note that indexes (i, j) refer to Gaussians in the grid and that indexes (a, b) refer to locations in the feature maps. The normalization constants Z_x, Z_y ensure $\sum_a F_X[i, a] = 1$ and $\sum_b F_Y[j, b] = 1$.

3.4 Implementation Details

We trained the LSTM and the attention module from scratch with the Adam optimizer [48], a mini-batch size of 128, and a learning rate of 0.001 sequentially decreased every 10 epochs by a factor of 10. All models are trained for 100 epochs, on the L2 distance between ground-truth and predicted trajectories. As in many sequence prediction tasks, the training and testing process is slightly different. At training time, the ground-truth positions are fed as inputs to the LSTM. In contrast, at test time, the predictions of positions (x_t, y_t) are re-injected as inputs to the LSTM at the next time step.

4 Experiments

We presented CAR-Net, a framework that provides accurate path predictions by leveraging spatial scene contexts. We perform a thorough comparison of our method to state-of-the-art techniques along with comprehensive ablation experiments. We then present insights on the interpretability of our method. We finally show the generality and robustness of CAR-Net by experimenting with different datasets.

4.1 Data

We tested our models on the following three datasets that all include trajectory data and top-view images of navigation scenes.

Stanford Drone Dataset (SDD). [37] To show that CAR-Net achieves state-of-the-art performance on path prediction, we tested the model on SDD, a standard benchmark for path prediction [16,35,37]. This large-scale dataset consists of top-view videos of various targets (*e.g.*, pedestrians, bicyclists, cars) navigating in many real-world outdoor environments in a university campus (20 different scenes). Trajectories were split into segments of 20 time steps each (8s total), yielding approximately 230 K trajectory segments. Each segment is composed of 8 past positions (3.2s), which are fed to the network as sequential inputs, and 12 future positions (4.8s) used to evaluate predictions. This is the standard temporal setup for path prediction on SDD. We use raw images to extract visual features, without any prior semantic labeling. We adopt the standard benchmark dataset split for SDD.

Formula One Dataset. Studying the influence of space on agents' trajectories is complex since agents' behaviors are influenced not only by the semantics of the navigation scene, but also by other factors such as interactions with other agents. For instance, a pedestrian could stop as they meet an acquaintance. We release a Formula One (F1) dataset, composed of real-world car racing tracks and their associated trajectories. This dataset provides a controlled environment to evaluate how well models can extract useful spatial information for trajectory prediction. In the F1 dataset, the agents' behaviors can be largely explained by the geometry of the tracks (*e.g.* the curve of an upcoming turn). As opposed to other popular datasets for trajectory prediction (*e.g.* SDD), F1 dataset allows for evaluations in static settings where future trajectories are not affected by confounding factors such as the behavior of other agents. This disentangles the contributions of the spatial information and of other agents interactions in the task of trajectory prediction.

The top-view racing track images were obtained from Google Maps. On top of them, we simulated trajectories corresponding to an optimal driving pattern, referred to as "optimal trajectories" and computed with the equations presented in [26]. We used hand-segmented roads as inputs for the computations of optimal trajectories. Note that those optimal trajectories illustrate complex navigational patterns that depend on far away scene dependencies. The F1 dataset includes 250 tracks and more than 100 K trajectories from different cities of Brazil, Canada, Columbia, Mexico, France, USA and other countries and will be available to the public for research purposes. Sample tracks are shown in Fig. 4. Car trajectories are split into 24 time step segments: 8 input past positions and 16 future positions used for evaluation. We opted for 16 future positions for evaluation, rather than 12 like in SDD, since the prediction task is simpler due to stronger agent-space dependencies. We split racing tracks in the F1 dataset into an 80% train set, 10% validation set, and 10% test set. The test racing tracks are totally unseen locations, they do not overlap with the training nor validation set racing tracks.

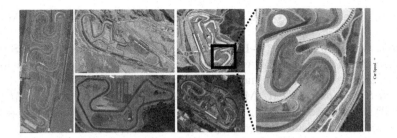

Fig. 4. Examples of scenes captured in the proposed F1 dataset. We annotated each track with the associated optimal racing trajectory.

Car-Racing Dataset [49]. In order to derive further insights on how agent-space dependencies influence our model's predictions, we experimented with the Car-Racing dataset, a simpler racing track dataset that we synthesized. The Car-Racing dataset is composed of 3,000 tracks of various curvatures and road widths that we generated with the Car-Racing-v0 simulator from the OpenAI gym. We simulated (1) the optimal trajectories for each circuits, and (2) trajectories following the middle of the road at constant speed. Racing trajectories were split into 24 time-step segments, 8 input past positions and 16 future positions used for evaluation, yielding approximately 500 K segments. We split racing tracks in this dataset into an 80% train set, 10% validation set, and 10% test set, which do not overlap.

Optimal Racing Trajectories. The ideal racing trajectory used in Car-Racing and F1 dataset is defined as the trajectory around a track that allows a given vehicle to traverse the track in minimum time. To calculate these optimal race trajectories, we segmented the roads by hand and computed the associated optimal racing paths using physics simulation. These simulations are based on 2D physical models from [26,50].

4.2   Evaluation Metrics and Baselines

We measure the performance of our models on the path prediction task using the following metrics: (i) average displacement error - the mean L2 distance (ML2) over all predicted points of the predicted trajectory and the ground-truth points, (ii) final L2 distance error (FL2) - the L2 distance between the final predicted position and the final ground-truth position.

To perform an ablation study in Sect. 4.3 and show that our model achieves state-of-the-art performance in Sect. 4.4, we compare CAR-Net to the following baselines and previous methods from literature:

- *Linear model* (**Lin.**) We use an off-the-shelf linear predictor to extrapolate trajectories under the assumption of linear velocity.
- *Social Forces* (**SF**) and *Social-LSTM* (**S-LSTM**). We use the implementation of the Social Forces model from [51] where several factors such as group affinity have been modeled. Since the code for Social-LSTM is not available

we compare our models with a self-implemented version of Social-LSTM from [35].

- *Trajectory only LSTM* (**T-LSTM**) and *Whole Image LSTM* (**I-LSTM**). These models are simplified versions of our model where we remove the image information and attention module, respectively.
- *Multi-Source only LSTM* (**MS-LSTM**) and *Single-Source only LSTM* (**SS-LSTM**). Our models using only multi-source attention and single-source attention mechanisms, respectively.
- *DESIRE*. A deep IOC framework model from [16]. We report the performance of the model *DESIRE-SI-IT0 Best* with top 1 sample.

Table 1. Quantitative results of our methods on the Car-Racing dataset with middle and optimal trajectories and the F1 dataset. We report the Mean L2 error (ML2) and the Final L2 error (FL2). CAR-Net outperforms all models by combining single-source and multi-source attention outputs.

Model	Car-racing middle		Car-racing optimal		Formula 1 optimal	
	ML2	FL2	ML2	FL2	ML2	FL2
T-LSTM	10.4	15.5	5.84	10.2	21.2	41.3
I-LSTM	9.71	14.1	5.62	9.5	20.8	40.1
MS-LSTM	7.35	12.7	5.30	8.71	18.9	37.8
SS-LSTM	6.36	9.91	4.64	7.63	14.7	28.9
CAR-Net	**5.0**	**8.87**	**3.58**	**6.79**	**13.3**	**25.8**

4.3   Ablation Study

We performed an ablation study to show that prediction accuracy improves when combining single-source and multi-source attention mechanisms, which suggests that they extract complementary semantic cues from raw images. We analyzed the performances of baseline models and of CAR-Net on the racing track datasets (Car-Racing and Formula One datasets). We present our results in Table 1.

We observe similar results on both racing track datasets. First, I-LSTM only slightly outperforms T-LSTM. This seems to be because the large feature maps extracted from each racing track are too complex to significantly complement the dynamic cues extracted from agents' past trajectories. Second, attention models (MS-LSTM, SS-LSTM, CAR-Net) greatly outperform I-LSTM. This suggests that visual attention mechanisms enhance performance by attending to specific areas of the navigation scenes. We show in Sect. 4.5 that these attended areas are relevant semantic elements of navigation scenes - *e.g.* an upcoming turn. Note that SS-LSTM achieves lower errors than MS-LSTM. This is due to racing track images being large, and relevant semantic cues being mostly located close to the car. Finally, CAR-Net outperforms both MS-LSTM and SS-LSTM on all datasets. We think it is due to robustly combining the outputs of single-source and multi-source attention mechanisms.

General Remarks. For the Car-Racing dataset, models perform better on the prediction of optimal trajectories than middle trajectories. This is due to the average pixel distance between consecutive positions being larger for middle trajectories than for the optimal trajectories. Also, we trained the models on 1 K tracks for middle trajectories, instead of 3 K for optimal trajectories.

Table 2. Performance of different baselines on predicting 12 future positions from 8 past positions on SDD. We report the Mean L2 error (ML2) and the Final L2 error (FL2) in pixel space of the original image. Our method, CAR-Net, achieves by far the lowest error.

Model	ML2	FL2
Lin.	37.11	63.51
SF [51]	36.48	58.14
DESIRE-SI-IT0 Best [16]	35.73	63.35
S-LSTM [35]	31.19	56.97
T-LSTM	31.96	55.27
I-LSTM	30.81	54.21
MS-LSTM	27.38	52.69
SS-LSTM	29.20	63.27
CAR-Net	**25.72**	**51.80**

4.4   Trajectory Forecasting Benchmark

CAR-Net outperforms state-of-the-art methods on the task of predicting 12 future positions (4.8s of motion) from 8 past positions (3.2s) on SDD benchmark, as reported in Table 2 (both lower ML2 and FL2 error). Note that the performance of *DESIRE-SI-IT0 Best* in [16] is provided for the task of predicting 4s of motion. We linearly interpolated this performance to obtain its performance on predicting 4.8s of motion and reported the interpolated number in Table 2.

The T-LSTM baseline achieves a lower ML2 error than Linear, SF, and S-LSTM models. However, the gaps between the FL2 errors of T-LSTM and SF or S-LSTM models are narrow, suggesting that the T-LSTM model tends to be relatively inaccurate when predicting the last future time-steps. We observe that S-LSTM performs poorly compared to MS-LSTM - especially in terms of FL2 error. We believe multi-source attention performs better due to scattered key semantics in SDD scenes. In all experiments, CAR-Net outperforms baselines methods regarding all metrics. Moreover, our model outperforms DESIRE with top 1 sample (DESIRE Best). This is consistent with [16] suggesting that regression-based models such as CAR-Net are a better fit for use cases where regression accuracy matters more than generating a probabilistic output.

Generalization to Unseen Locations. CAR-Net generalizes to unseen locations in all datasets. This suggests that our model leverages observable scene features, rather than location-specific information. First, CAR-Net achieves better accuracy than other baseline methods on F1 test set, which is exclusively composed of unseen F1 racing tracks. Second, 9/17 (53%) locations in the SDD test set are unseen. The remaining 8/17 (47%) locations in the SDD test set are visually similar to training locations (*seen* locations). We evaluate our trained model's performance on the seen and on the unseen SDD test locations, separately. CAR-Net achieves similar performances on both *seen* and *unseen* test SDD locations - mean L2 distance of 23.87 and 26.93 pixels on the seen and unseen locations, respectively - proving its ability to generalize to unseen SDD locations.

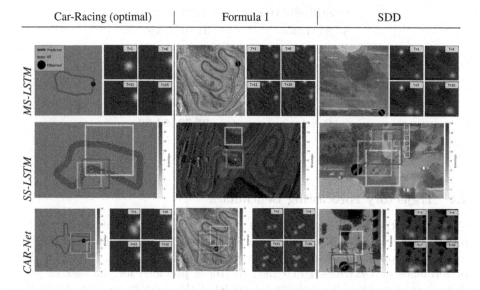

Fig. 5. Qualitative results of MS-LSTM, SS-LSTM, and CAR-Net (rows) predicting trajectories on Car-Racing, F1, and SDD datasets (columns). CAR-Net successfully leverages both single-source and multi-source attention mechanisms to predict future paths.

Quantitative Analysis of the Impact of Agent-Space Interactions. To analyze CAR-Net's ability to leverage agent-space interactions, we split the test set of SDD into scenes whose geometries are complex and likely to influence the trajectories of agents (*e.g.* scenes with grass lawns, pavements, buildings), and scenes whose observable context varies little across the top-view image (*e.g.* an open field with no roads, grass, etc.). We refer to these scenes as semantically *complex* and *simple*, respectively. We tested CAR-Net (that uses the scene context) and T-LSTM (that does not use any scene context) on SDD's semantically complex and simple test scenes. Our results are reported in Table 3. CAR-Net and T-LSTM achieve similar performance on *simple* scenes, where scene semantics should not typically affect the trajectories of agents. In contrast, CAR-Net achieves much better performance than T-LSTM on *complex* scenes, where scene semantics are likely to highly influence the trajectories of agents. This experiment shows CAR-Net's ability to successfully leverage scene context over T-LSTM.

Table 3. Performance of T-LSTM and CAR-Net on SDD semantically complex and simple scenes. We report the Mean L2 error (ML2) in pixels space of the original image. Our method, CAR-Net, is able to effectively use the scene context to predict future trajectories.

Model	Complex	Simple
T-LSTM	31.31	**30.48**
CAR-Net	**24.32**	**30.92**

4.5 Qualitative Analysis

Visualization Details. In all figures, ground-truth and predicted trajectories are plotted in red and blue, respectively. Past positions are circled in black. We display the weight maps of the multi-source attention mechanism over time by white highlights. The single-source attention grids are also displayed over time: yellow dots represent the centers of the grids, and rectangles represent bounding boxes of the attention grid.

Short-Term Predictions. Figure 5 shows sample trajectories predicted by our models on the datasets used in our experiments. On racing track datasets (Car-Racing and F1), we expect the region of the road close to the car to contain salient semantic elements. We observe that MS-LSTM successfully attends to the area around the car. On the mid-left and mid-center figures, we observe that the attention grid of SS-LSTM is initially off (white rectangle), before jumping to a small area close to the car, thereby identifying the relevant visual information. As shown in the bottom row, CAR-Net focuses on a narrow region of the image close to the car, using the single-source attention. It is also able to attend to further areas such as the next curve, using multi-source attention, proving its ability to leverage both attention mechanisms on racing track datasets.

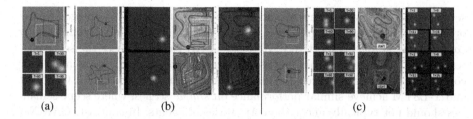

(a)   (b)   (c)

Fig. 6. Qualitative analysis: (a) Very long-term path prediction on the Car-Racing dataset. Predictions stay on track, showing that our model successfully uses scene context for path prediction. (b) By manually moving the attention to other parts of the image, we show that prediction heavily depends on the scene geometry. (c) When manually imposing the initial car position to be off-road, the predicted trajectory comes back on the road using the visual cues.

On SDD, where key semantic elements are scattered, the multi-source attention mechanism successfully attends to multiple relevant visual areas (top and bottom right images). We observe that on SDD the multi-source attention attends to regions that get larger over time. This may reflect a growing prediction uncertainty. The single-source attention grid attends to areas further ahead of the agent on SDD, compared to racing track datasets (*e.g.*, the mid-right figure). It shows that attending only close to the agent would not capture all salient semantics so attention grids reach ahead.

Very Long-Term Trajectory Prediction on Car-Racing Dataset. In this section we present qualitative results on the task of predicting future positions beyond 4.8s on the Car-Racing dataset, as a complementary result. We do not claim that our model achieves similar path prediction performance beyond 4.8s on real-world datasets. Figure 6(a) shows CAR-Net's predictions of 100 consecutive time steps of a middle trajectory on the Car-Racing dataset. We observe that predictions remain on the road over time. Note that the initial few positions of the agent are not helpful to predict future trajectories on very long time intervals (*e.g.* after a couple turns from the initial position). The fact that the predictions stay on the road proves that CAR-Net successfully extracts semantic understanding from the scene context in this case. We observe that both single and multi-source attention mechanisms are consistent with the predicted positions over time, as they attend to the salient parts of the scene - *e.g.*, the curve in front of the car.

Qualitative Analysis of Agent-Space Interactions. We further investigate the ability of our model to leverage agent-space dependencies on racing track datasets. First, we show that road geometry has a large influence on the prediction of future positions. As shown in Fig. 6(b) left, on the Car-Racing dataset, we manually place the visual attention on an irrelevant part of the road which is oriented along the top-right direction. We observe that the model predicts positions following a similar top-right axis, while the expected trajectory without any scene information would follow a top-left direction. We observe similar behaviors in the bottom-left image of Fig. 6(b). The same experiment on the real-world F1 dataset results in similar behaviors, as shown in Fig. 6(b) right.

Second, we study whether CAR-Net is robust enough to recover from errors or perturbations by manually setting the agent's past positions outside the road. The left image in Fig. 6(c) shows the result of this experiment on the Car-Racing dataset, using the model trained on the middle trajectories. The predicted future trajectory successfully comes back on the road and remains stable afterwards, showing our model's ability to recover from strong prediction errors on Car-Racing dataset. The right image in Fig. 6(c) shows a similar experiment on the real-world F1 dataset. Since this dataset is more challenging than the Car-Racing dataset, we apply a smaller perturbation to the past trajectory of the agent, moving it slightly off the road. We observe that this perturbation does not affect the predicted trajectory which follows the road.

5   Conclusions

In this paper, we tackle the trajectory prediction task with CAR-Net, a deep attention-based model that processes past trajectory positions and top-view images of navigation scenes. We propose an attention mechanism that successfully leverages multiple types of visual attention. To study our model's ability to leverage dependencies between agents' behaviors and their environment, we introduce a new dataset composed of top-view images of hundreds of F1 race tracks where the vehicles' dynamics are largely governed by specific regions within the images (*e.g.*, an upcoming curve). CAR-Net outperforms previous state-of-the-art approaches on the SDD trajectory forecasting benchmark by a large margin. By visualizing the output of the attention mechanism, we showed that our model leverages relevant scene semantic features in the prediction task.

Acknowledgement. The research reported in this publication was supported by funding from the SAIL-Toyota Center for AI Research (1186781-31-UDARO), ONR (1165419-10-TDAUZ), Nvidia, and MURI (1186514-1-TBCJE).

References

1. Walker, J., Gupta, A., Hebert, M.: Patch to the future: unsupervised visual prediction. In: Proceedings of the IEEE Conference on Computer Vision and Pattern Recognition, pp. 3302–3309 (2014)
2. Trautman, P., Krause, A.: Unfreezing the robot: navigation in dense, interacting crowds. In: 2010 IEEE/RSJ International Conference on Intelligent Robots and Systems (IROS), pp. 797–803. IEEE (2010)
3. Karasev, V., Ayvaci, A., Heisele, B., Soatto, S.: Intent-aware long-term prediction of pedestrian motion. In: 2016 IEEE International Conference on Robotics and Automation (ICRA), pp. 2543–2549. IEEE (2016)

178   A. Sadeghian et al.

4. Hirose, N., et al.: To go or not to go? A near unsupervised learning approach for robot navigation. arXiv preprint arXiv:1709.05439 (2017)
5. Sadeghian, A., Alahi, A., Savarese, S.: Tracking the untrackable: learning to track multiple cues with long-term dependencies. arXiv preprint arXiv:1701.01909 (2017)
6. Oh, S., et al.: A large-scale benchmark dataset for event recognition in surveillance video. In: 2011 IEEE conference on Computer vision and pattern recognition (CVPR), pp. 3153–3160. IEEE (2011)
7. Morris, B.T., Trivedi, M.M.: A survey of vision-based trajectory learning and analysis for surveillance. IEEE Trans. Circuits Syst. Video Technol. **18**(8), 1114–1127 (2008)
8. Xie, D., Shu, T., Todorovic, S., Zhu, S.C.: Learning and inferring "dark matter" and predicting human intents and trajectories in videos. IEEE Trans. Pattern Anal. Mach. Intell. **40**, 1639–1652 (2017)
9. Hirose, N., et al.: Gonet: a semi-supervised deep learning approach for traversability estimation. arXiv preprint arXiv:1803.03254 (2018)
10. Hirose, N., et al.: Gonet++: Traversability estimation via dynamic scene view synthesis. arXiv preprint arXiv:1806.08864 (2018)
11. Gong, H., Sim, J., Likhachev, M., Shi, J.: Multi-hypothesis motion planning for visual object tracking. In: 2011 IEEE International Conference on Computer Vision (ICCV), pp. 619–626. IEEE (2011)
12. Makris, D., Ellis, T.: Learning semantic scene models from observing activity in visual surveillance. IEEE Trans. Syst. Man Cybern. Part B (Cybern.) **35**(3), 397–408 (2005)
13. Kretzschmar, H., Kuderer, M., Burgard, W.: Learning to predict trajectories of cooperatively navigating agents. In: 2014 IEEE International Conference on Robotics and Automation (ICRA), pp. 4015–4020. IEEE (2014)
14. Kitani, K.M., Ziebart, B.D., Bagnell, J.A., Hebert, M.: Activity forecasting. In: Fitzgibbon, A., Lazebnik, S., Perona, P., Sato, Y., Schmid, C. (eds.) ECCV 2012. LNCS, vol. 7575, pp. 201–214. Springer, Heidelberg (2012). https://doi.org/10.1007/978-3-642-33765-9_15
15. Ballan, L., Castaldo, F., Alahi, A., Palmieri, F., Savarese, S.: Knowledge transfer for scene-specific motion prediction. In: Leibe, B., Matas, J., Sebe, N., Welling, M. (eds.) ECCV 2016. LNCS, vol. 9905, pp. 697–713. Springer, Cham (2016). https://doi.org/10.1007/978-3-319-46448-0_42
16. Lee, N., Choi, W., Vernaza, P., Choy, C.B., Torr, P.H., Chandraker, M.: Desire: distant future prediction in dynamic scenes with interacting agents. arXiv preprint arXiv:1704.04394 (2017)
17. Xu, K., et al.: Show, attend and tell: neural image caption generation with visual attention. In: International Conference on Machine Learning, pp. 2048–2057 (2015)
18. Bahdanau, D., Cho, K., Bengio, Y.: Neural machine translation by jointly learning to align and translate. arXiv preprint arXiv:1409.0473 (2014)
19. Sadeghian, A., Rodriguez, M., Wang, D.Z., Colas, A.: Temporal reasoning over event knowledge graphs (2016)
20. Sadeghian, A., Sundaram, L., Wang, D., Hamilton, W., Branting, K., Pfeifer, C.: Semantic edge labeling over legal citation graphs (2016)
21. Mnih, V., Heess, N., Graves, A., et al.: Recurrent models of visual attention. In: Advances in neural information processing systems, pp. 2204–2212 (2014)
22. Ba, J., Mnih, V., Kavukcuoglu, K.: Multiple object recognition with visual attention. arXiv preprint arXiv:1412.7755 (2014)
23. Gregor, K., Danihelka, I., Graves, A., Rezende, D.J., Wierstra, D.: Draw: a recurrent neural network for image generation. arXiv preprint arXiv:1502.04623 (2015)

24. Caba Heilbron, F., Escorcia, V., Ghanem, B., Carlos Niebles, J.: Activitynet: a large-scale video benchmark for human activity understanding. In: Proceedings of the IEEE Conference on Computer Vision and Pattern Recognition, pp. 961–970 (2015)
25. Bagautdinov, T., Alahi, A., Fleuret, F., Fua, P., Savarese, S.: Social scene understanding: end-to-end multi-person action localization and collective activity recognition. arXiv preprint arXiv:1611.09078 (2016)
26. Vesel, R.: Racing line optimization@ race optimal. ACM SIGEVOlution **7**(2–3), 12–20 (2015)
27. Kalman, R.E.: A new approach to linear filtering and prediction problems. J. Basic Eng. **82**(1), 35–45 (1960)
28. McCullagh, P.: Generalized linear models. Eur. J. Oper. Res. **16**(3), 285–292 (1984)
29. Williams, C.K.: Prediction with gaussian processes: from linear regression to linear prediction and beyond. In: Jordan, M.I. (ed.) Learning in Graphical Models. NATO ASI series D Behavioural and Social Sciences, vol. 89, pp. 599–621. Springer, Dordrecht (1998). https://doi.org/10.1007/978-94-011-5014-9_23
30. Quiñonero-Candela, J., Rasmussen, C.E.: A unifying view of sparse approximate Gaussian process regression. J. Mach. Learn. Res. **6**, 1939–1959 (2005)
31. Wang, J.M., Fleet, D.J., Hertzmann, A.: Gaussian process dynamical models for human motion. IEEE Trans. Pattern Anal. Mach. Intell. **30**(2), 283–298 (2008)
32. Pellegrini, S., Ess, A., Van Gool, L.: Improving data association by joint modeling of pedestrian trajectories and groupings. In: Daniilidis, K., Maragos, P., Paragios, N. (eds.) ECCV 2010. LNCS, vol. 6311, pp. 452–465. Springer, Heidelberg (2010). https://doi.org/10.1007/978-3-642-15549-9_33
33. Koppula, H.S., Saxena, A.: Anticipating human activities using object affordances for reactive robotic response. IEEE Trans. Pattern Anal. Mach. Intell. **38**(1), 14–29 (2016)
34. Helbing, D., Molnar, P.: Social force model for pedestrian dynamics. Phys. Rev. E **51**(5), 4282 (1995)
35. Alahi, A., Goel, K., Ramanathan, V., Robicquet, A., Fei-Fei, L., Savarese, S.: Social LSTM: human trajectory prediction in crowded spaces. In: Proceedings of the IEEE Conference on Computer Vision and Pattern Recognition, pp. 961–971 (2016)
36. Alahi, A., et al.: Learning to predict human behavior in crowded scenes. In: Group and Crowd Behavior for Computer Vision, pp. 183–207. Elsevier (2017)
37. Robicquet, A., Sadeghian, A., Alahi, A., Savarese, S.: Learning social etiquette: human trajectory understanding in crowded scenes. In: Leibe, B., Matas, J., Sebe, N., Welling, M. (eds.) ECCV 2016. LNCS, vol. 9912, pp. 549–565. Springer, Cham (2016). https://doi.org/10.1007/978-3-319-46484-8_33
38. Robicquet, A., et al.: Forecasting social navigation in crowded complex scenes. arXiv preprint arXiv:1601.00998 (2016)
39. Haque, A., Alahi, A., Fei-Fei, L.: Recurrent attention models for depth-based person identification. In: Proceedings of the IEEE Conference on Computer Vision and Pattern Recognition, pp. 1229–1238 (2016)
40. Sadeghian, A., Kosaraju, V., Sadeghian, A., Hirose, N., Savarese, S.: SoPhie: an attentive GAN for predicting paths compliant to social and physical constraints. arXiv preprint arXiv:1806.01482 (2018)
41. Zhao, B., Wu, X., Feng, J., Peng, Q., Yan, S.: Diversified visual attention networks for fine-grained object classification. IEEE Trans. Multimed. **19**(6), 1245–1256 (2017)

42. You, Q., Jin, H., Wang, Z., Fang, C., Luo, J.: Image captioning with semantic attention. In: Proceedings of the IEEE Conference on Computer Vision and Pattern Recognition, pp. 4651–4659 (2016)
43. Sharma, S., Kiros, R., Salakhutdinov, R.: Action recognition using visual attention. arXiv preprint arXiv:1511.04119 (2015)
44. Hochreiter, S., Schmidhuber, J.: Long short-term memory. Neural Comput. **9**(8), 1735–1780 (1997)
45. Simonyan, K., Zisserman, A.: Very deep convolutional networks for large-scale image recognition. arXiv preprint arXiv:1409.1556 (2014)
46. Russakovsky, O., et al.: Imagenet large scale visual recognition challenge. Int. J. Comput. Vis. (IJCV) **115**(3), 211–252 (2015)
47. Long, J., Shelhamer, E., Darrell, T.: Fully convolutional networks for semantic segmentation. In: Proceedings of the IEEE Conference on Computer Vision and Pattern Recognition, pp. 3431–3440 (2015)
48. Kingma, D., Ba, J.: Adam: a method for stochastic optimization. arXiv preprint arXiv:1412.6980 (2014)
49. OpenAI gym, published. https://gym.openai.com/envs/carracing-v0/. Accessed 01 Jan 2017
50. Graham, N.: Smoothing with periodic cubic splines. Bell Labs Tech. J. **62**(1), 101–110 (1983)
51. Yamaguchi, K., Berg, A.C., Ortiz, L.E., Berg, T.L.: Who are you with and where are you going? In: 2011 IEEE Conference on Computer Vision and Pattern Recognition (CVPR), pp. 1345–1352. IEEE (2011)

Evaluating Capability of Deep Neural Networks for Image Classification via Information Plane

Hao Cheng⬤, Dongze Lian⬤, Shenghua Gao⬤, and Yanlin Geng$^{(\boxtimes)}$⬤

ShanghaiTech University, Shanghai, China
{chenghao,liandz,gaoshh,gengyl}@shanghaitech.edu.cn

Abstract. Inspired by the pioneering work of information bottleneck principle for Deep Neural Networks (DNNs) analysis, we design an information plane based framework to evaluate the capability of DNNs for image classification tasks, which not only helps understand the capability of DNNs, but also helps us choose a neural network which leads to higher classification accuracy more efficiently. Further, with experiments, the relationship among the model accuracy, $I(X;T)$ and $I(T;Y)$ are analyzed, where $I(X;T)$ and $I(T;Y)$ are the mutual information of DNN's output T with input X and label Y. We also show the information plane is more informative than loss curve and apply mutual information to infer the model's capability for recognizing objects of each class. Our studies would facilitate a better understanding of DNNs.

Keywords: Information bottleneck · Mutual information
Neural networks · Image classification

1 Introduction

Deep Neural Networks (DNNs) have demonstrated their successes in many computer vision and natural language processing tasks [1–5], but the theoretical reasons that contribute to the successes of DNNs haven't been fully unveiled. Recently, information theory has shown its preponderance for DNNs understanding. Specifically, Tishby and Zaslavsky [6] note that layered neural networks can be represented as a Markov chain and analyze the neural network via the information bottleneck. Schwartz-Ziv and Tishby [7] calculate the mutual information $I(X;T)$, $I(T;Y)$ for each hidden layer, where X is the input data, Y is the label and T is the hidden layer output, respectively. Then they demonstrate the effectiveness of the visualization of neural networks. These works inspire us to leverage mutual information to evaluate the capability of DNNs.

Figure 1 depicts the evolution of the mutual information along with the training epochs in the information plane [7]. As can be seen, the green point, which is referred to as the **transition point**, in each mutual information path separates the learning process into two distinct phases: the 'fitting phase', which takes a

© Springer Nature Switzerland AG 2018
V. Ferrari et al. (Eds.): ECCV 2018, LNCS 11215, pp. 181–195, 2018.
https://doi.org/10.1007/978-3-030-01252-6_11

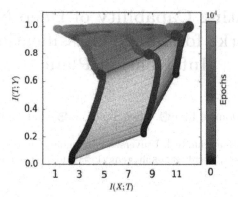

Fig. 1. This figure is adapted from [7]. The mutual information path is calculated based on a fully connected neural network. X is a 12-dimensional binary input and Y has 2 classes. Each hidden layer first reaches the green point (transition point), then converges at the yellow point. The leftmost path corresponds to the last hidden layer and the rightmost path corresponds to the first hidden layer. (best viewed in color) (Color figure online)

few hundred epochs, and the layers' information on the label, namely $I(T;Y)$, increases; the subsequent 'compression phase', which takes most of the training time and the layers' information on the input, i.e. $I(X;T)$, decreases (this means the layers remove irrelevant information until convergence).

The evolution of $I(X;T)$ and $I(T;Y)$ explains how DNNs work. However, the models used in [6,7] are some simple fully connected neural networks. In real applications, Convolutional Neural Networks (CNNs) are commonly used in computer vision. Pushing these works [6,7] forward, in this paper, we design an information plane based framework to study the capability of some classical CNN structures for image classification, including AlexNet [2], VGG [8]. The contributions of our work can be summarized as follows:

- Our work unveils that $I(X;T)$ also contributes to the training accuracy and the correlation grows stronger as the network gets deeper. We perform experiments to validate this claim.
- An evaluation framework based on the information plane is proposed. The framework is more 'informative' than the loss curve and would facilitate a better understanding of DNNs.
- We show that mutual information can be used to infer the DNN's capability of recognizing objects of each class in the image classification task.

2   Related Work

The most related topic is the information bottleneck (IB) principle [9]. IB provides a technique for extracting information in some *input* random variable that is relevant for predicting some different *output* random variable. [10] extends the original IB method to obtain continuous representations that preserve relevant information, rather than discrete clusters, for the special case of multivariate Gaussian variables. [11] introduces an alternative formulation called the deterministic IB (DIB), which replaces mutual information with entropy and better captures the notion which features are relevant. [12] theoretically analyzes the IB method and its relation to learning algorithms and minimal sufficient statistics. [13] shows that K-means and deterministic annealing algorithms for geometric clustering can be derived from a more general IB approach.

Recently, we have seen some applications of IB in deep learning. [14] presents a variational approximation to the IB method. This variational approach can parameterize the IB model using a neural network and leverage the reparameterization trick for efficient training. [15] proposes a method that allows IB to be used in more general domains, such as discrete or continuous inputs and outputs, nonlinear encoding and decoding maps. [16] proposes a Parametric IB (PIB) framework to jointly optimize the compression and relevance of all layers in stochastic neural networks for better exploiting the networks' representation capabilities. [17] introduces the Information Dropout method, which generalizes the dropout method in deep learning, rooted in information theoretic principles that automatically adapts to the data, and can better exploit architectures with limited capacity.

[6,7], which are most relevant to our work, visualize the mutual information of hidden layers and the input/output of a neural network in the information plane to understand the optimization process and the internal organization of DNNs. While in this paper, different from these works which study DNNs with fully connected layers, we propose to study the behavior of more commonly used CNNs in image classification.

3   Mutual Information and Deep Neural Networks

In this section, we first revisit the definition of mutual information and its properties relevant to DNNs analysis, then we interpret the representation learning in DNNs with mutual information and show how to calculate mutual information in DNNs.

3.1   Mutual Information

Given two random variables X and Y with a joint probability mass function $p(x, y)$ and marginal probability mass functions $p(x)$ and $p(y)$, the mutual information between two variables, $I(X; Y)$, is defined as:

$$I(X;Y) = \sum_{x,y} p(x,y) \log \frac{p(x,y)}{p(x)p(y)}. \tag{1}$$

The entropy of X, $H(X)$, can be defined using the mutual information:

$$H(X) = I(X;X) = -\sum_{x} p(x) \log p(x). \tag{2}$$

In general, the mutual information of two random variables is a measurement of the mutual dependence between the two variables. More specifically, it quantifies the amount of information obtained about one random variable, through the other one.

There are two properties (3) (4) of mutual information which are useful for analyzing DNNs:

- function transformation:

$$I(X;Y) = I(\psi(X); \phi(Y)) \tag{3}$$

for any invertible functions ψ and ϕ.
- Markov chain. Suppose $X \to Y \to Z$ forms a Markov chain, then we have the data processing inequality:

$$I(X;Y) \geq I(X;Z). \tag{4}$$

3.2   Optimal Representation of Learning Process

In representation learning, we want our model to learn an efficient representation of the original data X without losing prediction capability of the label Y, which means we want to learn a minimal sufficient statistics of X with respect to Y. A minimal sufficient statistics $T(X)$ is the solution to the following optimization problem:

$$T(X) = \underset{S(X):I(S(X);Y)=I(X;Y)}{\arg\min} I(S(X); X) \tag{5}$$

So, from the minimal sufficient statistics perspective, the goal of DNNs is to make $I(X; S(X))$ as small as possible, which means the representation is efficient; while $I(S(X);Y)$ should be the same value of $I(X;Y)$ which means the information on Y is not lost. In practice, the explicit minimal sufficient statistics only exist for very special distributions. The actual learning process is a tradeoff between $I(X; S(X))$ and $I(S(X);Y)$, and it leads to the IB method [9]. IB can be seen as a special case of Rate Distortion theory and provides a framework to find approximate minimal sufficient statistics. The efficient representation is a tradeoff between the compression of X and the prediction ability of Y.

Let x be an input point, and t be the corresponding model's output, or the compressed representation of x. This representation is defined by the probabilistic mapping $p(t|x)$. The information bottleneck tradeoff is formulated by the following optimization problem:

$$\underset{p(t|x),Y \to X \to T}{\min} \{I(X;T) - \beta I(T;Y)\}. \tag{6}$$

The Lagrange multiplier β determines the level of relevant information captured by the representation T. So given a joint distribution $p(x,y)$ and the parameter β, minimizing (6) yields the optimal $I(X;T)$ and $I(T;Y)$ (see (31) in [9]).

3.3   Calculating Mutual Information in DNNs

From Sect. 3.2, we know $I(X;T)$ and $I(T;Y)$ are essential to evaluate the representation learning algorithms, including DNNs, but the calculation in DNNs is a difficult problem.

[7] uses the hyperbolic tangent function as the hidden layer's activation function, and bins the neuron's output activation into 30 equal intervals between -1 and 1. Then they use these discretized values for each t, to directly calculate the joint distributions $p(x,t)$ and $p(t,y)$ over the equally likely patterns of the input data for every hidden layer. But when the number of neurons in the hidden layer is large (it happens when we visualize CNN layers), $I(X;T)$ and $I(T;Y)$ barely change. The reason is that the sample space of T is huge even if we decrease the number of intervals, and the output of a particular input data x falls into one interval of t with high probability. Thus $p(x|t)$ and $p(y|t)$ are approximately deterministic, $I(X;T) \approx H(X)$ and $I(T;Y) \approx H(Y)$ from (1) (2). So this issue makes it hard to analyze universal neural networks. Luckily our goal is to evaluate different network structures, so we just need to visualize the last hidden layer since it directly reveals the relationship among the model output T, input X and label Y. Since the number of neurons of the last hidden layer in the DNNs for image classification task is precisely the number of classes of input data, our method is only subject to the number of classes.

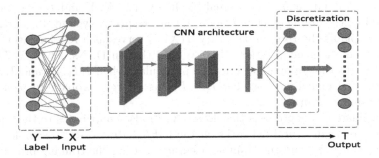

Fig. 2. This figure shows how we obtain T from the network for calculating $I(X;T)$ and $I(T;Y)$. $Y \to X \to T$ forms a Markov chain. The output of the last layer (blue circles) is the softmax probability. (Color figure online)

Suppose there are C classes, the outputs of the last hidden layer are scores of different classes which are unbounded. We use the normalized exponential function to squash a C dimensional real vector z of arbitrary real values to a C dimensional vector $\sigma(z)$ of real values in the range [0,1] that add up to 1. The function is given by

$$\sigma(z)_j = \frac{e^{z_j}}{\sum_{c=1}^{C} e^{z_c}} \quad \text{for } j = 1, \dots, C, \tag{7}$$

which is exactly what the softmax function does in the neural network. We bin the neuron's output $\sigma(z)$ into 10 equal intervals between 0 and 1 and get our final model output T. Then we can calculate $I(X;T)$ and $I(T;Y)$ for any network architecture. An advantage of this calculation is that the sample space of T is a bit smaller since we enforce the C dimensional vector $\sigma(z)$ add up to 1. This process is illustrated in Fig. 2.

4   Experiments

This section goes as follows: in Sect. 4.1, we analyze the relationship among the model accuracy, $I(X;T)$ and $I(T;Y)$; in Sect. 4.2, we propose a framework that can be used to evaluate DNNs; in Sect. 4.3, we show the evaluation framework is more informative than the loss curve when evaluating DNNs and how to use this framework to guide us on choosing networks efficiently; in Sect. 4.4, we show how to apply mutual information to infer the capability of a model for objects of each class in image classification tasks.

4.1   Relationship Among Classification Accuracy, $I(X;T)$ and $I(T;Y)$ in DNNs

In addition to developing the theory of deep learning, it is also important to empirically validate it. In the original IB theory [12], X, Y and T represent the *training* input, *training* label and model output, respectively; and [12] states that $I(T;Y)$ explains the *training* accuracy, $I(X;T)$ serves as a regularization term that controls the generalization. Here we find that in DNNs, low $I(X;T)$ also contributes to the training accuracy. In particular, when $I(T_1;Y)$ and $I(T_2;Y)$ are equal, the model with smaller $I(X;T)$ has a larger probability to achieve higher training accuracy.

To validate the hypothesis that low $I(X;T)$ also contributes to the training accuracy, we train neural networks on the CIFAR-10 dataset to sample values of $I(X;T)$, $I(T;Y)$ and the training accuracy. During the training process, the sampling is performed at every fixed iteration steps. For the i-th sample, we use $I(X;T_i)$, $I(T_i;Y)$ and Acc_i to denote the mutual information values and the training accuracy, respectively. A direct way to examine the rightness of our hypothesis is to find pairs (i,j) which satisfy $I(T_i;Y) = I(T_j;Y)$, then check the relationship of $I(X;T)$ and the training accuracy.

Since $I(T;Y)$ is a real number, it's hard to find a pair of samples who have the same value of $I(T;Y)$. Instead, we examine the hypothesis by checking inversions. An inversion is a pair of samples (i,j) which satisfy $I(T_i;Y) < I(T_j;Y)$ and $Acc_i > Acc_j$. Among all these inversion pairs, we calculate the percentage of pairs that satisfy $I(X;T_i) < I(X;T_j)$. This percentage is a proper indicator of the rightness of our hypothesis since if the percentage is near 0.5, then $I(X;T)$ almost has no relation to the training accuracy. Otherwise, if the percentage is high, then low $I(X;T)$ also contributes to the training accuracy. In our experiments,

Table 1. This table records the percentages with 600 samples for DNNs with different network structures and training methods on the training set. The percentage converges when we include 600 samples. CNN-9 is a deep convolutional neural network with 9 convolutional layers. Linear network is a feedforward network whose activation function is the identity function. SGD is short for Stochastic Gradient Descent, and BGD for Batch Gradient Descent. For computational limitation, we include 10000 training samples when performing BGD. Also BGD and SGD use the same training set.

Network structure	Training method	Percentages with 600 samples
CNN-9	SGD	**0.865**
	BGD	**0.821**
Linear network	SGD	**0.755**
	BGD	**0.594**

we set different training conditions to train neural networks. The percentages are listed in Table 1.

The results in Table 1 show that $I(X;T)$ also contributes to training accuracy since the percentages are over 0.5. Different network structures may end up with different percentages. Also SGD has higher percentage than BGD. We want to emphasize that the percentages may have a little deviation from the ground truth since the mutual information in DNNs was calculated approximately by binning. This is crucial especially when mutual information values do not vary too much. We believe the accurate mutual information will make our hypothesis more convincing. Table 1 can be further interpreted as follows:

First, notice that $I(T;Y)$ is not a monotonic function of the training accuracy. For example, suppose we have C classes in the dataset, and C_i denotes the i-th class. Consider two cases: In the first case, $T = \sigma(Y)$ where σ is an identity mapping which means T always predicts the true class. In the second case $T = \varphi(Y)$ where φ is a shift mapping which means if the true class is C_i, the prediction of T is C_{i+1}. In both two cases, since σ and φ are invertible functions, from (3), we have $I(T;Y) = I(\sigma(Y);Y) = I(\varphi(Y);Y) = H(Y)$. But in case 1, the training accuracy is 1, whereas in case 2 it is 0.

Second, unlike linear networks, the loss function of CNNs is highly non-convex. By using SGD or BGD to train neural networks, the training loss respect to all the training data does not decrease all the time during the training process which indicates the network sometimes is learning in the wrong direction. Since SGD only uses a mini-batch of samples for each iteration, the loss curve becomes more unstable. Only in the linear network (the loss function is convex) trained by BGD, with a proper learning rate, the training loss always decreases during the training process, which means the model always makes T closer to the true label Y (the model is stablest in this case). So $I(T;Y)$ can fully explain the training accuracy and $I(X;T)$ may not contribute to training accuracy very much.

Third, [18] defines that a learning algorithm is stable if its output does not depend too much on any individual training example. So when $I(T_1;Y)$ and

$I(T_2; Y)$ are equal, the model with low $I(X; T)$ has large stability, which may lead to a high training accuracy.

We also find that when trained by SGD, the percentages increase as more convolutional layers are considered, which can be seen from the columns in Table 2. This interesting phenomenon may reveal some inherent properties of CNNs which we would further explore in our future work.

Table 2. This table records the percentages with 600 samples for DNNs with different network structures on the training set. CNN-i is a deep convolutional neural network with i convolutional layers.

Network structure	CNN-2	CNN-4	CNN-9	CNN-16 (VGG)
Percentage with 600 samples	0.56	0.68	0.87	0.96

We also validate our hypothesis on the *validation* data where X and Y now represent the *validation* input and *validation* label, respectively. The percentages in Table 3 also show that low $I(X; T)$ contributes to validation accuracy. This result will be useful in the next subsection for evaluating DNNs.

Table 3. The percentages with numbers of samples on the validation set. The network is VGG-16 trained by SGD.

Number of samples	100	200	300	400	500	600
Percentage	0.905	0.921	0.912	0.924	0.924	**0.924**

4.2 Evaluating DNNs in the Information Plane

Evaluating the capability of DNNs during the training process is important because it would help us understand the training phase better. Section 3.2 shows that an optimal representation (a minimal sufficient statistics of X with respect to Y) is a tradeoff between $I(X; T)$ and $I(T; Y)$. We validate the hypothesis in Sect. 4.1 that, in DNNs trained by SGD, not only $I(T; Y)$ but also $I(X; T)$ is a measurement of validation accuracy where X and Y represent the *validation* input and *validation* label, respectively. So we use $\frac{\Delta I(T;Y)}{\Delta I(X;T)}$ (the slope of the curve) to represent the model's learning capability **at each moment** in the information plane.

Figure 1 shows two learning phases of the training process. The model begins to generalize in the second compression phase, and the first fitting phase takes very little time compared to the compression phase. So we just use $\frac{\Delta I(T;Y)}{\Delta I(X;T)}$ in the second compression phase to evaluate the model's capability of generalization. We expect that a good model has small (negative) $\frac{\Delta I(T;Y)}{\Delta I(X;T)}$ at the second phase. While for the first fitting phase, $I(T; Y)$ and $I(X; T)$ grow simultaneously (in order to fit the label, the model needs to remember X at first). So we use $I(T;Y)$ instead of $\frac{\Delta I(T;Y)}{\Delta I(X;T)}$ to represent the model's capability of fitting the label. Based on the discussion above, we propose our evaluation framework in Fig. 3.

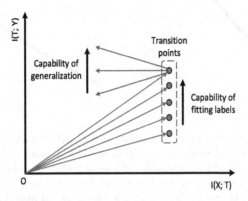

Fig. 3. Evaluation framework based on $I(X;T)$ and $I(T;Y)$. The height of transition point $(I(T;Y))$ represents the model's capability of fitting the label. The slope after transition point $(\frac{\Delta I(T;Y)}{\Delta I(X;T)})$ represents the model's capability of generalization.

We are interested in how different neural networks behave under the framework we propose in Fig. 3. So we run different network structures on MNIST and CIFAR-10 dataset (see Fig. 4). Notice that in this and the subsequent experiments, X and Y represent the *validation* input and *validation* label respectively. Mutual information curves are smoothed for better visualization since smoothing doesn't change the trend of the curve. Also, DNNs are just trained once until convergence without data augmentation or retraining since we want to compare networks in an equal way. We also record the mutual information, training epochs, model validation accuracy at the transition point and convergence point in Table 4. Figure 4 and Table 4 show some interesting phenomenons.

- Convolutional neural networks (CNNs) may have lower capabilities of fitting the label than fully connected networks (FCs) in the first fitting phase by comparing $I(T;Y)$ at the transition point (The reason may attribute to the large number of parameters of FCs), but CNNs have stronger capabilities of generalization (smaller $\frac{\Delta I(T;Y)}{\Delta I(X;T)}$) in the compression phase which lead to higher final validation accuracies.
- Some models may not have second compression phase. For MNIST, all models have exactly two learning phases, but for CIFAR-10, the models with fewer layers don't show second compression phase (see CNN-2, CNN-4, and FC-3 for CIFAR-10 in Fig. 4). It reveals that when the dataset is harder to classify, neural networks with fewer layers can not generalize well.
- For CIFAR-10, $I(X;T)$ and $I(T;Y)$ of FC-6 and FC-9 both drop down in the second phase indicating that increasing layers in FCs may lead to overfitting.

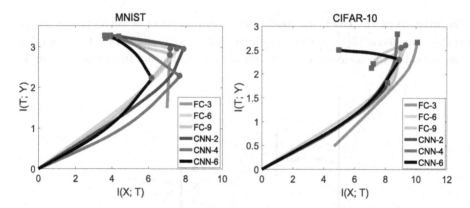

Fig. 4. The figures depict mutual information paths with training epochs in the information plane. The left and right figures represent MNIST and CIFAR-10, respectively. Both datasets are trained by fully connected neural networks and convolutional neural networks. FC-i denotes a fully connected neural network which has i layers including the input and output layers. CNN-i denotes a convolutional neural network which has i convolutional layers.

This evaluation framework allows us to visualize any CNN or FC in the information plane. In the next subsection, we will show this framework is more informative than the loss curve when evaluating neural networks.

4.3   Informativeness and Guidance of Information Plane

Usually, for a particular problem, the network structure is determined based on the exhausting search of different DNNs on the validation set which is time-consuming. Next, we will show our evaluation framework is more informative than the loss curve and would facilitate the model selection of DNNs.

Specifically, by comparing the number of training epochs at the transition point and convergence point, we can find that most of the training time is spent on the compression phase, as shown in Table 4. So we can visualize the information plane during training the network, and stop training once the model has crossed the transition point for several epochs. The height of the transition point ($I(T;Y)$) represents the model's capability of fitting the label. The slope ($\frac{\Delta I(T;Y)}{\Delta I(X;T)}$) after transition point represents the model's capability of generalization. These two indicators will give us a general prediction about the model's quality. Figure 5 shows the mutual information paths of different network structures on the CIFAR-10 dataset. Table 5 records the model validation accuracy and 'percentages' defined in Sect. 4.1.

Table 4. The table records $I(T;Y)$, $I(X;T)$, training epochs and validation accuracy of every network at the transition point and convergence point. For FC-3, CNN-2 and CNN-4 on CIFAR-10, the values on the transition point and convergence point are the same since they don't show the compression phase.

Dataset	Model	Transition point				Convergence point			
		$I(T;Y)$	$I(X;T)$	Epochs	Accuracy	$I(T;Y)$	$I(X;T)$	Epochs	Accuracy
MNIST	FC-3	2.96	7.183	1	0.836	3.259	4.358	51	0.983
	FC-6	2.962	7.532	1	0.846	3.249	3.746	56	0.988
	FC-9	2.803	7.166	1	0.774	3.214	3.647	54	0.988
	CNN-2	2.952	7.898	1	0.75	3.282	3.916	50	0.99
	CNN-4	2.286	7.683	1	0.451	3.284	3.621	53	0.994
	CNN-6	2.236	6.184	1	0.515	3.275	3.592	54	0.994
CIFAR-10	FC-3	2.671	10.085	65	0.534	2.671	10.085	65	0.534
	FC-6	2.604	9.321	20	0.537	2.218	7.197	66	0.575
	FC-9	2.55	9.02	21	0.555	2.218	7.197	66	0.56
	CNN-2	1.816	8.133	63	0.451	1.816	8.133	63	0.451
	CNN-4	2.840	8.761	67	0.705	2.840	8.761	67	0.705
	CNN-6	2.301	8.891	5	0.52	2.472	4.862	66	0.781

Table 5. The percentages of each network are from Table 2.

Network structure	CNN-2	CNN-4	CNN-9	CNN-16 (VGG)
Percentage of 600 samples	0.56	0.68	0.87	0.96
Final acc on validation set	0.45	0.70	0.77	0.89

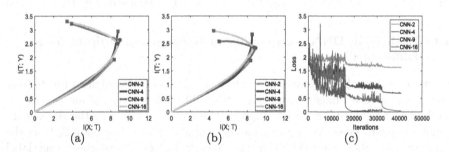

Fig. 5. (a) Mutual information path of each model with SGD optimization on the training set of CIFAR-10. (b) Mutual information path of each model on the validation set. (c) Training loss of each model with training iterations.

From Fig. 5(c), we can see the loss of each model continues to decrease with training iterations. While in the information plane, each model behaves differently. In Fig. 5(a) and (b), the models with few layers do not have clear second stage in the mutual information paths. Actually, we can visualize the information path of each model on the validation set to help us evaluate or select model efficiently. From Fig. 5(b), compared with CNN-9, the slope of information path of CNN-16 in the second stage is smaller (negative), which represents better generalization capability. The validation accuracy of each model in Table 5 is consistent with our analysis. Thus, the information plane is more 'informative' than loss curve when evaluating the DNN model. Since the first stage only takes little time compared to the second stage, we can choose a better model quickly given different model architectures by visualizing the information plane on the validation set.

It is worth noticing that our prediction may not always be true, since the mutual information path may have a larger slope change in the future. So it's a trade-off between training time and confidence of our prediction. The longer time we train the network, the more confident prediction about the model we can make. But it is still an efficient way to guide us on choosing neural network structure for a given task.

Figure 5(a), (b) and Table 5 also show that when CNNs have fewer layers, the information plane does not clearly show the second phase, and the percentages are low. Whereas for CNN-9 and CNN-16, the information plane clearly show the second phase and the percentages are high. This experiment shows that $I(X;T)$ contributes to training accuracy mostly at the second stage of information paths. One possible reason is that the model begins to 'compress' the information of the training set and learns to generalize (extract common features from each mini-batch) at the second stage. From the percentages, this process happens even when $I(T;Y)$'s remain the same. The correlation between accuracy and $I(X;T)$ grows stronger when the number of layers of DNN increases, since DNN with more layers has better generalization capability. We can view $I(X;T)$ and $I(T;Y)$ as: $I(T;Y)$ determines how much the knowledge T has about the label Y, and $I(X;T)$ determines how easy this knowledge can be learned by the network.

4.4 Evaluating DNN's Capability of Recognizing Objects from Different Classes

Furthermore, we also evaluate the model's capability of recognizing objects from each class for the image classification task. The information plane provides a method in an informative way. Suppose there are C classes in the dataset, C_i denotes the i-th class. To test the model's capability of recognizing C_i from the data, we can label other classes in the validation data as one class, thus label Y changes from $\mathbf{R}^C$ to $\mathbf{R}^2$. When calculating the mutual information, we make label Y balanced so that $H(Y)$ is equal to 1. Then $I(X;T)$ and $I(T;Y)$ can be calculated directly given a neural network. Note that the structure of the neural network does not change. The output T is still $\mathbf{R}^C$. We only alter the way how to test the data. Repeating this process for C times and the model's capability of recognizing each class can be visualized in the information plane. This method is similar to one-vs-all classifications [19]. It measures the model's capability of recognizing the true class from all the data.

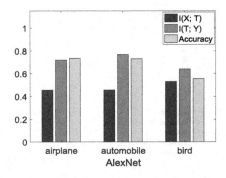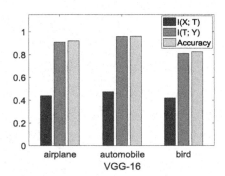

Fig. 6. Models' capabilities of recognizing objects from each class on the CIFAR-10 dataset. Models are well trained AlexNet and VGG-16. For each class, we show its $I(X;T)$, $I(T;Y)$ and validation accuracy. The validation accuracy of each class is the percentage of how many samples are correctly predicted out of all samples belonging to that class. Note that since $I(T;Y)$ is bounded by $H(Y)$ which is 1, the accuracy is also bounded by 1. To facilitate the visualization, we divide $I(X;T)$ by its upper-bound $H(X)$ so that $I(X;T)$, $I(T;Y)$ and the validation accuracy have the same magnitude.

For better visualization, we select the first 3 classes (airplane, automobile, bird) on CIFAR-10. Figure 7 shows how network recognizes objects from each class during the training stage in the information plane. Figure 6 compares different networks' recognizing capabilities for each class at the end of the training.

As shown in Fig. 7, Automobile has almost the same $I(T;Y)$ as airplane at the transition point, but automobile has smaller slop after that point. So we conclude that VGG-16 model has higher classification accuracy on automobile than airplane. For airplane and bird, model has almost equally generalization capabilities, but the capability of fitting the label of airplane is better than that of bird. So we conclude model has better classification accuracy on airplane than bird. The final classification accuracies for these three classes are 0.921, 0.961 and 0.825 which is consistent with our analysis.

Figure 6 shows that VGG-16 has stronger recognizing capability than AlexNet on each class. For each model, we can still use $I(X;T)$ and $I(T;Y)$ to compare each class. Like in AlexNet, after comparing $I(X;T)$ and $I(T;Y)$ of automobile and bird, we can conclude model has more recognizing capability on automobile rather than bird since automobile has a higher $I(T;Y)$ and lower $I(X;T)$.

Of course, 'model accuracy' can still be used to evaluate the model's recognizing capability for each class. But $I(X;T)$ and $I(T;Y)$ provide more information about the model's property in an informative way. Moreover, in some problems where the distribution of sample is unbalanced, we can use the information plane to test how many samples we need to train a neural network with balanced classification capability for each class.

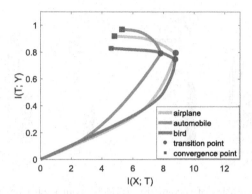

Fig. 7. Mutual information paths of different classes on CIFAR-10 dataset during the training phase for VGG-16.

5   Discussion

In this paper, we apply mutual information to evaluate the capability of DNNs for image classification tasks. We explore the relationship among model accuracy, $I(X;T)$ and $I(T;Y)$ in DNNs through extensive experiments. The results show that $I(X;T)$ also contributes to accuracy. We propose a general framework that can be used to evaluate DNNs in the information plane. This framework is more informative than the loss curve and can guide us on choosing network structures. We also apply mutual information to validate the network's recognizing capability for each class in the image classification tasks.

The datasets we use in the paper are MNIST and CIFAR. The difficulty of validating IB on large dataset like Imagenet is that Imagenet has 1000 classes. The sample space of T is huge and we can not calculate $I(X;T)$ and $I(T;Y)$ accurately by binning. Estimating accurate mutual information in high dimension space is still an open problem. Some future works can be done to develop more efficient ways to calculate mutual information and further explore the relationship between accuracy and $I(X;T)$ for understanding neural networks better.

Acknowledgements. This project is supported by NSFC (No. 61601288 and No. 61502304).

References

1. Graves, A., Mohamed, A., Hinton, G.: Speech recognition with deep recurrent neural networks. In: 2013 IEEE International Conference on Acoustics, Speech and Signal Processing (ICASSP), pp. 6645–6649. IEEE (2013)
2. Krizhevsky, A., Sutskever, I., Hinton, G.E.: Imagenet classification with deep convolutional neural networks. In: Advances in Neural Information Processing Systems, pp. 1097–1105 (2012)

3. Lotter, W., Kreiman, G., Cox, D.: Deep predictive coding networks for video prediction and unsupervised learning. arXiv preprint arXiv:1605.08104 (2016)
4. Silver, D., et al.: Mastering the game of go with deep neural networks and tree search. Nature **529**(7587), 484–489 (2016)
5. Zhang, X., LeCun, Y.: Text understanding from scratch. arXiv preprint arXiv:1502.01710 (2015)
6. Tishby, N., Zaslavsky, N.: Deep learning and the information bottleneck principle. In: 2015 IEEE Information Theory Workshop (ITW), pp. 1–5. IEEE (2015)
7. Shwartz-Ziv, R., Tishby, N.: Opening the black box of deep neural networks via information. arXiv preprint arXiv:1703.00810 (2017)
8. Simonyan, K., Zisserman, A.: Very deep convolutional networks for large-scale image recognition. arXiv preprint arXiv:1409.1556 (2014)
9. Tishby, N., Pereira, F.C., Bialek, W.: The information bottleneck method. arXiv preprint physics 0004057 (2000)
10. Chechik, G., Globerson, A., Tishby, N., Weiss, Y.: Information bottleneck for Gaussian variables. J. Mach. Learn. Res. **6**, 165–188 (2005)
11. Strouse, D.J., Schwab, D.J.: The deterministic information bottleneck. Neural Comput. **29**(6), 1611–1630 (2017)
12. Shamir, O., Sabato, S., Tishby, N.: Learning and generalization with the information bottleneck. Theor. Comput. Sci. **411**(29–30), 2696–2711 (2010)
13. Still, S., Bialek, W., Bottou, L.: Geometric clustering using the information bottleneck method. In: Advances in Neural Information Processing Systems, pp. 1165–1172 (2004)
14. Alemi, A.A., Fischer, I., Dillon, J.V., Murphy, K.: Deep variational information bottleneck. arXiv preprint arXiv:1612.00410 (2016)
15. Kolchinsky, A., Tracey, B.D., Wolpert, D.H.: Nonlinear information bottleneck. arXiv preprint arXiv:1705.02436 (2017)
16. Choi, J., Nguyen, T.T.: Layer-wise learning of stochastic neural networks with information bottleneck. arXiv preprint arXiv:1712.01272 (2018)
17. Achille, A., Soatto, S.: Information dropout: learning optimal representations through noisy computation. IEEE Trans. Pattern Anal. Mach. Intell. (PAMI) **PP**(99), 1 (2018)
18. Raginsky, M., Rakhlin, A., Tsao, M., Wu, Y., Xu, A.: Information-theoretic analysis of stability and bias of learning algorithms. In: 2016 IEEE Information Theory Workshop (ITW), pp. 26–30. IEEE (2016)
19. Bishop, C.M.: Pattern Recognition and Machine Learning. Springer, New York (2006)

Super-Identity Convolutional Neural Network for Face Hallucination

Kaipeng Zhang[1], Zhanpeng Zhang[2], Chia-Wen Cheng[1,3],
Winston H. Hsu[1(✉)], Yu Qiao[4], Wei Liu[5], and Tong Zhang[5]

[1] National Taiwan University, Taipei, Taiwan
whsu@ntu.edu.tw
[2] SenseTime Group Limited, Beijing, China
[3] The University of Texas at Austin, Austin, TX, USA
[4] Shenzhen Key Lab of Computer Vision and Pattern Recognition, Shenzhen
Institutes of Advanced Technology, CAS, Shenzhen, China
[5] Tencent AI Lab, Beijing, China

Abstract. Face hallucination is a generative task to super-resolve the facial image with low resolution while human perception of face heavily relies on identity information. However, previous face hallucination approaches largely ignore facial identity recovery. This paper proposes Super-Identity Convolutional Neural Network (SICNN) to recover identity information for generating faces closed to the real identity. Specifically, we define a super-identity loss to measure the identity difference between a hallucinated face and its corresponding high-resolution face within the hypersphere identity metric space. However, directly using this loss will lead to a Dynamic Domain Divergence problem, which is caused by the large margin between the high-resolution domain and the hallucination domain. To overcome this challenge, we present a domain-integrated training approach by constructing a robust identity metric for faces from these two domains. Extensive experimental evaluations demonstrate that the proposed SICNN achieves superior visual quality over the state-of-the-art methods on a challenging task to super-resolve 12×14 faces with an $8\times$ upscaling factor. In addition, SICNN significantly improves the recognizability of ultra-low-resolution faces.

Keywords: Face hallucination · Super identity
Domain-integrated training · Convolutional neural networks

1 Introduction

Face hallucination, which generates high-resolution (HR) facial images from low-resolution (LR) inputs, has attracted great interests in the past few years. However, most of existing works do not take the recovery of identity information into

Electronic supplementary material The online version of this chapter (https://doi.org/10.1007/978-3-030-01252-6_12) contains supplementary material, which is available to authorized users.

V. Ferrari et al. (Eds.): ECCV 2018, LNCS 11215, pp. 196–211, 2018.
https://doi.org/10.1007/978-3-030-01252-6_12

consideration such that they cannot generate faces closed to the real identity. Figure 1 shows some examples of hallucinated facial images generated by bicubic and several state-of-the-art methods. Though they generate clearer facial images than bicubic, the identity similarities are still low, which means that they cannot recover accurate identity-related facial details. On the other hand, human perception of face heavily relies on identity information [3]. Pixel-level cues cannot fully account for the perception process of the brain. These facts suggest that recovering identity information may improve both the recognizability and performance of hallucination.

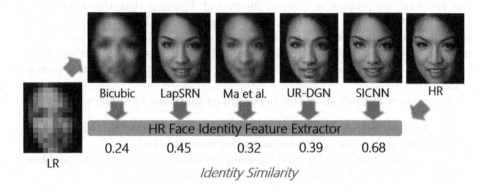

Fig. 1. Comparison of face hallucination visual quality and the performance of identity recovery over different hallucination methods. The identity similarity is computed by the cosine similarity of the identity feature.

Motivated by the above observations, this paper proposes Super-Identity Convolutional Neural Network (SICNN) for identity-enhanced face hallucination. Different from previous methods, we additionally minimize the identity difference between the hallucinated face and its corresponding high-resolution face. To do so, (i) we introduce a robust identity metric space in the training process; (ii) we define a super-identity loss to measure the identity difference; (iii) we propose a novel training approach to efficiently utilize the super-identity loss. More details as follows:

For identity metric space, we use a hypersphere space [18] as the identity metric space due to its state-of-the-art performance of facial identity representation. Specifically, our SICNN is composed of a face hallucination network cascaded with a recognition network to extract identity-related feature, and an Euclidean normalization operation to project the feature into the hypersphere space.

For loss function, perceptual loss [12], computed by feature Euclidean distance, can construct convincing HR images. Differently, in our work, we need to minimize the identity distance of face pairs in the metric space. Here, we modified the perceptual loss to the super-identity loss calculated by normalized Euclidean distance (equivalent to geodesic distance) between the hallucinated face and its corresponding high-resolution face in the hypersphere identity metric space. This also facilitates our analysis on the training process (see Sect. 3.5).

For training approach, using conventional training approaches to directly train the model with super-identity loss is difficult due to the large margin between the hallucination domain and the HR domain in the hypersphere identity metric space. This is critical during the early training stage when face hallucination network cannot predict high quality hallucinated face images. Moreover, the hallucination domain keeps changing during the hallucination network learning, which makes the training with super-identity loss unstable. We summarize this challenge as a *dynamic domain divergence* problem. To overcome this problem, we propose a Domain Integrated Training algorithm that alternately updates the face recognition network and the hallucination network by minimizing the different loss in each iteration. In this alterative optimization, the hallucinated face and HR face will gradually move closer to each other in the hypersphere identity metric space while keep the discrimination of this metric space.

The main contributions of this paper are as summarized as follows:

- We propose Super-identity Convolutional Neural Network (SICNN) for enhancing the identity information in face hallucination.
- We propose Domain-Integrated Training method to overcome the problem caused by dynamic domain divergence when training SICNN.
- Compared with existing state-of-the-art hallucination methods, the SICNN achieves superior visual quality and identity recognizability when super-resolving a facial image of size 12×14 pixels with an $8\times$ upscaling factor.

2   Related Works

Single image super-resolution (SR) aims at recovering a HR image from a LR one. Face hallucination is a kind of class-specific image SR, which exploits the statistical properties of facial images. We classify face hallucination methods into two categories: classical approaches and deep learning approach.

Classical Approaches. Subspace-based and facial components-based methods are two main kinds of classical face hallucination approaches.

For subspace-based methods. Liu et al. [17] employed a Principal Component Analysis (PCA) based global appearance model to hallucinate LR faces and a local non-parametric model to enhance the details. Ma et al. [21] used multiple local exemplar patches sampled from aligned HR facial images to hallucinate LR faces. Li et al. [16] resolved to sparse representation on local face patches. These subspace-based methods require precisely aligned reference HR and LR facial images with the same pose and facial expression.

Facial components based methods super-resolve facial parts rather than entire faces to address various poses and expressions. Tappen et al. [29] used SIFT flow to align LR images, and then deformed the reference HR images. However, the global structure is not preserved due to using local mapping.

Yang et al. [33] presented a structured face hallucination method which can maintain the facial structure. However, it relies on accurate facial landmarks.

Deep Learning Approaches. Recently, deep convolutional neural networks (DCNNs) achieve remarkable progresses in a variety of computer vision tasks, such as image classification [13], object detection [23], and face recognition [31]. Zhou et al. [37] proposed a bichannel CNN to hallucinate blurry facial images in the wild. For un-aligned faces, Zhu et al. [38] proposed to jointly learn face hallucination and facial dense spatial correspondence field estimation. The approach of [35] is a GAN-based method to generate realistic facial images. These works ignore the identity information recovery that is important for recognizability and hallucination quality. Johnson et al. [12] and Bruna et al. [2] relied on perceptual loss function closer to perceptual similarity to recover visually more convincing HR images for general image SR. In this paper we modified the perceptual loss to facilitate identity hypersphere space and propose a novel training approach to overcome the challenging while using the loss.

3   Super-Identity CNN

In this section, we will first describe the architecture of our face hallucination network. Then we will introduce the proposed super-resolution loss and super-identity loss for identity recovery. After that, we will analyze the challenge, dynamic domain divergence problem, in super-identity training. At the last, we introduce the proposed domain-integrated training algorithm to overcome this challenge.

3.1   Face Hallucination Network Architecture

As shown in Fig. 2(a), the face hallucination network can be decomposed into feature extraction, deconvolution, mapping, and reconstruction.

We use dense block [10] to extract semantic features from LR inputs. More specifically, in the dense block, we set the growth rate to 32 and the kernel size to 3×3. Deconvolution layer consists of learnable upscaling filters to enlarge the resolutions of input features. Mapping is implemented by a convolutional layer to reduce the dimension of features to reduce computational cost. Reconstruction also exploits a convolutional layer to predict HR images from semantic features.

Here, we denote a convolutional layer as $Conv(s, c)$ and a deconvolutional layer as $DeConv(s, c)$, where the variables s and c represent the filter size and the number of channels, respectively. In addition, PReLU [8] activation function achieves promising performance in CNN-based super-resolution [6] and we use it after each layer except the reconstruction stage.

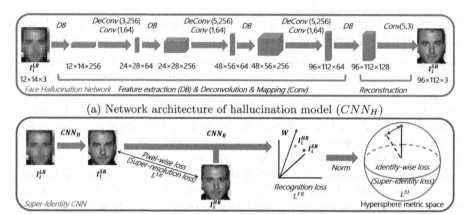

(a) Network architecture of hallucination model (CNN_H)

(b) Illustration of the proposed super-identity CNN

Fig. 2. Framework of our approach. (a) The network architecture of our hallucination network (CNN_H). DB denotes dense block [10]. (b) Illustration of our super-identity CNN. It uses super-resolution loss (L^{SR}), super-identity loss (L^{SI}), and recognition loss (L^{FR}) with domain-integrated training. Norm denotes Euclidean normalization, and CNN_R denotes the recognition network.

3.2 Super-Resolution Loss

We use the pixel-wise Euclidean loss, called super-resolution loss, to constrain the overall visual appearance. For LR face input I_i^{LR}, we penalize the pixel-wise Euclidean distance between the hallucinated face and its corresponding HR face:

$$L^{SR}(I_i^{LR}, I_i^{HR}) = \left\| CNN_H(I_i^{LR}) - I_i^{HR} \right\|_2^2, \tag{1}$$

where I_i^{LR} and I_i^{HR} are the i-th LR and HR facial image pair in the training data respectively, and $CNN_H(I_i^{LR})$ represents the output of hallucination network with input I_i^{LR}. For better understanding, we also denote $CNN_H(I_i^{LR})$ as I_i^{SR} in the following text.

3.3 Hypersphere Identity Metric Space

Super-resolution loss can constrain pixel-level appearance. And we further use a constrain on the identity level. To measure the identity level difference, the first step is to find a robust identity metric space. Here we employ the hypersphere space [18] due to its state-of-the-art performance on identity representation. As shown in Fig. 2(b), our hallucination network is cascaded with a face recognition network (i.e. CNN_R) and an Euclidean normalization operation that projects faces to the constructed hypersphere identity metric space.

CNN_R is a Resnet-like [9] CNN and more details about the network structure are introduced in our supplementary material. It is trained by A-Softmax loss function [18] which encourages the CNN to learn discriminate identity features (i.e. maximizing inter-class distance and minimizing intra-class distance) by an angular margin. In this paper, we denote this loss function as the recognition loss L^{FR}. For a face input I_i belonging to the y_i-th identity. The face recognition loss is represented as:

$$L^{FR}(I_i) = -\log\left(\frac{e^{\|CNN_R(I_i)\|\varphi(m\Theta_{y_i})}}{e^{\|CNN_R(I_i)\|\varphi(m\Theta_{y_i})} + \sum_{j \neq y_i} e^{\|CNN_R(I_i)\|\varphi(\Theta_j)}}\right), \quad (2)$$

where the Θ_{y_i} denotes the learned angle for identity y_i, $\varphi(\Theta_{y_i})$ is a monotonically decreasing function generalized from $\cos(\Theta_{y_i})$, and m is the hyper parameter of angular margin constrain. More details can be found in Sphereface [18].

3.4 Super-Identity Loss

To impose the identity information in the training process, one choice is to use a loss computed by features Euclidean distance between face pairs, such as perceptual loss [12]. However, in this paper, since our goal is to minimize identity distance in hypersphere metric space, the original perceptual loss, computed by L2 distance is not the best choice in our task. Therefore, we propose a modified perceptual loss, called Super-Identity (SI) loss, to compute the normalized Euclidean distance (equivalent to geodesic distance). This modification makes the loss directly related to identity in hypersphere space and facilitate our investigation in Sect. 3.5.

For a LR face input I_i^{LR}, we penalize the normalized Euclidean distance between the hallucinated face and its corresponding HR face in the constructed hypersphere identity metric space:

$$L^{SI}(I_i^{LR}, I_i^{HR}) = \left\|\widehat{CNN_R(I_i^{SR})} - \widehat{CNN_R(I_i^{HR})}\right\|_2^2 \quad (3)$$

where $CNN_R(I_i^{SR})$ and $CNN_R(I_i^{HR})$ are the identity features extracted from face recognition model (CNN_R) for facial images I_i^{SR} and I_i^{HR}, respectively. $\widehat{CNN_R(I_i^{SR})} = \frac{CNN_R(I_i^{SR})}{\|CNN_R(I_i^{SR})\|_2}$ is the identity representation projected to the unit hypersphere.

In addition to L^{SI}, we want to have some discussions about perceptual loss beyond our work. In general, the perceptual loss is computed by L2 distance. However, in most CNNs, inner-product operation is used in fully-connected and convolutional layers. These outputs are related to the feature's norm, weight's norm and the angular between them. Therefore, for different tasks and different metric space (e.g. [5,19,24]), some modifications about computational metric space of perceptual loss are necessary (L^{SI} is one of the cases).

3.5 Challenges of Training with Super-Identity Loss

Super-identity loss imposes an identity level constrain. We examine different training methods as follows:

Baseline Training Approach I. A straightforward way to train our framework is jointly using the L^{SR}, L^{SI} and L^{FR} to train both CNN_H and CNN_R from scratch. The optimization objective can be represented as:

$$\min_{\theta_{CNN_H}\theta_{CNN_R}} \frac{1}{n}\sum_{i=1}^{n} L^{SR}(I_i^{LR}, I_i^{HR}) + \alpha L^{SI}(I_i^{LR}, I_i^{HR}) + \beta L^{FR}(I_i^{SR}, I_i^{HR}), \quad (4)$$

where α and β denotes the loss weight of the L^{SI} and L^{FR} respectively, θ_{CNN_H} and θ_{CNN_R} denotes the learnable parameters.

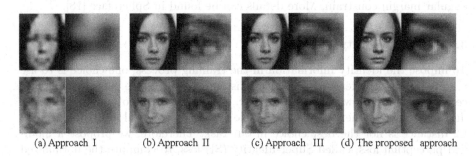

(a) Approach I   (b) Approach II   (c) Approach III   (d) The proposed approach

Fig. 3. Face hallucination examples produced by CNN_H trained by different training approaches. These four columns of results are produced by baseline training approach I, II, III and the proposed domain-integrated training approach respectively. It is clear that our approach achieves the best result while other results are noisy. This figure is best viewed in color. Please *zoom in* for better comparison.

Observation I. This training approach generates artifacts (see Fig. 3, first column) and the loss is too difficult to converge. The reasons may come from: (1) In the early training stage, the hallucinated faces are quite different from HR faces, so the CNN_R is too difficult to be optimized from scratch. (2) The objective of L^{FR} (i.e. minimizing the intra-class variance) is different from the objective of L^{SI} and L^{SR} loss (minimizing the pair-wise distance), which is disadvantageous to CNN_R and CNN_H learning. So, we cannot use the L^{SI} in CNN_R learning and also cannot use the L^{FR} in CNN_H learning.

Baseline Training Approach II. To solve above problems, one possible training approach used in perceptual loss [12] can be used. In particular, we train a CNN_R using HR faces and then jointly use the L^{SR} and the L^{SI} to train the CNN_H. The joint objective of L^{SI} and L^{SR} can be represented as:

$$\min_{\theta_{CNN_H}} \frac{1}{n}\sum_{i=1}^{n} L^{SR}(I_i^{LR}, I_i^{HR}) + \alpha L^{SI}(I_i^{LR}, I_i^{HR}), \quad (5)$$

Observation II. We have two observations while using this training approach: (1) The L^{SI} is difficult to converge. (2) The visual results are noisy (see Fig. 3, second column). To investigate these challenges, we first visualized the learned identity features (after Euclidean normalization, as shown in Fig. 4) and found that there exists a large margin between the hallucination domain and the HR domain. We formulate this challenge as domain divergence problem. It specifies the failure of the CNN_R, trained by HR faces, to project faces from hallucination domains to a measurable hypersphere identity metric space. In other words, this face recognition model cannot extract effective identity representation for hallucinated faces. This makes the L^{SI} very difficult to converge and easily get stuck in local minima (i.e. occur many noises in hallucination results).

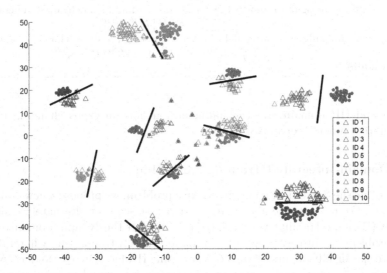

Fig. 4. The distribution of identity features (after Euclidean normalization) from hallucination domain (triangle) and HR domain (dot). These identities are randomly selected from the training set. Different colors denote different identities. We use t-SNE [30] to reduce the dimensions for better understanding. We can observe that there is a large gap between above two domains in the identity metric space.

Baseline Training Approach III. To overcome the domain divergence challenge, a straightforward alternately training strategy can be used. In particular, we first trained a CNN_H only using the L^{SR}. Then we trained a CNN_R using hallucinated faces and HR faces. Finally, we finetune the CNN_R jointly using the L^{SR} and the L^{SI} following baseline training approach II.

Observation III. Although this alternately training strategy seems able to overcome the domain divergence problem, it still produces artifacts (as shown in Fig. 3, third column). The reason is that the hallucination domain keeps changing when the CNN_H is being updated. If the hallucination domain has changed, the face recognition model cannot extract effective and measurable identity representation of hallucinated faces anymore.

In short, above observations can be concluded into a dynamic domain divergence problem as following: a large margin exists between the hallucination

---

Algorithm 1. Mini-batch SGD based domain-integrated training approach

---

Input: Face recognition model CNN_R trained by HR facial images, face hallucination model CNN_H trained by L^{SR}, minibatch size N, LR and HR facial image pairs $\{I_i^{LR}, I_i^{HR}\}$.
Output: SICNN.
1: **while** not converge **do**
2:     Choose one minibatch of N LR and HR image pairs $\{I_i^{LR}, I_i^{HR}\}$, $i = 1, ..., N$.
3:     Generate one minibatch of N hallucinated facial images I_i^{SR} from I_i^{LR}, $i = 1, ..., N$, where $I_i^{SR} = CNN_H(I_i^{LR})$.
4:     Update the recognition model CNN_R by descending its stochastic gradient:
        $$\nabla_{\theta_{CNN_R}} \frac{1}{N} \sum_{i=1}^{N} L^{FR}(\{I_i^{SR}, I_i^{HR}\})$$
5:     Update the hallucination model CNN_H by descending its stochastic gradient:
        $$\nabla_{\theta_{CNN_H}} \frac{1}{N} \sum_{i=1}^{N} L^{SR}(I_i^{LR}, I_i^{HR}) + \alpha L^{SI}(I_i^{LR}, I_i^{HR})$$
6: **end while**

---

domain and HR domain and the hallucination domain keeps changing if the hallucination model keeps learning.

3.6   Domain-Integrated Training Algorithm

To overcome the dynamic domain divergence problem, we propose a new training procedure. From above the above observations, we see that alternately training strategy (Baseline Training Approach III) can alleviate the dynamic domain divergence problem. We further propose to do this alternately training in each iteration.

More specifically, we first train a CNN_R using HR facial images and a CNN_H using the L^{SR}. Then, we propose to use domain-integrated training approach (Algorithm 1) to finetune CNN_R and CNN_H alternately in each iteration.

In particular, in each iteration, we first update the CNN_R using the recognition loss, which allows the CNN_R to perform accurate identity representation in this mini-batch of faces from different domains. Then, we jointly use the L^{SR} and the L^{SI} to update the CNN_H. This training approach can encourage the CNN_R to construct a robust mapping from faces to the measurable hypersphere identity metric space in each iteration for L^{SI} optimization whatever the CNN_H is changing. The alternative optimization process is conducted until converged. Some hallucination examples are shown in Fig. 3, fourth column, where we can observe a much better visual result with this training approach.

3.7   Comparison to Adversarial Training

Domain-Integrated (DI) training and adversarial training [7] can be related to their alternative learning strategy. But they are quite different in several aspects as follows:

(1) Generally speaking, DI training is essentially a cooperative process in which CNN_H collaborates with CNN_R to minimize the identity difference. The learning objective is the same in each sub-iteration. However, in adversarial

training, generator and discriminator compete against each other to improve the performance. The learning objective is alternatively challenging during two models learning.

(2) The loss functions and optimization style are different. In DI training, we minimize L^{FR} in CNN_R constructing a marginal identity metric space and then minimize L^{SI} for CNN_H reducing pair-wise identity difference. Differently, in adversarial training, the classification loss is minimized for discriminator learning and maximized for generator learning.

4   Experiments

In this section, we will first describe the training and testing details. Then we perform an ablation study to evaluate the effectiveness of the proposed Super-Identity loss and Domain-Integrated training. Further, we evaluate our proposed method with other state-of-the-art methods. At the last, we evaluate the benefit of our method for low-resolution face recognition. *More evaluations are included in our supplementary material.*

4.1   Training Details

Training Data. For a fair comparison with other state-of-the-art methods, we do face alignment in facial images. In particular, we use similarity transformation based on five landmarks detected by MTCNN [36]. *We have removed the images and identities overlap between training and testing.*

For face recognition training, we use web-collected facial images including CASIA-WebFace [34], CACD2000 [4], CelebA [20], VGG Faces [22] as *Set A*. It roughly goes to 1.5M images of 17,680 unique persons.

For face hallucination training, we select 1.1M HR facial images (larger than 96×112 pixels) from the same 1.5M images as *Set B*.

Training details. For recognition model training, we use *Set A* with the batch size of 512 and m (angular margin constrain in Eq. 2) of 4. The learning rate is started from 0.1 and divided by 10 at the 20K, 30K iterations. The training process is finished at 35K iterations.

For hallucination model training, we use *Set B* with the batch size of 128. The learning rate is started from 0.02 and divided by 10 at the 30K, 60K iterations. A complete training is finished at 80K iterations.

For domain-integrated training, we use *Set B* with the batch size of 128 for CNN_H and 256 for CNN_R. The learning rate is started from 0.01 and divided by 10 at the 6K iterations. A complete training is finished at 9K iterations.

4.2   Testing Details

Testing Data. We randomly select 1,000 identities with 10,000 HR facial images (larger than 96×112 pixels) from UMD-Face [1] dataset as *Set C*. The dataset is used for face hallucination and identity recovery evaluation.

Evaluation Protocols. In this section, we perform three kinds of evaluations: (1) Visual quality. (2) Identity recovery. (3) Identity recognizability. For visual quality evaluation, we report several visual examples results on *Set C*.

For identity recovery, we evaluate the performance of recovering identity information while super-resolving faces. In particular, we use the CNN_R trained by *Set A* as identity features extractor. And the identity features are taken from the output of the first fully connected layer. Then we compute the identity similarity (i.e. cosine similarity) between the hallucinated face and its corresponding HR faces on *Set C*. The average similarities over the testing set are reported.

For identity recognizability, we evaluate the recognizability of hallucinated faces. In particular, we first downsample *Set A* to 12×14 pixels as *Set A - LR*. Then we use different methods to super-resolve *Set A - LR* to 96×112 pixels as different *Set A - SR*. At last, we use the *Set A - SR* to train different CNN_R and evaluate them on LFW [11] and YTF [32].

4.3   Ablation Experiment

Loss Weight. The hyper parameter α (see Algorithm 1) dominates the identity recovery. To verify the effectiveness of the proposed Super-Identity loss, we vary α from 0 (i.e. only use super-resolution loss) to 32 to learn different models. From Table 1 and Fig. 5, we observe that larger α make the facial images sharper with more details and brings the better performance of identity recovery and recognizability. But too large α also makes the texture look slightly unnatural. And, since the performances of identity recovery and identity recognizability are stable when α is larger than 8, we fix α to 8 in other experiments.

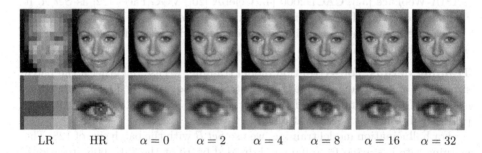

| LR | HR | $\alpha = 0$ | $\alpha = 2$ | $\alpha = 4$ | $\alpha = 8$ | $\alpha = 16$ | $\alpha = 32$ |

Fig. 5. Face hallucination examples generated by models trained with different loss weight α. It is clear that choosing larger α can make the facial images sharper with more details. Please *zoom in* for better comparison.

Training Approach. We evaluate different training approaches introduced in Sects. 3.5 and 3.6. Some visual results are shown in Fig. 3. We can see that Domain-Integrated training achieves the best visual results. Besides, from Table 2, Domain-Integrated training also achieves the best performance of identity recovery and identity recognizability.

Table 1. Quantitative comparison of different α on identity recovery and identity recognizability evaluation. Larger α brings better performance and it is stable when α is larger than 8.

α	0	2	4	8	16	32
Identity similarity	0.4418	0.5134	0.5639	0.5978	0.6041	0.6101
LFW accuracy	97.61%	97.88%	98.05%	98.25%	98.23%	98.16%
YTF accurarcy	93.20%	93.48%	93.56%	93.82%	93.84%	93.76%

Table 2. Quantitative comparison of different training approaches on identity recovery and identity recognizability evaluation. The results demonstrate the superiority of our proposed domain-integrated training.

Training approach	I	II	III	Domain-integrated training
Identity similarity	0.3875	0.4829	0.5132	**0.5978**
LFW accuracy	97.16%	97.46%	97.58%	**98.25%**
YTF accurarcy	92.98%	93.32%	93.34%	**93.84%%**

4.4 Evaluation on Face Hallucination

We compare SICNN with other state-of-the-art methods and bicubic interpolation on *Set C* for face hallucination. In particular, we follow EnhanceNet [25] training another UR-DGN, called UR-DGN*, with additional perceptual loss computed in end of the second and the last ResBlock in CNN_R. *All methods are re-trained in same training set - Set B.*

Some visual examples are shown in Fig. 6. More visual results are included in our supplementary material. We also report the results of average Peak Signal-to-Noise Ratio (PSNR) and Structural Similarity (SSIM) in Table 3. But as the claim of other works [12,15,25], PSNR and SSIM results are useless for sematic super-resolution evaluation while visual quality and recognizability are more valuable.

From the visual results, it is clear that our method achieves the best results over other methods. We analyze the results as follows:

(1) For Ma *et al.*'s method, exemplar patches based, the results are over-smooth and suffer from obvious blocking for such low low-resolution input with large up-sampling scale.
(2) For LapSRN [14], since it is based on L2 pixel-wise loss, it makes the hallucinated faces over-smooth.
(3) For UR-DGN [35], it jointly uses pixel-wise Euclidean loss and adversarial loss to generate a realistic facial image closest to the average of all potential images. Thus, though the generated facial images look realistic, they are quite different from the original HR images.

(4) For UR-DGN*, it uses an additional loss - perceptual loss computed in our CNN_R as the pair-wise semantic loss for identity recovery. Though this pixels-wise loss + adversarial loss + perceptual loss is the state-of-the-art super-resolution training approach (i.e. EnhancementNet [25]). It still achieves inferior results than ours.

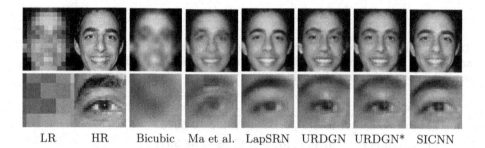

LR   HR   Bicubic   Ma et al.   LapSRN   URDGN   URDGN*   SICNN

Fig. 6. Comparison with the state-of-the-art methods on hallucination test dataset. It is clear that our method achieves the best hallucination visual quality. Please *zoom in* for better comparison. More visual results are included in our supplementary material.

Table 3. Quantitative hallucination comparison of different training approaches.

Method	Bicubic	Ma *et al.*	LapSRN	UR-DGN	UR-DGN*	SICNN
PSNR (db)	23.1323	23.8606	26.1451	24.1857	25.2859	26.8945
SSIM	0.6093	0.6571	0.7417	0.6764	0.7224	0.7689

Table 4. Quantitative comparison on identity recovery and identity recognizability evaluation. The results demonstrate the superiority of our proposed method.

Method	Bicubic	Ma *et al.*	LapSRN	UR-DGN	UR-DGN*	SICNN
Identity Similarity	0.2913	0.3823	0.4361	0.3682	0.5267	**0.5978**
LFW Acc	97.51%	97.58%	97.46%	97.20%	98.01%	**98.25%**
YTF Acc	93.08%	93.26%	93.10%	92.78%	93.54%	**93.82%**

4.5   Evaluation on Identity Recovery

We perform an evaluation on identity recovery with other state-of-the-art methods. All models for evaluation are the same as last experiment (i.e. Sect. 4.4).

From the Table 4, we observe that our method achieves the best performance. Besides, we also observe that UR-DGN, trained by pixels-wise loss and adversarial loss, even shows inferior performance than LapSRN though with sharper visual results (See Sect. 4.4). It means that UR-DGN will lose some identity information while super-resolving a face because the adversarial loss is not a pair-wise loss. And if add perceptual loss (i.e. UR-DGN*), pair-wise semantic loss, the results can be improved, but still inferior to our method.

4.6   Evaluation on Identity Recognizability

Follow last two experiments (i.e. Sects. 4.4 and 4.5)., we further perform an evaluation on identity recognizability with other state-of-the-art methods.

From the Table 4, we observe that our method achieves the best performance. We also obtain similar observations as last experiment. Besides, we also observe that though several methods (LapSRN. Ma *et al.*, and UR-DGN) obtain better visual results than Bicubic interpolation, the identity recognizability of super-resolved face is similar or even inferior. It means that these methods cannot generate discriminative faces with better identity recognizability.

4.7   Evaluation on Low-Resolution Face Recognition

To evaluate the benefit of our method for low-resolution face recognition, we compare our method $(SICNN + CNN_R)$ with other state-of-the-art recognition methods on LFW [11] and YTF [32] benchmark.

From the results in Table 5, we find that these methods' input sizes are relatively large (area size from 15.3× to 298× compared with our method). Moreover, using our face hallucination method, the recognition model can still achieve reasonable results in such ultra-low resolution. We also tried using un-aligned faces in training and testing and our proposed method still can achieve similar improvement of performance.

Table 5. Face verification performance of different methods on LFW [11] and YTF [32] benchmark. It shows that our method can help the recognition model to archive high accuracy with ultra-low-resolution inputs.

Method	Ours	CNN_R	Human	[28]	[27]	[26]	[22]	[31]	[18]
Input size	12 × 14	96 × 112	Original	152 × 152	47 × 55	224 × 224	224 × 224	96 × 112	96 × 112
LFW acc	98.25%	99.48%	97.53%	97.35%	98.70%	99.63%	98.95%	99.28%	99.42%
YTF acc	93.82%	95.38%	-	91.4%	93.2%	95.1%	97.3%	94.9%	95.0%

5   Conclusion

In this paper, we present Super-Identity CNN (SICNN) to enhance the identity information during super resolving face images of size 12 × 14 pixels with an 8× upscaling factor. Specifically, SICNN aims to minimize the identity difference between the hallucinated face and its corresponding HR face. In addition, we propose a domain-integrated training approach to overcome the dynamic domain divergence problem when training SICNN. Extensive experiments demonstrate that SICNN not only achieves superior hallucination results but also significantly improves the performance of low-resolution face recognition.

Acknowledgement. This work was supported in part by MediaTek Inc and the Ministry of Science and Technology, Taiwan, under Grant MOST 107-2634-F-002 -007. We also benefit from the grants from NVIDIA and the NVIDIA DGX-1 AI Supercomputer.

References

1. Bansal, A., Nanduri, A., Castillo, C., Ranjan, R., Chellappa, R.: UMDFaces: an annotated face dataset for training deep networks. arXiv:1611.01484 (2016)
2. Bruna, J., Sprechmann, P., LeCun, Y.: Super-resolution with deep convolutional sufficient statistics. In: ICLR (2016)
3. Chang, L., Tsao, D.Y.: The code for facial identity in the primate brain. Cell **169**(6), 1013–1028 (2017)
4. Chen, B.C., Chen, C.S., Hsu, W.H.: Face recognition and retrieval using cross-age reference coding with cross-age celebrity dataset. TMM **17**(6), 804–815 (2015)
5. Chunjie, L., Qiang, Y., et al.: Cosine normalization: Using cosine similarity instead of dot product in neural networks. arXiv (2017)
6. Dong, C., Loy, C.C., Tang, X.: Accelerating the super-resolution convolutional neural network. In: Leibe, B., Matas, J., Sebe, N., Welling, M. (eds.) ECCV 2016. LNCS, vol. 9906, pp. 391–407. Springer, Cham (2016). https://doi.org/10.1007/978-3-319-46475-6_25
7. Goodfellow, I., et al.: Generative adversarial nets. In: NIPS, pp. 2672–2680 (2014)
8. He, K., Zhang, X., Ren, S., Sun, J.: Delving deep into rectifiers: surpassing human-level performance on imagenet classification. In: ICCV, pp. 1026–1034 (2015)
9. He, K., Zhang, X., Ren, S., Sun, J.: Deep residual learning for image recognition. In: CVPR, pp. 770–778 (2016)
10. Huang, G., Liu, Z., Weinberge, K., Van Der Maaten, L.: Densely connected convolutional networks (2017)
11. Huang, G.B., Learned-Miller, E.: Labeled faces in the wild: updates and new reporting procedures. Dept. Comput. Sci., Univ. Massachusetts Amherst, Amherst, MA, USA, Technical report 14–003 (2014)
12. Johnson, J., Alahi, A., Fei-Fei, L.: Perceptual losses for real-time style transfer and super-resolution. In: Leibe, B., Matas, J., Sebe, N., Welling, M. (eds.) ECCV 2016. LNCS, vol. 9906, pp. 694–711. Springer, Cham (2016). https://doi.org/10.1007/978-3-319-46475-6_43
13. Krizhevsky, A., Sutskever, I., Hinton, G.E.: Imagenet classification with deep convolutional neural networks. In: NIPS, pp. 1097–1105 (2012)
14. Lai, W.S., Huang, J.B., Ahuja, N., Yang, M.H.: Deep laplacian pyramid networks for fast and accurate super-resolution. In: CVPR (2017)
15. Ledig, C., et al.: Photo-realistic single image super-resolution using a generative adversarial network (2017)
16. Li, Y., Cai, C., Qiu, G., Lam, K.M.: Face hallucination based on sparse local-pixel structure. PR **47**(3), 1261–1270 (2014)
17. Liu, C., Shum, H.Y., Freeman, W.T.: Face hallucination: theory and practice. IJCV **75**(1), 115–134 (2007)

18. Liu, W., Wen, Y., Yu, Z., Li, M., Raj, B., Song, L.: Sphereface: deep hypersphere embedding for face recognition (2017)
19. Liu, W., et al.: Deep hyperspherical learning. In: NIPS, pp. 3953–3963 (2017)
20. Liu, Z., Luo, P., Wang, X., Tang, X.: Deep learning face attributes in the wild. In: ICCV, pp. 3730–3738 (2015)
21. Ma, X., Zhang, J., Qi, C.: Hallucinating face by position-patch. PR **43**(6), 2224–2236 (2010)
22. Parkhi, O.M., Vedaldi, A., Zisserman, A.: Deep face recognition. In: BMVC, vol. 1, p. 6 (2015)
23. Ren, S., He, K., Girshick, R., Sun, J.: Faster R-CNN: towards real-time object detection with region proposal networks. In: NIPS, pp. 91–99 (2015)
24. Rippel, O., Paluri, M., Dollar, P., Bourdev, L.: Metric learning with adaptive density discrimination. In: ICLR (2016)
25. Sajjadi, M.S., Scholkopf, B., Hirsch, M.: Enhancenet: single image super-resolution through automated texture synthesis. In: ICCV, pp. 4491–4500 (2017)
26. Schroff, F., Kalenichenko, D., Philbin, J.: Facenet: a unified embedding for face recognition and clustering. In: CVPR, pp. 815–823 (2015)
27. Sun, Y., Wang, X., Tang, X.: Deeply learned face representations are sparse, selective, and robust. In: CVPR, pp. 2892–2900 (2015)
28. Taigman, Y., Yang, M., Ranzato, M., Wolf, L.: Deepface: closing the gap to human-level performance in face verification. In: CVPR, pp. 1701–1708 (2014)
29. Tappen, M.F., Liu, C.: A Bayesian approach to alignment-based image hallucination. In: Fitzgibbon, A., Lazebnik, S., Perona, P., Sato, Y., Schmid, C. (eds.) ECCV 2012. LNCS, vol. 7578, pp. 236–249. Springer, Heidelberg (2012). https://doi.org/10.1007/978-3-642-33786-4_18
30. Van Der Maaten, L.: Accelerating t-sne using tree-based algorithms. JMLR **15**(1), 3221–3245 (2014)
31. Wen, Y., Zhang, K., Li, Z., Qiao, Y.: A discriminative feature learning approach for deep face recognition. In: Leibe, B., Matas, J., Sebe, N., Welling, M. (eds.) ECCV 2016. LNCS, vol. 9911, pp. 499–515. Springer, Cham (2016). https://doi.org/10.1007/978-3-319-46478-7_31
32. Wolf, L., Hassner, T., Maoz, I.: Face recognition in unconstrained videos with matched background similarity. In: CVPR, pp. 529–534 (2011)
33. Yang, C.Y., Liu, S., Yang, M.H.: Structured face hallucination. In: ECVP, pp. 1099–1106 (2013)
34. Yi, D., Lei, Z., Liao, S., Li, S.Z.: Learning face representation from scratch. arXiv:1411.7923 (2014)
35. Yu, X., Porikli, F.: Ultra-resolving face images by discriminative generative networks. In: Leibe, B., Matas, J., Sebe, N., Welling, M. (eds.) ECCV 2016. LNCS, vol. 9909, pp. 318–333. Springer, Cham (2016). https://doi.org/10.1007/978-3-319-46454-1_20
36. Zhang, K., Zhang, Z., Li, Z., Qiao, Y.: Joint face detection and alignment using multitask cascaded convolutional networks. SPL **23**(10), 1499–1503 (2016)
37. Zhou, E., Fan, H., Cao, Z., Jiang, Y., Yin, Q.: Learning face hallucination in the wild. In: AAAI, pp. 3871–3877 (2015)
38. Zhu, S., Liu, S., Loy, C.C., Tang, X.: Deep cascaded bi-network for face hallucination. In: Leibe, B., Matas, J., Sebe, N., Welling, M. (eds.) ECCV 2016. LNCS, vol. 9909, pp. 614–630. Springer, Cham (2016). https://doi.org/10.1007/978-3-319-46454-1_37

What Do I Annotate Next? An Empirical Study of Active Learning for Action Localization

Fabian Caba Heilbron[1(✉)], Joon-Young Lee[2], Hailin Jin[2],
and Bernard Ghanem[1]

[1] King Abdullah University of Science and Technology (KAUST),
Thuwal, Saudi Arabia
{fabian.caba,bernard.ghanem}@kaust.edu.sa
[2] Adobe Research, San Jose, CA, USA
{jolee,hljin}@adobe.com
https://cabaf.github.io/what-to-annotate-next

Abstract. Despite tremendous progress achieved in temporal action localization, state-of-the-art methods still struggle to train accurate models when annotated data is scarce. In this paper, we introduce a novel active learning framework for temporal localization that aims to mitigate this data dependency issue. We equip our framework with active selection functions that can *reuse knowledge* from previously annotated datasets. We study the performance of two state-of-the-art active selection functions as well as two widely used active learning baselines. To validate the effectiveness of each one of these selection functions, we conduct simulated experiments on ActivityNet. We find that using previously acquired knowledge as a bootstrapping source is crucial for active learners aiming to localize actions. When equipped with the right selection function, our proposed framework exhibits significantly better performance than standard active learning strategies, such as uncertainty sampling. Finally, we employ our framework to augment the newly compiled Kinetics action dataset with ground-truth temporal annotations. As a result, we collect *Kinetics-Localization*, a novel large-scale dataset for temporal action localization, which contains more than 15K YouTube videos.

Keywords: Video understanding · Temporal action localization
Active learning · Video annotation

1 Introduction

Video data arguably dominates the largest portion of internet content. With more than 74% of total internet traffic being video [15], a need that arises

---

F. C. Heilbron—Work done during internship at Adobe Research.

Electronic supplementary material The online version of this chapter (https://doi.org/10.1007/978-3-030-01252-6_13) contains supplementary material, which is available to authorized users.

© Springer Nature Switzerland AG 2018
V. Ferrari et al. (Eds.): ECCV 2018, LNCS 11215, pp. 212–229, 2018.
https://doi.org/10.1007/978-3-030-01252-6_13

is to automatically understand and index such massive amounts of data. The computer vision community has embraced this problem, and during the last decade, several approaches for video analysis have been proposed [8,26,31,39,41, 48,52,58,76]. One of the most challenging tasks in this field, which has recently gained much attention, is to understand and temporally localize human actions in untrimmed videos. Such a task, which is widely known as temporal action localization, aims to produce temporal bounds in a video, during which human actions occur.

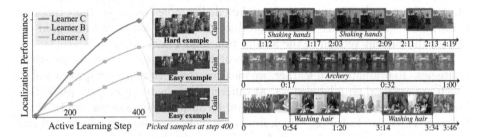

Fig. 1. Active Learning for Action Localization. We compare three different active learners for temporal action localization. We plot the localization performance (mAP) of each learner at different active learning steps. Each learner's aim is to use the least number of training samples as possible, which are obtained sequentially by annotating samples from an unlabeled set. The proposed method resembles Learner C, which minimizes the number of active learning steps to reach a target performance. Using our active learner, we construct Kinetics-Localization, a novel and large-scale dataset for temporal action localization.

Datasets such as Thumos14 [35], ActivityNet [8], and Charades [58] have enabled the development of innovative approaches addressing the temporal action localization problem [50,56,71,75,77]. These approaches have been successful in increasing localization performance while maintaining a low computational footprint [5,71]. For instance, current state-of-the-art approaches [44,77] have improved more than three times the first reported performance on datasets like Thumos14 and ActivityNet. However, despite those great achievements, a crucial limitation persists, namely the dependence of these models on large-scale annotated data for training. This limitation often prevents the deployment of action localization methods at scale, due to the large costs associated with video labeling (*e.g.* Charades authors [58] spent $1 per video).

Additionally, given that datasets for temporal action localization are relatively small, it is unclear whether existing methods will reach performances like the ones obtained in other vision tasks such as object detection [54]. To overcome some of these issues, Wang *et al.* [68] propose a new model that uses video-level annotations combined with an attention mechanism to pinpoint actions temporal bounds. Although it does not require temporal ground-truth, their performance is significantly lower than that achieved by fully-supervised approaches, thus, restricting its applications that do not require accurate detection.

In this paper, we propose an active learning method that aims to ease the large-scale data dependence of current temporal localization methods. As in every active learning setting [55], our goal is to develop a learner that selects samples (videos in this case) from unlabeled sets to be annotated by an oracle. As compared to traditional active learners [27,42] where heuristics such as uncertainty sampling are used to perform the sample selection, we explore novel selection functions [25,40] that reuse knowledge from a previously existing dataset. For instance, we study a learnable selection function that learns a mapping from a model-sample state pair to an expected improvement in performance. In doing so, such function learns to score the unlabelled samples based on the expected performance gain they are likely to produce if they are annotated and used to update the current version of the localization model being trained.

Figure 1 depicts the learning process of three different action localization strategies. To evaluate each learner, we measure the performance improvements, which are assessed on a labeled set, at different training dataset sizes (or learning stages). We associate traditional action localization approaches [5,71,77] to Learner A (passive learning), which randomly picks samples to be annotated for future training iterations. Learner A exhibits passive behavior in making smart selections of samples to augment its training set. Learner B is an active learner that uses uncertainty sampling [42] to select the samples (the learner chooses instances whose labels are most uncertain). Learner C is a learning-based active learner. Because it incorporates historical knowledge from previous dataset selections, Learner C enables a better learning process. In this paper, we introduce an active learning framework that minimizes the number of active learning steps required to reach the desired performance.

Contributions. The core idea of the paper is to develop an active learning framework for temporal action localization. Specifically, the contributions of this paper are threefold. (**1**) We introduce a new active learner for action localization (see Sect. 3). To develop our approach, we thoughtfully study different sampling functions, including those that can exploit previously labeled data to learn or bootstrap a selection function that chooses unlabelled samples with the aim of improving the localization model the most. (**2**) We conduct extensive experiments in Sect. 4 demonstrating the capabilities of the proposed framework. When compared to traditional learning (random sampling), our approach learns to detect actions significantly quicker. Additionally, we show that our active learner can be employed in batch-mode, and is robust to noisy ground-truth annotations. (**3**) We employ our active learner to construct a novel dataset for temporal action localization (see Sect. 5). Using videos from the Kinetics [39] dataset, we apply our learner to request temporal annotations from Amazon Mechanical Turk workers. We name this collected dataset *Kinetics-Localization* and it comprises more than 15*K* YouTube videos.

2   Related Work

This section briefly discusses the most relevant work to ours, namely those related to active learning and temporal action localization.

Active Learning tackles the problem of selecting samples from unlabeled sets to be annotated by an oracle. In the last decade, several active learning strategies have been proposed [27,42,63] and applied to several research fields, including speech recognition [32], natural language processing [62], chemistry [18], just to name a few. We refer the reader to the survey of Settles [55] for an extensive review of active learning methods. Active learning has also been used in traditional computer vision tasks, such as image classification [4,22,25,36,37,53] and object detection [64], or to construct large-scale image and video datasets [16,66,72]. Very recently, active learning approaches have emerged in more contemporary vision tasks, including human pose estimation [46] and visual question answering [45]. Most of the active learning approaches in computer vision have used the simple but effective uncertainty sampling query strategy [42,43], where unlabelled samples are selected based on the entropy of their scores generated by the current discriminative model (least confidence and margin based score selections are other popular query strategies). However, the main limitation of this strategy is its inability to handle complex scenarios where factors such as label noise, outliers, or shift in data distribution arise in the active learning setting [40]. Inspired by very recent ideas in active learning [1,25,40,70,74], our proposed active learning framework learns (or bootstrap) a function that selects samples for annotation based on knowledge extracted from a previous dataset. One variant of our approach estimates the effect of labeling a particular instance on the performance of the current discriminative model. As such, this learnable function is able to overcome the shortcomings of heuristic active learners, such as uncertainty sampling (see Sect. 4).

Temporal Action Localization. Many techniques have been developed over the years to recognize [11,12,49,59,67], and localize human activities, either in images [28,47,73] or videos [29,34,69]. Our work focuses on the temporal action localization problem in video, whose goal is to provide starting and ending times of an action occurring within an untrimmed video. Researchers have explored innovative ideas to efficiently and accurately address this problem. Earlier methods rely on applying action classifiers in a sliding window fashion [19,23,50]. To unburden the computational requirements of sliding windows, a new line of work studies the use of action proposals to quickly scan a video in an attempt to reduce the search space [6,7,10,20,24,56]. More recently, end-to-end approaches have boosted the performance of stage-wise methods, demonstrating the importance of jointly optimizing classifiers and feature extractors [13,71,75,77].

Despite the large body of work on action localization, most methods focus on either improving performance [77] or boosting speed [5], while very few investigate the use of active learning to mitigate the data dependency problem. To the best of our knowledge, only the work of Bandla and Grauman [2] has incorporated active learning to train an action detection model. However, their method relies on hand-crafted active selection functions such as uncertainty sampling [42], which works well in controlled scenarios where statistical properties of the dataset can be inferred. However, it fails when more complex shifts in data distribution are present. In contrast and inspired by recent works [25,40], our approach avoids predefined heuristics and instead *learns* or *bootstraps* the active selection function from existing data. We will show that learning such a function not only improves the learning process of an action localization model on a given dataset, but it is also adaptable for use when annotating new data.

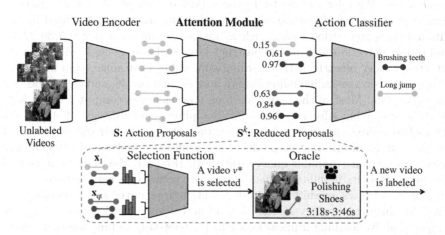

Fig. 2. Active Learner for Temporal Action Localization. Firstly, we train an action localization model with a labeled set of videos. Then, using the trained model, we generate video predictions in an unlabeled set and select one of the videos that is expected to improve the learner the most. Finally, an oracle temporally annotates the selected video and then added into the labeled set.

3   Active Learner for Temporal Action Localization

We propose an active learning framework for temporal action localization. Our goal is to train accurate detection models using a reduced amount of labeled data. At every learning step t, a set of labeled samples $\mathcal{L}_t$ is first used to train a model f_t. Then, from an unlabeled pool $\mathcal{U}_t$, a video instance v^* is chosen by a selection function g. Afterwards, an oracle provides temporal ground-truth for the selected instance, and the labeled set $\mathcal{L}_t$ is augmented with this new annotation. This process repeats until the desired performance is reached or the set $\mathcal{U}_t$ is empty. As emphasized in previous work [37,46], the key challenge in active learning is to design the proper selection function, which seeks to minimize the number of times an oracle is queried to reach a target performance. Accordingly, we empower our proposed framework with state-of-the-art selection functions that exploit previously labeled datasets as bootstrapping.

This section provides a complete walk-through of our approach (see Fig. 2). We describe our model for temporal action localization, elaborate on our proposed active selection function, and explain in detail the oracle's task.

3.1 Localization Model Training Step

Much progress has been made in designing accurate action detection models [5,24,71,77]. So ideally, any of these detectors can be used here. These detectors can be grouped into two categories, namely, stage-wise and end-to-end models. Models trained end-to-end have shown superior detection rates. However, such methods cannot decompose the localization problem into simpler tasks. We argue that decomposing the action localization task is key, specially for active learning methods that use previous knowledge to bootstrap the selection function learning process. As such, we opt for designing a stage-wise action localization model.

Our model takes as input a video v described by a set of n temporal segments, denoted by $\mathbf{S} = \{\mathbf{s}_1, \cdots, \mathbf{s}_n\}$ where $\mathbf{s_i} = [t^{start}, t^{end}]$ is a 2D vector containing starting and ending times of a segment. In this paper, these temporal segments are action proposals generated by DAPs [20]. Our localization model's goal is to select k temporal segments $\mathbf{S}^k$ from the initial set $\mathbf{S}$ and produce a vector of confidence scores $\mathbf{z}_c \in \mathbb{R}^k$ for each action class c in the dataset. In short, our model maps an input video described by a large set of candidate segments into a small set of temporal predictions: $f_t(v, \mathbf{S}) \rightarrow \{\mathbf{S}^k, \{\mathbf{z}_c\}_{c \in \mathcal{C}}\}$ where $\mathcal{C}$ is the set of action classes.

To that end, we organize our model into three modules: a *video encoder* whose goal is to describe temporal segments $\mathbf{S}$ in terms of a feature vector $\mathbf{o}$, an *attention module* which picks k segments based on a binary action classifier h_t, and an *action classifier* $\phi(\mathbf{S}^k)$ which generates the confidence scores $\mathbf{z}_c$ for each class in $\mathcal{C}$. Below, we provide design details for each component.

Video Encoder. Given a set of temporal segments $\mathbf{S}$, our aim is to encode each individual segment $\mathbf{s}_i$ with a compact representation. We first extract frame-level features using a CNN and then aggregate these representations into a single feature vector $\mathbf{o_i}$. In our experiments, we train an Inception V3 network [61] using the Kinetics dataset [39] and extract features from the *pool3* layer (a feature vector with 2048 dimensions). To reduce the temporal receptive field, we opt for average pooling, which beyond its simplicity has demonstrated competitive performance in various tasks [38,60]. Thus, our video encoder generates a matrix of visual observations, $\mathbf{O} = [\mathbf{o}_1 \cdots \mathbf{o}_n] \in \mathbb{R}^{2048 \times n}$.

Attention Module. This module receives a visual observation matrix $\mathbf{O}$ to pick k temporal segments $\mathbf{S}^k$ which are most likely to contain an action. We adopt a linear Support Vector Machine (SVM) [17,21] to learn a binary classifier that discriminates between actions and background. We employ Platt scaling [51] to obtain probabilistic scores from the SVM outputs. Finally, to select the output segments, we perform hard attention pooling and pick the *top-k* segments with high confidence scores. We set $k = 10$ in our experiments. Accordingly, our attention module h_t outputs a small number of segments $\mathbf{S}^k$, which are encoded with their corresponding visual representations in $\mathbf{O}$.

Action Classifier. Taking as input a reduced set of temporal segments $\mathbf{S}^k$, the action classifier aims to generate a set of confidence scores $\mathbf{z}_c$ for each action category in $\mathcal{C}$. Consciously, we build a model composed of a fully-connected layer and a soft-max classifier. Thus, our action classifier ϕ generates the final detection results $\{\mathbf{S}^k, \{\mathbf{z}_c\}_{c \in \mathcal{C}}\}$.

Training. We define the labeled set at learning step t of size p_t as $\mathcal{L}_t = \{(v_1^{train}, \mathbf{y}_1), (v_2^{train}, \mathbf{y}_2), \cdots (v_{p_t}^{train}, \mathbf{y}_{p_t})\}$, where $\mathbf{Y} = [\mathbf{y}_1|\cdots|\mathbf{y}_{p_t}] \in \mathbb{R}^{2 \times p_t}$ contains the temporal annotations of all action instances. We also define the set of temporal segments of size m as $\mathbf{S}_i^{(t)} = \{\mathbf{s}_1^{train}, \cdots, \mathbf{s}_m^{train}\}$, where $i \in \{1, 2, ..., p_t\}$ describes each video. We train our attention and action classifier modules separately. To train the attention module, we define instances in $\mathbf{S}_i^{(t)}$ as positives if the temporal Intersection over Union (tIoU) with any ground-truth instance is greater than 0.7. Similarly, for training the action classifier, we use temporal instances with tIoU greater than 0.7, but considering only the *top-k* segments chosen by our attention module.

3.2   Active Selection Step

Our aim is to design a selection function g that picks an instance v^* from the unlabeled set $\mathcal{U}_t$. Our primary challenge is to develop this function such that it selects the samples that are expected to improve the localization model the most. Additionally, we want the selection function to generalize to unseen action categories. Purposefully, instead of sampling directly from the f_t predictions, we cast the selection problem into a meta-learning task; *pick samples that improve attention module h_t the most*. Here, we focus the learner on the attention module as opposed to the action classifier, since the former deals with a more complex task (temporal boundary generation) and its output directly impacts the latter. Formally, our learnable selector g takes as input confidence scores produced by the action classifier h_t when applied to the unlabeled set $\mathcal{U}_t$: $\mathbf{X} = [\mathbf{x}_1, \mathbf{x}_2, \cdots, \mathbf{x}_{q_t}]$ where $\mathbf{X} \in \mathbb{R}^{l \times q_t}$ with l being the number of temporal segments and q_t the number of unlabeled videos. In this section, we introduce three different sampling functions, which are studied and diagnosed in Sect. 4.

Learning Active Learning (LAL). Here, we follow [40] and formulate the learning of the selection function as a regression problem, which predicts the improvement in performance of our attention module for all samples belonging to $\mathcal{U}_t$. We construct a feature matrix $\mathbf{F}$ from pairs of model state and sample description. We choose the model state to be the SVM weights defining h_t and the sample description to be the histogram of confidence scores in $\mathbf{X}$. The target vector used for regression is η, which corresponds to the improvement δ in localization performance (in practice mean Average Precision) after the model h_t is trained with each of the samples in a Set of previously labeled examples $\mathcal{K}_t$ individually. In our experiments, we refer to $\mathcal{K}_t$ as the Knowledge-Source

Set. To generate a matrix $\mathbf{F}$ that explores enough pairs of model and sample states, we follow the Monte-Carlo procedure used in [40]. Once matrix $\mathbf{F}$ and targets η are constructed, we learn g using Support Vector Regression (SVR). Once trained, we can apply g to the unlabelled set to select the sample with the highest predicted performance improvement: $g(\mathcal{U}_t) \rightarrow v^*$.

Maximum Conflict Label Equality (MCLE). This method leverages knowledge from past existing datasets. We closely follow [25] and devise a method that uses zero-shot learning as warm initialization for active learning. We opt for simplicity and implement a Video Search zero-shot learning approach, which uses top results from YouTube search as positive samples [14]. This approach's implementation is based on the code provided by [25].

Uncertainty Sampling (US). This baseline samples videos with the most uncertain predictions. Following standard uncertainty sampling approaches [42], we compute the entropy of the video predictions (*i.e.* the histogram of confidence scores in the columns of $\mathbf{X}$) and select the one with highest entropy value. This baseline is popularly used in computer vision applications such as image classification [53] or human pose estimation [46].

3.3 Annotation Step

The oracle's task is to annotate videos chosen by the selection function g. Specifically, the oracle is asked to provide temporal bounds of all instances of an intended action. Towards this goal, several researchers have proposed efficient strategies to collect such annotations [9,57]. Most of them have focused their approaches to exploit crowd-sourcing throughput and have used Amazon Mechanical Turk to annotate their large-scale video datasets. In this work, we experiment with two type of oracles: (i) simulated ones, which we emulate by using the ground-truth from existing and completely annotated datasets, and (ii) real human annotators, who are Amazon Mechanical Turk workers. We observe that the proposed framework is indiscriminately good in both cases.

4 Diagnostic Experiments

To evaluate our framework, we analyze its performance, including all its variants of selection functions, when oracles are simulated, *i.e.* we emulate an oracle's outcome by using the ground-truth from existing datasets that have already been completely annotated.

4.1 Experimental Settings

Dataset. We choose ActivityNet [8], the largest available dataset for temporal action localization, to conduct the diagnostic experiments in this section. Specifically, we use the training and validation sets of ActivityNet 1.3, which include 14950 videos from 200 activity classes.

Metrics. We use the mean Average Precision (mAP) metric to assess the performance of an action localization model. Following the standard evaluation of ActivityNet, we report mAP averaged in a range of tIoU thresholds, *i.e.* from 0.5 to 0.95 with an increment of 0.05. To quantify the merits of a sampling function, we are particularly interested in observing the rate of increase of mAP with increasing training set size (*i.e.* increasing percentage of the dataset used to train the localization model).

Setup. LAL and MCLE approaches (introduced in Sect. 3.2) leverage knowledge extracted from previous datasets to bootstrap the selection function learning process. To exploit each of these methods to their full extent, we extract two category-disjoint subsets from ActivityNet. The first subset, dubbed KNOWLEDGE-SOURCE, contains 2790 videos from 50 action categories. This subset is used to bootstrap the LAL and MCLE sampling functions. The second subset, dubbed ACTIVITYNET-SELECTION, consists of 11160 videos with 150 action categories, which do not overlap with the ones in KNOWLEDGE-SOURCE. We mainly conduct the active learning experiments on ACTIVITYNET-SELECTION. Additionally, to measure the performance of the localization model, we define a TESTING SET, which contains 3724 unseen videos from the same 150 categories as ACTIVITYNET-SELECTION. The TESTING SET videos do not overlap with ACTIVITYNET-SELECTION nor KNOWLEDGE-SOURCE videos.

We use the following protocol in our diagnostic experiments. We bootstrap LAL and MCLE using the labeled data in KNOWLEDGE-SOURCE by following the method described in Sect. 3.2. Note that US does not need previous knowledge to operate. Once the selection function is available, we randomly select 10% from ACTIVITYNET-SELECTION as a training set to build an initial action localization model (refer to Sect. 3.1). Then, we evaluate the model's mAP performance on the TESTING SET, and we apply our active learner onto the remaining videos of ACTIVITYNET-SELECTION to select one or more of them, which will be annotated in the next step. Subsequently, we probe the oracle, which is simulated in this case by using the ground-truth directly provided by ACTIVITYNET-SELECTION, to obtain temporal annotations for the selected videos. Finally, we augment the training set with the newly annotated samples, which in turn are used to re-train the localization model. This sequential process repeats until we have used 100% of the videos in ACTIVITYNET-SELECTION for training.

4.2 Selection Function Ablation Study

Comparison under Controlled Settings. Figure 3 (**Left**) compares mAP performance between the three selection functions introduced in Sect. 3.2 on the TESTING SET. We also report the performance of a Random Sampling baseline for reference. We report how the mAP of the localization model increases with the increase in training data, which is iteratively sampled according to the three active learning methods. These results help us investigate the effectiveness of each method in terms of how much improvement is obtained by adding a certain amount of training data. It is clear that LAL and MCLE significantly outperform

US and the random sampling baseline. For example, to achieve 80% of the final mAP (*i.e.* when all of ACTIVITYNET-SELECTION is used for training), LAL and MCLE require only 35% and 38% of the training data to be labelled respectively, while Uncertainty and Random Selection need 42% and 65% respectively to achieve the same performance. We attribute the superiority of LAL and MCLE to the fact that both approaches reuse information from labeled classes in the KNOWLEDGE-SOURCE Set. Additionally, LAL directly exploits the current state of the localization model to make its selection at every training step. As such, it has inherently broader knowledge about the dataset it is annotating as compared to the simple heuristics used by Uncertainty Selection.

Effect of Sampling Batch Size. Re-training a model whenever a single new sample is made available is prohibitively expensive. To alleviate this problem, researchers often consider active learning in batch-mode [3]. In batch-mode, our active learner selects groups of samples instead of just one. For LAL, we simply rank all the unlabelled samples and pick the top scoring ones based on LAL's predictions (*i.e.* the performance gain they are expected to cause when they are individually added to the training). For MCLE and Uncertainty Sampling, we select one unlabeled instance at a time until we completely fill the batch that will be annotated by the oracle. Figure 3 (**Center**) shows the Area Under the Learning Curve for different sampling batch sizes. The AULC value summarizes the performance of an active learner by computing the area under the *"percentage of full mAP vs ratio of labeled videos"* curve. For reference, we include the performance when using a single selection (*i.e.* batch size of 1). Uncertainty Sampling performance is poor after increasing the sampling batch size to 32. Interestingly, MCLE performance is strongly degraded at larger sampling batch sizes. The AULC score jumps from 0.75% down to 0.65% when the batch size is set to 64. On the other hand, we observe that LAL is relatively robust to larger sampling batch sizes. For instance, for a batch of size 64, the AULC drops only 0.05. We attribute the robustness of LAL to the fact that it estimates the selection score of each sample independently. Motivated by a trade-off between computational footprint and performance, we fix the selection batch size to 64 for the remaining experiments.

Effect of Noisy Annotations. Here, we analyze the performance of the selection functions when exposed to noisy oracles. To evaluate robustness against noisy annotations, we measure the performance of our active learner when different levels of noise are injected into the oracle responses. We quantify the noise in terms of how much an oracle response differs, in tIoU, from the original ground-truth. For example, at 5% noise level, the oracle returns temporal instances sampled from a Gaussian distribution with mean equal to 95% tIoU.

Similar to previous analysis, Fig. 3 (**Right**) reports the AULC at different noise levels. We observe that all sampling functions tolerate high levels of noise and in some cases (LAL) their performance can even improve when small (5%) noise levels are added. We conjecture that this improvement is due to the fact that such small levels of noise can be seen as adversarial examples, which previous works have demonstrated to be beneficial for training [30].

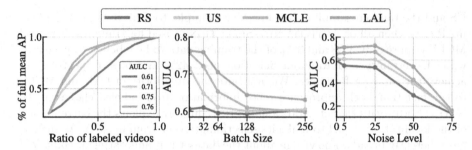

Fig. 3. Selection Function Ablation Study. Left. We show the % of full mAP (full training) achieved at different ratios of labeled videos. We report the Area Under the Learning Curve (AULC) for each sampling function. LAL and MCLE present steeper increases on mAP. **Center.** We report the AULC at different batch sizes. LAL is robust to large batch sizes. **Right.** We compute AULC against different level of noise from oracle annotations. All methods tolerate small levels of noise.

5   Online Experiments: Collecting Kinetics-Localization

In this section, we perform live experiments, where we employ our active learner to build a new dataset. Instead of collecting the dataset from scratch, we exploit Kinetics [39] videos (and its video-level labels) and enrich them with temporally localized annotations for actions. We call our novel dataset Kinetics-Localization. First, we run our active learner to collect temporal annotations from Kinetics videos. Then, we present statistics of the collected data. Finally, we evaluate the performance of models trained with the collected data.

5.1   Active Annotation Pipeline

The Kinetics dataset [39] is one of the largest available datasets for action recognition. To construct the dataset, the authors used Amazon Mechanical Turk (AMT) to decide whether a 10 seconds clip contains a target action. To gather the pool of clips to be annotated, first a large set of videos are obtained by matching YouTube titles with action names. Then, a classifier, which is trained with images returned by Google Image Search, decides where the 10 seconds clip to be annotated is extracted from. As a result, Kinetics provides more than $300K$ videos among 400 different action labels. There is only one annotated action clip in each video. The scale of the dataset has enabled the development of novel neural network architectures for video [12]. Unfortunately, despite the tremendous effort needed to build Kinetics, the dataset is not designed for the task of temporal action localization. Thus, we commit our active learner to collect temporal annotations for a portion of Kinetics.

We employ our active learner to gather temporal annotations for Kinetics videos from 75 action classes. It needs to select samples that will be annotated online by real human oracles. Following standard procedure for temporal video annotation, we design a user interface that allows people to determine the temporal bounds of actions in videos [9,57,65]. We rely on Amazon Mechanical Turk workers (turkers) to annotate the videos. Snapshots of the user interface and details about the annotation process are available in the *supplementary material.*

5.2 Kinetics-Localization at a Glance

As a result of our annotation campaign, we effectively compile a temporal action localization dataset comprising 15000 videos from 75 different action categories, resulting in more than 30000 temporal annotations. Figure 4 summarizes Kinetics-Localization properties. Figure 4 (**Top**) shows the number of videos and instances per class in the current version of the dataset. The distribution of number of videos/instances is close to uniform. Also notice that the ratio of instances per video is 2.2.

Figure 4 (**Middle**) shows the ground-truth distribution for three different inherent attributes of the dataset. (i) Coverage, which we measure as the fraction between an instance's length and the duration of the video it belongs to. We group instance coverage into five groups: Extra Small (XS: $(0, 0.2]$); Small (S: $(0.2, 0.4]$); Medium (M: $(0.4, 0.6]$); Large (L: $(0.6, 0.8]$); Extra Large (XL: $(0.8, 1.0]$). (ii) Length, measured as the duration, in seconds, of an instance. We define five bins to plot the distribution of this attribute: Extra Small (XS: $(0, 30]$), Small (S: $(30, 60]$), Medium (M: $(60, 120]$), Large (L: $(120, 180]$), and Extra Large (XL: >180). (iii) Number of instances in a video (# instances), which we cluster into five bins as well: Extra Small (XS: $[0, 1]$); Small (S: $(1, 4]$); Medium (M: $(4, 8]$); Large (L: $(8, 16]$); Extra Large (XL: >16). In terms of coverage, extra small and extra large instances have a large portion of ground-truth instances assigned. Also note that more than half of the instances have at most small coverage (<0.4). The dataset comprises 55.1% of instances that are relatively small. We hypothesize that such small instances will enable new challenges, as is the case in other fields such as face detection [33].

We also study the distribution between pairs of instance attributes (see Fig. 4 (**Bottom**)). We observe three major trends from the ground-truth distribution: (i) as expected, instances with high coverage tend to have no neighbours (single instance per video); (ii) 34.9% of instances have extra small coverage and extra small length, which we argue may be the hardest type of sample for current detectors; (iii) In summary, we find that the dataset exhibits challenging types of ground-truth instances, which may span ranges of difficulty.

5.3 Kinetics-Localization Benchmark

We evaluate two different temporal action localization models: (i) our temporal localization model (Stage-Wise), which we introduced in Sect. 3.1; (ii) the Structured Segmented Network (SSN) introduced by Zhao *et al.* [77] (we refer to this approach as End-to-End). Although we could have employed other action

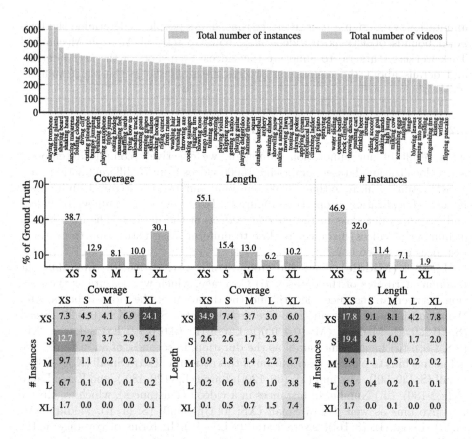

Fig. 4. Kinetics-Localization at a Glance. We introduce Kinetics-Localization, a novel dataset for temporal action localization. **Top:** Distribution of number of videos and instances per class. **Middle.** Kinetics-Localization attributes. We show the distribution of ground-truth instances for different attributes including Coverage, Length, and Number of Instances per video. **Bottom.** We analyze the distribution of ground-truth instances for pairwise interactions of attributes. Each bin reports the percentage of ground-truth that belongs to such bin.

detectors such as [5,71], we choose SSN because it registers state-of-the-art performance. We train each of the models either using Kinetics-Localization or the original Kinetics dataset. Table 1 summarizes the results. We use the provided 10 second clips to train the action localization models, and assume that all remaining content in the video is background information. Even though background might also contain some valid action instances, we argue there is no systematic way to add those for training without fully annotating them.

To properly quantify performance, we fully annotate a portion of the Kinetics validation subset with temporal annotations, which we refer from now on as Kinetics-Localization Validation Set. Table 1 shows the temporal localization performance of both approaches at different tIoU thresholds on the Kinetics-

Table 1. Kinetics-Localization benchmark. We report the mAP at different tIoU thresholds of the Stage-Wise and End-to-End models. We averaged mAP in a range of tIoU thresholds, *i.e.* from 0.5 to 0.95 with an increment of 0.05 (Avg. mAP). Notably, training with Kinetics-Localization dataset offers significant gains in performance as compared to using the original Kinetics dataset.

	mAP (%) at tIoU									
	0.1	0.2	0.3	0.4	0.5	0.6	0.7	0.8	0.9	Avg.
Kinetics-Localization										
Stage-Wise	72.1	59.2	52.8	48.7	45.1	31.0	26.4	17.7	3.9	21.3
End-to-End	72.8	61.3	54.9	52.3	49.6	32.7	28.2	19.5	5.2	22.8
Kinetics [39]										
Stage-Wise	43.2	34.7	22.8	15.1	13.7	11.0	8.9	5.7	2.9	8.2
End-to-End	59.4	40.1	28.3	20.8	15.0	11.8	9.4	5.2	1.2	8.3

Localization Validation Set. We observe that the performance at lower tIoU thresholds (*e.g.* 0.1) for both models is close to the achieved performance of previous work on the trimmed classification task [12]. However, when the tIoU threshold is increased to 0.2, the performance drastically drops. For example, the mAP of the End-to-End SSN model (trained on the original Kinetics) decreases from 59.4% to 40.1%. Also, once typical tIoU thresholds for localization are used (0.5 to 0.9), both approaches perform poorly. We attribute this behavior to the fact that Kinetics does not include accurate temporal action bounds, thus, preventing the localization models to reason about temporal configurations of actions. When comparing the performance of the Stage-Wise approach to that of the same model trained with the newly collected Kinetics-Localization data, an improvement of 13.1% mAP is unlocked on the validation set. This validates the need for accurate temporal annotations to train localization models as well as the need for cost effective frameworks to collect these annotations (like the active learner method we propose in this paper).

6   Conclusion

We introduced a novel active learning framework for temporal action localization. Towards this goal, we explored several state-of-the-art active selection functions and systematically analyzed their performance. We showed that our framework outperforms baseline approaches when the evaluation is conducted with simulated oracles. We also observed interesting properties of our framework when equipped with its LAL variant; (1) it exhibited good performance in batch-mode, and (2) is robust to noisy oracles. After validating the contributions of our active learner, we employed it to gather a novel dataset for temporal localization, which we called Kinetics-Localization. We presented statistics of the datasets as well as a novel established benchmark for temporal action localization. We hope that the collected Kinetics-Localization dataset helps to encourage the design of novel methods for action localization.

Acknowledgments. This publication is based upon work supported by the King Abdullah University of Science and Technology (KAUST) Office of Sponsored Research (OSR) under Award No. OSR-CRG2017-3405.

References

1. Bachman, P., Sordoni, A., Trischler, A.: Learning Algorithms for Active Learning. arXiv preprint arXiv:1708.00088 (2017)
2. Bandla, S., Grauman, K.: Active learning of an action detector from untrimmed videos. In: ICCV (2013)
3. Brinker, K.: Incorporating diversity in active learning with support vector machines. In: International Conference on Machine Learning (ICML) (2003)
4. Bruzzone, L., Marconcini, M.: Domain adaptation problems: a DASVM classification technique and a circular validation strategy. PAMI **32**(5), 770–787 (2010)
5. Buch, S., Escorcia, V., Ghanem, B., Fei-Fei, L., Niebles, J.C.: End-to-end, single-stream temporal action detection in untrimmed videos. In: BMVC (2017)
6. Buch, S., Escorcia, V., Shen, C., Ghanem, B., Niebles, J.C.: SST: single-stream temporal action proposals. In: CVPR (2017)
7. Caba Heilbron, F., Barrios, W., Escorcia, V., Ghanem, B.: SCC: semantic context cascade for efficient action detection. In: CVPR (2017)
8. Caba Heilbron, F., Escorcia, V., Ghanem, B., Carlos Niebles, J.: ActivityNet: a large-scale video benchmark for human activity understanding. In: CVPR (2015)
9. Caba Heilbron, F., Niebles, J.C.: Collecting and annotating human activities in web videos. In: Proceedings of International Conference on Multimedia Retrieval (ICMR) (2014)
10. Caba Heilbron, F., Niebles, J.C., Ghanem, B.: Fast temporal activity proposals for efficient detection of human actions in untrimmed videos. In: CVPR (2016)
11. Caba Heilbron, F., Thabet, A., Niebles, J.C., Ghanem, B.: Camera motion and surrounding scene appearance as context for action recognition. In: ACCV (2014)
12. Carreira, J., Zisserman, A.: Quo vadis, action recognition? A new model and the kinetics dataset. In: CVPR (2017)
13. Chao, Y.W., Vijayanarasimhan, S., Seybold, B., Ross, D.A., Deng, J., Sukthankar, R.: Rethinking the faster R-CNN architecture for temporal action localization. In: CVPR (2018)
14. Chen, X., Shrivastava, A., Gupta, A.: NEIL: extracting visual knowledge from web data. In: ICCV (2013)
15. Cisco: The Zettabyte Era: Trends and Analysis (2017). https://www.cisco.com/c/en/us/solutions/collateral/service-provider/visual-networking-index-vni/vni-hyperconnectivity-wp.html
16. Collins, B., Deng, J., Li, K., Fei-Fei, L.: Towards scalable dataset construction: an active learning approach. In: Forsyth, D., Torr, P., Zisserman, A. (eds.) ECCV 2008. LNCS, vol. 5302, pp. 86–98. Springer, Heidelberg (2008). https://doi.org/10.1007/978-3-540-88682-2_8
17. Cortes, C., Vapnik, V.: Support-vector networks. Mach. Learn. **20**(3), 273–297 (1995)

18. Cronin, L., et al.: Human vs robots in the discovery and crystallization of gigantic polyoxometalates. Angewandte Chemie (2017)
19. Duchenne, O., Laptev, I., Sivic, J., Bach, F., Ponce, J.: Automatic annotation of human actions in video. In: ICCV (2009)
20. Escorcia, V., Caba Heilbron, F., Niebles, J.C., Ghanem, B.: DAPs: deep action proposals for action understanding. In: Leibe, B., Matas, J., Sebe, N., Welling, M. (eds.) ECCV 2016. LNCS, vol. 9907, pp. 768–784. Springer, Cham (2016). https://doi.org/10.1007/978-3-319-46487-9_47
21. Fan, R.E., Chang, K.W., Hsieh, C.J., Wang, X.R., Lin, C.J.: LIBLINEAR: a library for large linear classification. J. Mach. Learn. Res. **9**(Aug), 1871–1874 (2008)
22. Freytag, A., Rodner, E., Denzler, J.: Selecting Influential examples: active learning with expected model output changes. In: Fleet, D., Pajdla, T., Schiele, B., Tuytelaars, T. (eds.) ECCV 2014. LNCS, vol. 8692, pp. 562–577. Springer, Cham (2014). https://doi.org/10.1007/978-3-319-10593-2_37
23. Gaidon, A., Harchaoui, Z., Schmid, C.: Actom sequence models for efficient action detection. In: CVPR (2011)
24. Gao, J., Yang, Z., Sun, C., Chen, K., Nevatia, R.: Turn tap: temporal unit regression network for temporal action proposals. In: ICCV (2017)
25. Gavves, S., Mensink, T., Tommasi, T., Snoek, C., Tuytelaars, T.: Active transfer learning with zero-shot priors: reusing past datasets for future tasks. In: ICCV (2015)
26. Giancola, S., Amine, M., Dghaily, T., Ghanem, B.: SoccerNet: a scalable dataset for action spotting in soccer videos. In: CVPR Workshops (2018)
27. Gilad-Bachrach, R., Navot, A., Tishby, N.: Query by committee made real. In: NIPS (2006)
28. Gkioxari, G., Hariharan, B., Girshick, R., Malik, J.: R-CNNs for pose estimation and action detection (2014)
29. Gkioxari, G., Malik, J.: Finding action tubes. In: CVPR (2015)
30. Goodfellow, I.J., Shlens, J., Szegedy, C.: Explaining and harnessing adversarial examples. In: ICLR (2014)
31. Gu, C., et al.: AVA: a video dataset of spatio-temporally localized atomic visual actions. In: CVPR (2018)
32. Hakkani-Tür, D., Riccardi, G., Gorin, A.: Active learning for automatic speech recognition. In: 2002 IEEE International Conference on Acoustics, Speech, and Signal Processing (ICASSP) (2002)
33. Hu, P., Ramanan, D.: Finding tiny faces. In: CVPR (2017)
34. Jain, M., van Gemert, J., Jegou, H., Bouthemy, P., Snoek, C.G.: Action localization with tubelets from motion. In: CVPR (2014)
35. Jiang, Y.G., et al.: THUMOS Challenge: Action Recognition with a Large Number of Classes (2014). http://crcv.ucf.edu/THUMOS14/
36. Joshi, A.J., Porikli, F., Papanikolopoulos, N.: Multi-class active learning for image classification. In: CVPR (2009)
37. Kapoor, A., Grauman, K., Urtasun, R., Darrell, T.: Active learning with Gaussian processes for object categorization. In: IEEE 11th International Conference on Computer Vision, ICCV 2007, pp. 1–8. IEEE (2007)
38. Karpathy, A., Toderici, G., Shetty, S., Leung, T., Sukthankar, R., Fei-Fei, L.: Large-scale video classification with convolutional neural networks. In: CVPR (2014)
39. Kay, W., et al.: The kinetics human action video dataset. arXiv preprint arXiv:1705.06950 (2017)
40. Konyushkova, K., Sznitman, R., Fua, P.: Learning active learning from data. In: Advances in Neural Information Processing Systems, pp. 4226–4236 (2017)

228   F. C. Heilbron et al.

41. Krishna, R., Hata, K., Ren, F., Fei-Fei, L., Niebles, J.C.: Dense-captioning events in videos. In: ICCV (2017)
42. Lewis, D.D., Catlett, J.: Heterogeneous uncertainty sampling for supervised learning. In: ICML (1994)
43. Lewis, D.D., Gale, W.A.: A sequential algorithm for training text classifiers. In: Proceedings of the 17th Annual International ACM SIGIR Conference on Research and Development in Information Retrieval (1994)
44. Lin, T., Zhao, X., Su, H., Wang, C., Yang, M.: BSN: boundary sensitive network for temporal action proposal generation. In: ECCV (2018)
45. Lin, X., Parikh, D.: Active learning for visual question answering: an empirical study. arXiv preprint arXiv:1711.01732 (2017)
46. Liu, B., Ferrari, V.: Active learning for human pose estimation. In: ICCV (2017)
47. Maji, S., Bourdev, L., Malik, J.: Action recognition from a distributed representation of pose and appearance. In: CVPR (2011)
48. Mehran, R., Oyama, A., Shah, M.: Abnormal crowd behavior detection using social force model. In: CVPR (2009)
49. Niebles, J.C., Chen, C.-W., Fei-Fei, L.: Modeling temporal structure of decomposable motion segments for activity classification. In: Daniilidis, K., Maragos, P., Paragios, N. (eds.) ECCV 2010. LNCS, vol. 6312, pp. 392–405. Springer, Heidelberg (2010). https://doi.org/10.1007/978-3-642-15552-9_29
50. Oneata, D., Verbeek, J., Schmid, C.: Efficient action localization with approximately normalized fisher vectors. In: CVPR (2014)
51. Platt, J., et al.: Probabilistic outputs for support vector machines and comparisons to regularized likelihood methods. Adv. Large Margin Classifiers 10(3), 61–74 (1999)
52. Poppe, R., et al.: A survey on vision-based human action recognition. Image Vis. Comput. 28(6), 976–990 (2010)
53. Qi, G.J., Hua, X.S., Rui, Y., Tang, J., Zhang, H.J.: Two-dimensional active learning for image classification. In: CVPR (2008)
54. Russakovsky, O., et al.: Imagenet large scale visual recognition challenge. Int. J. Comput. Vis. 115(3), 211–252 (2015)
55. Settles, B.: Active learning literature survey. Univ. Wis. Madison 52(55–66), 11 (2010)
56. Shou, Z., Wang, D., Chang, S.F.: Temporal action localization in untrimmed videos via multi-stage CNNS. In: CVPR (2016)
57. Sigurdsson, G.A., Russakovsky, O., Farhadi, A., Laptev, I., Gupta, A.: Much ado about time: exhaustive annotation of temporal data. In: AAAI Conference on Human Computation and Crowdsourcing (HCOMP) (2016)
58. Sigurdsson, G.A., et al.: Hollywood in homes: crowdsourcing data collection for activity understanding. In: Leibe, B., Matas, J., Sebe, N., Welling, M. (eds.) ECCV 2016. LNCS, vol. 9905, pp. 510–526. Springer, Cham (2016). https://doi.org/10.1007/978-3-319-46448-0_31
59. Simonyan, K., Zisserman, A.: Two-stream convolutional networks for action recognition in videos. In: Advances in Neural Information Processing Systems, pp. 568–576 (2014)
60. Simonyan, K., Zisserman, A.: Two-stream convolutional networks for action recognition in videos. In: NIPS (2014)
61. Szegedy, C., Vanhoucke, V., Ioffe, S., Shlens, J., Wojna, Z.: Rethinking the inception architecture for computer vision. In: CVPR (2016)
62. Thompson, C.A., Califf, M.E., Mooney, R.J.: Active learning for natural language parsing and information extraction

63. Tong, S., Chang, E.: Support vector machine active learning for image retrieval. In: Proceedings of the ninth ACM International Conference on Multimedia, pp. 107–118. ACM (2001)

64. Vijayanarasimhan, S., Grauman, K.: Large-scale live active learning: training object detectors with crawled data and crowds. Int. J. Comput. Vis. **108**(1–2), 97–114 (2014)

65. Vondrick, C., Patterson, D., Ramanan, D.: Efficiently scaling up crowdsourced video annotation. Int. J. Comput. Vis. **101**, 184–204 (2012)

66. Vondrick, C., Ramanan, D.: Video annotation and tracking with active learning. In: NIPS (2011)

67. Wang, H., Kläser, A., Schmid, C., Liu, C.L.: Action recognition by dense trajectories. In: CVPR (2011)

68. Wang, L., Xiong, Y., Lin, D., Van Gool, L.: UntrimmedNets for weakly supervised action recognition and detection. In: CVPR (2017)

69. Weinzaepfel, P., Harchaoui, Z., Schmid, C.: Learning to track for spatio-temporal action localization. In: ICCV (2015)

70. Woodward, M., Finn, C.: Active one-shot learning. In: NIPS (2016)

71. Xu, H., Das, A., Saenko, K.: R-C3D: region convolutional 3d network for temporal activity detection (2017)

72. Yang, J., et al.: Automatically labeling video data using multi-class active learning. In: ICCV (2003)

73. Yao, B., Jiang, X., Khosla, A., Lin, A.L., Guibas, L., Fei-Fei, L.: Human action recognition by learning bases of action attributes and parts. In: ICCV (2011)

74. Yeung, S., Ramanathan, V., Russakovsky, O., Shen, L., Mori, G., Fei-Fei, L.: Learning to learn from noisy web videos. In: CVPR (2017)

75. Yeung, S., Russakovsky, O., Mori, G., Fei-Fei, L.: End-to-end learning of action detection from frame glimpses in videos. In: CVPR (2016)

76. Yilmaz, A., Javed, O., Shah, M.: Object tracking: a survey. ACM Comput. Surv. (CSUR) **38**(4), 13 (2006)

77. Zhao, Y., Xiong, Y., Wang, L., Wu, Z., Lin, D., Tang, X.: Temporal action detection with structured segment networks. In: ICCV (2017)

Semi-supervised Adversarial Learning to Generate Photorealistic Face Images of New Identities from 3D Morphable Model

Baris Gecer[1]([✉]), Binod Bhattarai[1], Josef Kittler[2], and Tae-Kyun Kim[1]

[1] Department of Electrical and Electronic Engineering, Imperial College London, London, UK
{b.gecer,b.bhattarai,tk.kim}@imperial.ac.uk
[2] Centre for Vision, Speech and Signal Processing, University of Surrey, Guildford, UK
j.kittler@surrey.ac.uk
https://labicvl.github.io/
https://www.surrey.ac.uk/centre-vision-speech-signal-processing

Abstract. We propose a novel end-to-end semi-supervised adversarial framework to generate photorealistic face images of new identities with a wide range of expressions, poses, and illuminations conditioned by synthetic images sampled from a 3D morphable model. Previous adversarial style-transfer methods either supervise their networks with a large volume of paired data or train highly under-constrained two-way generative networks in an unsupervised fashion. We propose a semi-supervised adversarial learning framework to constrain the two-way networks by a small number of paired real and synthetic images, along with a large volume of unpaired data. A set-based loss is also proposed to preserve identity coherence of generated images. Qualitative results show that generated face images of new identities contain pose, lighting and expression diversity. They are also highly constrained by the synthetic input images while adding photorealism and retaining identity information. We combine face images generated by the proposed method with a real data set to train face recognition algorithms and evaluate the model quantitatively on two challenging data sets: LFW and IJB-A. The generated images by our framework consistently improve the performance of deep face recognition networks trained with the Oxford VGG Face dataset, and achieve comparable results to the state-of-the-art.

1 Introduction

Deep learning has shown a great improvement in performance of several computer vision tasks [13,14,17,18,22,41,66] including face recognition [34,37,47,62, 63] in the recent years. This was mainly thanks to the availability of large-scale

Electronic supplementary material The online version of this chapter (https://doi.org/10.1007/978-3-030-01252-6_14) contains supplementary material, which is available to authorized users.

datasets. Yet the performance is often limited by the volume and the variations of training examples. Larger and wider datasets improve the generalization and overall performance of the model [1,47].

The process of collecting and annotating training examples for every specific computer vision task is laborious and non-trivial. To overcome this challenge, additional synthetic training examples along with limited real training examples can be utilised to train the model. Some of the recent works such as 3D face reconstruction [42], gaze estimation [61,69], human pose, shape and motion estimation [58] *etc.* use additional synthetic images generated from 3D models to train deep networks. One can generate synthetic face images using a 3D morphable model (3DMM) [3] by manipulating identity, expression, illumination, and pose parameters. However, the resulting images are not photorealistic enough to be suitable for in-the-wild face recognition tasks. It is because the information of real face scans is compressed by the 3DMM and the graphical engine that models illumination and surface is not perfectly accurate. Thus, the main challenge of using synthetic data obtained from 3DMM model is the discrepancy in the nature and quality of synthetic and real images which poses the problem of domain adaptation [38]. Recently, adversarial training methods [12,48,51] have become popular to mitigate such challenges.

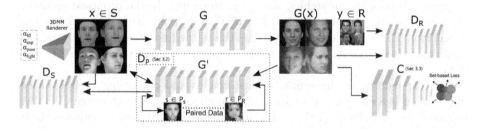

Fig. 1. Our approach aims to synthesize photorealistic images conditioned by a given synthetic image by 3DMM. It regularizes cycle consistency [71] by introducing an additional adversarial game between the two generator networks in an unsupervised fashion. Thus the under-constraint cycle loss is supervised to have correct matching between the two domains by the help of a limited number of paired data. We also encourage the generator to preserve face identity by a set-based supervision through a pretrained classification network.

Generative Adversarial Network (GAN), introduced by Goodfellow *et al.* [20], and its variants [2,15,28,39] are quite successful in generating realistic images. However, in practice, GANs are likely to stuck in mode collapse for large scale image generation. They are also unable to produce images that are 3D coherent and globally consistent [20]. To overcome these drawbacks, we propose a semi-supervised adversarial learning framework to synthesize photorealistic face images of new identities exhibiting extensive data variation supplied by a 3DMM. We address these shortcomings by exciting a generator network with synthetic images sampled from 3DMM and transforming them into photorealistic domain using adversarial training as a bridge. Unlike most of the existing works that excite their generators with a noise vector [2,39], we feed our generator network by synthetic face images. Such a strong constraint naturally helps in avoiding the mode collapse problem, one of the main challenges faced by the current GAN methods. Figure 1 shows a general overview of the proposed method. We discuss the proposed method in more details in Sect. 3.

In this paper, we address the challenge of generating photorealistic face images from 3DMM rendered faces of different identities with arbitrary poses, expressions, and illuminations. We formulate this problem as a domain adaptation problem *i.e.* aligning the 3DMM rendered face domain into realistic face domain. One of the previous works closest to ours [26] addresses the style transfer problem between a pair of domains with classical conditional GAN. The major bottleneck of this method is that it requires a large number of paired examples from both domains which are hard to collect. CycleGAN [71], another recent method and closest to our work, proposes a two-way GAN framework for unsupervised image-to-image translation. However, the cycle consistency loss proposed in their method is satisfied as long as the transitivity of the two mapping networks is maintained. Thus, the resulting mapping is not guaranteed to produce the intended transformation. To overcome the drawbacks of these methods [26,71], we propose to use a small amount of paired data to train an inverse mapping network as a matching aware discriminator. In the proposed method, the inverse mapping network plays the role of both the generator and the discriminator. To the best of our knowledge, this is the first attempt for adversarial semi-supervised style translation for an application with such limited paired data.

Adding realism to the synthetic face images and preserving their identity information is a challenging problem. Although synthetic input images, 3DMM rendered faces, contain distinct face identities, the distinction between them vanishes as a result of the inherent non-linear transformations induced by the discriminator to encourage realism. To tackle such a problem, prior works either employ a separate pre-trained network [65] or embed Identity labels (id) [55] into the discriminator. Unlike existing works, which are focused on generating new images of existing identities, we are interested in generating multiple images of new identities. Therefore, such techniques are not directly applicable to our problem. To address this challenge, we propose to use set-based center [59] and pushing loss functions [19] on top of a pre-trained face embedding network. This will keep track of the changing average of embeddings of generated images belonging to the same identity (i.e. centroids). In this way identity preservation becomes adaptive to the changing feature space during the training of the generator network unlike softmax layer that converges very quickly at the beginning of the training before meaningful images are generated.

Our contributions can be summarized as follows:

- We propose a novel end-to-end adversarial training framework to generate photorealistic face images of new identities constrained by synthetic 3DMM images with identity, pose, illumination and expression diversity. The resulting synthetic face images are visually plausible and can be used to boost face recognition as additional training data or any other graphical purposes.

- We propose a novel semi-supervised adversarial style transfer approach that trains an inverse mapping network as a discriminator with paired synthetic-real images.
- We employ a novel set-based loss function to preserve consistency among unknown identities during GAN training.

2   Related Works

In this Section we discuss the prior art that are closely related to the proposed method.

Domain Adaptation. As stated in the introduction, our problem of generating photorealistic face images from 3DMM rendered faces can be seen as a domain adaptation problem. A straightforward adaptation approach is to align the distributions at the feature level by simply adding a loss to measure the mismatch either through second-order moments [52] or with adversarial losses [16,56,57].

Recently, pixel level domain adaptation became popular due to practical breakthroughs on Kullback-Leibler divergence [20,21,39], namely GANs which optimize a generative and discriminative network through a mini-max game. It has been applied to a wide range of problems including fashion clothing [31], person specific avatar creation [60], text-to-image synthesis [67], face frontalization [65], and retinal image synthesis [12].

Pixel domain adaptation can be done in a supervised manner simply by conditioning the discriminator network [26] or directly the output of the generator [9] with the expected output when there is enough paired data from both domains. Please note collecting a large number of paired training examples is expensive, and often requires expert knowledge. [40] proposes a text-to-image synthesis GAN with a matching aware discriminator. They optimize their discriminator for image-text matching beside requiring realism with the information provided by additional mismatched text-image pairs.

For the cases where paired data is not available, many approaches adapt unsupervised learning such as imposing pixel-level consistency between input and output of the generator network [6,48], an encoder architecture that is shared by both domains [7] and adaptive instance normalization [24]. An interesting approach is to have two way translation between domains with two distinct generator and discriminator networks. They constrain the two mappings to be inverses of each other with either ResNet [71] or encoder-decoder network [33] as the generator.

Synthetic Training Data Generation. The usage of synthetic data as additional training data is shown to be helpful even if they are graphically rendered images in many applications such as 3D face reconstruction [42], gaze estimation [61,69], human pose, shape and motion estimation [58]. Despite the availability of almost infinite number of synthetic images, those approaches are limited due to the domain difference from that of in-the-wild images.

Many existing works utilize adversarial domain adaptation to translate images into photorealistic domain so that they are more useful as training data. [70] generates many unlabeled samples to improve person re-identification in a semi-supervised fashion. RenderGAN [51] proposes a sophisticated approach to refine graphically rendered synthetic images of tagged bees to be used as training data for a bee tag decoding application. WaterGAN [32] synthesizes realistic underwater images by modeling camera parameters and environment effects explicitly to be used as training data for a color correction task. Some studies deform existing images by a 3D model to augment diverse datasets [36] without adversarial learning.

One of the recent works, simGAN [48], generates realistic synthetic data to improve eye gaze and hand pose estimation. It optimizes the pixel level correspondence between input and output of the generator network to preserve the content of the synthetic image. This is in fact a limited solution since the pixel-consistency loss encourages the generated images to be similar to synthetic input images and it partially contradicts adversarial realism loss. Instead, we employ an inverse translation network similar to cycleGAN [71] with an additional pairwise supervision to preserve the initial condition without hurting realism. This network also behaves as a discriminator to a straight mapping network trained with real paired data to avoid possible biased translation.

Identity Preservation. To preserve the identity/category of the synthesized images, some of the recent works such as [10,55] keep categorical/identity information in discriminator network as an additional task. Some of the others propose to employ a separate classification network which is usually pre-trained [35,65]. In both these cases, the categories/identities are known beforehand and are fixed in number. Thus it is trivial to include such supervision in a GAN framework by training the classifier with real data. However such setup is not feasible in our case as images of new identities to-be-generated are not available to pre-train a classification network.

To address the limitation of existing methods of retaining identity/category information of synthesized images, we employ a combination of different set-based supervision approaches for unknown identities to be distinct in the pre-trained embedding space. We keep track of moving averages of same-id features by the momentum-like centroid update rule of center loss [59] and penalize distant same-id samples and close different-id samples by a simplified variant of the magnet loss [43] without its sophisticated sampling process and with only a single cluster per identity (see Sect. 3.3 for further discussions).

3   Adversarial Identity Generation

In this Section, we describe in details the proposed method. Figure 1 shows a schematic diagram of our method. Specifically, the synthetic image set $x \in$

$\mathcal{S}$ is formed by a graphical engine for the randomly sampled of 3DMM with its identity, pose and lighting parameters α. The generated images they are translated into a more photorealistic domain $G(x)$ through the network, G, and mapped back to its synthetic domain $(G'(G(x)))$ through the network, G', to retain x. The adversarial synthetic and real domain translation of G and G' networks are supervised by the discriminator networks D_R and D_S, with an additional adversarial game between G and G' as a generator and a discriminator respectively. During training, the identities generated by 3DMM are preserved with a set-based loss on a pre-trained embedding network C. In the following sub-sections, we further describe these components *i.e.* domain adaptation, real-synthetic pair discriminator, and identity preservation.

3.1 Unsupervised Domain Adaptation

Given a 3D morphable model (3DMM) [3], we synthesize face images of new identities sampled from its Principal Components Analysis (PCA) coefficients' space with random variation of expression, lighting and pose. Similar to [71], a synthetic input image $(x \in \mathcal{S})$ is mapped to a photorealistic domain by a residual network $(G : S \rightarrow \hat{R})$ and mapped back to the synthetic domain by a 3DMM fitting network $(G' : \hat{R} \rightarrow \hat{S})$ to complete the forward cycle only[1]. To preserve cycle consistency, the resulting image $G'(G(x))$ is encouraged to be the same as input x by a pixel level L_1 loss:

$$\mathcal{L}_{cyc} = \mathbb{E}_{x \in \mathcal{S}} \|G'(G(x)) - x\|_1 \tag{1}$$

In order to encourage the resulting images $G(x)$ and $G'(G(x))$ to have a similar distribution as real and synthetic domains respectively, those refiner networks are supervised by discriminator networks D_R and D_S with images of the respective domains. The discriminator networks are formed as auto-encoders as in the boundary equilibrium GAN (BEGAN) architecture [2] in which the generator and discriminator networks are trained by the following adversarial training formulation:

$$\mathcal{L}_G = \mathbb{E}_{x \in \mathcal{S}} \|G(x) - D_R(G(x))\|_1 \tag{2}$$

$$\mathcal{L}_{G'} = \mathbb{E}_{x \in \mathcal{S}} \|G'(G(x)) - D_S(G'(G(x)))\|_1 \tag{3}$$

$$\mathcal{L}_{D_R} = \mathbb{E}_{x \in \mathcal{S}, y \in \mathcal{R}} \|y - D_R(y)\|_1 - k_t^{D_R} \mathcal{L}_G \tag{4}$$

$$\mathcal{L}_{D_S} = \mathbb{E}_{x \in \mathcal{S}} \|x - D_S(x)\|_1 - k_t^{D_S} \mathcal{L}_{G'} \tag{5}$$

where for each training step t and the generator network (G for $k_t^{D_R}$, G' for $k_t^{D_S}$) we update the balancing term with $k_t^D = k_{t-1}^D + 0.001(0.5\mathcal{L}_D - \mathcal{L}_G)$. As suggested by [2], this term helps to maintain a balance between the interests of the generator and discriminator and stabilize the training.

---

[1] We empirically found that removing the backward cycle-loss improves performance when the task is to map from artificial images to real as also shown in Table 4 of [71].

3.2   Adversarial Pair Matching

The cycle consistency loss ensures the bijective transitivity of functions G and G' which means generated image $G(x) \in \hat{R}$ should be transformed back to $x \in \hat{S}$. Convolutional networks are highly under-constrained and they are free to make any unintended changes as long as the cycle consistency is satisfied. Therefore, without an additional supervision, it is not guaranteed to achieve the correct mapping that preserves shape, texture, expression, pose and lighting attributes of the face image from domains S to $\hat{R}$ and $\hat{R}$ to $\hat{S}$. This problem is often addressed by introducing pixel-level penalization between input and output of the networks [48,71] which is sub-optimal for domain adaptation as it encourages to stay in the same domain.

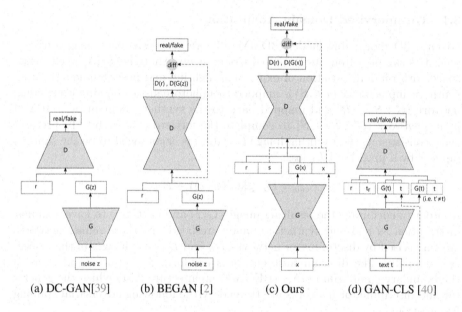

(a) DC-GAN[39]   (b) BEGAN [2]   (c) Ours   (d) GAN-CLS [40]

Fig. 2. Comparison of our pair matching method to the related work. (a) In the traditional GAN approach, the discriminator module aligns the distribution of real and synthetic images by means of a classification network. (b) BEGAN [2] and many others showed that the alignment of reconstruction error distributions offers a more stable training. (c) We propose to utilize this autoencoder approach to align the distribution of pairs to encourage generated images to be transformed to the realistic domain with a game between real and synthetic pairs. (d) An alternative to our method is to introduce wrongly labeled images to the discriminator to teach pair-wise matching as proposed by [40] for text to images synthesis.

To overcome this issue, we propose an additional pair-wise adversarial loss that assigns the G' network an additional role as a pair-wise discriminator to supervise the G network. Given a set of paired synthetic and real images $(\mathcal{P}_S, \mathcal{P}_R)$, the discriminator loss is computed by BEGAN as follows:

$$\mathcal{L}_{D_P} = \mathbb{E}_{s \in \mathcal{P}_S, r \in \mathcal{P}_R} \|s - G'(r)\|_1 - k_t^{D_P} \mathcal{L}_{cyc} \tag{6}$$

While the G' network is itself a generator network $(G' : \hat{R} \rightarrow \hat{S})$ with a separate discriminator (D_S), we use it as a third pair-matching discriminator to supervise G by means of a distribution of paired correspondence of real and synthetic images. Thus while cycle-loss optimizes for the biject correspondences, we expect the resulting pairs of $(x \in S, G(x) \in \hat{R})$ to have the similar correlation distribution as paired training data $(s \in \mathcal{P}_S, r \in \mathcal{P}_R)$. Figure 2 shows its relation to the previous related art and comparison to an alternative which is a matching aware discriminator with paired inputs for text to image synthesis, as suggested by [40]. Please note that how BEGAN autoencoder architecture is utilized to align the distribution of pairs of synthetic and real images with synthetic and generated images.

Alternatively, one could pretrain the G' network as a 3DMM fitting network as in [11,49,53,54]. However, we trained it from scratch to balance the adversarial zero-sum game between the generator (G) and the pair-wise discriminator (G'). Otherwise the gradient would vanish as there would be no success in fooling the discriminator. Moreover, those networks provide only fitted 3DMM parameters which then would need to be rendered into 3DMM images by a differentiable tensor operation.

3.3 Identity Preservation

Although identity information is provided by the 3DMM in shape and texture parameters, it may be lost to some extent by virtue of a non-linear transformation. Some studies [55,65] address this issue by employing identity labels of known subjects as additional supervision either with a pre-trained classification network or within the discriminator network. However, we intend to generate images of new identities sampled from the 3DMM parameter space and their photorealistic images simply do not exist yet. Furthermore, training a new softmax layer and the rest of the framework simultaneously becomes a chicken-egg problem and results in failed training.

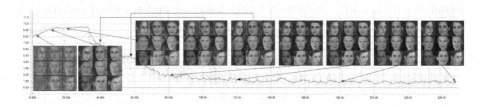

Fig. 3. Quality of 9 images of 3 identities (per row) during the training. Red plot shows the proposed identity preservation loss over the iterations. Note the changes of fine-details on the faces which is the main motivation of set-based identity preservation.

In order to preserve identity in the changing image space, we propose to adapt a set-based approach over a pre-trained face embedding network. We import the idea of pulling same-id samples as well as pushing close samples from different identities in the embedding space such that same-id images are gathered and distinct from other identities regardless of the quality of the images during the training. At the embedding layer of a pre-trained network C, the generator network (G) is supervised by a combination of the center [59] and pushing loss [19] (which is also a simplified version of the Magnet loss [43] formulation) defined for a given mini-batch (M) as:

$$\mathcal{L}_C = \mathbb{E}_{x \in \mathcal{S}, i_x \in \mathbb{N}+} \sum_x^M -log \frac{\exp(\frac{1}{2\sigma^2}\|C(G(x)) - c_{i_x}\|_2^2 - \eta)}{\sum_{j \neq i_x} \exp(\frac{1}{2\sigma^2}\|C(G(x)) - c_j\|_2^2)} \tag{7}$$

where i_x stands for the identity label of x provided by 3DMM sampling and c_j stands for the mean embedding of identity j. The margin term, η, is set to 1 and the variance is computed by $\sigma = \frac{\sum_x^M \|C(G(x)) - c_{i_x}\|_2^2}{M-1}$.

While the quality of images is improved during the training, i.e. better photo-realism, their projection on the embedding space is shifting. In order to adapt to those changes, we update identity centroids (c_j) with a momentum of $\beta = 0.95$ when new images of id j become available. Following [59], for a given x, the moving average of an identity centroid is calculated by $c_j^{t+1} = c_j^t - \beta \delta(i_x = j)(c_j^t - C(G(x)))$ where $\delta(condition) = 1$, if the condition is satisfied and $\delta(condition) = 0$ if not. Centroids (c_j) are initialized with zero and after few iterations, they converge to embedding centers and then continue updating to adapt to the changes caused by the simultaneous training of G. Figure 3 shows the quality of 9 images of 3 identities over training iterations. Please note the difference of the images after convergence with the images at the beginning of the training, produced by the Softmax layer which fails to supervise the forthcoming images in later iterations.

Full Objective

Overall, the framework is optimized by the following updates simultaneously:

$$\theta_G = \arg\min_{\theta_G} \mathcal{L}_G + \lambda_{cyc}\mathcal{L}_{cyc} + \lambda_C\mathcal{L}_C \tag{8}$$

$$\theta_{G'} = \arg\min_{\theta_{G'}} \mathcal{L}_{G'} + \lambda_{cyc}\mathcal{L}_{cyc} + \lambda_{D_P}\mathcal{L}_{D_P} \tag{9}$$

$$\theta_{D_R}, \theta_{D_S} = \arg\min_{\theta_{D_R}, \theta_{D_S}} \mathcal{L}_{D_R} + \mathcal{L}_{D_S} \tag{10}$$

where λ parameters balance the contribution of different modules. The selection of those parameters is discussed in the next section.

4   Implementation Details

Network Architecture: For the generator networks (G and G'), we use a shallow ResNet architecture as in [27] which supplies smooth transition without changing the global structure because of its limited capacity, having only 3 residual blocks. In order to benefit from 3DMM images fully, we also add skip connections to the network G. We also add dropout layers after each block in the forward pass with a 0.9 keep rate to introduce some noise that could be caused by uncontrolled environmental changes.

We construct the discriminator networks (D_R and D_S) as autoencoders trained by boundary equilibrium adversarial learning with Wasserstein distance as proposed by [2]. The classification network C, is a shallow FaceNet architecture [47], more specifically we use NN4 network with an input size of 96×96 where we randomly crop, rotate and flip generated images $G(x)$ which are of size 108×108.

Data: Our framework needs a large amount of real and synthetic face images. For real face images, we use CASIA-Web Face Dataset [64] that consists of $\sim$500K face images of $\sim$10K individuals.

The proposed method trains the G' network as a discriminator (D_P) with a small number of paired real and synthetic images. For that, we use a combination of 300W-3D [4,45,46] and AFLW2000-3D datasets as our paired training set [72] which consist of 5K real images with their corresponding 3DMM parameter annotations. We render synthetic images by those parameters and pair them with the matching real images. This dataset is relatively small, compared to the ones used by fully supervised transformation GANs (i.e. Amazon Handbag dataset used by [26] contains 137K bag images).

We randomly sample face images of new identities as our synthetic data set using Large Scale Face Model (LSFM) [5] for shape, Basel Face Model [25] for texture and Face Warehouse model [8] for expression. While the shape and texture parameters of new identities are sampled from the Gaussian distribution of the original model, expression, lighting and pose parameters are sampled with the same Gaussian distribution as that of synthetic samples of 300-3D [4,45,46] and AFLW2000-3D [72]. All images are aligned by MTCNN [68] and centre cropped to the size of 108×108 pixels.

Training Details: We train all the components of our framework together from scratch except for the classification network C which is pre-trained by using a subset of Oxford VGG Face Dataset [37]. The whole framework takes about 70 h to converge on a Nvidia GTX 1080TI GPU in 248K iterations with a batch size of 16. We start with a learning rate of 8×10^{-5} with ADAM solver [29] and halve it after 128Kth, 192Kth, 224Kth, 240Kth, 244Kth, 246Kth and 247Kth iterations.

As shown in Eqs.8 and 9, λ is a balancing factor which controls the contribution of each optimization. We set $\lambda_{cyc} = 0.5$, $\lambda_{D_P} = 0.5$, $\lambda_C = 0.001$ to achieve a balance between realism, cycle-consistency, identity preservation and the supervision by the paired data. We also add identity loss ($\mathcal{L}_{id} = \|x - G(x)\|$) as suggested by [71] to regularize the training with a balancing term $\lambda_{id} = 0.1$. During the training, we keep track of moving averages of the network parameters to generate images.

5   Results and Discussions

In this section, we show the qualitative and quantitative results obtained with the proposed framework. We also discuss and show the contribution of each module (i.e. $\mathcal{L}_{cyc}$, D_P, C) with an ablation study in the supplementary materials. For the experiments, we generate 500,000 and 5,000,000 images of 10,000 different identities with variations on expression, lighting and poses. We name this synthetic dataset **GANFaces**[2] (i.e. GANFaces-500K, GANFaces-5M).

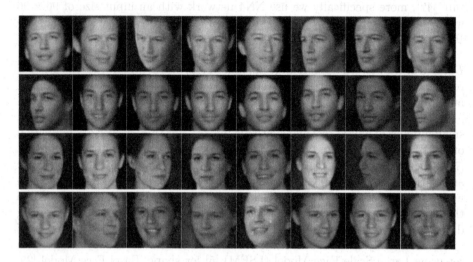

Fig. 4. Random samples from GANFaces dataset. Each row belongs to the same identity. Notice the variation in pose, expression and lighting.

5.1   Qualitative Evaluation

Please see Fig. 4 for random samples from the dataset. Figure 5 compares our results (left half of the Fig. 4) with the 3DMM inputs, the results with sim-GAN [6] and cycleGAN [71] settings, and our setup with the addition of the reconstruction loss of the paired data within the G network. We observe good correspondence when we compare first 4 columns of Fig. 4 to Fig. 5(a) in terms of identity, pose, expression and lighting. Compared to ours (Fig. 4), [6] suffers from the loss of identity-specific facial features (Fig. 5(b)) while [71] generates images visually less pleasant (Fig. 5(c)). An additional reconstruction loss used in our framework to train the G network with the paired data produces the results in Fig. 5(d). We achieved less clear images by this step probably because of the severity of the influence of the direct reconstruction loss on the adversarial balance. The superiority of the proposed framework is also confirmed by the quantitative experiments shown in Table 1.

---

[2] The dataset, training code, pre-trained models and face recognition experiments can be viewed at https://github.com/barisgecer/facegan.

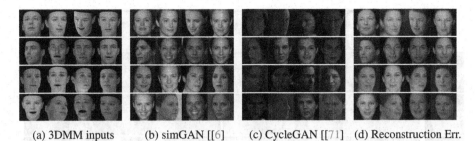

(a) 3DMM inputs   (b) simGAN [[6]   (c) CycleGAN [[71]   (d) Reconstruction Err.

Fig. 5. Comparison to (a) input 3DMM images, (b) results with simGAN settings [6], (c) results with cycleGAN settings [71] and (d) results with additional reconstruction loss. Figures correspond to left half of the Fig. 4 and each row belongs to the same identity.

One of the main goals of this work is to generate face images guided by the attributes of synthetic input images *i.e.* shape, expression, lighting, and poses. We can see from Fig. 6 that our model is capable of generating photorealistic images preserving the attributes conditioned by the synthetic input images. In the figure, top row shows the variations of pose and expression on input synthetic faces and the left column shows the input synthetic faces of different identities. The rest are the images generated by our model, conditioned on the corresponding attributes from the top row and the left column. We can clearly see that the conditioning attributes are preserved on the images generated by our model. We can also observe that fine-grained attributes such as shapes of chin, nose and eyes are also retained in the images generated by our model. In the case of extreme poses, the quality of the image generated by our model becomes less sharp as the CASIA-WebFace dataset, which we used to learn the parameters of discriminator network D_R, lacks a sufficient number of examples with extreme poses.

5.2   The Added Realism and Identity Preservation

In order to show that synthetic images are effectively transformed to the realistic domain with preserving identities, we perform a face verification experiments on GANFaces dataset. We took pre-trained face-recognition CNN network, namely FaceNet NN4 architecture [47] trained on CASIA-WebFace [64] to compute the features of the face images. The verification performance of the network on LFW is %95.6 accuracy and %95.5 1-EER which shows that the model is well optimized for in-the-wild face verification. We created 1000 similar (belonging to same identity) and 1000 dis-similar (belonging to different identities) face image pairs from GANFaces. Similarly, we also generated the same number of similar and dis-similar face image pairs from the VGG face dataset [37] and the synthetic 3DMM rendered faces dataset. Figure 7 shows the histograms of euclidean distances between similar and dis-similar images measured in the embedding space for the three datasets. The addition of realism and preservation of identities of the

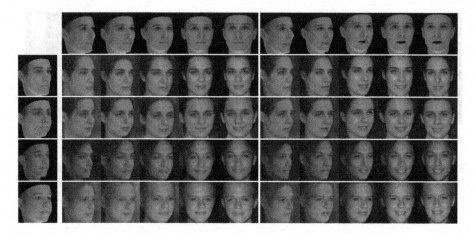

Fig. 6. Images generated by the proposed approach conditioned by identity variation in the vertical axis, normalized and mouth open expression in left and right blocks and pose variation in the horizontal axis. Images in this figure are not included in the training

GANFaces can be seen from the comparison of its distribution to the 3DMM synthetic dataset distribution. As the images become more realistic, they become better separable in the pre-trained embedding space. We also observe that the separation of positive and negative pairs of GANFaces is better than that of VGG faces pairs. The probable reason for VGG not achieving a better separation than GANFaces is noisy face labels as indicated in the original study [37].

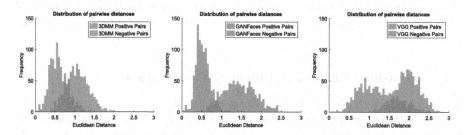

Fig. 7. Distances of 1000 positive and 1000 negative pairs from three different datasets (GANFaces, 3DMM synthetic images, Oxford VGG) embedded on a NN4 network that is trained with CASIA Face dataset

5.3   Face Recognition with GANFaces Dataset

We augmented GANFaces with real face dataset *i.e.* VGG Faces [37] and trained the VGG19 [50] network and tested its performance on two challenging datasets: LFW [23] and IJB-A [30]. We restrict ourselves from limited access to full access of real face dataset and train deep network on different combination of real and GANFaces. Following [36], we use a pre-trained VGGNet by [50] with 19 layers trained on the ImageNet dataset [44] and took these parameters as initial parameters. We train the network with different portions of the Oxford VGG Face dataset [37], augmented with the GANFaces dataset. We remove the last layer of the deep VGGNet and add two soft-max layers to the previous layer, one for each of the datasets. The learning rate is set to 0.1 for the soft-max layers and 0.01 to the pre-trained layers with the ADAM optimizer. Also we halve the gradient coming from the GANFaces soft-max. We decrease the learning rate exponentially and train for 80,000 iterations where all of our models converge well without overfitting. For a given input size of 108 × 108, we randomly crop and flip 96 × 96 patches and the overall training takes around 9 h on a GTX 1080TI GPU.

Table 1. Comparison with state-of-the-art studies on LFW performances

Method	Real	Synth	Test time Synth	Image size	Acc. (%)	100% - EER
FaceNet [47]	200M	-	No	220 × 220	98.87	-
VGG Face [37]	2.6M	-	No	224 × 224	98.95	99.13
Masi et al. [36]	495K	2.4M	Yes	224 × 224	98.06	98.00
Yin et al. [65]	495K	495K	Yes	100 × 100	96.42	-
VGG + Recons. Err.	1.8M	500K	No	96 × 96	94.7	94.8
VGG + simGAN [48]	1.8M	500K	No	96 × 96	94.7	94.8
VGG + cycleGAN [71]	1.8M	500K	No	96 × 96	94.5	94.7
VGG(%100)	1.8M	-	No	96 × 96	94.8	94.6
VGG(%100) + GANFaces-500K	1.8M	500K	No	96 × 96	**94.9**	**95.1**
VGG(%100) + GANFaces-5M	1.8M	5M	No	96 × 96	**95.2**	**95.1**

We train 6 models with %20, %50 and %100 of the VGG Face dataset with and without the augmentation of GANFaces-500K. As seen in Fig. 8, we evaluate the models on LFW and IJB-A datasets and the benchmark scores are improved with the addition of this dataset even though the image resolution is low. The contribution of GANFaces-500K increases inversely proportional to the number of images included from the VGG dataset, which indicates more synthetic images might improve the results even further.

We compare our best model trained by full VGG dataset and GANFaces to the other state of the art methods in Table 1. Despite the lower resolution, GANFaces was able to improve our baseline to the numbers comparable to the state-of-the-art. Note that generative methods, such as [36,65], do generation (i.e. pose augmentation and normalization) in the test time whereas we use only given test images. Together with the benefit of low resolution, this makes our models more efficient at test time.

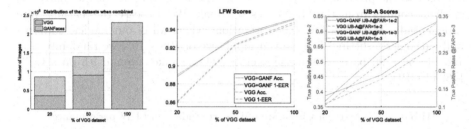

Fig. 8. Face recognition benchmark experiments. (Left) Number of images used from the two datasets in the experiments. The total number of images in the VGG data set is 1.8M since some images were removed from the URL (Middle) Performance on the LFW dataset with (solid) and without (dashed) the GANFaces-500K dataset. (Right) True Positive Rates on the IJB-A verification task with (solid) and without (dashed) the GANFaces-500K dataset.

6   Conclusions

This paper proposes a novel end-to-end semi-supervised adversarial training framework to generate photorealistic faces of new identities with wide ranges of poses, expressions, and illuminations from 3DMM rendered faces. Our extensive qualitative and quantitative experiments show that the generated images are realistic and identity preserving.

We generated a synthetic dataset of face images closer to a photorealistic domain and combined it with a real face image dataset to train a face recognition CNN and improved the performance in recognition and verification tasks. In the future, we plan to generate millions of high resolution images of thousands of new identities to boost the state-of-the-art face recognition.

The proposed framework helps to avoid some of the common GAN problems such as mode collapse and 3D coherency. It shows how the data generated by 3DMM or any other explicit model can be utilized to improve and control the behaviour of GANs.

Acknowledgments. This work was supported by the EPSRC Programme Grant 'FACER2VM' (EP/N007743/1). We would like to thank Microsoft Research for their support with Microsoft Azure Research Award. Baris Gecer is funded by the Turkish Ministry of National Education. This study is morally motivated to improve face recognition to help prediction of genetic disorders visible on human face in earlier stages.

References

1. Bansal, A., Castillo, C., Ranjan, R., Chellappa, R.: The do's and don'ts for CNN-based face verification. In: ICCVW (2017)
2. Berthelot, D., Schumm, T., Metz, L.: BEGAN: boundary equilibrium generative adversarial networks. arXiv preprint arXiv:1703.10717 (2017)
3. Blanz, V., Vetter, T.: A morphable model for the synthesis of 3d faces. In: Proceedings of the 26th Annual Conference on Computer Graphics and Interactive Techniques, pp. 187–194. ACM Press/Addison-Wesley Publishing Co. (1999)
4. Booth, J., Antonakos, E., Ploumpis, S., Trigeorgis, G., Panagakis, Y., Zafeiriou, S.: 3d face morphable models "in-the-wild". In: CVPR (2017)
5. Booth, J., Roussos, A., Zafeiriou, S., Ponniah, A., Dunaway, D.: A 3d morphable model learnt from 10,000 faces. In: CVPR (2016)
6. Bousmalis, K., Silberman, N., Dohan, D., Erhan, D., Krishnan, D.: Unsupervised pixel-level domain adaptation with generative adversarial networks. In: CVPR (2017)
7. Bousmalis, K., Trigeorgis, G., Silberman, N., Krishnan, D., Erhan, D.: Domain separation networks. In: NIPS (2016)
8. Cao, C., Weng, Y., Zhou, S., Tong, Y., Zhou, K.: FaceWarehouse: a 3d facial expression database for visual computing. IEEE Trans. Vis. Comput. Graph. $20(3)$, 413–425 (2014)
9. Chen, Q., Koltun, V.: Photographic image synthesis with cascaded refinement networks. In: ICCV (2017)
10. Chen, X., Duan, Y., Houthooft, R., Schulman, J., Sutskever, I., Abbeel, P.: Info-Gan: interpretable representation learning by information maximizing generative adversarial nets. In: NIPS (2016)
11. Cole, F., Belanger, D., Krishnan, D., Sarna, A., Mosseri, I., Freeman, W.T.: Synthesizing normalized faces from facial identity features. In: CVPR (2017)
12. Costa, P., et al.: Towards adversarial retinal image synthesis. arXiv preprint arXiv:1701.08974 (2017)
13. Dong, C., Loy, C.C., He, K., Tang, X.: Image super-resolution using deep convolutional networks. TPAMI $38(2)$, 295–307 (2016)
14. Dosovitskiy, A., et al.: FlowNet: learning optical flow with convolutional networks. In: ICCV (2015)
15. Dumoulin, V., et al.: Adversarially learned inference. arXiv preprint arXiv:1606.00704 (2016)
16. Ganin, Y., et al.: Domain-adversarial training of neural networks. J. Mach. Learn. Res. $17(59)$, 1–35 (2016)
17. Geçer, B.: Detection and classification of breast cancer in whole slide histopathology images using deep convolutional networks. Ph.D. thesis, Bilkent University (2016)
18. Gecer, B., Aksoy, S., Mercan, E., Shapiro, L.G., Weaver, D.L., Elmore, J.G.: Detection and classification of cancer in whole slide breast histopathology images using deep convolutional networks. In: Pattern Recognition (2018)
19. Gecer, B., Balntas, V., Kim, T.-K.: Learning deep convolutional embeddings for face representation using joint sample-and set-based supervision. In: ICCVW (2017)
20. Goodfellow, I.: NIPS 2016 tutorial: generative adversarial networks. In: NIPS (2016)
21. Goodfellow, I., et al.: Generative adversarial nets. In: NIPS (2014)

22. He, K., Gkioxari, G., Dollár, P., Girshick, R.: Mask R-CNN. In: ICCV (2017)
23. Huang, G.B., Ramesh, M., Berg, T., Learned-Miller, E.: Labeled faces in the wild: a database for studying face recognition in unconstrained environments. Technical report, Technical Report 07–49, University of Massachusetts, Amherst (2007)
24. Huang, X., Belongie, S.: Arbitrary style transfer in real-time with adaptive instance normalization. In: ICCV (2017)
25. IEEE: A 3D Face Model for Pose and Illumination Invariant Face Recognition, Genova, Italy (2009)
26. Isola, P., Zhu, J.-Y., Zhou, T., Efros, A.A.: Image-to-image translation with conditional adversarial networks. In: CVPR (2017)
27. Johnson, J., Alahi, A., Fei-Fei, L.: Perceptual losses for real-time style transfer and super-resolution. In: Leibe, B., Matas, J., Sebe, N., Welling, M. (eds.) ECCV 2016. LNCS, vol. 9906, pp. 694–711. Springer, Cham (2016). https://doi.org/10.1007/978-3-319-46475-6_43
28. Karras, T., Aila, T., Laine, S., Lehtinen, J.: Progressive growing of GANs for improved quality, stability, and variation. In: ICLR (2018)
29. Kingma, D., Ba, J.: Adam: a method for stochastic optimization. arXiv preprint arXiv:1412.6980 (2014)
30. Klare, B.F., et al.: Pushing the frontiers of unconstrained face detection and recognition: IARPA Janus benchmark A. In: CVPR (2015)
31. Lassner, C., Pons-Moll, G., Gehler, P.V.: A generative model of people in clothing. In: ICCV (2017)
32. Li, J., Skinner, K.A., Eustice, R.M., Johnson-Roberson, M.: WaterGAN: unsupervised generative network to enable real-time color correction of monocular underwater images. IEEE Robot. Autom. Lett. 3(1), 387–394 (2018)
33. Liu, M.-Y., Breuel, T., Kautz, J.: Unsupervised image-to-image translation networks. In: NIPS (2017)
34. Liu, W., Wen, Y., Yu, Z., Li, M., Raj, B., Song, L.: SphereFace: deep hypersphere embedding for face recognition. In: CVPR (2017)
35. Lu, Y., Tai, Y.-W., Tang, C.-K.: Conditional cycleGAN for attribute guided face image generation. arXiv preprint arXiv:1705.09966 (2017)
36. Masi, I., Tran, A.T., Hassner, T., Leksut, J.T., Medioni, G.: Do we really need to collect millions of faces for effective face recognition? In: Leibe, B., Matas, J., Sebe, N., Welling, M. (eds.) ECCV 2016. LNCS, vol. 9909, pp. 579–596. Springer, Cham (2016). https://doi.org/10.1007/978-3-319-46454-1_35
37. Parkhi, O.M., Vedaldi, A., Zisserman, A.: Deep face recognition. In: BMVC (2015)
38. Patel, V.M., Gopalan, R., Li, R., Chellappa, R.: Visual domain adaptation: a survey of recent advances. IEEE Signal Process. Mag. 32(3), 53–69 (2015)
39. Radford, A., Metz, L., Chintala, S.: Unsupervised representation learning with deep convolutional generative adversarial networks. arXiv preprint arXiv:1511.06434 (2015)
40. Reed, S., Akata, Z., Yan, X., Logeswaran, L., Schiele, B., Lee, H.: Generative adversarial text to image synthesis. In: ICML (2016)
41. Ren, S., He, K., Girshick, R., Sun, J.: Faster R-CNN: towards real-time object detection with region proposal networks. In: NIPS (2015)
42. Richardson, E., Sela, M., Kimmel, R.: 3d face reconstruction by learning from synthetic data. In: 3D Vision (3DV) (2016)
43. Rippel, O., Paluri, M., Dollar, P., Bourdev, L.: Metric learning with adaptive density discrimination. arXiv preprint arXiv:1511.05939 (2015)
44. Russakovsky, O., et al.: Imagenet large scale visual recognition challenge. Int. J. Comput. Vis. 115(3), 211–252 (2015)

45. Sagonas, C., Tzimiropoulos, G., Zafeiriou, S., Pantic, M.: 300 faces in-the-wild challenge: the first facial landmark localization challenge. In: Proceedings of the IEEE International Conference on Computer Vision Workshops, pp. 397–403 (2013)

46. Sagonas, C., Tzimiropoulos, G., Zafeiriou, S., Pantic, M.: A semi-automatic methodology for facial landmark annotation. In: Proceedings of the IEEE Conference on Computer Vision and Pattern Recognition Workshops, pp. 896–903 (2013)

47. Schroff, F., Kalenichenko, D., Philbin, J.: FaceNet: a unified embedding for face recognition and clustering. In: CVPR (2015)

48. Shrivastava, A., Pfister, T., Tuzel, O., Susskind, J., Wang, W., Webb, R.: Learning from simulated and unsupervised images through adversarial training. In: CVPR (2017)

49. Shu, Z., Yumer, E., Hadap, S., Sunkavalli, K., Shechtman, E., Samaras, D.: Neural face editing with intrinsic image disentangling. In: CVPR (2017)

50. Simonyan, K., Zisserman, A.: Very deep convolutional networks for large-scale image recognition. CoRR, abs/1409.1556 (2014)

51. Sixt, L., Wild, B., Landgraf, T.: RenderGAN: generating realistic labeled data. arXiv preprint arXiv:1611.01331 (2016)

52. Sun, B., Saenko, K.: Subspace distribution alignment for unsupervised domain adaptation. In: BMVC (2015)

53. Tewari, A., et al.: MOFA: model-based deep convolutional face autoencoder for unsupervised monocular reconstruction. In: ICCV (2017)

54. Tran, A.T., Hassner, T., Masi, I., Medioni, G.: Regressing robust and discriminative 3d morphable models with a very deep neural network. In: CVPR (2017)

55. Tran, L., Yin, X., Liu, X.: Disentangled representation learning GAN for pose-invariant face recognition. In: CVPR (2017)

56. Tzeng, E., Hoffman, J., Darrell, T., Saenko, K.: Simultaneous deep transfer across domains and tasks. In: ICCV (2015)

57. Tzeng, E., Hoffman, J., Saenko, K., Darrell, T.: Adversarial discriminative domain adaptation. In: CVPR (2017)

58. Varol, G., et al.: Learning from synthetic humans. In: CVPR (2017)

59. Wen, Y., Zhang, K., Li, Z., Qiao, Y.: A discriminative feature learning approach for deep face recognition. In: Leibe, B., Matas, J., Sebe, N., Welling, M. (eds.) ECCV 2016. LNCS, vol. 9911, pp. 499–515. Springer, Cham (2016). https://doi.org/10.1007/978-3-319-46478-7_31

60. Wolf, L., Taigman, Y., Polyak, A.: Unsupervised creation of parameterized avatars. In: ICCV (2017)

61. Wood, E., Baltrušaitis, T., Morency, L.-P., Robinson, P., Bulling, A.: Learning an appearance-based gaze estimator from one million synthesised images. In: Proceedings of the Ninth Biennial ACM Symposium on Eye Tracking Research & Applications, pp. 131–138. ACM (2016)

62. Xiong, C., Liu, L., Zhao, X., Yan, S., Kim, T.-K.: Convolutional fusion network for face verification in the wild. IEEE Trans. Circuits Syst. Video Technol. **26**(3), 517–528 (2016)

63. Xiong, C., Zhao, X., Tang, D., Jayashree, K., Yan, S., Kim, T.-K.: Conditional convolutional neural network for modality-aware face recognition. In: ICCV (2015)

64. Yi, D., Lei, Z., Liao, S., Li, S.Z.: Learning face representation from scratch. arXiv preprint arXiv:1411.7923 (2014)

65. Yin, X., Yu, X., Sohn, K., Liu, X., Chandraker, M.: Towards large-pose face frontalization in the wild. In: ICCV (2017)

66. Yuan, S., Ye, Q., Stenger, B., Jain, S., Kim, T.-K.: BigHand2. 2M benchmark: hand pose dataset and state of the art analysis. In: CVPR (2017)
67. Zhang, H., et al.: Text to photo-realistic image synthesis with stacked generative adversarial networks. In: ICCV (2017)
68. Zhang, K., Zhang, Z., Li, Z., Qiao, Y.: Joint face detection and alignment using multitask cascaded convolutional networks. IEEE Signal Process. Lett. **23**(10), 1499–1503 (2016)
69. Zhang, X., Sugano, Y., Fritz, M., Bulling, A.: Appearance-based gaze estimation in the wild. In: CVPR (2015)
70. Zheng, Z., Zheng, L., Yang, Y.: Unlabeled samples generated by GAN improve the person re-identification baseline in vitro. In: ICCV (2017)
71. Zhu, J.-Y., Park, T., Isola, P., Efros, A.A.: Unpaired image-to-image translation using cycle-consistent adversarial networks. In: ICCV (2017)
72. Zhu, X., Lei, Z., Liu, X., Shi, H., Li, S.Z.: Face alignment across large poses: a 3d solution. In: CVPR (2016)

HairNet: Single-View Hair Reconstruction Using Convolutional Neural Networks

Yi Zhou[1]([✉]), Liwen Hu[1], Jun Xing[2], Weikai Chen[2], Han-Wei Kung[3], Xin Tong[4], and Hao Li[1,2,3]

[1] University of Southern California, Los Angeles, USA
zhou859@usc.edu, huliwenkidkid@gmail.com
[2] USC Institute for Creative Technologies, Los Angeles, USA
junxnui@gmail.com, chenwk891@gmail.com
[3] Pinscreen, Santa Monica, USA
hanweikung@gmail.com, hao@hao-li.com
[4] Microsoft Research Asia, Beijing, China
xtong@microsoft.com

Abstract. We introduce a deep learning-based method to generate full 3D hair geometry from an unconstrained image. Our method can recover local strand details and has real-time performance. State-of-the-art hair modeling techniques rely on large hairstyle collections for nearest neighbor retrieval and then perform ad-hoc refinement. Our deep learning approach, in contrast, is highly efficient in storage and can run 1000 times faster while generating hair with 30K strands. The convolutional neural network takes the 2D orientation field of a hair image as input and generates strand features that are evenly distributed on the parameterized 2D scalp. We introduce a collision loss to synthesize more plausible hairstyles, and the visibility of each strand is also used as a weight term to improve the reconstruction accuracy. The encoder-decoder architecture of our network naturally provides a compact and continuous representation for hairstyles, which allows us to interpolate naturally between hairstyles. We use a large set of rendered synthetic hair models to train our network. Our method scales to real images because an intermediate 2D orientation field, automatically calculated from the real image, factors out the difference between synthetic and real hairs. We demonstrate the effectiveness and robustness of our method on a wide range of challenging real Internet pictures, and show reconstructed hair sequences from videos.

Keywords: Hair · Reconstruction · Real-time · DNN

Electronic supplementary material The online version of this chapter (https://doi.org/10.1007/978-3-030-01252-6_15) contains supplementary material, which is available to authorized users.

© Springer Nature Switzerland AG 2018
V. Ferrari et al. (Eds.): ECCV 2018, LNCS 11215, pp. 249–265, 2018.
https://doi.org/10.1007/978-3-030-01252-6_15

1   Introduction

Realistic hair modeling is one of the most difficult tasks when digitizing virtual humans [3,14,20,25,27]. In contrast to objects that are easily parameterizable, like the human face, hair spans a wide range of shape variations and can be highly complex due to its volumetric structure and level of deformability in each strand. Although [2,22,26,28,38] can create high-quality 3D hair models, but they require specialized hardware setups that are difficult to be deployed and populated. Chai et al. [5,6] introduced the first simple hair modeling technique from a single image, but the process requires manual input and cannot properly generate non-visible parts of the hair. Hu et al. [18] later addressed this problem by introducing a data-driven approach, but some user strokes were still required. More recently, Chai et al. [4] adopted a convolutional neural network to segment the hair in the input image to fully automate the modeling process, and [41] proposed a four-view approach for more flexible control.

Fig. 1. Hair reconstruction from a single view image using HairNet.

However, these data-driven techniques rely on storing and querying a huge hair model dataset and performing computationally-heavy refinement steps. Thus, they are not feasible for applications that require real-time performance or have limited hard disk and memory space. More importantly, these methods reconstruct the target hairstyle by fitting the retrieved hair models to the input image, which may capture the main hair shape well, but cannot handle the details nor achieve high accuracy. Moreover, since both the query and refinement of hair models are based on an undirected 2D orientation match, where a horizontal orientation tensor can either direct to the right or the left, this method may sometimes produce hair with incorrect growing direction or parting lines and weird deformations in the z-axis.

To speed up the procedure and reconstruct hairs that preserve better style w.r.t the input image and look more natural, we propose a deep learning based approach to generate the full hair geometry from a single-view image, as shown in Fig. 1. Different from recent advances that synthesize shapes in the form of volumetric grids [8] or point clouds [10] via neural networks, our method generates the hair strands directly, which are more suitable for non-manifold structures like hair and could achieve much higher details and precision.

Our neural network, which we call HairNet, is composed of a convolutional encoder that extracts the high-level hair-feature vector from the 2D orientation field of a hair image, and a deconvolutional decoder that generates 32×32 strand-features evenly distributed on the parameterized 2D scalp. The hair strand-features could be interpolated on the scalp space to get higher (30K) resolution and further decoded to the final strands, represented as sequences of 3D points. In particular, the hair-feature vector can be seen as a compact and continuous representation of the hair model, which enables us to sample or interpolate more plausible hairstyles efficiently in the latent space. In addition to the reconstruction loss, we also introduce a collision loss between the hair strands and a body model to push the generated hairstyles towards a more plausible space. To further improve the accuracy, we uses the visibility of each strand based on the input image as a weight to modulate its loss.

Obtaining a training set with real hair images and ground-truth 3D hair geometries is challenging. We can factor out the difference between synthetic and real hair data by using an intermediate 2D orientation field as network input. This enables our network to be trained with largely accessible synthetic hair models and also real images without any changes. For example, the 2D orientation field can be calculated from a real image by applying a Gabor filter on the hair region automatically segmented using the method of [42]. Specifically, we synthesized a hair data set composed of 40K different hairstyles and 160K corresponding 2D orientation images rendered from random views for training.

Compared to previous data-driven methods that could take minutes and terabytes of disk storage for a single reconstruction, our method only takes less than 1 second and 70 MB disk storage in total. We demonstrate the effectiveness and robustness of our method on both synthetic hair images and real images from the Internet, and show applications in hair interpolation and video tracking.

Our contributions can be summarized as follows:

1. We propose the first deep neural network to generate dense hair geometry from a single-view image. To the best of our knowledge, it is also the first work to incorporate both collision and visibility in a deep neural network to deal with 3D geometries.
2. Our approach achieves state-of-the-art resolution and quality, and significantly outperforms existing data-driven methods in both speed and storage.
3. Our network provides the first compact and continuous representation of hair geometry, from which different hairstyles can be smoothly sampled and interpolated.
4. We construct a large-scale database of around 40K 3D hair models and 160K corresponding rendered images.

2 Related Work

Hair Digitization. A general survey of existing hair modeling techniques can be found in Ward et al. [36]. For experienced artists, purely manual editing from scratch with commercial softwares such as XGen and Hairfarm is chosen for highest quality, flexibility and controllability, but the modeling of compelling and realistic hairstyles can easily take several weeks. To avoid tedious manipulations on individual hair fibers, some efficient design tools are proposed in [7,11,23,37,40].

Meanwhile, hair capturing methods have been introduced to acquire hairstyle data from the real world. Most hair capturing methods typically rely on high-fidelity acquisition systems, controlled recording sessions, manual assistance such as multi-view stereo cameras [2,9,17,22,26,28,38], single RGB-D camera [19] or thermal imaging [16].

More recently, Single-view hair digitization methods have been proposed by Chai et al. [5,6] but can only roughly produce the frontal geometry of the hair. Hu et al. [18] later demonstrated the first system that can model entire hairstyles at the strand level using a database-driven reconstruction technique with minimal user interactions from a single input image. A follow-up automatic method has been later proposed by [4], which uses a deep neural network for hair segmentation and augments a larger database for shape retrieval. To allow more flexible control of side and back views of the hairstyle, Zhang et al. [41] proposed a four-view image-based hair modeling method to fill the gap between multi-view and single-view hair capturing techniques. Since these methods rely on a large dataset for matching, speed is an issue and the final results depend highly on the database quality and diversity.

Single-View Reconstruction using Deep Learning. Generation of 3D data by deep neural networks has been attracting increasing attention recently. Volumetric CNNs [8,12,21,33] use 3D convolutional neural networks to generate voxelized shapes but are highly constrained by the volume resolution and computation cost of 3D convolution. Although techniques such as hierarchical reconstruction [15] and octree [31,32,35] could be used to improve the resolution, generating details like hair strands are still extremely challenging.

On the other hand, point clouds scale well to high resolution due to their unstructured representation. [29,30] proposed unified frameworks to learn features from point clouds for tasks like 3D object classification and segmentation, but not generation. Following the pioneering work of PointNet, [13] proposed the PCPNet to estimate the local normal and curvature from point sets, and [10] proposed a network for point set generation from a single image. However, point clouds still exhibit coarse structure and are not able to capture the topological structure of hair strands.

3   Method

The entire pipeline contains three steps. A preprocessing step is first adopted to calculate the 2D orientation field of the hair region based on the automatically estimated hair mask. Then, HairNet takes the 2D orientation fields as input and generates hair strands represented as sequences of 3D points. A reconstruction step is finally performed to efficiently generate a smooth and dense hair model.

3.1 Preprocessing

We first adopt PSPNet [42] to produce an accurate and robust pixel-wise hair mask of the input portrait image, followed by computing the undirected 2D orientation for each pixel of the hair region using a Gabor filter [26]. The use of undirected orientation eliminates the need of estimating the hair growth direction, which otherwise requires extra manual labeling [18] or learning [4]. However, the hair alone could be ambiguous due to the lack of camera view information and its scale and position with respect to the human body. Thus we also add the segmentation mask of the human head and body on the input image. In particular, the human head is obtained by fitting a 3D morphable head model to the face [20] and the body could be positioned accordingly via rigid transformation. All these processes could be automated and run in real-time. The final output is a $3 \times 256 \times 256$ image, whose first two channels store the color-coded hair orientation and third channel indicates the segmentation of hair, body and background.

3.2 Data Generation

Similar to Hu et al. [18], we first collect an original hair dataset with 340 3D hair models from public online repositories [1], align them to the same reference head, convert the mesh into hair strands and solve the collision between the hair and the body. We then populate the original hair set via mirroring and pair-wise blending.

Different from AutoHair [4] which simply uses volume boundaries to avoid unnatural combinations, we separate the hairs into 12 classes based on styles shown in Table 1 and blend each pair of hairstyles within the same class to generate more natural examples. In particular, we cluster the strands of each hair into five central strands, and each pair of hairstyles can generate $2^5 - 2$ additional combinations of central strands. The new central strands serve as a guidance to blend the detailed hairs. Instead of using all of the combinations, we randomly select the combination of them for each hair pair, leading to a total number over 40K hairs for our synthetic hair dataset.

Table 1. Hair classes and the number of hairs in each class. S refers to short, M refers to medium, L refers to long, X refers to very, s refers to straight and c refers to curly. Some hairs are assigned to multiple classes if its style is ambiguous.

XS_s	20	S_s	110	M_s	28	L_s	29	XL_s	27	XXL_s	4
XS_c	0	S_c	19	M_c	65	L_c	27	XL_c	23	XXL_c	1

In order to get the corresponding orientation images of each hair model, we randomly rotate and translate hair inside the view port of a fixed camera and render 4 orientation images at different views. The rotation ranges from $-90°$ to $+90°$ for the yaw axis and $-15°$ to $+15°$ for the pitch and roll axis. We also add Gaussian noises to the orientation to emulate the real conditions.

3.3   Hair Prediction Network

Hair Representation. We represent each strand as an ordered 3D point set $\zeta = \{s_i\}_{i=0}^{M}$, evenly sampled with a fixed number ($M = 100$ in our experiments) of points from the root to end. Each sample s_i contains attributes of position $\mathbf{p}_i$ and curvature c_i. Although the strands have large variance in length, curliness, and shape, they all grow from fixed roots to flexible ends. To remove the variance caused by root positions, we represent each strand in the local coordinate anchored at its root.

The hair model can be treated as a set of N strands $H = \zeta^N$ with fixed roots, and can be formulated as a matrix A_{N*M}, where each entry $A_{i,j} = (\mathbf{p}_{i,j}, c_{i,j})$ represents the jth sample point on the ith strand. In particular, we adopt the method in [34] to parameterize the scalp to a 32×32 grid, and sample hair roots at those grid centers ($N = 1024$).

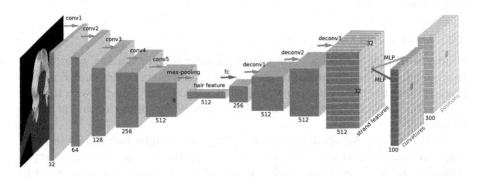

Fig. 2. Network Architecture. The input orientation image is first encoded into a high-level hair feature vector, which is then decoded to 32×32 individual strand-features. Each strand-feature is further decoded to the final strand geometry containing both sample positions and curvatures via two multi-layer perceptron (MLP) networks.

Network Architecture. As illustrated in Fig. 2, our network first encodes the input image to a latent vector, followed by decoding the target hair strands from the vector. For the encoder, we use the convolutional layers to extract the high-level features of the image. Different from the common practices that use a fully-connected layer as the last layer, we use the 2D max-pooling to spatially aggregate the partial features (a total number of 8×8) into a global feature vector z. This greatly reduces the number of network parameters.

The decoder generates the hair strands in two steps. The hair feature vector z is first decoded into multiple strand feature vectors $\{z_i\}_{i=0}^{M}$ via deconvolutional layers, and each z_i could be further decoded into the final strand geometry ζ via the same multi-layer fully connected network. This multi-scale decoding mechanism allows us to efficiently produce denser hair models by interpolating the strand features. According to our experiments, this achieves a more natural appearance than directly interpolating final strand geometry.

It is widely observed that generative neural networks often lose high frequency details, as the low frequency components often dominates the loss in training. Thus, apart from the 3D position $\{\mathbf{p}_i\}$ of each strand, our strand decoder also predicts the curvatures $\{c_i\}$ of all samples. With the curvature information, we can reconstruct the high frequency strand details.

Loss Functions. We apply three losses on our network. The first two losses are the L_2 reconstruction loss of the 3D position and the curvature of each sample. The third one is the collision loss between the output hair strand and the human body. To speed up the collision computation, we approximate the geometry of the body with four ellipsoids as shown in Fig. 3.

Given a single-view image, the shape of the visible part of the hair is more reliable than the invisible part, e.g. the inner and back hair. Thus we assign adaptive weights to the samples based on their visibility—visible samples will have higher weights than the invisible ones.

The final loss function is given by:

$$L = L_{pos} + \lambda_1 L_{curv} + \lambda_2 L_{collision}. \tag{1}$$

L_{pos} and L_{curv} are the loss of the 3D positions and the curvatures respectively, written as:

$$L_{pos} = \frac{1}{NM} \sum_{i=0}^{N-1} \sum_{j=0}^{M-1} w_{i,j} \| \mathbf{p}_{i,j} - \mathbf{p}_{i,j}^* \|_2^2$$

$$L_{curv} = \frac{1}{NM} \sum_{i=0}^{N-1} \sum_{j=0}^{M-1} w_{i,j} (c_{i,j} - c_{i,j}^*)^2 \tag{2}$$

$$w_{i,j} = \begin{cases} 10.0 & s_{i,j} \ is \ visible \\ 0.1 & otherwise \end{cases}$$

where $\mathbf{p}_{i,j}^*$ and $c_{i,j}^*$ are the corresponding ground truth position and curvature to $\mathbf{p}_{i,j}$ and $c_{i,j}$, and $w_{i,j}$ is the visibility weight.

Fig. 3. Ellipsoids for collision test.

The collision loss L_{col} is written as the sum of each collision error on the four ellipsoids:

$$L_{col} = \frac{1}{NM} \sum_{k=0}^{3} C_k \tag{3}$$

Each collision error is calculated as the sum of the distance of each collided point to the ellipsoid surface weighted by the length of strand that is inside the ellipsoid, written

$$C_k = \sum_{i=0}^{N-1} \sum_{j=1}^{M-1} \|\mathbf{p}_{i,j} - \mathbf{p}_{i,j-1}\| max(0, Dist_k) \tag{4}$$

$$Dist_k = 1 - \frac{(\mathbf{p}_{i,j,0} - x_k)^2}{a_k^2} - \frac{(\mathbf{p}_{i,j,1} - y_k)^2}{b_k^2} - \frac{(\mathbf{p}_{i,j,2} - z_k)^2}{c_k^2} \tag{5}$$

where $\|\mathbf{p}_{i,j} - \mathbf{p}_{i,j-1}\|$ is the L_1 distance between two adjacent samples on the strand. x_k, y_k, z_k, a_k, b_k, and d_k are the model parameters of the ellipsoid.

Training Details. The training parameters of Eq. 1 are fixed to be $\lambda_1 = 1.0$ and $\lambda_2 = 10^{-4}$. During training, we resize all the hair so that the hair is measured in the metric system. We use Relu for nonlinear activation, Adam [24] for optimization, and run the training for 500 epochs using a batch size of 32 and learning rate of 10^{-4} divided by 2 after 250 epochs.

(a) input image   (b) output orientation, training input   (c) 1K strands, training target

Fig. 4. The orientation image (b) can be automatically generated from a real image (a), or from a synthesized hair model with 9K strands. The orientation map and a down-sampled hair model with 1K strands (c) are used to train the neural network.

3.4 Reconstruction

The output strands from the network may contain noise, and sometimes lose high-frequency details when the target hair is curly. Thus, we further refine the smoothness and curliness of the hair. We first smooth the hair strands by using a Gaussian filter to remove the noise. Then, we compare the difference between the predicted curvatures and the curvatures of the output strands. If the difference is higher than a threshold, we add offsets to the strands samples. In particular, we first construct a local coordinate frame at each sample with one axis along the tangent of the strand, then apply an offset function along the other two axises by applying the curve generation function described in the work of Zhou et al. [39].

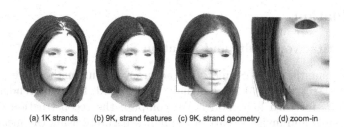

(a) 1K strands   (b) 9K, strand features (c) 9K, strand geometry   (d) zoom-in

Fig. 5. Hair strand upsampling in the space of (b) the strand-features and (c) the final strand geometry. (d) shows the zoom-in of (c).

The network only generates 1K hair strands, which is insufficient to render a high fidelity output. To obtain higher resolution, traditional methods build a 3D direction field from the guide strands and regrows strands using the direction field from a dense set of follicles. However, this method is time consuming and cannot be used to reconstruct an accurate hair model. Although directly interpolating the hair strands is fast, it can also produce an unnatural appearance. Instead, we bilinearly interpolate the intermediate strand features z_i generated by our network and decode them to strands by using the perceptron network, which enables us to create hair models with arbitrary resolution.

Figure 5 demonstrates that by interpolating in strand-feature space, we can generate a more plausible hair model. In contrast, direct interpolation of the final strands could lead to artifacts like collisions. This is easy to understand, as the strand-feature could be seen as a non-linear mapping of the strand, and could fall in a more plausible space.

Fig. 6. Reconstruction with and without using curliness.

Figure 6 demonstrates the effectiveness of adding curliness in our network. Without using the curliness as an extra constraint, the network only learns the dominant main growing direction while losing the high-frequency details. In this paper, we demonstrate all our results at a resolution of 9K to 30K strands.

4   Evaluation

4.1   Quantitative Results and Ablation Study

In order to quantitatively estimate the accuracy of our method, we prepare a synthetic test set with 100 random hair models and 4 images rendered from random views for each hair model. We compute the reconstruction errors on both the visible and invisible part of the hair separately using the mean square distance between points and the collision error using Eq. 3. We compare our result with Chai et al.'s method [4]. Their method first queries for the nearest neighbor in the database and then performs a refinement process which globally deforms the hair using the 2D boundary constraints and the 2D orientation constraints based on the input image. To ensure the fairness and efficiency of the comparison, we use the same database in our training set for the nearest neighbor query of [4] based on the visible part of the hair, and set the resolution at 1000 strands. We also compare with Hu et al.'s method [18] which requires manual strokes for generating the 3D hair model. But drawing strokes for the whole test set is too laborious, so in our test, we use three synthetic strokes randomly sampled from the ground-truth model as input. In Table 2, we show the error comparison with the nearest neighbor query results and the methods of both papers. We also perform an ablation test by respectively eliminating the visibility-adaptive weights, the collision loss and the curvature loss from our network.

From the experiments, we observe that our method outperforms all the ablation methods and Chai et al.'s method. Without the visibility-adaptive weights, the reconstruction error is about the same for both the visible and invisible parts, while the reconstruction error of the visible hair decreased by around 30% for all the networks that applies the visibility-adaptive weights. The curvature loss also helps decrease the mean square distance error of the reconstruction. The experiment also shows that using the collision loss will lead to much less error in collision. The nearest-neighbor method results have 0 collision error because the hairs in the database have no collisions.

In Table 3, we compare the computation time and hard disk usage of our method and the data-driven method at the resolution of 9K strands. It can be seen that our method can be about three magnitude faster faster and only uses a small amount of storage space. The reconstruction time differs from straight hair styles and curly hair styles because for straight hair styles which have less curvature difference, we skip the process of adding curves.

Table 2. Reconstruction Error Comparison. The errors are measured in metric. The Pos Error refers to the mean square distance error between the ground-truth and the predicted hair. "-VAW" refers to eliminating the visibility-adaptive weights. "-Col" refers to eliminating the collision loss, "-Curv" refers to eliminating the curvature loss. "NN" refers to nearest neighbor query based on the visible part of the hair.

	Visible Pos Error	Invisible Pos Error	Collision Error
HairNet	0.017	0.027	2.26×10^{-7}
HairNet - VAW	0.024	0.026	3.5×10^{-7}
HairNet - Col	0.019	0.027	3.26×10^{-6}
NairNet - Curv	0.020	0.029	3.3×10^{-7}
NN	0.033	0.041	0
Chai et al. [4]	0.021	0.040	0
Hu et al. [18]	0.023	0.028	0

Table 3. Time and space complexity.

Ours	Preprocessing	Inference	Reconstruction	Total time	Total space
	0.02 s	0.01 s	0.01–0.05 s	0.04–0.08 s	70 MiB
Chai et al. [4]	Preprocessing	NN query	Refinement	Total time	Total space
	3 s	10 s	40 s	53 s	1 TiB

4.2   Qualitative Results

To demonstrate the generality of our method, we tested with different real portrait photographs as input, as shown in the supplementary materials. Our method can handle different overall shapes (e.g. short hairstyles and long hairstyles). In addition, our method can also reconstruct different levels curliness within hairstyles (e.g. straight, wavy, and very curly) efficiently, since we learn the curliness as curvatures in the network and use it to synthesize our final strands.

In Figs. 8 and 9, we compare our results of single-view hair reconstruction with autohair [4]. We found that both methods can make rational inference of the overall hair geometry in terms of length and shape, but the hair from our method can preserve better local details and looks more natural, especially for curly hairs. This is because Chai et al.'s method depends on the accuracy and precision of the orientation field generated from the input image, but the orientation field generated from many curly hair images is noisy and the wisps overlap with each other. In addition, they use helix fitting to infer the depth of the hair, but it may fail for very curly hairs, as shown in the second row of Fig. 8. Moreover, Chai et al.'s method can only refine the visible part of the hair, so the reconstructed hair may look unnatural from views other than the view of the input image, while the hair reconstructed with our method looks comparatively more coherent from additional views.

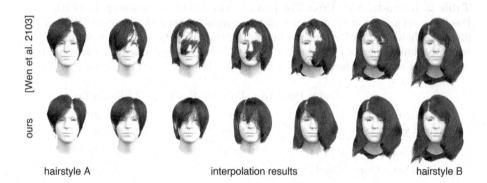

hairstyle A   interpolation results   hairstyle B

Fig. 7. Interpolation comparison.

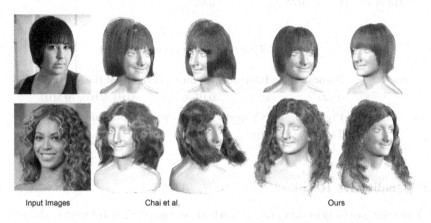

Input Images   Chai et al.   Ours

Fig. 8. Comparison with Autohair in different views [4].

Figure 7 shows the interpolation results of our method. The interpolation is performed between four different hair styles and the result shows that our method can smoothly interpolate hair between curly or straight and short or long hairs. We also compare interpolation with Weng et al.'s method [37]. In Fig. 7, Weng et al.'s method produces a lot of artifacts while our method generates more natural and smooth results. The interpolation results indicate the effectiveness of our latent hair representation. Please refer to the supplemental materials for more interpolation results.

We also show video tracking results (see Fig. 10 and supplemental video). It shows that our output may fail to achieve sufficient temporal coherence.

Input Images   Chai et al.   Ours

Fig. 9. Comparison with Autohair for local details [4].

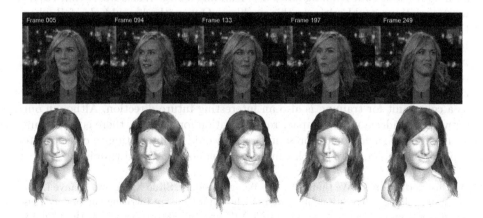

Fig. 10. Hair tracking and reconstruction on video.

Fig. 11. Failure cases.

5   Conclusion

We have demonstrated the first deep convolutional neural network capable of performing real-time hair generation from a single-view image. By training an end-to-end network to directly generate the final hair strands, our method can capture more hair details and achieve higher accuracy than current state-of-the-art. The intermediate 2D orientation field as our network input provides flexibility, which enables our network to be used for various types of hair representations, such as images, sketches and scans given proper preprocessing. By adopting a multi-scale decoding mechanism, our network could generate hairstyles of arbitrary resolution while maintaining a natural appearance. Thanks to the encoder-decoder architecture, our network provides a continuous hair representation, from which plausible hairstyles could be smoothly sampled and interpolated.

6   Limitations and Future Work

We found that our approach fails to generate exotic hairstyles like kinky, afro or buzz cuts as shown in Fig. 11. We think the main reason is that we do not have such hairstyles in our training database. Building a large hair dataset that covers more variations could mitigate this problem. Our method would also fail when the hair is partially occluded. Thus we plan to enhance our training in the future by adding random occlusions. In addition, we use face detection to estimate the pose of the torso in this paper, but it can be replaced by using deep learning to segment the head and body. Currently, the generated hair model is insufficiently temporally coherent for video frames. Integrating temporal smoothness as a constraint for training is also an interesting future direction. Although our network provides a more compact representation for the hair, there is no semantic meaning of such latent representation. It would be interesting to concatenate explicit labels (e.g. color) to the latent variable for controlled training.

Acknowledgments. We thank Weiyue Wang, Haoqi Li, Sitao Xiang and Tianye Li for giving us valuable suggestions in designing the algorithms and writing the paper. This work was supported in part by the ONR YIP grant N00014-17-S-FO14, the CONIX Research Center, one of six centers in JUMP, a Semiconductor Research Corporation (SRC) program sponsored by DARPA, the Andrew and Erna Viterbi Early Career

Chair, the U.S. Army Research Laboratory (ARL) under contract number W911NF-14-D-0005, Adobe, and Sony. The content of the information does not necessarily reflect the position or the policy of the Government, and no official endorsement should be inferred.

References

1. Electronic Arts: The Sims Resource (2017). http://www.thesimsresource.com/
2. Beeler, T., et al.: Coupled 3d reconstruction of sparse facial hair and skin. ACM Trans. Graph. **31**, 117:1–117:10 (2012). https://doi.org/10.1145/2185520.2185613. http://graphics.ethz.ch/publications/papers/paperBee12.php
3. Cao, X., Wei, Y., Wen, F., Sun, J.: Face alignment by explicit shape regression. Int. J. Comput. Vis. **107**(2), 177–190 (2014)
4. Chai, M., Shao, T., Wu, H., Weng, Y., Zhou, K.: Autohair: fully automatic hair modeling from a single image. ACM Trans. Graph. (TOG) **35**(4), 116 (2016)
5. Chai, M., Wang, L., Weng, Y., Jin, X., Zhou, K.: Dynamic hair manipulation in images and videos. ACM Trans. Graph. **32**(4), 75:1–75:8 (2013). https://doi.org/10.1145/2461912.2461990
6. Chai, M., Wang, L., Weng, Y., Yu, Y., Guo, B., Zhou, K.: Single-view hair modeling for portrait manipulation. ACM Trans. Graph. **31**(4), 116:1–116:8 (2012). https://doi.org/10.1145/2185520.2185612
7. Choe, B., Ko, H.: A statistical wisp model and pseudophysical approaches for interactivehairstyle generation. IEEE Trans. Vis. Comput. Graph. **11**(2), 160–170 (2005). https://doi.org/10.1109/TVCG.2005.20
8. Choy, C.B., Xu, D., Gwak, J., Chen, K., Savarese, S.: 3D–R2N2: a unified approach for single and multi-view 3D object reconstruction. CoRR abs/1604.00449 (2016). http://arxiv.org/abs/1604.00449
9. Echevarria, J.I., Bradley, D., Gutierrez, D., Beeler, T.: Capturing and stylizing hair for 3d fabrication. ACM Trans. Graph. **33**(4), 125:1–125:11 (2014). https://doi.org/10.1145/2601097.2601133
10. Fan, H., Su, H., Guibas, L.J.: A point set generation network for 3d object reconstruction from a single image. CoRR abs/1612.00603 (2016). http://arxiv.org/abs/1612.00603
11. Fu, H., Wei, Y., Tai, C.L., Quan, L.: Sketching hairstyles. In: Proceedings of the 4th Eurographics Workshop on Sketch-Based Interfaces and Modeling, SBIM 2007, pp. 31–36. ACM, New York (2007). https://doi.org/10.1145/1384429.1384439
12. Girdhar, R., Fouhey, D.F., Rodriguez, M., Gupta, A.: Learning a predictable and generative vector representation for objects. CoRR abs/1603.08637 (2016). http://arxiv.org/abs/1603.08637
13. Guerrero, P., Kleiman, Y., Ovsjanikov, M., Mitra, N.J.: PCPNET: learning local shape properties from raw point clouds. Comput. Graph. Forum (Eurographics) **37**, 75–85 (2017)
14. Hadap, S., et al.: Strands and hair: modeling, animation, and rendering. In: ACM SIGGRAPH 2007 Courses, pp. 1–150. ACM (2007)
15. Häne, C., Tulsiani, S., Malik, J.: Hierarchical surface prediction for 3d object reconstruction. CoRR abs/1704.00710 (2017). http://arxiv.org/abs/1704.00710
16. Herrera, T.L., Zinke, A., Weber, A.: Lighting hair from the inside: a thermal approach to hair reconstruction. ACM Trans. Graph. **31**(6), 146:1–146:9 (2012). https://doi.org/10.1145/2366145.2366165

17. Hu, L., Ma, C., Luo, L., Li, H.: Robust hair capture using simulated examples. ACM Trans. Graph. **33**(4), 126 (2014). Proceedings SIGGRAPH 2014

18. Hu, L., Ma, C., Luo, L., Li, H.: Single-view hair modeling using a hairstyle database. ACM Trans. Graph. (TOG) **34**(4), 125 (2015)

19. Hu, L., Ma, C., Luo, L., Wei, L.Y., Li, H.: Capturing braided hairstyles. ACM Trans. Graph. **33**(6), 225 (2014). Proceedings SIGGRAPH Asia 2014

20. Hu, L., et al.: Avatar digitization from a single image for real-time rendering. ACM Trans. Graph. (TOG) **36**(6), 195 (2017)

21. Jackson, A.S., Bulat, A., Argyriou, V., Tzimiropoulos, G.: Large pose 3d face reconstruction from a single image via direct volumetric CNN regression. In: International Conference on Computer Vision (2017)

22. Jakob, W., Moon, J.T., Marschner, S.: Capturing hair assemblies fiber by fiber. ACM Trans. Graph. **28**(5), 164:1–164:9 (2009). https://doi.org/10.1145/1618452.1618510

23. Kim, T.Y., Neumann, U.: Interactive multiresolution hair modeling and editing. ACM Trans. Graph. **21**(3), 620–629 (2002). https://doi.org/10.1145/566654.566627

24. Kingma, D., Ba, J.: Adam: a method for stochastic optimization. arXiv preprint arXiv:1412.6980 (2014)

25. Li, H., et al.: Facial performance sensing head-mounted display. ACM Trans. Graph. (TOG) **34**(4), 47 (2015)

26. Luo, L., Li, H., Rusinkiewicz, S.: Structure-aware hair capture. ACM Trans. Graph. **32**(4), 76 (2013). Proceedings SIGGRAPH 2013

27. Olszewski, K., Lim, J.J., Saito, S., Li, H.: High-fidelity facial and speech animation for VR HMDS. ACM Trans. Graph. **35**(6), 221 (2016). Proceedings SIGGRAPH Asia 2016

28. Paris, S., et al.: Hair photobooth: geometric and photometric acquisition of real hairstyles. ACM Trans. Graph. **27**(3), 30:1–30:9 (2008). https://doi.org/10.1145/1360612.1360629

29. Qi, C.R., Su, H., Mo, K., Guibas, L.J.: PointNet: deep learning on point sets for 3d classification and segmentation. arXiv preprint arXiv:1612.00593 (2016)

30. Qi, C.R., Yi, L., Su, H., Guibas, L.J.: Pointnet++: deep hierarchical feature learning on point sets in a metric space. arXiv preprint arXiv:1706.02413 (2017)

31. Riegler, G., Ulusoy, A.O., Geiger, A.: OctNet: learning deep 3d representations at high resolutions. In: Proceedings of the IEEE Conference on Computer Vision and Pattern Recognition, vol. 3 (2017)

32. Tatarchenko, M., Dosovitskiy, A., Brox, T.: Octree generating networks: efficient convolutional architectures for high-resolution 3d outputs. CoRR, arXiv:abs/1703.09438 (2017)

33. Tulsiani, S., Zhou, T., Efros, A.A., Malik, J.: Multi-view supervision for single-view reconstruction via differentiable ray consistency. CoRR abs/1704.06254 (2017). http://arxiv.org/abs/1704.06254

34. Wang, L., Yu, Y., Zhou, K., Guo, B.: Example-based hair geometry synthesis. ACM Trans. Graph. **28**(3), 56:1–56:9 (2009)

35. Wang, P.S., Liu, Y., Guo, Y.X., Sun, C.Y., Tong, X.: O-CNN: Octree-based convolutional neural networks for 3d shape analysis. ACM Trans. Graph. **36**(4), 72:1–72:11 (2017). https://doi.org/10.1145/3072959.3073608

36. Ward, K., Bertails, F., Kim, T.Y., Marschner, S.R., Cani, M.P., Lin, M.C.: A survey on hair modeling: styling, simulation, and rendering. IEEE Trans. Vis. Comput. Graph. **13**, 213–234 (2006)

37. Weng, Y., Wang, L., Li, X., Chai, M., Zhou, K.: Hair interpolation for portrait morphing. Comput. Graph. Forum (2013). https://doi.org/10.1111/cgf.12214
38. Xu, Z., Wu, H.T., Wang, L., Zheng, C., Tong, X., Qi, Y.: Dynamic hair capture using spacetime optimization. ACM Trans. Graph. **33**(6), 224:1–224:11 (2014). https://doi.org/10.1145/2661229.2661284
39. Yu, Y.: Modeling realistic virtual hairstyles. In: Proceedings of Ninth Pacific Conference on Computer Graphics and Applications, pp. 295–304. IEEE (2001)
40. Yuksel, C., Schaefer, S., Keyser, J.: Hair meshes. ACM Trans. Graph. **28**(5), 166:1–166:7 (2009). https://doi.org/10.1145/1618452.1618512
41. Zhang, M., Chai, M., Wu, H., Yang, H., Zhou, K.: A data-driven approach to four-view image-based hair modeling. ACM Trans. Graph. **36**(4), 156:1–156:11 (2017). https://doi.org/10.1145/3072959.3073627
42. Zhao, H., Shi, J., Qi, X., Wang, X., Jia, J.: Pyramid scene parsing network. In: Proceedings of IEEE Conference on Computer Vision and Pattern Recognition (CVPR) (2017)

Neural Network Encapsulation

Hongyang Li[1]([✉]), Xiaoyang Guo[1], Bo Dai[1], Wanli Ouyang[2],
and Xiaogang Wang[1]

[1] The Chinese University of Hong Kong, Shatin, Hong Kong
yangli@ee.cuhk.edu.hk
[2] SenseTime Computer Vision Research Group,
The University of Sydney, Sydney, Australia

Abstract. A capsule is a collection of neurons which represents different variants of a pattern in the network. The routing scheme ensures only certain capsules which resemble lower counterparts in the higher layer should be activated. However, the computational complexity becomes a bottleneck for scaling up to larger networks, as lower capsules need to correspond to each and every higher capsule. To resolve this limitation, we approximate the routing process with two branches: a master branch which collects primary information from its direct contact in the lower layer and an aide branch that replenishes master based on pattern variants encoded in other lower capsules. Compared with previous iterative and unsupervised routing scheme, these two branches are communicated in a fast, supervised and one-time pass fashion. The complexity and runtime of the model are therefore decreased by a large margin. Motivated by the routing to make higher capsule have agreement with lower capsule, we extend the mechanism as a compensation for the rapid loss of information in nearby layers. We devise a feedback agreement unit to send back higher capsules as feedback. It could be regarded as an additional regularization to the network. The feedback agreement is achieved by comparing the optimal transport divergence between two distributions (lower and higher capsules). Such an add-on witnesses a unanimous gain in both capsule and vanilla networks. Our proposed EncapNet performs favorably better against previous state-of-the-arts on CIFAR10/100, SVHN and a subset of ImageNet.

Keywords: Network architecture design · Capsule feature learning

1 Introduction

Convolutional neural networks (CNNs) [1] have been proved to be quite successful in modern deep learning architectures [2–5] and achieved better performance in various computer vision tasks [6–8]. By tying the kernel weights in convolution, CNNs have the translation invariance property that can identify the same pattern irrespective of the spatial location. Each neuron in CNNs is a scalar and can detect different (low-level details or high-level regional semantics) patterns

© Springer Nature Switzerland AG 2018
V. Ferrari et al. (Eds.): ECCV 2018, LNCS 11215, pp. 266–282, 2018.
https://doi.org/10.1007/978-3-030-01252-6_16

layer by layer. However, in order to detect the same pattern with various variants in viewpoint, rotation, shape, *etc.*, we need to stack more layers, which tends to "memorize the dataset rather than generalize a solution" [9].

A capsule [10,11] is a group of neurons whose output, in form of a vector instead of a scalar, represents various perspectives of an entity, such as pose, deformation, velocity, texture, object parts or regions, *etc.* It captures the existence of a feature *and* its variant. Not only does a capsule detect a pattern but also it is trained to learn the many variants of the pattern. This is what CNNs are incapable of. The concept of capsule provides a new perspective on feature learning via instance parameterization of entities (known as capsules) to encode different variants within a capsule structure, thus achieving the feature equivariance property[1] and being robust to adversaries. Intuitively, the capsule detects a pattern (say a face) with a certain variant (it rotates 20° clockwise) rather than realizes that the pattern matches a variant in the higher layer.

One basic capsule layer consists of two steps: *capsule mapping* and *agreement routing*, which is depicted in Fig. 1(a). The input capsules are first mapped into the space of their higher counterparts via a transform matrix. Then the routing process involves all capsules between adjacent layers to communicate by the routing co-efficients; it ensures only certain lower capsules which resemble higher ones (in terms of cosine similarity) can pass on information and activate the higher counterparts. Such a scheme can be seen as a feature clustering and is optimized by coordinate descent through several iterations. However, the computational complexity in the first mapping step is the main bottleneck to apply the capsule idea in CNNs; lower capsules have to generate correspondence for every higher capsule (*e.g.*, a typical choice [10] is 2048 capsules with 16 dimension, resulting in 8 million parameters in the transform matrix).

To tackle this drawback, we propose an alternative to estimate the original routing summation by introducing two branches: one is the `master` branch that serves as the primary source from the direct contact capsule in the lower layer; another is the `aide` branch that strives for searching other pattern variants along the channel and replenishes side information to `master`. These two branches are intertwined by their co-efficients so that feature patterns encoded in lower capsules could be fully leveraged and exchanged. Such a one-pass approximation is fast, light-weight and supervised, compared to the current iterative, short-lived and unsupervised routing scheme.

Furthermore, the routing effect in making higher capsule have agreement with lower capsule can be extended as a direct loss function. In deep neural networks, information is inevitably lost through stack of layers. To reduce the rapid loss of information in nearby layers, a loss function can be included to enforce that neurons or capsules in the higher layer can be used for reconstructing the counterparts in lower layers. Based on this motivation, we devise an agreement feedback unit which sends back higher capsules as a feedback signal to better supervise feature learning. This could be deemed as a regularization on network. Such a feedback agreement is achieved by measuring the distance between the

---

[1] Equivariance is the detection of feature patterns that can transform to each other.

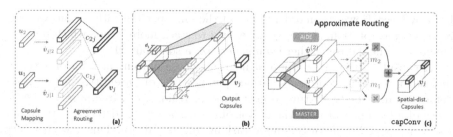

Fig. 1. (a) One capsule operation includes a capsule mapping and an agreement routing. (b) Capsule implemented in a convolutional manner by [10,11] where lower capsules are mapped into the space of *all* higher capsules and then routed to generate the output capsule. (c) Our proposed `capConv` layer: approximate routing with master and aide interaction to ease the computation burden in the current design in (b).

two distributions using optimal transport (OT) divergence, namely the Sinkhorn loss. The OT metric (*e.g.*, Wasserstein loss) is promised to be superior than other options to modeling data on general space. This add-on regularization is inserted during training and disposed of for inference. The agreement enforcement has witnessed a unanimous gain in both capsule and vanilla neural networks.

Altogether, bundled with the two mechanisms aforementioned, we (i) encapsulate the neural network in an approximate routing scheme with master/aide interaction, (ii) enforce the network's regularization by an agreement feedback unit via optimal transport divergence. The proposed capsule network is denoted as EncapNet and performs superior against previous state-of-the-arts for image recognition tasks on CIFAR10/100, SVHN and a subset of ImageNet. The code and dataset are available https://github.com/hli2020/nn_capsulation.

2   CapNet: Agreement Routing Analysis

2.1   Preliminary: Capsule Formulation

Let u_i, v_j denote the input and output capsules in a layer, where i, j indicates the index of capsules. The dimension and the number of capsules at input and output are d_1, d_2, n_1, n_2, respectively, *i.e.*, $\{u_i \in \mathbb{R}^{d_1}\}_{i=1}^{n_1}, \{v_j \in \mathbb{R}^{d_2}\}_{j=1}^{n_2}$. The first step is a mapping from lower capsules to higher counterparts: $\hat{v}_{j|i} = w_{ij} \cdot u_i$, where $w_{ij} \in \mathbb{R}^{d_1 \times d_2}$ is a transform matrix and we define the intermediate output $\hat{v}_{j|i} \in \mathbb{R}^{d_2}$ as *mapped activation* (called prediction vector in [10]) from i to j. The second step is an agreement routing process to aggregate all lower capsules into higher ones. The mapped activation is multiplied by a routing coefficient c_{ij} through several iterations in an unsupervised manner: $s_j^{(r)} = \sum_i c_{ij}^{(r)} \hat{v}_{j|i}$.

This is where the highlight of capsule idea resides in. It could be deemed as a voting process: the activation of higher capsules should be entirely dependent on the resemblance from the lower entities. Prevalent routing algorithms include the coordinate descent optimization [10] and the Gaussian mixture clustering via

Expectation-Maximum (EM) [11], to which we refer as `dynamic` and EM routing, respectively. For `dynamic` routing, given $b_{ij}^{(0)} \leftarrow 0, r \leftarrow 0$, we have:

$$b_{ij}^{(r+1)} \leftarrow b_{ij}^{(r)} + \hat{\boldsymbol{v}}_{j|i} \cdot \boldsymbol{v}_j^{(r)}, \tag{1}$$

where b is the softmax input to obtain c; $\boldsymbol{v}^{(r)}$ is computed from $\boldsymbol{s}^{(r)}$ via `squash`$(\cdot)$, i.e., $\boldsymbol{v} = \frac{\|\boldsymbol{s}\|^2}{1+\|\boldsymbol{s}\|^2} \frac{\boldsymbol{s}}{\|\boldsymbol{s}\|}$. The update of the routing co-efficient is conducted in a coordinate descent manner which optimizes c and $\boldsymbol{v}$ alternatively. For EM routing, given $c_{ij}^{(0)} \leftarrow 1/n_2, r \leftarrow 0$, and the activation response of input capsules a_i, we iteratively aggregate input capsules into d_2 Gaussian clusters:

$$a_j^{(r)}, \boldsymbol{\mu}_j^{(r)}, \boldsymbol{\sigma}_j^{(r)} \leftarrow \texttt{M-step}\big[a_i, c_{ij}^{(r)}, \hat{\boldsymbol{v}}_{j|i}\big], \tag{2}$$

$$c_{ij}^{(r+1)} \leftarrow \texttt{E-step}\big[a_j^{(r)}, p_{j|i}\big(\hat{\boldsymbol{v}}_{j|i}, \boldsymbol{\mu}_j^{(r)}, \boldsymbol{\sigma}_j^{(r)}\big)\big], \tag{3}$$

where the mean of cluster $\boldsymbol{\mu}_j$ is deemed as the output capsule $\boldsymbol{v}_j$. `M-step` generates the activation a_j alongside the mean and std w.r.t. higher capsules; these variables are further fed into `E-step` to update the routing co-efficients c_{ij}. The output from a capsule layer is thereby obtained after iterating R times.

2.2   Agreement Routing Analysis in CapNet

Effectiveness of the Agreement Routing. Figure 2 illustrates the training dynamics on routing between adjacent capsules as the network evolves. In essence, the routing process is a weighted average from all lower capsules to the higher entity (Eq. (4)). Intuitively, given a sample which belongs to the j-th class, the network tries to optimize capsule learning such that the length (existence probability) of $\boldsymbol{v}_j$ in the final capsule layer should be the largest. This requires the magnitude of its lower counterparts who resemble capsule j should occupy a majority and have a higher length compared to others that are dissimilar to j. Take the top row of Dynamic case for instance. At the first epoch, the kernel weights $\boldsymbol{w}_{ij}$ are initialized with Gaussian hence most capsules are orthogonal to each other and have the same length. As training goes (epoch 20 and 80), the percentage and length of "blurring" capsules, whose cosine similarity is around zero, goes down and the distribution evolves into a polarization: the most similar and dissimilar capsules gradually take the majority and hold a higher length than other i's. As training approaches termination (epoch 200), such a phenomenon is further polarized and the network is at a stable state where the most resembled and non-resembled capsules have a higher percentage and length than the others. The role of agreement routing is to adjust the magnitude and relevance from lower capsules to higher capsules, such that the activation of relevant higher counterparts could be appropriately turned on and the pattern information from lower capsules be passed on.

The analysis for EM routing draws a unanimous conclusion. The polarization phenomenon is further intensified (*c.f.* (h) vs (d) in Fig. (2)). The percentage of dissimilar capsules is lower (20% vs 37%) whilst the length of similar capsules is

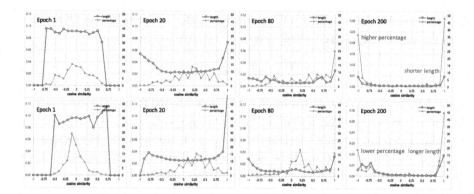

Fig. 2. Training dynamics as network evolves. Routing tends to magnify and pass on pattern variants of lower capsules to higher ones which mostly resemble the lower counterparts. **Top:** Dynamic routing. **Bottom:** EM routing. We show the cosine similarity between v_j and the mapped lower capsules, *i.e.*, $\texttt{cos\_sim}(v_j, \hat{v}_{j|i})$. Blue line represents the average (across all samples) length $\|\hat{v}_{j|i}\|$ and gray indicates the percentage (%) of how many lower capsules i's agree with j at a given resemblance. (Color figure online)

higher (0.02 vs 0.01): implying that EM is potentially a better routing solution than dynamic, which is also verified by (a) vs (b) in Table 1.

Moreover, it is observed that replacing scalar neurons in traditional CNNs with vector capsules and routing is effective, *c.f.* (a–b) vs (c) in Table 1. We adopt the same blob shape for each layer in vanilla CNNs for fair comparison. However, when we increase the parameters of CNNs to the same amount as that of CapNet, the former performs better in (d). Due to the inherent design, CapNet requires more parameters than the traditional CNNs, *c.f.* (a) vs (c) in Table 1 with around 152 Mb for CapNet vs 24 Mb for vanilla CNNs.

The capsule network is implemented in a group convolution fashion by [10,11], which is depicted in Fig. 1(b). It is assumed that the vector capsules are placed in the same way as the scalar neurons in vanilla CNNs. The *spatial* capsules in a channel share the same transform kernel since they search for the same patterns in different locations. The *channel* capsules own different kernels as they represent various patterns encapsulated in a group of neurons.

Computational Complexity in CapNet. From an engineering perspective, the original design for capsules in CNN structure (see Fig. 1(b)) is to save computation cost in the capsule mapping step; otherwise it would take 64× more kernel parameters (assuming spatial size is 8) to fulfill the mapping step. However, the burden is not eased effectively since step one has to generate a mapping for *each and every* capsule j in the subsequent layer. The output channel size of the transform kernel in Table 1(a–b) is 1,048,576 (16 × 32 × 2048). If we feed the network with a batch size of 128 (even smaller option, *e.g.*, 32), OOM (out-of-memory) occurs due to the super-huge volume of the transform kernel. The subtle difference of parameter size between dynamic and EM is that additionally the latter has a larger convolutional output before the first capsule operation to generate activations; and it has a set of trainable parameters in the EM routing. Another impact to consider is the routing co-efficient matrix of size $n_1 \times n_2$, the computation cost for this part is lightweight though and yet it takes longer runtime than traditional CNNs due to the routing iteration times R to update c, especially for EM method that involves two update alternations.

Table 1. Comparison of vanilla CNN, CapNet [10,11] and EncapNet. All models have a depth of six layers and are compared via (i) the number of model parameters (Mb), (ii) memory consumption (MB, at a given batch size), (iii) runtime (second per batch size) and (iv) performance (error rate %). 8 and 4 is the largest batch size that can fit in memory (A single Titan X GPU, which has a 12G memory.) for dynamic and EM routing. Metric (ii) and (iii) are measured on CIFAR-10.

Method	param #	mem. size	Runtime	CIFAR-10	MNIST
(a) CapNet, dynamic	151.24	3,961 (8)	0.444	14.28	0.37
(b) CapNet, EM	152.44	10,078 (4)	0.957	**12.66**	**0.31**
(c) vanilla CNN, same shape	24.44	1,652 (128)	0.026	14.43	0.38
(d) vanilla CNN, similar param	146.88	2,420 (128)	0.146	12.09	0.33
(e) EncapNet, master	25.76	1,433 (128)	0.039	13.87	0.31
(f) EncapNet, master/aide	60.68	1,755 (128)	0.061	**11.93**	**0.25**

Inspired by the routing-by-agreement scheme to aggregate feature patterns in the network and bearing in mind that the current solution has a large computation complexity, we resort to some alternative scheme stated below.

3   EncapNet: Neural Network Encapsulation

3.1   Approximate Routing with Master/aide Interaction

Recall that higher capsules are generated according to the voting co-efficient c_{ij} across all entities (capsules) in the lower layer:

$$s_j = \sum_{i=1}^{n_1} c_{ij} \cdot \hat{v}_{j|i} = c_{1j}\hat{v}_{j|1} + \cdots + c_{ij}\hat{v}_{j|i} + \cdots + c_{n_1j}\hat{v}_{j|n_1}, \tag{4}$$

$$= \underbrace{c_{ij}\hat{v}_{j|i}}_{i=j} + \sum_{i \neq j} c_{ij}\hat{v}_{j|i}. \tag{5}$$

Equation (4) can be grouped into two parts: one is a main mapping that directly receives knowledge from its lower counterpart i, whose spatial location is the same as j's; another is a side mapping which sums up all the remaining lower capsules, whose spatial location is different from j's. Hence the original unsupervised and short-lived routing process can be approximated in a supervised manner (see Fig. 1(c)):

$$s_j \approx m_1 \hat{v}^{(1)}_{|l(\mathcal{N}_j, k_1)} + m_2 \hat{v}^{(2)}_{|l(\overline{\mathcal{N}}_j, k_2)}, \tag{6}$$

where $\mathcal{N}_j$ is a location set along the channel dimension that *directly* maps lower capsules (there might be more than one) to higher j; $\overline{\mathcal{N}}_j$ is the complimentary set of $\mathcal{N}_j$ that contains the *remaining* locations along the channel; $k_{(*)}$ is the spatial kernel size; altogether $l(\cdot, \cdot)$ indicates the location set of all contributing lower capsules to create a higher capsule. Formally, we define $\hat{v}^{(1)}$ and $\hat{v}^{(2)}$ in Eq. (6) as the master and aide activation, respectively, with their co-efficients denoted as m_1 and m_2.

The `master` branch looks for the same pattern in two consecutive layers and thus only sees a window from its direct lower capsule. The `aide` branch, on the other hand, serves as a side unit to replenish information from capsules located in other channels. The convolution kernels in both branches use the spatial locality: kernels only attend to a small neighborhood of size $k_1 \times k_1$ and $k_2 \times k_2$ on the input capsule u to generate the intermediate activation $\hat{v}^{(1)}$ and $\hat{v}^{(2)}$. The master and aide activations in these two branches are communicated by their co-efficients in an interactive manner. Co-efficient $m_{(*)}$ is the output of group convolution; the input source is from both $\hat{v}^{(1)}$ and $\hat{v}^{(2)}$, leveraging information encoded in capsules from both the `master` and `aide` branches.

After the interaction as shown in Fig. 1(c), we append the batch normalization [12], rectified non-linearity unit [13] and `squash` operations at the end. These connectivities are not shown in the figure for brevity. To this end, we have encapsulated one layer of the neural network with each neuron being replaced by a capsule, where interaction among them is achieved by the `master/aide` scheme, and denote the whole pipeline as the `capConv` layer. An encapsulated module is illustrated in Fig. 3(a), where several `capConv` layers are cascaded with a skip connection. There are two types of `capConv`. Type I is to increase the dimension of capsules across modules and merge spatially-distributed capsules. The kernel size in the `master` branch is set to be 3 in this type. Type II is to increase the depth of the module for a length of N; the dimension of capsule is unchanged; nor does the number of spatial capsules. The kernel size for the `master` branch in this type is set to be 1. The `capFC` block is a per-capsule-dimension operation of the fully-connected layer as in standard neural network. Table 2 gives an example of the proposed network, called EncapNet.

Comparison to CapNet. Compared to the heavy computation of generating a huge number of mappings for each higher capsule in CapNet, our design only requires two mappings in the `master` and `aide` branch. The computational complexity is reduced by a large margin: the kernel size in the transform matrix in the first step is $\frac{n_2}{2}$ times fewer and the routing scheme in the second step is $\frac{S^4}{d_2}$ times fewer (S being the spatial size of feature map). Take the previous setting in Table 1 for instance, our design leads to 1024 and 256 times fewer parameters than the original 8,388,608 and 4,194,304 parameters in these two steps. To

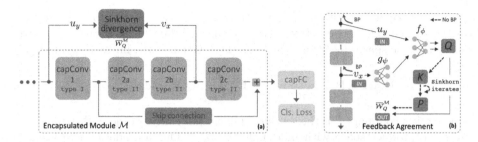

Fig. 3. (a) Connections inside one module of EncapNet, where several `capConv` layers (type I and II) are cascaded with skip connection and regularized by the Sinkhorn divergence. This is one type of design and in Sect. 5 we report other variants. (b) Pipeline and gradient flow in the Sinkhorn divergence. (Color figure online)

this end, we replace the unsupervised, iterative routing process [10,11] with a supervised, one-pass `master/aide` scheme. Compared with (a–b) in Table 1, our proposed method (e–f) has fewer parameters, less runtime, and better performance. It is also observed that the side information from the `aide` branch is a necessity to replenish the `master` branch, with baseline error 13.87% decreasing to 11.93% on CIFAR-10, *c.f.* (e) vs. (f) in Table 1.

3.2 Network Regularization by Feedback Agreement

Motivated by the agreement routing where higher capsules should be activated if there is a good 'agreement' with lower counterparts, we include a loss that requires the higher layer to be able to recover the lower layer. The influence of such a constraint (loss) is used during training and removed during inference.

To put the intuition aforementioned in math notation, let $v_x = \{v_j\}_{j=1}^{n_2}$ and $u_y = \{u_i\}_{i=1}^{n_1}$ be a sample in space $\mathcal{Z}$ and $\mathcal{U}$, respectively, where x, y are sample indices. Consider a set of observations, *e.g.* capsules at lower layer, $\mathcal{S}_1 = (u_1, \ldots, u_y, \ldots, u_{\mathcal{B}_1}) \in \mathcal{U}^{\mathcal{B}_1}$, we design a loss which enforces samples v on space $\mathcal{Z}$ as input (*e.g.*, capsules at higher layer) can be mapped to u' on space $\mathcal{U}$ through a differentiable function $g_\psi : \mathcal{Z} \to \mathcal{U}$, *i.e.*, $u' = g_\psi(v)$. The data distribution, denoted as $\mathbb{P}_\psi$, for the generated set of samples $\mathcal{S}_2 = (u'_1, \ldots, u'_x, \ldots, u'_{\mathcal{B}_2}) \in \mathcal{U}^{\mathcal{B}_2}$ should be as much *close* as the distribution $\mathbb{P}_r$ for $\mathcal{S}_1$. In summary, our goal is to find $\psi*$ that minimizes a certain loss or distance between two distributions $\mathbb{P}_\psi, \mathbb{P}_r \in \text{Prob}(\mathcal{U})^2$: $\arg\min_{\psi*} \mathcal{L}(\mathbb{P}_\psi, \mathbb{P}_r)$.

---

[2] In some literature, *i.e.*, [14,15], it is called the probability measure and commonly denoted as μ or ν; a coupling is the joint distribution (measure). We use distribution or measure interchangeably in the following context. $\text{Prob}(\mathcal{U})$ is the set of probability distributions over a metric space $\mathcal{U}$.

In this paper, we opt for an optimal transport (OT) metric to measure the distance. The OT metric between two joint probability distributions supported on two metric spaces $(\mathcal{U}, \mathcal{U})$ is defined as the solution of the linear program [16]:

$$\mathcal{W}_Q(\mathbb{P}_\psi, \mathbb{P}_r) = \inf_{\gamma \in \Gamma(\mathbb{P}_\psi, \mathbb{P}_r)} \mathbb{E}\left[\int_{\mathcal{U} \times \mathcal{U}} Q(u', u) d\gamma(u', u)\right], \tag{7}$$

where γ is a coupling; Γ is the set of couplings that consists of joint distributions over the product space with marginals $(\mathbb{P}_\psi, \mathbb{P}_r)$. Our formulation skips some mathematic notations; details are provided in [15,16]. Intuitively, $\gamma(u', u)$ implies how much "mass" must be transported from u' to u in order to transform the distribution $\mathbb{P}_\psi$ into $\mathbb{P}_r$; Q is the "ground cost" to move a unit mass from u' to u. As is well known, Eq. (7) becomes the p-Wasserstein distance (or loss, divergence) between probability measures when $\mathcal{U}$ is equipped with a distance $\mathcal{D}_\mathcal{U}$ and $Q = \mathcal{D}_\mathcal{U}(u', u)^p$, for some exponent p.

Note that the expectation $\mathbb{E}(\cdot)$ in Eq. (7) is used for mini-batches of size $(\mathcal{B}_1, \mathcal{B}_2)$. In our case, $\mathcal{B}_1$ and $\mathcal{B}_2$ are equal to the training batch size. Since both input measures are discrete for the indices x and y (capsules in the network), the coupling γ can be treated as a non-negative matrix P, namely $\gamma = \sum_{x,y} P_{x,y} \delta(v_x, u_y) \in \mathrm{Prob}(\mathcal{Z} \times \mathcal{U})$, where δ represents the Dirac unit mass distribution at point $(v, u) \in (\mathcal{Z} \times \mathcal{U})$. Rephrasing the continuous case of Eq. (7) into a discrete version, we have the desired OT loss:

$$\mathcal{W}_Q(\mathbb{P}_\psi, \mathbb{P}_r) \xleftarrow{\text{discrete}} \min_{P \in \mathbb{R}_+^{\mathcal{B}_2 \times \mathcal{B}_1}} \langle Q, P \rangle, \tag{8}$$

where P satisfies $P^\mathsf{T} \mathbb{1}_{\mathcal{B}_2} = \mathbb{1}_{\mathcal{B}_1}, P\mathbb{1}_{\mathcal{B}_1} = \mathbb{1}_{\mathcal{B}_2}$. $\langle \cdot, \cdot \rangle$ indicates the Frobenius dot-product for two matrices and $\mathbb{1}_m := (1/m, \ldots, 1/m) \in \mathbb{R}_+^m$. Now the problem boils down to computing P given some ground cost Q. We adopt the Sinkhorn algorithm [17] in an iterative manner, which is promised to have a differentiable loss function [16]. Starting with $b^{(0)} = \mathbb{1}_{\mathcal{B}_2}, l \leftarrow 0$, Sinkhorn iterates read:

$$a^{(l+1)} := \frac{\mathbb{1}_{\mathcal{B}_1}}{K^\mathsf{T} b^{(l)}}, \quad b^{(l+1)} := \frac{\mathbb{1}_{\mathcal{B}_2}}{K a^{(l)}}, \tag{9}$$

where the Gibbs kernel $K_{x,y}$ is defined as $\exp(-Q_{x,y}/\varepsilon)$; ε is a control factor. For a given budget of L iterations, we have:

$$P := P^{(L)} = \mathrm{diag}(b^{(L)}) \cdot K \cdot \mathrm{diag}(a^{(L)}), \tag{10}$$

which serves as a proxy for the OT coupling. Equipped with the computation of P and having some form of cost Q in hand, we can minimize the optimal transport divergence along with other loss in the network.

In practice, we introduce a bias fix to the original OT distance in Eq. (8), namely the Sinkhorn divergence [15]. Given two sets of samples v_x, u_y and accordingly distributions $\mathbb{P}_\psi, \mathbb{P}_r$, the revision is defined as:

$$\overline{\mathcal{W}}_Q^\mathcal{M}(\mathbb{P}_\psi, \mathbb{P}_r) = 2\mathcal{W}_Q(\mathbb{P}_\psi, \mathbb{P}_r) - \mathcal{W}_Q(\mathbb{P}_\psi, \mathbb{P}_\psi) - \mathcal{W}_Q(\mathbb{P}_r, \mathbb{P}_r), \tag{11}$$

where $\mathcal{M}$ is the module index. By tuning ε in K from 0 to ∞, the Sinkhorn divergence has the property of taking the best of both OT (non-flat geometry) and MMD [18] (high-dimensional rigidity) loss, which we find in experiments improves performance.

The overall workflow to calculate a Sinkhorn divergence[3] is depicted in Fig. 3(b). Note that our ultimate goal of applying OT loss is to make feature learning in the *mainstream* (blue blocks) better aligned across capsules in the network. It is added during training and abominated for inference. Therefore the design for Sinkhorn divergence has two principles: light-weighted and capsule-minded. Sub-networks g_ψ and f_ϕ should increase as minimal parameters to the model as possible; the generator should be encapsulated to match the data structure. Note that the Sinkhorn divergence is optimized to minimize loss w.r.t. both ϕ, ψ, instead of the practice in [14,15,19] via an adversarial manner.

Discussions. (i) There are alternatives besides the OT metric for $\mathcal{L}(\mathbb{P}_\psi, \mathbb{P}_r)$, *e.g.*, the Kullback-Leibler (KL) divergence, which is defined as $\sum_y \log \frac{d\mathbb{P}_\psi}{du'} u_y$ or Jenson-Shannon (JS) divergence. In [14], it is observed that these distances are not sensible when learning distributions supported by low dimensional manifolds on $\mathcal{Z}$. Often the model manifold and the "true" distribution's support often have a non-negligible intersection, implying that KL and JS are non-existent or infinite in some cases. In comparison, the optimal transport loss is continuous and differentiable on ψ under mild assumptions nonetheless. (ii) Our design of feedback agreement unit is not limited to the capsule framework. Its effectiveness on vanilla CNNs is also verified by experimental results in Sect. 5.1.

Design Choices in OT Divergence. We use a deconvolutional version of the capConv block as the mapping function g_ψ for reconstructing lower layer neurons from higher layer neurons. Before feeding into the cost function Q, samples from two distributions are passed into a feature extractor f_ϕ. The extractor is modeled by a vanilla neural network and can be regarded as a dimensionality reduction of $\mathcal{U}$ onto a lower-dimension space. There are many options to design the cost function Q, such as cosine distance or l_2 norm. Moreover, it is found in experiments that if the gradient flow in the Sinkhorn iterates process is ignored as does in [19], the result gets slightly better. Remind that $Q_{x,y} = \mathcal{D}\big(f_\phi(u'_x), f_\phi(u_y)\big)$ is dependent on ϕ, ψ (so does P, K, a, b); hence the whole OT unit can be trained in the standard optimizers (such as Adam [20]).

Overall Loss Function. The final loss of EncapNet is a weighted combination from both the Sinkhorn divergence across modules and the marginal loss [10] for capsule in the classification task: $\mathcal{L}_{margin}(t, v) + \lambda \sum_{\mathcal{M}} \overline{W}_Q^{\mathcal{M}}$, where t, v is the ground truth and class capsule outputs of the capFC layer, respectively; λ is a hyper-parameter to negotiate between these two losses (set to be 10).

---

[3] The term Sinkhorn used in this paper is two-folds: one is to indicate the computation of P via a Sinkhorn iterates; another is to imply the revised OT divergence.

4   Related Work

Capsule Network. Wang *et al.* [21] formulated the routing process as an optimization problem that minimizes the clustering-like loss and a KL regularization
term. They proposed a more general way to regularize the objective function,
which shares similar spirit as the agglomerative fuzzy k-means algorithm [22].
Shahroudnejad *et al.* [23] explained the capsule network inherently constructs
a relevance path, by way of dynamic routing in an unsupervised way, to eliminate the need for a backward process. When a group of capsules agree for a
parent one, they construct a part-whole relationship which can be considered
as a relevance path. A variant capsule network [24] is proposed where capsule's
activation is obtained based on the eigenvalue of a decomposed voting matrix.
Such a spectral perspective witnesses a faster convergence and a better result
than the EM routing [11] on a learning-to-diagnose problem.

Attention vs. Routing. In [25], Mnih *et al.* proposed a recurrent module to
extract information by adaptively selecting a sequence of regions and to only
attend the selected locations. DasNet [26] allows the network to iteratively focus
attention on convolution filters via feedback connections from higher layer to
lower ones. The network generates an observation vector, which is used by a
deterministic policy to choose an action, and accordingly changes the weights
of feature maps for better classifying objects. Vaswani *et al.* [27] formulated a
multi-head attention for machine translation task where attention coefficients
are calculated and parameterized by a compatibility function. Attention models
aforementioned tries to learn the attended weights from lower neurons to higher
ones. The lower activations are weighted by the learned parameters in attention
module to generate higher activations. However, the agreement routing scheme
[10,11] is a top-down solution: higher capsules should be activated if and only
if the most similar lower counterparts have a large response. The routing co-
efficients is obtained by recursively looking back at lower capsules and updated
based on the resemblance. Our approximate routing can be deemed as a bottom-
up approach which shares similar spirit as attention models.

5   Experiments

The experiments are conducted on CIFAR-10/100 [28], SVHN [29] and a large-
scale dataset called "h-ImageNet". We construct the fourth one as a subset of the
ILSVRC 2012 classification database [30]. It consists of 200 hard classes whose
top-1 accuracy, based on the prediction output of the ResNet-18 [5] model is
lower than other classes. The ResNet-18 baseline model on h-ImageNet has a
41.83% top-1 accuracy. The dataset has a collection of 255725, 17101 images for
training and validation, compared with CIFAR's 50000 for training and 10000
for test. We manually crop the object with some padding for each image (if the
bounding box is not provided) since the original image has too much background
and might be too large (over 1500 pixels); after the pre-processing, each image
size is around 50 to 500, compared with CIFAR's 32 input. "h-ImageNet" is

proposed for fast verifying ML algorithms on a large-scale dataset which shares similar distribution as ImageNet.

Implementation Details. The general settings are the same across datasets if not specified afterwards. Initial learning rate is set to 0.0001 and reduced by 90% with a schedule $[200, 300, 400]$ in epoch unit. Maximum epoch is 600. Adam [20] is used with momentum 0.9 and weight decay 5×10^{-4}. Batch size is 128.

5.1 Ablative Analysis

In this subsection we analyze the connectivity design in the encapsulated module and the many choices in the OT divergence unit. The depth of EncapNet and ResNet are the same 18 layers ($N = 3, n = 2$) for fair comparison. Their structures are depicted in Table 2. Remind that the comparison of capConv block with CapNet is reported in Table 1 and analyzed in Sect. 3.1.

Table 2. Network architecture of EncapNet and ResNet. The compared ResNet variant has the same input and output shape as EncapNet. '$x \rightarrow y$' indicates channel dimension from input to output. capConv(k, s, p) means the master capsule has a convolution of kernel size k, stride s and padding p. Similarly for the standard convolution conv() and residual block res(). The depth of the EncapNet and ResNet is $2 + \sum_i (N_i + 1)$ and $2 + \sum_i 2n_i$, respectively. Connection of OT divergence is omitted for brevity.

module	output size	cap dim.	EncapNet_v1	ResNet
$\mathcal{M}_0$	32×32	-	$3 \rightarrow 32$, conv$(3,1,1)$	$3 \rightarrow 32$, conv$(3,1,1)$
$\mathcal{M}_1$ I II	32×32	$1 \rightarrow 2$ 2	$32 \rightarrow 32$, capConv$(3,1,1)$ $[32 \rightarrow 32,$ capConv$(1,1,0)] \times N_1$	$32 \rightarrow 64$, res$(3,1,1)$ $[64 \rightarrow 64,$ res$(3,1,1)] \times (n_1 - 1)$
$\mathcal{M}_2$ I II	16×16	$2 \rightarrow 4$ 4	$32 \rightarrow 32$, capConv$(3,2,1)$ $[32 \rightarrow 32,$ capConv$(1,1,0)] \times N_2$	$64 \rightarrow 128$, res$(3,2,1)$ $[128 \rightarrow 128,$ res$(3,1,1)] \times (n_2 - 1)$
$\mathcal{M}_3$ I II	8×8	$4 \rightarrow 8$ 8	$32 \rightarrow 32$, capConv$(3,2,1)$ $[32 \rightarrow 32,$ capConv$(1,1,0)] \times N_3$	$128 \rightarrow 256$, res$(3,2,1)$ $[256 \rightarrow 256,$ res$(3,1,1)] \times (n_3 - 1)$
$\mathcal{M}_4$ I II	4×4	$8 \rightarrow 16$ 16	$32 \rightarrow 32$, capConv$(3,2,1)$ $[32 \rightarrow 32,$ capConv$(1,1,0)] \times N_4$	$256 \rightarrow 512$, res$(3,2,1)$ $[512 \rightarrow 512,$ res$(3,1,1)] \times (n_4 - 1)$
$\mathcal{M}_5$	$10/100/200$	16	capFC	avgPool, FC

Design in capConv Block. Table 3 (1–4) reports the different incoming sources of the co-efficients m in the master and aide branches. Without using aide, case (1) serves as baseline where higher capsules are only generated from the master activation. Note that the 9.83% result is already superior than all cases in Table 1, due to the increase of network depth. Result show that obtaining m_x from the activation $\hat{v}^{(x)}$ in its own branch is better than obtaining from the other activations, *c.f.*, cases (2) and (3). When the incoming source of co-efficient is from both branches, denoted as "maser/aide_v3" in (4), the pattern information from lower capsules is fully interacted by both master and aide branches; hence we achieve the best result of 7.41% when compared with cases (2) and (3). Table 3 (5–7) reports the result of adding skip connection based on case (4). It is observed that the skip connection used in both types of the capConv block make the network converge faster and get better performance (5.82%). Our final candidate model employs an additional OT unit with two Sinkhorn losses imposed on each module. One is the connectivity as shown in Fig. 3(a) where v_x is half the size of v_y; another connectivity is the same as the skip connection path shown in the figure, where v_x shares the same size with v_y; the "deconvolutional" generator in this connectivity has a stride of 1. It performances better (4.55%) than using one OT divergence alone (4.58%).

Network Regularization Design. Figure 4 illustrates the training loss curve with and without OT (Sinkhorn) divergence. It is found that the performance gain is more evident for EncapNet than ResNet (21% vs 4% increase on two networks, respectively). Moreover, we testify the KL divergence option as a distance measurement to substitute the Sinkhorn divergence, shown as case (b) in Table 3. The error rate decreases for both model, suggesting that the idea of imposing regularization on the network training is effective; such an add-on is to keep feature patterns better aligned across layers. The subtlety is that the gain clearly differs when we replace Sinkhorn with KL in EncapNet while these two options barely matter in ResNet.

Table 3. Ablative analysis on (**left**) the design in the capConv layer and (**right**) network regularization design. EncapNet and ResNet have the same 18 layers. "two OTs" indicates each module has two OT divergences coming from different sources. Experiments in series (d-*) are based on case (c) and conducted by removing or substituting each component in the OT unit while keeping the rest factors fixed (ResNet-20 reported in [5] has a 8.75% error rate; some online third party implementation (link anonymised for submission) obtains 6.98%; we run the 18-layer model in PyTorch with settings stated in the context.).

capConv Design	error (%)	Network Regularization	EncapNet	ResNet
(1) master (baseline)	9.83	(a) capConv block (baseline)	5.82	8.03[7]
(2) maser/aide_v1	8.05	(b) KL_loss	5.31	7.72
(3) maser/aide_v2	9.11	(c) OT_loss	**4.58**	7.67
(4) maser/aide_v3	7.41	(d1) remove bias fix	4.71	-
(5) skip_on_Type_I	6.81	(d2) do BP in P_L	4.77	-
(6) skip_on_Type_II	6.75	(d3) no extractor f_ψ	5.79	-
(7) skip_both	5.82	(d4) use vanilla g_ϕ	5.01	-
(8) two OTs	**4.55**	(d5) use l_2 in Q	4.90	-

Furthermore, we conduct a series of experiments (d-*) to prove the rationale of the Sinkhorn divergence design in Sect. 3.2. Without the bias fix, the result is inferior since it does not leverage both OT and MMD divergences (case d1); if we back-propagate the gradient in the P_L path, the error rate slightly increases; the role of feature extractor f_ψ is to down-sample both inputs to the same shape on a lower dimension for the subsequent pipeline to process. If we remove this functionality and directly compare the raw inputs (u, u') using cosine distance, the error increases by a large margin to 5.79%, compared with baseline 5.82%; if we adopt l_2 norm to measure the distance between raw inputs, loss will not converge (not shown in Table 3). This verifies the urgent necessity of having a feature extractor; if the generator recovering u' from v employs a standard CNN, the performance is inferior (5.01%) than the capsule version of the generator since data flows in form of capsules in the network; finally if we adopt l_2 norm to calculate P after the feature extractor, the performance degrades as well.

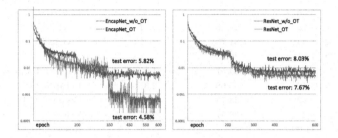

Fig. 4. Training losses with embedded optimal transport divergence for EncapNet and ResNet (*_OT). One OT unit is adopted as depicted in Fig. 3(a) for each module in the network.

5.2   Comparison to State-of-the-Arts

As shown in Table 4, (a) on CIFAR-10/100 and SVHN, we achieve a better performance of 3.10%, 24.01% and 1.52 % compared to previous entires. The multi-crop test is a key factor to further enhance the result, which is widely used by other methods as well. (b) on h-ImageNet, v1 is the 18-layer structure and has a reasonable top-1 accuracy of 51.77%. We further increase the depth of EncapNet (known as v2) by stacking more `capConv` blocks, making a depth of 101 to compare with the ResNet-101 model. To ease runtime complexity due to the `master/aide` intertwined communication, we replace some blocks in the shallow layers with `master` alone. v3 has a larger input size. Moreover, we have the ultimate version of EncapNet with data augmentation (v3^{++}) and obtain an error rate of 40.05%, compared with the runner-up WRN [31] 42.51%. Training on h-ImageNet roughly takes 2.9 days with 8 GPUs and batch size 256. (c) we have some preliminary results on the ILSVRC-CLS (`complete`-ImageNet) dataset, which are reported in terms of the top-5 error in Table 4.

Table 4. Classification errors (%) compared to state-of-the-arts. For state-of-the-arts, we show the best results available in their papers. $^+$ means mild augmentation while $^{++}$ stands for strong augmentation. For h-ImageNet, we train models and report results of other networks based on the same setting as EncapNet_v3^{++}.

Method	CIFAR-10	CIFAR-100	SVHN	h-ImageNet	
EncapNet	4.55	26.77	2.01	EncapNet_v1	48.23
EncapNet$^+$	3.13	**24.01**(24.85 ±0.11)	1.64	EncapNet_v2	43.15
EncapNet^{++}	**3.10** (3.56 ±0.12)	24.18	**1.52** (1.87 ±0.11)	EncapNet_v3	42.76
GoodInit [32]	5.84	27.66	-	EncapNet_v3$^+$	40.18
BayesNet [33]	6.37	27.40	-	EncapNet_v3^{++}	**40.05**
ResNet [5]	6.43	-	-	WRN [31]	42.51
ELU [34]	6.55	24.28	-	ResNet-101 [5]	44.13
Batch NIN [35]	6.75	28.86	1.81	VGG [3]	55.76
Rec-CNN [36]	7.09	31.75	1.77	GoogleNet [4]	60.18
Piecewise [37]	7.51	30.83	-		
DSN [38]	8.22	34.57	1.92	complete-ImageNet(top-5)	
NIN [39]	8.80	35.68	2.35	EncapNet-18	7.51
dasNet [26]	9.22	33.78	-	GoogleNet [4]	7.89
Maxout [40]	9.35	38.57	2.47	VGG [3]	8.43
AlexNet [2]	11.00	-	-	ResNet-101 [5]	6.21

6   Conclusions

In this paper, we analyze the role of routing-by-agreement to aggregate feature clusters in the capsule network. To lighten the computational load in the original framework, we devise an approximate routing scheme with master-aide interaction. The proposed alternative is light-weight, supervised and one-time pass during training. The twisted interaction ensures that the approximation can make best out of lower capsules to activate higher capsules. Motivated by the routing process to make capsules better aligned across layers, we send back higher capsules as feedback signal to better supervise the learning across capsules. Such a network regularization is achieved by minimizing the distance of two distributions using optimal transport divergence during training. This regularization is also found to be effective for vanilla CNNs.

Acknowledgment. We thank Jonathan Hui for the wonderful blog on capsule research, Gabriel Peyré and Yu Liu for helpful discussions. This work is supported by Hong Kong PhD Fellowship Scheme, SenseTime Group Limited, the Research Grants Council of Hong Kong under grant CUHK14213616, CUHK14206114, CUHK14205615, CUHK419412, CUHK14203015, CUHK14239816, CUHK14207814, CUHK14208417, CUHK14202217, and the Hong Kong Innovation and Technology Support Programme Grant ITS/121/15FX.

References

1. LeCun, Y., Bottou, L., Bengio, Y., Haffner, P.: Gradient-based learning applied to document recognition. Proc. IEEE **86**, 2278–2324 (1998)
2. Krizhevsky, A., Sutskever, I., Hinton, G.E.: ImageNet classification with deep convolutional neural networks. In: NIPS, pp. 1106–1114 (2012)
3. Simonyan, K., Zisserman, A.: Very deep convolutional networks for large-scale image recognition. In: ICLR (2015)
4. Szegedy, C., et al.: Going deeper with convolutions. In: CVPR (2015)
5. He, K., Zhang, X., Ren, S., Sun, J.: Deep residual learning for image recognition. In: CVPR (2016)
6. Li, H., Liu, Y., Ouyang, W., Wang, X.: Zoom out-and-in network with map attention decision for region proposal and object detection. Int. J. Comput. Vis. (IJCV), 1–14 (2018)
7. Li, H., et al.: Do we really need more training data for object localization. In: IEEE International Conference on Image Processing (2017)
8. Chi, Z., Li, H., Lu, H., Yang, M.H.: Dual deep network for visual tracking. IEEE Trans. Image Process. **26**(4), 2005–2015 (2017)
9. Hui, J.: Understanding Matrix capsules with EM Routing (2017). https://jhui.github.io/2017/11/14/Matrix-Capsules-with-EM-routing-Capsule-Network. Accessed 10 Mar 2018
10. Sabour, S., Frosst, N., Hinton, G.: Dynamic routing between capsules. In: NIPS (2017)
11. Hinton, G.E., Sabour, S., Frosst, N.: Matrix capsules with EM routing. In: ICLR (2018)
12. Ioffe, S., Szegedy, C.: Batch normalization: accelerating deep network training by reducing internal covariate shift. In: ICML (2015)
13. Nair, V., Hinton, G.E.: Rectified linear units improve restricted Boltzmann machines. In: ICML, pp. 807–814 (2010)
14. Arjovsky, M., Chintala, S., Bottou, L.: Wasserstein GAN. arXiv preprint arXiv:1701.07875 (2017)
15. Genevay, A., Peyr, G., Cuturi, M.: Learning generative models with Sinkhorn divergences. arXiv preprint: arXiv:1706.00292 (2017)
16. Cuturi, M.: Sinkhorn distances: lightspeed computation of optimal transport. In: NIPS (2013)
17. Sinkhorn, R.: A relationship between arbitrary positive matrices and doubly stochastic matrices. Ann. Math. Stat. **35**(2), 876–879 (1964)
18. Gretton, A., Borgwardt, K., Rasch, M.J., Scholkopf, B., Smola, A.J.: A kernel method for the two-sample problem. In: NIPS (2007)
19. Salimans, T., Zhang, H., Radford, A., Metaxas, D.: Improving GANs using optimal transport. In: International Conference on Learning Representations (2018)
20. Kingma, D.P., Ba, J.: Adam: a method for stochastic optimization. In: ICLR (2015)
21. Wang, D., Liu, Q.: An optimization view on dynamic routing between capsules. In: Submit to ICLR Workshop (2018)
22. Li, M.J., Ng, M.K., ming Cheung, Y., Huang, J.Z.: Agglomerative fuzzy k-means clustering algorithm with selection of number of clusters. IEEE Trans. Knowl. Data Eng. **20**, 1519–1534 (2008)
23. Shahroudnejad, A., Mohammadi, A., Plataniotis, K.N.: Improved explainability of capsule networks: relevance path by agreement. arXiv preprint: arXiv:1802.10204 (2018)

24. Bahadori, M.T.: Spectral capsule networks. In: ICLR workshop (2018)
25. Mnih, V., Heess, N., Graves, A., Kavukcuoglu, K.: Recurrent models of visual attention. In: NIPS (2014)
26. Stollenga, M.F., Masci, J., Gomez, F., Schmidhuber, J.: Deep networks with internal selective attention through feedback connections. In: NIPS, pp. 3545–3553 (2014)
27. Vaswani, A., et al.: Attention is all you need. arXiv preprint: arXiv:1706.03762 (2017)
28. Krizhevsky, A., Hinton, G.: Learning multiple layers of features from tiny images. Technical report (2009)
29. Netzer, Y., Wang, T., Coates, A., Bissacco, A., Wu, B., Ng, A.Y.: Reading digits in natural images with unsupervised feature learning. In: NIPS Workshop (2011)
30. Russakovsky, O., et al.: ImageNet large scale visual recognition challenge. Int. J. Comput. Vis. (IJCV) **115**(3), 211–252 (2015)
31. Zagoruyko, S., Komodakis, N.: Wide residual networks. In: BMVC (2016)
32. Mishkin, D., Matas, J.: All you need is a good init. arXiv preprint: arXiv:1511.06422 (2015)
33. Snoek, J., et al.: Scalable Bayesian optimization using deep neural networks. In: ICML (2015)
34. Clevert, D.A., Unterthiner, T., Hochreiter, S.: Fast and accurate deep network learning by exponential linear units. arXiv preprint: arXiv:1511.07289 (2015)
35. Chang, J.R., Chen, Y.S.: Batch-normalized maxout network in network. arXiv preprint: arXiv:1511.02583 (2015)
36. Liang, M., Hu, X.: Recurrent convolutional neural network for object recognition. In: The IEEE Conference on Computer Vision and Pattern Recognition (CVPR), June 2015
37. Agostinelli, F., Hoffman, M., Sadowski, P., Baldi, P.: Learning activation functions to improve deep neural networks. In: ICLR Workshop (2015)
38. Lee, C.Y., Xie, S., Gallagher, P., Zhang, Z., Tu, Z.: Deeply-supervised nets. arXiv preprint arXiv:1409.5185 (2014)
39. Lin, M., Chen, Q., Yan, S.: Network in network. In: ICLR (2014)
40. Goodfellow, I.J., Warde-farley, D., Mirza, M., Courville, A., Bengio, Y.: Maxout networks. In: ICML (2013)

Learning Deep Representations with Probabilistic Knowledge Transfer

Nikolaos Passalis$^{(\boxtimes)}$ (iD) and Anastasios Tefas

Aristotle University of Thessaloniki, 541 24 Thessaloniki, Greece
`passalis@csd.auth.gr,tefas@aiia.csd.auth.gr`

Abstract. Knowledge Transfer (KT) techniques tackle the problem of transferring the knowledge from a large and complex neural network into a smaller and faster one. However, existing KT methods are tailored towards classification tasks and they cannot be used efficiently for other representation learning tasks. In this paper we propose a novel probabilistic knowledge transfer method that works by matching the probability distribution of the data in the feature space instead of their actual representation. Apart from outperforming existing KT techniques, the proposed method allows for overcoming several of their limitations providing new insight into KT as well as novel KT applications, ranging from KT from handcrafted feature extractors to cross-modal KT from the textual modality into the representation extracted from the visual modality of the data.

Keywords: Knowledge transfer · Neural network distillation

1 Introduction

Deep Learning (DL) has been used to tackle many difficult problems [26], ranging from performing accurate object detection [36], to tackling challenging information retrieval problems [42], with great success. However, apart from developing more accurate models, the interest of the scientific community has also shifted into creating smaller and faster models that are able to run on devices with limited processing power, such as mobile phones, robots, embedded systems, etc. Several methods have been proposed to this end, including, but not limited to, model compression [20], and lightweight and more efficient neural network architectures [4,19,21,33].

Knowledge Transfer (KT) techniques have also been proposed to further improve the performance of lightweight neural networks [17,38]. KT works by transferring the knowledge from a powerful and complex model, called *teacher* model, to a smaller and simpler one, called *student* model. Usually, the knowledge is transferred between the models by having the student model to regress the output (or a transformed version of the output) of the teacher model. KT techniques allow for learning student networks that are more accurate and generalize better since the output of the teacher model implicitly encodes more

© Springer Nature Switzerland AG 2018
V. Ferrari et al. (Eds.): ECCV 2018, LNCS 11215, pp. 283–299, 2018.
https://doi.org/10.1007/978-3-030-01252-6_17

information about the similarity between the training samples and their distribution (which is usually ignored during the training when the hard binary labels of the training set are used). In that way, KT acts as a regularizer that improves the performance of the student model [44]. Note that KT methods are complementary to other techniques that allow for deploying smaller and faster networks, e.g., MobileNets that use depth-wise separable convolutions [19], or binarized networks [4], and they can be combined with them to further improve the accuracy of the models.

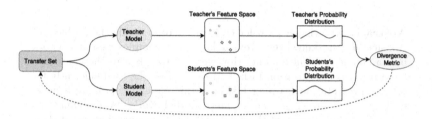

Fig. 1. Probabilistic Knowledge Transfer: The knowledge of the teacher model is modeled using a probability distribution. Then, the knowledge is transferred by minimizing the divergence between the probability distribution of the teacher and the student.

Even though existing KT techniques have been used with great success, they suffer from significant limitations. First, they are usually unable to directly transfer the knowledge between layers of different architecture/dimensionality. The reason for this is that KT methods are currently tailored towards classification tasks, where they are used to transfer the knowledge between the output classification layer of the networks (which has fixed size regardless the actual architecture of the networks). However, this renders most KT methods inappropriate for *representation learning* tasks that are needed for applications other than classification, such as text and multimedia information retrieval [8,29], learning convolutional feature extractors for object detectors [36]/trackers [31], or interactive exploratory data analysis [14]. Note that there is a growing demand for learning such lightweight feature extractors, e.g., extracting privacy-preserving representations (the user's data remain on the mobile device protecting his/her privacy) [41], lowering the energy and communication costs between mobile devices and the cloud [5], etc. Furthermore, existing KT techniques mostly ignore the *geometry* of the teacher's feature space, e.g., manifolds that are formed, similarities between neighboring samples, etc., since they merely regress the output of the teacher network. However, it has been shown that exploiting such kind of information can significantly increase the quality of the learned model regardless the domain of the application [2].

The aforementioned observations led us to a number of interesting questions. (a) Is it possible to use existing KT techniques for representation learning tasks instead of merely classification tasks? If this is indeed possible, how does existing KT techniques perform on these tasks? (b) Is there any way to learn a student model that directly regresses the geometry of the teacher's feature space instead of its output? This could possibly allow to effectively unwrap the manifolds formed in the feature space of the teacher model into the student's lower dimensional feature space increasing the accuracy of the student model. (c) Is it possible to transfer the knowledge from handcrafted features, e.g., SIFT [27], and HoG [10], into a neural network that can be then finetuned towards that task at hand? This could provide a way to exploit the large amount of the available unlabeled training samples and effectively use them in the process of training deep neural networks, overcoming a significant drawback of deep learning models, i.e., the enormous amount of labeled data that are needed for successfully training them. In that way, KT can also significantly boost DL on domains where there is knowledge on how to design good handcrafted representations, but large annotated collections of data do not exist yet, e.g., high-frequency trading analysis [23], predicting various properties of chemical compounds [30], etc. (d) Finally, can the knowledge of networks which were trained to solve other tasks, such as object detection [36], be effectively transferred into other smaller networks? This can be especially important since most deep object detectors rely on pre-trained deep convolutional neural networks, while training them from scratch is difficult and usually negatively affects their accuracy [40]. Therefore, transferring the knowledge from a larger, pre-trained network into a smaller one can significantly increase the accuracy of lightweight object detectors.

To overcome the limitations of existing KT techniques a probabilistic method for knowledge transfer is proposed in this paper. First, the interactions between the data samples in the feature space are modeled as a *probability distribution* that expresses the affinity between the data samples. In that way, it is possible to perform KT by learning a teacher model that directly regresses the probability distribution of the teacher representation instead of the actual output of the network. As it is demonstrated in Sect. 3, this process is connected to an information-theoretic measure, the Mutual Information (MI) [9], and provides several advantages over existing KT techniques. First, it allows for directly transferring the knowledge even when the output dimensionality of the networks does not match. Furthermore, even when the output dimensionality of the networks matches, directly regressing their outputs might not be the most effective strategy since the teacher network is expected to be less powerful than the student network. Using a method that is able to relax this constraint, e.g., by allowing to slightly distort the feature space, is expected to better facilitate the knowledge transfer process. Finally, note that the probability distribution can be also estimated or enhanced using any other information source, such as neural network ensembles, handcrafted feature extractors, supervised information or even qualitative information from domain experts or users, increasing the flexibility of the proposed method and allowing for using several new KT scenarios.

The main contribution of this paper is the proposal of a Probabilistic KT (PKT) technique that overcomes several limitations of existing KT methods by matching the probability distribution of the data in the feature space instead of their actual representation, as shown in Fig. 1. To the best of our knowledge the proposed technique is the first that is capable of (a) performing cross-modal knowledge transfer, (b) transferring the knowledge from handcrafted feature extractors into neural networks, (c) transferring the knowledge regardless the task at hand (e.g., object detection), and (d) incorporating domain-knowledge into the knowledge transfer procedure, providing new insight into KT. The proposed method is motivated by the fact that matching the probability density function of the teacher and student models maintains the teacher's *quadratic mutual information* (QMI) [45], between the feature representation of the data samples and a set of (possible unknown) label annotations. Also, the proposed method is capable of recreating the (local) geometry of the teacher's feature space into the feature space of the student model. Indeed, the proposed method embeds the manifolds formed in teacher's feature space into the student's space (regardless of the dimensionality of these spaces). The proposed method is extensively evaluated and compared to other KT techniques using four different evaluation setups (KT from deep neural networks, handcrafted feature extractors, different modalities and object detectors). Also, it is demonstrated that is possible to perform *cross-modal* KT by transferring the knowledge from the textual modality into the representation extracted from the visual modality. An easy to use implementation of the proposed method is available at https://github.com/passalis/probabilistic_kt to allow for easily using and extending the proposed method.

The rest of the paper is structured as follows. The related work is presented and compared to the proposed approach in Sect. 2. Then, the proposed method is presented in detail in Sect. 3 and evaluated in Sect. 4. Finally, conclusions are drawn in Sect. 5.

2   Related Work

The growing complexity of deep neural networks and the need to deploy them into mobile and embedded devices with limited computing capabilities have fueled the research on knowledge transfer techniques that are able to effectively train smaller and faster models. The vast majority of the proposed KT methods use the teacher model to generate soft-labels, e.g., by raising the temperature of the softmax activation function on the output layer of the network, that are then used to train the student model [3,6,17,44,47].

The first attempt for knowledge transfer using soft-labels was presented in [3], while the neural network distillation method [17], extends this approach by appropriately tuning the temperature of the softmax activation function. It has been demonstrated that the neural network distillation method can be used to efficiently regularize the smaller network and achieve better generalization than directly training the network using the labels of the training set [8,17,19]. Furthermore, the generated soft-targets can be used for pre-training a larger network, as in [43], for domain adaptation in combination with sparsely labeled data, as in [47], or for "compressing" the posterior predictive density in Bayesian methods [1]. Also, in [6], the knowledge is transferred from a recurrent neural network (RNN) to a deep neural network using a similar approach. It is worth mentioning a quite opposite approach followed in [44], where the knowledge is transferred from a weaker teacher model to a more powerful student network. It was demonstrated that this allows for training the student network using fewer labeled data and it highlights the regularization nature of the distillation process.

The aforementioned methods use soft-labels to train the student network. A vastly different approach is followed in [7], where the weights of the teacher model are used to initialize the student model allowing for faster convergence. Furthermore, in [38], the student network is trained not only using the soft-targets, but also using *hints* from the intermediate layers. Since the size of the student model is usually smaller, this is achieved by using a random projection to match the dimensionality of the targets and the output of the student model. A similar approach is also followed in [50], where instead of using hints, the *flow of solution procedure* (FSP) matrix is used to transfer the knowledge between some of the intermediate layers of a residual network. However, in contrast to the hint-based transfer method, the FSP-based method requires the intermediate layers of the networks to have the same size and number of filters, rendering the method unsuitable for representation learning when the dimensionality of the layers between the two networks is different (which is expected to be the case when learning a smaller network).

To the best of our knowledge the method proposed in this paper is the first probabilistic KT method for representation learning that works by directly matching the probability distribution of the data between the teacher's and the student's feature spaces using an appropriately defined divergence metric. The proposed method is simple and straightforward, without requiring careful domain-specific tuning of any hyper-parameter, such as the softmax temperature [17]. As we experimentally demonstrate in Sect. 4, this allows for directly using the proposed method for a wide range of different KT scenarios. Furthermore, the proposed method is capable of directly transferring the knowledge between spaces of different dimensionality by modeling the interactions between the data samples and, thus, avoiding the need for lossy low dimensional projections [38]. Also, the proposed method requires no knowledge about the teacher model, except for the probability distribution induced by the representation of the data samples, significantly increasing its flexibility and allowing for novel KT scenarios, such as transferring the knowledge from handcrafted feature extractors. This is in contrast with other methods that require having access to the weights of the teacher network [7]. The probability distribution can be also enhanced using domain knowledge or supervised information providing a straightforward way to directly incorporate such information into the KT procedure. Finally, the proposed method can be also used for classification tasks, similarly to other methods that regularize the distillation process by transferring the knowledge between intermediate layers, such as [34,38,50].

3   Probabilistic Knowledge Transfer

Let $\mathcal{T} = \{\mathbf{t}_1, \mathbf{t}_2, \ldots, \mathbf{t}_N\}$ denote a collection of N objects that are used to transfer the knowledge between two models. The set $\mathcal{T}$ is also called *transfer set*. Also, let $\mathbf{x} = f(\mathbf{t})$ denote the output representation of the teacher model and $\mathbf{y} = g(\mathbf{t}, \mathbf{W})$ denote the output representation of the student model, where $\mathbf{W}$ denotes the parameters of the student model. During the process of knowledge transfer the parameters $\mathbf{W}$ of the model $g(\cdot)$ are learned to "mimic" the behavior of $f(\cdot)$. Note that there is no constraint on what the functions $f(\cdot)$ and $g(\cdot)$ are as long as the output of $f(\cdot)$ is known for every element of $\mathcal{T}$ and $g(\cdot)$ is a differentiable function. The distributions of the teacher and student networks are modeled using two continuous random variables X and Y respectively, where X describes the representation extracted from the teacher model and Y describes the representation extracted from the student model.

Modeling the pairwise interactions between data samples allows for describing the geometry of the corresponding feature spaces [18,28]. To this end, the joint probability density of any two data points in the feature space, which models the probability of two data point being close together, can be used. To this end, the divergence between the joint density probability estimations for the teacher model $\mathcal{P}$ and the student model $\mathcal{Q}$ can be minimized. These joint density probability functions can be trivially estimated using Kernel Density Estimation (KDE) [39] as:

$$p_{ij} = p_{i|j} p_j = K(\mathbf{x}_i, \mathbf{x}_j; 2\sigma_t^2), \tag{1}$$

and

$$q_{ij} = q_{i|j} q_j = K(\mathbf{y}_i, \mathbf{y}_j; 2\sigma_s^2), \tag{2}$$

respectively, where $K(\mathbf{a}, \mathbf{b}; \sigma_t^2)$ is a symmetric kernel with width σ_t and $\mathbf{a}$ and $\mathbf{b}$ are two vectors. Note that class labels are not needed to minimize the divergence between these two distributions. Therefore, the proposed method can be used even when the class labels are unknown. Also note that minimizing the divergence between the probability distribution of the teacher model $\mathcal{P}$ and the probability distribution of the student model $\mathcal{Q}$ ensures that each transfer sample will have the same neighbors in both the student and teacher spaces as well as the relative distances between samples will be maintained. This, in turn, implies that the geometric relationships of the teacher's feature space are maintained in the lower dimensional feature space of the student.

Using the joint probability distribution to model the geometry of the data and perform knowledge transfer can overcome many of the drawbacks of traditional KT methods (as discussed in Sect. 2). However, learning a significantly smaller model that accurately recreates the whole geometry of a complex teacher model is often impossible. To overcome this issue, the joint probability density function can be replaced with the conditional probability distribution of the samples. Even in both cases the divergence between the probability distributions is minimized when the kernel similarities are equal for both models, using the conditional probability distribution allows for more accurately describing the local regions between the samples (the conditional probability distribution expresses the probability of each sample to select each of its neighbors [28]). The conditional probability distributions have been also used for the same reason in dimensionality reduction techniques that model data distributions in very high dimensions, such as the t-SNE algorithm [28]. The conditional probability distribution for the teacher model is defined as:

$$p_{i|j} = \frac{K(\mathbf{x}_i, \mathbf{x}_j; 2\sigma_t^2)}{\sum_{k=1,k\neq j}^{N} K(\mathbf{x}_k, \mathbf{x}_j; 2\sigma_t^2)} \in [0,1], \tag{3}$$

while for the student model as:

$$q_{i|j} = \frac{K(\mathbf{y}_i, \mathbf{y}_j; 2\sigma_t^2)}{\sum_{k=1,k\neq j}^{N} K(\mathbf{y}_k, \mathbf{y}_j; 2\sigma_s^2)} \in [0,1]. \tag{4}$$

The conditional probabilities are bounded to $[0,1]$ and sum to 1, i.e., $\sum_{i=0,i\neq j}^{N} p_{i|j} = 1$ and $\sum_{i=0,i\neq j}^{N} q_{i|j} = 1$.

Several choices exist to define the used kernel. Perhaps the most natural choice is the Gaussian kernel:

$$K_{Gaussian}(\mathbf{a}, \mathbf{b}; \sigma) = exp\left(-\frac{||\mathbf{a} - \mathbf{b}||_2^2}{\sigma}\right), \tag{5}$$

where $||\cdot||_2$ denotes the l^2 norm of a vector and σ is the scaling factor (width) of the kernel. Using the Gaussian kernel leads to the regular Kernel Density Estimation (KDE) method for estimating the conditional probabilities [39]. However, to ensure that a meaningful probability estimation is obtained the width of the kernels must be carefully tuned. This is not a straightforward task, with several heuristics proposed to tackle this problem [46]. To avoid this issue and derive a method that requires little domain-dependent tuning, a cosine similarity-based affinity metric is used in this work. Therefore, the employed similarity metric is defined as:

$$K_{cosine}(\mathbf{a}, \mathbf{b}) = \frac{1}{2}\left(\frac{\mathbf{a}^T\mathbf{b}}{||\mathbf{a}||_2||\mathbf{b}||_2} + 1\right) \in [0,1]. \tag{6}$$

Apart of avoiding the need for calculating the bandwidth of the kernel, using the cosine similarity as kernel metric allows for more robust affinity estimations, since it has been demonstrated that the cosine measure usually leads to improved performance over Euclidean measures (especially in high dimensional spaces) [29,48].

Also, several choices exist for the divergence metric that must be used for training the student model. In this work, the well known Kullback-Leibler (KL) divergence is used to this end:

$$KL(\mathcal{P}||\mathcal{P}) = \int_{-\infty}^{+\infty} \mathcal{P}(\mathbf{t}) \log \frac{\mathcal{P}(\mathbf{t})}{\mathcal{Q}(\mathbf{t})} d\mathbf{t}, \tag{7}$$

where $\mathcal{P}$ and $\mathcal{Q}$ are the probability distributions of the teacher and student models respectively. Since a finite number of points are used to approximate the distribution $\mathcal{P}$ and $\mathcal{Q}$, the loss function used for training the model is calculated as:

$$\mathcal{L} = \sum_{i=1}^{N} \sum_{j=1, i \neq j}^{N} p_{j|i} \log \left(\frac{p_{j|i}}{q_{j|i}} \right). \tag{8}$$

Note that the KL divergence is not a symmetric distance metric, giving higher weight to minimizing the divergence for neighboring pairs of points instead of distant ones. That means that maintaining the geometry of local neighborhoods is more important, during the optimization process, than recreating the global geometry of the whole feature space of the teacher, providing greater flexibility during the training of the student model. If maintaining the whole geometry of the feature space is equally important, then alternative symmetric divergence metrics, such as the quadratic divergence measure $D_Q(\mathcal{P}, \mathcal{Q}) = \int_{\mathbf{x}} (\mathcal{P}(\mathbf{t}) - \mathcal{Q}(\mathbf{t}))^2 d\mathbf{t}$, can be used. However, it should be noted that it is often infeasible to achieve this when training a student model with a significantly smaller number of parameters.

To learn the parameters of the student model $g(\mathbf{t}, \mathbf{W})$ gradient descent is used, i.e., $\Delta \mathbf{W} = -\eta \frac{\partial \mathcal{L}}{\partial \mathbf{W}}$, where $\mathbf{W}$ is the matrix with the parameters of the student model. The derivative of the loss function with respect to the parameters of the model can be easily derived as: $\frac{\partial \mathcal{L}}{\partial \mathbf{W}} = \sum_{i=1}^{N} \sum_{j=1, i \neq j}^{N} \frac{\partial \mathcal{L}}{\partial q_{j|i}} \sum_{l=1}^{N} \frac{\partial q_{j|i}}{\partial \mathbf{y}_l} \frac{\mathbf{y}_l}{\partial \mathbf{W}}$, where $\frac{\mathbf{y}_l}{\partial \mathbf{W}}$ is just the derivative of the student's output with respect to its parameters. Instead of using the plain stochastic gradient descent, a recently proposed method for stochastic optimization, the Adam algorithm [24], that calculates adaptive learning rates for each parameter of the model, is used for all the experiments conducted in this paper. Furthermore, the conditional probabilities are estimated using only a small batch of the data (64–128 samples) at each iteration, since it is usually intractable to calculate the full kernel matrix for the whole dataset. This process can be viewed as a Nyström-like approximation of the full similarity matrix [11], and it was experimentally established that it speeds up the training process, while it does not negatively impact the learned representation. The transfer samples are shuffled between the training epochs to ensure that different samples are used for estimating the conditional probability distributions during each epoch.

PKT and Mutual Information. In the following we provide a connection between the proposed method and maintaining the same amount of mutual information (MI) between the learned representation and a set of (possible unknown) labels as the teacher model. MI is a measure of dependence between random variables [9]. Let C be a discrete random variable that describes an attribute of the samples, e.g., their labels. For each feature vector $\mathbf{x}$ drawn from X there is an associated label c. The mutual information measures how much the uncertainty for the class label c is reduced after observing the feature vector $\mathbf{x}$ [45]. Let $p(c)$ be the probability of observing the class label c. Also, let $p(\mathbf{x}, c)$ denote the probability density function of the corresponding joint distribution. Then, the mutual information for the teacher is defined as $I(X, C) = \sum_c \int_{\mathbf{x}} p(\mathbf{x}, c) \log \frac{p(\mathbf{x}, c)}{p(\mathbf{x})P(c)} d\mathbf{x}$.

MI can be also expressed as the KL divergence between the joint probability density $p(\mathbf{x}, c)$ and the product of marginal probabilities $p(\mathbf{x})$ and $P(c)$. The Quadratic Mutual Information (QMI) is derived by replacing the KL divergence by a quadratic divergence measure, as proposed in [45]: $I_T(X, C) = \sum_c \int_{\mathbf{x}} (p(\mathbf{x}, c) - p(\mathbf{x})P(c))^2 d\mathbf{X}$. By expanding this definition, we obtain:

$$I_T(X, C) = \sum_c \int_{\mathbf{x}} p(\mathbf{x}, c)^2 d\mathbf{x} + \sum_c \int_{\mathbf{x}} (p(\mathbf{x})P(c))^2 d\mathbf{x} - 2\sum_c \int_{\mathbf{x}} p(\mathbf{x}, c)p(\mathbf{x})P(c) d\mathbf{x}, \quad (9)$$

where the following quantities, called *information potentials* of the teacher model, can be defined: $V_{IN}^{(t)} = \sum_c \int_{\mathbf{x}} p(\mathbf{x}, c)^2 d\mathbf{x}$, $V_{ALL}^{(t)} = \sum_c \int_{\mathbf{x}} (p(\mathbf{x})P(c))^2 d\mathbf{x}$, and $V_{BTW}^{(t)} = \sum_c \int_{\mathbf{x}} p(\mathbf{x}, c)p(\mathbf{x})P(c) d\mathbf{x}$. Thus, QMI can be expressed in terms of these information potentials as: $I_T(X, C) = V_{IN}^{(t)} + V_{ALL}^{(t)} - 2V_{BTW}^{(t)}$. Assuming that N_C different (and possible unknown) classes exist and each class is composed of J_p samples, the class prior probability for the c_p class is calculated as $P(c_p) = \frac{J_p}{N}$, where N is the total number of samples used to estimate the QMI. Also, Kernel Density Estimation [39], can be used to estimate the joint density probability as $p(\mathbf{x}, c_p) = \frac{1}{N} \sum_{j=1}^{J_p} K(\mathbf{x}, \mathbf{x}_{pj}; \sigma_t^2)$, where the notation $\mathbf{x}_{pj}$ is used to refer to the j-th sample of the p-th class, as well as probability density of X as $p(\mathbf{x}) = \sum_{p=1}^{J_p} p(\mathbf{x}, c_p) = \frac{1}{N} \sum_{j=1}^{N} K(\mathbf{x}, \mathbf{x}_j; \sigma_t^2)$.

The information potentials for the teacher model are derived using these probabilities [45]:

$$V_{IN}^{(t)} = \frac{1}{N^2} \sum_{p=1}^{N_c} \sum_{k=1}^{J_p} \sum_{l=1}^{J_p} K(\mathbf{x}_{pk}, \mathbf{x}_{pl}; 2\sigma_t^2), \quad (10)$$

$$V_{ALL}^{(t)} = \frac{1}{N^2} \left(\sum_{p=1}^{N_c} (\frac{J_p}{N})^2 \right) \sum_{k=1}^{N} \sum_{l=1}^{N} K(\mathbf{x}_k, \mathbf{x}_l; 2\sigma_t^2), \quad (11)$$

and

$$V_{BTW}^{(t)} = \frac{1}{N^2} \sum_{p=1}^{N_c} \frac{J_p}{N} \sum_{j=1}^{J_p} \sum_{k=1}^{N} K(\mathbf{x}_{pj}, \mathbf{x}_k; 2\sigma_t^2). \quad (12)$$

The interaction between two samples i and j is measured using the kernel function $K(\mathbf{x}_i, \mathbf{x}_j; \sigma^2)$ that expresses the similarity between them. Also, note that all the information potentials are expressed in terms of interactions between all the pairs of the data (weighted by a different factor). The potential V_{IN} expresses the in-class interactions, the potential V_{ALL} the interactions between all the samples, while the potential V_{BTW} the interaction of each class against all the other samples. Similarly, the information potentials can be calculated for the student network, e.g., $V_{IN}^{(s)} = \frac{1}{N^2} \sum_{p=1}^{N_c} \sum_{k=1}^{J_p} \sum_{l=1}^{J_p} K(\mathbf{y}_{pk}, \mathbf{y}_{pl}; 2\sigma_s^2)$. Different (and appropriately tuned) widths σ_t and σ_s must be used for the teacher and the student model.

If QMI is to be transferred between the models, then this implies that the respective information potentials must be equal between the two models. To have equal information potentials between the two models the values provided by the kernel function for each pair of data samples must be equal, i.e., $K(\mathbf{x}_i, \mathbf{x}_j; 2\sigma_t^2) = K(\mathbf{y}_i, \mathbf{y}_j; 2\sigma_s^2) \; \forall i, j$, which in turn implies that the joint densities defined in (1) and (2) must be equal to each other.

4   Experimental Evaluation

KT from Deep Neural Networks: First, the proposed method was evaluated using the CIFAR10. The knowledge was transferred from the penultimate layer of a deep neural network, the ResNet-18 network [16], that has over 11 million parameters, to a significantly smaller student network with the following architecture: 3×3 convolution with 8 filters, 2×2 max pooling, 3×3 convolution with 16 filters, 2×2 max pooling, 3×3 convolution with 32 filters, 2×2 max pooling and a fully connected layer with 64 neurons. Batch normalization was used after each convolutional layer [22], and the ReLU activation function was used for all the layers. The student network is composed of approximately 15,000 trainable parameters, i.e., more than 700 times less than the teacher ResNet model. The teacher network was trained for classifying the images of the CIFAR10 dataset (after adding a final classification layer with the softmax activation function) for 100 epochs with a learning rate of 0.001 for the first 50 epochs and a learning rate of 0.0001 for the last 50 epochs. A baseline teacher model was also trained and evaluated using the same setup.

The experimental results are reported in Table 1. All the methods were evaluated in a content-based retrieval setup, where the database is composed of the representation extracted from training images using the student network $g(\cdot)$, while the test set is used to query the database and evaluate each method. To evaluate the quality of the learned representation the (interpolated) mean Average Precision (mAP) at the standard 11-recall points and the top-k precision (abbreviated as "t-k") were used [29]. The cosine similarity was used to measure the similarity between the query and the database objects for all the conducted experiments. The penultimate layers (64-dimensional for the student model $g(\cdot)$ and 512-dimensional for the teacher model $f(\cdot)$) were used to extract the representation of the images and transfer the knowledge. The proposed method was compared to the hint-based knowledge transfer [38], abbreviated as "Hint", that supports directly transferring the knowledge between layers of different dimensionality (only the "hint" part of the method was used, since it is not possible to use the distillation approach between layers of different dimensionality). Note that neither the distillation approach [17], or the FSP transfer [50], can be employed when the dimensionality of the layers that are used for the knowledge transfer does not match [50]. To ensure a fair comparison between the evaluated

Table 1. CIFAR10 evaluation

Model	mAP	t-10	t-20	t-50	t-100
Student	38.96	68.30	65.35	61.89	59.17
Teacher	91.39	93.34	93.19	92.28	92.81
Distill.	40.13	68.81	65.95	62.55	59.93
Hint	21.40	33.20	30.10	27.16	24.89
PKT	**51.19**	**69.41**	**67.38**	**65.10**	**63.39**

Table 2. YouTube faces evaluation

Model	mAP	t-20	t-50	t-200
LBP	46.38 ± 0.88	98.78	95.66	81.02
Hint	52.31 ± 1.31	98.23	96.37	86.10
PKT	**54.84 ± 0.76**	**99.85**	**98.95**	**88.71**
S-PKT	70.11 ± 0.95	99.88	99.31	91.50

KT methods, the baseline student network was used for initializing the network for all the methods and the optimization process ran for 20 epoch with batch size 128 and learning rate 0.0001. The proposed method was also compared to the plain distillation approach (abbreviated as "Distill."), where the knowledge was transferred between the classification layers of the networks. However, it should be noted that this requires adding one extra classification layer to the student network and restricts the number of scenarios where the knowledge transfer can be used (since the knowledge must be transferred from a model that has been trained for classification tasks). Finally, the training data of the dataset were used as the transfer set (without using the supplied class labels).

Several conclusions can be drawn from the results reported in Table 1. First, it is confirmed that the proposed PKT method can indeed lead to significantly better results than directly training the network with the available hard labels of the training set. The hint-based method is capable of transferring some knowledge between the layers, but since it is based on random projections its power is severely limited in this application. As a result, the hint-based transfer actually decreases the retrieval precision. This phenomenon can be better understood if the regularization nature of the hint-based approach is considered, i.e., the hints were intended to regularize distillation process instead of being used for directly transferring the knowledge [38]. On the other hand, the proposed PKT method is capable of efficiently transferring the knowledge, significantly improving the mAP (51.19%) over the rest of the evaluated methods (40.13% for the next best performing method). Furthermore, note that the distillation approach cannot be used when the networks are not trained for classification and the dimensionality of the layers used for the transfer does match, while the proposed method can effectively overcome these limitations, as further demonstrated in the following experiments.

KT from Handcrafted Feature Extractors: Next, the proposed method was evaluated using the large-scale YouTube Faces dataset [49]. Before feeding each face image into the used networks it was resized to 64×64 pixels. An evaluation strategy, similar to those of celebrity face image retrieval tasks [15], is used. The persons that appear in more than 500 frames, i.e., 225 persons, are considered popular (celebrities). A total of 260,108 frames were extracted, where the 200,000 of them were used for training the method and building the database and 1,000 of them were used to query the database and evaluate the performance of the methods. The training/evaluation process was repeated five times and the mean and standard deviation of the evaluated metrics are reported.

A completely different evaluation setup was used for this dataset. Instead of transferring the knowledge from a larger neural network, the knowledge was transferred from a handcrafted feature extractor to a small neural network that also reduces the size of the extracted representation. More specifically, the representation extracted using the CS-LBP descriptors was used to perform the KT [49]. The dimensionality of the CS-LBP descriptors is 480, while the last layer of the network used to perform the knowledge transfer has only 64 neurons. Note that the distillation approach cannot be used in this case since there is no common classification layer and the dimensionality of the extracted representation differs. The following architecture was used for the student network: 3×3 convolution with 16 filters, 3×3 convolution with 32 filters, 2×2 max pooling, 3×3 convolution with 64 filters, 3×3 convolution with 64 filters, 2×2 max pooling, 3×3 convolution with 64 filters and a fully connected layer with 64 neurons. Again, batch normalization was used after each convolutional layer and the ReLU activation function was used for all the layers. All the knowledge transfer models were trained for 10 epochs using learning rate 0.0001 and batch size 128.

The evaluation results are reported in Table 2. The baseline model (LBP features) achieves a mAP of 46.38%, while the hint-based transfer increases the mAP to 52.31%. The proposed PKT again outperforms both the baseline and hint-based methods (54.84% mAP). Note that it is generally not expected the student models to achieve higher precision than the teacher model (the handcrafted feature extractor in our case). This behavior can be attributed to the completely different nature of the teacher model (convolutional neural network instead of a handcrafted feature extractor) in combination with the smaller dimensionality of the extracted representation that effectively regularize the learned representation.

Transferring the knowledge from a handcrafted feature extractor into a neural network also allows for finetuning the learned representation using supervised information (or any other kind of domain-specific knowledge). The proposed PKT method readily supports augmenting the transfer procedure with supervised information by simply constructing an appropriate probability distribution function. The most straightforward way to do so it to set $p_{i|j} = 1$ when the i-th and the j-th sample belong to the same class and $p_{i|j} = 0$ in any other case. This supervised probability distribution function can be combined with the probability distribution extracted from the representation of the teacher model or used standalone as a separate term in the loss function (by adding another divergence loss in Eq. (8)). The latter choice is followed in the proposed Supervised PKT (abbreviated as "S-PKT") with the supervised divergence weighted by 0.001. As it is demonstrated in Table 2 the S-PKT significantly increases the evaluated metrics over the unsupervised methods.

Cross-Modal KT: The proposed method was also evaluated on the SUN Attribute dataset [35], using an evaluation setup similar to this used for the Youtube Faces dataset, i.e., the knowledge is transferred from a handcrafted feature extractor (2×2 HoG features [10,35]). The SUN Attribute dataset is

Table 3. SUN attribute evaluation

Model	mAP	t-20	t-50
HoG	32.06 ± 1.20	42.65 ± 2.00	34.13 ± 1.64
Hint (HoG)	16.40 ± 0.58	19.04 ± 1.07	16.85 ± 0.86
PKT (HoG)	**26.84 ± 1.74**	**34.98 ± 2.42**	**28.96 ± 1.98**
Hint (attr)	26.08 ± 3.53	31.25 ± 4.38	27.11 ± 3.94
PKT (attr)	**47.26 ± 3.20**	**54.94 ± 4.18**	**48.72 ± 4.20**

Table 4. VOC2007 evaluation (object detection)

Initial Model	mAP
Random	18.39
Darknet	38.02
PKT	**44.14**

a large-scale scene attribute dataset that contains more than 700 categories of scenes and 14,000 images. Each image is also described by 102 discriminative textual attributes that were created by performing crowd-sourced human studies. The confidence for each textual attribute is provided. The multi-modal nature of the dataset makes it very appropriate for evaluating cross-modal and multi-modal techniques [32]. The SUN Attribute dataset was also used in this paper to evaluate the performance of cross-modal KT. Since a very small number of images exist for some categories, only images from the eight most common categories (for which at least 40 images exist) were used for training and evaluating the methods. Each image was resized in 128 × 128 pixels. The 80% of the extracted images was used for training the networks and building the database, while the rest 20% was used to query the database. The evaluation process was repeated 5 times and the mean and standard deviation of the evaluated metrics are reported.

The teacher network is also similar to the network used for the Youtube Faces dataset and it is composed of the following layers: 3 × 3 convolution with 16 filters, 2 × 2 max pooling, 3 × 3 convolution with 32 filters, 2 × 2 max pooling, 3 × 3 convolution with 64 filters, 3 × 3 convolution with 64 filters, 2 × 2 max pooling, 3 × 3 convolution with 64 filters and a fully connected layer with 64 neurons. All the knowledge transfer models were trained for 100 epochs using learning rate 0.0001 and batch size 128.

The evaluation results are reported in Table 3. First, the knowledge is transferred from 2 × 2 HoG features [10, 35] into the student network. Using the proposed PKT method leads to 26.84% mAP outperforming the hint-based transfer (16.40% mAP). As it was expected the student network performs slightly worse than the teacher model (HoG). This can be also attributed to the smaller representation extracted from the student network (64 dimensions instead of 300 dimensions for the HoG features).

The proposed method was also evaluated under a cross-modal KT setup where the knowledge is transferred from the textual modality (expressed in the form of a list of textual attributes) into the student neural network that operates within the visual modality. This setup is abbreviated as "attr" in Table 3. Transferring the knowledge from the textual modality improves the precision of the student network for both the hint-based KT method and the proposed PKT approach. Again, the proposed PKT method significantly outperforms the hint-based method leading to over 80% relative increase of the mAP.

KT from Object Detectors: Finally, the proposed method was evaluated on the PASCAL VOC 2007 and the PASCAL VOC 2012 datasets [12,13], following the experimental setup described in [36]. The Darknet framework was used for training and evaluating the object detectors [37] using the default parameters. The YOLO object detector is usually trained after initializing its convolutional layers using another network trained for solving a classification problem on the ImageNet dataset [25]. However, with the increasing need for more lightweight architectures this is not always possible, since usually pre-trained models exist only for a few architectures and it can be very tedious to successfully retrain every new model using such datasets [40]. The proposed PKT method can address this problem by directly transferring the knowledge from the 29-th layer (1280 filters) of the larger YOLOv2 model to the 13th layer of a smaller teacher model (a modified Tiny YOLO model with 512 filters instead of 1024 filters in its 13th layer). The proposed knowledge transfer method ran for 50 epochs with batch size 8 (due to memory constraints) and learning rate 10^{-4}.

The following networks were evaluated in the conducted experiments: (a) a randomly initialized network (abbreviated as "Random"), (b) a network initialized using the first 11 matching layers of the Darknet reference model trained on the ImageNet dataset (abbreviated as "Darknet") [37], and (c) the network trained using the proposed KT method (abbreviated as "PKT"). The networks were trained for 40,000 iterations with batch size 64 and the results are reported in Table 4. First, the importance of using a knowledge transfer technique (either direct or indirect) is highlighted. Using a randomly initialized network we were unable to train a useful object detector (mAP <19%), even though aggressive data augmentation techniques were used. This is expected, since it is well established that training deep object detectors from scratch it is not straightforward [40]. On the other hand, both directly using the weights of a network trained on another task and transferring the knowledge from another detector yield significantly better results. The proposed method also outperforms all the other evaluated methods leading to better object detection precision (44.14% mAP) demonstrating its ability to efficiently transfer the knowledge from an object detector into another one. Note that in contrast to the baseline ("Darknet") method, the proposed method is able to directly transfer the knowledge from a more powerful model that was trained for the task at hand (object detection) instead of using a smaller network that has been trained to extract representations for another task (classification). This can also significantly reduce the training time, since only the "useful" knowledge for the task at hand is transferred, instead of learning a generic object classifier using a huge dataset.

5   Conclusions

In this paper a Probabilistic KT technique that overcomes several limitations of existing KT methods by matching the probability distribution of the data in the feature space instead of their actual representation was proposed. The proposed method was extensively evaluated and it was demonstrated that outperforms several other KT techniques using different evaluation setups (KT from deep neural networks, handcrafted feature extractors, and different modalities).

References

1. Balan, A.K., Rathod, V., Murphy, K.P., Welling, M.: Bayesian dark knowledge. In: Proceedings of the Advances in Neural Information Processing Systems, pp. 3438–3446 (2015)
2. Belkin, M., Niyogi, P., Sindhwani, V.: Manifold regularization: a geometric framework for learning from labeled and unlabeled examples. J. Mach. Learn. Res. 7(Nov), 2399–2434 (2006)
3. Bucilu, C., Caruana, R., Niculescu-Mizil, A.: Model compression. In: Proceedings of the ACM SIGKDD International Conference on Knowledge Discovery and Data Mining, pp. 535–541 (2006)
4. Bulat, A., Tzimiropoulos, G.: Binarized convolutional landmark localizers for human pose estimation and face alignment with limited resources. In: Proceedings of the IEEE International Conference on Computer Vision, October 2017
5. Cao, Y., Chen, Y., Khosla, D.: Spiking deep convolutional neural networks for energy-efficient object recognition. Int. J. Comput. Vis. 113(1), 54–66 (2015)
6. Chan, W., Ke, N.R., Lane, I.: Transferring knowledge from a RNN to a DNN. arXiv preprint arXiv:1504.01483 (2015)
7. Chen, T., Goodfellow, I., Shlens, J.: Net2Net: accelerating learning via knowledge transfer. arXiv preprint arXiv:1511.05641 (2015)
8. Chitrakar, P., Zhang, C., Warner, G., Liao, X.: Social media image retrieval using distilled convolutional neural network for suspicious e-crime and terrorist account detection. In: Proceedings of the IEEE International Symposium on Multimedia, pp. 493–498 (2016)
9. Cover, T.M., Thomas, J.A.: Elements of Information Theory. Wiley, Hoboken (2012)
10. Dalal, N., Triggs, B.: Histograms of oriented gradients for human detection. Proc. IEEE Conf. Comput. Vis. Pattern Recognit. 1, 886–893 (2005)
11. Drineas, P., Mahoney, M.W.: On the Nyström method for approximating a gram matrix for improved kernel-based learning. J. Mach. Learn. Res. 6(Dec), 2153–2175 (2005)
12. Everingham, M., Van Gool, L., Williams, C.K.I., Winn, J., Zisserman, A.: The PASCAL Visual Object Classes Challenge 2007 (VOC2007) Results (2007). http://www.pascal-network.org/challenges/VOC/voc2007/workshop/index.html
13. Everingham, M., Van Gool, L., Williams, C.K.I., Winn, J., Zisserman, A.: The PASCAL Visual Object Classes Challenge 2012 (VOC2012) Results (2012). http://www.pascal-network.org/challenges/VOC/voc2012/workshop/index.html
14. Fisher, D., DeLine, R., Czerwinski, M., Drucker, S.: Interactions with big data analytics. ACM Interact. 19(3), 50–59 (2012)
15. Guo, Y., Zhang, L., Hu, Y., He, X., Gao, J.: MS-CELEB-1M: a dataset and benchmark for large-scale face recognition. In: Proceedings of the European Conference on Computer Vision, pp. 87–102 (2016)
16. He, K., Zhang, X., Ren, S., Sun, J.: Deep residual learning for image recognition. In: Proceedings of the IEEE Conference on Computer Vision and Pattern Recognition, pp. 770–778 (2016)

17. Hinton, G., Vinyals, O., Dean, J.: Distilling the knowledge in a neural network. In: Neural Information Processing System Deep Learning Workshop (2015)
18. Hinton, G.E., Roweis, S.T.: Stochastic neighbor embedding. In: Proceedings of the Advances in Neural Information Processing Systems, pp. 857–864 (2003)
19. Howard, A.G., et al.: MobileNets: efficient convolutional neural networks for mobile vision applications. arXiv preprint arXiv:1704.04861 (2017)
20. Hubara, I., Courbariaux, M., Soudry, D., El-Yaniv, R., Bengio, Y.: Binarized neural networks. In: Proceedings of the Advances in Neural Information Processing Systems, pp. 4107–4115 (2016)
21. Iandola, F.N., Han, S., Moskewicz, M.W., Ashraf, K., Dally, W.J., Keutzer, K.: SqueezeNet: Alexnet-level accuracy with 50x fewer parameters and <0.5 MB model size. arXiv preprint arXiv:1602.07360 (2016)
22. Ioffe, S., Szegedy, C.: Batch normalization: accelerating deep network training by reducing internal covariate shift. In: Proceedings of the International Conference on Machine Learning, pp. 448–456 (2015)
23. Kercheval, A.N., Zhang, Y.: Modelling high-frequency limit order book dynamics with support vector machines. Quant. Fin. **15**(8), 1315–1329 (2015)
24. Kingma, D., Ba, J.: Adam: a method for stochastic optimization. arXiv preprint arXiv:1412.6980 (2014)
25. Krizhevsky, A., Sutskever, I., Hinton, G.E.: ImageNet classification with deep convolutional neural networks. In: Proceedings of the Advances in Neural Information Processing Systems, pp. 1097–1105 (2012)
26. LeCun, Y., Bengio, Y., Hinton, G.: Deep learning. Nature **521**(7553), 436–444 (2015)
27. Lowe, D.G.: Distinctive image features from scale-invariant keypoints. Int. J. Comput. Vis. **60**(2), 91–110 (2004)
28. Maaten, L.V.D., Hinton, G.: Visualizing data using t-SNE. J. Mach. Learn. Res. **9**(Nov), 2579–2605 (2008)
29. Manning, C.D., Raghavan, P., Schtze, H.: Introduction to Information Retrieval. Cambridge University Press, Cambridge (2008)
30. Montavon, G., et al.: Machine learning of molecular electronic properties in chemical compound space. New J. Phys. **15**(9), 095003 (2013)
31. Nam, H., Han, B.: Learning multi-domain convolutional neural networks for visual tracking. In: IEEE Conference on Computer Vision and Pattern Recognition, pp. 4293–4302 (2016)
32. Ozdemir, B., Davis, L.S.: A probabilistic framework for multimodal retrieval using integrative Indian buffet process. In: Proceedings of the Advances in Neural Information Processing Systems, pp. 2384–2392 (2014)
33. Passalis, N., Tefas, A.: Learning bag-of-features pooling for deep convolutional neural networks. In: Proceedings of the IEEE International Conference on Computer Vision (2017)
34. Passalis, N., Tefas, A.: Unsupervised knowledge transfer using similarity embeddings. IEEE Trans. Neural Netw. Learn. Syst. **99**, 1–5 (2018)
35. Patterson, G., Hays, J.: Sun attribute database: discovering, annotating, and recognizing scene attributes. In: Proceedings of the IEEE Conference on Computer Vision and Pattern Recognition, pp. 2751–2758 (2012)
36. Redmon, J., Divvala, S., Girshick, R., Farhadi, A.: You Only Look Once: unified, real-time object detection. In: Proceedings of the IEEE Conference on Computer Vision and Pattern Recognition, pp. 779–788 (2016)
37. Redmon, J., Farhadi, A.: Yolo9000: Better, faster, stronger. arXiv preprint arXiv:1612.08242 (2016)

38. Romero, A., Ballas, N., Kahou, S.E., Chassang, A., Gatta, C., Bengio, Y.: FitNets: hints for thin deep nets. In: Proceedings of the International Conference on Learning Representations (2015)
39. Scott, D.W.: Multivariate Density Estimation: Theory, Practice, and Visualization. Wiley, Hoboken (2015)
40. Shen, Z., Liu, Z., Li, J., Jiang, Y.G., Chen, Y., Xue, X.: DSOD: learning deeply supervised object detectors from scratch. In: Proceedings of the IEEE International Conference on Computer Vision, October 2017
41. Shokri, R., Shmatikov, V.: Privacy-preserving deep learning. In: Proceedings of the ACM SIGSAC Conference on Computer and Communications Security, pp. 1310–1321 (2015)
42. Srivastava, N., Salakhutdinov, R.R.: Multimodal learning with deep Boltzmann machines. In: Pereira, F., Burges, C.J.C., Bottou, L., Weinberger, K.Q. (eds.) Proceedings of the Advances in Neural Information Processing Systems, pp. 2222–2230 (2012)
43. Tang, Z., Wang, D., Pan, Y., Zhang, Z.: Knowledge transfer pre-training. arXiv preprint arXiv:1506.02256 (2015)
44. Tang, Z., Wang, D., Zhang, Z.: Recurrent neural network training with dark knowledge transfer. In: Proceedings of the IEEE International Conference on Acoustics, Speech and Signal Processing, pp. 5900–5904. IEEE (2016)
45. Torkkola, K.: Feature extraction by non-parametric mutual information maximization. J. Machine Learn. Res. 3(Mar), 1415–1438 (2003)
46. Turlach, B.A., et al.: Bandwidth selection in kernel density estimation: a review. Université catholique de Louvain Louvain-la-Neuve (1993)
47. Tzeng, E., Hoffman, J., Darrell, T., Saenko, K.: Simultaneous deep transfer across domains and tasks. In: Proceedings of the IEEE International Conference on Computer Vision, pp. 4068–4076 (2015)
48. Wang, D., Lu, H., Bo, C.: Visual tracking via weighted local cosine similarity. IEEE Trans. Cybernet. 45(9), 1838–1850 (2015)
49. Wolf, L., Hassner, T., Maoz, I.: Face recognition in unconstrained videos with matched background similarity. In: Proceedings of the IEEE Conference on Computer Vision and Pattern Recognition, pp. 529–534 (2011)
50. Yim, J., Joo, D., Bae, J., Kim, J.: A gift from knowledge distillation: fast optimization, network minimization and transfer learning. In: Proceedings of the IEEE Conference on Computer Vision and Pattern Recognition, pp. 7130–7138 (2017)

Integrating Egocentric Videos in Top-View Surveillance Videos: Joint Identification and Temporal Alignment

Shervin Ardeshir$^{(\boxtimes)}$ and Ali Borji

Center for Research in Computer Vision (CRCV),
University of Central Florida, Orlando, FL, USA
ardeshir@cs.ucf.edu

Abstract. Videos recorded from first person (egocentric) perspective have little visual appearance in common with those from third person perspective, especially with videos captured by top-view surveillance cameras. In this paper, we aim to relate these two sources of information from a surveillance standpoint, namely in terms of identification and temporal alignment. Given an egocentric video and a top-view video, our goals are to: (a) identify the egocentric camera holder in the top-view video (self-identification), (b) identify the humans visible in the content of the egocentric video, within the content of the top-view video (re-identification), and (c) temporally align the two videos. The main challenge is that each of these tasks is highly dependent on the other two. We propose a unified framework to jointly solve all three problems. We evaluate the efficacy of the proposed approach on a publicly available dataset containing a variety of videos recorded in different scenarios.

1 Introduction

The widespread use of wearable devices such as GoPro cameras and smart glasses has created the opportunity to collect first person (egocentric) videos easily and in large scale. People tend to collect large amounts of visual data using their cell phones and wearable devices from the first person perspective. These videos are drastically different from traditional third person videos captured by static surveillance cameras, especially if the third person camera is recording top-down, as there could be very little overlap in the captured frames by the two cameras. Even though a lot of research has been done studying these two domains independently, relating the two views systematically has yet to be fully explored. From a surveillance standpoint, being able to relate these two sources of information and establishing correspondences between them could lead to additional beneficial information for law enforcement. In this work, we take a step towards this goal, by addressing three following problems:

Self-identification: The goal here is to identify the camera holder of an egocentric video in another reference video (here a top-view video). The main challenge

© Springer Nature Switzerland AG 2018
V. Ferrari et al. (Eds.): ECCV 2018, LNCS 11215, pp. 300–317, 2018.
https://doi.org/10.1007/978-3-030-01252-6_18

is that the egocentric camera holder is not visible in his/her egocentric video. Thus, there is often no information about the visual appearance of the camera holder (example in Fig. 1).

Human Re-identification: The goal here is to identify the humans seen in one video (here an egocentric video) in another reference video (here a top-view video). This problem has been studied extensively in the past. It is considered a challenging problem due to variability in lighting, view-point, and occlusion. Yet, existing approaches assume a high structural similarity between captured frames by the two cameras, as they usually capture humans from oblique or side views. This allows a rough spatial reasoning regarding parts (e.g., relating locations of head, torso and legs in the bounding boxes). In contrast, when performing human re-identification across egocentric and top-view videos, such reasoning is not possible (examples are shown in Figs. 1 and 2).

Fig. 1. A pair of top- (left) and egocentric (right) views. Self identification is to identify the egocentric camera holder (shown in red). Human re-identification is to identify people visible in the egocentric video, in the content of the top-view video (orange and purple). (Color figure online)

Temporal Alignment: Performing temporal alignment between the two videos directly is non-trivial as the top-view video contains a lot of content that is not visible in the egocentric video. We leverage the other two tasks (self identification and re-identification) to reason about temporal alignment and estimate the time-delay between them.

The interdependency of the three tasks mentioned above encourages designing a unified framework to address all simultaneously. To be able to determine the camera holder's identity within the content of the top-view video (task 1), it is necessary to know the temporal correspondence between the two videos (task 3). Identifying the people visible in the egocentric video in the content of the top-view video (task 2), would be easier if we already knew where the camera holder is in the top-view video at the corresponding time (tasks 1 and 3), since we can reason about who the camera holder is expected to see at any given moment. Further, knowing the correspondence between the people in ego and top views, and temporal alignment between two videos (tasks 2 and 3), could hint towards the identity of the camera holder (task 1). Finally, knowing who the camera holder is (task 1) and who he is seeing at each moment (task 2) can be an important cue to perform temporal alignment (task 3). The chicken-and-egg nature of these problems, encourage us to address them jointly. Thus, we formulate the problem as jointly minimizing the total cost $C_{tot}(l_s, L_r, \tau)$, where l_s is the identity of the camera holder (task 1), L_r is the set of identities of people visible in the egocentric video (task 2), and τ is the time offset between the two videos (task 3).

Assumptions: In this work, we hold assumptions similar to [1]. We assume that bounding boxes and trajectories in top-view are given (provided by the dataset). Therefore, an identity in top-view refers to a set of bounding boxes belonging to one person over time. We further assume that the top-view video contains all the people in the scene (including the ego-camera holder and other people visible in the ego video).

Fig. 2. Sample ego- and top-view bounding boxes. Unlike conventional re-identification instances, rough spatial alignment assumptions do not hold.

2   Related Work

Self-identification and self-localization of egocentric camera holder have been studied during the last few years. [2] uses the head motion of an egocentric viewer as a biometric signature to determine which videos have been captured by the same person. In [3], egocentric observers are identified in other egocentric videos by correlating their head motion with the egomotion of the query video. Authors in [4] localize the field of view of egocentric videos by matching them against Google street view. Landmarks and map symbols have been used in [5] to perform self localization on a map, and [6,7] use the geometric structure between different semantic entities (objects and semantic segments) for the problem of self-localization, by relating them to GIS databases. The closest works to ours are [1,8,9]. Please note that the mentioned works [1,8] do not address the other two problems of re-identification and temporal alignment. Our self-identification problem differs from [8] in three main aspects:

1. [8] self identifies the egocentric camera holder in a third person video using a fully supervised method. Please note that even though we perform unsupervised and supervised re-identification and use that as a prior, there is no supervision in the self-identification task. **2.** In [8]'s dataset, each egocentric video contains the majority of other identities, which could hold in settings such as sitting and having a conversation. As a result, cropping one person out from the third person video will have a lot in common with the content of that person's egocentric video. In our dataset, however, this is not the case, as many egocentric viewers do not observe each other at all. **3.** In [8]'s dataset, third person videos have a generic ground level viewpoints, which makes them have similar properties to the egocentric videos in terms of spatial reasoning. The difference between first and third person videos are more severe when the third person video is top-view like ours. Nonetheless, we evaluate [8] on our dataset as a baseline. [1,9] approached the problem of egocentric self-identification in top-view videos for the first time, leveraging the relationship among different egocentric videos. However, this method is highly dependent on the completeness of the egocentric set and performs poorly when there is only one egocentric video. We use this method as another baseline in our experiments.

Human Re-identification. This problem has been studied heavily in the past (e.g., [10–16]). Deep learning methods have recently been applied to person re-identification [17–19]. Yi [20] uses a Siamese network for learning appearance similarities. Similarly Ahmed [21] uses a two stream deep neural network to determine visual similarity between two bounding boxes. Cheng et al. [22] uses a multi-channel CNN in a metric learning based approach. Cho et al. [23] proposes using pose priors to perform comparison between different candidates, and Matsukawa et al. [24] uses a region descriptor based on hierarchical Gaussian distribution of pixel features for this task. In the egocentric domain, the study reported in [25] performs person re-identification in a network of wearable devices, and [26] addresses re-identification across time-synchronized wearable cameras. To the best of our knowledge, our work is the first attempt in addressing this problem across egocentric and top-view domains. Visual appearance is often the main cue for human re-identification. This cue can change from one camera to another due to occlusion, viewpoint, and lighting. However, the variation is often relatively low across different static surveillance cameras as the nature of the data is the same (both cameras being ground level or oblique viewpoints). In contrast, in situations where a set of surveillance and egocentric cameras are used, appearance variation is more severe due to egocentric camera motion, more drastic difference in field of views, lighting direction, etc. Thus, we propose a network to unify the representation of human detection bounding boxes across egocentric and top-view videos. In fact our visual re-identification network could be replaced with any other re-identification framework capable of measuring the visual similarity between the egocentric and top-view human detection bounding boxes. We compare and contrast our results with state of the art human identification methods in the experiments section.

Relating First- and Third-Person Vision: [27,28] have explored the relationship between mobile and static cameras for improving object detection. [29] fuses information from the first and third person static cameras and laser range data to improve depth perception and 3D reconstruction. Park et al. [30] predict gaze behavior in social scenes using first and third-person cameras. Soran et al.

[31] have addressed action recognition in presence of one egocentric and multiple static videos and [32] explores transfer learning across egocentric and exocentric actions.

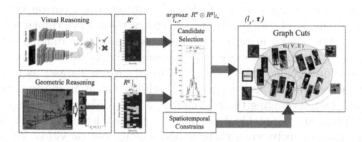

Fig. 3. The block diagram of our proposed method. We use three main cues: visual, geometrical, and spatiotemporal. Visual reasoning is used for initializing re-identification correspondences. Combining geometric and visual reasoning, we generate a set of candidate (l_s, τ) pairs. Finally, we evaluate the candidates using graph cuts while enforcing spatiotemporal consistency and find the optimum combination of labels and values.

3   Framework

We aim to address three different tasks jointly. To find the optimal values for all of the variables in a unified framework, we seek to optimize the following objective:

$$l_s^*, L_r^*, \tau^* = \underset{l_s, L_r, \tau}{argmin} \ C_{tot}(l_s, L_r, \tau) \tag{1}$$

Assuming a set of identities visible in the top-view video as $I^t = \{1, 2, ..., |I^t|\}$, our goal in task 1 is to identify the camera holder (assign a self-identity l_s). We assume that the camera holder is visible in the content of the top-view video, thus $l_s \in I^t$. In task 2, we aim to perform human re-identification for the visible humans in the egocentric video. Let $D^e = \{d_1^e, d_2^e, ..., d_{|D^e|}^e\}$ be the set of all human detection bounding boxes across all the frames of the egocentric video. In task 2, we find labeling $L_r = \{l_1^e, l_2^e, ..., l_{|D^e|}^e\} \in |I^t|^{|D^e|}$, which is the set of re-identification labels for human detection bounding boxes. Finally, τ is the time offset between the egocentric and top-view video, meaning that frame τ_0 in the top-view video corresponds to frame $\tau_0 + \tau$ in the egocentric video. We estimate τ in task 3. In our notation, we use superscripts to encode the view (t: top, e: ego).

The block diagram of our proposed method is shown in Fig. 3. Our method is based on three types of reasonings across the two views. First, we perform visual reasoning across the two videos by comparing the visual appearance of the people visible in the top video to the people visible in the egocentric video. This reasoning will provide us some initial probabilities for assigning the human detection bounding boxes in the ego-view to the identities in the top-view video. It gives an initial re-identification prior based on the likelihood of the human detections matching to top-view identities (Sect. 3.1). The second cue is designed to geometrically reason about the presence of different identities in each other's field of view in top-view over time (Sect. 3.2), providing us cues for re-identification based on self-identification. We then define two spatiotemporal constraints to enforce consistency among our re-identification labels (Sect. 3.3) in ego view. In the fusion step (Sect. 3.4), we combine visual and geometrical reasoning to narrow down the search space and generate a set of candidate (l_s, τ) pairs. Finally, we enforce spatiotemporal constraints and evaluate the candidates using graph cuts [33].

3.1   Visual Reasoning

The first clue for performing re-identification across the two views is to compare appearances of the bounding-boxes. Since in traditional re-identification works both cameras are static, and they have similar poses (oblique or ground level), there is an assumption of rough spatial correspondence between two human detection bounding boxes (i.e. the rough alignment in location of head-torso-leg between two bounding boxes). Since the viewpoints are drastically different in our problem, the rough spatial alignment assumption does not hold. A few examples are shown in Fig. 2. We perform this task in unsupervised and supervised settings. In the unsupervised setting, we extract some generic features from the two views and directly compare their features. In the supervised setting, we design a two stream network capable of measuring similarity across the two views.

Unsupervised Baseline: For each bounding box d_i^e in the ego-view, we extract VGG-19 deep neural network features [34] f_i^e (last fully connected layer, 4096 dimensional features). We perform L2 normalization on the features. As mentioned before, top-view bounding boxes are tracked and identities have been assigned to each track (set of bounding boxes belonging to each person). Therefore, for identity j in the top-view video, we extract VGG features from all of its bounding-boxes and represent identity j with the average of its feature vectors f_j^t.

To enforce the notion of probability, we measure the probability of ego-view bounding box d_i^e being assigned to label j in top-view ($l_i^e = j$) as:

$$P(l_i^e = j) = \frac{e^{-\|f_i^e - f_j^t\|}}{\sum_{m=1}^{|I^t|} e^{-\|f_i^e - f_m^t\|}}. \tag{2}$$

Supervised Approach: Training: We train a two stream convolutional neural network to match humans across the two views. As illustrated in Fig. 4, each stream consists of convolution and pooling layers, ending in fully connected layers. The output is defined as the Euclidean distance of the output of the last fully connected layers of each stream passed through a sigmoid activation. If the two bounding boxes belong to the same identity, the output is set to zero (and one, otherwise). This forces the network to find a distance measure across the two views.

Testing: We feed bounding box d_i^e to the ego stream of the network and extract f_i^e (We perform L2 normalization). In top-view, for identity j we feed all of its bounding-boxes to the top-view stream and represent identity j with the average of its feature vectors f_j^t. Similar to the unsupervised approach, we measure the probability of ego-view bounding box d_i^e being assigned to label j in top-view ($l_i^e = j$) according to Eq. 2.

Implementation Details of the CNN: We resize each of the top-view bounding boxes to 40×40, and each ego-view bounding box to 300×100 in the RGB format (3 channels). Each stream consists of 3 convolutional blocks, each having two convolutional layers and a pooling layer with 2×2 pooling. The number of filters for the convolutional layers in order are 16, 16, 32, 32, 64, and 64. Finally, each stream projects to two fully connected layers (top stream: 512, 128; ego-stream: 1024, 128). The euclidean distance of the output of the two streams is then passed through a sigmoid activation in order to enforce the notion of probability. We use Adam optimizer with learning rate of 0.001 and binary cross entropy loss, and train the network end-to-end. The hyper-parameters were fine-tuned on the validation set using grid search in logarithmic scale.

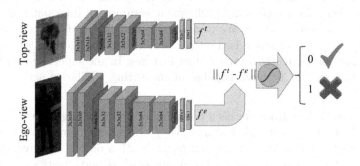

Fig. 4. The architecture of our two stream convolutional neural network trained on pairs of bounding boxes. The Euclidean distance between the output of the last fully connected layers (i.e., top and ego) passed through sigmoid activation is set to 0 when the pair belongs to the same person and 1, otherwise.

3.2 Geometric Reasoning

Here, we leverage the geometric arrangement of people with respect to each other in top-view and reason about their presence in each other's field of view. We iterate over different identities in top-view, and perform geometric reasoning assuming the identity is the camera-holder. In Fig. 5, we illustrate reasoning about the presence of the identities highlighted with blue and orange bounding boxes, assuming the person highlighted in the red bounding box is the camera holder.

Given the identity of the camera holder (l_s), we compute how likely it is for each person i to be present in l_s's field of view (FOV) at any given time. Following [1], we perform multiple object tracking [35] on the provided top-view bounding boxes (provided by the dataset). Knowing the direction of motion of each trajectory at each moment, we employ the same assumptions used in [1]. We estimate the head direction of each of the top-view camera holders by assuming that people often tend to look straight ahead while walking. Since the intrinsic parameters of the egocentric camera (e.g., focal length and sensor size) are unknown, we consider a lower and upper bound for the angle of the camera holder's FOV (θ_1 and θ_2 in Fig. 5) to estimate boundaries on l_s's field of view. As a result, we can determine the probability of each identity being present in the field of view of l_s (i.e., camera holder) at any given time ζ (Fig. 5, right side). We define the probability of identity i being present in the field of view of the camera holder (l_s) at time ζ as:

$$P_{g_\zeta}(i|l_s) = \begin{cases} 1, & \theta_i < \theta_1 \\ \frac{(\theta_2 - \theta_i)}{(\theta_2 - \theta_1)}, & \theta_1 < \theta_i < \theta_2 \\ 0, & \theta_2 < \theta_i \end{cases} \tag{3}$$

Intuitively, if the bounding box is within the lower bound of the FOV, we assign its presence probability to 1. If its orientation with respect to l_s is outside the upper-bound of the FOV range, we assign its presence probability to 0. For values in between the two bounds (e.g., the person at the bottom-left of Fig. 5), we assign its probability proportional to its orientation with respect to the camera holder. In our experiments, we empirically set θ_1 and θ_2 to 30° and 60°, respectively.

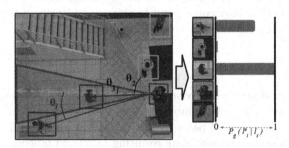

Fig. 5. Geometric reasoning in the top-view video. In this example (left), two identities are present in the field of view of the camera holder (the two red cones showing the lower and upper bound of field of view). Using their orientation (shown by blue arrows) with respect to the camera holder's direction of movement in the top-view (dashed green arrow), we estimate the probability of their presence in the content of the egocentric video. Right bar graph shows the probability of each person being present in the FOV of the camera holder. (Color figure online)

3.3   Spatiotemporal Reasoning

The third component of our approach enforces spatiotemporal constraints on the re-identification labels within the egocentric video. We define a cost for assigning the same identity label to a pair of human detection bounding boxes. We later incorporate this cost in our graph cuts formulation. Two constraints are defined as follows:

Constraint 1: Two different bounding boxes present in the same frame cannot belong to the same person. Note that non-maximum suppression is performed in the human detection process. Therefore the binary cost between any pair of co-occurring bounding boxes is set to infinity.

Constraint 2: If two bounding boxes have a high overlap in temporally nearby frames, their binary cost should be reduced, as they probably belong to the same identity. We incorporate two constraints in C_{st} cost as follows:

$$C_{st}(d_i^e, d_j^e) = \begin{cases} \infty, \text{ if } \zeta_{d_i^e} = \zeta_{d_j^e} \\ -1, \text{ if } 0 < |\zeta_{d_i^e} - \zeta_{d_j^e}| < \epsilon \text{ and } \frac{A_{d_i^e} \cap A_{d_j^e}}{A_{d_i^e} \cup A_{d_j^e}} > \sigma \\ 0, \text{ Otherwise} \end{cases} \tag{4}$$

where $A_{d_i^e}$ and $A_{d_j^e}$ correspond to the image area covered by human detection bounding boxes d_i^e and d_j^e, and $\zeta_{d_i^e}$ and $\zeta_{d_j^e}$ encode the time in which bounding boxes d_i^e and d_j^e are present. If d_i^e and d_j^e have been visible in the same frame, $C_{st}(d_i^e, d_j^e)$ will be set to infinity in order to prevent graph-cuts from assigning them to the same label (constraint 1). The negative cost of $C_{st}(i,j)$ in case of temporal neighborhood ($0 < |\zeta_{d_i} - \zeta_{d_j}| < \epsilon$) and high spatial overlap ($\frac{A_{d_i^e} \cap A_{d_j^e}}{A_{d_i^e} \cup A_{d_j^e}} > \sigma$) will encourage the graph cuts algorithm to assign them to the same label (constraint 2), as they may correspond to the same identity if they have a high overlap. Here, we empirically set ϵ to 5 frames and σ to 0.8.

3.4   Fusion

In this section we describe how visual, geometrical, and spatiotemporal reasonings are combined. First, we combine the visual and geometrical reasoning to find a set of candidate (l_s, τ) pairs. We then examine each candidate pair using graph cuts to measure the cost of its resulting (L_r, l_s, τ) labeling and select the one with the minimum cost.

Comparing Visual and Geometrical Priors: In Sect. 3.1, we described how an initial human re-identification prior can be obtained using visual reasoning. In Sect. 3.2, we described how an independent source of information (geometric reasoning) provides yet another set of human re-identification priors given each possible self-identity. In this section, we search over different self-identities and time delays, and choose the one whose patterns of geometric priors is consistent with his/her visual priors.

Temporal Representation: In Sect. 3.1, we described how we can compute $P_v(l_i^e = j)$ for any given egocentric human detection bounding box d_i^e and top-view identity j. We can form a $T^e \times |I^t|$ matrix R^v, where T^e is the number of frames in the egocentric video and $|I^t|$ is the number of identities visible in the top-view video. Intuitively, $R^v(\zeta, j)$ captures the probability of visibility of top-view identity j in the field of view of egocentric camera holder at time ζ. Let $D_\zeta^e = \{d_{\zeta_1}^e, d_{\zeta_2}^e, ..., d_{\zeta_{|D_\zeta^e|}}^e\}$ be the set of human detection bounding boxes visible in frame ζ of the egocentric video. We define $R^v(\zeta, j) = \sum_{i=1}^{|D_\zeta^e|} P_v(l_i^e = j)$. Since the sum of the probabilities might lead to a value higher than 1, we truncate the value at 1. In other words $R^v(\zeta, j) \leftarrow min(1, R(\zeta, j))$. An example R^v matrix is shown in Fig. 6 (center panel).

We can form a similar matrix based on the geometric reasoning for each self-identity. As described in Sect. 3.2, given the self identity of the camera holder (l_s), we can compute $P_g(l_i^e = j|l_s)$. Similar to R^v, we can form $T^t \times |I^t|$ matrix R^g where T^t is the number of frames in the top-view video, and $R^g(\zeta, j)|_{l_s} = P_{g_\zeta}(i|l_s)$, which is computed according to Eq. 3. Intuitively $R^g(\zeta, j)|_{l_s}$ is the probability of visibility of identity j in the field of view of self-identity l_s at time ζ of the top-vie video, geometrically (an example shown in Fig. 6-left). Forming R^v and $R^g|_{l_s}$ for different self-identities (l_s), we expect them to have similar patterns for the correct l_s. For each top-view identity l_s, we compute the cross correlation of its $R^g|_{l_s}$ matrix with R^v across the time dimension in order to evaluate their similarities across different time delays (τ). This cross correlation results in a 1D signal encoding the similarity score of the two matrices given different time offsets. As shown in Fig. 6, we estimate the time offset between the two videos (assuming self-identity l_s) by finding the maximum of that score. We search across all self identities and sort them based on their maximum cross correlation score.

$$l_s^*, \tau^* = \underset{l_s, \tau}{argmax} \ \ R^v \odot R^g|_{l_s} \tag{5}$$

where $\odot$ denotes element-wise multiplication. Please note that all the videos in our dataset are captured with the same frame rate. Thus, we can perform all of these computations in a frame-based manner. Otherwise, a pre-processing and quantization on the temporal domain would be necessary to correlate the two matrices.

Graph Cuts: Given a set of suggested (l_s, τ) pairs from the previous section, we evaluate the overall labeling cost as the cost of assigning l_s to the self identity, τ to the time delay, and L_r to the re-identification labels. Graph cuts allows the re-identification labels to adjust to the spatiotemporal constraint.

We form a graph $G(V, E)$ in which nodes are the human detection bounding boxes in ego-view $V = \{d_1^e, d_2^e, d_3^e, ..., d_{|D^e|}^e\}$ (See Fig. 7 for an illustration.). The goal is to assign each node to one of the top-view labels. Edges of the graph encode the spatiotemporal constraints between the nodes (as described in Sect. 3.3).

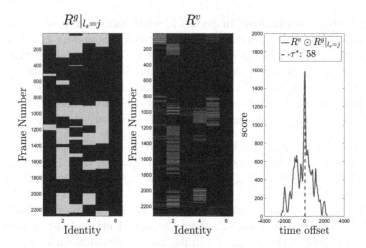

Fig. 6. An example of estimating the self-identity and temporal offset. For a certain self-identity (l_s), the geometric reasoning is performed and the suggested re-identification priors are stored in matrix $R^g|_{l_s}$ (values color-coded). The matrix acquired by visual reasoning (in this case the supervised CNN based method) is shown in the middle (R^v). The similarity between the patterns in two matrices suggests that the self identity (l_s) is a good candidate. By correlating the two matrices across the time domain (the rightmost panel), we can observe a peak at $\tau = 58$. This suggests that if the camera holder has in fact identity l_s, the time-offset of his egocentric video with respect to the top-view video is 58 frames. Also, the score of self-identity l_s is the maximum value of the cross correlation which is 1587 in this case. By computing this value for all of the possible self-identities, we can pick the most likely self identity as the one with the highest score. (Color figure online)

Given the self identification label and time delay, we can perform graph cuts with its cost defined as:

$$C_{tot}(l_s, \tau) = \sum_{i=1}^{|D^e|} \left[C_u(l_i^e|\tau, l_s) + \sum_{j=1, j\neq i}^{|D^e|} C_{st}(l_i^e, l_j^e) \right] \tag{6}$$

The first term in rhs of Eq. 6 encodes the unary cost for assigning d_i^e to its label l_i^e, given self-identity l_s and relative temporal offset (τ) between the two videos. We set C_u as:

$$C_u(l_i^e = j|\tau, l_s) = 1 - P^v(l_i^e = j)R^g(\zeta_i^e - \tau, j)|l_s \tag{7}$$

where ζ_i^e is the time in which human detection bounding box d_i^e appears in the ego-view. Intuitively Eq. 7 means that the probability of bounding box d_i^e (appearing at time ζ_i^e in the ego-view) being identity j in top-view, is the probability of the visibility of identity j at the field of view of l_s at time $\zeta_i^e - \tau$ in the top-view, multiplied by its likelihood of being identity j visually. The binary terms determine the costs of the edges and encode the spatiotemporal cost described in Sect. 3.3. The output of this method provides us with a cost for each (l_s, τ) pair, alongside with a set of labellings for the human detection bounding boxes L_r. The pair with the minimum cost and its corresponding L_r is the final solution of our method (i.e., l_s^*, L_r^*, τ^*).

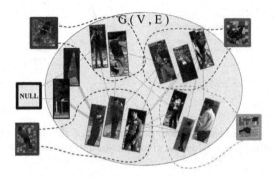

Fig. 7. An illustration of the graph formation. The silver oval contains the graph G(V, E) in which each node is one of the ego-view human detection bounding boxes. The squared bounding boxes highlight different top-view labels in different colors. The graph cuts are visualized using the dashed colored curves. We always consider an extra NULL class for all of the human detection bounding boxes that do not match any of the classes. (Color figure online)

4   Experimental Results

4.1   Dataset

We use the publicly available dataset [1]. It contains sets of videos shot in different indoor and outdoor environments. Each set contains one top-view and several egocentric videos captured by the people visible in top-view. Each ego-top pair is used as an input to our method. We used three sets for training our two stream neural network and the rest for testing. There are 47 ego-top test pairs and therefore 47 cases of self-identification and temporal alignment. The total number of human detection bounding boxes, and therefore human re-identification instances is 28,250. We annotated the labels for all the 28,250 human detection bounding boxes and evaluated the accuracy for re-identification and self-identification. The number of people visible in top-view videos vary from 3 to 6, and lengths of the videos vary from 1,019 frames (33.9 s) up to 3,132 frames (104.4 s).

4.2   Evaluation

We evaluate our proposed method in terms of addressing each objective and compare its performance in different settings. Moreover, we analyze the contribution of each component of our approach in the final results.

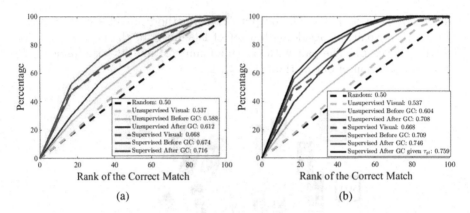

Fig. 8. (a) shows the re-identification performance of different components of our method. (b) shows the same evaluation given the ground truth self identification labels. (Color figure online)

4.2.1   Self-identification

We evaluate our proposed method in terms of identifying the camera holder in the content of the top-view video. Since we perform self-identification based on initial re-identification probabilities (visual reasoning), we evaluate self-identification based on supervised and unsupervised re-identification results, alongside with state-of-the-art baselines. We also evaluate the performance in each setting before and after the final graph cuts step to assess the contribution of the spatiotemporal reasoning. Upper-bounds of the proposed method are also evaluated by providing the ground-truth re-identification and temporal alignment. The cumulative matching curves are shown in Fig. 9 left. The solid yellow curve is the performance of [1]. As explained before, [1] highly relies on the relationship among multiple egocentric videos and does not perform well when it is provided with only one egocentric video. The dashed yellow curve shows the performance of [8]. The network provided by the authors was used. As explained in the related work section, this framework is not designed for scenarios such as ours. The cyan and blue curves show our self-identification accuracy in the unsupervised setting before and after the graph cuts step, respectively. The magenta and red curves show the performance in supervised setting, before and after the graph cuts step, respectively. The dashed black curve shows random ranking (performance of chance). The advantage of graph cuts and the spatiotemporal constraints can be observed by comparing before and after graph cuts curves. The contribution of our two stream visual reasoning is evident by comparing the unsupervised curves with their corresponding supervised settings. The effect of the geometrical reasoning could be seen by comparing visual reasoning results, and the before GC curves. The numbers in the figure legend show the area under each curve for quantitative comparison. The margin between the supervised and unsupervised approaches shows the effect of re-identification quality on self-identification performance, confirming the interconnectedness of the two tasks. The solid green and solid black curves show the upper-bounds of the proposed method. We evaluate self-identification, when providing ground-truth re-identification labels and the time-delay to the proposed approach.

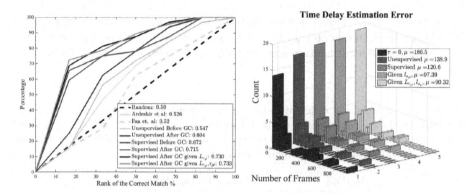

Fig. 9. Left shows the cumulative matching curves illustrating the performance in the self-identification task. Right shows the distribution of time-delay estimation errors using our supervised and unsupervised methods, compared to the baselines and upper-bounds. (Color figure online)

4.2.2 Cross-view Human Re-identification

We compute the human re-identification performance in supervised and unsupervised settings, before and after graph cuts (shown in Fig. 8a). In order to better assess the performance, we compute the performance of our proposed method given the ground truth self identification label ($l_{s_{gt}}$), and ground truth time delay τ_{gt} (Fig. 8b), which results in upper-bounds for re-identification performance. In both figures (a and b), the dashed black line shows the chance level performance. The dashed cyan and magenta curves show the performance of direct visual matching across the two views using our unsupervised and supervised visual reasonings, respectively. Solid cyan and magenta curves show the performance of our unsupervised and supervised visual cues combined with geometric reasoning. Which is re-identification solely based on unary confidences in Eq. 7 and before applying graph cuts. Finally, blue and red curves show performance of the unsupervised and supervised methods (in order) after the graph cuts step, which enforces the spatio-temporal constraints. Black solid curve in Fig. 8b shows the performance of the proposed method, given the ground truth time delay between the two videos in addition to the ground truth self-identity. Comparing the red curves of Fig. 8a and b shows the effect of knowing the correct self identity on re-identification performance and thus confirming the inter dependency of the two tasks. Comparing the red and black solid curves in Fig. 8b shows that once the self-identity is known, correct time-delay does not lead to a high boost in re-identification performance which is consistent with our results on self-identification and time delay estimation. Comparing Fig. 8a and b shows that knowing the correct self identity improves re-identification. As explained before, any re-identification method capable of producing a visual similarity measure could be plugged into our visual reasoning component. We evaluate the performance of two state of the art re-identification methods in Table 1. Before Fusion is the performance of each method in terms of Area under curve of cumulative matching curve (similar to Fig. 8a). After fusion is the overall performance after combining the re-identification method with our geometrical and spatiotemporal reasoning.

Table 1. Performance of different re-identification methods. Before Fusion is the performance of the re-identification method directly applied to the bounding boxes (only visual reasoning). After fusion shows the performance of our method if we replace our two stream network with the methods mentioned above.

Method	Before fusion	After fusion
Ours (Unsupervised)	0.537	0.612
Ahmed [21]	0.563	0.621
Cheng [22]	0.581	0.634
Ours (supervised)	**0.668**	**0.716**

4.2.3   Time-Delay Estimation

Defining τ_{gt} as the ground truth time offset between the egocentric and top-view videos, we compute the time-offset estimation error ($|\tau^* - \tau_{gt}|$) and compare its distribution with that of baselines and upper bounds. Figure 9b shows the distribution of time-offset estimation error. In order to measure the effectiveness of our time-delay estimation process, we measure the absolute value of the original time-offset. In other words, assuming $\tau^* = 0$ as a baseline, we compute the offset estimation error (shown in the dark blue histogram). The mean error is also added to the figure legend for quantitative comparisons. Please note that the time delay error is measured in terms of the number of frames (all the videos have been recorded at 30 fps). The baseline $\tau = 0$ leads to 186.5 frames error (6.21 s). Our estimated τ^* in the unsupervised setting, reduces this figure to 138.9 frames (4.63 s). Adding visual supervision reduces this number to an average of 120.6 frames (4.02 s). To have upper bounds and evaluate the performance of this task alone, we isolate it from the other two by providing the ground-truth self identification ($l_{s_{gt}}$) and human re-identification labels ($L_{r_{gt}}$). Providing $l_{s_{gt}}$ will lead to 97.39 frames error (3.24), and providing both $l_{s_{gt}}$ and $L_{r_{gt}}$ reduces the mean error to 90.32 (3.01 s). Similar to our re-identification upper-bounds, knowing the self-identity improves performance significantly. Once self-identity is known, the ground truth re-identification labels will improve the results by a small margin.

5   Conclusion

We explored three interconnected problems in relating egocentric and top-view videos namely human re-identification, camera holder self-identification, and temporal alignment. We perform visual reasoning across the two domains, geometric reasoning in top-view domain and spatiotemporal reasoning in egocentric domain. Our experiments show that solving these problems jointly improves the performance in each individual task, as the knowledge about each task can assist solving the other two.

References

1. Ardeshir, S., Borji, A.: Ego2Top: matching viewers in egocentric and top-view videos. In: Leibe, B., Matas, J., Sebe, N., Welling, M. (eds.) ECCV 2016. LNCS, vol. 9909, pp. 253–268. Springer, Cham (2016). https://doi.org/10.1007/978-3-319-46454-1_16

2. Poleg, Y., Arora, C., Peleg, S.: Head motion signatures from egocentric videos. In: Cremers, D., Reid, I., Saito, H., Yang, M.-H. (eds.) ACCV 2014. LNCS, vol. 9005, pp. 315–329. Springer, Cham (2015). https://doi.org/10.1007/978-3-319-16811-1_21

3. Yonetani, R., Kitani, K.M., Sato, Y.: Ego-surfing first person videos. In: 2015 IEEE Conference on Computer Vision and Pattern Recognition (CVPR). IEEE (2015)

4. Bettadapura, V., Essa, I., Pantofaru, C.: Egocentric field-of-view localization using firstperson point-of-view devices. In: IEEE Winter Conference on Applications of Computer Vision (WACV) (2015)

5. Kiefer, P., Giannopoulos, I., Raubal, M.: Where am i? Investigating map matching during selflocalization with mobile eye tracking in an urban environment. Trans. GIS **18**(5), 660–686 (2014)

6. Ardeshir, S., Malcolm Collins-Sibley, K., Shah, M.: Geo-semantic segmentation. In: Proceedings of the IEEE Conference on Computer Vision and Pattern Recognition, pp. 2792–2799 (2015)

7. Ardeshir, S., Zamir, A.R., Torroella, A., Shah, M.: GIS-assisted object detection and geospatial localization. In: European Conference on Computer Vision ECCV, pp. 602–617 (2014)

8. Fan, C., et al.: Identifying first-person camera wearers in third-person videos. In: Proceedings of the IEEE Conference on Computer Vision and Pattern Recognition, pp. 5125–5133 (2017)

9. Ardeshir, S., Borji, A.: Egocentric meets top-view. IEEE Trans. Pattern Anal. Mach. Intell. **PP**(99), 1 (2018)

10. Chen, D., Yuan, Z., Chen, B., Zheng, N.: Similarity learning with spatial constraints for person re-identification. In: The IEEE Conference on Computer Vision and Pattern Recognition (CVPR), June 2016

11. Cheng, D.S., Cristani, M., Stoppa, M., Bazzani, L., Murino, V.: Custom pictorial structures for re-identification. In: BMVC (2011)

12. Bak, S., Corvee, E., Bremond, F., Thonnat, M.: Multiple-shot human re-identification by mean Riemannian covariance grid. In: 8th IEEE International Conference on Advanced Video and Signal-Based Surveillance (AVSS) (2011)

13. Bazzani, L., Cristani, M., Murino, V.: Symmetry-driven accumulation of local features for human characterization and re-identification. Comput. Vis. Image Underst. **117**(2), 130–144 (2013)
14. Zhao, R., Oyang, W., Wang, X.: Person re-identification by saliency learning. IEEE Trans. Pattern Anal. Mach. Intell. **39**(2), 356–370 (2017)
15. Martinel, N., Foresti, G.L., Micheloni, C.: Person reidentification in a distributed camera network framework. IEEE Trans. Cybern. **47**(11), 3530–3541 (2016)
16. García, J., Martinel, N., Gardel, A., Bravo, I., Foresti, G.L., Micheloni, C.: Discriminant context information analysis for post-ranking person re-identification. IEEE Trans. Image Process. **26**(4), 1650–1665 (2017)
17. Li, W., Zhao, R., Xiao, T., Wang, X.: DeepReID: deep filter pairing neural network for person re-identification. In: 2014 IEEE Conference on Computer Vision and Pattern Recognition, June 2014, pp. 152–159 (2014)
18. Varior, R.R., Haloi, M., Wang, G.: Gated Siamese convolutional neural network architecture for human re-identification. CoRR abs/1607.08378 (2016)
19. Varior, R.R., Shuai, B., Lu, J., Xu, D., Wang, G.: A Siamese long short-term memory architecture for human re-identification. CoRR abs/1607.08381 (2016)
20. Yi, D., Lei, Z., Li, S.Z.: Deep metric learning for practical person re-identification. CoRR abs/1407.4979 (2014)
21. Ahmed, E., Jones, M., Marks, T.K.: An improved deep learning architecture for person re-identification. In: The IEEE Conference on Computer Vision and Pattern Recognition (CVPR), June 2015
22. Cheng, D., Gong, Y., Zhou, S., Wang, J., Zheng, N.: Person re-identification by multi-channel parts-based CNN with improved triplet loss function. In: The IEEE Conference on Computer Vision and Pattern Recognition (CVPR), June 2016
23. Cho, Y.J., Yoon, K.J.: Improving person re-identification via pose-aware multi-shot matching. In: The IEEE Conference on Computer Vision and Pattern Recognition (CVPR), June 2016
24. Matsukawa, T., Okabe, T., Suzuki, E., Sato, Y.: Hierarchical Gaussian descriptor for person re-identification. In: The IEEE Conference on Computer Vision and Pattern Recognition (CVPR), June 2016
25. Chakraborty, A., Mandal, B., Galoogahi, H.K.: Person re-identification using multiple first-person-views on wearable devices. In: 2016 IEEE Winter Conference on Applications of Computer Vision (WACV), pp. 1–8. IEEE (2016)
26. Zheng, K., Guo, H., Fan, X., Yu, H., Wang, S.: Identifying same persons from temporally synchronized videos taken by multiple wearable cameras
27. Alahi, A., Bierlaire, M., Kunt, M.: Object detection and matching with mobile cameras collaborating with fixed cameras. In: Workshop on Multi-camera and Multi-modal Sensor Fusion Algorithms and Applications-M2SFA2 (2008)
28. Alahi, A., Marimon, D., Bierlaire, M., Kunt, M.: A master-slave approach for object detection and matching with fixed and mobile cameras. In: 15th IEEE International Conference Image Processing, ICIP 2008 (2008)
29. Ferland, F., Pomerleau, F., Le Dinh, C.T., Michaud, F.: Egocentric and exocentric teleoperation interface using real-time, 3d video projection. In: 2009 4th ACM/IEEE International Conference on Human-Robot Interaction (HRI) (2009)
30. Soo Park, H., Jain, E., Sheikh, Y.: Predicting primary gaze behavior using social saliency fields. In: Proceedings of the IEEE International Conference on Computer Vision (2013)

31. Soran, B., Farhadi, A., Shapiro, L.: Action recognition in the presence of one egocentric and multiple static cameras. In: Cremers, D., Reid, I., Saito, H., Yang, M.-H. (eds.) ACCV 2014. LNCS, vol. 9007, pp. 178–193. Springer, Cham (2015). https://doi.org/10.1007/978-3-319-16814-2_12

32. Ardeshir, S., Borji, A.: An exocentric look at egocentric actions and vice versa. Comput. Vis. Image Underst. (2018)

33. Fulkerson, B., Vedaldi, A., Soatto, S.: Class segmentation and object localization with superpixel neighborhoods. In: 2009 IEEE 12th International Conference on Computer Vision, pp. 670–677. IEEE (2009)

34. Simonyan, K., Zisserman, A.: Very deep convolutional networks for large-scale image recognition. arXiv preprint arXiv:1409.1556 (2014)

35. Dicle, C., Camps, O.I., Sznaier, M.: The way they move: tracking multiple targets with similar appearance. In: Proceedings of the IEEE International Conference on Computer Vision (2013)

Visual-Inertial Object Detection
and Mapping

Xiaohan Fei$^{(\boxtimes)}$ and Stefano Soatto

UCLA Vision Lab, University of California, Los Angeles, USA
{feixh,soatto}@cs.ucla.edu

Abstract. We present a method to populate an unknown environment with models of previously seen objects, placed in a Euclidean reference frame that is inferred causally and on-line using monocular video along with inertial sensors. The system we implement returns a sparse point cloud for the regions of the scene that are visible but not recognized as a previously seen object, and a detailed object model and its pose in the Euclidean frame otherwise. The system includes bottom-up and top-down components, whereby deep networks trained for detection provide likelihood scores for object hypotheses provided by a nonlinear filter, whose state serves as memory. Additional networks provide likelihood scores for edges, which complements detection networks trained to be invariant to small deformations. We test our algorithm on existing datasets, and also introduce the VISMA dataset, that provides ground truth pose, point-cloud map, and object models, along with time-stamped inertial measurements.

1 Introduction

We aim to detect, recognize, and localize objects in the three-dimensional (3D) scene. We assume that previous views of the object are sufficient to construct a dense model of its shape, in the form of a closed and water-tight surface, and its appearance (a texture map). So, as soon as an object is detected from a monocular image, and localized in the scene, the corresponding region of space can be mapped with the object model, including the portion not visible in the current image (Figs. 4 and 5).

While single monocular images provide evidence of objects in the scene – in the form of a likelihood score for their presence, shape and pose – they should not be used to make a decision. Instead, evidence should be accumulated over time, and the likelihood at each instant combined into a posterior estimate of object pose and identity. This is often referred to as "semantic mapping," an early instance of which using depth sensors (RGB-D images) was given in [1]. Our method aims at the same goal, but using a monocular camera and inertial sensors, rather than a range sensor.

Electronic supplementary material The online version of this chapter (https://doi.org/10.1007/978-3-030-01252-6_19) contains supplementary material, which is available to authorized users.

© Springer Nature Switzerland AG 2018
V. Ferrari et al. (Eds.): ECCV 2018, LNCS 11215, pp. 318–334, 2018.
https://doi.org/10.1007/978-3-030-01252-6_19

Inertial sensors are increasingly often present in sensor suites with monocular cameras, from cars to phones, tablets, and drones. They complement vision naturally, in an information-rich yet cheap sensor package. Unlike RGB-D, they can operate outdoor; unlike stereo, they are effective at far range; unlike lidar, they are cheap, light, and provide richer photometric signatures. Inertial sensors provide a globally consistent orientation reference (gravity) and scale up to some drift. This allows reducing pose space to four dimensions instead of six. We leverage recent developments in visual-inertial sensor fusion, and its use for semantic mapping, an early instance of which was given in [2], where objects were represented by bounding boxes in 3D. Our method extends that work to richer object models, that allow computing fine-grained visibility and estimating accurate pose.

Contributions. We focus on applications to (indoor and outdoor) navigation, where many objects of interest are rigid and static: parked cars, buildings, furniture. Our contribution is a method and system that produces camera poses and a point-cloud map of the environment, populated with 3D shape and appearance models of objects recognized. It is semantic in the sense that we have identities for each object instance recognized. Also, all geometric and topological relations (proximity, visibility) are captured by this map.

We achieve this by employing some tools from the literature, namely visual-inertial fusion, and crafting a novel likelihood model for objects and their pose, leveraging recent developments in deep learning-based object detection. The system updates its state (memory) causally and incrementally, processing only the current image rather than storing batches.

Another contribution is the introduction of a dataset for testing visual-inertial based semantic mapping and 3D object detection. Using inertials is delicate as accurate time-stamp, calibration and bias estimates are needed. To this date, we are not aware of any dataset for object detection that comes with inertials.

We do not address intra-class variability. Having said that, the method is somewhat robust to modest changes in the model. For instance, if we have a model Aeron chair (Fig. 2) with arm rests, we can still detect and localize an Aeron chair without them, or with them raised or lowered.

Organization. In Sect. 2, we describe our method, which includes top-down (filter) and bottom-up (likelihood/proposals) components. In particular, Sect. 2.4 describes the novel likelihood model we introduce, using a detection and edge scoring network. Section 3 describes our implementation, which is tested in Sect. 4, where the VISMA dataset is described. We discuss features and limitations of our method in Sect. 5, in relation to prior related work.

2   Methodology

To facilitate semantic analysis in 3D, we seek to reconstruct a model of the scene sufficient to provide a Euclidean reference where to place object models. This cannot be done with a single monocular camera. Rather than using lidar (expensive, bulky), structured light (fails outdoors), or stereo (ineffective at large distances), we exploit inertial sensors frequently co-located with cameras in many modern sensor platforms, including phones and tablets, but also cars and drones. Inertial sensors provide a global and persistent orientation reference from gravity, and an estimate of scale, sufficient for us to reduce Euclidean motion to a four-dimensional group. In the next section we describe our visual-inertial simultaneous localization and mapping (SLAM) system.

2.1 Gravity-Referenced and Scaled Mapping

We wish to estimate $p(Z_t, X_t|y^t)$ the joint posterior of the state of the sensor platform X_t and objects in the scene $Z_t \doteq \{z\}_t^N$ given data $y^t = \{y_0, y_1, \cdots, y_t\}$ that consists of visual (image I_t) and inertial (linear acceleration α_t and rotational velocity ω_t) measurements, i.e., $y_t \doteq \{I_t, \alpha_t, \omega_t\}$. The posterior can be factorized as

$$p(Z_t, X_t|y^t) \propto p(Z_t|X_t, y^t)p(X_t|y^t) \tag{1}$$

where $p(X_t|y^t)$ is typically approximated as a Gaussian distribution whose density is estimated recursively with an EKF [3] in the visual-inertial sensor fusion literature [4,5]. Upon convergence where the density $p(X_t|y^t)$ concentrates at the mode $\hat{X}_t$, the joint posterior can be further approximated using a point estimate of $\hat{X}_t$.

Visual-inertial SLAM has been used for object detection by [2], whose notation we follow here. The state of a visual-inertial sensor platform is represented as

$$X_t \doteq [\Omega_{ib}^\top, T_{ib}^\top, \Omega_{bc}^\top, T_{bc}^\top, v^\top, \alpha_{\text{bias}}^\top, \omega_{\text{bias}}^\top, \gamma^\top, \tau]^\top$$

where $g_{ib}(t) \doteq (\Omega_{ib}, T_{ib}) \in \text{SE}(3)$ is the transformation of the body frame to the inertial frame, $g_{bc}(t) \doteq (\Omega_{bc}, T_{bc}) \in \text{SE}(3)$ is the camera-to-body alignment, $v \in \mathbb{R}^3$ is linear velocity, $\alpha_{\text{bias}}, \omega_{\text{bias}} \in \mathbb{R}^3$ are accelerometer and gyroscope biases respectively, $\gamma \in \mathbb{R}^3$ is the direction of gravity and $\tau \in \mathbb{R}$ is the temporal offset between visual and inertial measurements. The transformation from camera frame to inertial frame is denoted by $g_{ic} \doteq g_{ib}g_{bc}$. The implementation details of the visual-inertial SLAM system adopted are in Sect. 3. Next, we focus on objects.

2.2 Semantic Mapping

For each object $z_t \in Z_t$ in the scene, we simultaneously estimate its pose $g \in \text{SE}(3)$ and identify shape $S \subset \mathbb{R}^3$ over time. We construct beforehand a database of 3D models, which covers objects of interest in the scene. Thus the task of estimating shape of objects is converted to the task of determining shape label $k \in \{1, 2, \cdots, K\}$ of objects, which is a discrete random variable. Once the shape label k is estimated, its shape $S(k)$ can be simply read off from the database. Furthermore, given an accurate estimate of gravity direction γ from visual-inertial SLAM, the 6DoF (degrees of freedom) object pose can be reduced to a four-dimensional group element $g \doteq (t, \theta)$: Translation $t \in \mathbb{R}^3$ and rotation around gravity (azimuth) $\theta \in [0, 2\pi)$.

We formulate the semantic mapping problem as estimating the posterior $p(z_t = \{k, g\}_t | \hat{X}_t, I^t)$ conditioned on mode $\hat{X}_t$, which can be computed in a hypothesis testing framework, of which the hypothesis space is the Cartesian product of shape label and pose $\{k\} \times \{g\}$. To facilitate computation and avoid cluttered notations, we drop $\hat{X}_t$ behind the condition bar and introduce an auxiliary discrete random variable: Category $c \in \{1, 2, \cdots, C\}$.

$$p(\{k, g\}_t | I^t) = \sum_{c_t} p(\{k, g, c\}_t | I^t) \tag{2}$$

$$\propto \sum_{c_t} p(I_t | \{k, g, c\}_t) \int p(\{k, g, c\}_t | \{k, g, c\}_{t-1}) dP(\{k, g, c\}_{t-1} | I^{t-1}) \tag{3}$$

where marginalization is performed over all possible categories. By noticing that category c_t is a deterministic function of shape label k_t, i.e. $p(c_t | k_t) = \delta(c_t - c(k_t))$, the posterior $p(\{k, g\}_t | I^t)$ can be further simplified as follows:

$$\sum_{c_t} \delta(c_t - c(k_t)) p(I_t | \{k, g, c\}_t) \int p(\{k, g\}_t | \{k, g\}_{t-1}) dP(\{k, g\}_{t-1} | I^{t-1}) \tag{4}$$

where the first term in the summation is the likelihood (Sect. 2.4) and the second term can be approximated by numerical integration of weighted particles (Sect. 3).

2.3 Parameterization and Dynamics

Each object is parametrized locally and attached to a reference camera frame at time t_r with pose $g_{ic}(t_r)$ and the translational part of object pose is parameterized by a bearing vector $[x_c, y_c]^\top \in \mathbb{R}^2$ in camera coordinates and a log depth $\rho_c \in \mathbb{R}$ where $z_c = \exp(\rho_c) \in \mathbb{R}_+$. Log depth is adopted because of the positivity and cheirality it guarantees. Inverse depth [6], though often used by the SLAM community, has singularities and is not used in our system. The object centroid is then $T_{co} = \exp(\rho_c) \cdot [x_c, y_c, 1]^\top$ in the reference camera frame and $T_{io} = g_{ic}(t_r) T_{co}$ in the inertial frame. For azimuth θ, we parameterize it in the inertial frame and obtain the rotation matrix via Rodrigues' formula:

$$\mathbf{R}_{io}(\theta) = \mathbf{I} + \sin\theta \widehat{\gamma} + (1 - \cos\theta)\widehat{\gamma}^2$$

where γ is the direction of gravity and the hat operator $\widehat{\cdot}$ constructs a skew-symmetric matrix from a vector. Therefore the object pose in the inertial frame is $g_{io} = [\mathbf{R}_{io} | T_{io}] \in SE(3)$. Although the pose parameters are unknown constants instead of time varying quantities, we treat them as stochastic processes with trivial dynamics as a common practice: $[\dot{x}_c, \dot{y}_c, \dot{\rho}_c, \dot{\theta}]^\top = [n_x, n_y, n_\rho, n_\theta]^\top$ where n_x, n_y, n_ρ and n_θ are zero-mean Gaussian noises with small variance.

2.4   Measurement Process

In this section, we present our approximation to the log-likelihood $L(\{k, g, c\}_t | I_t) \doteq \log p(I_t | \{k, g, c\}_t)$ of the posterior (4). Given the prior distribution $p(\{k, g\}_{t-1} | I^{t-1})$, a hypothesis set $\{k, g\}_t$ can be constructed by a diffusion process around the prior $\{k, g\}_{t-1}$. To validate the hypothesis set, we use a log-likelihood function which consists of two terms:

$$L(\{k, g, c\}_t | I_t) = \alpha \cdot \Phi_{\text{CNN}}(\{k, g, c\}_t | I_t) + \beta \cdot \Phi_{\text{edge}}(\{k, g\}_t | I_t) \qquad (5)$$

where α and β are tuning parameters. The first term in the log-likelihood is a convolutional neural network which measures the likelihood of an image region is to contain a certain object. The second term scores the likelihood of an edge in the image. We describe them in order.

CNN as Likelihood Mechanism. Given a hypothesis $\{k, g\}_t$ in the reference frame, we first bring it to the current camera frame by applying a relative transformation and then project it to the current image plane via a rendering process. A minimal enclosing bounding box of the projection is found and then fed into an object detection network. The score of the hypothesis is simply read off from the network output (Fig. 1).

$$\Phi_{\text{CNN}}(k, g, c; I) = \text{Score}\left(I_{|b = \pi\left(g_{ic}^{-1}(t) g_{io}(t_r) \mathcal{S}(k)\right)}, c\right) \qquad (6)$$

where $\pi(\cdot)$ denotes the process to render the contour map of the object of which the minimal enclosing bounding box b is found; $g_{io}(t_r)$ is the transformation to bring the object from local reference frame at time t_r to the inertial frame and $g_{ic}^{-1}(t)$ is the transformation to bring the object from the inertial frame to current camera frame.

Either a classification network or a detection network can be used as our scoring mechanism. However, due to the size of the hypothesis set at each time instant, which is then mapped to bounding boxes sitting on the same support, it is more efficient to use a detection network where the convolutional features are shared by object proposals via ROI pooling: Once predicted, all the box coordinates are fed to the second stage of Faster R-CNN as object proposals in a single shot, where only one forward pass is carried out.

Edge Likelihood. An object detection network is trained to be invariant to viewpoint change and intra-class variabilities, which makes it ill-suited for pose estimation and shape identification. To that end, we train a network to measure the likelihood of edge correspondence:

$$\Phi_{\text{edge}}(k, g; I) = h\left(\pi\left(g_{ic}^{-1}(t) g_{io}(t_r) \mathcal{S}(k)\right), \text{EdgeNet}(I)\right) \qquad (7)$$

where $h(\cdot, \cdot)$ is some proximity function which measures the proximity of edge map constructed from pose and shape hypothesis via rendering (first argument of h) and edge map extracted from the image (second argument of h).

A popular choice for proximity function h is one-dimensional search [7-9], which we adopt (see Sup. Mat. for details). Such a method is geometric and more robust than appearance based methods which are photometric and subject to illumination change. However, due to its nature of locality, this method is also sensitive to background clutter and can be distracted by texture-rich image regions. Fortunately, these weaknesses are easily compensated by Φ_{CNN} which has a large receptive field and is trained on semantics. Also, instead of using Canny [10] or other non-learning-based edge features, we design an edge detection network (Sect. 3) on semantically relevant training sets. Figure 5 shows examples illustrating background distraction.

3   Implementation Details

System Overview. An overview of the system is illustrated in the system flowchart (Fig. 1). We perform Bayesian inference by interleaving bottom-up (the green pathway) and top-down (the blue pathway) processing over time, which both rely on CNNs. Faster R-CNN as a bottom-up proposal generation mechanism takes input image I_t and generates proposals for initialization of new objects. In the top-down hypothesis validation process, both geometric (edge net, takes object contour $\pi(S)$ and outputs likelihood Φ_{edge}) and semantic (Fast R-CNN, takes predicted bounding box b and class label c and outputs likelihood Φ_{CNN}) cues are used. Faster R-CNN consists of a region proposal network (RPN) and a Fast R-CNN, which share weights at early convolutional layers. RPN is only activated in the bottom-up phase to feed Fast R-CNN object proposals of which bounding box coordinates are regressed and class label is predicted. During top-down phase, proposals needed by Fast R-CNN are generated by first sampling from the prior distribution $p(z|y^{t-1})$ followed by a diffusion and then mapping each sample to a bounding box b and a class label c. Figure 1b illustrates the scoring process. The semantic filter (yellow box) is a variant of bootstrap algorithm [11] and recursively estimates the posterior $p(z|y^t)$ as a set of weighted particles. Point estimates of gravity γ and camera pose g are from the SLAM module.

SLAM and Network Modules. We implement the system in C++ and OpenGL Shading Language (GLSL, for rendering) and follow a modular design principle: Each major module runs in its own process and communicates via a publish/subscribe message transport system, which enables expandability and possible parallelism in the future. The visual-inertial SLAM is based on [5] which produces gravity-referenced and scaled camera pose estimates needed by the semantic mapping module. An off-the-shelf Faster R-CNN implementation [12] with weights pre-trained on Microsoft COCO is turned into a service running constantly in the background. Note we take the most generic object detector as it is *without fine-tuning on specific object instances*, which differs from other object instance detection systems. The benefit is scalability: No extra training is required when novel object instances are spotted. For the weakly semantic-aware edge detection network, we adapt SegNet [13] to the task of edge detection: The

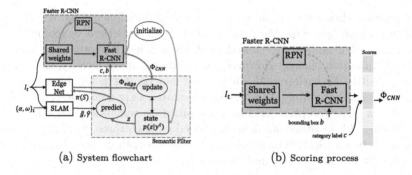

(a) System flowchart   (b) Scoring process

Fig. 1. Left *System flowchart.* Green pathway: Faster R-CNN as a bottom-up proposal generation mechanism. Blue pathway: Top-down hypothesis validation process. Pink box: Faster R-CNN. Yellow box: Semantic filter. **Right** *CNN as scoring mechanism.* Dashed pathway (proposal generation) is inactive during hypothesis testing. See system overview of Sect. 3 for details. (Color figure online)

last layer of SegNet is modified to predict the probability of each pixel being an edge pixel. Weights pre-trained on ImageNet are fine-tuned on BSDS [14]. Figure 4 shows sample results of our edge detection network.

Occlusion and Multiple Objects. We turn to some heuristics to handle occlusion due to its combinatorial nature. Fortunately, this is not a problem because we explicitly model the shape of objects, of which a Z-Buffer of the scene can be constructed with each object represented as its most likely shape at expected pose (Figs. 4 and 5). Only the visible portion of the edge map is used to measure the edge likelihood while Faster R-CNN still runs on the whole image, because object detectors should have seen enough samples with occlusion during the training phase and thus robust to occlusion.

Initialization. An object proposal from Faster R-CNN is marked as "explained" if it overlaps with the predicted projection mask by a large margin. For those "unexplained" proposals, we initialize an object attached to the current camera frame by spawning a new set of particles. For each particle: The bearing vector $[x_c, y_c]^\top$ is initialized as the direction from the optical center to the bounding box center with a Gaussian perturbation. The log depth is initialized at a nominal depth value with added Gaussian noise. Both the azimuth and the shape label are sampled from uniform priors. More informative priors enabled by data-driven approaches are left for future investigation.

The Semantic Filter. We summarize our joint pose estimation and shape identification algorithm in Algorithm 1, which is a hybrid bootstrap filter [11] with Gaussian kernel for dynamics and a discrete proposal distribution for shape identification: The shape label stays the same with high probability and jumps to other labels equally likely to avoid particle impoverishment. A breakdown of the computational cost of each component can be found in the Sup. Mat.

Algorithm 1. Semantic Filter

---

1. Initialization

When an unexplained bottom-up proposal is found at time $t = t_r$, sample $\{k, g\}_{t_r}^{(i)} \sim p(\{k, g\}_{t_r})$ and attach object to camera frame t_r. (Sect. 3, Initialization)

2. Importance Sampling

At time $t \geq t_r$, sample $\{k, g\}_t^{(i)} \sim q(k_t^{(i)}|k_{t-1}^{(i)})\mathcal{N}(g_t^{(i)}; g_{t-1}^{(i)}, \Sigma_{t-1})$ and compute weights $w_t^{(i)} = \exp\left(\alpha \cdot \Phi_{\text{CNN}} + \beta \cdot \Phi_{\text{edge}}\right)$. (Sect. 2.4)

3. Resampling

Resample particles $\{k, g\}_t^{(i)}$ with respect to the normalized importance weights $w_t^{(i)}$ to obtain equally weighted particles $\{k, g\}_t^{(i)}$.

4. Occlusion handling

Construct Z-Buffer at mean state to explain away bottom-up object proposals. (Sect. 3, Occlusion)

Set $t \leftarrow t + 1$ and go to step 1.

---

4 Experiments

We evaluate our system thoroughly in terms of mapping and object detection. While there are several benchmarks for each domain, very few allow measuring simultaneously localization and reconstruction accuracy, as well as 3D object detection.

In particular, [15,16] are popular for benchmarking RGB-D SLAM: one is real, the other synthetic. KITTI [17] enables benchmarking SLAM as well as object detection and optical flow. Two recent visual-inertial SLAM benchmarks are [18] and [19]. Unfortunately, we find these datasets unsuitable to evaluate the performance of our system: Either there are very few objects in the dataset [15,16,18,19], or there are many, but no ground truth shape annotations are available [17].

On the other hand, object detection datasets [20–22] focus on objects as regions of the image plane, rather than on the 3D scene. [23,24] are among the few exploring object attributes in 3D, but are single-image based. Not only does our method leverage video imagery, but it requires a Euclidean reference, in our case provided by inertial sensors, making single-image benchmarks unsuitable.

Therefore, to measure the performance of our method, we had to construct a novel dataset, aimed at measuring performance in visual-inertial semantic mapping. We call this the VISMA set, which will be made publicly available upon completion of the anonymous review process, together with the implementation of our method.

VISMA contains 8 richly annotated videos of several office scenes with multiple objects, together with time-stamped inertial measurements. We also provide ground truth annotation of several objects (mostly furniture, such as chairs, couches and tables) (Sect. 4.2). Over time we will augment the dataset with additional scanned objects, including moving ones, and outdoor urban scenes. The reason for selecting indoors at first is because we could use RGB-D sensors for cross-modality validation, to provide us with pseudo-ground truth. Nevertheless, to demonstrate the outdoor-applicability of our system, we provide illustrative results on outdoor scenes in Fig. 3.

We also looked for RGB-D benchmarks and datasets, where we could compare our performance with independently quantified ground truth. SceneNN [25] is a recently released RGB-D dataset, suitable for testing at least the semantic mapping module of our system, even though originally designed for deep learning. Section 4.3 describes the experiments conducted on SceneNN.

4.1 VISMA Dataset

A customized sensor platform is used for data acquisition: An inertial measurement unit (IMU) is mounted atop camera equipped with a wide angle lens. The IMU produces time-stamped linear acceleration and rotational velocity readings at 100 Hz. The camera captures 500×960 color images at 30 Hz. We have collected 8 sequences in different office settings, which cover ~ 200 m in trajectory length and consist of ~ 10K frames in total.

To construct the database of 3D models, we rely on off-the-shelf hardware and software, specifically an Occipital Structure Sensor[1] on an iPad, to reconstruct furniture objects in office scenes with the built-in 3D scanner application. This is a structured light sensor that acts as an RGB-D camera to yield watertight surfaces and texture maps. We place the 3D meshes in an object-centric canonical frame and simplify the meshes via quadratic edge collapse decimation using MeshLab[2]. Top row of Fig. 2 shows samples from our database. While the database will eventually be populated by numerous shapes, we use a small dictionary of objects in our experiments, following the setup of [1]. An optional shape retrieval [26] process can be adopted for larger dictionaries, but this is beyond the scope of this paper and not necessary given the current model library.

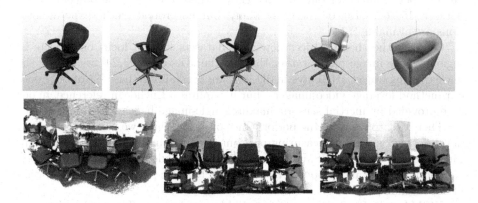

Fig. 2. Top *Sample objects in the VISMA dataset.* Each mesh has $\sim$5000 faces and is placed in an object-centric canonical frame, simplified, and texture-mapped. **Bottom** *(Pseudo) ground truth* from different viewpoints with the last panel showing an augmented view with models aligned to the original scene.

---

[1] http://www.structure.io.
[2] http://www.meshlab.net.

4.2 Evaluation

Comparing dense surface reconstruction is non-trivial, and several approaches have been proposed for RGB-D SLAM: Sturm et al. [15] use pose error (RPE) and absolute trajectory error (ATE) to evaluate RGB-D odometry. To ease the difficulty of ground truth acquisition, Handa et al. [16] synthesized a realistic RGB-D dataset for benchmarking both pose estimation and surface reconstruction, according to which, the state of the art RGB-D SLAM systems have typical ATE of $1.1 \sim 2.0$cm and average surface error of $0.7 \sim 2.8$cm [27], which renders RGB-D SLAM a strong candidate as our (pseudo) ground truth for the purpose of evaluating visual-inertial-semantic SLAM system.

Ground Truth. To obtain (pseudo) ground truth reconstruction of experimental scenes, we run ElasticFusion [27], which is at state-of-the-art in RGB-D SLAM, on data collected using a Kinect sensor. In cases where only partial reconstruction of objects-of-interest was available due to failures of ElasticFusion, we align meshes from our database to the underlying scene via the following procedure: Direction of gravity is first found by computing the normal to the ground plane which is manually selected from the reconstruction. Ground truth alignment of objects is then found by rough manual initialization followed by orientation-constrained ICP [28] where only rotation around gravity is allowed. Bottom row of Fig. 2 shows a reconstructed scene from different viewpoints where the last panel shows an augmented view.

Metrics and Results. We adopt the surface error metric proposed by [16] for quantitative evaluation. First, a scene mesh is assembled by retrieving 3D models from the database according to the most likely shape label, to which the pose estimate is applied. A point cloud is then densely sampled from the scene mesh and aligned to the ground truth reconstruction from RGB-D SLAM via ICP, because both our reconstructed scene and the ground truth scene are up to an arbitrary rigid-body transformation. Finally, for each point in the aligned scene mesh, the

Table 1. *Surface error and pose error* measured over 4 sequences from the VISMA dataset. Qualitative results on the other 4 sequences with coarse annotations can be found in the Sup. Mat. Translational error reads $\|T_{gt} - \hat{T}\|_2$ and rotational error reads $\| \log^\vee (\hat{R}^\top R_{gt}) \|_2$, where $\log : \mathrm{SO}(3) \mapsto \mathrm{so}(3)$ and $^\vee : \mathrm{so}(3) \mapsto \mathbb{R}^3$. (R_{gt}, T_{gt}) and $(\hat{R}, \hat{T})$ are ground truth and estimated object pose respectively.

Error metric		Clutter 1	Clutter 2	Occlusion 1	Occlusion 2
Surface	Median (cm)	1.37	1.11	1.30	2.01
	Mean (cm)	1.99	1.39	1.73	2.79
	Std. (cm)	1.96	1.12	1.45	2.54
	Max (cm)	17.6	9.88	14.3	17.9
Pose	Mean Trans. (cm)	4.39	2.42	3.94	13.64
	Mean Rot. (degree)	6.16	4.66	4.86	9.12

328   X. Fei and S. Soatto

closest triangle in the ground truth scene mesh is located and the normal distance between the point and the closest triangle is recorded. Following [16], four standard statistics are computed over the distances for all points in the scene mesh: Mean, median, standard deviation, and max (Table 1). In addition to surface error, Table 1 also includes pose estimation error which consists of translational and rotational part. Figure 4 shows how common failures of an image-based object detector have been resolved by memory (state of the semantic filter) and inference in a globally consistent spatial frame.

Fig. 3. *Exemplary outdoor results.* (best in color at 5×) In each panel, top inset shows (left to right): edge map, Z-buffer, projection masks; bottom shows input RGB with predicted mean object boundary and CNN detection. Rightmost panel shows a visual comparison of ours (top) against Fig. 1 of [2] (bottom), where we capture the boundaries of the cars better. Though only generic models from ShapeNet are used in these examples, pose estimates are fairly robust to shape variations.

4.3   Experiments on SceneNN Dataset

For independent validation, we turn to recent RGB-D scene understanding datasets to test at least the semantic mapping part of our system. Although co-located monocular and inertial sensors are ubiquitous, hence our choice of sensor suite, any SLAM alternative can be used in our system as the backbone localization subsystem as long as reliable metric scale and gravity estimation are provided. This makes SceneNN suitable for testing the semantic mapping part of our system, although originally designed for RGB-D scene understanding. It provides ground truth camera trajectories in a gravity-aligned reference frame. Raw RGB-D streams and ground truth meshes reconstructed from several object-rich real world scenes are provided in SceneNN.

To test the semantic mapping module on SceneNN, we take the ground truth camera trajectory and color images as inputs. *Note the depth images are not used in our experiments.* The database is constructed by manually selecting and cropping object meshes from the ground truth scene mesh. A subset scenes of SceneNN with various chairs is selected for our experiments. Except the fact that the camera trajectory and gravity are from the ground truth instead of from our visual-inertial SLAM, the rest of the experiment setup are the same as those in the experiment on our own dataset. Table 2 shows statistics of surface error of our semantic mapping on SceneNN. Typical mean surface error is around 3cm. Figure 5 shows some qualitative results on SceneNN.

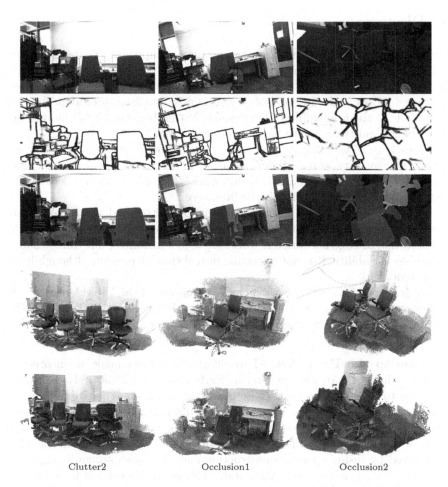

Clutter2   Occlusion1   Occlusion2

Fig. 4. *Qualitative results.* (best in color at 5×) Each column shows (top to bottom): One frame of the input video with CNN bounding box proposals with confidence > 0.8; Extracted edge map; Frame overlaid with predicted instance masks shaded according to Z-Buffer – darker indicates closer; Background reconstruction augmented with camera trajectory (orange dots) and semantic reconstruction from our visual-inertial-semantic SLAM; Ground truth dense reconstruction. Missed detections due to heavy occlusion (middle column) and indistinguishable background (right column) are resolved by memory and inference in a globally consistent spatial frame. (Color figure online)

Table 2. *Surface error* measured on a subset of the SceneNN dataset.

Sequence	005	025	032	036	043	047	073	078	080	082	084	096	273	522	249
Median (cm)	1.84	0.726	3.08	2.25	3.66	3.10	2.59	3.04	2.82	2.35	1.29	0.569	2.06	1.31	0.240
Mean (cm)	3.47	0.756	6.28	4.10	4.24	4.11	3.04	3.51	3.15	3.32	1.70	0.684	2.15	1.69	0.299
Std. (cm)	3.48	0.509	6.95	5.10	3.11	3.52	2.17	2.60	2.09	2.99	1.51	0.518	1.24	1.39	0.217
Max (cm)	13.7	3.07	36.3	34.3	11.9	18.5	8.72	17.4	13.9	22.7	8.33	4.41	5.75	5.60	1.27

5   Discussion

Our method exploits monocular images and time-stamped inertial measurements to construct a point-cloud model of the environment, populated by object models that were recognized, along with the camera trajectory in an Euclidean frame. We target indoor and outdoor mobility scenarios, and focus on indoor for evaluation due to the availability of benchmark. Yet no benchmark has inertial and semantic ground truth, so we have introduced VISMA.

We believe most mapping and navigation methods in the near future will utilize this modality as it is ubiquitous (e.g., in every smart phone or car, even some vacuum cleaners). Yet, at present, ours is one of few methods to exploit inertials for semantic mapping in the literature.

Our method has several limitations: It is limited to rigid objects and static scenes; it is susceptible to failure of the low-level processing modules, such as the detection or edge networks. It works for object instances, but cannot handle intra-class variability. It is not operating in real time at present, although it has the potential to.

Future extensions of this work include expansions of the VISMA dataset, the addition of synthetic scenes with rich ground truth. Extensions to independently moving objects, and deforming objects, is also an open area of investigation.

Relation to the Prior Art. Many efforts have been made to incorporate semantics into SLAM, and vice versa. Early attempts [29,30] rely on feature matching to register 3D objects to point clouds, which are sensitive to illumination and viewpoint changes, and most importantly, cannot handle texture-less objects. These issues are resolved by considering both semantic and geometric cues in our method (Figs. 4 and 5). In [31], voxel-wise semantic labeling is achieved by fusing sparse reconstruction and pixel-wise semantic segmentation with a CRF model over voxel grids. The same scheme has been adopted by [32–34] which explore different sensors to get better reconstruction. Although these methods produce visually pleasing semantic labeling at the level of voxels, object-level semantic understanding is missing without additional steps to group together the potentially over-segmented voxels. Our method treats objects in the scene as first-class citizens and places objects in the scene directly and immediately without post-processing. The works that are closest to ours are RGB-D based SLAM++ [1] and visual-inertial based [2] and [35], where the former models objects as generic parallelepipeds and the latter focuses on the data association problem and only estimates translation of objects, while ours estimates precise object shape and 6DoF pose.

This work is related to visual-inerital sensor fusion [4] and vision-only monocular SLAM [36] in a broader sense. While classic SLAM outputs a descriptor-attached point cloud for localization, ours also populates objects in the scene to enable augmented reality (AR) and robotic tasks.

This work, by its nature, also relates to recent advances in object detection, either in two stages [37–39], which consist of a proposal generation and a regres-

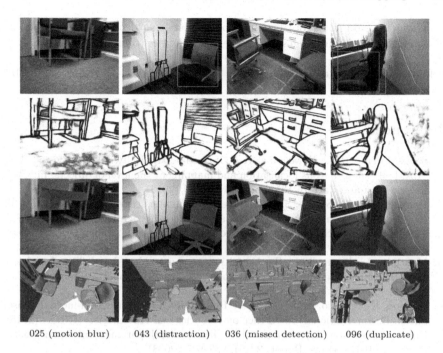

025 (motion blur)   043 (distraction)   036 (missed detection)   096 (duplicate)

Fig. 5. *Qualitative results on SceneNN.* (best in color at 5×) Each panel has the same meaning as Fig. 4. Last row shows estimated shape & pose (green) overlaid on ground truth mesh (gray). Partial projections due to broken models provided by SceneNN. 1st col: Moderate motion blur does not affect edge extraction. 2nd col: Background distraction does not affect shape & pose inference thanks to the holistic and semantic knowledge injected into low-level edge features. 3rd col: Missed detections due to truncation resolved by memory. 4th col: Duplicate detection from Faster R-CNN eliminated by memory and inference in a consistent spatial frame. (Color figure online)

sion/classification step, or in a single shot [40, 41], where pre-defined anchors are used. Though single-shot methods are in general faster than two-stage methods, the clear separation of the architecture in the latter suits our hypothesis testing framework better (Fig. 1). Image-based object detectors have encouraged numerous applications, however they are insufficient to fully describe the 3D attributes of objects. Efforts in making 2D detectors capable of 6DoF pose estimation include [23, 24], which are single image based and do not appreciate a globally consistent spatial reference frame, in which evidence can be accumulated over time as we did in our system.

The idea of using edge as a likelihood to estimate object pose dates back to the RAPiD algorithm [8] followed by [9, 42]. [43] is a recent survey on model-based tracking, which is a special and simplistic case of our system: In model-based tracking, the 3D model being tracked is selected and its pose initialized manually while in our setting, such quantities are found by the algorithm. Another line of work [44, 45] on model-based tracking relies on level-set and appearance modeling, which we do not adopt because appearance is subject to illumination and viewpoint changes while edges are geometric and more robust.

Acknowledgment. Research supported by ONR N00014-17-1-2072 and ARO W911NF-17-1-0304.

References

1. Salas-Moreno, R.F., Newcombe, R.A., Strasdat, H., Kelly, P.H., Davison, A.J.: SLAM++: simultaneous localisation and mapping at the level of objects. In: Computer Vision and Pattern Recognition (CVPR) (2013)
2. Dong, J., Fei, X., Soatto, S.: Visual-inertial-semantic scene representation for 3D object detection. In: Computer Vision and Pattern Recognition (CVPR) (2017)
3. Jazwinski, A.: Stochastic Processes and Filtering Theory. Academic Press, Cambridge (1970)
4. Mourikis, A., Roumeliotis, S.: A multi-state constraint kalman filter for vision-aided inertial navigation. In: International Conference on Robotics and Automation (ICRA) (2007)
5. Tsotsos, K., Chiuso, A., Soatto, S.: Robust inference for visual-inertial sensor fusion. In: International Conference on Robotics and Automation (ICRA) (2015)
6. Civera, J., Davison, A.J., Montiel, J.M.: Inverse depth parametrization for monocular slam. IEEE Trans. Robot. **24**(5), 932–945 (2008)
7. Blake, A., Isard, M.: The condensation algorithm-conditional density propagation and applications to visual tracking. In: Advances in Neural Information Processing Systems (NIPS) (1997)
8. Drummond, T., Cipolla, R.: Real-time visual tracking of complex structures. IEEE Trans. Pattern Anal. Mach. Intell. (PAMI) **24**(7), 932–946 (2002)
9. Klein, G., Murray, D.W.: Full-3D edge tracking with a particle filter. In: British Machine Vision Conference (BMVC) (2006)
10. Canny, J.: A computational approach to edge detection. In: Readings in Computer Vision, pp. 184–203. Elsevier (1987)
11. Gordon, N.J., Salmond, D.J., Smith, A.F.: Novel approach to nonlinear/non-gaussian bayesian state estimation. In: IEE Proceedings F (Radar and Signal Processing), vol. 140, pp. 107–113. IET (1993)
12. Girshick, R., Radosavovic, I., Gkioxari, G., Dollár, P., He, K.: Detectron. https://github.com/facebookresearch/detectron (2018)
13. Badrinarayanan, V., Kendall, A., Cipolla, R.: SegNet: A deep convolutional encoder-decoder architecture for image segmentation. IEEE Trans. Pattern Anal. Mach. Intell. (PAMI) **12**, 2481–2495 (2017)
14. Martin, D., Fowlkes, C., Tal, D., Malik, J.: A database of human segmented natural images and its application to evaluating segmentation algorithms and measuring ecological statistics. In: International Conference on Computer Vision (ICCV) (2001)
15. Sturm, J., Engelhard, N., Endres, F., Burgard, W., Cremers, D.: A benchmark for the evaluation of RGB-D slam systems. In: International Conference on Intelligent Robots and Systems (IROS) (2012)
16. Handa, A., Whelan, T., McDonald, J., Davison, A.J.: A benchmark for RGB-D visual odometry, 3D reconstruction and SLAM. In: International Conference on Robotics and Automation (ICRA) (2014)

17. Geiger, A., Lenz, P., Stiller, C., Urtasun, R.: Vision meets robotics: the KITTI dataset. Int. J. Robot. Res. (IJRR) **32**(11), 1231–1237 (2013)
18. Burri, M.: The EuRoC micro aerial vehicle datasets. Int. J. Robot. Res. (IJCV) **35**(10), 1157–1163 (2016)
19. Pfrommer, B., Sanket, N., Daniilidis, K., Cleveland, J.: Penncosyvio: a challenging visual inertial odometry benchmark. In: International Conference on Robotics and Automation (ICRA) (2017)
20. Everingham, M., Van Gool, L., Williams, C.K.I., Winn, J., Zisserman, A.: The pascal visual object classes (voc) challenge. Int. J. Comput. Vis. (IJCV) **88**(2), 303–338 (2010)
21. Russakovsky, O., et al.: ImageNet large scale visual recognition challenge. Int. J. Comput. Vis. (IJCV) **115**(3), 211–252 (2015)
22. Lin, T.-Y., et al.: Microsoft COCO: common objects in context. In: Fleet, D., Pajdla, T., Schiele, B., Tuytelaars, T. (eds.) ECCV 2014. LNCS, vol. 8693, pp. 740–755. Springer, Cham (2014). https://doi.org/10.1007/978-3-319-10602-1_48
23. Xiang, Y., Mottaghi, R., Savarese, S.: Beyond pascal: a benchmark for 3D object detection in the wild. In: Winter Conference on Applications of Computer Vision (WACV) (2014)
24. Leibe, B., Matas, J., Sebe, N., Welling, M. (eds.): ObjectNet3D: a large scale database for 3D object recognition. ECCV 2016. LNCS, vol. 9912, pp. 160–176. Springer, Cham (2016). https://doi.org/10.1007/978-3-319-46484-8_10
25. Hua, B.S., Pham, Q.H., Nguyen, D.T., Tran, M.K., Yu, L.F., Yeung, S.K.: Scenenn: a scene meshes dataset with annotations. In: 3D Vision (3DV) (2016)
26. Savva, M., et al.: Shrec16 track large-scale 3D shape retrieval from shapenet core55. In: Proceedings of the Eurographics Workshop on 3D Object Retrieval (2016)
27. Whelan, T., Leutenegger, S., Salas-Moreno, R.F., Glocker, B., Davison, A.J.: Elasticfusion: dense slam without a pose graph. In: Robotics: Science and Systems (RSS) (2015)
28. Zhou, Q.Y., Park, J., Koltun, V.: Open3D: a modern library for 3D data processing. arXiv:1801.09847 (2018)
29. Castle, R.O., Klein, G., Murray, D.W.: Combining monoslam with object recognition for scene augmentation using a wearable camera. Image Vis. Comput. **28**(11), 1548–1556 (2010)
30. Civera, J., Gálvez-López, D., Riazuelo, L., Tardós, J.D., Montiel, J.: Towards semantic slam using a monocular camera. In: International Conference on Intelligent Robots and Systems (IROS) (2011)
31. Kundu, A., Li, Y., Dellaert, F., Li, F., Rehg, J.: Joint semantic segmentation and 3D reconstruction from monocular video. In: European Conference Computer Vision (ECCV) (2014)
32. Hermans, A., Floros, G., Leibe, B.: Dense 3D semantic mapping of indoor scenes from RGB-D images. In: International Conference on Robotics and Automation (ICRA) (2014)
33. Vineet, V.E.A.: Incremental dense semantic stereo fusion for large-scale semantic scene reconstruction. In: International Conference on Robotics and Automation (ICRA) (2015)
34. McCormac, J., Handa, A., Davison, A., Leutenegger, S.: Semanticfusion: dense 3D semantic mapping with convolutional neural networks. In: International Conference on Robotics and Automation (ICRA) (2017)
35. Bowman, S.L., Atanasov, N., Daniilidis, K., Pappas, G.J.: Probabilistic data association for semantic slam. In: International Conference on Robotics and Automation (ICRA) (2017)

36. Klein, G., Murray, D.: Parallel tracking and mapping for small AR workspaces. In: International Symposium on Mixed and Augmented Reality (ISMAR) (2007)
37. Girshick, R.: Fast R-CNN. In: International Conference on Computer Vision (ICCV) (2015)
38. Ren, S., He, K., Girshick, R., Sun, J.: Faster R-CNN: towards real-time object detection with region proposal networks. In: Advances in Neural Information Processing Systems (NIPS) (2015)
39. He, K., Gkioxari, G., Dollár, P., Girshick, R.: Mask R-CNN. In: International Conference on Computer Vision (ICCV) (2017)
40. Liu, W., et al.: SSD: single shot multibox detector. In: Leibe, B., Matas, J., Sebe, N., Welling, M. (eds.) ECCV 2016. LNCS, vol. 9905, pp. 21–37. Springer, Cham (2016). https://doi.org/10.1007/978-3-319-46448-0_2
41. Redmon, J., Divvala, S., Girshick, R., Farhadi, A.: You only look once: Unified, real-time object detection. In: Computer Vision and Pattern Recognition (CVPR) (2016)
42. Choi, C., Christensen, H.I.: 3D textureless object detection and tracking: An edge-based approach. In: International Conference on Intelligent Robots and Systems (IROS) (2012)
43. Lepetit, V., Fua, P., et al.: Monocular model-based 3D tracking of rigid objects: a survey. In: Foundations and Trends® in Computer Graphics and Vision (2005)
44. Prisacariu, V.A., Reid, I.D.: Pwp3D: real-time segmentation and tracking of 3D objects. Int. J. Comput. Vis. (IJCV) 98(3), 335–354 (2012)
45. Tjaden, H., Schwanecke, U., Schömer, E.: Real-time monocular pose estimation of 3D objects using temporally consistent local color histograms. In: Computer Vision and Pattern Recognition (CVPR) (2017)

Actor-Centric Relation Network

Chen Sun[⊠], Abhinav Shrivastava, Carl Vondrick, Kevin Murphy,
Rahul Sukthankar, and Cordelia Schmid

Google Research, Mountain View, USA
chensun@google.com

Abstract. Current state-of-the-art approaches for spatio-temporal
action localization rely on detections at the frame level and model temporal context with 3D ConvNets. Here, we go one step further and model
spatio-temporal relations to capture the interactions between human
actors, relevant objects and scene elements essential to differentiate similar human actions. Our approach is weakly supervised and mines the
relevant elements automatically with an actor-centric relational network
(ACRN). ACRN computes and accumulates pair-wise relation information from actor and global scene features, and generates relation features
for action classification. It is implemented as neural networks and can be
trained jointly with an existing action detection system. We show that
ACRN outperforms alternative approaches which capture relation information, and that the proposed framework improves upon the state-of-
the-art performance on JHMDB and AVA. A visualization of the learned
relation features confirms that our approach is able to attend to the relevant relations for each action.

Keywords: Spatio-temporal action detection · Relation networks

1 Introduction

Robust human action understanding will have a large impact in applications
across robotics, security, and health. However, despite significant progress in
visual recognition for objects and scenes [16,27,41,63], performance on action
recognition remains relatively low. Now that we have large, diverse, and realistic datasets such as AVA [13], SLAC [61], and Charades [48], why has action
recognition performance not caught up?

Models for spatio-temporal action localization from the last few years have
been mainly based on architectures for recognizing objects [12,37,57], building
on the success of R-CNN style architectures [9,10,40]. However, unlike objects
which can be identified solely by their visual appearance, in many cases actions
can not be identified by the visual appearance of actors alone. Rather, action
recognition often requires reasoning about the actor's relationship with objects
and other actors, both spatially and temporally. To make this point, Fig. 1 shows
two actors performing different actions. Even for humans, by just looking at the

© Springer Nature Switzerland AG 2018
V. Ferrari et al. (Eds.): ECCV 2018, LNCS 11215, pp. 335–351, 2018.
https://doi.org/10.1007/978-3-030-01252-6_20

Fig. 1. Action detection is challenging even for humans without relation reasoning from the context. Only by extracting the relationship between the actor and the object (ball), and understanding how this relationship evolves over time, can one tell that the first action is catching a ball, while the second action is shooting a ball. The last column visualizes the relational heat maps generated by our algorithm.

cropped boxes, it is difficult to tell what actions are being performed. It is from the actors' interactions with a ball in the scene that we can tell that these are sports actions, and only by temporal reasoning of the relative positions, can we tell that the first actor is catching a ball and the second is shooting a ball.

Although the basic idea of exploiting context for action recognition is not new, earlier works [5,32,55] largely focused on the *classification* task (label each trimmed clip with an action label). For detection, where we want to assign different labels to different actors in the same scene, *actor-centric* relationships need to be extracted. Training this in a fully supervised manner would require detailed labeling of actors and relevant objects [4,15]; such annotations can be very expensive to obtain. Therefore, we aim to build an action detection system that can infer actor-object spatio-temporal relations automatically with only actor-level supervision.

In this paper, we propose an action detection model that learns spatio-temporal relationships between actors and the scene. Motivated by the recent work of Santoro et al. [44] on visual question answering, we use neural network to compute pair-wise relation information from the actor and scene features, which enables the module to be jointly trained with the action detector. We simplify the search space of scene features to be individual cells on a feature map, and pool the actor feature to be 1×1. These simplifications allow us to compute relation information efficiently with 1×1 convolutions. A set of 3×3 convolutions are then used to accumulate relation information from neighboring locations. We refer to this approach as actor-centric relation network (ACRN). Finally, we also use the temporal context as inputs to ACRN. Such context is captured by 3D ConvNets as suggested by [13].

We evaluate our approach on JHMDB [22] and the recently released AVA dataset [13]. Experimental results show that our approach consistently outperforms the baseline approach, which focuses on the actor, and alternative approaches that employ context information. We also visualize the relation heat maps with classification activation mapping [62]. Figure 1 shows two examples of such visualization. It is evident that ACRN learns to focus on the ball and its motion over time (flattened into 2D).

The primary contribution of this paper is to learn actor-centric spatio-temporal relationships for action detection in video. The rest of the paper describes our approach and experiments in detail. In Sect. 2, we first review related work. In Sect. 3, we present our approach to detect human actions. In Sect. 4, we discuss several experiments on two datasets where we obtain state-of-the-art action detection performance.

2   Related Work

Action Recognition. Action recognition has traditionally focused on classifying actions in short video clips. State-of-the-art methods rely either on two-stream 2D ConvNets [25,49], 2D ConvNets with LSTMs [7,34] or 3D ConvNets [3,53]. While action classification in videos has been successful, it is inherently limited to short trimmed clips. If we want to address long untrimmed videos, temporal localization is necessary in addition to action classification. This requires an additional step of determining the start and end time of each action instance. Many recent state-of-the-art methods [2,5,59] rely on temporal proposals and classification approaches similar in spirit to recent methods for object detection [40].

However, a more detailed understanding of actions in video requires localization not only in time, but also in space. This is particular true in the case of multiple actors [13]. Many existing state-of-the-art approaches for spatio-temporal action localization [11,37,43,50,56] employ state-of-the-art object detectors [28,40] to discriminate between action classes at the frame level. Recently, some approaches incorporate temporal context from multiple frames. This is particularly important for disambiguating actions such as "stand up" and "sit down", which may appear identical at the single frame level. The tubelet approach [24] concatenates SSD features [28] over spatio-temporal volumes and jointly estimates classification and regression over several frames. T-CNN [18] uses 3D convolutions to estimate short tubes, micro-tubes rely on two successive frames [42] and pose-guided 3D convolutions add pose to a two-stream approach [64]. Gu et al. [13] rely on inflated 3D ConvNet (I3D) convolutions [3] for Faster R-CNN [40] region proposals and show that the use of I3D over relatively long temporal windows [54] improves the performance. The spatio-temporal separable 3D ConvNet (S3D) [58] improves the I3D architecture by observing that the 3D convolutions can be replaced by separable spatial and temporal convolutions without loss in accuracy, and that using such convolutions in higher layers of the network results in faster and more accurate models. We use the S3D [58] model as the baseline approach in this paper.

Whereas several recent approaches for spatio-temporal action localization do take into account temporal information, they ignore spatial context such as interaction with humans, objects and the surrounding scene. This results in confusion

338   C. Sun et al.

of similar actions and interactions, such as jumping and shooting a basketball. We demonstrate that augmenting a state-of-the-art action localization approach with spatial context generates a significant performance improvement.

Context in Vision. The use of context information to improve visual recognition has been extensively studied in computer vision. Early work showed that context can help scene classification [35], object detection [15,17,33,39,52], and action recognition in images [60]. In these cases, context often provides a strong prior that enables more robust recognition. While these models of context were largely hand-designed, recent investigations have studied how to learn context with deep convolutional networks [46,47]. Spatial context has also been studied in self-supervised learning for learning unsupervised visual representations [6,36]. Beyond images, context has been leveraged in video, in particular for recognizing actions with hand-crafted features [32] and learned representations [8,45]. While we are also interested in recognizing human actions with context, this paper focuses on the role of context for *detection*. Importantly, since recognizing actions from crops is challenging even for humans, we believe context should play a critical role for learning robust action detection models.

Modeling the relations between objects [31,38] and more specifically between humans and objects [12,14] has been shown to improve the performance of recognizing relations in static images. Recent work [12] obtains state-of-the-art performance for human-action-object recognition on V-COCO [14] and HICO-DET [4]. In contrast to our approach, their model is only applied to static images and relies on full supervision of actor, action and objects as annotated in V-COCO [14] and HICO-DET [4].

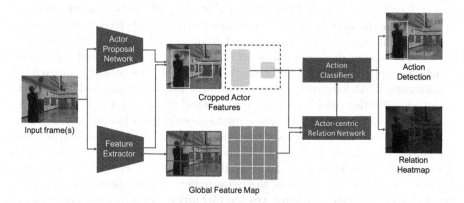

Fig. 2. Overview of our proposed action detection framework. Compared to a standard action detection approach, the proposed framework extracts pairwise relations from cropped actor features and a global feature map with the actor-centric relation network (ACRN) module. These relation features are then used for action classification.

3   Action Detection with Actor-Centric Relation Network

This section describes our proposed action detection framework. The framework builds upon the recent success of deep learning methods for object and action detection from static images [40] and videos [37]. We note that the relational information between the actor of interest and other actors or objects are important to identify actions, but are typically ignored by recent action detection methods [24,37]; such annotations could be time consuming to collect, and are not provided by many of the recent action recognition datasets [13,26,48]. Our proposed frameworks aims at explicitly modeling relations with weak actor-level supervision, with an actor-centric relation network module. Once trained, the framework can not only detects human actions with higher accuracy, but can also generate spatial heat maps of the relevant relations for each actor and action. An overview of the approach can be found in Fig. 2.

3.1   Action Detection Framework

Our goal is to localize actions in videos. We follow the popular paradigm of frame-based action detection, where the model produces bounding-box predictions for actions on each frame individually [11,37], and then links them into tubes as a post-processing step.

Action Detection Model. Our base model has two key components: actor localization and action classification. These two components are trained jointly in an end-to-end fashion. This action detection model was proposed in [13], motivated by the success of applying end-to-end object detection algorithms to action detection [24,37]. The inputs to the base model include the key frame to generate action predictions, and optionally neighboring frames of the key frame as temporal context. The outputs of the base model include 2D bounding boxes of localized actions for the key frame. The overall architecture of the base model largely resembles the Faster R-CNN detection algorithm. For actor localization, our method uses the region proposal network (RPN) from Faster R-CNN to generate 2D actor proposals. For action classification, we use deep representations extracted from the key frame and (optionally) neighboring frames. Unlike Faster R-CNN, we do not require the actor proposal network to share the same extracted features as the action classification network, although such sharing is possible. This allows more freedom to the choice of action classification features without adding much computation overhead, as classification feature computation is usually dominated by the neighboring frames.

Incorporating Temporal Context. We adopt 3D ConvNets [3,58] as used by [13] to incorporate larger temporal context from neighboring frames. We found that 3D ConvNets consistently outperform alternative approaches such as channel-wise stacking of frames at the input layer or average pooling at the output layer. The output feature map from 3D ConvNets has an extra time dimension, which is inconsistent with the 2D bounding box proposals generated by RPN. We address this issue by *flattening* the 3D feature map with a $t \times 1 \times 1$

temporal convolution, where t is the size of the time dimension. The flattened 2D feature map can then be provided to a standard differentiable ROIPooling operation [19,21] to produce cropped actor features. The cropped actor features are then inflated back to 3D, to allow reusing the pre-trained 3D ConvNets weights for classification. Empirically, we find that the flattening approach gives on par or better accuracy than keeping the temporal dimension with 3D ROIPooling.

Architecture Details. For accurate actor bounding-box locations, we follow [13] and use a 2D ResNet-50 model [16] trained on key frames with action bounding-box annotations. For action classification, we use gated separable 3D network (S3D-G) [58]. Compared with I3D [3] used in [13], S3D-G replaces full 3D convolutions with separable spatial and temporal convolutions, and employs spatio-temporal feature gating layers. Overall, S3D-G is faster, has fewer parameters, provides higher accuracy compared to other 3D ConvNet models, and has a flexible design which makes it ideal for the large-scale action detection setup.

Following the recommendation from [58], we use the *top-heavy* configuration and use 2D convolutions without gating until the Mixed_4b block (we follow the same naming conventions as the Inception networks [51]), and switch to separable 3D convolutions with gating onwards. To combine RGB and optical flow input modalities, we use early fusion at the Mixed_4f block instead of late fusion at the logits layer. With these changes, we observed a 1.8× speed-up in our action detection model without loosing performance. We use the features from the fused Mixed_4f (t × h × w × c) block for action classification. These features have a spatial output stride of 16 pixels and a temporal output stride of 4 frames. Regions in Mixed_4f corresponding to actor RPN proposals are temporally flattened and used as the input for the action classification network. We will refer to the h × w × c feature map as $\mathcal{F}$ going forward. For each RPN proposal generated by a potential actor $(b_i = (x_1^i, y_1^i, x_2^i, y_2^i)))$, we crop and resize the feature within b_i from $\mathcal{F}$ using ROIPooling to obtain a fixed-length representation $\mathcal{F}(b_i)$ of size $7 \times 7 \times 832$. This feature representation is used by the action classifier, which consists of Mixed_5b and Mixed_5c blocks (that output $7 \times 7 \times 1024$ feature), and an average pooling layer which outputs $1 \times 1 \times 1024$ feature. This feature is then used to learn a linear classifier for actions and a regressor for bounding-box offsets. We refer to the action detection model described above as our **Base-Model** throughout this paper. As shown in the experiments, the Base-Model by itself obtains state-of-the-art performance for action detection on the datasets explored in this work.

3.2 Actor-Centric Relations for Action Detection

A key component missing in the Base-Model is reasoning about relations outside the cropped regions. It is important to model such relations, as actions are in many cases defined by them (see Fig. 1). Here, we propose to extract actor-centric relation features and to input them to the action classification network. Our approach performs relation reasoning given only action annotations, and automatically retrieves the regions that are most related to the action. Thus, we refer to our approach as an actor-centric relation network (ACRN).

Actor-Centric Relations. Given an input example I with a set of actors $\mathcal{A} = \{A_1, A_2, ..., A_M\}$ and objects $\mathcal{O} = \{O_1, O_2, ..., O_N\}$, we define a pair-wise relation feature between actor A_i and object O_j as $g_\theta(a_i, o_j)$, where $g_\theta(\cdot)$ is a feature extractor function parameterized by θ, and a_i and o_j are the feature representations of actor A_i and object O_j respectively.

The actor-centric relation feature for actor A_i can be computed by

$$\mathrm{ACR}(A_i) = f_\phi\left(\left\{g_\theta(a_i, o_j) : O_j \in \mathcal{O}\right\}\right), \tag{1}$$

where $f_\phi(\cdot)$ is a function that aggregates features from all pair-wise relations, parameterized by ϕ.

To use actor-centric relations for action detection, we need to define actors, objects and their relations. We treat each actor proposal generated by RPN as one actor. However, objects and their relations are not explicitly defined or annotated for the action detection task. We adopt a workaround that treats each individual feature cell in the convolutional feature map $\mathcal{F}$ as an *object* O_i, which naturally gives the object representation o_i. This simplification avoids the need of generating object proposals, and has been shown to be effective for video classification [55] and question answering [44] tasks. However, as we show in the experiment section, directly applying this simplification does not improve the performance of the Base-Model. We compute $\mathrm{ACR}(A_i)$ with neural networks, this allows the module to be end-to-end trained with the Base-Model. In particular, both g_θ and f_ϕ can be implemented with standard convolutions and pooling operations.

Action Detection with Actor-Centric Relation Network (ACRN). We now discuss how to incorporate ACRN into our action detection framework. Given N frames from a video ($\mathcal{V}$), we first extract the fused feature map $\mathcal{F}_v$ of size $\mathtt{h} \times \mathtt{w} \times \mathtt{c}$ and a set of bounding-boxes generated by the actor RPN ($\mathcal{B} = (b_1, ..., b_R)$). For each box b_i, we follow the procedure described in Sect. 3.1 to get an actor feature f_i^a of size $1 \times 1 \times 1024$. Note that this is the same feature used by the Base-Model for action classification.

To extract pair-wise relation features, we follow the relation network module used by Santoro et al. [44] and implement g_θ as a single fully-connected layer. The inputs to g_θ are set as the concatenation of features from one actor proposal and one object location, along with their locations:

$$a_i = [f_i^a; b_i], \text{ and } o_{j,k} = [\mathcal{F}_v(j, k); l(j, k)], \tag{2}$$

where $\mathcal{F}_v(j, k)$ is the $1 \times 1 \times 832$ feature extracted at feature location (j, k), and $l = (j/H, k/W)$.

In practice, we can efficiently compute $g_\theta(a_i, o_{j,k})$ for all (j, k) locations using convolution operations. The actor appearance feature f_i^a is duplicated to $h \times w \times 1024$ feature and concatenated with $\mathcal{F}$ channel-wise, along with the box and location embeddings. Next, g_θ is computed using a 1×1 convolution layer, which outputs $\mathcal{F}^\theta(a_i)$ of size $\mathtt{h} \times \mathtt{w} \times 832$. These operations are illustrated in Fig. 3 (b).

Since a_i and $o_{j,k}$ come from different layers with varying feature amplitude, we follow the design decisions from [1,29,46] to normalize and scale the features when combining them as inputs to the relational reasoning modules.

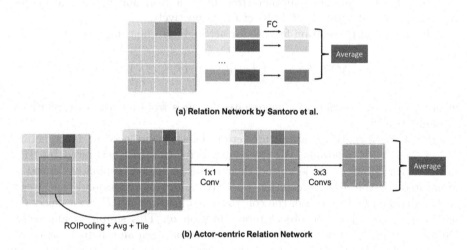

(a) Relation Network by Santoro et al.

ROIPooling + Avg + Tile

(b) Actor-centric Relation Network

Fig. 3. Comparison of our proposed ACRN (**b**) with the relation network used by Santoro et al. [44] (**a**). We compute relation feature maps by duplicating actor features and applying a 1×1 convolution. A set of 3×3 convolutions are then applied on relation feature map to accumulate information from neighboring relations.

After $\mathcal{F}^\theta(a_i)$ is computed, the model needs to aggregate all g_θ with f_ϕ. One option is to directly apply average pooling as in [44], which works for synthetic data with relative simple scene [23]. However, for action recognition the relevant relational information could be very sparse, and averaging will dilute such information. Moreover, since the relation features are computed locally, information about bigger objects could be lost after average pooling. Instead, we propose to apply convolution operations on $\mathcal{F}^\theta(a_i)$ before average pooling, which allows relational information to accumulate over neighboring locations. In practice, we use `Mixed_5b` and `Mixed_5c` blocks of the S3D-G network and an average pooling layer (similar to the action classifier network) to output a $1 \times 1 \times 1024$ feature (f_i^{RN}). Finally, we concatenate actor feature f_i^a and spatio-temporal relation feature f_i^{RN} to get a $1 \times 1 \times 2048$ representation which is used for action classification and bounding-box regression for a given actor box b_i (see Fig. 2). The same process is repeated for all proposed regions $\mathcal{B}$.

To handle objects of various scales, we further extend the ACRN module to allow feature maps other than $\mathcal{F}$ to be used, each of which can be resized to different scales. For example, smaller objects might be better represented in the earlier layers of the network at a larger scale feature map, while bigger objects might be better represented in the higher layers at a smaller scale. In Sect. 4.2, we study the impact of using different layers and their combination for relation reasoning.

4   Experiments

In this section, we perform design and ablation analysis of our method and visualize what relations are captured by the actor-centric relation network. Finally, we evaluate it on the task of spatio-temporal action localization and demonstrate consistent and significant gain across multiple benchmarks.

4.1   Experimental Setup

Datasets and Metrics. We report results on the JHMDB [22] and AVA [13] action detection benchmarks. JHMDB [22] consists of 928 temporally trimmed clips with 21 action classes and has three training/validation splits. Unless noted otherwise, we follow the standard setup and report results by averaging over all three splits. We report the frame-level and video-level mean average precision (frame-AP and video-AP) with an intersection-over-union (IOU) threshold of 0.5. For video-AP, we link per-frame action detection results into tubes using the algorithm from [13]. We use the AVA version 2.1 benchmark [13]. It consists of 211k training and 57k validation examples labeled at 1FPS over 80 action classes. We follow their baseline setup and report results on 60 action classes which have at least 25 validation examples per class. We report frame-AP for AVA.

Implementation Details. For the Base-Model, we use the ResNet-50 [16] RGB model for actor localization and the S3D-G [58] two-stream model for action classification. The detailed architecture is described in Sect. 3.1. Optical flow for the two-stream network is extracted using FlowNet2 [20]. As is standard practice, the ResNet-50 model is pre-trained on ImageNet and S3D-G RGB+Flow streams are pre-trained on Kinetics. The classification head (Mixed_5b, Mixed_5c) are initialized from RGB stream pre-trained on Kinetics for both RN and actor classification, but they are updated separately (weights are not shared). The whole pipeline (actor localization, actor-centric RN, and action classification) is trained jointly end-to-end.

We train the model for 200 K and 1.2M steps for JHMDB and AVA respectively, and use start asynchronous SGD with a batch-size of 1 per GPU (11 GPUs in total), mini-batch size of 256 for actor RPN and 64 for action classifier (following [13]). We warm-start the learning rate from 0.00001 to 0.001 in 40 K steps using linear annealing and then use cosine learning rate decay [30]. To stabilize training, the batch-norm updates are disabled during training and we apply a gradient multiplier of 0.01 to gradients from RN to the feature map.

4.2   Design and Ablation Analysis

We perform a number of ablation experiments to better understand the properties of our actor-centric relation network and its impact on the action detection performance. The results are shown in Tables 1 and 2.

Table 1. Frame-AP evaluating the impact of different parameters of ACRN on JHMDB dataset (3 splits).

Model	frame-AP
Base-Model	75.2
Resize+Concat [1, 29, 46]	74.8
Santoro et al. [44]	75.1
ACRN	**77.6**

(a) Relation reasoning modules.

Frames	Base-Model	ACRN
1	52.6	54.0
5	66.1	69.8
10	70.6	74.9
20	75.2	77.6

(b) Temporal context.

Feature	Conv1a	Conv2c	Mixed_3b	Mixed_4b	Mixed_4f	Conv2c, Mixed_3c, Mixed_4f
Scale 0.5	76.4	**77.2**	76.2	76.2	77.1	**77.9**
Scale 1.0	76.6	**77.9**	76.4	76.6	77.6	77.5

(c) Feature layers and scales.

Table 2. AVA actions with biggest performance gaps when different features are used by ACRN.

Action	Mixed_4f	Conv2c	Gap
answer phone	56.0	50.3	5.7
jump	6.8	4.0	2.8
swim	35.1	33.2	1.9
read	10.3	8.6	1.7
dance	32.7	31.6	1.1

Action	Mixed_4f	Conv2c	Gap
drive	15.3	19.5	-4.2
fight	36.2	40.4	-4.2
kiss	15.6	19.4	-3.8
play instrument	7.1	10.9	-3.8
touch	24.2	26.7	-2.5

Importance of Relation Reasoning Modules. Table 1a compare the performance between the Base-Model which only uses actor features, and three different relation reasoning modules which take global feature maps as additional inputs. We L2-normalize the actor appearance feature f_i^a and scene context feature Mixed_4f, concatenate the features together, scale the L2-norm of the concatenated feature back to the L2-norm of f_i^a, and use a 1×1 convolution layer to reduce the number of channels to be same as f_i^a. We study the following relational reasoning modules:

Resize+Concat [1,29,46]: resize the global feature map and actor feature map at Mixed_4f to have same size and directly concatenate channel-wise. The concatenated feature maps are fed into the classification head (Mixed_5b-5c).

Santoro et al. [44]: global and actor feature maps are used to compute g_θ, which are then averaged to compute f_ϕ with one fully-connected layer.

ACRN: global and actor feature maps are used to compute relation feature maps by ACRN, which are fed into the classification head.

Table 1a shows performance comparisons in frame-AP on JHMDB. Our proposed ACRN imrpoves by **2.4** over the Base-Model. However, Resize+Concat and Santoro et al. fail to outperform the baseline despite having access to global feature maps. The gap highlights the importance of designing an appropriate relation reasoning module.

Impact of Temporal Context. Table 1b studies the impact of temporal context on the Base-Model and the proposed ACRN framework by varying the number input frames, and show the results in. As observed by [13], using more input frames generally helps our models. ACRN consistently improves over the Base-Model across all temporal lengths.

Comparison of Feature Layers and Scales. ACRN can take feature maps from the different layers of a ConvNet as inputs. Each feature map can be resized to have different scales. Choices of feature layer and scale may have pros and cons: intuitively, features from higher layers (e.g. Mixed_4f) encode more semantic information, but have lower resolution; features from lower layers (e.g. Conv2c) have higher resolution but are less semantically meaningful. Similarly, feature map with larger scale potentially helps to identify interactions involving smaller objects, but also increases the number of relations to aggregate.

In Table 1c, we report frame-mAP on the JHMDB dataset by varying the feature layers and scales of the global feature map. We observe that Conv2c is the best performing single feature, followed by Mixed_4f. The performance is relatively stable for different scales. We note that combining features from multiple layers not necessarily results in better overall performance. In Table 2, we list the AVA categories with highest performance gap when using Mixed_4f and Conv2c. We can see that the two feature layers are clearly complimentary for many actions. In the following experiments, we report ACRN results based on the best single feature layer and scale.

4.3   Comparison with the State of the Art

We compare our best models with the state-of-the-art methods on JHMDB and AVA. For the state-of-the-art methods, we use the same experimental setup and quote the results as reported by the authors. We fix the number of input frames to 20 for I3D, Base-Model and ACRN.

As shown in Table 3, our Base-Model already outperforms all previous methods, and the proposed ACRN algorithm further achieves a gain over this Base-Model. We also look into the per-class performance breakdown: on the JHMDB dataset, ACRN outperforms the Base-Model significantly for catch (12%), jump (6%), shoot gun (5%) and wave (10%). The gain is smaller when the performance of the Base-Model is almost saturated (e.g. golf, pullup and pour). The Base-Model performs only slightly better on pick, throw and run. When visualizing the relation heatmaps, we can see that ACRN has difficulty attending to the right relations for these actions.

On the AVA dataset, the per-class performance breakdown for the 30 highest performing categories can be found in Fig. 4. We can discover that the biggest gains are achieved for answer phone (11%), fight (5%), swim (10%), dance (10%), touch (6%), kiss (8%) and play musical instruments (5%), most of which involve human-human or human-object interactions.

346   C. Sun et al.

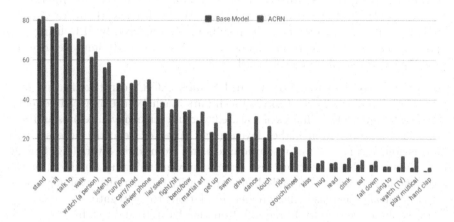

Fig. 4. Per-category frame-AP comparison between the Base-Model and ACRN on AVA. Labels are sorted by descending Base-Model performance, only the top 30 categories are shown.

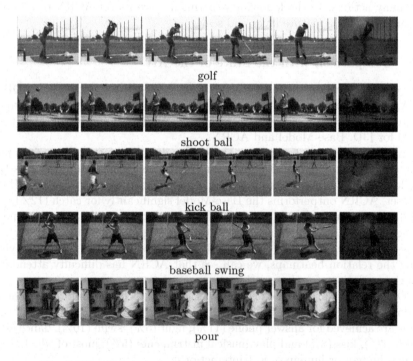

golf

shoot ball

kick ball

baseball swing

pour

Fig. 5. Visualization of relation heatmap on JHMDB dataset.

Table 3. Comparison with state of the art on (a) the JHMDB dataset and (b) AVA . For JHMDB, we report average precision over 3 splits.

Model	frame-AP	video-AP
Peng et al. [37]	58.5	73.1
ACT [24]	65.7	73.7
I3D [13]	73.3	78.6
Base-Model	75.2	78.8
ACRN	**77.9**	**80.1**

(a) JHMDB (3 splits)

Model	frame-AP
Single frame [13]	14.2
I3D [13]	15.1
Base-Model	15.5
ACRN	**17.4**

(b) AVA (version 2.1)

Fig. 6. Visualization of relation heatmap on AVA. The actor corresponding to the heatmap is marked in green, and its action is shown below the example. Notice how the heatmap varies depending on the action categories. (Color figure online)

4.4 Qualitative Results

To qualitatively verify what relations are learned by ACRN, we apply the class activation map (CAM) [62] method to visualize the per-category relation heatmaps based on ACRN outputs. We modify the inference network by removing the average pooling operation after the ACRN branch, and apply the final action classifier as 1×1 convolutions on the relation feature map. This allows us to generate spatially localized per-category activations, which illustrates the relations important to identify a certain action. Note that the spatial heatmaps also encode temporal information, as the input features are flattened from 3D to 2D.

Figures 5 and 6 show the visualizations of the top-1 and top-2 highest scoring detections on JHMDB and AVA respectively. We render the bounding boxes and their associated relation heatmap in green and red respectively. We can see that ACRN is able to capture spatio-temporal relations beyond the actor bounding box, and its output depends on actor and action. Finally, Fig. 7 illustrates examples for which the false alarms of the Base-Model are removed by ACRN (top row) and the missing detections are captured by ACRN (bottom row).

Fig. 7. (*Top row*) False alarm detections from the Base-Model (red boxes) that are removed by ACRN. (*Bottom row*) Miss detections (green) of the Base-Model captured by ACRN (blue). (Color figure online)

5   Conclusion

This paper presents a novel approach to automatically determine relevant spatio-temporal elements characterizing human actions in video. Experimental results for spatio-temporal action localization demonstrate a clear gain and visualizations show that the mined elements are indeed relevant. Future work includes a description of an actor by more than one feature, i.e., a number of features representing different human body parts. This will allow to model relations not only with an actor, but also the relations to relevant human parts. Another line of work could be to look at higher-order spatio-temporal relations.

Acknowledgement:. We thank Chunhui Gu, David Ross and Jitendra Malik for discussion and comments.

References

1. Bell, S., Lawrence Zitnick, C., Bala, K., Girshick, R.: Inside-outside net: detecting objects in context with skip pooling and recurrent neural networks. In: CVPR (2016)
2. Buch, S., Escorcia, V., Shen, C., Ghanem, B., Niebles, J.C.: SST: single-stream temporal action proposals. In: CVPR (2017)
3. Carreira, J., Zisserman, A.: Quo vadis, action recognition? a new model and the Kinetics dataset. In: CVPR (2017)
4. Chao, Y.W., Liu, Y., Liu, X., Zeng, H., Deng, J.: Learning to detect human-object interactions. In: WACV (2018)

5. Dai, X., Singh, B., Zhang, G., Davis, L.S., Chen, Y.Q.: Temporal context network for activity localization in videos. In: ICCV (2017)
6. Doersch, C., Gupta, A., Efros, A.A.: Unsupervised visual representation learning by context prediction. In: ICCV (2015)
7. Donahue, J., et al.: Long-term recurrent convolutional networks for visual recognition and description. In: CVPR (2015)
8. Girdhar, R., Ramanan, D.: Attentional pooling for action recognition. In: NIPS (2017)
9. Girshick, R.: Fast R-CNN. In: ICCV (2015)
10. Girshick, R., Donahue, J., Darrell, T., Malik, J.: Rich feature hierarchies for accurate object detection and semantic segmentation. In: CVPR (2014)
11. Gkioxari, G., Malik, J.: Finding action tubes. In: CVPR (2015)
12. Gkioxari, G., Girshick, R., Dollár, P., He, K.: Detecting and recognizing human-object intaractions. In: CVPR (2018)
13. Gu, C., et al.: AVA: a video dataset of spatio-temporally localized atomic visual actions. In: CVPR (2018)
14. Gupta, S., Malik, J.: Visual semantic role labeling. arXiv:1505.04474 (2015)
15. Gupta, S., Hariharan, B., Malik, J.: Exploring person context and local scene context for object detection. arXiv:1511.08177 (2015)
16. He, K., Zhang, X., Ren, S., Sun, J.: Deep residual learning for image recognition. In: CVPR (2016)
17. Heitz, G., Koller, D.: Learning spatial context: using stuff to find things. In: Forsyth, D., Torr, P., Zisserman, A. (eds.) ECCV 2008. LNCS, vol. 5302, pp. 30–43. Springer, Heidelberg (2008). https://doi.org/10.1007/978-3-540-88682-2_4
18. Hou, R., Chen, C., Shah, M.: Tube convolutional neural network (T-CNN) for action detection in videos. In: ICCV (2017)
19. Huang, J., et al.: Speed/accuracy trade-offs for modern convolutional object detectors. In: CVPR (2017)
20. Ilg, E., Mayer, N., Saikia, T., Keuper, M., Dosovitskiy, A., Brox, T.: FlowNet 2.0: evolution of optical flow estimation with deep networks. In: CVPR (2017)
21. Jaderberg, M., Simonyan, K., Zisserman, A., Kavukcuoglu, K.: Spatial transformer networks. In: NIPS (2015)
22. Jhuang, H., Gall, J., Zuffi, S., Schmid, C., Black, M.: Towards understanding action recognition. In: ICCV (2013)
23. Johnson, J., Hariharan, B., van der Maaten, L., Fei-Fei, L., Zitnick, C.L., Girshick, R.B.: CLEVR: a diagnostic dataset for compositional language and elementary visual reasoning. In: CVPR (2017)
24. Kalogeiton, V., Weinzaepfel, P., Ferrari, V., Schmid, C.: Action tubelet detector for spatio-temporal action localization. In: ICCV (2017)
25. Karpathy, A., Toderici, G., Shetty, S., Leung, T., Sukthankar, R., Fei-Fei, L.: Large-scale video classification with convolutional neural networks. In: CVPR (2014)
26. Kay, W., et al.: The Kinetics human action video dataset. arXiv:1705.06950 (2017)
27. Krizhevsky, A., Sutskever, I., Hinton, G.E.: Imagenet classification with deep convolutional neural networks. In: NIPS (2012)
28. Liu, W., et al.: SSD: single shot multibox detector. In: Leibe, B., Matas, J., Sebe, N., Welling, M. (eds.) ECCV 2016. LNCS, vol. 9905, pp. 21–37. Springer, Cham (2016). https://doi.org/10.1007/978-3-319-46448-0_2
29. Liu, W., Rabinovich, A., Berg, A.C.: Parsenet: looking wider to see better. arXiv:1506.04579 (2015)
30. Loshchilov, I., Hutter, F.: SGDR: stochastic gradient descent with restarts. In: ICLR (2017)

31. Lu, C., Krishna, R., Bernstein, M., Fei-Fei, L.: Visual relationship detection with language priors. In: ECCV (2016)
32. Marszalek, M., Laptev, I., Schmid, C.: Actions in context. In: CVPR (2009)
33. Mottaghi, R., et al.: The role of context for object detection and semantic segmentation in the wild. In: CVPR (2014)
34. Ng, J.Y., Hausknecht, M.J., Vijayanarasimhan, S., Vinyals, O., Monga, R., Toderici, G.: Beyond short snippets: deep networks for video classification. In: CVPR (2015)
35. Oliva, A., Torralba, A.: Modeling the shape of the scene: a holistic representation of the spatial envelope. IJCV **42**(3), 145–175 (2001)
36. Pathak, D., Krähenbühl, P., Donahue, J., Darrell, T., Efros, A.A.: Context encoders: feature learning by inpainting. In: CVPR (2016)
37. Peng, X., Schmid, C.: Multi-region two-stream R-CNN for action detection. In: ECCV (2016)
38. Peyre, J., Laptev, I., Schmid, C., Sivic, J.: Weakly-supervised learning of visual relations. In: ICCV (2017)
39. Rabinovich, A., Vedaldi, A., Galleguillos, C., Wiewiora, E., Belongie, S.: Objects in context. In: ICCV (2007)
40. Ren, S., He, K., Girshick, R., Sun, J.: Faster R-CNN: towards real-time object detection with region proposal networks. In: NIPS (2015)
41. Russakovsky, O., et al.: Imagenet large scale visual recognition challenge. IJCV textbf115(3), 211–252 (2015)
42. Saha, S., Sing, G., Cuzzolin, F.: AMTnet: action-micro-tube regression by end-to-end trainable deep architecture. In: ICCV (2017)
43. Saha, S., Singh, G., Sapienza, M., Torr, P., Cuzzolin, F.: Deep learning for detecting multiple space-time action tubes in videos. In: BMVC (2016)
44. Santoro, A., et al.: A simple neural network module for relational reasoning. In: NIPS (2017)
45. Sharma, S., Kiros, R., Salakhutdinov, R.: Action recognition using visual attention. arXiv:1511.04119 (2015)
46. Shrivastava, A., Gupta, A.: Contextual priming and feedback for faster R-CNN. In: Leibe, B., Matas, J., Sebe, N., Welling, M. (eds.) ECCV 2016. LNCS, vol. 9905, pp. 330–348. Springer, Cham (2016). https://doi.org/10.1007/978-3-319-46448-0_20
47. Shrivastava, A., Sukthankar, R., Malik, J., Gupta, A.: Beyond skip connections: top-down modulation for object detection. arXiv:1612.06851 (2016)
48. Sigurdsson, G.A., Varol, G., Wang, X., Farhadi, A., Laptev, I., Gupta, A.: Hollywood in homes: crowdsourcing data collection for activity understanding. In: Leibe, B., Matas, J., Sebe, N., Welling, M. (eds.) ECCV 2016. LNCS, vol. 9905, pp. 510–526. Springer, Cham (2016). https://doi.org/10.1007/978-3-319-46448-0_31
49. Simonyan, K., Zisserman, A.: Two-stream convolutional networks for action recognition in videos. In: NIPS (2014)
50. Singh, G., Saha, S., Sapienza, M., Torr, P., Cuzzolin, F.: Online real-time multiple spatiotemporal action localisation and prediction. In: ICCV (2017)
51. Szegedy, C., et al.: Going deeper with convolutions. In: CVPR (2015)
52. Torralba, A., Murphy, K.P., Freeman, W.T., Rubin, M.A.: Context-based vision system for place and object recognition. In: ICCV (2003)
53. Tran, D., Bourdev, L., Fergus, R., Torresani, L., Paluri, M.: Learning spatiotemporal features with 3D convolutional networks. In: ICCV (2015)
54. Varol, G., Laptev, I., Schmid, C.: Long-term temporal convolutions for action recognition. IEEE PAMI **40**(6), 1510–1517 (2017)

55. Wang, X., Girshick, R.B., Gupta, A., He, K.: Non-local neural networks. In: CVPR (2018)
56. Weinzaepfel, P., Harchaoui, Z., Schmid, C.: Learning to track for spatio-temporal action localization. In: ICCV (2015)
57. Weinzaepfel, P., Martin, X., Schmid, C.: Towards weakly-supervised action localization. arXiv:1605.05197 (2016)
58. Xie, S., Sun, C., Huang, J., Tu, Z., Murphy, K.: Rethinking spatiotemporal feature learning for video understanding. In: ECCV (2018)
59. Xu, H., Das, A., Saenko, K.: R-C3D: region convolutional 3D network for temporal activity detection. In: ICCV (2017)
60. Yao, B., Fei-Fei, L.: Modeling mutual context of object and human pose in human-object interaction activities. In: CVPR (2010)
61. Zhao, H., Yan, Z., Wang, H., Torresani, L., Torralba, A.: SLAC: a sparsely labeled dataset for action classification and localization. arXiv:1712.09374 (2017)
62. Zhou, B., Khosla, A., Lapedriza, A., Oliva, A., Torralba, A.: Learning deep features for discriminative localization. In: CVPR (2016)
63. Zhou, B., Lapedriza, A., Xiao, J., Torralba, A., Oliva, A.: Learning deep features for scene recognition using places database. In: NIPS (2014)
64. Zolfaghari, M., Oliveira, G., Sedaghat, N., Brox, T.: Chained multi-stream networks exploiting pose, motion, and appearance for action classification and detection. In: ICCV (2017)

Liquid Pouring Monitoring via Rich Sensory Inputs

Tz-Ying Wu[1], Juan-Ting Lin[1], Tsun-Hsuang Wang[1], Chan-Wei Hu[1],
Juan Carlos Niebles[2], and Min Sun[1(✉)]

[1] Department of Electrical Engineering, National Tsing Hua University,
Hsinchu, Taiwan
gina9726@gmail.com, brade31919@gmail.com, johnsonwang0810@gmail.com,
huchanwei1204@gmail.com, sunmin@ee.nthu.edu.tw
[2] Department of Computer Science, Stanford University, Stanford, USA
jniebles@cs.stanford.edu

Abstract. Humans have the amazing ability to perform very subtle manipulation task using a closed-loop control system with imprecise mechanics (i.e., our body parts) but rich sensory information (e.g., vision, tactile, etc.). In the closed-loop system, the ability to monitor the state of the task via rich sensory information is important but often less studied. In this work, we take liquid pouring as a concrete example and aim at learning to continuously monitor whether liquid pouring is successful (e.g., no spilling) or not via rich sensory inputs. We mimic humans' rich sensories using synchronized observation from a chest-mounted camera and a wrist-mounted IMU sensor. Given many success and failure demonstrations of liquid pouring, we train a hierarchical LSTM with late fusion for monitoring. To improve the robustness of the system, we propose two auxiliary tasks during training: inferring (1) the initial state of containers and (2) forecasting the one-step future 3D trajectory of the hand with an adversarial training procedure. These tasks encourage our method to learn representation sensitive to container states and how objects are manipulated in 3D. With these novel components, our method achieves ~8% and ~11% better monitoring accuracy than the baseline method without auxiliary tasks on unseen containers and unseen users respectively.

Keywords: Monitoring manipulation · Multimodal fusion
Auxiliary tasks

1 Introduction

Researchers in cognitive science community have conducted several studies [1,2] of mental simulation, and proved that humans have some internal mechanisms to reason daily life physics with relative ease. Some robotics research borrows a

---

T.-Y. Wu and J.-T. Lin—Equally contributed.

© Springer Nature Switzerland AG 2018
V. Ferrari et al. (Eds.): ECCV 2018, LNCS 11215, pp. 352–369, 2018.
https://doi.org/10.1007/978-3-030-01252-6_21

hand from human demonstrations to tackle manipulation problems; for example, recently, Edmonds et al. [3] leverage multimodal sensor to capture poses and contact forces to learn the manipulation of opening medicine bottles. Humans can be viewed as closed-loop control systems with imprecise mechanics (i.e., our body parts) but rich sensory information (e.g., vision, tactile, etc.). The sensory feedback helps us continuously reason the environment, and plan our next action according to it. In the closed-loop system, the ability to monitor the state of the task via rich sensory information is important but often less studied. Monitoring subtle manipulation task is useful for both in-home elder care system and virtual training in medical scenarios (e.g., training surgical operation), since a system with this kind of ability can further assist people to accomplish subtle tasks.

Liquid pouring is a subtle manipulation task that humans learn during childhood and can easily perform on a daily basis. This task requires continuously monitoring environmental states such as the liquid level in containers and the relative position and motion between containers in order to adjust future actions toward not spilling. For instance, if the receiver container is empty and the source container is tilting slowly, one should speed-up the tilting action. In contrast, if the receiver container is almost full and the source container is tilting fast, one should slow down the tilting action to prevent overflow. This suggests that both object states, relative position and motion are very important cues for subtle manipulation tasks such as liquid pouring. With the ability to monitor liquid pouring, an intelligent system can either stop the user from spilling, or bring a duster to the user when the liquid is spilled.

Monitoring liquid pouring activity is a very subtle task compared to mainstream activity recognition tasks such as action classification or temporal detection [4,5]. Hence, only a few works have made progress toward this direction in computer vision. Alayrac et al. [6] propose to discover object states and manipulation actions in videos. However, they only consider empty versus full (binary) container states and multiple discrete actions where pouring is one of them. Recently, Mottaghi et al. [7] propose to reason about volume and content in liquid containers to predict how much liquid will remain in the container if we tilt it by x degrees (referred to as pouring prediction). However, we argue that such prediction target has limited application since it does not directly answer how to pour liquid successfully or whether the pouring action results in success or failure.

In this work, we take liquid pouring as a concrete example and aim at learning to continuously monitor whether liquid pouring is successful (e.g., not spilling) or not via rich sensory inputs. Cognitive scientists suggest that people have the ability to simulate pouring behaviors in their mind, which is mentioned in [1]. However, there remain discrepancies between the simulation and the real results. By continuously observe current environmental states, people can adjust their ways to manipulate the object (e.g. the angle of the container) in order to reach their goal. This process can be viewed as a closed-loop control. In order to borrow a hand from humans' physical reasoning ability, we mimic humans' rich sensors using synchronized observation from a chest-mounted camera and a wrist-mounted IMU sensor as the input (details in Sect. 5). The target output for monitoring is a binary class: a success or a failure pouring trial. To study liquid pouring monitoring in the real world by leveraging human demonstrations, we collect a liquid pouring dataset containing both successful and failed demonstrations with all inputs and outputs information mentioned above. To the best of our knowledge, this is the first dataset with multimodal sensor information for studying monitoring in a subtle liquid pouring task (Fig. 1).

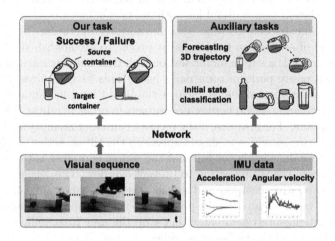

Fig. 1. Overview. From a series of visual observations and IMU data, our model can monitor if this sequence is a success or failure with two auxiliary tasks: initial object state classification (different containers with different initial liquid levels) to ensure the recurrent model encode states sensitive features; forecasting 3D trajectory requires the ability to model hand dynamics during the pouring process, providing a strong cue for our monitoring task. The details of auxiliary tasks are described in Sect. 4

Given many success and failure demonstrations of liquid pouring, we train a hierarchical LSTM [8] with late fusion to incorporate rich sensories inputs without significantly increasing the model parameters as compared to early fusion models. To further improve the generalizability of our method, we introduce two auxiliary tasks during training: (1) predicting the initial state of containers and (2) forecasting the one-step future 3D trajectory of the hand with an adversarial training procedure. These auxiliary tasks encourage our method to learn representation sensitive to container states and how objects are manipulated in 3D. In our experiments, our method achieves ~8% and ~11% better monitoring accuracy than the baseline method without auxiliary tasks on unseen containers and unseen users respectively.

2   Related Work

Activity Recognition. Activity recognition has received lots of attention from the computer vision community and already has many released datasets

[4,5,9–11] containing diverse actions. Many prior works on activity recognition focus on understanding human activity through observing body poses [12–14], scenes [15,16] or objects interacting with human [17–20]. There are also many works [21–23] considering recognizing activity through egocentric videos, some of which use depth sensor [24,25] as well in attempt to enhance the perception of the changes in the environment. There are also methods [26] and datasets [27,28] utilizing multimodal sensor inputs to perform activity recognition. These established datasets mainly focus on diverse activity recognition and do not include failure cases. However, we focus more on distinguishing subtle differences among behaviors targeting on the same objective (liquid pouring). Therefore, we collect our own liquid pouring dataset with multimodal sensor data which includes both success and failure cases (details in Sect. 5).

Fine-Grained Activity Recognition. Many methods focused on interacting and manipulating motions between human and objects. Lei *et al.* [25] applied RGB-D camera to achieve the robust object and action recognition. There are also methods utilizing spatiotemporal information [29–33]. By combining spatiotemporal and object semantic features, Yang *et al.* [29] find key interaction without using further object annotations. In this work, rather than designing special procedures to mine unique spatiotemporal features, we introduce auxiliary tasks to learn feature good for multiple tasks.

Environmental State Estimation. In liquid pouring sequences, container and the liquid state can be estimated from RGB inputs. Alayrac *et al.* [6] model the interaction between actions and objects in a discrete manner. Some methods further demonstrate that liquid amount can be estimated by combining semantic segmentation CNN and LSTM [7,34]. In contrast, our main goal is not to explicitly recognize environmental states. We aim at implicitly learning environmental state sensitive features such that our performance in monitoring can be improved. Recently, Sermanet *et al.* [35] also propose to learn states sensitive feature in a self-supervised manner.

Robot Liquid Pouring. In the robotics community, there are a number of works [36–42] directly tackle the manipulating task of liquid pouring without considering the monitoring task. [36] build a liquid dynamic model using optical flow. [41,42] are developed in synthetic environments. Tamosiunaite *et al.* [37] apply model-based reinforcement learning. Rozo *et al.* [38] propose a parametric hidden Markov model to direct regress control commands. Brandl *et al.* [39] learn to generalize pouring to unseen containers by warping the functional parts of the unseen containers to mimic the functional parts of a seen container. Schenck and Fox [40] propose to first estimate the volume of liquid in a container; then, a simple PID controller is used to pour specific amounts of liquid. However, all of the methods above are not evaluated on generalization jointly across users, containers states, container instances.

3   Overview

In this section, we first formulate the problem of monitoring liquid pouring. Next, we describe our recurrent model for fusing multimodal data. Our method with two auxiliary tasks will be mainly described in Sect. 4.

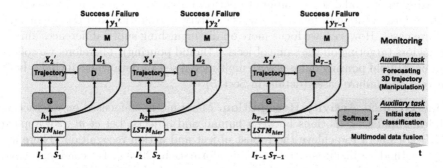

Fig. 2. Model architecture. Our model consists of a hierarchical LSTM $LSTM_{hier}$ (details in Subsect. 3.2), a generator G, a discriminator D and a monitoring module M (details in Sect. 4). There are two auxiliary tasks in our method, which are 3D trajectory forecasting (green shading) and initial state classification (blue shading). At each time step t, $LSTM_{hier}$ will encode visual observation I_t and IMU data S_t to h_t (red shading). G will generate a trajectory X'_{t+1} according to hidden encoding h_t. D will distinguish if the input trajectory is generated or not corresponding to h_t, which models the dynamics during the manipulation. M will predict if this pouring sequence is a success or failure based on the discriminator score d_t and hidden encoding h_t. At the end of the sequence, the model will classify 36 initial states as an auxiliary task (Color figure online)

3.1   Problem Formulation

Notations. For all of our notations, general font style stands for ground truth data, and prime stands for predictions. For example, y_t is the ground truth label for whether the sequence is a success and y'_t is the prediction. Notations with boldface denote a sequence of data. t denotes a certain time step, and T stands for the total time steps of the sequence.

Observation. To capture visual and motion information like liquid content, container type and dynamics of the demonstrator's hand during the pouring process, we use a multimodal sensing system including a camera on the front chest and an IMU sensor on the wrist. At each time step t, the camera observes visual observation I_t, and the 6DOF IMU sensor captures motion observation $S_t = \{\mathbf{a}^1, \mathbf{a}^2, ..., \mathbf{a}^N\}$, where $\mathbf{a}^i$ is the i'th sample in the current time step, $i \in 1 \sim N$, and N denotes the number of samples in this time step. In practice, $N = 38$, i.e., IMU sensor will capture 38 samples within two consecutively captured camera frames. $\mathbf{a} = \{a_1, a_2, a_3, a_4, a_5, a_6\}$ is a single piece of real-valued data from the IMU, where (a_1, a_2, a_3) is the acceleration and (a_4, a_5, a_6) is the angular velocity corresponding to x, y, and z axis. Simultaneously, at each time step t, we obtain hand 3D trajectory ground truth $X_t = (P, R)$ by a HTC Vive tracker mounted on the wrist, where $P = (p_x, p_y, p_z)$ and $R = (r_x, r_y, r_z)$ stand for the position part and rotation part in world coordinate respectively. Note that HTC Vive system is only used in training.

Goal. In our task, we aim at learning to monitor whether the pouring liquid sequence is a success or failure with two auxiliary tasks, which are initial object state classification (IOSC) and next-step hand 3D trajectory forecasting (TF). Considering the input sequence containing visual images $\mathbf{I} = \{I_1, I_2, ..., I_T\}$ and IMU data $\mathbf{S} = \{S_1, S_2, ..., S_T\}$, the output of our model for each time step t are the prediction y'_t indicating whether the sequence is a success for our monitoring task and next-step trajectory prediction X'_{t+1} for 3D trajectory forecasting, where $t \in 1 \sim T - 1$, T denotes the total time steps of the sequence. In the end of the whole sequence, our model will predict the initial object state z' of the sequence among the 36 variations (details in Sect. 5).

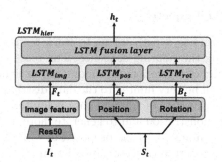

Fig. 3. LSTM encoder. Our hierarchical LSTM encoder $LSTM_{hier}$ consists of 3 LSTM cells ($LSTM_{img}$, $LSTM_{pos}$, $LSTM_{rot}$) at the first level and a LSTM fusion layer to fuse these hidden encodings at the second level, fusing multimodal inputs containing image feature F_t, hand position feature A_t and hand rotation feature B_t computed from IMU sensor

3.2 Multimodal Data Fusion

To catch and combine the temporal sequence of input from image and IMU sensor, we adopt a hierarchical LSTM proposed by [8] to handle scale differences among multimodal inputs. In the first layer of our module $LSTM_{hier}$ (see Fig. 3), there are 3 LSTM cells ($LSTM_{img}$, $LSTM_{pos}$, $LSTM_{rot}$) with different hidden layer sizes to encode the inputs from three different sources: (1) image feature $F_t = \mathbf{Res50}(I_t)$ extracted from the pool5 layer of ResNet50 [43] with dimension of 1×2048, (2) hand position feature: the aggregation of acceleration along 3 axis $A_t = \{(a_1^i, a_2^i, a_3^i)\}_{i=1}^N \subset S_t$ with dimension of $1 \times 3N$ and (3) hand rotation feature: the aggregation of angular velocity along 3 axis $B_t = \{(a_4^i, a_5^i, a_6^i)\}_{i=1}^N \subset S_t$ with dimension of $1 \times 3N$. Then the encoded features are concatenated as the input to the second layer consisting of a single LSTM cell. The output encoded feature $h_t = LSTM_{hier}(F_t, A_t, B_t)$ of the hierarchical LSTM will be passed to the generator G, discriminator D and the monitor module (please refer to Sect. 4).

4   Monitoring with Auxiliary Tasks

Monitoring the success of a pouring sequence is a challenging task since subtle changes in states of the environment are hard to perceive. Intuitively, the initial object state and the hand dynamics are the strong cues for monitoring pouring process. We model the object and manipulator (i.e., hand) states implicitly by a hierarchical LSTM $LSTM_{hier}$ and introduce two auxiliary tasks, 3D trajectory forecasting (TF) and initial object state classification (IOSC). In this section, we describe the details of the two auxiliary tasks and our monitoring module.

4.1   Forecasting 3D Trajectory

Forecasting 3D trajectory is a path for us to learn to model the dynamics of the manipulator during the pouring sequence. The most naive way to predict trajectory is to train direct regression on demonstration sequences; however, the generated trajectory will be very limited to the data distribution of training data as the amount and the diversity of training data is limited. To model the distribution of successful demonstration and to generate more diverse trajectories, we introduce adversarial training loss L_{adv} proposed by Goodfellow et al. [44] here with a generator G to generate trajectory prediction and a discriminator D to distinguish if the input trajectory is generated or not (see Fig. 2).

Generator. Taking the encoded feature h_t from $LSTM_{hier}$ as input, our generator predicts next-step trajectory $X'_{t+1} = G_{\theta_G}(h_t)$ as output, where G_{θ_G} is a three-layer fully-connected feed-forward network parametrized by θ_G. Our generator has two objectives:

(1) Generate the trajectory which is close to the ground truth demonstration. (modeled by the regression loss). (2) Fool discriminator with the generated trajectory (modeled by the adversarial loss).

Thus, our loss function for the generator can be derived as follows,

$$L_{Gen} = L_{reg} + \lambda * L_{adv}, \tag{1}$$

where λ is the weighting between the two different losses (we empirically set λ to 1), L_{reg} is the regression loss, and L_{adv} stands for the adversarial loss.

The regression loss is defined as follows,

$$L_{reg} = \frac{1}{T-1} \sum_{t=1}^{T-1} dist(X_{t+1}, G_{\theta_G}(h_t)), \tag{2}$$

where $dist()$ is the distance function, X_{t+1} is the ground truth trajectory, $G_{\theta_G}(h_t)$ is the generated trajectory, and T denotes the total time steps of the sequence. Recall the trajectory X_{t+1} is composed of two parts, position $P = (p_x, p_y, p_z)$ and rotation $R = (r_x, r_y, r_z)$; likewise $G_{\theta_G}(h_t) = (P', R')$, where $P' = (p'_x, p'_y, p'_z)$, $R' = (r'_x, r'_y, r'_z)$.

The distance function is defined as

$$dist(X_{t+1}, G_{\theta_G}(h_t)) = MSE(P, P') + \sum_{k=x,y,z} (1 - \cos(r_k - r'_k)), \tag{3}$$

where MSE denotes Mean Squared Error. Here we use different distance metrics for rotation and translation because adopting cosine distance in angular difference is more reasonable. In particular, the cosine distance between $359°$ and $0°$ is small, but its mean square error is large. Note that we empirically adopt the same weighting for the position loss and rotation loss since the effect of different weightings is marginal on the performance.

The adversarial loss is defined as follows,

$$L_{adv} = \frac{1}{T-1} \sum_{t=1}^{T-1} -\log D_{\theta_D}(h_t, G_{\theta_G}(h_t)), \tag{4}$$

where D_{θ_D} is the discriminator of our model and will be elaborated later.

Discriminator. In training time, the discriminator takes both the encoded feature at that time step h_t and the predicted trajectory $X'_{t+1} = G_{\theta_G}(h_t)$ from the generator or ground truth trajectory X_{t+1} as inputs with the objective of catching generated trajectory from the generator. Adopting similar design from the generator, our discriminator D_{θ_D} is also modeled with a three-layer fully-connected feed-forward network parameterized by θ_D. The discriminator loss is defined as follows,

$$L_{Dis} = \frac{1}{T-1} \sum_{t=1}^{T-1} [-\log(D_{\theta_D}(h_t, X_{t+1})) - \log(1 - D_{\theta_D}(h_t, G_{\theta_G}(h_t)))] \tag{5}$$

In testing time, given the encoded feature h_t and generated trajectory X'_{t+1} of the certain time step t, the discriminator will predict the score $d_t = D_{\theta_D}(h_t, X'_{t+1}), t \in 1 \sim T-1$ of whether the input sequence is generated or not.

4.2   Initial Object State Classification

As we mention above, hand motion and initial object states are the two strong cues for monitoring pouring sequences. Learning the embedding of the data sequence is critical since the amount of training data is limited. To learn a good representation for monitoring, we train the classification on the initial object state based on the hidden encoding from the hierarchical LSTM $LSTM_{hier}$ in the end of each successful demonstration sequence (see Fig. 2) as follows,

$$q = \text{Softmax}(\theta_q, h_{T-1}), \tag{6}$$

$$z' = \arg\max_{c \in \mathcal{Z}} q(c), \tag{7}$$

$$L_{cls} = -\log q(z), \tag{8}$$

where h_{T-1} is the hidden encoding at the last time step of the sequence, θ_q is the parameter of the classifier and $q \in R^{|\mathcal{Z}|}$ is the softmax probability of initial object states in $\mathcal{Z}$. z' is the prediction of the initial object state and z denotes the ground truth initial object state. In our case, $|\mathcal{Z}| = 36$, which means there are 36 variations of initial object states (details can be referred to Sect. 5).

4.3   Monitoring Module

We propose a monitoring module M, which is designed as a single-layer network to predict whether a pouring sequence is a success or not given the hidden representation h_t from $LSTM_{hier}$ and the discriminator score d_t as inputs (see Fig. 2). The output of the monitoring module is defined as,

$$y'_t = M_{\theta_M}(h_t, d_t), \tag{9}$$

where θ_M is the parameter of M and y'_t is the prediction of success or failure. We train our monitoring module with cross-entropy loss. The architecture of our monitoring module is compact and effective since our model has already learned powerful feature that can capture the appearance changes and hand dynamics during the pouring process through auxiliary tasks.

4.4   Implementation Details

We use ResNet50 [43] trained on ImageNet [45] as the visual feature extractor. The input size of $LSTM_{img}$ is 2048, and the input size of both $LSTM_{pos}$ and $LSTM_{rot}$ are $3N$ ($N = 38$ in our case). $LSTM_{img}$ hidden size is 512, and both $LSTM_{pos}$ and $LSTM_{rot}$ hidden size are 128. The second layer of hierarchical LSTM has its hidden size 512. Generator G and discriminator D are the 3-layered fully-connected network with each layer of size 128. Monitor module is a fully-connected layer of size 256. We train our model for 3000 epochs with batch size 24. Learning rate is $1e^{-4}$. We optimize all objectives with equal weightings.

5   Dataset

In order to examine our method on monitoring whether the pouring sequence belongs to successful/failure sequences, we collect both successful and failure pouring sequences with our multimodal sensing system. We have one chest-mounted camera to capture the first-person view observation; one wrist-mounted

6DOF IMU sensor and one tracker of the HTC Vive motion tracking system on the right wrist to catch both the motion observation and the ground truth trajectory simultaneously. Figure 4a is the illustration of the devices on the demonstrator. We illustrate how we collect different kinds of demonstrations below.

Variations of Pouring Sequences. Our single pouring sequence consists of pouring liquid from the source container with initial liquid amount α to target container with β amount of liquid. Similar to [7], we roughly divide the container states into discrete labels. In successful sequences, the demonstrator tries to fill target container with the liquid in the source container without spilling out any liquid. If target container is filled to about 80% full, the demonstration will stop even if there is still liquid left in the source container. For single demonstrator, we will record the demonstrations with different kinds of containers and different initial liquid amounts to obtain more diverse demonstrations. For source container, we use 4 different containers b, c, d, e in Fig. 4b with three different initial liquid amount α: {10%, 50%, 80%}. We use container a in Fig. 4b as the target container with three different initial liquid amount β: {0%, 30%, 50%}. Combining the different settings in source container, α, and β, we can obtain total 36 different initial object states. In practice, we will record 5 repeated sequences for each initial object state setting. As a result, for a single demonstrator, we can obtain 180 demonstration sequences.

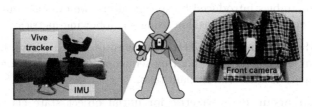

(a) Our multimodal sensing systema

(b) Variations of initial settings

Fig. 4. Settings to collect our dataset. (a) A camera is mounted on the chest to capture visual images. On the wrist, there is a vive tracker and an IMU sensor. (b) We use these containers to create variations of initial settings (details in Sect. 5)

Pouring Styles. In addition to different variations in the liquid amount and container appearances, we collect demonstrations conducted by 5 different demonstrators to ensure the diversity in pouring styles from person to person.

Failure Sequences. In general, there can be many ways to conduct a failure sequence. However, to model the monitoring tasks, we choose one of the most common mistakes made by humans during the pouring sequences: *Spill out* (The demonstrator accidentally spill out some liquid during the pouring action.) Regarding the variations and pouring styles, we use the same settings from the successful sequences: (1) 5 repeated sequences for each of 36 variations. (2) 5 different demonstrators to ensure diverse pouring behaviors. Hence, the total amount of demonstration is $2 * 5 * 5 * 36 = 1800$.

6   Experiments

In this section, we introduce the evaluation metrics and settings used in our experiments. We then describe our monitoring experiments and discuss our experimental results with ablation studies.

6.1   Metrics

In our experiments, we observe that prediction varies a lot across users and thus, to eliminate bias introduced by specific users, we evaluate our model in a leave-one-out cross-validation fashion using the following metrics:

Success/Failure accuracy — metric for monitor task. It shows how well the model discriminates a successful pouring sequence from a failed one. It directly indicates the performance of our main task.

Classification accuracy — metric for initial object state classification. It shows how well the model recognizes what kinds of container and amount of liquid in the containers in a pouring sequence.

Regression error — metric for trajectory forecasting. It is the error between 6-dimensional 3D trajectories recorded by HTC Vive and predicted 3D trajectories. Note that due to distinct properties of position and rotation error, the two errors are calculated separately.

6.2   Setting Variants

To study the effectiveness of each independent component in our network, we evaluate different settings described below in the following experiments.

Vanilla RNN: Our fusion RNN without auxiliary tasks. The model is a LSTM encoder (see Subsect. 3.2) followed by fully-connected layers. The fully-connected layers perform success/failure classification based on the encoded features.

RNN w/ IOSC: Our fusion RNN with an auxiliary task, initial object state classification (IOSC). The details of IOSC are described in Subsect. 4.2.

RNN w/ TF: Our fusion RNN with an auxiliary task, trajectory forecasting (TF). The details of TF are described in Subsect. 4.1.

Ours w/o adv.: Our fusion RNN with two proposed auxiliary tasks, initial object state classification and trajectory forecasting. In this setting, we treat one-step trajectory forecasting as a regression task (see Eq. 2).

Ours: Our fusion RNN with two proposed auxiliary tasks, initial object state classification and trajectory forecasting. In this setting, we introduce the adversarial training loss (see Eq. 4) to generate more diverse trajectories.

6.3 Monitoring Liquid Pouring

We consider 3 scenarios to test our method's generalization ability. Firstly, we assume that our model is used to monitor a specific group of users with a specific set of containers. Then, in a more challenging scenario, we assume the model need to monitor unseen containers as well. Finally, we consider that the model needs to monitor unseen users. More details are described below.

Cross Trial Experiment. This experiment is the most simple case. Models are trained and tested on data of the same group of users with the same container set, but training data and testing data are collected from different trials of pouring. In this easiest scenario, success/failure classification poses minor challenge here and is well solved. From Table 1, we can see that our method generates better performance on monitoring than the baseline method (i.e. *vanilla RNN*), which lacks two auxiliary tasks.

Cross Container Experiment. This is a common scenario that may occur in the real use case. When using different containers to pour liquid, the whole pouring sequences may be very different. For instance, there are huge changes in the appearance and the pouring trajectories between the case of the teapot and the bottle. We run leave-one-out cross-validation on the 4 different source containers to test whether our model can generalize to unseen containers. The initial states are only related to the liquid amount in the source (10%, 50%, 80%) and target container (0%, 30%, 50%), so we have 9 initial states (rather than 36 states) in total. The results in Table 2 show that our method achieves better performance on monitoring than the baseline method, since it successfully catches the change of states and the hand dynamics during the pouring sequence.

Cross User Experiment. This is the most challenging scenario, since different demonstrators may have very different pouring styles. Considering a specific set of containers, models are trained on data of 4 different users and tested on 1 user other than the 4 users in training set. The main difference among cross-user data is the variance in pouring styles. To be more precise, this experiment examines generalization ability in IMU sensor data sequences. By looking at success/failure accuracy shown in Table 3, we can find that both auxiliary tasks, initial-state classification and trajectory forecasting, brings considerable improvement in monitoring object manipulation. From Fig. 6, we can observe that our model's prediction correctly follows the visual cues. Initial object state classification helps the model know what the source container and the target container are, and the amount of liquid in both containers. Trajectory forecasting helps the model learn local dynamics of pouring sequences. Remarkably, by comparing our method and *Ours w/o adv.*, we can find that adversarial training introduced in our method significantly boosts initial state classification and slightly improves trajectory forecasting. From the results, we infer that there is implicitly-shared knowledge between the two auxiliary tasks and a more robust trajectory forecasting may enhance initial state classification. Adversarial training does help regarding obtaining a better understanding of pouring behaviors and increase the performance of our model in monitoring task.

Table 1. The results of cross trial experiments

	Succ./fail. acc.	Classification acc.	Position error	Rotation error
Vanilla RNN	99.65%	*N/A*	*N/A*	*N/A*
Ours w/o adv.	100%	96.50%	0.020 m	7.58°
Ours	100%	96.07%	0.020 m	**6.80°**

Table 2. The results of cross container experiments

	Succ./fail. acc.	Classification acc.	Position error	Rotation error
Vanilla RNN	89.16%	*N/A*	*N/A*	*N/A*
Ours w/o adv.	96.45%	63.92%	0.040 m	11.11°
Ours	**97.11%**	**67.69%**	**0.038 m**	11.30°

Table 3. The results of cross user experiments

	Succ./fail. acc.	Classification acc.	Position error	Rotation error
Vanilla RNN	81.95%	*N/A*	*N/A*	*N/A*
RNN w/ IOSC	89.25%	68.51%	*N/A*	*N/A*
RNN w/ TF	90.82%	*N/A*	0.033 m	14.15°
Ours w/o adv.	92.97%	64.15%	0.033 m	14.20°
Ours	**93.25%**	**75.69 %**	0.033 m	**14.06°**

6.4   Discussion

In this section, we further discuss each component in our network and the future feasibilities. Firstly, we do ablation study on LSTM architecture under the cross-user scenario, comparing the hierarchical LSTM (see Subsect. 3.2) to a 2-layer LSTM. The latter one is an early fusion method that data from different modalities is directly concatenated together and fed into the 2-layer LSTM. The results

Table 4. Ablation study on LSTM architecture

LSTM architecture	Succ./fail. acc.	Classification acc.	Position error	Rotation error
2-*layer*	87.06%	58.92%	0.033 m	14.72°
hierachical	**93.25%**	**75.69%**	0.033 m	**14.06°**

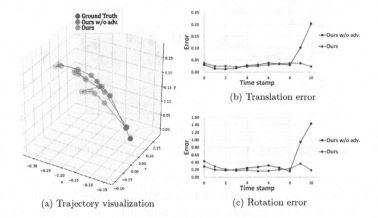

(a) Trajectory visualization   (b) Translation error

(c) Rotation error

Fig. 5. Trajectory forecasting comparison between "*Ours w/o adv.*" and "*Ours*". (a) Ground truth, "*Ours w/o adv.*" and "*Ours*" are shown in blue, orange and green, respectively. Time is visualized as color intensity goes from dark to light. Apparently, "*Ours w/o adv.*" failed to forecast the trajectory at a later stage of liquid pouring, while "*Ours*" can still follow the trend. (b)(c) "*Ours*" and "*Ours w/o adv.*" have comparable errors at early steps, but the former one performs better in later steps (Color figure online)

in Table 4 show that the hierarchical LSTM with late fusion outperforms the naive 2-layer LSTM in all tasks and this may be due to the capability of the hierarchical LSTM to handle scale difference and imbalanced dimension among multimodal inputs.

Secondly, we study the effect of the adversarial loss to the whole network. Recall that we introduce adversarial loss since there are multiple feasible trajectories for each data sample. However, these errors assume that there is only one truth position and rotation of each testing sample. As mentioned above, our model learns a more general concept and will predict trajectory based on common knowledge considering pouring, whereas prediction of "*Ours w/o adv.*" heavily relies on knowledge of seen trajectories and will drastically fail if testing pouring sequences have little in common with training data. This can be observed in Fig. 5a. Also, the adversarial loss will allow the model to generate more diverse trajectories, which means the model will observe more diverse hidden states in later steps. The trajectory forecasting errors in Fig. 5b and c show that "*Ours*" and "*Ours w/o adv.*" have comparable errors at early steps, but the former one perform better in later steps.

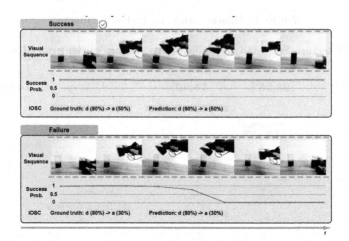

Fig. 6. Monitoring along time. The prediction correctly follows the visual cues

Our experiments show that introducing auxiliary tasks is beneficial for understanding the subtle liquid pouring task. By implicitly modeling the environmental states and hand dynamics, we improve liquid pouring monitoring significantly. We believe the general idea applies to other subtle manipulating tasks like opening doors, driving nails and cutting bread. Intuitively speaking, opening doors also involves mapping visual (e.g., what types of doors) and non-visual (e.g., hand motion) observations into environmental states to facilitate monitoring whether the door is opened. Monitoring different tasks may need different auxiliary tasks to make use of rich sensories in order to learn both visual and non-visual signals.

7   Conclusion

In this work, we aim at learning to monitor whether liquid pouring is successful (e.g., not spilling) or not using synchronized visual and IMU signals. We propose a novel method containing two auxiliary tasks during training: inferring (1) the initial state of containers and (2) forecasting the one-step future 3D trajectory of the hand with an adversarial training procedure. These tasks encourage our method to learn representation sensitive to container states and how objects are manipulated in 3D. On our newly collected liquid pouring dataset, our method achieves ∼8% and ∼11% better monitoring accuracy than the baseline method without auxiliary tasks on unseen containers and unseen users respectively.

Acknowledgement. We thank Stanford University for collaboration. We also thank MOST 107-2634-F-007-007, Panasonic and MediaTeK for their support.

References

1. Kubricht, J., Jiang, C., Zhu, Y., Zhu, S.C., Terzopoulos, D., Lu, H.: Probabilistic simulation predicts human performance on viscous fluid-pouring problem. In: CogSci (2016)
2. Bates, C.J., Yildirim, I., Tenenbaum, J.B., Battaglia, P.W.: Humans predict liquid dynamics using probabilistic simulation. In: CogSci (2015)
3. Edmonds, M., et al.: Feeling the force: integrating force and pose for fluent discovery through imitation learning to open medicine bottles. In: IROS (2017)
4. Abu-El-Haija, S., et al.: Youtube-8m: a large-scale video classification benchmark. arXiv:1609.08675 (2016)
5. Heilbron, F.C., Escorcia, V., Ghanem, B., Niebles, J.C.: Activitynet: a large-scale video benchmark for human activity understanding. In: CVPR (2015)
6. Alayrac, J.B., Sivic, J., Laptev, I., Lacoste-Julien, S.: Joint discovery of object states and manipulating actions. In: ICCV (2017)
7. Mottaghi, R., Schenck, C., Fox, D., Farhadi, A.: See the glass half full: Reasoning about liquid containers, their volume and content. In: ICCV (2017)
8. Nishida, N., Nakayama, H.: Multimodal gesture recognition using multi-stream recurrent neural network. In: Bräunl, T., McCane, B., Rivera, M., Yu, X. (eds.) PSIVT 2015. LNCS, vol. 9431, pp. 682–694. Springer, Cham (2016). https://doi.org/10.1007/978-3-319-29451-3_54
9. Soomro, K., Zamir, A.R., Shah, M.: Ucf101: a dataset of 101 human actions classes from videos in the wild. arXiv:1212.0402 (2012)
10. Kuehne, H., Jhuang, H., Garrote, E., Poggio, T., Serre, T.: Hmdb: a large video database for human motion recognition. In: ICCV (2011)
11. Gu, C., et al.: AVA: a video dataset of spatio-temporally localized atomic visual actions. In: CVPR (2018)
12. Rohrbach, M., Amin, S., Andriluka, M., Schiele, B.: A database for fine grained activity detection of cooking activities. In: CVPR (2012)
13. Chéron, G., Laptev, I., Schmid, C.: P-CNN: pose-based CNN features for action recognition. In: ICCV (2015)
14. Jhuang, H., Gall, J., Zuffi, S., Schmid, C., Black, M.J.: Towards understanding action recognition. In: ICCV (2013)
15. Vu, T.-H., Olsson, C., Laptev, I., Oliva, A., Sivic, J.: Predicting actions from static scenes. In: Fleet, D., Pajdla, T., Schiele, B., Tuytelaars, T. (eds.) ECCV 2014. LNCS, vol. 8693, pp. 421–436. Springer, Cham (2014). https://doi.org/10.1007/978-3-319-10602-1_28
16. Zhang, Y., Qu, W., Wang, D.: Action-scene model for human action recognition from videos (2014)
17. Moore, D.J., Essa, I.A., Hayes, M.H.: Exploiting human actions and object context for recognition tasks. In: ICCV (1999)
18. Delaitre, V., Sivic, J., Laptev, I.: Learning person-object interactions for action recognition in still images. In: NIPS (2011)
19. Gupta, A., Kembhavi, A., Davis, L.S.: Observing human-object interactions: using spatial and functional compatibility for recognition. In: TPAMI (2009)
20. Gupta, A., Davis, L.S.: Objects in action: an approach for combining action understanding and object perception. In: CVPR (2007)

21. Fathi, A., Rehg, J.M.: Modeling actions through state changes. In: CVPR (2013)
22. Bambach, S., Lee, S., Crandall, D.J., Yu, C.: Lending a hand: detecting hands and recognizing activities in complex egocentric interactions. In: ICCV (2015)
23. Ma, M., Fan, H., Kitani, K.M.: Going deeper into first-person activity recognition. In: CVPR (2016)
24. Hu, J.F., Zheng, W.S., Lai, J., Zhang, J.: Jointly learning heterogeneous features for RGB-D activity recognition. In: CVPR (2015)
25. Lei, J., Ren, X., Fox, D.: Fine-grained kitchen activity recognition using RGB-D. In: UbiComp (2012)
26. Song, S., Cheung, N.M., Chandrasekhar, V., Mandal, B., Liri, J.: Egocentric activity recognition with multimodal fisher vector. In: Acoustics, Speech and Signal Processing (ICASSP). IEEE (2016)
27. de la Torre, F., Hodgins, J.K., Montano, J., Valcarcel, S.: Detailed human data acquisition of kitchen activities: the cmu-multimodal activity database (cmu-mmac). In: CHI Workshop (2009)
28. Roggen, D., et al.: Collecting complex activity datasets in highly rich networked sensor environments. In: INSS. IEEE (2010)
29. Zhou, Y., Ni, B., Hong, R., Wang, M., Tian, Q.: Interaction part mining: a mid-level approach for fine-grained action recognition. In: CVPR (2015)
30. Zhou, Y., Ni, B., Yan, S., Moulin, P., Tian, Q.: Pipelining localized semantic features for fine-grained action recognition. In: Fleet, D., Pajdla, T., Schiele, B., Tuytelaars, T. (eds.) ECCV 2014. LNCS, vol. 8692, pp. 481–496. Springer, Cham (2014). https://doi.org/10.1007/978-3-319-10593-2_32
31. Peng, X., Zou, C., Qiao, Y., Peng, Q.: Action recognition with stacked fisher vectors. In: Fleet, D., Pajdla, T., Schiele, B., Tuytelaars, T. (eds.) ECCV 2014. LNCS, vol. 8693, pp. 581–595. Springer, Cham (2014). https://doi.org/10.1007/978-3-319-10602-1_38
32. Sun, S., Kuang, Z., Sheng, L., Ouyang, W., Zhang, W.: Optical flow guided feature: a fast and robust motion representation for video action recognition. In: CVPR (2018)
33. Tran, D., Wang, H., Torresani, L., Ray, J., LeCun, Y., Paluri, M.: A closer look at spatiotemporal convolutions for action recognition. In: CVPR (2018)
34. Schenck, C., Fox, D.: Detection and tracking of liquids with fully convolutional networks. In: RSS workshop (2016)
35. Sermanet, P., Lynch, C., Hsu, J., Levine, S.: Time-contrastive networks: Self-supervised learning from multi-view observation. arXiv:1704.06888 (2017)
36. Yamaguchi, A., Atkeson, C.G.: Stereo vision of liquid and particle flow for robot pouring. In: Humanoids (2016)
37. Tamosiunaite, M., Nemec, B., Ude, A., Wrgtter, F.: Learning to pour with a robot arm combining goal and shape learning for dynamic movement primitives. In: IEEE-RAS (2011)
38. Rozo, L., Jimnez, P., Torras, C.: Force-based robot learning of pouring skills using parametric hidden markov models. In: 9th International Workshop on Robot Motion and Control (2013)
39. Brandi, S., Kroemer, O., Peters, J.: Generalizing pouring actions between objects using warped parameters. In: Humanoids (2014)
40. Schenck, C., Fox, D.: Visual closed-loop control for pouring liquids. In: ICRA (2017)
41. Yamaguchi, A., Atkeson, C.G.: Differential dynamic programming with temporally decomposed dynamics. In: IEEE-RAS (2015)

42. Kunze, L., Beetz, M.: Envisioning the qualitative effects of robot manipulation actions using simulation-based projections. Artif. Intell. **247**, 352–380 (2017)
43. He, K., Zhang, X., Ren, S., Sun, J.: Deep residual learning for image recognition. In: CVPR (2016)
44. Goodfellow, I., et al.: Generative adversarial nets. In: NIPS (2014)
45. Deng, J., Dong, W., Socher, R., Li, L.J., Li, K., Fei-Fei, L.: ImageNet: a large-scale hierarchical image database. In: CVPR (2009)

Weakly Supervised Region Proposal Network and Object Detection

Peng Tang[1], Xinggang Wang[1], Angtian Wang[1], Yongluan Yan[1],
Wenyu Liu[1(✉)], Junzhou Huang[2,3], and Alan Yuille[4]

[1] School of EIC, Huazhong University of Science and Technology, Wuhan, China
{pengtang,xgwang,angtianwang,yongluanyan,liuwy}@hust.edu.cn
[2] Tencent AI lab, Shenzhen, China
[3] Department of CSE, University of Texas at Arlington, Arlington, USA
jzhuang75@gmail.com
[4] Department of Computer Science, The Johns Hopkins University, Baltimore, USA
alan.l.yuille@gmail.com

Abstract. The Convolutional Neural Network (CNN) based region proposal generation method (*i.e.* region proposal network), trained using bounding box annotations, is an essential component in modern fully supervised object detectors. However, Weakly Supervised Object Detection (WSOD) has not benefited from CNN-based proposal generation due to the absence of bounding box annotations, and is relying on standard proposal generation methods such as selective search. In this paper, we propose a weakly supervised region proposal network which is trained using only image-level annotations. The weakly supervised region proposal network consists of two stages. The first stage evaluates the objectness scores of sliding window boxes by exploiting the low-level information in CNN and the second stage refines the proposals from the first stage using a region-based CNN classifier. Our proposed region proposal network is suitable for WSOD, can be plugged into a WSOD network easily, and can share its convolutional computations with the WSOD network. Experiments on the PASCAL VOC and ImageNet detection datasets show that our method achieves the state-of-the-art performance for WSOD with performance gain of about 3% on average.

Keywords: Object detection · Region proposal
Weakly supervised learning · Convolutional neural network

1 Introduction

Convolutional Neural Networks (CNNs) [22,24] in conjunction with large scale datasets with detailed bounding box annotations [14,26,32] have contributed

---

Electronic supplementary material The online version of this chapter (https://doi.org/10.1007/978-3-030-01252-6_22) contains supplementary material, which is available to authorized users.

V. Ferrari et al. (Eds.): ECCV 2018, LNCS 11215, pp. 370–386, 2018.
https://doi.org/10.1007/978-3-030-01252-6_22

to a giant leap forward for object detection [15,16,30,37,43]. However, it is very laborious and expensive to collect bounding box annotations. By contrast, images with only image-level annotations, indicating whether an image belongs to an object class or not, are much easier to acquire (*e.g.*, using keywords to search on the Internet). Inspired by this fact, in this paper we focus on training object detectors with only image-level supervisions, *i.e.*, Weakly Supervised Object Detection (WSOD).

The most popular pipeline for WSOD has three main steps [4,5,9,12,20,21, 25,34,38,39,42]: region proposal generation (shortened to proposal generation) to generate a set of candidate boxes that may cover objects, proposal feature extraction to extract features from these proposals, and proposal classification to classify each proposal as an object class, or background. Various studies focus on proposing better proposal classification methods [4,9,41,42]. Recently, some methods have trained the last two steps jointly and have achieved great improvements [5,21,38,39].

But most of the previous studies only use standard methods, *e.g.* selective search [40] and Edge Boxes [46], to generate proposals. A previous work [17] has shown that the quality of the proposals has great influence on the performance of fully supervised object detection (*i.e.*, using bounding box annotations for training). In addition, the CNN-based region proposal generation method (*i.e.* region proposal network) [30] is an essential component in the state-of-the-art fully supervised object detectors. These motivate us to improve the proposal generation method, in particular to propose CNN-based methods for WSOD.

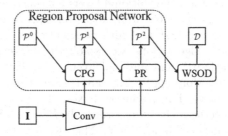

Fig. 1. The overall network architecture. "**I**": input image; "$\mathcal{P}^0$": the initial proposals by sliding window, "$\mathcal{P}^1$": the proposals from the first stage of the network, "$\mathcal{P}^2$": the proposals from the second stage of the network, "$\mathcal{D}$": the detection results, "Conv": convolutional layers, "CPG": coarse proposal generation, "PR": proposal refinement, "WSOD": weakly supervised object detection

In this paper, we focus on proposal generation for WSOD, and propose a novel weakly supervised region proposal network which generates proposals by CNNs trained under weak supervisions. Due to the absence of bounding box annotations, we are unable to train a region proposal network end-to-end as in Faster RCNN [30]. Instead, we decompose the proposal network into two stages, where the first stage is coarse proposal generation which generates proposals $\mathcal{P}^1$

from sliding window boxes $\mathcal{P}^0$ ($|\mathcal{P}^0| > |\mathcal{P}^1|$), and the second stage is proposal refinement which refines proposals $\mathcal{P}^1$ to generate more accurate proposals $\mathcal{P}^2$ ($|\mathcal{P}^1| > |\mathcal{P}^2|$). The proposals $\mathcal{P}^2$ are fed into the WSOD network to produce detection results $\mathcal{D}$. In addition, the proposal network and the WSOD network are integrated into a single three-stage network, see Fig. 1.

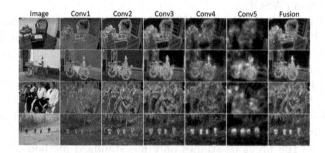

Fig. 2. The responses of different convolutional layers from the VGG16 [36] network trained on the ImageNet [32] dataset using only image-level annotations. Results from left to right are original images, response from the first to the fifth layers, and the fusion of responses from the second layer to the fourth layer

The first stage of our method is motivated by the intuition that CNNs trained for object recognition contain latent object location information. For example, as shown in Fig. 2, the early convolutional layers concentrate on low-level vision features (*e.g.* edges) and the later layers focus on more semantic features (*e.g.* object itself). Because the first and fifth convolutional layers also have high responses on many non-edge regions, we exploit the low-level information only from the second to the fourth convolutional layers to produce edge-like responses, as illustrated in Fig. 2. More specifically, after generating initial proposals $\mathcal{P}^0$ from an exhaustive set of sliding window boxes, these edge-like responses are used to evaluate objectness scores of proposals $\mathcal{P}^0$ (*i.e.* the probability of a proposal being an object), following [46]. Then we obtain some proposals $\mathcal{P}^1$ accordingly.

However, the proposals generated above are still very coarse because the early convolutional layers also fire on background regions. To address this, we refine the proposals $\mathcal{P}^1$ in the second stage. We train a region-based CNN classifier, which is a small WSOD network [38], using $\mathcal{P}^1$, and adapt the network to distinguish whether $\mathcal{P}^1$ are object or background regions instead of to detect objects. The objectness scores of proposals in $\mathcal{P}^1$ are re-evaluated using the classifier. Proposals with high objectness scores are more likely to be objects, which generates the refined proposals $\mathcal{P}^2$. We do not use the region-based CNN classifier on the sliding window boxes directly, because this requires an enormous number of sliding window boxes to ensure high recall and it is hard for a region-based CNN classifier to handle such a large number of boxes efficiently.

The proposals $\mathcal{P}^2$ are used to train the third stage WSOD network to produce detection results $\mathcal{D}$. To make the proposal generation efficient for WSOD, we adapt the alternating training strategy in Faster RCNN [30] to integrate the proposal network and the WSOD network into a single network. More precisely, we alternate the training of the proposal network and the WSOD network, and share the convolutional features between the two networks. After that, the convolutional computations for proposal generation and WSOD are shared, which improves the computational efficiency.

Elaborate experiments are carried out on the challenging PASCAL VOC [14] and ImageNet [32] detection datasets. Our method obtains the state-of-the-art performance on all these datasets, e.g., 50.4% mAP and 68.4% CorLoc on the PASCAL VOC 2007 dataset which surpass previous best performed methods by more than 3%.

In summary, the main contributions of our work are listed as follows.

- We confirm that CNNs contain latent object location information which we exploit to generate proposals for WSOD.
- We propose a two-stage region proposal network for proposal generation in WSOD, where the first stage exploits the low-level information from the early convolutional layers to generate proposals and the second stage is a region-based CNN classifier to refine the proposals from the first stage.
- We adapt the alternating training strategy [30] to share convolutional computations among the proposal network and WSOD network for testing efficiency, and thus the proposal network and WSOD network are integrated into a single network.
- Our method obtains the state-of-the-art performance on the PASCAL VOC and ImageNet detection datasets for WSOD.

2   Related Work

Weakly Supervised Object Detection/Localization. WSOD has attracted a great deal of attention in recent years [4,5,9,12,20,21,34,38,39,41,42]. Most methods adopt a three step pipeline: proposal generation, proposal feature extraction, and proposal classification. Based on this pipeline, many variants have been introduced to give better proposal classification, e.g., multiple instance learning based approaches [4,9,34,39,42]. Recently, inspired by the great success of CNNs, many methods train a WSOD network by integrating the last two steps (i.e. proposal feature extraction and proposal classification) into a single network [5,12,21,38]. These networks show more promising results than the step-by-step ones. However, most of these methods use off-the-shelf methods [40,46] for the proposal generation step. Unlike them, we propose a better proposal generation method for WSOD. More specifically, we propose a weakly supervised region proposal network which generates object proposals by CNN trained under weak supervisions, and integrate the proposal network and WSOD network into a single network. This relates to the work by Diba et al. [12] who propose a cascaded convolutional network to select some of the most reliable proposals for WSOD.

They first generate a set of proposals by Edge Boxes [46], and then choose a few most confident proposals according to class activation map from [44] or segmentation map from [2]. These chosen proposals are used to train multiple instance learning classifiers. Unlike them, we use CNN to generate proposals, and refine proposals using region-based CNN classifiers. In fact, their network can be used as our WSOD network.

Recently, some studies show a similar intuition that CNNs trained under weak supervisions contain object location information and try to localize objects without proposals [10,18,27,35,44,45]. For example, Oquab et al. [27] train a max-pooling based multiple instance learning network to localize objects. But they can only give coarse locations of objects which are independent of object sizes and aspect ratios. The methods in [10,35,44,45] localize objects by first generating object score heatmaps and then placing bounding boxes around the high response regions. However, they mainly test their methods on the ImageNet localization dataset which contains a large portion of iconic-object images (i.e., a single large object located in the center of an image). Considering that natural images (e.g. images in PASCAL VOC) contain several different objects located anywhere in the image, the performance of these methods can be limited compared with the proposal-based methods [5,12,21,38]. Zhu et al. [45] also suggest a soft proposal method for weakly supervised object localization. They use a graph-based method to generate an objectness map that indicates whether each point on the map belongs to an object or not. However, the method cannot generate "real" proposals, i.e., generate boxes which cover as many as possible objects in images. Our method differs from these methods in that we generate a set of proposals using CNNs which potentially cover objects tightly (i.e., have high Intersection-over-Union with groundtruth object boxes) and use the proposals for WSOD in complex images. In addition, all these methods focus on the later convolutional layers that contain more semantic information, whereas our method exploits the low-level information from the early layers.

Region Proposal Generation. There are many works focusing on region proposal generation [6,29,40,46], where Selective Search (SS) [40] and Edge Boxes (EB) [46] are two most commonly used proposal generation methods for WSOD. The SS generates proposals based on a superpixel merging method. The EB generates proposals by first extracting image edges and then evaluating the objectness scores of sliding window boxes. Our method follows the EB for objectness score evaluation in the first stage. But unlike EB which adopts edge detectors trained on datasets with pixel-level edge annotations [13] to ensure high proposal recall, we exploit the low-level information in CNNs to generate edge-like responses, and use a region-based CNN classifier to refine the proposals. Experimental results show that our method obtains much better WSOD performance.

There are already some CNN-based proposal generation methods [23,28,30]. For example, the Region Proposal Network (RPN) [30] uses bounding box annotations as supervisions to train a proposal network, where the training targets are to classify some sliding window style boxes (*i.e.* anchor boxes) as object or background and regress the box locations to the real object locations. These RPN-like proposals are standard for recent fully supervised object detectors. However, to ensure their high performance, these methods require bounding box annotations [23,31] and even pixel-level annotations [28] to train their networks, which deviates from the requirement of WSOD that only image-level annotations are available during training. Instead, we show that CNNs trained under weak supervisions have the potential to generate very satisfactory proposals.

Others. The works by [3,33] also show that the different CNN layers contain different level visual information. Unlike our approach, Bertasius *et al.* [3] aim to fuse information from different layers for better edge detection which requires pixel-level edge annotations for training. Saleh *et al.* [33] choose more semantic layers (*i.e.* later layers) as foreground priors to guide the training of weakly supervised semantic segmentation, whereas we show that the low-level cues can be used for proposal generation.

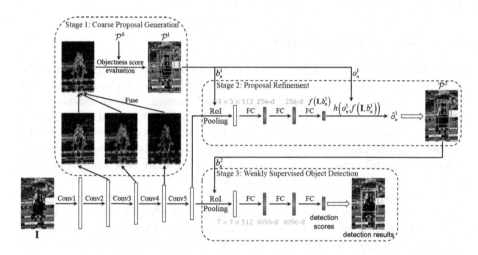

Fig. 3. The detailed architecture of our network. The first stage "Coarse Proposal Generation" produces edge-like responses which can evaluate objectness scores of sliding window boxes $\mathcal{P}^0$ to generate coarse proposals $\mathcal{P}^1$. The second stage "Proposal Refinement" uses a small region-based CNN classifier to re-evaluate the objectness scores of each proposal in $\mathcal{P}^1$ to get refined proposals $\mathcal{P}^2$. The third stage "Weakly Supervised Object Detection" uses a large region-based CNN classifier to classify each proposal in $\mathcal{P}^2$ as different object classes or background, to produce the object detection results. The proposals $\mathcal{P}^t, t \in \{0,1,2\}$ consist of boxes $\{b_n^t\}_{n=0}^{N^t}$ and objectness scores $\{o_n^t\}_{n=0}^{N^t}$

3   Method

The architecture of our network is shown in Figs. 1 and 3. Our architecture consists of three stages during testing, where the first and second stages are the region proposal network for proposal generation and the third stage is a WSOD network for object detection. For an image $\mathbf{I}$, given initial proposals $\mathcal{P}^0$ which are an exhaustive set of sliding window boxes, the coarse proposal generation stage generates some coarse proposals $\mathcal{P}^1$ from $\mathcal{P}^0$, see Sect. 3.1. The proposal refinement stage refines the proposals $\mathcal{P}^1$ to generate more accurate proposals $\mathcal{P}^2$, see Sect. 3.2. The WSOD stage classifies the proposals $\mathcal{P}^2$ to produce the detection results, see Sect. 3.3. The proposals consist of bounding boxes and objectness scores, $i.e.$, $\mathcal{P}^t = \{(b_n^t, o_n^t)\}_{n=1}^{N^t}, t \in \{0, 1, 2\}$, where b_n^t and o_n^t are the box coordinates and the objectness score of the n-th proposal respectively. $o_n^0 = 1, n \in \{1, ..., N^0\}$ because we have no prior knowledge on the locations of objects so we consider that all initial proposals have equal probability to cover objects. To share the conv parameters among different stages, we use an alternating training strategy, see Sect. 3.4.

3.1   Coarse Proposal Generation

Given the initial proposals $\mathcal{P}^0 = \{(b_n^0, o_n^0)\}_{n=1}^{N^0}$ of image $\mathbf{I}$ which are an exhaustive set of sliding window boxes with various sizes and aspect ratios, together the conv features of the image, the coarse proposal generation stage evaluates the objectness scores of these proposals coarsely and filters out most of the proposals that correspond to background. This stage needs to be very efficient because the number of initial proposals is usually very large (hundreds of thousands or even millions). Here we exploit the low-level information, more specifically the edge-like information from the CNN for this stage.

Let us start from Fig. 2. This visualizes the responses from different conv layers of the VGG16 network [36] trained on the ImageNet classification dataset (with only image-level annotations). Other networks have similar results and could also be chosen as alternates. Specially, we pass images forward through the network and compute the average value over the channel dimension for each conv layer to obtain five response maps (as there are five conv layers). Then these maps are resized to the original image size and are visualized as the second to the sixth columns in Fig. 2. As we can see, the early layers fire on low-level vision features such as edges. By contrast, the later layers tend to respond to more semantic features such as objects or object parts, and the response maps from these layers are similar to the saliency map. Obviously, these response maps provide useful information to localize objects. Here we propose to make use of the second to the fourth layers to produce edge-like response maps for proposal generation, as shown in Fig. 3.

More specifically, suppose the output feature map from a conv layer is $\mathbf{F} \in \mathbb{R}^{C \times W \times H}$, where C, W, H are the channel number, weight, and height of the feature map respectively. Then the response map $\mathbf{R} \in \mathbb{R}^{W \times H}$ of this layer is obtained by Eq. (1) which computes the average over the channels first and the normalization then, where f_{cwh} and r_{wh} are elements in $\mathbf{F}$ and $\mathbf{R}$ respectively.

$$r_{wh} = \frac{1}{C} \sum_{c=1}^{C} f_{cwh}, \; r_{wh} \leftarrow \frac{r_{wh}}{\max\limits_{w',h'} r_{w'h'}}. \tag{1}$$

As we can see in Fig. 2, both the second to the fourth conv layers have high responses on edges and relative low responses on other parts of the image. Hence we fuse the response maps from the second to the fourth conv layers by first resizing them to the original image size and sum them up, see the 7th column in Fig. 2 for examples. Accordingly we obtain the edge-like response map. We do not choose the response maps from the first and the fifth conv layers, because the former has high responses on most of the image regions and the later tends to fire on the whole object instead of the edges.

After obtaining the edge-like response map, we evaluate the objectness scores of the initial proposals $\mathcal{P}^0$ by using the Edge Boxes (EB) [46] to count the number of edges that exist in each initial proposal. More precisely, we follow the strategies in EB to generate $\mathcal{P}^0$, evaluate objectness scores, and perform Non-Maximum Suppression (NMS), so this stage is as efficient as Edge Boxes. Finally, we rank the proposals according to the evaluated objectness scores and choose N^1 ($N^1 < N^0$) proposals with the highest objectness scores. Accordingly we obtain the first stage proposals $\mathcal{P}^1 = \{(b_n^1, o_n^1)\}_{n=1}^{N^1}$.

In fact, the edge-like response map generated here is not the "real" edge in the sense of the edges generated by a fully supervised edge detector [13]. Therefore, directly using EB may not be optimal. We suspect that this stage can be further improved by designing more sophisticated proposal generation methods that consider the characteristics of the edge-like response map. In addition, responses from other layers can also be used as cues to localize objects, such as using saliency based methods [1]. Exploring these variants is left to future works and in this paper we show that our simple method is sufficient to generate satisfactory proposals for the following stages.

No direct loss is required in this stage and any trained network can be chosen.

3.2 Proposal Refinement

Proposals generated by the coarse proposal generation stage are still very noisy because there are also high responses on the background regions of the edge-like response map. To address this, we refine proposals using a region-based CNN classifier to re-evaluate the objectness scores, as shown in Figs. 1 and 3.

Given the proposals $\mathcal{P}^1 = \{(b_n^1, o_n^1)\}_{n=1}^{N^1}$ from the first stage and the conv features of the image, the task of the proposal refinement stage is to compute the probability that each proposal box b_n^1 covers an object using a region-based CNN classifier $f(\mathbf{I}, b_n^1)$, to re-evaluate the objectness score $\tilde{o}_n^1 = h\left(o_n^1, f(\mathbf{I}, b_n^1)\right)$, and to reject proposals with low scores. To do this, we first extract the conv feature map of b_n^1 and resize it to $512 \times 3 \times 3$ using the RoI pooling method [15]. After that, we pass the conv feature map through two 256-dimension Fully Connected (FC) layers to obtain the object proposal feature vector. Finally, an FC layer and a soft-max layer are used to distinguish whether the proposal is object or background (we omit the softmax layer in Fig. 3 for simplification). Accordingly we obtain proposals $\tilde{\mathcal{P}}^1 = \{(b_n^1, \tilde{o}_n^1)\}_{n=1}^{N^1}$ with re-evaluated objectness score $\tilde{o}_n^1$. Here we use a simple multiplication to compute $h(\cdot, \cdot)$ as in Eq. (2).

$$\tilde{o}_n^1 = h\left(o_n^1, f(\mathbf{I}, b_n^1)\right) = o_n^1 \cdot f(\mathbf{I}, b_n^1). \tag{2}$$

There are other possible choices like addition, but we find that multiplication works well in experiments.

To get final proposals we can simply rank the proposals according to the objectness score $\tilde{o}_n^1$ and select some proposals with top objectness scores. But there are many redundant proposals (i.e. highly overlapped proposals) in $\tilde{\mathcal{P}}^1$. Therefore, we apply NMS on $\tilde{\mathcal{P}}^1$ and keep N^2 proposals with the highest object-ness scores. Accordingly we obtain our refined proposals $\mathcal{P}^2 = \{(b_n^2, o_n^2)\}_{n=1}^{N^2}$.

To train the network using only image-level annotations, we train the state-of-the-art WSOD network given in [38], and adapt the network to compute $f(\mathbf{I}, b_n^1)$ instead of to detect objects. The network in [38] has a multiple instance learning stream which is trained by an image classification loss, and some instance clas-sifier refinement streams which encourage category coherence among spatially adjacent proposals. The loss to train the network in the second stage network has the form of $L^2(\mathbf{I}, \mathbf{y}, \mathcal{P}^1; \mathbf{\Theta}^2)$, where $\mathbf{y}$ is the image-level annotation and $\mathbf{\Theta}^2$ represents the parameters of the network. Please see [38] for more details. Other WSOD networks [5,12,21] can also be chosen as alternates. Specially, the output of proposal box b_n^1 by [38] is a probability vector $\mathbf{p}_n^1 = [p_{n0}^1, ..., p_{nK}^1]$, where p_{n0}^1 is for background, $p_{nk}^1, k > 0$ is for the k-th object class, and K is the number of object classes. We transfer this probability to the probability that b_n^1 covers an object by $f(\mathbf{I}, b_n^1) = 1 - p_{n0}^1 = \sum_{k=1}^{K} p_{nk}^1$. We use a smaller network than the original network in [38] to ensure the efficiency.

3.3   Weakly Supervised Object Detection

The final stage, i.e. WSOD, classifies proposals $\mathcal{P}^2$ into different object classes, or background. This is our ultimate goal. Similar to the previous stage, we use a region-based CNN for classification, see Fig. 3.

Given the proposals $\mathcal{P}^2 = \{(b_n^2, o_n^2)\}_{n=1}^{N^2}$ from the second stage and the conv features of the image, for each proposal box b_n^2, $512 \times 7 \times 7$ feature map and two 4096-dimension FC layers are used to extract the proposal features. Then a $\{K + 1\}$-dimension FC layer is used to classify the b_n^2 as one of the K object classes or background. Finally, NMS is used to remove redundant detection boxes and produces object detection results.

Here we also train the WSOD network given in [38] and make some improvements. Then the loss to train the third stage network has the form of $L^3(\mathbf{I}, \mathbf{y}, \mathcal{P}^2; \mathbf{\Theta}^3)$, where $\mathbf{\Theta}^3$ represents the parameters of the network. Both of the multiple instance detection stream and instance classifier refinement streams in

---

Algorithm 1. Proposal network training

Input: Training images with image-level annotations; an initial CNN network M^{init}.
Output: Proposal networks M^1, M^2; proposals $\mathcal{P}^2$.
1: Generate initial proposals $\mathcal{P}^0$ for each image and initialize M^1 by M^{init}.
2: Generate proposals $\mathcal{P}^1$ for each image using $\mathcal{P}^0$ and M^1.
3: Train the proposal network M^2 on M^{init} using $\mathcal{P}^1$.
4: Generate $\mathcal{P}^2$ for each image using $\mathcal{P}^1$ and M^2.

Algorithm 2. The alternating network training

Input: Training images with image-level annotations; M^{pre}.
Output: Proposal networks M^1, M^2; WSOD network M.
1: Train proposal networks M^1, M^2 on M^{pre} and generate proposals $\mathcal{P}^2$ for each image, see Algorithm 1.
2: Train WSOD network M' on M^{pre} using $\mathcal{P}^2$.
3: Re-train proposal networks M^1, M^2 on M', fix the parameters of conv layers, and re-generate proposals $\mathcal{P}^2$ for each image, see Algorithm 1.
4: Re-train WSOD network M on M' using $\mathcal{P}^2$ and fix the parameters of conv layers.

---

[38] produce proposal classification probabilities. Given a proposal box b_n^2, suppose the proposal classification probability vector from the multiple instance detection stream is φ_n, then similar to [5], we multiply φ_n by the objectness score o_n^2 during the training to exploit the prior object/background knowledge from the objectness score. More improvements are described in the supplementary material. We use the original version network in [38] rather than the smaller version in Sect. 3.2 for better detection performance.

3.4 The Overall Network Training

If we do not share the parameters of the conv layers among the different stages, then each proposal generation stage and the WSOD stage has its own separate network. Suppose M^{pre}, M^1, M^2, and M are the ImageNet pre-trained network, the proposal network for the first stage, the proposal network for the second stage, and the WSOD network for the third stage, respectively, we train the proposal networks and the WSOD network step-by-step, because in our architecture each network requires outputs generated from its previous network for training. That is, we first initialize M^1 by M^{pre} and generate $\mathcal{P}^1$, then use $\mathcal{P}^1$ to train M^2 and generate $\mathcal{P}^2$, and finally use $\mathcal{P}^2$ to train M.

Although we can use different networks for different stages, this would be very time-consuming during testing, because it requires passing image through three different networks. Therefore, w adapt the alternating network training strategy in Faster RCNN [30] in order to share parameters of conv layers among all stages. That is, after training the separate networks M^1, M^2, and M, we re-train proposal networks M^1 and M^2 on M, fixing the parameters of the conv layers. Then we generate proposals to train the WSOD network on M, also fixing the parameters of the conv layers. Accordingly the conv computations of all stages are shared. We summarize this procedure in Algorithm 2. It is obvious that the shared method is more efficient than the unshared method because it computes the conv features only one time rather than three times.

4 Experiments

In this section we will give experiments to analysis different components of our method and compare our method with previous state of the arts.

4.1 Experimental Setups

Datasets and Evaluation Metrics. We choose the challenging PASCAL VOC 2007, 2012 [14], and ImageNet [32] detection datasets for evaluation. We only use image-level annotations for training.

Table 1. Result comparison (AP and mAP in %) for different methods on the PASCAL VOC 2007 test set. The upper/lower part are results by single/multiple model. Our method obtains the best mAP. See Sect. 4.2 for definitions of the Ours-based methods

Method	aero	bike	bird	boat	bottle	bus	car	cat	chair	cow	table	dog	horse	mbike	person	plant	sheep	sofa	train	tv	mAP
WSDDN-VGG16 [5]	39.4	50.1	31.5	16.3	12.6	64.5	42.8	42.6	10.1	35.7	24.9	38.2	34.4	55.6	9.4	14.7	30.2	40.7	54.7	46.9	34.8
WSDDN+context [21]	57.1	52.0	31.5	7.6	11.5	55.0	53.1	34.1	1.7	33.1	49.2	**42.0**	47.3	56.6	15.3	12.8	24.8	48.9	44.4	47.8	36.3
OICR-VGG16 [38]	**58.0**	62.4	31.1	**19.4**	13.0	65.1	62.2	28.4	**24.8**	44.7	30.6	25.3	37.8	65.5	15.7	24.1	41.7	46.9	**64.3**	**62.6**	41.2
Ours-VGG16	57.9	**70.5**	**37.8**	5.7	**21.0**	66.1	69.2	**59.4**	3.4	57.1	**57.3**	35.2	**64.2**	68.6	**32.8**	28.6	50.8	49.5	41.1	30.0	**45.3**
WSDDN-Ens. [5]	46.4	58.3	35.5	25.9	14.0	66.7	53.0	39.2	8.9	41.8	26.6	38.6	44.7	59.0	10.8	17.3	40.7	49.6	56.9	50.8	39.3
OM+MIL+FRCNN [25]	54.5	47.4	41.3	20.8	17.7	51.9	63.5	46.1	**21.8**	57.1	22.1	34.4	50.5	61.8	16.2	**29.9**	40.7	15.9	55.3	40.2	39.5
WCCN [12]	49.5	60.6	38.6	**29.2**	16.2	**70.8**	56.9	42.5	10.9	44.1	29.9	**42.2**	47.9	64.1	13.8	23.5	45.9	54.1	**60.8**	54.5	42.8
HCP+DSD+OSSH3 [20]	54.2	52.0	35.2	25.9	15.0	59.6	67.9	**58.7**	10.1	**67.4**	27.3	37.8	54.8	67.3	5.1	19.7	52.6	43.5	56.9	**62.5**	43.7
OICR-Ens.+FRCNN [38]	**65.5**	67.2	**47.2**	21.6	22.1	68.0	68.5	35.9	5.7	63.1	49.5	30.3	64.7	66.1	13.0	25.6	50.0	**57.1**	60.2	59.0	47.0
Ours-Ens.	60.3	66.2	45.0	19.6	26.6	68.1	68.4	49.4	8.0	56.9	55.0	33.6	62.5	68.2	20.6	29.0	49.0	54.1	58.8	58.4	47.9
Ours-Ens.+FRCNN	63.0	**69.7**	40.8	11.6	**27.7**	70.5	**74.1**	58.5	10.0	66.7	**60.6**	34.7	**75.7**	**70.3**	25.7	26.5	**55.4**	56.4	55.5	54.9	**50.4**

There are $9,962$ and $22,531$ images for 20 object classes in the PASCAL VOC 2007 and 2012 respectively. The datasets are divided into the train, val, and test sets. Following [5,21,38], we train our network on the trainval set. For evaluation, the Average Precision (AP) and mean of AP (mAP) [14] is used to evaluate our network on the test set; the Correct Localization (CorLoc) [11] is used to evaluate the localization accuracy on the trainval set.

There are hundreds of thousands of images for 200 object classes in the ImageNet detection dataset which is divided into the train, val, and test sets. Following [16], we divide the val set into val1 and val2 sets, randomly choose no more than 1000 images per-class from the train set (train$_{1k}$ set), combine the train$_{1k}$ and val1 sets for training, and report mAP on the val2 set.

Implementation Details. We choose the VGG16 network [36] pre-trained on ImageNet classification dataset [32] as our initial CNN network $\mathbb{M}^{\text{pre}}$ in Sect. 3.4. The two 256-dimension FC layers in Sect. 3.2 are initialized by subsampling the parameters of the FC parameters in the original VGG16 network, following [8]. Other new added layers are initialized by sampling from a Gaussian distribution with mean 0 and standard deviation 0.01.

During training, we choose Stochastic Gradient Descent and set the batchsize to 2 and 32 for PASCAL VOC and ImageNet respectively. We train each network 50K, 80K, and 20K iterations for the PSACAL VOC 2007, 2012, and ImageNet datasets, respectively, where the learning rates are 0.001 for the first 40K, 60K, and 15K iterations and 0.0001 for the other iterations. We set the momentum and weight decay to 0.9 and 0.0005 respectively.

As stated in Sects. 3.2 and 3.3, we choose the best performed WSOD network by Tang et al. [38] for region classification, while other WSOD networks can also be chosen. We use five image scales $\{480, 576, 688, 864, 1024\}$ along with horizontal flipping for data augmentation during training and testing, and train a Fast RCNN (FRCNN) [15] using top-scoring proposals by our method as pseudo groundtruths following [12,25,38]. For the FRCNN training, we also use our proposal network through replacing the "WSOD network" in the second line and fourth line of Algorithm 2 by the FRCNN network. Other hyper-parameters are as follows: the number of proposals from the first stage of the network is set to 10K (i.e. $N^1 = 10K$), the number of proposals from the second stage of the network is set to 2K (i.e. $N^2 = 2K$) which is the same scale as the Selective Search [40], and the NMS thresholds for three stages are set to 0.9, 0.75, and 0.3, respectively. We only report results from the method that shares conv features, because there is no performance difference between the shared and unshared methods.

All of our experiments are carried out on an NIVDIA GTX 1080Ti GPU, using the Caffe [19] deep learning framework.

Table 2. Result comparison (CorLoc in %) among different methods on the PASCAL VOC 2007 `trainval` set. The upper/lower part are results by single/multiple model. Our method obtains the best mean of CorLoc. See Sect. 4.2 for definitions of the Ours-based methods

Method	aero	bike	bird	boat	bottle	bus	car	cat	chair	cow	table	dog	horse	mbike	person	plant	sheep	sofa	train	tv	mean
WSDDN-VGG16 [5]	65.1	58.8	58.5	33.1	39.8	68.3	60.2	59.6	34.8	64.5	30.5	43.0	56.8	82.4	25.5	41.6	61.5	55.9	65.9	63.7	53.5
WSDDN+context [21]	83.3	68.6	54.7	23.4	18.3	73.6	74.1	54.1	8.6	65.1	47.1	59.5	67.0	83.5	35.3	39.9	67.0	49.7	63.5	65.2	55.1
OICR-VGG16 [38]	81.7	80.4	48.7	**49.5**	32.8	81.7	85.4	40.1	**40.6**	79.5	35.7	33.7	60.5	88.8	21.8	57.9	76.3	59.9	75.3	**81.4**	60.6
SP-VGG16 [43]	**85.3**	64.2	**67.0**	42.0	16.4	71.0	64.7	**88.7**	20.7	63.8	58.0	**84.1**	84.7	80.0	**60.0**	29.4	56.3	**68.1**	**77.4**	30.5	60.6
Ours-VGG16	77.5	**81.2**	55.3	19.7	**44.3**	80.2	86.6	69.5	10.1	**87.7**	**68.4**	52.1	84.4	**91.6**	57.4	**63.4**	**77.3**	58.1	57.0	53.8	**63.8**
OM+MIL+FRCNN [25]	78.2	67.1	61.8	38.1	36.1	61.8	78.8	55.2	28.5	68.8	18.5	49.2	64.1	73.5	21.4	47.4	64.6	22.3	60.9	52.3	52.4
WSDDN-Ens. [5]	68.9	68.7	**65.2**	42.5	40.6	72.6	75.2	53.7	29.7	68.1	33.5	45.6	65.9	86.1	27.5	44.9	76.0	62.4	66.3	66.8	58.0
WCCN [12]	83.9	72.8	64.5	44.1	40.1	65.7	82.5	58.9	**33.7**	72.5	25.6	53.7	67.4	77.4	26.8	49.1	68.1	27.9	64.5	55.7	56.7
HCP+DSD+OSSH3 [20]	72.7	55.3	53.0	27.8	35.2	68.6	81.9	60.7	11.6	71.6	29.7	**54.3**	64.3	88.2	22.2	53.7	72.2	52.6	68.9	75.5	56.1
OICR-Ens.+FRCNN [38]	**85.8**	**82.7**	62.8	**45.2**	43.5	**84.8**	87.0	46.8	15.7	82.2	51.0	45.6	83.7	91.2	22.2	59.7	75.3	65.1	**76.8**	**78.1**	64.3
Ours-Ens.	81.2	81.2	60.7	36.7	52.3	80.7	**89.0**	65.1	20.5	**86.3**	61.6	49.5	86.4	92.4	41.4	**62.6**	79.4	62.4	73.0	75.6	66.9
Ours-Ens.+FRCNN	83.8	**82.7**	60.7	35.1	**53.8**	82.7	88.6	**67.4**	22.0	86.3	**68.8**	50.9	**90.8**	**93.6**	44.0	61.2	**82.5**	65.9	71.1	76.7	**68.4**

4.2 Experimental Results

The result comparisons among our method and other methods on the PASCAL VOC datasets are shown in Tables 1, 2, and 3. As we can see, using our proposals (Ours-VGG16 in tables), we obtain much better performance than other methods that use a single model [5,21,38], in particular the OICR-VGG16 method [38] which is our WSOD network. Following other methods which combine multiple models through model ensemble or training FRCNN [5,12,20,38], we also

Table 3. Result comparison (mAP and CorLoc in %) for different methods on the PASCAL VOC 2012 dataset. Our method obtains the best mAP and CorLoc

Method	mAP	CorLoc
WSDDN+context [21]	35.3	54.8
WCCN [12]	37.9	-
HCP+DSD+OSSH3 [20]	38.3	58.8
OICR-Ens.+FRCNN [38]	42.5	65.6
Ours-VGG16	40.8	64.9
Ours-VGG16-Ens	43.4	67.2
Ours-VGG16-Ens.+FRCNN	**45.7**	**69.3**

Table 4. Result comparison (mAP in %) for different methods on the ImageNet detection dataset. Our method obtains the best mAP

Method	Results
Wang et al. [41]	6.0
OM+MIL+FRCNN [25]	10.8
WCCN [12]	16.3
Ours-VGG16	**18.5**

do model ensemble for our proposal results and selective search proposal results (Ours-VGG16-Ens. in tables). As the tables show, performance is improved a lot, which show that our proposals and selective search proposals are complementary to some extent. We also train a FRCNN network using the top-scoring proposals from Ours-VGG16-Ens. as pseudo labels (Ours-VGG16-Ens.+FRCNN in tables). It is clear that the results are boosted further. Importantly, our results outperform the results of the state-of-the-art proposal-free method (i.e., localize objects without proposals) [45], which confirms that the proposal-based method can localize objects better in complex images. Some qualitative results can be found in the supplementary material.

We also report the Ours-VGG16 result on the ImageNet detection dataset in Table 4. Using a single model already outperforms all previous state-of-the-arts [12,25,41]. Confidently, our result can be further improved by combining multiple models.

4.3   Ablation Experiments

We conduct some ablation experiments on the PASCAL VOC 2007 dataset to analyze different components of our method, including proposal recall, detection results of different proposal methods, and the influence of the proposal refinement. Also see the supplementary material for more ablation experiments.

Proposal Recall. We first compute the proposal recall at different IoU thresholds with groundtruth boxes. Although the recall to IoU metric is loosely correlated to detection results [7,17], it can give a reliable result to diagnose whether proposals cover objects of desired categories well [30]. In Fig. 4, we observe that our method obtains higher recall than the Selective Search (SS) and Edge Boxes (EB) methods for IoU<0.9, especially when the number of proposals is small

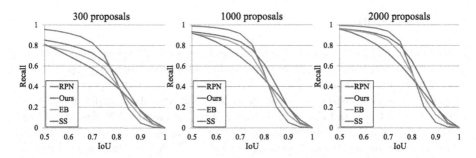

Fig. 4. Recall *vs.* IoU for different proposal methods on the VOC 2007 `test` set. Our method outperforms all methods except the RPN [30] which uses bounding box annotations for training

(*e.g.* 300 proposals). This is because our region-based classifier refines proposals. It is not strange that the recall of Region Proposal Network (RPN) [30] is higher than ours, because they train their network using the bounding box annotations. But we do not use the bounding box information because we do weakly supervised learning.

Detection Results of Different Proposal Methods. Here we compare the detection results of different proposal methods, using the same WSOD network [38] (with the improvements in this paper). For fair comparison, we generate about 2K proposals for each method. The results are as follows: 41.6% mAP and 60.7% CorLoc for EB, 42.2% mAP and 60.9% CorLoc for SS, and 46.2% mAP and 65.7% for RPN [30]. Our results (45.3% mAP and 63.8% CorLoc) are much better than the results of EB and SS which were used by most previous WSOD methods. The results demonstrates the effectiveness of our method for WSOD. As before, the RPN obtains the best results because it uses the bounding box annotations for training. These results also show that better proposals can contribute to better WSOD performance.

The Influence of the Proposal Refinement. Finally, we study whether the proposal refinement stage improves the WOSD performance or not. If we only perform the coarse proposal generation stage, we obtain mAP 37.5% and CorLoc 57.3% which are much worse than the results after proposal refinement, and even worse than the EB and SS. This is because the early conv layers also fire on background regions, and the responses of the early conv layers are not "real" edges, thus directly applying EB may not be optimal. The results demonstrates that it is necessary to refine the proposals. It is also possible to perform more proposal generation stages by using more proposal refinement stages. We plan to explore this in the future.

5   Conclusion

In this paper, we focus on the region proposal generation step for weakly supervised object detection and propose a weakly supervised region proposal network which generates proposals by CNN trained under weak supervisions. Our proposal network consists of two stages where the first stage exploits low-level information in CNN and the second stage is a region-based CNN classifier which distinguishes whether proposals are object or background regions. We further adapt the alternating training strategy in Faster RCNN to share convolutional computations among all proposal stages and the weakly supervised object detection network, which contributes to a three-stage network. Experimental results show that our method obtains the state-of-the-art weakly supervised object detection performance with performance gain of about 3% on average. In the future, we will explore better ways to use both low-level and high-level information in CNN for proposal generation.

Acknowledgements. We really appreciate the enormous help from Yan Wang, Wei Shen, Zhishuai Zhang, Yuyin Zhou, and Baoguang Shi during the paper writing and rebuttal. This work was partly supported by NSFC (No.61733007, No.61503145, No.61572207), ONR N00014-15-1-2356, and China Scholarship Council. Xinggang Wang was sponsored by CCF-Tencent Open Research Fund, Hubei Scientific and Technical Innovation Key Project, and the Program for HUST Academic Frontier Youth Team.

References

1. Alexe, B., Deselaers, T., Ferrari, V.: Measuring the objectness of image windows. TPAMI **34**(11), 2189–2202 (2012)
2. Bearman, A., Russakovsky, O., Ferrari, V., Fei-Fei, L.: What's the point: semantic segmentation with point supervision. In: Leibe, B., Matas, J., Sebe, N., Welling, M. (eds.) ECCV 2016. LNCS, vol. 9911, pp. 549–565. Springer, Cham (2016). https://doi.org/10.1007/978-3-319-46478-7_34
3. Bertasius, G., Shi, J., Torresani, L.: Deepedge: a multi-scale bifurcated deep network for top-down contour detection. In: CVPR, pp. 4380–4389 (2015)
4. Bilen, H., Pedersoli, M., Tuytelaars, T.: Weakly supervised object detection with convex clustering. In: CVPR, pp. 1081–1089 (2015)
5. Bilen, H., Vedaldi, A.: Weakly supervised deep detection networks. In: CVPR, pp. 2846–2854 (2016)
6. Carreira, J., Sminchisescu, C.: CPMC: automatic object segmentation using constrained parametric min-cuts. TPAMI **7**, 1312–1328 (2011)
7. Chavali, N., Agrawal, H., Mahendru, A., Batra, D.: Object-proposal evaluation protocol is 'gameable'. In: CVPR, pp. 835–844 (2016)
8. Chen, L.C., Papandreou, G., Kokkinos, I., Murphy, K., Yuille, A.L.: Semantic image segmentation with deep convolutional nets and fully connected CRFS. In: ICLR (2015)
9. Cinbis, R.G., Verbeek, J., Schmid, C.: Weakly supervised object localization with multi-fold multiple instance learning. TPAMI **39**(1), 189–203 (2017)

10. Dabkowski, P., Gal, Y.: Real time image saliency for black box classifiers. In: NIPS, pp. 6970–6979 (2017)
11. Deselaers, T., Alexe, B., Ferrari, V.: Weakly supervised localization and learning with generic knowledge. IJCV **100**(3), 275–293 (2012)
12. Diba, A., Sharma, V., Pazandeh, A., Pirsiavash, H., Van Gool, L.: Weakly supervised cascaded convolutional networks. In: CVPR, pp. 914–922 (2017)
13. Dollár, P., Zitnick, C.L.: Fast edge detection using structured forests. TPAMI **37**(8), 1558–1570 (2015)
14. Everingham, M., Eslami, S.A., Van Gool, L., Williams, C.K., Winn, J., Zisserman, A.: The pascal visual object classes challenge: a retrospective. IJCV **111**(1), 98–136 (2015)
15. Girshick, R.: Fast R-CNN. In: ICCV, pp. 1440–1448 (2015)
16. Girshick, R., Donahue, J., Darrell, T., Malik, J.: Region-based convolutional networks for accurate object detection and segmentation. TPAMI **38**(1), 142–158 (2016)
17. Hosang, J., Benenson, R., Dollár, P., Schiele, B.: What makes for effective detection proposals? TPAMI **38**(4), 814–830 (2016)
18. Huang, Z., Wang, X., Wang, J., Liu, W., Wang, J.: Weakly-supervised semantic segmentation network with deep seeded region growing. In: CVPR, pp. 7014–7023 (2018)
19. Jia, Y., et al.: Caffe: convolutional architecture for fast feature embedding. In: ACM MM, pp. 675–678 (2014)
20. Jie, Z., Wei, Y., Jin, X., Feng, J., Liu, W.: Deep self-taught learning for weakly supervised object localization. In: CVPR, pp. 1377–1385 (2017)
21. Kantorov, V., Oquab, M., Cho, M., Laptev, I.: Contextlocnet: context-aware deep network models for weakly supervised localization. In: ECCV, pp. 350–365 (2016)
22. Krizhevsky, A., Sutskever, I., Hinton, G.E.: Imagenet classification with deep convolutional neural networks. In: NIPS, pp. 1097–1105 (2012)
23. Kuo, W., Hariharan, B., Malik, J.: Deepbox: learning objectness with convolutional networks. In: ICCV, pp. 2479–2487 (2015)
24. LeCun, Y., Bottou, L., Bengio, Y., Haffner, P.: Gradient-based learning applied to document recognition. Proc. IEEE **86**(11), 2278–2324 (1998)
25. Li, D., Huang, J.B., Li, Y., Wang, S., Yang, M.H.: Weakly supervised object localization with progressive domain adaptation. In: CVPR, pp. 3512–3520 (2016)
26. Lin, T.-Y., et al.: Microsoft COCO: common objects in context. In: Fleet, D., Pajdla, T., Schiele, B., Tuytelaars, T. (eds.) ECCV 2014. LNCS, vol. 8693, pp. 740–755. Springer, Cham (2014). https://doi.org/10.1007/978-3-319-10602-1_48
27. Oquab, M., Bottou, L., Laptev, I., Sivic, J.: Is object localization for free?-weakly-supervised learning with convolutional neural networks. In: CVPR, pp. 685–694 (2015)
28. Pinheiro, P.O., Lin, T.Y., Collobert, R., Dollár, P.: Learning to refine object segments. In: ECCV, pp. 75–91 (2016)
29. Pont-Tuset, J., Arbelaez, P., Barron, J.T., Marques, F., Malik, J.: Multiscale combinatorial grouping for image segmentation and object proposal generation. TPAMI **39**(1), 128–140 (2017)
30. Ren, S., He, K., Girshick, R., Sun, J.: Faster R-CNN: towards real-time object detection with region proposal networks. TPAMI **39**(6), 1137–1149 (2017)
31. Ren, W., Huang, K., Tao, D., Tan, T.: Weakly supervised large scale object localization with multiple instance learning and bag splitting. TPAMI **38**(2), 405–416 (2016)

32. Russakovsky, O., et al.: Imagenet large scale visual recognition challenge. IJCV **115**(3), 211–252 (2015)
33. Saleh, F., Aliakbarian, M.S., Salzmann, M., Petersson, L., Alvarez, J.M., Gould, S.: Incorporating network built-in priors in weakly-supervised semantic segmentation. TPAMI **40**(6), 1382–1396 (2018)
34. Shi, M., Caesar, H., Ferrari, V.: Weakly supervised object localization using things and stuff transfer. In: ICCV, pp. 3381–3390 (2017)
35. Simonyan, K., Vedaldi, A., Zisserman, A.: Deep inside convolutional networks: visualising image classification models and saliency maps. arXiv preprint arXiv:1312.6034 (2013)
36. Simonyan, K., Zisserman, A.: Very deep convolutional networks for large-scale image recognition. In: ICLR (2015)
37. Tang, P., Wang, C., Wang, X., Liu, W., Zeng, W., Wang, J.: Object detection in videos by short and long range object linking. arXiv preprint arXiv:1801.09823 (2018)
38. Tang, P., Wang, X., Bai, X., Liu, W.: Multiple instance detection network with online instance classifier refinement. In: CVPR, pp. 2843–2851 (2017)
39. Tang, P., Wang, X., Huang, Z., Bai, X., Liu, W.: Deep patch learning for weakly supervised object classification and discovery. Pattern Recogn. **71**, 446–459 (2017)
40. Uijlings, J.R., van de Sande, K.E., Gevers, T., Smeulders, A.W.: Selective search for object recognition. IJCV **104**(2), 154–171 (2013)
41. Wang, C., Ren, W., Huang, K., Tan, T.: Weakly supervised object localization with latent category learning. In: ECCV, pp. 431–445 (2014)
42. Wang, X., Zhu, Z., Yao, C., Bai, X.: Relaxed multiple-instance svm with application to object discovery. In: ICCV, pp. 1224–1232 (2015)
43. Zhang, Z., Qiao, S., Xie, C., Shen, W., Wang, B., Yuille, A.L.: Single-shot object detection with enriched semantics. In: CVPR, pp. 5813–5821 (2018)
44. Zhou, B., Khosla, A., Lapedriza, A., Oliva, A., Torralba, A.: Learning deep features for discriminative localization. In: CVPR, pp. 2921–2929 (2016)
45. Zhu, Y., Zhou, Y., Ye, Q., Qiu, Q., Jiao, J.: Soft proposal networks for weakly supervised object localization. In: ICCV, pp. 1814–1850 (2017)
46. Zitnick, C.L., Dollár, P.: Edge boxes: locating object proposals from edges. In: Fleet, D., Pajdla, T., Schiele, B., Tuytelaars, T. (eds.) ECCV 2014. LNCS, vol. 8693, pp. 391–405. Springer, Cham (2014). https://doi.org/10.1007/978-3-319-10602-1_26

Zero-Annotation Object Detection
with Web Knowledge Transfer

Qingyi Tao[1,2(✉)], Hao Yang[3], and Jianfei Cai[1]

[1] Nanyang Technological University, Singapore, Singapore
qtao002@e.ntu.edu.sg, asjfcai@ntu.edu.sg
[2] NVIDIA AI Technology Center, Singapore, Singapore
[3] Amazon Rekognition, Seattle, USA
lancelot365@gmail.com

Abstract. Object detection is one of the major problems in computer vision, and has been extensively studied. Most of the existing detection works rely on labor-intensive supervision, such as ground truth bounding boxes of objects or at least image-level annotations. On the contrary, we propose an object detection method that does not require any form of human annotation on target tasks, by exploiting freely available web images. In order to facilitate effective knowledge transfer from web images, we introduce a multi-instance multi-label domain adaption learning framework with two key innovations. First of all, we propose an instance-level adversarial domain adaptation network with attention on foreground objects to transfer the object appearances from web domain to target domain. Second, to preserve the class-specific semantic structure of transferred object features, we propose a simultaneous transfer mechanism to transfer the supervision across domains through pseudo strong label generation. With our end-to-end framework that simultaneously learns a weakly supervised detector and transfers knowledge across domains, we achieved significant improvements over baseline methods on the benchmark datasets.

Keywords: Object detection · Domain adaptation
Web knowledge transfer

1 Introduction

In recent years, with the advances of deep convolutional neural networks (DCNN), object detection tasks have attracted significant attention and have achieved great improvements in performance and efficiency. State-of-the-art works such as Faster R-CNN [25], SSD [21], FPN [20] achieve high accuracy but require labour-intensive bounding box annotations for training. To alleviate the large labour cost for annotating ground truth bounding boxes, weakly supervised object detection methods that only rely on image-level human annotations have

---

This work was done when Hao Yang was at NTU, Singapore.

© Springer Nature Switzerland AG 2018
V. Ferrari et al. (Eds.): ECCV 2018, LNCS 11215, pp. 387–403, 2018.
https://doi.org/10.1007/978-3-030-01252-6_23

also been extensively studied [2–4,8,14–16,27]. However, for large-scale multi-object detection problem, even annotating just image-level labels could deem to be too expensive. This motivates us to develop an object detection method with no human annotations involved. Our basic idea is to transfer knowledge from free web resources to the target tasks.

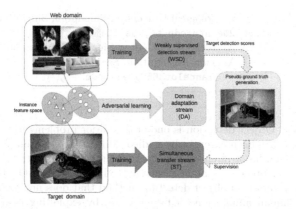

Fig. 1. Overall idea of object detection without human annotations. First of all, we mine freely available web images through automatic retrieval with respect to a given set of object categories. Our framework then facilitates knowledge transfer from these web images to the target task using a multi-stream network with three major components: (1) a weakly supervised detection stream (WSD) to train the detection model from web images; (2) an instance-level domain adaptation (DA) stream to minimize the feature discrepancy across domains at instance-level feature space; (3) a simultaneous transfer (ST) stream that learns to discriminate unsupervised target examples by transferring supervision from web detection model. These three streams are trained simultaneously to effectively transfer the learning of web images to the target task.

With the similar motivation, zero-shot learning (ZSL) problem has been proposed for unsupervised learning. Many works [1,10,11,17,18,24] have been proposed to utilize side information such as attributes, Wikipedia or WordNet to jointly encode semantic space and image feature space for solving zero-shot recognition problems. However, although textual side information could help zero-shot object recognition with exploiting the intrinsic semantic relations between categories, it is hard to learn a class-specific object detector that can accurately differentiate objects from the background as well as different objects with just semantic descriptions. In contrast, our direction is to exploit freely available web images as a much stronger side information to solve the object detection problem without human annotations, considering that there are huge amount of image resources from the web and plenty of works studying the automatic collection of these web imagery resources [7,19,28,34].

One baseline approach for learning detectors with web images is to simply use the web images and their image "labels" (essentially the pre-defined labels used as search phrases to retrieve the images) to train a web object detector using some weakly supervised detection (WSD) methods and apply them on target images. This naive learning scheme is referred as webly supervised learning in previous works [6,9]. However, directly applying the web models to the target data produces poor results. The major reason is that it ignores the domain discrepancies between web images and target images. As shown in Fig. 1, web images from image search engines are mostly studio-shot images, which are simple, clear and unblocked. In contrast, the target images (e.g. Pascal VOC images) usually contain multiple objects of different classes that are often occluded with cluttered scenes. Hence it is necessary to properly transfer the models learned from web images to the target images.

To address this domain discrepancy problem, we need to adapt the source (i.e. web domain) and target domain object appearances, for which unsupervised domain adaptation is the common way [5,12,22,29,30]. Although many unsupervised domain adaptation methods have been proposed, they all focus on image-level domain adaptation for image classification problems. What we consider here is the domain adaptation at instance level (i.e. object proposal level), which is non-trivial to solve. Inspired by the recent adversarial domain adaptation works [12,29,30], we propose an instance-level adversarial domain adaptation network to reduce the domain discrepancies particularly at instance level. Our adversarial domain adaptation network includes a domain discriminator that differentiates object features from web domain and target domain, and a feature generator that projects source and target objects to the same manifold in the feature space so that the discriminator can no longer tell their differences.

In addition, we introduce an innovative component in our domain adaptation network: attention on foreground objects. As weakly supervised detection is essentially a multi-instance multi-label learning problem, each image actually is a bag of instances, where each instance corresponds to a bounding box proposal. Equally treating all proposals in each image when training adversarial domain adaptation network will lead to sub-par results, as we care more about proposals containing objects than proposals that are largely background. Therefore, we introduce an attention mechanism to emphasize the transfer of object proposals and suppress the transfer of background proposals.

However, the introduced instance-level domain adaptation network brings in a side effect, i.e. the feature generator is likely to ignore the semantic structure of different object classes, since there is no class-specific constraint. As a result, it not only brings features from different domains together to the same manifold, but also mixes up the sub-manifolds from different classes. For example, the "cow" from web domain will be confused with the "sheep" from target domain through the domain adaptation. To address this issue, we further introduce simultaneous learning towards class-specific pseudo labels to preserve the semantic structure during the domain adaptation. This component compensates the side effect of the domain adaptation component so that the domain shift will be guided in a class-specific manner. In this way, our overall architecture including the web object detector, the domain adaptation component and the simultaneous transfer component significantly boosts up the object detection results on unsupervised target data.

We would like to highlight that the rationale of studying this problem lies in that such detector can be trained without any human labour and therefore the whole process could be fully automated. Different from fully supervised and weakly supervised object detection, our object detector allows the training of the detection models to be highly scalable in term of categories. For example, in the Pascal VOC dataset, if we want to add the object class "keyboard", which exists in some of the images but is not annotated, we need to re-annotate all the images in the training data by providing respective labels at bounding box level (for supervised detector) or image level (for weakly supervised detector). Another example is that if we want to further break down the "bird" class into multiple classes such as "parrot", "goose", "hawk" and etc., we also need to revise the annotations for all images containing "bird" objects. In contrast, our solution can automatically search the web and progressively transfer the web knowledge to learn the detector without any human intervention or any modification in the target domain dataset. The training of such detector can be a completely self-taught process. Hence, we think this problem is highly meaningful and worth to be studied.

Overall, the main contributions of our work can be summarized as follows:

- We propose a new problem of knowledge transfer in object detection for *unsupervised* data, which enables learning an object detector from free web images and alleviates any forms of human annotations for target domain. By studying this problem, the learning of object detectors can be fully automated and highly scalable with categories.
- We propose an *instance-level* domain adaptation method to transfer web knowledge to unsupervised target dataset. The proposed domain adaptation framework includes: (1) an instance-level adversarial domain adaptation network with attention on foreground objects; (2) a simultaneous transfer stream to preserve the semantic structure of classes by transferring the pseudo labels obtained from the web domain detector to the target domain detector.
- Our method significantly reduces the gap between unsupervised object detection (i.e. train a detector using only web images and then directly apply it on target images) and the upper bound (i.e. train a detector using image-level labels of target data) by 3.6% in detection mAP.

2   Related Works

Our work is related to a few computer vision and machine learning areas. We will review these related topics in this section.

Weakly Supervised Object Detection: Recent works on weakly supervised object detection aim to reduce the intensive human labour cost by using only image-level labels instead of bounding box annotations [2,3,8]. They are more cost-effective than the fully supervised object detection methods since image-level labels are easier to obtain compared with the bounding box annotations.

These works formulate the weakly supervised object detection task as a multi-instance learning (MIL) problem in which the model will be learned alternatively to recognize the object categories and to find the object locations of each category. The recent work [4] is the first one introducing an end-to-end network with two separate branches for object recognition and localization respectively. Later, [15] introduced context information to the weakly supervised detection network in the localization stream. [27] proposed online classifier refinement to refine the instance classification based on image-level labels.

Our work is related to these works as the web data will be trained in a weakly supervised way with their weak labels. In this paper, we use WSDDN in [4] as the base model for our work.

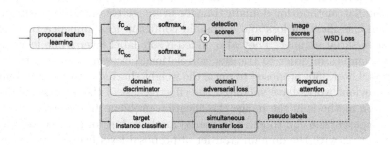

Fig. 2. The proposed network branches into three streams after the proposal feature learning layers. The first stream (in blue) is the weakly supervised detection (WSD) network which is further divided into recognition and localization streams. The middle stream (in yellow) is the instance-level domain adaptation (DA) stream that optimizes an adversarial loss to enforce domain invariant feature representation. The last stream (in purple) is the simultaneous transfer (ST) stream to preserve semantic structure of target data with pseudo labels. (Color figure online)

Learning from Web Data: Web data is a free source of training samples that can be collected automatically for various tasks [6,9,26,35]. Previous works [6,9,35] study the web data collection approaches and further evaluate their data collection methods by training those web data for different tasks. They focus on reducing the effects of noises from web images and thereby construct robust and clean web datasets. While learning for the target tasks, these prior works simply treat the web dataset as the substitute of the training dataset in the target task without considering the domain shifts between web data and target data, which is similar as our baseline approach. Apart from that, web data are often used as complementary data to improve the training of target dataset. In [33], web images are used to produce pseudo masks for pre-training the semantic segmentation network. In [32], an object interaction dataset with web images is created to facilitate the semantic segmentation task as additional data. In their approaches, the image-level labels (in [33]) or pixel-level ground truth masks (in [32]) of target images are required and web images are utilized as additional knowledge to improve the segmentation model performance. In our work, we attempt to solve the detection problem using only the web images without any forms of annotations from target dataset.

Domain Adaptation: Our work is also closely related to the domain adaptation works [5,12,29,30,36]. [12] introduced the domain adversarial training of neural networks. The domain adaptation is achieved by introducing a domain classifier to classify features to their corresponding domains and applying a gradient reversal layer between the feature extractor and the domain classifier. With this reversal layer, when the domain classifier learns to distinguish the features from different domains, the feature extractor learns in the reverse way to make the feature distributions as indistinguishable as possible. Hence, this domain adversarial training can result in a domain-invariant feature representation. [29] also uses a similar method for domain transfer in image classification task. In [29], a domain classification loss and a domain confusion loss influence the training in an adversarial manner. They also added a soft label layer while learning the source examples in order to transfer correlations between classes to the target examples. Later, [30] proposed to untie the weight sharing between two domains. These previous works have validated the effectiveness of the adversarial domain adaptation methods in the image classification problem. In our work, we follow the principles of the end-to-end adversarial methods but for our zero-annotation detection task with the domain transfer of proposal-level features to reduce the domain mismatch between web data and target data.

3   Problem Definition and Notations

In this section, we formally define our problem of zero-annotation object detection with web knowledge transfer. Essentially, we define this problem as an unsupervised multi-instance multi-label domain adaptation problem. Specifically, we consider two domains, the web domain D^w representing web images and target domain D^t representing target tasks (e.g. Pascal VOC and MS COCO). The source data $\{X_j^w, y_j\}_{j=1}^{n_w}$ is sampled from D^w, where X_j^w is the j-th image, $y_j \in \mathbb{R}^C$ sampled from label space Y is the corresponding C dimensional binary label vector and n_w is the number of source images. For object detection problems, it is natural to decompose each image to a bag of instances, i.e., object proposals, through dense sampling or objectness techniques. Thus, X_j^w can be represented as $X_j^w = \{x_i^{w,j}\}_{i=1}^{m_j^w}$, where $x_i^{w,j}$ is the i-th proposal in X_j^w and m_j^w is the number of total proposals of X_j^w. Similarly, the target data sampled from D^t can be denoted as $\{X_j^t\}_{j=1}^{n_t}$, and $X_j^t = \{x_i^{t,j}\}_{i=1}^{m_j^t}$. Note that since we do not have annotations for target data, effective knowledge transfer from the web domain is necessary.

Traditional domain adaptation methods usually optimize an objective function $f : X^w, X^t \to Y$, which jointly learns a classifier for source/web domain and transfers the knowledge to target domain at *image-level*. However, for object detection, we need to go deeper to *instance-level*. In particular, we need to learn

$f : x^w, x^t \to Y$. Therefore, we will need a backbone structure to learn from image-level labels and propagate knowledge to instances, and an effective way to transfer knowledge from the web domain to the target domain at instance-level.

4 Methodology

Figure 2 shows the diagram of the proposed framework for zero-annotation object detection with web knowledge transfer. The entire framework branches into three streams after feature representation, including WSD, DA, and ST. In the following, we describe each stream one by one.

4.1 Weakly Supervised Detection Trained on Web Images

Our weakly supervised detection backbone is based on the basic WSDDN [4] (blue region in Fig. 2). Note that other end-to-end WSD methods can be easily applied as well. Specifically, for WSSDN, the proposal features $x_i \in \mathbb{R}^d$ are obtained through an ROI pooling layer on the feature map of the image, followed by two fully connected layers, similar to Fast-RCNN [13]. Then we represent each image X as the concatenation of its proposal features, i.e., $X = \text{concat}(x_i), \forall i \in [1, m]$, thus $X \in \mathbb{R}^{m \times d}$, where m denotes the number of proposals in the image. Note that here we abuse the notation x_i to represent both proposal and its corresponding feature, and X to represent both image and its corresponding concatenated feature matrix.

Following the proposal feature learning, the WSD network breaks into two branches of fully connected (fc) layers to produce two score matrices S^{cls} and $S^{loc} \in \mathbb{R}^{m \times C}$, where C is the number of object classes. Then S^{cls} and S^{loc} are passed to two $softmax$ layers with different axes, i.e. S^{cls} is normalized in the class dimension to produce the class probability of each proposal and S^{loc} is normalized in the proposal dimension to find the most responsive proposal for each class among all candidate proposals. For proposal i and class c, we respectively denote the outputs of these two $softmax$ layers as $p_{i,c}^{cls}$ and $p_{i,c}^{loc}$, which are defined as

$$p_{i,c}^{cls} = \frac{e^{s_{i,c}^{cls}}}{\sum_{k=1}^{C} e^{s_{i,k}^{cls}}}, \quad p_{i,c}^{loc} = \frac{e^{s_{i,c}^{loc}}}{\sum_{k=1}^{m} e^{s_{k,c}^{loc}}} \tag{1}$$

Then the detection probability $p_{i,c}$ of each proposal can be computed by element-wise products of the normalized probabilities from the two branches:

$$p_{i,c} = p_{i,c}^{cls} \cdot p_{i,c}^{loc}. \tag{2}$$

The image classification probability p_c is calculated by summing up the detection probabilities of all proposals:

$$p_c = \sum_{i=1}^{m} p_{i,c}. \tag{3}$$

Finally, the multi-class cross entropy loss is adopted as the loss function of WSD, which is defined as

$$L_{WSD} = -\sum_{c=1}^{C}[y(c)log(p_c) + (1 - y(c))log(1 - p_c)] \tag{4}$$

where $y(c) \in \{0, 1\}$ is the web image label for class c.

Note that since we do not have any label in the target domain, this WSD loss is only optimized by training with web images.

4.2 Instance-Level Adversarial Domain Adaptation

The purpose of this instance-level domain adaptation (DA) stream (yellow region in Fig. 2) is to close the feature discrepancies between the two domains. Figure 3 gives the detailed structure of this DA stream. In particular, it includes two players with adversarial goals: a discriminator trained to differentiate the domains where input features come from, and a feature learner shared with the WSD stream trained to align features from both domains so as to confuse the discriminator.

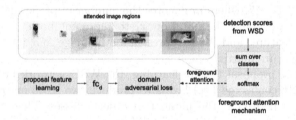

Fig. 3. Instance-level domain adaptation stream with foreground attention. We visualize the attended image regions produced by the foreground attention mechanism. The examples show that the foreground object regions are well attended and the background regions are suppressed during domain adversarial learning.

In particular, the proposed discriminator consists of a fully connected layer fc_d that classifies the input proposal features x_i in i-th row of X to their domains $y_i^t \in \{0, 1\}$. Here we define $y_i^t = 0$ for x_i from the web domain D^w and $y_i^t = 1$ for x_i from target domain D^t. Through a *softmax* operation, we can compute the domain probability as p_i^t, i.e. $prob(y_i^t = 1)$. The adversarial loss can then be written as

$$\min_{\phi_f^w} \max_{\phi_{fc_d}} \mathbb{E}_{x \sim D^t}[\log(p^t)] + \mathbb{E}_{x \sim D^w}[\log(1 - p^t)],$$

$$\mathbb{E}_{x \sim D^t}[\log(p^t)] = \sum_i \mathbb{1}[y_i^t = 1]log(p_i^t),$$

$$\mathbb{E}_{x \sim D^w}[\log(1 - p^t)] = \sum_i \mathbb{1}[y_i^t = 0]\log(1 - p_i^t), \tag{5}$$

where ϕ_f^w denotes the parameters of the feature learner, ϕ_{fc_d} denotes the parameters of the discriminator fc_d, and $\mathbb{1}[]$ is the indication function.

The optimization of the minimax domain adversarial loss in (5) is achieved by training alternatively between the following two steps. First, we update ϕ_{fc_d} to distinguish proposal features from D^w and D^t to seek for maximizing the loss. Then we fix ϕ_{fc_d} and learn the feature representation ϕ_f^w to minimize the loss so as to confuse the discriminator. In practice, we only shift the web domain D^w towards the target domain and ϕ_f^w is updated by training only web images.

Moreover, unlike the existing domain adaptation works for image classification [12,29], which focus on aligning image-level features, here we need to align instance-level features instead, especially for important instances that are more likely to contain objects. Specifically, while adapting the instance-level features, we care more about the foreground features than those background features in order to learn common object appearances. Therefore, we introduce an attention mechanism to focus on the adaptation of foreground features and suppress the effects for background features. As shown in Fig. 3, our foreground attention model uses the detection scores from the WSD stream and computes the foreground probability p_i^f for proposal i by summing up $p_{i,c}$ in (2) over all the classes (i.e. $\sum_{c=1}^{C} p_{i,c}$) followed by a *softmax* operation for the normalization over all the proposals. This is to find out the most responsive proposals regardless which object classes they belong to, and the responsive proposals with high p^f scores are highly likely to be foreground. Finally, we use the foreground probability as the attention weight, and modify the minimax adversarial loss as

$$\min_{\phi_f^w} \max_{\phi_{fc_d}} \mathbb{E}_{x \sim D^t}[p^f \cdot \log(p^t)] + \mathbb{E}_{x \sim D^w}[p^f \cdot \log(1 - p^t)]. \tag{6}$$

4.3 Simultaneous Transfer by Pseudo Supervision

Ideally, the domain adaptation stream should produce domain invariant features and improve the detection results while applying on the target dataset. However, it is observed that it fails to perform domain shift with class-specific directions. Specifically, it could encourage the features to be indistinguishable across not only domains but also classes. This ill effect of DA stream eventually makes features to be non-discriminative. Therefore, to preserve the semantic structure across different categories, we introduce the simultaneous transfer (ST) stream (purple part in Fig. 2) and use the pseudo labels generated from the WSD network as the supervision to preserve or even enhance the discriminative power of the learned features. The network details are shown in Fig. 4.

To generate the pseudo ground truth for each target image, we use the detection scores $p_{i,c}$ in (2) from the WSD stream. We select to highest scoring proposal for each object class c, denoted as $i_c = \text{argmax}_i \, p_{i,c}$. We set a threshold t to determine the presence of a class in an image. If $p_{i_c,c} >= t$, the corresponding proposal i_c is selected as the pseudo ground truth bounding box. Given the pseudo ground truth boxes, we then sample the boxes with large overlaps with the pseudo ground truth boxes as positive examples and randomly sample a few background examples from the remaining bounding boxes.

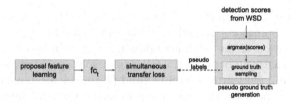

Fig. 4. Simultaneous transfer stream with pseudo ground truth generation.

Finally, we use the *softmaxloss* as the ST loss function:

$$L_{ST} = -\sum_{i \in P} \sum_{c=0}^{C} \mathbb{1}[y_i^{ST} = c] log(p_{i,c}^{ST}), \tag{7}$$

where $y^{ST} \in \{0, 1, 2, ...C\}$ are the class labels (0 is the class label of background), P is the set of the selected proposals, and $p_{i,c}^{ST}$ is the class probability output from the fully connected layer fc_t followed by a *softmax* operation.

Conditional adversarial loss is also a common way in GAN to enable class-specific domain adaptation. However, here the conditions are instance-level pseudo labels, which are noisy labels. It will be more stable to detach the class conditional learning with the domain adversarial learning.

5   Experiments

In this section, we conduct various experiments to evaluate the effectiveness of our proposed zero-annotation object detection with web knowledge transfer.

5.1   Datasets and Experiment Setup

We evaluate our method on two object detection benchmark datasets: Pascal VOC 2007 and 2012. These two datasets contain images of 20 object classes. The web images we used are from the STC dataset [33], whose images can be freely obtained from Internet without human labour. Similar as most supervised detection works, mean average precision (mAP) is used as the evaluation metric. Following the common standard, the IoU threshold is set to be 0.5 between ground truths and correctly predicted boxes.

Implementation Details. Our method is built upon two pre-trained networks on imagenet: VGG_M and VGG 16. We use selective search [31] to generate proposals for source and target images. In the WSD stream, we follow the details in the basic model of WSDDN as described in Sect. 4.1. The ROI features from the web domain are passed to the WSD stream to optimized the WSD loss whereas the ROI features from the target domain are only forwarded up to the detection score layer to generate foreground attention weights for the DA stream and pseudo labels for the ST stream. The DA stream takes the inputs from both source and target domains. It alternates between training the discriminator and the feature generator each time after training 5000 images. Lastly, the ST stream takes the inputs from the target domain and uses the detection scores generated from the WSD stream to generate pseudo ground truths as described in Sect. 4.3.

5.2 Baseline and Upper Bound

The baseline of our method is the basic WSD network [4] trained using only web images with web image labels. As shown in Table 1, due to the domain mismatch, the results are only 21.5 for VGG_M and 21.8 for VGG16.

The upper bound of our method is to train the basic WSD network with VOC image-level labels similar as [4]. Our obtained upper bound result for VGG_M is quite close to that reported in [4] with selective search proposals, while our result of 29.3 for VGG16 is higher than that of 24.3 reported in [4] with selective search proposals. Also, we have the same finding as [4] that VGG 16 performs slightly worse than VGG_M. This could be because the image level labels might not give sufficient supervision for a very deep network for the MIL problem.

Overall, there are significant gaps between the results without VOC labels and those with VOC labels. We aim to reduce the gap between the unsupervised and weakly supervised detection by transferring the knowledge of web domain to target domain with our proposed method.

Table 1. Baseline(wt.web data) and upper-bound(wt.VOC labels) on VOC 2007.

Method	mAP
WSD(wt.web data)-VGG_M	21.5
WSD(wt.web data)-VGG16	21.8
WSD(wt.VOC labels)-VGG_M	30.2
WSD(wt.VOC labels)-VGG16	29.3

5.3 Detailed Results and Analysis

Table 2 shows the detailed detection results of different combinations of the three streams developed in our method on VOC2007 test set. All of these methods are evaluated against the baseline,'WSD(Baseline)', that uses web images to train the WSD network alone. Before training the DA and ST streams, we train the WSD for one epoch first. This will give a more stable initialization to get the foreground attention weights for DA and pseudo labels for ST.

From Table 2, we can see that adding DA alone, 'WSD + DA', results in a slight drop in mAP. As discussed in Sect. 4.2, DA could result in an unexpected feature confusion among object classes with similar appearance, such as vehicle classes and animal classes. Only for classes that are different from all the other classes, such as "tv monitor", DA shows its contribution to the detection results.

Table 2. Average precision results (%) of different component combinations on VOC2007 test set.

	aero	bike	bird	boat	bottle	bus	car	cat	chair	cow	table	dog	horse	mbike	person	plant	sheep	sofa	train	tv	mean
WSD(Baseline)-VGG_M	31.1	27.1	18.6	10.0	9.1	29.9	37.7	21.5	2.7	15.8	21.5	27.8	30.0	35.7	10.8	9.9	17.6	28.9	23.1	21.1	21.5
WSD+DA-VGG_M	30.3	24.1	15.6	13.8	9.1	32.7	39.0	21.4	2.9	19.0	26.4	25.5	24.7	32.9	4.3	8.2	15.6	28.7	24.5	25.1	21.2
WSD+DA+ST-VGG_M	33.3	31.5	16.9	13.8	10.8	39.5	36.2	30.8	8	19.9	33.4	18.4	26.4	37.8	8.3	13.1	15.5	32.1	25.0	33.8	24.2
WSD+DA+2ST-VGG_M	34.3	31.3	18.5	9.4	10.6	39.6	37.7	17.9	10.2	16.7	34.7	19.8	31.8	40.7	7.4	12.5	18.6	33.0	26.8	34.6	24.3
WSD+DA+3ST-VGG_M	35.6	31.3	18.2	7.7	9.1	40.4	38.4	23.8	9.7	20.1	33.4	22.5	30.9	41.4	9.8	10.8	18.7	28.7	27.1	34.7	24.6
WSD(Baseline)-VGG16	45.8	28.2	11.1	8.5	2.5	42.8	41.5	25.9	4.2	15.9	13.0	16.9	28.0	40.8	3.6	5.5	11.0	38.5	28.4	23.2	21.8
WSD+DA-VGG16	33.8	22.4	13.1	13.4	9.1	38.1	36.5	25.8	9.2	20.1	12.6	19.8	19.9	34.4	4.4	10.8	13.8	30	26.8	25.1	21.0
WSD+DA+ST-VGG16	43.7	30.8	15.7	10.6	13.4	41.3	39.5	23.9	12.8	20.7	27.9	13.9	23.4	39.7	10.3	12.7	21.3	39.6	28.1	30.7	25.0
WSD+DA+2ST-VGG16	44.7	31.0	12.1	15.7	11.8	38.8	40.6	29.1	12.0	17.9	32.2	9.1	24.1	42.8	7.6	13.7	17.0	33.4	30.6	33.5	24.9
WSD+DA+3ST-VGG16	40.6	30.1	17.8	15.9	6.4	42.9	40.5	31.5	11.4	20.3	27.4	15.7	24.1	43.8	8.9	12.2	17.7	37.3	32.1	31.0	25.4

Table 3. Average precision results (%) on VOC2012 test set.

	aero	bike	bird	boat	bottle	bus	car	cat	chair	cow	table	dog	horse	mbike	person	plant	sheep	sofa	train	tv	mean
WSD(Baseline)-VGG_M	39.7	25.4	12.6	5.8	2.3	32.3	25.0	20.7	1.6	17.9	9.6	29.0	24.3	42.4	3.8	4.6	10.6	16.6	22.5	11.4	17.9
WSD+DA+3ST-VGG_M	44.3	29.8	15.6	6.6	6.0	34.4	24.2	25.1	5.7	20.3	22.3	24.9	29.1	45.2	7.8	9.4	12.4	21.4	22.6	26.0	21.7
WSD(Baseline)-VGG16	47.9	29.2	14.8	7.9	3.5	39.6	27.3	24.6	2.3	15.9	4.9	18.3	25.5	47.5	3.8	4.3	9.4	22.2	19.3	16.0	19.2
WSD+DA+3ST-VGG16	48.8	32.8	16.6	6.3	7.7	39.0	26.2	32.6	7.8	18.3	12.4	22.1	29.7	45.9	9.6	9.0	14.5	24.0	26.8	28.1	22.9

It can be seen that by further adding the ST stream, 'WSD + DA + ST', the detection results improve significantly, by 2.7% for VGG_M and 3.2% for VGG16, compared with the baselines. In addition, inspired by the idea of [27], we also evaluate the performance of adding multiple pseudo label transfer streams one by one. Specifically, the pseudo labels generated by the first ST stream are used as the supervision of the second ST stream, whose generated pseudo labels are then used as the supervision of the third ST stream. The results of appending multiple ST streams, 'WSD + DA + 2ST' and 'WSD + DA + 3ST', are also shown in Table 2. We can see that adding one additional ST stream generally leads to slight improvements. Overall, by adding the ST streams, our method brings up the results for most categories, especially difficult classes such as "chairs" and "dining tables". These classes are usually in cluttered scenes and the single WSD learned from clean web images can hardly capture the objects from the environment.

The overall performance gains from the best combinations are 3.1% for VGG_M and 3.6% for VGG16. These results show that our proposed method improves the baseline webly supervised detection model significantly by introducing the DA and ST streams. In VGG16, it brings up the unsupervised results to 25.4% without any labels from the target dataset, much closer to the weakly supervised result of 29.3% that requires image-level labels from the target dataset.

In addition to the mAP results for detection, we also measured the correct localization (CorLoc) result on the VOC 2007 trainval set (see Table 5) and compare it with the best reported CorLoc results of the WSD works [3,4,27]. Note that all of these WSD methods use image labels of VOC trainval set during the training and CorLoc is measured on these training images. In our method, we do not include any VOC training labels and we can still achieve a good localization model, 44.3% images are with correctly localized objects, which is even better than [3].

Table 4. Comparing the results (mAP in %) on VOC 2007 test set with different settings of the DA stream.

Method	mAP
WSD+3ST-VGG_M	23.5
WSD+DA(w/o.FA)+3ST-VGG_M	23.3
WSD+DA+3ST-VGG_M	**24.6**

Table 5. CorLoc results on VOC 2007 compared with WSD methods.

Method	CorLoc
Bilen et al. [3]	43.7
Bilen et al. [4]	56.1
Tang et al. [27]	60.6
WSD+DA+3ST-VGG16	44.3

5.4 Ablation Experiments

In the following sections, we analyze the effectiveness of each component, including the domain adaptation stream and the simultaneous transfer streams.

Analysis of the DA Stream. To further verify the effects of the DA stream, we visualizing the feature distributions of 'WSD+DA' in 2D space by t-SNE [23] in Fig. 5. Although this visualization of high dimensional features in 2D space may not be accurate, we can still have some ideas that the DA stream does help shift the features closer to the same region across domains.

We further examine the results by removing the DA stream from the overall structure. As shown in Table 4, the WSD with the ST streams only cannot achieve as high detection mAP as our overall network with the DA stream, which demonstrates the contribution of DA to the overall network. In Table 4, we also evaluate the effectiveness of the foreground attention mechanism (FA) for the DA stream. It can be seen that the result of DA without FA, 'WSD+DA(w/o.FA)+3ST', is even worse than of no DA, 'WSD+3ST', which suggests that treating all proposals equally during DA does not help.

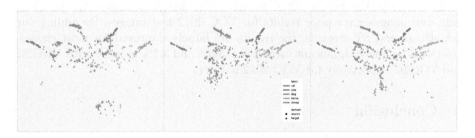

Fig. 5. Visualization of features in 2D space by t-SNE [23]. We randomly sample some object proposals from target and web domains and extract fc7 features (VGG_M) using different methods. Then we use PCA and t-SNE to reduce the dimension to 2. We plot the scatter diagrams for all mammal animal classes. Left: WSD (baseline). Middle: WSD+DA. Right: WSD+DA+3ST.

Analysis of the ST Stream. We also visualized the features of WSD+DA+3ST in 2D space in Fig. 5. It can be seen that by adding both DA and ST, we are able to move the cross-domain features closer while making the classes in target domain more separable.

We would like to point out that the incremental gains of our method with multiple ST streams are not as much as [27] that also use multiple refinement streams. This is due to the following reason. In [27], the positive samples are selected by image-level labels of target dataset and their purpose is to refine the instance classifier for multiple times. However, our method does not use the image labels of VOC dataset and our purpose is to prevent the unexpected distribution shift among similar classes. In other words, the gain of pseudo label transfer in our scenario is mainly from the effects of preserving the semantic structure among classes rather than refining the instance classifiers again and again.

One insight of the ST stream is that our framework trains the WSD model from web domain and selects pseudo ground truth samples of target domain based on the current WSD model at the same time. In other words, the ST stream is trained simultaneously with the WSD stream. In this way, it shares the feature learning between the WSD stream for web image training and the ST stream for target dataset training. An alternative way of transferring the pseudo labels is to train on the two datasets in an isolated way. In particular, we can first pre-train the WSD using web images, then use this pre-trained WSD model to generate the pseudo ground truths for the target dataset and finally use these pseudo ground truths to train a detector for target dataset. We conduct the experiment using such isolated method and obtain an mAP of 22.5%. This implies that the simultaneous weights sharing is important for the learning transfer across domains.

5.5 More Results

We also evaluate our method on VOC 2012 dataset and the results are shown in Table 3. The baseline result shows that the detection model trained using only web images gives poor results for VOC 2012 test images. By adding our DA stream and ST streams, the results are largely improved for most classes. Overall, we achieve significant increases of 3.8% and 3.7% in mAP with VGG_M and VGG16 respectively for VOC 2012 dataset.

6   Conclusion

In conclusion, we introduced an annotation-free object detection method by learning from web image resources. Particularly, to solve the domain mismatch problem between the web domain objects and the target domain objects, we proposed an instance-level domain adaptation stream with foreground attention, together with a simultaneous transfer stream that simultaneously learns target data from pseudo labels. Through these novel components, we achieved significant improvements in detection results and successfully reduced the performance gap between the baseline detectors trained with and without human annotations.

Acknowledgments. This project is partially supported by MoE Tier-2 Grant (MOE2016-T2-2-065).

References

1. Al-Halah, Z., Stiefelhagen, R.: Automatic discovery, association estimation and learning of semantic attributes for a thousand categories. arXiv preprint arXiv:1704.03607 (2017)
2. Bilen, H., Pedersoli, M., Tuytelaars, T.: Weakly supervised object detection with posterior regularization. In: Proceedings BMVC 2014, pp. 1–12 (2014)
3. Bilen, H., Pedersoli, M., Tuytelaars, T.: Weakly supervised object detection with convex clustering. In: Proceedings of the IEEE Conference on Computer Vision and Pattern Recognition, pp. 1081–1089 (2015)
4. Bilen, H., Vedaldi, A.: Weakly supervised deep detection networks. In: Proceedings of the IEEE Conference on Computer Vision and Pattern Recognition, pp. 2846–2854 (2016)
5. Bousmalis, K., Silberman, N., Dohan, D., Erhan, D., Krishnan, D.: Unsupervised pixel-level domain adaptation with generative adversarial networks. In: The IEEE Conference on Computer Vision and Pattern Recognition (CVPR), vol. 1, p. 7 (2017)
6. Chen, X., Gupta, A.: Webly supervised learning of convolutional networks. In: Proceedings of the IEEE International Conference on Computer Vision, pp. 1431–1439 (2015)
7. Chen, X., Shrivastava, A., Gupta, A.: Neil: extracting visual knowledge from web data. In: Proceedings of the IEEE International Conference on Computer Vision, pp. 1409–1416 (2013)
8. Cinbis, R.G., Verbeek, J., Schmid, C.: Weakly supervised object localization with multi-fold multiple instance learning. IEEE Trans. Pattern Anal. Mach. Intell. **39**(1), 189–203 (2017)
9. Divvala, S.K., Farhadi, A., Guestrin, C.: Learning everything about anything: webly-supervised visual concept learning. In: Proceedings of the IEEE Conference on Computer Vision and Pattern Recognition, pp. 3270–3277 (2014)
10. Ferrari, V., Zisserman, A.: Learning visual attributes. In: Advances in Neural Information Processing Systems, pp. 433–440 (2008)
11. Fu, Z., Xiang, T., Kodirov, E., Gong, S.: Zero-shot object recognition by semantic manifold distance. In: Proceedings of the IEEE Conference on Computer Vision and Pattern Recognition, pp. 2635–2644 (2015)
12. Ganin, Y., Lempitsky, V.: Unsupervised domain adaptation by backpropagation. In: International Conference on Machine Learning, pp. 1180–1189 (2015)
13. Girshick, R.: Fast R-CNN. In: Proceedings of the IEEE International Conference on Computer Vision, pp. 1440–1448 (2015)
14. Jie, Z., Wei, Y., Jin, X., Feng, J., Liu, W.: Deep self-taught learning for weakly supervised object localization. arXiv preprint arXiv:1704.05188 (2017)

15. Kantorov, V., Oquab, M., Cho, M., Laptev, I.: ContextLocNet: context-aware deep network models for weakly supervised localization. In: Leibe, B., Matas, J., Sebe, N., Welling, M. (eds.) ECCV 2016. LNCS, vol. 9909, pp. 350–365. Springer, Cham (2016). https://doi.org/10.1007/978-3-319-46454-1_22

16. Kumar Singh, K., Xiao, F., Jae Lee, Y.: Track and transfer: watching videos to simulate strong human supervision for weakly-supervised object detection. In: Proceedings of the IEEE Conference on Computer Vision and Pattern Recognition, pp. 3548–3556 (2016)

17. Lampert, C.H., Nickisch, H., Harmeling, S.: Learning to detect unseen object classes by between-class attribute transfer. In: IEEE Conference on Computer Vision and Pattern Recognition CVPR 2009, pp. 951–958. IEEE (2009)

18. Lampert, C.H., Nickisch, H., Harmeling, S.: Attribute-based classification for zero-shot visual object categorization. IEEE Trans. Pattern Anal. Mach. Intell. **36**(3), 453–465 (2014)

19. Li, L.J., Fei-Fei, L.: Optimol: automatic online picture collection via incremental model learning. Int. J. Comput. Vis. **88**(2), 147–168 (2010)

20. Lin, T.-Y., Dollár, P., Girshick, R., He, K., Hariharan, B., Belongie, S.: Feature pyramid networks for object detection. In: 2017 IEEE Conference on Computer Vision and Pattern Recognition (CVPR), pp. 936–944 (2017). IEEE

21. Liu, W., et al.: SSD: single shot multibox detector. In: Leibe, B., Matas, J., Sebe, N., Welling, M. (eds.) ECCV 2016. LNCS, vol. 9905, pp. 21–37. Springer, Cham (2016). https://doi.org/10.1007/978-3-319-46448-0_2

22. Long, M., Zhu, H., Wang, J., Jordan, M.I.: Deep transfer learning with joint adaptation networks. arXiv preprint arXiv:1605.06636 (2016)

23. Maaten, L.V.D., Hinton, G.: Visualizing data using T-SNE. J. Mach. Learn. Res. **9**(Nov), 2579–2605 (2008)

24. Pennington, J., Socher, R., Manning, C.: Glove: global vectors for word representation. In: Proceedings of the 2014 Conference on Empirical Methods in Natural Language Processing (EMNLP), pp. 1532–1543 (2014)

25. Ren, S., He, K., Girshick, R., Sun, J.: Faster R-CNN: towards real-time object detection with region proposal networks. In: Advances in Neural Information Processing Systems, pp. 91–99 (2015)

26. Sultani, W., Shah, M.: What if we do not have multiple videos of the same action? video action localization using web images. In: 2016 IEEE Conference on Computer Vision and Pattern Recognition (CVPR), pp. 1077–1085. IEEE (2016)

27. Tang, P., Wang, X., Bai, X., Liu, W.: Multiple instance detection network with online instance classifier refinement. In: CVPR (2017)

28. Tao, Q., Yang, H., Cai, J.: Exploiting web images for weakly supervised object detection. arXiv preprint arXiv:1707.08721 (2017)

29. Tzeng, E., Hoffman, J., Darrell, T., Saenko, K.: Simultaneous deep transfer across domains and tasks. In: Proceedings of the IEEE International Conference on Computer Vision, pp. 4068–4076 (2015)

30. Tzeng, E., Hoffman, J., Saenko, K., Darrell, T.: Adversarial discriminative domain adaptation. In: Computer Vision and Pattern Recognition (CVPR), vol. 1, p. 4 (2017)

31. Uijlings, J.R., Van De Sande, K.E., Gevers, T., Smeulders, A.W.: Selective search for object recognition. Int. J. Comput. Vis. **104**(2), 154–171 (2013)

32. Wang, G., Luo, P., Lin, L., Wang, X.: Learning object interactions and descriptions for semantic image segmentation. In: Proceedings of the IEEE Conference on Computer Vision and Pattern Recognition, pp. 5859–5867 (2017)

33. Wei, Y., et al.: STC: a simple to complex framework for weakly-supervised semantic segmentation. IEEE Trans. Pattern Anal. Mach. Intell. **39**(11), 2314–2320 (2017)
34. Xia, Y., Cao, X., Wen, F., Sun, J.: Well begun is half done: generating high-quality seeds for automatic image dataset construction from web. In: Fleet, D., Pajdla, T., Schiele, B., Tuytelaars, T. (eds.) ECCV 2014. LNCS, vol. 8692, pp. 387–400. Springer, Cham (2014). https://doi.org/10.1007/978-3-319-10593-2_26
35. Xu, Z., Huang, S., Zhang, Y., Tao, D.: Augmenting strong supervision using web data for fine-grained categorization. In: Proceedings of the IEEE International Conference on Computer Vision, pp. 2524–2532 (2015)
36. Yang, X., Zhang, H., Cai, J.: Shuffle-then-assemble: learning object-agnostic visual relationship features. In: ECCV (2018)

Receptive Field Block Net for Accurate and Fast Object Detection

Songtao Liu, Di Huang$^{(\boxtimes)}$ (iD), and Yunhong Wang

Beijing Advanced Innovation Center for Big Data and Brain Computing,
Beihang University, Beijing 100191, China
{liusongtao,dhuang,yhwang}@buaa.edu.cn

Abstract. Current top-performing object detectors depend on deep CNN backbones, such as ResNet-101 and Inception, benefiting from their powerful feature representations but suffering from high computational costs. Conversely, some lightweight model based detectors fulfil real time processing, while their accuracies are often criticized. In this paper, we explore an alternative to build a fast and accurate detector by strengthening lightweight features using a hand-crafted mechanism. Inspired by the structure of Receptive Fields (RFs) in human visual systems, we propose a novel RF Block (RFB) module, which takes the relationship between the size and eccentricity of RFs into account, to enhance the feature discriminability and robustness. We further assemble RFB to the top of SSD, constructing the RFB Net detector. To evaluate its effectiveness, experiments are conducted on two major benchmarks and the results show that RFB Net is able to reach the performance of advanced very deep detectors while keeping the real-time speed. Code is available at https://github.com/ruinmessi/RFBNet.

Keywords: Real-time object detection · Receptive Field Block (RFB)

1 Introduction

In recent years, Region-based Convolutional Neural Networks (R-CNN) [8], along with its representative updated descendants, *e.g.* Fast R-CNN [7] and Faster R-CNN [26], have persistently promoted the performance of object detection on major challenges and benchmarks, such as Pascal VOC [5], MS COCO [21], and ILSVRC [27]. They formulate this issue as a two-stage problem and build a typical pipeline, where the first phase hypothesizes category-agnostic object proposals within the given image and the second phase classifies each proposal according to CNN based deep features. It is generally accepted that in these methods, CNN representation plays a crucial role, and the learned feature is expected to deliver a high discriminative power encoding object characteristics and a good robustness especially to moderate positional shifts (usually incurred by inaccurate boxes). A number of very recent efforts have confirmed such a fact. For instance, [11] and [15] extract features from deeper CNN backbones,

© Springer Nature Switzerland AG 2018
V. Ferrari et al. (Eds.): ECCV 2018, LNCS 11215, pp. 404–419, 2018.
https://doi.org/10.1007/978-3-030-01252-6_24

like ResNet [11] and Inception [31]; [19] introduces a top-down architecture to construct feature pyramids, integrating low-level and high-level information; and the latest top-performing Mask R-CNN [9] produces an RoIAlign layer to generate more precise regional features. All these methods adopt improved features to reach better results; however, such features basically come from deeper neural networks with heavy computational costs, making them suffer from a low inference speed.

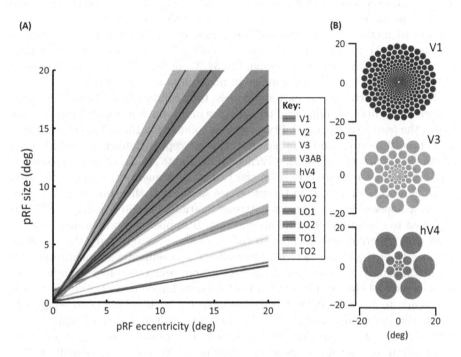

Fig. 1. Regularities in human population Receptive Field (pRF) properties. **(A)** pRF size as a function of eccentricity in some human retinotopic maps, where two trends are evident: (1) the pRF size increases with eccentricity in each map and (2) the pRF size differs between maps. **(B)** The spatial array of the pRFs based on the parameters in **(A)**. The radius of each circle is the apparent RF size at the appropriate eccentricity. Reproduced from [36] with the permission from J. Winawer and H. Horiguchi (https://archive.nyu.edu/handle/2451/33887).

To accelerate detection, a single-stage framework is investigated, where the phase of object proposal generation is discarded. Although the pioneering attempts, namely You Look Only Once (YOLO) [24] and Single Shot Detector (SSD) [22], illustrate the ability of real-time processing, they tend to sacrifice accuracies, with a clear drop ranging from 10% to 40% relative to state-of-the-art two-stage solutions [20]. More recently, Deconvolutional SSD (DSSD) [6] and RetinaNet [20] substantially ameliorate the precision scores, which are comparable to the top ones reported by the two-stage detectors. Unfortunately their performance gains are credited to the very deep ResNet-101 [11] model as well, which limits the efficiency.

According to the discussion above, to build a fast yet powerful detector, a reasonable alternative is to enhance feature representation of the lightweight network by bringing in certain hand-crafted mechanisms rather than stubbornly deepening the model. On the other side, several discoveries in neuroscience reveal that in human visual cortex, the size of population Receptive Field (pRF) is a function of eccentricity in their retinotopic maps, and although varying between maps, it increases with eccentricity in each map [36], as illustrated in Fig. 1. It helps to highlight the importance of the region nearer to the center and elevate the insensitivity to small spatial shifts. A few shallow descriptors coincidentally make use of this mechanism to design [14,34,37] or learn [1,29,38] their pooling schemes, and show good performance in matching image patches.

Regarding current deep learning models, they commonly set RFs at the same size with a regular sampling grid on a feature map, which probably induces some loss in the feature discriminability as well as robustness. Inception [33] considers RFs of multiple sizes, and it implements this concept by launching multi-branch CNNs with different convolution kernels. Its variants [16,31,32] achieve competitive results in object detection (in the two-stage framework) and classification tasks. However, all kernels in Inception are sampled at the same center. A similar idea appears in [3], where an Atrous Spatial Pyramid Pooling (ASPP) is exploited to capture multi-scale information. It applies several parallel convolutions with different atrous rates on the top feature map to vary the sampling distance from the center, which proves effective in semantic segmentation. But the features only have a uniform resolution from previous convolution layers of the same kernel size, and compared to the daisy shaped ones, the resulting feature tends to be less distinctive. Deformable CNN [4] attempts to adaptively adjust the spatial distribution of RFs according to the scale and shape of the object. Although its sampling grid is flexible, the impact of eccentricity of RFs is not taken into account, where all pixels in an RF contribute equally to the output response and the most important information is not emphasized.

Inspired by the structure of RFs in the human visual system, this paper proposes a novel module, namely Receptive Field Block (RFB), to strengthen the deep features learned from lightweight CNN models so that they can contribute to fast and accurate detectors. Specifically, RFB makes use of multi-branch pooling with varying kernels corresponding to RFs of different sizes, applies dilated convolution layers to control their eccentricities, and reshapes them to generate final representation, as in Fig. 2. We then assemble the RFB module to the top of SSD [22], a real-time approach with a lightweight backbone, and construct an advanced one-stage detector (RFB Net). Thanks to such a simple module, RFB Net delivers relatively decent scores that are comparable to the ones of up-to-date deeper backbone network based detectors [18–20] and retains the fast speed of the original lightweight detector. Additionally, the RFB module is generic and imposes few constraints on the network architecture.

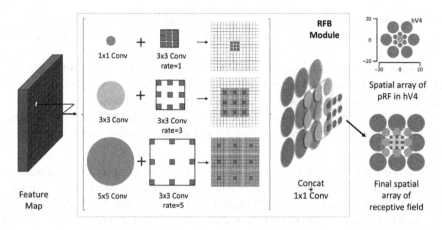

Fig. 2. Construction of the RFB module by combining multiple branches with different kernels and dilated convolution layers. Multiple kernels are analogous to the pRFs of varying sizes, while dilated convolution layers assign each branch with an individual eccentricity to simulate the ratio between the size and eccentricity of the pRF. With a concatenation and 1×1 conv in all the branches, the final spatial array of RF is produced, which is similar to that in human visual systems, as depicted in Fig. 1.

Our main contributions can be summarized as follows:

1. We propose the RFB module to simulate the configuration in terms of the size and eccentricity of RFs in human visual systems, aiming to enhance deep features of lightweight CNN backbones.
2. We present the RFB Net based detector, and by simply replacing the top convolution layers of SSD [22] with RFB, it shows significant performance gain while still keeping the computational cost under control.
3. We show that RFB Net achieves state-of-the-art results on Pascal VOC and MS COCO at a real time processing speed, and demonstrate the generalization ability of RFB by linking it to MobileNet [12].

2   Related Work

Two-Stage Detector: R-CNN [8] straightforwardly combines the steps of cropping box proposals like Selective Search [35] and classifying them through a CNN model, yielding a significant accuracy gain compared to traditional methods, which opens the deep learning era in object detection. Its descendants (*e.g.*, Fast R-CNN [7], Faster R-CNN [26]) update the two-stage framework and achieve dominant performance. Besides, a number of effective extensions are proposed to further improve the detection accuracy, such as R-FCN [17], FPN [19], Mask R-CNN [9].

One-Stage Detector: The most representative one-stage detectors are YOLO [24,25] and SSD [22]. They predict confidences and locations for multiple objects based on the whole feature map. Both the detectors adopt lightweight backbones for acceleration, while their accuracies apparently trail those of top two-stage methods.

Recent more advanced single-stage detectors (*e.g.*, DSSD [6] and RetinaNet [20]) replace their original lightweight backbones by the deeper ResNet-101 and apply certain techniques, such as deconvolution [6] or Focal Loss [20], whose scores are comparable and even superior to the ones of state-of-the-art two-stage methods. However, such performance gains largely consume their advantage in speed.

Receptive Field: Recall that in this study, we aim to improve the performance of high-speed single-stage detectors without incurring too much computational burden. Therefore, instead of applying very deep backbones, RFB, imitating the mechanism of RFs in the human visual system, is used to enhance lightweight model based feature representation. Actually, there exist several studies that discuss RFs in CNN, and the most related ones are the Inception family [31–33], ASPP [3], and Deformable CNN [4].

The Inception block adopts multiple branches with different kernel sizes to capture multi-scale information. However, all the kernels are sampled at the same center, which requires much larger ones to reach the same sampling coverage and thus loses some crucial details. For ASPP, dilated convolution varies the sampling distance from the center, but the features have a uniform resolution from the previous convolution layers of the same kernel size, which treats the clues at all the positions equally, probably leading to confusion between object and context. Deformable CNN [4] learns distinctive resolutions of individual objects, unfortunately it holds the same downside as ASPP. RFB is indeed different from them, and it highlights the relationship between RF size and eccentricity in a daisy-shape configuration, where bigger weights are assigned to the positions nearer to the center by smaller kernels, claiming that they are more important than the farther ones. See Fig. 3 for differences of the four typical spatial RF structures. On the other side, Inception and ASPP have not been successfully exploited to improve one-stage detectors, while RFB shows an effective way to make use of their advantages in this issue.

3   Method

In this section, we revisit the human visual cortex, introduce our RFB components and the way to simulate such a mechanism, and describe the architecture of the RFB Net detector as well as its training/testing schedule.

3.1   Visual Cortex Revisit

During the past few decades, it has come true that functional Magnetic Resonance Imaging (fMRI) non-invasively measures human brain activities at a resolution in millimeter, and RF modeling has become an important sensory science tool used to predict responses and clarify brain computations. Since human

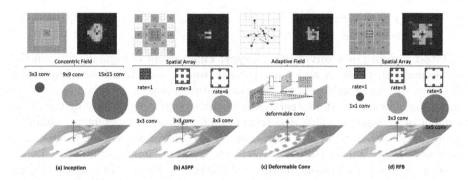

Fig. 3. Four typical structures of Spatial RFs. (a) shows the kernels of multiple sizes in Inception. (b) demonstrates the daisy-like pooling configuration in ASPP. (c) adopts deformable conv to produce an adaptive RF according to object characteristics. (d) illustrates the mechanism of RFB. The color map of each structure is the effective RF derived from one correspondent layer in the trained model, depicted by the same gradient back-propagation method in [23]. In (a) and (b), we adjust the RF sizes in original Inception and ASPP for fair comparison.

neuroscience instruments often observe the pooled responses of many neurons, these models are thus commonly called pRF models [36]. Based on fMRI and pRF modeling, it is possible to investigate the relation across many visual field maps in the cortex. At each cortical map, researchers find a positive correlation between pRF size and eccentricity [36], while the coefficient of correlation varies in visual field maps, as shown in Fig. 1.

3.2 Receptive Field Block

The proposed RFB is a multi-branch convolutional block. Its inner structure can be divided into two components: the multi-branch convolution layer with different kernels and the trailing dilated pooling or convolution layers. The former part is identical to that of Inception, responsible for simulating the pRFs of multiple sizes, and the latter part reproduces the relation between the pRF size and eccentricity in the human visual system. Figure 2 illustrates RFB along with its corresponding spatial pooling region maps. We elaborate the two parts and their functions in detail in the following.

Multi-branch Convolution Layer: According to the definition of RF in CNNs, it is a simple and natural way to apply different kernels to achieve multi-size RFs, which is supposed to be superior to the RFs that share a fixed size.

We adopt the latest changes in the updated versions, *i.e.*, Inception V4 and Inception-ResNet V2 [31] in the Inception family. To be specific, first, we employ the bottleneck structure in each branch, consisting of a 1×1 conv-layer, to decrease the number of channels in the feature map plus an $n \times n$ conv-layer. Second, we replace the 5×5 conv-layer by two stacked 3×3 conv-layers to reduce parameters and deeper non-linear layers. For the same reason, we use a $1 \times n$

plus an $n \times 1$ conv-layer to take place of the original $n \times n$ conv-layer. Ultimately, we apply the shortcut design from ResNet [11] and Inception-ResNet V2 [31].

Dilated Pooling or Convolution Layer: This concept is originally introduced in Deeplab [2], which is also named the astrous convolution layer. The basic intention of this structure is to generate feature maps of a higher resolution, capturing information at a larger area with more context while keeping the same number of parameters. This design has rapidly proved competent at semantic segmentation [3], and has also been adopted in some reputable object detectors, such as SSD [22] and R-FCN [17], to elevate speed or/and accuracy.

In this paper, we exploit dilated convolution to simulate the impact of the eccentricities of pRFs in the human visual cortex. Figure 4 illustrates two combinations of multi-branch convolution layer and dilated pooling or convolution layer. At each branch, the convolution layer of a particular kernel size is followed by a pooling or convolution layer with a corresponding dilation. The kernel size and dilation have a similar positive functional relation as that of the size and eccentricity of pRFs in the visual cortex. Eventually, the feature maps of all the branches are concatenated, merging into a spatial pooling or convolution array as in Fig. 1.

The specific parameters of RFB, *e.g.*, kernel size, dilation of each branch, and number of branches, are slightly different at each position within the detector, which are clarified in the next section.

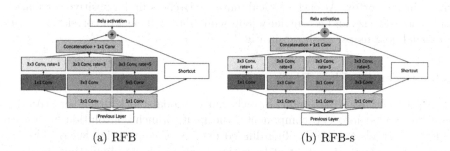

| (a) RFB | (b) RFB-s |

Fig. 4. The architectures of RFB and RFB-s. RFB-s is employed to mimic smaller pRFs in shallow human retinotopic maps, using more branches with smaller kernels. Following [32], we use two layers of 3×3 conv replacing 5×5 to reduce parameters, which is not shown for better visualization.

3.3   RFB Net Detection Architecture

The proposed RFB Net detector reuses the multi-scale and one-stage framework of SSD [22], where the RFB module is embedded to ameliorate the feature extracted from the lightweight backbone so that the detector is more accurate and still fast enough. Thanks to the property of RFB for easily being integrated into CNNs, we can preserve the SSD architecture as much as possible. The main

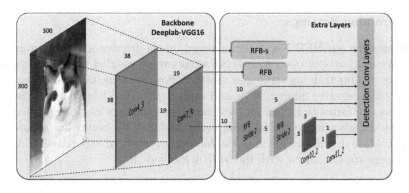

Fig. 5. The pipeline of RFB-Net300. The conv4_3 feature map is tailed by RFB-s which has smaller RFs and an RFB module with stride 2 is produced by operating 2-stride multi-kernel conv-layers in the original RFB.

modification lies in replacing the top convolution layers with RFB, and some minor but active ones are given in Fig. 5.

Lightweight Backbone: We use exactly the same backbone network as in SSD [22]. In brief, it is a VGG16 [30] architecture pre-trained on the ILSVRC CLS-LOC dataset [27], where its fc6 and fc7 layers are converted to convolutional layers with sub-sampling parameters, and its pool5 layer is changed from 2×2-s2 to 3×3-s1. The dilated convolution layer is used to fill holes and all the dropout layers and the fc8 layer are removed. Even though many accomplished lightweight networks have recently been proposed (*e.g.* DarkNet [25], MobileNet [12], and ShuffleNet [39]), we focus on this backbone to achieve direct comparison to the original SSD [22].

RFB on Multi-scale Feature Maps: In the original SSD [22], the base network is followed by a cascade of convolutional layers to form a series of feature maps with consecutively decreasing spatial resolutions and increasing fields of view. In our implementation, we keep the same cascade structure of SSD, but the front convolutional layers with feature maps of relatively large resolutions are replaced by the RFB module. In the primary version of RFB, we use a single structure setting to imitate the impact of eccentricity. As the rate of the size and eccentricity of pRF differs between visual maps, we correspondingly adjust the parameters of RFB to form an RFB-s module, which mimics smaller pRFs in shallow human retinotopic maps, and put it behind the conv4_3 features, as illustrated in Figs. 4 and 5. The last few convolutional layers are preserved since the resolutions of their feature maps are too small to apply filters with large kernels like 5×5.

3.4   Training Settings

We implement our RFB Net detector based on the framework of Pytorch[1], utilizing several parts of open source infrastructures provided by the ssd.pytorch repository[2]. Our training strategies mostly follow SSD, including data augmentation, hard negative mining, scale and aspect ratios for default boxes, and loss functions (e.g., smooth L1 loss for localization and softmax loss for classification), while we slightly change our learning rate scheduling for better accommodation of RFB. More details are given in the following section of experiments. All new conv-layers are initialized with the MSRA method [10].

4   Experiments

We conduct experiments on the Pascal VOC 2007 [5] and MS COCO [21] datasets, which have 20 and 80 object categories respectively. In VOC 2007, a predicted bounding box is positive if its Intersection over Union (IoU) with the ground truth is higher than 0.5, while in COCO, it uses various thresholds for more comprehensive calculation. The metric to evaluate detection performance is the mean Average Precision (mAP).

4.1   Pascal VOC 2007

In this experiment, we train our RFB Net on the union of 2007 *trainval* set and 2012 *trainval* set. We set the batch size at 32 and the initial learning rate at 10^{-3} as in the original SSD [22], but it makes the training process not so stable as the loss drastically fluctuates. Instead, we use a "warmup" strategy that gradually ramps up the learning rate from 10^{-6} to 4×10^{-3} at the first 5 epochs. After the "warmup" phase, it goes back to the original learning rate schedule, divided by 10 at 150 and 200 epochs. The total number of training epochs is 250. Following [22], we utilize a weight decay of 0.0005 and a momentum of 0.9.

Table 1 shows the comparison between our results and the state of the art ones on the VOC2007 *test* set. SSD300* and SSD512* are the updated SSD results with an expansion of data augmentation [22], which zooms out the images to create more small examples. For fair comparison, we reimplement SSD with Pytorch-0.3.0 and CUDNN V6, the same environment as that of RFB Net. By integrating the RFB layers, our basic model, *i.e.* RFB Net300, outperforms SSD and YOLO with an mAP of 80.5%, while keeping the real-time speed as SSD300. It even reaches the same accuracy with R-FCN [17], the advanced model under the two-stage framework. RFB Net512 achieves the mAP of 82.2% with a larger input size, better than most one stage and two stage object detection systems equipped with very deep base backbone networks, while still running at a high speed.

---

[1] https://pytorch.org/.

[2] https://github.com/amdegroot/ssd.pytorch.

Table 1. Comparison of detection methods on the PASCAL VOC 2007 *test* set. All runtime information is computed on a Graphics card of Geforce GTX Titan X (Maxwell architecture).

Method	Backbone	Data	mAP(%)	FPS
Faster [26]	VGG	07 + 12	73.2	7
Faster [11]	ResNet-101	07 + 12	76.4	5
R-FCN [17]	ResNet-101	07 + 12	80.5	9
YOLOv2 544 [25]	Darknet	07 + 12	78.6	40
R-FCN w Deformable CNN [4]	ResNet-101	07 + 12	**82.6**	8[a]
SSD300* [22]	VGG	07 + 12	77.2	**120**[b]
DSSD321 [6]	ResNet-101	07 + 12	78.6	9.5
RFB Net300	VGG	07 + 12	**80.5**	**83**
SSD512* [22]	VGG	07 + 12	79.8	50[b]
DSSD513 [6]	ResNet-101	07 + 12	81.5	5.5
RFB Net512	VGG	07 + 12	**82.2**	**38**

[a]Extrapolated time
[b]Tested in Pytorch-0.3.0 and CUDNN V6 for fair comparison

4.2 Ablation Study

RFB Module: For better understanding RFB, we investigate the impact of each component in its design and compare RFB with some similar structures. The results are summarized in Tables 2 and 3. As displayed in Table 2, the original SSD300 with new data augmentation achieves a 77.2% mAP. By simply replacing the last convolution layer with the RFB-max pooling, we can see that the result is improved to 79.1%, delivering a gain of 1.9%, which indicates that the RFB module is effective in detection.

Cortex Map Simulation: As described in Sect. 3.3, we tune our RFB parameters to simulate the ratio between the size and eccentricity of pRFs in cortex maps. This adjustment boosts the performance by 0.5% (from 79.1% to 79.6%) for RFB max pooling and 0.4% for RFB dilated conv (from 80.1% to 80.5%), which validates the mechanism in human visual systems (Table 2).

More Prior Anchors: The original SSD associates only 4 default boxes at conv4_3, conv10_2, and conv11_2 feature map locations and 6 default anchors for all the other layers. Recent research [13] claims that low level features are critical to detecting small objects. We thus suppose that performance, especially that of small instances, tends to increase if more anchors are added in low level feature maps like conv4_3. In the experiment, we put 6 default priors at conv4_3, and it has no influence on the original SSD, while it further improves 0.2% (from 79.6% to 79.8%) for our RFB model (Table 2).

Dilated Convolutional Layer: In early experiments, we choose dilated pooling layers for RFB to avoid incurring additional parameters, but these stationary

S. Liu et al.

pooling strategies limit feature fusion of RFs of multiple sizes. When picking the dilated convolutional layer, we find that it raises the accuracy by 0.7% (from 79.8% to 80.5%) without slowing down the inference speed (Table 2).

Table 2. Effectiveness of various designs on the VOC 2007 *test* set (refer to Sects. 3.3 and 4.2 for more details).

	SSD*						RFB
RFB-max pooling?		✓	✓	✓			
Add RFB-s?			✓	✓	✓		✓
More Prior?				✓	✓	✓	✓
RFB-avg pooling?					✓		
RFB-dilated conv?						✓	✓
	77.2	79.1	79.6	79.8	79.8	80.1	**80.5**

Comparison with Other Architectures: We also compare our RFB with Inception [33], ASPP [3] and Deformable CNN [4]. For Inception, besides the original version, we change its parameters so that it has the same RF size as RFB does (termed "Inception-L"). For ASPP, its primary parameters are tuned in image segmentation [3] and the RFs are too large for detection, and in our experiment, we set it at the same size as in RFB as well (termed "ASPP-S"). Figure 3 shows a visualized comparison in their structures. Simply, we individually mount these structures on the top layer of the detector as in Fig. 5 and keep the same training schedule and almost the same number of parameters. Their evaluations on Pascal VOC and MS COCO are recorded in Table 3, and we can see that our RFB performs best. It points out that the dedicated RFB structure indeed contributes to the detection precision, as it has a larger effective RF than the counterparts (see an example in Fig. 3).

Table 3. Comparison of different blocks on VOC 2007 *test* and MS COCO *minival2014*.

Architecture	#parameters	VOC 2007 mAP (%)	COCO minival mAP (%)
RFB	34.5M	**80.1**	**29.7**
Inception [33]	32.9M	78.4	27.3
Inception-L	33.3M	79.5	28.5
ASPP-S	33.4M	79.7	28.1
Deformable CNN [4]	35.2M	79.5	27.6

4.3   Microsoft COCO

To further validate the proposed RFB module, we carry out experiments on the MS COCO dataset. Following [20,22], we use the *trainval35k* set (*train* set + *val 35k* set) for training and set the batch size at 32. We keep the original SSD strategy that decreases the size of default boxes, since objects in COCO are smaller than those in PASCAL VOC. At the begin of training, we still apply the "warmup" technique that progressively increases the learning rate from 10^{-6} to 2×10^{-3} at the first 5 epochs, then decrease it after 80 and 100 epochs by the factor of 10, and end up at 120.

From Table 4, it can be seen that RFB Net300 achieves 30.3%/49.3% on the *test-dev* set, which surpasses the baseline score of SSD300* with a large margin, and even equals to that of R-FCN [17] which employs ResNet-101 as the base net with a larger input size (600 × 1000) under the two stage framework.

Regarding the bigger model, the result of RFB Net512 is slightly inferior to but still comparable to the one of the recent advanced one-stage model RetinaNet500 (33.8% vs. 34.4%). However, it should be noted that RetinaNet employs the deep ResNet-101-FPN backbone and a new loss to make learning focus on hard examples, while our RFB Net is only built on a lightweight VGG model. On the other hand, we can see that RFB Net500 averagely consumes 30 ms per image, while RetinaNet needs 90 ms.

One may notice that RetinaNet800 [20] reports the top accuracy (39.1%) based on a very high resolution up to 800 pixels. Although it is well known that a larger input image size commonly yields higher performance, it is out of the scope of this study, where an accurate and fast detector is pursued. Instead, we consider two efficient updates: (1) to up-sample the conv7_fc feature maps and concat it with the conv4_3 before applying the RFB-s module, sharing a similar strategy as in FPN [19]; and (2) to add a branch with a 7 × 7 kernel in all RFB layers. As we can see in Table 4, they further increase the performance, making the best score in this study at 34.4% (denoted as RFB Net512-E), while the computational cost only marginally ascends.

5   Discussion

Inference Speed Comparison: In Table 1 and Fig. 6, we show speed comparison to other recent top-performing detectors. In our experiments, the inference speeds in different datasets have slight variations, since MS COCO has 80 categories and average dense instances consume more time on the NMS process. Table 1 shows that our RFB Net300 is the most accurate one (80.5% mAP) among the real-time detectors and runs at 83 fps in Pascal VOC, and RFB Net512 provides more accurate results still with a speed of 38 fps. In Fig. 6, we follow [20] to plot the speed/accuracy trade-off curve for RFB Net, and compare it to RetinaNet [20] and other recent methods on the MS COCO *test-dev* set. This plot displays that our RFB Net forms an upper envelope among all the real-time detectors. In particular, RFB Net300 keeps a high speed (66 fps)

Table 4. Detection performance on the COCO *test-dev* 2015 dataset. Almost all the methods are measured on the Nvidia Titan X (Maxwell architecture) GPU, except RetinaNet, Mask R-CNN and FPN (Nvidia M40 GPU).

Method	Backbone	Time	Avg. Precision, IoU:			Avg. Precision, Area:		
			0.5:0.95	0.5	0.75	S	M	L
Faster [26]	VGG	147 ms	24.2	45.3	23.5	7.7	26.4	37.1
Faster+++ [11]	ResNet-101	3.36 s	34.9	55.7	37.4	15.6	38.7	50.9
Faster w FPN [19]	ResNet-101-FPN	240 ms	36.2	59.1	39.0	18.2	39.0	48.2
Faster by G-RMI [15]	Inception-Resnet-v2 [31]	–	34.7	55.5	36.7	13.5	38.1	52.0
R-FCN [17]	ResNet-101	110 ms	29.9	51.9	–	10.8	32.8	45.0
R-FCN w Deformable CNN [4]	ResNet-101	125ms[a]	34.5	55.0	–	14.0	37.7	50.3
Mask R-CNN [9]	ResNext-101-FPN	210 ms	37.1	60.0	39.4	16.9	39.9	53.5
YOLOv2 [25]	darknet	25 ms	21.6	44.0	19.2	5.0	22.4	35.5
SSD300* [22]	VGG	12 ms[b]	25.1	43.1	25.8	–	–	–
SSD512* [22]	VGG	28 ms[b]	28.8	48.5	30.3	–	–	–
DSSD513 [6]	ResNet-101	182 ms	33.2	53.3	35.2	13.0	35.4	51.1
RetinaNet500 [20]	ResNet-101-FPN	90 ms	34.4	53.1	36.8	14.7	38.5	49.1
RetinaNet800 [20]	ResNet-101-FPN	198 ms	**39.1**	59.1	42.3	21.8	42.7	50.2
RFB Net300	VGG	**15 ms**	**30.3**	49.3	31.8	11.8	31.9	45.9
RFB Net512	VGG	**30 ms**	**33.8**	54.2	35.9	16.2	37.1	47.4
RFB Net512-E	VGG	**33 ms**	**34.4**	55.7	36.4	17.6	37.0	47.6

[a]Extrapolated time
[b]Tested in Pytorch-0.3.0 and CUDNN V6 for fair comparison

while outperforming all the high frame rate counterparts. Note that they are measured on the same Titan X (Maxwell architecture) GPU, except RetinaNet (Nvidia M40 GPU).

Other Lightweight Backbone: Although the base backbone we use is a reduced VGG16 version, it still has a large number of parameters compared with those recent advanced lightweight networks, *e.g.*, MobileNet [12], DarkNet [25], and ShuffleNet [39]. To further test the generalization ability of the RFB module, we link RFB to MobileNet-SSD [12]. Following [12], we train it on the MS COCO *train+val35k* dataset with the same schedule and make evaluation on *minival*. Table 5 shows that RFB still increases the accuracy of the MobileNet backbone with limited additional layers and parameters. This suggests its great potential for applications on low-end devices.

Training from Scratch: We also notice another interesting property of the RFB module, *i.e.* efficiently training the object detector from scratch. Recently, according to [28], training without using pre-trained backbones is discovered to be a hard task, where all the structures of base nets fail to be trained from scratch in the two-stage framework and the prevalent CNNs (ResNet or VGG) in the one-stage framework successfully converge with much worse results. Deeply Supervised Object Detectors (DSOD) [28] proposes a lightweight structure which achieves a 77.7% mAP on the VOC 2007 *test* set without pre-training, but it does not promote the performance when using pre-trained network. We train our RFB Net300 on the VOC 07 + 12 *trainval* set from scratch and reach a 77.6%

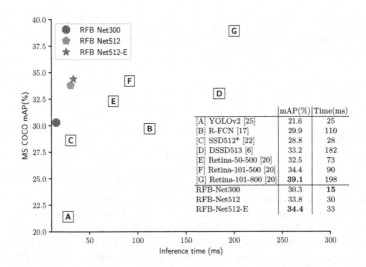

Fig. 6. Speed (ms) vs. accuracy (mAP) on MS COCO *test-dev*. Enabled by the proposed RFB module, our single one-stage detector surpasses all existing high frame rate detectors, including the best reported one-stage system Retina-50-500 [20].

mAP on the same test set, which is comparable to DSOD. It is worth noting that our pre-trained version boosts the performance to 80.5%.

Table 5. Accuracies on MS COCO *minival2014* using MobileNet as the backbone.

Framework	Model	mAP (%)	#parameters
SSD 300	MobileNet [12]	19.3%	6.8M
SSD 300	MobileNet + RFB	**20.7%**	7.4M

6   Conclusion

In this paper, we propose a fast yet powerful object detector. In contrast to the widely employed way that greatly deepens the backbone, we choose to enhance feature representation of lightweight networks by bringing in a hand-crafted mechanism, namely Receptive Field Block (RFB), which imitates the structure of RF in human visual systems. RFB measures the relationship between the size and eccentricity of RFs, and generates more discriminative and robust features. RFB is equipped on the top of lightweight CNN based SSD, and the resulting detector delivers a significant performance gain on the Pascal VOC and MS COCO databases, where the final accuracies are even comparable to those of existing top-performing deeper model based detectors. In addition, it retains the advantage in processing speed of lightweight models.

Acknowledgment. This work was partly supported by the National Key Research and Development Plan (Grant No. 2016YFC0801002) and the National Natural Science Foundation of China (No. 61421003).

References

1. Brown, M., Hua, G., Winder, S.: Discriminative learning of local image descriptors. TPAMI **33**(1), 43–57 (2011)
2. Chen, L.C., Papandreou, G., Kokkinos, I., Murphy, K., Yuille, A.L.: Deeplab: Semantic image segmentation with deep convolutional nets, atrous convolution, and fully connected CRFS. arXiv preprint arXiv:1606.00915 (2016)
3. Chen, L.C., Papandreou, G., Schroff, F., Adam, H.: Rethinking atrous convolution for semantic image segmentation. arXiv preprint arXiv:1706.05587 (2017)
4. Dai, J., et al.: Deformable convolutional networks. In: ICCV (2017)
5. Everingham, M., Van Gool, L., Williams, C.K., Winn, J., Zisserman, A.: The PASCAL visual object classes (voc) challenge. IJCV **88**(2), 303–338 (2010)
6. Fu, C.Y., et al.: DSSD: deconvolutional single shot detector. arXiv preprint arXiv:1701.06659 (2017)
7. Girshick, R.: Fast R-CNN. In: ICCV (2015)
8. Girshick, R., Donahue, J., Darrell, T., Malik, J.: Rich feature hierarchies for accurate object detection and semantic segmentation. In: CVPR (2014)
9. He, K., Gkioxari, G., Dollár, P., Girshick, R.: Mask R-CNN. In: ICCV (2017)
10. He, K., Zhang, X., Ren, S., Sun, J.: Delving deep into rectifiers: surpassing human-level performance on imagenet classification. In: ICCV (2015)
11. He, K., Zhang, X., Ren, S., Sun, J.: Deep residual learning for image recognition. In: CVPR (2016)
12. Howard, A.G., et al.: Mobilenets: efficient convolutional neural networks for mobile vision applications. arXiv preprint arXiv:1704.04861 (2017)
13. Hu, P., Ramanan, D.: Finding tiny faces. In: CVPR (2017)
14. Huang, D., Zhu, C., Wang, Y., Chen, L.: HSOG: a novel local image descriptor based on histograms of the second-order gradients. IEEE Trans. Image Process. **23**(11), 4680–4695 (2014)
15. Huang, J., et al.: Speed/accuracy trade-offs for modern convolutional object detectors. In: CVPR (2017)
16. Kim, K.H., Hong, S., Roh, B., Cheon, Y., Park, M.: PVANET: deep but lightweight neural networks for real-time object detection. arXiv preprint arXiv:1608.08021 (2016)
17. Li, Y., He, K., Sun, J., et al.: R-FCN: object detection via region-based fully convolutional networks. In: NIPS (2016)
18. Li, Y., Qi, H., Dai, J., Ji, X., Wei, Y.: Fully convolutional instance-aware semantic segmentation. In: CVPR (2017)
19. Lin, T.Y., Dollár, P., Girshick, R., He, K., Hariharan, B., Belongie, S.: Feature pyramid networks for object detection. In: CVPR (2017)
20. Lin, T.Y., Goyal, P., Girshick, R., He, K., Dollár, P.: Focal loss for dense object detection. In: ICCV (2017)
21. Lin, T.-Y., et al.: Microsoft COCO: common objects in context. In: Fleet, D., Pajdla, T., Schiele, B., Tuytelaars, T. (eds.) ECCV 2014. LNCS, vol. 8693, pp. 740–755. Springer, Cham (2014). https://doi.org/10.1007/978-3-319-10602-1_48

22. Liu, W., et al.: SSD: single shot multibox detector. In: Leibe, B., Matas, J., Sebe, N., Welling, M. (eds.) ECCV 2016. LNCS, vol. 9905, pp. 21–37. Springer, Cham (2016). https://doi.org/10.1007/978-3-319-46448-0_2

23. Luo, W., et al.: Understanding the effective receptive field in deep convolutional neural networks. In: NIPS (2016)

24. Redmon, J., Divvala, S., Girshick, R., Farhadi, A.: You only look once: unified, real-time object detection. In: CVPR (2016)

25. Redmon, J., Farhadi, A.: Yolo9000: better, faster, stronger. In: CVPR (2017)

26. Ren, S., He, K., Girshick, R., Sun, J.: Faster R-CNN: towards real-time object detection with region proposal networks. In: NIPS (2015)

27. Russakovsky, O., et al.: Imagenet large scale visual recognition challenge. IJCV 115(3), 211–252 (2015)

28. Shen, Z., Liu, Z., Li, J., Jiang, Y.G., Chen, Y., Xue, X.: DSOD: learning deeply supervised object detectors from scratch. In: ICCV (2017)

29. Simonyan, K., Vedaldi, A., Zisserman, A.: Learning local feature descriptors using convex optimisation. TPAMI 36(8), 1573–1585 (2014)

30. Simonyan, K., Zisserman, A.: Very deep convolutional networks for large-scale image recognition. In: NIPS (2014)

31. Szegedy, C., Ioffe, S., Vanhoucke, V., Alemi, A.A.: Inception-v4, inception-resnet and the impact of residual connections on learning. In: AAAI (2017)

32. Szegedy, C., Vanhoucke, V., Ioffe, S., Shlens, J., Wojna, Z.: Rethinking the inception architecture for computer vision. In: CVPR (2016)

33. Szegedy, C., et al.: Going deeper with convolutions. In: CVPR (2015)

34. Tola, E., Lepetit, V., Fua, P.: A fast local descriptor for dense matching. In: CVPR (2008)

35. Uijlings, J.R., Van De Sande, K.E., Gevers, T., Smeulders, A.W.: Selective search for object recognition. IJCV 104(2), 154–171 (2013)

36. Wandell, B.A., Winawer, J.: Computational neuroimaging and population receptive fields. In: Trends in Cognitive Sciences (2015)

37. Weng, D., Wang, Y., Gong, M., Tao, D., Wei, H., Huang, D.: DERF: distinctive efficient robust features from the biological modeling of the P Ganglion cells. IEEE Trans. Image Process. 24(8), 2287–2302 (2015)

38. Winder, S.A., Brown, M.: Learning local image descriptors. In: CVPR (2007)

39. Zhang, X., Zhou, X., Lin, M., Sun, J.: Shufflenet: an extremely efficient convolutional neural network for mobile devices. arXiv preprint arXiv:1707.01083 (2017)

Deep Adversarial Attention Alignment for Unsupervised Domain Adaptation: The Benefit of Target Expectation Maximization

Guoliang Kang[1], Liang Zheng[1,2], Yan Yan[1], and Yi Yang[1(✉)]

[1] CAI, University of Technology Sydney, Ultimo, Australia
{Guoliang.Kang,Yan.Yan-3}@student.uts.edu.au, Yi.Yang@uts.edu.au
[2] Research School of Computer Science, Australian National University,
Canberra, Australia
liangzheng06@gmail.com

Abstract. In this paper, we make two contributions to unsupervised domain adaptation (UDA) using the convolutional neural network (CNN). First, our approach transfers knowledge in all the convolutional layers through attention alignment. Most previous methods align high-level representations, *e.g.,* activations of the fully connected (FC) layers. In these methods, however, the convolutional layers which underpin critical low-level domain knowledge cannot be updated directly towards reducing domain discrepancy. Specifically, we assume that the discriminative regions in an image are relatively invariant to image style changes. Based on this assumption, we propose an attention alignment scheme on all the target convolutional layers to uncover the knowledge shared by the source domain. Second, we estimate the posterior label distribution of the unlabeled data for target network training. Previous methods, which iteratively update the pseudo labels by the target network and refine the target network by the updated pseudo labels, are vulnerable to label estimation errors. Instead, our approach uses category distribution to calculate the cross-entropy loss for training, thereby ameliorating the error accumulation of the estimated labels. The two contributions allow our approach to outperform the state-of-the-art methods by +2.6% on the Office-31 dataset.

Keywords: Domain adaptation · CycleGAN · Attention · EM

1 Introduction

This paper focuses on unsupervised domain adaptation (UDA) for visual classification task. We aim to adapt the knowledge from a source network, trained

---

Electronic supplementary material The online version of this chapter (https://doi.org/10.1007/978-3-030-01252-6_25) contains supplementary material, which is available to authorized users.

© Springer Nature Switzerland AG 2018
V. Ferrari et al. (Eds.): ECCV 2018, LNCS 11215, pp. 420–436, 2018.
https://doi.org/10.1007/978-3-030-01252-6_25

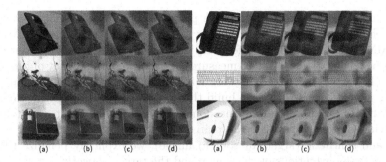

Fig. 1. Attention visualization of the last convolutional layer of ResNet-50. The original *target* input images are illustrated in (**a**). The corresponding attentions of the source network, the target network trained on labeled target data, and the target network adapted with adversarial attention alignment are shown in (**b**), (**c**), and (**d**) respectively.

by the source domain data, to the training of a target network, which will be used for making predications in the target domain. Note that in UDA the *target domain is unlabeled*. The increasing popularity of UDA arises from the fact that the performance of a model trained on one domain may degenerate heavily on another when their underlying data distributions are different.

In the community of UDA, many deep learning methods attempt to minimize the discrepancy across domains on the top layers, such as the fully connected layers, of the neural network via explicitly imposing penalty terms [16,17,23,26] or in an adversarial way [7,24,25]. While the modifications at the fully connected layers can be back-propagated in principle, it may decay after a few layers, especially when gradient explosion or vanishing takes place. Consequently, the convolutional layers may be under-constrained. However, the domain discrepancy may emerge at the start from the convolutional layers, which makes any adjustment purely at the tail of the network less effective.

We investigate the domain discrepancy of the convolutional layers by visualizing their attention mechanisms. In essence, the attention mechanism is emphasized as a key ingredient for CNN, suggested by a number of studies [20,22,27–30,32]. Zagoruyko *et al.* [28] find that the model performance is highly correlated with the attention mechanism: a stronger model always owns better aligned attention than a weaker one. From Fig. 1, suppose we have networks trained on labeled data from source and target domains respectively, we observe distinct attention patterns exhibited by the convolutional layers for the same target domain image. The attention mechanism degenerates when directly applying the source network to the target domain data, which may exert negative influence on the classification performance. Therefore, this paper expects the attention of the convolutional layers to be *invariant to the domain shift*.

Based on the above discussions, this paper takes the domain discrepancy of the convolutional layers directly into account by aligning the attention of the target network with the source network. Our assumption is that no matter how domain varies, the discriminative parts of an image should be insensitive to the changes of image style. Previous discrepancy measures (*e.g.*, MMD [16] and JMMD [17]) which work effectively on high-level *semantic* representations cannot be trivially transferred to measure the attention discrepancy of the convolutional layers where low-level *structure* information is critical. In this paper, we propose using CycleGAN [33] to build the data correspondence across domains, *i.e.*, translating the data from one domain to another without modifying its underlying content. Then, for the paired samples (*e.g.* real source (or target) image and synthetic target (or source) image), we explicitly penalize the distances between attentions of the source and the target networks.

Additionally, we train our target network with real and synthetic data from both source and target domains. For source domain and its translated data, we impose the cross-entropy loss between the predictions and the ground-truth labels. For target domain and its translated source domain data, due to the lack of ground-truth labels, we make use of their underlying category distributions which provide insight into the target data. In a nutshell, we adopt the modified Expectation Maximization (EM) steps to maximize the likelihood of target domain images and update the model. Training iterations improve both the label posterior distribution estimation and the discriminative ability of the model.

Our contributions are summarized below,

- We propose a deep attention alignment method which allows the target network to mimic the attention of the source network. Taking advantage of the pairing nature of CycleGAN, no additional supervision is needed.
- We propose using EM algorithm to exploit the unlabeled target data to update the network. Several modifications are made to stabilize training and improve the adaptation performance.
- Our method outperforms the state of art in all the six transfer tasks, achieving +2.6% improvement in average on the real-world domain adaptation dataset Office-31.

2 Related Work

Unsupervised Domain Adaptation. Various methods have been proposed for unsupervised domain adaptation [7,16,17,26]. Many works try to make the representations at the tail of neural networks invariant across domains. Tzeng *et al.* [26] propose a kind of domain confusion loss to encourage the network to learn both semantically meaningful and domain invariant representations. Similarly, Long *et al.* [16] minimize the MMD distance of the fully-connected activations between source and target domain while sharing the convolutional features. Ganin *et al.* [7] enable the network to learn domain invariant representations in an adversarial way by adding a domain classifier and back-propagating inverse gradients. JAN [17] penalizes the JMMD over multiple fully-connected layers to minimize the domain discrepancy coming from both the data distribution and the label distribution. Further, JAN-A [17], as a variant of JAN, trains the network in an adversarial way with JMMD as the domain adversary.

DSN [3] explicitly models domain-specific features to help improve networks' ability to learn domain-invariant features. Associative domain adaptation (ADA) [8] reinforces associations across domains directly in embedding space to extract statistically domain-invariant and class discriminative features. Few works pay attention to the domain shift coming from the convolutional layers. In this paper, we notice that the attention mechanism cannot be preserved when directly applying the model trained on the source domain to the target domain. To alleviate this problem, we constrain the training of convolutional layers by imposing the attention alignment penalty across domains.

Attention of CNNs. There exist many ways to define and visualize the attention mechanisms learned by CNNs. Zeiler and Fergus [29] project certain features back onto the image through a network called "deconvnet" which shares the same weights as the original feed-forward network. Simonyan *et al.* [22] propose using the gradient of the class score *w.r.t* the input image to visualize the CNN. Class activation maps (CAMs), proposed by [32], aim to visualize the class-discriminative image regions used by a CNN. Grad-CAM [20] combines gradient based attention method and CAM, enabling to obtain class-discriminative attention maps without modifying the original network structure as [32].

Zagoruyko *et al.* [28] define attention as a set of spatial maps indicating which area the network focuses on to perform a certain task. The attention maps can also be defined *w.r.t* various layers of the network so that they are able to capture both low-, mid-, and high-level representation information. They propose that attention mechanism should be a kind of knowledge transferred across different *network architectures*. Zaogruyko *et al.* [28] align the attention across different architectures for exactly the same image during the training process and aim to transfer the knowledge from a large model to a smaller one. Different to [28], our method aligns the attention across different *data domains* where images across domains are unpaired and aims to promote the model adaptation performance.

Unpaired Image-to-Image Translation. Unpaired image-to-image translation aims to train a model to map image samples across domains, under the absence of pairing information. It can be realized through GAN to pair the real source (or target) and synthetic target (or source) images [2,11,12,14,15,19, 21,33]. Generating synthetic images can be beneficial for various vision tasks [5,6,18,31]. In this paper, we concentrate on maximizing the utility of given paired real and synthetic samples. And we choose CycleGAN [33] to perform such adversarial data pairing.

3   Deep Adversarial Attention Alignment

Our framework is illustrated in Fig. 2. We train a source CNN which guides the attention alignment of the target CNN whose convolutional layers have the same architecture as the source network. The target CNN is trained with a mixture of real and synthetic images from both source and target domains. For source and synthetic target domain data, we have ground-truth labels and use them to train the target network with cross-entropy loss. On the other hand, for the target and synthetic source domain data, due to the lack of ground-truth labels, we optimize the target network through an EM algorithm.

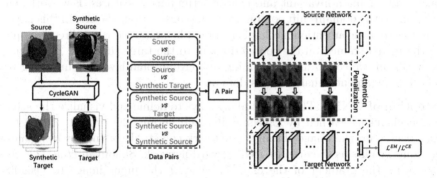

Fig. 2. The framework of deep adversarial attention alignment. We train a source network and fix it. The source network guides the attention alignment of the target network. The target network is trained with real and synthetic images from both domains. For labeled real source and synthetic target data, we update the network by computing the cross-entropy loss between the predictions and the ground-truth labels. For unlabeled real target and synthetic source images, we maximize the likelihood of the data with EM steps. The attention distance for a pair of images (as illustrated in the "Data Pairs" block) passing through the source network and the target network, respectively, is minimized.

3.1 Adversarial Data Pairing

We use CycleGAN to translate the samples in the source domain S to those in the target domain T, and vice versa. The underlying assumption to obtain meaningful translation is that there exist some relationships between two domains. For unsupervised domain adaptation, the objects of interest across domains belong to the same set of category. So it is possible to use CycleGAN to map the sample in the source domain to that in the target domain while maintaining the underlying object-of-interest.

The Generative Adversarial Network (GAN) aims to generate synthetic images which are indistinguishable from real samples through an adversarial loss,

$$\mathcal{L}^{GAN}(G^{ST}, D^T, X^S, X^T) = \mathbb{E}_{x^T}[\log D^T(x^T)] + \mathbb{E}_{x^S}[1 - \log D^T(G^{ST}(x^S))], \tag{1}$$

where x^S and x^T are sampled from source domain S and target domain T, respectively. The generator G^{ST} mapping X^S to X^T strives to make its generated synthetic outputs $G^{ST}(x^S)$ indistinguishable from real target samples x^T for the domain discriminator D^T.

Because the training data across domains are unpaired, the translation from source domain to target domain is highly under-constrained. CycleGAN couples the adversarial training of this mapping with its inverse one, *i.e.* the mapping from S to T and that from T to S are learned concurrently. Moreover, it introduces a cycle consistency loss to regularize the training,

$$\mathcal{L}^{cyc}(G^{ST}, G^{TS}) = \mathbb{E}_{x^S}[\|G^{TS}(G^{ST}(x^S)) - x^S\|_1] + \mathbb{E}_{x^T}[\|G^{ST}(G^{TS}(x^T)) - x^T\|_1], \quad (2)$$

Formally, the full objective for CycleGAN is,

$$\mathcal{L}^{cyc}(G, F, D_X, D_Y) = \mathcal{L}^{GAN}(G^{ST}, D^T, X^S, X^T) + \mathcal{L}^{GAN}(G^{TS}, D^S, X^T, X^S)$$
$$+ \lambda \mathcal{L}^{cyc}(G^{ST}, G^{TS}), \quad (3)$$

where the constant λ controls the strength of the cycle consistency loss. Through CycleGAN, we are able to translate an image in the source domain to that in the target domain in the context of our visual domain adaptation tasks (Fig. 3).

(a)   (b)   (c)   (d)

Fig. 3. Paired data across domains using CycleGAN. (**a**) and (**c**): real images sampled from source and target domain, respectively. (**b**): a synthetic target image paired with (**a**) through G^{ST}. (**d**): a synthetic source image paired with a real target image (**c**) through G^{TS}.

As illustrated in Fig. 1, the target model pays too much attention to the irrelevant background or less discriminative parts of the objects of interest. This attention misalignment will degenerate the model's performance. In this paper, we propose to use the style-translated images as natural image correspondences to guide the attention mechanism of the target model to mimic that of the source model, to be detailed in Sect. 3.2.

3.2 Attention Alignment

Based on the paired images, we propose imposing the attention alignment penalty to reduce the discrepancy of attention maps across domains. Specifically, we represent attention as a function of spatial maps *w.r.t* each convolutional layer [28]. For the input x of a CNN, let the corresponding feature maps *w.r.t* layer l be represented by $F_l(x)$. Then, the attention map $A_l(x)$ *w.r.t* layer l is defined as

$$A_l(x) = \sum_c |F_{l,c}(x)|^2, \quad (4)$$

where $F_{l,c}(x)$ denotes the c-th channel of the feature maps. The operations in Eq. (4) are all element-wise. Alternative ways to represent the attention maps include $\sum_c |F_{l,c}|$, and $\max |F_{l,c}|$, *etc.* We adopt Eq. (4) to emphasize the salient parts of the feature maps.

We propose using the source network to guide the attention alignment of the target network, as illustrated in Fig. 2. We penalize the distance between the vectorized attention maps between the source and the target networks to minimize their discrepancy. In order to make the attention mechanism invariant to the domain shift, we train the target network with a mixture of real and synthetic data from both source and target domains.

Formally, the attention alignment penalty can be formulated as,

$$
\mathcal{L}^{AT} = \sum_l \{ \sum_i \| \frac{A_l^S(x_i^S)}{\|A_l^S(x_i^S)\|_2} - \frac{A_l^T(x_i^S)}{\|A_l^T(x_i^S)\|_2} \|_2 + \sum_j \| \frac{A_l^S(x_j^S)}{\|A_l^S(x_j^S)\|_2} - \frac{A_l^T(\tilde{x}_j^T)}{\|A_l^T(\tilde{x}_j^T)\|_2} \|_2
$$
$$
+ \sum_m \| \frac{A_l^S(\tilde{x}_m^S)}{\|A_l^S(\tilde{x}_m^S)\|_2} - \frac{A_l^T(\tilde{x}_m^S)}{\|A_l^T(\tilde{x}_m^S)\|_2} \|_2 + \sum_n \| \frac{A_l^S(\tilde{x}_n^S)}{\|A_l^S(\tilde{x}_n^S)\|_2} - \frac{A_l^T(x_n^T)}{\|A_l^T(x_n^T)\|_2} \|_2 \},
$$

$$(5)$$

where the subscript l denotes the layer and i, j denote the samples. The A_l^S and A_l^T represent the attention maps *w.r.t* layer l for the source network and the target network, respectively. x^S and x^T are real source and real target domain data, respectively. The synthetic target data $\tilde{x}_i^T$ and synthetic source data $\tilde{x}_n^S$ satisfy $\tilde{x}_i^T = G^{ST}(x_i^S)$ and $\tilde{x}_n^S = G^{TS}(x_n^T)$, respectively.

Through Eq. (5), the distances of attention maps for the paired images (*i.e.*, $(x_j^S, \tilde{x}_j^T)$ and $(x_n^T, \tilde{x}_n^S)$) are minimized. Moreover, we additionally penalize the attention maps of the same input (*i.e.*, x_i^S and $\tilde{x}_m^S$) passing through different networks. The attention alignment penalty $\mathcal{L}^{AT}$ allows the attention mechanism to be gradually adapted to the target domain, which makes the attention mechanism of the target network invariant to the domain shift.

Discussion. On minimizing the discrepancy across domains, our method shares similar ideas with DAN [16] and JAN [17]. The difference is that our method works on the convolutional layers where the critical structure information is captured and aligned across domains; in comparison, DAN and JAN focus on the FC layers where high-level semantic information is considered. Another notable difference is that our method deals with the image-level differences through CycleGAN data pairing, whereas DAN and JAN consider the discrepancy of feature distributions.

In DAN and JAN, MMD and JMMD criteria are adopted respectively to measure the discrepancy of feature distributions across domains. Technically, MMD and JMMD can also be used as attention discrepancy measures. However, as to be shown in the experiment part, MMD and JMMD yield inferior performance to the L_2 distance enabled by adversarial data pairing in our method. The reason is that MMD and JMMD are distribution distance estimators: they map the attention maps to the Reproducing Kernel Hilbert Space (RKHS) and lose the structure information. So they are not suitable for measuring the attention discrepancy across domains.

3.3   Training with EM

To make full use of the available data (labeled and unlabeled), we train the target-domain model with a mixture of real and synthetic data from both source and target domains, as illustrated in Fig. 2. For the source and its translated synthetic target domain data, we compute the cross-entropy loss between the predictions and ground-truth labels to back-propagate the gradients through the target network. The cross-entropy loss for the source and corresponding synthetic target domain data can be formulated as follows,

$$\mathcal{L}^{CE} = -[\sum_i \log p_\theta(y_i^S|x_i^S) + \sum_j \log p_\theta(y_j^S|\tilde{x}_j^T)], \tag{6}$$

where $y^S \in \{1, 2, \cdots, K\}$ denotes the label for the source sample x^S and the translated synthetic target sample $\tilde{x}^T$. The probability $p_\theta(y|x)$ is represented by the y-th output of the target network with parameters θ given the input image x. $\tilde{x}_j^T = G^{ST}(x_j^S)$.

For the unlabeled target data, due to the lack of labels, we employ the EM algorithm to optimize the target network. The EM algorithm can be split into two alternative steps: the (**E**)xpectation computation step and the expectation (**M**)aximization step. The objective is to maximize the log-likelihood of target data samples,

$$\sum_i \log p_\theta(x_i^T), \tag{7}$$

In image classification, our prior is that the target data samples belong to K different categories. We choose the underlying category $z_i \in \{1, 2, \cdots, K\}$ of each sample as the hidden variable, and the algorithm is depicted as follows (we omit the sample subscript and the target domain superscript for description simplicity).

(i) **The Expectation step.** We first estimate $p_{\theta_{t-1}}(z|x)$ through,

$$p_{\theta_{t-1}}(z|x) = \frac{p_{\theta_{t-1}}(x|z)p(z)}{\sum_z p_{\theta_{t-1}}(x|z)p(z)}, \tag{8}$$

where the distribution $p_{\theta_{t-1}}(z|x)$ is modeled by the target network. θ_{t-1} is the parameters of the target-domain CNN at last training step $t-1$. We adopt the uniform distributions to depict $p(z)$ (*i.e.*, assuming the occurrence probabilities of all the categories are the same) and $p(x)$ (*i.e.*, assuming all possible image instantiations are distributed uniformly in the manifold of image gallery). In this manner, $p_{\theta_{t-1}}(z|x) = \alpha p_{\theta_{t-1}}(x|z)$ where α is a constant.

(ii) The Maximization step. Based on the computed posterior $p_{\theta_{t-1}}(z|x)$, our objective is to update θ_t to improve the lower bound of Eq. (7),

$$\sum_z p_{\theta_{t-1}}(z|x) \log p_{\theta_t}(x|z) \tag{9}$$

Note that we omit $\sum_z p_{\theta_{t-1}}(z|x) \log p(z)$ because we assume $p(z)$ subjects to the uniform distribution which is irrelevant to θ_t. Also, because $p_\theta(z|x) = p_\theta(x|z)$, Eq. (9) is equivalent to,

$$\sum_z p_{\theta_{t-1}}(z|x) \log p_{\theta_t}(z|x). \tag{10}$$

Moreover, we propose to improve the effectiveness and stability of the above EM steps through three aspects

(A) Asynchronous update of $p(z|x)$. We adopt an independent network M^{post} to estimate $p(z|x)$ and update M^{post} asynchronously, *i.e.*, M^{post} synchronizes its parameters θ^{post} with the target network every N steps: $\theta_t^{post} = \theta_{\lfloor t/N \rfloor \times N}$. In this manner, we avoid the frequent update of $p(z|x)$ and make the training process much more stable.

(B) Filtering the inaccurate estimates. Because the estimate of $p(z|x)$ is not accurate, we set a threshold p_t and discard the samples whose maximum value of $p(z|x)$ over z is lower than p_t.

(C) Initializing the learning rate schedule after each update of M^{post}. To accelerate the target network adapting to the new update of the distribution $p(z|x)$, we choose to initialize the learning rate schedule after each update of M^{post}.

Note that for synthetic source data $\tilde{x}^S = G^{TS}(x^T)$, we can also apply the modified EM steps for training. Because G^{TS} is a definite mapping, we assume $p(z|\tilde{x}^S) = p(z|x^T)$.

To summarize, when using the EM algorithm to update the target network with target data and synthetic source data, we first compute the posterior $p(z|x^T)$ through network M^{post} which synchronizes with the target network every N steps. Then we minimize the loss,

$$\mathcal{L}^{EM} = -\{\sum_i \sum_{z_i} p_{\theta^{post}}(z_i|x_i^T) \log p_\theta(z_i|x_i^T) + \sum_j \sum_{z_j} p_{\theta^{post}}(z_j|x_j^T) \log p_\theta(z_j|\tilde{x}_j^S)\}. \tag{11}$$

In our experiment, we show that these modifications yield consistent improvement over the basic EM algorithm.

3.4 Deep Adversarial Attention Alignment

Based on the above discussions, our full objective for training the target network can be formulated as,

$$\min_\theta \mathcal{L}^{full} = \mathcal{L}^{CE} + \mathcal{L}^{EM} + \beta \mathcal{L}^{AT} \tag{12}$$

where β determines the strength of the attention alignment penalty term $\mathcal{L}^{AT}$.

Discussion. Our approach mainly consists of two parts: attention alignment and EM training. On the one hand, attention alignment is crucial for the success of EM training. For EM training, there originally exists no constraint that the estimated hidden variable Z is assigned with the semantic meaning aligned with the ground-truth label, *i.e.* there may exist label shift or the data is clustered in an undesirable way. Training with labeled data (*e.g.* source and synthetic target data) and synchronizing θ^{post} with θ, the above issue can be alleviated. In addition, attention alignment further regularizes the training process by encouraging the network to focus on the desirable discriminative information.

On the other hand, EM benefits attention alignment by providing label distribution estimations for target data. EM approximately guides the attention of target network to fit the target domain statistics, while attention alignment regularizes the attention of target network to be not far from source network. These two seemingly adversarial counterparts cooperate to make the target network acquire the attention mechanism which is invariant to the domain shift.

Note that both parts are promoted by the use of adversarial data pairing which provides natural image correspondences to perform attention alignment. Thus our method is named "deep adversarial attention alignment".

4   Experiment

4.1   Setup

Datasets. We use the following two UDA datasets for image classification.

(1) Digit datasets from **MNIST** [13] (60,000 training + 10,000 test images) to **MNIST-M** [7] (59,001 training + 90,001 test images). MNIST and MNIST-M are treated as the source domain and target domain, respectively. The images of MNIST-M are created by combining MNIST digits with the patches randomly extracted from color photos of BSDS500 [1] as their background.

(2) **Office-31** is a standard benchmark for real-world domain adaptation tasks. It consists of 4,110 images subject to 31 categories. This dataset contains three distinct domains, (1) images which are collected from the Amazon website (**A**mazon domain), (2) web camera (**W**ebcam domain), and (3) digital SLR camera (**D**SLR domain) under different settings, respectively. The dataset is also imbalanced across domains, with 2,817 images in **A** domain, 795 images in **W** domain, and 498 images in **D** domain. We evaluate our algorithm for six transfer tasks across these three domains, including $\mathbf{A} \rightarrow \mathbf{W}$, $\mathbf{D} \rightarrow \mathbf{W}$, $\mathbf{W} \rightarrow \mathbf{D}$, $\mathbf{A} \rightarrow \mathbf{D}$, $\mathbf{D} \rightarrow \mathbf{A}$, and $\mathbf{W} \rightarrow \mathbf{A}$.

Competing Methods. We compare our method with some representative and state-of-the-art approaches, including RevGrad [7], JAN [17], JAN-A [17], DSN [3] and ADA [8] which minimize domain discrepancy on the FC layers of CNN. We compare with the results of these methods reported in their published papers with identical evaluation setting. For the task MNIST $\rightarrow$ MNIST-M, we also compare with PixelDA [2], a state-of-the-art method on this task. Both Cycle-GAN and PixelDA transfer the source style to the target domain without modifying its content heavily. Therefore, PixelDA is an alternative way to generate paired images across domains and is compatible to our framework. We emphasize that a model capable of generating more genuine paired images will probably lead to higher accuracy using our method. The investigation in this direction can be parallel and reaches beyond the scope of this paper.

4.2 Implementation Details

MNIST → MNIST-M. The source network is trained on the MNIST training set. When the source network is trained, it is fixed to guide the training of the target network. The target and the source network are made up of four convolutional layers, where the first three are for feature extraction and the last one acts as a classifier. We align the attention between the source and target network for the three convolutional layers.

Office-31. To make a fair comparison with the state-of-the-art domain adaptation methods [17], we adopt the ResNet-50 [9,10] architecture to perform the adaptation tasks on Office-31 and we start from the model pre-trained on ImageNet [4]. We first fine-tune the model on the source domain data and fix it. The source model is then used to guide the attention alignment of the target network. The target network starts from the fine-tuned model and is gradually trained to adapt to the target domain data. We penalize the distances of the attention maps $w.r.t$ all the convolutional layers except for the first convolutional layer.

Detailed settings of training are demonstrated in the supplementary material.

4.3 Evaluation

MNIST → MNIST-M. The classification results of transferring MNIST to MNIST-M are presented in Table 1. We arrive at four observations. First, our method outperforms a series of representative domain adaptation methods (*e.g.*, RevGrad, DSN, ADA) with a large margin, all of which minimize the domain discrepancy at the FC layers of neural networks. Moreover, we achieve competitive accuracy (95.6%) to the state-of-the-art result (98.2%) reported by PixelDA. Note that technically, PixelDA is compatible to our method, and can be adopted to improve the accuracy of our model. We will investigate this in the future. Second, we observe that the accuracy of the source network drops heavily when transferred to the target domain (from 99.3% on source test set to 45.6% on target test set), which implies the significant domain shift from MNIST to MNIST-M. Third, we can see that the distribution of synthetic target data is much closer to real target data than real source data, by observing that training with synthetic target data improves the performance over the source network by about +30%. Finally, training with a mixture of source and synthetic target data is beneficial for learning domain invariant features, and improves the adaptation performance by +3.5% over the model trained with synthetic target data only.

Table 1 demonstrates that our EM training algorithm is an effective way to exploit unlabeled target domain data. Moreover, imposing the attention alignment penalty $\mathcal{L}^{AT}$ always leads to noticeable improvement.

Table 1. Classification accuracy (%) for MNIST → MNIST-M. "CNN" denotes the source and target network (Sect. 4.2). The "S" and "T_f" represent labeled source data and synthetic target data, respectively. The "T" and "S_f" denote unlabeled target data and synthetic source data, respectively

Method	Train Data	Accuracy (%)	Method	Train Data	Accuracy (%)
RevGrad [7]	S+T	81.5	CNN	S	45.6
DSN [3]	S+T	83.2	CNN	T_f	75.0
ADA [8]	S+T	85.9	CNN	S+T_f	78.5
PixelDA [2]	S+T+T_f	**98.2**	CNN + $\mathcal{L}^{AT}$	S+T_f	85.7
Ours (wo $\mathcal{L}^{AT}$)	S+T_f+T+S_f	93.5	Ours (wo $\mathcal{L}^{AT}$)	S+T_f+T+S_f	93.5
Ours (w $\mathcal{L}^{AT}$)	S+T_f+T+S_f	**95.6**	Ours (w $\mathcal{L}^{AT}$)	S+T_f+T+S_f	**95.6**

Table 2. Classification accuracy (%) on the Office-31 dataset based on ResNet-50

Method	Train Data	A → W	D → W	W → D	A → D	D → A	W → A	Average
ResNet-50	S	68.4 ± 0.2	96.7 ± 0.1	99.3 ± 0.1	68.9 ± 0.2	62.5 ± 0.3	60.7 ± 0.3	76.1
RevGrad [7]	S+T	82.0 ± 0.4	96.9 ± 0.2	99.1 ± 0.1	79.7 ± 0.4	68.2 ± 0.4	67.4 ± 0.5	82.2
JAN [17]	S+T	85.4 ± 0.3	97.4 ± 0.2	99.8 ± 0.2	84.7 ± 0.3	68.6 ± 0.3	70.0 ± 0.4	84.3
JAN-A [17]	S+T	86.0 ± 0.4	96.7 ± 0.3	99.7 ± 0.1	85.1 ± 0.4	69.2 ± 0.4	70.7 ± 0.5	84.6
ResNet-50	T_f	81.1 ± 0.2	98.5 ± 0.2	99.8 ± 0.0	83.3 ± 0.3	61.0 ± 0.2	60.2 ± 0.3	80.6
ResNet-50	S+T_f	81.9 ± 0.2	98.5 ± 0.2	99.8 ± 0.0	83.7 ± 0.3	66.5 ± 0.2	64.8 ± 0.3	82.5
Ours (wo $\mathcal{L}^{AT}$)	T_f+T	86.2 ± 0.2	**99.3 ± 0.1**	100 ± 0.0	86.5 ± 0.6	69.9 ± 0.6	70.2 ± 0.2	85.4
Ours (w $\mathcal{L}^{AT}$)	T_f+T	86.8 ± 0.2	**99.3 ± 0.1**	100 ± 0.0	87.2 ± 0.5	71.7 ± 0.5	71.8 ± 0.1	86.1
Ours (wo $\mathcal{L}^{AT}$)	S+T_f+T+S_f	**87.1 ± 0.3**	**99.3 ± 0.1**	100 ± 0.0	87.1 ± 0.2	72.3 ± 0.2	72.2 ± 0.2	86.3
Ours (w $\mathcal{L}^{AT}$)	S+T_f+T+S_f	86.8 ± 0.2	**99.3 ± 0.1**	100 ± 0.0	**88.8 ± 0.4**	**74.3 ± 0.2**	**73.9 ± 0.2**	**87.2**

Office-31. The classification results based on ResNet-50 are shown in Table 2. With identical evaluation setting, we compare our methods with previous transfer methods and variants of our method. We have three major conclusions.

First, from Table 2, it can be seen that our method outperforms the state of art in all the transfer tasks with a large margin. The improvement is larger on harder transfer tasks, where the source domain is substantially different from and has much less data than the target domain, e.g. **D → A**, and **W → A**.

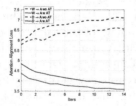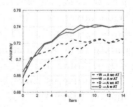

Fig. 4. Analysis of the training process (EM is implemented). **Left:** The trend of $\mathcal{L}^{AT}$ during training with and without imposing the $\mathcal{L}^{AT}$ penalty term. **Right:** The curves of test accuracy on the target domain. The results of tasks **W → A** and **D → A** are presented. The results for other tasks are similar. One iteration here represents one update of the network M^{post} (see Sect. 3.3).

Table 3. Variants of the EM algorithm with and without $\mathcal{L}^{AT}$. The EM algorithm without asynchronous update of M^{post} is denoted by EM-A, while that without filtering the noisy data is denoted by EM-B. EM-C represents EM training without initializing the learning rate schedule when M^{post} is updated

Method	Train Data	A → W	A → D	D → A	W → A	Average
ResNet-50	S	68.4 ± 0.2	68.9 ± 0.2	62.5 ± 0.3	60.7 ± 0.3	65.1
EM-A	S+T$_f$+T+S$_f$	68.6 ± 0.3	73.5 ± 0.3	62.7 ± 0.3	52.8 ± 0.3	64.4
EM-A + $\mathcal{L}^{AT}$	S+T$_f$+T+S$_f$	80.4 ± 0.2	79.1 ± 0.2	66.4 ± 0.2	58.4 ± 0.2	71.1
EM-C	S+T$_f$+T+S$_f$	86.4 ± 0.3	87.0 ± 0.3	69.5 ± 0.3	71.4 ± 0.3	78.6
EM-C + $\mathcal{L}^{AT}$	S+T$_f$+T+S$_f$	86.2 ± 0.2	86.6 ± 0.3	71.8 ± 0.3	73.7 ± 0.2	79.6
EM-B	S+T$_f$+T+S$_f$	*very low*	*very low*	*very low*	*very low*	*very low*
EM-B + $\mathcal{L}^{AT}$	S+T$_f$+T+S$_f$	*very low*	*very low*	*very low*	*very low*	*very low*
Ours (wo $\mathcal{L}^{AT}$)	S+T$_f$+T+S$_f$	**87.1** ± 0.3	87.1 ± 0.2	72.3 ± 0.2	72.2 ± 0.2	79.7
Ours (w $\mathcal{L}^{AT}$)	S+T$_f$+T+S$_f$	86.8 ± 0.2	**88.8** ± 0.4	**74.3** ± 0.2	**73.9** ± 0.2	**80.9**

Table 4. Comparison of different attention discrepancy measures on Office-31

Measure	A → W	A → D	D → A	W → A	Average
L_1-norm	*very low*	*very low*	*very low*	*very low*	*very low*
MMD	84.7	84.1	66.2	64.5	74.9
JMMD	85.9	85.3	70.1	71.1	78.1
Ours	**86.8**	**88.8**	**74.3**	**73.9**	**80.9**

Specifically, we improve over the state of art result by +2.6% on average, and by +5.1% for the difficult transfer task **D → A**.

Second, we also compare our method with and without the adversarial attention alignment loss $\mathcal{L}^{AT}$. Although for easy transfer tasks, the performance of these two variants are comparable, when moving to much harder tasks, we observe obvious improvement brought by the adversarial attention alignment, *e.g.*, training with adversarial attention alignment outperforms that without attention alignment by +2% for the task **D → A**, and +1.7% for the task **W → A**. This implies that adversarial attention alignment helps reduce the discrepancy across domains and regularize the training of the target model.

Third, we validate that augmenting with synthetic target data to facilitate the target network training brings significant improvement of accuracy over source network. This indicates that the discrepancy between synthetic and real target data is much smaller. We also notice that in our method, the accuracy of the network trained with real and synthetic data from both domains is much better than the one purely trained with real and synthetic target data. This verifies the knowledge shared by the source domain can be sufficiently uncovered by our framework to improve the target network performance.

Figure 4 illustrates how the attention alignment penalty $\mathcal{L}^{AT}$ changes during the training process with and without this penalty imposed. Without attention alignment, the discrepancy of the attention maps between the source and target network is significantly larger and increases as the training goes on. The improvement of accuracy brought by adding $\mathcal{L}^{AT}$ penalty to the objective can be attributed to the much smaller discrepancy of attention maps between the source and the target models, *i.e.*, better aligned attention mechanism. The testing accuracy curves on the target domain for tasks $\mathbf{D} \rightarrow \mathbf{A}$ and $\mathbf{D} \rightarrow \mathbf{A}$ are also drawn in Fig. 4. It can be seen that the test accuracy steadily increases and the model with $\mathcal{L}^{AT}$ converges much faster than that without any attention alignment.

Visualization of the attention maps of our method is provided in Fig. 1. We observe that through attention alignment, the attention maps of the target network adapt well to the target domain images, and are even better than those of the target model trained on labeled target images.

4.4   Ablation Study

Table 3 compares the accuracy of different EM variants. We conduct ablation studies by removing one component from the system at a time (three components are considered which are defined in Sect. 3.3). For each variant of EM, we also evaluate the effect of imposing $\mathcal{L}^{AT}$ by comparing training with and without $\mathcal{L}^{AT}$. By comparing the performances of EM-A, EM-B, EM-C and full method we adopted, we find that the three modifications all contribute considerably to the system. Among them, filtering the noisy data is the most important factor. We also notice that for EM-A and EM-C, training along with $\mathcal{L}^{AT}$ always leads to a significant improvement, implying performing attention alignment is an effective way to improve the adaptation performance.

4.5   Comparing Different Attention Discrepancy Measures

In this section, we provide a method comparison in measuring the attention discrepancy across domains which is discussed in Sect. 3.2. This paper uses the L_2 distance, and the compared methods include the L_1 distance, MMD [16] and JMMD [17]. Results are presented in Table 4.

We find that our method achieves the best results among the four measures. The L_1 distance fails in training a workable network because it is misled by the noise in the attention maps. Our method outperforms MMD/JMMD by a large margin, because our method preserves the structure information, as discussed in Sect. 3.2.

5   Conclusion

In this paper, we make two contributions to the community of UDA. First, from the *convolutional layers*, we propose to align the attention maps of the source network and target network to make the knowledge from source network better adapted to the target one. Second, from an *EM perspective*, we maximize the likelihood of unlabeled target data, which enables target network to leverage more training data for better domain adaptation. Both contributions benefit from the unsupervised image correspondences provided by CycleGAN. Experiment demonstrates that the two contributions both have positive effects on the system performance, and they cooperate together to achieve competitive or even state-of-the-art results on two benchmark datasets.

Acknowledgement. We acknowledge the Data to Decisions CRC (D2D CRC) and Cooperative Research Centres Programme for funding the research.

References

1. Arbelaez, P., Maire, M., Fowlkes, C., Malik, J.: Contour detection and hierarchical image segmentation. IEEE Trans. Pattern Anal. Mach. Intell. **33**(5), 898–916 (2011)
2. Bousmalis, K., Silberman, N., Dohan, D., Erhan, D., Krishnan, D.: Unsupervised pixel-level domain adaptation with generative adversarial networks. In: The IEEE Conference on Computer Vision and Pattern Recognition (CVPR) (2017)
3. Bousmalis, K., Trigeorgis, G., Silberman, N., Krishnan, D., Erhan, D.: Domain separation networks. In: Advances in Neural Information Processing Systems, pp. 343–351 (2016)
4. Deng, J., Dong, W., Socher, R., Li, L.J., Li, K., Fei-Fei, L.: ImageNet: a large-scale hierarchical image database. In: IEEE Conference on Computer Vision and Pattern Recognition, CVPR 2009, pp. 248–255. IEEE (2009)
5. Ding, M., Fan, G.: Multilayer joint gait-pose manifolds for human gait motion modeling. IEEE Trans. Cybern. **45**(11), 2413–2424 (2015)
6. Dong, X., Yan, Y., Ouyang, W., Yang, Y.: Style aggregated network for facial landmark detection. In: Proceedings of the IEEE Conference on Computer Vision and Pattern Recognition (CVPR), pp. 379–388, June 2018
7. Ganin, Y., Lempitsky, V.: Unsupervised domain adaptation by backpropagation. In: International Conference on Machine Learning, pp. 1180–1189 (2015)
8. Haeusser, P., Frerix, T., Mordvintsev, A., Cremers, D.: Associative domain adaptation. In: International Conference on Computer Vision (ICCV), vol. 2, p. 6 (2017)
9. He, K., Zhang, X., Ren, S., Sun, J.: Deep residual learning for image recognition. In: Proceedings of the IEEE Conference on Computer Vision and Pattern Recognition, pp. 770–778 (2016)
10. He, K., Zhang, X., Ren, S., Sun, J.: Identity mappings in deep residual networks. In: Leibe, B., Matas, J., Sebe, N., Welling, M. (eds.) ECCV 2016. LNCS, vol. 9908, pp. 630–645. Springer, Cham (2016). https://doi.org/10.1007/978-3-319-46493-0_38
11. Hoffman, J., et al.: Cycada: Cycle-consistent adversarial domain adaptation. arXiv preprint arXiv:1711.03213 (2017)
12. Kim, T., Cha, M., Kim, H., Lee, J., Kim, J.: Learning to discover cross-domain relations with generative adversarial networks. In: International Conference on Machine Learning (2017)
13. LeCun, Y., Bottou, L., Bengio, Y., Haffner, P.: Gradient-based learning applied to document recognition. Proc. IEEE **86**(11), 2278–2324 (1998)
14. Liu, M.Y., Breuel, T., Kautz, J.: Unsupervised image-to-image translation networks. In: Advances in Neural Information Processing Systems, pp. 700–708 (2017)

15. Liu, M.Y., Tuzel, O.: Coupled generative adversarial networks. In: Advances in Neural Information Processing Systems, pp. 469–477 (2016)

16. Long, M., Cao, Y., Wang, J., Jordan, M.: Learning transferable features with deep adaptation networks. In: International Conference on Machine Learning, pp. 97–105 (2015)

17. Long, M., Wang, J., Jordan, M.I.: Deep transfer learning with joint adaptation networks. In: ICML (2017)

18. Luc, P., Couprie, C., Chintala, S., Verbeek, J.: Semantic segmentation using adversarial networks. In: NIPS Workshop on Adversarial Training (2016)

19. Russo, P., Carlucci, F.M., Tommasi, T., Caputo, B.: From source to target and back: symmetric bi-directional adaptive GAN. arXiv preprint arXiv:1705.08824 (2017)

20. Selvaraju, R.R., Cogswell, M., Das, A., Vedantam, R., Parikh, D., Batra, D.: Grad-CAM: visual explanations from deep networks via gradient-based localization. In: ICCV, pp. 618–626 (2017)

21. Shrivastava, A., Pfister, T., Tuzel, O., Susskind, J., Wang, W., Webb, R.: Learning from simulated and unsupervised images through adversarial training. In: CVPR (2017)

22. Simonyan, K., Vedaldi, A., Zisserman, A.: Deep inside convolutional networks: visualising image classification models and saliency maps. arXiv preprint arXiv:1312.6034 (2013)

23. Sun, B., Saenko, K.: Deep CORAL: correlation alignment for deep domain adaptation. In: Hua, G., Jégou, H. (eds.) ECCV 2016. LNCS, vol. 9915, pp. 443–450. Springer, Cham (2016). https://doi.org/10.1007/978-3-319-49409-8_35

24. Tzeng, E., Hoffman, J., Darrell, T., Saenko, K.: Simultaneous deep transfer across domains and tasks. In: Proceedings of the IEEE International Conference on Computer Vision, pp. 4068–4076 (2015)

25. Tzeng, E., Hoffman, J., Saenko, K., Darrell, T.: Adversarial discriminative domain adaptation. In: Computer Vision and Pattern Recognition (CVPR) (2017)

26. Tzeng, E., Hoffman, J., Zhang, N., Saenko, K., Darrell, T.: Deep domain confusion: maximizing for domain invariance. arXiv preprint arXiv:1412.3474 (2014)

27. Wei, Y., Feng, J., Liang, X., Cheng, M.M., Zhao, Y., Yan, S.: Object region mining with adversarial erasing: a simple classification to semantic segmentation approach. In: IEEE CVPR (2017)

28. Zagoruyko, S., Komodakis, N.: Paying more attention to attention: improving the performance of convolutional neural networks via attention transfer. In: ICLR (2017)

29. Zeiler, M.D., Fergus, R.: Visualizing and understanding convolutional networks. In: Fleet, D., Pajdla, T., Schiele, B., Tuytelaars, T. (eds.) ECCV 2014. LNCS, vol. 8689, pp. 818–833. Springer, Cham (2014). https://doi.org/10.1007/978-3-319-10590-1_53

30. Zhang, X., Wei, Y., Feng, J., Yang, Y., Huang, T.: Adversarial complementary learning for weakly supervised object localization. In: IEEE CVPR (2018)

31. Zheng, Z., Zheng, L., Yang, Y.: Unlabeled samples generated by gan improve the person re-identification baseline in vitro. In: Proceedings of the IEEE International Conference on Computer Vision (2017)

32. Zhou, B., Khosla, A., Lapedriza, A., Oliva, A., Torralba, A.: Learning deep features for discriminative localization. In: Proceedings of the IEEE Conference on Computer Vision and Pattern Recognition, pp. 2921–2929 (2016)

33. Zhu, J.Y., Park, T., Isola, P., Efros, A.A.: Unpaired image-to-image translation using cycle-consistent adversarial networkss. In: 2017 IEEE International Conference on Computer Vision (ICCV) (2017)

MultiPoseNet: Fast Multi-Person Pose Estimation Using Pose Residual Network

Muhammed Kocabas$^{(\boxtimes)}$, Salih Karagoz , and Emre Akbas

Department of Computer Engineering, Middle East Technical University,
Ankara, Turkey
{muhammed.kocabas,e234299,eakbas}@metu.edu.tr

Abstract. In this paper, we present *MultiPoseNet*, a novel bottom-up multi-person pose estimation architecture that combines a multi-task model with a novel assignment method. MultiPoseNet can jointly handle person detection, person segmentation and pose estimation problems. The novel assignment method is implemented by the *Pose Residual Network (PRN)* which receives keypoint and person detections, and produces accurate poses by assigning keypoints to person instances. On the COCO keypoints dataset, our pose estimation method outperforms all previous bottom-up methods both in accuracy (+4-point mAP over previous best result) and speed; it also performs on par with the best top-down methods while being at least 4x faster. Our method is the fastest real time system with $\sim$ 23 frames/sec.

Keywords: Multi-task learning · Multi-person pose estimation
Semantic segmentation · MultiPoseNet · Pose residual network

1 Introduction

This work is aimed at estimating the two-dimensional (2D) poses of multiple people in a given image. Any solution to this problem has to tackle a few sub-problems: (i) detecting body joints (or keypoints, as they are called in the widely used COCO [36] dataset) such as wrists, ankles, etc., (ii) grouping these joints into person instances, or detecting people and (iii) assigning joints to person instances. Depending on which sub-problem is tackled first, there have been two major approaches in multi-person 2D estimation: *bottom-up* and *top-down*. Bottom-up methods [5,6,25,26,37,39,42] first detect body joints without having any knowledge as to the number of people or their locations. Next, detected joints are grouped to form individual poses for person instances. On the other hand, top-down methods [10,18,23,40] start by detecting people first and then for each person detection, a single-person pose estimation method (e.g. [12,24,38,48]) is

Electronic supplementary material The online version of this chapter (https://doi.org/10.1007/978-3-030-01252-6_26) contains supplementary material, which is available to authorized users.

© Springer Nature Switzerland AG 2018
V. Ferrari et al. (Eds.): ECCV 2018, LNCS 11215, pp. 437–453, 2018.
https://doi.org/10.1007/978-3-030-01252-6_26

executed. Single-person pose estimation, i.e. detecting body joints conditioned on the information that there is a single person in the given input (the top-down approach), is typically a more costly process than grouping the detected joints (the bottom-up approach). Consequently, the top-down methods tend to be slower than the bottom-up methods, since they need to repeat the single-person pose estimation for each person detection; however, they usually yield better accuracy than bottom-up methods.

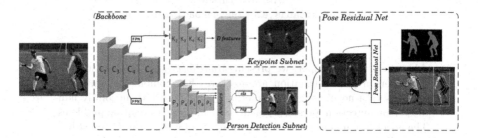

Fig. 1. MultiPoseNet is a multi-task learning architecture capable of performing human keypoint estimation, detection and semantic segmentation tasks altogether efficiently.

In this paper, we present a new bottom-up method (with respect to the categorization given above) for multi-person 2D pose estimation. Our method is based on a multi-task learning model, which can jointly handle the person detection, person segmentation and pose estimation problems. To emphasize its multi-person and multi-task aspects of our model, we named it as "MultiPoseNet. Our model (Fig. 1) consists of a shared backbone for feature extraction, detection subnets for keypoint and person detection/segmentation, and a final network which carries out the pose estimation, i.e. assigning detected keypoints to person instances. Our major contribution lies in the pose estimation step where the network implements a novel assignment method. This network receives keypoint and person detections, and produces a pose for each detected person by assigning keypoints to person boxes using a learned function. In order to put our contribution into context, here we briefly describe the relevant aspects of the state-of-the-art (SOTA) bottom-up methods [6,37]. These methods attempt to group detected keypoints by exploiting lower order relations either between the group and keypoints, or among the keypoints themselves. Specifically, Cao et al. [6] model pairwise relations (called part affinity fields) between two nearby joints and the grouping is achieved by propagating these pairwise affinities. In the other SOTA method, Newell et al. [37] predict a real number called a *tag* per detected keypoint, in order to identify the group the detection belongs to. Hence, this model makes use of the unary relations between a certain keypoint and the group it belongs to. Our method generalizes these two approaches in the sense that we achieve the grouping in a single shot by considering all joints together at the same time. We name this part of our model which achieves the grouping as the *Pose Residual Network* (PRN) (Fig. 2). PRN takes a region-of-interest (RoI) pooled keypoint detections and then feeds them into a residual multilayer perceptron (MLP). PRN considers all joints simultaneously and learns configurations of joints. We illustrate this capability of PRN by plotting a sample set of learned configurations. (Fig. 2 right). Our experiments (on the COCO dataset, using no external data) show that our method outperforms all previous bottom-up methods: we achieve a 4-point mAP increase over the previous best result. Our method performs on par with the best performing top-down methods while being at least 4x faster than them. To the best of our knowledge, there are only two top-down methods that we could not outperform. Given the fact that bottom-up methods have always performed less accurately than the top-down methods, our results are remarkable. In terms of running time, our method appears to be the fastest of all multi-person 2D pose estimation methods. Depending on the number of people in the input image, our method runs at between 27 frames/sec (FPS) (for one person detection) and 15 FPS (for 20 person detections). For a typical COCO image, which contains ~ 3 people on average, we achieve ~ 23 FPS (Fig. 6). Our contributions in this work are four fold. (1) We propose the *Pose Residual Network* (PRN), a simple yet very effective method for the problem of assigning/grouping body joints. (2) We outperform all previous bottom-up methods and achieve comparable performance with top-down methods. (3) Our method works faster than all previous methods, in real-time at ~ 23 frames/sec. (4) Our network architecture is extendible; we show that using the same backbone, one can solve other related problems, too, e.g. person segmentation.

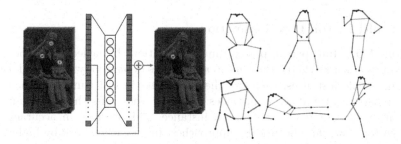

Fig. 2. Left: Pose Residual Network (PRN). The PRN is able to disambiguate which keypoint should be assigned to the current person box. **Right:** Six sample poses obtained via clustering the structures learned by PRN.

2   Related Work

2.1   Single Person Pose Estimation

Single person pose estimation is to predict individual body parts given a cropped person image (or, equivalently, given its exact location and scale within an image). Early methods (prior to deep learning) used hand-crafted HOG features [14] to detect body parts and probabilistic graphical models to represent the pose structure (tree-based [2,28,41,51]; non-tree based [15,21]). Deep neural networks based models [3,7,13,24,33,38,45,46,48,51] have quickly dominated the pose estimation problem after the initial work by Toshev et al. [46] who used the AlexNet architecture to directly regress spatial joint coordinates. Tompson et al. [45] learned pose structure by combining deep features along with graphical models. Carreira et al. [7] proposed the Iterative Error Feedback method to train Convolutional Neural Networks (CNNs) where the input is repeatedly fed to the network along with current predictions in order to refine the predictions. Wei et al. [48] were inspired by the pose machines [43] and used CNNs as feature extractors in pose machines. *Hourglass blocks*, (HG) developed by Newell et al. [38], are basically convolution-deconvolution structures with residual connections. Newell et al. stacked HG blocks to obtain an iterative refinement process and showed its effectiveness on single person pose estimation. Stacked Hourglass (SHG) based methods made a remarkable performance increase over previous results. Chu et al. [13] proposed adding visual attention units to focus on keypoint regions of interest. Pyramid residual modules by Yang et al. [51] improved the SHG architecture to handle scale variations. Lifshitz et al. [33] used a probabilistic keypoint voting scheme from image locations to obtain agreement maps for each body part. Belagiannis et al. [3] introduced a simple recurrent neural network based prediction refinement architecture. Huang et al. [24] developed a coarse-to-fine model with Inception-v2 [44] network as the backbone. The authors calculated the loss in each level of the network to learn coarser to finer representations of parts.

2.2   Multi Person Pose Estimation

Bottom-Up. Multi person pose estimation solutions branched out as bottom-up and top-down methods. Bottom-up approaches detect body joints and assign them to people instances, therefore they are faster in test time and smaller in size compared to top-down approaches. However, they miss the opportunity to zoom into the details of each person instance. This creates an accuracy gap between top-down and bottom-up approaches. In an earlier work by Ladicky et al. [32], they proposed an algorithm to jointly predict human part segmentations and part locations using HOG-based features and probabilistic approach. Gkioxari et al. [20] proposed k-poselets to jointly detect people and keypoints. Most of the recent approaches use Convolutional Neural Networks (CNNs) to detect body parts and relationships between them in an end-to-end manner [6,25,37,41,42,47], then use assignment algorithms [6,25,42,47] to form individual skeletons. Pischulin et al. [42] used deep features for joint prediction of part locations and relations between them, then performed correlation clustering. Even though [42] doesn't use person detections, it is very slow due to proposed clustering algorithm and processing time is in the order of hours. In a follow-up work by Insafutdinov et al. [25], they benefit from deeper ResNet architectures as part detectors and improved the parsing efficiency of a previous approach with an incremental optimization strategy. Different from Pischulin and Insa-futdinov, Iqbal et al. [27] proposed to solve the densely connected graphical model locally, thus improved time efficiency significantly. Cao et al. [6] built a model that contains two entangled CPM [48] branches to predict keypoint heatmaps and pairwise relationships (part affinity fields) between them. Key-points are grouped together with fast Hungarian bipartite matching algorithm according to conformity of part affinity fields between them. This model runs in realtime. Newell et al. [37] extended their SHG idea by outputting associative vector embeddings which can be thought as tags representing each keypoint's group. They group keypoints with similar tags into individual people.

Top-Down. Top-down methods first detect people (typically using a top per-forming, off-the-shelf object detector) and then run a single person pose esti-mation (SPPEN) method per person to get the final pose predictions. Since a SPPEN model is run for each person instance, top-down methods are extremely slow, however, each pose estimator can focus on an instance and perform fine localization. Papandreou et al. [40] used ResNet with dilated convolutions [22] which has been very successful in semantic segmentation [8] and computing key-point heatmap and offset outputs. In contrast to Gaussian heatmaps, the authors estimated a disk-shaped keypoint masks and 2-D offset vector fields to accurately localize keypoints. Joint part segmentation and keypoint detection given human detections approach were proposed by Xia et al. [49] The authors used separate PoseFCN and PartFCN to obtain both part masks and locations and fused them with fully-connected CRFs. This provides more consistent predictions by elimi-nating irrelevant detections. Fang et al. [18] proposed to use spatial transformer networks to handle inaccurate bounding boxes and used *stacked hourglass* blocks [38]. He et al. [23] combined instance segmentation and keypoint prediction in their *Mask-RCNN* model. They append keypoint heads on top of *RoI aligned* feature maps to get a one-hot mask for each keypoint. Chen et al. [10] developed *globalnet* on top of *Feature Pyramid Networks* [34] for multiscale inference and refined the predictions by using hyper-features [31].

3   The Method and Models

The architecture of our proposel model, MultiPoseNet, can be found in Fig. 1. In the following, we describe each component in detail.

3.1   The Shared Backbone

The backbone of MultiPoseNet serves as a feature extractor for keypoint and person detection subnets. It is actually a ResNet [22] with two Feature Pyra-mid Networks (FPN)[34] (one for the keypoint subnet, the other for the person detection subnet) connected to it, FPN creates pyramidal feature maps with top-down connections from all levels of CNNs feature hierarchy to make use of inherent multi-scale representations of a CNN feature extractor. By doing so, FPN compromises high resolution, weak representations with low resolution, strong representations. Powerful localization and classification properties of FPN proved to be very successful in detection, segmentation and keypoint tasks recently [10,23,34,35]. In our model, we extracted features from the last residual blocks C_2, C_3, C_4, C_5 with strides of (4,8,16,32) pixels and compute corresponding FPN features per subnet.

3.2   Keypoint Estimation Subnet

Keypoint estimation subnet (Fig. 3) takes hierarchical CNN features (outputted by the corresponding FPN) and outputs keypoint and segmentation heatmaps. Heatmaps represent keypoint locations as Gaussian peaks. Each heatmap layer belongs to a specific keypoint class (nose, wrists, ankles etc.) and contains arbitrary number of peaks that pertain to person instances. Person segmentation mask at the last layer of heatmaps encodes the pixelwise spatial layout of people in the image. A set of features specific to the keypoint detection task are computed similarly to [34] with top-down and lateral connections from the bottom-up pathway. $K_2 - K_5$ features have the same spatial size corresponding to $C_2 - C_5$ blocks but the depth is reduced to 256. K features are identical to P features in the original FPN paper, but we denote them with K to distinguish from person detection subnet layers. The depth of P features is downsized to 128 with 2 subsequent 3×3 convolutions to obtain D_2, D_3, D_4, D_5 layers. Since D features still have different strides, we upsampled D_3, D_4, D_5 accordingly to match 4-pixel stride as D_2 features and concatenated them into a single depth-512 feature map. Concatenated features are smoothed by a 3×3 convolution with ReLU. Final heatmap which has $(K + 1)$ layers obtained via 1×1 convolutions without activation. The final output is multiplied with a binary mask of $\mathbf{W}$ which has $\mathbf{W}(\mathbf{p}) = 0$ in the area of the persons without annotation. K is the number of human keypoints annotated in a dataset and +1 is person segmentation mask. In addition to the loss applied in the last layer, we append a loss at each level of K features to benefit from intermediate supervision. Semantic person segmentation masks are predicted in the same way with keypoints.

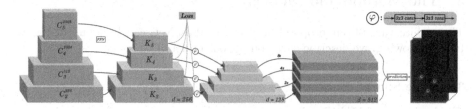

Fig. 3. The architecture of the keypoint subnet. It takes hierarchical CNN features as input and outputs keypoint and segmentation heatmaps.

3.3 Person Detection Subnet

In order to design a faster and simpler person detection model which is compatible with FPN backbone, we have adopted RetinaNet. Same strategies to compute anchors, losses and pyramidal image features are followed. Classification and regression heads are modified to handle only person annotations.

Fig. 4. Bounding box overlapping scenarios.

3.4 Pose Residual Network (PRN)

Assigning keypoint detections to person instances (bounding boxes, in our case) is straightforward if there is only one person in the bounding box as in Fig. 4 a–b. However, it becomes non-trivial if there are overlapping people in a single box as in Fig. 4 c–d. In the case of an overlap, a bounding box can contain multiple keypoints not related to the person in question, and this creates ambiguity in constructing final pose predictions. We solve these ambiguities by learning pose structures from data. The input to PRN is prepared as follows. For each person box that the person detection subnet detected, the region from the keypoint detection subnet's output, corresponding to the box, is cropped and resized to a fixed size, which ensures that PRN can handle person detections of arbitrary sizes and shapes. Specifically, let $\mathbf{X}$ denote the input to the PRN, where $\mathbf{X} = \{\mathbf{x}_1, \mathbf{x}_2, \ldots, \mathbf{x}_k\}$ in which $\mathbf{x}_k \in \mathbb{R}^{W \times H}$, k is the number of different keypoint types. The final goal of PRN is to output $\mathbf{Y}$ where $\mathbf{Y} = \{\mathbf{y}_1, \mathbf{y}_2, \ldots, \mathbf{y}_k\}$, in which $\mathbf{y}_k \in \mathbb{R}^{W \times H}$ is of the same size as $\mathbf{x}_k$, containing the correct position for each keypoint indicated by a peak in that keypoints channel. PRN models the mapping from $\mathbf{X}$ to $\mathbf{Y}$ as

$$\mathbf{y}_k = \phi_k(\mathbf{X}) + \mathbf{x}_k \tag{1}$$

where the functions $\phi_1(\cdot), \ldots, \phi_K(\cdot)$ apply a *residual correction* to the pose in $\mathbf{X}$, hence the name pose residual network. We implement Eq. 1 using a residual multilayer perceptron (Fig. 2). Activation of the output layer uses softmax to obtain a proper probability distribution and binary cross-entropy loss is used during training. Before we came up with this residual model, we experimented with two naive baselines and a non-residual model. In the first baseline method, which we call *Max*, for each keypoint channel k, we find the location with the highest value and place a Gaussian in the corresponding location of the kth channel in $\mathbf{Y}$. In the second baseline method, we compute $\mathbf{Y}$ as

$$\mathbf{y}_k = \mathbf{x}_k * \mathbf{P}_k \tag{2}$$

where $\mathbf{P}_k$ is a prior map for the location of the kth joint, learned from ground-truth data and $*$ is element-wise multiplication. We named this method as Unary Conditional Relationship (UCR). Finally, in our non-residual model, we implemented

$$\mathbf{y}_k = \phi_k(\mathbf{X}). \tag{3}$$

Performances of all these models can be found in Table 3. In the context of the models described above, both SOTA bottom up methods learn lower order grouping models than the PRN. Cao et al. [6] model pairwise channels in $\mathbf{X}$ while Newell et al. [37] model only unary channels in $\mathbf{X}$. Hence, our model can be considered as a generalization of these lower order grouping models. We hypothesize that each node in PRN's hidden layer encodes a certain body configuration. To show this, we visualized some of the representative outputs of PRN in Fig. 2. These poses are obtained via reshaping PRN outputs and selecting the maximum activated keypoints to form skeletons. All obtained configurations are clustered using k-means with OKS (object keypoint similarity) [36] and cluster means are visualized in Fig. 2. OKS (object keypoint similarity) is used as k-means distance metric to cluster the meaningful poses.

3.5   Implementation Details

Training. Due to different convergence times and loss imbalance, we have trained keypoint and person detection tasks separately. To use the same backbone in both task, we first trained the model with only keypoint subnet Fig. 3. Thereafter, we froze the backbone parameters and trained the person detection subnet. Since the two tasks are semantically similar, person detection results were not adversely affected by the frozen backbone. We used the Tensorflow [1] and Keras [11] deep learning libraries. For person detection, we made use of open-source Keras RetinaNet [19] implementation.

Keypoint Estimation Subnet: For keypoint training, we used 480 × 480 image patches, that are centered around the crowd or the main person in the scene. Random rotations between ±40 degrees, random scaling between 0.8 − 1.2 and vertical flipping with a probability of 0.3 were used during training. We have transferred the ImageNet [16] pretrained weights for each backbone before training. We optimize the model with Adam [30] starting with a learning rate of 1e-4 and decreased it by a factor of 0.1 in plateaux. We used the Gaussian peaks located at the keypoint locations as the ground truth to calculate L_2 loss, and we masked (ignored) people that are not annotated. We appended the segmentation masks to ground-truth as an extra layer and trained along with keypoint heatmaps. The cost function that we minimize is

$$L_{kp} = \mathbf{W} \cdot \|\mathbf{H}_t - \mathbf{H}_p\|_2^2, \tag{4}$$

where $\mathbf{H}_t$ and $\mathbf{H}_p$ are the ground-truth and predicted heatmaps respectively, and $\mathbf{W}$ is the mask used to ignore non-annotated person instances.

Person Detection Subnet: We followed a similar person detection training strategy as Lin et al. [35]. Images containing persons are used, they are resized such that shorter edge is 800 pixels. We froze backbone weights after keypoint training and not updated them during person detection training. We optimized subnet with Adam [30] starting with a learning rate of 1e-5 and is decreased by a factor of 0.1 in plateaux. We used Focal loss with ($\gamma = 2, \alpha = 0.25$) and smooth L_1 loss for classification and bbox regression, respectively. We obtained final proposals using NMS with a threshold of 0.3.

Pose Residual Network: During training, we cropped input and output pairs and resized heatmaps according to bounding-box proposals. All crops are resized to a fixed size of 36×56 (height/width $= 1.56$). We trained the PRN network separately and Adam optimizer [30] with a learning rate of 1e-4 is used during training. Since the model is shallow, convergence takes 1.5 hours approximately. We trained the model with person instances having at least 2 keypoints. We utilized a sort of curriculum learning [4] by sorting annotations based on number of keypoints and bounding box areas. In each epoch, model is started to learn easy-to-predict instances, hard examples are given in later stages.

Inference. The whole architecture (see in Fig. 1) behaves as a monolithic, end-to-end model during test time. First, an image ($W \times H \times 3$) is processed through backbone model to extract the features in multi-scales. Person and keypoint detection subnets compute outputs simultaneously out of extracted features. Keypoints are outputted as $W \times H \times (K+1)$ sized heatmaps. K is the number of keypoint channels, and $+1$ is for the segmentation channel. Person detections are in the form of $N \times 5$, where N is the number of people and 5 channel corresponds to 4 bounding box coordinates along with confidence scores. Keypoint heatmaps are cropped and resized to form RoIs according to person detections. Optimal RoI size is determined as $36 \times 56 \times K$ in our experiments. PRN takes each RoI as separate input, then outputs same size RoI with only one keypoint selected in each layer of heatmap. All selected keypoints are grouped as a person instance.

4   Experiments

4.1   Datasets

We trained our keypoint and person detection models on COCO keypoints dataset [36] (without using any external/extra data) in our experiments. We used COCO for evaluating the keypoint and person detection, however, we used PASCAL VOC 2012 [17] for evaluating person segmentation due to the lack of semantic segmentation annotations in COCO. Backbone models (ResNet-50 and ResNet-101) were pretrained on ImageNet and we finetuned with COCO-keypoints. COCO train2017 split contains 64 K images including 260 K person instances which 150 K of them having keypoint annotations. Keypoints of persons with small area are not annotated in COCO. We did ablation experiments on COCO val2017 split which contains 2693 images with person instances. We made comparison to previous methods on the test-dev2017 split which has 20 K test images. We evaluated test-dev2017 results on the online COCO evaluation server. We use the official COCO evaluation metric average precision (AP) and average recall (AR). OKS and IoU based scores were used for keypoint and person detection tasks, respectively. We performed person segmentation evaluation in PASCAL VOC 2012 test split with PASCAL IoU metric. PASCAL VOC 2012 person segmentation test split contains 1456 images. We obtained test results using the online evaluation server.

4.2   Multi Person Pose Estimation

The overall AP results of our method along with top-performing bottom-up (BU) and top-down (TD) methods are given in Table 1. MultiPoseNet outperforms all bottom-up methods and most of the top-down methods. We outperform the previously best bottom-up method [37] by a 4-point increase in mAP. In addition, the runtime speed (see the FPS column Table 1 and Fig. 6) of our system is far better than previous methods with 23 FPS on average[1]. This proves the effectiveness of PRN for assignment and our multitask detection approach while providing reasonable speed-accuracy tradeoff. To get these results (Table 1) on test-dev, we have utilized test time augmentation and ensembling (as also done in all previous studies). Multi scale and multi crop testing was performed during test time data augmentation. Two different backbones and a single person pose refinement network similar to our keypoint detection model was used for ensembling. Results from different models are gathered and redundant detections was removed via OKS based NMS [40]. With ablation experiments we have inspected the effect of different backbones, keypoint detection architectures, and PRN designs. Tables 2 and 3 present the ablation analysis results on the COCO validation set. We present the recall-precision curves of our method for different scales *all, large, medium* in the supplementary material.

Different Backbones. We used ResNet models [22] as shared backbone to extract features. Table 2 shows the impact of deeper features and dilated features. R101 improves the result by 1.6 mAP over R50. Dilated convolutions [8] which are very successful in dense detection tasks increase accuracy by 2 mAP over the R50 architecture. However, dilated convolutional filters add more computational complexity, consequently hinder realtime performance. We showed that concatenation of K features and intermediate supervision (Sect. 3.2) is crucial for good perfomance. The results demonstrate that performance of our system can be further enhanced with stronger feature extractors like recent ResNext [50] architectures.

---

[1] We obtained the FPS results by averaging the inference time using images containing 3 people on a 1080Ti GPU. We got CFNs and Mask RCNNs FPS results from their respective papers.

Table 1. Results on COCO **test-dev**, excluding systems trained with external data. Top-down methods are shown separately to make a clear comparison between bottom-up methods.

		FPS	AP	AP_{50}	AP_{75}	AP_M	AP_L	AR	AR_{50}	AR_{75}	AR_M	AR_L
BU	Ours	23	**69.6**	86.3	**76.6**	65.0	76.3	73.5	88.1	**79.5**	68.6	80.3
BU	Newell et al. [37]	6	65.5	**86.8**	72.3	60.6	72.6	70.2	**89.5**	76.0	64.6	78.1
BU	CMU-Pose [6]	10	61.8	84.9	67.5	57.1	68.2	66.5	87.2	71.8	60.6	74.6
TD	Megvii [10]	-	73.0	91.7	80.9	69.5	78.1	79.0	95.1	85.9	74.8	84.6
TD	CFN [24]	3	72.6	86.7	69.7	78.3	64.1	-	-	-	-	-
TD	Mask R-CNN [23]	5	69.2	90.4	76.0	64.9	76.3	75.2	93.7	81.1	70.3	81.8
TD	SJTU [18]	0.4	68.8	87.5	75.9	64.6	75.1	73.6	91.0	79.8	68.9	80.2
TD	GRMI-2017 [40]	-	66.9	86.4	73.6	64.0	72.0	71.6	89.2	77.6	66.1	79.1
TD	G-RMI-2016 [40]	-	60.5	82.2	66.2	57.6	66.6	66.2	86.6	71.4	61.9	72.2

Different Keypoint Architectures. Keypoint estimation requires dense prediction over spatial locations, so its performance is dependent on input and output resolution. In our experiments, we used 480×480 images as inputs and outputted $120 \times 120 \times (K+1)$ heatmaps per input. K is equal to 17 for COCO dataset. The lower resolutions harmed the mAP results while higher resolutions yielded longer training and inference complexity. We have listed the results of different keypoint models in Table 2.

Table 2. Comparison of different keypoint models. *(no concat: no concatenation, no int: no intermediate supervision, dil: dilated, concat: concatenation)*

Models	AP	AP_{50}	AP_{75}	AP_M	AP_L
R50	62.3	86.2	71.9	57.7	70.4
R101$_{\text{no int.}}$	61.3	83.7	69.6	56.6	67.4
R101$_{\text{no concat}}$	62.1	84.3	70.9	57.3	68.8
R101	63.9	87.1	73.2	58.1	72.2
R101$_{\text{dil}}$	**64.3**	**88.2**	**75**	**59.6**	**73.9**

The intermediate loss which is appended to the outputs of K blocks enhanced the precision significantly. Intermediate supervision acts as a refinement process among the hierarchies of features. As previously shown in [6,38,48], it is an essential strategy in most of the dense detection tasks. We have applied a final loss to the concatenated D features which is downsized from K features. This additional stage ensured us to combine multi-level features and compress them into a uniform space while extracting more semantic features. This strategy brought +2 mAP gain in our experiments.

Pose Residual Network Design. PRN is a simple yet effective assignment strategy, and is designed for fast inference while giving reasonable accuracy. To design an accurate model we have tried different configurations. Different PRN models and corresponding results can be seen in Table 3. These results indicate the scores obtained from the assignment of ground truth person bounding boxes and keypoints.

Table 3. Left: Performance of different PRN models on COCO validation set. *N: nodes, D: dropout and R: residual connection.* **Right:** Ablation experiments of PRN with COCO validation data.

PRN Models	AP	AP_{50}	AP_{75}	AP_M	AP_L
1 Layer 512 N, D	84.1	94.2	85.3	82	86.2
2 Layers 512 N, D	81.9	91.1	82.6	79.8	84.3
2 Layer 512 N, D+R	83.5	95.7	86.2	82.3	86.4
1 Layer 1024 N, D	84.6	95.7	87.6	82.1	88.7
1 Layer 1024 N, D+R	**89.4**	**97.1**	**91.2**	**87.9**	**91.8**

PRN Ablations	AP	AP_{50}	AP_{75}	AP_M	AP_L
Both GT	89.4	97.1	91.2	87.9	91.8
GT keypoints + Our bbox	75.3	82.1	78	70.1	84.5
Our keypoints + GT bbox	65.1	89.2	76.2	60.3	74.7
PRN	64.3	88.2	75	59.6	73.9
UCR	49.7	59.5	52.4	44.1	51.6
Max	45.3	55.1	48.8	40.6	46.9

We started with a primitive model which is a single hidden-layer MLP with 50 nodes, and added more nodes, regularization and different connection types to balance speed and accuracy. We found that 1024 nodes MLP, dropout with 0.5 probability and residual connection between input and output boosts the PRN performance up to 89.4 mAP on ground truth inputs.

In ablation analysis of PRN (Table 3), we compared *Max*, *UCR* and *PRN* implementations (see Sect. 3.4 for descriptions) along with the performance of PRN with ground truth detections. We found that lower order grouping methods could not handle overlapping detections; both of them per-

Table 4. PRN assignment results with non-grouped keypoints obtained from two bottom-up methods.

Models	AP	AP_{50}	AP_{75}	AP_M	AP_L
Cao et al. [6]	58.4	81.5	62.6	**54.4**	65.1
PRN + [6]	**59.2**	**82.2**	**64.4**	54.1	**67.0**
Newell et al. [37]	56.9	80.8	61.3	49.9	**68.8**
PRN + [37]	**58.1**	**81.4**	**63.0**	**51.3**	68.1

formed poorly. As we hypothesized, PRN could overcome ambiguities by learning meaningful pose structures (Fig. 2 (right)) and improved the results by ∼ 20 mAP over naive assignment techniques. We evaluated the impact of keypoint and person subnets to the final results by alternating inputs of PRN with ground truth detections. With ground truth keypoints and our person detections, we obtained 75.3 mAP, it shows that there is a large room for improvement in the keypoint localization part. With our keypoints and ground truth person detections, we obtained 65.1 mAP. This can be interpreted as our person detection subnet is performing quite well. Both ground truth detections got 89.4 mAP, which is a good indicator of PRN performance. In addition to these experiments, we tested PRN on the keypoints detected by previous SOTA bottom-up models [6,37]. Consequently, PRN performed better grouping (Table 4) than *Part Affinity Fields* [6] and *Associative Embedding* [37] by improving both detection results by ∼ 1 mAP. To obtain results in Table 4, we have used COCO val split, our person bounding box results and the keypoint results from the official source code of the papers. Note that running PRN on keypoints that were not generated by MultiPoseNet is unfair to PRN because it is trained with our detection architecture. Moreover original methods use image features for assignment coupled with their detection scheme, nonetheless, PRN is able to outperform the other grouping methods.

4.3   Person Detection

We trained the person detection subnet only on COCO person instances by freezing the backbone with keypoint detection parameters. The person category results of our network with different backbones can be seen in Table 5. Our model with both ResNet-50 and ResNet-101 backends outperformed the original implementations. This is not a surprising result since our network is only dealing with a single class whereas the original implementations handle 80 object classes.

Table 5. Left: Person detection results on COCO dataset. **Right:** Person semantic segmentation results on PASCAL VOC 2012 test split.

Person Detectors	AP	AP_{50}	AP_{75}	AP_S	AP_M	AP_L	Segmentation	IoU
Ours - R101	**52.5**	**81.5**	**55.3**	**35.2**	59	71	DeepLab v3 [9]	**92.1**
Ours - R50	51.3	81.4	53.6	34.9	58	68.1	DeepLab v2 [8]	87.4
RetinaNet [35]	50.2	77.7	53.5	31.6	**59**	**71.5**	SegNet [29]	74.9
FPN [34]	47.5	78	50.7	28.6	55	67.4	Ours	87.8

4.4   Person Semantic Segmentation

Person segmentation output is an additional layer appended to the keypoint outputs. We obtained the ground truth labels by combining person masks into single binary mask layer, and we jointly trained segmentation with keypoint task. Therefore, it adds a very small complexity to the model. Yet, producing segmentation masks didn't affect the keypoint results. Evaluation was performed on PASCAL VOC 2012 test set with PASCAL IoU metric. We obtained final segmentation results via multi-scale testing and thresholding. We did not apply any additional test-time augmentation or ensembling. Table 5 shows the test results of our system in comparison with previous successful semantic segmentation algorithms. Our model outperformed most of the successful baseline models such as SegNet [29] and Deeplab-v2 [8], and got comparable performance to the state-of-the-art Deeplab v3 [9] model. This demonstrates the capacity of our model to handle different tasks altogether with competitive performance. Some qualitative segmentation results are given in Fig. 5.

Fig. 5. Some qualitative results for COCO test-dev dataset.

4.5   Runtime Analysis

Our system consists of a backbone, keypoint & person detection subnets, and the pose residual network. The parameter sizes of each block is given in the supplementary material. Most of the parameters are required to extract features in the backbone network, subnets and PRN are relatively lightweight networks. By using a shallow feature extractor like ResNet-50, we can achieve realtime performance. To measure the perfor-

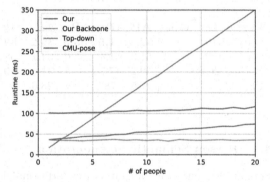

Fig. 6. Runtime analysis of MultiPoseNet with respect to number of people.

mance, we have built a model using ResNet-50 with 384×576 sized inputs which contain 1 to 20 people. We measured the time spent during the inference of 1000 images, and averaged the inference times to get a consistent result (Fig. 6). Keypoint and person detections take 35 ms while PRN takes 2 ms per instance. Our model runs in between 15–27 FPS depending on the number of people in the image (15 FPS @ 1 person, 27 FPS @ 20 persons).

5   Conclusion

In this work, we introduced the Pose Residual Network which can accurately assign keypoints to person detections outputted by a multi task learning architecture (MultiPoseNet). Our pose estimation method achieved state-of-the-art performance among bottom-up methods and comparable results with top-down methods. Our method has the fastest inference time compared to previous methods. We showed the assignment performance of pose residual network ablation analysis. We demonstrated the representational capacity of our multi-task learning model by jointly producing keypoints, person bounding boxes and person segmentation results.

Acknowledgement.. We gratefully acknowledge the support of NVIDIA Corporation with the donation of the Tesla K40 GPU used for this research. The experiments reported in this paper were partially performed at TUBITAK ULAKBIM, High Performance and Grid Computing Center (TRUBA resources).

References

1. Abadi, M., et al.: Tensorflow: large-scale machine learning on heterogeneous systems (2015). software available from tensorflow.org
2. Andriluka, M., Roth, S., Schiele, B.: Pictorial structures revisited: People detection and articulated pose estimation. In: IEEE Conference on Computer Vision and Pattern Recognition (2009)
3. Belagiannis, V., Zisserman, A.: Recurrent human pose estimation. In: International Conference on Automatic Face and Gesture Recognition (2017)
4. Bengio, Y., Louradour, J., Collobert, R., Weston, J.: Curriculum learning. In: International Conference on Machine Learning (2009)
5. Bulat, A., Tzimiropoulos, G.: Human pose estimation via convolutional part heatmap regression. In: Leibe, B., Matas, J., Sebe, N., Welling, M. (eds.) ECCV 2016. LNCS, vol. 9911, pp. 717–732. Springer, Cham (2016). https://doi.org/10.1007/978-3-319-46478-7_44
6. Cao, Z., Simon, T., Wei, S.E., Sheikh, Y.: Realtime multi-person 2D pose estimation using part affinity fields. In: IEEE Conference on Computer Vision and Pattern Recognition (2017)
7. Carreira, J., Agrawal, P., Fragkiadaki, K., Malik, J.: Human pose estimation with iterative error feedback. In: IEEE Conference on Computer Vision and Pattern Recognition (2016)
8. Chen, L.C., Papandreou, G., Kokkinos, I., Murphy, K., Yuille, A.L.: DeepLab: semantic image segmentation with deep convolutional nets, atrous convolution, and fully connected CRFs. IEEE Trans. Pattern Anal. Mach. Intell. (2017)
9. Chen, L.C., Zhu, Y., Papandreou, G., Schroff, F., Adam, H.: Encoder-decoder with atrous separable convolution for semantic image segmentation. In: arXiv preprint arXiv:1802.02611 (2018)
10. Chen, Y., Wang, Z., Peng, Y., Zhang, Z., Yu, G., Sun, J.: Cascaded pyramid network for multi-person pose estimation. In: arXiv preprint arXiv:1711.07319 (2017)
11. Chollet, F., et al.: Keras (2015). https://github.com/keras-team/keras
12. Chou, C.J., Chien, J.T., Chen, H.T.: Self adversarial training for human pose estimation. arXiv preprint arXiv:1707.02439 (2017)
13. Chu, X., Yang, W., Ouyang, W., Ma, C., Yuille, A.L., Wang, X.: Multi-context attention for human pose estimation. In: IEEE Conference on Computer Vision and Pattern Recognition (2017)
14. Dalal, N., Triggs, B.: Histograms of oriented gradients for human detection. In: IEEE Conference on Computer Vision and Pattern Recognition (2005)
15. Dantone, M., Gall, J., Leistner, C., Van Gool, L.: Human pose estimation using body parts dependent joint regressors. In: IEEE Conference on Computer Vision and Pattern Recognition (2013)

16. Deng, J., Dong, W., Socher, R., Li, L.J., Li, K., Fei-Fei, L.: ImageNet: a large-scale hierarchical image database. In: IEEE Conference on Computer Vision and Pattern Recognition (2009)

17. Everingham, M., Eslami, S.M.A., Van Gool, L., Williams, C.K.I., Winn, J., Zisserman, A.: The pascal visual object classes challenge: a retrospective. Int. J. Comput. Vis. **111**, 98–136 (2015)

18. Fang, H., Xie, S., Tai, Y., Lu, C.: RMPE: regional multi-person pose estimation. In: International Conference on Computer Vision (2017)

19. Gaiser, H., et al.: Keras-RetinaNet (2018). https://github.com/fizyr/keras-retinanet

20. Gkioxari, G., Arbelaez, P., Bourdev, L., Malik, J.: Articulated pose estimation using discriminative armlet classifiers. In: IEEE Conference on Computer Vision and Pattern Recognition (2013)

21. Gkioxari, G., Hariharan, B., Girshick, R., Malik, J.: Using k-poselets for detecting people and localizing their keypoints. In: IEEE Conference on Computer Vision and Pattern Recognition (2014)

22. He, K., Zhang, X., Ren, S., Sun, J.: Deep residual learning for image recognition. In: IEEE Conference on Computer Vision and Pattern Recognition (2016)

23. He, K., Gkioxari, G., Dollr, P., Girshick, R.: Mask R-CNN. In: International Conference on Computer Vision (2017)

24. Huang, S., Gong, M., Tao, D.: A coarse-fine network for keypoint localization. In: International Conference on Computer Vision (2017)

25. Insafutdinov, E., Pishchulin, L., Andres, B., Andriluka, M., Schiele, B.: DeeperCut: a deeper, stronger, and faster multi-person pose estimation model. In: European Conference on Computer Vision (2016)

26. Iqbal, U., Gall, J.: Multi-person pose estimation with local joint-to-person associations. In: Hua, G., Jégou, H. (eds.) ECCV 2016. LNCS, vol. 9914, pp. 627–642. Springer, Cham (2016). https://doi.org/10.1007/978-3-319-48881-3_44

27. Iqbal, U., Milan, A., Gall, J.: PoseTrack: joint multi-person pose estimation and tracking. In: IEEE Conference on Computer Vision and Pattern Recognition (2017)

28. Johnson, S., Everingham, M.: Clustered pose and nonlinear appearance models for human pose estimation. In: British Machine Vision Conference (2010)

29. Kendall, A., Badrinarayanan, V., Cipolla, R.: Bayesian SegNet: model uncertainty in deep convolutional encoder-decoder architectures for scene understanding. In: British Machine Vision Conference (2017)

30. Kingma, D.P., Ba, J.: Adam: a method for stochastic optimization. In: International Conference on Learning Representations (2015)

31. Kong, T., Yao, A., Chen, Y., Sun, F.: HyperNet: towards accurate region proposal generation and joint object detection. In: IEEE Conference on Computer Vision and Pattern Recognition (2016)

32. Ladicky, L., Torr, P.H., Zisserman, A.: Human pose estimation using a joint pixel-wise and part-wise formulation. In: IEEE Conference on Computer Vision and Pattern Recognition (2013)

33. Lifshitz, I., Fetaya, E., Ullman, S.: Human pose estimation using deep consensus voting. In: Leibe, B., Matas, J., Sebe, N., Welling, M. (eds.) ECCV 2016. LNCS, vol. 9906, pp. 246–260. Springer, Cham (2016). https://doi.org/10.1007/978-3-319-46475-6_16

34. Lin, T.Y., Dollr, P., Girshick, R., He, K., Hariharan, B., Belongie, S.: Feature pyramid networks for object detection. In: IEEE Conference on Computer Vision and Pattern Recognition (2017)

35. Lin, T.Y., Goyal, P., Girshick, R., He, K., Dollr, P.: Focal loss for dense object detection. In: International Conference on Computer Vision (2017)
36. Lin, T.-Y., et al.: Microsoft COCO: common objects in context. In: Fleet, D., Pajdla, T., Schiele, B., Tuytelaars, T. (eds.) ECCV 2014. LNCS, vol. 8693, pp. 740–755. Springer, Cham (2014). https://doi.org/10.1007/978-3-319-10602-1_48
37. Newell, A., Huang, Z., Deng, J.: Associative embedding: end-to-end learning for joint detection and grouping. In: Advances in Neural Information Processing (2017)
38. Newell, A., Yang, K., Deng, J.: Stacked hourglass networks for human pose estimation. In: Leibe, B., Matas, J., Sebe, N., Welling, M. (eds.) ECCV 2016. LNCS, vol. 9912, pp. 483–499. Springer, Cham (2016). https://doi.org/10.1007/978-3-319-46484-8_29
39. Ning, G., Zhang, Z., He, Z.: Knowledge-guided deep fractal neural networks for human pose estimation. In: IEEE Transactions on Multimedia (2017)
40. Papandreou, G., et al.: Towards accurate multi-person pose estimation in the wild. In: IEEE Conference on Computer Vision and Pattern Recognition (2017)
41. Pishchulin, L., Andriluka, M., Gehler, P., Schiele, B.: Poselet conditioned pictorial structures. In: IEEE Conference on Computer Vision and Pattern Recognition (2013)
42. Pishchulin, L., et al.: DeepCut: joint subset partition and labeling for multi person pose estimation. In: IEEE Conference on Computer Vision and Pattern Recognition (2016)
43. Ramakrishna, V., Munoz, D., Hebert, M., Andrew Bagnell, J., Sheikh, Y.: Pose machines: articulated pose estimation via inference machines. In: Fleet, D., Pajdla, T., Schiele, B., Tuytelaars, T. (eds.) ECCV 2014. LNCS, vol. 8690, pp. 33–47. Springer, Cham (2014). https://doi.org/10.1007/978-3-319-10605-2_3
44. Szegedy, C., Vanhoucke, V., Ioffe, S., Shlens, J., Wojna, Z.: Rethinking the inception architecture for computer vision. In: IEEE Conference on Computer Vision and Pattern Recognition (2016)
45. Tompson, J., Jain, A., LeCun, Y., Bregler, C.: Joint training of a convolutional network and a graphical model for human pose estimation. In: Advances in Neural Information Processing (2014)
46. Toshev, A., Szegedy, C.: DeepPose: human pose estimation via deep neural networks. In: IEEE Conference on Computer Vision and Pattern Recognition (2014)
47. Varadarajan, S., Datta, P., Tickoo, O.: A greedy part assignment algorithm for realtime multi-person 2D pose estimation. arXiv preprint arXiv:1708.09182 (2017)
48. Wei, S.E., Ramakrishna, V., Kanade, T., Sheikh, Y.: Convolutional pose machines. In: IEEE Conference on Computer Vision and Pattern Recognition (2016)
49. Xia, F., Wang, P., Yuille, A., Angeles, L.: Joint multi-person pose estimation and semantic part segmentation in a single image. In: IEEE Conference on Computer Vision and Pattern Recognition (2017)
50. Xie, S., Girshick, R., Dollr, P., Tu, Z., He, K.: Aggregated residual transformations for deep neural networks. In: IEEE Conference on Computer Vision and Pattern Recognition (2017)
51. Yang, Y., Ramanan, D.: Articulated pose estimation with flexible mixtures-of-parts. In: IEEE Transaction on Pattern Analysis and Machine Intelligence (2013)

TS²C: Tight Box Mining with Surrounding Segmentation Context for Weakly Supervised Object Detection

Yunchao Wei[1(✉)], Zhiqiang Shen[1,2], Bowen Cheng[1], Honghui Shi[3],
Jinjun Xiong[3], Jiashi Feng[4], and Thomas Huang[1]

[1] University of Illinois at UrbanaChampaign, Urbana, IL, USA
{yunchao,shen54,bcheng9,t-huang1}@illinois.edu
[2] Fudan University, Shanghai, China
[3] IBM T.J. Watson Research Center, Yorktown Heights, USA
Honghui.Shi@ibm.com, jinjun@us.ibm.com
[4] National University of Singapore, Singapore, Singapore
elefjia@nus.edu.sg

Abstract. This work provides a simple approach to discover *tight* object bounding boxes with only image-level supervision, called **T**ight box mining with **S**urrounding **S**egmentation **C**ontext (TS²C). We observe that object candidates mined through current multiple instance learning methods are usually trapped to discriminative object parts, rather than the entire object. TS²C leverages surrounding segmentation context derived from weakly-supervised segmentation to suppress such low-quality distracting candidates and boost the high-quality ones. Specifically, TS²C is developed based on two key properties of desirable bounding boxes: (1) high purity, meaning most pixels in the box are with high object response, and (2) high completeness, meaning the box covers high object response pixels comprehensively. With such novel and computable criteria, more tight candidates can be discovered for learning a better object detector. With TS²C, we obtain 48.0% and 44.4% mAP scores on VOC 2007 and 2012 benchmarks, which are the new state-of-the-arts.

Keywords: Weakly-supervised learning · Object detection Semantic segmentation

1 Introduction

Weakly Supervised Object Detection (WSOD) [3,7,10,17,18,20,21,23,32,33,35, 42–44] aims to detect objects only using image-level annotations for supervision. Despite remarkable progress, existing approaches still have difficulties in accurately identifying tight boxes of target objects with only image-level annotations, thus their performance is inferior to the fully supervised counterparts [6,13,22,25,28–30].

Z. Shen and B. Cheng—Equal contribution.

© Springer Nature Switzerland AG 2018
V. Ferrari et al. (Eds.): ECCV 2018, LNCS 11215, pp. 454–470, 2018.
https://doi.org/10.1007/978-3-030-01252-6_27

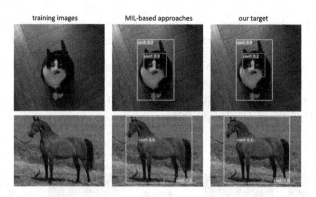

Fig. 1. Comparison of MIL-based approaches and our target. MIL-based approaches tend to assign high confidence to discriminative parts (blue boxes) of target objects. Our target is to alleviate such cases and lift the confidence of the tight ones (yellow boxes). Best viewed in color. (Color figure online)

To localize objects with weak supervision information, one popular solution is to apply Multiple Instance Learning (MIL) for mining high-confidence region proposals [34,47] with positive image-level annotations. However, MIL usually discovers the most discriminative part of the target object (*e.g.* the head of a cat) rather than the entire object region, as shown in Fig. 1. This inability of providing the complete object severely limits its effectiveness for WSOD. To address this issue, Li *et al.* [21] exploited the contrastive relationship between a selected region and its mask-out image for proposal selection. Nevertheless, the mask-out strategy fails for multi-instance cases. The selector is easily confused by remained instances with high responses, even though the correct object has been masked out.

Recently, some weakly supervised semantic segmentation approaches [19,36, 38,40] have demonstrated promising performance. Utilizing the inferred segmentation confidence maps, Diba *et al.* [10] presented a cascaded approach that leverages segmentation knowledge to filter noisy proposals and achieves competitive detection results. However, we argue that their solution is sub-optimal and insufficient as it only considers the segmentation confidence *inside* the proposal boxes, thus is unable to filter high-response fragments of object parts, as the magenta boxes shown in Fig. 2 (b).

In this work, we propose a principled and more effective approach, compared with [10], to mine tight object boxes by exploiting segmentation confidence maps in a creative way, aiming for addressing the challenging WSOD problems. Our approach is motivated by the following observations, as illustrated by two examples in Fig. 2 (a). We use blue and yellow to encode two kinds of boxes, which partially and tightly cover objects respectively. Based on the semantic segmentation confidence maps obtained in a weakly supervised manner, many pixels surrounding the blue boxes have high predicted segmentation confidence, while very few high-confidence pixels are included in the surrounding context for the

yellow ones of higher tightness. We find that a desirable tight object box generally needs to satisfy two properties based on segmentation context:

- *Purity*: most pixels inside the box should have high confidence scores, which
  guarantees that the box is located around the target object;
- *Completeness*: very few pixels are with high confidence scores in the surrounding context of the target box.

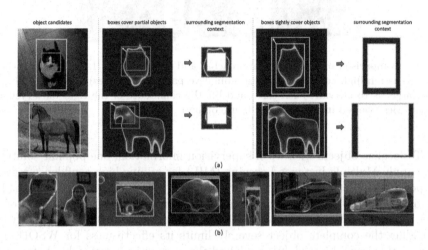

Fig. 2. (a) Motivation of the proposed TS^{2}C: fewer high response pixels on the segmentation confidence map are included by enlarging higher-quality boxes of object
candidates (the yellow one) compared with partial bounding boxes (the blue one). (b)
Comparison of the rank 1 proposal using the strategy proposed by [10] (magenta boxes)
and ours (yellow boxes). Best viewed in color. (Color figure online)

Based on these properties, we devise a simple yet effective approach, named
Tight box mining with Surrounding Segmentation Context (TS^{2}C), to efficiently
select object candidates of high quality from thousands of candidates. Specifically, the proposed TS^{2}C examines two kinds of regions for evaluating the tightness of bounding boxes: (1) the region included in the box and (2) the region
surrounding the box. It computes objectness scores of the two regions by averaging the corresponding pixel confidence values on the segmentation maps. Tight
boxes are expected to be with high and low objectness values of the two kinds
of regions simultaneously. Thus, the difference of two objectness scores is then
taken as the quality metric on the final tightness for ranking object candidates.
Figure 2 (b) shows the top 1 object candidate inferred by the proposed TS^{2}C.
We can see that our approach is more effective for mining tight object boxes
than [10]. Moreover, our proposed TS^{2}C is generic and can be easily integrated
into any WSOD framework by introducing a parallel semantic segmentation
branch for class-specific confidence map prediction. Benefiting from our TS^{2}C,

we achieve 48.0% and 44.4% mAP scores on the challenging Pascal VOC 2007 and VOC 2012 benchmarks, which are the new state-of-the-arts in the WSOD community.

2 Related Work

Multiple Instance Learning (MIL) provides a suitable way for formulating and solving WSOD. In specific, if an image is annotated with a specific class, at least one proposal instance from the image is positive for this class; and no proposal instance is positive for unlabeled classes. Previous works on applying MIL to WSOD can be roughly categorized into two-step [7,17,21,35] and end-to-end [3,10,18,20,32,33] based approaches.

Two-Step Approaches. First extract proposal representation leveraging hand-crafted features or pre-trained CNN models and employ MIL to select the best object candidate for learning the object detector. For instance, Wang et al. [35] presented a latent semantic clustering approach to select the most discriminative cluster for each category. Cibis et al. [7] learned a multi-fold MIL detector by re-labeling proposals and re-training the object classifier iteratively. Li et al. [21] first trained a multi-label classification network on entire images and then selected class-specific proposal candidates using a mask-out strategy, followed by MIL for learning a Fast R-CNN detector. Recently, Jie et al. [17] took a similar strategy as Li et al. [21] and proposed a more robust self-taught approach to learn a detector by harvesting more accurate supportive proposals in an online manner. However, splitting the WSOD into two steps results in a non-convex optimization problem, making such approaches trapped in local optima.

End-to-End Approaches. Combine CNNs and MIL into a unified framework for addressing WSOD. Oquab et al. [27] and Wei et al. [39] adopted a similar strategy to learn a multi-label classification network with max-pooling MIL. The learned classification model was then applied to coarse object localization [27]. Bilen et al. [3] proposed a novel Weakly Supervised Deep Detection Network (WSDDN) including two key streams, one for classification and the other for object localization. The outputs of these two streams are then combined for better rating the objectness of proposals. Based on WSDDN, Kantorov et al. [18] proposed to learn a context-aware CNN with contrast-based contextual modeling. Both [18] and our approach employ proposal context to identify high-quality proposals. However, [18] exploits inside/outside context features of each bounding box for learning to classification, in contrast, we leverage objectness scores obtained by segmentation confidence maps to pick out tight candidates. Recently, Tang et al. [32] also employed WSDDN as the basic network and augmented it with several Online Instance Classifier Refinement (OICR) branches, which is the state-of-the-art on the challenging WSOD task. In this work, we employ both WSDDN and OICR to develop our framework where the proposed TS^{2}C is leveraged to further improve performance. Both [10] and our approach utilizes object segmentation knowledge to benefit WSOD. However, Diba et al. [10] only considered the confidence of pixels included in the bounding box for rating the proposal objectness, which is not as effective as ours.

Beyond the above mentioned related works, some fully-supervised object detection approaches [5,12,22,46] also exploit contextual information of bounding boxes for benefiting object detection. Both Chen *et al.* [5] and Li *et al.* [22] leveraged information of enlarged contextual proposals to enhance the accuracy of the classifier. Zhu *et al.* [46] proposed to use a pool of segments obtained in the bottom-up manner to obtain better detection boxes. Our TS^{2}C is totally different from these works in terms of both motivation and methodology. In particular, our motivation is to employ surrounding segmentation context to suppress these false positive objects parts. In addition, our approach can be easily embedded into any WSOD framework to make a further performance improvement.

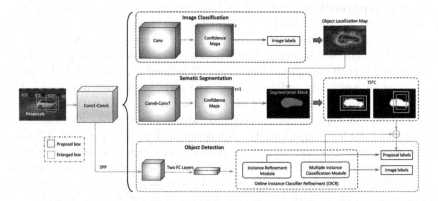

Fig. 3. Overview of the proposed TS^{2}C for weakly supervised object detection. Several convolutional layers are leveraged to extract the intermediate features of an input image. The entire feature maps are firstly fed into a *Classification* branch to produce object localization maps corresponding to image-level labels. We then employ the localization maps to generate the segmentation masks, which serve as supervision to learn the *Segmentation* branch. Based on the segmentation confidence maps, we utilize TS^{2}C to evaluate the objectness scores of proposals according to their purity and completeness, which collaborates with the OICR [32] for training the *Detection* branch.

3   The Proposed Approach

We show the overall architecture of the proposed approach in Fig. 3. It consists of three key branches, *i.e.* image classification, semantic segmentation and object detection. In particular, the *Classification* branch is employed to generate class-specific localization maps. Following the previous weakly supervised semantic segmentation approaches [37], we leverage the inferred localization maps to produce pseudo segmentation masks of training images, which are then used as supervision to train the *Segmentation* branch. The segmentation confidence maps from the *Segmentation* branch are then employed to evaluate objectness scores of the proposals according to the proposed TS^{2}C, which finally collaborates with the *Detection* branch for learning an improved object detector. The overall framework is trained by minimizing the following composite loss functions from the three branches using stochastic gradient descent:

$$L = L_{cls} + L_{seg} + L_{det}. \tag{1}$$

We will introduce each branch below and then elaborate on details of TS^{2}C.

3.1 Classification for Object Localization

Inspired by [10,24,45], the fully convolutional network along with the Global Average Pooling (GAP) operation is able to generate class-specific activation maps, which can provide coarse object localization prior. We conduct experiments on Pascal VOC benchmarks, in which each training image is annotated with one or several labels. We thus treat the classification task as a separate binary classification problem for each class. Following [27], the loss function L_{cls} is thus defined as a sum of C binary logistic regression losses.

3.2 Weakly Supervised Semantic Segmentation

The *Classification* branch can produce localization cues for foreground objects. We assign the pixels with values on the class-specific confidence map larger than a pre-defined normalized threshold (*i.e.* ≥ 0.78) with the corresponding class label. Beyond the object regions, background localization cues are also needed for training the segmentation branch. Motivated by [19,36,38,40], we leverage the saliency detection technology [41] to produce the saliency map for each training image. Based on the generated saliency map, we choose the pixels with low normalized saliency values (*i.e.* ≤ 0.06) as background. However, both the class-specific confidence map and the saliency map are not accurate enough to guarantee a high-quality segmentation mask. To alleviate the negative effect caused by falsely assigned pixels, we ignore the ambiguous pixels during training the *Segmentation* branch, including (1) pixels that are not assigned semantic labels, (2) foreground pixels of different categories that are in conflict, and (3) low-saliency pixels that fall in the foreground pixels. With the produced pseudo segmentation mask, we train the *Segmentation* branch with pixel-wise cross-entropy loss L_{seg}, which is widely adopted by fully-supervised schemes [4,26].

3.3 Learning Object Detection with TS^{2}C

For each training or test image, Selective Search [34] is employed to generate object proposals and Spatial Pyramid Pooling (SPP) [15] is leveraged to generate constant size feature maps for different proposals. Our TS^{2}C aims to select high-quality object candidates from thousands of candidates to improve the effectiveness of training, which can be easily implanted into any WSOD framework.

We choose the state-of-the-art Online Instance Classifier Refinement (OICR) [32] as the backbone of the *Detection* branch, which collaborates with the proposed TS^{2}C for learning a better object detector. In the following, we will first make a brief introduction of OICR, and then explain how to leverage our TS^{2}C to benefit the learning process of WSOD.

OICR. As shown in Fig. 3, the OICR mainly includes two modules, *i.e.* multiple instance classification and instance refinement. In particular, the multiple instance classification module is inspired from [3], which includes two branches to extract parallel data streams from the input features pooled by SPP, as shown in Fig. 4 (a). The upper stream conducts softmax operation on each individual proposal for classification. The bottom stream estimates a probability distribution over all candidate proposals using softmax, which indicates the contribution of each proposal to classifier decision for each class. Therefore, these two streams provide classification-based and localization-based features for each proposal. Both inferred scores are then fused with element-wise product operation and finally aggregated into image-level prediction by sum-pooling over all proposals. With the supervision of image-level annotations, the multiple instance classification module can be learned with binary logistic regression losses as detailed in Sect. 3.1.

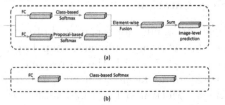

(a)

(b)

Fig. 4. Details of (a) multiple instance classification module and (b) instance refinement module in TS^{2}C.

By leveraging multiple instance classification module as a basic classifier for obtaining initial classification scores for each proposal, progressive refinement is then conducted via the instance refinement module, as detailed in Fig. 4 (b). In particular, the instance refinement module first selects the top-scoring proposal of each image-level label. Those proposals with high spatial overlap scores over the top-scoring one are then labeled correspondingly. The idea behind such a module is that the top-scoring proposal may only contain part of a target object and its adjacent proposals may cover more object regions. Benefiting from both two modules embedded in the OICR, each proposal is assigned with a pseudo class label, which is then employed as supervision for learning detection with the softmax cross-entropy loss [13,14,29]. To address the initialization issue (*i.e.* the classifier cannot well recognize proposals with randomly initialized parameters at the beginning of training), OICR adopts a weighted loss by assigning different weights to different proposals during different training iterations. Thus, the L_{det} is composed of binary logistic regression losses for image-level classification and softmax cross-entropy loss for proposal-level classification. Please refer to [32] for more details.

Problems. However, such progressive refinement operation of OICR highly relies on the quality of initial object candidates from the multiple instance classification module. This means without reasonable object candidates received from the multiple instance classification module for initialization, the following progressive refinement strategy of OICR cannot find the correct proposals with high IoU scores over ground-truth bounding boxes. This brings a critical risk: if the multiple instance classification module fails to produce reasonable object candidates then the OICR cannot recall the missed object with any hope. We propose to reduce such a risk by designing an objectness rating approach from a totally new perspective. In particular, we detail our proposed TS^{2}C that rates the proposals' objectness from the segmentation view in the following.

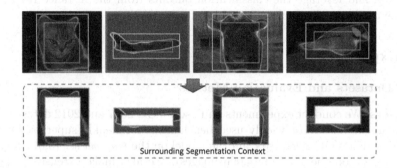

Surrounding Segmentation Context

Fig. 5. Motivation of the conditional average strategy: only a small number of pixels belong to objects in the surrounding regions. To promote the objectness score of surrounding context, we only employ pixels with large confidence values (highlighted by red color) for conducting average calculation. Best viewed in color. (Color figure online)

TS^{2}C for Learning Detection. As shown in Fig. 3, TS^{2}C uses the segmentation confidence maps from the *Segmentation* branch to rate the proposal objectness. We consider $x_i (i = 1 \cdots n)$ as one proposal from a given training image annotated by class c. Let H_c denote the confidence map of category c predicted by the semantic *Segmentation* branch. For x_i, we calculate objectness scores of both the region inside the box P_I and the surrounding context P_S between x_i and the corresponding enlarged one. Let $avg(H_c, x_i)$ denote the operation of computing P_I, which takes all pixel values included in x_i into account. P_I of a large value can guarantee that x_i is around the target object. To obtain a robust surrounding objectness score P_S, we adopt a conditional average strategy $a\hat{v}g(H_c, x_i)$. As shown in Fig. 5, many surrounding regions of negative candidates include a large number of un-related (*i.e.* background) pixels, which are with low confidence scores. Therefore, the resulted objectness score will be small if we average all the pixel values for computing P_S, in a similar way as for P_I. However, we expect the value of P_S to be large, so that negative candidates of such cases can be suppressed by $P_I - P_S$. To this end, we first rank the pixels in the surrounding region according to their confidence scores and the conditional average strategy only employs the first 50% pixels for calculating the objectness score. Then, the objectness score $O(x_i)$ of the proposed TS^{2}C is finally calculated as

$$O(x_i) = P_I - P_S = avg(H_c, x_i) - a\hat{v}g(H_c, x_i).$$

We rank all the object candidates according to $O(x_i)$ and build a candidate pool by selecting the top two hundred proposals, collaborating with the OICR for learning a better detector. As shown in Fig. 3, $\oplus$ means the OICR will only select object candidates from the pool produced by TS^{2}C for the following training process.

During the testing stage, we ignore the *Classification* and *Segmentation* branches, and leverage the classification outputs from the instance refinement module to obtain the final detection results.

4   Experiments

4.1   Datasets and Evaluation Metrics

Datasets. We conduct experiments on Pascal VOC 2007 and 2012 datasets [11], which are the two most widely used benchmarks for weakly supervised object detection. For VOC 2007, we train the model on the *trainval* set (5,011 images) and evaluate on the *test* set (4,096 images). We also make extensive ablation analysis on VOC 2007 to verify the effectiveness of some settings. For VOC 2012, we train the model on the *trainval* set (11,540 images) and evaluate on *test* set (10,991 images) by submitting the testing result to the evaluation server.
Metrics. Following [10, 17, 32], we adopt two metrics for evaluation, *i.e.* mean average precision (mAP) and correct localization (CorLoc) [9], for evaluation on *test* and *trainval* sets, respectively. Both two metrics employ the same threshold of bounding box overlaps with ground-truth boxes, *i.e.* IoU >=0.5.

4.2   Implementation Details

We use the object proposals generated by Selective Search [34], and adopt the VGG16 network [31] pre-trained on ImageNet [8] as the backbone of the proposed framework. We employ the Deeplab-CRF-LargeFOV [4] model to initialize the corresponding layers in the segmentation branch. For the newly added layers, the parameters are randomly initialized with a Gaussian distribution $\mathcal{N}(\mu, \delta)(\mu = 0, \delta = 0.01)$. We take a mini-batch size of 2 images and set the learning rates of the first 40 K and the following 30 K iterations as 0.001 and 0.0001 respectively. During training, we take five image scales $\{480, 576, 688, 864, 1200\}$ for data augmentation. For TS^{2}C, we adopt an enlarged ratio of 1.2 to obtain the surrounding context, which is further employed for evaluating completeness of object candidates. Our experiments use the OICR [32] code, which is implemented based on the publicly available Caffe [16] deep learning framework. All of our experiments are run on NVIDIA TITAN X PASCAL GPUs.

Table 1. Comparison of detection average precision (AP) (%) on PASCAL VOC.

Method	plane	bike	bird	boat	bottle	bus	car	cat	chair	cow	table	dog	horse	motor	person	plant	sheep	sofa	train	tv	mAP
Comparisons on VOC 2007:																					
Bilen [1]	42.2	43.9	23.1	9.2	12.5	44.9	45.1	24.9	8.3	24.0	13.9	18.6	31.6	43.6	7.6	20.9	26.6	20.6	35.9	29.6	26.4
Bilen [2]	46.2	46.9	24.1	16.4	12.2	42.2	47.1	35.2	7.8	28.3	12.7	21.5	30.1	42.4	7.8	20.0	26.8	20.8	35.8	29.6	27.7
Cinbis [7]	39.3	43.0	28.8	20.4	8.0	45.5	47.9	22.1	8.4	33.5	23.6	29.2	38.5	47.9	20.3	20.0	35.8	30.8	41.0	20.1	30.2
Wang [35]	48.8	41.0	23.6	12.1	11.1	42.7	40.9	35.5	11.1	36.6	18.4	35.3	34.8	51.3	17.2	17.4	26.8	32.8	35.1	45.6	30.9
Li [21]	54.5	47.4	41.3	20.8	17.7	51.9	63.5	46.1	21.8	57.1	22.1	34.4	50.5	61.8	16.2	29.9	40.7	15.9	55.3	40.2	39.5
Bilen [3]	46.4	58.3	35.5	25.9	14.0	66.7	53.0	39.2	8.9	41.8	26.6	38.6	44.7	59.0	10.8	17.3	40.7	49.6	56.9	50.8	39.3
Teh [33]	48.8	45.9	37.4	26.9	9.2	50.7	43.4	43.6	10.6	35.9	27.0	38.6	48.5	43.8	24.7	12.1	29.0	23.2	48.8	41.9	34.5
Tang [32]	58.0	62.4	31.1	19.4	13.0	65.1	62.2	28.4	24.8	44.7	30.6	25.3	37.8	65.5	15.7	24.1	41.7	46.9	64.3	62.6	41.2
Jie [17]	52.2	47.1	35.0	26.7	15.4	61.3	66.0	54.3	3.0	53.6	24.7	43.6	48.4	65.8	6.6	18.8	51.9	43.6	53.6	62.4	41.7
Diba [10]	49.5	60.6	38.6	29.2	16.2	70.8	56.9	42.5	10.9	44.1	29.9	42.2	47.9	64.1	13.8	23.5	45.9	54.1	60.8	54.5	42.8
Lai [20]	48.4	61.5	33.3	30.0	15.3	72.4	62.4	59.1	10.9	42.3	34.3	53.1	48.4	65.0	20.5	16.6	40.6	46.5	54.6	55.1	43.5
TS²C	59.3	57.5	43.7	27.3	13.5	63.9	61.7	59.9	24.1	46.9	36.7	45.6	39.9	62.6	10.3	23.6	41.7	52.4	58.7	56.6	44.3
Comparisons on VOC 2012:																					
Kantorov [18]	64.0	54.9	36.4	8.1	12.6	53.1	40.5	28.4	6.6	35.3	34.4	49.1	42.6	62.4	19.8	15.2	27.0	33.1	33.0	50.0	35.3
Tang [32]	-	-	-	-	-	-	-	-	-	-	-	-	-	-	-	-	-	-	-	-	37.9
Jie [17]	60.8	54.2	34.1	14.9	13.1	54.3	53.4	58.6	3.7	53.1	8.3	43.4	49.8	69.2	4.1	17.5	43.8	25.6	55.0	50.1	38.3
TS²C	67.4	57.0	37.7	23.7	15.2	56.9	49.1	64.8	15.1	39.4	19.3	48.4	44.5	67.2	2.1	23.3	35.1	40.2	46.6	45.8	40.0

Table 2. Comparison of detection AP (%) by training FRCNN detectors.

Method	VOC 2007	VOC 2012
TS²C + FRCNN	48.0	44.4
OICR-Ens. + FRCNN [32]	47.0	42.5

Fig. 6. Examples of our object detection results on VOC 2007 test set. Ground-truth annotations, predictions of OICR and ours are indicated by red, green and blue bounding boxes respectively. Best viewed in color. (Color figure online)

Table 3. Comparison of correct localization (CorLoc) (%) on PASCAL VOC.

Method	plane	bike	bird	boat	bottle	bus	car	cat	chair	cow	table	dog	horse	motor	person	plant	sheep	sofa	train	tv	mean
Comparisons on VOC 2007:																					
Bilen [2]	66.4	59.3	42.7	20.4	21.3	63.4	74.3	59.6	21.1	58.2	14.0	38.5	49.5	60.0	19.8	39.2	41.7	30.1	50.2	44.1	43.7
Cinbis [7]	65.3	55.0	52.4	48.3	18.2	66.4	77.8	35.6	26.5	67.0	46.9	48.4	70.5	69.1	35.2	35.2	69.6	43.4	64.6	43.7	52.0
Wang. [35]	80.1	63.9	51.5	14.9	21.0	55.7	74.2	43.5	26.2	53.4	16.3	56.7	58.3	69.5	14.1	38.3	58.8	47.2	49.1	60.9	48.5
Li [21]	78.2	67.1	61.8	38.1	36.1	61.8	78.8	55.2	28.5	68.8	18.5	49.2	64.1	73.5	21.4	47.4	64.6	22.3	60.9	52.3	52.4
Bilen [3]	65.1	63.4	59.7	45.9	38.5	69.4	77.0	50.7	30.1	68.8	34.0	37.3	61.0	82.9	25.1	42.9	79.2	59.4	68.2	64.1	56.1
Jie [17]	72.7	55.3	53.0	27.8	35.2	68.6	81.9	60.7	11.6	71.6	29.7	54.3	64.3	88.2	22.2	53.7	72.2	52.6	68.9	75.5	56.1
Diba [10]	83.9	72.8	64.5	44.1	40.1	65.7	82.5	58.9	33.7	72.5	25.6	53.7	67.4	77.4	26.8	49.1	68.1	27.9	64.5	55.7	56.7
Tang [32]	81.7	80.4	48.7	49.5	32.8	81.7	85.4	40.1	40.6	79.5	35.7	33.7	60.5	88.8	21.8	57.9	76.3	59.9	75.3	81.4	60.6
Lai [20]	71.0	76.5	54.9	49.7	54.1	78.0	87.4	68.8	32.4	75.2	29.5	58.0	67.3	84.5	41.5	49.0	78.1	60.3	62.8	78.9	62.9
Teh [33]	84.0	64.6	70.0	62.4	25.8	80.7	73.9	71.5	35.7	81.6	46.5	71.3	79.1	78.8	56.7	34.3	69.8	56.7	77.0	72.7	64.6
TS^{2}C	84.2	74.1	61.3	52.1	32.1	76.7	82.9	66.6	42.3	70.6	39.5	57.0	61.2	88.4	9.3	54.6	72.2	60.0	65.0	70.3	61.0
Comparisons on VOC 2012:																					
Kantorov [18]	78.3	70.8	52.5	34.7	36.6	80.0	58.7	38.6	27.7	71.2	32.3	48.7	76.2	77.4	16.0	48.4	69.9	47.5	66.9	62.9	54.8
Jie [17]	82.4	68.1	54.5	38.9	35.9	84.7	73.1	64.8	17.1	78.3	22.5	57.0	70.8	86.6	18.7	49.7	80.7	45.3	70.1	77.3	58.8
Tang [32]	-	-	-	-	-	-	-	-	-	-	-	-	-	-	-	-	-	-	-	-	62.1
TS^{2}C	79.1	83.9	64.6	50.6	37.8	87.4	74.0	74.1	40.4	80.6	42.6	53.6	66.5	88.8	18.8	54.9	80.4	60.4	70.7	79.3	64.4

4.3   Comparison with Other State-of-the-arts

We compare our approach with both two-step [7,17,21,35] and end-to-end [3,10, 18,20,32,33] approaches. Top-3 results are indicated by **green**, *red* and *blue* colors. Table 1 shows the comparison in terms of AP on the VOC 2007. It can be observed that the proposed TS^{2}C is effective and outperforms all the other approaches. In particular, we adopt OICR proposed by Tang et al. [32] as the detection backbone in the proposed framework. Our approach outperforms OICR by 3.1%. The gains are mainly from using both purity and completeness metrics for filtering noisy object candidates. We also show the comparison between our approach and other state-of-the-arts on PASCAL VOC 2012 in terms of AP. Our result[1] outperforms the baseline (i.e. Tang et al.[32]) and the state-of-the-art approach (i.e. Jie et al.[17]) by 2.1% and 1.7%, respectively.

Following [32], we also train a FRCNN [13] detector using top-scoring proposals produced by TS^{2}C as pseudo ground-truth bounding boxes. As shown in Table 2, the performance can be further enhanced to 48.0% and 44.4%[2] on VOC 2007 and 2012, respectively. Our results from a single model are much better than those of [32] obtained by models (e.g. VGG16 and VGG-M) fusion. In addition, we conduct additional experiments using CorLoc as the evaluation metric. Table 3 shows the comparison on the VOC 2007 and 2012. Our approach achieves 61.0% and 64.4% in terms of CorLoc score, which are competitive compared with the state-of-the-arts. We visualize some successful detection results (blue boxes) on VOC 2007, as shown in Fig. 6. Results from OICR (green boxes) and ground truth (red boxes) are employed for comparison. It can be seen that our approach effectively reduces false positives including partial objects.

---

[1] http://host.robots.ox.ac.uk:8080/anonymous/GDNUDG.html.
[2] http://host.robots.ox.ac.uk:8080/anonymous/ECKWR7.html.

4.4 Ablation Experiments

We conduct extensive ablation analyses of the proposed TS^{2}C, including the influence of the enlarged scale for obtaining surrounding context and the proposed tightness criteria (*i.e.* purity and completeness). All experiments are based on VOC 2007 benchmark.

Table 4. Ablation study on PASCAL VOC 2007.

Method	plane	bike	bird	boat	bottle	bus	car	cat	chair	cow	table	dog	horse	motor	person	plant	sheep	sofa	train	tv	mAP
P_I vs. $P_I - P_S$:																					
P_I	54.8	64.3	37.5	28.7	13.9	63.7	62.4	47.3	16.7	45.5	29.6	26.6	41.4	63.1	10.1	23.0	42.5	50.5	63.3	57.9	42.2
$P_I - P_S$	59.3	57.5	43.7	27.3	13.5	63.9	61.7	59.9	24.1	46.9	36.7	45.6	39.9	62.6	10.3	23.6	41.7	52.4	58.7	56.6	**44.3**
Enlarged scales:																					
baseline	58.0	62.4	31.1	19.4	13.0	65.1	62.2	28.4	24.8	44.7	30.6	25.3	37.8	65.5	15.7	24.1	41.7	46.9	64.3	62.6	41.2
scale (1.4)	61.3	58.1	44.7	26.2	10.1	65.0	60.5	37.2	28.3	49.8	40.9	24.2	38.9	62.1	9.4	23.9	41.7	51.0	60.8	58.8	42.6
scale (1.3)	61.2	60.2	39.7	29.0	9.8	65.2	59.5	53.3	24.5	48.3	41.0	33.9	40.4	61.4	12.2	22.5	42.1	52.5	59.4	60.9	43.8
scale (1.2)	59.3	57.5	43.7	27.3	13.5	63.9	61.7	59.9	24.1	46.9	36.7	45.6	39.9	62.6	10.3	23.6	41.7	52.4	58.7	56.6	**44.3**
scale (1.1)	59.6	58.1	41.3	29.1	13.3	64.0	60.6	52.9	25.7	49.9	45.6	29.2	40.4	61.4	11.6	22.9	40.8	48.3	60.3	60.7	43.8
Conditional average strategy:																					
top 30%	60.8	58.7	39.7	33.2	11.2	64.3	60.5	52.6	24.8	48.1	37.2	25.6	45.5	63.7	11.4	23.8	40.9	49.1	58.4	59.9	43.5
top 50%	59.3	57.5	43.7	27.3	13.5	63.9	61.7	59.9	24.1	46.9	36.7	45.6	39.9	62.6	10.3	23.6	41.7	52.4	58.7	56.6	**44.3**
top 70%	60.9	61.5	41.8	31.8	12.8	64.8	60.3	46.5	22.8	49.7	38.7	26.3	50.2	63.2	12.7	22.4	41.6	49.4	60.0	60.3	43.9
all pixels	60.8	60.3	38.2	31.2	11.3	63.6	60.1	55.6	20.9	51.9	40.0	33.4	41.2	64.6	11.1	23.2	43.0	47.7	59.6	59.3	43.8

Purity and Completeness. One of our main contributions is the proposed criteria of purity and completeness for measuring the tightness of object candidates based on the semantic segmentation confidence maps. To validate the effectiveness of our approach (*i.e.* $P_I - P_S$), we test the other popular setting where only the purity (*e.g.* P_I) is taken into account. Specifically, we firstly leverage the two metrics to rank object candidates for annotated class(es). For example, if the image is annotated with two labels, we will produce two rankings according to segmentation confidence maps of the two classes, which are then employed for evaluating recall scores. As shown in Fig. 7, we vary the top number of object candidates based on the rankings from two metrics. Since our evaluation method only takes one object candidate for each annotated category in the top-1 case, the upper bound of the recall is 57.9% due to the existence of multi-instance images. Despite the apparent simplicity, the recall scores of our proposed $P_I - P_S$ significantly outperform those of P_I under different settings according to the top number, which demonstrates that the completeness metric is effective for reducing noisy object candidates. More visualizations of rank 1 boxes produced by $P_I - P_S$ and P_I are shown in Fig. 8. We can observe that our approach can successfully discover the tight ones from thousands of candidates. To further validate the effectiveness of the proposed TS^{2}C, we also conduct experiments using purity *i.e.* P_I for ranking object candidates as adopted in [10] for proposal selection, which results in 42.2% in mAP. By simultaneously taking purity and completeness into account, *i.e.* $P_I - P_S$, the result surpasses the baseline by 2.1% as shown in Table 4.

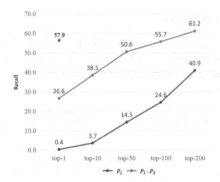

Fig. 7. Comparison of recall scores (%) between the proposed TS^{2}C ($P_I - P_S$) and the purity strategy (P_I).

Influence of Enlarged Scale. To evaluate the completeness of object candidates, we need to enlarge the original box with a specific ratio. As shown in Table 4, we examine four ratios (*i.e.* from 1.1 to 1.4) for obtaining the surrounding context of object candidates, which are then employed to calculate objectness scores with the proposed TS^{2}C. We can observe that all the models trained with the proposed TS^{2}C can outperform the baseline by more than 1.4%. In particular, the best result is achieved by adopting the ratio of 1.2. By continually enlarging the ratio, the performance will be decreased. The reason may be that some training images include multiple instances with the same semantics, and the completeness score of each object candidate will be influenced by adjacent instances in the case of using larger ratios.

Influence of Conditional Averaging Strategy. As shown in Table 4, we also examine the threshold of conditional average strategy. The best result is achieved by employ the first 50% largest pixels to calculate the objectness score of surrounding region.

Discussion. Some failure cases are shown in the last row of Fig. 8. These samples share some similar characteristics: low-quality segmentation predictions or many semantically identical instances are linked together. For instance (the middle image of the last row), the semantic segmentation branch makes a false prediction for the object under the *bird*, leading to incorrect inference of our approach. It is believed that such a case can be well addressed with the development of weakly supervised semantic segmentation techniques. For other failure samples, although the segmentation branch can provide high quality confidence maps, the overlap between objects results in false prediction of our TS^{2}C. In this case, we may need to develop effective instance-level semantic segmentation approaches in a weakly supervised manner.

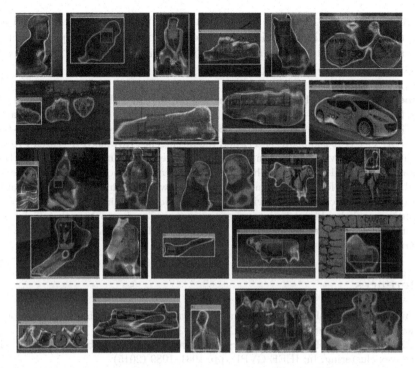

Fig. 8. Rank 1 object candidates inferred by the proposed TS²C (yellow boxes) and the strategy only using purity metric for ranking (magenta boxes). Some failure cases are given in the last row. Best viewed in color. (Color figure online)

However, the limitation of our TS²C to deal with overlapping objects with the same semantics does not affect its good performance on WSOD. We do not employ the top-1 proposal according to the objectness score as the object candidate, but build a candidate pool by selecting the top two hundred proposals. In this case, these tight boxes may still be recalled even without the largest tightness score. The effectiveness of our TS²C can be well proved by the performance gains on VOC 2007 and 2012 compared with [32].

5   Conclusion and Future Work

In this work, we proposed a simple approach, *i.e.* TS²C, for mining tight boxes by exploiting surrounding segmentation context. The TS²C is effective for suppressing low quality object candidates and promoting high quality ones tightly covering the target object. Based on the segmentation confidence map, TS²C introduces two simple criteria, *i.e.* purity and completeness, to evaluate objectness scores of object candidates. Despite apparent simplicity, the proposed TS²C can effectively filter thousands of noisy candidates and be easily embedded into any end-to-end weakly supervised framework for performance improvement. In the future, we plan to design more effective metrics for mining tight boxes by further boosting our current approach.

Acknowledgements. This work is in part supported by IBM-ILLINOIS Center for Cognitive Computing Systems Research (C3SR) - a research collaboration as part of the IBM AI Horizons Network, NUS IDS R-263-000-C67-646, ECRA R-263-000-C87-133, MOE Tier-II R-263-000-D17-112 and the Intelligence Advanced Research Projects Activity (IARPA) via Department of Interior/ Interior Business Center (DOI/IBC) contract number D17PC00341. The U.S. Government is authorized to reproduce and distribute reprints for Governmental purposes notwithstanding any copyright annotation thereon. Disclaimer: The views and conclusions contained herein are those of the authors and should not be interpreted as necessarily representing the official policies or endorsements, either expressed or implied, of IARPA, DOI/IBC, or the U.S. Government.

References

1. Bilen, H., Pedersoli, M., Tuytelaars, T.: Weakly supervised object detection with posterior regularization. In: BMVC, pp. 1–12 (2014)
2. Bilen, H., Pedersoli, M., Tuytelaars, T.: Weakly supervised object detection with convex clustering. In: IEEE CVPR, pp. 1081–1089 (2015)
3. Bilen, H., Vedaldi, A.: Weakly supervised deep detection networks. In: IEEE CVPR, pp. 2846–2854 (2016)
4. Chen, L.C., Papandreou, G., Kokkinos, I., Murphy, K., Yuille, A.L.: Semantic image segmentation with deep convolutional nets and fully connected CRFs. preprint arXiv:1412.7062 (2014)
5. Chen, X., et al.: 3D object proposals for accurate object class detection. In: NIPS, pp. 424–432 (2015)
6. Cheng, B., Wei, Y., Shi, H., Feris, R., Xiong, J., Huang, T.: Revisiting RCNN: on awakening the classification power of faster RCNN. In: ECCV (2018)
7. Cinbis, R.G., Verbeek, J., Schmid, C.: Weakly supervised object localization with multi-fold multiple instance learning. IEEE TPAMI **39**(1), 189–203 (2017)
8. Deng, J., Dong, W., Socher, R., Li, L.J., Li, K., Fei-Fei, L.: ImageNet: a large-scale hierarchical image database. In: IEEE CVPR, pp. 248–255 (2009)
9. Deselaers, T., Alexe, B., Ferrari, V.: Weakly supervised localization and learning with generic knowledge. IJCV **100**(3), 275–293 (2012)
10. Diba, A., Sharma, V., Pazandeh, A., Pirsiavash, H., Van Gool, L.: Weakly supervised cascaded convolutional networks. In: IEEE CVPR (2017)
11. Everingham, M., Eslami, S.A., Van Gool, L., Williams, C.K., Winn, J., Zisserman, A.: The pascal visual object classes challenge: a retrospective. IJCV **111**(1), 98–136 (2014)
12. Gidaris, S., Komodakis, N.: Object detection via a multi-region and semantic segmentation-aware CNN model. In: IEEE ICCV, pp. 1134–1142 (2015)
13. Girshick, R.: Fast R-CNN. In: IEEE ICCV, pp. 1440–1448 (2015)
14. Girshick, R., Donahue, J., Darrell, T., Malik, J.: Rich feature hierarchies for accurate object detection and semantic segmentation. In: IEEE CVPR, pp. 580–587 (2014)

15. He, K., Zhang, X., Ren, S., Sun, J.: Spatial pyramid pooling in deep convolutional networks for visual recognition. In: Fleet, D., Pajdla, T., Schiele, B., Tuytelaars, T. (eds.) ECCV 2014. LNCS, vol. 8691, pp. 346–361. Springer, Cham (2014). https://doi.org/10.1007/978-3-319-10578-9_23
16. Jia, Y., et al.: Caffe: convolutional architecture for fast feature embedding. In: ACM Multimedia, pp. 675–678 (2014)
17. Jie, Z., Wei, Y., Jin, X., Feng, J., Liu, W.: Deep self-taught learning for weakly supervised object localization. In: IEEE CVPR (2017)
18. Kantorov, V., Oquab, M., Cho, M., Laptev, I.: ContextLocNet: context-aware deep network models for weakly supervised localization. In: Leibe, B., Matas, J., Sebe, N., Welling, M. (eds.) ECCV 2016. LNCS, vol. 9909, pp. 350–365. Springer, Cham (2016). https://doi.org/10.1007/978-3-319-46454-1_22
19. Kolesnikov, A., Lampert, C.H.: Seed, expand and constrain: Three principles for weakly-supervised image segmentation. In: ECCV, pp. 695–711 (2016)
20. Lai, B., Gong, X.: Saliency guided end-to-end learning for weakly supervised object detection. In: IJCAI (2017)
21. Li, D., Huang, J.B., Li, Y., Wang, S., Yang, M.H.: Weakly supervised object localization with progressive domain adaptation. In: IEEE CVPR, pp. 3512–3520 (2016)
22. Li, J., et al.: Attentive contexts for object detection. IEEE Trans. Multimedia 19(5), 944–954 (2017)
23. Liang, X., Liu, S., Wei, Y., Liu, L., Lin, L., Yan, S.: Towards computational baby learning: a weakly-supervised approach for object detection. In: IEEE ICCV, pp. 999–1007 (2015)
24. Lin, M., Chen, Q., Yan, S.: Network in network. In: ICLR (2013)
25. Liu, W., et al.: SSD: single shot multibox detector. In: Leibe, B., Matas, J., Sebe, N., Welling, M. (eds.) ECCV 2016. LNCS, vol. 9905, pp. 21–37. Springer, Cham (2016). https://doi.org/10.1007/978-3-319-46448-0_2
26. Long, J., Shelhamer, E., Darrell, T.: Fully convolutional networks for semantic segmentation. In: IEEE CVPR (2015)
27. Oquab, M., Bottou, L., Laptev, I., Sivic, J.: Is object localization for free?-weakly-supervised learning with convolutional neural networks. In: IEEE CVPR, pp. 685–694 (2015)
28. Redmon, J., Farhadi, A.: Yolo9000: better, faster, stronger. In: IEEE CVPR (2017)
29. Ren, S., He, K., Girshick, R., Sun, J.: Faster R-CNN: towards real-time object detection with region proposal networks. In: NIPS, pp. 91–99 (2015)
30. Shen, Z., Liu, Z., Li, J., Jiang, Y.G., Chen, Y., Xue, X.: DSOD: learning deeply supervised object detectors from scratch. In: IEEE ICCV (2017)
31. Simonyan, K., Zisserman, A.: Very deep convolutional networks for large-scale image recognition. In: International Conference on Learning Representations (2015)
32. Tang, P., Wang, X., Bai, X., Liu, W.: Multiple instance detection network with online instance classifier refinement. In: IEEE CVPR (2017)
33. Teh, E.W., Rochan, M., Wang, Y.: Attention networks for weakly supervised object localization. In: BMVC (2016)
34. Uijlings, J.R., van de Sande, K.E., Gevers, T., Smeulders, A.W.: Selective search for object recognition. IJCV 104(2), 154–171 (2013)
35. Wang, C., Ren, W., Huang, K., Tan, T.: Weakly supervised object localization with latent category learning. In: Fleet, D., Pajdla, T., Schiele, B., Tuytelaars, T. (eds.) ECCV 2014. LNCS, vol. 8694, pp. 431–445. Springer, Cham (2014). https://doi.org/10.1007/978-3-319-10599-4_28

36. Wei, Y., Feng, J., Liang, X., Cheng, M.M., Zhao, Y., Yan, S.: Object region mining with adversarial erasing: a simple classification to semantic segmentation approach. In: IEEE CVPR (2017)
37. Wei, Y., et al.: Learning to segment with image-level annotations. Pattern Recogn. (2016)
38. Wei, Y., et al.: STC: a simple to complex framework for weakly-supervised semantic segmentation. IEEE TPAMI (2016)
39. Wei, Y., et al.: HCP: a flexible cnn framework for multi-label image classification. IEEE TPAMI **38**(9), 1901–1907 (2016)
40. Wei, Y., Xiao, H., Shi, H., Jie, Z., Feng, J., Huang, T.S.: Revisiting dilated convolution: a simple approach for weakly-and semi-supervised semantic segmentation. In: IEEE CVPR, pp. 7268–7277
41. Xiao, H., Feng, J., Wei, Y., Zhang, M., Yan, S.: Deep salient object detection with dense connections and distraction diagnosis. IEEE Trans. Multimedia (2018)
42. Zhang, X., Wei, Y., Feng, J., Yang, Y., Huang, T.: Adversarial complementary learning for weakly supervised object localization. In: IEEE CVPR (2018)
43. Zhang, X., Wei, Y., Kang, G., Yang, Y., Huang, T.: Self-produced guidance for weakly-supervised object localization. In: ECCV (2018)
44. Zhao, F., Li, J., Zhao, J., Feng, J.: Weakly supervised phrase localization with multi-scale anchored transformer network. In: IEEE CVPR, pp. 5696–5705 (2018)
45. Zhou, B., Khosla, A.A.L., Oliva, A., Torralba, A.: Learning Deep Features for Discriminative Localization. IEEE CVPR (2016)
46. Zhu, Y., Urtasun, R., Salakhutdinov, R., Fidler, S.: segDeepM: exploiting segmentation and context in deep neural networks for object detection. In: IEEE CVPR, pp. 4703–4711 (2015)
47. Zitnick, C.L., Dollár, P.: Edge boxes: locating object proposals from edges. In: Fleet, D., Pajdla, T., Schiele, B., Tuytelaars, T. (eds.) ECCV 2014. LNCS, vol. 8693, pp. 391–405. Springer, Cham (2014). https://doi.org/10.1007/978-3-319-10602-1_26

Hierarchy of Alternating Specialists for Scene Recognition

Hyo Jin Kim$^{(\boxtimes)}$ and Jan-Michael Frahm

Department of Computer Science, University of North Carolina at Chapel Hill,
Chapel Hill, USA
{hyojin,jmf}@cs.unc.edu

Abstract. We introduce a method for improving convolutional neural networks (CNNs) for scene classification. We present a hierarchy of specialist networks, which disentangles the intra-class variation and inter-class similarity in a coarse to fine manner. Our key insight is that each subset within a class is often associated with different types of inter-class similarity. This suggests that existing network of experts approaches that organize classes into coarse categories are suboptimal. In contrast, we group images based on high-level appearance features rather than their class membership and dedicate a specialist model per group. In addition, we propose an alternating architecture with a global ordered- and a global orderless-representation to account for both the coarse layout of the scene and the transient objects. We demonstrate that it leads to better performance than using a single type of representation as well as the fused features. We also introduce a mini-batch soft k-means that allows end-to-end fine-tuning, as well as a novel routing function for assigning images to specialists. Experimental results show that the proposed approach achieves a significant improvement over baselines including the existing tree-structured CNNs with class-based grouping.

Keywords: Deep learning · Hierarchy of specialists · Scene recognition

1 Introduction

Accurately identifying the background in an image (e.g. beach, mountains, candy store) is an important task in computer vision because it provides us with strong contextual information as to what is happening in the scene. The major challenge that needs to be addressed is the severe intra-class variation and inter-class similarity. Not only there are many visually diverse instances within one scene category (e.g. Notre-Dame de Paris vs. Saint Basil's Cathedral), but there is also a significant visual overlap between different scene categories (e.g. airports vs. modern train stations). Several approaches have been proposed to address

Electronic supplementary material The online version of this chapter (https://doi.org/10.1007/978-3-030-01252-6_28) contains supplementary material, which is available to authorized users.

V. Ferrari et al. (Eds.): ECCV 2018, LNCS 11215, pp. 471–488, 2018.
https://doi.org/10.1007/978-3-030-01252-6_28

this problem by designing or learning better visual features [8,9,18,45,50,59]. Newer end-to-end deep neural networks were able to achieve state-of-the-art classification accuracy [1,63]. However, it becomes increasingly hard to find a distinctive representation when the classes become visually nearly indistinguishable as the number of classes increases [40]. Downweighting the representations for commonly shared visual elements can help reduce the inter-class similarity. However, these elements are sometimes the key to distinguish a class from others, as illustrated in Fig. 1.

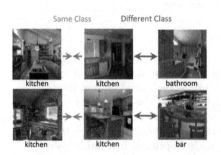

Fig. 1. Examples of intra-class variation and inter-class similarity. While base cabinets and bars characterize the kitchen class, they cause overlap with other classes with similar furnishings.

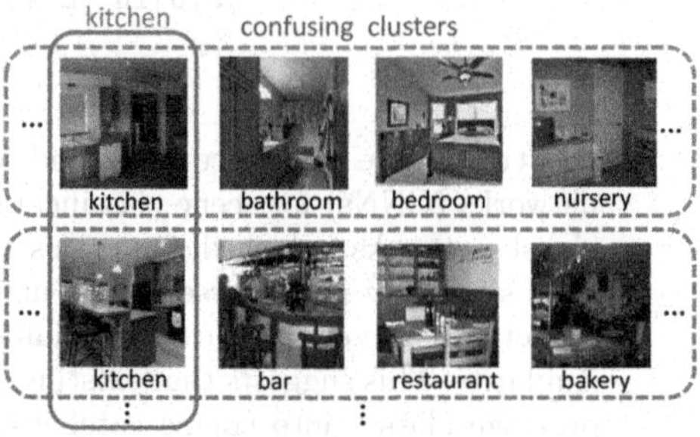

Fig. 2. There are subsets of images in each class that are often confused with those of other classes. We discover *confusing clusters* in the feature space to disentangle intra-class variation and inter-class similarity.

Thus, a sensible way to handle this issue is to apply a divide and conquer [48] strategy to dedicate different CNNs to separable subproblems. Existing methods organize classes into coarse categories, either based on the semantic hierarchy [12,15,22,58] or the confusion matrix of a trained classifier [53,57]. However, we observe that there are multiple modes of intra-class appearance variation, and that each of these modes typically causes overlap with different subsets of categories. As depicted in Fig. 2, some images of a kitchen with cabinets can be confused with a bathroom or a bedroom with similar furnishings, while other kitchen images showing the dining area are easily mistaken as a bar or a restaurant. In this case, grouping the whole kitchen class with the whole bathroom or restaurant class into a coarse category is suboptimal. Instead, it would be more effective to group confusable images below the category level, such as the images of different classes with similar furnishings as shown in Fig. 2.

Hence, we aim to identify such *confusing clusters* of images in a coarse to fine manner based on high-level appearance. The key idea is to disentangle intra-class variation and inter-class similarity by limiting the intra-class variation within each cluster. With reduced intra-class variation, a specialist model can focus on finding the subtle differences between the categories within the cluster. To this end, we introduce a Hierarchy of Alternating Specialists model, which automatically builds a hierarchical network of specialists based on the unsupervised discovery of confusing clusters. For a given specialist CNN, we find its corresponding confusing cluster by performing clustering in the feature space of its parent model that handles a more general task. This groups images that are visually similar and likely to be confused by the parent model. For assigning images to a model in the hierarchy, we propose a simple routing function which invokes only a small fraction of the models in the whole tree for an input image.

On the other hand, we notice that the spatial layout and the objects in the scene are complementary features for scene categorization (Fig. 4). This seems natural because the scene class is often determined by the way humans use objects in a certain spatial context. For example, the different rooms in a house are typically similar in structure with walls, doors, and windows. However, the objects, such as sofas, books, and dining ware, determine their function as being a living room, office, or dinning room. Another notable fact is that the objects do not necessarily stay in the same configuration. To account for this fact, we use two different types of representations in our model: One that is robust to transient local visual elements, and the other that preserves spatial layout. In particular, we propose an alternating architecture, where the architecture of a specialist alternates between the two representations based on its level in the hierarchy. We show that it achieves better performance than the fused features as well as the hierarchical models with a single type of representation.

In summary, our innovations are as follows: (1) We present a hierarchical generalist-specialist model that automatically builds itself based on the unsupervised discovery of confusing clusters in a coarse to fine manner. The confusing clusters allow specialists to focus on subtle differences between images that are visually similar and confusable to their parents. We experimentally validate that our method significantly outperforms baselines including the tree-structured CNNs based on coarse categories. (2) We propose a novel alternating architecture that effectively takes advantage of two complementary representations that capture spatial layouts and transient objects. As minor innovations, we introduce a novel routing function as well as mini-batch soft k-means for end-to-end fine tuning. Beyond the detailed innovations, our proposed algorithm is generalizable to other categorization tasks, and is applicable to any CNN architecture.

2   Related Work

Our method takes the hierarchical mixture of experts approach [7,23], where each expert in the tree structure learns to handle splits of the input space. In light of recent advances in deep neural networks, many researchers have revisited the concept for various recognition tasks [4,21,46,53]. In particular, our method adopts the generalist and specialist model from the work of Hinton et al. [21], which is similar to the mixture of experts, in the sense that each specialist focuses on a confusable subset of the classes, but it has a generalist that takes care of the classes that are not handled by specialists. It also does not require the training of a gating function, allowing models to be trained in parallel. Defining the areas of expertise can be done using a pre-defined semantic hierarchy [11,15], but in this work, we focus on unsupervised approaches [2,37,53,57]. Yan et al. [57]

and Murthy et al. [37] use the confusion matrix of a trained classifier to group classes into coarse categories. Ahmed et al. [2] randomly initialize the grouping of classes, then iteratively optimize the grouping as well as the model parameters jointly. In the context of transfer learning, Srivastava and Salakhutdinov [46] take a Bayesian approach to organize the classes into a tree hierarchy.

However, all these approaches partition the input space by grouping categories, while our method partitions the feature space that captures high-level appearance information regardless of class membership, based on the observation that there are visually drastically different sub-classes within each class. This also frees our method from the risk of misclassification in specialties due to severe inter-class similarity and intra-class variation in appearance, from which, the methods using class-based grouping can not recover [2,37,53,57]. Moreover, our method only invokes a limited number of models during testing, which leads to significant computational efficiency gains over existing methods.

In contrast to organizing multiple CNN models, there have been efforts to separate visual features of a single CNN in a tree structure [3,26,31,36,42]. This is especially useful for parallel and distributed learning as demonstrated in Kim et al. [26], where disjoint sets of features, as well as disjoint sets of classes are automatically discovered. In the same spirit of parallelization, but on a much larger scale, Gross et al. [16] deal with a mixture of experts model that does not fit in the memory. Similar to their work, our learned submodels are local in the feature space, and the image-to-model assignment is determined by the distance of the image to the corresponding submodel cluster center.

Numerous work has been done on scene categorization as being one of the fundamental problems in computer vision [17,25,30,38,41,51,55,56,62]. Our work is related to recent attempts to leverage object information within the scene [10,13,14,20,52,63]. However, we do not explicitly detect objects using pre-trained networks or perform rigorous clustering offline to find such visual elements [24,54]. Instead, we let the network capture such information during the end-to-end training process through a network architecture that accounts for objects that can freely move within the scene. Global orderless pooling of convolutional features has a high degree of invariance for encoding local visual elements such as objects. In this way, high-level convolutional filters perform like an object detector [6,60]. Furthermore, we also leverage a global ordered pooling representation which preserves coarse spatial information [35].

3   Method

We first describe our proposed hierarchy of specialists with alternating architecture in Sect. 3.1. We then illustrate how to discover a specialist's area of expertise in an unsupervised manner in Sect. 3.2. Lastly, we describe the learning objectives as well as the overall training procedure in Sect. 3.3.

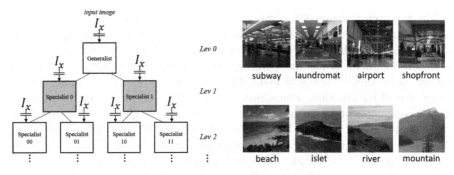

Fig. 3. Hierarchy of alternating specialists. The white and the blue boxes denote network architectures with different global pooling strategy. The assignment of images to models is determined by our routing function, depicted as switches.

Fig. 4. (top) Similar layouts make these scenes confusing, but different objects within them can help determine the correct scene class. (bottom) When scenes are similar in terms of content, their layouts can help distinguish between them.

3.1 Hierarchy of Alternating Specialists

We propose a hierarchical version of the generalist-specialist models [21], where the child specialist focuses on the task that is more specific than its parents. To achieve this, we begin with a generalist model and then incrementally add specialist models in the next level of the hierarchy, after reaching convergence at the current level. We initialize a new specialist with its parent, or the nearest ancestor that share the network architecture, to inherit its parent's knowledge as they encode important commonalities of the classes. Note that a specialist model outputs predictions for the same set of categories as the generalist model does. A specialist refines the inherited model towards the finer details to distinguish the classes for images that fall into its specialty. The overall architecture is depicted in Fig. 3. The algorithm stops extending the hierarchy when there is no further improvement, or if the network reaches a pre-specified maximum depth. In this paper, we use a binary tree structure where each parent model has two child models. Every model within this tree shares the low level layers for computational efficiency.

We design this hierarchy of specialists to have an alternating architecture such that specialists at each level have a different model architecture than their parents or children. In particular, we use the global ordered pooling architecture for capturing the rough geometry of the scene, and the global orderless pooling architecture for capturing transient visual elements such as objects. The key idea is that the scene layout and the objects in the scene are complementary for scene classification. Objects can often disambiguate the two images belonging to different categories with similar layouts, while the scene layouts can help distinguish two images, which share the same objects (Fig. 4).

The two architectures differ from each other in how they pool the features in the last convolutional layer before the fully connected layers for the class prediction. First is the global ordered pooling architecture, where the orderless pooling operation (i.e., max- or average-pooling) is performed only within a local spatial window, as in AlexNet [29] and VGG [44]. Thus, the representation preserves the coarse spatial information. The second is the global orderless pooling architecture, in which convolutional features are pooled through global average-pooling, global max-pooling, or VLAD [5], as in NIN [32] and ResNet [19] architecture. This has a high degree of invariance for encoding local visual elements such as objects, analogous to the widely adopted bag-of-words representation.

Our model uses the original pooling strategy of the base architecture for the generalist at the root node, and alternates between the two architectures for all other elements of our tree structure. To convert one architecture from the other, we either substitute global average pooling with a fully-connected layer (global orderless $\rightarrow$ global ordered), or replace a fully connected layer with global average pooling (global orderless $\leftarrow$ global ordered).

Routing: In order to decide which model in the hierarchy should tackle the input image, we use a simple routing function inspired by the SIFT ratio test [34]. The idea is to let the parent handle the image unless the image has a good membership to any of its children's area of expertise. We define the routing function to produce a k-dimensional binary vector γ, where the k is the number of children at the current node and $\sum_i \gamma_i \le 1$. $\gamma_i = 1$ indicates the routing to the i-th child is valid. In the feature space of the current node f_p, given its childs' corresponding *confusing cluster* (Sect. 3.2) centroids μ_k's, we compute the distance between the input image I and its nearest centroid μ_i, where $i = \operatorname*{argmin}_k \|f_p(I) - \mu_k\|$. We also compute the second nearest centroid μ_j. We then take the ratio of the two distances. If the ratio is less than a threshold τ, the image is assigned to the child node i. Otherwise, the image is assigned to the current node (Eq. (1)). Then the same routing procedure is performed at the child node i. The decision boundary of the routing function consists of two Apollonius circles where the foci's are the centroids μ_i and μ_j [4].

$$\gamma_i{}^{train}(I) = \begin{cases} 1, & \frac{\|f_p(I)-\mu_i\|}{\|f_p(I)-\mu_j\|} < \tau \\ 0, & otherwise \end{cases} \tag{1}$$

During testing, we put an additional constraint based on the relative confidence of the prediction between a parent and its child. Intuitively, for those images that are within the specialty of the child ($\gamma_i{}^{train}(x) = 1$), we trust the prediction of the child as our answer, when the confidence of the child model is greater than that of its parent model on the given image. Otherwise, we accept the parent model's prediction and regard the prediction of the child model as unreliable.

$$\gamma_i{}^{test}(I) = \begin{cases} 1, & \gamma_i{}^{train}(I) \wedge (conf_i(I) > conf_p(I)) \\ 0, & otherwise \end{cases}, \tag{2}$$

where $conf_t(I) = \max_c P(c|I, \theta_t)$. Since the distance to the clusters is computed in the feature space of the parent models at each level, the total number of models that needs to be invoked is $n_l + 1$ where n_l is the hierarchical level of the selected model ($n_l = 0$ for the generalist). The procedure can also be computed in parallel, at the expense of the number of invoked models (Sect. 4.7).

3.2   Discovering the Areas of Confusion

We want to partition the input data based on their high-level appearance features, and not by their categorization, thus allowing samples belonging to the same class to fall into different clusters. Our key insight is that each subset within a class is often associated with different types of inter-class similarity. We perform clustering in the feature space of a parent model to discover *confusing clusters*, the groups of images that are both visually similar and likely to be confused by the parent. This can be interpreted as disentangling intra-class variation and inter-class similarity, as the resulting cluster has limited intra-class variation, and a child model can focus on finding the subtle differences between each categories within the cluster. Also, due to our alternating architecture, we obtain confusing clusters that are both confusing in terms of scene layout and the transient scene objects as we go deeper in the hierarchy.

Feature for Clustering: The features from the penultimate layer of a parent model encodes high-level appearance as perceived by the parent. On the other hand, the features from the last fully-connected layer directly encode the class scores by the parent model. The distance of images in these two embedding spaces indicates how likely they are to be distinguished by the parent. In the dataset we tested, the combination of these embeddings produced a marginally better results compared to using each of them separately. In the experiments, we report the result using the combined features, unless otherwise specified.

Incremental Hard Clustering: As described in Sect. 3.1, we build our hierarchical model in an incremental manner, where the models in the next hierarchical level are added when their parent models have converged. As such, we discover confusing clusters by performing hard k-means clustering on the features of a converged parent model. Once initialized with these clusters, we can further fine-tune them end-to-end using the soft k-means layer described below.

Soft k-Means Layer for Fine-Tuning: We propose to use mini-batch-based soft k-means that allows end-to-end fine-tuning. For each model θ, we update the centroids μ_k through back-propagation to optimize the following objective function:

$$L_{clust}(\theta, \mu; I_i) = \sum_{k=1}^{K} \sum_{i=1}^{N} w_{ik} \| f_\theta(I_i) - \mu_k \|^2, \tag{3}$$

where

$$w_{ik} = \frac{e^{-m\|f_\theta(I_i) - \mu_k\|^2}}{\sum_{k=1}^{K} e^{-m\|f_\theta(I_i) - \mu_k\|^2}}, \tag{4}$$

and $f_\theta(I_i)$ denotes an image representation in the mini-batch. The parameter m decides the softness of the membership w_{ik} of x_i belonging to cluster k. We set m to $1/(8\sigma^2)$ where σ is the average of the standard deviation to the cluster center, which is computed during the hard k-means clustering.

3.3   Training

Classification Loss: As we allow the samples belonging to the same class to be in different clusters, it may introduce class imbalance in the training set of the specialists. Thus, we weigh the cross-entropy loss with the inverted document frequency similar to [33]. This better accounts for under-represented classes within the cluster. We computed the inverted document frequency as a running average to allow changes caused by clustering.

$$L_{class}(\theta; x) = -\sum_c \left(\log \frac{N}{n_c} \right) \log(P[c|x, \theta])$$ (5)

Training Objective: Our final training objective consists of clustering loss and classification loss as follows:

$$L_{total}(\theta; x) = \sum_{d \in \mathcal{D}} L_{class}(\theta_d; x) + \sum_{d \in \mathcal{D}, d \notin \mathcal{L}} L_{clust}(\theta_d; x).$$ (6)

$\mathcal{D}$ and $\mathcal{L}$ denote the sets of all nodes and leaf nodes in the hierarchy, respectively.

Implementation Details: The parameters of the shared low-level layers and the layers of the parents are kept frozen until the fine-tuning stage of the overall network. As the architecture of the specialist model alternates between the levels in the hierarchy, a specialist is initialized with its grandparent model whom it shares the architecture with. We initialized our base models with the models pre-trained on ImageNet, then fine-tuned them on the target dataset, with an exception in the experiment on CIFAR-100, where the base model is trained from the scratch until its accuracy reached the performance for the same model reported in [3,57]. The number of confusing clusters K are set to 2. The threshold τ for the routing function is empirically selected as 0.96. We used stochastic gradient descent for the optimization. The deployed learning rate was 0.001, and was reduced by a factor of 10 when the loss plateaus. To combat overfitting, data augmentation techniques such as random cropping, scaling, aspect ratio setting [47], and color jittering [49] were applied. We used an image resolution of 224×224. Our models are implemented using PyTorch [39].

4   Experiments

We perform quantitative comparison to evaluate our approach and its components (Sects. 4.2–4.3). For a direct comparison with other tree-structured networks, we show the results of our method on a general image classification task (Sect. 4.4). We then show how regions of interest are changed in the specialists as compared to that of the generalist (Sect. 4.5). We also visualize the learned hierarchy, which qualitatively validates our premises on feature-based grouping (Sect. 4.6).

4.1   Datasets and Evaluation Methodology

Dataset: We performed experiments on the widely used SUN database [55]. The original number of scene categories in this dataset is 397. However, the majority of categories contain just around 100 example images. To alleviate the potential overfitting problem, we create a subset of SUN-397 [55], the *(1) SUN-190 dataset*, which consist of classes that contains at least 200 examples, resulting in 48 K images in total. Following Agrawal et al. [1], we randomly divide the data for training, test, and validation with the proportion of 60%, 30%, and 10%. We used this dataset for comprehensive study, as its size allows us to evaluate a variety of design choices. We also performed experiments on another publicly available dataset, the *(2) Places-205 dataset* [63], which contains 2.5M images. For the Places-205 dataset, we treated the validation set as our test set. Finally, for the comparison with the existing tree-structured networks, we also report our results on the *(3) CIFAR-100 dataset* [28], a standard image classification benchmark which contains 60 K images in total.

Evaluation Metric: Following the standard protocol [1,63], we report one-vs.-all classification accuracy averaged over all classes. We report both top-1 accuracy and top-5 accuracy for SUN-190 and Places-205 [63], and top-1 for the CIFAR-100 dataset [28]. In all our experiments, test images for evaluation were resized to a resolution of 224×224 and we perform single-view testing, i.e., no averaging of multiple crops [1,29,63] were performed.

Base Model: On the SUN-190 and Places-205 [63] datasets, we used AlexNet* [27] as our base model, which is a slimmer version of the original AlexNet [29]. We let the specialists share the parameters with the lower layers of the generalist up to `conv4`. For the global ordered representation, we use the AlexNet* architecture as is. For the global orderless representation, we keep the layers of AlexNet* up to `conv5` and add a `conv6` layer with 768 3×3 filters, with a global average pooling layer between `conv6` and `fc7`. On CIFAR-100 [28] dataset, NIN-C100 [32] is used as our base model. It is used as is for the global orderless representation. For the global ordered representation, the global average pooling layer was replaced with two fully-connected layers, each with 1024 and 100 dimensional output.

4.2   Scene Classification Results

In order to evaluate our premise that specialists trained on *confusing clusters* are better than those trained on coarse categories, we compare with a network of experts based on coarse categories. In particular, we compare a two-level hierarchical model similar to HD-CNN [57], but with AlexNet* [27] (HD-CNN*) as a baseline for a fair comparison with our method. For this baseline method, spectral clustering was performed on the covariance matrix of class predictions of the generalist model for discovering the groups of confusing categories as in [21]. The final prediction is made using the weighted average of predictions as in [57]. We experimented with a different number of clusters of 2, 4, and 8 for this model. Furthermore, we compare our approach with a simple ensemble model, where the models are trained with different initializations and the predictions are averaged. We also report the performance of the fine-tuned single AlexNet* [27] model, which is also our generalist model at the root of the hierarchy.

In Table 1, we compare our performance with the aforementioned baselines on the SUN-190 dataset. All of our models outperform the baselines, where our best model with a 3-level hierarchy achieved a classification accuracy of 66.41% for the Top-1 prediction, exceeding the accuracy of the coarse-category-based model (HD-CNN*) by 2.76%. The performance of our proposed model consistently improves as we increase the number of levels in the hierarchy. In contrast, HD-CNN* only has marginal improvements in the Top-1 accuracy, while the Top-5 accuracy drops as the number of clusters increases. This demonstrates the effectiveness of our model in discovering the correct hierarchical organization of image data while overcoming the intra-class variation issues inherent in conventional tree-structured models. We also observe that while our model achieves well-balanced clusters, the spectral clustering resulted in high bias in the number of classes per coarse category. The simple ensembles is also inferior to our approach which outputs the prediction of a single specialist model.

We also show the scene classification performance on the Places-205 [63] dataset on Table 2. Our approach provides an improvement of 2.87% over the base model at Top-1 accuracy. Similarly as in SUN-190, we observe that the accuracy of the proposed model increases as we increment the number of levels in the hierarchy.

Table 1. Scene classification accuracy on the Sun-190 dataset. All compared models are based on AlexNet* [27]. The statistics are based on single-view testing. (Lev: the hierarchical levels, K: the number of clusters, N: the number of ensembles).

Method		Top-1	Top-5	Method		Top-1	Top-5
Proposed	Lev 1	66.13	89.66	AlexNet*[27] (Ordered)	Lev 0	63.46	89.18
	Lev 2	66.37	89.85	AlexNet*-Orderless	Lev 0	61.79	88.14
	Lev 3	**66.41**	**89.96**	Fusion	Lev 0	64.45	89.36
	K = 2	63.11	88.81	Model 1:	Lev 1	64.02	89.27
HD-CNN* [57]	K = 4	63.62	87.64	global ordered	Lev 2	64.33	89.44
	K = 8	63.65	84.08	pooling only	Lev 3	64.43	89.48
	N = 2	64.19	89.47	Model 2:	Lev 1	62.71	88.54
Simple Ensembles	N = 4	64.66	89.72	global orderless	Lev 2	63.14	88.76
	N = 8	64.99	89.96	pooling only	Lev 3	63.08	88.69

4.3   Benefits of Alternating Architecture

The performance of architectures with global ordered pooling (AlexNet* [27]) and global orderless pooling (AlexNet*-Orderless) are shown in Tables 1 and 2, for the SUN-190 and Places-205 datasets, respectively. Both models achieve similar accuracy, while global ordered pooling shows slightly better performance. Meanwhile, the IoU of the correct prediction was 78.1% (with the overall prediction overlap ratio being and 73.2%). This quantitatively validates our assumption that the two representations are complementary. We also evaluated the performance of fused features, one with early fusion that concatenates two representations before the last fully connected layer, and the other with late fusion where the predictions of the two architectures are averaged. The early fusion did not yield competitive classification accuracy. On the other hand, the late fusion (Fusion in Tables 1 and 2) achieves better performance than using each representation separately, however, does not reach the classification accuracy of our proposed alternating architecture.

Table 2. Scene classification accuracy on the Places-205 [63] dataset using single-view testing. All models are based on AlexNet* [27].

Method		Top-1	Top-5
AlexNet*[27] (Ordered)	Lev 0	48.67	79.24
Proposed:	Lev 1	50.21	79.82
Alternating	Lev 2	51.42	80.67
Architecture	Lev 3	**51.54**	**80.76**
Model 1:	Lev 1	49.99	80.09
Global ordered	Lev 2	50.21	80.30
Pooling only	Lev 3	50.28	80.26
AlexNet*-Orderless	Lev 0	48.19	78.23
Model 2:	Lev 1	48.99	79.01
Global orderless	Lev 2	49.31	79.48
Pooling only	Lev 3	49.25	79.49
Fusion	Lev 0	49.19	79.54

Table 3. Image classification accuracy on CIFAR-100 with single-view testing. All models are based on NIN-C100 [32].

Method		Top-1
NIN-C100 [32] (Orderless)	Lev 0	64.73
Proposed:	Lev 1	67.32
Alternating	Lev 2	67.61
Architecture	Lev 3	**67.70**
Model A:	Lev 1	66.92
Global orderless	Lev 2	66.70
Pooling only	Lev 3	66.62
NIN-C100-Ordered	Lev 0	64.67
Model B:	Lev 1	65.64
Global ordered	Lev 2	65.74
Pooling only	Lev 3	65.48
Fusion	Lev 0	66.83

Table 4. Comparison with other tree-structured models on CIFAR-100 [28]. All models are based on NIN-C100 [32]. The accuracies are based on single-view testing.

Method	Hierarchy levels	#model Choices	#model Selected	#models Invoked	Accuracy (%)
NIN-C100 [32]	0	1	1	1	64.73
Proposed	1	3	1	1–2	67.32
	2	7	1	1–3	67.61
	3	15	1	1–4	**67.70**
HD-CNN (best) [57]	1	9	9	10	65.64
NofE [2]	1	10	1	2	65.91
BranchConnect [3]	1	10	1	10	66.10
			5	10	66.45

Furthermore, in Tables 1 and 2, we compare with other versions of our method—hierarchy of specialists *without* the alternating architecture, that is, using only a single type of representation. In particular, we report the results of Model 1 that uses global ordered pooling architecture, and Model 2 with global orderless pooling architecture. Both models were trained with the same training protocol as our proposed model. While the performance of our proposed model with its alternating architecture improves with an increasing depth of the hierarchy, models with a non-alternating architecture have marginal or no observable performance gain. We suspect that this is due to the fact that our alternating architecture is better at yielding confusing clusters, in terms of both coarse spatial layout and the objects in the scene, by using two different types of feature sets.

To show the observation holds for other networks, we repeated the same experiments using the NIN-C100 [32] architecture on CIFAR-100 [28] in Table 3. Unlike AlexNet* [27], which has a global ordered pooling architecture, NIN-C100 [32] has a global-orderless-pooling architecture by default. We observe that our alternating architecture clearly outperforms other strategies. The Model A and B denote the hierarchy of specialists with a single type of representation, using global orderless- and global ordered- pooling, respectively.

4.4   Comparison with Existing Tree-Structured CNNs on CIFAR-100

For a direct comparison with other tree-structured networks, we show the results of our architecture on the image classification task of the CIFAR-100 [28] dataset in Table 4. We compare with HD-CNN [57], NofE [2], and BranchConnect [3]. All these methods train their experts on coarse categories (class-based grouping) while our method alone uses *confusing clusters*. Furthermore, they require additional networks or layers to be used for gating. We show the recalls reported in their original paper, except for NofE [2] in which we used the recalls reported in [3] in order to match the performance of the base model for a fair comparison. All models are based on the NIN-C100 [32] architecture. We also illustrate the number of models to choose from, the number of selected models, and the total number of invoked models on the same table. Our approach outperforms all other methods despite the fact that it outputs the prediction of a single specialist network, rather than averaging predictions of multiple networks. It also invokes the least number of models. In particular, our method outperforms the best baseline BranchConnect [3] with significantly fewer models invoked.

4.5   Comparison of Regions of Interest (ROI)

The benefit of our proposed architecture lies in the specialists' ability to discriminate between classes based on subtle details for images that falls into their specialty. As specialists are trained on the subset of data which reflects their specialty, it evolves to focus on such details to better accommodate the classification task at hand. To illustrate these changes in activation patterns, we investigated how the regions of interest (ROI) of the specialist models differ from those of the generalist models. We visualize the corresponding class activation maps (CAM) [43,61] for the specialists and the generalists. Since CAMs show the regions that contributed to the prediction of the class in question, we are able to tell which regions in the image contributed to the correct (or the incorrect) prediction.

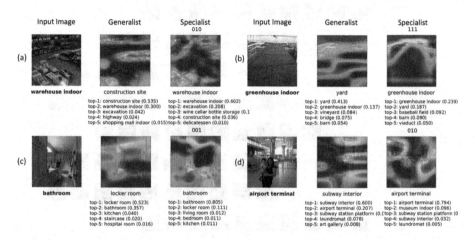

Fig. 5. (left) Input images and ground-truth category. The top-5 predictions and the visualization of class activation maps (CAM) of the top predicted class for the generalist (center) and the selected specialist (right). (See supplementary for more results.)

Figure 5 shows the CAMs of the top predicted class for both the generalist and the specialists. We only show examples where the specialists with the depicted results are invoked by our routing function. We observe that the specialists are good at focusing on fine-grain details as compared to the generalist. For example, in Fig. 5 (a), the generalist reasonably predicted the scene category as construction site, based on the construction materials on the right side of the image. However, the specialist was able to focus more on the boxes, predicting the correct scene class of warehouse indoor. In Fig. 5 (b), generalist predicted yard for the scene class, based on the grass field in the center of the image. However, the specialist payed more attention to plants and frames on the sides to predict the correct class of greenhouse indoors.

4.6   Visualization of Learned Hierarchy of Specialties

We visualize the learned hierarchy of images in Fig. 6. For each centroid of the discovered confusing clusters that the specialists were trained on, we depict the top 10 nearest neighbor images in the feature space for SUN-190. We observe that each cluster consists of visually coherent and easily confusable images from different scene classes. At the same time, different instances of the same class appear in multiple clusters that are visually distinct. For example, a subset of the kitchen images, which are visually similar to bathrooms with base cabinets, appear in the cluster of the Specialist 001, while the subset of the same category that look similar to restaurants and bars are found in the cluster of the Specialist 10. This visualization strongly supports our underlying idea of *confusing clusters*.

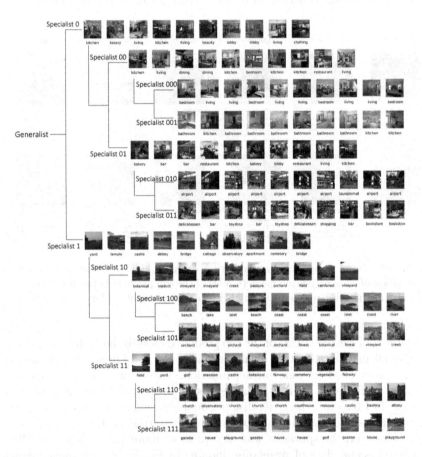

Fig. 6. Visualization of the learned hierarchy on the SUN-190 dataset. A three level hierarchy is shown, with the 10 top images associated with each specialist.

4.7   Computational Time

Our model can be run in parallel or sequentially. Running sequentially minimizes the number of invoked models, thus saving memory at the expense of time. The opposite is true when running in parallel. Let $t_A = t_l + t_u$ be the execution time for the base model, where t_u and t_l denote the time spent on the upper layers and the shared lower layers. Let t_r be the time spent for routing and L the hierarchical levels. When run sequentially, the best case is $t_A + t_r$ when routed to the generalist, while the worst is $t_l + L \cdot (t_u + t_r)$ when routed to a leaf specialist.

On an NVIDIA GTX1080Ti with batch size 512 using AlexNet*, it takes 105, 121, and 138 ms for our models with $L = 1, 2, 3$, respectively. AlexNet* takes 87 ms. When fully parallelized, each model is run in parallel, then a model is selected, which takes $t_A + t_r$. It takes 89 ms for all our models ($L = 1, 2, 3$).

5   Conclusion

We introduced a novel hierarchy of alternating specialists for tackling inter-class similarity and intra-class variation in scene categories. The global feature pooling strategy of the specialist model alternates at each level to account for both coarse scene layout and transient objects, which are both essential for accurate scene classification. For defining the area of expertise for each child model, we discover confusing image clusters by performing clustering based on the learned features of the parent model, thereby obtaining image clusters that are visually coherent and confusing at the same time. Our method invokes only a small fraction of the models in the whole tree for an input image. We experimentally show that our method achieves significant improvement over baselines including existing tree-structured models that use class-based grouping. Our algorithm is applicable to a variety of CNN models and visual category recognition tasks.

Acknowledgment. Partially supported by NSF grant No. CNS-1405847.

References

1. Agrawal, P., Girshick, R., Malik, J.: Analyzing the performance of multilayer neural networks for object recognition. In: Fleet, D., Pajdla, T., Schiele, B., Tuytelaars, T. (eds.) ECCV 2014. LNCS, vol. 8695, pp. 329–344. Springer, Cham (2014). https://doi.org/10.1007/978-3-319-10584-0_22
2. Ahmed, K., Baig, M.H., Torresani, L.: Network of experts for large-scale image categorization. In: Leibe, B., Matas, J., Sebe, N., Welling, M. (eds.) ECCV 2016. LNCS, vol. 9911, pp. 516–532. Springer, Cham (2016). https://doi.org/10.1007/978-3-319-46478-7_32
3. Ahmed, K., Torresani, L.: Branchconnect: Large-scale visual recognition with learned branch connections. In: WACV (2018)
4. Aljundi, R., Chakravarty, P., Tuytelaars, T.: Expert gate: Lifelong learning with a network of experts. In: CVPR (2017)
5. Arandjelović, R., Gronat, P., Torii, A., Pajdla, T., Sivic, J.: NetVLAD: CNN architecture for weakly supervised place recognition. In: CVPR (2016)
6. Bau, D., Zhou, B., Khosla, A., Oliva, A., Torralba, A.: Network dissection: quantifying interpretability of deep visual representations. In: CVPR (2017)
7. Bishop, C.M., Svenskn, M.: Bayesian hierarchical mixtures of experts. In: Uncertainty in Artificial Intelligence (2002)
8. Chen, W., Chen, X., Zhang, J., Huang, K.: Beyond triplet loss: a deep quadruplet network for person re-identification. In: CVPR (2017)
9. Cheng, G., Zhou, P., Han, J.: RIFD-CNN: Rotation-invariant and fisher discriminative convolutional neural networks for object detection. In: CVPR (2016)

10. Cheng, X., Lu, J., Feng, J., Yuan, B., Zhou, J.: Scene recognition with objectness. Pattern Recogn. (2018)
11. Deng, J., Berg, A.C., Fei-Fei, L.: Hierarchical semantic indexing for large scale image retrieval. In: CVPR (2011)
12. Deng, J., et al.: Large-scale object classification using label relation graphs. In: ECCV (2014)
13. Dixit, M., Chen, S., Gao, D., Rasiwasia, N., Vasconcelos, N.: Scene classification with semantic fisher vectors. In: CVPR (2015)
14. Dixit, M.D., Vasconcelos, N.: Object based scene representations using fisher scores of local subspace projections. In: NIPS (2016)
15. Goo, W., Kim, J., Kim, G., Hwang, S.J.: Taxonomy-regularized semantic deep convolutional neural networks. In: Leibe, B., Matas, J., Sebe, N., Welling, M. (eds.) ECCV 2016. LNCS, vol. 9906, pp. 86–101. Springer, Cham (2016). https://doi.org/10.1007/978-3-319-46475-6_6
16. Gross, S., Ranzato, M., Szlam, A.: Hard mixtures of experts for large scale weakly supervised vision. In: CVPR (2017)
17. Guo, S., Huang, W., Wang, L., Qiao, Y.: Locally supervised deep hybrid model for scene recognition. TIP (2017)
18. Guo, Y., Zhao, G., Pietikäinen, M., Xu, Z.: Descriptor learning based on fisher separation criterion for texture classification. In: Kimmel, R., Klette, R., Sugimoto, A. (eds.) ACCV 2010. LNCS, vol. 6494, pp. 185–198. Springer, Heidelberg (2011). https://doi.org/10.1007/978-3-642-19318-7_15
19. He, K., Zhang, X., Ren, S., Sun, J.: Deep residual learning for image recognition. In: CVPR (2016)
20. Herranz, L., Jiang, S., Li, X.: Scene recognition with CNNs: objects, scales and dataset bias. In: CVPR (2016)
21. Hinton, G., Vinyals, O., Dean, J.: Distilling the knowledge in a neural network. Arxiv preprint arXiv:1503.02531 (2015)
22. Hwang, S.J., Sigal, L.: A unified semantic embedding: Relating taxonomies and attributes. In: NIPS (2014)
23. Jordan, M.I., Jacobs, R.A.: Hierarchical mixtures of experts and the EM algorithm. Neural Comput. (1994)
24. Juneja, M., Vedaldi, A., Jawahar, C., Zisserman, A.: Blocks that shout: distinctive parts for scene classification. In: CVPR (2013)
25. Khan, S.H., Hayat, M., Porikli, F.: Scene categorization with spectral features. In: CVPR (2017)
26. Kim, J., Park, Y., Kim, G., Hwang, S.J.: SplitNet: learning to semantically split deep networks for parameter reduction and model parallelization. In: ICML (2017)
27. Krizhevsky, A.: One weird trick for parallelizing convolutional neural networks. arXiv preprint arXiv:1404.5997 (2014)
28. Krizhevsky, A., Hinton, G.: Learning multiple layers of features from tiny images (2009)
29. Krizhevsky, A., Sutskever, I., Hinton, G.E.: ImageNet classification with deep convolutional neural networks. In: NIPS (2012)
30. Lazebnik, S., Schmid, C., Ponce, J.: Beyond bags of features: Spatial pyramid matching for recognizing natural scene categories. In: CVPR (2006)
31. Li, F., Neverova, N., Wolf, C., Taylor, G.: Modout: learning multi-modal architectures by stochastic regularization. In: FG (2017)
32. Lin, M., Chen, Q., Yan, S.: Network in network. arXiv preprint arXiv:1312.4400 (2013)

33. Lin, T.Y., Goyal, P., Girshick, R., He, K., Dollár, P.: Focal loss for dense object detection. In: ICCV (2017)
34. Lowe, D.G.: Object recognition from local scale-invariant features. In: ICCV (1999)
35. Mousavian, A., Kosecka, J.: Deep convolutional features for image based retrieval and scene categorization. arXiv preprint arXiv:1509.06033 (2015)
36. Murdock, C., Li, Z., Zhou, H., Duerig, T.: Blockout: dynamic model selection for hierarchical deep networks. In: CVPR (2016)
37. Murthy, V.N., Singh, V., Chen, T., Manmatha, R., Comaniciu, D.: Deep decision network for multi-class image classification. In: CVPR (2016)
38. Oliva, A., Torralba, A.: Modeling the shape of the scene: a holistic representation of the spatial envelope. IJCV (2001)
39. Paszke, A., Gross, S., Chintala, S., Chanan, G.: PyTorch: tensors and dynamic neural networks in python with strong GPU acceleration (2017). http://pytorch.org/
40. Qian, Q., Jin, R., Zhu, S., Lin, Y.: Fine-grained visual categorization via multi-stage metric learning. In: CVPR (2015)
41. Quattoni, A., Torralba, A.: Recognizing indoor scenes. In: CVPR (2009)
42. Sabour, S., Frosst, N., Hinton, G.E.: Dynamic routing between capsules. In: NIPS (2017)
43. Selvaraju, R.R., Das, A., Vedantam, R., Cogswell, M., Parikh, D., Batra, D.: Grad-CAM: why did you say that? Visual explanations from deep networks via gradient-based localization. In: ICCV (2017)
44. Simonyan, K., Zisserman, A.: Very deep convolutional networks for large-scale image recognition. In: ICLR (2015)
45. Somanath, G., Kambhamettu, C.: Abstraction and generalization of 3D structure for recognition in large intra-class variation. In: ACCV (2010)
46. Srivastava, N., Salakhutdinov, R.R.: Discriminative transfer learning with tree-based priors. In: NIPS (2013)
47. Szegedy, C., et al.: Going deeper with convolutions. In: CVPR (2015)
48. Tu, Z.: Probabilistic boosting-tree: learning discriminative models for classification, recognition, and clustering. In: CVPR (2005)
49. Urban, G., et al.: Do deep convolutional nets really need to be deep and convolutional? arXiv preprint arXiv:1603.05691 (2016)
50. Wang, J., Liu, Z., Wu, Y., Yuan, J.: Mining actionlet ensemble for action recognition with depth cameras. In: CVPR (2012)
51. Wang, L., Guo, S., Huang, W., Xiong, Y., Qiao, Y.: Knowledge guided disambiguation for large-scale scene classification with multi-resolution CNNs. TIP (2017)
52. Wang, Z., Wang, L., Wang, Y., Zhang, B., Qiao, Y.: Weakly supervised patchnets: describing and aggregating local patches for scene recognition. TIP (2017)
53. Warde-Farley, D., Rabinovich, A., Anguelov, D.: Self-informed neural network structure learning. arXiv preprint arXiv:1412.6563 (2014)
54. Wu, R., Wang, B., Wang, W., Yu, Y.: Harvesting discriminative meta objects with deep CNN features for scene classification. In: ICCV (2015)
55. Xiao, J., Hays, J., Ehinger, K.A., Oliva, A., Torralba, A.: Sun database: large-scale scene recognition from abbey to zoo. In: CVPR (2010)
56. Xiao, Y., Wu, J., Yuan, J.: mCENTRIST: a multi-channel feature generation mechanism for scene categorization. TIP (2014)
57. Yan, Z., et al.: HD-CNN: hierarchical deep convolutional neural networks for large scale visual recognition. In: ICCV (2015)
58. Zhao, B., Li, F., Xing, E.P.: Large-scale category structure aware image categorization. In: NIPS (2011)

59. Zheng, W.S., Gong, S., Xiang, T.: Person re-identification by probabilistic relative distance comparison. In: CVPR (2011)
60. Zhou, B., Khosla, A., Lapedriza, A., Oliva, A., Torralba, A.: Object detectors emerge in deep scene CNNs. In: ICLR (2014)
61. Zhou, B., Khosla, A., Lapedriza, A., Oliva, A., Torralba, A.: Learning deep features for discriminative localization. In: CVPR (2016)
62. Zhou, B., Lapedriza, A., Khosla, A., Oliva, A., Torralba, A.: Places: A 10 million image database for scene recognition. PAMI (2017)
63. Zhou, B., Lapedriza, A., Xiao, J., Torralba, A., Oliva, A.: Learning deep features for scene recognition using places database. In: NIPS (2014)

Move Forward and Tell: A Progressive Generator of Video Descriptions

Yilei Xiong$^{(\boxtimes)}$, Bo Dai, and Dahua Lin

CUHK-SenseTime Joint Lab, The Chinese University of Hong Kong,
Hong Kong, China
{xy014,db014,dhlin}@ie.cuhk.edu.hk

Abstract. We present an efficient framework that can generate a coherent paragraph to describe a given video. Previous works on video captioning usually focus on video clips. They typically treat an entire video as a whole and generate the caption conditioned on a single embedding. On the contrary, we consider videos with rich temporal structures and aim to generate paragraph descriptions that can preserve the story flow while being coherent and concise. Towards this goal, we propose a new approach, which produces a descriptive paragraph by assembling temporally localized descriptions. Given a video, it selects a sequence of distinctive clips and generates sentences thereon in a coherent manner. Particularly, the selection of clips and the production of sentences are done jointly and progressively driven by a recurrent network – what to describe next depends on what have been said before. Here, the recurrent network is learned via self-critical sequence training with both sentence-level and paragraph-level rewards. On the ActivityNet Captions dataset, our method demonstrated the capability of generating high-quality paragraph descriptions for videos. Compared to those by other methods, the descriptions produced by our method are often more relevant, more coherent, and more concise.

Keywords: Video captioning · Move forward and tell
Recurrent network · Reinforcement learning · Repetition evaluation

1 Introduction

Textual descriptions are an important way to characterize images and videos. Compared to class labels or semantic tags, descriptions are usually more informative and distinctive. In recent years, image captioning, a task to generate short descriptions for given images, becomes an active research topic [1,8,25,30] and has seen remarkable progress thanks to the wide adoption of recurrent neural networks. However, how to extend the captioning techniques to describe videos remains an open question.

Electronic supplementary material The online version of this chapter (https://doi.org/10.1007/978-3-030-01252-6_29) contains supplementary material, which is available to authorized users.

Over the past several years, various methods have been proposed for generating video descriptions. Early efforts [28] simply extend the encoder-decoder paradigm in image captioning to videos. Such methods follow a similar pipeline, namely embedding an entire video into a feature vector, feeding it to a decoding network to obtain a descriptive sentence. However, for a video with rich temporal structures, a single sentence is often not enough to capture all important aspects of the underlying events. Recently, a new stream of efforts emerge [10,20], which attempt to use multiple sentences to cover a video. Whereas such methods can provide more complete characterization of a video, they are still subject to various issues, *e.g.* lack of coherence among sentences and high redundancy. These issues, to a large extent, are ascribed to two reasons: (1) failing to align the temporal structure of the given video with the narrative structure of the generated description; and (2) neglecting the dependencies among sentences (Fig. 1).

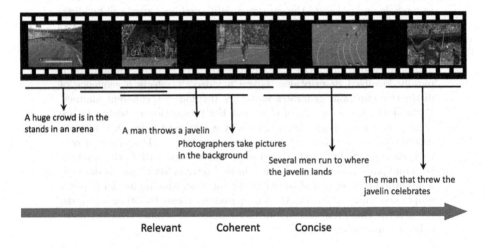

Fig. 1. As shown in this figure, our framework localizes important events in a video, and picks a sequence of coherent and independent events, on which generates a coherent and concise descriptive paragraph for the video.

In this work, we aim to develop a new framework for generating *paragraph* descriptions for videos with rich temporal structures. The goal is to generate descriptions that are *relevant, coherent,* and *concise*. According to the discussion above, the key to achieving this goal lies in two aspects: (1) associate the temporal structures in the given video with the linguistic generation process; and (2) encourage coherence among sentences in an effective way.

Specifically, our approach is based on two key observations. First, a natural video is usually composed of multiple short and meaningful segments that reflect a certain step in a procedure or an episode of a story. We refer to such video segments as *events*. While a single sentence may not be enough to describe a long video, it often suffices to characterize an individual event. Second, when people describe a video with a paragraph, there exist strong logical and linguistic relations among consecutive sentences. What to describe in a sentence depends strongly on what have been said.

Inspired by these observations, we devise a two-stage framework. This framework first localizes candidate events from the video through video action detection. On top of these candidates, the framework then generate a coherent paragraph in a *progressive* manner. At each step, it selects the next event to describe and produces a sentence therefor, both conditioned on what have been said before. The progressive generation process is driven by a variant of LSTM network that takes into account both temporal and linguistic structures. To effectively learn this network, we adopt the *self-critical sequence training* method and introduce rewards in two different levels, namely the sentence level and the paragraph level. On ActivityNet Captions [10], the proposed framework outperforms previous ones under multiple metrics. Qualitatively, the descriptions produced by our method are generally more relevant, more coherent, and more concise.

The key contribution of this work lies in a new framework for generating descriptions for given videos. This framework is distinguished from previous ones in three key aspects: (1) It aligns the temporal structure of the given video and the narrative structure of the generated description via a recurrent network. (2) It maintains coherence among the sentences in a paragraph by explicitly conditioning *what to say next* on both the temporal structures and *what have been said*. (3) It is learned via reinforcement learning, guided by rewards in both the sentence level and the paragraph level.

2   Related Work

Image Captioning. Early attempts of image captioning rely on visual concept detection, followed by templates filling [11] or nearest neighbour retrieving [6]. Recently, Vinyals *et al.* [24] proposed the encoder-decoder paradigm, which extracts image features using a CNN, followed by an RNN as the decoder to generate captions based on the features. This model outperforms classical methods and becomes the backbone of state-of-the-art captioning models. Many variants [2,3,27] are proposed following the encoder-decoder paradigm, For example, Xu *et al.* [27] improved it by introducing an attention mechanism to guide the decoding process.

While many methods for image captioning can be seamlessly converted into methods for video captioning, video contains richer semantic content that spreads on the temporal dimension, directly applying methods for image captioning often lead to the loss of temporal information.

Video Dense Captioning. Video dense captioning, is a topic that closely related to video captioning, where it densely generates multiple sentences, covering different time spans of the input video. Specifically, Krishna *et al.* [10] proposed a method that obtains a series of proposals from the input video and uses a captioning model to generate a sentence for each, where the temporal relationships among the proposals are taken into account. On the other hand, Shen *et al.* [20] proposed a weakly-supervised method, which uses multi-instance multi-label learning to detect words from the input video and then uses these words to select spatial regions to form region sequences. Finally, it employs a sequence-to-sequence submodule to transfer region sequences into captions.

Although closely related, video dense captioning is different from video captioning. Particularly, a model for video dense captioning could generate multiple captions, each covers a small period of the input video, where the periods can be overlapped with each other, leading to a lot of redundancy in the corresponding captions. On the contrary, a model for video captioning should generate a *single* description consisting of several *coherent* sentences for the *entire* input video.

Video Captioning. Our method targets the topic of video captioning. Related works can be roughly divided into two categories based on whether a single sentence or a paragraph is generated for each input video. In the first category, a single sentence is generated. Among all the works in this category, Rohrbach *et al.* [18] detected a set of visual concepts at first, including verbs, objects and places, and then applied an LSTM net to fuse these concepts into a caption. Yu *et al.* [30] and Pan *et al.* [13] followed a similar way, but respectively using a semantic attention model and a transfer unit to select detected concepts and generate a caption. Instead of relying on visual concepts, Hori *et al.* [8] and Venugopalan *et al.* [23] use features from multiple sources including appearance and motion to improve quality of the generated caption. There are also efforts devoted to improving the decoder side. Wang *et al.* [25] added a memory network before the LSTM net during the decoding process to share features at different timestamps. Baraldi *et al.* [1] applied a boundary detecting module to share features hierarchically. While they are able to produce great captions, a single sentence is difficult to capture all semantic information in a video, as one video usually contains several distinctive events.

The second category is to generate a paragraph to describe a video. Our method belongs to this category. In this category, Yu *et al.* [29] applied hierarchical recurrent neural networks, where a sentence generator is used to generate a single sentence according to a specific *topic*, and a paragraph generator is used to capture inter-sentence statistics and feed the sentence generator with a series of topics. The most similar work to our method is the one presented in [19]. This method first select a subset of clips from the input video, and then use a decoder to generate sentence from these clips to form a paragraph summary of the entire video. Our method is different from these existing works from two aspects. (1) When generating each sentence of the paragraph, the method in [29] requires the features from the entire video, which is expensive for very long videos, while our method only requires features in selected proposals. (2) In [19], the clips are selected according to frame quality *in advance* as a preprocessing step, without taking into account the coherence of narration. This way will lead to redundancy in the resulting paragraph. On the contrary, our method selects key events *along with* the generation of captions in a progressive way. The selection of the next key event depends on what has been said before in preceding captions. Also, this process takes into account temporal and semantic relationships among the selected events in order to ensure the coherence of the resultant paragraph.

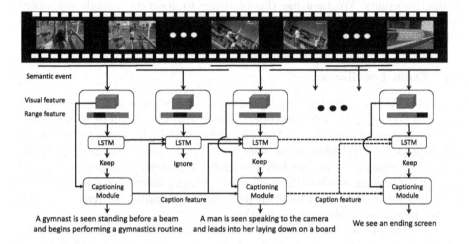

Fig. 2. An overview of our framework, which at first localize important events from the entire video. It then generates a coherent and concise descriptive paragraph upon these localized events. Specifically, an LSTM net, serves as a selection module, will pick out a sequence of coherent and semantically independent events, based on appearances, temporal locations of events, as well as their semantic relationships. And based on this selected sequence, another LSTM net, serves as a captioning module, will generate a single sentence for each event in the sequence conditioned on previous generated sentences, which are then concatenated sequentially as the output of our framework.

3   Generation Framework

Our task is to develop a framework that can generate coherent paragraphs to describe given videos. Specifically, a good description should possess three properties: (1) *Relevant*: the narration aligns well with the events in their temporal order. (2) *Coherent*: the sentences are organized into a logical and fluent narrative flow. (3) *Concise*: each sentence conveys a distinctive message, without repeating what has been said.

3.1   Overview

A natural video often comprises multiple events that are located sparsely along the temporal range. Here, *events* refer to those video segments that contain distinctive semantics that need to be conveyed. Taking the entire video as input for generating the description is inefficient, and is likely to obscure key messages when facing numerous noisy clips. Therefore, we propose a framework as shown in Fig. 2, which generates a descriptive paragraph in two stages, namely *event localization* and *paragraph generation*. In event localization, we localize *candidate events* in the video with a high recall. In paragraph generation, we first filter out redundant or trivial candidates, so as to get a sequence of important and distinctive events. We then use this sequence to generate a single descriptive paragraph for the entire video in a progressive manner, taking into account the coherence among sentences.

3.2   Event Localization

To localize event candidates, we adopted the clip proposal generation scheme presented in [31], using the released codes. This scheme was shown to be effective in locating important clips from untrimmed videos with high accuracy. Specifically, following [31], we calculate frame-wise importance scores, and then group the frames into clips of via a watershed procedure. This method outputs a collection of clips as *event candidates*. These clips have varying durations and can overlap with each other. As our focus is on paragraph generation, we refer readers to [31] for more details of event localization.

Note that not all the candidates derived in this stage is worthy of description. The paragraph generation will select a subset of candidates that contain important and distinctive messages, *along with* the generation process.

3.3   Progressive Event Selection and Captioning

Given a sequence of events, there are various ways to generate a descriptive paragraph. While the most straightforward way is to generate a single sentence for each event in the sequence, it is very likely to introduce a large amount of redundancy. To generate coherent and concise description, we can select a subset of distinctive events and generate sentences thereon. The key challenge here is to stride a good balance between sufficient coverage and conciseness.

In this work, we develop a *progressive* generation framework that couples two recurrent networks, one for event selection and the other for caption generation.

Event Selection. With all event candidates arranged in the chronological order, denoted as $(e_1, \ldots, e_T)$, the event selection network begins with the first candidate in the sequence and moves forward gradually as follows:

$$\mathbf{h}_0 = \mathbf{0}, \ \mathbf{h}_t = \mathrm{LSTM}(\mathbf{h}_{t-1}, \mathbf{v}_t, \mathbf{r}_t, \mathbf{c}_{k_t}), \tag{1}$$

$$p_t = \mathrm{sigmoid}(\mathbf{w}_p^T \mathbf{h}_t), \ \ y_t = 1[p_t > \delta]. \tag{2}$$

Specifically, it initializes the latent state vector $\mathbf{h}_0$ to be zeros. At each step t, it updates the latent state $\mathbf{h}_t$ with an LSTM cell and computes p_t, the probability of e_t containing relevant and distinctive information, by applying a sigmoid function to $\mathbf{w}_p^T \mathbf{h}_t$. If p_t is above a threshold δ, y_t would be set to 1, indicating that the candidate e_t will be selected for sentence generation.

The updating of $\mathbf{h}_t$ depends on four different inputs: (1) $\mathbf{h}_{t-1}$: the latent state at the preceding step. (2) $\mathbf{v}_t$: the visual feature of e_t, extracted using a Temporal Segmental Network (TSN) [26]. (3) $\mathbf{r}_t$: the range feature, similar as the image mask in [4], represented by a binary mask that indicates the normalized time span of e_t relative to the entire duration. (4) $\mathbf{c}_{k_t}$: the caption feature of e_{k_t}, where k_t is the index of the *last* selected event candidate (before t). Here, the caption feature is from the *caption generation network*, which we will present next. Particularly, $\mathbf{c}_{k_t}$ is chosen to be the latent state of the caption generation network at the final decoding step when generating the description for e_{k_t}.

With the previous caption feature $\mathbf{c}_{k_t}$ incorporated, the event selection network is aware of what have been said in the past when making a selection. This allows it to avoid selecting the candidates that are semantically redundant.

Caption Generation. On top of the selected events, the *caption generation network* will produce a sequence of sentences, one for each event, as follows:

$$\mathbf{g}_0^{(k)} = \begin{cases} \mathbf{0}, & k = 1 \\ \mathbf{g}_*^{(k-1)}, & k > 1 \end{cases}, \quad \mathbf{g}_l^{(k)} = \mathrm{LSTM}(\mathbf{g}_{l-1}^{(k)}, \mathbf{u}_l^{(k)}, w_{l-1}^{(k)}), \tag{3}$$

$$\mathbf{s}_l^{(k)} = \mathbf{W}_s \mathbf{g}_l^{(k)}, \quad w_l^{(k)} \sim \mathrm{softmax}(\mathbf{s}_l^{(k)}). \tag{4}$$

Here, $\mathbf{g}_l^{(k)}$ denotes the latent state at the l-th step of the caption generation network when describing the k-th selected event. $\mathbf{u}_l^{(k)}$ denotes a visual feature of a subregion of the event. Here, the computation of $\mathbf{u}_l^{(k)}$ follows the scheme presented in [16], which allows the network to dynamically attend to different subregions as it proceeds[1]. $w_l^{(k)}$ is the word produced at the l-th step, which is sampled from $\mathrm{softmax}(\mathbf{s}_l^{(k)})$.

This network is similar to a standard LSTM for image captioning except for an important difference: When $k > 1$, the latent state is initialized to $\mathbf{g}_*^{(k-1)}$, the latent state at the last decoding step while generating the previous sentence. This means that the generation of each sentence (except the first one) is conditioned on the preceding one, which allows the generation to take into account the coherence among sentences.

Discussions. The event selection network and the caption generation network work hand in hand with each other when generating a description for a given video. On one hand, the selection of next event candidate depends on what has been said. Particularly, one input to the event selection network is $\mathbf{c}_{k_t}$, which is set to the $\mathbf{g}_*^{(k_t)}$, the last latent state of the caption generation network in generating the previous sentence. On the other hand, the caption generation network is invoked only when the event selection network outputs $y_t = 1$, and the generation of the current sentence depends on those that come before. The collaboration

---

[1] We provide more details of the computation of $\mathbf{u}_l^{(k)}$ in the supplemental materials.

between both networks allows the framework to produce paragraphs that can cover major messages, while being coherent and concise.

Note that one may also use Non-Maximum Suppression (NMS) to directly remove temporal overlapped events. This simple way is limited compared to ours, as it only considers temporal overlap while ignoring the semantic relevance. Another way is to first generate sentences for all events and then select a subset of important ones based on text summarization [19]. This approach, however, does not provide a mechanism to encourage linguistic coherence among sentences, which is crucial for generating high-quality descriptions.

4   Training

Three modules in our framework need to be trained, namely *event localization, caption generation*, and *event selection*. In particular, we train the event localization module simply following the procedure presented in [31]. The other two modules, the caption generation network and the event selection network, are trained separately. We first train the caption generation network using the ground-truth event captions. Thereon, we then train the event selection network, which requires the caption generation states as input.

4.1   Training Caption Generation Network.

The caption generation network models the distribution of each word conditioned on previous ones and other inputs, including the visual features of the corresponding event $\mathbf{u}^{(k)}$ and the final latent state of for the preceding sentence $\mathbf{g}_*^{(k-1)}$. Hence, this distribution can be expressed as $p_\theta(w_l | w_{1:l-1}; \mathbf{u}^{(k)}, \mathbf{g}_*^{(k-1)})$, where θ denotes the network parameters. We train this network through two stages: (1) initial supervised training, and (2) reinforcement learning.

The initial supervised training is performed based on pairs of events and their corresponding ground-truth descriptions, with the standard cross entropy loss. Note that this network requires $\mathbf{g}_*^{(k-1)}$ as input, which is provided *on the fly* during training. In particular, we feed the ground-truth sentences for each video one by one. At each iteration, we cache the final latent state for the current sentence and use it as an input for the next one.

Supervised training encourages the caption generation network to emulate the training sentences word by word. To further improve the quality of the resultant sentences, we resort to reinforcement learning. In this work, we employ the *Self-Critical Sequence Training (SCST)* [16] technique. Particularly, we consider the caption generation network as an *"agent"*, and choosing a word an *"action"*. Following the practice in [16], we update the network parameters using approximated policy gradient in the reinforcement learning stage.

The key to reinforcement learning is the design of the rewards. In our design, we provide *rewards* at two levels, namely the *sentence-level* and the *paragraph-level*. As mentioned, the network takes in the ground-truth events of a video sequentially, producing one sentence for each event (conditioned on the previous state). These sentences together form a paragraph. When a sentence is generated, it receives a sentence-level reward. When the entire paragraph is completed, it receives a paragraph-level reward. The reward is defined to be the CIDEr [22] metric between the generated sentence/paragraph and the ground truth.

4.2 Training Event Selection Network

The event selection network is a recurrent network that takes a sequence of candidate events as input and produces a sequence of binary indicators (for selecting a subset of candidates to retain). We train this network in a supervised manner. Here, the key question is how to obtain the training samples. We accomplish this in two steps: (1) labeling and (2) generating training sequences.

First, for each video, we use the event localization module to produce a series of event candidates as $(e_1, \ldots, e_T)$. At the same time, we also have a set of ground-truth events provided by the training set, denoted as $(e_1^*, \ldots, e_{T^*}^*)$. For each ground-truth event e_j^*, we find the candidate e_i that has the highest overlap with it, in terms of the temporal IoU, and label it as positive, *i.e.* setting $y_i = 1$. All the other event candidates are labeled as negative.

Second, to generate training sequences, we consider three different ways:

- *(S1) Complete sequences*, which simply uses the whole sequence of candidates for every video, *i.e.* $(e_1, e_2, \cdots, e_m)$.
- *(S2) Subsampling at intervals*, which samples event candidates at varying intervals, *e.g.* $(e_2, e_4, \cdots, e_m)$, to obtain a larger set of sequences.
- *(S3) Subsampling negatives*, which keeps all positive candidates, while randomly sampling the same number of negative candidates in between.

Note that the positive and negative candidates are highly imbalanced. For each video, positive candidates are sparsely located, while negative ones are abundant. The scheme (S3) explicitly rebalances their numbers. Our experiment shows that (S3) often yields the best performance.

The event selection network is trained with the help of the caption generation network. To be more specific, whenever the event selection network yields a positive prediction, the caption feature $\mathbf{c}_{k_t}$ will be updated based on the caption generation network, which will be fed as an input to the next recurrent step.

5 Experiment

We report our experiments on ActivityNet Captions [10], where we compared the proposed framework to various baselines, and conducted ablation studies to investigate its characteristics.

5.1 Experiment Settings

The ActivityNet Captions dataset [10] is the largest publicly available dataset for video captioning. This dataset contains $10,009$ videos for training, and $4,917$

for validation. Compared to previous datasets [7,15,17], it has two orders of magnitude more videos. The videos in this dataset are 3 minutes long on average. Each video in the training set has one set of human labeled annotations, and each video in the validation set has two such sets. Here, a set of annotations is a series of sentences, each aligned with a long or short segment in the video. About 10% of all segments have overlaps with each other. On average, each set of annotations contains 3.65 sentences.

While ActivityNet Captions was originally designed for the task of video dense captioning, we adapt it to our task with the ground-truth paragraphs derived by sequentially concatenating the sentences within each set of segment-based annotations. As a result, for each video in the training set, there is one ground-truth paragraph, and for each video in the validation set, there are two ground-truth paragraphs. Since the annotations for testing videos are not publicly accessible, we randomly split the validation set in half, resulting in 2,458 videos for tuning hyperparameters, and 2,459 videos for performance evaluation.

We set $\delta = 0.3$, $L = 100$ in the event selection module, and $N = 10$ in the captioning module. We separately train the three modules in our framework. In particular, the event localization module is trained according to [31], where the localized events have a recall of 63.77% at 0.7 tIoU threshold. For captioning module, the LSTM hidden size is fixed to 512. As discussed in Sect. 4, we first train the model under the cross-entropy objective using ADAM [9] with an initial learning rate of 4×10^{-4}. We choose the model with best CIDEr score on the validation set. We then run SCST training initialized with this model. The reward metric is CIDEr, for both sentence and paragraph reward. SCST training uses ADAM with a learning rate 5×10^{-5}. One batch contains at least 80 events, since events in the same video are fed into a batch simultaneously. For the event selection module, we train it on a collection of labeled training sequences prepared as described in Sect. 4, where each training sequence contains 64 candidate events. We use cross-entropy as the loss function and SGD with momentum as the optimizer. The learning rate is initialized to 0.1 and scaled down by a factor of 0.1 every 10,000 iterations. We set the SGD momentum to 0.9, weight decay to 0.0005, and batch size to 80. [2]

5.2   Evaluation

We evaluate the performance using multiple metrics, including BLEU [14], METEOR [5], CIDEr [22] and Rouge-L [12]. Besides, we notice there exists a general problem for video captioning results, i.e., repetition or redundancy. This may be due to that captioning module can't distinguish detailed events. For example, the captioner may take both ironing collar and ironing sleeve as ironing. Describing repeated things definitely hurts the coherence of the descriptions. However this can not reflect in the above metrics.

To measure this effect, a recent work proposes Self-BLEU [32] by evaluating how one sentence resembles the rest a generated paragraph. We also propose

---

[2] Code will be made publicly available soon.

another metric, called Repetition Evaluation (RE). Given a generating description c_i, the number of time an n-gram w_k occurs in it is denoted as $h_k(c_i)$. The Repetition Evaluation computes a redundancy score for every description c_i:

$$RE(c_i) = \frac{\sum_k \max\left(h_k(c_i) - 1, 0\right)}{\sum_k h_k(c_i)}, \tag{5}$$

where the gram length, n, takes a large number, like 4 in our experiments. The corpus-level score is the mean score across all descriptions. Ideally, a description with n repetitions would get a score around $(n-1)/n$.

5.3   Comparison with Other Methods

We compared our framework with various baselines, which we describe as below.

(1) *Sentence-Concat*: a simple baseline that equally splits a video into four disjoint parts, and describes each part with a single sentence using the captioning model as ours. The final paragraph is derived by concatenating these four sentences. Using this baseline, we are able to study the effect of localizing events in the input video.

(2) *Hierarchical-RNN* [29]: a more sophisticated way to generate paragraphs from a video, where a topic RNN generates a sequence of topics to control the generation of each individual sentence. With the topic embeddings as input, a sentence RNN generates a sentence for each topic in the sequence.

(3) *Dense-Caption* [10]: one of the state-of-the-art methods for video dense captioning, which generates a single sentence for each candidate event and then concatenate them all into a paragraph, regardless of their similarities. This baseline is used to demonstrate the differences between *video dense captioning* and *video captioning*.

(4) *Dense-Caption-NMS*: a method based on the above Dense-Caption. It selects events from candidate events of Dense-Caption using Non-Maximum Suppression (NMS), removing those that are highly overlapped with others on temporal range.

(5) *Semantic-Sum* [19]: a recent method that also identifies the video segments as ours. We find that this method gets best performance when setting sentence length as 3 and using Latent Semantic Analysis [21] in summarization module.

(6) *Move Forward and Tell (MFT)*: our proposed framework which progressively select events and produce sentences conditioned on what have been said before.

(7) *GT-Event*: this baseline directly applies our captioning module on *ground-truth events*. In principle, this should serve as a performance upper bound, as it has access to the ground-truth event locations.

Table 1 presents the results for different methods on ActivityNet Captions, from which we have the following observations: (1) *Dense-Caption* performs very poorly since there are many redundant proposals and therefore repeated sentences indicating by RE and Self-BLEU metrics. The RE score is terribly

Table 1. Comparison results of video captioning. The last method GT-Event uses ground truth information and can be seen as the upper bound of event selecting. The value is in %. For metrics RE and Self-BLEU, the lower is better. For the others, the higher is bette

Model	CIDEr	BLEU@4	BLEU@3	BLEU@2	BLEU@1	Rouge-L	METEOR	RE	Self-BLEU
Sentence-Concat	4.51	4.18	6.45	10.41	17.52	22.59	8.79	18.41	49.40
Hierarchical-RNN [29]	6.99	7.32	12.13	21.23	39.02	25.53	10.79	18.79	54.38
Dense-Caption [10]	0.29	0.99	1.51	2.33	3.52	8.63	6.75	64.05	89.79
Dense-Caption-NMS	3.52	4.45	6.96	11.21	18.09	21.41	12.08	23.98	62.46
Semantic-Sum [19]	10.43	6.44	11.21	20.36	37.22	25.44	12.66	29.94	67.49
MFT (Ours)	**14.15**	**8.45**	**13.52**	**22.26**	**39.11**	**25.88**	**14.75**	**17.59**	**45.80**
GT-Event	19.56	10.33	16.44	27.24	46.77	29.70	15.09	15.88	42.95

high, meaning two thirds of the descriptions are likely redundant. This clearly shows the differences between video dense captioning and video captioning. (2) *Sentence-Concat* and *Dense-Caption-NMS* are at a comparable level, much better than *Dense-Caption*. These two methods may benefit from a common aspect, *i.e.* their events are almost not overlapped. But some important events may not be localized here. (3) *Hierarchical-RNN* improves the result to the next level, achieving 25.53% Rouge-L. This suggests that it produces more coherent result by modelling the sentence relationships. (4) *Semantic-Sum* further improves the result, achieving 10.43% CIDEr. This shows the effect of localizing video events for captioning. (5) Our method *MFT* significantly outperforms all above methods, *e.g.* it attains 14.15% for CIDEr, compared to 10.43% from *Semantic-Sum*. It also performs comparably well with *GT-Event*, a method utilizing ground-truth events.

5.4   Ablation Studies

Training Scheme. In Sect. 4, we introduce our training strategies. For caption generation network, the training includes two phases – (P1) *initial supervised training* and (P2) *reinforcement learning*. For event selection network, we propose three different ways to generate training sequences. (S1) *complete sequences*, (S2) *subsampling at intervals* and (S3) *subsampling negatives* where our model adopts scheme (S3).

Table 2 shows the performance under different training schemes. First of all, among all three schemes of generating training sequences for event selection network, (S3) *subsampling negatives* performs best. (S1) scheme only gets 9.25% CIDEr while (S2) scheme gets 8.04% CIDEr, a considerable drop from our model. This indicates the importance of balancing the positive candidates and negative candidates. Besides, by utilizing the *reinforcement learning* for caption generation network, our model gains performance improvement, especially for the target metric, CIDEr. Our model yields 14.15% CIDEr score while only using *supervised training* yields 12.81%. Other metrics get consistent improvement with reinforcement learning, including RE and Self-BLEU metrics.

Table 2. This table compares different training schemes for our model. See Sect. 4 for the detail of schemes

Training Scheme	CIDEr	BLEU@4	BLEU@3	BLEU@2	BLEU@1	Rouge-L	METEOR	RE	Self-BLEU
(S1) Complete sequences	9.25	7.12	11.56	19.18	33.80	23.84	11.06	26.11	51.41
(S2) Subsampling at intervals	8.04	6.49	10.52	17.58	31.16	21.27	10.16	24.09	46.19
(P1) Supervised training only	12.81	**8.53**	13.25	21.76	37.68	25.53	13.24	19.10	46.77
(P1 + P2 & S3) Ours	**14.15**	8.45	**13.52**	**22.26**	**39.11**	**25.88**	**14.75**	**17.59**	**45.80**

Feature for Event Selection. In this part, we study the effect of using different features for event selection. Specifically, the following combinations are tested. (1) *visual*: using visual features **v** in isolation, which serves as a baseline for other combinations. (2) *visual + range*: combining visual features **v** with range features **t**, which provides the temporal ranges in the original videos in addition to visual features. (3) *visual + caption*: combining visual features **v** with caption feature **c**, which provides event selection module the ability to know *what have been said*. (4) *visual + range + caption*: using all features.

Table 3. This table lists the results of using different feature combinations for event selection, where the full combination is shown to be the best configuration

Feature	CIDEr	BLEU@4	BLEU@3	BLEU@2	BLEU@1	Rouge-L	METEOR	RE	Self-BLEU
Visual	10.19	6.41	10.41	17.50	31.47	25.74	12.05	29.00	56.57
Visual + range	10.54	7.53	12.16	20.32	36.58	25.42	11.86	27.62	54.11
Visual + caption	11.29	7.90	12.61	20.83	36.55	23.82	13.24	18.92	49.14
Visual + range + caption	**14.15**	**8.45**	**13.52**	**22.26**	**39.11**	**25.88**	**14.75**	**17.59**	**45.80**

As shown in Table 3, compared to *visual*, both *visual + range* and *visual + caption* outperforms it by a significant margin, indicating both the temporal range features and the caption features are complementary to the visual information. It is reasonable as the visual features contain no temporal information, which is explicitly captured in temporal range features, and semantically captured in caption features. Moreover, caption features and temporal range features are also complementary to each other, as the full combination *visual + range + caption* outperforms both *visual + range* and *visual + caption*.

5.5   Human Study

To have a more pertinent assessment, we also conduct a human study, where 20 users are asked to pick the best descriptive paragraph among those generated by the proposed MFT, Hierarchical-RNN, and Semantic-Sum, in terms of relevance, coherence and conciseness respectively. Figure 3 shows that MFT generates the best ones across all aspects.

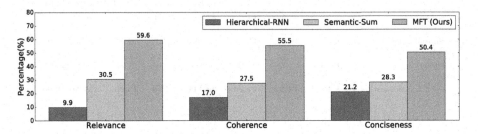

Fig. 3. The figure shows the results of human evaluation, which compares paragraphs generated by different methods, with respect to relevance, coherence and conciseness.

5.6   Qualitative Example

In Fig. 4, we also include one qualitative example, where a video is shown with paragraphs generated by *Dense-Caption-NMS*, *Hierarchical-RNN*, *Semantic-*

Dense-Caption-NMS	A gymnast is seen walking ready to a beam and leads into her performing a routine. The girl then begins to do a routine and flips flips and flips and flips off the beam. He mounts his arms up and down on the mat. A woman is seen standing on a horse and begins walking around. A girl is seen standing on a beam beam with her arms around and performing flips… (remaining skipped)
Hierarchical-RNN	A gymnast is seen performing a routine and leads into several people performing a gymnastics routine. The gymnast performs a routine on a beam. The gymnast dismounts and lands on the pommel horse.
Semantic-Sum	A gymnast is seen standing ready with her arms up in the air. A man is seen standing before a beam and begins performing a gymnastics routine. A man is seen standing ready to perform a routine on the bars.
MFT (ours)	**A gymnast is seen standing ready to a beam and performing a gymnastics routine on a beam. The girl performs several flips and flips around the beam and ends by jumping off the beam.**
Ground-Truth	A girl jumps onto a balance beam. She does a gymnastics routine on the balance beam. She does a flip off the balance beam and lands on a mat.

Fig. 4. This figure lists a qualitative example, where paragraphs generated by *Dense-Caption-NMS*, *Hierarchical-RNN*, *Semantic-Sum* and our method *MFT* are shown.

Sum and our method *MFT*. As shown in Fig. 4, compared to the baselines, our method produces more concise and more coherent paragraphs. We will provide more qualitative results in the supplementary materials.

6   Conclusion

We presented a new framework for generating coherent descriptions for given videos. The generated paragraphs well align with the temporal structure of the given video, covering major semantics without redundancy. Specifically, it sequentially locates important events via an LSTM net, which selects events from a candidate pool, based on their appearances, temporal locations and mutual semantic relationships. When respectively describing events in the acquired sequence, it explicitly decides *what to say next* based on temporal structure and *what have been said*. On ActivityNet Captions, our method significantly outperformed others on a wide range of metrics, while producing more coherent and more concise paragraphs.

Acknowledgement. This work is partially supported by the Big Data Collaboration Research grant from SenseTime Group (CUHK Agreement No. TS1610626), the Early Career Scheme (ECS) of Hong Kong (No. 24204215).

References

1. Baraldi, L., Grana, C., Cucchiara, R.: Hierarchical boundary-aware neural encoder for video captioning. arXiv preprint arXiv:1611.09312 (2016)
2. Dai, B., Fidler, S., Urtasun, R., Lin, D.: Towards diverse and natural image descriptions via a conditional GAN. In: International Conference on Computer Vision (ICCV), pp. 2989–2998. IEEE (2017)
3. Dai, B., Lin, D.: Contrastive learning for image captioning. In: Advances in Neural Information Processing Systemsr (NIPS), pp. 898–907 (2017)
4. Dai, B., Zhang, Y., Lin, D.: Detecting visual relationships with deep relational networks. In: IEEE Conference on Computer Vision and Pattern Recognition (CVPR), pp. 3298–3308. IEEE (2017)
5. Denkowski, M., Lavie, A.: Meteor universal: language specific translation evaluation for any target language. In: Proceedings of the Ninth Workshop on Statistical Machine Translation, pp. 376–380 (2014)
6. Farhadi, A., et al.: Every picture tells a story: generating sentences from images. In: Daniilidis, K., Maragos, P., Paragios, N. (eds.) ECCV 2010. LNCS, vol. 6314, pp. 15–29. Springer, Heidelberg (2010). https://doi.org/10.1007/978-3-642-15561-1_2
7. Geiger, A., Lenz, P., Stiller, C., Urtasun, R.: Vision meets robotics: the kitti dataset. Int. J. Rob. Res. **32**(11), 1231–1237 (2013)
8. Hori, C., Hori, T., Lee, T.Y., Sumi, K., Hershey, J.R., Marks, T.K.: Attention-based multimodal fusion for video description. arXiv preprint arXiv:1701.03126 (2017)
9. Kingma, D.P., Ba, J.: Adam: A method for stochastic optimization. arXiv preprint arXiv:1412.6980 (2014)

10. Krishna, R., Hata, K., Ren, F., Fei-Fei, L., Niebles, J.C.: Dense-captioning events in videos. In: International Conference on Computer Vision (ICCV) (2017)
11. Kulkarni, G., et al.: Babytalk: understanding and generating simple image descriptions. IEEE Trans. Pattern Anal. Mach. Intell. **35**(12), 2891–2903 (2013)
12. Lin, C.Y.: Rouge: a package for automatic evaluation of summaries. In: Text Summarization Branches Out: Proceedings of the ACL-04 workshop, vol. 8, Barcelona, Spain (2004)
13. Pan, Y., Yao, T., Li, H., Mei, T.: Video captioning with transferred semantic attributes. arXiv preprint arXiv:1611.07675 (2016)
14. Papineni, K., Roukos, S., Ward, T., Zhu, W.J.: BLEU: a method for automatic evaluation of machine translation. In: Proceedings of the 40th Annual Meeting on Association for Computational Linguistics, pp. 311–318. Association for Computational Linguistics (2002)
15. Regneri, M., Rohrbach, M., Wetzel, D., Thater, S., Schiele, B., Pinkal, M.: Grounding action descriptions in videos. Trans. Assoc. Comput. Linguist. **1**, 25–36 (2013)
16. Rennie, S.J., Marcheret, E., Mroueh, Y., Ross, J., Goel, V.: Self-critical sequence training for image captioning. arXiv preprint arXiv:1612.00563 (2016)
17. Rohrbach, A., Rohrbach, M., Qiu, W., Friedrich, A., Pinkal, M., Schiele, B.: Coherent multi-sentence video description with variable level of detail. In: Jiang, X., Hornegger, J., Koch, R. (eds.) GCPR 2014. LNCS, vol. 8753, pp. 184–195. Springer, Cham (2014). https://doi.org/10.1007/978-3-319-11752-2_15
18. Rohrbach, A., Rohrbach, M., Schiele, B.: The long-short story of movie description. In: Gall, J., Gehler, P., Leibe, B. (eds.) GCPR 2015. LNCS, vol. 9358, pp. 209–221. Springer, Cham (2015). https://doi.org/10.1007/978-3-319-24947-6_17
19. Sah, S., Kulhare, S., Gray, A., Venugopalan, S., Prud'Hommeaux, E., Ptucha, R.: Semantic text summarization of long videos. In: 2017 IEEE Winter Conference on Applications of Computer Vision (WACV), pp. 989–997. IEEE (2017)
20. Shen, Z., et al.: Weakly supervised dense video captioning. arXiv preprint arXiv:1704.01502 (2017)
21. Steinberger, J., Jezek, K.: Using latent semantic analysis in text summarization and summary evaluation. Proc. ISIM **4**, 93–100 (2004)
22. Vedantam, R., Lawrence Zitnick, C., Parikh, D.: CIDEr: consensus-based image description evaluation. In: Proceedings of the IEEE Conference on Computer Vision and Pattern Recognition, pp. 4566–4575 (2015)
23. Venugopalan, S., Rohrbach, M., Donahue, J., Mooney, R., Darrell, T., Saenko, K.: Sequence to sequence-video to text. In: Proceedings of the IEEE International Conference on Computer Vision, pp. 4534–4542 (2015)
24. Vinyals, O., Toshev, A., Bengio, S., Erhan, D.: Show and tell: a neural image caption generator. In: Proceedings of the IEEE Conference on Computer Vision and Pattern Recognition, pp. 3156–3164 (2015)
25. Wang, J., Wang, W., Huang, Y., Wang, L., Tan, T.: Multimodal memory modelling for video captioning. arXiv preprint arXiv:1611.05592 (2016)
26. Wang, L., et al.: Temporal segment networks: towards good practices for deep action recognition. In: Leibe, B., Matas, J., Sebe, N., Welling, M. (eds.) ECCV 2016. LNCS, vol. 9912, pp. 20–36. Springer, Cham (2016). https://doi.org/10.1007/978-3-319-46484-8_2
27. Xu, K., et al.: Show, attend and tell: Neural image caption generation with visual attention. In: International Conference on Machine Learning, pp. 2048–2057 (2015)
28. Yao, L., et al.: Describing videos by exploiting temporal structure. In: Proceedings of the IEEE International Conference on Computer Vision, pp. 4507–4515 (2015)

29. Yu, H., Wang, J., Huang, Z., Yang, Y., Xu, W.: Video paragraph captioning using hierarchical recurrent neural networks. In: Proceedings of the IEEE Conference on Computer Vision and Pattern Recognition, pp. 4584–4593 (2016)
30. Yu, Y., Ko, H., Choi, J., Kim, G.: End-to-end concept word detection for video captioning, retrieval, and question answering. In: Proceedings of the IEEE Conference on Computer Vision and Pattern Recognition, pp. 3165–3173 (2017)
31. Zhao, Y., Xiong, Y., Wang, L., Wu, Z., Tang, X., Lin, D.: Temporal action detection with structured segment networks. In: ICCV (2017)
32. Zhu, Y., et al.: Texygen: a benchmarking platform for text generation models. arXiv preprint arXiv:1802.01886 (2018)

Learning Monocular Depth by Distilling Cross-Domain Stereo Networks

Xiaoyang Guo[1], Hongsheng Li[1(✉)], Shuai Yi[2], Jimmy Ren[2],
and Xiaogang Wang[1]

[1] CUHK-SenseTime Joint Laboratory, The Chinese University of Hong Kong,
Hong Kong, China
{xyguo,hsli,xgwang}@ee.cuhk.edu.hk
[2] SenseTime Research, Beijing, China
{yishuai,rensijie}@sensetime.com

Abstract. Monocular depth estimation aims at estimating a pixelwise depth map for a single image, which has wide applications in scene understanding and autonomous driving. Existing supervised and unsupervised methods face great challenges. Supervised methods require large amounts of depth measurement data, which are generally difficult to obtain, while unsupervised methods are usually limited in estimation accuracy. Synthetic data generated by graphics engines provide a possible solution for collecting large amounts of depth data. However, the large domain gaps between synthetic and realistic data make directly training with them challenging. In this paper, we propose to use the stereo matching network as a proxy to learn depth from synthetic data and use predicted stereo disparity maps for supervising the monocular depth estimation network. Cross-domain synthetic data could be fully utilized in this novel framework. Different strategies are proposed to ensure learned depth perception capability well transferred across different domains. Our extensive experiments show state-of-the-art results of monocular depth estimation on KITTI dataset.

Keywords: Monocular depth estimation · Stereo matching

1 Introduction

Depth estimation is an important computer vision task, which is a basis for understanding 3D geometry and could assist other vision tasks including object detection, tracking, and recognition. Depth can be recovered by varieties of methods, such as stereo matching [14,27], structure from motion [1,40,44], SLAM systems [7,28,29], and light field [38]. Recently, monocular depth prediction from a single image [6,9,11] was investigated with deep Convolutional Neural Networks (CNN).

Electronic supplementary material The online version of this chapter (https://doi.org/10.1007/978-3-030-01252-6_30) contains supplementary material, which is available to authorized users.

© Springer Nature Switzerland AG 2018
V. Ferrari et al. (Eds.): ECCV 2018, LNCS 11215, pp. 506–523, 2018.
https://doi.org/10.1007/978-3-030-01252-6_30

Deep CNNs could inherently combine local and global contexts of a single image to learn depth maps. The methods are mainly divided into two categories, supervised and unsupervised methods. For deep CNN based supervised methods [5,6], neural networks are directly trained with ground-truth depths, where conditional random fields (CRF) are optionally used to refine the final results. For unsupervised methods, the photometric loss is used to match pixels between images from different viewpoints by warping-based view synthesis. Some methods [9,11] learn to predict depth maps by matching stereo images, while some other ones [47,50] learn depth and camera poses simultaneously from video frame sequences.

There are several challenges for existing monocular depth estimation methods. Supervised learning methods require large amounts of annotated data, and depth annotations need to be carefully aligned and calibrated. Ground truth captured by LIDAR is generally sparse, and structured light depth sensors do not work in strong light. Unsupervised learning methods [9,11] suffer from low texture, repeated pattern, and occlusions. It is hard to recover depth in occlusion regions with only the photometric loss because of the lack of cross-image correspondences at those regions.

Learning from synthetic data with accurate depth maps could be a potential way to tackle the above problems, but this requires synthetic data to be similar as realistic data in contents, appearance and viewpoints to ensure the model transferability. Otherwise, it is hard to adapt the model to realistic data due to the large domain gap (Fig. 1). For example, a monocular depth estimation network pretrained with indoor synthetic data will have a bad performance in driving scenes, but it will perform better if pretrained with synthetic driving scene datasets like virtual KITTI [8]. As a result, a lot of works are needed to build up corresponding synthetic datasets if the algorithm needs to be deployed in different scenes. On the other hand, we find that for state-of-the-art stereo matching algorithms [2,27], the stereo networks pretrained on cross-domain synthetic stereo images generalize much better to new domains compared with monocular depth networks, because the network learns the concept of matching pixels across stereo images instead of understanding high-level semantic meanings. Recently, stereo matching algorithms have achieved great success with the introduction of deep CNNs and synthetic datasets like Scene Flow datasets [27], which inspires us to use stereo matching as a proxy task to learn depth maps from stereo image pairs, which can better utilize synthetic data and alleviate domain transfer problem compared with directly training monocular depth networks.

In this paper, we propose a new pipeline for monocular depth learning with the guidance of stereo matching networks pretrained with cross-domain synthetic datasets. Our pipeline consists of three steps. First, we use a variant of DispNet [27] to predict disparity maps and occlusion masks with synthetic Scene Flow datasets. Then, the stereo matching network is finetuned with realistic data in a supervised or our novel unsupervised way. Finally, the monocular depth estimation network is trained under the supervision of the stereo network.

Using stereo matching network as a proxy to learn depth has several advantages. On the one hand, stereo networks could efficiently make full use of cross-domain synthetic data and can be easier adapted to new domains compared to learning monocular depth. The synthetic datasets do not need to be separately designed for different scenes. On the other hand, the input data for stereo networks could be augmented by cropping and resizing to avoid over-fitting, while monocular depth networks usually fail to learn augmented images because it is sensitive to viewpoint changes. The experiment results show that our stereo matching network trained with synthetic data provides strong guidance for training monocular depth network, which could capture sharp boundaries and clear thin structures.

Our method achieves state-of-the-art results on the KITTI [10] dataset. Our contributions are as follows. (1) We propose a novel monocular depth learning pipeline, which takes advantages of the power of stereo matching networks and synthetic data. By using stereo matching as a proxy task, the synthetic-to-realistic cross-domain problem could be effectively alleviated. (2) A novel unsupervised fine-tuning method is proposed based on the pretrained network to avoid occlusion problem and improve smoothness regularization. Visualization results show shaper boundaries and better occlusion predictions compared with previous unsupervised methods. (3) Our proposed pipeline achieves state-of-the-art monocular depth estimation performance in both unsupervised and semi-supervised settings.

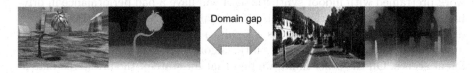

Fig. 1. Illustration of the large domain gap between synthetic and realistic data. Directly training monocular depth networks with cross-domain synthetic and realistic data results in inferior performance.

2   Related Work

Existing depth estimation methods can be mainly categorized into two types: estimation from stereo images and estimation from single monocular images. For depth from stereo images, disparity maps are usually estimated and then converted into depth maps with focal length and baseline (distance between two cameras).

Monocular Depth Estimation. Monocular depth estimation aims to estimate depth values from a single image, instead of stereo images or multiple frames in a video. This problem is ill-posed because of the ambiguity of object sizes. However, humans could estimate the depth from a single image with prior knowledge of the scenes. Recently, learning based methods were explored to learn depth values by supervised or unsupervised learning.

Saxena et al. [32,33] first incorporated multi-scale local and global features using Markov Random Field (MRF) to predict depth maps. Saxena et al. [34] then extended to model locations and orientations of superpixels to obtain precise 3D structures from single images. Liu et al. [25] formulated depth estimation as a discrete-continuous graphic model.

Eigen et al. [6] first employed Convolutional Neural Networks (CNN) to predict depth in a coarse-to-fine manner and further improved its performance by multi-task learning [5]. Liu et al. [24] presented deep convolutional neural fields model by combining deep model with continuous CRF. Li et al. [22] refined deep CNN outputs with a hierarchical CRF. Multi-scale continuous CRF was formulated into a deep sequential network by Xu et al. [45] to refine depth estimation.

Unsupervised methods tried to train monocular depth estimation with stereo image pairs or image sequences and test on single images. Garg et al. [9] used novel image view synthesis loss to train a depth estimation network in an unsupervised way. Godard et al. [11] introduced left-right consistency regularization to improve the performance of view synthesis loss. Kuznietsov et al. [21] combined supervised and unsupervised losses to further boost the performance. There were also works [41–43,47,50] that try to recover depth maps and egomotion from consecutive video frames.

Stereo Matching. The target of stereo matching is to compute the disparity map given left-right image pairs. Usually, the input image pairs are rectified to make epipolar lines horizontal to simplify the matching problem.

Stereo algorithms generally consist of all or some of the following four steps [35]: matching cost computation, cost aggregation, disparity optimization, and refinement. Local stereo methods [15–17] generally compute matching cost for all possible disparities and take the *winner-take-all* strategy to generate the final disparities. Global methods, including graph cut [20], belief propagation [37,46] and semi-global matching (SGM) [14], take smoothness prior into consideration but are usually time-consuming. Higher level prior is investigated in Displets [12], which takes object shape into account in a superpixel-based CRF framework.

Recently, deep learning has been successfully applied to stereo matching. Usually, these methods first train on large amounts of synthetic data, such as Scene Flow datasets [27], and then finetune on realistic data. Zbontar and LeCun [48] proposed to train a patch comparing network to compute the matching cost of stereo images. Mayer et al. [27] generalized the idea of Flownet [4] and proposed a network structure with 1D correlation layer named DispnetC, which directly regresses disparity maps in an end-to-end way. Pang et al. [30] and Liang et al. [23] extended DispnetC with cascade refinement structures. Recently, GC-Net [18] and PSMNet [2] incorporated contextual information using 3-D convolutions over cost volume to improve the performance.

For unsupervised learning, Zhou et al. [49] presented a framework to learn stereo matching by iterative left-right consistency check. Tonioni et al.

[39] combined off-the-shelf stereo algorithms and confidence measures to fine-tune stereo matching network.

3   Method

This section describes details of our method. For supervised monocular depth estimation methods [6,24], the accurate ground truth is usually limited and hard to obtain. For warping-based unsupervised methods [11,50], the performance is usually limited due to the ambiguity of pixel matching. Directly training with synthetic data could only partly solve the problems, because it requires lots of works to design different synthetic datasets for different scenes, and there is a large domain gap between synthetic and realistic data. Since the stereo matching network learns pixelwise matching instead of directly deducing depth from semantic features, it generalizes much better from synthetic domain to realistic domain compared with learning-based monocular depth methods. Inspired by the good generalization ability of stereo matching algorithms, we propose a novel pipeline for monocular depth learning to tackle the above limitations.

Our method uses stereo matching as a proxy task for monocular depth learning and consists of three steps, as shown in Fig. 2. In Sect. 3.1, we train a stereo matching network with synthetic data to predict occlusion masks and disparity maps of stereo image pairs simultaneously. In Sect. 3.2, the stereo network is finetuned on realistic data in supervised or unsupervised settings, depending on the availability of realistic data. In supervised settings, only 100 sampled training images are used to simulate the situation of limited ground truth. For unsupervised settings, a novel unsupervised loss is proposed to achieve better performance in occlusion regions. In Sect. 3.3, we train the monocular depth estimation network by distilling the stereo network. In this way, with the proxy stereo network as a bridge from synthetic to realistic data, monocular depth estimation could better benefit from synthetic data, and much freedom is allowed for choosing synthetic data.

3.1   Training Proxy Stereo Matching Network with Synthetic Data

Synthetic data can be used for pre-training to improve the performance of stereo matching. However, directly training monocular networks with synthetic data generally leads to inferior performance, because monocular depth estimation is sensitive to viewpoints and objects of the input scenes. Usually, synthetic datasets need to be carefully designed to narrow the domain gap, such as Virtual KITTI [8] for driving scenes, which requires manually designing 3D scenes with large labor costs. However, we observe that stereo matching networks trained with only general-propose synthetic data can produce acceptable disparity map predictions on cross-domain realistic stereo image pairs. This inspires us to train stereo networks as a proxy to learn from synthetic data and a bridge between two data domains and two related tasks.

Step 1: Train a stereo network with synthetic data, supervised with ground truth M^*, D^*

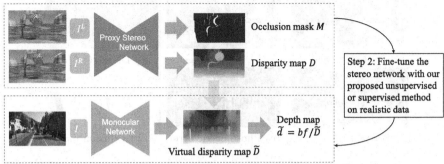

Step 3: Train monocular depth network by distilling stereo network

Fig. 2. The pipeline of our proposed method. The proxy stereo network is pre-trained with synthetic data and then finetuned on realistic data in supervised or unsupervised settings. The cross-domain gap problem could be mitigated by our stereo-to-monocular distillation approach.

We use a variant of DispnetC [27] as our proxy stereo matching network. DispnetC employs a 1-D correlation layer to extract the matching cost over all possible disparities and uses an encoder-decoder structure to obtain multi-scale coarse-to-fine disparity predictions. Different from the original structure, our stereo network estimates multiscale occlusion masks in addition to disparity maps, as shown in Step 1 of Fig. 2. Occlusion masks indicate whether the corresponding points of left image pixels are occluded in the right image. Figure 3(f) shows an example of occlusion masks. The occlusion masks will be used by our proposed unsupervised fine-tuning in Sect. 3.2 to avoid wrong photometric supervisions.

The ground truth of occlusion masks is deduced from ground-truth disparity maps using left-right disparity consistency check,

$$M_{ij}^* = \mathbb{1}\left(\left|D_{ij}^{*L} - D_{ij}^{*wR}\right| \leq 1\right) = \mathbb{1}\left(\left|D_{ij}^{*L} - D_{i(j-D_{ij}^{*R})}^{*R}\right| \leq 1\right), \tag{1}$$

where the subscript ij represents the value at the ith row and the jth column. $D^{*L/R}$ denotes the left/right disparity map, and D^{*wR} is the right image which is warped to the left viewpoint. In occlusion regions, the values of D^{*L} and D^{*wR} are inconsistent. The threshold for the consistency check is set to 1-pixel length. The occlusion mask is set to 0 in occlusion regions and 1 in non-occlusion regions.

The loss is defined as $\mathcal{L}_{\text{stereo}} = \sum_{m=0}^{M-1} w_m \mathcal{L}_{\text{stereo}}^m$ for M scales of predictions, where w_m denotes the weighting factor for the mth scale. The loss function consists of two parts, disparity loss and occlusion mask loss,

$$\mathcal{L}_{\text{stereo}}^m = \mathcal{L}_{disp} + \mathcal{L}_{occ}. \tag{2}$$

(a) Left image   (b) Right image   (c) Disparity Map

(d) Warped right image (e) Photometric error   (f) Occlusion mask

Fig. 3. Illustration of image warping and occlusion masks. The occlusion regions of the warped right image are not consistent with those of the left image even if the disparity map is correct. As a result, in the unsupervised fine-tuning, predicted occlusion masks are used to mask out the wrong supervision of photometric loss (see red rectangles) in occlusion regions. (Color figure online)

To train disparity maps, $L1$ regression loss is used to alleviate the impact of outliers and make the training process more robust. Occlusion masks are trained with binary cross-entropy loss as a classification task,

$$\mathcal{L}_{occ} = -\frac{1}{N} \sum_{i,j} M^*_{ij}\log(M_{ij}) + (1 - M^*_{ij})\log(1 - M_{ij}), \tag{3}$$

where N is the total number of pixels.

3.2 Supervised and Unsupervised Fine-Tuning Stereo Matching Network on Realistic Data

The stereo matching network can be finetuned on realistic data depending on the availability of realistic depth data. In this paper, we investigate two ways to finetune the stereo matching network on realistic data, supervised learning with a very limited amount of depth data and our proposed unsupervised fine-tuning method.

Supervised Fine-Tuning. For supervised fine-tuning, only a multiscale $L1$ disparity regression loss is employed to refine the errors of pretrained models. The fine-tuning loss for the mth scale is defined as $\mathcal{L}^m_{stereo(supft)} = \mathcal{L}_{disp}$. Good results can be obtained with only a small amount of depth data, for example, 100 images. The stereo network can adapt from the synthetic domain to the realistic domain and fix most of the errors.

Unsupervised Fine-Tuning. For unsupervised fine-tuning, we tried the unsupervised method of Godard et al. [11] to finetune our stereo networks with warping-based view synthesis loss but found that disparity predictions tended to become blurred, and the performance dropped, as shown in Fig. 4(a). We argue that this is because of the matching ambiguity of the unsupervised loss and lack of occlusion handling. As a result, we propose to introduce additional occlusion handling terms and new regularization terms to improve the matching quality of unsupervised loss.

Our proposed unsupervised loss requires the occlusion mask and disparity map predictions on realistic data from the un-finetuned stereo network, which is got in Sect. 3.1. The predictions are denoted as M_{un} and D_{un} respectively. The unsupervised fine-tuning loss consists of three parts, the photometric loss, the absolute regularization term, and the relative regularization term,

$$\mathcal{L}^m_{stereo(unsupft)} = \mathcal{L}_{photo} + \gamma_1 \mathcal{L}_{abs} + \gamma_2 \mathcal{L}_{rel}, \tag{4}$$

where γ_1 and γ_2 are weighting factors.

 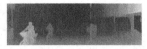

(a) Finetuned with [11]   (b) Finetuned with proposed method

Fig. 4. Illustration of unsupervised finetuned predictions of stereo matching networks with the method of Godard et al. [11] and our proposed method. (a) Finetuned with [11]. (b) Finetuned with proposed method

The photometric loss $\mathcal{L}_{photo}$ follows [9, 11] and uses warping-based view synthesis to learn disparity values by image reconstruction. The right image I^R is first warped to the left viewpoint by bilinear sampling to obtain the warped right image I^{wR}, which is an estimate of the left image except for occlusion regions, which is illustrated in Fig. 3(d). Since there is no pixelwise correspondence for pixels in occlusion regions, as shown in Fig. 3(e), we use the occlusion mask M_{un} to mask out the photometric supervision in occlusion regions to avoid incorrect supervisions. Then our photometric loss is given by

$$\mathcal{L}_{photo} = \frac{1}{N} \sum_{i,j} M_{un(ij)} \left| I^L_{ij} - I^{wR}_{ij} \right| = \frac{1}{N} \sum_{i,j} M_{un(ij)} \left| I^L_{ij} - I^R_{i(j-D^L_{ij})} \right|. \tag{5}$$

The absolute regularization term $\mathcal{L}_{abs}$ tries to make the newly-predicted disparity values close to the un-finetuned predictions especially in occlusion regions,

$$\mathcal{L}_{abs} = \frac{1}{N} \sum_{i,j} \left(1 - M_{un(ij)} + \gamma_3 \right) \left| D^L_{ij} - D^L_{un(ij)} \right|, \tag{6}$$

where D_{un} is the disparity prediction of the un-finetuned stereo network, and γ_3 is a small regularization coefficient.

The relative regularization term $\mathcal{L}_{rel}$ regularizes the prediction smoothness by the gradients of D_{un}, instead of input image gradients used in [11],

$$\mathcal{L}_{rel} = \frac{1}{N} \sum_{i,j} \left| \nabla D^L_{ij} - \nabla D^L_{un(ij)} \right|. \tag{7}$$

Figure 4 compares the finetuned predictions using [11] and our unsupervised fine-tuning method, which shows that our method is able to preserve sharp boundaries and accurate predictions in occlusion regions. In the experiment section, we will show that our method also achieves better quantitative results.

3.3   Train Monocular Depth Network by Distilling Stereo Network

By using a stereo network as a proxy, a large amount of synthetic data are fully utilized to train the stereo network without the cross-domain problem. To train the final monocular depth estimation network, we need to distill the knowledge of the stereo matching network. The monocular network also outputs multiscale predictions, and the loss is given by $\mathcal{L}_{\mathrm{mono}} = \sum_{m=0}^{M-1} w_m \mathcal{L}_{mono}^m$. For each scale,

$$\mathcal{L}_{\mathrm{mono}}^m = \frac{1}{N} \sum_{i,j} \left| \tilde{D}_{ij}^L - D_{ij}^L \right|, \tag{8}$$

where $\tilde{D}$ represents the virtual disparity maps predicted by monocular networks, and D denotes the predictions of the stereo matching network from Sect. 3.2.

After getting the virtual disparity map $\tilde{D}$ from the monocular depth estimation network, the final depth map $\tilde{d}$ is then given by $\tilde{d} = bf/\tilde{D}$, where b is the baseline distance between two cameras, and f is the focal length of the lenses.

4   Experiments

4.1   Datasets and Evaluation Metrics

The synthetic Scene Flow Datasets [27] are used to pre-train our proxy stereo matching network, which is then finetuned on KITTI dataset [10] in supervised or unsupervised ways. The monocular network is then trained on the KITTI dataset under the supervision of the proxy stereo network.

Scene Flow Datasets are a collection of synthetic datasets, containing more than 39,000 stereo pairs for training and 4,000 for testing. The datasets are rendered by computer graphics in low cost and provide accurate disparity. The occlusion masks can be easily deduced from the ground-truth disparity maps by left-right consistency check.

The KITTI Dataset is collected by moving vehicles in several outdoor scenes. We use the raw data of the KITTI dataset, which provide rectified stereo sequences, calibration information, and 3D LIDAR point clouds. Ground truth depth maps are inferred by mapping LIDAR points to the coordinate of the left camera. Our methods are all trained and tested on the Eigen split [6] of the KITTI dataset, which contains 22,600 image pairs for training, 888 for validation and 697 for testing. The Cityscapes dataset [3] also provides driving scene stereo pairs and can be used to pre-train the monocular depth network.

Evaluation Metrics. The evaluation metrics in [6] are adopted to compare with the previous works. The metrics consist of absolute relative difference (Abs Rel), squared relative difference (Sq Rel), root mean square error (RMS), root mean square error in log scale (Log RMS), and threshold-based metrics. The threshold metric is defined as the percentage of pixels that satisfy $\delta = max(d_{ij}/d_{ij}^*, d_{ij}^*/d_{ij}) < thr$, where d_{ij} and d_{ij}^* are the depth prediction and depth ground truth for a pixel, and thr is the threshold value. We cap the maximum depth values to 80 m following previous works.

4.2 Implementation Details

Proxy Stereo Matching Network. We implement our proxy stereo matching network with the structure of DispNetC [27], extra branch is added along with the disparity map output to predict occlusion masks. Equal weights are assigned for training disparity maps and occlusion masks. During training, the left-right image pairs are randomly flipped and then swapped to obtain the mirrored stereo pairs. Random resizing is then performed with a scaling factor between [0.8, 1.2] and followed by random cropping to generate stereo image patches. When performing image resizing, the corresponding ground-truth disparity values are multiplied by the scaling factor to ensure the correctness of stereo correspondences. Following [11], the cropped images are then augmented by adjusting gamma in the range of [0.8, 1.2], illuminations in [0.8, 1.2], and color jitting in [0.95, 1.05], respectively. The network is optimized using Adam algorithm [19]. The parameters for Adam are set to $\beta_1 = 0.9$, $\beta_2 = 0.999$, and $\epsilon = 10^{-8}$. The weighting factors w_m for 4 multiscale predictions are set as $w_m = 2^{-m}$ for both pre-training and fine-tuning, and w_0 corresponds to the final prediction.

When pre-training on Scene Flow datasets, the stereo network is trained for 50 epochs with a batch size of 4. The crop size for training is 768×384, and original images without any augmentation are used for testing. The initial learning rate is 10^{-4} and is downgraded by half at epoch 20, 35, 45. The network is trained for two rounds to achieve better performance, following [30]. For each round, the learning rate restarts at 10^{-4}. The stereo network trained with only synthetic data is denoted as *StereoNoFt*.

Fine-tuning the stereo network is performed on the KITTI dataset. The input size for KITTI is 832×256 for training and 1280×384 for testing. Similar augmentation is performed on KITTI as those on Scene Flow datasets. The learning rate starts at 2×10^{-5} and stops at 2.5×10^{-6}. For unsupervised fine-tuning, the whole training set of the Eigen Split is used, and the network is trained for 10 epochs. The weighting factors γ_1, γ_2 are set as 0.05 and 0.1, and γ_3 is 0.1. For supervised fine-tuning, only 100 images sampled from the training set are used to simulate the scenarios when ground truth depth maps are limited. The stereo models with unsupervised fine-tuning and supervised fine-tuning are denoted as *StereoUnsupFt* and *StereoSupFt100* respectively.

Monocular Depth Estimation Network. The structure of our monocular depth estimation network follows [11] with several important modifications. As shown in Fig. 5, the encoder adopts the VGG-16 [36] structure, and the decoder uses stacked deconvolutions and shortcut encoder features to recover multiscale depth predictions. The Leaky Rectified Linear Unit (LReLU) [26] with coefficient 0.1 is used in the decoder. The input images are randomly flipped and swapped. No cropping and scaling is used since the monocular depth estimation network is sensitive to viewpoint changes. The input images and disparity supervision from the stereo network are resized to 512×256 to fit the input size of the monocular network. Gamma, illumination, and color augmentations are performed in the same way as the stereo network. The network is trained on the KITTI training set for 50 epochs with an initial learning rate of 10^{-4}, which is then decreased by half at epoch 20, 35 and 45. If the monocular depth estimation model is supervised by *StereoNoFt*, the name for this model is denoted as *StereoNoFt → Mono*, and the naming rule is similar for other models. If the encoder of a model is initialized with weights pretrained for the ImageNet [31] classification task, the suffix *pt* is added to the model name.

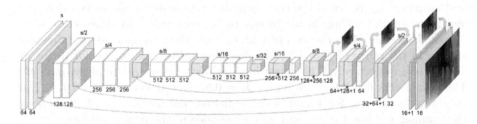

Fig. 5. The architecture of our monocular depth estimation network. The encoder is chosen as VGG-16 model. White blocks: 3×3 convolution with ReLU. Red blocks: max pooling. Blue blocks: 4×4 stride 2 deconvolution with Leaky ReLU. Yellow blocks: 3×3 convolution with Leaky ReLU. (Color figure online)

4.3   Comparison with State-of-the-Arts

In Table 1, we compare the performance of our models with previous supervised and unsupervised methods. Depth results are visualized in Fig. 6 to compare with previous methods. We can see that our models can capture more detailed structures of the scenes. More visualization results can be found in the supplementary material.

First, we demonstrate the way we use stereo matching as a proxy task is crucial for utilizing cross-domain synthetic data. In the second part of Table 1, we showed some results of monocular networks which were directly trained with synthetic data. We can get some conclusions. (1) The monocular network does not work on the KITTI dataset if only trained with Scene Flow datasets. Stereo networks generalize much better and have smaller synthetic-to-real domain transfer problems. (2) The performance of monocular networks has no apparent difference with or without pre-training on Scene Flow datasets. It is difficult for monocular depth networks to utilize cross-domain synthetic data by directly pre-training due to the large domain gap. (3) The monocular depth network requires a large amount of depth data to achieve good performance, while our method achieves better performance without or with only a limited number of depth maps. Therefore, our method, stereo-to-monocular distillation, could make better use of the large amount of cross-domain synthetic data to improve the performance of monocular depth estimation.

Comparison with Unsupervised Methods. Our unsupervised model $StereoNoFt \rightarrow Mono$ and $StereoUnsupFt \rightarrow Mono$ are in similar settings with previous unsupervised methods [11] since they do not use ground truth depth of realistic data, and synthetic data can be obtained free of charge by rendering engines. From Table 1, we can see that the monocular depth model supervised by the un-finetuned proxy stereo network ($StereoNoFt \rightarrow Mono$) even surpasses the state-of-the-art unsupervised method [11], which is based on warping-based view synthesis and difficult to obtain sharp boundaries and handle occlusion parts. In contrast, our method can take advantages of synthetic data to provide rich depth supervisions and infer the depth values in occlusion parts. We also observe that monocular depth estimation can benefit from ImageNet pretrained weights (with postfix *pt* in experiment names) and pre-training on street scene datasets like the Cityscapes dataset under the supervision of the stereo model $StereoNoFt$. Our best unsupervised model $StereoUnsupFt \rightarrow Mono$ *pt* trained on Cityscapes and KITTI outperforms the method of [11] by 0.62 meters in terms of root mean squared error and decreases the squared relative error by 21.7%.

Comparison with Supervised Methods. For supervised fine-tuning, instead of using all ground truth in the training set of KITTI, our model $StereoSupFt100 \rightarrow Mono$ only used 100 sampled images with LIDAR depths in the training set for fine-tuning. Results show that our method also works when only a limited number of accurate depth maps is available. We compare our results with the method of Kuznietsov et al. [21], which combines supervised and unsupervised losses to estimate monocular depth. However, although their method uses all ground truth data, we can see from Table 1 that all evaluation metrics of our model $StereoSupFt100 \rightarrow Mono$ *pt*, surpass [21] and all other previous supervised methods. We also provide the results of fine-tuning the proxy stereo network with all supervised data ($StereoSupFtAll \rightarrow Mono$) for reference.

We also evaluate with a maximum depth cap of 50 meters in the bottom part of Table 1. Similarly, our method beats all of the state-of-the-art methods.

Table 1. Quantitative results on KITTI [10] using the split of Eigen et al. [6]. All results are evaluated with the crop of [9] except [6]. The results of [6,24] are from the paper of [11] for fair comparision. *Sup.* means supervised and 100 represents only using 100 ground truth depth maps. S, C, K denote Scene Flow datasets [27], Cityscapes dataset [3] and KITTI dataset [10] respectively. *res* denotes using Resnet [13] as the encoder structure, and *pt* denotes using model weights pretrained on ImageNet [31].

Method	Sup.	Dataset	Lower is better				Higher is better		
			Abs Rel	Sq Rel	RMS	Log RMS	$\delta < 1.25$	$\delta < 1.25^2$	$\delta < 1.25^3$
Eigen et al. Fine [6]	Yes	K	0.203	1.548	6.307	0.282	0.702	0.890	0.958
DCNF-FCSP FT [24]	Yes	K	0.201	1.584	6.471	0.273	0.680	0.898	0.967
Godard et al. [11]	No	K	0.148	1.344	5.927	0.247	0.803	0.922	0.964
Godard et al. [11] res pp	No	C,K	0.114	0.898	4.935	0.206	0.861	0.949	0.976
Zhou et al. [50]	No	K	0.208	1.768	6.856	0.283	0.678	0.885	0.957
Kuznietsov et al. [21] res pt	Yes	K	0.113	0.741	4.621	0.189	0.862	0.960	0.986
Direct Sup	No	S	0.662	9.502	16.03	1.407	0.053	0.124	0.209
Direct Sup. (All of K)	Yes	K	0.105	0.717	4.422	0.183	0.874	0.959	0.983
Direct Sup. pt(S) (All of K)	Yes	S,K	0.106	0.723	4.506	0.185	0.871	0.958	0.983
Direct Sup. (100 of K)	100	K	0.187	1.563	6.283	0.273	0.732	0.889	0.953
Direct Sup. pt(S) (100 of K)	100	S,K	0.194	1.560	6.001	0.267	0.737	0.896	0.956
StereoNoFt → Mono	No	S → K	0.109	0.822	4.656	0.192	0.868	0.958	0.981
StereoUnsupFt → Mono	No	S,K → K	0.105	0.811	4.634	0.189	0.874	0.959	0.982
StereoUnsupFt → Mono pt	No	S,K → K	0.099	0.745	4.424	0.182	0.884	0.963	0.983
StereoUnsupFt → Mono pt	No	S,K → C,K	**0.095**	**0.703**	**4.316**	**0.177**	**0.892**	**0.966**	**0.984**
StereoSupFt100 → Mono pt	100	S,K → K	0.101	0.690	4.254	0.173	0.884	0.966	**0.986**
StereoSupFtAll → Mono pt	Yes	S,K → K	0.097	0.653	4.170	0.170	0.889	**0.967**	**0.986**
StereoSupFt100 → Mono pt	100	S,K → C,K	**0.096**	**0.641**	**4.095**	**0.168**	**0.892**	**0.967**	**0.986**
cap 50m									
Garg et al. [16] L12 Aug 8x	No	K	0.169	1.080	5.104	0.273	0.740	0.904	0.962
Godard et al. [11] res pp	No	C,K	0.108	0.657	3.729	0.194	0.873	0.954	0.979
Kuznietsov et al. [21] res pt	Yes	K	0.108	0.595	3.518	0.179	0.875	0.964	0.988
StereoUnsupFt → Mono pt	No	S,K → K	0.094	0.555	3.347	0.172	0.895	0.968	0.985
StereoUnsupFt → Mono pt	No	S,K → C,K	**0.090**	**0.522**	**3.258**	**0.168**	**0.902**	**0.969**	**0.986**
StereoSupFt100 → Mono pt	100	S,K → K	0.097	0.549	3.259	0.164	0.895	0.970	**0.988**
StereoSupFt100 → Mono pt	100	S,K → C,K	**0.092**	**0.515**	**3.163**	**0.159**	**0.901**	**0.971**	**0.988**

4.4 Analysis of Fine-Tuning for Proxy Stereo Models

We first compared our proposed unsupervised fine-tuning method with the unsupervised method of [11] (*StereoUnsupFt* and *StereoUnsupFt* ([11])) in Table 2). The method of [11] didn't explicitly handle the occlusion regions, so the predictions in the occlusion parts tended to be blurred. Our unsupervised fine-tuning method removed the incorrect supervision in occlusion regions and improved the regularization terms. From Fig. 4 and Table 2, we can see our unsupervised fine-tuning method surpasses the method of [11] quantitatively and qualitatively.

We then compare the performance of our stereo models *StereoNoFt*, *StereoUnsupFt*, *StereoSupFt100*, and corresponding distilled monocular depth estimation models. By comparing *StereoUnsupFt* and *StereoSupFt100* with *StereoNoFt*, we can see that both supervised and unsupervised fine-tuning improve

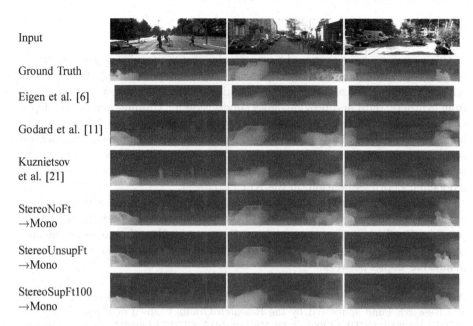

Fig. 6. Visualization of depth maps of different methods on KITTI test set. Results of [11] are shown without post-processing.

Table 2. Comparison of our proxy stereo models and corresponding monocular depth models on the KITTI dataset (Eigen split) and Scene Flow datasets.

Method	KITTI (Eigen split)							Scene Flow		
	Abs Rel	Sq Rel	RMS	Log RMS	$\delta < 1.25$	$\delta < 1.25^2$	$\delta < 1.25^3$	MAE (px)	> 1px %	> 3px %
StereoNoFt	0.072	0.665	3.836	0.153	0.936	0.973	0.986	**3.41**	**0.241**	**0.096**
StereoUnsupFt([11])	0.076	0.691	4.076	0.173	0.915	0.960	0.979	13.3	0.515	0.365
StereoUnsupFt	**0.061**	0.612	3.553	0.144	**0.948**	0.975	0.986	4.23	0.293	0.124
StereoSupFt100	0.063	**0.562**	**3.325**	**0.137**	**0.948**	**0.978**	**0.988**	5.27	0.430	0.181
StereoNoFt → Mono	0.109	0.822	4.656	0.192	0.868	0.958	0.981	-	-	-
StereoUnsupFt([11]) → Mono	0.116	0.877	4.996	0.210	0.845	0.943	0.975	-	-	-
StereoUnsupFt → Mono	**0.105**	0.811	4.634	0.189	**0.874**	**0.959**	0.982	-	-	-
StereoSupFt100 → Mono	0.111	**0.771**	**4.449**	**0.185**	0.868	0.958	**0.983**	-	-	-

the performance on the KITTI dataset. Although only 100 images are used for supervised fine-tuning, it still surpasses the model with unsupervised fine-tuning. The performance of monocular depth networks improves with the performance of corresponding proxy stereo networks. Fine-tuning of stereo networks brings performance improvement for monocular depth estimation. The performance of our pipeline improves if the proxy stereo network is replaced with PSMNet [30], and detailed results are reported in the supplementary material. As a result, if more advanced stereo matching networks and better fine-tuning strategies are employed, the performance of our method could be further improved.

5   Conclusion

In this paper, we have proposed a new pipeline for monocular depth estimation to tackle the problems existing in previous supervised and unsupervised methods. Our method utilizes deep stereo matching network as a proxy to learn depth from synthetic data and provide dense supervision for training monocular depth estimation network. Multiple strategies for fine-tuning the proxy stereo matching network are investigated, and the proposed unsupervised fine-tuning method successfully keeps detailed structures of predictions and improves the final performance. Our extensive experimental results show state-of-the-art results of monocular depth estimation on the KITTI dataset.

For future works, more advanced stereo matching algorithms and better fine-tuning strategies can be investigated to further improve the performance of the pipeline. Confidence measurement is another way to filter the noises of the outputs of stereo matching networks and provide better supervision for training monocular depth network.

Acknowledgements. This work is supported by SenseTime Group Limited, the General Research Fund sponsored by the Research Grants Council of Hong Kong (Nos. CUHK14213616, CUHK14206114, CUHK14205615, CUHK14203015, CUHK14239816, CUHK419412, CUHK14207814, CUHK14208417, CUHK14202217), the Hong Kong Innovation and Technology Support Program (No. ITS/121/15FX).

References

1. Agarwal, S., et al.: Building rome in a day. Communi. ACM **54**(10), 105–112 (2011)
2. Chang, J.R., Chen, Y.S.: Pyramid stereo matching network. In: Proceedings of the IEEE Conference on Computer Vision and Pattern Recognition, pp. 5410–5418 (2018)
3. Cordts, M., et al.: The cityscapes dataset for semantic urban scene understanding. In: Proceedings of the IEEE Conference on Computer Vision and Pattern Recognition (CVPR) (2016)
4. Dosovitskiy, A., et al.: FlowNet: learning optical flow with convolutional networks. In: Proceedings of the IEEE International Conference on Computer Vision, pp. 2758–2766 (2015)
5. Eigen, D., Fergus, R.: Predicting depth, surface normals and semantic labels with a common multi-scale convolutional architecture. In: Proceedings of the IEEE International Conference on Computer Vision, pp. 2650–2658 (2015)
6. Eigen, D., Puhrsch, C., Fergus, R.: Depth map prediction from a single image using a multi-scale deep network. In: Advances in Neural Information Processing Systems, pp. 2366–2374 (2014)
7. Engel, J., Schöps, T., Cremers, D.: LSD-SLAM: large-scale direct monocular SLAM. In: Fleet, D., Pajdla, T., Schiele, B., Tuytelaars, T. (eds.) ECCV 2014. LNCS, vol. 8690, pp. 834–849. Springer, Cham (2014). https://doi.org/10.1007/978-3-319-10605-2_54
8. Gaidon, A., Wang, Q., Cabon, Y., Vig, E.: Virtual worlds as proxy for multi-object tracking analysis. In: CVPR (2016)

9. Garg, R., B.G., V.K., Carneiro, G., Reid, I.: Unsupervised CNN for single view depth estimation: geometry to the rescue. In: Leibe, B., Matas, J., Sebe, N., Welling, M. (eds.) ECCV 2016. LNCS, vol. 9912, pp. 740–756. Springer, Cham (2016). https://doi.org/10.1007/978-3-319-46484-8_45

10. Geiger, A., Lenz, P., Stiller, C., Urtasun, R.: Vision meets robotics: the kitti dataset. Int, J. Rob. Res. (IJRR) (2013)

11. Godard, C., Mac Aodha, O., Brostow, G.J.: Unsupervised monocular depth estimation with left-right consistency. In: CVPR, vol. 2, p. 7 (2017)

12. Guney, F., Geiger, A.: Displets: resolving stereo ambiguities using object knowledge. In: Proceedings of the IEEE Conference on Computer Vision and Pattern Recognition, pp. 4165–4175 (2015)

13. He, K., Zhang, X., Ren, S., Sun, J.: Deep residual learning for image recognition. In: Proceedings of the IEEE Conference on Computer Vision and Pattern Recognition, pp. 770–778 (2016)

14. Hirschmuller, H.: Stereo processing by semiglobal matching and mutual information. IEEE Trans. Pattern Anal. Mach. Intell. **30**(2), 328–341 (2008)

15. Hosni, A., Bleyer, M., Gelautz, M., Rhemann, C.: Local stereo matching using geodesic support weights. In: 2009 16th IEEE International Conference on Image Processing (ICIP), pp. 2093–2096. IEEE (2009)

16. Hosni, A., Rhemann, C., Bleyer, M., Rother, C., Gelautz, M.: Fast cost-volume filtering for visual correspondence and beyond. IEEE Trans. Pattern Anal. Mach. Intell. **35**(2), 504–511 (2013)

17. Kanade, T., Okutomi, M.: A stereo matching algorithm with an adaptive window: theory and experiment. IEEE Trans. Pattern Anal. Mach. Intell. **16**(9), 920–932 (1994)

18. Kendall, A., et al.: End-to-end learning of geometry and context for deep stereo regression. CoRR, vol. arXiv:1703.04309 (2017)

19. Kingma, D.P., Ba, J.: Adam: a method for stochastic optimization. arXiv preprint arXiv:1412.6980 (2014)

20. Kolmogorov, V., Zabih, R.: Computing visual correspondence with occlusions using graph cuts. In: Eighth IEEE International Conference on Computer Vision, ICCV 2001. Proceedings, vol. 2, pp. 508–515. IEEE (2001)

21. Kuznietsov, Y., Stückler, J., Leibe, B.: Semi-supervised deep learning for monocular depth map prediction. In: Proceedings of the IEEE Conference on Computer Vision and Pattern Recognition, pp. 6647–6655 (2017)

22. Li, B., Shen, C., Dai, Y., van den Hengel, A., He, M.: Depth and surface normal estimation from monocular images using regression on deep features and hierarchical CRFs. In: Proceedings of the IEEE Conference on Computer Vision and Pattern Recognition, pp. 1119–1127 (2015)

23. Liang, Z., Feng, Y., Chen, Y.G.H.L.W., Zhang, L.Q.L.Z.J.: Learning for disparity estimation through feature constancy. In: Proceedings of the IEEE Conference on Computer Vision and Pattern Recognition, pp. 2811–2820 (2018)

24. Liu, F., Shen, C., Lin, G., Reid, I.: Learning depth from single monocular images using deep convolutional neural fields. IEEE Trans. Pattern Anal. Mach. Intell. **38**(10), 2024–2039 (2016)

25. Liu, M., Salzmann, M., He, X.: Discrete-continuous depth estimation from a single image. In: 2014 IEEE Conference on Computer Vision and Pattern Recognition (CVPR), pp. 716–723. IEEE (2014)

26. Maas, A.L., Hannun, A.Y., Ng, A.Y.: Rectifier nonlinearities improve neural network acoustic models. In: Proceedings ICML, vol. 30, p. 3 (2013)

27. Mayer, N., et al.: A large dataset to train convolutional networks for disparity, optical flow, and scene flow estimation. In: Proceedings of the IEEE Conference on Computer Vision and Pattern Recognition, pp. 4040–4048 (2016)

28. Mur-Artal, R., Montiel, J.M.M., Tardos, J.D.: ORB-SLAM: a versatile and accurate monocular slam system. IEEE Trans. Rob. **31**(5), 1147–1163 (2015)

29. Newcombe, R.A., Lovegrove, S.J., Davison, A.J.: DTAM: dense tracking and mapping in real-time. In: 2011 IEEE International Conference on Computer Vision (ICCV), pp. 2320–2327. IEEE (2011)

30. Pang, J., Sun, W., Ren, J., Yang, C., Yan, Q.: Cascade residual learning: a two-stage convolutional neural network for stereo matching. In: International Conference on Computer Vision-Workshop on Geometry Meets Deep Learning (ICCVW 2017), vol. 3 (2017)

31. Russakovsky, O., et al.: ImageNet large scale visual recognition challenge. Int. J. Comput. Vis. (IJCV) **115**(3), 211–252 (2015). https://doi.org/10.1007/s11263-015-0816-y

32. Saxena, A., Chung, S.H., Ng, A.Y.: Learning depth from single monocular images. In: Advances in Neural Information Processing Systems, pp. 1161–1168 (2006)

33. Saxena, A., Chung, S.H., Ng, A.Y.: 3-d depth reconstruction from a single still image. Int. J. Comput. Vis. **76**(1), 53–69 (2008)

34. Saxena, A., Sun, M., Ng, A.Y.: Make3D: learning 3D scene structure from a single still image. IEEE Trans. Pattern Anal. Mach. Intell. **31**(5), 824–840 (2009)

35. Scharstein, D., Szeliski, R.: A taxonomy and evaluation of dense two-frame stereo correspondence algorithms. Int. J. Comput. Vis. **47**(1–3), 7–42 (2002)

36. Simonyan, K., Zisserman, A.: Very deep convolutional networks for large-scale image recognition. CoRR arXiv:1409.1556 (2014)

37. Sun, J., Zheng, N.N., Shum, H.Y.: Stereo matching using belief propagation. IEEE Trans. Pattern Anal. Mach. Intell. **25**(7), 787–800 (2003)

38. Tao, M.W., Hadap, S., Malik, J., Ramamoorthi, R.: Depth from combining defocus and correspondence using light-field cameras. In: 2013 IEEE International Conference on Computer Vision (ICCV), pp. 673–680. IEEE (2013)

39. Tonioni, A., Poggi, M., Mattoccia, S., Di Stefano, L.: Unsupervised adaptation for deep stereo. In: Proceedings of the IEEE Conference on Computer Vision and Pattern Recognition, pp. 1605–1613 (2017)

40. Torr, P.H.S., Zisserman, A.: Feature based methods for structure and motion estimation. In: Triggs, B., Zisserman, A., Szeliski, R. (eds.) IWVA 1999. LNCS, vol. 1883, pp. 278–294. Springer, Heidelberg (2000). https://doi.org/10.1007/3-540-44480-7_19

41. Ummenhofer, B., et al.: DeMoN: depth and motion network for learning monocular stereo. In: IEEE Conference on Computer Vision and Pattern Recognition (CVPR), vol. 5 (2017)

42. Vijayanarasimhan, S., Ricco, S., Schmid, C., Sukthankar, R., Fragkiadaki, K.: SfM-Net: learning of structure and motion from video. arXiv preprint arXiv:1704.07804 (2017)

43. Wang, C., Buenaposada, J.M., Zhu, R., Lucey, S.: Learning depth from monocular videos using direct methods. arXiv preprint arXiv:1712.00175 (2017)

44. Wu, C., et al.: VisualSFM: a visual structure from motion system (2011)

45. Xu, D., Ricci, E., Ouyang, W., Wang, X., Sebe, N.: Multi-scale continuous CRFs as sequential deep networks for monocular depth estimation. In: Proceedings of CVPR (2017)

46. Yang, Q., Wang, L., Ahuja, N.: A constant-space belief propagation algorithm for stereo matching. In: 2010 IEEE Conference on Computer Vision and Pattern Recognition (CVPR), pp. 1458–1465. IEEE (2010)
47. Yang, Z., Wang, P., Xu, W., Zhao, L., Nevatia, R.: Unsupervised learning of geometry with edge-aware depth-normal consistency. arXiv preprint arXiv:1711.03665 (2017)
48. Zbontar, J., LeCun, Y.: Computing the stereo matching cost with a convolutional neural network. In: Proceedings of the IEEE Conference on Computer Vision and Pattern Recognition, pp. 1592–1599 (2015)
49. Zhou, C., Zhang, H., Shen, X., Jia, J.: Unsupervised learning of stereo matching. In: Proceedings of the IEEE Conference on Computer Vision and Pattern Recognition, pp. 1567–1575 (2017)
50. Zhou, T., Brown, M., Snavely, N., Lowe, D.G.: Unsupervised learning of depth and ego-motion from video. In: CVPR, vol. 2, p. 7 (2017)

Video Object Segmentation by Learning Location-Sensitive Embeddings

Hai Ci[1](✉), Chunyu Wang[2], and Yizhou Wang[1,3]

[1] EECS, Peking University, Beijing, China
{cihai,yizhou.wang}@pku.edu.cn
[2] Microsoft Research Asia, Beijing, China
chnuwa@microsoft.com
[3] Deepwise AI Lab, Beijing, China

Abstract. We address the problem of video object segmentation which outputs the masks of a target object throughout a video given only a bounding box in the first frame. There are two main challenges to this task. First, the background may contain similar objects as the target. Second, the appearance of the target object may change drastically over time. To tackle these challenges, we propose an end-to-end training network which accomplishes foreground predictions by leveraging the location-sensitive embeddings which are capable to distinguish the pixels of similar objects. To deal with appearance changes, for a test video, we propose a robust model adaptation method which pre-scans the whole video, generates pseudo foreground/background labels and retrains the model based on the labels. Our method outperforms the state-of-the-art methods on the DAVIS and the SegTrack v2 datasets.

Keywords: Video object segmentation
Location-sensitive embeddings

1 Introduction

Video Object Segmentation (VOS) [3,6,16,17,24,31] is an important problem in video understanding which estimates the masks of an object in a video given the masks in the first frame. The estimated masks can be used by higher level applications such as video editing. If only a bounding box of which object to segment is provided for the first frame, we denote the task as Box-based Video Object Segmentation (BVOS). Compared to VOS, BVOS provides an easier interface for users because it doesn't require cumbersome labelings.

BVOS is related to foreground extraction (FE) [2,27] in static images which extracts the mask of the foreground object in a complex environment. The target of FE is to minimize the interactive efforts on the part of users. If only a bounding box of the foreground object is provided, it is similar to BVOS except that BVOS also needs to extract foreground masks for the consecutive frames without

© Springer Nature Switzerland AG 2018
V. Ferrari et al. (Eds.): ECCV 2018, LNCS 11215, pp. 524–539, 2018.
https://doi.org/10.1007/978-3-030-01252-6_31

bounding boxes. BVOS is also related to object tracking [1,14] which aims to localize the target object by bounding boxes in a video. In contrast, BVOS needs to generate sharp foreground masks.

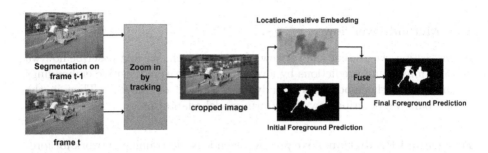

Fig. 1. The pipeline of the proposed method. (1) Based on the segmentation results of the previous frame, the method first zooms in to the probable foreground region by cropping and resizing in the current image. (2) The cropped image is fed to a network to predict the location-sensitive embeddings and initial foreground predictions. (3) The embeddings are fused with the foreground predictions to obtain final segmentation.

The FE methods such as [2,27] model foreground and background distributions by low level features. For many cases, they can give satisfying results. But as shown in their work, failures may occur when the foreground and background have low contrast. This is because these methods use low level features and lack high level understandings of objects.

Recently, convolutional neural networks have demonstrated outstanding performance in many areas of computer vision. In particular, it is shown in [5,21] that the pixel-wise semantic segmentation can be achieved by Fully Convolutional Networks (FCN) which are robust to appearance variations. The success inspires [12] to estimate the (dominant) foreground pixels directly from a detected image patch which tightly contains the object.

In VOS, the authors in [3] propose to estimate the foreground pixels in an image without first detecting the object. Since the target object may not be dominant in the image, this is more difficult than estimating from patches [12]. They [3] propose to retrain the model based on the first frame of the video, which helps to learn the specific features of the target object and alleviate this problem. However, this model has limited power to distinguish the objects of the same class especially when new objects enter the scene. The main reason is that the first frame lacks sufficient negative training data, i.e., the other objects of the same class.

Another challenge in VOS is that the appearance of the target object may vary drastically over time, for example, due to scale changes, occlusions and viewpoint changes. The authors in [30] propose to update their model in an online manner where the estimated foreground/background pixels in the current frame are used to retrain the network before applying to the following frame.

This enables the network to adapt to the new features in the video sequence. However, it is a challenge for the method to choose the appropriate pixels and the predicted labels for finetuning the network as erroneous labels may mislead the network to learn wrong features.

1.1   Method Overview

In this section, we present an overview of our approach. We first describe how we perform foreground predictions by leveraging the location-sensitive embeddings assuming that the model has already been learned or adapted. Then in the second part, we describe how to perform model adaptation.

Foreground Predictions. We present an end-to-end training network for foreground predictions which leverages location-sensitive embeddings (LSEs) to distinguish the pixels of different objects. The framework is shown in Fig. 1. First, given a bounding box in the previous frame (obtained from foreground predictions), we first zoom in to the highly probable foreground region in the current frame in order to improve the predictions for small objects. Then the cropped image is fed to a fully convolutional network to generate foreground predictions and location-sensitive embeddings. Finally, the two branches are combined to generate the final foreground predictions.

The LSEs are targetted to distinguish objects with similar appearance. We learn the embeddings by an FCN network aiming that the pixels of the same object are pushed closer and those of different objects are pulled further. Since FCN is translation invariant, it is not trivial to learn distinct embeddings for very similar objects in different locations of an image. So we propose to jointly regress the center of the object to which the pixel belongs. By fusing the appearance and location features, we obtain LSEs with improved discriminative power. Different from foreground predictions, the LSEs can be learned on the large scale static image datasets and transferred to the video segmentation dataset.

Model Adaptation. Adapting the model to the consecutive frames of a video is important. To robustly adapt the model, we propose an approach which scans a video twice and adapts the model once. In the first scan, we obtain coarse object segmentations which are used as pseudo-labels to retrain the network. The retrained model will be applied to each frame without adaptation any more. This alleviates the problem of error accumulation which is common for online update. Note that a very small portion of erroneous labels would not significantly degrade the performance of the network. The method is simple and has few hyperparameters to tune. But it outperforms the state-of-the-arts on two datasets.

2   Related Work

On Feature Embeddings. Learning embeddings resembles a particular type of clustering methods where the pixels of the same label are pushed closer and those of different labels are pulled apart. This has been extensively explored in the area of clustering [28], human pose estimation [23], segmentation [11] and instance segmentation [4,8].

In [28], the authors propose to embed a face image into a vector (on a unit sphere). The training data are in the form of triplets where the distance between a positive pair is smaller than that of a negative pair by a margin. Then the authors in [8,20] extend the work to learn pixel-wise embeddings for instance segmentation. They use the embeddings to group the pixels into segments which are postprocessed for instance segmentation. The differences between our work and [8,20] are two folds. First, our embeddings are location sensitive, which provide enhanced power to distinguish very similar objects in different locations. To the best of our knowledge, this hasn't been explored before. Second, we combine the embeddings with foreground predictions in an end-to-end way, rather than using the embeddings as postprocessing.

On Model Update. Online model adaptation has been extensively studied for bounding box level tracking [9,18,26]. But the online adaptation for pixel level models has been rarely touched. In [30], the authors select the pixels for which the predicted foreground probability exceeds a certain threshold as positive examples. The negative examples are carefully selected to be those which are very far away (based on a threshold) from the last predicted object mask. The reason for applying such a complex rule-based selection method is that the erroneous supervisions may bias the network to learn wrong features. The online adaptation method differs from ours in that they update the model at each time step. In contrast, we update the model only once which is more robust to small portions of inaccurate supervisions and less dependent on parameter choices.

3   Location-Sensitive Embeddings

The LSE of a pixel not only relies on its appearance but also relies on its spatial location relative to the object it belongs to. This allows the embedding to distinguish very similar objects in different locations. We jointly learn the appearance embedding x_i and location embedding l_i for each pixel p_i which are fused to generate location-sensitive embeddings.

Denote the instance labels for the two pixels p_i and p_j as y_i and y_j, respectively. If p_i and p_j are from the same instance, then $y_i = y_j$. Denote the location embeddings for the two pixels as l_i and l_j, respectively. A location embedding l_i encodes the spatial offset between the pixel and the center of the object to which the pixel belongs. In addition, $c_i = l_i + p_i$ gives the object center where p_i presents the pixel location in the image in this context. We can imagine that c_i is the same as c_j if two pixels belong to the same object.

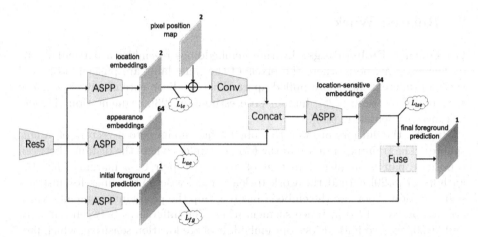

Fig. 2. The figure shows the overall network structure of the proposed method. *ASPP* represents the Atrous Spatial Pyramid Pooling layer introduced in [5].

We propose to jointly learn the appearance and location embeddings, which are fused to generate LSEs. In the following subsections, we will introduce the details for learning appearance and location embeddings.

3.1 Appearance Embeddings

If two pixels are from the same object in an image, they form a positive training pair. Otherwise, they form a negative training pair. The appearance embedding branch is the same as [8]. We measure the similarity between two appearance embeddings x_i and x_j using the following similarity: $s_{i,j} = \frac{2}{1+\exp(\|x_i-x_j\|_2^2)}$.

The goal is to learn an embedding so that the pixels of the same object $(y_i = y_j)$ have similar embeddings $(s_{i,j} = 1)$. To avoid a trivial solution where all the embeddings are the same, we use an additional term which requires that the embeddings of different objects $(y_i \neq y_j)$ are far apart. The total loss over all pairs and training images is:

$$L_{ae} = -\frac{1}{|S|} \sum_{i,j \in S} \omega_{ij}[1_{\{y_i=y_j\}}\log(s(i,j)) + 1_{\{y_i \neq y_j\}}\log(1 - s(i,j))] \qquad (1)$$

where S is the set of the selected training positive and negative pairs. Involving all pixels of an image for loss computation is not practical due to the limitations in GPU memories. We randomly choose K pixels for each object instance in the image. ω_{ij} is the weight for that particular pair which is set to be a value inversely proportional to the size of the instance which the pixels belong to. This is to guarantee that the loss will not ignore the small instances.

3.2 Location Embeddings

We measure the distance between the predicted location embedding $\hat{l}_i$ and the groundtruth l_i using Euclidean distance: $d_i = \|l_i - \hat{l}_i\|_2$. Note that adding the location of each pixel p_i to the embedding $c_i = p_i + l_i$ gives the location of the object center. The pixels of the same object have the same c rather than l. But we don't directly estimate c because it is difficult to learn for a fully convolutional network which is translation invariant.

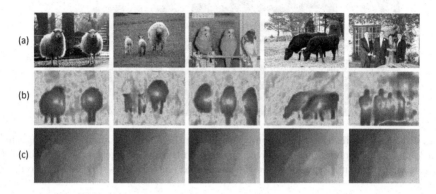

Fig. 3. Sample location embeddings on the PASCAL dataset. (a) shows five challenging test images. (b) shows the magnitude maps of the estimated spatial offsets ($\|l_i\|_2$). Ideally, the values in object centers are zero and increase gradually towards boundary. (c) shows the object center maps c_i. Pixels of the same object should have similar colors and those of different objects should have different colors. (Color figure online)

Loss Function. Different from appearance embeddings, we don't need to construct pairs of data for training because every foreground pixel has a fixed location embedding. The embeddings of background pixels are set to zero during training. The total loss over all training images is:

$$L_{le} = \frac{1}{M} \sum_{k=1}^{M} \frac{1}{U_k} \sum_{i=1}^{U_k} d_i, \tag{2}$$

where M is the number of training images and U_k is the number of non-background pixels in one image. Figure 3 demonstrates several samples for location embeddings.

3.3 Combine Appearance and Location Embeddings for LSEs

We first add a convolution layer to embed the object center map into a higher dimensional space which is then concatenated with the appearance embeddings. The concatenations are fed to an ASPP layer to generate the LSEs. See Fig. 2. We add a loss L_{lse} which is similar to L_{ae} after the outputs of LSEs.

We learn the embeddings by jointly optimizing $L_{em} = L_{ae} + L_{le} + L_{lse}$. We show several LSE examples in Fig. 4. For visualization purposes, we project the 64-dimensional embeddings to RGB space. Similar embeddings are mapped to have similar colors. We can see from the camel and car examples that the method is capable to distinguish the objects of the same class.

Fig. 4. LSEs visualization by randomly projecting the 64-dimensional embeddings into RGB space. The embeddings can preserve the details around edges and can distinguish objects with similar appearance. See the camel and car examples. (Color figure online)

4   Video Object Segmentation Method

The framework of the proposed segmentation method is shown in Fig. 1. First, given the estimated bounding box in the previous frame, we first zoom in to the probable foreground regions in the current frame. Second, the cropped image is fed to a network to generate initial foreground predictions and LSEs which are combined to obtain the foreground.

4.1   Zooming in to See Clearer

The benefits of zooming into a tight region surrounding the object are two folds. First, the target object becomes more dominant. Second, the size of the target object is increased and more details can be preserved which improves the sharpness of the predicted masks.

Since we don't have groundtruth bounding boxes (except for the first frame) for a video, we propose to take advantage of the foreground predictions of the previous frame to coarsely estimate a bounding box for the current frame. Suppose the foreground predictions for frame t are o_t. Then we can get a bounding box $b_t^{(i)}$ by identifying the left/right/top/bottom most foreground pixels. Figure 7 shows some estimated bounding boxes. The estimations generally have high qualities. Then we propagate $b_t^{(i)}$ to frame $t + 1$ as $b_{t+1}^{(p)}$. Considering the objects move smoothly in a video, we simply require $b_{t+1}^{(p)}$ is an enlarged version of $b_t^{(i)}$. It is worth noting that the estimated bounding box is not necessarily very accurate as long as all object pixels are within the box.

We crop frame $t+1$ according to $b_{t+1}^{(p)}$ and resize it to 321×321. After feeding it to the network, we obtain the foreground prediction from which we infer a tight box $b_{t+1}^{(i)}$ and propagate it to frame $t+2$. We repeat the procedure until reaching the last frame.

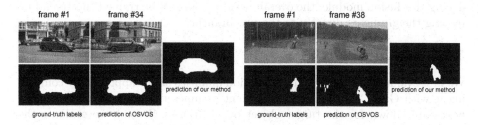

Fig. 5. Example foreground predictions without instance embeddings (OSVOS) and with instance embeddings (our method). Joint learning instance embeddings improves the model's capability to distinguish pixels of different objects.

4.2 Learning Foreground Predictions

Inspired by the previous work of [3,12], we propose to estimate the foreground pixels from an image using a network. Let o_i be the predicted probability or confidence of pixel i being the foreground and z_i be the binary groundtruth foreground label. We use the pixel-wise cross-entropy loss for binary classification which is defined as:

$$L_{fg} = -\sum_{k=1}^{M}\sum_{i=1}^{W_k} \frac{1}{M \times W_k} z_i \log(o_i) + (1 - z_i)\log(1 - o_i) \qquad (3)$$

We jointly learn the foreground predictions and location-sensitive embeddings by summing the two loss functions $L_{em} + L_{fg}$. The joint training enables the network to focus more on the image details which are important to obtain sharp masks and distinguish objects of the same class. In particular, we will show in experiments that the joint training significantly improves the accuracy of the foreground prediction branch.

4.3 Combining Foreground Predictions and Embeddings

In this section, we present a fusion module to combine the LSEs and foreground predictions. We first obtain a set of foreground embeddings $\mathbb{F}$ according to the labels in the foreground predictions. Then we compute a representative r by identifying the median for each dimension of the embeddings in $\mathbb{F}$.

Then for each embedding p, we compute a foreground probability by $\frac{2}{1+\exp^{\|r-p\|_2^2}}$. It is worth noting that the metric was previously used for computing the similarity between two embeddings when optimizing the embedding loss. So it is favorable to use the same metric here because it is suitable to the distributions of the learned embeddings. If an embedding has large distance with the representative, it is less likely to be a foreground pixel. Finally, after getting the foreground map from the embeddings, we compute the average of the two foreground predictions as the fused results. It is worth noting that, after introducing this fusion module, the overall network can still be trained end-to-end by passing the gradients directly to the two branches.

5   Experiments

We first evaluate the foreground extraction qualities of our approach by comparing it with GrabCut [27]. The experiment assumes the groundtruth bounding boxes are known for the target object on all frames. Second, we evaluate the proposed method for video object segmentation where only a bounding box in the first frame is known. We perform extensive ablation studies to evaluate the influences of each component and compare with the state-of-the-arts.

5.1   Dataset

The DAVIS dataset [25] consists of 50 high quality videos and 3455 frames. The dense foreground annotations are provided for each frame. We test our approach on the validation set as most of the previous work. The SegTrack-v2 dataset consists of 14 videos with 24 objects and 947 frames. The dense annotations are provided for the foreground object. Different from the DAVIS dataset, they provide instance annotations for images with multiple objects. Following [24], each object is treated as a separate target to segment.

On DAVIS, we use the officially provided measures to evaluate the segmentation result: region similarity $\mathcal{J}$ and contour accuracy $(\mathcal{F})$. The region similarity $\mathcal{J}$ is defined as the intersection-over-union of the estimated mask and the groundtruth mask. In particular, given an estimated mask M and the corresponding ground-truth mask G, it is defined as $\mathcal{J} = \frac{M \cap G}{M \cup G}$. The contour accuracy $\mathcal{F}$ interprets M as a set of closed contours $c(M)$ delimiting the spatial extent of the mask. The contour-based precision P_c and recall R_c between the contour points of $c(M)$ and $c(G)$ are computed by morphology operators. The contour accuracy reflects the sharpness of the extracted masks. Please refer to [25] for the precise definitions. On SegTrack-v2 we use $\mathcal{J}$ as our measure.

5.2   Implementation Details

Network. Our model is based on the semantic segmentation network DeepLab [5] which is based on the ResNet-101 [13]. The atrous spatial pyramid pooling (ASPP) layer is extensively used in our model which shows better performance in capturing the details than using a single convolution. In particular, we use the ASPP layer to predict location embeddings, appearance embeddings and foreground probability, respectively, as shown in Fig. 2. To get the object center map, we add the pixel coordinates to the predicted location embedding vectors for each pixel. The center map is fed to a 1 × 1 convolution layer and then concatenated with the 64-channel appearance embeddings. The concatenations are fed to another ASPP layer to obtain the location sensitive embeddings.

Training. We pretrain our network on the augmented PASCAL VOC2012 segmentation dataset [7,10]. There are three training stages: (1) we first jointly train the location embedding and appearance embedding branches ($L_{ae} + L_{le}$) for $20K$ iterations. The batchsize and learning rate are set to be 7 and $1.5e^{-4}$, respectively. We scale the location embedding with a factor of $1/321$. (2) then we fix the two branches and train the following layers associated with LSE (L_{lse}). The parameters are set to be the same as step (1). (3) finally, we jointly train the whole network, including the foreground predictions and the LSEs, with a smaller learning rate of $1e^{-4}$.

For a test video, we also train our model on the first frame. Given the bounding box, we directly apply the pretrained model to the corresponding region and obtain a set of highly confident (≥ 0.6) foreground pixels. The pixels outside the bounding box are the background pixels. We retrain our model based on these pseudo-labels for 20 epochs with the learning rate of $2.5e^{-5}$.

5.3   Foreground Extraction

Since the core of our approach is to predict the foreground pixels from an image, it is natural to compare with the classic FE method GrabCut [27]. We assume the bounding boxes of the target in every frame are known and extract the foreground masks. The results are shown in Table 1.

Table 1. Foreground extraction results on the DAVIS dataset

	Measure	GrabCut [27]	FP	Ours
$\mathcal{J}$	Mean M ↑	61.5	80.4	80.9
	Recall O ↑	73.4	96.3	96.7
	Decay D ↓	1.3	3.1	2.1
$\mathcal{F}$	Mean M ↑	59.0	80.2	80.8
	Recall O ↑	72.8	90.6	90.2
	Decay D ↓	3.7	3.1	1.3

We propose a baseline *FP* which only learns the *F*oreground *P*rediction branch (by minimizing L_{fg} in Fig. 2). This can be regarded as a simplified version of OSVOS [3] without boundary snapping. From the Table 1, we can see that FP significantly outperforms GrabCut in terms of both region similarity and contour accuracy. This is mainly because the FP is based on deep networks which are learned to extract higher level cues of objects which are robust to cluttered backgrounds. In addition, our approach which learns both foreground predictions and LSEs improves over FP by about 0.5. The improvement is marginal because the power of LSE is not fully revealed when groundtruth bounding boxes are known. This is because most background objects have already been suppressed and have negligible influence on the results.

534   H. Ci et al.

Fig. 6. Foreground extraction results on the DAVIS dataset. (a) shows five testing images. (b) shows the results of GrabCut. (c) shows the results of FP. (d) shows the results of our method.

Figure 6 shows some examples from the DAVIS dataset. GrabCut obtains coarse foreground extractions for most cases. This is because GrabCut lacks higher level cues for objects and the performance is degraded when the background is cluttered. In particular, for the dancing and camel examples, it cannot differentiate the background pixels from the foreground objects. The FP method faces a similar problem. See Fig. 6(c). Although it learns the concept of objects by using a deep network, it cannot distinguish objects of the same class with similar appearance. For example, see the background person in a red shirt and the small camel. In contrast, our approach successfully suppresses the background objects by learning the LSEs.

Table 2. Video object segmentation results on the DAVIS dataset

	Measure	FP (no-zoom)	FP	FPLSE	Ours	Ours + CRF	Ours (static)
$\mathcal{J}$	Mean $M \uparrow$	70.5	76.2	80.0	81.0	82.9	80.0
	Recall $O \uparrow$	83.5	90.0	95.6	96.4	96.7	95.6
	Decay $D \downarrow$	9.1	7.0	5.9	5.4	5.4	6.4
$\mathcal{F}$	Mean $M \uparrow$	69.1	75.0	79.1	80.3	80.1	79.6
	Recall $O \uparrow$	77.4	82.2	87.7	89.1	88.9	87.0
	Decay $D \downarrow$	8.2	7.3	5.9	5.7	5.4	6.2

5.4 Ablation Study on Video Object Segmentation

We investigate the influences of different components in our method on the video object segmentation task. We experiment on the DAVIS dataset and report the region similarity and contour accuracy.

Ablation Study on LSEs. We first evaluate the influences of LSEs by designing three baselines. The first baseline FP only learns the foreground prediction branch, which actually is a simplified version of OSVOS [3] without boundary snapping. The second baseline FPLSE jointly learns the foreground prediction branch and the location sensitive embedding branch. But it doesn't fuse the two branches and only uses the foreground prediction branch. The third baseline is our method which fuses the two branches for foreground prediction.

Table 2 shows the results. The baseline FP achieves the mIoU of 76.2 which is similar to the result in [3] without boundary snapping. FPLSE increases the mIoU to 80.0 although we don't fuse the two branches. The reason for the improvement may be because the joint training encourages the network to focus more on the appearance details (which are required for learning LSEs) and strikes a good balance between abstraction (high level cues of objects) and details (low level appearance cues). In addition, the boundary accuracy is improved from 75.0 to 79.1 which indicates the predictions are more precise. Fusing the two branches further improves the accuracy (from 80.0 to 81.0) which demonstrates the effectiveness of learning LSEs. It is worth noting that the fusion is trained end-to-end without manually setting the model parameters.

Table 3 shows an evaluation with respect to different attributes annotated in the DAVIS dataset. We can see that our method has the best performance on most attributes, and it has a significant resilience to these challenges.

Ablation Study on Other Factors. We first evaluate the proposed model adaptation method. We compare with a baseline *Static* which only trains the model on the first frame and doesn't perform adaptation on the video. The results are shown in Table 2. We can see that if we don't perform model adaptation, the mIoU drops from 81.0 to 80.0 due to the degraded power to handle appearance variations. In particular, the boundary recall decreases significantly from 89.1 to 87.0 indicating that, without adaptation, model has degraded capability to generate sharp and accurate masks for the video.

We also evaluate the influences of the zooming in operation. See Table 2. By comparing FP(no-zoom) and FP, we can see that the zooming in operation increases the mIoU by about 5.7. There are two reasons for the improvement. First, zooming in decreases the influence of background objects. Second, zooming in allows the method to capture the finer details of an object.

Table 3. Attribute-based performance: quality of the methods on sequences with a certain attribute. See DAVIS [25] for the meanings of the acronyms

Attribute	OSVOS [3]	Lucid [19]	Ours	FP	FPLSE
AC	0.81	0.74	*0.86*	0.77	0.83
BC	*0.83*	*0.83*	*0.83*	0.78	0.81
DB	0.74	0.51	*0.75*	0.60	0.70
EA	0.77	0.71	*0.80*	0.76	0.78
FM	0.76	0.70	*0.82*	0.74	0.78
HO	0.75	0.75	*0.79*	0.71	0.76
IO	0.75	*0.80*	0.78	0.71	0.74
LR	0.77	0.64	*0.83*	0.79	0.81
OV	0.72	*0.83*	*0.83*	0.70	0.78
ROT	0.81	0.80	*0.87*	0.77	0.84
SC	0.71	*0.74*	*0.74*	0.68	0.70
SV	0.74	0.68	*0.80*	0.73	0.77

Table 4. The state-of-the-art results on the DAVIS dataset

Measure	OnAVOS [30]	OSVOS [3]	Lucid Tracker [19]	Mask Track [24]	Mask RNN [15]	MaskTrack Box [24]	Ours
$\mathcal{J}_M \uparrow$	86.1	79.8	80.5	79.7	80.4	73.7	82.9
$\mathcal{J}_O \uparrow$	96.1	93.6	90.2	93.1	96.0	–	96.7
$\mathcal{J}_D \downarrow$	5.2	14.9	6.1	8.9	4.4	–	5.6
$\mathcal{F}_M \uparrow$	84.9	80.6	77.6	75.4	82.3	–	80.3
$\mathcal{F}_O \uparrow$	89.7	92.6	82	87.1	93.2	–	89.1
$\mathcal{F}_D \downarrow$	5.8	15.0	6.9	9.0	8.8	–	5.7

5.5   Comparison to the State-of-the-Arts

Table 4 compares the proposed method to the state-of-the-arts on the DAVIS dataset. The methods [3, 15, 19, 24, 30] use the precise masks in the first frame as inputs. The MaskTrack-Box method uses only a bounding box in the first frame which is the same as our method.

We can see that our method outperforms most of the state-of-the-arts except [30]. But the method [30] uses additional training dataset from the DAVIS, which according to their experiments, increases the mIoU by about 3. In this case, our result is comparable with [30] although we only use a bounding box as inputs. MaskTrack-Box is one of the state-of-art methods which take a box as input. The result of it is obtained on the train-val dataset without CRF. For fair comparison, we also report the result on this dataset without CRF. The number is 80.7. Its mIoU is about 7.0 lower than that of our method.

Table 5 shows the results on the SegTrack v2 dataset. The methods [15,19, 24] use the precise masks in the first frame as inputs. We can see that our method is comparable to the state-of-the-arts. The core contribution in [19] is the generation of new training data based on the first frame which can also be combined with our method to further improve the performance.

Table 5. The state-of-the-art results on the SegTrack v2 dataset

Method	MaskTrack [24]	OBJFlow [29]	MaskRNN [15]	LucidTracker [19]	BVS [22]	MaskTrack Box [24]	Ours
mIoU	70.3	67.5	72.1	78.0	58.4	62.4	69.7

5.6 Qualitative Evaluation

Figure 7 shows five sample results of our method from the DAVIS and the Seg-Track v2 datasets. We can see that the method deals well with situations such as occlusions, scale changes, cluttered backgrounds, background with the same class of objects as the target. The green rectangles are the estimated bounding boxes for the current frame. We can see that in most cases, the bounding boxes are accurate and tight.

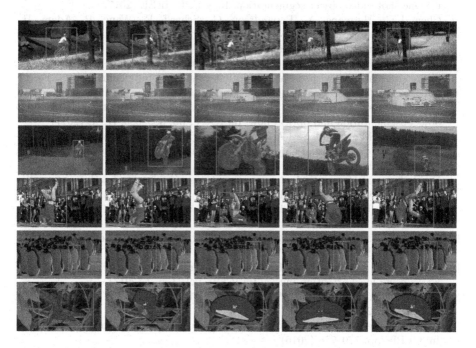

Fig. 7. Sample segmentation results on the DAVIS and the SegTrack v2 datasets. (Color figure online)

6 Conclusion

We present an end-to-end training method for video object segmentation. The main contribution of this work is to propose a method to learn location-sensitive embeddings which have enhanced power to distinguish very similar objects in different locations of an image. We validate the effectiveness of the approach by extensive numerical and qualitative experiments on the DAVIS and SegTrack v2 datasets. The method is simple and has fewer hyperparameters to tune, but it achieves the state-of-the-art performance on the datasets.

Acknowledgements. This work is supported in part by NSFC-61625201, 61527804, 61650202.

References

1. Bertinetto, L., Valmadre, J., Henriques, J.F., Vedaldi, A., Torr, P.H.S.: Fully-convolutional siamese networks for object tracking. In: Hua, G., Jégou, H. (eds.) ECCV 2016. LNCS, vol. 9914, pp. 850–865. Springer, Cham (2016). https://doi.org/10.1007/978-3-319-48881-3_56
2. Boykov, Y.Y., Jolly, M.P.: Interactive graph cuts for optimal boundary & region segmentation of objects in ND images. In: ICCV, vol. 1, pp. 105–112 (2001)
3. Caelles, S., Maninis, K.K., Pont-Tuset, J., Leal-Taixé, L., Cremers, D., Van Gool, L.: One-shot video object segmentation. In: CVPR. IEEE (2017)
4. Chen, L.C., Hermans, A., Papandreou, G., Schroff, F., Wang, P., Adam, H.: MaskLab: instance segmentation by refining object detection with semantic and direction features. arXiv preprint arXiv:1712.04837 (2017)
5. Chen, L.C., Papandreou, G., Kokkinos, I., Murphy, K., Yuille, A.L.: Semantic image segmentation with deep convolutional nets and fully connected CRFs. In: ICLR (2015)
6. Cheng, J., Tsai, Y.H., Wang, S., Yang, M.H.: Segflow: joint learning for video object segmentation and optical flow. In: ICCV, pp. 686–695. IEEE (2017)
7. Everingham, M., Eslami, S.M.A., Van Gool, L., Williams, C.K.I., Winn, J., Zisserman, A.: The pascal visual object classes challenge: a retrospective. IJCV **111**(1), 98–136 (2015)
8. Fathi, A., et al.: Semantic instance segmentation via deep metric learning. arXiv preprint arXiv:1703.10277 (2017)
9. Grabner, H., Bischof, H.: On-line boosting and vision. In: CVPR, vol. 1, pp. 260–267 (2006)
10. Hariharan, B., Arbelaez, P., Bourdev, L., Maji, S., Malik, J.: Semantic contours from inverse detectors. In: ICCV (2011)
11. Harley, A.W., Derpanis, K.G., Kokkinos, I.: Segmentation-aware convolutional networks using local attention masks. In: ICCV, vol. 2, p. 7 (2017)
12. He, K., Gkioxari, G., Dollár, P., Girshick, R.: Mask R-CNN. In: ICCV, pp. 2980–2988. IEEE (2017)
13. He, K., Zhang, X., Ren, S., Sun, J.: Deep residual learning for image recognition. In: CVPR, pp. 770–778 (2016)
14. Henriques, J.F., Caseiro, R., Martins, P., Batista, J.: High-speed tracking with kernelized correlation filters. TPAMI **37**(3), 583–596 (2015)

15. Hu, Y.T., Huang, J.B., Schwing, A.: MaskRNN: instance level video object segmentation. In: NIPS, pp. 324–333 (2017)
16. Jampani, V., Gadde, R., Gehler, P.V.: Video propagation networks. In: Proceedings of the CVPR, vol. 6, p. 7 (2017)
17. Jang, W.D., Kim, C.S.: Online video object segmentation via convolutional trident network. In: CVPR, vol. 1, p. 7 (2017)
18. Kalal, Z., Mikolajczyk, K., Matas, J.: Tracking-learning-detection. TPAMI **34**(7), 1409–1422 (2012)
19. Khoreva, A., Benenson, R., Ilg, E., Brox, T., Schiele, B.: Lucid data dreaming for object tracking. arXiv preprint arXiv:1703.09554 (2017)
20. Li, S., Seybold, B., Vorobyov, A., Fathi, A., Huang, Q., Kuo, C.C.J.: Instance embedding transfer to unsupervised video object segmentation. arXiv preprint arXiv:1801.00908 (2018)
21. Long, J., Shelhamer, E., Darrell, T.: Fully convolutional networks for semantic segmentation. In: CVPR, pp. 3431–3440 (2015)
22. Märki, N., Perazzi, F., Wang, O., Sorkine-Hornung, A.: Bilateral space video segmentation. In: CVPR, pp. 743–751 (2016)
23. Newell, A., Huang, Z., Deng, J.: Associative embedding: end-to-end learning for joint detection and grouping. In: NIPS, pp. 2274–2284 (2017)
24. Perazzi, F., Khoreva, A., Benenson, R., Schiele, B., Sorkine-Hornung, A.: Learning video object segmentation from static images. In: CVPR (2017)
25. Perazzi, F., Pont-Tuset, J., McWilliams, B., Van Gool, L., Gross, M., Sorkine-Hornung, A.: A benchmark dataset and evaluation methodology for video object segmentation. In: CVPR, pp. 724–732 (2016)
26. Ren, X., Malik, J.: Tracking as repeated figure/ground segmentation. In: CVPR, pp. 1–8 (2007)
27. Rother, C., Kolmogorov, V., Blake, A.: GrabCut: interactive foreground extraction using iterated graph cuts. ACM Trans. Graph. (TOG) **23**, 309–314 (2004)
28. Schroff, F., Kalenichenko, D., Philbin, J.: FaceNet: a unified embedding for face recognition and clustering. In: CVPR, pp. 815–823 (2015)
29. Tsai, Y.H., Yang, M.H., Black, M.J.: Video segmentation via object flow. In: CVPR, pp. 3899–3908 (2016)
30. Voigtlaender, P., Leibe, B.: Online adaptation of convolutional neural networks for video object segmentation. In: BMVC (2017)
31. Xiao, F., Jae Lee, Y.: Track and segment: an iterative unsupervised approach for video object proposals. In: CVPR, pp. 933–942 (2016)

DPP-Net: Device-Aware Progressive Search for Pareto-Optimal Neural Architectures

Jin-Dong Dong[1]([✉]), An-Chieh Cheng[1]([✉]), Da-Cheng Juan[2]([✉]), Wei Wei[2]([✉]), and Min Sun[1]([✉])

[1] National Tsing -Hua University, Hsinchu, Taiwan
mark840205@gmail.com, anjiezheng@gapp.nthu.edu.tw, sunmin@ee.nthu.edu.tw
[2] Google, Mountain View, CA, USA
{dacheng,wewei}@google.com

Abstract. Recent breakthroughs in Neural Architectural Search (NAS) have achieved state-of-the-art performances in applications such as image classification and language modeling. However, these techniques typically ignore device-related objectives such as inference time, memory usage, and power consumption. Optimizing neural architecture for device-related objectives is immensely crucial for deploying deep networks on portable devices with limited computing resources. We propose DPP-Net: Device-aware Progressive Search for Pareto-optimal Neural Architectures, optimizing for both device-related (e.g., inference time and memory usage) and device-agnostic (e.g., accuracy and model size) objectives. DPP-Net employs a compact search space inspired by current state-of-the-art mobile CNNs, and further improves search efficiency by adopting progressive search (Liu et al. 2017). Experimental results on CIFAR-10 are poised to demonstrate the effectiveness of Pareto-optimal networks found by DPP-Net, for three different devices: (1) a workstation with Titan X GPU, (2) NVIDIA Jetson TX1 embedded system, and (3) mobile phone with ARM Cortex-A53. Compared to CondenseNet and NASNet (Mobile), DPP-Net achieves better performances: higher accuracy & shorter inference time on various devices. Additional experimental results show that models found by DPP-Net also achieve considerably-good performance on ImageNet as well.

Keywords: Architecture search · Multi-objective optimization

1 Introduction

Deep Neural Networks (DNNs) have demonstrated impressive performance on many machine-learning tasks such as image recognition [2], speech recognition [3], and language modeling [4]. Despite the great successes achieved by DNNs, crafting neural architectures is usually a manual, time-consuming process that requires profound domain knowledge. Recently, automating neural architecture

© Springer Nature Switzerland AG 2018
V. Ferrari et al. (Eds.): ECCV 2018, LNCS 11215, pp. 540–555, 2018.
https://doi.org/10.1007/978-3-030-01252-6_32

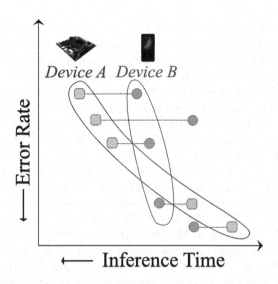

Fig. 1. Different devices share different Pareto-Optimality. An optimal point on Device A's Pareto front may not lie on Device B's Pareto front. Given multiple device-related (e.g., inference time and memory usage) and device-agnostic (e.g., accuracy and model size) objectives. Our DPP-Net can efficiently find various network architectures at the Pareto-front for the corresponding device.

search (NAS) has drawn lots of attention from both industry and academia [5,6]. Approaches for NAS can mainly be categorized into two branches: based on Reinforcement Learning (RL) [6–10] or Genetic Algorithm (GA) [11–14]. There are also works not based on RL or GA, such as [15], achieving comparable performance by using other efficient search algorithms. However, most of these works mentioned above focus on optimizing one single objective (e.g., accuracy), and other objectives have been largely ignored, especially thoses related to devices (e.g., latency).

On the other hand, while designing complex, sophisticated architectures have already been treated more like an art than science, searching for neural architectures optimized for multiple objectives has posed an even more significant challenge. To this end, new architectures leveraging novel operations [16–18] have been developed to achieve higher computing efficiency than conventional convolution. Not surprisingly, designing such architectures requires, again, profound domain knowledge and much effort. Therefore, how to automatically search for network architectures jointly considering high accuracy and other objectives (e.g., inference time, model size, etc. to conforms to device-related constraints) remains a critical yet less addressed question. To the best of our knowledge, there is one previous work [19] that searches network architectures by considering both accuracy and inference time. Nevertheless, the computational power required during training by their algorithm is very significant, and their search space is naively small.

We propose *DPP-Net*: *D*evice-aware *P*rogressive Search for *P*areto-optimal Neural Architectures given multiple device-related (e.g., inference time and memory usage) and device-agnostic (e.g., accuracy and model size) objectives. It is an efficient search algorithm to find various network architectures at the Pareto-front (Fig. 1) in the multiple objectives space to explore the trade-off among these objectives. In this way, a deep learning practitioner can select the best architecture under the specific use case. We define our search space by taking inspirations from state-of-the-art handcrafted mobile CNNs, which is more compact and efficient comparing to usual NAS architectures. For search efficiency, we have also adopted the progressive search strategy used in [15] to speed up the search process. Experimental results on CIFAR-10 demonstrate that DPP-Net can find various Pareto-optimal networks on three devices: (1) a workstation with Titan X GPU, (2) NVIDIA Jetson TX1 embedded system, and (3) a mobile phone with ARM Cortex-A53. Most importantly, DPP-Net achieves better performances in both (a) higher accuracy and (b) shorter inference time, comparing to the state-of-the-art CondenseNet on three devices. Finally, our searched DPP-Net achieves considerably good performance on ImageNet as well.

2 Related Work

Recent advancements on neural architecture search can be classified into three basic categories: Reinforcement Learning (RL) based approaches, Genetic Algorithm (GA) based ones and the third category of methods that involve optimization techniques other than those two. In addition to architecture search techniques, we will also focus on those methods that work on multiple objectives.

RL-Based Approach. Seminal work by [6] proposed "Neural Architecture Search (NAS)" using REINFORCE algorithm [20] to learn a network architecture called "controller" RNN that generates a sequence of actions representing the architecture of a CNN. Classification accuracies of the generated bypass CNN models on a validation dataset are used as rewards for the controller. NASNet [9] further improves NAS by replacing REINFORCE with proximal policy-optimization (PPO) [21] and search architectures of a "block" which repeatedly concatenated itself to form a complete model. This techniques has not only reduced the search space but also managed to incorporate empirical knowledge when designing a CNN. Other works in the field including approach used in [22] which searches model architectures by manipulating the depth of the width of the layers using policy gradient, and the methods proposed by [8,10] which search network architectures using Q-learning. A concurrent work [7] proposed a model to force all child networks to share weights, which largely reduced the computational costs needed to search in a space as defined by [9].

GA-Based Approach. Except for RL-based methods, Genetic Algorithm based methods [11–13] are also popular in architecture search research. One of the recent work in this field [14] achieves state-of-the-art performance on CIFAR-10 image classification task over RL-based method.

Other Approaches. Methods using either RL-based or GA-based algorithm usually requires a significant amount of computational power and are therefore infeasible in certain situations. Many approaches are proposed to specifically address this issue by proposing their search strategies that cannot be categories using methods that belong to the previous two families. [5] use Monte Carlo Tree Search (MCTS) to search through the space of CNN architectures in a shallow-to-deep manner and randomly select which branch to expand at each node. A sequential Model-based Optimization (SMBO) [23] that learns a predictive model is further adopted to help the decision making of node expansion. [15] also use SMBO as the search algorithm and have achieved comparable performance to NASNet using significantly less computational resources while operated on the same search space. [24] proposed to predict performance to reduce the effort of searching model architectures. A concurrent work [25] proposed to train a network to predict the weights of another network and combine this method with random search to search for good candidate models. Despite the small number of resources required in each search, the performance of the model is hard to compete with state-of-the-art approaches.

Architecture Search with Multiple Objectives. All the previously mentioned works focus on searching models that achieve highest performance (e.g.classification accuracy) regardless of the model complexity. [19] proposed to treat neural network architecture search as a multi-objective optimization task and adopt an evolutionary algorithm to search models with two objectives, run-time speed, and classification accuracy. However, the performances of the searched models are not comparable to handcrafted small CNNs, and the numbers of GPUs they required are enormous.

Handcrafted Models with Multiple Objectives. The machine learning and computer vision community are rich in handcrafted neural architectures. Here we will list some of the most recent work that involves multiple objectives. [16] and ShuffleNet [17] have utilized depth-wise convolution and largely reduced computational resources required but remained comparably accurate. However, the real-world implementation of depth-wise convolution in most of the deep learning framework have not reached the theoretical efficiency and results in much inferior inference time. CondenseNet [18] proposed to use a group convolution [2] variant in order to achieve state-of-the-art computational efficiency.

3   Search Architecture

In Fig. 2 we illustrate the overall architectures. We repeat an identical "cell" (Dense Cell) numerous of times following the connecting rules of CondenseNet [18]. We take inspirations from CondenseNet, which optimizes both classification

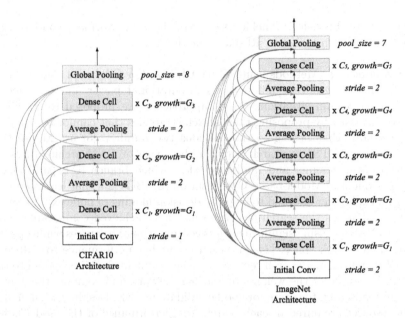

Fig. 2. Network architecture for CIFAR-10 and ImageNet. Our final network structure is fully specified by defining the Dense Cell topology. The number of Dense Cell repetitions C and the growth rate G are different for CIFAR-10 and ImageNet architecture. Note that in ImageNet Architecture we set the stride value of initial convolution 2 and the pool size in global pooling to 7 due to the scale of the input image.

accuracy and inference speed for mobile devices. The feature maps are directly connected even with different resolution and the growth rate is doubled whenever the size of the feature maps reduces. The strategy to make fully dense connections encourage feature re-use and the exponentially increased growth rate reduces computational costs. These characteristics are beneficial when deploying models on energy constrained devices. As we conduct our searching on CIFAR-10, transferring the searched model to ImageNet, requires more stride 2 pooling layers and Dense Cells since the size of the input images (224×224) is way larger than CIFAR10 (32×32). Finally, a global average pooling layer is appended to the last Dense Cell to obtain the final output.

The overall architectures (e.g., how many cells are connected, initial output feature map size, growth rate) are fixed before searching, the only component we are going to search is the cell structure, this idea follows the heuristics of searching for a "block" similar to [9,15]. Each cell to be searched consists of multiple layers of two types - normalization (Norm) and convolutional (Conv) layers. We progressively add layers following the Norm-Conv-Norm-Conv order (Fig. 3(a)-Right). The operations available for Norm (yellow boxes) and Conv (green boxes) layers are shown in the left and right column below, respectively:

1. Batch Normalization + Relu
2. Batch Normalization
3. No op (Identity)

1. 1×1 Convolution
2. 3×3 Convolution
3. 1×1 Group Convolution
4. 3×3 Group Convolution
5. 1×1 Learned Group Convolution
6. 3×3 Depth-wise Convolution

DPP-Net	DenseNet	MobileNet	CondenseNet	ShuffleNet
Norm	BN-Relu	3x3 DWConv	BN-Relu	1x1 GConv
Conv	1x1 Conv	BN-Relu	1x1 LGConv	BN-Relu
Norm	BN-Relu	1x1 Conv	BN-Relu	3x3 DWConv
Conv	3x3 Conv	BN-Relu	3x3 GConv	BN
•				1x1 GConv
•				BN-Relu

(a)   (b)

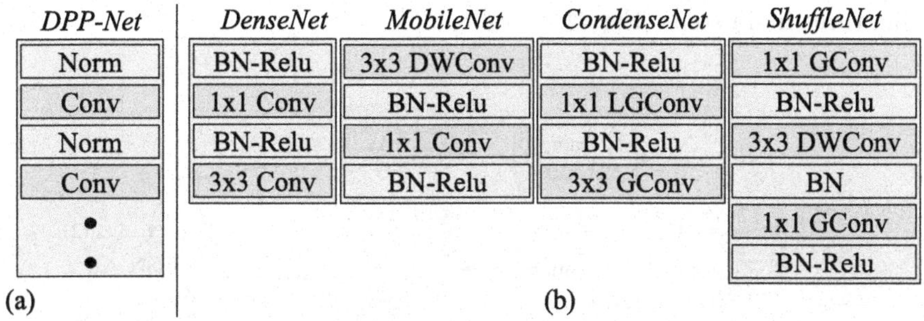

Fig. 3. Search Space Design. Panel (a): We show the cell structure of our DPP-Net. Panel (b): cells of efficient CNNs. BN, DW, LG, G stands for Batch Norm, Depth-wise, Learned Group, Group, respectively. All the group convolutions are implicitly followed by channel shuffle operation. (Color figure online)

4   Search Space

Our search space covers well-designed efficient operations (e.g., Depth-wise Convolution [26], Learned Group Convolution [18]) to take advantages of empirical knowledge when designing efficient CNNs. This not only ensures the robustness and efficiency of our searched architectures but also reduces the training time of the searched model, therefore reduce the search time as well. Finally, the block of other efficient CNNs, e.g., MobileNet [16], ShuffleNet [17] are also shown in Fig. 3(b) for a more thorough comparison.

We now measure the complexity of our search space to have an intuition of the size of the search problem. For a ℓ-layer cell, the total number of possible cell structures is $O_0 \times O_1 \times ... \times O_i \times ... \times O_\ell$ where $O_i = |Norm|$ if i mod $2 = 0$ or $O_i = |Conv|$. As shown above, the number of operations in the Norm set is 3 and the number of operations in the Conv set is 6. Therefore, a 3-layer cell structure has $3 \times 6 \times 3 = 54$ possibilities, a 4-layer cell will have $54 \times 6 = 324$ possible structures. As the number of layer increases, it is hardly pragmatic to train all the architectures. This search space is undersized comparing to the search space of [9,15] because we discarded the operations that are rarely used in modern mobile CNNs and we do not need to search for which layer to connect to. Nevertheless, this search space is still versatile enough to cover a wide variety of possible mobile models.

5   Search Algorithm

5.1   Overview

Many architecture search approaches intuitively search on the complete search space which requires significant computing power. Inspired by [15], which progressively search the architectures from a small search space to a large one, we adopt Sequential Model-Based Optimization ([23]) algorithm to navigate through the search space efficiently. Our search algorithm consists of the following three main steps (Fig. 4).

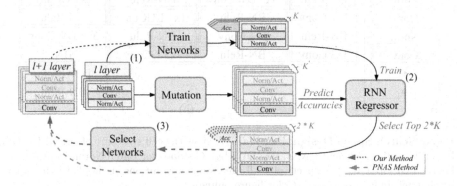

Fig. 4. Flow Diagram of Our Search Algorithm. We adopt Sequential Model-Based Optimization [23] algorithm to search efficiently with the following three steps: **(1) Train and Mutation, (2) Update and Inference,** and **(3) Model Selection.** Note that ℓ is the layers in a cell, K is the number of models to train, and K' is the number of models after *Mutation*.

1. **Train and Mutation.** In this stage, we train K ℓ-layer models and acquire their accuracies after N epochs. Meanwhile, for each ℓ-layer model, we mutate it and acquire a $\ell + 1$-layer model by exploring all possible combinations. Assuming that we have K models before mutation, the number of models after mutation K' process will be the following.

$$K' = \begin{cases} K \times |Norm|, & \text{if } \ell + 1 \bmod 2 = 0 \\ K \times |Conv|, & \text{otherwise} \end{cases} \tag{1}$$

2. **Update and Inference.** In **Train and Mutation** step, the algorithm will generate a large number of candidate models that are usually beyond our ability to evaluate. We use a surrogate function to predict the networks' accuracies with the given architectures. The surrogate function is updated with the evaluation accuracies (output) and the architectures (inputs) of the K ℓ-layer models from the **Train and Mutation** step. After the surrogate function is updated, we predict the accuracies of the mutated $\ell + 1$-layer models. Using a surrogate function avoids time-consuming training to obtain true accuracy of a network with only a slight drawback of regression error.

3. **Model Selection.** There are two ways we can select $\ell + 1$-layers models.

PNAS Method. [15] adopted the SMBO algorithm to search for block architectures of increasing complexity. During the search process, SMBO simply selects top K performing models based on predicted accuracies. This approach is inconsiderate of the heterogeneity of real-world portable device, which is only equipped with limited power supply.

Our Method. Our method considers not only the accuracy of the models but also the device-aware characteristics. Those characteristics include QoS (Quality of Service) and hardware requirements (e.g., memory size), which are critical metrics to be considered on mobile and embedded devices. Given the device we are searching on, multiple hard constraints μ and soft constraints ξ are set. A hard constraint μ is considered to be the minimal requirement of the model. A model that does not meet the hard constraint will be removed from the candidate list. On the other hand, a soft constraint ξ is treated as one of the objectives to be optimized which will be eventually selected using Pareto Optimality selection.

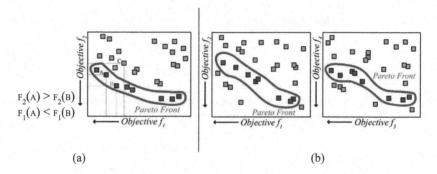

(a)   (b)

Fig. 5. A symbolic figure for Pareto Optimality. Panel (a) illustrates an example of two objectives Pareto front. Every box represents a feasible choice. In this case, our goal is to minimize both objectives. Since box C is dominated by both box A and box B, it is not on the Pareto front. While box A and box B both lie on the front because none of them dominated another. Panel (b) demonstrates that when the number of objectives is more than two, the Pareto front becomes more complicated.

5.2 Pareto Optimality

Since we are optimizing the problem using multiple objectives, no single solution will optimize each objective simultaneously and compromises will have to be made. We treat neural network architecture search as a multi-objective optimization problem and use Pareto Optimality over a set of pre-defined objectives to select models. Using Pareto Optimization, it is likely that there exists a number of optimal solutions. A solution is said to be Pareto optimal if none of the objectives can be improved without worsening some of the other objectives, and the solutions achieve Pareto-optimality are said to be in the Pareto front.

5.3   Surrogate Function

To accurately predict the classification accuracy of an architecture, a surrogate function is used. The surrogate function is able to learn efficiently from a few data points and handle variable-sized inputs (models with different number of layers). Hence, we choose a Recurrent Neural Network (RNN), the last hidden state of the RNN is followed by a fully connected layer with sigmoid nonlinearity to regress accuracy. The reason for choosing RNN as the surrogate function is because of its high sampling efficiency and the ability to handle different length of inputs. The input to the RNN is the one-hot encoding of our cell structure and each structure has its own embedding.

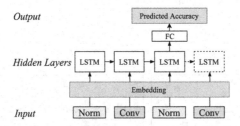

Fig. 6. The architecture diagram of our Recurrent Neural Network (RNN). The dashed block indicates we progressively search for more layers architectures.

6   Experiments and Results

6.1   Experimental Details

We conduct our search on the CIFAR-10 dataset with standard augmentation, the training set consists of 50,000 images and the testing set consists of 10,000 images. After the search is done, we use the cell structure to form a larger model and train on ImageNet [27] classification task to see how well the search performs. For the surrogate function, we use a standard LSTM with layer normalization [28], the hidden state size and the embedding size are both set to 128. Bias in the fully connected layer is initialized to 2, and the embeddings use random uniform initializer in range 0 to 1. To train the surrogate function, we use Adam Optimizer [29] with learning rate 0.008.

During the search, the number of repeated blocks C_1, C_2, C_3 are set to 14, 14, 14, G_1, G_2, G_3 are set to 8, 16, 32 for CIFAR-10 and the searching end at $\ell = 4$. Each sampled architecture is trained for 10 epochs with batch size 256 using Stochastic Gradient Descent and Nesterov momentum weight 0.9. The learning rate is set to 0.1 with cosine decay [30]. At each iteration of the search algorithm, our number of models to train, K, is set to 128. After searching is done, we train the final models on ImageNet with batch size 256 for 120 epochs, the number of repeated blocks C_1, C_2, C_3, C_4, C_5 are set to 4, 6, 8, 10, 8 and G_1, G_2, G_3, G_4, G_5 are set to 8, 16, 32, 64, 128.

The detail settings of the devices to search on are shown in Table 1. When searching models on WS and ES, we consider 4 objectives, evaluation error rate, number of parameters, FLOPs, and actual inference time on different computing devices. While on Mobile Phone, we consider an additional metric, memory usage, as our 5th objective.

Table 1. Hardware Specifications and Numbers of Objectives. For WS, 64 GB is the CPU memory and 12 GB is the GPU memory. In ES, memory space is shared among CPU and GPU

	Workstation (WS)	Embedded System (ES)	Mobile Phone (M)
Instance	Desktop PC	NVIDIA Jetson TX1	Xiaomi Redmi Note 4
CPU	Intel i5-7600	ARM Cortex57	ARM Cortex53
Cores	4	4	8
GHz	3.5	1.9	2.0
CUDA	Titan X (Pascal)	Maxwell 256	–
Memory	64 GB/12 GB	4 GB	3 GB
Objectives	4	4	5

6.2 Results on CIFAR-10

We first provide the results about the Pareto-optimal candidates (each trained for 10 epochs) found during the search process, and then demonstrate the evaluations of final models (trained for 300 epochs).

Figure 7 shows the candidates extracted from the Pareto front during the search process. In Fig. 7(a, b), no clear pattern (or association) is observed between the error rate and the number of parameters (or FLOPs). Similarly, from Fig. 7(c), the inference time couldn't be simply associated with the device-agnostic objectives (FLOPs and number of parameters). As we will show later in Table 2 and Fig. 9, not surprisingly, inference time is device-dependent since, in addition to modeling, the hardware implementation also affects the inference time. For a better comparison and also to showcase our DPP-Net, we evaluate and plot the performance of CondenseNet (reproduce 10 epochs performance), which is also included in our search space but not on the Pareto front.

During the searching process, the surrogate function was updated several times. The best regression error (on the validation set) is around 12%. At the first glance, this number is a bit large in terms of predicting the true accuracy.

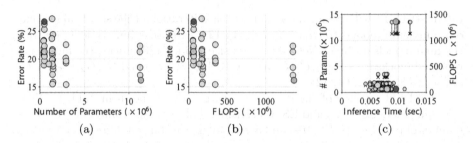

(a)   (b)   (c)

Fig. 7. Pareto-optimal candidates on WS (trained with 10 epochs) evaluated with Cifar10 dataset. (a) is the scatter plot between error rate (Y-axis) and the number of parameters (X-axis), whereas (b) stands for error rate v.s. FLOPs. (c) is the number of parameters (left Y-axis) and FLOPs (right Y-axis) v.s. actual inference time (X-axis), where the dot represents params v.s. inference time and the cross is FLOPs v.s. inference time. Each model is color-coded: green (DPP-Net-PNAS), yellow (DPP-Net-WS), and cyan (DPP-Net-Panacea). Notice that each candidate here represents a neural architecture that achieves Pareto optimality. Finally, CondenseNet (red dots) is included for comparison. (Color figure online)

Table 2. Cifar10 Classification Results. Missing values are the metrics not reported in their original papers. Pareto front visualizations of our searched networks can also be found in Fig. 7. The standard deviation of the metrics of DPP-Net-Panacea are calculated across 10 runs

Model from previous works	Device-agnostic metrics			Device-aware metrics			
	Error rate	Params	FLOPs	Time-WS	Time-ES	Time-M	Mem-M
Real et al. [11]	5.4	5.4M	–	–	–	–	–
NASNet-B [9]	3.73	2.6M	–	–	–	–	–
PNASNet-1 [15]	4.01	1.6M	–	–	–	–	–
DenseNet-BC (k=12) [31]	4.51	0.80M	–	–	–	0.273	79 MB
CondenseNet-86 [18]	5.0	0.52M	65.8M	0.009	0.090	0.149	113 MB

Model from DPP-Net	Device-agnostic metrics			Device-aware metrics			
	Error rate	Params	FLOPs	Time-WS	Time-ES	Time-M	Mem-M
DPP-Net-PNAS	**4.36**	11.39M	1364M	0.013	0.062	0.912	213 MB
DPP-Net-WS	4.78	1.00M	137M	**0.006**	0.075	0.210	129 MB
DPP-Net-ES	4.93	2.04M	270M	0.007	**0.044**	0.381	100 MB
DPP-Net-M	5.84	**0.45M**	**59.27M**	0.008	0.065	**0.145**	**58 MB**
DPP-Net-Panacea	4.62 ± 0.23	0.52M	63.5M	0.009 ± 7.4e-5	0.082 ± 0.011	0.149 ± 0.017	104 MB

However, it is important to clarify that the purpose of using the surrogate function is to suggest what kind of models may have a relatively good accuracy instead of exactly how accurate the models are. For the search time, we use 4 GTX 1080 GPUs and search for two days (around 48 hours).

After searching process is done, we select two architectures (from others on the Pareto front) for detailed evaluation: DPP-Net-*Device* and DPP-Net-

Panacea. DPP-Net-*Device* has a small error rate and the shortest inference time when running on certain *Device* (WS or ES), whereas DPP-Net-Panacea also has a small error rate and performs relatively well on every objective (but longer inference time than DPP-Net-*Device*). These two best models, in terms of Pareto Optimality, are trained for 300 epochs and the evaluation metrics are reported in Table 2 (bottom half). We also include the results of the neural architecture searched by DPP-Net with PNAS [15] criterion: the highest classification accuracy among all the candidates. Furthermore, for the completeness and comprehensive study, in the top half of Table 2, we include the results from the best models of previous NAS works [9,11,15], as well as the current state-of-the-art handcrafted mobile CNN models (bottom half) [18,31]. The architectures of these models are shown in Fig. 8.

DPP-Net-PNAS results in finding models with possible large number of parameters and very slow inference time. Our results are compared with state-of-the-art handcrafted mobile CNNs (second group) and models designed using architecture search methods (first group). Our DPP-Net clearly strikes better trade-off among multiple objectives.

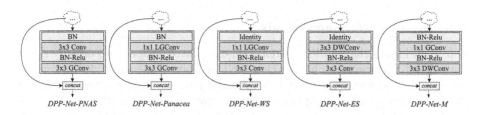

Fig. 8. The result of our searched dense cell topology.

6.3   Results on ImageNet

We further transfer our searched architecture to test the performance on ImageNet classification task. The cell structures searched using CIFAR-10 dataset are directly used for ImageNet with only a slight modification on the number of repeated Dense Cells. The hyper-parameters for training DPP-Net on ImageNet are nearly identical to training DPP-Net on CIFAR-10, except for the parameter of group lasso regularizer which we set to 1e-5. This regularization induces group-level sparsity for Learned Group Convolution as suggested in [18].

The results of ImageNet training is shown in Table 3. DPP-Net-Panacea performs better in nearly every aspect than Condensenet-74. Moreover, DPP-Net-Panacea outperforms NASNet (Mobile), a state-of-the-art mobile CNN designed by an architecture search method [9] in every metrics. We further argue that the sophisticated architecture makes NASNet (Mobile) not practical on mobile devices although it has a relatively small number of parameters compared to traditional CNNs. These results again show the versatility and robustness of our device-aware search method.

Table 3. ImageNet Classification Results. Time-M and Mem-M is the inference time and memory usage of the corresponding model on our mobile phone using ONNX and Caffe2. Due to operations not supported on this framework, we cannot measure the inference time and memory usage of NASNet (Mobile) on our mobile phone

Model	Top-1	Top-5	Params	FLOPs	Time-ES	Time-M	Mem-M
Densenet-121 [31]	25.02	7.71	–	–	0.084	1.611	466 MB
Densenet-169 [31]	23.80	6.85	–	–	0.142	1.944	489 MB
Densenet-201 [31]	22.58	6.34	–	–	0.168	2.435	528 MB
ShuffleNet 1x (g = 8)	32.4	–	5.4M	140M	0.051	0.458	243 MB
MobileNetV2	28.3	–	1.6M	–	0.032	0.777	270 MB
Condensenet-74 (G = 4) [18]	26.2	8.30	4.8M	529M	0.072	0.694	238 MB
NASNet (Mobile)	26.0	8.4	5.3M	564M	0.244	–	–
DPP-Net-PNAS	24.16	7.13	77.16M	9276M	0.218	5.421	708 MB
DPP-Net-Panacea	25.98	8.21	4.8M	523M	0.069	0.676	238 MB

6.4 Device Performance Study

Our main idea is that models searched on one device does not necessarily guarantee good performance on the other devices when it comes to device-related metrics, such as actual inference time. A small number of parameters or FLOPs does not always indicate fast inference time, this is due to existing problems of hardware optimization and software implementations (e.g., implementation of depth-wise convolution is inefficient and group convolution cannot reach theoretical speedups). To prove that inference time is device-aware, we measured the inference time of all 4-layers models (measuring only the network forward time can be done very efficiently) on 3 devices and plot them in Fig. 9. For WS and ES environments, we test our models on PyTorch 0.3.0 [32] built with Python 3.5, CUDA-8.0, and CUDNN-6.0, as for M, we follow the instructions from the PyTorch official guide and port the models to Caffe2 for deployment. The X-axis in Fig. 9 is the inference time of all the 4-layer cell structures sorted by WS (green line/bottom line) in ascending order. The red line and the blue line is the inference time on ES and M, respectively.

The plot shows that even on similar devices with identical software settings (WS v.s. ES), the inference time can be sensitive to particular devices. Moreover, inference time on M is significantly disparate to that of WS. Therefore, we conclude that only searching models on an actual device can ensure the robustness of the searched results.

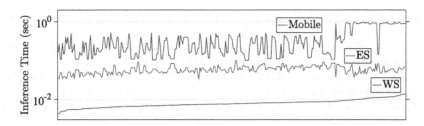

Fig. 9. Models inference time on different devices. We show that the inference time is highly device-related. The X-axis is the index of all 4-layers models, sorted by inference time on WS in ascending order. (Color figure online)

7   Conclusions

Our proposed *DPP-Net* is the first device-aware neural architecture search approach outperforming state-of-the-art handcrafted mobile CNNs. Experimental results on CIFAR-10 demonstrate the effectiveness of Pareto-optimal networks found by DPP-Net, for three different devices: (1) a workstation with NVIDIA Titan X GPU, (2) NVIDIA Jetson TX1 embedded system, and (3) mobile phone with ARM Cortex-A53. Compared to CondenseNet and NASNet (Mobile), DPP-Net achieves better performances: higher accuracy & shorter inference time on these various devices. Additional experimental results also show that models found by DPP-Net achieve state-of-the-art performance on ImageNet.

Acknowledgement. We are grateful to the National Center for High-performance Computing for computer time and facilities, and Google Research, MediaTek, MOST 107-2634-F-007-007 for their support. This research is also supported in part by the Ministry of Science and Technology of Taiwan (MOST 107-2633-E-002-001), National Taiwan University, Intel Corporation, and Delta Electronics.

References

1. Krizhevsky, A., Hinton, G.: Learning multiple layers of features from tiny images (2009)
2. Krizhevsky, A., Sutskever, I., Hinton, G.E.: Imagenet classification with deep convolutional neural networks. In: Advances in Neural Information Processing Systems, pp. 1097–1105 (2012)
3. Hannun, A., et al.: Deep speech: scaling up end-to-end speech recognition. arXiv preprint arXiv:1412.5567 (2014)
4. Sutskever, I., Vinyals, O., Le, Q.V.: Sequence to sequence learning with neural networks. In: Advances in Neural Information Processing Systems, pp. 3104–3112 (2014)
5. Negrinho, R., Gordon, G.: Deeparchitect: automatically designing and training deep architectures. arXiv preprint arXiv:1704.08792 (2017)
6. Zoph, B., Le, Q.V.: Neural architecture search with reinforcement learning. In: ICLR 2017 (2016)

7. Pham, H., Guan, M.Y., Zoph, B., Le, Q.V., Dean, J.: Efficient neural architecture search via parameter sharing. arXiv preprint arXiv:1802.03268 (2018)
8. Baker, B., Gupta, O., Naik, N., Raskar, R.: Designing neural network architectures using reinforcement learning. In: ICLR 2017 (2016)
9. Zoph, B., Vasudevan, V., Shlens, J., Le, Q.V.: Learning transferable architectures for scalable image recognition. arXiv preprint arXiv:1707.07012 (2017)
10. Zhong, Z., Yan, J., Liu, C.L.: Practical network blocks design with q-learning. In: AAAI 2018 (2017)
11. Real, E., et al.: Large-scale evolution of image classifiers. In: ICML 2017 (2017)
12. Xie, L., Yuille, A.: Genetic CNN. In: ICCV 2017 (2017)
13. Liu, H., Simonyan, K., Vinyals, O., Fernando, C., Kavukcuoglu, K.: Hierarchical representations for efficient architecture search. In: ICLR 2018 (2017)
14. Real, E., Aggarwal, A., Huang, Y., Le, Q.V.: Regularized evolution for image classifier architecture search. arXiv preprint arXiv:1802.01548 (2018)
15. Liu, C., et al.: Progressive neural architecture search. arXiv preprint arXiv:1712.00559 (2017)
16. Howard, A.G., et al.: Mobilenets: efficient convolutional neural networks for mobile vision applications. arXiv preprint arXiv:1704.04861 (2017)
17. Zhang, X., Zhou, X., Lin, M., Sun, J.: Shufflenet: an extremely efficient convolutional neural network for mobile devices. arXiv preprint arXiv:1707.01083 (2017)
18. Huang, G., Liu, S., van der Maaten, L., Weinberger, K.Q.: Condensenet: an efficient densenet using learned group convolutions. arXiv preprint arXiv:1711.09224 (2017)
19. Kim, Y.H., Reddy, B., Yun, S., Seo, C.: Nemo: neuro-evolution with multiobjective optimization of deep neural network for speed and accuracy. In: ICML 2017 AutoML Workshop (2017)
20. Williams, R.J.: Simple statistical gradient-following algorithms for connectionist reinforcement learning. Mach. Learn. **8**(3–4), 229–256 (1992)
21. Schulman, J., Wolski, F., Dhariwal, P., Radford, A., Klimov, O.: Proximal policy optimization algorithms. arXiv preprint arXiv:1707.06347 (2017)
22. Cai, H., Chen, T., Zhang, W., Yu, Y., Wang, J.: Efficient architecture search by network transformation. In: AAAI 2018 (2017)
23. Hutter, F., Hoos, H.H., Leyton-Brown, K.: Sequential model-based optimization for general algorithm configuration. In: Coello, C.A.C. (ed.) LION 2011. LNCS, vol. 6683, pp. 507–523. Springer, Heidelberg (2011). https://doi.org/10.1007/978-3-642-25566-3_40
24. Baker, B., Gupta, O., Raskar, R., Naik, N.: Accelerating neural architecture search using performance prediction (2018)
25. Brock, A., Lim, T., Ritchie, J.M., Weston, N.: Smash: one-shot model architecture search through hypernetworks. In: ICLR 2018 (2017)
26. Chollet, F.: Xception: deep learning with depthwise separable convolutions. arXiv preprint (2016)
27. Deng, J., Dong, W., Socher, R., Li, L.J., Li, K., Fei-Fei, L.: Imagenet: a large-scale hierarchical image database. In: 2009 IEEE Conference on Computer Vision and Pattern Recognition, CVPR 2009, pp. 248–255. IEEE (2009)
28. Ba, J.L., Kiros, J.R., Hinton, G.E.: Layer normalization. arXiv preprint arXiv:1607.06450 (2016)
29. Kingma, D.P., Ba, J.: Adam: a method for stochastic optimization. arXiv preprint arXiv:1412.6980 (2014)
30. Loshchilov, I., Hutter, F.: SGDR: stochastic gradient descent with restarts. arXiv preprint arXiv:1608.03983 (2016)

31. Huang, G., Liu, Z., Weinberger, K.Q., van der Maaten, L.: Densely connected convolutional networks. In: CVPR 2017 (2017)
32. Paszke, A., et al.: Automatic differentiation in pytorch (2017)

Riemannian Walk for Incremental Learning: Understanding Forgetting and Intransigence

Arslan Chaudhry, Puneet K. Dokania, Thalaiyasingam Ajanthan$^{(\boxtimes)}$, and Philip H. S. Torr

University of Oxford, Oxford, UK
{arslan.chaudhry,puneet.dokania,thalaiyasingam.ajanthan, philip.torr}@eng.ox.ac.uk

Abstract. Incremental learning (IL) has received a lot of attention recently, however, the literature lacks a precise problem definition, proper evaluation settings, and metrics tailored specifically for the IL problem. One of the main objectives of this work is to fill these gaps so as to provide a common ground for better understanding of IL. The main challenge for an IL algorithm is to update the classifier whilst preserving existing knowledge. We observe that, in addition to *forgetting*, a known issue while preserving knowledge, IL also suffers from a problem we call *intransigence*, its inability to update knowledge. We introduce two metrics to quantify *forgetting* and *intransigence* that allow us to understand, analyse, and gain better insights into the behaviour of IL algorithms. Furthermore, we present RWalk, a generalization of EWC++ (our efficient version of EWC [6]) and Path Integral [25] with a theoretically grounded KL-divergence based perspective. We provide a thorough analysis of various IL algorithms on MNIST and CIFAR-100 datasets. In these experiments, RWalk obtains superior results in terms of accuracy, and also provides a better trade-off for forgetting and intransigence.

1 Introduction

Realizing human-level intelligence requires developing systems capable of learning new tasks continually while preserving *knowledge* about the old ones. This is precisely the objective underlying incremental learning (IL) algorithms. By definition, IL has ever-expanding output space, and no or limited access to data from the previous tasks while learning a new one. This makes it more challenging and fundamentally different from the classical learning paradigm where the entire dataset is available and the output space is fixed. Recently, there have been several works in IL [6,14,19,25] with varying evaluation settings and metrics

---

A. Chaudhry, P. K. Dokania, T. Ajanthan—Joint first authors

Electronic supplementary material The online version of this chapter (https:// doi.org/10.1007/978-3-030-01252-6_33) contains supplementary material, which is available to authorized users.

© Springer Nature Switzerland AG 2018
V. Ferrari et al. (Eds.): ECCV 2018, LNCS 11215, pp. 556–572, 2018.
https://doi.org/10.1007/978-3-030-01252-6_33

making it difficult to establish fair comparisons. The first objective of this work is to rectify these issues by providing precise definitions, evaluation settings, and metrics for IL for the classification task.

Let us now discuss the key points to consider while designing IL algorithms. The first question is 'how to define knowledge: factors that quantify what the model has learned'. Usually, knowledge is defined either using the input-output behaviour of the network [4,19] or the network parameters [6,25]. Once the knowledge is defined, the objective then is to preserve and update it to counteract two inherent issues with IL algorithms: (1) forgetting: catastrophically forgetting knowledge of previous tasks; and (2) intransigence: inability to update the knowledge to learn the new task. Both of these problems require contradicting solutions and pose a trade-off for any IL algorithm.

To capture this trade-off, we advocate the use of measures that evaluate an IL algorithm based on its performance on the past and the present tasks in the hope that this will reflect in its behaviour in the future unseen tasks. Taking this into account we introduce two metrics to evaluate forgetting and intransigence. These metrics together with the standard multi-class average accuracy allow us to understand, analyse, and gain better insights into the behaviour of various IL algorithms.

In addition, we present a generalization of two recently proposed incremental learning algorithms, Elastic Weight Consolidation (EWC) [6], and Path Integral (PI) [25]. In particular, first we show that in EWC, while learning a new task, the model's likelihood distribution is regularized using a well known second-order approximation of the KL-divergence [1,17], which is equivalent to computing distance in a Riemannian manifold induced by the Fisher Information Matrix [1]. To compute and update the Fisher matrix, we use an efficient (in terms of memory) and online (in terms of computation) approach, leading to a faster and online version of EWC which we call EWC++. Note that, a similar extension to EWC, called online-EWC, is concurrently proposed by Schwarz et al. [21]. Next, we modify the PI [25] where instead of computing the change in the loss per unit distance in the Euclidean space between the parameters as the measure of sensitivity, we use the approximate KL divergence (distance in the Riemannian manifold) between the output distributions as the distance to compute the sensitivity. This gives us the parameter importance score which is accumulated over the optimization trajectory encoding information about the previous tasks as well. Finally, RWalk is obtained by combining EWC++ and the modified PI.

Furthermore, in order to counteract intransigence, we study different sampling strategies that store a small representative subset ($\leq 5\%$) of the dataset from the previous tasks. This not only allows the network to recall information about the previous tasks but also helps in learning to discriminate current and previous tasks. Finally, we present a thorough analysis to better understand the behaviour of IL algorithms on MNIST [10] and CIFAR-100 [7] datasets. To summarize, our main contributions are:

1. New evaluation metrics - Forgetting and Intransigence - to better understand the behaviour and performance of an incremental learning algorithm.

2. EWC++: An efficient and online version of EWC.
3. RWalk: A generalization of EWC++ and PI with theoretically grounded KL-divergence based perspective providing new insights.
4. An analysis of different methods in terms of accuracy, forgetting, and intransigence.

2   Problem Set-Up and Preliminaries

Here we define the IL problem and discuss the practicality of two different evaluation settings: (a) single-head; and (b) multi-head. In addition, we review the probabilistic interpretation of neural networks and the connection of KL-divergence with the distance in the Riemannian manifold, both of which are crucial to our approach.

2.1   Single-Head vs Multi-head Evaluations

We consider a stream of tasks, each corresponding to a set of labels. For the k-th task, let $\mathcal{D}_k = \{(\mathbf{x}_i^k, y_i^k)\}_{i=1}^{n_k}$ be the dataset, where $\mathbf{x}_i^k \in \mathcal{X}$ is the input and $y_i^k \in \mathbf{y}^k$ the ground truth label, and $\mathbf{y}^k$ is the set of labels specific to the task. The main distinction between the single-head and the multi-head evaluations is that, at test time, in *single-head*, the task identifier (k) is unknown, whereas in *multi-head*, it is given. Therefore, for the single-head evaluation, the objective at the k-th task is to learn a function $f_\theta : \mathcal{X} \to \mathcal{Y}^k$, where $\mathcal{Y}^k = \cup_{j=1}^k \mathbf{y}^j$ corresponds to all the known labels. For multi-head, as the task identifier is known, $\mathcal{Y}^k = \mathbf{y}^k$. For example, consider MNIST with 5 tasks: $\{\{0,1\}, \cdots, \{8,9\}\}$; trained in an incremental manner. Then, at the 5-th task, for a given image, the *multi-head* evaluation is to predict a class out of two labels $\{8, 9\}$ for which the 5-th task was trained. However, the *single-head* evaluation at 5-th task is to predict a label out of all the ten classes $\{0, \cdots, 9\}$ that the model has seen thus far.

Why Is Single-Head the Right Evaluation for il? In the case of *single-head*, used by [12,19], the output space consists of all the known labels. This requires the classifier to learn to distinguish labels from different tasks as well. Since, the tasks are supplied in a sequence in IL, while learning a task, the classifier must also learn the inter-task discrimination with no or limited access[1] to the previous data. This is a much harder problem compared to multi-head where the output space contains labels of the current task only. Furthermore, single-head is more practical as knowing a priori the subset of labels to look at is a big assumption. For instance, if the task contains only one label, multi-head evaluation would be equivalent to knowing the ground truth label itself.

---

[1] Since the number of tasks are potentially unlimited in IL, it is impossible to store all the previous data in a scalable manner.

2.2   Probabilistic Interpretation of Neural Network Output

If the final layer of a neural network is a soft-max layer and the network is trained using cross entropy loss, then the output may be interpreted as a probability distribution over the categorical variables. Thus, at a given θ, the conditional likelihood distribution learned by a neural network is actually a conditional multinoulli distribution defined as $p_\theta(\mathbf{y}|\mathbf{x}) = \prod_{j=1}^{K} p_{\theta,j}^{[y=j]}$, where $p_{\theta,j}$ is the soft-max probability of the j-th class, K are the total number of classes, $\mathbf{y}$ is the one-hot encoding of length K, and $[\cdot]$ is Iverson bracket. A prediction can then be obtained from the likelihood distribution $p_\theta(\mathbf{y}|\mathbf{x})$. Typically, instead of sampling, a label with the highest soft-max probability is chosen as the network's prediction. Note that, if $\mathbf{y}$ corresponds to the ground-truth label then the log-likelihood is exactly the same as the negative of the cross-entropy loss, i.e., if the ground-truth corresponds to the t-th index of the one-hot representation of $\mathbf{y}$, then $\log p_\theta(\mathbf{y}|\mathbf{x}) = \log p_{\theta,t}$. More insights can be found in the supplementary material.

2.3   KL-Divergence as the Distance in the Riemannian Manifold

Let $D_{KL}(p_\theta \| p_{\theta+\Delta\theta})$ be the KL-divergence [8] between the conditional likelihoods of a neural network at θ and $\theta + \Delta\theta$, respectively. Then, assuming $\Delta\theta \to 0$, the second-order Taylor approximation of the KL-divergence can be written as $D_{KL}(p_\theta \| p_{\theta+\Delta\theta}) \approx \frac{1}{2}\Delta\theta^\top F_\theta \Delta\theta = \frac{1}{2}\|\Delta\theta\|_{F_\theta}^2$, where F_θ, known as the *empirical Fisher Information Matrix* [1,17] at θ, is defined as:

$$F_\theta = \mathbb{E}_{(\mathbf{x},\mathbf{y})\sim\mathcal{D}} \left[\left(\frac{\partial \log p_\theta(\mathbf{y}|\mathbf{x})}{\partial \theta} \right) \left(\frac{\partial \log p_\theta(\mathbf{y}|\mathbf{x})}{\partial \theta} \right)^\top \right], \tag{1}$$

where $\mathcal{D}$ is the dataset. Note that, as mentioned earlier, the log-likelihood $\log p_\theta(\mathbf{y}|\mathbf{x})$ is the same as the negative of the cross-entropy loss function, thus, F_θ can be seen as the *expected loss-gradient covariance matrix*. By construction (outer product of gradients), F_θ is positive semi-definite (PSD) which makes it highly attractive for second-order optimization techniques [1,2,9,15,17]. Thus, when $\Delta\theta \to 0$, computing KL-divergence $\frac{1}{2}\|\Delta\theta\|_{F_\theta}^2$ is equivalent to computing the *distance* in a Riemannian manifold[3] [11] induced by the Fisher information matrix at θ. Since $F_\theta \in \mathbb{R}^{P\times P}$ and P is usually in the order of millions for neural networks, it is practically infeasible to store F_θ. To handle this, similar to [6], we assume parameters to be independent of each other (diagonal F_θ) which results in the following approximation of the KL-divergence:

$$D_{KL}(p_\theta \| p_{\theta+\Delta\theta}) \approx \frac{1}{2} \sum_{i=1}^{P} F_{\theta_i} \Delta\theta_i^2, \tag{2}$$

---

[2] Proof and insights are provided in the supplementary material.
[3] Since F_θ is PSD, this makes it a pseudo-manifold.

where θ_i is the i-th entry of θ. Notice, the diagonal entries of F_θ are the expected square of the gradients, where the expectation is over the entire dataset. Thus, F_θ is expensive to compute as it requires a full forward-backward pass over the dataset.

3   Forgetting and Intransigence

Since the objective is to continually learn new tasks while preserving knowledge about the previous ones, an IL algorithm should be evaluated based on its performance both on the *past* and the *present* tasks in the hope that this will reflect in its behaviour on the *future* unseen tasks. To achieve this, along with average accuracy, there are two crucial components that must be quantified (1) *forgetting*: how much an algorithm forgets what it learned in the past; and (2) *intransigence*: inability of an algorithm to learn new tasks. Intuitively, if a model is heavily regularized over previous tasks to preserve knowledge, it will forget less but have high intransigence. If, in contrast, the regularization is too weak, while the intransigence will be small, the model will suffer from catastrophic forgetting. Ideally, we want a model that suffers less from both, thus efficiently utilizing the finite model capacity. In contrast, if one observes high negative correlation between forgetting and intransigence, which is usually the case, then, it suggests that either the model capacity is saturated or the method does not effectively utilize it. Before defining metrics for quantifying forgetting and intransigence, we first define the multi-class average accuracy which will be the basis for defining the other two metrics. Note, some other task specific measure of correctness (*e.g.*, IoU for object segmentation) can also be used while the definitions of forgetting and intransigence remain the same.

Average Accuracy (A). Let $a_{k,j} \in [0, 1]$ be the accuracy (fraction of correctly classified images) evaluated on the held-out test set of the j-th task ($j \leq k$) after training the network incrementally from tasks 1 to k. Note that, to compute $a_{k,j}$, the output space consists of either $\mathbf{y}^j$ or $\cup_{j=1}^{k}\mathbf{y}^j$ depending on whether the evaluation is multi-head or single-head (refer Sect. 2.1). The average accuracy at task k is then defined as $A_k = \frac{1}{k}\sum_{j=1}^{k} a_{k,j}$. The higher the A_k the better the classifier, but this does not provide any information about forgetting or intransigence profile of the IL algorithm which would be crucial to judge its behaviour.

Forgetting Measure (F). We define forgetting for a particular task (or label) as the difference between the *maximum* knowledge gained about the task throughout the learning process in the past and the knowledge the model currently has about it. This, in turn, gives an estimate of how much the model forgot about the task given its current state. Following this, for a classification problem, we quantify forgetting for the j-th task after the model has been incrementally trained up to task $k > j$ as:

$$f_j^k = \max_{l \in \{1, \cdots, k-1\}} a_{l,j} - a_{k,j}, \quad \forall j < k. \tag{3}$$

Note, $f_j^k \in [-1, 1]$ is defined for $j < k$ as we are interested in quantifying forgetting for *previous* tasks. Moreover, by normalizing against the number of tasks seen previously, the average forgetting at k-th task is written as $F_k = \frac{1}{k-1} \sum_{j=1}^{k-1} f_j^k$. Lower F_k implies less forgetting on previous tasks. Here, instead of max one could use *expectation* or $a_{j,j}$ in order to quantify the knowledge about a task in the past. However, taking max allows us to estimate forgetting along the learning process as explained below.

Positive/Negative Backward Transfer ((P/N)BT): Backward transfer (BT) is defined in [14] as the influence that learning a task k has on the performance on a previous task $j < k$. Since our objective is to measure forgetting, negative forgetting ($f_j^k < 0$) implies positive influence on the previous task or positive backward transfer (PBT) and the opposite for NBT. Furthermore, in [14], $a_{j,j}$ is used in place of $\max_{l \in \{1, \cdots, k-1\}} a_{l,j}$ (refer Eq. (3)) which makes the measure agnostic to the IL process and does not effectively capture forgetting. To understand this, let us consider an example with 4 tasks trained in an incremental manner and we are interested in measuring forgetting of task 1 after training up to task 4. Let the accuracies be $\{a_{1,1}, a_{1,2}, a_{1,3}, a_{1,4}\} = \{0.7, 0.8, 0.6, 0.5\}$. Here, forgetting measured based on Eq. (3) is $f_1^4 = 0.3$, whereas [14] would measure it as 0.2 (irrespective of the variations in $a_{1,2}$ and $a_{1,3}$). Hence, it does not capture the fact that there was a PBT in the learning process and, we believe, it is vital that an evaluation metric of an IL algorithm considers such behaviour along the learning process.

Intransigence Measure (I). We define *intransigence* as the inability of a model to learn new tasks. The effect of intransigence is more prominent in the single-head setting especially in the absence of previous data, as the model is expected to learn to differentiate the current task from the previous ones. Experimentally we show that storing just a few representative samples (refer Sect. 4.2) from the previous tasks improves intransigence significantly. Since we wish to quantify the *inability* to learn, we compare to the standard classification model which has access to all the datasets at all times. We train a reference/target model with dataset $\bigcup_{l=1}^{k} \mathcal{D}_l$ and measure its accuracy on the held-out set of the k-th task, denoted as a_k^*. We then define the intransigence for the k-th task as:

$$I_k = a_k^* - a_{k,k}, \tag{4}$$

where $a_{k,k}$ denotes the accuracy on the k-th task when trained up to task k in an incremental manner. Note, $I_k \in [-1, 1]$, and lower the I_k the better the model. A reasonable reference/target model can be defined depending on the feasibility to obtain it. In situations where it is highly expensive, an approximation can be proposed.

Positive/Negative Forward Transfer ((P/N)FT): Since intransigence is defined as the gap between the accuracy of an IL algorithm and the reference model, negative intransigence ($I_k < 0$) implies learning incrementally up to task k positively influences model's knowledge about it, *i.e.*, positive forward transfer (PFT). Similarly, $I_k > 0$ implies NFT. However, in [14], FT is quantified as the gain in accuracy compared to the random guess (not a measure of intransigence) which is complementary to our approach.

4   Riemannian Walk for Incremental Learning

We first describe EWC++, an efficient version of the well known EWC [6], and then RWalk which is a generalization of EWC++ and PI [25]. Briefly, RWalk has three key components: (1) a KL-divergence-based regularization over the conditional likelihood $p_\theta(\mathbf{y}|\mathbf{x})$ (EWC++); (2) a parameter importance score based on the sensitivity of the loss over the movement on the Riemannian manifold (similar to PI); and (3) strategies to obtain a few representative samples from the previous tasks. The first two components mitigate the effects of catastrophic forgetting, whereas the third handles intransigence.

4.1   Avoiding Catastrophic Forgetting

KL-Divergence Based Regularization (ewc++). We learn parameters for the current task such that the new conditional likelihood is close (in terms of KL) to the one learned until previous tasks. To achieve this, we regularize over the conditional likelihood distributions $p_\theta(\mathbf{y}|\mathbf{x})$ using the approximate KL-divergence, Eq. (2), as the distance measure. This would preserve the inherent properties of the model about previous tasks as the learning progresses. Thus, given parameters θ^{k-1} trained sequentially from task 1 to $k-1$, and dataset $\mathcal{D}_k$ for the k-th task, our objective is:

$$\underset{\theta}{\operatorname{argmin}} \tilde{L}^k(\theta) := L^k(\theta) + \lambda\, D_{KL}\left(p_{\theta^{k-1}}(\mathbf{y}|\mathbf{x}) \| p_\theta(\mathbf{y}|\mathbf{x})\right), \qquad (5)$$

where, λ is a hyperparameter. Substituting Eq. (2), the KL-divergence component can be written as $D_{KL}\left(p_{\theta^{k-1}} \| p_\theta\right) \approx \frac{1}{2} \sum_{i=1}^{P} F_{\theta_i^{k-1}}(\theta_i - \theta_i^{k-1})^2$. Note that, for two tasks, the above regularization is exactly the same as that of EWC [6]. Here we presented it from the KL-divergence based perspective. Another way to look at it would be to consider Fisher[4] for each parameter to be its importance score. The intuitive explanation for this is as follows; since Fisher captures the local curvature of the KL-divergence surface of the likelihood distribution (as it is the second-derivative component of the Taylor approximation, refer Sect. 2.3), higher Fisher implies higher curvature, thus suggests to move less in that direction in order to preserve the likelihood.

---

[4] By Fisher we always mean the empirical Fisher information matrix.

In the case of multiple tasks, EWC requires storing Fisher for each task independently ($\mathcal{O}(kP)$ parameters), and regularizing over all of them jointly. This is practically infeasible if there are many tasks and the network has millions of parameters. Moreover, to estimate the empirical Fisher, EWC requires an additional pass over the dataset of each task (see Eq. (1)). To address these two issues, we propose EWC++ that (1) maintains single diagonal Fisher matrix as the training over tasks progresses, and (2) uses moving average for its efficient update similar to [15]. Given F_θ^{t-1} at $t-1$, Fisher in EWC++ is updated as:

$$F_\theta^t = \alpha F_\theta^t + (1-\alpha)F_\theta^{t-1}, \tag{6}$$

where F_θ^t is the Fisher matrix obtained using the *current batch* and $\alpha \in [0,1]$ is a hyperparameter. Note, t represents the training iterations, thus, computing Fisher in this manner contains information about previous tasks, and also eliminates the additional forward-backward pass over the dataset. At the end of each task, we simply store F_θ^t as $F_{\theta^{k-1}}$ and use it to regularize the next task, thus storing only two sets of Fisher at any instant during training, irrespective of the number of tasks. Similar to EWC++, an efficient version of EWC referred to as online-EWC is concurrently developed in [21].

In EWC, Fisher is computed at a local minimum of $\tilde{L}^k$ using the gradients of L^k, which is nearly zero whenever $\tilde{L}^k \approx L^k$ (*e.g.*, smaller λ or when $k = 1$). This results in negligible regularization leading to catastrophic forgetting. This issue is partially addressed in EWC++ using moving average. However, to improve it further and to capture model's behaviour not just at the minimum but also during the entire training process, we augment each element of the diagonal Fisher with a positive scalar as described below. This also ensures that the augmented Fisher is always positive-definite.

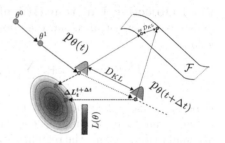

Fig. 1. Parameter importance accumulated over the optimization trajectory.

Optimization-Path Based Parameter Importance. Since Fisher captures the intrinsic properties of the model and it only depends on L^k, it is blinded towards the influence of parameters over the optimization path on the loss surface of $\tilde{L}^k$. Similar to [25], we accumulate parameter importance based on $\tilde{L}^k$ over the entire training trajectory. This score is defined as the ratio of the change in the loss function to the distance between the conditional likelihood distributions per step in the parameter space.

More precisely, for a change of parameter from $\theta_i(t)$ to $\theta_i(t+1)$ (where t is the time step or training iteration), we define parameter importance as the ratio of the change in the loss to its influence in $D_{KL}(p_{\theta(t)}\|p_{\theta(t+1)})$. Intuitively, importance will be higher if a small change in the distribution causes large improvement over the loss. Formally, using the first-order Taylor approximation, the change in loss L can be written as:

$$L(\theta(t + \Delta t)) - L(\theta(t)) \approx - \sum_{i=1}^{P} \sum_{t=t}^{t+\Delta t} \frac{\partial L}{\partial \theta_i} (\theta_i(t+1) - \theta_i(t)) = - \sum_{i=1}^{P} \Delta L_t^{t+\Delta t}(\theta_i), \quad (7)$$

where $\frac{\partial L}{\partial \theta_i}$ is the gradient at t, and $\Delta L_t^{t+\Delta t}(\theta_i)$ represents the accumulated change in the loss caused by the change in the parameter θ_i from time step t to $t + \Delta t$. This change in parameter would cause a corresponding change in the model distribution which can be computed using the approximate KL-divergence (Eq. (2)). Thus, the importance of the parameter θ_i from training iteration t_1 to t_2 can be computed as $s_{t_1}^{t_2}(\theta_i) = \sum_{t=t_1}^{t_2} \frac{\Delta L_t^{t+\Delta t}(\theta_i)}{\frac{1}{2} F_{\theta_i}^t \Delta \theta_i(t)^2 + \epsilon}$, where $\Delta \theta_i(t) = \theta_i(t+\Delta t) - \theta_i(t)$ and $\epsilon > 0$. The denominator is computed at every discrete intervals of $\Delta t \geq 1$ and $F_{\theta_i}^t$ is computed efficiently at every t-th step using moving average as described while explaining EWC++. The computation of this importance score is illustrated in Fig. 1. Since we care about the positive influence of the parameters, negative scores are set to zero. Note that, if the Euclidean distance is used instead, the score $s_{t_1}^{t_2}(\theta_i)$ would be similar to that of PI [25].

Final Objective Function (RWalk). We now combine Fisher information matrix based importance and the optimization-path based importance scores as follows:

$$\tilde{L}^k(\theta) = L^k(\theta) + \lambda \sum_{i=1}^{P} (F_{\theta_i^{k-1}} + s_{t_0}^{t_{k-1}}(\theta_i))(\theta_i - \theta_i^{k-1})^2. \quad (8)$$

Here, $s_{t_0}^{t_{k-1}}(\theta_i)$ is the score accumulated from the first training iteration t_0 until the last training iteration t_{k-1}, corresponding to task $k-1$. Since the scores are accumulated over time, the regularization gets increasingly rigid. To alleviate this and enable continual learning, after each task the scores are averaged: $s_{t_0}^{t_{k-1}}(\theta_i) = \frac{1}{2} \left(s_{t_0}^{t_{k-2}}(\theta_i) + s_{t_{k-2}}^{t_{k-1}}(\theta_i) \right)$. This continual averaging makes the tasks learned far in the past less influential than the tasks learned recently. Furthermore, while adding, it is important to make sure that the scales of both $F_{\theta_i^{k-1}}$ and $s_{t_0}^{t_{k-1}}(\theta_i)$ are in the same order, so that the influence of both the terms is retained. This can be ensured by individually normalizing them to be in the interval $[0, 1]$. *This, together with score averaging, have a positive side-effect of the regularization hyperparameter λ being less sensitive to the number of tasks.* However, EWC [6] and PI [25] are highly sensitive to λ, making them relatively less reliable for IL. Note, during training, the space complexity for RWalk is $\mathcal{O}(P)$, independent of the number of tasks.

4.2   Handling Intransigence

Experimentally, we observed that training k-th task with $\mathcal{D}_k$ leads to a poor test accuracy for the current task compared to previous tasks in the *single-head* evaluation setting (refer Sect. 2.1). This happens because during training the model has access to $\mathcal{D}_k$ which contains labels only for the k-th task, $\mathbf{y}^k$. However, at test time the label space is over all the tasks seen so far $\mathcal{Y}^k = \cup_{j=1}^{k} \mathbf{y}^j$, which is much larger than $\mathbf{y}^k$. This in turn increases *confusion* at test time as the predictor function has no means to differentiate the samples of the current task from the ones of previous tasks. An intuitive solution to this problem is to store a small subset of representative samples from the previous tasks and use it while training the current task [19]. Below we discuss different strategies to obtain such a subset. Note that we store m points from each task-specific dataset as the training progresses, however, it is trivial to have a fixed total number of samples for all the tasks similar to iCaRL [19].

Uniform Sampling. A naïve yet highly effective (shown experimentally) approach is to sample uniformly at random from the previous datasets.

Plane Distance-Based Sampling. In this case, we assume that samples closer to the decision boundary are more representative than the ones far away. For a given sample $\{\mathbf{x}_i, y_i\}$, we compute the pseudo-distance from the decision boundary $d(\mathbf{x}_i) = \phi(\mathbf{x}_i)^\top w^{y_i}$, where $\phi(\cdot)$ is the feature mapping learned by the neural network and w^{y_i} are the last fully connected layer parameters for class y_i. Then, we sample points based on $q(\mathbf{x}_i) \propto \frac{1}{d(\mathbf{x}_i)}$. Here, the intuition is, since the change in parameters is regularized, the feature space and the decision boundaries do not vary much. Hence, the samples that lie close to the boundary would act as *boundary defining samples*.

Entropy-Based Sampling. Given a sample, the entropy of the output softmax distribution measures the uncertainty of the sample which we used to sample points. The higher the entropy the more likely is that the sample would be picked.

Mean of Features (MoF). iCaRL [19] proposes a method to find samples based on the feature space $\phi(\cdot)$. For each class y, m number of points are found whose mean in the feature space closely approximate the mean of the entire dataset for that class. However, this subset selection strategy is inefficient compared to the above sampling methods. In fact, the time complexity is $\mathcal{O}(nfm)$ where n is dataset size, f is the feature dimension and m is the number of required samples.

5   Related Work

One way to address catastrophic forgetting is by dynamically expanding the network for each new task [18,20,23,24]. Though intuitive and simple, these approaches are not scalable as the size of the network increases with the number of tasks. A better strategy would be to exploit the over-parametrization of neural networks [3]. This entails regularizing either over the activations (output) [13,19] or over the network parameters [6,25]. Even though activation-based approach allows more flexibility in parameter updates, it is memory inefficient if the activations are in millions, *e.g.*, semantic segmentation. On the contrary, methods that regularize over the parameters - weighting the parameters based on their individual *importance* - are suitable for such tasks. Our method falls under the latter category and we show that our method is a generalization of EWC++ and PI [25], where EWC++ is our efficient version of EWC [6], very similar to the concurrently developed online-EWC [21]. Similar in spirit to regularization over the parameters, Lee *et al.* [12] use moment matching to obtain network weights as the combination of the weights of all the tasks, and Nguyen *et al.* [16] enforce the distribution over the model parameters to be close via a Bayesian framework. Different from the above approaches, Lopez-Paz *et al.* [14] update gradients such that the losses of the previous tasks do not increase, while Shin *et al.* [22] resort to a retraining strategy where the samples of the previous tasks are generated using a learned generative model.

6 Experiments

Datasets. We evaluate baselines and our proposed model - RWalk - on two datasets:

1. *Incremental MNIST*: The standard MNIST dataset is split into five disjoint subsets (tasks) of two consecutive digits, *i.e.*, $\cup_k \mathbf{y}^k = \{\{0,1\}, \ldots, \{8,9\}\}$.
2. *Incremental CIFAR*: To show that our approach scales to bigger datasets, we use incremental CIFAR where CIFAR-100 dataset is split into ten disjoint subsets such that $\cup_k \mathbf{y}^k = \{\{0-9\}, \ldots, \{90-99\}\}$.

Architectures. The architectures used are similar to [25]. For MNIST, we use an MLP with two hidden layers each having 256 units with ReLU nonlinearites. For CIFAR-100, we use a CNN with four convolutional layers followed by a single dense layer (see supplementary for more details). In all experiments, we use Adam optimizer [5] (learning rate $= 1 \times 10^{-3}$, $\beta_1 = 0.9$, $\beta_2 = 0.999$) with a fixed batch size of 64.

Baselines. We compare RWalk against the following baselines:

- Vanilla: Network trained without any regularization over past tasks.
- EWC [6] and PI [25]: Both use parameter based regularization. Note, we observed that EWC++ performed at least as good as EWC and therefore, in all the experiments, by EWC we mean the stronger baseline EWC++.
- iCaRL [19]: Uses regularization over the activations and a nearest-exemplar-based classifier. Here, iCaRL-hb1 refers to the *hybrid1* version, which uses the standard neural network classifier. Both the versions use previous samples.

Note, we use a few samples from the previous tasks to consolidate our baselines further in the single-head setting.

6.1   Results

We report the results in Table 1 where RWalk outperforms all the baselines in terms of average accuracy and provides better trade-off between forgetting and intransigence. We now discuss the results in detail.

Table 1. Comparison with different baselines on MNIST and CIFAR in both multi-head and single-head evaluation settings. Baselines where samples are used are appended with '-S'. For MNIST and CIFAR, 10 (0.2%) and 25 (5%) samples are used from the previous tasks using mean of features (MoF) based sampling strategy (refer Sect. 4.2).

Methods	MNIST				CIFAR			
	λ	$A_5(\%)$	F_5	I_5	λ	$A_{10}(\%)$	F_{10}	I_{10}
Multi-head evaluation								
Vanilla	0	90.3	0.12	6.6×10^{-4}	0	44.4	0.36	0.02
EWC	75000	**99.3**	0.001	0.01	3×10^6	72.8	0.001	0.07
PI	0.1	**99.3**	0.002	0.01	10	73.2	0	0.06
RWalk (Ours)	1000	**99.3**	0.003	0.01	1000	**74.2**	0.004	0.04
Single-head evaluation								
Vanilla	0	38.0	0.62	0.29	0	10.2	0.36	−0.06
EWC	75000	55.8	0.08	0.77	3×10^6	23.1	0.03	0.17
PI	0.1	57.6	0.11	0.8	10	22.8	0.04	0.2
iCaRL-hb1	–	36.6	0.68	−0.01	–	7.4	0.40	0.06
iCaRL	–	55.8	0.19	0.46	–	9.5	0.11	0.35
Vanilla-S	0	73.7	0.30	0.03	0	12.9	0.64	−0.3
EWC-S	75000	79.7	0.14	0.22	15×10^5	33.6	0.27	−0.05
PI-S	0.1	78.7	0.24	0.05	10	33.6	0.27	−0.03
RWalk (Ours)	1000	**82.5**	0.15	0.14	500	**34.0**	0.28	−0.06

In the multi-head evaluation setting [14,25], except Vanilla, all the methods provide state-of-the-art accuracy with *almost zero* forgetting and intransigence (top row of Fig. 2). *This gives an impression that* IL *problem is solved.* However, as discussed in Sect. 2.1, this is an easier evaluation setting and does not capture the essence of IL.

However, in the single-head evaluation, *forgetting* and *intransigence* increase substantially due to the the inability of the network to differentiate among tasks. Hence, the performance significantly drops for all the methods (refer Table 1 and the middle row of Fig. 2). For instance, on MNIST, forgetting and intransigence of Vanilla deteriorates from 0.12 to 0.62, and 6.6×10^{-4} to 0.29, respectively, causing the average accuracy to drop from 90.3% to 38.0%. Although, regularized methods, EWC and PI, designed to counter catastrophic forgetting, result in less

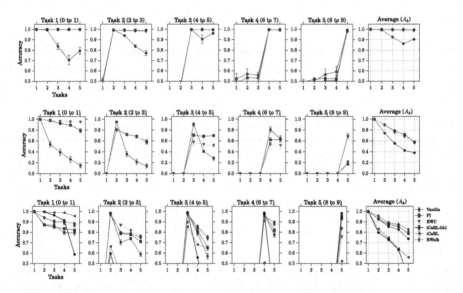

Fig. 2. Accuracy on incremental MNIST with multi-head evaluation (**top**), and single-head evaluation without (**middle**) and with samples (**bottom**). First five columns show the variation in performance for different tasks, *e.g.*, the first plot depicts the performance variation on Task 1 when trained incrementally over five tasks. The last column shows the accuracy (A_k, refer Sect. 3). Mean of features (MoF) sampling is used.

degradation of forgetting, their accuracy is still significantly worse - compare 99.3% of PI in multi-head against 57.6% in single-head. In Table 1, a similar performance decrease is observed on CIFAR-100 as well. Such a degradation in accuracy even with less forgetting shows that it is not only important to preserve knowledge (quantified by forgetting) but also to update knowledge (captured by intransigence) to achieve better performance. Task-level analysis for CIFAR dataset, similar to Fig. 2, is presented in the supplementary material.

We now show that even with a few representative samples intransigence can be mitigated. For example, in the case of PI on MNIST with only 10 ($\approx$0.2%) samples for each previous class, the intransigence drops from 0.8 to 0.05 which results in improving the average accuracy from 57.6% to 78.7%. Similar improvements can be seen for other methods as well. On CIFAR-100, with only 5% representative samples, almost identical behaviour is observed.

In our CIFAR-100 experiments (CNN instead of ResNet32), we note that the performance of iCaRL [19] is significantly worse than what has been reported by the authors. We believe this is due to the dependence of iCaRL on a highly expressive feature space, as both the regularization and the classifier depend on it. Perhaps, this reduced expressivity of the feature space due to the smaller network resulted in the performance loss.

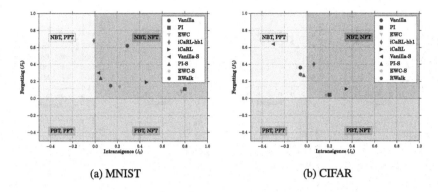

(a) MNIST   (b) CIFAR

Fig. 3. Interplay between forgetting and intransigence

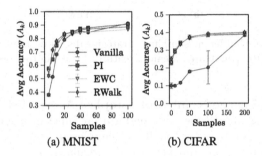

(a) MNIST   (b) CIFAR

Fig. 4. Comparison by increasing the number of samples. On MNIST and CIFAR each class has around 5000 and 500 samples, respectively. With increasing number of samples, the performance of Vanilla improved, but in the range where Vanilla is poor, RWalk consistently performs the best. Uniform sampling is used

Interplay of Forgetting and Intransigence. In Fig. 3 we study the interplay of forgetting and intransigence in the single-head setting. Ideally we would like a model to be in the quadrant marked as *PBT, PFT* (*i.e.*, positive backward transfer and positive forward transfer). On MNIST, since all the methods, except iCaRL-hb1, lie on the top-right quadrant, hence for models with comparable accuracy, a model which has the smallest distance from $(0,0)$ would be better. As evident, RWalk is closest to $(0,0)$, providing a better trade-off between forgetting and intransigence compared to all the other methods. On CIFAR-100, the models lie on both the top quadrants and with the introduction of samples, all the regularized methods show positive forward transfer. Since the models lie on different quadrants, their comparison of forgetting and intransigence becomes application specific. In some cases, we might prefer a model that performs well on new tasks (better intransigence), irrespective of its performance on the old ones (can compromise forgetting), and vice versa. Note that, RWalk maintains comparable performance to other baselines while yielding higher average accuracy on CIFAR-100.

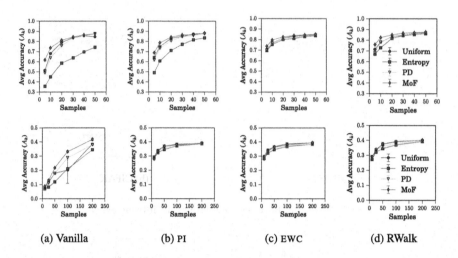

Fig. 5. Comparison of different sampling strategies discussed in Sect. 4.2 on MNIST (**top**) and CIFAR-100 (**bottom**). Mean of features (MoF) outperforms others

Effect of Increasing the Number of Samples. As expected, for smaller number of samples, regularized methods perform far superior compared to Vanilla (refer Fig. 4). However, once the number of samples are sufficiently large, Vanilla starts to perform better or equivalent to the regularized models. The reason is simple because now the Vanilla has access to enough samples of the previous tasks to relearn them at each step, thereby obviating the need of regularized models. However, in an IL problem, a fixed small-sized memory budget is usually assumed. Therefore, one cannot afford to store large number of samples from previous tasks. Additionally, for a simpler dataset like MNIST, Vanilla quickly catches up to the regularized models with small number of samples (20, 0.4% of total samples) but on a more challenging dataset like CIFAR it takes considerable amount of samples (200, 40% of total samples) of previous tasks for Vanilla to match the performance of the regularized models.

Comparison of Different Sampling Strategies. In Fig. 5 we compare different subset selection strategies discussed in Sect. 4.2. It can be observed that for all the methods Mean-of-Features (MoF) subset selection procedure, introduced in iCaRL [19], performs the best. Surprisingly, *uniform* sampling, despite being simple, is as good as more complex MoF, Plane Distance (PD) and entropy-based sampling strategies. Furthermore, the regularized methods remain insensitive to different sampling strategies, whereas in Vanilla, performance varies a lot against different strategies. We believe this is due to the unconstrained change in the last layer weights of the previous tasks.

7   Discussion

In this work, we analyzed the challenges in the incremental learning problem, namely, catastrophic forgetting and intransigence, and introduced metrics to quantify them. Such metrics reflect the interplay between *forgetting* and *intransigence*, which we believe will encourage future research for exploiting model capacity, such as, sparsity enforcing regularization, and exploration-based methods for incremental learning. In addition, we have presented an efficient version of EWC referred to as EWC++, and a generalization of EWC++ and PI with a KL-divergence-based perspective. Experimentally, we observed that these parameter regularization methods suffer from high intransigence in the practical *single-head* setting and showed that this can be alleviated with a small subset of representative samples. Since these methods are memory efficient compared to knowledge distillation-based algorithms such as iCaRL, future research in this direction would enable the possibility of incremental learning on segmentation tasks.

Acknowledgements. This work was supported by The Rhodes Trust, EPSRC, ERC grant ERC-2012-AdG 321162-HELIOS, EPSRC grant Seebibyte EP/M013774/1 and EPSRC/MURI grant EP/N019474/1.

References

1. Amari, S.I.: Natural gradient works efficiently in learning. Neural Comput. **10**, 251–276 (1998)
2. Grosse, R., Martens, J.: A kronecker-factored approximate fisher matrix for convolution layers. In: ICML (2016)
3. Hecht-Nielsen, R., et al.: Theory of the backpropagation neural network. Neural Netw. **1**(Supplement–1), 445–448 (1988)
4. Hinton, G., Vinyals, O., Dean, J.: Distilling the knowledge in a neural network. In: NIPS (2014)
5. Kingma, D., Ba, J.: Adam: a method for stochastic optimization. In: ICLR (2015)
6. Kirkpatrick, J., et al.: Overcoming catastrophic forgetting in neural networks. In: Proceedings of the National Academy of Sciences of the United States of America (PNAS) (2016)
7. Krizhevsky, A., Hinton, G.: Learning multiple layers of features from tiny images (2009). https://www.cs.toronto.edu/~kriz/cifar.html
8. Kullback, S., Leibler, R.A.: On information and sufficiency. Ann. Math. Stat. **22**, 79–86 (1951)
9. Le Roux, N., Pierre-Antoine, M., Bengio, Y.: Topmoumoute online natural gradient algorithm. In: NIPS (2007)
10. LeCun, Y.: The MNIST database of handwritten digits (1998). http://yann.lecun.com/exdb/mnist/
11. Lee, J.M.: Riemannian Manifolds: An Introduction to Curvature, vol. 176. Springer, New York (2006). https://doi.org/10.1007/b98852
12. Lee, S.W., Kim, J.H., Ha, J.W., Zhang, B.T.: Overcoming catastrophic forgetting by incremental moment matching. In: NIPS (2017)
13. Li, Z., Hoiem, D.: Learning without forgetting. In: Leibe, B., Matas, J., Sebe, N., Welling, M. (eds.) ECCV 2016. LNCS, vol. 9908, pp. 614–629. Springer, Cham (2016). https://doi.org/10.1007/978-3-319-46493-0_37

14. Lopez-Paz, D., Ranzato, M.: Gradient episodic memory for continuum learning. In: NIPS (2017)
15. Martens, J., Grosse, R.: Optimizing neural networks with kronecker-factored approximate curvature. In: ICML (2015)
16. Nguyen, C.V., Li, Y., Bui, T.D., Turner, R.E.: Variational continual learning. In: ICLR (2018)
17. Pascanu, R., Bengio, Y.: Revisiting natural gradient for deep networks. In: ICLR (2014)
18. Rebuffi, S.A., Bilen, H., Vedaldi, A.: Learning multiple visual domains with residual adapters. In: NIPS (2017)
19. Rebuffi, S.V., Kolesnikov, A., Lampert, C.H.: iCaRL: incremental classifier and representation learning. In: CVPR (2017)
20. Rusu, A.A., et al.: Progressive neural networks. arXiv preprint arXiv:1606.04671 (2016)
21. Schwarz, J., et al.: Progress & compress: a scalable framework for continual learning. In: ICML (2018)
22. Shin, H., Lee, J.K., Kim, J., Kim, J.: Continual learning with deep generative replay. In: NIPS (2017)
23. Terekhov, A.V., Montone, G., O'Regan, J.K.: Knowledge transfer in deep block-modular neural networks. In: Wilson, S.P., Verschure, P.F.M.J., Mura, A., Prescott, T.J. (eds.) LIVINGMACHINES 2015. LNCS (LNAI), vol. 9222, pp. 268–279. Springer, Cham (2015). https://doi.org/10.1007/978-3-319-22979-9_27
24. Yoon, J., Yang, E., Lee, J., Hwang, S.J.: Lifelong learning with dynamically expandable networks. In: ICLR (2018)
25. Zenke, F., Poole, B., Ganguli, S.: Continual learning through synaptic intelligence. In: ICML (2017)

Dependency-Aware Attention Control for Unconstrained Face Recognition with Image Sets

Xiaofeng Liu[1]($\boxtimes$)(iD), B. V. K. Vijaya Kumar[1](iD), Chao Yang[2](iD),
Qingming Tang[3](iD), and Jane You[4](iD)

[1] Carnegie Mellon University, Pittsburgh, PA 15213, USA
liuxiaofeng@cmu.edu
[2] University of Southern California, Los Angeles, CA 90089, USA
[3] Toyota Technological Institute at Chicago, Chicago, IL 60637, USA
[4] The Hong Kong Polytechnic University, Hong Kong, Hong Kong

Abstract. This paper targets the problem of image set-based face verification and identification. Unlike traditional single media (an image or video) setting, we encounter a set of heterogeneous contents containing orderless images and videos. The importance of each image is usually considered either equal or based on their independent quality assessment. How to model the relationship of orderless images within a set remains a challenge. We address this problem by formulating it as a Markov Decision Process (MDP) in the latent space. Specifically, we first present a dependency-aware attention control (DAC) network, which resorts to actor-critic reinforcement learning for sequential attention decision of each image embedding to fully exploit the rich correlation cues among the unordered images. Moreover, we introduce its sample-efficient variant with off-policy experience replay to speed up the learning process. The pose-guided representation scheme can further boost the performance at the extremes of the pose variation.

Keywords: Deep reinforcement learning · Actor-critic
Face recognition · Set-to-set · Attention control

1 Introduction

Recently, unconstrained face recognition (FR) has been rigorously researched in computer vision community [1,2]. In its initial days, the single image setting is used for FR evaluations, e.g., Labeled Faces in the Wild (LFW) verification task [3]. The trend of visual media explosion pushes the research into the next phase, where the video face verification attracts much attention, such as the YouTube Faces (YTF) dataset [4]. Since the LFW and YTF have a well-known frontal pose selection bias, the unconstrained FR is still considered an unsolved problem [5,6]. In addition, the open-set face identification is actually more challenging compared to the verification popularized by the LFW and YTF datasets [7,8].

© Springer Nature Switzerland AG 2018
V. Ferrari et al. (Eds.): ECCV 2018, LNCS 11215, pp. 573–590, 2018.
https://doi.org/10.1007/978-3-030-01252-6_34

The IARPA Janus Benchmark A (IJB-A) [9] provides a more practical uncon-strained face verification and identification benchmark. It takes a set (containing orderless images and/or videos with extreme head rotations, complex expressions and illuminations) as the smallest unit for representation. The set of a subject can be sampled from the mugshot history of a criminal, lifetime enrollment images for identity documents, different check points, and trajectory of a face in the video. This kind of setting is more similar to the real-world biometric scenarios [10]. Capturing human faces from multiple views, background envi-ronments, camera parameters, does result in the large inner-set variations, but also incorporates more complementary information hopefully leading to higher accuracy in practical applications [11].

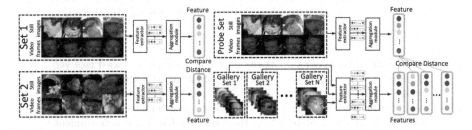

Fig. 1. Illustration of the image set-based 1:1 face verification (left) and open-set 1:N identification (right) using the typical aggregation method.

A commonly adopted strategy to aggregate identity information in each image is the average/max pooling [12–15]. Since the images vary in quality, a neural network-based assessment module has been introduced to independently assign the weight for each frame [11,16]. By doing this, the frontal and clear faces are favored by their model. However, this may result in redundancy and sacrifice the diversity in a set. As shown in Fig. 2, these inferior frontal images are given relatively high weights in a set, sometimes as high as the weight given to the most discriminative one. There is little additional information that can be extracted from the blurry version of the same pose, while the valuable profile information *etc.*, are almost ignored by the system. We argue that the desired weighting decision should depends on the other images within a set.

Instead, we propose to formulate the attention scheme as a Markov Deci-sion Process and resort to the actor-critic reinforcement learning (RL) to har-ness model learning. The dependency-aware attention control (DAC) module learns a policy to decide the importance of each image step-by-step with the observation of the other images in a set. In this way, we adaptively aggregate the feature vectors into a highly-compact representation inside the convex hull spanned by them. It not only explicitly learns to advocate high-quality images while repelling low-quality one, but also considers the inner-set dependency to reduce the redundancy and maintains the benefit of diversity information.

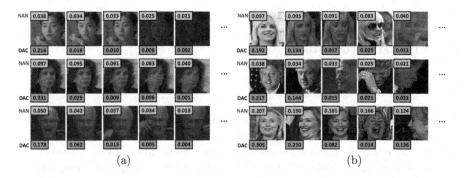

Fig. 2. Typical examples on the test set of (a) YTF and (b) IJB-A dataset showing the weights of images calculated by the previous method NAN [16], and proposed DAC.

Moreover, extracting a set-level invariable feature can be always challenging to incorporate all of the potential information in varying poses, illumination conditions, resolutions *etc*. Some approaches aggregate the image-level pair-wise similarity scores of two compared sets to fully use all images [17–20]. Given n as the average number of images in a set, then this corresponds to the $\mathcal{O}(n^2)$ computational complexity per match operation and $\mathcal{O}(n)$ space complexity per set are not desirable. More recently, [21–23] are proposed to trade-off between speed and accuracy of processing paired video inputs using value-based Q-learning methods. These configurations focus on the verification, and cannot be scaled well for large scale identification tasks [16]. Conventionally, the feature extraction of the probe and gallery samples are independent processes [8].

We notice that pose is the primary challenge in the IJB-A dataset and real applications [7,24,25], and there is a prior that the structures of frontal and profile face are significantly different. Therefore, we simply utilize a pose-guided representation (PGR) scheme with stochastic routing to model the inter-set dependency. It well balances the computation cost and information utilization.

Considering the above factors, we propose to fully exploit both the inner- and inter-set relationship for the unified set-based face verification and identification. (1) To the best of our knowledge, this is the first effort to introduce deep actor-critic RL into visual recognition problem. (2) The DAC can potentially be a general solution to incorporate rich correlation cues among orderless images. Its coefficients can be trained in a normal recognition training task given only set-level identity annotation, without the need of extra supervision signals. (3) To further improve the sample-efficiency, the trust region-based experience replay is introduced to speedup the training and achieve a stronger convergence property. (4) The PGR scheme well balances the computation cost and information utilization at the extremes of pose variation with the prior domain knowledge of human face. (5) The module-based feature-level aggregation also inherits the advantage of conventional pooling strategies *e.g.*, taking varied number of inputs as well as offering time and memory efficiency.

We show that our method leads to the state-of-the-art accuracy on IJB-A dataset and also generalizes well in several video-based face recognition tasks, *e.g.*, YTF and Celebrity-1000.

2   Related Work

Image Set/Video-Based Face Recognition has been actively studied in recent years [2]. The multi-image setting in the template-based dataset is similar to the multiple frames in the video-base recognition task. However, the temporal structure within a set is usually disordered, and the inner/inter-set variations are more challenging [9]. We will not cover the methods which exploit the temporal dynamics here. There are two kinds of conventional solutions, *i.e.*, manifold-based and image-based methods. In the first category, each set/video is usually modeled as a manifold, and the similarity or distance is measured in the manifold-level. In previous works, the affine hull, SPD model, Grassmann manifolds, n-order statistics and hyperplane similarity have been proposed to describe the manifolds [26–30]. In these methods, images are considered as equal importance. They usually cannot handle the large appearance variations in the unconstrained FR task. For the second category, the pairwise similarities between probe and gallery images are exploited for verification [17,18,20,31,32]. The quadratic number of comparisons make them not scale well for identification tasks. Yang *et al.* [16] propose an attention model to aggregate a set of features to a single representation with an independent quality assessment module for each feature. Reference [33] further up-sampled the aggregated features to an image, then fed it to an image-based FR network. However, weighting decision for an image does not take the other images into account as discussed in Sect. 1. Since the frequently used RNN in video task [22,34,35] is not fit for the image set, in this work, we consider the dependency within a set of features in a different way, where we use deep reinforcement learning to suggest the attention of each feature.

Reinforcement Learning (RL) trains an agent to interact (by trail and error) with a dynamic environment with the objective to maximize its accumulated reward. Recently, deep RL with convolutional neural networks (CNN) achieved human-level performance in Atari Games [36]. The CNN is an ideal approximate function to address the infinite state space [37]. There are two main streams to solve RL problems: methods based on value function and methods based on policy gradient. The first category, *e.g.*, Q-learning, is the common solution for discrete action tasks [36]. The second category can be efficient for continuous action space [38,39]. There is also a hybrid actor-critic approach in which the parameterized policy is called an actor, and the learned value-function is called a critic [40,41]. As it is essentially a policy gradient method, it can also be used for continuous action space [42].

Besides, policy-based and actor-critic methods have faster convergence characteristics than value-based methods [43], but they usually suffer from low sample-efficiency, high variance and often converge to local optima, since they typically learn via on-policy algorithms [44,45]. Even the Asynchronous Advantage Actor-Critic [40,41] also requires new samples to be collected for each gradient step on the policy. This quickly becomes extravagantly expensive, as the number of gradient steps to learn an effective policy increases with task complexity. Off-policy learning instead aims to reuse past experiences. This is not directly feasible with conventional policy gradient formulations, despite it relatively straightforward for value-based methods [37]. Hence in this paper, we focus on combining the stability of actor-critic methods with the efficiency of off-policy RL, which capitalizes in recent advances on deep RL [40], especially off-policy algorithms [46,47].

In addition to its traditional applications in robotics and control, recently RL has been successfully applied to a few visual recognition tasks. Mnih *et al.* [48] introduce the recurrent attention model to focus on selected regions or locations from an image for digits detection and classification. This idea is extended to identity alignment by iteratively removing irrelevant pixels in each image [49]. The value-based Q-learning methods are used for object tracking [50] and the video verification in a computationally efficient view by dropping inefficient probe-gallery pairs [22] or stopping the comparison after receiving sufficient pairs [21,23]. However, this will inevitably result in information loss of the unused pairs and only applicable for verification. There has been little progress made in policy gradient/actor-critic RL for visual recognition.

3 Proposed Methods

The flow chart of our framework is illustrated in Fig. 3. It takes a set of face images as input and processes them with two major modules to output a single (w/o PGR)/three (with PGR) feature vectors as its representation for recognition. We adopt a modern CNN module to embed an image into a latent space, which can largely reduce the computation costs and offer a practicable state space for RL. Then, we cascade the DAC, which works as an attention model reads all feature vectors and linearly combines them with adaptive weighting at the feature-level. Following the memory attention mechanism described in [16,34,35], the features are treated as the memory and the feature weighting is cast as a memory addressing procedure.These two modules can be trained in a one-by-one or end-to-end manner. We choose the first option, which makes our system benefit from the sufficient training data of the image-based FR datasets. The PGR scheme can further utilize the prior knowledge of human face to address a set with large pose variants.

3.1 Inner-Set Dependency Control

In the set-based recognition task, we are given M sets/videos $(\mathcal{X}^m, y^m)_{m=1}^{M}$, where $\mathcal{X}^m$ is a image set/video sequence with varying number of images T^m (*i.e.*, $\mathcal{X}^m = \{x_1^m, x_2^m, \cdots, x_{T^m}^m\}$, x_t^m is the t-th image in a set) and the y^m is the corresponding set-level identity label. We feed each image x_t^m to our model, and its corresponding feature representation f_t^m are extracted using our neural embedding network. Here, we adopt the GoogLeNet [51] with Batch Normalization [52] to produce a 128-dimensional feature as our encoding of each image. With a relatively simple architecture, GoogLeNet has shown superior performance on several FR benchmarks. It can be easily replaced by other advanced CNNs for better performance. In the rest of the paper, we will simply refer to our neural embedding network as CNN, and omit the upper index (identity) where appropriate for better readability.

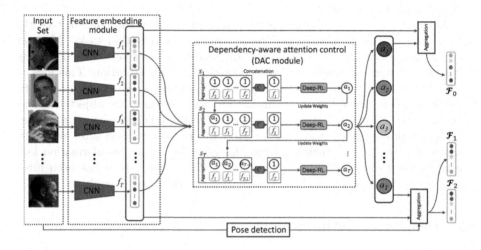

Fig. 3. Our network architecture for image set-based face recognition.

Since the features are deterministically computed from the images, they also inherit and display large variations. Simply discarding some of them using the hard attention scheme may result in loss of too much information in a set [16, 22]. Our attention control can be seen as the task of reinforcement learning to find the optimal weights of soft attention, which defines how much of them are focused by the memory attention mechanism. Moreover, the principle of taking different number of images without temporal information, and having trainable parameters through standard recognition training are fully considered.

Our solution of inner-set dependency modeling is to formulated as a MDP. At each time step t, the agent receives a state s_t in a state space $\mathcal{S}$ and chooses an action a_t from an action space $\mathcal{A}$, following a policy $\pi(a_t \mid s_t)$, which is the behavior of the agent. Then the action will determine the next state i.e., s_{t+1} or termination, and receive a reward $r_t(s_t, a_t) \in \mathcal{R} \subseteq \mathbb{R}$ from the environment. The goal is to find an optimal policy π^* that maximizes the discounted total return $R_t = \sum_{i \geq 0}^{T} \gamma^i r_{t+i}(s_t, a_t)$ in expectation, where $\gamma \in [0, 1)$ is the discount factor to trade-off the importance of immediate and future rewards [37].

In the context of image-set based face recognition, we define the actions, i.e., $\{a^1, a^2, \cdots, a^T\}$, as the weights of each feature representation $\{f\}_{i=1}^{T}$.

The weights of soft attention $\{a\}_{i=1}^{T}$ are initialized to be 1, and are updated step-by-step. The state s_t is related to the $t-1$ weighted features and $T-(t-1)$ to-be weighted features. In contrast to image-level dependency modeling, the compact embeddings largely shrink the state space and make our RL training feasible. In our practical applications, s_t is the concatenation of f_t and the aggregation of the remaining features with their updated weights at time step t. The termination means all of the images in this set have been successfully traversed.

$$s_t = \left\{ \frac{(\sum_{i=1}^{T} a_i f_i) - f_t}{(\sum_{i=1}^{T} a_i) - 1} \right\} Concatenate\{f_t\} \tag{1}$$

We define the global reward for RL by the overall recognition performance of the aggregated embeddings, which drives the RL network optimization. In practice, we add on the top of the DAC few fully connected layers h and followed by a softmax to calculate the cross-entropy loss $L_m = -\log\left(\{e^{o_{y^m}}\}/\sum_{j}^{M} e^{o_j}\right)$ to calculate the reward at this time step. We use the notation o_j to mean the j-th element of the vector of class scores o. $g(\cdot)$ is the weighted average aggregation function, h maps the aggregated feature with the updated weights $g(\mathcal{X}^m \mid s_t)$ to the o. The reward are defined as follows:

$$g(\mathcal{X}^m \mid s_t, CNN) = \sum_{i=1}^{T^m} \frac{a_i f_i^m}{\sum a_i} \quad \text{(with updated } a_i \text{ at step } t) \tag{2}$$

$$r_t = \{L_m[h(g(\mathcal{X}^m \mid s_t))] - L_m[h(g(\mathcal{X}^m \mid s_{t+1}))]\} + \lambda\max[0, (1 - a_t)] \tag{3}$$

where the hinge loss term serves as a regularization to encourage redundancy elimination and is balanced with the λ. It also contributes to stabilize training. The aggregation operation essentially selects a point inside of the convex hull spanned by all feature vectors [26].

Considering that the action space here is a continuous space $\mathcal{A} \in \mathbb{R}^+$, the value-based RL (e.g., Q-Learning) cannot tackle this task. We adapt the actor-critic network to directly grade each feature dependent on the observation of the other features. In a policy-based method, the training objective is to find a parametrized policy $\pi_\theta(a_t \mid s_t)$ that maximizes the expected reward $J(\theta)$ over all possible aggregation trajectories given a starting state. Following the Policy Gradient Theorem [43], the gradient of the parameters given the objective function has the form:

$$\nabla_\theta J(\theta) = \mathbb{E}[\nabla_\theta \log\pi_\theta(a_t \mid s_t)(Q(s_t, a_t) - b(s_t))] \tag{4}$$

where $Q(s_t, a_t) = \mathbb{E}[R_t \mid s_t, a_t]$ is the state-action value function, in which the initial action a_t is provided to calculate the expected return when starting in the state s_t. A baseline function $b(s_t)$ is typically subtracted to reduce the variance while not changing the estimated gradient [44,53]. A natural candidate for this baseline is the state only value function $V(s_t) = \mathbb{E}[R_t \mid s_t]$, which is similar to

$Q(s_t, a_t)$, except the a_t is not given here. The advantage function is defined as $A(s_t, a_t) = Q(s_t, a_t) - V(s_t)$ [37]. Equation (4) then becomes:

$$\nabla_\theta J(\theta) = \mathbb{E}[\nabla_\theta \log \pi_\theta(a_t \mid s_t) A(s_t, a_t)] \tag{5}$$

This can be viewed as a special case of the actor-critic model, where $\pi_\theta(a_t \mid s_t)$ is the actor and the $A(s_t, a_t)$ is the critic. To reduce the number of required parameters, the parameterized temporal difference (TD) error $\delta_\omega = r_t + \gamma V_\omega(S_{s+1}) - V_\omega(S_s)$ can be used to approximate the advantage function [45]. We use two different symbols θ and ω to denote the actor and critic function, but most of these parameters are shared in a main stream neural network, then separated to two branches for policy and value predictions, respectively.

3.2   Off-Policy Actor-Critic with Experience Replay

On-policy RL methods update the model with the samples collected via the current policy. The experience replay (ER) can be used to improve the sample-efficiency [54], where the experiences are randomly sampled from a replay pool $\mathcal{P}$. This ensure the training stability by reducing the data correlation. Since these past experiences were collected from different policies, the use of ER leads to off-policy updates.

When training models with RL, ε-greedy action selection is often used to trade-off between exploitation and exploration, whereby a random action is chosen with a probability otherwise the top-ranking action is selected. A policy used to generate a training weight is referred to as a behavior policy μ, in contrast to the policy to-be optimized which is called the target policy π.

The basic advantage actor-critic (A2C) training algorithm described in Sect. 3.1 is on-policy, as it assume the actions are drawn from the same policy as the target to-be optimized (i.e., $\mu = \pi$). However, the current policy π is updated with the samples generated from old behavior policies μ in off-policy learning. Therefore, an importance sampling (IS) ratio is used to rescale each sampled reward to correct the sampling bias at time-step t: $\rho_t = \pi(a_t \mid s_t)/\mu(a_t \mid s_t)$ [55]. For A2C, the off-policy gradient for the parametrized state only value function V_ω thus has the form:

$$\Delta \omega^{\text{off}} = \sum_{t=1}^{T} (\bar{R}_t - \hat{V}_\omega(s_t)) \nabla_\omega \hat{V}_\omega(s_t) \prod_{i=1}^{t} \rho_i \tag{6}$$

where $\bar{R}_t$ is the off-policy Monte-Carlo return [56]:

$$\bar{R}_t = r_t + \gamma r_{t+1} \prod_{i=1}^{1} \rho_i + \cdots + \gamma^{T-t} r_T \prod_{i=1}^{T-t} \rho_{t+i} \tag{7}$$

Likewise, the updated gradient for policy π_θ is:

$$\Delta \theta^{\text{off}} = \sum_{t=1}^{T} \rho_t \nabla_\theta \log \pi_\theta(a_t \mid s_t) \hat{\delta}_\omega \tag{8}$$

where $\hat{\delta}_\omega = r_t + \gamma \hat{V}_\omega(s_{t+1} - \hat{V}_\omega(s_t)$ is the TD error using the estimated value of $\hat{V}_\omega$.

Here, we introduce a modified Trust Region Policy Optimization method [46,47]. In addition to maximizing the cumulative reward $J(\theta)$, the optimization is also subject to a Kullback-Leibler (KL) divergence limit between the updated policy θ and an average policy θ_a to ensure safety. This average policy represents a running average of past policies and constrains the updated policy from deviating too far from the average $\theta_a \leftarrow [\alpha \theta_a + (1 - \alpha)\theta]$ with a weight α. Thus, given the off-policy policy gradient $\Delta \theta^{\text{off}}$ in Eq. (8), the modified policy gradient with trust region z is calculated as follows:

$$\begin{array}{c} \underset{z}{minimize} \quad \dfrac{1}{2}\|\Delta \theta^{\text{off}} - z\|_2^2, \\ \text{Subject to:} \nabla_\theta D_{KL}[\pi_{\theta_a}(s_t)\|\pi_\theta(s_t)]^{\mathrm{T}} \, z \leq \xi \end{array} \tag{9}$$

where π is the policy parametrized by θ or θ_a, and ξ controls the magnitude of the KL constraint. Since the constraint is linear, a closed form solution to this quadratic programming problem can be derived using the KKT conditions. Setting $k = \nabla_\theta D_{KL}[\pi_{\theta_a}(s_t)\|\pi_\theta(s_t)]$, we get:

$$z_{tr}^* = \Delta \theta^{\text{off}} - max\left\{\frac{k^{\mathrm{T}}\Delta \theta^{\text{off}} - \xi}{\|k\|_2^2}, 0\right\}k \tag{10}$$

This direction is also shown to be closely related to the natural gradient [57, 58]. The above enhancements speed up and stabilize our A2C network training.

3.3   Pose-Guided Inter-set Dependency Model

To model the inter-set dependency without paired-input, we propose a pose-guided stochastic routing scheme. Such a divide-and-conquer idea originated in [59], which constructs several face detectors to charge each view. Given a set of face image, we extract its general feature aggregation $\mathcal{F}_0$, as well as the aggregation of the frontal face features $\mathcal{F}_1$ and profile face feature $\mathcal{F}_2$. The $\mathcal{F}_1$ and $\mathcal{F}_2$ are the weighted average of the features from the near-frontal face images ($\leq 30°$) and profile face images ($> 30°$) respectively, in which the attention is assigned with the observation of full set. We use PIFA [60] to estimate the yaw angle. The sum of weights of the frontal and profile features p_1 and p_2 are with respect to the quality of each pose group. Considering the mirror transforms in data augmentation and the symmetry property of human faces, we do not discriminate the right face and the left face. With PGR, the distance d between two sets of samples is computed as:

$$d = \frac{1}{2}S(\mathcal{F}_0^1, \mathcal{F}_0^2) + \frac{1}{2}\sum_{i=1}^{2}\sum_{j=1}^{2}S(\mathcal{F}_i^1, \mathcal{F}_j^2)p_i^1 p_j^2 \tag{11}$$

where S is the L2 distance function to measure the distance between two feature vectors. We treat the generic features and pose-specific features equally, and fuse them for evaluations. The number of distance evaluations is decreased to $\mathcal{O}(5n)$. This achieves promising verification performance requiring fewer comparisons than conventional image-level similarity measurements. It is also readily applied to the other variations.

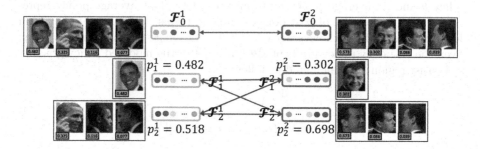

Fig. 4. Illustration of the pose-guided representation scheme.

4   Numerical Experiments

We evaluated the performance of the proposed method on three Set/video-based FR datasets: the IJB-A [9], YTF [4], and Celebrity-1000 [61]. To utilize the millions of available still images, we train our CNN embedding module separately. As in [16], 3M face images from 50K identities are detected with the JDA [62] and aligned using the LBF [63] method for our GoogleNet training. This part is fixed when we train the DAC module on each set/video face dataset. Benefiting from the highly-compact 128-d feature representation and the simple neural network of the DAC, the training time of our DAC(off) on IJB-A dataset with a single Xeon E5 v4 CPU is about 3 h, the average testing time per each set-pair for verification is 62 ms. We use Titan Xp for CNN processing.

As our baseline methods, CNN + Mean L2 measures the average L2 distances of all image pairs of two sets, while the CNN + AvePool uses average pooling along each feature dimension for aggregation. The previous work NAN [16] uses the same CNN structure as our framework, but adopts a neural network module for independently quality assessment of each image. Therefore, NAN can be also regarded as our baseline. We refer the vanilla A2C as DAC(on), and use DAC(off) for the actor-critic with trust region-based experience replay scheme. The DAC(off) + PGR is the combination of the DAC(off) and PGR.

4.1   Results on IJB-A Dataset

IJB-A [9] is a face *verification* and *identification* dataset, containing images captured from unconstrained environments with wide variations of pose and imaging conditions. There are 500 identities with a total of 25,813 images (5,397 still images and 20,412 video frames sampled from 2,042 videos). A set of images for a particular identity is called a template. Each template can be a mixture of still images and sampled video frames. The number of images (or frames) in a template ranges from 1 to 190 with approximately 11.4 images and 4.2 videos per subject on average. It provides a ground truth bounding box for each face with 3 landmarks. There are 10 training and testing splits. Each split contains 333 training and 167 testing identities.

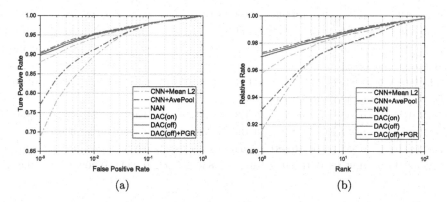

Fig. 5. Average ROC (Left) and CMC (Right) curves of the proposed method and its baselines on the IJB-A dataset over 10 splits.

We compare the proposed framework with the existing methods on both face verification and identification following the standard evaluation protocol on IJB-A dataset. Metrics for the 1:1 compare task are evaluated using the receiver operating characteristics (ROC) curves in Fig. 5(a). We also report the true accept rate (TAR) *vs.* false positive rates (FAR) in Table 1. For the 1:N search task, the performance is evaluated in terms of a Cumulative Match Characteristics (CMC) curve as shown in Fig. 5(b). It is an information retrieval metric, which plots identification rates corresponding to different ranks. A rank-k identification rate is defined as the percentage of probe searches whose gallery match is returned with in the top-k matches. The true positive identification rate (TPIR) *vs.* false positive identification rate (FPIR) as well as the rank-1 accuracy are also reported in Table 1.

These results show that both the verification and the identification performance are largely improved compared to our baseline methods. The RL networks have learned to be robust to low-quality and redundant image. The DAC(on) outperforms the previous approaches in most of the operating points, showing that our representation is more discriminative than the weighted feature in [11,16] without considering the inner-set dependency. The experience replay can further help the stabilization of our training and the state-of-the-art performance is achieved. Combining the off-policy DAC and pose-guide representation scheme also contributes to the final results in an efficient way.

Table 1. Performance evaluation on the IJB-A dataset. For verification, the true accept rates (TAR) vs. false positive rates (FAR) are reported. For identification, the true positive identification rate (TPIR) vs. false positive identification rate (FPIR) and the Rank-1 accuracy are presented.

Method	1:1 Verification TAR		1:N Identification TPIR		
	FAR = 0.01	FAR = 0.1	FPIR = 0.01	FPIR = 0.1	Rank-1
B-CNN [15]	–	–	0.143 ± 0.027	0.341 ± 0.032	0.588 ± 0.02
LSFS [64]	0.733 ± 0.034	0.895 ± 0.013	0.383 ± 0.063	0.613 ± 0.032	0.820 ± 0.024
DCNN [14]	0.787 ± 0.043	0.947 ± 0.011	–	–	0.852 ± 0.018
Pose-model [65]	0.826 ± 0.018	–	–	–	0.840 ± 0.012
Masi *et al.* [66]	0.886	–	–	–	0.906
Adaptation [6]	0.939 ± 0.013	0.979 ± 0.004	0.774 ± 0.049	0.882 ± 0.016	0.928 ± 0.010
QAN [11]	0.942 ± 0.015	0.980 ± 0.006	–	–	–
NAN [16]	0.941 ± 0.008	0.978 ± 0.003	0.817 ± 0.041	0.917 ± 0.009	0.958 ± 0.005
DAC(on)	0.951 ± 0.014	0.980 ± 0.016	0.852 ± 0.048	0.931 ± 0.012	0.970 ± 0.011
DAC(off)	0.953 ± 0.009	$\mathbf{0.981 \pm 0.013}$	0.853 ± 0.033	0.933 ± 0.006	0.972 ± 0.012
DAC(off)PGR	$\mathbf{0.954 \pm 0.01}$	$\mathbf{0.981 \pm 0.008}$	$\mathbf{0.855 \pm 0.042}$	$\mathbf{0.934 \pm 0.009}$	$\mathbf{0.973 \pm 0.011}$

4.2 Results on YouTube Face Dataset

The YouTube Face (YTF) dataset [4] is a widely used video face *verification* dataset, which contains 3,425 videos of 1,595 different subjects. In this dataset, there are many challenging videos, including amateur photography, occlusions, problematic lighting, pose and motion blur. The length of face videos in this dataset varies from 48 to 6,070 frames, and the average length of videos is 181.3 frames. In experiments, we follow the standard verification protocol as in [16,22, 33], which test our method for unconstrained face 1:1 verification with the given 5,000 video pairs. These pairs are equally divided into 10 splits, and each split has around 250 intra-personal pairs and 250 inter-personal pairs.

Table 2 presents the results of our DAC and previous methods. It can be seen that the DAC outperforms all the previous state-of-the-art methods following the setting that without fine-tuning the feature embedding module on YTF. Since this dataset has frontal face bias [6] and the face variations in this dataset are relatively small as shown in Fig. 2, we have not used the pose-guided representation scheme. It is obvious that the video sequences are redundant, considering the inner-video relationship does contribute to the improvement over [16]. The comparable performance with temporal representation-based methods suggests the DAC could be a potential substitute for RNN in some specific areas. Actually, the RNN itself is computationally expensive and sometimes difficult to train [67]. We directly model the dependency in the feature-level, which is faster than the temporal representation of original images [22], and more effective than the adversarial face generation-based method [33].

It also indicates that DAC achieves a very competitive performance without highly-engineered CNN models. Note that the FaceNet [18], NAN [16] also

Table 2. Comparisons of the average verification accuracy with the recently state-of-the-art results on the YTF dataset. † fine-tuned the CNN model with YTF.

Method	Accuracy	†Accuracy	Year
FaceNet [18]	0.9512 ± 0.0039	–	2015
Deep FR [13]	0.915	0.973	2015
CenterLoss [20]	0.949	–	2016
TBE-CNN [68]	0.9384 ± 0.0032	0.9496 ± 0.0031	2017
TR [22]	0.9596 ± 0.0059	0.9652 ± 0.0054	2017
NAN [16]	0.9572 ± 0.0064	–	2017
DAN [33]	0.9428 ± 0.0069	–	2017
DAC(on)	0.9597 ± 0.0041		
DAC(off)	**0.9601 ± 0.0048**		

use the GoogleNet style structure. We show that DAC outperforms them on both the verification accuracy and the standard variation. The Deep FR, TBE-CNN and TR methods have additional fine-tuning of the CNN-model with YTF dataset, and the residual constitutional networks are used in TR. Considering our module-based structure, these advanced CNNs can be easily added on the DAC and boost its performance. We see that the DAC can generalizes well in video-based face verification datasets.

4.3   Results on Celebrity-1000 Dataset

We then test our method on the Celebrity-1000 dataset [61], which is designed for the unconstrained video-based face *identification* problem. 2.4M frames from 159,726 face videos (about 15 frames per sequence) of 1,000 subjects are contained in this dataset. It is released with two standard evaluation protocols: open-set and closed-set. We follow the standard $1 : N$ identification setting as in [61] and report the result of both protocols.

For the closed-set protocol, we use the softmax outputs from the reward network, and the subject with the maximum score as the result. Since the baseline methods do not have a multi-class prediction unit, we simply compare the L2 distance as in [16]. We present the results in Table 3, and show the CMC curves in Fig. 6(a). With the help of end-to-end learning and large volume training data for CNN model, deep learning methods outperform [12,61] by a large margin. It can be seen that the state-of-the-art is achieved by the DAC. We can also benefit from the experience replay to achieve improvements over the baselines.

For the open-set testing, we take multiple image sequences of each gallery subject to extract a highly compact feature representation as in NAN [16]. Then the open-set identification is performed by comparing the L2 distance of the aggregated probe and gallery representations. Figure 6(b) and Table 3 show the results of different methods in our experiments. We see that our proposed methods outperform the previous methods again, which clearly shows that DAC is effective and robust.

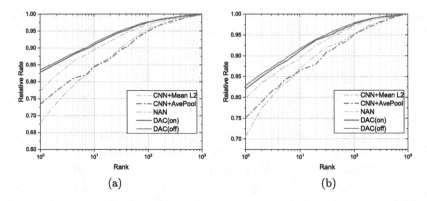

Fig. 6. The CMC curves of different methods on Celebrity 1000. (a) Close-set tests on 1000 subjects, (b) Open-set tests on 800 subjects

Table 3. Identification performance (rank-1 accuracies), on the Celebrity-1000 dataset for the closed-set tests (left) and open-set tests (right).

Method	Number of Subjects(*closed*)				Number of subjects(*open*)			
	100	200	500	1000	100	200	500	800
MTJSR [61]	0.506	0.408	0.3546	0.3004	0.4612	0.3984	0.3751	0.3350
Eigen-PEP [12]	0.506	0.4502	0.3997	0.3194	0.5155	0.4615	0.4233	0.2590
CNN+Mean L2	0.8526	0.7759	0.7457	0.6791	0.8488	0.7988	0.7676	0.7067
CNN+AvePool	0.8446	0.7893	0.7768	0.7341	0.8411	0.7909	0.7840	0.7512
NAN [16]	0.9044	0.8333	0.8227	0.7717	0.8876	0.8521	0.8274	0.7987
DAC(on)	0.9125	0.8722	0.8475	0.8278	0.8986	0.8706	0.8395	0.8205
DAC(off)	**0.9137**	**0.8783**	**0.8523**	**0.8353**	**0.9004**	**0.8715**	**0.8428**	**0.8264**

5   Conclusions

We have introduced the actor-critic RL for visual recognition problem. We cast the inner-set dependency modeling to a MDP, and train an agent DAC to make attention control for each image in each step. The PGR scheme well balances the computation cost and information utilization. Although we only explore their ability in set/video-based face recognition tasks, we believe it is a general and practicable methodology that could be easily applied to other problems, such as Re-ID, action recognition and event detection *etc.*

Acknowledgement. This work was supported in part by the National Key R&D Plan 2016YFB0501003, Hong Kong Government General Research Fund GRF 152202/14E, PolyU Central Research Grant G-YBJW, Youth Innovation Promotion Association, CAS (2017264), Innovative Foundation of CIOMP, CAS (Y586320150).

References

1. Chen, J.C., et al.: Unconstrained still/video-based face verification with deep convolutional neural networks. Int. J. Comput. Vis., 1–20 (2017)
2. Learned-Miller, E., Huang, G.B., RoyChowdhury, A., Li, H., Hua, G.: Labeled faces in the wild: a survey. In: Kawulok, M., Celebi, M., Smolka, B. (eds.) Advances in Face Detection and Facial Image Analysis, pp. 189–248. Springer, Cham (2016). https://doi.org/10.1007/978-3-319-25958-1_8
3. Huang, G.B., Ramesh, M., Berg, T., Learned-Miller, E.: Labeled faces in the wild: a database for studying face recognition in unconstrained environments. Technical report, Technical Report 07–49, University of Massachusetts, Amherst (2007)
4. Wolf, L., Hassner, T., Maoz, I.: Face recognition in unconstrained videos with matched background similarity. In: 2011 IEEE Conference on Computer Vision and Pattern Recognition (CVPR), pp. 529–534 (2011)
5. Phillips, P.J., Hill, M.Q., Swindle, J.A., O'Toole, A.J.: Human and algorithm performance on the PaSC face recognition challenge. In: 2015 IEEE 7th International Conference on Biometrics Theory, Applications and Systems (BTAS), pp. 1–8. IEEE (2015)
6. Crosswhite, N., Byrne, J., Stauffer, C., Parkhi, O., Cao, Q., Zisserman, A.: Template adaptation for face verification and identification. In: FG, pp. 1–8. IEEE (2017)
7. Hayat, M., Khan, S.H., Werghi, N., Goecke, R.: Joint registration and representation learning for unconstrained face identification. In: IEEE CVPR, pp. 2767–2776 (2017)
8. Liu, W., Wen, Y., Yu, Z., Li, M., Raj, B., Song, L.: Sphereface: Deep hypersphere embedding for face recognition. In: IEEE CVPR, vol. 1 (2017)
9. Klare, B.F., et al.: Pushing the frontiers of unconstrained face detection and recognition: IARPA Janus benchmark A. In: Proceedings of the IEEE Conference on Computer Vision and Pattern Recognition, pp. 1931–1939 (2015)
10. Grother, P., Ngan, M.: Face recognition vendor test (FRVT). Performance of face identification algorithms (2014)
11. Liu, Y., Yan, J., Ouyang, W.: Quality aware network for set to set recognition. In: Proceedings of the IEEE Conference on Computer Vision and Pattern Recognition, pp. 5790–5799 (2017)
12. Li, H., Hua, G., Shen, X., Lin, Z., Brandt, J.: Eigen-PEP for video face recognition. In: Cremers, D., Reid, I., Saito, H., Yang, M.-H. (eds.) ACCV 2014. LNCS, vol. 9005, pp. 17–33. Springer, Cham (2015). https://doi.org/10.1007/978-3-319-16811-1_2
13. Parkhi, O.M., Vedaldi, A., Zisserman, A.: Deep face recognition. In: BMVC, vol. 1, p. 6 (2015)
14. Chen, J.C., Ranjan, R., Kumar, A., Chen, C.H., Patel, V.M., Chellappa, R.: An end-to-end system for unconstrained face verification with deep convolutional neural networks. In: IEEE CVPRW, pp. 118–126 (2015)
15. Chowdhury, A.R., Lin, T.Y., Maji, S., Learned-Miller, E.: One-to-many face recognition with bilinear CNNs. In: WACV, pp. 1–9. IEEE (2016)
16. Yang, J., Ren, P., Zhang, D., Chen, D., Wen, F., Li, H., Hua, G.: Neural aggregation network for video face recognition. In: IEEE CVPR, pp. 4362–4371 (2017)
17. Taigman, Y., Yang, M., Ranzato, M., Wolf, L.: Deepface: closing the gap to human-level performance in face verification. In: Proceedings of the IEEE Conference on Computer Vision and Pattern Recognition, pp. 1701–1708 (2014)

18. Schroff, F., Kalenichenko, D., Philbin, J.: Facenet: a unified embedding for face recognition and clustering. In: Proceedings of the IEEE Conference on Computer Vision and Pattern Recognition, pp. 815–823 (2015)
19. Sun, Y., Wang, X., Tang, X.: Deeply learned face representations are sparse, selective, and robust. In: 2015 IEEE Conference on Computer Vision and Pattern Recognition (CVPR), pp. 2892–2900. IEEE (2015)
20. Wen, Y., Zhang, K., Li, Z., Qiao, Y.: A discriminative feature learning approach for deep face recognition. In: Leibe, B., Matas, J., Sebe, N., Welling, M. (eds.) ECCV 2016. LNCS, vol. 9911, pp. 499–515. Springer, Cham (2016). https://doi.org/10.1007/978-3-319-46478-7_31
21. Zhang, J., Wang, N., Zhang, L.: Multi-shot pedestrian re-identification via sequential decision making. arXiv preprint arXiv:1712.07257 (2017)
22. Rao, Y., Lu, J., Zhou, J.: Attention-aware deep reinforcement learning for video face recognition. In: IEEE ICCV, pp. 3931–3940 (2017)
23. Janisch, J., Pevný, T., Lisý, V.: Classification with costly features using deep reinforcement learning. arXiv preprint arXiv:1711.07364 (2017)
24. Zhu, Z., Luo, P., Wang, X., Tang, X.: Multi-view perceptron: a deep model for learning face identity and view representations. In: Advances in Neural Information Processing Systems, pp. 217–225 (2014)
25. Wright, J., Yang, A.Y., Ganesh, A., Sastry, S.S., Ma, Y.: Robust face recognition via sparse representation. IEEE Trans. Pattern Anal. Mach. Intell. 31(2), 210–227 (2009)
26. Cevikalp, H., Triggs, B.: Face recognition based on image sets. In: 2010 IEEE Conference on Computer Vision and Pattern Recognition (CVPR), pp. 2567–2573. IEEE (2010)
27. Huang, Z., Wu, J., Van Gool, L.: Building deep networks on Grassmann manifolds. arXiv preprint arXiv:1611.05742 (2016)
28. Huang, Z., Van Gool, L.J.: A Riemannian network for SPD matrix learning. In: AAAI, vol. 2, p. 6 (2017)
29. Wang, R., Guo, H., Davis, L.S., Dai, Q.: Covariance discriminative learning: a natural and efficient approach to image set classification. In: 2012 IEEE Conference on Computer Vision and Pattern Recognition (CVPR), pp. 2496–2503. IEEE (2012)
30. Lu, J., Wang, G., Moulin, P.: Image set classification using holistic multiple order statistics features and localized multi-kernel metric learning. In: 2013 IEEE International Conference on Computer Vision (ICCV), pp. 329–336. IEEE (2013)
31. Sivic, J., Everingham, M., Zisserman, A.: Who are you?-Learning person specific classifiers from video. In: 2009 IEEE Conference on Computer Vision and Pattern Recognition, CVPR 2009, pp. 1145–1152. IEEE (2009)
32. Lu, J., Wang, G., Deng, W., Moulin, P., Zhou, J.: Multi-manifold deep metric learning for image set classification. In: Proceedings of the IEEE Conference on Computer Vision and Pattern Recognition, pp. 1137–1145 (2015)
33. Rao, Y., Lin, J., Lu, J., Zhou, J.: Learning discriminative aggregation network for video-based face recognition. In: IEEE ICCV, pp. 3781–3790 (2017)
34. Graves, A., Wayne, G., Danihelka, I.: Neural turing machines. arXiv preprint arXiv:1410.5401 (2014)
35. Vinyals, O., Bengio, S., Kudlur, M.: Order matters: sequence to sequence for sets. arXiv preprint arXiv:1511.06391 (2015)
36. Mnih, V., et al.: Human-level control through deep reinforcement learning. Nature 518(7540), 529 (2015)
37. Li, Y.: Deep reinforcement learning: an overview. arXiv preprint arXiv:1701.07274 (2017)

38. Silver, D., Lever, G., Heess, N., Degris, T., Wierstra, D., Riedmiller, M.: Deterministic policy gradient algorithms. In: ICML (2014)
39. Lillicrap, T.P., et al.: Continuous control with deep reinforcement learning. arXiv preprint arXiv:1509.02971 (2015)
40. Mnih, V., et al.: Asynchronous methods for deep reinforcement learning. In: International Conference on Machine Learning, pp. 1928–1937 (2016)
41. Babaeizadeh, M., Frosio, I., Tyree, S., Clemons, J., Kautz, J.: Reinforcement learning through asynchronous advantage actor-critic on a GPU (2017)
42. Arulkumaran, K., Deisenroth, M.P., Brundage, M., Bharath, A.A.: Deep reinforcement learning: a brief survey. IEEE Sig. Process. Mag. **34**(6), 26–38 (2017)
43. Sutton, R.S., McAllester, D.A., Singh, S.P., Mansour, Y.: Policy gradient methods for reinforcement learning with function approximation. In: NIPS, pp. 1057–1063 (2000)
44. Williams, R.J.: Simple statistical gradient-following algorithms for connectionist reinforcement learning. Mach. Learn. **8**, 229–256 (1992)
45. Schulman, J., Moritz, P., Levine, S., Jordan, M., Abbeel, P.: High-dimensional continuous control using generalized advantage estimation (2017)
46. Schulman, J., Levine, S., Abbeel, P., Jordan, M., Moritz, P.: Trust region policy optimization. In: ICML, pp. 1889–1897 (2015)
47. Wang, Z., et al.: Sample efficient actor-critic with experience replay (2017)
48. Mnih, V., Heess, N., Graves, A., et al.: Recurrent models of visual attention. In: Advances in Neural Information Processing Systems, pp. 2204–2212 (2014)
49. Lan, X., Wang, H., Gong, S., Zhu, X.: Identity alignment by noisy pixel removal. arXiv preprint arXiv:1707.02785 (2017)
50. Huang, C., Lucey, S., Ramanan, D.: Learning policies for adaptive tracking with deep feature cascades. arXiv preprint arXiv:1708.02973 (2017)
51. Szegedy, C., Vanhoucke, V., Ioffe, S., Shlens, J., Wojna, Z.: Rethinking the inception architecture for computer vision. In: Proceedings of the IEEE Conference on Computer Vision and Pattern Recognition, pp. 2818–2826 (2016)
52. Ioffe, S., Szegedy, C.: Batch normalization: Accelerating deep network training by reducing internal covariate shift. In: International Conference on Machine Learning, pp. 448–456 (2015)
53. Andrew, A.M.: Reinforcement learning: an introduction by Richard S. Sutton and Andrew G. Barto, adaptive computation and machine learning series, MIT Press (Bradford book), Cambridge, Mass., 1998, xviii+ 322 pp, ISBN 0-262-19398-1, (hardback, £ 31.95). Robotica **17**(2), 229–235 (1999)
54. Lin, L.J.: Self-improving reactive agents based on reinforcement learning, planning and teaching. Mach. Learn. **8**(3–4), 293–321 (1992)
55. Meuleau, N., Peshkin, L., Kaelbling, L.P., Kim, K.E.: Off-Policy Policy Search. MIT Artifical Intelligence Laboratory, Cambridge (2000)
56. Precup, D., Sutton, R.S., Dasgupta, S.: Off-policy temporal-difference learning with function approximation. In: ICML, pp. 417–424 (2001)
57. Amari, S.I.: Natural gradient works efficiently in learning. Neural Comput. **10**(2), 251–276 (1998)
58. Peters, J., Schaal, S.: Policy gradient methods for robotics. In: 2006 IEEE/RSJ International Conference on Intelligent Robots and Systems, pp. 2219–2225. IEEE (2006)
59. Li, Y., Zhang, B., Shan, S., Chen, X., Gao, W.: Bagging based efficient kernel fisher discriminant analysis for face recognition. In: 2006 18th International Conference on Pattern Recognition, ICPR 2006, vol. 3, pp. 523–526. IEEE (2006)

60. Jourabloo, A., Liu, X.: Pose-invariant face alignment via CNN-based dense 3D model fitting. Int. J. Comput. Vis. **124**(2), 187–203 (2017)
61. Liu, L., Zhang, L., Liu, H., Yan, S.: Toward large-population face identification in unconstrained videos. IEEE Trans. Circuits Syst. Video Technol. **24**(11), 1874–1884 (2014)
62. Chen, D., Ren, S., Wei, Y., Cao, X., Sun, J.: Joint cascade face detection and alignment. In: Fleet, D., Pajdla, T., Schiele, B., Tuytelaars, T. (eds.) ECCV 2014. LNCS, vol. 8694, pp. 109–122. Springer, Cham (2014). https://doi.org/10.1007/978-3-319-10599-4_8
63. Ren, S., Cao, X., Wei, Y., Sun, J.: Face alignment at 3000 fps via regressing local binary features. In: Proceedings of the IEEE Conference on Computer Vision and Pattern Recognition, pp. 1685–1692 (2014)
64. Wang, D., Otto, C., Jain, A.K.: Face search at scale: 80 million gallery. arXiv preprint arXiv:1507.07242 (2015)
65. Masi, I., Rawls, S., Medioni, G., Natarajan, P.: Pose-aware face recognition in the wild. In: IEEE CVPR, pp. 4838–4846 (2016)
66. Masi, I., et al.: Do we really need to collect millions of faces for effective face recognition? In: Leibe, B., Matas, J., Sebe, N., Welling, M. (eds.) ECCV 2016. LNCS, vol. 9909, pp. 579–596. Springer, Cham (2016). https://doi.org/10.1007/978-3-319-46454-1_35
67. Zhang, Y., Pezeshki, M., Brakel, P., Zhang, S., Bengio, C.L.Y., Courville, A.: Towards end-to-end speech recognition with deep convolutional neural networks. arXiv preprint arXiv:1701.02720 (2017)
68. Ding, C., Tao, D.: Trunk-branch ensemble convolutional neural networks for video-based face recognition. IEEE Trans. Pattern Anal. Mach. Intell. (2017)

Volumetric Performance Capture from Minimal Camera Viewpoints

Andrew Gilbert[1(✉)], Marco Volino[1], John Collomosse[1,2], and Adrian Hilton[1]

[1] Centre for Vision Speech and Signal Processing, University of Surrey,
Guildford, UK
a.gilbert@surrey.ac.uk
[2] Creative Intelligence Lab, Adobe Research, San Jose, USA

Abstract. We present a convolutional autoencoder that enables high fidelity volumetric reconstructions of human performance to be captured from multi-view video comprising only a small set of camera views. Our method yields similar end-to-end reconstruction error to that of a probabilistic visual hull computed using significantly more (double or more) viewpoints. We use a deep prior implicitly learned by the autoencoder trained over a dataset of view-ablated multi-view video footage of a wide range of subjects and actions. This opens up the possibility of high-end volumetric performance capture in on-set and prosumer scenarios where time or cost prohibit a high witness camera count.

Keywords: Multi-view reconstruction · Deep autoencoders
Visual hull

1 Introduction

Image based model reconstruction from multi-view video acquisition is enabling new forms of content production across the creative industries. In particular, the capture of human performance in three dimensions (3D) enables rendering from an arbitrary viewpoint (free-viewpoint video rendering - FVVR) [1–3] and photo-realistic replay within immersive VR/AR experiences. Commercial studios now operate for the capture of volumetric ("holographic") performance capture e.g. implementations of at Mixed Reality Capture Studios (San Francisco, London) [4] and Intel Studios (Los Angeles) both utilising over 100 camera views of a ~2.5 m^3 capture volume. Whilst able to reconstruct detailed 3D models of performance, such configurations do not scale to on-set deployments where practical constraints limit the number of deployable witness cameras (e.g. due to cost or rigging overheads). The contribution of this paper is to explore whether a deeply learned prior can be incorporated into volumetric reconstruction to minimise the number of views required at acquisition. Specifically, we investigate for the first time whether convolutional autoencoder architectures, commonly applied to visual content for de-noising and up-scaling (super-resolution), may be adapted to enhance the fidelity of volumetric reconstructions derived from

© Springer Nature Switzerland AG 2018
V. Ferrari et al. (Eds.): ECCV 2018, LNCS 11215, pp. 591–607, 2018.
https://doi.org/10.1007/978-3-030-01252-6_35

just a few wide-baseline camera viewpoints. We describe a symmetric autoencoder with 3D convolutional stages capable of refining a probabilistic visual hull (PVH) [5] i.e. voxel occupancy data derived from a small set of views. Hallucinating a PVH of approximately equal fidelity to that obtainable from the same performance captured with significantly greater (double or more) camera viewpoints (Fig. 1). This extends the space of use scenarios for volumetric capture to stages with low camera counts, prosumer scenarios where cost similarly limits the number of available camera views, or settings where volumetric capture is not possible due to restrictions on camera placement and cost such as sports events [6].

Fig. 1. Two high fidelity character models (JP, Magician) where 3D geometry was fully reconstructed using only two wide-baseline camera views via our proposed method.

2   Related Work

Volumetric performance capture pipelines typically fuse imagery from multiple wide baseline viewpoints [1,7] equispaced around the capture volume. Initially, an estimate of volume occupancy is obtained by fusing silhouettes across views to yield a volumetric [8] or polyhedral [9] "visual hull" of the performer. Stereomatching and volume optimisation subsequently fuse appearance data to refine the volume estimate ultimately yielding a textured mesh model [3,10]. In the case of video, a 4D alignment step is applied to conform 3D mesh topology over time [11]. Reconstruction error can be mitigated by temporally propagating error through a soft i.e. probabilistic visual hull (PVH) [5] estimate. Or where practical by increasing the number of camera views since view sparsity limits the ability to resolve fine volume detail leading to the introduction of phantom volumes. Shape refinement and hole filling has been explored with a LSTM and 3D convolutional model [12] for objects. 3D ShapeNets by Wu [13], learnt the distribution of 3D objects across arbitrary poses and was able to discover hierarchical compositional part representation automatically for object recognition and shape completion while Sharma learnt the shape distribution of objects to enhance corrupted 3D shapes [14].

Our work is inspired by contemporary super-resolution (SR) algorithms that apply learned priors to enhance visual detail in images. Classical approaches to image restoration and SR combine multiple data sources (e.g. multiple images obtained at sub-pixel misalignments [15], fusing these within a regularisation constraint e.g. total variation [16]. SR has been applied also to volumetric data in microscopy [17] via depth of field, and multi-spectral sensing data [18] via sparse coding. Most recently, deep learning has been applied in the form of convolutional neural network (CNN) autoencoders for image [19,20] and video-upscaling [21]. Symmetric autoencoders effectively learn an image transformation between clean and synthetically noisy images [22] and are effective at noise reduction e.g. due to image compression. Similarly, Dong [23] trained end-to-end networks to learn image up-scaling.

Whilst we share the high-level goal of learning deep models for detail enhancement, our work differs from prior work including deep autoencoders in several respects. We are dealing with volumetric (PVH) data and seek not to up-scale (increase resolution) as in SR, but instead, enhance detail within a constant-sized voxel grid to simulate the benefit of having additional viewpoints available during the formation of the PVH. This motivates the exploration of alternative (3D) convolutional architectures and training methodologies.

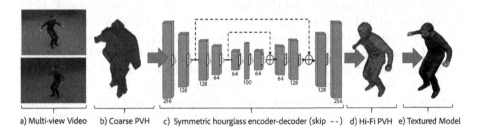

a) Multi-view Video   b) Coarse PVH   c) Symmetric hourglass encoder-decoder (skip --)   d) Hi-Fi PVH   e) Textured Model

Fig. 2. Overview and autoencoder architecture. A coarse PVH (b) captured using minimal camera views (a) is encoded into a latent representation via 3D convolutional and full-connected layers (c). The decoder uses the latent representation to synthesise an output PVH of identical size but improved fidelity (d) which is subsequently meshed and textured to yield the performance capture model; meshing/texturing (e) is not a contribution of this paper. The encoder-decoder is optimised during training using exemplar PVH pairs of the coarse and Hi-Fi PVH volumes.

3   Minimal Camera Volumetric Reconstruction

The goal of our method is to learn a generative model for high fidelity 3D volume reconstruction given a low number of wide baseline camera views. We first describe the convolutional autoencoder architecture used to learn this model using a training set of sub-volume pairs sampled from full volumetric reconstructions (PVHs) of performance obtained using differing camera counts (Sect. 3.1). By using a PVH we are able to process wide baseline views, that would cause failure for a correspondence based method. Our process for refining the PVH echos the stages employed in traditional image de-noising. First, a pre-processing step (adapted from [5]) reconstructs a coarse PVH using a limited number of cameras. This low quality result will contain phantom limbs and blocky false positive voxels (Fig. 2b). Next, a latent feature representation of the PVH (akin to the low-fidelity image in traditional pipelines) is deeply encoded via a series of convolution layers. We then perform non-linear mapping decoding the latent feature space to a high fidelity PVH (akin to the high-fidelity image). The reconstruction is performed in a piece-wise fashion using densely overlapping sub-volumes, This mitigates the instabilities and memory constraints of training and inference on a network with a large receptive (volumetric) field (Sect. 3.2). The high fidelity PVH is then meshed and textured with appearance data from the camera views yielding a video-realistic character model (Sect. 3.3). Note that the final stage *is not a contribution of this paper*, rather we demonstrate the benefits of the PVH refinement using the method of Casas *et al.* [3] but any textured meshing pipeline could be substituted as a post-process.

3.1 Volumetric Autoencoder

We wish to learn a deep representation given input tensor $\mathbf{V_L} \in \mathbb{R}^{X \times Y \times Z \times 1}$, where the single channel encodes the probability of volume occupancy $p(X, Y, Z)$ derived from a PVH obtained using a low camera count (Eq. 5). We wish to train a deep representation to solve the prediction problem $\mathbf{V_H} = \mathcal{F}(\mathbf{V_L})$ for similarly encoded tensor $\mathbf{V_H} \in \mathbb{R}^{X \times Y \times Z \times 1}$ derived from a higher fidelity PVH of identical dimension obtained using a higher camera count. Function $\mathcal{F}$ is learned using a CNN specifically a convolutional autoencoder consisting of successive three-dimensional (3D) alternate convolutional filtering operations and down- or up-sampling with non linear activation layers. Figure 2 illustrates our architecture which has symmetric structure with skip connections bridging hourglass encoder-decoder stages, the full network parameters are:

$$n_e = [64, 64, 128, 128, 256]$$
$$n_d = [256, 128, 128, 64, 64]$$
$$k_e = [3, 3, 3, 3, 3]$$
$$k_d = [3, 3, 3, 3, 3]$$
$$k_s = [0, 1, 0, 1, 0]$$
$$\text{NumEpoch} = 10$$

where $k[i]$ indicates the kernel size and $n[i]$ is the number of filters at layer i for the encoder (e) and decoder (d) parameters respectively. The location of the two skip connections are indicated by s and link two groups of convolutional layers to their corresponding mirrored up-convolutional layer. The passed convolutional feature maps are summed to the up-convolutional feature maps element-wise and passed to the next layer after rectification. The central fully-connected layer encodes the 100-D latent representation.

Learning the end-to-end mapping from blocky volumes generated from a small number of camera viewpoints to cleaner high fidelity volumes, as if made by a greater number of camera viewpoints, requires estimation of the weights ϕ in $\mathcal{F}$ represented by the convolutional and deconvolutional kernels. Specifically, given a collection of N training sample pairs x^i, z^i, where $x^i \in \mathbf{V_L}$ is an instance of a low camera count volume and $z^i \in \mathbf{V_H}$ is the high camera count output volume provided as a groundtruth, we minimise the Mean Squared Error (MSE) at the output of the decoder across $N = X \times Y \times Z$ voxels:

$$\mathcal{L}(\phi) = \frac{1}{N} \sum_{i=1}^{N} \|\mathcal{F}(x^i : \phi) - z^i\|_2^2. \tag{1}$$

To train $\mathcal{F}$ we use Adadelta [24] an extension of Adagrad that seeks to reduce it's aggressive, radically diminishing learning rates, restricting the window of accumulated past gradients to some fixed size w. Given the amount of data and variation in it due to the use of patches the number of epochs required for the approach to converge is small at around 5 to 10 epochs.

Skip Connections. Deeper networks in image restoration tasks can suffer from performance degradation. Given the increased number of convolutional layers, finer image details can be lost or corrupted, as given a compact latent feature abstraction, the recovery of all the image detail is an under-determined problem. This issue is exasperated by the need to reconstruct the additional dimension in volumetric data. Deeper networks also often suffer from vanishing gradients and become much harder to train. In the spirit of highway [25] and deep residual networks [26], we add skip connections between two corresponding convolutional and deconvolutional layers as shown in Fig. 2. These connections mitigate detail loss by feeding forward higher frequency content to enable up-convolutional stages to recover a sharper volume. Skip connections also benefit back-propagation to lower layers, enhancing the stability of training. Our proposed skip connections differ from that proposed in recent image restoration work [25,26] which concern only smoother optimisation. Instead, we pass the feature activation's at intervals of every two convolutional layers to their mirrored up-convolutional layers to enhance reconstruction detail.

3.2   Volumetric Reconstruction and Sampling

The low-fidelity input PVH ($\mathbf{V_L}$) is reconstructed using a variant of [5]. We assume a capture volume observed by a limited number C of camera views $c = [1, C]$ for which extrinsic parameters $\{R_c, COP_c\}$ (camera orientation and focal point) and intrinsic parameters $\{f_c, o_c^x, o_c^y\}$ (focal length, and 2D optical centre) are known, and for which soft foreground mattes are available from each camera image I_c using background subtraction $\mathcal{BG}$.

The studio capture volume is finely decimated into voxels $\mathbf{V_L}^i = \begin{bmatrix} v_x^i & v_y^i & v_z^i \end{bmatrix}$ for $i = [1, \ldots, |\mathbf{V_L}|]$; each voxel is approximately 5mm^3 in size. The point (x_c, y_c) is the point within I_c to which $\mathbf{V_L}^i$ projects in a given view:

$$x[\mathbf{V_L}^i] = \frac{f_c v_x^i}{v_z^i} + o_c^x \quad \text{and} \quad y[\mathbf{V_L}^i] = \frac{f_c v_y^i}{v_z^i} + o_c^y, \quad \text{where} \tag{2}$$

$$\begin{bmatrix} v_x^i & v_y^i & v_z^i \end{bmatrix} = COP_c - R_c^{-1} V_L^i. \tag{3}$$

The probability of the voxel being part of the performer in a given view c is:

$$p(\mathbf{V_L}^i|c) = \mathcal{BG}(x[\mathbf{V_L}^i], y[\mathbf{V_L}^i]). \tag{4}$$

The overall likelihood of occupancy for a given voxel $p(\mathbf{V_L}^i)$ is:

$$p(\mathbf{V_L}^i) = \prod_{i=1}^{C} 1/(1 + e^{p(\mathbf{V_L}^i|c)}). \tag{5}$$

We compute $p(\mathbf{V_L}^i)$ for all voxels to create the PVH for volume $\mathbf{V_L}$.

In practice, the extent of $\mathbf{V_L}$ is limited to a sub-volume (a 3D "patch") of the capture volume. Patches are densely sampled to cover the capture volume, each of which is processed through $\mathcal{F}$ independently at both training and inference time. Similar to prior image super-resolution and de-noising work [23] this makes tractable the processing of large capture volumes without requiring excessively large receptive fields or up-convolutional layer counts in the CNN. In Sect. 4.1 we evaluate the impact of differing degrees of patch overlap during dense sampling. For efficiency we ignore any patches where $\sum_i p(\mathbf{V_L}^i) = 0$.

3.3   Meshing and Texturing

Given $\mathbf{V_H}$ inferred from the network we produce a "4D" (i.e. moving 3D) performance capture. To generate the mesh for a given frame, the PVH is converted to a vertex and face based mesh using the marching-cubes algorithm. The iterative process fits vertices to the PVH output by the CNN using the marching cubes algorithm [27] with a dynamically chosen threshold, thus producing a high-resolution triangle mesh, that is used as the geometric proxy for resampling of the scene appearance onto the texture. Without loss of generality, we texture the mesh using the approach of Casas *et al.* [3] where a virtual camera view I_{c*} is synthesised in the renderer by compositing the appearance sampled from the camera views $I_{1,...,C}$ closest to that virtual viewpoint.

TotalCapture [30]   Human3.6m [31]   Dan:JumpLong [3]   JP:Flashkick[32]   JP:Lock2pop[32]   Magician[33]

Fig. 3. Samples of the multi-view video datasets used to evaluate our method.

4   Experiments and Discussion

We evaluate the quantitative improvement in reconstruction accuracy, as well
as the qualitative improvement in visual fidelity, due to the proposed method.
Reconstruction accuracy is evaluated using two public multi-view video datasets
of human performance; *TotalCapture* [28] (8 camera dataset of 5 subjects
performing 4 actions with 3 repetitions at 60 Hz in 360° arrangement) and
Human3.6M [29] (4 camera view dataset of 10 subjects performing 210 actions
at 50 Hz in a 360° arrangement). Perceptual quality of textured models is
evaluated using the public 4D datasets *Dan:JumpLong* [3], *JP:Flashkick* [30],
JP:Lock2Pop [30], and *Magician* [31][1] (see Fig. 3 for samples of each dataset).

2cam PVH   4cam PVH   8cam PVH G.Truth   2cam PVH   4cam PVH   8cam PVH G.Truth

Fig. 4. Visualisation of raw PVH occupancy volumes estimated with C=2,4,8 views
using standard method (i.e. without enhancement via our approach). PVH is a probability between 0 and 1 of the subject's occupancy. This data forms the input to our
auto-encoder and illustrates the phantom volumes and artefacts to contend with at
$C = \{2, 4\}$ versus the $C = 8$ ground-truth (GT) for this dataset (*TotalCapture*).

4.1   Evaluating Reconstruction Accuracy

We study the accuracy gain due to our method by ablating the set of camera
views available on *TotalCapture*. The autoencoder model is trained using high
fidelity PVHs obtained using all $(C = 8)$ views of the dataset, and corresponding
low fidelity PVHs obtained using fewer views (we train for $C = 2$ and $C = 4$
random neighbouring views). The model is then tested on held-out footage to
determine the degree to which it can reconstruct a high fidelity PVH from the
ablated set of camera views. The dataset consists of a total of four male and
one female subjects each performing four diverse performances, repeated three
times: *ROM, Walking, Acting and Freestyle*, and each sequence lasts around
3000–5000 frames. The train and test partitions are formed wrt. to the subjects
and sequences, the training consists of *ROM1,2,3; Walking1,3; Freestyle1,2* and
Acting1,2 on subjects 1, 2 and 3. The test set is the performances Freestyle3

---

[1] We use the datasets released publicly at http://cvssp.org/data/cvssp3d/.

(**FS3**), Acting (**A3**) and Walking2 (**W2**) on subjects 1, 2, 3, 4 and 5. This split allows for separate evaluation on unseen and on seen subjects but always on unseen sequences.

The PVH is set to $z \in \mathbb{R}^{256 \times 256 \times 256}$. The sub-volume ('patch') size i.e. receptive field of the autoencoder ($\mathbf{V_L}$ and $\mathbf{V_H} \in \mathbb{R}^{n \times n \times n}$ is varied across $n = \{16, 32, 64\}$ the latter being a degenerate case where the entire volume is scaled and passed through the CNN in effect a global versus patch based filter of the volume. Patches are sampled with varying degrees of overlap; overlapping densely every 8, 16 or 32 voxels (Table 1). The PVH at $C = 8$ provides a ground-truth for comparison, whilst the $C = \{2, 4\}$ input covers at most a narrow 90° view of the scene. Prior to refinement via the autoencoder, the ablated view PVH data exhibits phantom extremities and lacks fine-grained detail, particularly at $C = 2$ (Fig. 4). These crude volumes would be unsuitable for reconstruction with texture as they do not reflect the true geometry and would cause severe visual misalignments when camera texture is projected onto the model. Applying our autoencoder method to clean up and hallucinate a volume equivalent to one produced by the unabated $C = 8$ camera viewpoints solves this issue.

Table 1 quantifies error between the unablated ($C = 8$) and the reconstructed volumes for $C = \{2, 4\}$ view PVH data, baselining these against $C = \{2, 4\}$ PVH prior to enhancement via the auto-encoder (*input*). To measure the performance we compute the average per-frame MSE of the probability of occupancy across each sequence. The 2 and 4 camera PVH volume prior to enhancement is also shown and our results indicate a reduction in MSE of around 4 times through our approach when 2 cameras views are used for the input and a halving of MSE for a PVH formed from 4 cameras. We observe that $C = 4$ in a 180° arc around the subject perform slightly better than $C = 2$ neighbouring views in a 90° arc. However, the performance decrease is minimal for the greatly increased operational flexibility that a 2 camera deployment provides. In all cases, MSE is more than halved (up to 34% lower) using our refined PVH for a reduced number of views. Using only 2 cameras, a comparable volume to that reconstructed from a full 360° $C = 8$ setup can be produced. Qualitative results of using only 2 and 4 camera viewpoint to construct the volume are shown in Fig. 5, where high quality reconstructions are possible despite the presence of phantom limbs and extensive false volumes in the input PVH. The bottom line includes results, from increasingly wide baseline cameras, separated by 45°, 90°, and 135°. Furthermore, the patch overlap is examined with the steps of 8, 16 and 32. When sampled at 32 voxel increments i.e. without any overlap, performance is noticeably worse. This distinction between the patch overlap (16) and not (32) is visualised in Fig. 7. In all cases, performance is slightly better when testing on seen versus unseen subjects.

Cross-Dataset Generalisation. Given that the learned model on *TotalCapture* can improve the fidelity of a PVH acquired with 2–4 views to approximate a PVH reconstructed from 8 views, we explore the performance of the same model on a second dataset (*Human3.6M*) which only has on $C = 4$ views.

Fig. 5. Qualitative visual comparison of a PVH before (left) and after (right) enhancement, showing detail improvement from $C = \{2,4\}$ views *(TotalCapture)*. False colour volume occupancy (PVH) and groundtruth $C = 8$ PVH. Bottom line indicates performance for different pairs of cameras separated by increased amounts

Table 1. Quantitative performance of volumetric reconstruction on the *TotalCapture* dataset using 2–4 cameras prior to our approach (Input) and after, versus unablated groundtruth using 8 cameras (error as MSE $\times 10^{-3}$). Patch size is 32^3 voxels; patch overlap of 32 implies no overlap. Our method reduces reconstruction error to 34% of the baseline (Input) for 2 views.

Patch	NumCams	SeenSubjects(S1,2,3)			UnseenSubjects(S4,5)			Mean
Overlap	C	W2	FS3	A3	W2	FS3	A3	
Input	2	19.1	28.5	23.9	23.4	27.5	25.2	24.6
Input	4	11.4	16.5	12.5	12.0	15.2	14.2	11.6
8	2	5.49	9.98	6.94	5.46	9.86	8.79	7.75
16	2	5.43	10.03	6.70	5.34	10.05	8.71	7.71
32	2	6.21	12.75	8.08	5.98	11.88	10.30	9.20
8	4	5.01	9.07	6.48	4.98	9.81	8.61	7.33
16	4	5.49	9.56	6.58	5.12	10.01	8.81	7.60
32	4	5.98	10.02	7.85	5.32	10.85	9.21	8.28

The *Human3.6M* PVH models are poor quality as there are only 4 cameras at body height in four corners of a studio covering a relatively large capture area. This causes phantom parts and ghosting to occur. Examples of the PVH reconstructed using $C = \{2,4\}$ views on *Human3.6M* are shown in Fig. 6 (red). These volumes are of poorer quality, even for 4 camera reconstructions, primarily due to the cameras being closer to the ground causing greater occlusion. However, we are able to transfer our trained CNN models for $2 \mapsto 8$ and $4 \mapsto 8$ views on *TotalCapture* without any further training, to hallucinate volumes as if 8 cameras were used at acquisition. Figure 6 visualises the enhanced fidelity due to significantly reduced phantom volumes that would otherwise frustrate efforts to render the volume. $C = 4$ result provides a more complete volume but slightly enlarged. Quantitatively, the MSE of the input PVH with $C = 2$ against the *groundtruth* $C = 4$ PVH across the test datasets of S9 and S11 is 17.4×10^{-3}. However, after using our trained CNN model on the $C = 2$ input PVH this MSE is reduced to 12.3×10^{-3}, mirroring the qualitative improvement shown in Fig. 6.

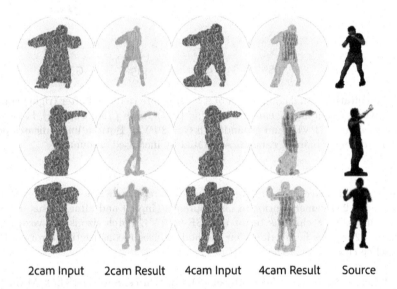

2cam Input   2cam Result   4cam Input   4cam Result   Source

Fig. 6. Qualitative visual comparison of a PVH before (left) and after (right) enhancement, showing detail improvement from $C = \{2,4\}$ views *(Human3.6M)*. False colour volume occupancy (PVH) and source footage.

Receptive Field Size. The use of densely sampled sub-volumes (patches) rather than global processing of the PVH is necessary for computational tractability of volumes at $\mathbb{R}^{256 \times 256 \times 256}$, since the 3D convolutional stages greatly increase the number of network parameters and GPU memory footprint for batches during training. However, a hypothesis could be that the use of patches ignores the global context that the network could be learning about the subjects thus increasing error. Therefore we performed an experiment on the *TotalCapture* dataset using the network with a modified input vector of $z \in \mathbb{R}^{64 \times 64 \times 64}$, therefore making each voxel around $30\,\text{mm}^3$, against standard $p \in \mathbb{R}^{32 \times 32 \times 32}$, $p \in \mathbb{R}^{16 \times 16 \times 16}$ and $p \in \mathbb{R}^{8 \times 8 \times 8}$ patches sampled from the same $z \in \mathbb{R}^{64 \times 64 \times 64}$ vector, with a patch sampling overlap of 8, 16 and 32. Quantitative results of the average MSE against the groundtruth 8 camera reconstruction volume are shown in Table 2 and qualitative results are shown in Fig. 7.

Table 2. Quantifying the effect of patch (sub-volume) size and patch overlap during dense sampling of the PVH; *TotalCapture* dataset (error as MSE $\times 10^{-3}$).

Patch Size	Patch Overlap	NumCams C	SeenSubjects(S1,2,3)			UnseenSubjects(S4,5)			Mean
			W2	FS3	A3	W2	FS3	A3	
Input	–	2	20.1	24.2	22.3	23.5	25.7	26.8	23.8
Input	–	4	9.9	14.2	13.5	11.8	14.1	13.9	12.9
64	–	2	4.34	6.45	5.78	5.01	7.45	6.98	6.00
16	8	2	4.43	6.42	5.65	4.99	7.56	7.23	6.05
16	16	2	5.45	7.03	6.03	6.56	8.02	7.98	6.85
32	8	2	4.56	6.47	5.48	5.13	7.98	6.90	6.10
32	16	2	4.42	6.52	5.63	5.23	7.78	6.97	6.10
32	32	2	5.67	7.34	6.34	7.02	8.87	8.03	7.20

Comparing the performance of the whole volume against patch based methods shows little change both quantitatively and qualitatively, providing that overlapping patches are utilised (therefore an overlap of 8 and 8 or 16 for $p \in \mathbb{R}^{16 \times 16 \times 16}$ and $p \in \mathbb{R}^{32 \times 32 \times 32}$ respectively. Therefore we can conclude that there is no requirement for global semantics to be learned as separate patches provide a measured compromise against the computational costs of training using a single global volume. However, the benefit of using patches is that much larger PVH can be processed, as in our experiments (256^3 voxels).

4.2 4D Character Reconstruction

We explore the efficacy of our approach as a pre-process to a state of the art 4D model reconstruction technique [3]. We use three popular 4D datasets (*J-P, Dan, Magician*) intended to be reconstructed from a PVH derived from 8 cameras in a 360° configuration. We pick a subset of 2 neighbouring views at random from the set of 8, compute the low fidelity PVH from those views, and use our proposed method to enhance the fidelity of the PVH prior to running the reconstruction process [3] and obtaining model geometry (Sect. 3.3). The geometric proxy recovered via [3] is then textured using all views. The purpose of the test is to assess the impact of any incorrect geometry on texture alignment.

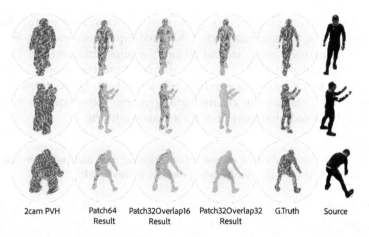

2cam PVH   Patch64   Patch32Overlap16   Patch32Overlap32   G.Truth   Source
              Result   Result   Result

Fig. 7. Visual comparison accompanying quantitative data in Table 2 comparing the efficacy of different patch sizes and overlaps (where a patch size of 64 implies whole volume processing).

The datasets all comprise a single performer indoors in a $3\,m^2$ capture volume. The cameras are HD resolution running at 30 Hz. Across all datasets, there are a total of 20 sequences of duration 80–3000 frames. We randomly select for test sequences: *Dan:JumpLong, JP:FlashKick, JP:Lock2Pop* and *Magician*; the remaining 16 sequences and a total of 5000 frames used as training. Given the lower number of frames available for training, the autoencoder is initially trained on *TotalCapture* dataset per Sect. 4.1 then fine-tuned (with unfixed weights) using these 5000 frames. We quantify the visual fidelity of our output by rendering it from a virtual viewpoint coinciding with one of the 6 ablated viewpoints (picked randomly). This enables a direct pixel comparison between our rendering and the original camera data for that ablated view. As a baseline, we also compare our rendering against a baseline built using all 8 views using Casas [3] with identical parameters. Each frame of test data thus yields a triplet of results for comparison; 2-view PVH, 8-view PVH, and real footage from the viewpoint.

Figure 8 presents a visual comparison for a representative triplet from each of the 4 test data. In particular, we are examining the differences in geometry which would manifest e.g. via texture misalignment or spurious mesh facets that would cause texture artefacts. The results are nearly indistinguishable with only minor texture artefacts present; a high quality result considering only 2 views are used for estimate the geometry. Table 3 quantifies performance using two metrics; PSNR and structural similarity (SSIM) [32], which closely correlates with perceptual quality. The metrics compare the 2-view and 8-view reconstructions to the camera footage which is considered to be the ground truth.

The main sources of error between the rendered frames and the original images are found in the high frequency areas such as the face and hands, where

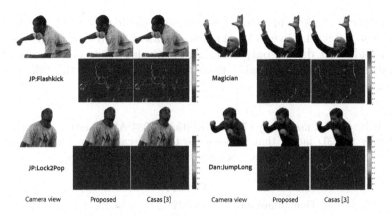

Fig. 8. Visual comparison of reconstructions from 2- (our) and 8-view (baseline) PVHs rendered from the viewpoint of an unused camera. The difference images (SSIM) show only minor differences relative to the real camera footage, with 2- and 8- reconstructions near identical. The error is quantified in Table 3 and AMT user study (Table 4).

Table 3. Quantifying 4D reconstruction fidelity in terms of PSNR and SSIM averaged across frames of the sequence. We compare running [3] over our proposed output; a PVH recovered from 2 views via the autoencoder, against a baseline reconstructed directly from an 8 view PVH. The reconstruction errors are very similar, indicating our model correctly learns to hallucinate structure from the missing views.

Method	Dan		JP		JP		Magic		Mean	
	JumpLong		flashkick		lock2pop		Magician			
	PSNR	SSIM	PSNR	SSIM	PSNR	SSIM	PSNR	SSIM	PSNR	SSIM
Casas [3]	38.0	0.903	31.8	0.893	32.4	0.893	38.1	90.4	35.1	0.898
Proposed	37.5	0.902	33.6	0.896	32.3	0.893	36.1	90.3	34.9	0.899

additional vertices could provide greater detail. However, the overall reconstruction is impressive considering the poor quality of the input PVH due to the minimal camera view count.

Perceptual User Study. We conducted a study via Amazon Mechanical Turk (AMT) to compare the performance of our rendering to the 8-view baseline. A total of 500 frames sampled from the four 4D test sequences is reconstructed as above, yielding 500 image triplets. The camera view was presented to the participant alongside the 2- and 8-view reconstructions in random order. Participants were asked to "identify the 3D model that is closest to the real camera image". Each result was presented 15 times, gathering in total 7763 annotations, from 343 unique users. Table 4 reports the preferences expressed. It was our expectation that the preference would be around random at 50%, and over the 7.8K results, yet our approach was chosen as most similar to the real camera view

50.7% of the time. An unpaired t-test indicates the likelihood of identical preference is $p > 0.9984$. Given also the near-identical SSIM and PSNR scores we can conclude that despite only using 2 camera viewpoints our reconstructions are statistically indistinguishable from those sourced using the full 8 camera viewpoints.

Table 4. Perceptual user study (7.8k annotations). 334 AMT participants were asked to "identify the 3D model that is closest to the real camera image" and could not perceive a difference between the 2- an 8-view reconstructed models.

Sequence	Our approach	Casas [3]
Dan:JumpLong	43.5 %	56.3%
JP:Flashkick	53.2 %	46.7%
JP:Lock2Pop	57.7%	42.2%
Magician	48.2%	51.7%
Mean	50.7	49.2%
Standard deviation	6.15%	6.11%

4.3   Failure Cases

Despite the excellent performance of our approach at reconstructing view impoverished scenes, Fig. 9 highlights failure cases sometimes encountered by the proposed method. The use of the soft mattes from the 2D images to form the PVH can limit performance e.g. in Fig. 9(a) the initial coarse PVH input has a large horizontal hole and this isn't compensated for by the deeply learned prior; in general we find the prior learns to erode phantom volumes instead of dilating existing volumes. Figure 9(b) illustrates that sometimes the extremities of the arms are missed, due to ambiguities in the input PVH. Finally, Fig. 9(c), indicates a reconstruction failure due to incomplete removal of a phantom limb, caused by inaccurate geometry created from the PVH volume.

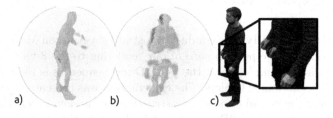

Fig. 9. Illustrative failure cases. Large holes due to errors in multiple 2D mattes can cause holes in the PVH that are non-recoverable. Texture misalignments can occur in areas of phantom geometry. Discussion in Sect. 4.3.

5 Conclusion

Volumetric performance capture from multi-view video is becoming increasingly popular in the creative industries, but reconstructing high fidelity models requires many wide-baseline views. We have shown that high fidelity 3D models can be built with as few as a couple of views, when accompanied by a deep representation prior learned via our novel autoencoder framework. We demonstrated that the models reconstructed via our method are quantitatively similar (Tables 1 and 2) and perceptually indistinguishable (AMT study, Table 4) from models reconstructed from considerably more camera views via existing volumetric reconstruction techniques. An additional feature of our approach is that we are able to greatly reduce the computational cost of 4D character reconstruction. Whilst training the autoencoder takes several hours, computing the PVH and passing it through the trained network for inference of a higher fidelity volume is comfortably achievable at 25 fps on commodity GPU hardware. Furthermore, the cross-data set performance of the autoencoder appears strong without (Sect. 4.1) or with minimal (Sect. 4.2) fine-tuning.

Future work could include exploring the efficacy of our deep prior beyond the domain of human performance capture, or inference of meshes directly from a coarse PVH. Nevertheless, we believe these findings are promising first steps toward the commoditisation of volumetric video, unlocking broader use cases for volumetric characters in immersive content.

Acknowledgements. The work was supported by InnovateUK via the TotalCapture project, grant agreement 102685. The work was supported in part through the donation of GPU hardware by the NVidia corporation.

References

1. Starck, J., Kilner, J., Hilton, A.: A free-viewpoint video renderer. J. Graph. GPU Game Tools **14**(3), 57–72 (2009)
2. Tsiminaki, V., Franco, J., Boyer, E.: High resolution 3D shape texture from multiple videos. In: Proceedings of the Computer Vision and Pattern Recognition (CVPR) (2014)
3. Volino, M., Casas, D., Collomosse, J., Hilton, A.: 4D for interactive character appearance. In: Computer Graphics Forum (Proceedings of Eurographics 2014) (2014)
4. Collet, A., et al.: High-quality streamable free-viewpoint video. ACM Trans. Graph. (TOG) **34**(4), 69 (2015)
5. Grauman, K., Shakhnarovich, G., Darrell, T.: A Bayesian approach to image-based visual hull reconstruction. In: Proceedings of the CVPR (2003)
6. Guillemaut, J.Y., Hilton, A.: Joint multi-layer segmentation and reconstruction for free-viewpoint video applications. Int. J. Comput. Vis. **93**(1), 73–100 (2011)
7. Casas, D., Huang, P., Hilton, A.: Surface-based character animation. In: Magnor, M., Grau, O., Sorkine-Hornung, O., Theobalt, C. (eds.) Digital Representations of the Real World: How to Capture, Model, and Render Visual Reality, pp. 239–252. CRC Press (2015)

8. Laurentini, A.: The visual hull concept for silhouette-based image understanding. IEEE Trans. Pattern Anal. Mach. Intell. **16**(2), 150–162 (1994)
9. Franco, J., Boyer, E.: Exact polyhedral visual hulls. In: Proceedings of the British Machine Vision Conference (BMVC) (2003)
10. Volino, M., Casas, D., Collomosse, J., Hilton, A.: Optimal representation of multiple view video. In: Proceedings of the British Machine Vision Conference. BMVA Press (2014)
11. Budd, C., Huang, P., Klaudinay, M., Hilton, A.: Global non-rigid alignment of surface sequences. Int. J. Comput. Vis. (IJCV) **102**(1–3), 256–270 (2013)
12. Han, X., Li, Z., Huang, H., Kalogerakis, E., Yu, Y.: High-resolution shape completion using deep neural networks for global structure and local geometry inference. In: Proceedings of the International Conference on Computer Vision (ICCV 2017) (2017)
13. Wu, Z., et al.: 3D shapenets: a deep representation for volumetric shapes. In: IEEE Conference on Computer Vision and Pattern Recognition (CVPR 2015) (2015)
14. Sharma, A., Grau, O., Fritz, M.: VConv-DAE: deep volumetric shape learning without object labels. In: Hua, G., Jégou, H. (eds.) ECCV 2016. LNCS, vol. 9915, pp. 236–250. Springer, Cham (2016). https://doi.org/10.1007/978-3-319-49409-8_20
15. Fattal, R.: Image upsampling via imposed edge statistics. In: Proceedings of the ACM SIGGRAPH (2007)
16. Rudin, L.I., Osher, S., Fatemi, E.: Non-linear total variation based noise removal algorithms. Phys. D **60**(1–4), 259–268 (1992)
17. Abrahamsson, S., Blom, H., Jans, D.: Multifocus structured illumination microscopy for fast volumetric super-resolution imaging. Biomed. Opt. Express **8**(9), 4135–4140 (2017)
18. Aydin, V., Foroosh, H.: Volumetric super-resolution of multispectral data. In: CORR arXiv:1705.05745v1 (2017)
19. Xie, J., Xu, L., Chen, E.: Image denoising and inpainting with deep neural networks. In: Proceedings of the Neural Information Processing Systems (NIPS), pp. 350–358 (2012)
20. Wang, Z., Liu, D., Yang, J., Han, W., Huang, T.S.: Deep networks for image super-resolution with sparse prior. In: Proceedings of the International Conference on Computer Vision (ICCV), pp. 370–378 (2015)
21. Shi, W., et al.: Real-time single image and video super-resolution using an efficient sub-pixel convolutional neural network. In: Proceedings of the Computer Vision and Pattern Recognition (CVPR) (2016)
22. Jain, V., Seung, H.: Natural image denoising with convolutional networks. In: Proceedings of the Neural Information Processing Systems (NIPS), pp. 769–776 (2008)
23. Dong, C., Loy, C.C., He, K., Tang, X.: Image super-resolution using deep convolutional networks. IEEE Trans. Pattern Anal. Mach. Intell. **38**(2), 295–307 (2016)
24. Zeiler, M.D.: Adadelta: an adaptive learning rate method. arXiv preprint arXiv:1212.5701 (2012)
25. Srivastava, R.K., Greff, K., Schmidhuber, J.: Training very deep networks. In: Advances in Neural Information Processing Systems, pp. 2377–2385 (2015)
26. He, K., Zhang, X., Ren, S., Sun, J.: Deep residual learning for image recognition. In: Proceedings of the IEEE Conference on Computer Vision and Pattern Recognition, pp. 770–778 (2016)
27. Lorensen, W., Cline, H.: Marching cubes: a high resolution 3D surface construction algorithm. ACM Trans. Graph. (TOG) **21**(4), 163–169 (1987)

28. Trumble, M., Gilbert, A., Malleson, C., Hilton, A., Collomosse, J.: Total capture: 3D human pose estimation fusing video and inertial sensors. In: Proceedings of 28th British Machine Vision Conference, pp. 1–13 (2017)
29. Ionescu, C., Papava, D., Olaru, V., Sminchisescu, C.: Human3.6m: large scale datasets and predictive methods for 3D human sensing in natural environments. IEEE Trans. Pattern Anal. Mach. Intell. **36**(7), 1325–1339 (2014)
30. Starck, J., Hilton, A.: Surface capture for performance-based animation. IEEE Comput. Graph. Appl. **27**(3) (2007)
31. Mustafa, A., Volino, M., Guillemaut, J.Y., Hilton, A.: 4D temporally coherent light-field video. In: 3DV 2017 Proceedings (2017)
32. Wang, Z., Bovik, A.C., Sheikh, H.R., Simoncelli, E.P.: Image quality assessment: from error visibility to structural similarity. IEEE Tran. Image Process. (TIP) **13**(4), 600–612 (2004)

A Framework for Evaluating 6-DOF Object Trackers

Mathieu Garon$^{(\boxtimes)}$ (iD), Denis Laurendeau (iD), and Jean-François Lalonde (iD)

Université Laval, Quebec City, Canada
mathieu.garon.2@ulaval.ca, {denis.laurendeau,jflalonde}@gel.ulaval.ca

Abstract. We present a challenging and realistic novel dataset for evaluating 6-DOF object tracking algorithms. Existing datasets show serious limitations—notably, unrealistic synthetic data, or real data with large fiducial markers—preventing the community from obtaining an accurate picture of the state-of-the-art. Using a data acquisition pipeline based on a commercial motion capture system for acquiring accurate ground truth poses of real objects with respect to a Kinect V2 camera, we build a dataset which contains a total of 297 calibrated sequences. They are acquired in three different scenarios to evaluate the performance of trackers: *stability*, robustness to *occlusion* and accuracy during challenging *interactions* between a person and the object. We conduct an extensive study of a deep 6-DOF tracking architecture and determine a set of optimal parameters. We enhance the architecture and the training methodology to train a 6-DOF tracker that can robustly generalize to objects never seen during training, and demonstrate favorable performance compared to previous approaches trained specifically on the objects to track.

Keywords: 3D object tracking · Databases · Deep learning

1 Introduction

With the recent emergence of 3D-enabled augmented reality devices, tracking 3D objects in 6 degrees of freedom (DOF) is a problem that has received increased attention in the past few years. As opposed to SLAM-based camera localization techniques—now robustly implemented on-board various commercial devices—that can use features from the entire scene, 6-DOF object tracking approaches have to rely on features present on a (typically small) object, making it a challenging problem. Despite this, recent approaches have demonstrated tremendous performance both in terms of speed and accuracy [1–3].

Unfortunately, obtaining an accurate assessment of the performance of 6-DOF object tracking approaches is becoming increasingly difficult since accuracy on the main dataset used for this purpose has now reached closed to

Electronic supplementary material The online version of this chapter (https://doi.org/10.1007/978-3-030-01252-6_36) contains supplementary material, which is available to authorized users.

© Springer Nature Switzerland AG 2018
V. Ferrari et al. (Eds.): ECCV 2018, LNCS 11215, pp. 608–623, 2018.
https://doi.org/10.1007/978-3-030-01252-6_36

100%. Introduced in 2013 by Choi and Christensen [4], their dataset consists of 4 short sequences of purely synthetic scenes. The scenes are made of unrealistic, texture-less backgrounds with a single colored object to track, resulting in noiseless RGBD images (see Fig. 1-(a)). The object is static and the camera rotates around it in wide motions, occasionally creating small occlusions (at most 20% of the object is occluded). While challenging at first, the dataset has now essentially been solved for the RGBD case. For example, the method of Kehl et al. [1] reports an average error in translation/rotation of 0.5 mm/0.26°, which is an improvement of 0.3 mm/0.1° over the work of Tan et al. [5], who have themselves reported a 0.01 mm/1° improvement to the approach designed by Krull et al. [6]. The state of the art on the dataset has reached a near-perfect error of 0.1 mm/0.07° [2], which highlights the need for a new dataset with more challenging scenarios.

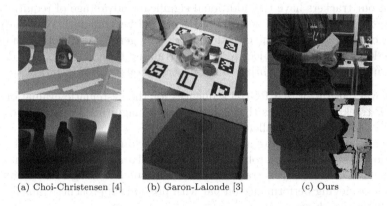

(a) Choi-Christensen [4]   (b) Garon-Lalonde [3]   (c) Ours

Fig. 1. Comparison of datasets for evaluating 6-DOF tracking algorithms. Typical RGB (top) and depth (bottom) frames for (a) the synthetic dataset of Choi and Christensen [4], (b) the real dataset of Garon and Lalonde [3], and (c) ours. Compared to the previous work, our dataset contains real objects captured by a sensor, and does not use a calibration board, therefore mimicking realistic real-world scenarios.

Another dataset, introduced by Garon and Lalonde [3], includes 12 sequences of real objects captured with real sensors. While a significant improvement over the synthetic dataset of [4], dealing with real data raises the issue of providing accurate ground truth pose of the object at all times. To obtain this ground truth information, their strategy (also adopted in 6-DOF *detection* datasets [7,8]) is to use calibration boards with fiducial markers. While useful to accurately and easily determine an object pose, this has the unfortunate consequence of constraining the object to lie on a large planar surface (Fig. 1-(b)).

In this paper, we present a novel dataset allowing the systematic evaluation of 6-DOF tracking algorithms in a wide variety of real scenarios without requiring calibration boards (Fig. 1-(c)). Our dataset is one order of magnitude larger than the previous work: it contains 297 sequences of 11 real objects. The sequences are split into 3 different scenarios, which we refer to as *stability, occlusion,* and *interaction.* The *stability* scenario aims at quantifying the degree of jitter in a tracker. The object is kept static and placed at various angles and distances from the camera. The *occlusion* scenario, inspired by [3], has the object rotating on a turntable and being progressively occluded by a flat panel. Occlusion ranges from 0% (unoccluded) to 75%, thereby testing trackers in very challenging situations. Finally, in the *interaction* scenario, a person is moving the object around freely in front of the camera (Fig. 1-(c)), creating occlusions and varying object speed.

In addition, we also introduce two new 6-DOF real-time object trackers based on deep learning. The first, trained for a specific object, achieves state-of-the-art performance on the new dataset. The second, trained *without a priori knowledge of the object to track,* is able to achieve an accuracy that is comparable with previous work trained specifically on the object. These two trackers rely on the same deep learning architecture and only differ in the training data. Furthermore, both of our trackers have the additional significant advantage of requiring only *synthetic* training data (i.e. no real data is needed for training). We believe this is an exciting first step in the direction of training generic trackers which do not require knowledge of the object to track at training time.

In summary, this paper brings 3 key contributions to 6-DOF object tracking:

1. A novel dataset of real RGBD sequences for the systematic evaluation of 6-DOF tracking algorithms that is one order of magnitude larger than existing ones, and contains 3 challenging scenarios;
2. A real-time deep learning architecture for tracking objects in 6-DOF which is more stable and more robust to occlusions than previous approaches;
3. A generic 6-DOF object tracker trained without knowledge of the object to track, achieving performance on par with previous approaches trained specifically on the object.

2   Related Work

There are two main relevant aspects in 6-DOF pose estimation: single frame object detection and multi-frame temporal trackers. The former has received a lot of attention in the literature and benefits from a large range of public datasets. The most notorious dataset is arguably *Linemod* [7], which provide 15 objects with their mesh models and surface colors. To obtain the ground truth object pose, a calibration board with fiducial markers is used. Since then, many authors created similar but more challenging benchmarks [8–10]. However these datasets do not contain temporal and displacement correlation between each frame, which makes them inadequate for evaluating temporal trackers.

In the case of temporal tracking, only a few datasets exist to evaluate the approaches. As mentioned in the introduction, the current, widely used standard dataset is the synthetic dataset of Choi and Christensen [4], which contains 4 sequences with 4 objects rendered in a texture-less virtual scene. Another available option is the one provided by Akkaladevi et al. [11] who captured a single sequence of a scene containing 4 different objects with a Primesense sensor.

However, the 3D models are not complete and do not include training data that could be exploited by learning-based methods. Finally, recent work by Garon and Lalonde [3] proposed a public dataset of 4 objects containing 4 sequences with clutter and an additional set of 8 sequences with controlled occlusion on a specific object. Fiducial markers are used to generate the ground truth pose of the model, which limits the range of displacements that can be achieved. In contrast, we propose a new method to collect ground truth pose data that makes the acquisition simpler without the need for fiducial markers.

There is an increasing interest in 6-DOF temporal trackers since they were shown to be faster and more robust than single frame detection methods. In the past, geometric methods based on ICP [4, 12–14] were used for temporal tracking, but they lack robustness for small objects and are generally computationally expensive. Data-driven approaches such as the ones reported in [5, 6, 15] can learn more robust features and the use of the Random Forest regressor [16] decreases the computing overhead significantly. Other methods show that the contours of the objects in RGB and depth data provide important cues for estimating pose [1, 2, 17]. While their optimization techniques can be accurate, many assumptions are made on the features which restrict the type of object and the type of background that can be dealt with. Recently, Garon and Lalonde [3] proposed a deep learning framework which can learn robust features automatically from data. They use a feedback loop by rendering the 3D model at runtime at the previous pose, and regress the pose difference between the rendered object and the real image. While their method compares to the previous work with respect to accuracy, their learned features are more robust to higher level of occlusion and noise. A downside is that their method needs a dataset of real images and a specific network has to be trained for each object which can be time consuming. We take advantage of their architecture but introduce novel ideas to provide a better performing tracker that can be trained entirely on synthetic data. In addition, our network can be trained to generalize to previously unseen objects.

3   Dataset Capture and Calibration

Building a dataset with calibrated object pose w.r.t the sensor at each frame is a challenging task since it requires an accurate method to collect ground truth object pose. Until now, the most practical method to achieve this task was to use fiducial markers and calibrate the object pose w.r.t these markers [3, 7–9]. However, this method suffers from two main drawbacks. First, the object cannot be moved independently of the panel so this restricts the camera to move around the object of interest. Second, the scene always contains visual cues (the markers) which could involuntarily "help" the algorithms.

Our approach eliminates these limitations. A Vicon^{TM} MX-T40 motion capture system is used to collect the ground truth pose of the objects in the scene. The retroreflective Vicon markers that must be used are very small in size (3 mm diameter) and can be automatically removed in a post-processing step. In this section, we describe the capture setup and the various calibration steps needed to align the object model and estimate its ground truth pose. The resulting RGBD video sequences captured using this setup are presented in Sect. 4.

3.1 Capture Setup

The motion capture setup is composed of a set of 8 calibrated cameras that track retro-reflective markers of 3 mm in diameter installed on the objects of interest in a $3 \times 3 \times 3\,m^3$ work area. Vicon systems can provide a marker detection accuracy of up to 0.15 mm on static objects and 2 mm on moving objects according to [18]. A Kinect V2 is used to acquire the RGBD frames, and is calibrated with the Vicon to record the ground truth pose of the objects in the Kinect coordinate system. The actual setup used to capture the dataset is shown in Fig. 2-(a).

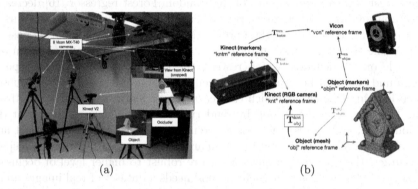

(a)   (b)

Fig. 2. Acquisition setup used to capture our novel dataset. (a) Actual setup, which includes an 8-camera Vicon motion capture system and a Kinect V2. The resulting view from the Kinect is shown in the inset. Here, an occluder is placed in front of the object. (b) The various transformations that must be calibrated in order to obtain the object pose in the Kinect RGB camera reference frame $\mathbf{T}^{knt}_{obj}$. The transformations shown in black are obtained from the motion capture system directly, while the gray ones need a specific calibration procedure described in the main body of the paper.

3.2 Calibration

With an RGB-D sensor such as the Kinect V2, color and depth values are projected onto two different planes. We define the Kinect reference frame ("knt") as the origin of its RGB camera, and align the depth data by reprojecting it to the color plane using the factory calibration parameters. We calibrate the depth correction as in Hodan et al. [8]. In this section, the notation $\mathbf{T}^{b}_{a}$ is used to denote a rigid transformation from reference frame "a" to "b".

   We aim to recover the pose of the object in the Kinect reference frame $\mathbf{T}^{knt}_{obj}$ (Fig. 2-(b)). To do so, we first rely on the Vicon motion capture system, which has its own reference frame "vcn". The set of retroreflective markers installed on the object define the local reference frame "objm". Similarly, the set of markers placed on the Kinect define the local reference frame "kntm". The Vicon system provides the transformations $\mathbf{T}_{objm}^{vcn}$ and $\mathbf{T}_{kntm}^{vcn}$ directly, that is, the mappings between the object and Kinect markers and the Vicon reference frame respectively. The transformation between the object markers and the Kinect markers is obtained by chaining the previous transformations:

$$\mathbf{T}_{objm}^{kntm} = (\mathbf{T}_{kntm}^{vcn})^{-1}\mathbf{T}_{objm}^{vcn}. \tag{1}$$

The pose $\mathbf{T}_{obj}^{knt}$ is recovered with the transformations between the local frames defined by the markers and the object/Kinect reference frames $\mathbf{T}_{obj}^{objm}$ and $\mathbf{T}_{knt}^{kntm}$:

$$\mathbf{T}_{obj}^{knt} = (\mathbf{T}_{knt}^{kntm})^{-1}\mathbf{T}_{objm}^{kntm}\mathbf{T}_{obj}^{objm}. \tag{2}$$

The calibration procedures needed to obtain these two transformations, also shown in gray in Fig. 2-(b), are detailed next.

Kinect Calibration. In order to find the transformation $\mathbf{T}_{kntm}^{knt}$ between the local frame defined by the markers installed on the Kinect and its RGB camera, we rely on a planar checkerboard target on which Vicon markers are randomly placed. Then, the position of each corner of the checkerboard is determined with respect to the markers with the following procedure. A 15 cm-long pen-like probe that has a 1 cm Vicon marker attached at one end was designed for this purpose. The sharp end is placed on the corner to be detected, and the probe is moved in a circular motion around that point. A sphere is then fit (using least-squares) to the resulting marker positions (achieving an average radius estimation error of 0.7 mm), and the center of the sphere is kept as the location for the checkerboard corner. The checkerboard target was then moved in the capture volume and corners were detected by the Kinect RGB camera, thereby establishing 2D-3D correspondences between these points. The perspective-n-points algorithm [19] was finally used to compute $\mathbf{T}_{kntm}^{knt}$.

Object Calibration. To estimate the transformation between the local frame defined by the markers placed on the object and its mesh coordinate system $\mathbf{T}_{objm}^{obj}$, we rely on the Kinect pose calibrated with the method described previously. As a convention, we define the origin of the object local coordinate system at the center of mass of the markers, the same convention is used for the mesh by using the center of mass of the vertices. We roughly align the axis and use ICP to refine its position (based on the Kinect depth values). Finally, with the help of a visual interface where a user can move and visualize the alignment of the object, fine-scale adjustments can be performed manually from several viewpoints to minimize the error between the observed object and the reprojected mesh.

Synchronization. In addition to spatial calibration, precise temporal alignment must be achieved to synchronize Vicon and Kinect frames. Unfortunately, the Kinect does not offer hardware synchronization capabilities, therefore we adopt the following software solution. We assume that the sequences are short enough to neglect clock drift. We also assume a stable sampling of the Vicon system on a high bandwidth closed network. In this setup, synchronization can be achieved by estimating the (constant) time difference δt between the Vicon and the Kinect frame timestamps. By moving the checkboard of Sect. 3.2 with varying speed, we estimate the δt that minimizes the reprojection error between the checkerboard corners from Sect. 3.2 and the Vicon markers.

Removing the Markers. The 3 mm markers used to track the object are retro-reflective and, despite their small size and their low number (7 per object on average), they nevertheless create visible artifacts in the depth data measured by the Kinect, see Fig. 3. We propose a post-processing algorithm for automatically removing them in all the sequences. First, to ensure that the marker can be observed by the Kinect we reproject the (known) marker positions onto the depth image and compute the median distance between the depth in a small window around the reprojected point and its ground truth depth. If the difference is less than 1 cm, the point is considered as not occluded, and will be processed. Finally, we render the depth values of the 3D model at the given pose and replace the 10×10 pixel window from the original image with the rendered depth values. For more realism, a small amount of gaussian noise is added. Pixels from the background are simply ignored. On average, only 3.4% of the object pixels are corrected. We also minimize the chances of affecting the geometric structure of the object by placing the markers on planar surfaces. Figure 3 shows a comparison of the error between a Kinect depth image captured with markers, and another image of the same scene with markers that have been corrected with our algorithm. The RMSE of the pixel patches around the markers is 139.8 mm without the correction, and 4.7 mm with the correction.

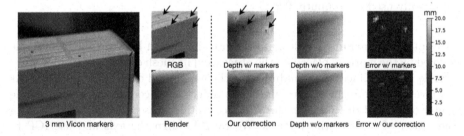

Fig. 3. Example of an RGB and depth frame containing 2 markers on a flat surface, and 2 markers near an edge. We take advantage of our knowledge of the object mesh and pose to replace patches of 10×10 pixels around the marker by the depth values of a render at the same pose. We capture an image without the markers to compare the error. On the modified patches we report a RMSE of 139.8 mm on the depth with the markers, and 4.7 with the corrected version.

4   Dataset Scenarios, Metrics, and Statistics

This section defines novel ways to evaluate 6-DOF trackers using calibrated sequences captured with the setup presented in Sect. 3. We provide an evaluation methodology that will reflect the overall performance of a tracker in different scenarios. To attain this objective, we captured 297 sequences of 11 different objects of various shapes in 3 scenarios: *stability*, *occlusion*, and *interaction*. We also provide quantitative metrics to measure the performance in each scenario. Our dataset and accompanying code is available at http://www.jflalonde.ca/ projects/6dofObjectTracking.

4.1   Performance Metrics

Before we describe each scenario, we first introduce how we propose to evaluate the difference between two poses $\mathbf{P}_1$ and $\mathbf{P}_2$. Here, a pose $\mathbf{P} = \begin{bmatrix} \mathbf{R} \ \mathbf{t} \end{bmatrix}$ is described by a rotation matrix $\mathbf{R}$ and a translation vector $\mathbf{t}$. Previous works consider the average of each axis component in translation and rotation separately. The side effect of this metric is that a large error on a single component is less penalized. To overcome this limitation, the translation error is simply defined as the L2 norm between the two translation vectors:

$$\delta_t(\mathbf{t}_1, \mathbf{t}_2) = ||\mathbf{t}_1 - \mathbf{t}_2||_2. \tag{3}$$

The distance between two rotation matrices is computed using:

$$\delta_{\mathbf{R}}(\mathbf{R}_1, \mathbf{R}_2) = \arccos\left(\frac{\mathrm{Tr}(\mathbf{R}_1^T \mathbf{R}_2) - 1}{2}\right), \tag{4}$$

where $\mathrm{Tr}(\cdot)$ denotes the matrix trace.

4.2   Scenarios

The *Stability* Scenario. In this first scenario, we propose to quantify the degree of pose jitter when tracking a static object. To evaluate this, we captured 5-second sequences of the object under 4 different viewpoints and with 3 configurations: at a distance of 0.8 m from the sensor ("near"), of 1.5 m from the sensor ("far"), and of 0.8 m from the sensor, but this time with distractor objects partly occluding the object of interest ("occluded"). To measure the stability, Tan et al. [2] use the standard deviation of the pose parameters on a sequence. We propose a different metric inspired from [20] that penalizes variation from frame to frame instead of the general distribution across the sequence. We compute the distance between poses $\mathbf{P}_{i-1}$ and $\mathbf{P}_i$ at time i. In other words, we report the distribution of $\delta_t(\mathbf{t}_{i-1}, \mathbf{t}_i)$ and $\delta_{\mathbf{R}}(\mathbf{R}_{i-1}, \mathbf{R}_i)$ for all frames of the stability scenario.

The *Occlusion* Scenario. To evaluate the robustness to occlusion, we follow [3] and place the object on a turntable at 1.2 m from the sensor, and a static occluder is placed in front of the object in a vertical and horizontal position. We compute the amount of occlusion based on the largest dimension of the object, and provide sequences for each object from 0% to 75% occlusion in 15% increments, which results in a total of 11 sequences per object. Here, we compute errors by comparing the pose $\mathbf{P}_i$ at time i with the ground truth $\mathbf{P}_i^*$ for that same frame, i.e., $\delta_\mathbf{t}(\mathbf{t}_i^*, \mathbf{t}_i)$ and $\delta_\mathbf{R}(\mathbf{R}_i^*, \mathbf{R}_i)$. Temporal trackers may lose tracking on difficult frames. This can affect the overall score depending on the moment where the tracker fails. To bypass this limitation, we initialize the tracker at the ground truth pose $\mathbf{P}_i^*$ every 15 frames as in [3].

The *Interaction* Scenario. In this last scenario, the experimenter holds the object in his hands and manipulates it in 4 different ways: (1) by moving the object around but without rotating it ("translation-only"); (2) by rotating the object on itself without translating it ("rotation-only"); (3) by freely moving and rotating the object around at low speeds ("free-slow"); and (4) by freely moving and rotating the object at higher speeds and by voluntarily generating more occlusions ("free-hard"). In all situations but the "free-hard", we reset the tracker every 15 frames and we report $\delta_\mathbf{t}(\mathbf{t}_i^*, \mathbf{t}_i)$ and $\delta_\mathbf{R}(\mathbf{R}_i^*, \mathbf{R}_i)$ as in Sect. 4.2. Since the object speed varies, we also compute the translational and rotational inter-frame displacement $(\delta_\mathbf{t}(\mathbf{t}_{i-1}^*, \mathbf{t}_i^*), \delta_\mathbf{R}(\mathbf{R}_{i-1}^*, \mathbf{R}_i^*))$ and report the performance metric above as a function of that displacement. In addition, it is also informative to count the number of times the tracker has failed. We consider a tracking failure when either $\delta_\mathbf{t}(\mathbf{t}_i^*, \mathbf{t}_i) > 3\,\mathrm{cm}$ or $\delta_\mathbf{R}(\mathbf{R}_i^*, \mathbf{R}_i) > 20°$ for more than 7 consecutive frames. When a failure is detected, the tracker is reset at the ground truth pose $\mathbf{P}^*$. We report these failures on the "free-hard" sequences only.

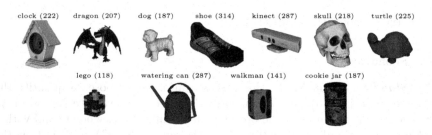

Fig. 4. Overview of the 11 objects in our dataset, with their maximum distance between two vertices in mm shown above.

4.3   Dataset Statistics

We selected 11 different objects to obtain a wide variety of object geometries and appearance, as shown in Fig. 4. To obtain a precise 3D model of each object in the database, each of them was scanned with a Creaform GoScan™ handheld 3D scanner at a 1 mm voxel resolution. The scans were manually cleaned using Creaform VxElements™ to remove background and spurious vertices.

Overall, the dataset contains 297 sequences: 27 sequences for each object. The breakdown is the following: 12 sequences for *stability* (4 viewpoints, 3 configurations: "near", "far", "occluded"); 11 sequences for *occlusion* (0% to 75% in 15% increment for both horizontal and vertical occluders); and 4 sequences for *interaction* ("rotation-only", "translation-only", "free-slow", "free-hard"). It also contains high resolution textured 3D models for each object.

Input: x_{pred}	Input: x_{obs}
conv3-96	conv3-96
fire-48-96	fire-48-96
concatenation	
fire-96-384	
fire-192-768	
fire-384-768	
FC-500	
FC-6	

Output: y

Fig. 5. The deep learning architecture used to track 3D objects in this work, inspired by [3]. The notation "conv$x$-y" indicates a convolution layer of y filters of dimension $x \times x$, "fire-x-y" indicates a "fire" module [21] which reduces the number of channels to x and expands to y, and "FC-x" is a fully-connected layer of x units. Each layer have a skip link similar to DenseNet [22] and is followed by a max pooling 2×2 operation. We use a dropout of 50% on the input connections to the FC-500 layer. All layers (except the last FC-6) have batch normalization and the ELU activation function [23].

5   Analyzing a Deep 6-DOF Tracker with Our Dataset

As a testbed to evaluate the relevance of the new dataset, we borrow the technique of Garon and Lalonde [3] who train a 6-DOF tracker using deep learning, but propose changes to their architecture and training methodology. We evaluate several variants of the network on our dataset and show that it can be used to accurately quantify the performance of a tracker in a wide variety of scenarios.

5.1   Training an Object-Specific Tracker

We propose improvements over the previous work of [3] by adding 5 main changes: 2 to the network architecture, and 3 to the training procedure. The new proposed network architecture is shown in Fig. 5. As in [3], the network accepts two inputs: an image of the object rendered at its predicted position (from the previous timestamp in the video sequence) x_{pred}, and an image of the observed object at the current timestamp x_{obs}. The last layer outputs the 6-DOF (3 for translation, 3 for rotation in Euler angles) representing the pose change between the two inputs. We first replace convolution layers by the "fire" modules proposed in [21]. The second change, inspired by DenseNet [22], is to concatenate the input features of each layers to the outputs before being max-pooled. Our improvement requires the same runtime as [3], which is 6 ms on a Nvidia GTX-970M. As in [3], the loss used is the MSE between the predicted and ground truth pose change. Note that we experimented with the reprojection loss [24], but found it did not help in our context.

We also propose changes to the training procedure of [3]. Their approach consists in generating pairs of synthetic views of the object with random pose changes between them. To sample the random pose changes, they proposed to independently sample a random translation $t_{x,y,z} \sim U(20\,\mathrm{mm}, 20\,\mathrm{mm})$ and rotation $r_{\alpha,\beta,\gamma} \sim U(-10°, 10°)$ in Euler angle notation, with $U(a,b)$ referring to a uniform distribution on interval $[a,b]$. Doing so unfortunately biases the resulting pose changes. For example, small amplitude translations are quite unlikely to be generated (since this requires *all* three translation components to be small simultaneously). Our first change is to sample a random translation *vector* and *magnitude* separately. The translation vector $\mathbf{v}_t$ is sampled in spherical coordinates (θ_t, ϕ_t), where $\theta_t \sim U(-180°, 180°)$ and $\phi_t = \cos^{-1}(x)$ with $x \sim U(-1,1)$. The translation magnitude m_t is drawn from a Gaussian distribution $m_t \sim \mathcal{N}(0, \Delta t)$. The same process is repeated for rotations, where the rotation axis $\mathbf{v}_r$ and angle $m_r \sim \mathcal{N}(0, \Delta r)$ are sampled similarly. Here, we intentionally parameterize the translation magnitude m_t and rotation angle m_r distributions with Δt and Δr, since the range of these parameters may influence the behavior of the network. Our second change is to downsample the depth channel to better match the resolution of the Kinect V2. Our third change consists in a data augmentation method for RGBD images where we randomly set a modality (depth or RGB) to zero during training, which has the effect of untangling the features of both modalities. With these changes, we can now rely purely on synthetic data to train the network (in [3] a set of real frames was required to fine-tune the network).

5.2   Training a Generic Tracker

To train a generic 6-DOF object tracker, we experimented with two ways of generating a training dataset, using the same network architecture, loss, and training procedure described in Sect. 5.1. First, we generate a training set of images that contain all 11 objects from our dataset, as well as 30 other objects. These other objects, downloaded from 3D Warehouse[1] and from "Linemod" [7], show a high diversity in geometry and texture and are roughly of the same size. We name the network trained on this dataset the "multi-object" network. Second, we generate a training set of images that contain only the 30 *other* objects—the actual objects to track are *not* included. We call this network "generic", since it never saw any of the objects in our dataset during training. Note that all these approaches require the 3D model of the object to track at test time, however.

---

[1] Available at: https://3dwarehouse.sketchup.com.

Table 1. Applying our evaluation methodology for determining the best range of translations Δt and rotations Δr for generating synthetic data when training a deep 6-DOF tracker. We show (a) the impact of varying Δt on the error δ_t, and (b) the impact of varying Δr on the error δ_R for all three scenarios (from top to bottom: *stability*, *occlusion*, and *interaction*).

Stability Scenario

Δt	Translation (mm/frame)			Δr	Rotation (degree/frame)		
	Near	Far	Occluded		Near	Far	Occluded
10	0.42	0.53	0.48	15	0.35	0.51	0.63
20	0.62	0.77	0.71	20	0.55	0.68	0.88
30	0.72	0.84	0.89	25	0.53	0.66	0.97
40	0.75	0.89	1.00	30	0.61	0.74	1.04
50	0.95	1.03	1.16	35	0.68	0.87	1.10

Occlusion scenario

Δt	Translation (mm)						Δr	Rotation (degrees)					
Occlusion %	0	15	30	45	60	75		0	15	30	45	60	75
10	14.8	12.5	13.1	15.5	20.0	25.3	15	2.1	2.9	5.4	8.1	15.7	26.0
20	7.5	7.6	12.5	15.5	22.3	29.5	20	3.3	4.8	7.5	9.9	17.2	48.0
30	11.0	11.5	17.4	21.5	26.6	33.9	25	3.3	4.8	8.7	16.8	30.6	41.1
40	12.7	14.8	17.9	26.0	36.0	68.1	30	2.7	3.9	6.9	12.3	26.9	62.9
50	10.4	11.1	17.7	30.6	43.8	73.7	35	3.2	4.6	9.1	16.1	36.7	66.1

Interaction scenario

Δt	Translation (mm)				Δr	Rotation (degrees)			
Speed (per frame)	(0, 10]	(10, 20]	(20, 30]	(30, 40]		(0, 4]	(4, 8]	(8, 12]	(12, 16]
10	10.1	11.8	16.4	18.8	15	2.9	3.8	4.2	4.4
20	6.5	8.7	11.0	18.0	20	3.7	4.7	4.9	5.0
30	9.7	9.9	11.5	9.5	25	5.7	5.9	5.8	6.1
40	10.8	11.4	11.7	6.6	30	4.3	4.6	4.7	4.7
50	10.5	11.4	10.9	7.2	35	4.7	4.8	5.4	5.1

(a) Impact of Δt on δ_t (b) Impact of Δr on δ_R

6 Experiments

In this section, we perform an exhaustive evaluation of the various approaches presented in Sect. 5 using our novel dataset and framework proposed in Sect. 4. First, we analyze the impact of varying the training data generation hyper-parameters Δt and Δr for the object-specific case. Then, we proceed to compare our object-specific, "multi-object", and "generic" trackers with two existing methods: Garon and Lalonde [3] and Tan et al. [5].

6.1 Analysis to Training Data Generation Parameters

We now apply the evaluation methodology proposed in Sect. 4 on the method presented above and evaluate the influence of the Δr and Δt hyper-parameters on the various metrics and sequences from our dataset. We experiment by varying $\Delta t \in \{10, 20, 30, 40, 50\}$ mm and $\Delta r \in \{15, 20, 25, 30, 35\}°$ one at a time (the other parameter is kept at its lowest value). For each of these parameters, we synthesize 200,000 training image pairs per object using [3] and the modifications proposed in Sect. 5.1. We then train a network for each object, for each set of parameters, and evaluate each network on our dataset. A subset of the results of this analysis is shown in Table 1. Note that, for the *interaction* scenario, the "free-hard" sequences (Sect. 4.2) were left out since they are much harder than the others and would bias the results. In particular, we show the impact that varying Δt has on δ_t, as well as that of varying Δr has on δ_R for all 3 scenarios. Here, we drop the parentheses for the $\delta_{\{t,R\}}$ error metrics for ease of notation (see Sect. 4 for the definitions). The figure reveals a clear trend: increasing Δr (Table 1-(b)) systematically results in worse performance in rotation. This is especially visible for the high occlusion cases (45% and 60%), where the rotation error δ_R increases significantly as a function of Δr. The situation is not so simple when Δt is increased (Table 1-(a)). Indeed, while increasing Δt negatively impacts δ_t in the *stability* and *occlusion* scenarios, performance actually *improves* when the object speed is higher, as seen in the *interaction* scenario. Therefore, to achieve a good balance between stability and accuracy at higher speeds, a value of $\Delta t = 30$ mm seems to be a good trade-off. The remainder of the plots for this analysis, as well as plots evaluating the impact of the resolution of the crop and the size of the bounding box w.r.t the object are shown in the supplementary material.

Table 2. Comparison of our networks with the previous work of [3,5]. Our "object-specific" networks outperform the state of the art in almost all scenarios, and performs remarkably well at predicting the rotation. Our "generic" tracker shows great promise: although not as good as the "object-specific" version, it results in slightly lower error compared with [3], even if it has not seen any of these objects during training. See the supplementary video for a visual qualitative comparison of the trackers.

Stability scenario	Translation (mm/frame)			Rotation (degree/frame)		
	Near	Far	Occluded	Near	Far	Occluded
Ours specific	0.56	0.68	0.72	**0.52**	**0.59**	**0.76**
Ours multi-object	**0.38**	**0.41**	**0.57**	0.69	0.79	1.09
Ours generic	0.72	0.75	1.19	0.95	0.98	1.67
Garon and Lalonde [1]	0.93	1.06	1.24	1.13	1.23	1.49
Tan et al [5]	1.20	1.31	1.53	1.30	1.44	1.92

Occlusion scenario	Translation (mm)						Rotation (degrees)					
Occlusion %	0	15	30	45	60	75	0	15	30	45	60	75
Ours specific	7.4	9.8	11.5	12.5	15.5	24.2	3.6	5.9	7.9	10.0	12.6	22.2
Ours multi-object	23.3	16.9	14.6	14.3	**13.2**	**13.4**	4.0	8.6	12.3	12.1	14.7	**15.4**
Ours generic	**6.7**	11.1	18.9	25.9	34.4	47.4	5.3	8.4	16.1	26.8	43.7	50.6
Garon and Lalonde [1]	7.4	11.2	18.9	26.8	38.1	55.0	5.3	8.8	17.7	28.2	41.7	49.8
Tan et al [5]	8.2	**8.5**	15.9	138	186	213	4.0	7.4	33.1	70.3	89.5	88.0

Interaction scenario	Translation (mm)				Rotation (degrees)				
Speed (per frame)	(0, 12.5]	(12.5, 25]	(25, 37.5]	(37.5, 50]	(0, 19]	(19, 37]	(37, 56]	(56, 75]	Fail
Ours specific	8.2	10.3	11.1	13.4	**3.7**	5.8	**3.6**	**5.8**	37
Ours multi-object	22.1	27.3	26.0	41.9	6.0	8.6	2.9	6.1	127
Ours generic	9.3	9.9	11.7	13.4	6.3	6.8	8.8	7.0	38
Garon and Lalonde [1]	9.5	10.2	**10.3**	12.4	7.8	9.5	13.4	11.8	53
Tan et al [5]	**8.1**	**8.5**	10.7	67.1	4.5	6.0	8.1	10.1	86

6.2   Comparison with Previous Work

Our trackers yields a 1.7 mm/0.6° error on the 4 sequences of [4] which is slightly above [5] who obtain 0.81 mm/0.37°. However, as reported in Table 2, more interesting differences between the trackers can be observed when using our new dataset. We compare with object-specific versions of the work of Garon and Lalonde [3] as well as the Random Forest approach of Tan et al. [5]. For [3], we use the training parameters reported in their paper. For our trackers, the Δm and Δr hyper-parameters were obtained with leave-one-out cross-validation to ensure no training/test overlap. As before, the "free-hard" sequences were left out for the *interaction* experiments.

Overall, as can be observed in Table 2, the proposed deep learning methods perform either on par or better than the previous work. The "object-specific" networks outperform almost all the other techniques, except for the case of translational error in the interaction scenario. It performs remarkably well at predicting rotations, and is on par with the other methods for translation. In comparison, [5] performs well at low occlusions, but fails when the occlusion level is 30% or greater (particularly in rotation). [3] shows improved robustness to occlusions, but still achieves high rotation errors at 45% occlusion, and is also much less stable (esp. in rotation) than our "object-specific" networks. Interestingly, our "generic" tracker, which has seen none of these objects in training, performs similarly to the previous works that were trained specifically on these objects. Indeed, it shows a stability, robustness to occlusions and behavior at higher speeds that is similar to [3,5], demonstrating that learning generic features that are useful for tracking objects can be achieved. Finally, we use the "free-hard" *interaction* sequences to count the number of times the tracking is lost (Sect. 4.2). In this case, the "object-specific" and "generic" networks outperforms the other methods. Qualitative videos showing side-by-side comparisons of these methods are available in the supplementary material.

7   Discussion

The recent evolution in 6-DOF tracking performance on the popular dataset of Choi et al. [4] highlights the need for a new dataset containing real data and more challenging scenarios. In this paper, we provide such a dataset, which we hope will spur further research in the field. Our dataset contains 297 sequences containing 11 objects of various shapes and textures. The sequences are grouped into 3 scenarios: *stability, occlusion,* and *interaction.* The dataset and companion evaluation code is released publicly[2]. Additionally, we build on the framework of [3] with an improved architecture and training procedure which allows the network to learn purely from synthetic data, yet generalize well on real data. In addition, the architecture allows for training on multiple objects and test on *different* objects it has never seen in training. To the best of our knowledge, we are the first to propose such a generic learner for the 6-DOF object tracking task. Finally, our approach is extensively compared with recent work and is shown to achieve better performance.

A current limitation is that the Vicon markers must be removed in a post-processing step, which may leave some artifacts behind. While the markers are very small (3 mm) and the resulting marker-free images have low error (see Fig. 3), there might still be room for improvement. Finally, our "generic" tracker is promising, but it still does not perform quite as well as "object-specific" models, especially for rotations. In addition, a 3D model of the object is still required

---

[2] http://www.jflalonde.ca/projects/6dofObjectTracking.

at test time, so exploring how this constraint can be removed would make for an exciting future research direction.

Acknowledgements. The authors wish to thank Jonathan Gilbert for his help with data acquisition and Sylvain Comtois for the Vicon setup. This work was supported by the NSERC/Creaform Industrial Research Chair on 3D Scanning: CREATION 3D. We gratefully acknowledge the support of Nvidia with the donation of the Tesla K40 and Titan X GPUs used for this research.

References

1. Kehl, W., Tombari, F., Ilic, S., Navab, N.: Real-time 3D model tracking in color and depth on a single CPU core. In: IEEE Conference on Computer Vision and Pattern Recognition (2017)
2. Tan, D.J., Navab, N., Tombari, F.: Looking beyond the simple scenarios: combining learners and optimizers in 3D temporal tracking. IEEE Trans. Vis. Comput. Graph. **23**(11), 2399–2409 (2017)
3. Garon, M., Lalonde, J.F.: Deep 6-DOF tracking. IEEE Trans. Comput. Graph. Vis. **23**(11) (2017)
4. Choi, C., Christensen, H.I.: RGB-D object tracking: a particle filter approach on GPU. In: International Conference on Intelligent Robots and Systems (2013)
5. Tan, D.J., Tombari, F., Ilic, S., Navab, N.: A versatile learning-based 3D temporal tracker: scalable, robust, online. In: IEEE International Conference on Computer Vision (2015)
6. Krull, A., Michel, F., Brachmann, E., Gumhold, S., Ihrke, S., Rother, C.: 6-DOF model based tracking via object coordinate regression. In: Cremers, D., Reid, I., Saito, H., Yang, M.-H. (eds.) ACCV 2014. LNCS, vol. 9006, pp. 384–399. Springer, Cham (2015). https://doi.org/10.1007/978-3-319-16817-3_25
7. Hinterstoisser, S., et al.: Model based training, detection and pose estimation of texture-less 3D objects in heavily cluttered scenes. In: Lee, K.M., Matsushita, Y., Rehg, J.M., Hu, Z. (eds.) ACCV 2012. LNCS, vol. 7724, pp. 548–562. Springer, Heidelberg (2013). https://doi.org/10.1007/978-3-642-37331-2_42
8. Hodan, T., Haluza, P., Obdržálek, Š., Matas, J., Lourakis, M., Zabulis, X.: T-LESS: an RGB-D dataset for 6D pose estimation of texture-less objects. In: IEEE Winter Conference on Applications of Computer Vision (2017)
9. Tejani, A., Tang, D., Kouskouridas, R., Kim, T.-K.: Latent-class hough forests for 3D object detection and pose estimation. In: Fleet, D., Pajdla, T., Schiele, B., Tuytelaars, T. (eds.) ECCV 2014. LNCS, vol. 8694, pp. 462–477. Springer, Cham (2014). https://doi.org/10.1007/978-3-319-10599-4_30
10. Doumanoglou, A., Kouskouridas, R., Malassiotis, S., Kim, T.K.: Recovering 6D object pose and predicting next-best-view in the crowd. In: IEEE Conference on Computer Vision and Pattern Recognition (2016)
11. Akkaladevi, S., Ankerl, M., Heindl, C., Pichler, A.: Tracking multiple rigid symmetric and non-symmetric objects in real-time using depth data. In: IEEE International Conference on Robotics and Automation (2016)
12. Aldoma, A., Tombari, F., Prankl, J., Richtsfeld, A., Di Stefano, L., Vincze, M.: Multimodal cue integration through hypotheses verification for RGB-D object recognition and 6DOF pose estimation. In: IEEE International Conference on Robotics and Automation, pp. 2104–2111. IEEE (2013)

13. Kwon, J., Choi, M., Park, F.C., Chun, C.: Particle filtering on the Euclidean group: framework and applications. Robotica **25**(6), 725–737 (2007)
14. Chitchian, M., van Amesfoort, A.S., Simonetto, A., Keviczky, T., Sips, H.J.: Adapting particle filter algorithms to many-core architectures. In: 2013 IEEE 27th International Symposium on Parallel and Distributed Processing (IPDPS), pp. 427–438. IEEE (2013)
15. Tan, D.J., Ilic, S.: Multi-forest tracker: a chameleon in tracking. In: Proceedings of the IEEE Conference on Computer Vision and Pattern Recognition (2014)
16. Breiman, L.: Random forests. Mach. Learn. **45**(1), 5–32 (2001)
17. Tjaden, H., Schwanecke, U., Schömer, E.: Real-time monocular pose estimation of 3D objects using temporally consistent local color histograms. In: IEEE Conference on Computer Vision and Pattern Recognition (2017)
18. Merriaux, P., Dupuis, Y., Boutteau, R., Vasseur, P., Savatier, X.: A study of vicon system positioning performance. Sensors **17**(7), 1591 (2017)
19. Zhang, Z.: A flexible new technique for camera calibration. IEEE Trans. Pattern Anal. Mach. Intell. **22**(11), 1330–1334 (2000)
20. Niehorster, D.C., Li, L., Lappe, M.: The accuracy and precision of position and orientation tracking in the HTC vive virtual reality system for scientific research. i-Perception **8**(3) (2017)
21. Iandola, F.N., Han, S., Moskewicz, M.W., Ashraf, K., Dally, W.J., Keutzer, K.: Squeezenet: Alexnet-level accuracy with 50x fewer parameters and <0.5MB model size. arXiv:1602.07360 (2016)
22. Huang, G., Liu, Z., van der Maaten, L., Weinberger, K.Q.: Densely connected convolutional networks. In: IEEE Conference on Computer Vision and Pattern Recognition (2017)
23. Clevert, D.A., Unterthiner, T., Hochreiter, S.: Fast and accurate deep network learning by exponential linear units (ELUs). arXiv preprint arXiv:1511.07289 (2015)
24. Kendall, A., Cipolla, R.: Geometric loss functions for camera pose regression with deep learning. In: IEEE Conference on Computer Vision and Pattern Recognition (2017)

Variable Ring Light Imaging: Capturing Transient Subsurface Scattering with an Ordinary Camera

Ko Nishino[1,3]([✉]), Art Subpa-asa[2], Yuta Asano[2], Mihoko Shimano[3],
and Imari Sato[3]

[1] Kyoto University, Kyoto, Japan
kon@i.kyoto-u.ac.jp
[2] Tokyo Institute of Technology, Tokyo, Japan
{art.s.aa,asano.y.ac}@m.titech.ac.jp
[3] National Institute of Informatics, Tokyo, Japan
{miho,imarik}@nii.ac.jp

Abstract. Subsurface scattering plays a significant role in determining the appearance of real-world surfaces. A light ray penetrating into the subsurface is repeatedly scattered and absorbed by particles along its path before reemerging from the outer interface, which determines its spectral radiance. We introduce a novel imaging method that enables the decomposition of the appearance of a fronto-parallel real-world surface into images of light with bounded path lengths, i.e., transient subsurface light transport. Our key idea is to observe each surface point under a variable ring light: a circular illumination pattern of increasingly larger radius centered on it. We show that the path length of light captured in each of these observations is naturally lower-bounded by the ring light radius. By taking the difference of ring light images of incrementally larger radii, we compute transient images that encode light with bounded path lengths. Experimental results on synthetic and complex real-world surfaces demonstrate that the recovered transient images reveal the subsurface structure of general translucent inhomogeneous surfaces. We further show that their differences reveal the surface colors at different surface depths. The proposed method is the first to enable the unveiling of dense and continuous subsurface structures from steady-state external appearance using ordinary camera and illumination.

1 Introduction

Subsurface scattering, the light transport inside a surface near its external interface, has a significant effect on the appearance of real-world surfaces. Once incident light penetrates into the subsurface, it bounces off particles (e.g., pigments)

Electronic supplementary material The online version of this chapter (https://doi.org/10.1007/978-3-030-01252-6_37) contains supplementary material, which is available to authorized users.

V. Ferrari et al. (Eds.): ECCV 2018, LNCS 11215, pp. 624–639, 2018.
https://doi.org/10.1007/978-3-030-01252-6_37

in the medium multiple times. In addition to the absorption by the surface medium itself, each of these bounces causes absorption and scattering, leading to the unique color and direction of light reemerging from the interface.

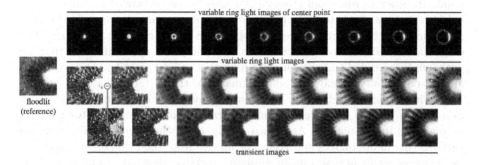

Fig. 1. We propose an imaging method that enables the decomposition of the appearance of subsurface scattering into a set of images of light with bounded path lengths, and proportionally a limited number of bounces with particles inside the surface, i.e., transient light transport in the surface. These transient images collectively reveal the internal structure and color of the surface.

The longer the light travels the more bounces it experiences. If we can decompose the appearance of a subsurface scattering surface into a set of images, each of which captures light that has traveled a limited range of distance (i.e., path length) or probabilistically proportionally a limited number of bounces with particles in the surface, the results would tell us a great deal about the otherwise unobservable internal surface structure underneath the external interface.

Imaging path length or bounce decomposed light has been studied primarily for interreflection as part of scene-wide global light transport analysis. Subsurface scattering is distinct from interreflection as it concerns light transport inside a surface and is governed by the statistically distributed particles rather than much larger-scale 3D scene geometry. As we review in Sect. 2, past methods fundamentally rely on frequency and geometric characteristics that are unique to interreflection, and cannot be applied to decompose subsurface scattering.

This paper introduces the first method for subsurface scattering decomposition, the recovery of path length (and proportionally bounce) dependent light that make up the appearance of real-world translucent surfaces. Our key contribution lies in the use of a natural lower bound on the shortest path length defined by the external interface of a surface. When lit and viewed orthographically from the top, the surface defines a halfspace and the shortest path length of light incident at a single surface point, referred to as impulse illumination, observed at distance r from the point of incidence would naturally be r.

We exploit this lower bound on light path length by observing the same surface point while varying the distance of an impulse illumination. Instead of using impulse illuminations at an arbitrary point, we use a radius-r ring light around each surface point, i.e., all surface points at surface distance r

illuminated with impulse illuminations. We obtain variable ring light images, each of which encodes the appearance of each surface point captured with ring lights of varying radii. We show that taking the difference of two ring light images of slightly different radii bounds the light path length observed at each surface point. In other words, from steady-state appearance captured as variable ring light images, we compute surface appearance with varying degrees of subsurface scattering. i.e., transient images of subsurface light transport. We also show empirical evidence based on simulation and analytical approximation that the path length-bounded transient images may also be interpreted as approximately and proportionally bounded n-bounce images of the surfaces.

We implement variable ring light imaging by capturing N impulse illumination images, where N is the number of surface points (i.e., projector pixels in an observed image region). As shown in Fig. 1, we then synthetically compute variable ring lights images and transient images from their differences. We show extensive experimental results of applying variable ring light imaging to both synthetic and real-world complex surfaces. The results show that the method successfully decomposes subsurface scattering and demonstrate that the recovered transient images reveal the internal surface structure including its color variation and lateral and along-depth configurations for general inhomogeneous surfaces. We further show that the differences of the transient images reveal the colors of the surface at different depths.

Our method is simple requiring only a regular projector and camera. Most important, it is model-free, making no restrictive assumptions about the subsurface light transport. To our knowledge, the proposed method is the first to enable the dense recovery of the continuous variation of inner surface structures from external observation of the steady-state appearance using ordinary imaging components. Variable ring light imaging complements past transient imaging methods especially those for bounce decomposition of scene-wide global light transport, by providing an unprecedented means for deciphering subsurface scattering and consequently for visually probing intrinsic surface structures. We believe the method opens new avenues for richer radiometric understanding of real-world scenes and materials.

2   Related Work

Recently, a number of approaches have been proposed to capture the transient light transport of real-world scenes. Many of these transient imaging methods directly sample the temporal light transport with time-of-flight or ultra-fast cameras in the pico- to femtosecond range [3,5,11,20,21], which enable separation of large-scale light transport events including reflection and interreflection. It is, however, unclear how such temporal sampling can be applied to disentangle subsurface scattering, where the light interaction happens at a much smaller scale and is not openly accessible from an external view.

Other approaches leverage ordinary or moderately high-speed cameras and programmable illumination (e.g., projectors) to control the light transport itself for capturing its distinct components. Seitz et al. [17] recover n-bounce images of a scene with successive multiplications of "interreflection cancellation operators" to the observed image. Here, a bounce is defined as light interaction between scene geometry, not with minute particles in a surface that we are interested in. The method specifically requires diffuse interreflection so that the light transport matrix is full-rank and can be inverted to construct the cancellation operator. For subsurface scattering, the light transport viewed and illuminated from the outside will be rank-deficient or worse yet rank-one for completely homogeneous surfaces. For this, the inverse light transport theory [1,17] does not apply to subsurface scattering.

Nayar et al. [9] introduced the use of spatial high-frequency illumination patterns to decouple 1-bounce and 2-and-higher bounces of light in the scene which are referred to as direct and global light transport, respectively. The method relies on the fact that the first light bounce is essentially an impulse function in the angular space resulting in all-frequency light transport, and the rest of the scene-wide light bounces are of comparatively lower frequency. This is generally true for direct reflection and other light transport components including diffuse interreflection and subsurface scattering. The method, however, can only separate the first bounce (direct) from the rest, and cannot further decompose subsurface scattering or interreflection into their components. Although various subsequent techniques extend the original high-frequency illumination method [2,6,18], for instance, to decompose the global light transport into spatially near- and far-range components [15], they are all limited by this fundamental frequency requirement of separable components and cannot be applied to decompose subsurface scattering.

O'Toole et al. [13,14] introduced the idea of modulating both the illumination and image capture to realize selective probing of the light transport matrix in a coaxial imaging setup, which was later extended to exploit epipolar geometry in non-coaxial systems for realtime direct-indirect imaging [12] and further combined with rolling shutter for efficiency [10]. Our goal is to decompose the indirect light into its constituents based on path length (and proportional number of bounces) of subsurface scattering, and primal-dual imaging cannot be used for this as the intensity of each bounce would be too low to probe with pixel masking. Most important, subsurface scattering does not obey the geometric two-view constraint cleverly exploited in these methods. Similarly, high-frequency temporal light transport sampling can only separate subsurface scattering as a whole and cannot decompose it further [21]. When viewed in light of the categorization of [12], our novel imaging method can be viewed as successive co-axial "long-range indirect imaging" applied to subsurface scattering. The key ideas lie in varying this "range" and to bound path lengths by taking their differences.

A few recent works concern light transport analysis of subsurface scattering. Mukaigawa et al. [7] achieves n-bounce imaging of subsurface scattering by directly observing a side slice of the surface illuminated with high-frequency illumination on its top interface. The parameters of an analytical scattering model is recursively estimated from the observation to compute n-bounce scattering. The method requires physical slicing of the surface to gain a view of the actual light propagation in depth and is restricted to a specific analytical scattering model. As a result, the method cannot be applied to general surfaces including even homogeneous ones of unknown materials. Our method does not assume either—the imaging setup does not require any modification to the surface of interest and it is model-free, enabling the application to arbitrary surfaces.

Tanaka et al. [19] propose a method for decomposing the appearance of a surface seen from above into a few layers at different depths. The surface is captured with high-frequency illumination of varying pitches whose direct component images [9] are then deblurred with known kernels corresponding to each depth. Subsurface light transport captured with an external illuminant, however, cannot be expressed with the radiative transfer model they use [8] which does not account for scattering of incident light. Furthermore, depth-dependent appearance of subsurface scattering neither results in distinctive texture patterns nor is its component frequencies distinct enough to disentangle with high-frequency illumination. More recently, Redo-Sanchez et al. [16] demonstrated similar discrete layer extraction with sub-picosecond imaging using terahertz time-domain spectroscopy. In contrast, our method is model-free and does not assume any frequency characteristics of the subsurface light transport, and is specifically aimed at decomposing the continuous appearance variation both across the surface extent and along its depth including its colors with an ordinary camera-projector imaging setup.

Diffuse optical tomography temporarily samples transmitted light through a scattering volume, whereas our method bounds the light path length by spatial differentiation on a flat surface, which makes them complementary both in application and methodology.

Our method, for the first time to the best our knowledge, provides access to the transient light transport of subsurface scattering. The resulting bounded path length images, or proportionally approximate n-bounce images, would likely find use in a wide range of applications. As we demonstrate, they reveal the complex internal subsurface structures including their colors and provide novel means for real-world surface appearance understanding.

3   Variable Ring Light Imaging

In this section, we describe the intuition and theoretical underpinnings of our novel imaging method.

3.1   Preliminaries

A surface at a microscopic scale, i.e., smaller than an image pixel but larger than the wavelength, consists of a medium and particles. An incident light ray, after penetrating through the outer interface, travels straight in the medium and every time it hits a suspended particle it is scattered until eventually reemerging from the interface. Each of these bounces causes the light ray to change its direction while some portion of its energy is absorbed. The degree of absorption by both the medium and the particles vary across the wavelength, causing the light ray to accumulate a unique color depending on its traveled path. The appearance of a surface point consists of such light rays that have undergone various number of bounces in the subsurface.

Due to this subsurface scattering, light travels on a zigzag path inside the surface. As a result, the *surface distance* of a light ray, i.e., the Euclidean distance on the surface between its entry and exit points, is not the same as its *light path length*, the actual geometric distance the light ray traveled inside the surface. Note that the *optical* path length is the product of the light path length and the index of refraction of the medium. The incident light may have traveled straight right beneath the interface or it may have traveled deep through the surface before reemerging from the interface.

We consider an imaging setup consisting of an orthographic camera and directional light collinear with each other and both perpendicular to the surface of interest. The following theoretical discussion is valid for non-parallel line of sight and illumination, and in practice the camera and illuminant can be tilted with respect to the surface as they will only scale the path length range corresponding to each transient image. Nevertheless, for simplicity both in theory and practice, we will assume a collinear and perpendicular imaging setup.

The surface of interest is assumed to be flat to safely ignore interreflection at its external interface. The surface distance for a non-flat surface would be the geodesic distance which reduces to the geometric distance for a flat surface. It is important to note that, in this paper, our focus is on real-world surfaces that exhibit subsurface scattering. The path length lower bound will not necessarily apply to general scattering without a surface that defines a halfspace, such as smoke and general scene interreflection.

3.2 Impulse Subsurface Scattering

Let us consider a directional light source illuminating a surface point corresponding to a single pixel in the image. We refer to this as impulse illumination [17]. In practice, impulse illumination is achieved by calibrating the correspondences between projector pixels and image pixels and the finest resolution we use is usually the projector pixel (which equates roughly 4 image pixels in our later real experiments). Figure 2a depicts the isophotes of a subsurface scattering radiance distribution inside the surface.

The radiance of a surface point at distance r, which we denote with $E(r)$, from an impulse illumination point is the sum of the radiance of each light ray, denoted with $L(\cdot)$, that traveled through the surface before reemerging from the interface at surface distance r. Instead of considering each individual light ray ℓ, we will instead distinguish each by its path length $|\ell|$:

$$E(r) = \sum_{|\ell_i| \in \mathfrak{L}(r)} L(|\ell_i|), \tag{1}$$

where $\mathfrak{L}(r)$ is the set of path length of light rays that we observe at surface distance r,

$$\mathfrak{L}(r) = \{|\ell_i| \; : \; |\Pi(\ell_i)| = r\}. \tag{2}$$

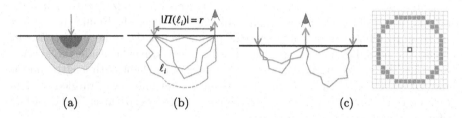

(a)   (b)   (c)

Fig. 2. (a) Isophotes of subsurface scattering. (b) Surface appearance of subsurface scattering consists of light rays that have traveled various path lengths which are naturally bounded by the surface distance between the points of incident and observation. (c) Illuminating the surface with variable ring light, a circular impulse illumination centered on the surface point of interest of different radii, and taking their differences lets us bound the path length of light observed at each surface point.

Here, $\Pi(\ell)$ is an operator that returns the entry and exit surface points of a light ray ℓ, $|\Pi(\ell)|$ is the surface distance the light ray traveled, and although it is not denoted explicitly, the set only includes light rays whose paths are contained inside the halfspace defined by the surface. In other words, as Fig. 2b depicts, the light ray set $\mathfrak{L}(r)$ consists of those light rays that entered a surface and exited from a surface point of distance r from entry. We assume that the impulse illuminant is of unit radiance and the camera is calibrated for linear radiance capture.

We are now ready to state a key observation of subsurface scattering:

$$\min \mathfrak{L}(r) \geq r. \tag{3}$$

The proof of this observation is trivial; the shortest path between two points on a surface is the geodesic between them, which we have defined as the surface distance r for our flat surface, and the observed light cannot have traveled a shorter distance to reemerge from the surface.

We rewrite Eq. 2 to make this property explicit:

$$\mathfrak{L}(r) = \{|\ell_i| \; : \; |\ell_i| \geq r, |\Pi(\ell_i)| = r\}. \tag{4}$$

3.3   Ring Light Subsurface Scattering

Given the lower bound on the light path length, observations of a surface point with impulse illuminations would likely let us extract light of bounded path lengths (i.e., transient light). Before we discuss how exactly we achieve this transient image computation in Sect. 3.4, let us first address fundamental issues of using impulse illumination for it. Using single impulse illumination is inefficient for two reasons. First, the radiance of subsurface scattering decays exponentially with the light path length and the transient light computed from impulse subsurface scattering will have low fidelity. Second, the light paths of these transient lights, especially for inhomogeneous surfaces would be different depending on which surface point at distance r is used for impulse illumination. Preserving this directionality of subsurface scattering might be of interest for some surfaces, but achieving this with high fidelity is challenging and beyond the scope of our current work.

We resolve these inefficiencies with a special illuminant-observation configuration which we refer to as variable ring light. As depicted in Fig. 2c, consider impulse illuminating all surface points at distance r from the surface point of interest. The normalized radiance of the observed surface point can then be written as the linear combination of all the radiance values due to each of the impulse illuminants (Eq. 1)

$$E(r) = \frac{1}{K} \sum_k^K E(r_k) = \frac{1}{K} \sum_k^K \sum_{|\ell_i| \in \mathfrak{L}(r_k)} L(|\ell_i|), \tag{5}$$

where K is the number of impulse illuminant points (i.e., projector pixels corresponding to image pixels lying at distance r as depicted in Fig. 2c right). We are abusing the notion E to avoid clutter by representing both the normalized ring light radiance and the unnormalized impulse illumination radiance, but since $r_k = r$ for all k this notational overwrite should be intuitive. Ring light illumination improves the SNR by K, where K increases with larger r.

Ring light subsurface scattering also effectively averages all the possible light paths in the spatial vicinity of the point of observation. This leads to a more robust observation of internal structures surrounding the observed point as it does not rely on a single arbitrary selected point of incident impulse illumination. Note that any point other than the center of the ring light (i.e., the point of observation) would have superimposed impulse subsurface scattering of different distances. It is only the radiance of the center point that we consider. In practice, we virtually construct ring lights of varying radii around each of the surface points as we discuss in Sect. 4.

3.4 Transient Images from Ring Light Images

Let us consider illuminating the surface with another ring light of slightly larger radius $r + \Delta r$

$$\mathfrak{L}(r + \Delta r) = \{|\ell_i| : |\ell_i| \geq r + \Delta r, |\Pi(\ell_i)| = r + \Delta r\}. \tag{6}$$

The actual instantiation of the light rays in these two sets Eqs. 4 and 6 are disjoint, because even though they are observed at the same surface point, the entry points are slightly different.

Let us instead assume that the two sets Eqs. 4 and 6 approximately overlap for all light with path length longer than $r + \Delta r$

$$\mathfrak{L}(r) \cap \mathfrak{L}(r + \Delta r) \approx \mathfrak{L}(r + \Delta r). \tag{7}$$

This key assumption implies that the radiances of light rays with path length longer than $r + \Delta r$ observed at the same surface point with an impulse illumination at surface distance r are the same as those with an impulse illumination at surface distance $r + \Delta r$. In other words, the only difference is the light rays of path length shorter than $r + \Delta r$ due to lower bounds on the two sets. This property holds exactly for homogeneous surfaces, as the light rays would accumulate the same spectral radiance regardless of their incident points from the observed surface point for the same path length. Strictly speaking the number of bounces a light ray experiences for a given path length would vary, but statistically speaking (i.e., on average with a tight variance), we may safely assume this to be true.

When Eq. 7 holds, the difference of the normalized observed radiance at the same surface point but illuminated with ring lights of slightly different radii becomes

$$E(r) - E(r + \Delta r) \approx \sum_{|l_i| \in \mathcal{L}(r) \backslash \mathcal{L}(r+\Delta r)} L(|l_i|), \tag{8}$$

where

$$\mathcal{L}(r) \backslash \mathcal{L}(r + \Delta r) = \{|\ell_i| : r + \Delta r > |\ell_i| \geq r, |\Pi(\ell_i)| = r\}. \tag{9}$$

Note that $\backslash$ denotes set difference. This means that, as Fig. 1 depicts, by illuminating each surface point with a variable ring light of incrementally increasing radius, which are then assembled into ring light images each of whose imaged surface points encode the radiance for a given ring light radius, and then by taking the difference of them across radius increments, we recover images of light with bounded path lengths, i.e., transient images of subsurface light transport.

When the surface is volumetrically inhomogeneous, i.e., consists of different material regions distributed both in space and depth, Eq. 7 would not necessarily hold, since the path length difference between the two can include integration of subsurface scattering in additional material regions. The discrepancy of spectral radiance of light with path length longer than $r + \Delta r$ between the two observations can, however, be minimized by keeping Δr small—sufficiently smaller than the minimum size of a distinct material region in either the depth or spatial direction. In this case, the resolution of the bounded path lengths would be smaller than the distinct material regions. In other words, the discrete resolution of transient light transport recovered from the ring light image differences is finer than the material composition of the surface volume. As a result, the transient images would still capture important subsurface scattering events sufficiently fine enough to reveal the intrinsic surface structure. It is also important to note that the radiance of longer path length light decays exponentially and thus the discrepancy is usually small in brightness in any case.

Figure 3 shows transient images computed from variable ring light images and path-length limited renderings for two synthetic inhomogeneous surfaces. Each transient image is normalized in its brightness independently to show its intricate structure, as otherwise they become exponentially darker for longer path lengths. We rendered these synthetic surfaces using Mitsuba renderer [4]. For variable ring light imaging, we first render impulse illumination images using an idealized single-ray light source orthogonal to the surface pointed at each pixel center. By reassembling these impulse illumination images, we compute ring light images of varying radii of a pixel increment, and take the difference of ring light images of adjacent radii to compute the transient images. Mitsuba only includes limited bounce rendering, where each bounce occurs at sampled rendering nodes, not statistically distributed particles in the surface. To achieve path-length limited rendering with Mitsuba, we modified its bidirectional path tracing integrator to limit the longest path length of light in the rendering. By taking the difference of these images of upper-bounded path length light, we obtain bounded path length images that can be considered as ground truth.

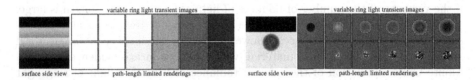

Fig. 3. Top: Transient images computed from synthetic ring light images for two example scenes rendered with Mitsuba [4]. Bottom: Bounded path length images rendered by Mitsuba. The ring light transient images visually match the rendered bounded path length images except for discrepancies expected from its theory and also stemming from rendering noise and aliasing (the dark rim around the white glow in the red bead case). (Color figure online)

Unfortunately, rendering subsurface scattering, especially for a complex inhomogeneous surface and also with limits on the path length is challenging as they require almost unrealistically large numbers of samples to properly simulate their light transport. We used 262, 144 samples for the path-limited rendering, which takes a day to render and still suffers from excessive noise. For this, the variable ring light imaging results also become noisy. The results in Fig. 3, however, still show that the recovered transient images match the path-length-limited renderings well for both surfaces. For the layered color surface, the integrated light color in each transient image agree, and for the surface with an immersed red bead, the light propagation from the bead (white light expanding out from the red bead due to specular reflection at its surface, followed by red light glowing out of the bead after bouncing inside it[1]) match between the variable ring light and the ground truth. There is a small but noticeable discrepancy for the red bead surface, where the first few images from path-limited renderings do not show the full internal red bead, while the variable ring light result includes light from the entire red bead from the first transient image. For the ring light images the first few ring light images have red light from the bead contributing less for the larger radius $(r + \Delta r)$, since the bead is spherical resulting in residual red light in their differences. In contrast, red light would only gradually be observed

---

[1] The white glow in the path length limited renderings are difficult to see due to contrast with the dark noise, but they are present.

in the first few path-length limited renderings as light has not reached the red bead. Other than this expected difference and noise, these synthetic results show that variable ring light imaging captures transient subsurface light transport.

If the surface is homogeneous in which the scatterers are uniformly distributed in the surface volume, the number of particles along the path is directly proportional to the light path length. Even if the surface is inhomogeneous in its composition, statistically speaking, the number of bounces will monotonically increase with the path length. As a result, we may safely assume that the mean number of bounces a light ray experiences is proportional to the path length. As a result, the radiance difference of two ring light images of different radii bound the mean number of bounces of light. The bound is, however, on the mean, and if the variance of the number of bounces of light for a given path length is large, variable ring light images would not be able to sift out the progression of subsurface scattering. This variance is, however, usually small for general real-world surfaces. In the supplemental material, we provide empirical evidence based on Monte Carlo simulation of the ratio of radiance of n-bounce light of ring light observation as well as theoretical analysis using its analytical approximation that show that this variance is indeed tight and we can safely assume that the recovered transient images approximately correspond to bounded n-bounce light.

4   Experimental Results

In addition to the synthetic surfaces in Fig. 3, we experimentally validate our theory of variable ring light by examining recovered transient images of real-world surfaces.

4.1   Spatial Light Transport in Transient Images

We implement variable ring light imaging with a USB camera (Point Grey Grasshopper3) and a DLP projector (TI DLP Light Commander). The lines of sight and projection are roughly aligned and made perpendicular to the target surface by placing together the projector and camera sufficiently far from the surface. We use telephoto lenses for both the camera and the projector to realize orthographic projection and directional light. We calibrate the projector and camera to associate each projector pixel to image pixels. In our experiments, roughly one projector pixel corresponds to a 2×2 image pixel region. We capture an impulse illumination image for each projector pixel and compute variable ring light images from these images.

The path lengths of light in each transient image is determined by the thickness and spacing of the variable ring light radii. The thicker the ring light, the brighter the observed radiance and thus better fidelity in the recovered transient images. Thick ring lights, however, directly compound the bound on the path length (i.e., r will have a large range in Eq. 9). For this, we set the thickness to be a single projector pixel (e.g., Fig. 2c) to ensure sharp bounds on the path length. The spacing between the different ring light radii, Δr, controls the range of light path lengths we capture in one transient image. We also set this to one projector pixel to recover the highest possible path length resolution. Note that, for inhomogeneous surfaces, the condition on Δr regarding Eq. 7 that we discussed can be controlled by ensuring that this single projector pixel is sufficiently smaller than the finest material region. This can be achieved by changing the distance of the projector from the surface.

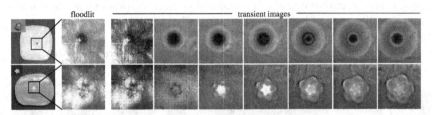

(a) Spatial propagation of light in the subsurface

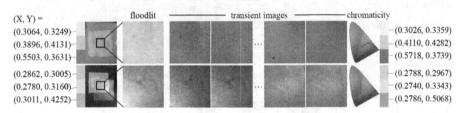

(b) Color variation in subsurface depth

Fig. 4. The transient images, in their pixels that encode bounded integration of light interactions in the subsurface, reveal the volumetric composition of the surface and their colors that are unclear from its outer interface appearance. The difference of the transient images, i.e., the difference of the difference of variable ring light images, reveal the surface color at different depth.

As shown in Fig. 4a, for spatially inhomogeneous subsurface structures, the recovered transient images capture interesting spatial propagation of light as the corresponding ring light radius increases. For these results and all others, the brightness of each transient image is normalized independently to visualize the details independent of decreasing radiance of longer path length light. The results show, for a red translucent bead inserted in white plastic clay, concentric propagation of white light specularly reflecting off the red bead followed by red light glowing out from the bead, and for a star shape plastic embedded in pink polymer, star shaped light emanating and interreflecting creating petal-like light propagation shapes as the path length increases. These subsurface structures are unclear from the outer surface as shown in the left most images taken with ordinary room light.

4.2   Color from Transient Images

When the surface has subsurface structures that vary across its depth, the recovered transient images will provide appearance samples of its continuous depth variation. Furthermore, as the bounded path length light directly encodes the accumulated color along its path, each of the transient images would reveal the integrated color variation along depth. This spectral integration of transient light suggests that we may reveal the true color at each corresponding surface depth by taking the difference of light with incrementally increasing path lengths. In other words, by taking the difference of the difference of variable ring light images, we are able to reconstruct the color of the subsurface at different depth.

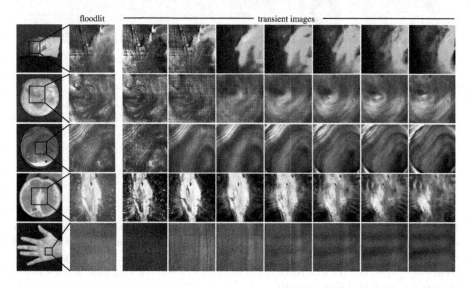

Fig. 5. Variable ring light imaging reveals complex intrinsic surface structures in its recovered transient images in which light that has traveled deeper and longer is captured with larger radius ring light. For the skin, wrinkles fade out, deeper red of skin appear, and the arteries become prominent, and for the marble pendant, spatial extents of different color regions emerge as the radius increases.

Figure 4b shows transient images and chromaticity values recovered from their difference for surfaces made of various color layers in depth. The chromaticity trajectories of the transient images reveal the spectral integration of subsurface scattering. We manually selected three transient images at equal spacings, so that each of them likely corresponds to light path length roughly of each layer depth, and computed the mean chromaticities of each image and then their differences to recover the colors at each depth. The recovered colors shown in the right most column match the ground truth shown in the left most image very well. Note that these color variations are not accessible from simple external observation, and worse yet, the same outer surface color could have been made of infinite color combinations inside the subsurface.

4.3   Transient Images of Complex Real Surfaces

Figures 1 and 5 show recovered transient images of real surfaces with complex subsurface structures and color compositions including those of natural objects. The transient images of each example reveal the subsurface composition both in its volumetric structure as well as its color variation that are otherwise invisible from the outer surface. Notice the colorless surface reflection and early scattering as well as the complex volumetric propagation and richer color of longer path length light in transient images of larger radius. The supplemental material contains more results and movies of transient images.

Our current implementation of variable ring light imaging is suboptimal in speed, as it requires impulse illumination capture. Note that HDR capture significantly adds to image capture time. This limits us to the 64×64 transient images for reasonable computation time (i.e., around an hour for all image capture and computation). For high resolution image capture of larger surface regions, we can speed up the imaging with parallel impulse illumination capture of surface points at far distances but by limiting the maximum ring light radius to avoid accidently picking up light from a concurrently illuminated point. Figure 6 shows example results of variable ring light imaging for large object regions in high resolution. In future work, we plan to fundamentally speed up our implementation by combining spatial and dynamic range multiplexing with ring light imaging.

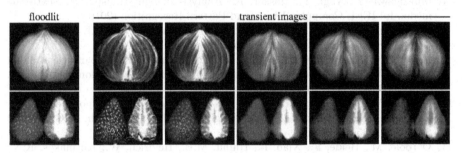

floodlit   transient images

Fig. 6. Variable ring light imaging of whole objects with parallel impulse illumination capture. Each transient image is about 800 pixels in width.

5   Conclusion

In this paper, we introduced variable ring light imaging for disentangling subsurface scattering light into varying bounded path lengths, and proportionally number of bounces, from external observations. The method does not assume any restrictive analytical scattering model and can be applied to arbitrary real-world surfaces that exhibit subsurface scattering. The theory and its experimental validation demonstrate the effectiveness of variable ring light imaging for unveiling subsurface structures and their colors. We believe the method has significant implications for visual probing of surfaces and for deciphering light transport for richer scene understanding. We plan to derive a radiometrically and computationally efficient implementation in our future work.

Acknowledgements. This work was supported in part by JSPS KAKENHI Grant Numbers JP15K21742, JP15H05918, and JP17K20143.

References

1. Bai, J., Chandraker, M., Ng, T.-T., Ramamoorthi, R.: A dual theory of inverse and forward light transport. In: Daniilidis, K., Maragos, P., Paragios, N. (eds.) ECCV 2010. LNCS, vol. 6312, pp. 294–307. Springer, Heidelberg (2010). https://doi.org/10.1007/978-3-642-15552-9_22
2. Gu, J., Kobayashi, T., Gupta, M., Nayar, S.K.: Multiplexed illumination for scene recovery in the presence of global illumination. In: IEEE International Conference on Computer Vision (2011)
3. Heide, F., Hullin, M.B., Gregson, J., Heidrich, W.: Low-budget transient imaging using photonic mixer devices. ACM Trans. Graph. **32**(4), 45:1–45:10 (2013)
4. Jakob, W.: Mitsuba: Physically based renderer 0.5.0 (2014). http://www.mitsuba-renderer.org/
5. Jarabo, A., Masia, B., Marco, J., Gutierrez, D.: Recent advances in transient imaging: a computer graphics and vision perspective. Vis. Inform. **1**(1), 65–79 (2017)
6. Li, D., Nair, A.S., Nayar, S.K., Zheng, C.: AirCode: unobtrusive physical Tags for Digital Fabrication. In: ACM Symposium on User Interface Software and Technology (2017)
7. Mukaigawa, Y., Yagi, Y., Raskar, R.: Analysis of light transport in scattering media. In: IEEE Computer Vision and Pattern Recognition (2010)
8. Narasimhan, S., Nayar, S.: Shedding light on the weather. In: IEEE Conference on Computer Vision and Pattern Recognition, pp. 665–672 (2003)
9. Nayar, S.K., Krishnan, G., Grossberg, M.D., Raskar, R.: Fast separation of direct and global components of a scene using high frequency illumination. ACM Trans. Graph. **25**(3), 935–944 (2006)
10. O'Toole, M., Achar, S., Narasimhan, S.G., Kutulakos, K.N.: Homogeneous codes for energy-efficient illumination and imaging. ACM Trans. Graph. (SIGGRAPH) **34**(4), 35:1–35:13 (2015)
11. O'Toole, M., Heide, F., Xiao, L., Hullin, M.B., Heidrich, W., Kutulakos, K.N.: Temporal frequency probing for 5D transient analysis of global light transport. ACM Trans. Graph. **33**(4), 87:1–87:11 (2014)
12. O'Toole, M., Mather, J., Kutulakos, K.N.: 3D shape and indirect appearance by structured light transport. In: IEEE Conference on Computer Vision and Pattern Recognition (2014)
13. O'Toole, M., Mather, J., Kutulakos, K.N.: 3D shape and indirect appearance by structured light transport. IEEE Trans. Pattern Anal. Mach. Intell. **38**(7), 1298–1312 (2016)
14. O'Toole, M., Raskar, R., Kutulakos, K.N.: Primal-dual coding to probe light transport. ACM Trans. Graph. (SIGGRAPH) (2012)
15. Reddy, D., Ramamoorthi, R., Curless, B.: Frequency-space decomposition and acquisition of light transport under spatially varying illumination. In: Fitzgibbon, A., Lazebnik, S., Perona, P., Sato, Y., Schmid, C. (eds.) ECCV 2012. LNCS, vol. 7577, pp. 596–610. Springer, Heidelberg (2012). https://doi.org/10.1007/978-3-642-33783-3_43
16. Redo-Sanchez, A., et al.: Terahertz time-gated spectral imaging for content extraction through layered structures. Nature Communi. (2016)

17. Seitz, S.M., Matsushita, Y., Kutulakos, K.N.: A theory of inverse light transport. In: IEEE International Conference on Computer Vision (2005)
18. Subpa-asa, A., Fu, Y., Zheng, Y., Amano, T., Sato, I.: Direct and global component separation from a single image using basis representation. In: Lai, S.-H., Lepetit, V., Nishino, K., Sato, Y. (eds.) ACCV 2016. LNCS, vol. 10113, pp. 99–114. Springer, Cham (2017). https://doi.org/10.1007/978-3-319-54187-7_7
19. Tanaka, K., Mukaigawa, Y., Kubo, H., Matsushita, Y., Yagi, Y.: Recovering inner slices of layered translucent objects by multi-frequency illumination. IEEE Trans. Pattern Anal. Mach. Intell. **39**(4), 746–757 (2017)
20. Velten, A., et al.: Femto-photography: capturing and visualizing the propagation of light. ACM Trans. Graph. **32**(4), 44:1–44:8 (2013)
21. Wu, D., et al.: Decomposing global light transport using time of flight imaging. Int. J. Comput. Vis. **107**, 123–138 (2014)

Large Scale Urban Scene Modeling from MVS Meshes

Lingjie Zhu[1,2], Shuhan Shen[1,2(✉)], Xiang Gao[1,2], and Zhanyi Hu[1,2]

[1] NLPR, Institute of Automation, Chinese Academy of Sciences, Beijing, China
{lingjie.zhu,shshen,xiang.gao,huzy}@nlpr.ia.ac.cn
[2] University of Chinese Academy of Sciences, Beijing, China

Abstract. In this paper we present an efficient modeling framework for large scale urban scenes. Taking surface meshes derived from multi-view-stereo systems as input, our algorithm outputs simplified models with semantics at different levels of detail (LODs). Our key observation is that urban building is usually composed of planar roof tops connected with vertical walls. There are two major steps in our framework: segmentation and building modeling. The scene is first segmented into four classes with a Markov random field combining height and image features. In the following modeling step, various 2D line segments sketching the roof boundaries are detected and slice the plane into faces. Through assigning each face with a roof plane, the final model is constructed by extruding the faces to the corresponding planes. By combining geometric and appearance cues together, the proposed method is robust and fast compared to the state-of-the-art algorithms.

Keywords: Urban reconstruction · Building modeling
Markov random field · Segment based modeling

1 Introduction

Modeling urban environment has been the core part for many applications including navigation, simulation and virtual reality. Although detailed models can be created with modern interactive softwares, it is inevitably tedious and not applicable to large city scale. Actually, automatic generation of urban models from physical measurements remains an open problem [23]. Typically, there are two types of data sources used in the reconstruction: aerial LiDAR (light detection and ranging) and aerial imagery.

Airborne LiDAR point cloud was once the first choice for city-scale modeling [17,27,35]. It is pure geometric data and usually in the form of 2.5D, *i.e.*, the LiDAR sensor captures roof structures well but fails to collect sufficient points

Electronic supplementary material The online version of this chapter (https://doi.org/10.1007/978-3-030-01252-6_38) contains supplementary material, which is available to authorized users.

V. Ferrari et al. (Eds.): ECCV 2018, LNCS 11215, pp. 640–655, 2018.
https://doi.org/10.1007/978-3-030-01252-6_38

on facade. By contrast, meshes derived from oblique images using structure from motion (SfM) and multi-view stereo (MVS) workflows contain walls with details and have rich texture information [2,8,9,11,12]. Although LiDAR point cloud is more accurate, images are much cheaper and more approachable. With advanced automated SfM and MVS workflows like Pix4D [26] and Acute3D [1], people can obtain faithful meshes with realistic textures at large scale. However, these triangulated meshes are particularly dense and noisy because they do not convey any high level semantic or structural information (*e.g.*, road, building, tree, roof and wall). Therefore reconstructing them into more compact models with abstracted semantics has gained increasing attention [14,18,19,25,31,36].

Fig. 1. Modeling of a large urban area. Our input is textured surface meshes generated from 3720 oblique aerial images. It has 92 M triangle faces covering an area of $12.2\,\mathrm{km}^2$. The output model (in the middle) has 4343 buildings with 0.25M faces, enhanced with regularity and semantics. Two close-ups are shown on left and right sides

In the context of urban modeling, practitioners usually wish to present the data with semantics and levels of detail (LODs). Although classic simplification or approximation algorithms [7,13] can generate models of different complexity via controllable parameters. Herein LOD is not only in the sense of data storage or rendering, but also a simplified semantic abstraction of the scene. One aspect of our system is to generate models with LODs conforming to the CityGML [6] standard, which is a widely accepted open data model for representing and exchanging virtual 3D city models. Figure 2 shows the basic semantics and LOD abstractions defined by CityGML [6].

The proposed pipeline takes urban MVS meshes as input and outputs simplified building models with meaningful LODs adhering to the CityGML [6] standard. We utilize the 2.5D characteristic of building structures and cast the modeling as a shape labeling problem. Specifically, we first segment the scene on the orthograph into 4 classes: ground, grass, tree and building. Then various roof boundary segments are detected for each building. The segments slice the plane into pieces of faces. Built on the faces of the segment arrangement, each face is assigned with a roof plane via a Markov random field (MRF) formulation. Extruding the face to their designated plane gives the final model.

Fig. 2. Modeling semantics and LODs defined by CityGML [6]. From left to right are LODs from 0 to 3 with increasing details: LOD1 is LOD0 rising to the averaged height, LOD2 models the roof top shapes and LOD3 is decorated with superstructures. Semantics are color coded: ground in brown, facade in light yellow and roof top in blue (Color figure online)

The main contributions of our work include:

- A novel line segment based 2D shape labeling method for LOD modeling taking both appearance and geometry cues into consideration.
- A prior embedded shape detection approach, which enhances the regularity of the model with orthogonal facades and symmetric roofs.
- An efficient pipeline to generate LOD models of large urban scene from noisy MVS meshes, and validated on our real-world dataset.

2   Related Work

Two major steps of the proposed pipeline are covered in our review of previous work: urban scene segmentation and modeling.

Segmentation. Although surface mesh segmentation and image segmentation have been around for a long time in computer graphics and computer vision communities respectively. Little literature is devoted to the segmentation of meshes reconstructed from images. Verdie *et al.* [31] compute different geometric features on the surface and classify it by constructing a MRF labeling on the superfacet graph. Similarly, Rouhani *et al.* [28] add other photometric features and using a random forest to compute the MRF pair-wise potentials. Liu *et al.* [21] partition the urban surfaces into structural elements by iteratively clustering faces into bigger primitives with a high-order conditional random field.

Modeling. Speaking of urban modeling, building is of the most interest. Two categories of building modeling have been proposed recently.

Candidate selection is a common modeling strategy, which usually follows the *generation and selection* pattern. Both [19,31] slice the bounding space into candidate 3D cells with planes and transform the modeling into a binary inside/outside labeling problem. Comparing to [19,31] is restricted to Manhattan scene. Apart from the cell selection method, Nan *et al.* [24] formulate the modeling as a cell face selection problem. By putting constraints on the faces sharing an edge, the model is guaranteed to be 2-manifold by solving a linear programing problem.

Contour based modeling is another category. In [18], the authors simplify the boundaries of the pixel-wise labeled height map and generate the model by lifting the boundary polygons to 3D spaces. Given street-level imagery, GIS footprint and MVS meshes, Kelly *et al.* [15] detect the profiles of the footprint contour and generate detailed models with procedural extrusion [16]. Although the generated model is of high-quality, the input data is not always available. Zhu *et al.* [36] extend the variational shape approximation (VSA) [7] algorithm for the urban scene and model the facade contour with regularity.

LOD generation is another concern in city modeling. General mesh simplification [13] or shape approximation [7] methods can generate models of different complexity. However they are essentially geometric error driven, which are not aware of the higher-level structure or regularity presented in the scene. Build upon the detected structure primitive graph, Salinas *et al.* [29] try to preserve the structure when conducting the mesh decimation. None of them could generate LODs with respect to the semantic abstraction.

3   Overview

Taking noisy MVS meshes of large urban scene as input, our method outputs manifold models of low complexity and strong regularity in the form of semantic LODs. The proposed framework consists of two main phases: semantic segmentation and building modeling. Figure 3 shows the overview of the pipeline.

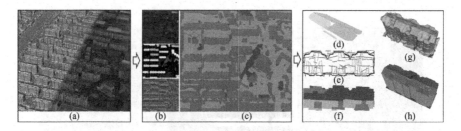

Fig. 3. Large urban scene modeling pipeline of two major steps: semantic segmentation (b)(c) and building modeling (d)–(h). (a) The input raw MVS meshes in terrestrial coordinate, rendered with (right) and without (left) texture; (c) semantic segmentation on the orthographs of (b); (d) plane detection on the roof top; (e) various line segments outlining the roof patch boundaries; (f) line segments arrangement shape labeling; (h) an example of the final model with semantics and LODs of building (g)

For city scale reconstruction, aerial oblique images acquired at high altitude are often used. Although the images are of high resolution and quality, the output MVS surface meshes still suffer from occlusion, shade, weak and repetitive texture. Compared with LiDAR point clouds, MVS meshes are more noisy as we can see in Fig. 3(a)(g).

Memory issues also arise when dealing with city scale data. Rendering such dense and large scene alone can be challenging. To curb the computation burden, we cut the input mesh into several memory manageable blocks and each block can be processed in parallel. In the segmentation part, we fuse both geometry and appearance information on the orthographs, Fig. 3(b)(c). Then we model each building with a segment based modeling method as demonstrated in Fig. 3(d)–(f).

4   Segmentation

Our segmentation step relies on a MRF built on the orthographs to distinguish four classes of urban objects: *ground, grass, tree* and *building*. Through combining a specialized supervised tree classifier and geometric attributes, we can achieve decent result that meets our need with a simple formulation.

Raw MVS surfaces usually contain many geometric and topological defects such as self-intersections, non-manifold edges and floating parts. Instead of operating on the 3D meshes directly like [28,31], we sample the textured mesh into a 2D orthograh representation. Given a grid sampling step, a vertical ray is cast from above at each grid center. Recording the texture color, height and normal of the first intersected point gives us an orthophoto, a depth map and a normal map respectively, as shown in Fig. 4. The obvious advantages of the orthogonal grid sampling are: (1) data are evenly distributed with efficient access, (2) both geometric and texture information are in the same image form, (3) many off-the-shelf image processing algorithms are available.

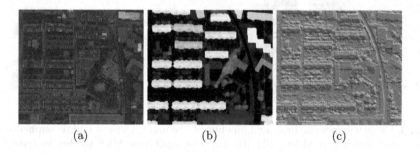

Fig. 4. Orthogonal grid sampling of a block, step size is set to $0.2m$. (a) Orthophoto. (b) Height map (linearly mapped into range [0, 255]). (c) Normal map colored by treating x, y, z components as RGB channels respectively, the blueish color shows that normals are mostly facing upwards (Color figure online)

Recent CNN-based segmentation methods [22,32] have impressive performances. Despite that we choose a traditional boosting and MRF combined method over them because: (1) the large amount of training data is hard to acquire, (2) they are unable to integrate orthophoto features with geometric data (*e.g.*, height or normal) effectively [22], (3) the segmentation here is more treated as a building isolation step rather than a pixel-level precision labeling task, and it serves the subsequent modeling step well in our experiments, Sect. 6.

4.1   Tree Probability

Although buildings may have various textures and colors, trees generally have distinguishable color and similar pattern (Fig. 4). Based on the specialized orthophoto tree detection algorithm [34], we give each pixel a value measuring the tree probability. To be more specific, we compute visual features x_i at each pixel p_i of (1) color: CIE L*a*b* color and the illumination-invariant color [5], (2) texture: Gaussian derivative filter-bank at 3 scales (with $\sigma = 1, \sqrt{2}, 2$) and 6 uniform sampled directions in $[0, \pi)$, (3) entropy of L channel: with window sizes of 5, 9 and 17. With these features, we use the boosting algorithm [10] to train a strong classifier $F(x_i)$ from T basic decision stump $f_t(x_i)$:

$$F(x_i) = \sum_{t=1}^{T} \alpha_t f_t(x_i), \tag{1}$$

where T is set to 200 across our experiments and the weights α_t is learned in the training process. Then a tree probability $t(p_i)$ is given by the sigmoid function:

$$t(p_i) = \frac{1}{1 + e^{-F(x_i)}}. \tag{2}$$

We trained our model on a small area of about $300\,\mathrm{m} \times 300\,\mathrm{m}$, Fig. 5(a) shows the predicted tree probability of the same block in Fig. 4.

4.2   MRF Labeling

With the tree probability and the observation that only trees and buildings rise above the ground of few meters, our label set is $l^p = \{ground, grass, tree, building\}$. Since ground is almost flat in a block, we measure the height with a normalized value defined as:

$$h_n(p_i) = L(max(h(p_i) - h_{ground}, 0)), \tag{3}$$

where $L(x) = 1/(1 + e^{-2(x - h_{trunc})})$ is a logistic function with "S"-shaped curve and its midpoint is modulated by a truncation value h_{trunc}. h_{ground} is the height of block ground. Figure 5(b) shows the normalized height map.

With the tree probability $t(p_i)$ and the normalized height $h_n(p_i)$, each pixel p_i is defined with a likelihood data term:

$$D^p(l_i^p) = \begin{cases} h_n(p_i) \cdot t(p_i) & \text{if } l_i^p = ground \\ h_n(p_i) \cdot (1 - t(p_i)) & \text{if } l_i^p = grass \\ (1 - h_n(p_i)) \cdot (1 - t(p_i)) & \text{if } l_i^p = tree \\ (1 - h_n(p_i)) \cdot t(p_i) & \text{if } l_i^p = building \end{cases} \tag{4}$$

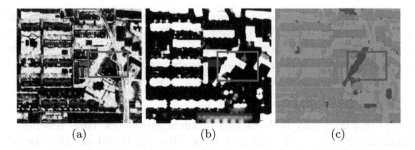

(a)   (b)   (c)

Fig. 5. (a) Tree probability learned from the boosting algorithm. (b) Normalized height map. (c) Result of segmentation: *ground*, *grass*, *tree* and *building* are colored with brown, light green, dark green and blue respectively. Notice the adjacent tree and building are correctly separated in red rectangle (Color figure online)

The pairwise smooth relation is measured by their clamped height difference:

$$V^p(l_i^p, l_j^p) = (1 - [h(p_i) - h(p_j)]_0^1) \cdot \mathbf{1}_{\{l_i^p \neq l_j^p\}}, \tag{5}$$

where $\mathbf{1}_{\{.\}}$ denotes the characteristic function. Then the objective function on the image grid graph $\mathcal{G}^p = \{\mathcal{V}^p, \mathcal{E}^p\}$ can be written as:

$$E^p(l^p) = \sum_{i \in \mathcal{V}^p} D^p(l_i^p) + \mu \sum_{\{i,j\} \in \mathcal{E}^p} V^p(l_i^p, l_j^p), \tag{6}$$

where l is the label configuration of the orthophoto. μ is the balance and set to 1 in all experiments shown in this paper. The proposed energy function can be efficiently minimized by graph-cuts [3,4].

To start the segmentation, we use the lowest point in the block as an initial estimation of h_{ground}. After running MRF once, all ground pixels are averaged to give better estimation of h_{ground}. With updated h_{ground}, the normalized heights h_n are recomputed and the MRF formulation is solved again. This iterative technique will give more accurate ground height estimation and thus better segmentation of the scene.

In our experiment, h_{ground} typically converges after 3 iterations and h_{trunc} is set to $3m$ as the height of an one story building. After the segmentation, we apply a morphology open operation to break weakly connected buildings followed by a close operation to eliminate small holes. An example of the labeling result is shown in Fig. 5(c).

5   Modeling

With the labeled block, each connected *building* region is isolated from the scene. The objective of this section is to reconstruct buildings into LOD models with enhanced regularity.

Since images for urban reconstruction are usually obtained from aerial vehicles, facades suffer more from occlusion and shade than the roofs. Therefore, quite a few works [18,27,35] take advantage of the 2.5D nature of the buildings and mainly use the roof information for modeling. Here 2.5D means buildings can be viewed as piece-wise planar roofs connected with vertical walls. Both [27,35] deal with LiDAR point clouds and extract roof contours by analysing the point geometric features, making them vulnerable to noise and outliers. Li *et al.* [18] uses a pixel-wise labeling to extract the contours of the roof patches. However none of them tries to model the regularity (*e.g.*, symmetry, orthogonality and parallelism) or is capable of generating models with LODs.

In this section, we propose a segment based modeling approach. We first construct a roof boundary segment arrangement on the ground plane, then assign each arrangement face a roof plane label. Extruding each face to the assigned plane gives the model. Comparing to previous work, we consolidate different data sources together, producing models with LODs and enhanced regularity.

5.1 Facade Directions

One common regularity of urban building is that its facade has two orthogonal directions. We detect the local orthogonal directions of the facade with the RANSAC algorithm.

Specifically, the input data $\{n_f\}$ is a set of 2D unit normals constructed from the horizontal projections of face normals that are within an angle threshold ang_{thre} to the ground plane. Each time a hypothesis normal n_o is generated. Together with its orthogonal counterpart n'_o, the inlier set is defined as:

$$\{n|min(cos^{-1}(n \cdot n_o), cos^{-1}(n \cdot n'_o)) < ang_{thre}, n \in \{n_f\}\}. \tag{7}$$

Then, the maximum consensus set is considered as the facade orthogonal directions. Figure 6(a)(b) show the detection of the facade directions on a small house provided by Pix4D [26] open data set.

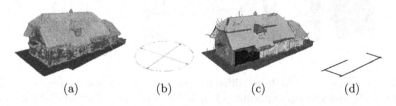

(a)   (b)   (c)   (d)

Fig. 6. Facade directions and segments detection on the Pix4D [26] house. (a) Z component of face normals with the jet color map. (b) The near horizontal unit normal circle $\{n_f\}$, two orthogonal (red and blue arrows) directions are detected. (c) VSA [7] segmentation on the mesh with color coded proxies and unit normal of short red line. (d) The facade segments detection by projecting near vertical proxies on the ground. Notice the boundary is not closed due to occlusion (Color figure online)

5.2   Line Segments

Generally roof tops are piece-wise planar and their boundaries projected on the ground are polygons. This inspires us to detect line segments that outline the roof patches. With the orthogonal sampling in Sect. 4, each building has an orthophoto, a normal map and a height map. We utilize these complementary data sources to detect various edge segments.

Image Segments. The most straight forward boundary cue is line segments from orthophoto. Due to the noise and mismatch, MVS mesh generation algorithms generally perform some smoothing operations, making the reconstructed surface corner rounded (Fig. 3(g)). Although it is difficult to locate the edges from geometric data, it can be easily spotted in the image. Therefore, we use the line segment detection (LSD) [33] algorithm to detect line segments from the orthophoto, as illustrated in Fig. 7(a).

Facade Segments. Apart from the visual cues, we also detect segments from geometry data. The facade contouring segments is detected with the plane approximation method VSA [7]. Specifically, a minimum area (set to $10\,\mathrm{m}^2$) is used to estimate the number of proxies used to approximate the building shape. And we use the random seeding to give a rough and fast segmentation of the mesh. By projecting vertical proxies (controlled by ang_{thre}) onto the ground, we have facade line segments bounding the roofs, as shown in Fig. 7(c)(d).

Height Map Segments. When the building facade is touching a tree, there is no mesh at the facade thus VSA [7] is unable to detect any proxy here. To solve this problem, we treat height map as an intensity image and use the same LSD [33] algorithm to detect height discontinuity segments as shown in Fig. 7(c).

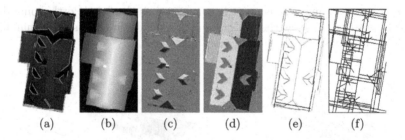

| (a) | (b) | (c) | (d) | (e) | (f) |

Fig. 7. Segments detected from different sources of the house in Fig. 6. (a) Image segments. (b) Height map segments. (c)(d) *Directional normal variation* maps and the detected ridge segments. (e) The stacked segments from (a)–(d) and facade segments in Fig. 6(d). (f) The regularized line segments slices the plane into faces

Normal Map Segments. While height map segments is evident where sufficient height disparity exists, it is unable to detect the ridge lines where two roof patches meet. In contrast, ridges are quite noticeable in the normal map as shown in Fig. 4(c). Unfortunately, there is no clear definition of the gradient of a 3-channel image, so we can not apply the LSD [33] on it directly.

One important structural characteristic of the building is that roof normals are in the planes constructed by the z axis and facade normals [15, 16], as depicted in Fig. 8(a). We construct two *directional normal variation* maps by computing the dot products of the normal map and two orthogonal facade directions in Sect. 5.1 respectively, highlighting the normal changes along each direction. Then we can apply the LSD [33] on the two generated intensity images and spot the ridge lines easily, as illustrated in Fig. 7(c)(d).

Stacking all these line segments together, we can outline the complete contours of major roof patches, as shown in Fig. 5(e). To enhance the regularity of the contours, we employ the two step regularization technique described in [36]: (1) segments parallel to the facade directions are reoriented to the facade directions first, (2) then coplanar segments are repositioned and merged into one longer segment. Figure 7(f) shows the regularized segments slice the plane into smaller polygon faces. The collinear threshold is set to $0.5m$ in our experiment.

5.3   Shape Detection

An often underestimated obstacle in modeling from MVS data is the detection of shape primitives that are complete and with regularity. Unlike previous works [17, 20] using the *first-detect-then-regularize* strategy, we extend the RANSAC [30] algorithm to model regularities into the shape detection process.

Roof Direction Detection. Before detecting roof planes, we detect prominent roof directions on the normal map first. All normals are collected in $\{n_r\}$ as the input for the RANSAC. When a hypothesis direction n_s is proposed, it is snapped to the nearest roof direction plane (based on the characteristic discussed in normal map segments). Similar to Sect. 5.1, the inlier set is defined as

$$\{n|min(cos^{-1}(n \cdot n_s), cos^{-1}(n \cdot n'_s)) < ang_{thre}, n \in \{n_r\}\}, \qquad (8)$$

where n'_s is the z-symmetry counter part of n_s. Figure 8(a)(b) shows the roof principal direction detection.

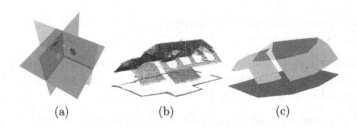

(a)   (b)   (c)

Fig. 8. Roof shape detection of the building in Fig. 6. (a) The normal sphere $\{n_r\}$ and roof direction planes. (b) Detected symmetric roof direction inliers (blue points). (c) 5 detected shapes: 2 pairs of z-symmetric/parallel planes and a horizontal plane (Color figure online)

Roof Plane Detection. Based on the RANSAC shape detection [30], we detect planes along the roof principal directions on the height map. In the same spirit to roof direction detection, each hypothesis plane is snapped to the nearest roof principal directions. Figure 8(c) shows the detected roof planes along the roof directions. With the direction constraints stemmed from facades, the detected planes $\{P_i\}$ is inherently encoded with parallelism and z-symmetry.

5.4 LOD Modeling

With the regularized segment arrangement in Sect. 5.2, we have a dual graph $\mathcal{G}^f = \{\mathcal{V}^f, \mathcal{E}^f\}$, where each face f_i is a vertex and adjacent faces is connected with an edge. Another MRF is build on $\mathcal{G}^f$ with the detected roof planes as the label set $l^f = \{P_i\}$.

MRF Formulation. In the height map in Sect. 4, each pixel p_i is treated as a 3D point p_i'. To measure how well a plane is fitted to the points bounded by face f_i, each face f_i is defined with a data term:

$$D^f(l_i^f) = \sum_{p_k \in f_i} \|p_k', l_i^f\|. \tag{9}$$

The pairwise smooth relation between two adjacent faces f_i, f_j is weight by their shared edge length $len_{i,j}$:

$$V^f(l_i^f, l_j^f) = len_{i,j} \cdot \left(1 - \frac{3\lambda_0}{\lambda_0 + \lambda_1 + \lambda_2}\right) \cdot \mathbf{1}_{\{l_i^f \neq l_j^f\}}, \tag{10}$$

where λ_0 denotes the minimum eigenvalues of the covariance matrix of points $\{p_i' | p_i \in f_i \vee f_j\}$ measuring the planarity of two faces [31]. $\mathbf{1}_{\{.\}}$ is the characteristic function. With the data and smooth terms balanced by β, the objective function of a labeling configuration l^f is:

$$E^f(l^f) = \sum_{i \in \mathcal{V}^f} D^f(l_i^f) + \beta \sum_{\{i,j\} \in \mathcal{E}^f} V^f(l_i^f, l_j^f). \tag{11}$$

We use the same graph-cut [3,4] algorithm to solve the above problem, and β is set to 10 in our experiments.

LOD Generation. Given the 2D faces labeled with roof planes, models of LODs can be extracted by projecting the face vertices to the corresponding plane, as illustrated in Fig. 9 (same house in Fig. 6):

- LOD0: the outer boundary of non-ground face is the building's footprint,
- LOD1: each face is extruded to the plane's averaged height,
- LOD2: each face is extruded to the corresponding roof planes.

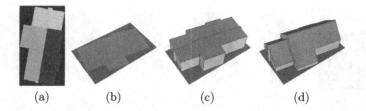

(a)   (b)   (c)   (d)

Fig. 9. LOD generation. (a) Segment arrangement color coded with the plane labels in Fig. 8(c). (b) LOD0 model of the outer most boundary. (c) LOD1 model extruded to the averaged heights. (d) LOD2 model extruded to the corresponding 3D roof planes

6   Results and Discussion

Our method is implemented in C++ with the CGAL and the max-flow library [3, 4]. In this section, we test our method on both open data set and our own large urban scene data. Experiments show that our modeling workflow can generate regular and accurate building models with different LODs. Both qualitative and quantitative assessments are conducted.

Modeling Quality. Three aspects are considered in evaluating the modeling quality: reconstruction error, model complexity and regularity. In Fig. 10, we compare the modeling results on the public Pix4D [26] house model in Fig. 6. Two recent *candidate selection* methods [24,31] and two classic shape simplification algorithms [7,13] are compared with our method.

Generally, geometric error driven methods like VSA [7] and QEM [13] can generate models of LODs with controllable parameters. Although both methods are able to reduce the complexity of the model dramatically while keeping the error low, they are more sensitive to noise and outliers and unable to convey the global regularity of the model.

More recent approaches [19,24,31] employ the *slice and selection* strategy. While [19,31] choose a cell based selection and assembly method, Nan *et al.* [24] take the edge selection approach. As illustrated in Fig. 10, both methods can produce models of high regularity but the accuracy is low. One common difficulty of the 3D slicing methods is that they suffer from noise and incomplete primitives. For example, facades can be severely occluded because the images are captured from above. Without the complete structures of the model, both [24,31] failed in Fig. 10 (in rectangles). In the proposed method, we consolidate various complementary information from appearance to geometry into one modeling framework. We are able to infer the incomplete structures from the scene.

The proposed workflow can reach the balance of model complexity, accuracy and regularity. In Table 1, our LOD2 model has slightly higher error than [7,13] but much lower complexity and more regular surfaces.

Scalability and Performances. By orthogonal grid sampling, we simplify the 3D modeling into a 2D shape labeling problem, making the modeling relatively fast. In fact, the modeling speed is more affected by the sampling step size. In

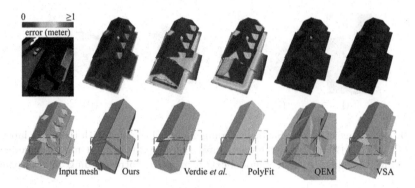

Fig. 10. Modeling quality comparison of accuracy and regularity to our LOD2 model. At each column we have the reconstructed model below and the corresponding modeling error to the input mesh on the top. The accuracy is measured by the Hausdorff distance from the output models to the input mesh, color scaled from blue to red. Both Verdie *et al.* [31] and Polyfit [24] suffer from incomplete primitives of the protruded parts (in red and orange rectangle). QEM [13] and VSA [7] have higher quality but less regularity (Color figure online)

Table 1. Comparison of modeling accuracy and complexity. The accuracy is measured by the RMS of the Hausdorff distance to the input mesh. The generated model complexity is accessed by the number of triangle faces. Our LOD2 model can reach the balance of accuracy and complexity

Method	Our LOD1	Our LOD2	Verdie *et al.* [31]	PolyFit [24]	QEM [13]	VSA [7]
RMS	2.25	0.21	1.16	1.27	0.14	0.11
#Face	24	24	153	52	149	830

Table 2. Running time on different data sets. Data complexity measured by the number of triangles. We run all modeling in a sequential implementation, except for the large city district in Fig. 1

Input	Segmentation	Modeling
Pix4D house (418.6 k faces, Fig. 10)	5 s	8 s
Apartment (92 k faces, second row in Fig. 11)	4 s	3 s
Block (588 k faces, Fig. 3)	25 s	42 s
City district (92 M faces, Fig. 1)	22 min	49.5 min

Table 2, we list the timing of different sizes of data set. All timings are measured on a PC with a 4 cores Intel Xeon CPU clocked at 3.7 GHz. VSA [7] and QEM [13] are either iterative method or sequential, neither of them scales well with data. The computational speed of PolyFit [24] relies on the linear programming solver. When there are too many intersections in the model, the solver may take really long time.

As Table 2 shows our pipeline scales well with data and can deal with input meshes with up to a hundred million triangles. Figure 1 shows a large urban area reconstructed from 356 high-resolution oblique aerial images by Pix4D [26]. The flight height is 750 m and the averaged definition is 0.1 m. The input mesh has 94M triangles covering an area of 12.2 km². We cut the data into 16 × 16 blocks and run them in parallel. The orthogonal sampling step is set to 0.2 m. Buildings that are cut at the block borders are later merged to avoid unnatural seams. On the left and right sides of Fig. 1 are two close-ups. Although obvious defects are visible in the input building's mesh model, we can still recover the sharp structures of roof tops and small protrusions on facades with the parallelism, coplanarity and z-symmetry regularity. Figure 11 shows some other modeling results. More results are available in the supplementary materials.

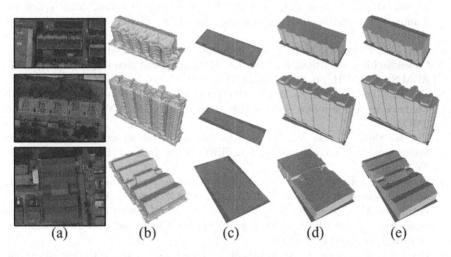

(a)   (b)   (c)   (d)   (e)

Fig. 11. LOD modeling on typical urban buildings. From top to bottom rows are ordinary residential building, high rising apartment and low connecting houses. From left to right at each row are: (a) orthograph, (b) isolated input building mesh, (c)–(e) LOD0, LOD1, LOD2 models respectively

7   Conclusions

In this paper we present a complete framework of LOD modeling from MVS meshes of large urban scene. We first segment the scene with a simple yet effective MRF formulation by fusing the visual and geometry features. The subsequent modeling method take advantage of the structure characteristics of the urban building and transform the 3D modeling into a 2D shape labeling problem. With line segments detected from complementary data sources, we are able to model the scene with strong regularity and low complexity. The result of our method is regular polygon models with LODs conforming to the CityGML standard [6], which can be used for presentation or further processing.

Acknowledgment. This work was supported by the Natural Science Foundation of China under Grants 61632003, 61333015 and 61421004. We also thank China TOPRS Technology Co. Ltd. for the city dataset in the paper.

References

1. Acute3D: Acute3D. https://www.acute3d.com/
2. Agarwal, S., et al.: Building Rome in a day. Commun. ACM **54**(10), 105–112 (2011)
3. Boykov, Y., Kolmogorov, V.: An experimental comparison of min-cut/max- flow algorithms for energy minimization in vision. IEEE Trans. Pattern Anal. Mach. Intell. **26**(9), 1124–1137 (2004)
4. Boykov, Y., Veksler, O., Zabih, R.: Fast approximate energy minimization via graph cuts. IEEE Trans. Pattern Anal. Mach. Intell. **23**(11), 1222–1239 (2001)
5. Chong, H.Y., Gortler, S.J., Zickler, T.: A perception-based color space for illumination-invariant image processing. In: ACM SIGGRAPH, pp. 61:1–61:7 (2008)
6. CityGML: CityGML. http://www.opengeospatial.org/standards/citygml
7. Cohen-Steiner, D., Alliez, P., Desbrun, M.: Variational shape approximation. In: ACM SIGGRAPH, pp. 905–914 (2004)
8. Cui, H., Gao, X., Shen, S., Hu, Z.: HSfM: hybrid structure-from-motion. In: IEEE Conference on Computer Vision and Pattern Recognition (CVPR), pp. 2393–2402 (2017)
9. Cui, H., Shen, S., Gao, W., Hu, Z.: Efficient large-scale structure from motion by fusing auxiliary imaging information. IEEE Trans. Image Process. **22**(11), 3561–3573 (2015)
10. Freund, Y., Schapire, R.E.: A decision-theoretic generalization of on-line learning and an application to boosting. J. Comput. Syst. Sci. **55**(1), 119–139 (1997)
11. Furukawa, Y., Curless, B., Seitz, S.M., Szeliski, R.: Towards internet-scale multi-view stereo. In: IEEE Conference on Computer Vision and Pattern Recognition (CVPR), pp. 1434–1441 (2010)
12. Furukawa, Y., Ponce, J.: Accurate camera calibration from multi-view stereo and bundle adjustment. Int. J. Comput. Vis. **84**(3), 257–268 (2009)
13. Garland, M., Heckbert, P.S.: Surface simplification using quadric error metrics. In: ACM SIGGRAPH, pp. 209–216 (1997)
14. Hofer, M., Maurer, M., Bischof, H.: Efficient 3D scene abstraction using line segments. Comput. Vis. Image Underst. **157**(4), 167–178 (2017)
15. Kelly, T., Femiani, J., Wonka, P., Mitra, N.J.: BigSUR: large-scale structured urban reconstruction. ACM Trans. Graph. **36**(6), 204:1–204:16 (2017)
16. Kelly, T., Wonka, P.: Interactive architectural modeling with procedural extrusions. ACM Trans. Graph. **30**(2), 14:1–14:15 (2011)
17. Lafarge, F., Mallet, C.: Building large urban environments from unstructured point data. In: IEEE International Conference on Computer Vision (ICCV), pp. 1068–1075 (2011)
18. Li, M., Nan, L., Smith, N., Wonka, P.: Reconstructing building mass models from UAV images. Comput. Graph. **54**, 84–93 (2016)
19. Li, M., Wonka, P., Nan, L.: Manhattan-world urban reconstruction from point clouds. In: Leibe, B., Matas, J., Sebe, N., Welling, M. (eds.) ECCV 2016. LNCS, vol. 9908, pp. 54–69. Springer, Cham (2016). https://doi.org/10.1007/978-3-319-46493-0_4

20. Li, Y., Wu, X., Chrysathou, Y., Sharf, A., Cohen-Or, D., Mitra, N.J.: GlobFit: consistently fitting primitives by discovering global relations. In: ACM SIGGRAPH, pp. 52:1–52:12 (2011)
21. Liu, J., Wang, J., Fang, T., Tai, C.L., Quan, L.: Higher-order CRF structural segmentation of 3D reconstructed surfaces. In: IEEE International Conference on Computer Vision (ICCV), pp. 2093–2101 (2015)
22. Liu, Y., Piramanayagam, S., Monteiro, S.T., Saber, E.: Dense semantic labeling of very-high-resolution aerial imagery and LiDAR with fully-convolutional neural networks and higher-order CRFs. In: IEEE Conference on Computer Vision and Pattern Recognition Workshops (CVPRW), pp. 1561–1570 (2017)
23. Musialski, P., Wonka, P., Aliaga, D.G., Wimmer, M., Gool, L.V., Purgathofer, W.: A survey of urban reconstruction. Comput. Graph. Forum 32(6), 146–177 (2013)
24. Nan, L., Wonka, P.: PolyFit: polygonal surface reconstruction from point clouds. In: IEEE International Conference on Computer Vision (ICCV), pp. 2372–2380 (2017)
25. Nguatem, W., Mayer, H.: Modeling urban scenes from pointclouds. In: IEEE International Conference on Computer Vision (ICCV), pp. 3857–3866 (2017)
26. Pix4D: Pix4D. https://pix4d.com/
27. Poullis, C.: A framework for automatic modeling from point cloud data. IEEE Trans. Pattern Anal. Mach. Intell. 35(11), 2563–2575 (2013)
28. Rouhani, M., Lafarge, F., Alliez, P.: Semantic segmentation of 3D textured meshes for urban scene analysis. ISPRS J. Photogramm. Remote. Sens. 123, 124–139 (2017)
29. Salinas, D., Lafarge, F., Alliez, P.: Structure-aware mesh decimation. Comput. Graph. Forum 34(6), 211–227 (2015)
30. Schnabel, R., Wahl, R., Klein, R.: Efficient RANSAC for point-cloud shape detection. Comput. Graph. Forum 26(2), 214–226 (2007)
31. Verdie, Y., Lafarge, F., Alliez, P.: LOD generation for urban scenes. ACM Trans. Graph. 34(3), 30:1–30:14 (2015)
32. Volpi, M., Tuia, D.: Dense semantic labeling of subdecimeter resolution images with convolutional neural networks. IEEE Trans. Geosci. Remote. Sens. 55(2), 881–893 (2017)
33. Von Gioi, R.G., Jakubowicz, J., Morel, J.M., Randall, G.: LSD: A fast line segment detector with a false detection control. IEEE Trans. Pattern Anal. Mach. Intell. 32(4), 722–732 (2010)
34. Yang, L., Wu, X., Praun, E., Ma, X.: Tree detection from aerial imagery. In: ACM GIS, pp. 131–137 (2009)
35. Zhou, Q.-Y., Neumann, U.: 2.5D dual contouring: a robust approach to creating building models from aerial LiDAR point clouds. In: Daniilidis, K., Maragos, P., Paragios, N. (eds.) ECCV 2010. LNCS, vol. 6313, pp. 115–128. Springer, Heidelberg (2010). https://doi.org/10.1007/978-3-642-15558-1_9
36. Zhu, L., Shen, S., Hu, L., Hu, Z.: Variational building modeling from urban MVS meshes. In: IEEE International Conference on 3D Vision (3DV), pp. 318–326 (2017)

Dynamic Multimodal Instance Segmentation Guided by Natural Language Queries

Edgar Margffoy-Tuay[✉], Juan C. Pérez, Emilio Botero, and Pablo Arbeláez

Universidad de los Andes, Bogotá, Colombia
{ea.margffoy10,jc.perez13,e.botero10,pa.arbelaez}@uniandes.edu.co

Abstract. We address the problem of segmenting an object given a natural language expression that describes it. Current techniques tackle this task by either (i) directly or recursively merging linguistic and visual information in the channel dimension and then performing convolutions; or by (ii) mapping the expression to a space in which it can be thought of as a filter, whose response is directly related to the presence of the object at a given spatial coordinate in the image, so that a convolution can be applied to look for the object. We propose a novel method that integrates these two insights in order to fully exploit the recursive nature of language. Additionally, during the upsampling process, we take advantage of the intermediate information generated when downsampling the image, so that detailed segmentations can be obtained. We compare our method against the state-of-the-art approaches in four standard datasets, in which it surpasses all previous methods in six of eight of the splits for this task.

Keywords: Referring expressions · Instance segmentation
Multimodal interaction · Dynamic convolutional filters
Natural language processing

1 Introduction

Consider the task of retrieving specific object instances from an image based on natural language descriptions, as illustrated in Fig. 1. In contrast to traditional instance segmentation, in which the goal is to label all pixels belonging to instances in the image for a set of predefined semantic classes [1,2], segmenting instances described by a natural language expression is a task that humans are able to perform without specifically focusing on a limited set of categories: we simply associate a referring expression such as "Man on the right" with what we see, as shown in Fig. 1. To learn such an association is the main goal of this paper.

In this task, the main labels to be assigned are *related to query* and *background*. Thus, the set of possible segmentation masks has few constraints, as a mask can be anything one might observe in the image, in all the ways natural

© Springer Nature Switzerland AG 2018
V. Ferrari et al. (Eds.): ECCV 2018, LNCS 11215, pp. 656–672, 2018.
https://doi.org/10.1007/978-3-030-01252-6_39

language allows an object to be referred to. An algorithm to tackle this problem must then make sense of the query and relate it to what it sees and recognizes in the image, to finally output an instance segmentation map. Therefore, attempting to naively use Convolutional Neural Networks (CNNs) for this task falls short, since such networks do not model sequential information by nature, as is required when processing natural language. Given that the cornerstone of this task is the proper *combination* of information retrieved from multiple, dissimilar domains, we expect traditional architectures, like CNNs and Recurrent Neural Networks (RNNs), to be useful modules, but we still need to design an overall architecture that fully exploits their complementary nature.

(a) Original image.   (b) Output based on query *guy.*   (c) Output based on query *girl.*

Fig. 1. Example of *segmentation based on a natural language expression.* A single mask is the output, in which the only two labels are *member of query* and *background.* Here, we show the raw output of our system, which is the pixelwise probability of belonging to the referred object instance.

In this paper, we introduce a modular neural network architecture that divides the task into several sub-tasks, each handling a different type of information in a specific manner. Our approach is similar to [3–5] in that we extract visual and natural language information in an independent manner by employing networks commonly used for these types of data, *i.e.*, CNNs and RNNs, and then focus on processing this multi-domain information by means of another neural network, yielding an end-to-end trainable architecture. However, our method also introduces the usage of Simple Recurrent Units (SRUs) for efficient segmentation based on referring expressions, a Synthesis Module that processes the linguistic and visual information jointly, and an Upsampling Module that outputs highly detailed segmentation maps.

Our network, which we refer to as Dynamic Multimodal Network (DMN), is composed of several modules, as depicted in Fig. 2: *(i)* a Visual Module (VM) that produces an adequate representation of the image, *(ii)* a Language Module (LM) that outputs an appropriate representation of the meaning of the query up to a given word, *(iii)* a Synthesis Module (SM) that merges the information provided by the VM and LM at each time step and produces a single output for the whole expression and, finally, *(iv)* an Upsampling Module (UM) that incrementally upsamples the output of the SM by using the feature maps produced by the VM. Our approach is a fully differentiable, end-to-end trainable neural network for segmentation based on natural language queries. Our main contributions are the following:

- The use of Simple Recurrent Units (SRUs) [6] as language *and* multi-modal processors instead of standard LSTMs [7]. We empirically show that they are efficient while providing high performance for the task at hand.
- A Synthesis Module that takes visual and linguistic information and merges them by generating "scores" for the referring expression in a visual space.
- The Synthesis Module then takes this representation as well as additional features, and exploits the spatial and sequential nature of both types of information to produce a low resolution segmentation map.
- A high resolution upsampling module that takes advantage of visual features during the upsampling procedure in order to recover fine scale details.

We validate our method by performing experiments on all standard datasets, and show that DMN outperforms all the previous methods in various splits for instance segmentation based on referring expressions, and obtains state-of-the art results. Additionally, in order to ensure reproducibility, we provide full implementation of our method and training routines, written in PyTorch[1] [8].

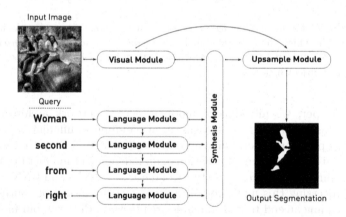

Fig. 2. Overview of our Dynamic Multimodal Network (DMN), involving four different modules: Visual Module (VM), Language Module (LM), Synthesis Module (SM), and Upsampling Module (UM).

---

[1] https://github.com/BCV-Uniandes/query-objseg.

2   Related Work

The intersection of Computer Vision (CV) and Natural Language Understanding (NLU) is an active area of research that includes multiple tasks such as object detection based on natural language expressions [9,10], image captioning [11–14] and visual question answering (VQA) [15–19]. Since visual and linguistic data have properties that make them fundamentally different, *i.e.*, the former has spatial meaning and no sequentiality while the latter does not contemplate space but has a sequential nature, optimally processing both types of information is still an open question. Hence, each work in this sub-field has proposed a particular way of addressing each task.

The task studied in this paper is closest in nature to object detection based on natural language expressions, mirroring how semantic segmentation arose from object detection [20]. Indeed, in [3], object detection with NLU evolved into instance segmentation using referring expressions. We review the state-of-the-art on the task of segmentation based on natural language expressions [3–5], highlighting the main contributions in the fusion of multimodal information, and then compare them against our approach.

Segmentation from Natural Language Expressions [3]. This work processes visual and natural language information through separate neural networks: a CNN extracts visual features from the image while an LSTM scans the query. Strided convolutions and pooling operations in the CNN downsample the feature maps to a low resolution output while producing large receptive fields for neurons in the final layers. Additionally, to explicitly model spatial information, relative coordinates are concatenated at each spatial location in the feature map obtained by the CNN. Merging of visual and natural language information is done by concatenating the LSTM's output to the visual feature map at each spatial location. Convolution layers with ReLU [21] nonlinearities are applied for final classification. The loss is defined as the average over the per-pixel weighed logistic regression loss. Training has two stages: a low resolution stage, in which the ground truth mask is downsampled to have the same dimensions as the output, and a high resolution stage that trains a deconvolution layer to upsample the low resolution output to yield the final segmentation mask [3]. This seminal method does not fully exploit the sequential nature of language, as it does not make use of the learned word embeddings, it merges visual and linguistic information by concatenation, and it uses deconvolution layers for upsampling, which have been shown to introduce checkerboard artifacts in images [22].

Recurrent Multimodal Interaction [4]. This paper argues that segmenting the image based only on a final, memorized representation of the sentence does not fully take advantage of the sequential nature of language. Consequently, the paper proposes to perform segmentation multiple times in the pipeline. The method produces image features at every time step by generating a representation that involves visual, spatial and linguistic features. Such multimodal representation is obtained by concatenating the hidden state of the LSTM that processed the query at every spatial location of the visual representation. The segmentation mask is obtained by applying a multimodal LSTM (mLSTM) to the joint representation and then performing regular convolutions to combine the channels that were produced by the mLSTM. The mLSTM is defined as a convolutional LSTM that shares weights both across spatial location and time step, and is implemented as a 1×1 convolution that merges all these types of information. Bilinear upsampling is performed to the network's output at test time to produce a mask with the same dimensions of the ground-truth mask. This method reduces strides of convolutional layers and uses atrous convolution in the final layers of the CNN to compensate for the downsampling. Such modification reduces the upsampling process to bilinear interpolation, but can decrease the CNN's representation capacity while also increasing the number of computations that must be performed by the mLSTM.

Tracking by Natural Language Specification [5]. In this paper, the main task is object tracking in video sequences. A typical user interaction in tracking consists in providing the bounding box of the object of interest in the first frame. However, this type of interaction has the issue that, for the duration of the video, the appearance and location of objects may change, rendering the initial bounding box useless in some cases. The main idea is to provide an alternative to this approach, by noting that *(i)* the semantic meaning of the object being tracked does not vary for the duration of the video as much as the appearance, and *(ii)* this semantic meaning may be better defined by a linguistic expression. This approach is substantially different from [4] and [3]: visual and linguistic information is never merged *per se*, but rather the linguistic information is mapped to a space in which it can be interpreted as having visual meaning. The visual input is thus processed by a modified VGG [23] to yield a feature map. An LSTM scans the linguistic input, and a single layer perceptron is applied to the LSTM's last hidden state to generate a vector that can be interpreted as being a *filter for a 2D convolution* that is to be performed on the feature map. The *dynamic convolutional visual filter*, generated based on the expression, is computed to produce a strong response to the elements being referred to the expression, and a weak response to those *not* being referred to. This response is interpreted as a "score" for the referring expression, so that a segmentation can be produced. This method proposes a new paradigm for combining information from the visual and linguistic domains, but assumes a non linear combination of the last hidden state is sufficient for modeling a filter that responds to the query.

Our approach. The approach of [3] merges multi-domain information by concatenation of linguistic information, subsequent 1×1 convolutions for segmentation and a deconvolution layer to perform upsampling. The method in [4] follows the same logic as [3] but introduces *recursion* into the approach, exploiting the linguistic information further; however, the upsampling module is an interpolation that produces rather coarse results, to which the authors apply a post-processing DenseCRF, making the architecture not trainable end-to-end. Finally, [5] has a different approach, in which linguistic information is never merged with feature maps, but is rather transformed so that it can detect the locations in the image to which the referring expression has strong response; nonetheless, like [3], it does not fully exploit linguistic information in a sequential manner. Moreover, all these methods fail to utilize information acquired in the downsampling process in the upsampling process.

Our approach takes advantage of the previous insights, and consists of a modularized network that exploits both the possibility of segmentation based on combinations of multi-domain information, and the feasibility of producing filters that respond to objects being referred to by processing the linguistic information. Following the spirit of [24–26], we use skip connections between the downsampling process and the upsampling module to output finely-defined segmentations. We employ the concatenation strategy of [3] but include richer visual and language features. Furthermore, we make use of dynamic filter computation, like [5], but in a sequential manner. Lastly, we introduce the use of a more efficient alternative to LSTMs in this domain, namely SRUs. We demonstrate empirically that SRUs can be used for modeling language *and* multimodal information for this task, and that they can be up to 3× faster than LSTMs, allowing us to train more expressive models.

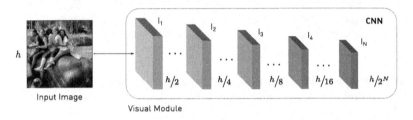

Fig. 3. The Visual Module outputs feature maps at N different scales with the aim of using them in the segmentation process and in the upsampling.

3   Dynamic Multimodal Network

3.1   Overall Architecture

Figure 2 illustrates our overall architecture. Given an input consisting of an image I, and a query composed of T words, $\{w_t\}_{t=1}^{T}$, the Visual Module (VM) takes I as input and produces feature maps at N different scales: $\{I_n\}_{n=1}^{N}$. The Language Module (LM) processes $\{w_t\}_{t=1}^{T}$ and yields a set of features $\{r_t\}_{t=1}^{T}$ and a set of dynamic filters $\{\{f_{k,t}\}_{k=1}^{K}\}_{t=1}^{T}$. Given the VM's last output, I_N, $\{r_t\}_{t=1}^{T}$, and $\{\{f_{k,t}\}_{k=1}^{K}\}_{t=1}^{T}$, the Synthesis Module (SM) processes this information and produces a single feature map for the entire referring expression. This output, along with the feature maps given by the VM, is processed by the Upsampling Module (UM), that outputs a heatmap with a single channel, to which a sigmoid activation function is applied in order to produce the final prediction.

3.2 Visual Module (VM)

Figure 3 depicts the Visual Module. We extract deep visual features from the image using as backbone a Dual Path Network 92 (DPN92) [27], which has shown competitive performance in various tasks, and is efficient in parameter usage. The VM can be written as a function returning a tuple:

$$\{I_n\}_{n=1}^{N} = \text{VM}(I) \tag{1}$$

Where I is the original image, and $I_n, n \in \{1, \dots, N\}$ are the downsampled feature maps of dimensions equal to $\frac{1}{2^n}$ of the dimensions of I. In the experiments, we use $N = 5$, which considers all convolutional layers in the visual encoder. Note that, since our architecture is fully convolutional, we are not restricted to a fixed image size.

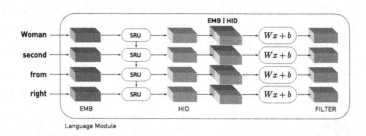

Language Module

Fig. 4. The Language Module uses an SRU, instead of the traditional LSTM, to output enriched features of the query and dynamic filters based on such features.

3.3 Language Module (LM)

Figure 4 shows a diagram of the Language Module. Given an expression consisting of T words $\{w_t\}_{t=1}^{T}$, each word is represented by an embedding (WE), $e_t = WE(w_t)$ (*EMB* in Fig. 4), and the sentence is scanned by an RNN to produce a hidden state h_t for each word (*HID* in Fig. 4). Instead of using LSTMs as recurrent cells, we employ SRUs [6], which allow the LM to process the natural language queries more efficiently than when using LSTMs. The SRU is defined by:

$$\tilde{x}_t = W x_t \tag{2}$$
$$f'_t = \sigma\left(W_f x_t + b_f\right) \tag{3}$$
$$r_t = \sigma\left(W_r x_t + b_r\right) \tag{4}$$
$$c_t = f'_t \odot c_{t-1} + (1 - f'_t) \odot \tilde{x}_t \tag{5}$$
$$h_t = r_t \odot g(c_t) + (1 - r_t) \odot x_t \tag{6}$$

Where $\odot$ is the element-wise multiplication. The function $g(\cdot)$ can be selected based on the task; here we choose $g(\cdot)$ to be the sigmoid function. For further details regarding the SRU definition and implementation, please refer to [6].

We concatenate the hidden state h_t with the word embedding e_t to produce the final language output: $r_t = [e_t, h_t]$. This procedure yields an enriched language representation of the concept of the sentence up to word t. Moreover, we compute a set of dynamic filters $f_{k,t}$ based on r_t, defined by:

$$f_{k,t} = \sigma \left(W_{f_k} r_t + b_{f_k} \right), k = 1, ..., K \tag{7}$$

thus, we define the LM formally as:

$$\left(\{r_t\}_{t=1}^T, \{\{f_{k,t}\}_{k=1}^K\}_{t=1}^T \right) = \text{LM} \left(\{w_t\}_{t=1}^T \right) \tag{8}$$

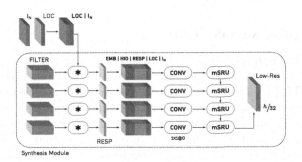

Fig. 5. The Synthesis Module takes into account the response to dynamic filters, language features, spatial coordinates representation, and visual features in a recurrent manner to output a single response map.

3.4   Synthesis Module (SM)

Figure 5 illustrates the Synthesis Module. The SM is the core of our architecture, as it is responsible for merging multimodal information. We first concatenate I_N and a representation of the spatial coordinates (LOC in Fig. 5), following the implementation of [3], and convolve this result with each of the filters computed by the LM to generate a response map ($RESP$ in Fig. 5) consisting of K channels: $F_t = \{f_{k,t} * I_N\}_{k=1}^K$. Next, we concatenate I_N, LOC, and F_t along the channel dimension to obtain a representation I', to which r_t is concatenated *at each spatial location*, as to have all the multimodal information in a single tensor. Finally, we apply a 1×1 convolutional layer that merges all the multimodal information, providing tan output corresponding to each time step t, denoted by M_t. Formally, M_t is defined by:

$$M_t = \text{Conv}_{1 \times 1}([I_N, F_t, LOC, r_t]) \tag{9}$$

Next, in the pursuit of performing a recurrent operation that takes into account the sequentiality of the set and also the information of each of the channels in M_t, we propose the use of a multimodal SRU (mSRU), which we define as a 1×1 convolution, similar to [4] but using SRUs. We apply the mSRU to the whole set $\{M_t\}_{t=1}^T$, so that all the information in each M_t, including the sequentiality of the set, is used in the segmentation process. The final hidden states are gathered to produce a 3D tensor that is interpreted as a feature map. This tensor, which we denominate R_N, due to its size being $\frac{1}{2^N}$ of the image's original size, has the same dimensions as M_t and has as many channels as there are entries in the hidden state of the mSRU. We define the SM as a function returning R_N:

$$R_N = \text{SM}\left(\{M_t\}_{t=1}^T\right) = \text{mSRU}\left(\{M_t\}_{t=1}^T\right), \tag{10}$$

where M_t is reshaped appropriately to make sense of the sequential nature of the information at each time step.

3.5   Upsampling Module (UM)

Finally, the Upsampling Module is shown in Fig. 6. Inspired by skip connections [24,25,28], we construct an upsampling architecture that takes into account the feature maps $\{I_n\}_{n=1}^N$ at all stages in order to recover fine-scale details. At each stage we concatenate R_n with I_n, perform 3×3 convolution over this result, and then scale the size by a factor of 2 via bilinear interpolation to generate R_{n-1}. We apply this process $\log_2(N)$ times, to produce an output mask of the same size of the input R_1. We apply 1×1 convolution over R_1 to generate a single channel and, finally, a sigmoid layer to obtain scores between 0 and 1.

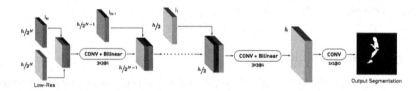

Fig. 6. The Upsampling Module makes use of all the feature maps that were generated in the feature extraction process to provide more detailed segmentations.

4   Experimental Setup

4.1   Datasets

We conduct experiments on the four standard datasets for this task: ReferIt, UNC, UNC+ [29], and GRef [30]. UNC, UNC+ and GRef are based on MS COCO [1]. The type of objects that appear in the referring expressions, length of the expressions, and relative size of the referred objects are the main differences between the datasets. The high variability of those characteristics across the datasets evidences the challenge of constructing models for this task that are capable of generalization.

ReferIt [29] is a crowd-sourced database that contains images and referring expressions to objects in those images. Currently it has 130,525 expressions, referring to 96,654 distinct objects, in 19,894 photographs of natural scenes.

UNC [31], was collected interactively in the ReferIt game, with images that were selected to contain two or more objects of the same object category [31], which means that an expression making reference to a determined type of object will need to be further analysed to determine *which* object the query is referring to, since ambiguity arises when only guided by semantic instance class cues. It consists of 142,209 referring expressions for 50,000 objects in 19,994 images.

UNC+ [31], is similar to UNC but has an additional restriction regarding words describing location: expressions must be based only on appearance rather than location. Such restriction implies that the expression will depend on the perspective of the scene and the semantic class of the object.

GRef [30], was collected on Amazon's Mechanical Turk and contains 85,474 referring expressions for 54,822 objects in 26,711 images selected to contain between two and four objects of the same class, and thus, it presents similar challenges to those of UNC.

4.2 Performance Metrics

We use the standard metrics from the literature to allow for direct comparison with respect to the state-of-the-art. We perform experiments with the proposed method on the four standard datasets described above by training on the training set and evaluating the performance in each of the validation or test sets. We evaluate results by using two standard metrics: *(i)* mean Intersection over Union (mIoU), defined as the total intersection area between the output and the Ground Truth (GT) mask, divided by the total union area between the output and the GT mask, added over all the images in the evaluation set, and *(ii) Precision@X*, or *Pr@X*, ($X \in \{0.5, 0.6, 0.7, 0.8, 0.9\}$), defined as the percentage of images with IoU higher than X. We report mIoU in the validation and test splits of each dataset, when available, using optimal thresholds from the training or validation splits, respectively.

4.3 Implementation Details

All the models are defined and trained with DPN92 [27] as the backbone, which outputs 2688 channels in the last layer. We use $N = 5$ scales in the VM. We use the following hyperparameters, which we optimized on the UNC+ *val* set: WE size of 1000, 2-layered SRU with hidden state size of 1000, $K = 10$ filters, 1000 1×1 convolution filters in the SM, 3-layered mSRU's hidden state size of 1000. The increased number of layers presented here in both the SRU and the mSRU, with respect to usual number of layers in LSTMs, are in response to the increased need of layers for an SRU to work as expected, according to [6]. We train our method in two stages: at low resolution (*i.e.*, without using the UM) and then finetune the UM to obtain high resolution segmentation maps.

Training is done with Adam optimizer [32] with an initial learning rate of 1×10^{-5}, a scheduler that waits 2 epochs for loss stagnation to reduce the learning rate by a factor of 10, and batch size of 1 image-query pair.

5   Results

5.1   Control Experiments

We assess the relative importance of our modules in the final result by performing ablation experiments. The control experiments were trained until convergence on the UNC dataset. Accordingly, we compare them to a version of our full method trained for a similar amount of time. Table 1 presents the results.

The "Only VM" experiment in row 1 consists on training only the VM and upsampling the low resolution output with bilinear interpolation, without using the query. At test time, the VM processes the image and the resulting segmentation map is upsampled using the UM and compared to the GT mask. Results show how this method performs poorly in comparison to our full approach, which confirms our hypothesis that naively using a CNN falls short for the task addressed in this paper. However, it is interesting that performance is rather high for a method that does not use linguistic information at all. This result reveals that many of the objects annotated in this dataset are salient, and so the network is able to learn to segment salient objects without help from the query.

The experiment in row 2 consists of defining $r_t = h_t$, instead of using the concatenation of h_t and e_t, which affects both the LM (when computing the dynamic filters) and the SM. Results show that using the learned embeddings provides a small gain in the full method, particularly for stricter overlap thresholds.

Next, in row 3 we assess the importance of skip connections in the UM, which is a measure of the usefulness of features extracted in the downsampling process for the upsampling module. The large drop in performance with respect to the full method shows that the skip connections allow the network to exploit finer details that are otherwise lost, showing how the upsampling strategy can benefit from performing convolutions followed by bilinear interpolations instead of deconvolutions, as done in [3].

We next study the effects of removing features from M_t. In rows 4 and 5 we remove the set of responses to the dynamic filters F, as well as the concatenation of r_t in the SM, respectively. We observe that the dynamic filters generate useful scores for the natural language queries in the visual space, and that reusing features from the LM in the SM does not help the network significantly.

Our results show that the key components of our network have significant impact in overall performance. High performance is not achieved by either using only linguistic information (r_t) or the response to filters (F): both must be properly combined. Additionally, the UM allows the network to properly exploit features from the downsampling stage and perform detailed segmentation.

Table 1. Precision@X and mIoU for ablation study in the UNC testA split

Method	Pr@0.5	Pr@0.6	Pr@0.7	Pr@0.8	Pr@0.9	mIoU
Only VM	15.26	6.36	2.96	0.91	0.14	30.92
Only h_t in LM and SM	65.38	**57.99**	**47.07**	27.38	4.63	54.80
No skip connections in UM	56.58	42.77	26.32	9.22	1.07	49.26
No dynamic filters	57.53	48.70	38.27	20.64	3.00	50.34
No concatenation of r_t	64.52	56.69	45.16	25.56	4.38	54.69
DMN	**65.83**	57.82	46.80	**27.64**	**5.12**	**54.83**

5.2 Comparison with the State-of-the-Art

Next, we proceed to compare our full method with the state-of-the-art, for which we evaluate on all the datasets described above. Table 2 compares the mIoU of our method with the state-of-the-art in this task [3–5]. The results show that our method outperforms all other methods in six out of eight splits of the datasets. By including enriched linguistic features at several stages of the process, and by combining them in different ways, our network learns appropriate associations between queries and the instances they refer to.

Interestingly, the performance gain in the *testB* splits of UNC and UNC+ is not as large as in *testA*. One possible reason for the smaller performance gain across splits is their difference: visual inspection of results shows how *testA* splits are biased towards queries related to segmenting persons. The *testB* splits, however, contain more varied queries and objects, which is why the increase in mIoU is not as marked. This behavior can also be observed for the method proposed by [4], as shown in the second-to-last line of Table 2.

Table 2. Comparison with the state-of-the-art in mIoU performance across the different datasets. Blank entries where authors do not report performance

Method	Referit test	GRef val	UNC			UNC+		
			val	testA	testB	val	testA	testB
[3]	48.03	28.14	-	-	-	-	-	-
[33]	49.91	34.06	-	-	-	-	-	-
[5]	54.30	-	-	-	-	-	-	-
[4]	**58.73**	34.52	45.18	45.69	**45.57**	29.86	30.48	29.50
DMN	52.81	**36.76**	**49.78**	**54.83**	45.13	**38.88**	**44.22**	**32.29**

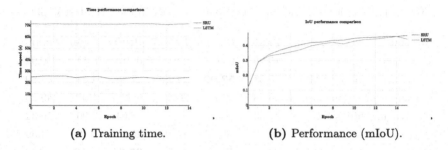

(a) Training time.   (b) Performance (mIoU).

Fig. 7. SRUs *vs.* LSTMs comparison on UNC *testA* (at low resolution).

5.3   Efficiency Comparison: SRU *vs.* LSTM

In order to assess the efficiency and the performance of SRUs when compared to the more commonly used LSTMs, both as language *and* multi-modal processors, we conduct an experiment in which we replaced the SRUs with LSTMs in our final system, both in the LM and the SM, we trained on the UNC dataset, and we measured performance on the *testA* split. In terms of model complexity, when using SRUs, the LM and the SM have 9M and 10M trainable parameters, respectively. When switching to LSTMs, the number of parameters increases to 24M and 24.2M, respectively, multiplying training time by a factor of three, as shown in Fig. 7a. Regarding accuracy, Fig. 7b shows that both systems perform similarly, with a small advantage for SRUs. Therefore, when compared to LSTMs, SRUs allow us to design architectures that are more compact, train significantly faster, and generalize better.

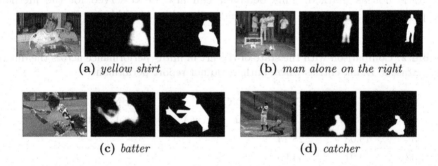

(a) *yellow shirt*   (b) *man alone on the right*

(c) *batter*   (d) *catcher*

Fig. 8. Qualitative examples of the output of the network. From left to right in each subfigure: original image, heatmap produced by our method, and ground-truth mask. Each caption is the query that produced the output.

5.4   Qualitative Results

Figure 8 shows qualitative results in which the network performed well. These examples demonstrate DMN's flexibility for segmenting based on different information about a particular class or instance: attributes, location or role. We emphasize that understanding a role is not trivial, as it is related to the object's context and appearance. Additionally, a semantic difficulty that our network seems to overcome is that the role coexists with the object's class: an instance can be "batter" and be "person". Notice in Fig. 8 that thanks to the upsampling module, our network segments fine details such as legs, heads and hands. In Fig. 8a the query refers to the kid by one of his *attributes*: the color of his shirt; in Fig. 8b the man is defined by his *location* and the fact that he is alone (although that could be dropped, as there is no ambiguity); in Figs. 8c and d the reference is based on the person's *role*.

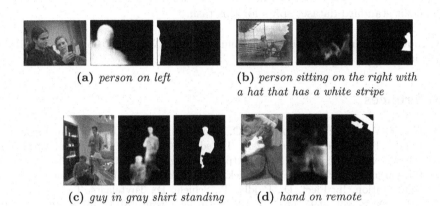

(a) *person on left*

(b) *person sitting on the right with a hat that has a white stripe*

(c) *guy in gray shirt standing*

(d) *hand on remote*

Fig. 9. Negative examples of the output of the network. From left to right in each Subfigure: original image, heatmap produced by our method, and ground-truth mask. Each caption is the query that produced the output.

Typical failure cases are depicted in Fig. 9. In Fig. 9a the network segments (arguably) the incorrect person, since the correct segmentation was the person at the border of the image whose face is partially shown. Several failure cases we found had exactly the same issue: ambiguity in the expression that could confuse even a human. Fig. 9b shows an example of strong failure, in which a weak segmentation is produced. The model appears to have only focused on the word "right". We attribute this failure to the network's inability to make sense of such a relatively long sentence, which, while unambiguously defining an object, is a confusing way of referring to it. Fig. 9c is an interesting example of the network's confusion. While the woman is not segmented, two subjects that share several attributes (*guy, gray* and *shirt*) are confused and are *both* segmented. However, the network does not manage to use the word "standing" to resolve the ambiguity. Finally, in Fig. 9d a failure is observed, where nothing related to the query is segmented. The mask that is produced only reflects a weak attempt of segmenting the red object, while ignoring the upper part of the image, in which both the hand *and* the remote were present.

6 Conclusions

We propose Dynamic Multimodal Network, a novel approach for segmentation of instances based on natural language expressions. DMN integrates insights from previous works into a modularized network, in which each module has the responsibility of handling information from a specific domain. Our Synthesis Module combines the outputs from previous modules and handles this multimodal information to produce features that can be used by the Upsampling Module. Thanks to the incremental use of feature maps obtained in the encoding part of the network, the Upsampling Module delivers great detail in the final segmentations. Our method outperforms the state-of-the-art methods in six of the eight standard dataset splits for this task.

Acknowledgments. The authors gratefully thank NVIDIA for donating the GPUs used in this work.

References

1. Lin, T.-Y., et al.: Microsoft COCO: common objects in context. In: Fleet, D., Pajdla, T., Schiele, B., Tuytelaars, T. (eds.) ECCV 2014. LNCS, vol. 8693, pp. 740–755. Springer, Cham (2014). https://doi.org/10.1007/978-3-319-10602-1_48
2. Hariharan, B., Arbeláez, P., Girshick, R., Malik, J.: Simultaneous detection and segmentation. In: Fleet, D., Pajdla, T., Schiele, B., Tuytelaars, T. (eds.) ECCV 2014. LNCS, vol. 8695, pp. 297–312. Springer, Cham (2014). https://doi.org/10.1007/978-3-319-10584-0_20
3. Hu, R., Rohrbach, M., Darrell, T.: Segmentation from natural language expressions. In: Leibe, B., Matas, J., Sebe, N., Welling, M. (eds.) ECCV 2016. LNCS, vol. 9905, pp. 108–124. Springer, Cham (2016). https://doi.org/10.1007/978-3-319-46448-0_7
4. Liu, C., Lin, Z.L., Shen, X., Yang, J., Lu, X., Yuille, A.L.: Recurrent multimodal interaction for referring image segmentation. In: International Conference on Computer Vision (ICCV), pp. 1280–1289 (2017)
5. Li, Z., Tao, R., Gavves, E., Snoek, C.G.M., Smeulders, A.W.M.: Tracking by natural language specification. In: Conference on Computer Vision and Pattern Recognition (CVPR) (2017)
6. Lei, T., Zhang, Y., Artzi, Y.: Training RNNs as fast as CNNs. CoRR abs/1709.02755 (2017)
7. Hochreiter, S., Schmidhuber, J.: Long short-term memory. Neural Comput. 9(8), 1735–1780 (1997)
8. Paszke, A., et al.: Automatic differentiation in pytorch. In: Conference on Neural Information Processing Systems (NIPS) (2017)
9. Hu, R., Xu, H., Rohrbach, M., Feng, J., Saenko, K., Darrell, T.: Natural language object retrieval. In: Conference on Computer Vision and Pattern Recognition (CVPR) (2016), pp. 4555–4564
10. Guadarrama, S., Rodner, E., Saenko, K., Darrell, T.: Understanding object descriptions in robotics by open-vocabulary object retrieval and detection. Int. J. Robot. Res. 35(1–3), 265–280 (2016)

11. Hendricks, L.A., Venugopalan, S., Rohrbach, M., Mooney, R.J., Saenko, K., Darrell, T.: Deep compositional captioning: Describing novel object categories without paired training data. In: Conference on Computer Vision and Pattern Recognition (CVPR), pp. 1–10 (2016)
12. Gan, Z., et al.: Semantic compositional networks for visual captioning. In: Conference on Computer Vision and Pattern Recognition (CVPR), pp. 1141–1150 (2017)
13. Johnson, J., Karpathy, A., Fei-Fei, L., Li, C., Li, Y.W., fei Li, F.: Densecap: Fully convolutional localization networks for dense captioning. In: Conference on Computer Vision and Pattern Recognition (CVPR), pp. 4565–4574 (2016)
14. Yang, Z., Yuan, Y., Wu, Y., Cohen, W.W., Salakhutdinov, R.: Review networks for caption generation. In: Conference on Neural Information Processing Systems (NIPS) (2016)
15. Goyal, Y., Khot, T., Summers-Stay, D., Batra, D., Parikh, D.: Making the V in VQA matter: elevating the role of image understanding in visual question answering. In: 2017 IEEE Conference on Computer Vision and Pattern Recognition (CVPR), pp. 6325–6334 (2017)
16. Li, C., Groth, O., Bernstein, M.S., Fei-Fei, L., Li, Y.W., Li, F.F.: Visual7w: grounded question answering in images. In: Conference on Computer Vision and Pattern Recognition (CVPR), pp. 4995–5004 (2016)
17. Krishna, R., Li, C., Groth, O., Johnson, J., Hata, K., Kravitz, J., Chen, S., Kalantidis, Y., Shamma, D.A., Bernstein, M.S., Fei-Fei, L.: Visual genome: connecting language and vision using crowdsourced dense image annotations. Int. J. Comput. Vis. (IJCV) **123**, 32–73 (2016)
18. Agrawal, A., et al.: VQA: visual question answering. In: International Conference on Computer Vision (ICCV), pp. 2425–2433 (2015)
19. Teney, D., Liu, L., van den Hengel, A.: Graph-structured representations for visual question answering. In: Conference on Computer Vision and Pattern Recognition (CVPR), pp. 3233–3241 (2017)
20. Everingham, M., Van Gool, L., Williams, C.K.I., Winn, J., Zisserman, A.: The pascal visual object classes (voc) challenge. Int. J. Comput. Vis. **88**(2), 303–338 (2010)
21. Nair, V., Hinton, G.E.: Rectified linear units improve restricted boltzmann machines. In: Proceedings of the 27th International Conference on Machine Learning (ICML-10), pp. 807–814 (2010)
22. Odena, A., Dumoulin, V., Olah, C.: Deconvolution and checkerboard artifacts. Distill (2016)
23. Simonyan, K., Zisserman, A.: Very deep convolutional networks for large-scale image recognition. In: International Conference on Learning Representations (ICLR) (2015)
24. Ronneberger, O., Fischer, P., Brox, T.: U-Net: convolutional networks for biomedical image segmentation. In: Navab, N., Hornegger, J., Wells, W.M., Frangi, A.F. (eds.) MICCAI 2015. LNCS, vol. 9351, pp. 234–241. Springer, Cham (2015). https://doi.org/10.1007/978-3-319-24574-4_28
25. Shelhamer, E., Long, J., Darrell, T.: Fully convolutional networks for semantic segmentation. In: Conference on Computer Vision and Pattern Recognition (CVPR), pp. 3431–3440 (2015)
26. Hariharan, B., Arbeláez, P., Girshick, R., Malik, J.: Object instance segmentation and fine-grained localization using hypercolumns. IEEE Trans. Pattern Anal. Mach. Intell. (TPAMI) **39**(4), 627–639 (2017)
27. Chen, Y., Li, J., Xiao, H., Jin, X., Yan, S., Feng, J.: Dual path networks. In: Conference on Neural Information Processing Systems (NIPS) (2017)

28. Huang, G., Liu, Z., Weinberger, K.Q.: Densely connected convolutional networks. In: Conference on Computer Vision and Pattern Recognition (CVPR), pp. 2261–2269 (2017)

29. Kazemzadeh, S., Ordonez, V., Matten, M., Berg, T.L.: Referit game: referring to objects in photographs of natural scenes. In: EMNLP (2014)

30. Mao, J., Huang, J., Toshev, A., Camburu, O., Yuille, A.L., Murphy, K.: Generation and comprehension of unambiguous object descriptions. In: Conference on Computer Vision and Pattern Recognition (CVPR), pp. 11–20 (2016)

31. Yu, L., Poirson, P., Yang, S., Berg, A.C., Berg, T.L.: Modeling context in referring expressions. In: Leibe, B., Matas, J., Sebe, N., Welling, M. (eds.) ECCV 2016. LNCS, vol. 9906, pp. 69–85. Springer, Cham (2016). https://doi.org/10.1007/978-3-319-46475-6_5

32. Kingma, D.P., Ba, J.: Adam: a method for stochastic optimization. In: International Conference on Learning Representations (ICLR) (2015)

33. Hu, R., Rohrbach, M., Venugopalan, S., Darrell, T.: Utilizing large scale vision and text datasets for image segmentation from referring expressions. In: European Conference on Computer Vision (ECCV) (2016)

Learning Shape Priors for Single-View 3D Completion And Reconstruction

Jiajun Wu[1(✉)], Chengkai Zhang[1], Xiuming Zhang[1], Zhoutong Zhang[1],
William T. Freeman[1,2], and Joshua B. Tenenbaum[1]

[1] MIT CSAIL, Cambridge, MA 02139, USA
`jiajunwu@mit.edu`
[2] Google Research, Cambridge, MA 02139, USA

Abstract. The problem of single-view 3D shape completion or reconstruction is challenging, because among the many possible shapes that explain an observation, most are implausible and do not correspond to natural objects. Recent research in the field has tackled this problem by exploiting the expressiveness of deep convolutional networks. In fact, there is another level of ambiguity that is often overlooked: among plausible shapes, there are still multiple shapes that fit the 2D image equally well; *i.e.*, the ground truth shape is non-deterministic given a single-view input. Existing fully supervised approaches fail to address this issue, and often produce blurry mean shapes with smooth surfaces but no fine details. In this paper, we propose *ShapeHD*, pushing the limit of single-view shape completion and reconstruction by integrating deep generative models with adversarially learned shape priors. The learned priors serve as a regularizer, penalizing the model only if its output is unrealistic, not if it deviates from the ground truth. Our design thus overcomes both levels of ambiguity aforementioned. Experiments demonstrate that ShapeHD outperforms state of the art by a large margin in both shape completion and shape reconstruction on multiple real datasets.

Keywords: Shape priors · Shape completion · 3D reconstruction

1 Introduction

Let's start with a game: each of the two instances in Fig. 1 shows a depth or color image and two different 3D shape interpretations. Which one looks better?

We asked this question to 100 people on Amazon Mechanical Turk. 59% of them preferred interpretation A of the airplane, and 35% preferred interpretation A of the car. These numbers suggest that people's opinions diverge on these two cases, indicating that these reconstructions are close in quality, and their perceptual differences are relatively minor.

J. Wu and C. Zhang contributed equally to this work.

© Springer Nature Switzerland AG 2018
V. Ferrari et al. (Eds.): ECCV 2018, LNCS 11215, pp. 673–691, 2018.
https://doi.org/10.1007/978-3-030-01252-6_40

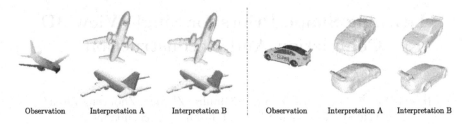

Observation   Interpretation A   Interpretation B   Observation   Interpretation A   Interpretation B

Fig. 1. Our model completes or reconstructs the object's full 3D shape with fine details from a single depth or RGB image. In this figure, we show two examples, each consisting of an input image, two views of its ground truth shape, and two views of our results. Our reconstructions are of high quality with fine details, and are preferred by humans 41% and 35% of the time in behavioral studies, respectively. Our model takes a single feed-forward pass without any post-processing during testing, and is thus highly efficient ($< 100 \, \text{ms}$) and practically useful. Answers are available in the footnote.

Actually, for each instance, one of the reconstructions is the output of the model introduced in this paper, and the other is the ground truth shape. Answers are available in the footnote.

In this paper, we aim to push the limits of 3D shape completion from a single depth image, and of 3D shape reconstruction from a single color image. Recently, researchers have made impressive progress on the these tasks [7,8,52], making use of gigantic 3D datasets [5,59,60]. Many of these methods tackle the ill-posed nature of the problem by using deep convolutional networks to regress possible 3D shapes. Leveraging the power of deep generative models, their systems learn to avoid producing implausible shapes (Fig. 2b).

However, from Fig. 2c we realize that there is still ambiguity that a supervis-edly trained network fails to model. From just a single view, there exist multiple natural shapes that explain the observation equally well. In other words, there is no deterministic ground truth for each observation. Through pure supervised learning, the network tends to generate mean shapes that minimize its penalty precisely due to this ambiguity.

To tackle this, we propose ShapeHD, which completes or reconstructs a 3D shape by combining deep volumetric convolutional networks with adversarially learned shape priors. The learned shape priors penalize the model only if the generated shape is unrealistic, not if it deviates from the ground truth. This overcomes the difficulty discussed above. Our model characterizes this natural-ness loss through adversarial learning, a research topic that has received immense attention in recent years and is still rapidly growing [14,37,57].

Experiments on multiple synthetic and real datasets suggest that ShapeHD performs well on single-view 3D shape completion and reconstruction, achieving better results than state-of-the-art systems. Further analyses reveal that the network learns to attend to meaningful object parts, and the naturalness module indeed helps to characterize shape details over time.[1]

---

[1] Our reconstructions: B, A**

2   Related Work

3D Shape Completion. Shape completion is an essential task in geometry processing and has wide applications. Traditional methods have attempted to complete shapes with local surface primitives, or to formulate it as an optimization problem [35,44], *e.g.*, Poisson surface reconstruction solves an indicator function on a voxel grid via the Poisson equation [28,29]. Recently, there have also been a growing number of papers on exploiting shape structures and regularities [34,51], and papers on leveraging strong database priors [4,32,46]. These methods, however, often require the database to contain exact parts of the shape, and thus have limited generalization power.

With the advances in large-scale shape repositories like ShapeNet [5], researchers began to develop fully data-driven methods, some building upon deep convolutional networks. To name a few, Voxlets [12] employs random forests for predicting unknown voxel neighborhoods. 3D ShapeNets [58] uses a deep belief network to obtain a generative model for a given shape database, and Nguyen *et al.* [50] extend the method for mesh repairing.

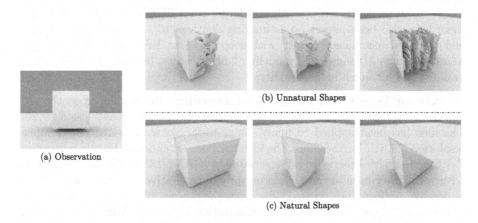

(a) Observation

(b) Unnatural Shapes

(c) Natural Shapes

Fig. 2. Two levels of ambiguity in single-view 3D shape perception. For each 2D observation (a), there exist many possible 3D shapes that explain this observation equally well (b, c), but only a small fraction of them correspond to real, daily shapes (c). Methods that exploit deep networks for recognition reduce, to a certain extent, ambiguity on this level. By using an adversarially learned naturalness model, our ShapeHD aims to model ambiguity on the next level: even among the realistic shapes, there are still multiple shapes explaining the observation well (c).

Probably the most related paper to ours is the 3D-EPN from Dai *et al.* [8]. 3D-EPN achieves impressive results on 3D shape completion from partial depth scans by levering 3D convolutional networks and nonparametric patch-based shape synthesis methods. Our model has advantages over 3D-EPN in two aspects. First, with naturalness losses, ShapeHD can choose among multiple hypotheses that explain the observation, therefore reconstructing a high-quality 3D shape with fine details; in contrast, the output from 3D-EPN without non-parametric shape synthesis is often blurry. Second, our completion takes a single feed-forward pass without any post-processing, and is thus much faster (<100 ms) than 3D-EPN.

Single-image 3D Reconstruction. The problem of recovering the object shape from a single image is challenging, as it requires both powerful recognition systems and prior shape knowledge. As an early attempt, Huang *et al.* [21] propose to borrows shape parts from existing CAD models. With the development of large-scale shape repositories like ShapeNet [5] and methods like deep convolutional networks, researchers have built more scalable and efficient models in recent years [7,13,18,27,36,38,48,52,56,57,62]. While most of these approaches encode objects in voxels from vision, there have also been attempts to reconstruct objects in point clouds [11,15] or octave trees [39,40,49], or using tactile signals [53].

A related direction is to estimate 2.5D sketches (*e.g.*, depth and surface normal maps) from an RGB image. In the past, researchers have explored recovering 2.5D sketches from shading, texture, or color images [2,3,20,47,55,63]. With the development of depth sensors [23] and larger-scale RGB-D datasets [33,42,43], there have also been papers on estimating depth [6,10], surface normals [1,54], and other intrinsic images [25,41] with deep networks. Inspired by MarrNet [56], we reconstructs 3D shapes via modeling 2.5D sketches, but incorporating a naturalness loss for much higher quality.

Perceptual Losses and Adversarial Learning. Researchers recently proposed to evaluate the quality of 2D images using perceptual losses [9,26]. The idea has been applied to many image tasks like style transfer and super-resolution [26,31]. Furthermore, the idea has been extended to learn a perceptual loss function with generative adversarial nets (GAN) [14]. GANs incorporate an adversarial discriminator into the procedure of generative modeling, and achieve impressive performance on tasks like image synthesis [37]. Isola *et al.* [22] and Zhu *et al.* [65] use GANs for image translation with and without supervision, respectively.

In 3D vision, Wu *et al.* [57] extends GANs for 3D shape synthesis. However, their model for shape reconstruction (3D-VAE-GAN) often produces a noisy, incomplete shape given an RGB image. This is because training GANs jointly with recognition networks could be highly unstable. Many other researchers have also noticed this issue: although adversarial modeling of 3D shape space may resolve the ambiguity discussed earlier, its training could be challenging [8]. Addressing this, when Gwak *et al.* [17] explored adversarial nets for single-image 3D reconstruction and chose to use GANs to model 2D projections instead of 3D shapes. This weakly supervised setting, however, hampers their reconstructions. In this paper, we develop our naturalness loss by adversarial modeling of the 3D shape space, outperforming the state-of-the-art significantly.

3   Approach

Our model consists of three components: a 2.5D sketch estimator and a 3D shape estimator that predicts a 3D shape from an RGB image via 2.5D sketches (Fig. 3-I,II, inspired by MarrNet [56]), and a deep naturalness model that penalizes the shape estimator if the predicted shape is unnatural (Fig. 3-III). Models trained with a supervised reconstruction loss alone often generate blurry mean shapes. Our learned naturalness model helps to avoid this issue.

2.5D Sketch Estimation Network. Our 2.5D sketch estimator has an encoder-decoder structure that predicts the object's depth, surface normals, and silhouette from an RGB image (Fig. 3-I). We use a ResNet-18 [19] to encode a 256×256 image into 512 feature maps of size 8×8. The decoder consists of four transposed convolutional layers with a kernel size of 5×5 and a stride and padding of 2. The predicted depth and surface normal images are then masked by the predicted silhouette and used as the input to our shape completion network.

3D Shape Completion Network. Our 3D estimator (Fig. 3-II) is an encoder-decoder network that predicts a 3D shape in the canonical view from 2.5D sketches. The encoder is adapted from ResNet-18 [19] to encode a four-channel 256×256 image (one for depth, three for surface normals) into a 200-D latent vector. The vector then goes through a decoder of five transposed convolutional and ReLU layers to generate a $128 \times 128 \times 128$ voxelized shape. Binary cross-entropy losses between predicted and target voxels are used as the supervised loss L_{voxel}.

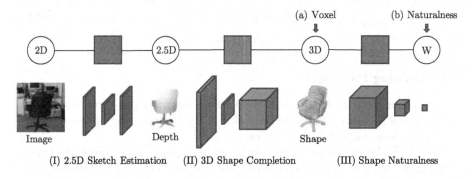

(I) 2.5D Sketch Estimation   (II) 3D Shape Completion   (III) Shape Naturalness

Fig. 3. For single-view shape reconstruction, ShapeHD contains three components: (I) a 2.5D sketch estimator that predicts depth, surface normal and silhouette images from a single image; (II) a 3D shape completion module that regresses 3D shapes from silhouette-masked depth and surface normal images; (III) an adversarially pretrained convolutional net that serves as the naturalness loss function. While fine-tuning the 3D shape completion net, we use two losses: a supervised loss on the output shape, and a naturalness loss offered by the pretrained discriminator. (Color figure online)

3.1 Shape Naturalness Network

Due to the inherent uncertainty of single-view 3D shape reconstruction, shape completion networks with only a supervised loss usually predict unrealistic mean shapes. By doing so, they minimize the loss when there exist multiple possible ground truth shapes. We instead introduce an adversarially trained deep naturalness regularizer that penalizes the network for such unrealistic shapes.

We pre-train a 3D generative adversarial network [14] to determine whether a shape is realistic. Its generator synthesizes a 3D shape from a randomly sampled vector, and its discriminator distinguishes generated shapes from real ones. Therefore, the discriminator has the ability to model the real shape distribution and can be used as a naturalness loss for the shape completion network. The generator is not involved in our later training process. Following 3D-GAN [57], we use 5 transposed convolutional layers with batch normalization and ReLU for the generator, and 5 convolutional layers with leaky ReLU for the discriminator.

Due to the high dimensionality of 3D shapes ($128 \times 128 \times 128$), training a GAN becomes highly unstable. To deal with this issue, we follow Gulrajani $et\ al.$ [16] and use the Wasserstein GAN loss with a gradient penalty to train our adversarial generative network. Specifically,

$$L_{\text{WGAN}} = \underset{\tilde{x} \sim P_g}{\mathbb{E}} [D(\tilde{x})] - \underset{x \sim P_r}{\mathbb{E}} [D(x)] + \lambda \underset{\hat{x} \sim P_x}{\mathbb{E}} [(\|\nabla_{\hat{x}} D(\hat{x})\|_2 - 1)^2], \qquad (1)$$

where D is the discriminator, P_g and P_r are distributions of generated shapes and real shapes, respectively. The last term is the gradient penalty from Gulrajani $et\ al.$ [16]. During training, the discriminator attempts to minimize the overall loss L_{WGAN} while the generator attempts to maximize the loss via the first term in Eq. 1, so we can define our naturalness loss as $L_{\text{natural}} = - \underset{\tilde{x} \sim P_c}{\mathbb{E}} [D(\tilde{x})]$, where P_c are the reconstructed shapes from our completion network.

3.2 Training Paradigm

We train our network in two stages. We first pre-train the three components of our model separately. The shape completion network is then fine-tuned with both voxel loss and naturalness losses.

Our 2.5D sketch estimation network and 3D completion network are trained with images rendered with ShapeNet [5] objects (see Sects. 4.1 and 5 for details). We train the 2.5D sketch estimator using a L2 loss and SGD with a learning rate of 0.001 for 120 epochs. We only use the supervised loss L_{voxel} for training the 3D estimator at this stage, again with SGD, a learning rate of 0.1, and a momentum of 0.9 for 80 epochs. The naturalness network is trained in an adversarial manner, where we use Adam [30] with a learning rate of 0.001 and a batch size of 4 for 80 epochs. We set $\lambda = 10$ as suggested in Gulrajani $et\ al.$ [16].

We then fine-tune our completion network with both voxel loss and natural-ness losses as $L = L_{\text{voxel}} + \alpha L_{\text{natural}}$. We compare the scale of gradients from the losses and train our completion network with $\alpha = 2.75 \times 10^{-11}$ using SGD for 80 epochs. Our model is robust to these parameters; they are only for ensuring gradients of various losses are of the same magnitude.

An alternative is to jointly train the naturalness module with the completion network from scratch using both losses. It seems tempting, but in practice we find that Wasserstein GANs have large losses and gradients, resulting in unstable outputs. We therefore choose to use our pre-training and fine-tuning setup.

4   Single-View Shape Completion

For 3D shape completion from a single depth image, we only use the last two modules of the model: the 3D shape estimator and deep naturalness network.

4.1   Setup

Data. We render each of the ShapeNet Core55 [5] objects from the aeroplane, car and chair categories in 20 random, fully unconstrained views. For each view, we randomly set the azimuth and elevation angles of the camera, but the camera up vector is fixed to be the world $+y$ axis, and the camera always looks at the object center. The focal length is fixed at 50 mm with a 35 mm film. We use Mitsuba [24], a physically-based graphics engine, for all our renderings. We used 90% of the data for training and 10% for testing.

We render the ground-truth depth image of each object in all 20 views. Depth values are measured from the camera center (*i.e.*, ray depth), rather than from the image plane. To approximate depth scanner data, we also generate the accompanying ground-truth surface normal images from the raw depth data, as surface normal maps are the common by-products of depth scanning. All our rendered surface normal vectors are defined in the camera space.

Baselines. We compare with the state of the art: 3D-EPN [8]. To ensure a fair comparison, we convert depth maps to partial surfaces registered in a canonical global coordinate defined by ShapeNet Core55 [5], which is required by 3D-EPN. While the original 3D-EPN paper generates their partial observations by rendering and fusing multi-view depth maps, our method takes a single-view depth map as input and is solving a more challenging problem.

Metrics. We use two standard metrics for quantitative comparisons: Intersection over Union (IoU) and Chamfer Distance (CD). In particular, Chamfer distance can be applied to various shape representations including voxels (by sampling points on the isosurface) and point clouds.

4.2   Results on ShapeNet

Qualitative Results. In Fig. 4, we show 3D shapes predicted by ShapeHD from single-view depth images. While common encoder-decoder structure usually

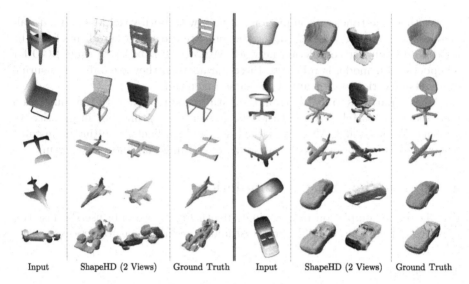

| Input | ShapeHD (2 Views) | Ground Truth | Input | ShapeHD (2 Views) | Ground Truth |

Fig. 4. Results on 3D shape completion from single-view depth. From left to right: input depth maps, shapes reconstructed by ShapeHD in the canonical view and a novel view, and ground truth shapes in the canonical view. Assisted by the adversarially learned naturalness losses, ShapeHD recovers highly accurate 3D shapes with fine details. Sometimes the reconstructed shape deviates from the ground truth, but can be viewed as another plausible explanation of the input (*e.g.*, the airplane on the left, third row).

generates mean shapes with few details, our ShapeHD predicts shapes with large variance and fine details. In addition, even when there is strong occlusion in the depth image, our model can predict a high-quality, plausible 3D shape that looks good perceptually, and infer parts not present in the input images.

Ablation. When using naturalness loss, the network is penalized for generating mean shapes that are unreasonable but minimize the supervised loss. In Fig. 5, we show reconstructed shapes from our ShapeHD with and without naturalness loss (*i.e.* before fine-tuning with $L_{natural}$), together with ground truth shapes and shapes predicted by 3D-EPN [8]. Our results contain finer details compared with those from 3D-EPN. Also, the performance of ShapeHD improves greatly with the naturalness loss, which predicts more reasonable and complete shapes.

Quantitative Results. We present quantitative results in Table 1. Our ShapeHD outperforms the state of the art by a margin in all metrics. Our method outputs shapes at the resolution of 128^3, while shapes produced by 3D-EPN are of resolution 32^3. Therefore, for a fair comparison, we downsample our predicted shapes to 32^3 and report results of both methods in that resolution. The original 3D-EPN paper suggests a post-processing step that retrieves similar patches from a shape database for results of a higher resolution. Practically, we find

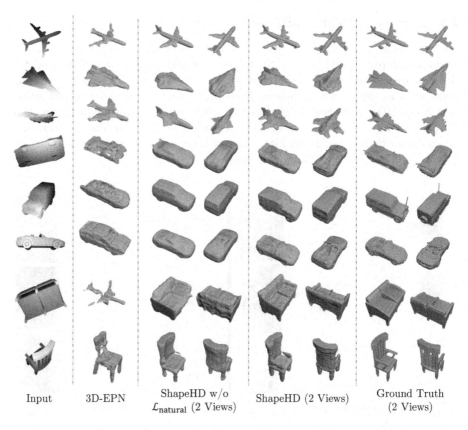

| Input | 3D-EPN | ShapeHD w/o $\mathcal{L}_{\mathrm{natural}}$ (2 Views) | ShapeHD (2 Views) | Ground Truth (2 Views) |

Fig. 5. Our results on 3D shape completion, compared with the state of the art, 3D-EPN [8], and our model but without naturalness losses. Our results contain more details than 3D-EPN. We observe that the adversarially trained naturalness losses help fix errors, add details (*e.g.*, the plane wings in row 3, car seats in row 6, and chair arms in row 8), and smooth planar surfaces (*e.g.*, the sofa back in row 7).

this steps takes 18 hours for a single image. We therefore report results without post-processing for both methods.

Table 1 also suggests the naturalness loss improve the completion results, achieving comparable IoU scores and better (lower) CDs. CD has been reported to be better at capturing human perception of shape quality [45].

Table 1. Average IoU scores (32^3) and CDs for 3D shape completion on ShapeNet [5]. Our model outperforms the state of the art by a large margin. The learned naturalness losses consistently improve the CDs between our results and ground truth.

Methods	IoU				CD			
	chair	car	plane	avg	chair	car	plane	avg
3D-EPN [8]	.147	.274	.155	.181	.227	.200	.125	.192
ShapeHD w/o $\mathcal{L}_{\mathrm{natural}}$	.466	**.698**	**.488**	**.529**	.112	.083	.071	.093
ShapeHD	**.488**	**.698**	.452	**.529**	**.096**	**.078**	**.068**	**.084**

4.3   Results on Real Depth Scans

We now show results of ShapeHD on real depth scans. We capture six depth maps of different chairs using a Structure sensor (http://structure.io) and use the captured depth maps to evaluate our model. All the corresponding normal maps used as inputs are estimated from depth measurements. Figure 6 shows that ShapeHD completes 3D shapes well given a single-view depth map. Our ShapeHD is more flexible than 3D-EPN, as we do not need any camera intrinsics or extrinsics to register depth maps. In our case, none of these parameters are known and thus 3D-EPN cannot be applied.

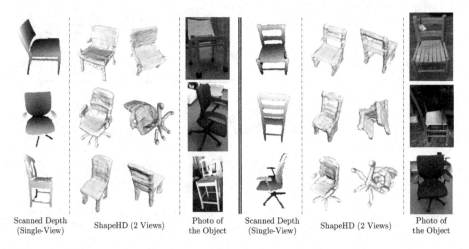

| Scanned Depth (Single-View) | ShapeHD (2 Views) | Photo of the Object | Scanned Depth (Single-View) | ShapeHD (2 Views) | Photo of the Object |

Fig. 6. Results of 3D shape completion on depth data from a physical scanner. Our model is able to reconstruct the shape well from just a single view. From left to right: input depth, two views of our completion results, and a color image of the object.

5   3D Shape Reconstruction

We now evaluate ShapeHD on 3D shape reconstruction from a single color image.

RGB Image Preparation. For the task of single-image 3D reconstruction, we need to render RGB images that correspond to the depth images for training. We follow the same camera setup specified earlier. Additionally, to boost the realism of the rendered RGB images, we put three different types of backgrounds behind the object during rendering. One third of the images are rendered in a clean white background; one third are rendered in high-dynamic-range backgrounds with illumination channels that produce realistic lighting. We render the remaining one third images with backgrounds randomly sampled from the SUN database [61].

Baselines. We compare our ShapeHD with the state-of-the-art in 3D shape reconstruction, including 3D-R2N2 [7], point set generation network

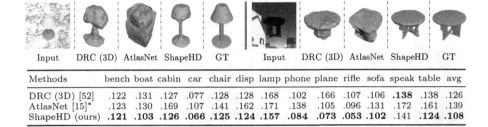

Methods	bench	boat	cabin	car	chair	disp	lamp	phone	plane	rifle	sofa	speak	table	avg
DRC (3D) [52]	.122	.131	.127	.077	.128	.128	.168	.102	.166	.107	.106	**.138**	.138	.126
AtlasNet [15]*	.123	.130	.169	.107	.141	.162	.171	.138	.105	.096	.131	.172	.161	.139
ShapeHD (ours)	**.121**	**.103**	**.126**	**.066**	**.125**	**.124**	**.157**	**.084**	**.073**	**.053**	**.102**	.141	**.124**	**.108**

Fig. 7. Qualitative results and CDs for 3D shape reconstruction on ShapeNet [5]. Our rendering of ShapeNet is more challenging than that from Choy *et al.* [7]; as such, the numbers of the other methods may differ from those in the original paper. All methods are trained with full 3D supervision on our rendering of the largest 13 ShapeNet categories. *DRC and ShapeHD take a single image as input, while AltasNet requires ground truth object silhouettes as additional input.

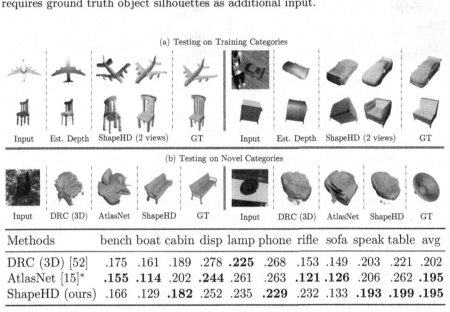

Methods	bench	boat	cabin	disp	lamp	phone	rifle	sofa	speak	table	avg
DRC (3D) [52]	.175	.161	.189	.278	**.225**	.268	.153	.149	.203	.221	.202
AtlasNet [15]*	**.155**	**.114**	.202	**.244**	.261	.263	**.121**	**.126**	.206	.262	**.195**
ShapeHD (ours)	.166	.129	**.182**	.252	.235	**.229**	.232	.133	**.193**	**.199**	**.195**

Fig. 8. Qualitative results and CDs for 3D shape reconstruction on novel categories from ShapeNet [5]. All methods are trained with full 3D supervision on our rendering of ShapeNet cars, chairs, and planes, and tested on the next 10 largest categories. *DRC and ShapeHD take a single image as input, while AltasNet requires ground truth object silhouettes as additional input.

(PSGN) [11], differentiable ray consistency (DRC) [52], octree generating network (OGN) [49], and AtlasNet [15]. 3D-R2N2, DRC, OGN, and our ShapeHD take a single image as input, while PSGN and AltasNet require object silhouettes as additional input.

Results on Synthetic Data. We first evaluate on renderings of ShapeNet objects [5]. We present reconstructed 3D shapes and quantitative results in Fig. 7.

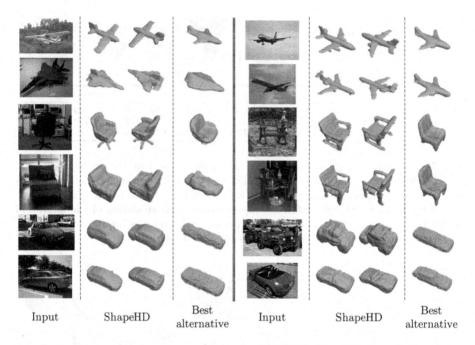

| Input | ShapeHD | Best alternative | Input | ShapeHD | Best alternative |

Fig. 9. Single-view 3D shape reconstruction on PASCAL 3D+ [60]. From left to right: input, two views of reconstructions from ShapeHD, and reconstructions by the best alternative in Table 2. Assisted by the learned naturalness losses, ShapeHD recovers accurate 3D shapes with fine details.

All these models are trained on our rendering of the largest 13 ShapeNet categories (those have at least 1,000 models) with ground truth 3D shapes as supervision. In general, our ShapeHD is able to predict 3D shapes that closely resemble the ground truth shapes, giving fine details that make the reconstructed shapes more realistic. It also performs better quantitatively.

Generalization on Novel Categories. An important aspect of evaluating shape reconstruction methods is on how well they generalize. Here we train our model and baselines on the largest three ShapeNet classes (cars, chairs, and planes), again with ground truth shapes as supervision, and test them on the next largest ten. Figure 8 shows our ShapeHD performs better than DRC (3D) and is comparable to AtlasNet; however, note that AtlasNet requires ground truth silhouettes as additional input, while ShapeHD works on raw images.

Results on Real Data. We then evaluate on two real datasets, PASCAL 3D+ [60] and Pix3D [45]. Here, we train our model on synthetic ShapeNet renderings and use the pre-trained models released by the authors as baselines. All methods take ground truth 3D shapes as supervision during training. As shown in Figs. 9 and 10, ShapeHD works well, inferring a reasonable shape even in the presence of strong self-occlusions. In particular, in Fig. 9, we compare our reconstructions with the best-performing alternatives (DRC on chairs and airplanes, and AtlasNet on cars). In addition to preserving details, our model captures the shape variations of the objects, while the competitors produce similar reconstructions across instances.

Quantitatively, Tables 2 and 3 suggest that ShapeHD performs significantly better than the other methods in almost all metrics. The only exception is the CD on PASCAL 3D+ cars, where OGN performs the best. However, as PASCAL 3D+ only has around 10 CAD models for each object category as ground truth 3D shapes, the ground truth labels and the scores can be inaccurate, failing to reflect human perception [52].

We therefore conduct an additional user study, where we show an input image and its two reconstructions (from ShapeHD and from OGN, each in two views) to users on Amazon Mechanical Turk, and ask them to choose the shape that looks closer to the object in the image. For each image, we collect 10 responses from "Masters" (workers who have demonstrated excellence across a wide range of HITs). Table 2b suggests that on most images, most users prefer our reconstruction to OGN's. In general, our reconstructions are preferred 64.5% of the time.

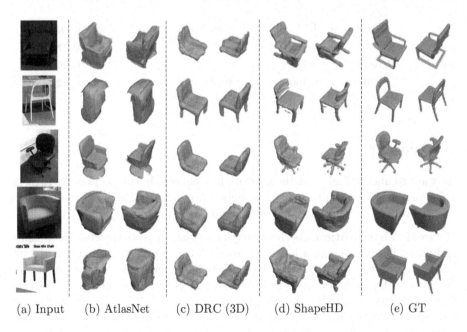

(a) Input   (b) AtlasNet   (c) DRC (3D)   (d) ShapeHD   (e) GT

Fig. 10. Single-view 3D reconstruction on Pix3D [45]. For each input image, we show reconstructions by AtlasNet, DRC, our ShapeHD, and ground truth. Our ShapeHD reconstructs complete 3D shapes with fine details that resemble the ground truth.

Table 2. Results for 3D shape reconstruction on PASCAL 3D+ [60]. (a) We compare our ShapeHD with 3D-R2N2, DRC, and OGN. PSGN and AtlasNet are not evaluated, because they require object masks as additional input, but PASCAL 3D+ has only inaccurate masks. (b) In the behavioral study, most users prefer our constructions on most images. Overall, our reconstructions are preferred 64.5% of the time to OGN's.

Methods	CD			
	chair	car	plane	avg
3D-R2N2 [7]	0.238	0.305	0.305	0.284
DRC (3D) [52]	0.158	0.099	0.112	0.122
OGN [49]	-	**0.087**	-	-
ShapeHD (ours)	**0.137**	0.129	**0.094**	**0.119**

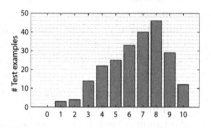

(a) CDs on PASCAL 3D+ [60]   (b) Human Study results

Table 3. 3D shape reconstruction results on Pix3D [45]. All methods were trained with full 3D supervision on rendered images of ShapeNet objects. *3D-R2N2, DRC, and ShapeHD take a single image as input, while PSGN and AtlasNet require the ground truth mask as input. Also, PSGN and AtlasNet generate surface point clouds without guaranteeing watertight meshes and therefore cannot be evaluated in IoU.

	3D-R2N2 [7]	DRC (3D) [52]	PSGN [11]*	AtlasNet [15]*	ShapeHD
IoU (32^3)	0.136	0.265	-	-	**0.284**
IoU (128^3)	0.089	0.185	-	-	**0.205**
CD	0.239	0.160	0.199	0.126	**0.123**

6   Analyses

We want to understand what the network has learned. In this section, we present a few analyses to visualize what the network is learning, analyze the effect of the naturalness loss function over time, and discuss common failure modes.

Network Visualization. As the network successfully reconstructs object shape and parts, it is natural to ask if it learns object or part detectors implicitly. To this end, we visualize the top activating regions across all validation images for units in the last convolutional layer of the encoder in our 3D completion network, using the method proposed by Zhou et al. [64]. As shown in Fig. 11, the network indeed learns a diverse and rich set of object and part detectors. There are detectors that attend to car wheels, chair backs, chair arms, chair legs, and airplane engines. Also note that many detectors respond to certain patterns (e.g., strided) in particular, which is probably contributing to the fine details in the reconstruction. Additionally, there are units that respond to generic shape patterns across categories, like the curve detector in the bottom right.

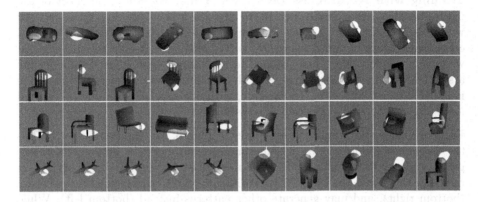

Fig. 11. Visualizations on how ShapeHD attends to details in depth maps. Row 1: car wheel detectors. Row 2: chair back and leg detectors. The left responds to the strided pattern in particular. Row 3: chair arm and leg detectors. Row 4: airplane engine and curved surface detectors. The right responds to a specific pattern across classes.

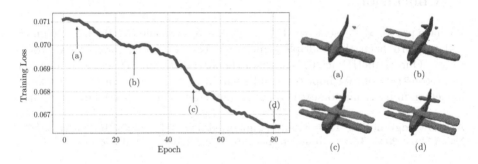

Fig. 12. Visualizations on how ShapeHD evolves over time with naturalness losses: the predicted shape becomes increasingly realistic as details are being added.

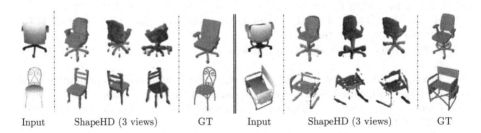

Input   ShapeHD (3 views)   GT   Input   ShapeHD (3 views)   GT

Fig. 13. Common failure modes of our system. Top left: the model sometimes gets confused by deformable object parts (*e.g.*, wheels). Top right: the model might miss uncommon object parts (the ring above the wheels). Bottom row: the model has difficulty in recovering very thin structure, and may generate other structure patterns instead.

Training with Naturalness Loss Over Time. We study the effect of the naturalness loss over time. In Fig. 12, we plot the loss of the completion network with respect to fine-tuning epochs. We realize the voxel loss goes down slowly but consistently. If we visualize the reconstructed examples at different timestamps, we clearly see details are being added to the shapes. These fine details occupy a small region in the voxel grid, and thus training with supervised loss alone is unlikely to recover them. In contrast, with adversarially training perceptual losses, our model recovers details successfully.

Failure Cases. We present failure cases in Fig. 13. We observe our model has these common failing modes: it sometimes gets confused by deformable object parts (*e.g.*, wheels on the top left); it may miss uncommon object parts (top right, the ring above the wheels); it has difficulty in recovering very thin structure (bottom right), and may generate other patterns instead (bottom left). While the voxel representation makes it possible to incorporate the naturalness loss, intuitively, it also encourages the network to focus on thicker shape parts, as they carry more weights in the loss function.

7   Conclusion

We have proposed to use learned shape priors to overcome the 2D-3D ambiguity and to learn from the multiple hypotheses that explain a single-view observation. Our ShapeHD achieves state-of-the-art results on 3D shape completion and reconstruction. We hope our results will inspire further research in 3D shape modeling, in particular on explaining the ambiguity behind partial observations.

Acknowledgements. This work is supported by NSF #1231216, ONR MURI N00014-16-1-2007, Toyota Research Institute, Shell Research, and Facebook.

References

1. Bansal, A., Russell, B.: Marr revisited: 2D–3D alignment via surface normal prediction. In: CVPR (2016)
2. Barron, J.T., Malik, J.: Shape, illumination, and reflectance from shading. IEEE TPAMI **37**(8), 1670–1687 (2015)
3. Bell, S., Bala, K., Snavely, N.: Intrinsic images in the wild. ACM TOG **33**(4), 159 (2014)
4. Brock, A., Lim, T., Ritchie, J.M., Weston, N.: Generative and discriminative voxel modeling with convolutional neural networks. In: NIPS Workshop (2016)
5. Chang, A.X., et al.: Shapenet: an information-rich 3D model repository. arXiv:1512.03012 (2015)
6. Chen, W., Fu, Z., Yang, D., Deng, J.: Single-image depth perception in the wild. In: NIPS (2016)
7. Choy, C.B., Xu, D., Gwak, J.Y., Chen, K., Savarese, S.: 3D-R2N2: a unified approach for single and multi-view 3D object reconstruction. In: Leibe, B., Matas, J., Sebe, N., Welling, M. (eds.) ECCV 2016. LNCS, vol. 9912, pp. 628–644. Springer, Cham (2016). https://doi.org/10.1007/978-3-319-46484-8_38

8. Dai, A., Qi, C.R., Nießner, M.: Shape completion using 3D-encoder-predictor CNNS and shape synthesis. In: CVPR (2017)
9. Dosovitskiy, A., Brox, T.: Generating images with perceptual similarity metrics based on deep networks. In: NIPS (2016)
10. Eigen, D., Fergus, R.: Predicting depth, surface normals and semantic labels with a common multi-scale convolutional architecture. In: ICCV (2015)
11. Fan, H., Su, H., Guibas, L.: A point set generation network for 3D object reconstruction from a single image. In: CVPR (2017)
12. Firman, M., Aodha, O.M., Julier, S., Brostow, G.J.: Structured Completion of Unobserved Voxels from a Single Depth Image. In: CVPR (2016)
13. Girdhar, R., Fouhey, D.F., Rodriguez, M., Gupta, A.: Learning a predictable and generative vector representation for objects. In: Leibe, B., Matas, J., Sebe, N., Welling, M. (eds.) ECCV 2016. LNCS, vol. 9910, pp. 484–499. Springer, Cham (2016). https://doi.org/10.1007/978-3-319-46466-4_29
14. Goodfellow, I., et al.: Generative adversarial nets. In: NIPS (2014)
15. Goueix, T., Fisher, M., Kim, V.G., Russel, B.C., Aubry, M.: Atlasnet: a papier-mch approach to learning 3D surface generation. In: CVPR (2018)
16. Gulrajani, I., Ahmed, F., Arjovsky, M., Dumoulin, V., Courville, A.: Improved training of wasserstein gans. In: NIPS (2017)
17. Gwak, J., Choy, C.B., Chandraker, M., Garg, A., Savarese, S.: Weakly supervised 3D reconstruction with adversarial constraint. In: 3DV (2017)
18. Häne, C., Tulsiani, S., Malik, J.: Hierarchical surface prediction for 3D object reconstruction. In: 3DV (2017)
19. He, K., Zhang, X., Ren, S., Sun, J.: Deep residual learning for image recognition. In: CVPR (2015)
20. Horn, B.K., Brooks, M.J.: Shape from Shading. MIT Press, Cambridge (1989)
21. Huang, Q., Wang, H., Koltun, V.: Single-view reconstruction via joint analysis of image and shape collections. ACM TOG **34**(4), 87 (2015)
22. Isola, P., Zoran, D., Krishnan, D., Adelson, E.H.: Learning visual groups from co-occurrences in space and time. In: ICLR Workshop (2016)
23. Izadi, S., et al.: Kinectfusion: real-time 3D reconstruction and interaction using a moving depth camera. In: UIST (2011)
24. Jakob, W.: Mitsuba renderer (2010). http://www.mitsuba-renderer.org
25. Janner, M., Wu, J., Kulkarni, T., Yildirim, I., Tenenbaum, J.B.: Self-Supervised Intrinsic Image Decomposition. In: NIPS (2017)
26. Johnson, J., Alahi, A., Fei-Fei, L.: Perceptual losses for real-time style transfer and super-resolution. In: Leibe, B., Matas, J., Sebe, N., Welling, M. (eds.) ECCV 2016. LNCS, vol. 9906, pp. 694–711. Springer, Cham (2016). https://doi.org/10.1007/978-3-319-46475-6_43
27. Kar, A., Tulsiani, S., Carreira, J., Malik, J.: Category-specific object reconstruction from a single image. In: CVPR (2015)
28. Kazhdan, M., Bolitho, M., Hoppe, H.: Poisson surface reconstruction. In: SGP. SGP 2006 (2006)
29. Kazhdan, M., Hoppe, H.: Screened poisson surface reconstruction. ACM TOG **32**(3), 29 (2013)
30. Kingma, D.P., Ba, J.: Adam: a method for stochastic optimization. In: ICLR (2015)
31. Ledig, C., et al.: Photo-realistic single image super-resolution using a generative adversarial network. arXiv:1609.04802 (2016)
32. Li, Y., Dai, A., Guibas, L., Nießner, M.: Database-assisted object retrieval for real-time 3D reconstruction. CGF **34**(2), 435–446 (2015)

690	J. Wu et al.

33. McCormac, J., Handa, A., Leutenegger, S., Davison, A.J.: Scenenet RGB-D: Can 5m synthetic images beat generic imagenet pre-training on indoor segmentation? In: ICCV (2017)
34. Mitra, N.J., Guibas, L.J., Pauly, M.: Partial and approximate symmetry detection for 3d geometry. ACM TOG **25**(3), 560–568 (2006)
35. Nealen, A., Igarashi, T., Sorkine, O., Alexa, M.: Laplacian mesh optimization. In: Proceedings of the 4th international conference on Computer graphics and interactive techniques in Australasia and Southeast Asia. pp. 381–389. ACM (2006)
36. Novotny, D., Larlus, D., Vedaldi, A.: Learning 3D object categories by looking around them. In: ICCV (2017)
37. Radford, A., Metz, L., Chintala, S.: Unsupervised representation learning with deep convolutional generative adversarial networks. In: ICLR (2016)
38. Rezende, D.J., Eslami, S., Mohamed, S., Battaglia, P., Jaderberg, M., Heess, N.: Unsupervised learning of 3D structure from images. In: NIPS (2016)
39. Riegler, G., Ulusoy, A.O., Bischof, H., Geiger, A.: Octnetfusion: Learning depth fusion from data. In: 3DV (2017)
40. Riegler, G., Ulusoys, A.O., Geiger, A.: Octnet: learning deep 3D representations at high resolutions. In: CVPR (2017)
41. Shi, J., Dong, Y., Su, H., Yu, S.X.: Learning non-lambertian object intrinsics across shapenet categories. In: CVPR (2017)
42. Silberman, Nathan, Hoiem, Derek, Kohli, Pushmeet, Fergus, Rob: Indoor segmentation and support inference from RGBD images. In: Fitzgibbon, Andrew, Lazebnik, Svetlana, Perona, Pietro, Sato, Yoichi, Schmid, Cordelia (eds.) ECCV 2012. LNCS, vol. 7576, pp. 746–760. Springer, Heidelberg (2012). https://doi.org/10.1007/978-3-642-33715-4_54
43. Song, S., Yu, F., Zeng, A., Chang, A.X., Savva, M., Funkhouser, T.: Semantic scene completion from a single depth image. In: CVPR (2017)
44. Sorkine, O., Cohen-Or, D.: Least-squares meshes. In: Shape Modeling Applications (2004)
45. Sun, X., et al.: Pix3D: Dataset and methods for single-image 3D shape modeling. In: CVPR (2018)
46. Sung, M., Kim, V.G., Angst, R., Guibas, L.: Data-driven structural priors for shape completion. ACM TOG **34**(6), 175 (2015)
47. Tappen, M.F., Freeman, W.T., Adelson, E.H.: Recovering intrinsic images from a single image. In: NIPS (2003)
48. Tatarchenko, Maxim, Dosovitskiy, Alexey, Brox, Thomas: Multi-view 3D models from single images with a convolutional network. In: Leibe, Bastian, Matas, Jiri, Sebe, Nicu, Welling, Max (eds.) ECCV 2016. LNCS, vol. 9911, pp. 322–337. Springer, Cham (2016). https://doi.org/10.1007/978-3-319-46478-7_20
49. Tatarchenko, M., Dosovitskiy, A., Brox, T.: Octree generating networks: efficient convolutional architectures for high-resolution 3D outputs. In: ICCV (2017)
50. Thanh Nguyen, D., Hua, B.S., Tran, K., Pham, Q.H., Yeung, S.K.: A field model for repairing 3D shapes. In: CVPR (2016)
51. Thrun, S., Wegbreit, B.: Shape from symmetry. In: ICCV (2005)
52. Tulsiani, S., Zhou, T., Efros, A.A., Malik, J.: Multi-view supervision for single-view reconstruction via differentiable ray consistency. In: CVPR (2017)
53. Wang, S., Wu, J., Sun, X., Yuan, W., Freeman, W.T., Tenenbaum, J.B., Adelson, E.H.: 3d shape perception from monocular vision, touch, and shape priors. In: IROS (2018)
54. Wang, X., Fouhey, D., Gupta, A.: Designing deep networks for surface normal estimation. In: CVPR (2015)

55. Weiss, Y.: Deriving intrinsic images from image sequences. In: ICCV (2001)
56. Wu, J., Wang, Y., Xue, T., Sun, X., Freeman, W.T., Tenenbaum, J.B.: MarrNet: 3D shape reconstruction via 2.5D sketches. In: NIPS (2017)
57. Wu, J., Zhang, C., Xue, T., Freeman, W.T., Tenenbaum, J.B.: Learning a probabilistic latent space of object shapes via 3D generative-adversarial modeling. In: NIPS (2016)
58. Wu, Z., et al.: 3D shapenets: a deep representation for volumetric shapes. In: CVPR (2015)
59. Xiang, Yu., et al.: ObjectNet3D: a large scale database for 3D object recognition. In: Leibe, Bastian, Matas, Jiri, Sebe, Nicu, Welling, Max (eds.) ECCV 2016. LNCS, vol. 9912, pp. 160–176. Springer, Cham (2016). https://doi.org/10.1007/978-3-319-46484-8_10
60. Xiang, Y., Mottaghi, R., Savarese, S.: Beyond pascal: a benchmark for 3d object detection in the wild. In: WACV (2014)
61. Xiao, J., Hays, J., Ehinger, K.A., Oliva, A., Torralba, A.: Sun database: Large-scale scene recognition from abbey to zoo. In: CVPR (2010)
62. Yan, X., Yang, J., Yumer, E., Guo, Y., Lee, H.: Perspective transformer nets: learning single-view 3D object reconstruction without 3D supervision. In: NIPS (2016)
63. Zhang, R., Tsai, P.S., Cryer, J.E., Shah, M.: Shape-from-shading: a survey. IEEE TPAMI **21**(8), 690–706 (1999)
64. Zhou, B., Khosla, A., Lapedriza, A., Oliva, A., Torralba, A.: Object detectors emerge in deep scene CNNs. In: ICLR (2014)
65. Zhu, Jun-Yan, Krähenbühl, Philipp, Shechtman, Eli, Efros, Alexei A.: Generative visual manipulation on the natural image manifold. In: Leibe, Bastian, Matas, Jiri, Sebe, Nicu, Welling, Max (eds.) ECCV 2016. LNCS, vol. 9909, pp. 597–613. Springer, Cham (2016). https://doi.org/10.1007/978-3-319-46454-1_36

AGIL: Learning Attention from Human for Visuomotor Tasks

Ruohan Zhang[1]([✉])(iD), Zhuode Liu[2], Luxin Zhang[3], Jake A. Whritner[4],
Karl S. Muller[4], Mary M. Hayhoe[4], and Dana H. Ballard[1]

[1] Department of Computer Science, University of Texas at Austin, Austin, USA
{zharu,danab}@utexas.edu
[2] Google Inc., Mountain View, USA
zhuodel@google.com
[3] Department of Intelligence Science, Peking University, Beijing, China
zhangluxin@pku.edu.cn
[4] Center for Perceptual Systems, University of Texas at Austin, Austin, USA
{jake.whritner,karl.muller,hayhoe}@utexas.edu

Abstract. When intelligent agents learn visuomotor behaviors from human demonstrations, they may benefit from knowing where the human is allocating visual attention, which can be inferred from their gaze. A wealth of information regarding intelligent decision making is conveyed by human gaze allocation; hence, exploiting such information has the potential to improve the agents' performance. With this motivation, we propose the AGIL (Attention Guided Imitation Learning) framework. We collect high-quality human action and gaze data while playing Atari games in a carefully controlled experimental setting. Using these data, we first train a deep neural network that can predict human gaze positions and visual attention with high accuracy (the gaze network) and then train another network to predict human actions (the policy network). Incorporating the learned attention model from the gaze network into the policy network significantly improves the action prediction accuracy and task performance.

Keywords: Visual attention · Eye tracking · Imitation learning

1 Introduction

In end-to-end learning of visuomotor behaviors, algorithms such as imitation learning, reinforcement learning (RL), or a combination of both, have achieved remarkable successes in video games [28], board games [37,38], and robot manipulation tasks [24,30]. One major issue of using RL alone is its sample efficiency, hence in practice human demonstration can be used to speedup learning [6,15,37].

Electronic supplementary material The online version of this chapter (https://doi.org/10.1007/978-3-030-01252-6_41) contains supplementary material, which is available to authorized users.

© Springer Nature Switzerland AG 2018
V. Ferrari et al. (Eds.): ECCV 2018, LNCS 11215, pp. 692–707, 2018.
https://doi.org/10.1007/978-3-030-01252-6_41

Imitation learning, or learning from demonstration, follows a student-teacher paradigm, in which a learning agent learns from the demonstration of human teachers [1]. A popular approach is behavior cloning, i.e., training an agent to predict (imitate) demonstrated behaviors with supervised learning methods. Imitation learning research mainly focuses on the student–advancing our understanding of the learning agent–while very little effort is made to understand the human teacher. In this work, we argue that understanding and modeling the human teacher is also an important research issue in this paradigm. Specifically, in visuomotor learning tasks, a key component of human intelligence–the visual attention mechanism–encodes a wealth of information that can be exploited by a learning algorithm. Modeling human visual attention and guiding the learning agent with a learned attention model could lead to significant improvement in task performance.

We propose the *Attention Guided Imitation Learning (AGIL)* framework, in which a learning agent first learns a visual attention model from human gaze data, then learns how to perform the visuomotor task from human decision data. The motivation is that for deep imitation learning tasks where the decision state is often in raw pixel space, the introduction of attention could help resolve two issues:

1. Humans have a unique sensory system that is different from machines' and this leads to different perceived decision states.
2. The traits of this sensory system lead to gaze behaviors and visual attention–intelligent mechanisms that are not yet available to the learning agent. Without these mechanisms, it is difficult for the agent to infer which visual features are being attended and are relevant for the decision at a given moment in a high dimensional feature space.

To elaborate the first point, humans have high acuity foveal vision in the central 1–2 visual degrees of the visual field (i.e., covering the width of a finger at arms length), with resolution decreasing in the periphery. This leads to a discrepancy in the perceived states of a human and a machine, where the machine perceives full resolution images like in Fig. 1a while a human would see Figs. 1b if the stimulus is 64.6×40.0 cm and the distance to the subjects' eyes is 78.7 cm. A foveal visual system may seem inferior compared to a full resolution camera, but it leads to an outstanding property of human intelligence: Visual attention, which can be seen as a feature selection mechanism. Humans manage to move their foveae to the correct place at the right time in order to emphasize important task-relevant features [8,36]. In this way, a wealth of information is encoded in human gaze behaviors–for example, the priority of one object over another in performing an action.

Given the rich information encoded in human gaze, we hypothesize that a promising approach to strengthen an imitation learning algorithm is to model human visual attention through gaze, and subsequently include such a model in the decision-learning process. Doing so would allow the learning agent to use gaze information to help decipher the internal state representation used by the human teacher. By extracting features that are most important for tasks, the learning agent can better understand and imitate a human teachers' behaviors.

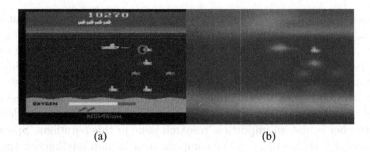

(a)   (b)

Fig. 1. An original game frame for Atari Seaquest with a red circle indicating the gaze position (a). The gaze position is used to generate foveated images (b) that are biologically plausible retinal representations of the visual stimulus (the stimulus as perceived by the human).

We start by extracting the large amount of high-quality training data necessary for training. With modern high-speed eye trackers we collect human game playing data and gaze data for various Atari games. We first train a deep neural network that can predict human gaze positions and visual attention (the gaze network). Second, we train another deep neural network–guided by visual attention information–to predict human actions (the policy network). Finally, we evaluate the imitation learning results in terms of both behavior matching accuracy and game playing performance.

2   Related Work

Modeling Visual Attention: Bottom-up vs. Top-Down. Previous work in computer vision has formalized visual attention modeling as a saliency prediction problem where saliency is derived from image statistics, such as intensity, color, and orientation in the classic Itti-Koch model [17]. In recent years, this approach has made tremendous progress due to large benchmark datasets and deep neural networks [5,19,21,22,25,42]. Many saliency datasets collect human eye tracking data in a "free-viewing" manner due to their task-free nature [19].

In contrast to this approach, top-down models emphasizes the effects of task-dependent variables on visual attention [2,12,33,39]. [36] have shown that varying task instructions drastically alters the gaze distributions on different categories of objects (e.g., task-irrelevant objects are ignored even though they are salient from a bottom-up perspective). [20] has shown that in an urban driving environment, attention shifts can be accurately predicted by changing both the relative reward of different tasks and the level of uncertainty in the state estimation. The top-down attention model is hence closely related to reinforcement learning since they both concern visual state features that matter the most for acquiring the reward [12,23].

Regardless of their approaches, these works argue that there is much valuable information encoded in gaze behaviors. It should be said that the two approaches are not mutually exclusive, since attention is modulated in both saliency-driven and volition-controlled manners [17]. As mentioned before, deep neural networks have been a standard approach to predict bottom-up saliency. In contrast, top-down gaze models often rely on manually defined task variables. Our approach seeks to combine these approaches and use the representation learning power of deep networks to extract task-relevant visual features, given task-driven gaze data. A recent work that also takes this approach is [31], where they predict human gaze while driving from raw images using a multi-channel deep network.

Attention in Visuomotor Learning Tasks. While visual attention models have shown very promising results in several visual learning tasks, including visual question answering [43], image generation [11], image caption generation [41], and spatial transformer networks [18], incorporating visual attention models into visuomotor learning is yet to be explored.

The relation between attention and reinforcement learning has been revealed by neuroscience researchers [9,16,23,35]. [29] attempts to jointly learn attention and control, and show that a learned attention model can predict visual attention much better than bottom-up saliency models. [40] show that different network components learn to attend to different visual features, but they do not explicitly model visual attention. [27] pioneered efforts to combine deep reinforcement learning and visual attention, where attention is treated as a sequential decision problem (where to look) and is jointly trained with the control policy (what to do) via deep reinforcement learning. Therefore their attention model is a non-differentiable (or "hard") attention model which leads to a computationally expensive training procedure. In contrast, saliency approaches in general prefer a differentiable (or "soft") attention model that could be trained more efficiently. Our work treats visual attention as an auxiliary component for visuomotor learning tasks and chooses to use the more efficient soft attention model.

3   Data Acquisition

We collected human game-playing actions using Atari games in the Arcade Learning Environment [3], a rich environment with games of very different dynamics, visual features, and reward functions. These games capture many interesting aspects of the natural visuomotor tasks meanwhile allow better experimental control than real-world tasks.

At each time step t, the raw image frame I_t, the human keystroke action a_t, and the gaze position g_t were recorded. The gaze data was recorded using an EyeLink 1000 eye tracker at 1000 Hz. The game screen is 64.6 × 40.0 cm and the distance to the subjects' eyes was 78.7cm. The visual angle of an object is a measure of the size of the object's image on the retina. The visual angle of the screen was 44.6 × 28.5 visual degrees. Standard eye tracking calibration and validation techniques were implemented, resulting in an average gaze positional error of 0.44 visual degrees (covering the half width of a finger at arms length).

Our goal is to obtain the best possible control policy from human subjects, hence we take into account the limitations of human reaction time and fatigue. For visuomotor tasks like playing Atari games, human response time to visual stimulus is on average 250 ms, so running the game at the original speed is too challenging for most human subjects. To allow for enough response time, the games only proceed when the subject makes an action (presses a key or keeps a key pressed down). To reduce fatigue, players play for 15 minutes and rest for at least 20 min.

We carefully chose eight Atari games from [28] that each represent a different genre. The data are from three amateur human players that contains a total length of 1,335 min and 1,576,843 image frames. The frames without gaze–due to blinking, off-screen gaze, or tracker error–are marked as bad data and excluded from training and testing (5.04%). Data belong to a single trajectory (an episode in Atari game) will not be split into training and testing set. Due to the high sampling frequency of the data recording device, two adjacent frames/actions/gazes are highly similar so we avoid putting one in training and another in testing. The sample size information for training and testing can be found in Appendix 1.

The data is collected under a different setting compared to the human experiments reported in the previous deep imitation learning and RL literature [15,28,40]. Even though human players are recruited students who are familiar with these games but non-experts, our experimental settings resulted in significantly better human performance; see Appendix 1 for a human game score comparison. The high human game scores pave the way for a more insightful comparison between human and deep RL performances in terms of decision making. The dataset is available upon request to encourage future research in vision science, visuomotor behaviors, imitation learning, and reinforcement learning.

4   Gaze Network

Computer vision research has formalized visual attention modeling as an end-to-end saliency prediction problem, whereby a deep network can be used to predict a probability distribution of the gaze (saliency map). The ground truth saliency map is generated by converting discrete gaze positions to a continuous distribution using a Gaussian kernel with σ equals to 1 visual degree, as suggested by [4].

We use the same deep neural network architecture and hyperparameters for all eight games (this is true for all models used in this work). The network architecture we use (shown in Fig. 2) is a three-channel convolution-deconvolution network. The inputs to the top channel are the images where the preprocessing procedure follows [28] and hence consist of a sequence of 4 frames stacked together where each frame is 84×84 in grayscale. The reason to use 4 frames is because a single image state is non-Markovian in Atari games, e.g., the direction of a flying bullet is ambiguous if we only see a single frame. The mid channel models motion information (optical flow) which is included since human gaze is sensitive to movement, and motion information has been used to improve gaze prediction accuracy [26]. Optical flow vectors of two continuous frames are calculated using the algorithm in [10] and fed into the network. The bottom channel includes bottom-up saliency map computed by the classic Itti-Koch model [17]. The output of the network is a gaze saliency map trained with Kullback-Leibler divergence as the loss function:

$$KL(P,Q) = \sum_i Q_i \log \left(\epsilon + \frac{Q_i}{\epsilon + P_i} \right)$$ (1)

where P denotes the predicted saliency map and Q denotes the ground truth. The regularization constant ϵ is set to $1e - 10$.

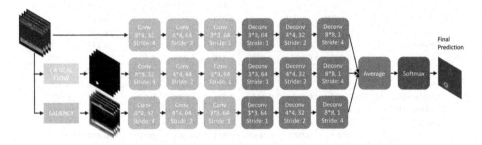

Fig. 2. The three-channel gaze network. The top channel takes in images, the mid channel takes in the corresponding optical flow, and the bottom channel takes in the bottom-up image saliency. We then average the output of three channels. The final output is a gaze saliency map that indicates the predicted probability distribution of the gaze. The design of the convolutional layers follows the Deep Q-network [28].

For a performance comparison we use the classic bottom-up saliency model [17] as the first baseline (Saliency(S) in Table 1). Then we compute optical flow (Motion(M) in Table 1) of the current image as the second baseline, since motion is a reasonable indicator of visual attention. Then an ablation study is performed where the model consists only one or two channels of the original network in Fig. 2, i.e., Image(I), Image+Saliency(I+S), or Image+Motion(I+M). The performance of the algorithms are evaluated using four standard metrics in the visual saliency literature [34]: Normalized Scanpath Saliency (NSS), Area Under the Curve (AUC), Kullback-Leibler divergence (KL), and Correlation Coefficient (CC).

The quantitative results are shown in Table 1. Overall, the prediction results of our models are highly accurate across all games and largely outperform the saliency and motion baselines, indicated by the high AUC (above 0.93 for all games) obtained. A two-channel model (Image+Motion) in general achieves the best results. Further removing the motion information (having only the image) results in only slightly less accuracy–with the exception of the game Venture in which the speed of the monsters matters the most, hence removing motion decreases prediction accuracy. Including bottom-up saliency into the model does not improve the performance overall. This indicates that in the given tasks, the top-down visual attention is different than and hard to be inferred from the traditional bottom-up image saliency.

Table 1. Quantitative results of predicting human gaze across eight games. Random prediction baseline: NSS = 0.000, AUC = 0.500, KL = 6.159, CC = 0.000. For comparison, the classic [17] model (Saliency) and optical flow (Motion) are compared to versions of our model. All our models are accurate in predicting human gaze (AUC>0.93). In general the Image+Motion (I+M) model achieves the best prediction accuracy across games and four metrics.

		Break-out	Free-way	Enduro	River-raid	Sea-quest	Ms-Pacman	Centi-pede	Ven-ture
Saliency(S)	NSS↑	−0.075	−0.175	−0.261	0.094	−0.208	−0.376	0.665	0.422
Motion(M)		2.306	1.015	0.601	1.200	2.016	0.891	1.229	1.004
Image(I)		6.336	6.762	8.455	5.776	6.417	4.522	5.147	5.429
I+S		6.363	6.837	8.379	5.746	6.384	4.518	5.215	5.469
I+M		**6.432**	**6.874**	**8.481**	5.834	6.485	**4.600**	**5.445**	**6.222**
I+S+M		6.429	6.852	8.435	**5.873**	**6.510**	4.571	5.369	6.125
Saliency(S)	AUC↑	0.494	0.560	0.447	0.494	0.352	0.426	0.691	0.607
Motion(M)		0.664	0.697	0.742	0.738	0.779	0.664	0.729	0.643
Image(I)		**0.970**	**0.973**	**0.988**	**0.962**	0.963	0.932	0.956	0.957
I+S		0.969	**0.973**	**0.988**	0.961	0.963	0.933	0.957	0.956
I+M		**0.970**	0.972	**0.988**	**0.962**	**0.964**	0.935	**0.961**	**0.964**
I+S+M		0.969	**0.973**	**0.988**	**0.962**	**0.964**	**0.936**	0.960	**0.964**
Saliency(S)	KL↓	4.375	4.289	4.517	4.235	4.744	4.680	3.774	3.868
Motion(M)		13.097	10.638	8.312	9.151	9.133	12.173	10.810	12.853
Image(I)		1.304	1.261	0.834	1.609	1.464	1.985	1.711	1.749
I+S		1.301	1.260	0.834	1.613	1.470	1.995	1.709	1.727
I+M		**1.294**	**1.257**	**0.832**	1.593	1.438	**1.959**	**1.622**	1.512
I+S+M		1.299	1.260	0.835	**1.592**	**1.437**	1.961	1.645	**1.510**
Saliency(S)	CC↑	−0.009	−0.023	−0.033	−0.008	−0.035	−0.048	0.065	0.048
Motion(M)		0.205	0.099	0.077	0.125	0.190	0.092	0.132	0.105
Image(I)		0.583	0.588	0.705	0.505	0.558	0.439	0.481	0.483
I+S		0.583	0.588	0.702	0.503	0.555	0.436	0.479	0.488
I+M		**0.584**	**0.591**	**0.706**	0.509	**0.564**	**0.441**	**0.499**	**0.543**
I+S+M		**0.584**	0.589	0.704	**0.511**	0.562	0.440	0.492	0.541

We encourage readers to view the video demo of the prediction results at https://www.youtube.com/watch?v=-zTX9VFSFME. Example predictions for all games are shown in Fig. 3 where the predicted gaze saliency map and ground truth human gaze positions are overlayed on top of the game frames. It is worth noticing that the prediction could be multimodal as in Figs. 3d and 3g, indicating the task requires divided attention in these situations which our model successfully captured.

Sample Efficiency. In imitation learning tasks, sample efficiency is a major concern since human demonstration data could be expensive to collect. The proposed AGIL framework cannot be claimed to have an advantage over previous imitation learning or RL approaches if learning the attention model requires

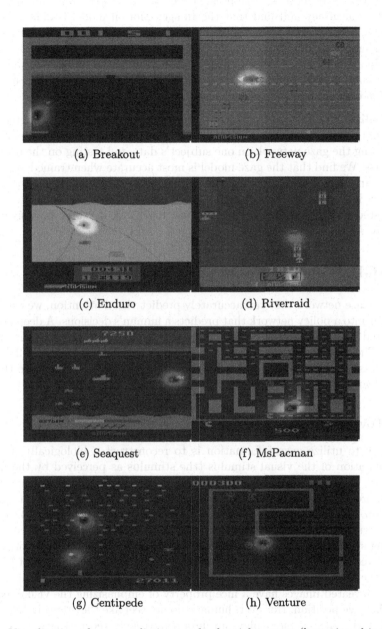

(a) Breakout   (b) Freeway

(c) Enduro   (d) Riverraid

(e) Seaquest   (f) MsPacman

(g) Centipede   (h) Venture

Fig. 3. Visualization of gaze prediction results for eight games (best viewed in color). The solid red dot indicates the ground truth human gaze position. The heatmap shows the model's prediction as a saliency map, computed using the Image+Motion gaze network. (Color figure online)

significantly more data. We study the effect of varying training sample size on prediction accuracy and find that the Image+Motion model is able to achieve high AUC values (above 0.88 for MsPacman and above 0.94 for 7 other games) with a single trial of human gaze data (15-minute)–although additional data can still help. The learning curves plotted against training sample size for all games can be found in Appendix 2. Therefore, training the gaze network does not incur a burden on sample size for the given task.

Generalization Across Subjects. Do human subjects exhibit different gaze behaviors when performing the same task? This question is further investigated by training the gaze network on one subject's data and testing on the others for all games. We find that the gaze model is most accurate when trained and tested on the same subject. When tested on a different subject, the average prediction accuracy loss, in terms of correlation coefficient, is 0.091 comparing to trained and tested on the same subject (0.387 vs. 0.478). A detailed analysis can be found in Appendix 3.

5   AGIL: Policy Network with Attention

Given a gaze network that can accurately predict visual attention, we can incorporate it into a policy network that predicts a human's decisions. A deep network is trained with supervised learning to classify human actions given the current frame. The baseline network architecture follows the Deep Q-Network [28]. Here, we discuss two models that incorporate visual attention information to the imitation learning process.

5.1   Foveated Rendering

One way to utilize gaze information is to reconstruct a biologically plausible representation of the visual stimulus (the stimulus as perceived by the human subject). We hypothesize that training the network with realistic retinal images may improve prediction, since these images are closer to the true human representation. We fed the visual angle of the game screen (44.58×28.50), a single ground truth human gaze position, and the original image into the Space Variant Imaging system [32]. The algorithm provides a biologically plausible simulation of foveated retinal images as shown in Fig. 1b by down-sampling and blurring the image according to the distribution of ganglion cells on the human retina.

The foveated images have a nice property of emphasizing the visual features near the gaze position. However, humans do not feel like they perceive the world like Figs. 1b, since memory plays an important role in reconstructing the visual world. A foveated image highlights the visual information being perceived at the moment, but it may lose other task-relevant information stored in memory. To compensate for this effect, we feed both the original image and the foveated image into a two-channel deep network. The model is referred as the Foveated model.

The prediction results are shown in Table 2. As expected, the Foveated model consistently achieves better or comparable performance over the plain imitation model.

5.2 Masking with Attention

The foveated rendering approach directly incorporates human ground truth gaze into imitation learning. However, we argue that using the gaze heatmap learned by the gaze network might be better for two reasons: (1) While the ground truth gaze position is a single location, the human attention may be distributed on multiple objects (e.g., in Figs. 3d, e, and g); (2) The ground truth human gaze could be noisy but the predicted attention is accurate and clean. In addition, when the agent actually plays the game the ground truth human gaze will not be available.

We treat the predicted gaze heatmap as a saliency mask and multiply the mask with image frame element-wise. Similar to foveated rendering, the mask has the effect of emphasizing the stimulus being attended. For the same reason as in the Foveated model, we add a second channel that also takes the original image as the input and call this the Attention model. The final architecture is shown in Fig. 4. The prediction results are shown in Table 2. It is evident that the incorporating attention model has an advantage over the baseline. In particular, results for the four games that often require multitasking show large improvements: 15.6% on Seaquest, 16% on MsPacman, 5.1% on Centipede, and 6.6% on Venture. We conclude that including gaze information–either by foveated rendering or masking–can significantly improves the performance in terms of policy matching accuracy.

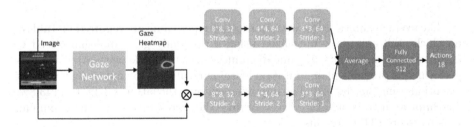

Fig. 4. The policy network architecture for imitating human actions. The top channel takes in the current image frame and the bottom channel takes in the masked image which is an element-wise product of the original image and predicted gaze saliency map by the gaze network. We then average the output of the two channels.

6   Evaluating the Learned Policy

The behavior matching accuracy is not the sole performance evaluation metric, since the ultimate goal of imitation learning is to learn a good policy to actually perform the task. When playing the games, the AGIL framework takes game images as input to the trained gaze network, and passes gaze network's predicted attention mask to the policy network to make decisions. The agent chooses an action a probabilistically using a softmax function with Gibbs (Boltzmann) distribution according to policy network's prediction $P(a)$:

$$\pi(a) = \frac{\exp(\eta P(a))}{\sum_{a' \in \mathcal{A}} \exp(\eta P(a'))} \qquad (2)$$

where $\mathcal{A}$ denotes the set of all possible actions, $\exp(.)$ denotes the exponential function, and the temperature parameter η is set to 1.

Table 2. Percentage accuracy (mean $\pm$ standard deviation) in predicting human actions across eight games using different models. Random prediction baseline: 5.56. The model in Fig. 4 (+Attention) yields the best prediction accuracy.

	Imitation	+Foveated	+Attention
Breakout	81.5 ± 0.3	84.2 ± 0.1	$\mathbf{86.2 \pm 0.2}$
Freeway	$\mathbf{96.7 \pm 0.0}$	96.4 ± 0.1	96.4 ± 0.2
Enduro	60.6 ± 0.4	60.5 ± 0.4	$\mathbf{61.9 \pm 0.3}$
Riverraid	$\mathbf{72.5 \pm 0.3}$	72.4 ± 0.4	$\mathbf{72.5 \pm 0.4}$
Seaquest	46.0 ± 1.8	51.4 ± 1.0	$\mathbf{61.6 \pm 0.2}$
MsPacman	54.6 ± 1.0	65.1 ± 1.0	$\mathbf{70.6 \pm 0.3}$
Centipede	61.9 ± 0.2	64.8 ± 0.3	$\mathbf{67.0 \pm 0.3}$
Venture	46.7 ± 0.2	48.7 ± 0.1	$\mathbf{53.3 \pm 0.3}$

The average games scores over 100 episodes per game are reported in Table 3, in which each episode is initialized using a randomly generated game seed to ensure enough variability in game dynamics [13]. Our model with attention outperforms the previous plain imitation learning results of [15] and the one without attention using our dataset. The improvement over the latter is 3.4% to 1143.8%. The improvement is minor for Freeway since the scores are close to the maximum possible score (34.0) for this task.

An advantage of imitation learning comparing to RL is its sample efficiency. We show performance of deep Q-learning [28] implemented using the standard OpenAI DQN benchmark [7] trained for the same sample size (training sample size for each game can be found in Appendix 1). It is evident that DQN's performance is not at the same level with imitation learning given the same amount of training data. Remarkably, after 200 million training samples (corresponds to about 38.58 days of play experience when playing at 60 Hz), our method is still better than or comparable to DQN in four games: Freeway, Enduro, Centipede, and Venture. In fact, our method achieves the state-of-the-art result on Centipede comparing to any RL methods or their combinations [14].

Table 3. A comparison of game scores (mean ± standard deviation) between plain imitation learning from a previous work [15], plain imitation learning using our dataset, AGIL, and deep reinforcement learning (DQN) [7,28]. The DQN scores are recorded at two different training sample sizes: one at the same sample size with our dataset (114K-223K depends on the game) and the other one at 200 million samples. The "Improvement" column indicates AGIL's performance increase over the plain imitation learning using our dataset.

	Imitation [15]	Imitation our data	AGIL our data	Improvment	DQN Same N	DQN N = 200M
Breakout	3.5	1.6 ± 1.2	**19.9 ± 14.1**	1143.8%	1.52	401.2
Freeway	22.7	29.6 ± 1.2	**30.6 ± 1.2**	3.4%	0	30.3
Enduro	134.8	239.8 ± 90.8	**295.7 ± 99.5**	23.3%	0	301.8
Riverraid	2148.5	2419.7 ± 655.8	**3338.5 ± 1485.9**	38.0%	1510	8316
Seaquest	195.6	252.2 ± 109.2	**788.9 ± 609.2**	212.8%	100	5286
MsPacman	692.4	1069.9 ± 810.5	**1755.1 ± 1000.9**	64.0%	230	2311
Centipede	N/A	5543.0 ± 3509.5	**9515.4 ± 5626.8**	71.7%	2080	8309
Venture	N/A	363.0 ± 133.2	**468.0 ± 176.6**	28.9%	0	380.0

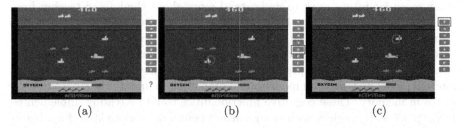

(a)   (b)   (c)

Fig. 5. Human gaze information helps the learning agent correctly infer the underlying reason for the chosen action. The red circles indicate human teacher's gaze position.

Why does the learned visual attention model improve action prediction accuracy and task performance? First, attention highlights task-relevant visual features in a high-dimensional state space, even though the features may only occupy a few pixels in that space, as observed in Fig. 3. Hence, attention can be seen as a feature selection mechanism that biases the policy network to focus on the selected features. Second, attention could help to identify and disambiguate the goal of current action when multiple task-relevant objects are present. For example, in Fig. 5b and c the gaze indicates that the goal of current action involves the enemy to the left or above the yellow submarine. The corresponding actions would be moving left for the first case and moving up for the second. The two enemies are visually identical hence the learning agent cannot predict the correct action without gaze information – an issue further exacerbated by convolutional layers of the network due to their spatial invariant nature. For these reasons, modeling human attention helps the agent infer the correct decision state of the human teacher and understand the underlying reason for that decision.

7   Conclusion and Future Work

A research question for imitation learning in visuomotor tasks is: what should be learned from the human teacher? The agent could learn the policy (behavior cloning), the reward function (inverse RL), or some high-level cognitive functionality such as visual attention. To our knowledge, the proposed AGIL framework represents the first attempt to learn visual attention for imitation learning tasks. Through modeling the human teacher's visual attention the student agent gains a deeper understanding of *why* a particular decision is made by the teacher. We show that it is feasible to learn an accurate task-driven human visual attention model, and that combining this with deep imitation learning yields promising results.

The high accuracy achieved in predicting gaze in our work implies that, given a cognitively demanding visuomotor task, human gaze can be modeled accurately using an end-to-end learning algorithm. This suggests that popular deep saliency models could be used to learn visual attention, given task-driven data.

In this student-teacher paradigm, a better learning framework is possible when we have more knowledge on both the student and the teacher. There is much room for future work to understand more about the human teacher from a psychological perspective. Due to human visuomotor reaction time, action a_t may not be conditioned on the image and gaze at time t, but on images and gazes several hundreds milliseconds prior. More importantly, the human memory system allows for states of previously attended objects to be preserved, and an internal model may perform model-based prediction to update the environmental states in memory. These cognitive functionalities could be readily implemented by deep networks models, such as a recurrent neural network to allow for a better prediction of human actions.

The results of [28] have demonstrated the effectiveness of end-to-end learning of visuomotor tasks, where the DQN excels at games that involve a single task. However, for games such as Seaquest and MsPacman–which typically involve multiple tasks–the performance is still below human levels, even though human reaction time was limited in their setting. In addition, DQN takes millions of samples to train. The above issues could be potentially alleviated by combining AGIL and deep RL where attention model can help extract features to speedup learning and to indicate task priority. By making our dataset available we encourage future research towards the combined approach.

Acknowledgement. We would like to thank Wilson Geisler's lab for providing data collection tools. We would like to thank Calen Walshe and Prabhat Nagarajan for helpful discussions and suggestions. The work is supported by NIH Grant EY05729, NIH Grant T32 EY21462-6, NSF Grant CNS-1624378, and Google AR/VR Research Award.

References

1. Argall, B.D., Chernova, S., Veloso, M., Browning, B.: A survey of robot learning from demonstration. Robot. Auton. Syst. **57**(5), 469–483 (2009)
2. Baldauf, D., Wolf, M., Deubel, H.: Deployment of visual attention before sequences of goal-directed hand movements. Vis. Res. **46**(26), 4355–4374 (2006)
3. Bellemare, M.G., Naddaf, Y., Veness, J., Bowling, M.: The arcade learning environment: an evaluation platform for general agents. J. Artif. Intell. Res. **47**, 253–279 (2012)
4. Bylinskii, Z., Judd, T., Oliva, A., Torralba, A., Durand, F.: What do different evaluation metrics tell us about saliency models? arXiv preprint arXiv:1604.03605 (2016)
5. Bylinskii, Z., Recasens, A., Borji, A., Oliva, A., Torralba, A., Durand, F.: Where should saliency models look next? In: Leibe, B., Matas, J., Sebe, N., Welling, M. (eds.) ECCV 2016. LNCS, vol. 9909, pp. 809–824. Springer, Cham (2016). https://doi.org/10.1007/978-3-319-46454-1_49
6. Cruz Jr., G.V., Du, Y., Taylor, M.E.: Pre-training neural networks with human demonstrations for deep reinforcement learning. arXiv preprint arXiv:1709.04083 (2017)
7. Dhariwal, P., et al.: Openai baselines (2017). https://github.com/openai/baselines
8. Diaz, G., Cooper, J., Rothkopf, C., Hayhoe, M.: Saccades to future ball location reveal memory-based prediction in a virtual-reality interception task. J. Vis. **13**(1), 20–20 (2013)
9. Eldar, E., Cohen, J.D., Niv, Y.: The effects of neural gain on attention and learning. Nat. Neurosci. **16**(8), 1146–1153 (2013)
10. Farnebäck, G.: Two-frame motion estimation based on polynomial expansion. In: Bigun, J., Gustavsson, T. (eds.) SCIA 2003. LNCS, vol. 2749, pp. 363–370. Springer, Heidelberg (2003). https://doi.org/10.1007/3-540-45103-X_50
11. Gregor, K., Danihelka, I., Graves, A., Rezende, D., Wierstra, D.: Draw: a recurrent neural network for image generation. In: Proceedings of the 32nd International Conference on Machine Learning (ICML 2015), pp. 1462–1471 (2015)
12. Hayhoe, M., Ballard, D.: Eye movements in natural behavior. Trends Cogn. Sci. **9**(4), 188–194 (2005)
13. Henderson, P., Islam, R., Bachman, P., Pineau, J., Precup, D., Meger, D.: Deep reinforcement learning that matters. arXiv preprint arXiv:1709.06560 (2017)
14. Hessel, M., et al.: Rainbow: Combining improvements in deep reinforcement learning. arXiv preprint arXiv:1710.02298 (2017)
15. Hester, T., et al.: Deep Q-learning from demonstrations. In: Association for the Advancement of Artificial Intelligence (AAAI) (2018)
16. Holroyd, C.B., Coles, M.G.: The neural basis of human error processing: reinforcement learning, dopamine, and the error-related negativity. Psychol. Rev. **109**(4), 679 (2002)
17. Itti, L., Koch, C., Niebur, E.: A model of saliency-based visual attention for rapid scene analysis. IEEE Trans. Pattern Anal. Mach. Intell. **20**(11), 1254–1259 (1998)
18. Jaderberg, M., Simonyan, K., Zisserman, A., et al.: Spatial transformer networks. In: Advances in Neural Information Processing Systems, pp. 2017–2025 (2015)
19. Jiang, M., Huang, S., Duan, J., Zhao, Q.: Salicon: saliency in context. In: Proceedings of the IEEE Conference on Computer Vision and Pattern Recognition, pp. 1072–1080 (2015)

20. Johnson, L., Sullivan, B., Hayhoe, M., Ballard, D.: Predicting human visuomotor behaviour in a driving task. Philos. Trans. R. Soc. Lond. B: Biol. Sci. **369**(1636), 20130044 (2014)
21. Krafka, K., et al.: Eye tracking for everyone. In: Proceedings of the IEEE Conference on Computer Vision and Pattern Recognition, pp. 2176–2184 (2016)
22. Kruthiventi, S.S., Ayush, K., Babu, R.V.: Deepfix: a fully convolutional neural network for predicting human eye fixations. IEEE Trans. Image Process. **26**(9), 4446–4456 (2017)
23. Leong, Y.C., Radulescu, A., Daniel, R., DeWoskin, V., Niv, Y.: Dynamic interaction between reinforcement learning and attention in multidimensional environments. Neuron **93**(2), 451–463 (2017)
24. Levine, S., Finn, C., Darrell, T., Abbeel, P.: End-to-end training of deep visuomotor policies. J. Mach. Learn. Res. **17**(1), 1334–1373 (2016)
25. Li, G., Yu, Y.: Visual saliency based on multiscale deep features. In: Proceedings of the IEEE Conference on Computer Vision and Pattern Recognition, pp. 5455–5463 (2015)
26. Marat, S., Phuoc, T.H., Granjon, L., Guyader, N., Pellerin, D., Guérin-Dugué, A.: Modelling spatio-temporal saliency to predict gaze direction for short videos. Int. J. Comput. Vis. **82**(3), 231 (2009)
27. Mnih, V., Heess, N., Graves, A., et al.: Recurrent models of visual attention. In: Advances in Neural Information Processing Systems, pp. 2204–2212 (2014)
28. Mnih, V., et al.: Human-level control through deep reinforcement learning. Nature **518**(7540), 529–533 (2015)
29. Mousavi, S., Borji, A., Mozayani, N.: Learning to predict where to look in interactive environments using deep recurrent Q-learning. arXiv preprint arXiv:1612.05753 (2016)
30. Nair, A., McGrew, B., Andrychowicz, M., Zaremba, W., Abbeel, P.: Overcoming exploration in reinforcement learning with demonstrations. arXiv preprint arXiv:1709.10089 (2017)
31. Palazzi, A., Abati, D., Calderara, S., Solera, F., Cucchiara, R.: Predicting the driver's focus of attention: the dr (eye) ve project. arXiv preprint arXiv:1705.03854 (2017)
32. Perry, J.S., Geisler, W.S.: Gaze-contingent real-time simulation of arbitrary visual fields. In: Electronic Imaging 2002, pp. 57–69. International Society for Optics and Photonics (2002)
33. Peters, R.J., Itti, L.: Beyond bottom-up: Incorporating task-dependent influences into a computational model of spatial attention. In: IEEE Conference on Computer Vision and Pattern Recognition, 2007. CVPR 2007, pp. 1–8. IEEE (2007)
34. Riche, N., Duvinage, M., Mancas, M., Gosselin, B., Dutoit, T.: Saliency and human fixations: State-of-the-art and study of comparison metrics. In: Proceedings of the IEEE International Conference on Computer Vision, pp. 1153–1160 (2013)
35. Roelfsema, P.R., van Ooyen, A.: Attention-gated reinforcement learning of internal representations for classification. Neural Comput. **17**(10), 2176–2214 (2005)
36. Rothkopf, C.A., Ballard, D.H., Hayhoe, M.M.: Task and context determine where you look. J. Vis. **7**(14), 16–16 (2007)
37. Silver, D., et al.: Mastering the game of go with deep neural networks and tree search. Nature **529**(7587), 484–489 (2016)
38. Silver, D., et al.: Mastering the game of go without human knowledge. Nature **550**(7676), 354 (2017)
39. Tatler, B.W., Hayhoe, M.M., Land, M.F., Ballard, D.H.: Eye guidance in natural vision: reinterpreting salience. J. Vis. **11**(5), 5–5 (2011)

40. Wang, Z., Schaul, T., Hessel, M., Hasselt, H., Lanctot, M., Freitas, N.: Dueling network architectures for deep reinforcement learning. In: International Conference on Machine Learning, pp. 1995–2003 (2016)
41. Xu, K., et al.: Show, attend and tell: Neural image caption generation with visual attention. In: International Conference on Machine Learning, pp. 2048–2057 (2015)
42. Zhao, R., Ouyang, W., Li, H., Wang, X.: Saliency detection by multi-context deep learning. In: Proceedings of the IEEE Conference on Computer Vision and Pattern Recognition, pp. 1265–1274 (2015)
43. Zhu, Y., Groth, O., Bernstein, M., Fei-Fei, L.: Visual7w: grounded question answering in images. In: Proceedings of the IEEE Conference on Computer Vision and Pattern Recognition, pp. 4995–5004 (2016)

Deep Imbalanced Attribute Classification Using Visual Attention Aggregation

Nikolaos Sarafianos$^{(\boxtimes)}$, Xiang Xu, and Ioannis A. Kakadiaris

Computational Biomedicine Lab, University of Houston, Houston, USA
{nsarafia,xxu18,ikakadia}@central.uh.edu

Abstract. For many computer vision applications, such as image description and human identification, recognizing the visual attributes of humans is an essential yet challenging problem. Its challenges originate from its multi-label nature, the large underlying class imbalance and the lack of spatial annotations. Existing methods follow either a computer vision approach while failing to account for class imbalance, or explore machine learning solutions, which disregard the spatial and semantic relations that exist in the images. With that in mind, we propose an effective method that extracts and aggregates visual attention masks at different scales. We introduce a loss function to handle class imbalance both at class and at an instance level and further demonstrate that penalizing attention masks with high prediction variance accounts for the weak supervision of the attention mechanism. By identifying and addressing these challenges, we achieve state-of-the-art results with a simple attention mechanism in both PETA and WIDER-Attribute datasets without additional context or side information.

Keywords: Visual attributes · Deep imbalanced learning
Visual attention

1 Introduction

We set out to develop a method that, given an image of a human, predicts its visual attributes. We posed the following questions: (i) what are the challenges of this problem? (ii) what have other people done? and (iii) how should a simple yet effective solution to this problem look like? Human attributes are imbalanced in nature. Bald individuals with a mustache wearing glasses are 14 to 43 times less likely to appear in the CelebA dataset [1] compared to people without these characteristics. Large-scale imbalanced datasets can lead to biased models, optimized to favor the majority classes while failing to identify the subtle discriminant features that are required to recognize the under-represented classes. Setting the class imbalance aside, an additional challenge is identifying which areas in the

---

Electronic supplementary material The online version of this chapter (https:// doi.org/10.1007/978-3-030-01252-6_42) contains supplementary material, which is available to authorized users.

V. Ferrari et al. (Eds.): ECCV 2018, LNCS 11215, pp. 708–725, 2018.
https://doi.org/10.1007/978-3-030-01252-6_42

image provide class-discriminant information. Giving emphasis to the upper part of an image, where the face is located, for attributes such as "glasses" and to the bottom part for attributes such as "long pants" can increase the recognition performance as well as the interpretability of our models [2]. This challenge is usually addressed using visual attention techniques that output saliency maps. However, in the human attribute estimation domain, attention ground-truth annotations are not available to learn such spatial attributions.

Learning from imbalanced data is a well-studied problem in machine learning and computer vision. Traditional solutions include over-sampling the minority classes [3,4] or under-sampling the majority classes [5] to compensate for the imbalanced class ratio and cost-sensitive learning [6] where classification errors are penalized differently. Such approaches have been extensively used in the past but they suffer from some limitations. For example, over-sampling introduces redundant information making the models prone to over-fitting, whereas under-sampling may remove valuable discriminative information. Recent works with deep convolutional neural networks [7–9] introduced a sampling procedure of triplets, quintuplets or clusters of samples that satisfy some properties in the feature-space and used them to regularize their models. However, sampling triplets is a computationally expensive procedure and the characteristics of the triplets in a batch-mode setup might vary significantly.

Fig. 1. Visual attribute classification challenges from left to right: (i) the face mask is under the head, (ii) are there sunglasses in the image? (iii) extreme pose variation, and (iv) large class imbalance.

Modern visual attribute classification techniques rely either on contextual information [10,11], side information [12], curriculum learning strategies [13] or visual attention mechanisms [14] to accomplish their task. Although context and side information can increase the recognition accuracy, we believe that a simple solution should not rely on those. We argue that a solution to the deep imbalanced attribute classification problem should: (i) extract discriminative information, (ii) leverage visual information that is specific for each attribute, and (iii) handle class imbalance. Since, to the best of our knowledge, there is no method available with such characteristics, we developed an approach that uses (i) a pre-trained network for feature extraction, (ii) a weakly-supervised visual attention mechanism at multiple scales for attribute specific information, and (iii) a loss function that handles class imbalance and focuses on hard and uncertain samples. By simplifying the problem and addressing each one of its challenges, we were able to achieve state-of-the-art results in both WIDER-Attribute [10] and PETA [15] datasets, which are the most widely used in this domain.

In the deep learning era, most models are overly-complicated for what they aspire to achieve. Carefully developed, well established, accurate baselines are essential to measure our progress over time. Towards this direction, there have been a few works recently with well-performing yet simple baseline approaches in the fields of 3D human pose estimation [16], image classification [17], and person re-identification [18]. Our main contribution is the design and analysis of an end-to-end neural-network architecture that can be easily reproduced, is easy to train and achieves state-of-the-art visual attribute classification results. This performance improvement originates from extracting and aggregating visual attention masks at different scales as well as establishing a loss function for imbalanced attributes as well as hard or uncertain samples. Through experiments, ablation studies and qualitative results we demonstrate that:

- A simple visual attention mechanism with only attribute-level supervision (no ground-truth attention masks) can improve the classification performance by guiding the network to focus its resources to those spatial parts that contain information relevant to the input image.
- Extracting visual attention masks from more than one stage of the network and aggregating the information at a score-level enables the model to learn more discriminant feature representations.
- Accounting for class imbalance is essential during learning from large datasets. While assigning prior class weights can alleviate part of this problem, we observed that a weighted-variant of the focal loss works consistently better by handling imbalanced classes and at the same time focusing on hard examples.
- Due to the lack of strong supervision, the attention masks result in attribute predictions with high variance across subsequent epochs. To prevent this from destabilizing training and degrading the performance we introduce an attention loss function, which penalizes predictions that originate from attention masks with high prediction variance.

Since this work aspires to serve as a bar in the visual attribute classification domain that future works may improve upon, we identify some sources of error that still prevail, and point out future research directions to address them that require further exploration.

2   Related Work

Visual Attributes: When we are interested in providing a description of an object or a human, we tend to rely on visual attributes to accomplish this task. From early works [19–21] to more recent ones [10–12,14,22,23] visual attributes have been studied extensively in computer vision. Due to its commercial applications and the abundance of available data, the clothing domain has received significant attention recently with methods ranging from transfer learning and domain adaptation [24–26] to retrieval [27] and forecasting [28]. Some works rely on contextual information [10,11], or leverage side information (e.g., viewpoint) to improve the recognition performance [12]. Others [29], assume the existence of a predefined connection between parts and attributes (e.g., hats are usually above the head and in the upper 20% of the image) which does not always hold true as depicted in Fig. 1. Zhu *et al.* [14] proposed to learn spatial regularizations using an attention mechanism on a final ResNet [30] representation. Their attention module outputs an attention tensor per attribute which is then fed to a multi-label classification sub-network. However, none of the aforementioned approaches consider the class imbalance that exists in such datasets, which prevents them from accurately recognizing under-represented attributes such as wearing sunglasses.

Visual Attention: Visual attention can be interpreted as a mechanism of guiding the network to focus its resources on those spatial parts that contain information relevant to the input image. In computer vision applications, visual attribution is usually implemented as a gating function represented with a sigmoid activation or a spatial softmax and is placed on top of one or more convolutional layers with small kernels extracting high-level information. Several interesting works have appeared recently that demonstrate the efficiency of visual attention [14,31–37]. For example, the harmonious attention of Li *et al.* [33] consists of four subparts that extract hard-regional attention, soft-spatial, and channel attention to perform person re-identification. Deciding where to place the attention mechanism in the network is a topic of active research with several single-scale and multi-scale attention techniques in the literature. Das *et al.* [38], opted for a single attention module, whereas others [31,36,39] extract saliency heatmaps at multiple-scales to build richer feature representations.

Deep Imbalanced Classification: Two works that address this problem in an attribute classification framework are the large margin local embedding (LMLE) method [7] and the class rectification loss (CRL) [9]. In LMLE, quintuplets were sampled that preserve locality across clusters and discrimination between classes and a new loss was introduced. Dong *et al.* [9] demonstrated that a careful hard mining of triplets within the batch acts as an effective regularization which improves the recognition performance of imbalanced attributes. However, LMLE is prohibitively computationally expensive as it comprises an alternating scheme for cluster refinement and classification. In a follow-up work [8] the authors address this limitation by replacing the quintuplets with clusters. CRL on the other hand, samples triplets within the batch, complicating the training process significantly, as the convergence and the performance heavily rely on the triplet selection. In addition, CRL adds a fully-connected layer for each attribute before the final classification layer, which increases the number of parameters that need to be learned. Both methods approach class imbalance purely as a machine learning problem without focusing on the visual traits of the images that correspond to these attributes. Class imbalance arises also in detection problems [31,40], where the foreground object (or face) covers a small part of the image. A simple yet very effective solution is focal loss [40], which uses a weighting scheme at an instance-level within the batch to penalize hard misclassified samples and assign near-zero weights to easily classified samples.

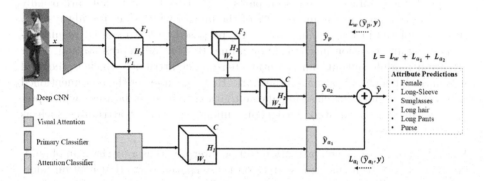

Fig. 2. Given an image of a human we aspire to predict C visual attributes. Visual attention mechanisms are placed at two different levels of the network to identify spatial information that is relevant to each attribute with only attribute-level supervision. The predictions from the attention and the primary classifiers are aggregated at a score level and the whole network is trained end-to-end with two loss functions: $\mathcal{L}_w$ that handles class imbalance and hard samples and $\mathcal{L}_a$ which penalizes attention masks with high prediction variance.

3   Methodology

3.1   Multi-scale Visual Attention and Aggregation

Given an image of a human our goal is to predict its visual attributes. Specifically, our input consists of an image x along with its corresponding labels $y = [y^1, y^2, \ldots, y^C]^T$ where C is the total number of attributes and y^c a binary label that indicates the presence or absence of a particular attribute in the image. In this work, we experimented with both ResNets [30] and DenseNets [41] as backbone architectures and thus, we opted for the representations after the third and the fourth stage/block of layers. The concept of extracting attention information can be expanded to more spatial resolutions/scales besides two at the expense of learning additional parameters. We will thus refer to the first part of the networks (up to stage/block three) as $\phi_1(\cdot)$ and to the part from there and until the classifier as $\phi_2(\cdot)$. In our primary network, which unless otherwise specified is a ResNet-101 architecture (deep CNN module in Fig. 2), given an image x, we obtain three-dimensional feature representations:

$$k_1(x) = \phi_1(x), \quad k_1(x) \in \mathcal{R}^{H_1 \times W_1 \times F_1},$$
$$k_2(x) = \phi_2(k_1(x)), \quad k_2(x) \in \mathcal{R}^{H_2 \times W_2 \times F_2}. \tag{1}$$

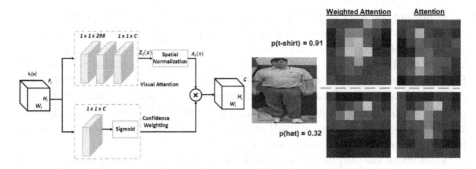

Fig. 3. Our attention mechanism (upper-left) maps feature representations of spatial resolution $H_i \times W_i$ and F_i channels to C channels (one for each attribute) with the same size which are then spatially normalized to force the model to focus its resources to the most relevant region of the image. The attention masks are weighted by attribute confidences (lower-left) which as we demonstrate on the right, apply larger weights to the attribute-corresponding areas. For example, more emphasis is given in the middle-upper part when looking for a t-shirt and to the upper part of the image when looking for a hat (even when it is not there).

For 224×224 images the attention mechanism is placed on features of channel size F_i equal to $1,024$ and $2,048$ with spatial resolutions $H_i \times W_i$ equal to 14×14 and 7×7, respectively. Finally, the classifier of the primary network outputs logits $\hat{y}_p(x) = W_p k_2(x) + b_p$ where (W_p, b_p) are the parameters of the classification layer.

With simplicity in mind, our attention mechanism, depicted in Fig. 3, consists of three stacked convolutional layers (along with batch-normalization and ReLU) with a kernel size equal to one. Due to the multi-label nature of the problem, the last convolutional layer maps the channels to the C number of classes (i.e., attributes). This is different than most attention works (with one label per image) that extract saliency maps of the same spatial/channel size of the given feature representation. The attribute-specific attention maps $z_{h,w}^c$ are then spatially normalized to $a_{h,w}^c$ using a spatial softmax operation:

$$a_{h,w}^c = \frac{\exp(z_{h,w}^c)}{\sum_{h,w} \exp(z_{h,w}^c)}, \tag{2}$$

where h, w correspond to the height and width dimension and c to the corresponding attribute label. The spatial softmax operation results in attention masks with the property $\sum_{h,w} a_{h,w}^c = 1$ for each attribute c and is used to force the model to focus its resources to the most relevant region of the image. We will refer to the attention mechanism comprising the three convolutional layers as $\mathcal{A}$ and thus, for each spatial resolution i we first obtain unnormalized attentions $Z_i(x) = \mathcal{A}(k_i(x))$, which are then spatially normalized using Eq. (2) resulting in normalized attention masks $A_i(x)$.

Following the work of Zhu *et al.* [14], we concurrently pass the feature representations to a single convolutional layer with C channels (same as the number of classes) followed by a sigmoid function. The role of this branch is to assign weights to the attention maps based on label confidences and avoid learning from the attention masks when the label is absent. The weighted attention maps reflect both attribute information at different spatial locations and label confidences. We observed in our experiments that this confidence-weighting branch boosts the performance by a small amount and helps the attention mechanism learn better saliency heatmaps (Fig. 3 right).

Combining the output saliency masks from different scales can be done either at a prediction level (i.e., averaging the logits) or at a feature level [42]. However, aggregating the attention masks at a feature level provided consistently inferior performance. We believe that this is because the two attention mechanisms extract masks that give emphasis to different spatial regions which, when added together, fail to provide the classifier with attribute-discriminative information. Thus, we opted for the former approach and fed each confidence-weighted attention mask to a classifier to obtain logits $\hat{y}_{a_i}$ of the attention module i. The final attribute predictions of dimensionality $1 \times C$ for an image x are then defined as $\hat{y} = (\hat{y}_p + \hat{y}_{a_1} + \hat{y}_{a_2})/3$.

3.2 Deep Imbalanced Classification

Using the output predictions of the primary model $\hat{y}_p$ which have the same dimensionality $1 \times C$ (i.e., one for each attribute), a straight-forward approach adopted by Zhu *et al.* [14] is to train the whole network using the binary cross-entropy loss $\mathcal{L}_b$ as:

$$\mathcal{L}_b(\hat{y}_p, y) = -\sum_{c=1}^{C} \log(\sigma(\hat{y}_p^c))y^c + \log(1 - \sigma(\hat{y}_p^c))(1 - y^c), \tag{3}$$

where $(\hat{y}_p^c, y^c)$ correspond to the logit and ground-truth labels for attribute c, and $\sigma(\cdot)$ is the sigmoid activation function. However, such a loss function ignores completely the class imbalance. Aiming to alleviate this problem both at a class- and at an instance-level, we propose to use for our primary model a weighted-variant of the focal loss [40] defined as:

$$\mathcal{L}_w(\hat{y}_p, y) = -\sum_{c=1}^{C} w_c \Big((1 - \sigma(\hat{y}_p^c))^\gamma \log\left(\sigma(\hat{y}_p^c)\right) y^c + \sigma(\hat{y}_p^c)^\gamma \log(1 - \sigma(\hat{y}_p^c))(1 - y^c) \Big), \tag{4}$$

where γ is a hyper-parameter (set to 0.5), which controls the instance-level weighting based on the current prediction giving emphasis to the hard misclassified samples, and $w_c = e^{-a_c}$, where a_c the prior class distribution of the cth attribute as in [12].

Unlike the face attention networks [31], which learn the attention masks based on ground-truth facial bounding boxes, in the human attribute domain such information is not available. This means that the attention masks will be learned based on attribute-level supervisions y. The attention masks of dimensionality $H_i \times W_i \times F_i$ are fed to a classifier which outputs logits $\hat{y}_{a_i}$ for each spatial resolution i. To account for the weak supervision of the attention network, we decided to focus on the attention masks with high prediction variance. Similar to the work of Chang et al. [43], after some burn-in epochs in which $\mathcal{L}_b$ is used, we start collecting the history H of the predictions $p_H(y_s|x_s)$ for the sth sample and compute the standard deviation across time for each sample within the batch:

$$\widehat{std}_s(H) = \sqrt{\widehat{var}\big(p_{H^{t-1}}(y_s|x_s)\big) + \frac{\widehat{var}\big(p_{H^{t-1}}(y_s|x_s)\big)^2}{|H_s^{t-1}| - 1}}, \tag{5}$$

where t corresponds to the current epoch, $\widehat{var}$ to the prediction variance estimated in history H^{t-1} and $|H_s^{t-1}|$ the number of stored prediction probabilities. The loss for the attention-masks at level i with attribute-level supervision for each sample s is defined as:

$$\mathcal{L}_{a_i}(\hat{y}_{a_i}, y) = \big(1 + \widehat{std}_s(H)\big)\mathcal{L}_b(\hat{y}_{a_i}, y) . \tag{6}$$

Attention mask predictions with high standard deviation across time will be given higher weights in order to guide the network to learn those uncertain samples. Note that for memory reasons, our history comprises only the last five epochs and not the entire history of predictions. We believe that such a scheme makes intuitively more sense in a weakly-supervised application rather than the fully-supervised scenarios (such as MNIST or CIFAR) in the original paper [43]. Finally, the total loss that is used to train our network end-to-end (the primary network and the two attention modules) is defined as:

$$\mathcal{L} = \mathcal{L}_w + \mathcal{L}_{a_1} + \mathcal{L}_{a_2}, \tag{7}$$

where $\mathcal{L}_{a_1}$ is applied to the first attention module that extracts saliency maps of spatial resolution 14×14, and $\mathcal{L}_{a_2}$ is similarly applied to the second attention module after the fourth stage of the primary network with spatial resolution of 7×7. Disentangling the two loss functions enables us to focus on different types of challenges separately. The weighted focal loss $\mathcal{L}_w$, handles the prior class imbalance per attribute using the weight w_c and at the same time focuses on hard misclassified positive samples via the instance-level weights of the focal loss. The attention loss $\mathcal{L}_a$ penalizes predictions that originate from attention masks with high prediction variance.

4   Experiments

To assess our method, we performed experiments and ablation studies on the publicly available WIDER-Attribute [10] and PETA [15] datasets, which are the most widely used in this domain. The training details for both datasets are provided in the supplementary material.

4.1 Results on WIDER-Attribute

Dataset Description and Evaluation Metrics: The WIDER-Attribute [10] dataset contains 13,789 images with 57,524 bounding boxes of humans with 14 binary attribute annotations each. Besides "gender", which is balanced, the rest of the attributes demonstrate class imbalance, which can reach 1 : 18 and 1 : 28 for attributes such as "face-mask" and "sunglasses". Following the training protocol of [12,14], we used the human bounding box as an input to our model and mean average precision (mAP) results are reported.

Table 1. Evaluation of the proposed approach against nine different methods. The asterisk next to SRN indicates that it is our re-implementation due to the fact that the validation set was included in the original work which is not the case for the rest of the methods.

Method	Male	Long hair	Sunglasses	Hat	T-shirt	Long sleeve	Formal	Shorts	Jeans	Long Pants	Skirt	Face Mask	Logo	Plaid	mAP
Imbalance Ratio	1:1	1:3	1:18	1:3	1:4	1:1	1:13	1:6	1:11	1:2	1:9	1:28	1:3	1:18	
RCNN [44]	94	81	60	91	76	94	78	89	68	96	80	72	87	55	80.0
R*CNN [45]	94	82	62	91	76	95	79	89	68	96	80	73	87	56	80.5
DHC [10]	94	82	64	92	78	95	80	90	69	96	81	76	88	55	81.3
VeSPA [12]	-	-	-	-	-	-	-	-	-	-	-	-	-	-	82.4
CAM [46]	95	85	71	**94**	78	96	81	89	75	96	81	73	88	60	82.9
ResNet-101 [30]	94	85	69	91	80	96	83	91	78	95	82	74	89	65	83.7
ResNet-101+MTL	94	86	68	91	81	**96**	83	91	79	95	83	74	**90**	65	83.8
ResNet-101+MTL+CRL [9]	94	86	71	91	81	**96**	83	92	79	96	84	76	**90**	66	84.7
SRN [14]*	95	87	72	92	82	95	84	92	80	**96**	84	76	**90**	66	85.1
Ours	**96**	**88**	**74**	93	**83**	**96**	**85**	**93**	**81**	**96**	**85**	**78**	**90**	**68**	**86.4**

Baselines: We evaluate our approach against all the methods that have been tested on the WIDER-Attribute dataset, namely R-CNN [44], R*CNN [45], DHC [10], CAM [46], VeSPA [12], SRN [14], and a fine-tuned ResNet-101 network [30]. In addition, we transform the last part of the network to perform multi-task classification (MTL) by adding a fully-connected layer with 64 units for each attribute. This enables us to additionally evaluate against CRL [9] by forming triplets within the batch using class-level hard samples. Note that DHC and R*CNN leverage additional contextual information (e.g., scene context or image parts) that intuitively should boost the performance and VeSPA, which jointly predicts the viewpoint along with the attributes, did not train its viewpoint prediction sub-network on the WIDER-Attribute dataset. In SRN [14], the validation set was included in the training (which results in 20% more training data) and samples from the test set were used to obtain an idea about the training performance. In order to allow for a fair comparison with the rest of the methods, we re-implemented their method (which is why there is an asterisk next to their work in Table 1) and trained it only on the training set of the WIDER-Attribute [10] dataset. The difference between the reported results and our re-implementation is 1.2 in terms of mAP which is reasonable given the access to approximately 20% less training data.

Evaluation Results: Our proposed approach achieves state-of-the-art results on the WIDER dataset by improving upon the second best work by 1.3 in terms of mAP and by 2.7 over ResNet-101 [30] which was our primary network. The larger improvements achieved by our algorithm are in imbalanced attributes such as "Sunglasses" or "Plaid" that have visual cues in the image which demonstrates the importance of handling class imbalance and using visual attention to identify important visual information in the image. DHC and R*CNN that use additional context information performed significantly worse but this is partially because they utilize smaller primary networks. Overall the proposed approach performs better than or equal than the rest of the literature in all but one attributes and comes second behind CAM [46] at recognizing hats.

Table 2. Ablation studies on the WIDER dataset to assess the impact of individual modules on the final performance of our method. On the left, we report mAP results just for the primary network (w/o adding any attention mechanisms) using different backbone architectures. On the right, we investigate the additions in terms of performance for attention at a single- and multi-scale level as well as the two loss functions we introduced.

Primary Net	Params	mAP
ResNet-50	25.6×10^6	82.3
DenseNet-121	8.1×10^6	82.9
ResNet-101	44.7×10^6	83.7
ResNet-152	60.4×10^6	84.2
DenseNet-201	20.2×10^6	84.5

Primary Net	$\mathcal{L}_w$	Attention	$\mathcal{L}_a$	Multi-scale	mAP
ResNet-101					83.7
ResNet-101	✓				84.4
ResNet-101	✓	✓			85.0
ResNet-101	✓	✓	✓		85.7
ResNet-101	✓	✓		✓	85.9
ResNet-101	✓	✓	✓	✓	86.4

4.2 Ablation Studies on WIDER

In our first ablation study (Table 2 - left), we investigate to what extent the primary network affects the final performance. This is because it is commonplace that as architectures become deeper, the impact of individual add-on modules becomes less significant. We observe that (i) the difference between a ResNet-50 and a DesneNet-201 architecture is more than 2% in terms of mAP, (ii) DenseNet-201, which is the highest performing primary network, is almost as good as SRN [14] due to its effective feature aggregation and reuse, and (iii) the mAP of the proposed approach is 2.1 more than the best performing primary network. In our second ablation study (Table 2 - right), we assess how each proposed component of our approach contributes to the final mAP. Our ResNet-101 baseline (w/o any class weighting) achieves 83.7% mAP which increases to 84.0% when the class weights are added. When the instance-level weighting is added (i.e., L_w) the total performance increases to 84.4%. These results indicate that it is important to take both class-level and instance-level weighting into consideration during imbalanced learning. Handling class imbalance using the weighted focal loss and adding our attention mechanism just at a single scale result in mAP equal to 85.0 which performs almost as well as the existing state-of-the-art. Adding the attention loss that penalizes attention masks with high prediction variance and expanding our attention module to two scales improves the final mAP to 86.4.

Qualitative Results: Figure 4, depicts attention masks for six successful (left) and three failure cases (right). We observe that for imbalanced attributes such as sunglasses that have discriminant visual cues, our attention mechanism locates successfully the corresponding regions, which explains the 7% relative improved mAP for this attribute compared to our primary ResNet architecture.

4.3   Results on PETA

Dataset Description and Evaluation Metrics: The PETA [15] dataset is a collection of 10 person surveillance datasets and consists of 19,000 cropped images along with 61 binary and 5 multi-value attributes. We used the same train/validation/test splits with the method of Sarfraz *et al.* [12] and followed the established protocol of this dataset by reporting results on the 35 attributes for which the ratio of positive labels is higher than 5%. For the PETA dataset,

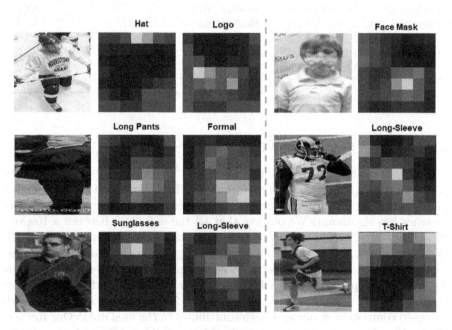

Fig. 4. Successful attention masks (left) and failure cases (right) for attributes of the WIDER dataset. The attention masks of our method try to find formal clothes and long pants in the bottom part of the image, logos in the middle and sunglasses or hats at the top. However, due to their weakly-supervised training, there are examples in which they fail to identify the correct locations (face mask in the bottom) or make completely wrong guesses as in the T-shirt example in the bottom right.

two different types of metrics are reported namely label-based and example-based [51]. For the label-based metrics due to the imbalanced class distribution, we used the balanced mean accuracy (mA) for each attribute that computes separately the classification accuracy of the positive and the negative examples and then computes the average. For the label-based metrics, we report accuracy, precision, recall, and F1-score averaged across all examples in the test set.

Table 3. Evaluation of the proposed approach against nine different approaches on the PETA dataset ranked by F1-score. The asterisk next to SRN indicates that it is our re-implementation due to the fact that the validation set was included in the original work which is not the case for the rest of the methods. The loss next to it corresponds to the loss function used in each case.

Method	mA	Acc	Prec	Rec	F1
ACN [47]	81.15	73.66	84.06	81.26	82.64
SRN [14]* (w/ $\mathcal{L}_b$)	80.55	74.24	84.04	82.48	83.25
WPAL-FSPP [48]	84.16	74.62	82.66	85.16	83.40
DeepMAR [49]	82.89	75.07	83.68	83.14	83.41
GoogleNet [50]	81.98	76.06	84.78	83.97	84.37
ResNet-101 [30]	82.67	76.63	85.13	84.46	84.79
WPAL-GMP [48]	**85.50**	76.98	84.07	85.78	84.90
SRN [14]* (w/ $\mathcal{L}_w$)	82.36	75.69	85.25	84.59	84.92
VeSPA [12]	83.45	77.73	86.18	84.81	85.49
Ours	84.59	**78.56**	**86.79**	**86.12**	**86.46**

Baselines: We compared our approach with all the methods that have been tested on the PETA dataset, namely the ACN [47], DeepMAR [49], two variations of WPAL [48], VeSPA [12], the GoogleNet [50] baseline reported by Sarfraz et al. [12], ResNet-101 [30] and SRN [14].

Evaluation Results: From the complete evaluation results in Table 3, we observe that the proposed approach achieves state-of-the-art results in all example-based metrics and comes second to WPAL [48] in terms of balanced mean accuracy (mA). We believe this is due to the fact that different methods use different metrics, based on which they optimize their models. For example, our approach is optimized based on the F1 score which balances between precision and recall and is applicable in search applications. Our approach improves upon a fine-tuned ResNet-101 architecture by approximately 2% in terms of F1 score which demonstrates the importance of the visual attention mechanisms. Notably, we improve upon VeSPA [12] in all evaluation metrics despite the fact that they utilize additional viewpoint information to train their model. Finally, we observe that by using the weighted variant of focal loss ($\mathcal{L}_w$) instead of the binary-cross entropy loss ($\mathcal{L}_b$), the F1 score of SRN [14] increases by 1.7%. This demonstrates why failing to account for class imbalance affects the performance of deep attribute classification models.

4.4 Ablation Studies on PETA

Based on our analysis an important question arises: can we achieve similar results with significantly fewer parameters? Aiming to find out the impact of large back-bone architectures in the final performance, we investigated how each component of our work performs using a pre-trained DenseNet-121 [41] architecture. DenseNet-121 contains 7.5× less parameters compared to ResNet-101 due to efficient feature propagation and reuse. To our surprise, when all components are included (last row in Table 4), the performance drop in terms of F1 score is less than 2%. In addition, we explored a variety of feature aggregations by either up-sampling the smaller attention masks, max-pooling the larger or mapping the larger to the smaller using a convolutional layer with a stride equal to two. Although the latter approach performed better than up-sampling/down-sampling, we observed that the aggregation of the attention information at a logit level is superior compared to feature level aggregation. We believe that this is because the two attention mechanisms extract masks that give emphasis to different spatial regions that when added together fail to provide the classifier with attribute-discriminative information.

Table 4. Ablation studies to assess the impact of each submodule to the final result using DenseNet-121 as a light-weight backbone architecture.

Primary Net	Class Weight	$\mathcal{L}_w$	Attention	Multi-scale (feature aggr.)	Multi-scale (score aggr.)	**F1**
DenseNet-121	✓					82.1
DenseNet-121	✓	✓				82.9
DenseNet-121	✓	✓	✓			83.8
DenseNet-121	✓	✓	✓	✓		84.1
DenseNet-121	✓	✓	✓		✓	84.7

4.5 Sources of Error and Further Improvements

Where does the proposed method fail and what are the characteristics of the failure cases? Aiming to gain a better understanding we will discuss separately the errors originating from the noise inherent to the input data and the errors related to modeling. A significant limitation of most pedestrian attribute classification methods (including ours) is that they resize the input data to a fixed square-size resolution (e.g., 224 × 224) in order to feed them to deep pre-trained architectures. Human crops are usually rectangular captured from different viewpoints and thus, when they are resized to a square, important spatial information is lost. One possible solution to this would be feeding the whole image (before performing the human crop) at a fixed resolution that does not destroy the spatial relations and then extract human-related features using ROI-pooling at a stage within the network. To cope with the high viewpoint variance, the spatial transformer networks of Jaderberg *et al.* [52] could be employed to align the input image before feeding it to the network, a practice which is very common in face recognition applications [53–55]. A second source of error is the very low resolution of several images especially in the PETA dataset, which makes it hard even for the human eye to identify the attribute traits of the depicted human. Some training examples that demonstrate these sources of error are depicted in Fig. 5. In addition, the provided annotations contain a third unspecified/uncertain class, which is used as negative during training in the literature, that further dilutes the learning process. Applying modern super-resolution techniques [56,57] could alleviate this issue but only to some extent. Regarding errors due to modeling richer feature representations could be extracted using feature pyramid networks [58] since they extract high-level semantic feature maps at multiple scales. Because the goal of this paper was to introduce a simple yet effective attribute classification solution, we refrained from building a complicated attention mechanism with a high number of parameters. Modern visual attention mechanisms [33,34,59] could be adapted to a multi-label setup and applied to achieve superior performance at the expense of a larger parameter space.

Fig. 5. Pedestrian attribute datasets contain images with large inherent noise and variation. Images can be out of focus, occluded, wrongly cropped, resized to fixed squared higher resolutions, blurry or even grayscale.

5   Conclusion

Learning the visual attributes of humans is a multi-label classification problem that suffers from large class imbalance and lack of semantic/spatial attribute annotations. To address these challenges, we developed a simple yet effective and easy-to-reproduce architecture that outputs visual attention masks at multiple scales and handles effectively class imbalance and samples with high prediction variance. We introduced a weighted variant of focal loss that handles the prior class imbalance per attribute and focuses on hard misclassified positive samples. In addition, we observed that the weakly-supervised attention masks result in high prediction variance and thus, we introduced an attention loss that penalizes accordingly such predictions. By simplifying the problem and addressing each one of its challenges, we achieve state-of-the-art results in both the WIDER-Attribute and PETA datasets, which are the most widely used in this domain. This work aspires to serve as a bar in the visual attribute classification domain that future works can improve upon. To facilitate this process, we performed ablation studies, identified some sources of error that still exist and pointed out possible future research directions that require further exploration.

Acknowledgments. This work has been funded in part by the UH Hugh Roy and Lillie Cranz Cullen Endowment Fund. All statements of fact, opinion or conclusions contained herein are those of the authors and should not be construed as representing the official views or policies of the sponsors.

References

1. Liu, Z., Luo, P., Wang, X., Tang, X.: Deep learning face attributes in the wild. In: Proceedings of the International Conference on Computer Vision, Santiago, Chile, 13–16 December 2015 (2015)
2. Olah, C., et al.: The building blocks of interpretability. Distill **3**, e10 (2018)
3. Chawla, N.V., Bowyer, K.W., Hall, L.O., Kegelmeyer, W.P.: Smote: synthetic minority over-sampling technique. J. Artif. Intell. Res. **16**, 321–357 (2002)
4. Maciejewski, T., Stefanowski, J.: Local neighbourhood extension of smote for mining imbalanced data. In: Proceedings of the Computational Intelligence and Data Mining, Paris, France, 11–15 April 2011
5. Drummond, C., Holte, R.C., et al.: Class imbalance, and cost sensitivity: why under-sampling beats over-sampling. In: Proceedings of the Workshop on Learning from Imbalanced Datasets II, Washington, DC, 21 August 2003 (2003)
6. Khan, S.H., Hayat, M., Bennamoun, M., Sohel, F.A., Togneri, R.: Cost-sensitive learning of deep feature representations from imbalanced data. Trans. Neural Netw. Learn. Syst. **29**, 3573–3587 (2017)
7. Huang, C., Li, Y., Change Loy, C., Tang, X.: Learning deep representation for imbalanced classification. In: Proceedings of the Conference on Computer Vision and Pattern Recognition, Las Vegas, NV, 26 June–1 July 2016 (2016)
8. Huang, C., Li, Y., Loy, C.C., Tang, X.: Deep imbalanced learning for face recognition and attribute prediction. arXiv preprint arXiv:1806.00194 (2018)
9. Dong, Q., Gong, S., Zhu, X.: Class rectification hard mining for imbalanced deep learning. In: Proceedings of the International Conference on Computer Vision, Venice, Italy 22–29 October 2017 (2017)
10. Li, Y., Huang, C., Loy, C.C., Tang, X.: Human attribute recognition by deep hierarchical contexts. In: Leibe, B., Matas, J., Sebe, N., Welling, M. (eds.) ECCV 2016. LNCS, vol. 9910, pp. 684–700. Springer, Cham (2016). https://doi.org/10.1007/978-3-319-46466-4_41
11. Gkioxari, G., Girshick, R., Malik, J.: Actions and attributes from wholes and parts. In: Proceedings of the International Conference on Computer Vision, Santiago, Chile, 13–16 December 2015 (2015)
12. Sarfraz, M.S., Schumann, A., Wang, Y., Stiefelhagen, R.: Deep view-sensitive pedestrian attribute inference in an end-to-end model. In: Proceedings of the British Machine Vision Conference, London, UK, 4–7 September 2017 (2017)

13. Sarafianos, N., Giannakopoulos, T., Nikou, C., Kakadiaris, I.A.: Curriculum learning of visual attribute clusters for multi-task classification. Pattern Recognit. **80**, 94–108 (2018)

14. Zhu, F., Li, H., Ouyang, W., Yu, N., Wang, X.: Learning spatial regularization with image-level supervisions for multi-label image classification. In: Proceedings of the Conference on Computer Vision and Pattern Recognition, Honolulu, HI, 21–26 July 2017 (2017)

15. Deng, Y., Luo, P., Loy, C.C., Tang, X.: Pedestrian attribute recognition at far distance. In: Proceedings of the ACM Multimedia, Orlando, FL 3–7 November 2014 (2014)

16. Martinez, J., Hossain, R., Romero, J., Little, J.J.: A simple yet effective baseline for 3D human pose estimation. In: Proceedings of the International Conference on Computer Vision, Venice, Italy, 22–29 October 2017 (2017)

17. Chan, T.H., Jia, K., Gao, S., Lu, J., Zeng, Z., Ma, Y.: PCANet: a simple deep learning baseline for image classification? Trans. Image Process. **24**, 5017–5032 (2015)

18. Zheng, Z., Zheng, L., Yang, Y.: Unlabeled samples generated by gan improve the person re-identification baseline in vitro. In: Proceedings of the Conference on Computer Vision and Pattern Recognition, Honolulu, HI, 21–26 July 2017 (2017)

19. Ferrari, V., Zisserman, A.: Learning visual attributes. In: Proceedings of the Advances in Neural Information Processing Systems, Vancouver, Canada, 3–6 December 2007 (2007)

20. Kumar, N., Berg, A., Belhumeur, P.N., Nayar, S.: Describable visual attributes for face verification and image search. Transactions on Pattern Analysis and Machine Intelligence (2011)

21. Chen, H., Gallagher, A., Girod, B.: Describing clothing by semantic attributes. In: Proceedings of the European Conference on Computer Vision, Florence, Italy, 7–13 October 2012 (2012)

22. Sarafianos, N., Giannakopoulos, T., Nikou, C., Kakadiaris, I.A.: Curriculum learning for multi-task classification of visual attributes. In: Proceedings of the International Conference on Computer Vision Workshops, Venice, Italy, 22–29 October 2017 (2017)

23. Zhang, N., Paluri, M., Ranzato, M., Darrell, T., Bourdev, L.: PANDA: Pose aligned networks for deep attribute modeling. In: Proceedings of the Conference on Computer Vision and Pattern Recognition, Columbus, OH, 23–28 June 2014 (2014)

24. Dong, Q., Gong, S., Zhu, X.: Multi-task curriculum transfer deep learning of clothing attributes. In: Proceedings of the Winter Conference on Applications of Computer Vision, Santa Rosa, CA, 27–29 March 2017 (2017)

25. Sarafianos, N., Vrigkas, M., Kakadiaris, I.A.: Adaptive SVM+: learning with privileged information for domain adaptation. In: Proceedings of the International Conference on Computer Vision Workshops, Venice, Italy, 22–29 October 2017 (2017)

26. Chen, Q., Huang, J., Feris, R., Brown, L.M., Dong, J., Yan, S.: Deep domain adaptation for describing people based on fine-grained clothing attributes. In: Proceedings of the Conference on Computer Vision and Pattern Recognition, Boston, MA 8–10 June 2015 (2015)

27. Liu, Z., Luo, P., Qiu, S., Wang, X., Tang, X.: Deepfashion: Powering robust clothes recognition and retrieval with rich annotations. In: Proceedings of the Conference on Computer Vision and Pattern Recognition, Las Vegas, NV, 26 June-1 July 2016 (2016)

28. Al-Halah, Z., Stiefelhagen, R., Grauman, K.: Fashion forward: Forecasting visual style in fashion. In: Proceedings of the International Conference on Computer Vision, Venice, Italy, 22–29 October 2017 (2017)

29. Zhu, J., Liao, S., Lei, Z., Li, S.Z.: Multi-label convolutional neural network based pedestrian attribute classification. Image Vis. Comput. **58**, 224–229 (2016)

30. He, K., Zhang, X., Ren, S., Sun, J.: Deep residual learning for image recognition. In: Proceedings of the Conference on Computer Vision and Pattern Recognition, Las Vegas, NV, 26 June–1 July 1 2016 (2016)

31. Wang, J., Yuan, Y., Yu, G.: Face attention network: an effective face detector for the occluded faces. arXiv preprint arXiv:1711.07246 (2017)

32. Liu, X., Xia, T., Wang, J., Yang, Y., Zhou, F., Lin, Y.: Fully convolutional attention networks for fine-grained recognition. arXiv preprint arXiv:1603.06765 (2016)

33. Li, W., Zhu, X., Gong, S.: Harmonious attention network for person re-identification. In: Proceedings of the Conference on Computer Vision and Pattern Recognition, Salt Lake City, UT, 18–22 June 2018 (2018)

34. Wang, F., et al.: Residual attention network for image classification. In: Proceedings of the Conference on Computer Vision and Pattern Recognition, Honolulu, HI, 21–26 July 2017 (2017)

35. Hu, J., Shen, L., Sun, G.: Squeeze-and-excitation networks. arXiv preprint arXiv:1709.01507 (2017)

36. Chu, X., Yang, W., Ouyang, W., Ma, C., Yuille, A.L., Wang, X.: Multi-context attention for human pose estimation. In: Proc. Conference on Computer Vision and Pattern Recognition, Honolulu, HI, 21–26 July 2017 (2017)

37. Chen, S.F., Chen, Y.C., Yeh, C.K., Wang, Y.C.F.: Order-free RNN with visual attention for multi-label classification. In: Proceedings of the AAAI Conference on Artificial Intelligence, New Orleans, LA, 2–7 February 2018 (2018)

38. Das, A., Agrawal, H., Zitnick, L., Parikh, D., Batra, D.: Human attention in visual question answering: do humans and deep networks look at the same regions? Comput. Vis. Image Underst. **163**, 90–100 (2017)

39. Rodrguez, P., Gonfaus, J.M., Cucurull, G., Roca, X., Gonzalez, J.: Attend and rectify: a gated attention mechanism for fine-grained recovery. In: Proceedings of the European Conference on Computer Vision, Munich, Germany, 8–14 September 2018 (2018)

40. Lin, T.Y., Goyal, P., Girshick, R., He, K., Dollár, P.: Focal loss for dense object detection. In: Proceedings of the International Conference on Computer Vision, Venice, Italy, 22–29 October 2017 (2017)

41. Huang, G., Liu, Z., Weinberger, K.Q., van der Maaten, L.: Densely connected convolutional networks. In: Proceedings of the Conference on Computer Vision and Pattern Recognition, Honolulu, HI, 21–26 July 2017 (2017)

42. Wang, W., Shen, J.: Deep visual attention prediction. Trans. Image Process. **27**, 2368–2378 (2018)

43. Chang, H.S., Learned-Miller, E., McCallum, A.: Active bias: Training more accurate neural networks by emphasizing high variance samples. In: Proceedings of the Neural Information Processing Systems, Long Beach, CA, 4–9 December 2017 (2017)

44. Girshick, R.: Fast R-CNN. In: Proceedings of the International Conference on Computer Vision, Santiago, Chile, 13–16 December 2015 (2015)

45. Gkioxari, G., Girshick, R., Malik, J.: Contextual action recognition with R*CNN. In: Proceedings of the International Conference on Computer Vision, Santiago, Chile, 13–16 December 2015 (2015)

46. Guo, H., Fan, X., Wang, S.: Human attribute recognition by refining attention heat map. Pattern Recognit. Lett. **94**, 38–45 (2017)
47. Sudowe, P., Spitzer, H., Leibe, B.: Person attribute recognition with a jointly-trained holistic CNN model. In: Proceedings of the International Conference on Computer Vision Workshops, Santiago, Chile, 13–16 December 2015 (2015)
48. Yu, K., Leng, B., Zhang, Z., Li, D., Huang, K.: Weakly-supervised learning of mid-level features for pedestrian attribute recognition and localization. arXiv preprint arXiv:1611.05603 (2016)
49. Li, D., Chen, X., Huang, K.: Multi-attribute learning for pedestrian attribute recognition in surveillance scenarios. In: Proceedings of the Asian Conference on Pattern Recognition, Kuala Lumpur, Malaysia, 3–6 November 2015 (2015)
50. Szegedy, C., et al.: Going deeper with convolutions. In: Proceedings of the Conference on Computer Vision and Pattern Recognition, Boston, MA, 7–12 June 2015 (2015)
51. Li, D., Zhang, Z., Chen, X., Ling, H., Huang, K.: A richly annotated dataset for pedestrian attribute recognition. arXiv preprint arXiv:1603.07054 (2016)
52. Jaderberg, M., Simonyan, K., Zisserman, A., et al.: Spatial transformer networks. In: Proceedings of the Neural Information Processing Systems, Montreal, Canada, 7–12 December 2015 (2015)
53. Peng, X., Feris, R.S., Wang, X., Metaxas, D.N.: A recurrent encoder-decoder network for sequential face alignment. In: Leibe, B., Matas, J., Sebe, N., Welling, M. (eds.) ECCV 2016. LNCS, vol. 9905, pp. 38–56. Springer, Cham (2016). https://doi.org/10.1007/978-3-319-46448-0_3
54. Tuzel, O., Marks, T.K., Tambe, S.: Robust face alignment using a mixture of invariant experts. In: Leibe, B., Matas, J., Sebe, N., Welling, M. (eds.) ECCV 2016. LNCS, vol. 9909, pp. 825–841. Springer, Cham (2016). https://doi.org/10.1007/978-3-319-46454-1_50
55. Jeni, L.A., Cohn, J.F., Kanade, T.: Dense 3D face alignment from 2D video for real-time use. Image Vis. Comput. **58**, 13–24 (2017)
56. Kim, J., Kwon Lee, J., Mu Lee, K.: Accurate image super-resolution using very deep convolutional networks. In: Proceedings of the Conference on Computer Vision and Pattern Recognition, Las Vegas, NV, 26 June–1 July 2016 (2016)
57. Dahl, R., Norouzi, M., Shlens, J.: Pixel recursive super resolution. In: Proceedings of the International Conference on Computer Vision, Venice, Italy, 22–29 October 2017 (2017)
58. Lin, T.Y., Dollár, P., Girshick, R., He, K., Hariharan, B., Belongie, S.: Feature pyramid networks for object detection. In: Proceedings of the Conference on Computer Vision and Pattern Recognition, Honolulu, HI, 21–26 July 2017 (2017)
59. Liang, J., Jiang, L., Cao, L., Li, L.J., Hauptmann, A.: Focal visual-text attention for visual question answering. In: Proceedings of the Conference on Computer Vision and Pattern Recognition, Salt Lake City, UT, 18–22 June 2018 (2018)

Sub-GAN: An Unsupervised Generative Model via Subspaces

Jie Liang[1], Jufeng Yang[1(✉)], Hsin-Ying Lee[2], Kai Wang[1],
and Ming-Hsuan Yang[2,3]

[1] Nankai University, Tianjin, China
yangjufeng@nankai.edu.cn
[2] University of California, Merced, USA
[3] Google Cloud, Merced, USA

Abstract. The recent years have witnessed significant growth in constructing robust generative models to capture informative distributions of natural data. However, it is difficult to fully exploit the distribution of complex data, like images and videos, due to the high dimensionality of ambient space. Sequentially, how to effectively guide the training of generative models is a crucial issue. In this paper, we present a subspace-based generative adversarial network (Sub-GAN) which simultaneously disentangles multiple latent subspaces and generates diverse samples correspondingly. Since the high-dimensional natural data usually lies on a union of low-dimensional subspaces which contain semantically extensive structure, Sub-GAN incorporates a novel clusterer that can interact with the generator and discriminator via subspace information. Unlike the traditional generative models, the proposed Sub-GAN can control the diversity of the generated samples via the multiplicity of the learned subspaces. Moreover, the Sub-GAN follows an unsupervised fashion to explore not only the visual classes but the latent continuous attributes. We demonstrate that our model can discover meaningful visual attributes which is hard to be annotated via strong supervision, *e.g.*, the writing style of digits, thus avoid the mode collapse problem. Extensive experimental results show the competitive performance of the proposed method for both generating diverse images with satisfied quality and discovering discriminative latent subspaces.

1 Introduction

Significant progress has been made in deep generative modeling, of which the ability to synthesize data requires a deep understanding of the data structure. Recently, generative adversarial network (GAN) [1] has emerged as a promising framework for generating complex data distribution in a data-driven manner. GAN is composed of a generator and a discriminator, where the generator maps

Electronic supplementary material The online version of this chapter (https://doi.org/10.1007/978-3-030-01252-6_43) contains supplementary material, which is available to authorized users.

© Springer Nature Switzerland AG 2018
V. Ferrari et al. (Eds.): ECCV 2018, LNCS 11215, pp. 726–743, 2018.
https://doi.org/10.1007/978-3-030-01252-6_43

samples from an arbitrary latent distribution to ambient data space and the adversarial discriminator attempts to distinguish between real and generated samples. Both modules are optimized via adversarial training.

While GAN has shown promising results in simulating complex data distribution like images and videos, the realistic distribution is not fully exploited. The complexity of real data makes it difficult for generative models to learn useful and detailed attributes without any guidance. Sequentially, the conditional GAN [2] proposes to provide direct clustering guidance in a supervised manner where the labels of data are given. However, the requirements of annotations constrain the generative models to limited applications with strong prior of the distinctive classes, e.g., the 10 digits in the MNIST dataset. Furthermore, there are far more intrinsic patterns which are hard to be labeled, such as the various styles of the hand-written digits. Full exploitations on these latent structures can obviously alleviate the mode collapse problem in the generation process.

Research has shown that high-dimensional data can always be modeled as a union of low-dimensional subspaces [3]. Numerous subspace clustering methods have been developed to explore the high-dimensional data distribution [3,4]. The disentangling of the underlying low-dimensional subspaces serves as a guidance on approximate the data distribution and can facilitate the generation on complex data space.

In this work, we propose a joint framework, i.e., subspace-based generative adversarial network (Sub-GAN), to simultaneously discover intrinsic subspaces in an unsupervised manner and generate realistic samples from each of them. Sub-GAN consists of three modules, a clusterer, a generator and a discriminator. The clusterer aims to discover distinctive subspaces of high-dimensional data in an unsupervised fashion. It is updated on each epoch based on the feedback from the discriminator. The generator produces samples conditioned on a one-hot vector indicating the belonged cluster and a base vector of subspace derived from the clusterer. The discriminator not only needs to distinguish between real and fake samples, but also requires to classify them to belonged subspaces. It also provides distinctive representations of data samples for updating the clusterer. We conduct extensive experiments to validate the effectiveness of the proposed framework. Specifically, based on both visualized and quantitative results, we demonstrate that the generated samples are not only visually appealing but diverse with multiple latent attributes. We also show that our model achieves favorable performance on image clustering tasks.

Our contributions are of two folds. First, we present a joint unsupervised framework to simultaneously learn the subspaces of the ambient space and generating instances accordingly, where both tasks are mutually optimized. Second, we address the mode collapse problem by specifying the number of distinct subspaces, from which we generate meaningful and diverse images with informative visual attributes. Extensive experiments demonstrate the effectiveness of the proposed Sub-GAN model.

2 Related Work

Deep Generative Models. Deep generative frameworks have recently drawn significant attention due to the ability of modeling large-scale unlabeled data [5–10]. The generative models can be applied to various low-level vision problems, e.g., image super-resolution [11,12] and semantic segmentation [13,14].

Generative models aim to fit the space of real data samples, e.g., a set of natural images [15–17]. To capture the real distribution, most generative models optimize an aggregated probabilistic problem conditioned on latent noises over multiple variables. They assume that all data samples are drawn from a single low-dimensional latent space. Early studies focused on learning embedded representations in an unsupervised manner, e.g., the restricted Boltzmann machines (RBM [18,19]) and the stacked auto-encoders (AE [20]). For instance, Hinton et al. [21] propose to efficiently train the deep belief nets (DBN) by using the contrastive divergence algorithm. Both DBN and AE learn a low-dimensional representation for each data sample on a single latent space, followed by generating new instances via a decoding network [22]. However, these methods suffer from the difficulty to disentangle an intractable probabilistic optimization problem while maximizing the training data likelihood, especially for the data of high-dimensionality [23]. More recently, Goodfellow et al. [1] propose GAN as an alternative adversarial strategy for training the generative models. The minimax game between the generator and the discriminator induces a data-driven approximation process from a low-dimensional latent distribution, e.g., standard Gaussian, to a high-dimensional real distribution. During training, the adversarial module is used to optimize a loss function and sidesteps the requirement to explicitly calculate or approximate the complicated ambient space. Nevertheless, due to the high-dimensional and contradictory nature of the two counterparts, traditional GANs suffer from the mode collapse problem as well as the instable training [24,25], which are crucial for further improvement.

Built upon these generative models, various conditional image generation methods (e.g., CGAN [2]) are proposed to generate a specific deterministic output from a given conditioning latent vector, which somehow controls the diversity of the generation. In particular, the latent variable is designed to encode the object class by concatenating the ground-truth labels so that the generator can produce samples from specific visual category [26,27]. The CGAN has the advantage of providing better representations for multi-modal data generation, but such inference process relies on the extensively annotated training data, some of which is hard to explicitly labeled, e.g., the writing styles of the digits [28]. Recently, InfoGAN [29] optimizes the mutual information of latent codes, which is constructed by a mixture of Gaussian instead of uniform noise. However, it lacks explicit categorical assignments as well as distinctive embedding vectors of samples. In this paper, we present a joint model to simultaneously learn the informative latent category of the real samples and conduct the generation from each subspace, the inference and generation process are totally unsupervised and mutually optimized.

Subspace Learning. Modeling high-dimensional data has been one of the most critical issues in computer vision [30]. As the high-dimensional data is usually distributed in a union of low-dimensional subspaces [4,31], numerous deep subspace clustering methods [32–35] have been developed in the literature.

The goal of subspace learning methods is to find a given number of disentangled low-dimensional subspaces [34]. Traditional algorithms focus on calculating the similarity/dissimilarity relationship among instances [36], followed by constructing graphs and conducting spectral clustering [37]. Recently, researchers propose to extract more distinctive representations of each sample via a deep embedding network [38]. Xie *et al.* [39] propose the deep embedding clustering (DEC) algorithm for learning a non-linear mapping from data space to a latent feature space with a denoising stacked autoencoder (DAE), followed by refining the clustering assignments. The DEC framework first pre-trains the DAE and then fine-tunes it stacked by iteratively optimizing a clustering objective function based on the Kullback-Leibler (KL) divergence with a self-training target distribution. However, it requires the layer-wise pre-training and a non-joint embedding and clustering [34]. In this paper, we propose a joint model for training all modules simultaneously with an adversarial strategy, which is demonstrated to be effective to extract distinctive subspaces.

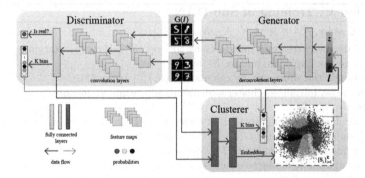

Fig. 1. Main steps of the proposed Sub-GAN method. The three boxes represent the clusterer C (*purple*), generator G (*green*) and discriminator D (*blue*), respectively. We design C to disentangle K subspaces $\{S_i\}_{i=1}^{K}$ for the given dataset X (when initializing) or the deep features derived from D (during training). For G, the input l consists of three components, *i.e.*, e and y derived from C, and the noise vector $z \in \mathcal{N}(0,1)$. The D can not only discriminate the real or fake images by outputting a binary prediction, but also calculate probabilities of each subspace to refine the C. The K bins from both C and D are unified for comprehensive prediction. (Color figure online)

3   Subspace-Based GAN

Given a set of unlabeled high-dimensional data $X = \{x_i\}_{i=1}^N$, the goal of generative models is to approximate the real distribution $p_x(x)$ via a mapping $G(\cdot)$ from a low-dimensional latent variable $z \sim p_z(z)$, i.e., $x = G(z)$. However, directly modeling the raw space may suffer from the problem of mode collapse, i.e., the generated samples are of similar pattern which caters the objective function [40]. It also leads to an instable training [41].

The data samples X could be drawn from multiple subspaces $\{S_i\}_{i=1}^K$, which depict informative attributes and are easier to be approximated than the high-dimensional ambient space. Hence, we present a joint unsupervised framework termed as Sub-GAN, to seek auxiliary distributions which effectively cover multiple modes of the multi-modal data X. In the rest of this section, we first describe the deep clustering module C, which disentangles the $\{S_i\}_{i=1}^K$ of the ambient space X. Afterwards, we explain the formulation of deep generative modules, including a generator G and discriminator D which alternate between updating model parameters for both generation and clustering. Figure 1 shows the pipeline of Sub-GAN and Algorithm 1 illustrates the training process, where N_i and N_b denote the number of iterations and batch size, respectively.

Algorithm 1 . Training of Sub-GAN

Input: $X = \{x_i\}_{i=1}^N \in \mathbb{R}^{d_x}$, K, N_i, N_b.

1: Calculate the correlation matrix C by solving the self-representation problem (1);
2: Compute the Laplacian matrix M by (2);
3: Disentangle the subspaces by calculating $\{e_i\}_{i=1}^K$ using (3);
4: Calculate an initialized cluster assignment $\hat{y}_{ini}$ using K-means;
5: **while** $I < N_i$ **do**
6:      Calculate comprehensive latent codes $L = \{l_i\}_{i=1}^K$ for each subspace using (8);
7:      Update the generator $G(L)$ by optimizing (6);
8:      Update the discriminator D by optimizing (9);
9:      Calculate new distinctive representations for each sample x;
10:     **if** $I\%(\frac{N}{N_b}) = 0$ **then**
11:          Calculate and update C and e;
12:          Update C according to (12);
13:     **end if**
14: **end while**

Output: Cluster assignment $\hat{y}$; Generator G.

3.1   Clusterer for Subspace Disentangling

We consider the task of clustering a set of N samples $X = \{x_i\}_{i=1}^N \in \mathbb{R}^{d_x}$ into K clusters $\{S_i\}_{i=1}^K$, where d_x denotes the dimension of X and K is fixed based on the diversity and intrinsic structure of the X. Note we allow the user control on K to generate either diverse or compact samples. To satisfy the requirement on subspace disentangling, we design a clusterer C which is jointly learned in the adversarial framework. We first initialize the soft assignments $\hat{P}$ via subspace clustering [30]. Then, we minimize the KL divergence between predicted assignment P and an auxiliary target distribution T. During training of Sub-GAN, we iteratively map the raw data samples into a distinctive embedding space $U \in \mathbb{R}^{d_u}$ where we have $d_u \ll d_x$. Meanwhile, the adversarial process can provide gradients for refining the soft assignment.

For initializing the assignment with raw data samples, we follow a two-step subspace clustering approach. Specifically, we disentangle the multiple affine subspaces $\{S_i\}_{i=1}^{K}$ using self-representation and graph clustering techniques. We first tackle the following ℓ_1-norm optimization problem [4] to calculate the self-representation of the data samples:

$$\min_{C} \|X - XC\|_2^2 + \lambda\|C\|_1, \quad s.t. \ \text{diag}(C) = 0, \tag{1}$$

where $\|\cdot\|_1$ denotes the ℓ_1-norm and the constraint $\text{diag}(C) = 0$ eliminates the trivial solution of representing sample x as a linear combination of itself. Here, C denotes the coefficient matrix where each entry c_{ij} reflects the similarity between samples x_i and x_j. Afterwards, the C is used to define a directed graph $G = (V, E)$ where the each vertex in V represents a data sample and the edge $(v_i, v_j) \in E$ is weighted by c_{ij}. We construct a balanced graph $\hat{G}$ with the adjacency matrix W where we have $W = |C| + |C^\top|$. Then, the Laplacian matrix M of the graph is calculated by

$$M = D - W, \tag{2}$$

where $D \in \mathbb{R}^{N \times N}$ is computed as $D_{ii} = \sum_j W_{ij}$. Given the Laplacian matrix M, we calculate the first K eigenvectors as

$$[e_1, e_2, \cdots, e_K] = \text{eig}(M), \tag{3}$$

where $\text{eig}(\cdot)$ is the decomposition function to extract the eigenvectors of a matrix. Note the multiplicity of the zero eigenvalues of M reflects the number of connected components in G [4], thus the eigenvectors are distinguishable in the latent spectral space. We finally use the K-means to calculate the initialized clustering assignment $\hat{P}$ [42].

Given $\hat{P}$, we refine the model predictions iteratively in the following training process. In each iteration I, we feed the G and D with both data sample x_i and the current predicted subspace assignment $\hat{p}_i^I$. On top of the deep network of the discriminator which is illustrated in Sect. 3.3, we generate the deep embedding feature f_i^I of each sample x_i which is distinguishable on discriminating the K subspaces. Given f, we calculate the soft assignment P_b for each local training set X_b, where X_b is composed of images in each batch. We then define a clustering objective function $\mathcal{L}_C$ for each iteration I by using the Kullback-Leibler (KL) divergence to minimize the distance between the prediction $\boldsymbol{P}^I$ and a target variable $\boldsymbol{Q}^I$:

$$\mathcal{L}_C^I = \mathrm{KL}(\boldsymbol{Q}^I \| \boldsymbol{P}^I) = \frac{1}{N_b} \sum_{i=1}^{N} \sum_{k=1}^{K} q_{ik} \log \frac{q_{ik}}{p_{ik}}, \tag{4}$$

where N_b denotes the batch size, N is the number of training samples and K is the number of subspaces. Here, we induce a sparse prediction matrix $\boldsymbol{P}$ where each $\boldsymbol{p}_i$ is a one-hot vector, i.e., $p_{ik} = 1$ for $\boldsymbol{x}_i \in \boldsymbol{S}_k$ and $\{p_{ij}\}_{j \neq k} = 0$. In the clusterer C, we update the target distribution $\boldsymbol{Q}$ by normalizing based on the frequency for each cluster:

$$q_{ik} = \frac{p_{ik}^2 / f_k}{\sum_m (p_{im}^2 / f_m)}, \tag{5}$$

where $f_k = \sum_i p_{ik}$ denotes the predicted frequency of each cluster. Figure 1 shows that in each iteration, the predicted K bins in C is refined by the dense K bins derived from D.

3.2   Generator for Subspace Approximation

Deep generative models aim to approximate the real data space $\boldsymbol{X}$ from a latent space $\boldsymbol{L}$. Consequently, they optimize a non-linear mapping function $f_\theta : \boldsymbol{l} \to \boldsymbol{x}$, where $\boldsymbol{l}$ denotes the latent vector which encodes the intrinsic attributes of the ambient space, θ denotes the set of parameters.

Traditional generative frameworks approximate a single ambient space by optimizing an aggregated posterior $p_\theta(\boldsymbol{x}|\boldsymbol{z})$, where $\boldsymbol{z}$ denotes the source of incompressible noise in the latent space. In this section, we design a generator $G(\boldsymbol{l})$ to realize the non-linear mapping of $f_\theta : \boldsymbol{l} \to \boldsymbol{x}$. We demonstrate that the proposed $G(\boldsymbol{l})$ captures informative intrinsic structures, i.e., generates diverse samples from multiple subspaces. More concretely, we express $G(\boldsymbol{l})$ as a deterministic feed forward network $G : \Omega_L \to \Omega_S$, where Ω. denotes the corresponding distribution, $\boldsymbol{L} = \{\boldsymbol{l}_i\}_{i=1}^{K}$ denotes the latent space and $\boldsymbol{S} = \{\boldsymbol{S}_i\}_{i=1}^{K}$ denotes the K subspaces of the data $\boldsymbol{X}$. We formulate the optimization process as:

$$p_G(\boldsymbol{x} \in \boldsymbol{S}_i) = \mathbb{E}_{\boldsymbol{l}_i \sim p_L}[p_G(\boldsymbol{x}|\boldsymbol{l}_i)], \tag{6}$$

where $p_G(\boldsymbol{x}|\boldsymbol{l}_i) = \mathcal{L}(\boldsymbol{x} - G(\boldsymbol{l}_i))$ and $\boldsymbol{l}_i$ denotes the latent code induced from $\boldsymbol{S}_i$. We finally train the $G(\boldsymbol{l})$ via an adversarial manner such that

$$p_G(\boldsymbol{x}) \approx p_{\boldsymbol{S}_i}(\boldsymbol{x}), \quad \forall \boldsymbol{S}_i \in \boldsymbol{S}. \tag{7}$$

Given the disentangled subspaces $\{\boldsymbol{S}_i\}_{i=1}^{K}$, we design $\boldsymbol{l}$ to depict the independent attributes of each $\boldsymbol{S}_i$ with a comprehensive combination, i.e.,

$$\boldsymbol{l} = \boldsymbol{z} \oplus \boldsymbol{e} \oplus \hat{\boldsymbol{y}}. \tag{8}$$

Here, $\oplus$ denotes the concatenation operation and $\hat{\boldsymbol{y}} \in \mathbb{R}^K$ denotes the one-hot vector in current assignment. The eigenvector $\boldsymbol{e}$ in (3) reflects intrinsic base of a subspace derived from C, where C is updated in each iteration. We set the prior on the noise variable $p_z(\boldsymbol{z}) = \mathcal{N}[0,1]$ where $\mathcal{N}$ denotes normal distribution. The green box in Fig. 1 provides a visualization of this concatenation operation.

3.3 Discriminator for Adversarial Training

GAN [1] is an adversarial framework which trains a deep generative model via a minimax game. Traditional GAN is composed of a generator G and a discriminator D of which the ability of generation or discrimination are mutually improved during training. The G always non-linearly maps a latent noise variable $z \sim p_z(\boldsymbol{z})$ to the data space $x \sim p_x(\boldsymbol{x})$. Meanwhile, the discriminator D calculates a probability of belief $p = D(\boldsymbol{x}) \in [0,1]$ for real samples and assigns a probability of $1-p$ when for generated samples $G(\boldsymbol{z})$. During training, a minimax objective is used to alternatively train both networks:

$$\min_G \max_D \; \mathcal{L}(G,D) \;=\; \mathbb{E}_{x \sim p_x(x)}[\log D(\boldsymbol{x})] + \mathbb{E}_{z \sim p_z(z)}[\log(1-D(G(\boldsymbol{z})))]. \quad (9)$$

Here D is optimized to be a binary classifier which provides the optimal probability estimation between real and fake samples, $i.e.$, x and $G(\boldsymbol{z})$. Simultaneously, G is encouraged to resemble the data distribution, $i.e.$, $G(\boldsymbol{z}) \sim p_x(\boldsymbol{x})$, followed by challenging the discriminator D with $G(\boldsymbol{z})$. Both G and D are updated alternatively via back-propagation.

For refining the subspace assignment, we incorporate the adversarial loss with the clustering loss, $i.e.$, $\mathcal{L}_C$ in (4) which discriminates whether the samples are generated from a single $\boldsymbol{S}$. The hybrid Sub-GAN training objective is defined as a minimax optimization:

$$\min_{G,C} \max_D \; \mathcal{L}(D,G,C), \quad (10)$$

where we have

$$\mathcal{L}(D,G,C) = \mathbb{E}_{x \sim p_S(x)}[\log D(\boldsymbol{x})] + \mathbb{E}_{l \sim p_L(l)}[\log(1-D(G(l)))]$$
$$+ \mathrm{KL}(\boldsymbol{Q_S} \| \boldsymbol{P_S}). \quad (11)$$

Here, $\boldsymbol{S} = \{\boldsymbol{S}_k\}_{k=1}^K$ denotes the predicted subspaces in each iteration.

In the training process, we followed the alternating gradient based optimization technique as is used in [1]. Specifically, each module in Sub-GAN is a parametric function with parameters θ_D, θ_G and θ_C, respectively. We jointly optimize the Sub-GAN framework using an alternating stochastic gradient step. For each iteration I, we update the θ_D for the discriminator by calculating the single or multiple steps of the positive gradient direction, $i.e.$, $\nabla_{\theta_D} \mathcal{L}^{I-1}(D,G,C)$. Then, we simultaneously update the parameter θ_G and θ_C for the G and C, respectively. We take a single step in the negative gradient direction $-\nabla_{\theta_G,\theta_C} \mathcal{L}^{I-1}(D,G,C)$. In particular, for the clusterer C, we have

$$\theta_C^I = \{\boldsymbol{C}^I, \boldsymbol{P}^I, \boldsymbol{Q}^I\}. \quad (12)$$

To update the coefficient matrix C, we calculate the ℓ_1-norm optimization in (1) in each epoch on top of favorable data features derived from D^{I-1}. Consequently, for the generator G, we update the eigenvector e_i^I for representing each subspace S_i through C^{I-1}. For all modules, the first two terms of $\mathcal{L}(D, G, C)$ are calculated based on the mini-batches of n samples $\{x_i \sim p_S\}_{i=1}^n$ and the latent codes $\{l_i \sim p_L\}_{i=1}^n$ drawn from the underlying subspaces.

4   Experimental Results

4.1   Datasets and Methods

We conduct experiments on the MNIST and CIFAR-10 datasets. The MNIST is a standard handwritten digits dataset which is composed of $70,000$ images of 28×28 grayscale. We use this dataset to demonstrate the comprehensive characteristics of the proposed Sub-GAN. The CIFAR-10 dataset consists of $60,000$ 32×32 color images in 10 classes, which cover common objects such as airplanes or automobiles. Both datasets are of informative intrinsic attributes apart from the existing label, *e.g.*, the writing style of each digits in MNIST, the various scene of the automobiles in CIFAR-10.

For evaluating the generation quality, we compare the proposed Sub-GAN with various state-of-the-art generative models, *i.e.*, CGAN [2], Improved GAN (IGAN, [43]), Improved WGAN (IWGAN, [44]), DCGAN [45] and InfoGAN [29]. Furthermore, we perform experiments to evaluate the unsupervised clustering performance of the Sub-GAN. We make the comparison with K-means, SSC [4], LSR [46], SMR [47], NSN [48], SSC-OMP [35], ORGEN [31], iPursuit [49], DEC [39], CatGAN [50] and InfoGAN [29]. Here, the SSC, LSR, SMR, NSN,

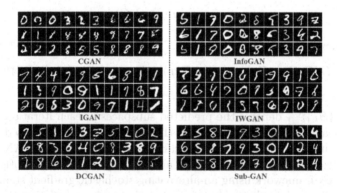

Fig. 2. Generated images on the MNIST dataset by the CGAN [2], InfoGAN [29], IGAN [43], IWGAN [44], DCGAN [45] and the proposed Sub-GAN. The first two methods explore the class information during the generation, however, the generated digits do not look visually appealing. While the the samples from the others look better, the diversity is hard to control. In contrast, the proposed Sub-GAN can simultaneously discover the subspaces $\{S_i\}_{i=1}^K$ and generate diverse samples from each S_i.

SSC-OMP, ORGEN and iPursuit are subspace clustering algorithms. The DEC concentrate on deep embedding clustering while the CatGAN and InfoGAN are based on the generative models.

4.2   Evaluation Metrics

We employ various metrics to quantitatively evaluate the proposed Sub-GAN in terms of both generation and clustering capacity. Specifically, we assess the image quality by using the Inception Score [43] and Diversity Score [51]. We then quantify the clustering assignments by calculating the Adjusted Accuracy [52].

Inception Score: The inception score [43] is widely adopted in evaluating generative tasks which uses a pre-trained neural network classifier to capture both highly classifiable and diverse properties with respect to class labels. For evaluated samples, it calculates average KL divergences between conditional label distributions (expected to have low entropy for easily classifiable samples) and marginal distribution (expected to have high entropy if all classes are equally presented). We follow the same routine in [53] for evaluation, *i.e.*, using the Inception network [54] trained on the ImageNet dataset [55].

Diversity Score: The diversity score [51] is based on the cosine distances among features (the maximum score is 5). In this paper, we use it to quantitatively evaluate the diversity of generated samples thus validate the alleviation on mode collapse problem in GAN training.

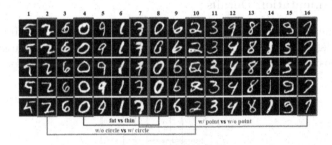

Fig. 3. Samples generated from joint unsupervised training on the MNIST dataset using the proposed Sub-GAN. Here, we set $K = 16$ (*top row*) to disentangle diverse subspaces $\{S_i\}_{i=1}^{16}$. Note we construct this figure according to the sequence derived from the clusterer C. The *bottom* illustrates three pairs of different writing styles of digits $2, 0$ and 7. The Sub-GAN can discover not only the 10 subspaces with the digits $0 - 9$, but the different writing style, *e.g.*, the fat and thin '0' in the 4-th and 8-th, respectively. The brown box reflects the failure case which confuses between 4 and 9. (Color figure online)

Adjusted Accuracy for Clustering: The Adjusted Accuracy [52] is a common metric for evaluating the clustering performance when $K \neq K_g$ where K_g denotes the ground-truth number of clusters. For each cluster S_k, we found the validation example x_i that maximizes $q(y_k|x_i)$, and assigned the label of x_i to all the points in the cluster S_k. We then compute the test accuracy based on the assigned class labels. Note it is identical to standard clustering accuracy when $K = K_g$.

4.3   Network Architecture

The generator G is mainly composed of two deconvolution layers (deconv) and two fully connected layers (FC). Specifically, the input latent vector is $l \in \mathbb{R}^{110}$. Afterwards, the network architecture of G is: (1) $FC.1024$ w/ ReLU and batch-norm; (2) $FC.6272$ w/ ReLU and batch-norm; (3) reshape to $7 \times 7 \times 128$; (4) deconv.4×4, stride $= 2$, feature maps $= 64$, w/ ReLU and batch-norm; (5) deconv.4×4, stride $= 2$, feature maps $= 1$.

The discriminator D is mainly composed of two convolution layers (conv) and two fully connected layers. In particular, the input image size is 28×28 with 1 gray channel. The network architecture of D is: (1) conv.4×4, stride $= 2$, feature maps $= 64$, w/ lReLU; (2) conv.4×4, stride $= 2$, feature maps $= 128$, w/ lReLU and batch-norm; (3) $FC.1024$ w/ lReLU and batch-norm; (4) $FC.1$ for classifying whether the image is real.

The clusterer C shares a similar structure with D. However, the last layer of C, i.e., $FC.K$, is designed to calculate a K-bins probabilities of the K subspaces.

4.4   Implementation Details

To setup the experiments of the proposed joint framework, we first initialize the soft assignments of the subspaces $\{\hat{S}_i\}_{i=1}^{K}$ by employing an unsupervised subspace clustering termed SMR [47] on the raw data space. Then, for stabilizing

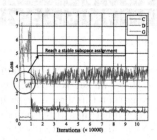

Fig. 4. Optimization losses of three modules, i.e., C (*blue*), D (*green*) and G (*red*), over training iterations on the MNIST dataset. The $\mathcal{L}_C$ demonstrates a downward trend before around $10,000$-th iteration. Sequentially, the training of G and D is unstable, e.g., D can easily discriminate the fake images from the real one so that the $\mathcal{L}_D$ is low. After C reaches a stable subspace assignment, the framework begins a normal adversarial training of G, D and C.

the training of Sub-GAN, we design G and D based on state-of-the-art techniques in DCGAN [45] and InfoGAN [29]. Specifically, we construct both networks with multiple convolution and deconvolution layers, followed by ReLU and leaky RelU (lReLU) activations in G and D, respectively. We also incorporate batch normalizations in both networks. We train the proposed joint model for $100,000$ iterations, with the batch size 100. We provide more training details in the supplementary material.

4.5   Generated Images by Sub-GAN

In this section, we analyze the generation performance of the proposed Sub-GAN on both MNIST and CIFAR-10 datasets.

Different K's on MNIST. We first conduct experiments on the MNIST dataset. Figure 2 shows the visualized comparison among samples derived from five contrastive generative models and the proposed Sub-GAN. The CGAN and InfoGAN generate samples from a union of subspaces. However, the samples derived from CGAN have unsatisfied consistency to human judgments, e.g., the components of the digits are broken in several cases. In addition, CGAN relies on the strong supervision of the annotations, which can only accessed on limited applications. The generated digits from IGAN, DCGAN or IWGAN have satisfied quality, yet the algorithm can not discover informative subspaces of the ambient space. As a result, the attribute of generated samples is hard to control. With $K = 10$, the proposed Sub-GAN framework generates diverse samples from each subspace, which alleviate the mode collapse problem in training GANs.

Table 1. Comparison of the diversity scores on both MNIST and CIFAR datasets with $K = 10$. The proposed Sub-GAN achieves best performance against contrastive methods, which alleviates the mode collapse problem in training GANs. The column of 'Real' indicates the diversity scores of real images from respective datasets.

Datasets	Real	CGAN [2]	IGAN [43]	IWGAN [44]	DCGAN [45]	InfoGAN [29]	Sub-GAN
MNIST	2.96	0.92	1.81	1.78	1.63	2.11	**2.36**
CIFAR	3.21	1.02	2.20	2.03	1.95	2.48	**2.72**

In Fig. 3, we also demonstrate that the proposed Sub-GAN can discover informative visual attributes which can hardly be annotated by strong supervision. As a result, the algorithm handles the mode collapse problem in an unsupervised way. In the experiment, we set $K = 16$ and generate images on the MNIST dataset. We can see that the Sub-GAN discovers multiple writing styles for the digits, and thus generates diverse new samples for different attributes. For example, the red boxes reflects that the digit '0' are divided into two types, i.e., the fat '0' and the thin one. It also finds several writing styles for other digits such as

'2 and '7'. We provide more results of different attributes in the supplementary material.

Furthermore, for quantitatively evaluating the diversity of the generated digits, we calculate the diversity scores among contrastive methods and report them in Table 1. While Sub-GAN achieves the best performance on this metric, it demonstrate that the proposed method alleviates the mode collapse problem due to the incorporation of subspace analysis.

To exposure the training process, we visualize the optimization loss in Fig. 4. The clusterer is iteratively optimized in about the first 10^4 iterations. During this process, the training of both generator and discriminator is unstable, $i.e.$, the loss of G is high and unstable while the loss of D is close to 0. It reflects that the generated samples are not visually appealing and can be easily discriminate by D. After reaching a stable subspace assignment, the joint unsupervised model starts a normal adversarial training of all modules.

CIFAR-10. In this section, we conduct experiments on the CIFAR-10 dataset. We set $K = 10$ in the training procedure and show the example results in Fig. 5. We also collect the generated samples from existing frameworks and calculate the inception score for each of them.

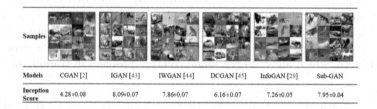

Models	CGAN [2]	IGAN [43]	IWGAN [44]	DCGAN [45]	InfoGAN [29]	Sub-GAN
Inception Score	4.28±0.08	8.09±0.07	7.86±0.07	6.16±0.07	7.26±0.05	7.95±0.04

Fig. 5. Inception scores for samples derived from various generative models on the CIFAR-10 dataset. Higher score indicates more consistence with human judgment. The experimental results demonstrate that the proposed Sub-GAN generates favorable samples against other state-of-the-art methods in terms of both visual expression and diversity. The IGAN achieves state-of-the-art inception score, however, the red boxes in the figure shows that it suffers from the mode collapse problem, which is tackled by Sub-GAN via subspace analysis. (Color figure online)

The Sub-GAN achieves favorable performance on the metric of inception score, which demonstrates the consistency to human judgments and thus the effectiveness of our method in terms of the generation ability. The proposed model can also generate samples from each subspace, which handles the mode collapse problem. The samples generated from the IGAN get a slight higher score than Sub-GAN, however, the samples in red boxes reflect the mode collapse problem of IGAN, $i.e.$, many generated samples are very similar. The other methods suffer from the same problem, while the quality of generated images is lower than ours. We provide more comparisons of the generated samples derived from the contrasted methods in the supplementary material.

We also quantitatively evaluate the diversity of generated samples on CIFAR dataset in Table 1, where the proposed Sub-GAN shows favorable performance against contrastive methods. The results of diversity scores show consistency to the visualized results in Fig. 5. For example, the diversity score of IGAN is lower than the proposed Sub-GAN (2.20 vs 2.72).

4.6 Image Clustering Performance

The clusterer is an auxiliary module which disentangles the subspaces to facilitate the generation. An effective interaction among G, D and C is important for both generating samples and clustering. In this section, we analyze the clustering performance of the proposed Sub-GAN on both MNIST and CIFAR datasets.

In this paper, the clusterer updates the clustering assignment of the whole dataset in each epoch, while the D refine the assignment of one mini-batch in each iteration. Some samples might be wrongly grouped based on the global similarity to all others, hence we refine the assignment in D based on the similarity of samples in local batches. We have conducted an ablation studies on the MNIST dataset with $K = 10$ and reported the clustering accuracy (%) in Table 2, which demonstrates the effectiveness of the refinement operation.

We report the adjusted accuracy of contrastive methods on both datasets in Table 3. The K-means method does not perform well on this task, since it lacks the ability on handling the high-dimensional large-scale data. In contrast, the subspace clustering (SSC, LSR, SMR, NSN, SSC-OMP, ORGEN and iPursuit), the deep embedding based clustering method (DEC) and the generation based methods (CatGAN and InfoGAN) show better performance due to the distinctive representation or iteratively optimization. In contrast, the proposed Sub-GAN achieves favorable performance against contrastive methods under all configurations, since the deep representation is iteratively updated according to the guidance of adversarial training process.

Note in the experiment with $K = 10$, the accuracy of initialized assignment using SMR is 73.39% for MNIST and 56.24% for CIFAR, while the joint training of three modules induces about 12% and 22% improvement, respectively. Consequently, the information interaction facilitates not only the generation of diverse samples but also the clustering performance. In addition, for both datasets, the Sub-GAN shows better performance with increasing K's, since the model can disentangle informative subspace structure with a large number of clusters.

Table 2. Clustering accuracy (%) on the MNIST dataset under $K = 10$ with/without the refinement operation in the discriminator.

Refinement in D	1st Epoch	20th Epoch	40th Epoch	Last Epoch
W/o	75.23	82.96	83.11	83.87
W/	**77.12**	**83.45**	**84.24**	**85.32**

Table 3. Unsupervised clustering performance (adjusted clustering accuracy) of the contrasted methods on the MNIST and CIFAR datasets with different K's. The clusterer in Sub-GAN shows favorable performance against various clustering algorithms.

Methods	MNIST			CIFAR		
	$K = 10$	$K = 16$	$K = 20$	$K = 10$	$K = 16$	$K = 20$
K-means	53.49	60.36	62.55	42.62	46.81	51.02
SSC [4]	62.71	66.82	70.19	50.31	52.77	53.98
LSR [46]	66.85	70.21	73.83	53.97	55.80	59.24
SMR [47]	73.39	81.27	83.63	56.24	59.02	62.73
NSN [48]	68.75	71.04	73.67	52.29	56.55	59.03
SSC-OMP [35]	76.33	79.25	82.52	51.21	53.02	57.84
ORGEN [31]	71.04	74.07	78.65	52.29	55.61	58.08
iPursuit [49]	61.35	64.28	68.84	59.21	62.53	65.66
DEC [39]	84.30	83.28	83.02	61.03	65.29	67.31
CatGAN [50]	80.21	84.92	90.30	67.42	67.85	68.76
InfoGAN [29]	70.63	73.77	78.69	71.02	73.64	74.07
Sub-GAN	**85.32**	**90.36**	**90.81**	**78.95**	**81.35**	**82.44**

5   Conclusions

In this work, we present an unsupervised Sub-GAN model for jointly learning the latent subspaces of the ambient space and generating instances correspondingly. We incorporate a novel clusterer into the GAN framework, where the clusterer disentangles the subspaces and is updated based on the deep representations of the samples derived from the discriminator. Meanwhile, the generator is fed with both random vectors of a normal distribution and low-dimensional eigenvectors derived from the clusterer. Here, the eigenvectors reflect latent structures of the disentangled subspaces. The discriminator is sequentially designed to reward high scores for samples which fit a specific subspace distribution, and provide feedbacks to refine the cluster assignment. Both quantitative evaluation and the visualization demonstrate that Sub-GAN can not only discover meaningful latent subspaces of the datasets but also generate photo-realistic and diverse images.

Acknowledgments. This work was supported in part by NSFC under Grants 61620106008, 61572264, NSF CAREER under Grant 1149783, the Open Project Program of the National Laboratory of Pattern Recognition and the Natural Science Foundation of Tianjin, China, under Grant 18JCYBJC15400.

References

1. Goodfellow, I., et al.: Generative adversarial nets. In: NIPS (2014)
2. Mirza, M., Osindero, S.: Conditional generative adversarial nets. arXiv preprint arXiv:1411.1784 (2014)
3. Vidal, R.: Subspace clustering. IEEE Sig. Process. Mag. **28**(2), 52–68 (2011)
4. Elhamifar, E., Vidal, R.: Sparse subspace clustering. In: CVPR (2009)
5. Yu, L., Zhang, W., Wang, J., Yu, Y.: SeqGAN: sequence generative adversarial nets with policy gradient. In: AAAI (2017)
6. Shen, W., Liu, R.: Learning residual images for face attribute manipulation. In: CVPR (2017)
7. Dong, H., Yu, S., Wu, C., Guo, Y.: Semantic image synthesis via adversarial learning. In: ICCV (2017)
8. Mao, X., Li, Q., Xie, H., Lau, R.Y., Wang, Z., Smolley, S.P.: Least squares generative adversarial networks. In: ICCV (2017)
9. Deng, Z., et al.: Structured generative adversarial networks. In: NIPS (2017)
10. Li, C., Wand, M.: Precomputed real-time texture synthesis with markovian generative adversarial networks. In: Leibe, B., Matas, J., Sebe, N., Welling, M. (eds.) ECCV 2016. LNCS, vol. 9907, pp. 702–716. Springer, Cham (2016). https://doi.org/10.1007/978-3-319-46487-9_43
11. Zhang, H., et al.: StackGAN: text to photo-realistic image synthesis with stacked generative adversarial networks. In: ICCV (2017)
12. Ledig, C., et al.: Photo-realistic single image super-resolution using a generative adversarial network. In: CVPR (2017)
13. Luc, P., Couprie, C., Chintala, S., Verbeek, J.: Semantic segmentation using adversarial networks. In: NIPS (2016)
14. Wei, Y., Feng, J., Liang, X., Cheng, M.M., Zhao, Y., Yan, S.: Object region mining with adversarial erasing: a simple classification to semantic segmentation approach. In: CVPR (2017)
15. Donahue, J., Krähenbühl, P., Darrell, T.: Adversarial feature learning. In: ICLR (2017)
16. Nguyen, A., Yosinski, J., Bengio, Y., Dosovitskiy, A., Clune, J.: Plug & play generative networks: conditional iterative generation of images in latent space. In: CVPR (2017)
17. Wang, X., Gupta, A.: Generative image modeling using style and structure adversarial networks. In: Leibe, B., Matas, J., Sebe, N., Welling, M. (eds.) ECCV 2016. LNCS, vol. 9908, pp. 318–335. Springer, Cham (2016). https://doi.org/10.1007/978-3-319-46493-0_20
18. Nair, V., Hinton, G.E.: Rectified linear units improve restricted boltzmann machines. In: ICML (2010)
19. Tieleman, T.: Training restricted boltzmann machines using approximations to the likelihood gradient. In: ICML (2008)
20. Rifai, S., Vincent, P., Muller, X., Glorot, X., Bengio, Y.: Contractive auto-encoders: explicit invariance during feature extraction. In: ICML (2011)
21. Hinton, G.E., Osindero, S., Teh, Y.W.: A fast learning algorithm for deep belief nets. Neural Comput. **18**(7), 1527–1554 (2006)
22. Lee, H., Ekanadham, C., Ng, A.Y.: Sparse deep belief net model for visual area V2. In: NIPS (2008)
23. Hinton, G.E., Salakhutdinov, R.R.: Reducing the dimensionality of data with neural networks. Science **313**(5786), 504–507 (2006)

24. Arjovsky, M., Chintala, S., Bottou, L.: Wasserstein GAN. In: ICLR (2017)
25. Arjovsky, M., Bottou, L.: Towards principled methods for training generative adversarial networks. In: ICLR (2017)
26. van den Oord, A., Kalchbrenner, N., Espeholt, L., Vinyals, O., Graves, A., et al.: Conditional image generation with pixelCNN decoders. In: NIPS (2016)
27. Odena, A., Olah, C., Shlens, J.: Conditional image synthesis with auxiliary classifier GANs. In: ICML (2017)
28. Yan, X., Yang, J., Sohn, K., Lee, H.: Attribute2Image: conditional image generation from visual attributes. In: Leibe, B., Matas, J., Sebe, N., Welling, M. (eds.) ECCV 2016. LNCS, vol. 9908, pp. 776–791. Springer, Cham (2016). https://doi.org/10.1007/978-3-319-46493-0_47
29. Chen, X., Duan, Y., Houthooft, R., Schulman, J., Sutskever, I., Abbeel, P.: InfoGAN: interpretable representation learning by information maximizing generative adversarial nets. In: NIPS (2016)
30. Parsons, L., Haque, E., Liu, H.: Subspace clustering for high dimensional data: a review. ACM SIGKDD Explor. Newsl. **6**(1), 90–105 (2004)
31. You, C., Li, C.G., Robinson, D.P., Vidal, R.: Oracle based active set algorithm for scalable elastic net subspace clustering. In: CVPR (2016)
32. Patel, V.M., Van Nguyen, H., Vidal, R.: Latent space sparse subspace clustering. In: CVPR (2013)
33. Yang, J., Parikh, D., Batra, D.: Joint unsupervised learning of deep representations and image clusters. In: CVPR (2016)
34. Dizaji, K.G., Herandi, A., Huang, H.: Deep clustering via joint convolutional autoencoder embedding and relative entropy minimization. ICCV (2017)
35. You, C., Robinson, D., Vidal, R.: Scalable sparse subspace clustering by orthogonal matching pursuit. In: CVPR (2016)
36. Elhamifar, E., Vidal, R.: Sparse subspace clustering: algorithm, theory, and applications. IEEE Trans. Pattern Anal. Mach. Intell. **35**(11), 2765–2781 (2013)
37. Ng, A.Y., Jordan, M.I., Weiss, Y.: On spectral clustering: Analysis and an algorithm. In: NIPS (2002)
38. Peng, X., Xiao, S., Feng, J., Yau, W.Y., Yi, Z.: Deep subspace clustering with sparsity prior. In: IJCAI (2016)
39. Xie, J., Girshick, R., Farhadi, A.: Unsupervised deep embedding for clustering analysis. In: ICML (2016)
40. Nguyen, T.D., Le, T., Vu, H., Phung, D.: Dual discriminator generative adversarial nets. In: NIPS (2017)
41. Roth, K., Lucchi, A., Nowozin, S., Hofmann, T.: Stabilizing training of generative adversarial networks through regularization. In: NIPS (2017)
42. Von Luxburg, U.: A tutorial on spectral clustering. Statist. Comput. **17**(4), 395–416 (2007)
43. Salimans, T., Goodfellow, I., Zaremba, W., Cheung, V., Radford, A., Chen, X.: Improved techniques for training GANs. In: NIPS (2016)
44. Gulrajani, I., Ahmed, F., Arjovsky, M., Dumoulin, V., Courville, A.: Improved training of wasserstein GANs. In: NIPS (2017)
45. Radford, A., Metz, L., Chintala, S.: Unsupervised representation learning with deep convolutional generative adversarial networks. arXiv preprint arXiv:1511.06434 (2015)
46. Lu, C.-Y., Min, H., Zhao, Z.-Q., Zhu, L., Huang, D.-S., Yan, S.: Robust and efficient subspace segmentation via least squares regression. In: Fitzgibbon, A., Lazebnik, S., Perona, P., Sato, Y., Schmid, C. (eds.) ECCV 2012. LNCS, vol. 7578, pp. 347–360. Springer, Heidelberg (2012). https://doi.org/10.1007/978-3-642-33786-4_26

47. Hu, H., Lin, Z., Feng, J., Zhou, J.: Smooth representation clustering. In: CVPR (2014)
48. Park, D., Caramanis, C., Sanghavi, S.: Greedy subspace clustering. In: NIPS (2014)
49. Rahmani, M., Atia, G.K.: Innovation pursuit: A new approach to subspace clustering. In: ICML (2017)
50. Springenberg, J.T.: Unsupervised and semi-supervised learning with categorical generative adversarial networks. In: ICLR (2016)
51. Zhu, J.Y., et al.: Toward multimodal image-to-image translation. In: NIPS (2017)
52. Makhzani, A., Shlens, J., Jaitly, N., Goodfellow, I.: Adversarial autoencoders. In: ICLR (2016)
53. Rosca, M., Lakshminarayanan, B., Warde-Farley, D., Mohamed, S.: Variational approaches for auto-encoding generative adversarial networks. arXiv preprint arXiv:1706.04987 (2017)
54. Szegedy, C., Vanhoucke, V., Ioffe, S., Shlens, J., Wojna, Z.: Rethinking the inception architecture for computer vision. In: CVPR (2016)
55. Deng, J., Dong, W., Socher, R., Li, L.J., Li, K., Fei-Fei, L.: Imagenet: a large-scale hierarchical image database. In: CVPR (2009)

Pyramid Dilated Deeper ConvLSTM
for Video Salient Object Detection

Hongmei Song[1], Wenguan Wang[1] ⓘ, Sanyuan Zhao[1(✉)], Jianbing Shen[1,2],
and Kin-Man Lam[3]

[1] Beijing Lab of Intelligent Information Technology, School of Computer Science,
Beijing Institute of Technology, Beijing, China
{songhongmei,zhaosanyuan,shenjianbing}@bit.edu.cn,
wenguanwang.ai@gmail.com
[2] Inception Institute of Artificial Intelligence, Abu Dhabi, UAE
[3] The Hong Kong Polytechnic University, Kowloon, Hong Kong
enkmlam@polyu.edu.hk
https://github.com/shenjianbing/PDB-ConvLSTM

Abstract. This paper proposes a fast video salient object detection
model, based on a novel recurrent network architecture, named Pyramid
Dilated Bidirectional ConvLSTM (PDB-ConvLSTM). A Pyramid Dilated
Convolution (PDC) module is first designed for simultaneously extracting spatial features at multiple scales. These spatial features are then
concatenated and fed into an extended Deeper Bidirectional ConvLSTM
(DB-ConvLSTM) to learn spatiotemporal information. Forward and backward ConvLSTM units are placed in two layers and connected in a cascaded
way, encouraging information flow between the bi-directional streams and
leading to deeper feature extraction. We further augment DB-ConvLSTM
with a PDC-like structure, by adopting several dilated DB-ConvLSTMs
to extract multi-scale spatiotemporal information. Extensive experimental results show that our method outperforms previous video saliency models in a large margin, with a real-time speed of **20 fps** on a single GPU.
With unsupervised video object segmentation as an example application,
the proposed model (with a CRF-based post-process) achieves state-of-
the-art results on two popular benchmarks, well demonstrating its superior
performance and high applicability.

1 Introduction

Video saliency detection aims at finding the most interesting parts in each video
frame that mostly attract human attention. It can be applied as a fundamental
module in many visual tasks, such as video object segmentation, scene rendering,
object tracking, and so on. Similar to visual saliency detection in static images,
research on video saliency detection can also be divided into two categories, *i.e.*,
eye fixation prediction [39,41] and salient object detection [47,49]. The purpose

---

H. Song and W. Wang—Contributed equally.

V. Ferrari et al. (Eds.): ECCV 2018, LNCS 11215, pp. 744–760, 2018.
https://doi.org/10.1007/978-3-030-01252-6_44

of eye fixation prediction is to locate the focus of human eyes when looking at a scene, which is helpful for understanding the mechanism of biological visual attention. Salient object detection focuses on uniformly highlighting the most salient objects with clear contour. In this paper, we focus on the latter task.

Most existing video saliency methods [8,11,42,43], are built upon shallow, hand-crafted features (e.g., color, edge, etc.), and especially rely on motion information from optical flow. These methods are typically heuristic and suffer from slow speed (due to time-consuming optical flow computation) and low prediction accuracy (due to the limited representability of low-level features). Currently, only a few works [24,44] on video saliency detection, based on deep learning, can be found in the literature. For example, Wang et al. [44] proposed a fully convolutional network (FCN) based video saliency model, as a very early attempt towards an end-to-end deep learning solution for this problem, achieves a speed of 2 fps. In their method, temporal dynamics between only two adjacent video frames are considered. Clearly, it faces difficulties to achieve a real-time speed and lacks exploration of motion information from a longer time span.

To employ deep learning techniques for video saliency detection, two problems should be considered [44]. The first problem is how to describe the temporal and spatial information and how to combine them together. Optical flow offers explicit motion information, but also incurs significant computational cost, which severely limits the applicability of current video saliency models. The second problem is data. A sufficiently large, densely labeled video saliency training data is desirable, but hard to obtain. Wang et al. [44] synthesize motion frames from static images to enrich the video training data. However, the quality of the synthesized data is unsatisfactory.

To address above issues, first, we base our model upon a convolutional LSTM (ConvLSTM) structure [32], which captures the long and short-term memory of video sequences and contains both temporal and spatial information, for implicitly learning temporal dynamics and efficiently fusing temporal and spatial features. For encouraging information exchange between LSTM units in bi-directions, we propose a Deeper Bidirectional ConvLSTM (DB-ConvLSTM) structure which learns temporal characteristics in a cascaded and deeper way, i.e., the ConvLSTM units in the backward layer are built upon the forward layer (instead of directly connecting to the inputs). Thus the forward ConvLSTM units, each of which corresponds to a specific input frame, can exchange their sequential knowledge with the backward layers. For further improving the spatial learning ability of DB-ConvLSTM, we introduce a multi-scale receptive field module, called Pyramid Dilated Convolution (PDC), into ConvLSTM to obtain more spatial details. Second, we train our model with massive static-image saliency data, in addition to video saliency data. In this way, our network could capture different object appearances which are important for video saliency prediction. Above designs lead to a powerful and very fast deep video saliency model, which achieves state-of-the-art performance on three video datasets [2,31,43] with fast speed of 20 fps (all steps on one GPU). With unsupervised video object segmentation as an example application task, we further show that the proposed video saliency model, equipped with a CRF segmentation module, gains best performance over two popular video segmentation benchmarks (*e.g.*, DAVIS [31] and FBMS [2]), which clearly demonstrates the high applicability of our model.

2 Related Work

Image/Video Salient Object Detection. Recently, with the popularity of deep neural network, various deep learning based image salient object detection models were proposed, *e.g.*, multi-stream network with embedded super-pixels [22,25], recurrent module [26,40], and multi-scale and hierarchical feature fusion [16,36,51], *etc.*. These models generally achieve far better performance compared with traditional static saliency models [45,49].

Conventional video salient object detection methods [8,9,28,42] extract spatial and temporal features separately and then integrate them together to generate a spatiotemporal saliency map. The spatiotemporal result can be refined by various mechanisms [27,43]. The computational cost, especially for temporal features, is usually expensive. Recently, Wang *et al.* [44] introduced FCN to video salient object detection by using adjacent pairs of frames as input, which substantially improves the precision and achieves a speed of 2 fps. However, this speed is still so slow for real-time processing, and more spatiotemporal information should be explored by considering more frames in video sequences.

Unsupervised Video Segmentation. Some unsupervised video segmentation tasks, like temporal superpixel/supervoxel over-segmentation [3,48] and motion segmentation [2], are typically based on clustering methods with low-level appearance and motion information. The unsupervised video primary object segmentation [46], which is the most related video segmentation topic to our approach, aims at extracting the primary object(s) in video sequences with the use of object-level information (*e.g.*, object proposal) and various heuristics [7,10,38]. Those models have similar goal with video salient object detection, aside from they seeking to get a binary fore-/background mask for each video frame. As demonstrated in [42], video saliency models are able to offer valuable information for guiding video object segmentation. Recent unsupervised video object segmentation methods are mainly based on deep learning models, such as two-stream architecture [19], recurrent neural network [34], bottom-up top-down model [33], FCN network [5], *etc.*. In this work, we show our model is well applicable to unsupervised video object segmentation task.

3 Our Approach

This section elaborates on the details of the proposed video salient object detection model, which consists of two key components. The first one, named *Pyramid Dilated Convolution* (PDC) module, is used for explicitly extracting spatial saliency features on multi-scales (as shown in Fig. 2). This is achieved via a set of parallel dilated convolution layers with different sampling rates (Sect. 3.1). The second module, named *Pyramid Dilated Bidirectional ConvLSTM* (PDB-ConvLSTM), which augments the *vanilla* ConvLSTM with the powerful structure of PDC module and is improved with a cascaded bi-directional feature learning process, *i.e.*, learning deeper, backward information upon forward features. PDB-ConvLSTM takes the spatial features learnt from the PDC module as inputs, and outputs improved spatiotemporal saliency representations for final video salient object prediction (Sect. 3.2). In Sect. 3.3, detailed implementations of our model are presented.

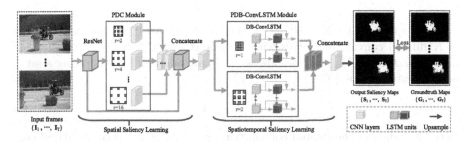

Fig. 1. Architecture overview of the proposed video salient object detection model, which consists of two components, *e.g.*, a spatial saliency learning module based on Pyramid Dilated Convolution (PDC) (Sect. 3.1) and a spatiotemporal saliency learning module via Pyramid Dilated Bidirectional ConvLSTM (PDB-ConvLSTM) (Sect. 3.2).

3.1 Spatial Saliency Learning via PDC Module

A typical CNN model is comprised of a stack of convolution layers, interleaved with non-linear downsampling operation (*e.g.*, max pooling) and point-wise non-linearity (*e.g.*, *ReLU*). Downsampling operation is effective for enlarging the receptive field, but quite harmful for pixel-wise prediction tasks, such as video salient object detection, since too many spatial details are lost. The recently proposed dilated convolution [50] provides a good alternative that efficiently computes dense CNN features at any receptive field sizes without loss of resolution. This is achieved by a specially designed 'hole' kernel which has sparsely aligned weights.

Additionally, multi-scale information often plays an important role for many computer vision tasks, such as image classification [13] and semantic segmentation [4,53]. Previous studies [18,39] in cognitive psychology also emphasized the multi-scale nature as an essential element of visual saliency. Motivated by above research, we utilize a PDC module, which consists of a set of dilated convolutions with different dilation rates, for emphasizing multi-scale spatial saliency representation learning (see Fig. 2).

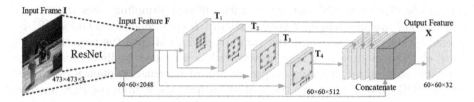

Fig. 2. Illustration of PDC module, where features from 4 parallel dilated convolution branches with different dilated rates are concatenated with the input features for emphasizing multi-scale spatial feature learning. See Sect. 3.1 for details.

More specially, let $\mathbf{F} \in \mathbb{R}^{W \times H \times M}$ denote the input 3D feature tensor, a set of K dilated convolution layers with kernels $\{\mathbf{C}_k \in \mathbb{R}^{c \times c \times C}\}_{k=1}^K$ and different dilation factors $\{r_k\}_{k=1}^K$ (strides are set as 1) are adopted for generating a set of output feature maps $\{\mathbf{T}_k \in \mathbb{R}^{W \times H \times C}\}_{k=1}^K$:

$$\mathbf{T}_k = \mathbf{C}_k \circledast \mathbf{F}. \tag{1}$$

Here '$\circledast$' indicates the dilated convolution operation. For a certain dilated convolution layer with $c \times c$ kernel and r_k dilation rate, it could preserve a receptive field with size of $[(c-1)r_k + 1]^2$. Thus the dilated convolution increases receptive field size exponentially while with linear parameter accretion. Although the sizes of the output features are identical, the receptive field sizes $[(c-1)r_k + 1]^2$ differ significantly with the change of the dilation rate r_k, sometimes even being much larger than the input frame size. This is similar to observing the image from different distances. A region will be reasonably salient if only we see it from a proper distance and see its proper spatial context.

After that, multi-scale spatial features $\{\mathbf{T}_k\}_{k=1}^K$ are concatenated together and fed into PDB-ConvLSTM (detailed in next section), thus the network is able to learn the importance of the scales automatically (such as learning saliency feature from a proper distance). The combined feature $\mathbf{X} \in \mathbb{R}^{W \times H \times KC}$ is calculated as:

$$\mathbf{X} = [\mathbf{T}_1, \ \mathbf{T}_2, \ldots, \ \mathbf{T}_K], \tag{2}$$

where '$[., .]$' represents the concatenation operation.

Inspired by the residual connection [14], we further combine the original input feature $\mathbf{F}$ into $\mathbf{X}$ to address the degradation problem. Thus $\mathbf{X} \in \mathbb{R}^{W \times H \times (KC+M)}$ in above equation is improved in a residual form:

$$\mathbf{X} = [\mathbf{F}, \ \mathbf{T}_1, \ \mathbf{T}_2, \ldots, \ \mathbf{T}_K]. \tag{3}$$

In comparison, [4] proposes an *Atrous Spatial Pyramid Pooling* (ASPP) module, which applies multiple parallel atrous (dilated) convolutions with different sampling rates. Our PDC module has similar structure. However, ASPP simply performs element-wise sum operation (denoted by '$\oplus$') on the output features from dilated convolution layers: $\mathbf{X} = \mathbf{T}_1 \oplus \mathbf{T}_2 \oplus \ldots \oplus \mathbf{T}_K$, treating the features from different scales equally. Differently, PDC lets the network automatically learn the weights of different features. Our design is more intuitive and effective, which will be further quantitatively verified in Sect. 4.4. With above definition, we build a powerful spatial feature learning model that emphasizes multi-scales. In next section, we will improve traditional ConvLSTM with deeper spatiotemporal information extraction and a PDC-like structure.

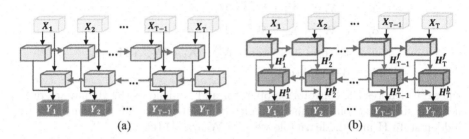

Fig. 3. Illustration of (a) Bidirectional ConvLSTM and (b) the proposed DB-ConvLSTM module. In PDB-ConvLSTM module, two DB-ConvLSTMs with different dilate rates are adopted for capturing multi-scale information and encouraging information flow between bi-directional LSTM units. See Sect. 3.2 for details.

3.2 Spatiotemporal Saliency Learning via PDB-ConvLSTM Module

Given an input video sequence $\{\mathbf{I}_t\}_{t=1}^{T}$ with T frames, we adopt PDC Module to produce a corresponding sequence of multi-scale spatial saliency features $\{\mathbf{X}_t\}_{t=1}^{T}$. Then these spatial features are fed into a modified ConvLSTM structure, called Pyramid Dilated Bidirectional ConvLSTM (PDB-ConvLSTM), for interpreting the temporal characteristics of video frames and fusing spatial and temporal features automatically. The PDB-ConvLSTM is improved in two ways. First, previous shallow, parallel bi-directional feature extraction strategy is replaced with a deeper and cascaded learning process, $i.e.$, building backward LSTM unit upon spatiotemporal features learnt in forward process. Second, incorporating pyramid dilated convolutions into LSTM for learning saliency features in multi-scales. Before detailing the proposed PDB-ConvLSTM module, we first give a brief introduction of classic ConvLSTM.

Vanilla ConvLSTM. ConvLSTM [32], as a convolutional counterpart of conventional fully connected LSTM (FC-LSTM) [15], introduces convolution operation into input-to-state and state-to-state transitions. ConvLSTM preserves spatial information as well as modeling temporal dependency. Thus it has been well applied in many spatiotemporal pixel-level tasks, such as dynamic visual attention prediction [41], video super-resolution [12]. Similar to FC-LSTM, ConvLSTM unit consists of a memory cell $\mathbf{c}_t$, an input gate $\mathbf{i}_t$, an output gate $\mathbf{o}_t$ and a forget gate $\mathbf{f}_t$. The memory cell $\mathbf{c}_t$, acting as an accumulator of the state information, is accessed, updated and cleared by self-parameterized controlling gates: $\mathbf{i}_t$, $\mathbf{o}_t$ and $\mathbf{f}_t$. As soon as an input arrives, the new data will be accumulated to the memory cell if the input gate is activated. Similarly, the past cell status $\mathbf{c}_{t-1}$ could be forgotten if the forget gate $\mathbf{f}_t$ is switched on. Whether the latest memory cell's value $\mathbf{c}_t$ will be transmitted to the final state $\mathbf{h}_t$ is further controlled by the output gate $\mathbf{o}_t$. With above definitions, ConvLSTM can be formulated as follows:

$$
\begin{aligned}
\mathbf{i}_t &= \sigma(\mathbf{W}_i^X * \mathbf{X}_t + \mathbf{W}_i^H * \mathbf{H}_{t-1}), \\
\mathbf{f}_t &= \sigma(\mathbf{W}_f^X * \mathbf{X}_t + \mathbf{W}_f^H * \mathbf{H}_{t-1}), \\
\mathbf{o}_t &= \sigma(\mathbf{W}_o^X * \mathbf{X}_t + \mathbf{W}_o^H * \mathbf{H}_{t-1}), \\
\mathbf{c}_t &= \mathbf{f}_t \circ \mathbf{c}_{t-1} + \mathbf{i}_t \circ \tanh(\mathbf{W}_c^X * \mathbf{X}_t + \mathbf{W}_c^H * \mathbf{H}_{t-1}), \\
\mathbf{H}_t &= \mathbf{o}_t \circ \tanh(\mathbf{c}_t),
\end{aligned}
\tag{4}
$$

where '$*$' denotes the convolution operator and '$\circ$' denotes the Hadamard product. For simplicity, bias terms are omitted. All the gates $\mathbf{i}, \mathbf{f}, \mathbf{o}$, memory cell $\mathbf{c}$, hidden state $\mathbf{H}$ and the learnable weights $\mathbf{W}$ are 3D tensors.

It can be seen that above ConvLSTM simply 'remembers' the past sequences, since it accumulates the past information in the memory cells. However, in video sequences, information from both the forward and backward frames are important and complementary for predicting video saliency. Thus Bidirectional ConvLSTM (B-ConvLSTM) should be used for capturing temporal characteristics in bi-directions (see Fig. 3(a)):

$$
\mathbf{Y}_t = \tanh(\mathbf{W}_y^{H^f} * \mathbf{H}_t^f + \mathbf{W}_y^{H^b} * \mathbf{H}_{t-1}^b),
\tag{5}
$$

where $\mathbf{H}^f$ and $\mathbf{H}^b$ indicates the hidden states from forward and backward ConvLSTM units, and $\mathbf{Y}_t$ indicates the final output considering bidirectional spatiotemporal information.

Deeper Bidirectional ConvLSTM. In B-ConvLSTM, there is no information exchange between the forward and backward directional LSTM units. We first improve B-ConvLSTM by organizing the forward and backward ConvLSTM units in a cascaded and tighter way, called Deeper Bidirectional ConvLSTM (DB-ConvLSTM). The DB-ConvLSTM has two layers, a shallow, forward layer and a deeper, backward layer (see Fig. 3(b)). The ConvLSTM units in the forward layer receive spatial feature maps $\{\mathbf{X}_t\}_{t=1}^T$ from T frames as inputs, and output forward sequential feature maps $\{\mathbf{H}_t^f\}_{t=1}^T$ (according to Eq. 4). The deeper layer is constituted of the backward units that receive the output features from the forward layer $\{\mathbf{H}_t^f\}_{t=1}^T$ as inputs. Formally, the backward ConvLSTM unit is formulated as:

$$
\begin{aligned}
\mathbf{i}_t^b &= \sigma(\mathbf{W}_i^{H^f} * \mathbf{H}_t^f + \mathbf{W}_i^{H^b} * \mathbf{H}_{t+1}^b), \\
\mathbf{f}_t^b &= \sigma(\mathbf{W}_f^{H^f} * \mathbf{H}_t^f + \mathbf{W}_f^{H^b} * \mathbf{H}_{t+1}^b), \\
\mathbf{o}_t^b &= \sigma(\mathbf{W}_o^{H^f} * \mathbf{H}_t^f + \mathbf{W}_o^{H^b} * \mathbf{H}_{t+1}^b), \\
\mathbf{c}_t^b &= \mathbf{f}_t^b \circ \mathbf{c}_{t+1}^b + \mathbf{i}_t^b \circ \tanh(\mathbf{W}_c^{H^f} * \mathbf{H}_t^f + \mathbf{W}_c^{H^b} * \mathbf{H}_{t+1}^b), \\
\mathbf{H}_t^b &= \mathbf{o}_t^b \circ \tanh(\mathbf{c}_t^b).
\end{aligned}
\tag{6}
$$

Then the forward features $\{\mathbf{H}_t^f\}_{t=1}^T$ and the backward features $\{\mathbf{H}_t^b\}_{t=1}^T$ are combined for final outputs: $\{\mathbf{Y}_t\}_{t=1}^T$, using Eq. 5. In this way, information are encouraged to flow between the forward and backward ConvLSTM units, and deeper spatiotemporal features can be extracted by the backward units.

Deeper Bidirectional ConvLSTM with Pyramid Dilated Convolution. In order to extract more powerful spatiotemporal information and let the network adapt to salient targets at different scales, we further extend DB-ConvLSTM with a PDC-like structure. Specifically, the outputs $\{\mathbf{X}_t\}_{t=1}^T$ from the spatial PDC module are fed into several parallel DB-ConvLSTMs (see Fig. 1). In these DB-ConvLSTM modules, convolution operation '$*$' is further replaced by dilated convolution '$\circledast$' and different dilation factors are adopted. Such designs lead to a more powerful ConvLSTM structure, named Pyramid Dilated Bidirectional ConvLSTM (PDB-ConvLSTM). It is able to utilize different features from different receptive fields for capturing more complementary spatiotemporal features.

3.3 Detailed Network Architecture

Base Network. At the bottom the suggested model resides a stack of convolutional layers, which are borrowed from the first five convolution blocks of the model in [53] (a ResNet-50 [14]-like model). Given an input frame $\mathbf{I}$ with resolution of 473×473, the feature $\mathbf{F} \in \mathbb{R}^{60 \times 60 \times 2048}$ extracted from the last convolution block is fed into our PDC module for multi-scale spatial feature learning.

PDC Module. In PDC module, four parallel dilated convolution layers ($K = 4$) are adopted, where the size of the kernel is set as $c = 3, C = 512$, and the four dilation factors are set as $r_k = 2^k$ ($k = \{1, \ldots, 4\}$). Thus the PDC module is able to extract features on four different scales. Following Eq. 3, the outputs $\{\mathbf{T}_k \in \mathbb{R}^{60 \times 60 \times 512}\}_{k=1}^4$ of the four dilated convolution branches and the inputs $\mathbf{F} \in \mathbb{R}^{60 \times 60 \times 2048}$ of the PDC module are further concatenated for generating a multi-scale spatial saliency feature $\mathbf{X} \in \mathbb{R}^{60 \times 60 \times 4096}$. A 1×1 convolution layer with 32 channels is then applied for feature dimension reduction. Therefore, for the input video $\{\mathbf{I}_t\}_{t=1}^T$, PDC module produces a sequence of multi-scale spatial features $\{\mathbf{X}_t \in \mathbb{R}^{60 \times 60 \times 32}\}_{t=1}^T$, which will be further fed into the PDB-ConvLSTM module for spatiotemporal saliency prediction.

PDB-ConvLSTM Module. PDB-ConvLSTM module consists of two DB-ConvLSTMs, which are equipped with 3×3 kernels (32 channels). The dilation factors are set as 1 and 2 respectively, due to our limited computational resources. Note that, when the dilation factor is set as 1, the dilation kernel can be viewed as a normal convolution kernel without any 'holes'. For each frame, the outputs of the two DB-ConvLSTM branches in the PDB-ConvLSTM module are further concatenated as a multi-scale spatiotemporal saliency feature with $60 \times 60 \times 64$ dimensions. Then the output features from the PDB-ConvLSTM module are fed into a 1×1 convolution layer with 1 channel and *sigmoid* activation for producing final saliency map. The saliency map is upsampled into the original input frame size, *i.e.*, 473×473, via bilinear interpolation.

Loss Function. For producing better saliency prediction and training the suggested model more efficiently, we propose here a fused loss function that accounts for multiple evaluation metrics, inspired by [40]. Let $\mathbf{G} \in \{0,1\}^{473 \times 473}$ and $\mathbf{S} \in [0,1]^{473 \times 473}$ denote the groundtruth saliency map and predicted saliency respectively, the overall loss $\mathcal{L}$ can be formulated as follows:

$$\mathcal{L}(\mathbf{S}, \mathbf{G}) = \mathcal{L}_{cross\_entropy}(\mathbf{S}, \mathbf{G}) + \mathcal{L}_{MAE}(\mathbf{S}, \mathbf{G}), \tag{7}$$

where $\mathcal{L}_{cross\_entropy}$ and $\mathcal{L}_{MAE}$ indicate cross entropy loss and MAE loss respectively. $\mathcal{L}_{cross\_entropy}$ is computed as:

$$\mathcal{L}_{cross\_entropy}(\mathbf{S}, \mathbf{G}) = -\frac{1}{N} \sum_{i=1}^{N} [g_i log(s_i) + (1 - g_i)log(1 - s_i)] \tag{8}$$

where $g_i \in \mathbf{G}$, and $s_i \in \mathbf{S}$. N indicates the total pixel number, *i.e.*, $N = 473 \times 473$.

$\mathcal{L}_{MAE}$ is based on MAE metric, which is widely used in salient object detection. $\mathcal{L}_{MAE}$ computes the absolute difference between the predicted saliency map $\mathbf{S}$ and the corresponding ground truth $\mathbf{G}$:

$$\mathcal{L}_{MAE}(\mathbf{S}, \mathbf{G}) = \frac{1}{N} \sum_{i=1}^{N} |g_i - s_i|. \tag{9}$$

Training Settings. During training, with training batch size H, the network can be fed with H video frames or H copies of the same image. The latter one can be interpreted as using the PDB-ConvLSTM to refine the single-image saliency map for $2H$ times in each DB-ConvLSTM branch. This means we can utilize the massive static-image saliency data to let the network capture more appearances of the objects and the scenes. Therefore, our training procedure has three steps. First, we pre-train the spatial-learning part (including PDC module and base network) using two image saliency datasets: MSRA10K [6], and DUT-OMRON [49], and one video dataset: the training set of DAVIS dataset [31]. Initial learning rate of SGD algorithm is 10^{-8}. Then we set the learning rate of spatiotemporal learning part (PDB-ConvLSTM module) as 10^{-6}, and use above static and video data to train the whole model. After that, we fix the weights of the spatial-learning part and fine-tune the spatiotemporal learning part with the training set of DAVIS dataset only (learning rate is set as 10^{-6}). In this way, although the densely labelled video saliency data is scarce, our video saliency detection model still achieves good generalization performance for unseen videos. Quantitative experiments regarding to our training strategy can be found in Sect. 4.4. The proposed videos saliency model is implemented using PYTHON, with the Caffe toolbox. Momentum and weight decay are set to 0.9 and 0.0005 respectively. The length of the training video frames H is set to 5.

Data Augmentation. We use data augmentation by mirror reflection, rotation (four rotation angles, 0°, 90°, 180°, and 270°) and image cropping to relieve overfitting. For each training sample instance (static images or video frames), we crop out the most top, bottom, left, and right slices of the border. Meanwhile, considering the video sequences may have different frame rates, we utilize different sampling steps in time axis to increase training samples. Specifically, for each video training iteration, we first randomly select a video frame from video data as the first frame in the training batch. Then we pick up following frames with a certain sampling step $(= \{1, 2, 3, 4, 5, 6\})$ until obtaining a training batch of 5 frames. The total training time is about 40 hours on one GTX 1080Ti GPU (11G Memory).

4   Experiments

In this section, two sets of experiments are first performed. One is for examining the performance of the proposed model for the main purpose, video salient object detection (Sect. 4.1). The other one is for evaluating the effectiveness of the proposed model on unsupervised video object segmentation, as salient object detection has been shown as an essential preprocessing step for unsupervised segmentation task (Sect. 4.2). After that, in Sect. 4.3, we present runtime analysis. Finally, an ablation study is performed to gain a deeper insight into the proposed model (Sect. 4.4).

For video salient object detection, we evaluate the performance on three public datasets, *i.e.*, Densely Annotated VIdeo Segmentation (DAVIS) [31], Freiburg-Berkeley Motion Segmentation (FBMS) [2] and the Video Salient object detection (ViSal) [43]. **DAVIS** consists of 50 high-quality videos, totaling 3455 frames with fully annotated pixel-level ground truths. We utilize its training set that consists of 30 videos, totaling 2079 frames, to train our model. We test the models on the test set, which contains 20 videos, totaling 1376 frames. **FBMS** contains 59 natural video sequences, in which 29 are for training and 30 are for testing. We report the performance of our method on the test set. **ViSal** is the first dataset specially designed for video salient object detection and includes 17 challenging video clips. The length of videos in ViSal ranges from 30 to 100 frames, and totally 193 frames are manually annotated. The whole ViSal dataset is used for evaluation. For unsupervised video object segmentation task, we perform experiments on the test sets of DAVIS and FBMS datasets, which are the most popular benchmarks currently.

4.1   Performance on Video Salient Object Detection

We compared our model with 18 famous saliency methods, including 11 image salient object detection models: Amulet [51], SRM [36], UCF [52], DSS [16], MSR [23], NLDF [29], DCL [25], DHS [26], ELD [22], RFCN [35], KSR [37]; and 7 video salient object detection approaches: SGSP [27], GAFL [43], SAGE [42], STUW [8], SP [28], FCNS [44], and FGRNE [24]. Note that FCNS and FGRNE are deep learning based video salient object detection models.

For quantitative evaluation, we employ three widely used metrics, namely PR curve, F-measure and MAE score. We refer readers to [44] for more details. Figure 4 plots the PR curves on the test sets of DAVIS and FBMS datasets,

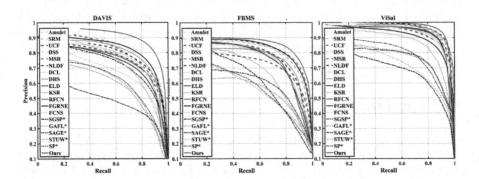

Fig. 4. Quantitative comparison against 18 saliency methods using PR curve on DAVIS [31], FBMS [2] and ViSal [43] datasets. Please see Sect. 4.1 for more details.

Table 1. Quantitative comparison results against 18 saliency methods using MAE and maximum F-measure on DAVIS [31], FBMS [2] and ViSal [43]. The best scores are marked in **bold**. See Sect. 4.1 for more details.

	Methods	Year	DAVIS		FBMS		ViSal	
			MAE↓	F^{max} ↑	MAE↓	F^{max} ↑	MAE↓	F^{max} ↑
Image Saliency Models	Amulet [51]	ICCV'17	0.082	0.699	0.110	0.725	0.032	0.894
	SRM [36]	ICCV'17	0.039	0.779	0.071	0.776	0.028	0.890
	UCF [52]	ICCV'17	0.107	0.716	0.147	0.679	0.068	0.870
	DSS [16]	CVPR'17	0.062	0.717	0.083	0.764	0.028	0.906
	MSR [23]	CVPR'17	0.057	0.746	**0.064**	0.787	0.031	0.901
	NLDF [29]	CVPR'17	0.056	0.723	0.092	0.736	0.023	0.916
	DCL [25]	CVPR'16	0.070	0.631	0.089	0.726	0.035	0.869
	DHS [26]	CVPR'16	0.039	0.758	0.083	0.743	0.025	0.911
	ELD [22]	CVPR'16	0.070	0.688	0.103	0.719	0.038	0.890
	KSR [37]	ECCV'16	0.077	0.601	0.101	0.649	0.063	0.826
	RFCN [35]	ECCV'16	0.065	0.710	0.105	0.736	0.043	0.888
Video Saliency Models	FGRNE [24]	CVPR'18	0.043	0.786	0.083	0.779	0.040	0.850
	FCNS [44]	TIP'18	0.053	0.729	0.100	0.735	0.041	0.877
	SGSP* [27]	TCSVT'17	0.128	0.677	0.171	0.571	0.172	0.648
	GAFL* [43]	TIP'15	0.091	0.578	0.150	0.551	0.099	0.726
	SAGE* [42]	CVPR'15	0.105	0.479	0.142	0.581	0.096	0.734
	STUW* [8]	TIP'14	0.098	0.692	0.143	0.528	0.132	0.671
	SP* [28]	TCSVT'14	0.130	0.601	0.161	0.538	0.126	0.731
	Ours	ECCV'18	**0.030**	**0.849**	0.069	**0.815**	**0.022**	**0.917**

* Non-deep learning model

as well as the whole ViSal dataset. It can be observed that our model outperforms other competitors. The maximum F-measures and MAE scores on above three datasets are reported in Table 1. Overall, our model achieves the best performance over three datasets using all the evaluation metrics. Figure 5 presents some visual comparison results on three example video sequences: *horsejump-high* (from DAVIS), *tennis* (from FBMS), and *bird* (from ViSal). As seen, our model consistently produces accurate salient object estimations with various challenging scenes.

4.2 Performance on Unsupervised Video Object Segmentation

Video salient object detection model produces a sequence of probability maps that highlight the most visually important object(s). As demonstrated in [42], such salient object estimation could offer meaningful cue for unsupervised video primary object segmentation, which seeks to a binary foreground/background classification of each pixel. Thus video salient object detection can be used as a pre-processing step for unsupervised video segmentation. For better demonstrating the advantages of the proposed video saliency model, we extend our model for unsupervised video object segmentation and test it on DAVIS and FBMS datasets in segmentation settings.

Given an input frame I_t and corresponding saliency estimation S_t, we formulate the segmentation task as an energy function minimization problem. The

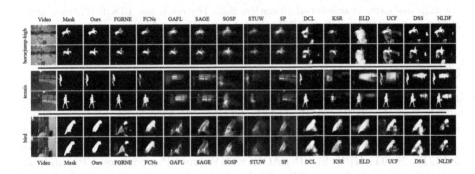

Fig. 5. Qualitative comparison against other top-performing saliency methods with groundtruths on three example video sequences. Zoom-in for details.

Table 2. Comparison with 7 representative unsupervised video object segmentation methods on the test sets of DAVIS and FBMS datasets. The best scores are marked in **bold**. See Sect. 4.2 for details.

Dataset	Metric	Method								
		ARP* [20]	LVO [34]	FSEG [19]	LMP [33]	SFL* [5]	FST* [30]	SAGE* [42]	Ours	Ours+
DAVIS	$\mathcal{J}$ ↑	76.2	75.9	70.7	70.0	67.4	55.8	41.5	74.3	**77.2**
	$\mathcal{F}$ ↑	70.6	72.1	65.3	65.9	66.7	51.1	36.9	72.8	**74.5**
FBMS	$\mathcal{J}$ ↑	59.8	65.1	68.4	35.7	55.0	47.7	61.2	72.3	**74.0**

* Non-deep learning model

segmentation energy function is based on fully connected CRF model [21], where the foreground (or background) label assignment probability in binary term is $\mathbf{S}_t$ (or $1 - \mathbf{S}_t$). The pairwise potential is defined as [21]. With the publicly available implementation of [21], our model takes about $0.5 \sim 1\,$s per frame to generate a segmentation mask.

We compare our segmentation results with 7 representative unsupervised video segmentation methods [5,19,20,30,33,34,42], on the test sets of DAVIS and FBMS datasets. Following the experimental settings of DAVIS dataset, we employ the intersection-over-union metric $(\mathcal{J})$ and contour accuracy $(\mathcal{F})$ metrics for quantitative evaluation. For FBMS dataset, we adopted intersection-over-union score, as done by previous methods. Table 2 summarizes the results, where *Ours* indicates the results obtained via a simple thresholding strategy $(= 0.42$, validated on the training set of DAVIS) and *Ours+* indicates the results obtained via the CRF optimization. It can be observed that our model is able to produce more accurate segmentation results. This is mainly because the proposed PDB-ConvLSTM offers a powerful spatiotemporal learning framework that captures multi-scale features efficiently.

Table 3. Runtime comparison with 6 existing video saliency methods.

Method	SGSP [27]	SAGE [42]	GAFL [43]	STUW [8]	SP [28]	FCNS [44]	Ours
Time(s)	1.70*(+)	0.88*(+)	1.04*(+)	0.78*(+)	6.05*(+)	0.47	**0.05**

* CPU time.

(+) indicates extra computation of optical flow. For reference, LDOF [1] takes about 49.64 s per frame, Flownet v2.0 [17] takes about 0.05 s per frame

4.3   Runtime Analysis

In Table 3, we report the runtime comparison results with other 6 video saliency models, namely SGSP, SAGE, GAFL, STUW, SP, FCNS. For all the methods, we exclude their computation time of optical flow and the I/O time. All timings are measured on the same computer configuration Intel Core i7-6700 @3.4GHz and GTX 1080Ti GPU. SGSP, SAGE, STUW and SP are run on CPU and take optical flow as extra input. FCNS needs to calculate static saliency first. In comparison, our model extracts spatial features for each input frame independently, and leans temporal dynamics via the efficient PDB-ConvLSTM module without optical flow. Additionally, our model does not need any pre-/post-processing. For a 353×353 input frame, our model achieves the fastest speed of 20 fps.

4.4   Ablation Study

PDC Module. In order to analyze the effect of PDC module, we derive four variants, each of which only adopts one single dilate rate, *i.e.*, r is set to $2, 4, 8$, or 16. We also replace our PDC module with ASPP [4], which adopts element-wise sum operation, instead of concatenation, over all the features from different

Table 4. Ablation study for PDC module on DAVIS and FBMS datasets.

Dataset	Metric	PDC Module					ASPP [4]
		$r = 2$	$r = 4$	$r = 8$	$r = 16$	$r = \{2, 4, 8, 16\}$	
DAVIS	$F^{max} \uparrow$	0.703	0.704	0.715	0.708	**0.774**	0.769
	MAE $\downarrow$	0.079	0.077	0.074	0.074	0.047	**0.045**
FBMS	$F^{max} \uparrow$	0.707	0.702	0.714	0.716	**0.744**	0.730
	MAE $\downarrow$	0.110	0.109	0.107	0.108	**0.103**	0.111

scales. The experimental results are summarized in Table 4. We can observe performance drops when only considering single scale and features extracted from different scales would have different impacts on the final results. Confusing multi-scale features (baseline: $r = \{2, 4, 8, 16\}$) brings the best performance. The results also demonstrate that the proposed PDC module is more favored, compared with ASPP, since PDC module lets the network automatically learn the importance of each scale via concatenation operation.

PDB-ConvLSTM Module. Four baselines are used to discuss the contribution of our PDB-ConvLSTM module in spatiotemporal information learning, namely Fully Connected LSTM (FC-LSTM), Convolutional LSTM (ConvLSTM), Bidirectional ConvLSTM (B-ConvLSTM), and Deeper Bidirectional ConvLSTM (DB-ConvLSTM). In comparison, we replace our PDB-ConvLSTM module with above variants and report the corresponding performance using maximum F-score and MAE over the DAVIS and FBMS datasets. The results are summarized in Table 5. It can be observed that, no surprisingly, FC-LSTM gains worst performance since it totally loses spatial details. DB-LSTM performs better than ConvLSTM and B-ConvLSTM due to its deeper fusion of bidirectional information. PDB-ConvLSTM further advances the performance by considering multi-scales.

Table 5. Ablation study for PDB-ConvLSTM on DAVIS and FBMS datasets.

Dataset	Metric	FC-LSTM	ConvLSTM	B-ConvLSTM	DB-ConvLSTM	PDB-ConvLSTM
DAVIS	$F^{max} \uparrow$	0.705	0.783	0.786	0.809	**0.849**
	MAE $\downarrow$	0.056	0.043	0.039	0.036	**0.030**
FBMS	$F^{max} \uparrow$	0.672	0.755	0.757	0.799	**0.815**
	MAE $\downarrow$	0.121	0.096	0.094	0.072	**0.069**

Training Protocol. Now we assess the our training strategy, *i.e.*, using massive data from static images and video frames. On DAVIS dataset, we find *Our w. static data* ($F^{max} \uparrow$: 0.849, MAE $\downarrow$: 0.030) outperforms *Our w/o. static data* ($F^{max} \uparrow$: 0.753, MAE $\downarrow$: 0.049). This demonstrates that using static data to train the model can avoid the risk of over-fitting on relatively small amount of video data and improve the generalization ability of our model.

5   Conclusions

This paper proposed a deep video salient object detection model which consists of two essential components: PDC module and PDB-ConvLSTM module. In the PDC module, a set of parallel dilated convolutions are adopted for extracting multi-scale spatial features through different receptive fields. In the PDB-ConvLSTM module, conventional ConvLSTM is extended with deeper information extraction and parallel two dilated ConvLSTMs to extract sequential features at different scales. The proposed model leverages both labeled video data and also the massive amount of labeled static-image data for training, so as to increase its generalization to diverse videos. The proposed model generates high-quality saliency maps with a real-time processing speed of 20 fps. The experiments also demonstrate the proposed model is well applicable to unsupervised segmentation task and achieves most accurate segmentation results.

Acknowledgments. This research was supported in part by the Beijing Natural Science Foundation under Grant 4182056, the Fok Ying Tung Education Foundation under Grant 141067, and the Specialized Fund for Joint Building Program of Beijing Municipal Education Commission.

References

1. Brox, T., Malik, J.: Large displacement optical flow: descriptor matching in variational motion estimation. IEEE TPAMI **33**(3), 500–513 (2011)
2. Brox, T., Malik, J.: Object segmentation by long term analysis of point trajectories. In: Daniilidis, K., Maragos, P., Paragios, N. (eds.) ECCV 2010. LNCS, vol. 6315, pp. 282–295. Springer, Heidelberg (2010). https://doi.org/10.1007/978-3-642-15555-0_21
3. Chang, J., Wei, D., Fisher, J.W.: A video representation using temporal superpixels. In: IEEE CVPR, pp. 2051–2058 (2013)
4. Chen, L.C., Papandreou, G., Kokkinos, I., Murphy, K., Yuille, A.L.: DeepLab: semantic image segmentation with deep convolutional nets, atrous convolution, and fully connected CRFs. IEEE TPAMI **40**(4), 834–848 (2018)
5. Cheng, J., Tsai, Y.H., Wang, S., Yang, M.H.: SegFlow: Joint learning for video object segmentation and optical flow. In: IEEE CVPR, pp. 686–695 (2017)
6. Cheng, M.M., Mitra, N.J., Huang, X., Torr, P.H.S., Hu, S.M.: Global contrast based salient region detection. IEEE TPAMI **37**(3), 569–582 (2015)
7. Cong, R., Lei, J., Fu, H., Huang, Q., Cao, X., Hou, C.: Co-saliency detection for rgbd images based on multi-constraint feature matching and cross label propagation. IEEE TIP **27**(2), 568–579 (2018)
8. Fang, Y., Wang, Z., Lin, W., Fang, Z.: Video saliency incorporating spatiotemporal cues and uncertainty weighting. IEEE TIP **23**(9), 3910–3921 (2014)
9. Fu, H., Cao, X., Tu, Z.: Cluster-based co-saliency detection. IEEE TIP **22**(10), 3766–3778 (2013)
10. Fu, H., Xu, D., Zhang, B., Lin, S., Ward, R.K.: Object-based multiple foreground video co-segmentation via multi-state selection graph. IEEE TIP **24**(11), 3415–3424 (2015)
11. Guo, F., et al.: Video saliency detection using object proposals. IEEE TCYB (2018)

12. Guo, J., Chao, H.: Building an end-to-end spatial-temporal convolutional network for video super-resolutiong. In: AAAI, pp. 4053–4060 (2017)
13. He, K., Zhang, X., Ren, S., Sun, J.: Spatial pyramid pooling in deep convolutional networks for visual recognition. IEEE TPAMI **37**(9), 1904–1916 (2015)
14. He, K., Zhang, X., Ren, S., Sun, J.: Deep residual learning for image recognition. In: IEEE CVPR, pp. 770–778 (2016)
15. Hochreiter, S., Schmidhuber, J.: Long short-term memory. Neural Comput. **9**(8), 1735–1780 (1997)
16. Hou, Q., Cheng, M.M., Hu, X., Borji, A., Tu, Z., Torr, P.H.S.: Deeply supervised salient object detection with short connections. In: IEEE CVPR, pp. 5300–5309 (2017)
17. Ilg, E., Mayer, N., Saikia, T., Keuper, M., Dosovitskiy, A., Brox, T.: Flownet 2.0: evolution of optical flow estimation with deep networks. In: IEEE CVPR, pp. 2462–2470 (2017)
18. Itti, L., Koch, C.: Computational modelling of visual attention. Nat. Rev. Neurosci. **2**(3), 194–203 (2001)
19. Jain, S., Xiong, B., Grauman, K.: Fusionseg: Learning to combine motion and appearance for fully automatic segmention of generic objects in videos. In: IEEE CVPR (2017)
20. Koh, Y.J., Kim, C.S.: Primary object segmentation in videos based on region augmentation and reduction. In: IEEE CVPR, pp. 7417–7425 (2017)
21. Krahenbuhl, P., Koltun, V.: Efficient inference in fully connected CRFs with Gaussian edge potentials. In: NIPS (2011)
22. Lee, G., Tai, Y.W., Kim, J.: Deep saliency with encoded low level distance map and high level features. In: IEEE CVPR, pp. 660–668 (2016)
23. Li, G., Xie, Y., Lin, L., Yu, Y.: Instance-level salient object segmentation. In: IEEE CVPR, pp. 247–256 (2017)
24. Li, G., Xie, Y., Wei, T., Wang, K., Lin, L.: Flow guided recurrent neural encoder for video salient object detection. In: IEEE CVPR, pp. 3243–3252 (2018)
25. Li, G., Yu, Y.: Deep contrast learning for salient object detection. In: IEEE CVPR, pp. 478–487 (2016)
26. Liu, N., Han, J.: Dhsnet: Deep hierarchical saliency network for salient object detection. In: IEEE CVPR, pp. 678–686 (2016)
27. Liu, Z., Li, J., Ye, L., Sun, G., Shen, L.: Saliency detection for unconstrained videos using superpixel-level graph and spatiotemporal propagation. IEEE TCSVT **27**(12), 2527–2542 (2017)
28. Liu, Z., Zhang, X., Luo, S., Meur, O.L.: Superpixel-based spatiotemporal saliency detection. IEEE TCSVT **24**(9), 1522–1540 (2014)
29. Luo, Z., Mishra, A.K., Achkar, A., Eichel, J.A., Li, S., Jodoin, P.M.: Non-local deep features for salient object detection. In: IEEE CVPR, pp. 6593–6601 (2017)
30. Papazoglou, A., Ferrari, V.: Fast object segmentation in unconstrained video. In: IEEE ICCV, pp. 1777–1784 (2013)
31. Perazzi, F., Pont-Tuset, J., McWilliams, B., Gool, L.J.V., Gross, M.H., Sorkine-Hornung, A.: A benchmark dataset and evaluation methodology for video object segmentation. In: IEEE CVPR, pp. 724–732 (2016)
32. Shi, X., Chen, Z., Wang, H., Yeung, D.Y., Wong, W.K., Woo, W.C.: Convolutional LSTM network: a machine learning approach for precipitation nowcasting. In: NIPS (2015)
33. Tokmakov, P., Alahari, K., Schmid, C.: Learning motion patterns in videos. In: IEEE CVPR, pp. 531–539 (2017)

34. Tokmakov, P., Alahari, K., Schmid, C.: Learning video object segmentation with visual memory. In: IEEE ICCV (2017)

35. Wang, L., Wang, L., Lu, H., Zhang, P., Ruan, X.: Saliency detection with recurrent fully convolutional networks. In: Leibe, B., Matas, J., Sebe, N., Welling, M. (eds.) ECCV 2016. LNCS, vol. 9908, pp. 825–841. Springer, Cham (2016). https://doi.org/10.1007/978-3-319-46493-0_50

36. Wang, T., Borji, A., Zhang, L., Zhang, P., Lu, H.: A stagewise refinement model for detecting salient objects in images. In: IEEE ICCV, pp. 4039–4048 (2017)

37. Wang, T., Zhang, L., Lu, H., Sun, C., Qi, J.: Kernelized subspace ranking for saliency detection. In: Leibe, B., Matas, J., Sebe, N., Welling, M. (eds.) ECCV 2016. LNCS, vol. 9912, pp. 450–466. Springer, Cham (2016). https://doi.org/10.1007/978-3-319-46484-8_27

38. Wang, W., Shen, J., Li, X., Porikli, F.: Robust video object cosegmentation. IEEE TIP 24(10), 3137–3148 (2015)

39. Wang, W., Shen, J.: Deep visual attention prediction. IEEE TIP 27(5), 2368–2378 (2018)

40. Wang, W., Shen, J., Dong, X., Borji, A.: Salient object detection driven by fixation prediction. In: IEEE CVPR, pp. 1171–1720 (2018)

41. Wang, W., Shen, J., Guo, F., Cheng, M.M., Borji, A.: Revisiting video saliency: a large-scale benchmark and a new model. In: IEEE CVPR, pp. 4894–4903 (2018)

42. Wang, W., Shen, J., Porikli, F.: Saliency-aware geodesic video object segmentation. In: IEEE CVPR, pp. 3395–3402 (2015)

43. Wang, W., Shen, J., Shao, L.: Consistent video saliency using local gradient flow optimization and global refinement. IEEE TIP 24(11), 4185–4196 (2015)

44. Wang, W., Shen, J., Shao, L.: Video salient object detection via fully convolutional networks. IEEE TIP 27(1), 38–49 (2018)

45. Wang, W., Shen, J., Shao, L., Porikli, F.: Correspondence driven saliency transfer. IEEE TIP 25(11), 5025–5034 (2016)

46. Wang, W., Shen, J., Xie, J., Fatih, P.: Super-trajectory for video segmentation. In: IEEE ICCV, pp. 1671–1679 (2017)

47. Wang, W., Shen, J., Yang, R., Porikli, F.: Saliency-aware video object segmentation. IEEE TPAMI 40(1), 20–33 (2018)

48. Xu, C., Corso, J.J.: Evaluation of super-voxel methods for early video processing. In: IEEE CVPR, pp. 1202–1209 (2012)

49. Yang, C., Zhang, L., Lu, H., Ruan, X., Yang, M.H.: Saliency detection via graph-based manifold ranking. In: IEEE CVPR, pp. 3166–3173 (2013)

50. Yu, F., Koltun, V.: Multi-scale context aggregation by dilated convolutions. In: ICLR (2016)

51. Zhang, P., Wang, D., Lu, H., Wang, H., Ruan, X.: Amulet: aggregating multi-level convolutional features for salient object detection. In: IEEE ICCV, pp. 202–211 (2017)

52. Zhang, P., Wang, D., Lu, H., Wang, H., Yin, B.: Learning uncertain convolutional features for accurate saliency detection. In: IEEE ICCV, pp. 212–221 (2017)

53. Zhao, H., Shi, J., Qi, X., Wang, X., Jia, J.: Pyramid scene parsing network. In: IEEE CVPR, pp. 6230–6239 (2017)

Where Will They Go? Predicting Fine-Grained Adversarial Multi-agent Motion Using Conditional Variational Autoencoders

Panna Felsen[1,2]([✉]), Patrick Lucey[2], and Sujoy Ganguly[2]

[1] BAIR, UC Berkeley, Berkeley, USA
panna@eecs.berkeley.edu
[2] STATS, Chicago, USA
{plucey,sganguly}@stats.com

Abstract. Simultaneously and accurately forecasting the behavior of many interacting agents is imperative for computer vision applications to be widely deployed (*e.g.*, autonomous vehicles, security, surveillance, sports). In this paper, we present a technique using conditional variational autoencoder which learns a model that "personalizes" prediction to individual agent behavior within a group representation. Given the volume of data available and its adversarial nature, we focus on the sport of basketball and show that our approach efficiently predicts context-specific agent motions. We find that our model generates results that are *three times* as accurate as previous state of the art approaches (5.74 ft vs. 17.95 ft).

Keywords: Forecasting · Motion prediction · Multi-agent tracking Context aware prediction · Conditional variational autoencoders

1 Introduction

Humans continuously anticipate the future states of their surroundings. Someone extending a hand to another is likely initiating a handshake. A couple entering a restaurant is likely looking for a table for two. A basketball player on defense is likely trying to stay between their opponent and the basket. These predictions are critical for shaping our daily interactions, as they enable humans to navigate crowds, score in sports matches, and generally follow social mores. As such, computer vision systems that are successfully deployed to interact with humans must be capable of forecasting human behavior.

In practice, deploying a computer vision system to make a fine-grain prediction is difficult. Intuitively, people rely on context to make more accurate

Electronic supplementary material The online version of this chapter (https://doi.org/10.1007/978-3-030-01252-6_45) contains supplementary material, which is available to authorized users.

© Springer Nature Switzerland AG 2018
V. Ferrari et al. (Eds.): ECCV 2018, LNCS 11215, pp. 761–776, 2018.
https://doi.org/10.1007/978-3-030-01252-6_45

predictions. For example, a basketball player may be known to stay back in the lane to help protect the rim. The ability to leverage specific information, or *personalize*, should improve the prediction of fine-grained human behavior.

The primary challenge of personalizing prediction of multi-agent motion is to develop a representation that is simultaneously robust to the number of possible permutations arising in a situation and sufficiently fine-grained, so the output prediction is at the desired level of granularity. One typically employees one of two approaches: (i) *bottom-up* – where each trajectory has the same model applied to it individually, or (ii) *top-down* – where a group representation of all trajectories has one model applied to it all at once. The data and target application mainly drive the choice of approach. Typically, in settings with a variable number of agents, *e.g.*, autonomous vehicles or surveillance, one uses a bottom-up approach [1–3]. When the number of agents is fixed, *e.g.*, sports, faces, and body pose one prefers a top-down approach [4–7].

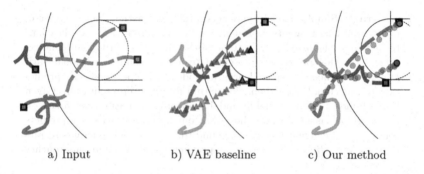

a) Input   b) VAE baseline   c) Our method

Fig. 1. (a) Given a 2D trajectory history of moving agents (solid lines), and the future motion of a subset of the agents (blue dashed lines); our **prediction task** (b) is to generate the most likely motion of the other agents (orange, purple dashed lines). Standard approaches are unable to capture the influence of the group motion (triangles). (c) Our method improves performance by incorporating context-specific information (circles). (Color figure online)

While efficient for heavily structured problems, current top-down methods cannot incorporate the necessary context to enable *personalized* prediction, and often require pre-computing some heuristic group representation. Whereas, bottom-up approaches can personalize via a large refinement module [1]. In this paper, we show that by using a conditional variational autoencoder (CVAE), we can create a generative model that simultaneously learns the latent representation of multi-agent trajectories and can predict the agents' context-specific motion.

Due to the vast amount of data available and its adversarial, multi-agent nature, we focus on predicting the motion paths of basketball players. Specifically, we address the problem of forecasting the motion paths of players during a game (Fig. 1a). We demonstrate the effectiveness of our approach on a new basketball dataset consisting of sequences of play from over 1200 games, which contains position data of players and the ball.

To understand the function of initial data representation, context, personalization of agent trajectory prediction and generative modeling, we divide our problem into three parts. First, to understand the role of data representation on prediction, we predict the offense given the motion history of all players (Fig. 1b). By applying *alignment* to the multi-agent trajectories we minimize the problem of permutation allowing our group representation of player motion to outperform the current state of the art methods. Next, to understand the role of context, we compare the prediction of offensive agents given the motion of the defense, player and team identities. We use separate encoders for context and player/team identity which we connect to the variational layer, as opposed to being used in a ranking and refinement layer, and thus act directly as conditionals. By conditioning on context with alignment and identity, we can generate a very accurate, fine-grained, prediction of any group of agents without the need for an additional refinement module (Fig. 1c). Finally, we tackle the challenge of forecasting the motion of subsets of players (a mixture of offense and defense), given the motion of the other remaining players. Again we find that our CVAE far outperforms the previous state of the art methods by a factor of two and that it can make reasonable predictions given only the motion history and the player and team identities when predicting the future motion of all ten players.

Our primary contributions are:

1. How to use context and identity as conditionals in CVAE thus removing the need for ranking and refinement modules.
2. Utilizing multi-agent alignment to personalize prediction
3. A dataset of fine-grained, personalized, adversarial multi-agent tracking data which will be made publicly available for research purposes.

2   Related Work

Forecasting Multi-Agent Motion. Lee et al. [1] provide an excellent review of recent path prediction methods, in which they chronicle previous works that utilize classical methods, inverse reinforcement learning, interactions, sequential prediction and deep generative models. For predicting multi-agent motion paths, there are two primary bodies of work: *bottom-up* and *top-down* approaches.

Regarding bottom-up approaches, where the number of agents varies, Lee *et al.* [1] recently proposed their DESIRE framework, which consisted of two main modules. First, they utilized a CVAE-based RNN encoder-decoder which generated multiple plausible predictions. These predictions, along with context, were fed to a ranking and refinement module that assigns a reward function. The predictions are then iteratively refined to obtain a maximum accumulated future reward. They demonstrated the approach on data from autonomous vehicles and aerial drones and outperformed other RNN-based methods [3]; however, in the absence of the refinement module, the predictions were poor.

For predicting variable numbers of humans moving in crowded spaces, Alahi et al. [2] introduced the idea of "Social LSTMs" which connected neighboring

LSTMs in a social pooling layer. The intuition behind this approach is that instead of utilizing all possible information in the scene, the model only focuses on people who are near each other. The model will then learn that behavior from data, which was shown to improve over traditional approaches which use hand-crafted functions such as social forces [8]. Many authors have applied similar methods for multi-agent tracking using trajectories [9–11].

Nearly all work that considers multiple agents via a top-down approach is concerned with modeling behaviors in sports. Kim et al. [12] used the global motion of all players to predict the future location of the ball in soccer. Chen et al. [13] used an occupancy map of noisy player detections to predict the camera-motion of a basketball broadcast. Zheng et al. [14] used an image-based representation of player positions over time to simulate the future location of a basketball. Lucey et al. [5] learned role representations from raw positional data, while Le et al. [7] utilized a similar representation with a deep neural network to imitate the motion paths of an entire soccer team. Felsen et al. [15] used hand-crafted features to predict future events in water polo and basketball. Lastly Su et al. [16] used ego-centric appearance and joint attention to model social dynamics and predict the motion of basketball players. In this paper, we utilize the representation which most closely resembles Le et al. [7], the CVAE approach utilized by [1], and a prediction task similar to [16].

Personalization to Tracking Data. Recommendation systems, which provide *personalized* predictions for various tasks often use matrix factorization techniques [17]. However, such techniques operate under the assumption that one can decompose the data linearly, using hand-crafted features to capture the non-linearities. However, in conjunction with deep models and the vast amount of vision data, recommendation engines based on vision data are starting to emerge. Recently, Deng et al. [18] used a factorized variational autoencoder to model audience reaction to full-feature length movies. Charles et al. [19] proposed using a CNN to personalize pose estimation to a person's appearance over time. Insafutdinov et al. [6] used a graph partitioning to group similar body-parts to enable effective body-pose tracking. In all of these works, they use their deep networks to find the low-dimensional embedding at the encoder state which they use to personalize their predictions. In this work, we followed a similar strategy but included the embedding in a variational module.

Conditional Variational Autoencoders. Variational Autoencoders [20] are similar to traditional autoencoders, but have an added regularization of the latent space, which allows for the generation of new examples in a variety of contexts [21,22]. Since the task of fine-grained prediction is naturally one in which history and context determine the future motions, we utilize a conditional variational autoencoder (CVAE) [23,24]. In computer vision, CVAEs have recently been used for inpainting [25,26], and for predicting the future motion of agents in complex scenes [1,27]. In this paper, we apply the idea of conditioning on the history and the surrounding context to predict the personalized adversarial motion of multiple agents without ranking or refinement.

3   Basketball Tracking Dataset

Team sports provide an ideal setting for evaluating personalized behavior models. Firstly, there is a vast amount of labeled data in sports, including potentially thousands of data points for each player. Furthermore, the behaviors in team sports are well-defined and complex, with multiple agents simultaneously interacting collaboratively and adversarially. Therefore, sports tracking data is a good compromise between completely unstructured tracking data (*e.g.*, pedestrian motion where the number of agents is unconstrained) and highly structured data (*e.g.*, body pose or facial tracking where the number of agents is both fixed and physically connected). To that end, we present basketball as a canonical example of a team goal sport, and we introduce a new basketball dataset.

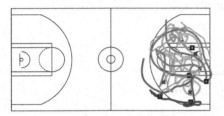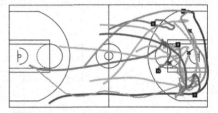

Fig. 2. Dataset Example plays from our basketball dataset, which contains 95,002 12-second sequences of offense (color), defense (gray), and ball (orange) 2D overhead-view trajectories. The identity, team, and canonical position of each player are known. (Color figure online)

Our proposed dataset is composed of 95,002 12-second sequences of the 2D basketball player and ball overhead-view point trajectories from 1247 games in the 2015/16 NBA season. The trajectories are obtained from the STATS in-venue system of six stationary, calibrated cameras, which projects the 3D locations of players and the ball onto a 2D overhead view of the court. Figure 2 visualizes two example sequences. Each sequence, sampled at 25 Hz, has the same team on offense for the full duration, ends in either a shot, turnover or foul. By eliminating transition plays where teams switch from defense to offense mid-sequence, we constrain the sequences to contain persistent offense and defense. Each sequence is zero-centered to the court center and aligned, so the offense always shoots toward the court's right-side basket. In our experiments, we sub-sample the trajectory data at 5 Hz, thereby reducing the data dimensionality without compromising information about quick changes of direction.

Personalization. We label each sequence with its player identity, team, canonical position (*i.e.*, point/shooting guard, small/power forward, center), and aligned position (Sect. 4.3). Only the 210 players with the most playing time across all sequences are assigned unique identities. The remaining players are labeled by their canonical position, thus limiting the set of player identities.

Data Splits. The data is randomly split into train, validation, and test sets with 60 708, 15 244, and 19 050 sequences in each respective split.

4   Methods

We frame the multi-agent trajectory prediction problem as follows: In a 2D environment, a set $\mathcal{A}$ of interacting agents are observed over the time history $[t_0, t_q]$ to have trajectories $X_{\mathcal{A}}^{[t_0,t_q]} = \{X_i^{[t_0,t_q]}\}|_{\forall i \in \mathcal{A}}$. The trajectory history of the ith agent is defined as $X_i^{[t_0,t_q]} = \{x_i^{t_0}, x_i^{t_0+1}, \cdots, x_i^{t_q}\}$, where x_i^t represents the 2D coordinates of the trajectory at time t. We wish to predict the subsequent future motion, to time t_f, of a subset of agents $\mathcal{P} \subseteq \mathcal{A}$. In other words, our objective is to learn the posterior distribution $P(Y_{\mathcal{P}}^{(t_q,t_f]}|X_{\mathcal{A}}^{[t_0,t_q]}, \mathcal{O})$ of the future trajectory motion of the agents in subset $\mathcal{P}$, specifically $Y_{\mathcal{P}}^{(t_q,t_f]} = \{Y_j^{(t_q,t_f]}\}|_{\forall j \in \mathcal{P}}$.

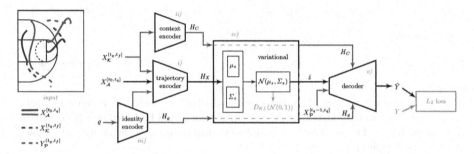

Fig. 3. Model architecture. The inputs to the *(i)* trajectory encoder are the tracking history of all players $X_{\mathcal{A}}^{[t_0,t_q]}$, the identity ϱ, and the context $X_{\mathcal{K}}^{(t_q,t_f]}$. The trajectory context $X_{\mathcal{K}}^{(t_q,t_f]}$ is *(ii)* encoded as H_C. The one-hot-encoded player or team identity ϱ is *(iii)* encoded as H_ρ. The *(iv)* variational module predicts the mean μ_z and standard deviation Σ_z of the latent variable distribution $\mathcal{N}(\mu_z, \Sigma_z)$. A random sample $\hat{z}$ from $\mathcal{N}(\mu_z, \Sigma_z)$ is input to the decoder, along with the conditionals H_C, H_ρ, and the last one second of player motions $X_{\mathcal{A}}^{[t_q-fps,t_q]}$. The *(v)* decoder then predicts the future paths $\hat{Y}$. At train time the KL divergence and L_2 loss are minimized.

In addition to the observed trajectory history, we also condition our learned future trajectory distribution on other available observations $\mathcal{O}$. In particular, $\mathcal{O}$ may consist of: (1) the identities ϱ of the agents in $\mathcal{P}$, and (2) the future context C, represented by the future trajectories $X_{\mathcal{K}}^{(t_q,t_f]} = \{X_\ell^{(t_q,t_f]}\}|_{\forall \ell \in \mathcal{K}}$ of agents in the set $\mathcal{K} \subset \mathcal{A}$ s.t. $\mathcal{K} \cup \mathcal{P} = \mathcal{A}$, $\mathcal{K} \cap \mathcal{P} = \{\}$. One of the main contributions of this work is how to include various types of information into $\mathcal{O}$, and the influence of each information type on the prediction accuracy of $Y_{\mathcal{P}}^{(t_q,t_f]}$ (Sect. 5.1).

The conditionals and inputs to our model are each encoded in their encoders. To learn the posterior, we use a CVAE, which allows for the conditional generation of trajectories while modeling the uncertainty of future prediction. In our case, the CVAE learns to approximate the distribution $P(Y_{\mathcal{P}}^{(t_q,t_f)} \mid X_{\mathcal{A}}^{[t_0,t_q]}, \mathcal{O})$ by introducing a random D_z-dimensional latent variable z. The CVAE enables solving one-to-many problems, such as prediction, by learning a distribution $Q(z = \hat{z} \mid X_{\mathcal{A}}^{[t_0,t_q]}, \mathcal{O})$ that best reconstructs $Y_{\mathcal{P}}^{(t_q,t_f)}$.

Figure 3 shows our overall model architecture, which is divided into the five modules: (i) the trajectory encoder with $X_{\mathcal{A}}^{[t_0,t_q]}$ and O as input, (ii) the context encoder with $X_{\mathcal{K}}^{(t_q,t_f)}$ as input, (iii) the identity encoder with ϱ as input, (iv) a variational module, and (v) the trajectory decoder with sampled latent variable $\hat{z}$ and encoded conditionals as input. The input to the variational module is the joint encoding of the trajectory history $X_{\mathcal{A}}^{[t_0,t_q]}$ with the context and identity. The trajectory history, context, and identity serve as our conditionals in the CVAE, where the context and identity are each separately encoded before being concatenated with $\hat{z}$ as input to the decoder. The trajectory history *conditional* $X_{\mathcal{P}}^{[t_q-1,\hat{t}_q]}$ for $\hat{z}$ is the last one second of observed trajectory history of the agents in $\mathcal{P}$. This encourages the model predictions to be consistent with the observed history, as our decoder outputs $X_{\mathcal{P}}^{[t_q-1,t_q]}$ concatenated with $Y_{\mathcal{P}}^{(t_q,t_f)}$.

4.1 Training Phase

We have modeled the latent variable distribution as a normal distribution

$$Q\left(z = \hat{z} \mid X_{\mathcal{A}}^{[t_0,t_q]}, X_{\mathcal{K}}^{(t_q,t_f)}, \varrho\right) = Q\left(z = \hat{z} \mid H_x, H_C, H_\varrho\right)$$
$$\sim \mathcal{N}\left(\mu_z, \Sigma_z\right). \tag{1}$$

Therefore, at train time the variational module minimizes the Kullback-Leibler (KL) divergence (D_{KL}) and the trajectory decoder minimizes Euclidean distance $\left\| Y - \hat{Y} \right\|_2^2$. For simplicity, let $Y = (X_{\mathcal{P}}^{[t_q-1,t_q]}, Y_{\mathcal{P}}^{(t_q,t_f)})$. The total loss is

$$L = \left\| Y - \hat{Y} \right\|_2^2 + \beta D_{KL}(P||Q), \tag{2}$$

where $P\left(z \mid X_{\mathcal{A}}^{[t_0,t_q]}, X_{\mathcal{K}}^{(t_q,t_f)}, \varrho\right) = \mathcal{N}(0,1)$ is a prior distribution and β is a weighting factor to control the relative scale of the loss terms. We found that for $\beta = 1$, our model without the conditionals (VAE) would roughly predict the mean trajectory, whereas when $\beta \ll 1$ we were able to predict input-dependent motion. In our proposed model, we observed that $\beta = 1$ performed as well as $\beta \ll 1$, so in all our experiments except for the vanilla VAE, we use $\beta = 1$.

4.2 Testing Phase

At test time, the input into the trajectory encoder is the trajectory history of all agents $X_{\mathcal{A}}^{[t_0,t_q]}$, the future trajectories of the agents not predicted $X_{\mathcal{K}}^{(t_q,t_f)}$, and the encoded agent identities ϱ. The variational module takes the encoded trajectory H_X, which is also conditioned on the context $X_{\mathcal{K}}^{(t_q,t_f)}$ and the player identities

ϱ, and returns a sample of the random latent variable $\hat{z}$. The trajectory decoder then infers the tracks of the agents to be predicted $Y_{\mathcal{P}}^{(t_q, t_f]}$ given a sampled $\hat{z}$, the encoded context H_C, the encoded identities H_ϱ, and the final one second of trajectory history for the agents to be predicted, $X_{\mathcal{P}}^{[t_q-1, t_q]}$.

4.3 Trajectory Alignment

The network inputs are a concatenation of each 2D agent trajectories. For example, the input $X_{\mathcal{A}}^{[t_0, t_q]}$ forms an $|\mathcal{A}| \times (t_q \cdot 5) \times 2$ array, where $|\mathcal{A}|$ is the number of agents, $t_q \cdot 5$ is the total number of temporal samples over t_q seconds sampled at 5 Hz. One of the significant challenges in encoding multi-agent trajectories is the presence of permutation disorder. In particular, when we concatenate the trajectories of all agents in $\mathcal{A}$ to form $X_{\mathcal{A}}^{[t_0, t_q]}$, we need to select a natural and consistent ordering of the agents. If we concatenate them in a random order, then two similar plays with similar trajectories will have considerably different representations. To minimize the permutation disorder, we need an agent ordering that is consistent from one play to another.

If we have a variable number of agents, it is natural to use an image-based representation of the agent tracks. In our case, where we have a fixed number of agents, we instead align tracks using a tree-based role alignment [28]. This alignment has recently been shown to minimize reconstruction error; therefore it provides an optimal representation of the multi-agent trajectories.

In brief, the tree-based role alignment uses two alternating steps, (i) an Expectation-Maximization (EM) based alignment of agent positions to a template and (ii) K-means clustering of the aligned agent positions, where cluster centers form the templates for the next EM step. Alternating between EM and clustering leads to a splitting of leaf nodes in a tree until either there are fewer than M frames in a cluster or the depth of the tree exceeds D. For our experiments we used $D = 6$ and trained separate trees for offense ($M = 400$) and defense ($M = 4000$). To learn a per-frame alignment tree, we used 120 K randomly sampled frames from 10 NBA games from the 2014/15 season.

4.4 Implementation Details

Architecture. All encoders consist of N fully connected layers, where each layer has roughly half the number of units as its input layer. We experimented with different input histories, prediction horizons, and player representations, so we dynamically set the layer structure for each experiment, while maintaining 64 and 16 units in the final layer of the trajectory and context encoders, respectively. For the identity encoder, the final output size depended on the identity representation ϱ, which was either: (1) a (concatenated) one-hot encoding of the team(s) of the players in $\mathcal{P}$ (output dimension 5 for single team and 16 for mixed), and (2) a (concatenated) one-hot encoding of each player identity in $\mathcal{P}$. See the supplementary for the full architecture details.

Learning. At train time we minimize the loss via backpropagation with the ADAM optimizer, batch size 256, initial learning rate 0.001, and 0.5 learning rate decay every 10 epochs of size 200K. We also randomly sample the training set so that the number of times a sequence appears in an epoch is proportional to the number of players it has with unique identity.

5   Experiments

We evaluate the effect on prediction performance of: (1) each information type input in our proposed model architecture (Sect. 5.1); (2) the number and types of agents in the input and output, *i.e.*, offense only, defense only, and both offense and defense (Sect. 5.2); (3) the predicted agents' during-play role (Sect. 5.3); (4) the length of the history input (Sect. 5.4); and (5) the length of the prediction horizon (Sect. 5.5).

Baselines. Our baselines are: velocity-based extrapolation, nearest neighbor retrieval, vanilla and Social LSTMs, and a VAE. Retrieval was performed using nearest neighbor search on the aligned (Sect. 4.3) trajectory history of the agents we wish to predict, matching the evaluation track histories to the training track histories based on minimum Euclidean distance. Then, we compare the error of the future trajectories of the top-k results to the ground truth. We found that these predictions are very poor, performing significantly worse than velocity-based extrapolation. Next, we compared our performance with the previous state of the art recurrent prediction methods, namely a vanilla LSTM and the Social LSTM. We found that the vanilla LSTM performed poorly with around 25 ft error for 4 s prediction horizon. The inclusion of social pooling improved the performance of the LSTM with 18 ft error for 4 s prediction horizon. However, the Social LSTM still performed significantly worse than simple velocity extrapolation at time horizons less than 6 s. The poor performances of the vanilla LSTM method and the Social LSTM method agrees with previous work on predicting basketball player trajectories conducted on a different data set [16]. As such, for most experiments, we use velocity-based extrapolation as our baseline, since it has the best performance.

Performance Metrics. We report three metrics. First, the L_2 distance (ft) between predicted trajectories and the ground truth, averaged over each time step for each agent. Second is the maximum distance between the prediction and ground truth for an agent trajectory, averaged over all agent trajectories. Last is the miss rate, calculated as the fraction of time the L_2 error exceeds 3 ft.

5.1   What Information Gives Us the Best Prediction?

In our proposed problem, there are four sources of information with the potential to improve prediction: (i) the trajectory history $X_{\mathcal{A}}^{[t_0, t_q]}$ of all agents, (ii) the future motion $X_{\mathcal{K}}^{(t_q, t_f]}$ of the players not predicted, *i.e.*, context, (iii) the player/team identities, *i.e.*, personalization and (iv) the agent alignment. The

Table 1. Offense prediction error for 4 s history and prediction horizon.
We test three different trajectory alignments (i) random, (ii) canonical position, and
(iii) role. We also test 3 conditionals: (a) the previous one second of player motions
(history), (b) the next 4 s of the defensive motions (context), and (c) one-hot encoded
player or team (identity). The miss rate is calculated with threshold 3 ft.

Method	Alignment	Conditional			Error (Offense, 4 s in future)		
		History	Context	Identity	Avg dist [ft] / (Top-5)	Max dist	Miss rate
Velocity	-	-	-	-	7.77	14.45	82.18
Retrieval	Role	-	-	-	11.41 / (8.80)	28.57	86.77
VAE	Random	-	-	-	7.10	19.24	74.90
VAE	Role	-	-	-	6.85	18.84	72.78
CVAE	Random	1 s	None	None	6.90	18.98	73.83
CVAE	Random	None	Encoded	None	6.97	18.46	75.29
CVAE	Random	None	None	Team	7.05	19.25	74.15
CVAE	Random	None	None	Player	7.02	19.17	75.15
CVAE	Random	None	Encoded	Team	6.98	18.46	75.65
CVAE	Random	1 s	None	Team	6.91	18.95	74.18
CVAE	Random	1 s	Encoded	None	6.73	18.11	74.64
CVAE	Random	1 s	Encoded	Team	6.76	18.15	74.97
CVAE	Random	1 s	Encoded	Player	6.64	18.00	74.29
CVAE	Position	1 s	Encoded	Team	6.09	16.87	70.37
CVAE	**role**	**1 s**	**encoded**	**none**	5.81	**16.41**	66.67
CVAE	**role**	**1 s**	**encoded**	**team**	**5.80**	16.45	**66.39**
CVAE	Role	1 s	Encoded	Player	5.96	17.03	67.07

observed trajectory history serves as the input to the model and is fixed to 4 s.
The final 1 second of trajectory history of the players we predict, the context,
and the identity are treated as conditionals (Fig. 3), whereas the agent alignment
enables efficient trajectory encoding. For this section (Table 1), we only predict
the offense, which avoids conflating the effect of agent type with the effect of the
information sources. We also fix the prediction horizon at 4 s.

To understand the influence of alignment alone, we compare the result of
the baseline VAE with random versus role aligned agents. In the absence of
the alignment the VAE has moderate performance, outperforming baselines. For
example, in the first row of Fig. 4 the VAE captures co-movement of players (red
and purple) that velocity-based extrapolation does not. However, the VAE does
not capture the two agents crossing.

To understand the influence of each conditional, we randomly order the input
trajectories and perform a set of ablation studies using a variety of conditions.
We apply each conditional separately to compare their individual effects on
performance, including comparing the use of team versus player identity.

Interestingly, the VAE and the CVAE using a single conditional perform
similarly. However, if we combine conditionals, we create an even stronger co-
movement signal, *e.g.*, red and purple players in the first row in Fig. 4. Still, with
all the conditionals and random agent ordering, we fail to get the crossing of the
trajectories.

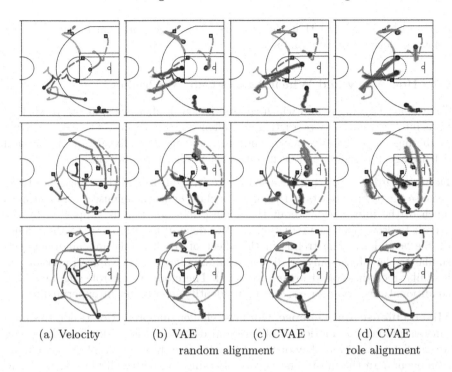

| (a) Velocity | (b) VAE | (c) CVAE | (d) CVAE |
| | random alignment | | role alignment |

Fig. 4. Offense player predictions. Given a 4 s trajectory history (gray) for all players (defense not pictured), we predict (solid lines) the next 4 s of offense player motion. Dashed lines are ground truth. Each row represents the same play, and each trajectory color corresponds to a player. The color intensity is proportional to the likelihood. **Column (a)** velocity-based extrapolation. **Column (b)** VAE with random trajectory alignment. **Column (c)** CVAE with random trajectory alignment and all conditionals (player ID). **Column (d)** adding role alignment to the CVAE (team ID).

When we both align and condition, we are able to correctly predict tracks crossing (red and purple players first row in Fig. 4d). In particular, we see the greatest improvement in our prediction by including the context, history, and team identity (bold in Table 1). These results imply that alignment, context, and history contain complementary information. Though alignment and conditioning improve our predictions, we struggle to predict sudden changes in movement (red player in row 3 of Fig. 4d), and stationary players (green players in row 1 and blue player in row 3 of Fig. 4d).

The modest improvements found by including team identity vanish when we use multi-template tree-based role alignment; implying that the alignment contains the added information provided by conditioning on the team identity. In other words, the clusters in latent space that the variational module finds with canonical alignment are team sensitive. This sensitivity to the team implies that certain teams perform certain collective motions. However, after tree-alignment, this vanishes, implying that the clusters found given optimal alignment exist below the level of player combinations.

5.2   How Many and Which Agents Can We Predict?

To evaluate how many and which agents we can predict, we split our prediction tasks into (i) exclusively predicting all 5 offense agents (Sect. 5.1), (ii) exclusively predicting all 5 defense agents, and (iii) predicting a mixture of offense and defense agents, from one of each (mix 1v1) to all 10 agents (mix 5v5).

Defense Only. Predicting defense is more straightforward than our other tasks because the defense reacts to the offense's play. Thus, the offense motion encodes much of the information about the defense motion. This is supported by the overall improvement in prediction for the defense as compared to the offense (Table 2a and b). The trends in the effect of conditionals and alignment are similar to the offense-only prediction results, indicating the value of information is similar regardless of adversary predicted. Therefore, we use role alignment and conditionals history, context, and team identity in subsequent experiments.

Mixed Offense and Defense. Our most challenging prediction task is to simultaneous predict the motion of offense and defense. This is akin to asking: can we predict the motion of unobserved agents given the motion of the remaining seen agents? In the most general case of trying to predict all players, we found that the prediction performance splits the difference between the prediction of the offense and defense alone (Table 2a).

Table 2. Prediction error ablation. (a) We vary the observed history for a 4 s prediction, and observe that the optimal trajectory history is 4 s, though marginally so. (b) We vary the prediction horizon given a 4 s observed history, and observe that the prediction error monotonically increases as a function of time horizon. (c) We vary the number of players to predict for a 4 s horizon given a 4 s history, and observe an increase in average prediction error as we increase the number of agents per team from 1 to 5. For all experiments, we conditioned on the previous 1 s, the future motion of all agents not predicted, and the selected player or team identities. All errors are in feet.

Method-Align-Pl.	Personnel	Error: Avg dist [ft]		
		1 s	4 s	8 s
Velocity	offense	7.74	7.72	7.74
CVAE-rand-ID	offense	7.06	**6.64**	6.86
CVAE-role-none	offense	6.04	**5.81**	6.21
CVAE-role-team	offense	6.05	**5.80**	6.16
CVAE-role-team	defense	4.23	**4.10**	4.31
CVAE-role-team	mix 5v5	5.75	**5.74**	5.76

(a) observed history

Method-Align-Pl.	Personnel	Error: Avg dist [ft] (4 s history)				
		1 s	2 s	4 s	6 s	8 s
Velocity	offense	**1.93**	4.10	7.72	11.50	24.02
CVAE-rand-ID	offense	2.66	4.23	6.64	8.14	9.41
CVAE-role-none	offense	2.38	4.00	5.81	7.07	8.28
CVAE-role-team	offense	2.35	**3.95**	**5.80**	**7.08**	**8.07**
CVAE-role-team	defense	2.08	3.01	4.10	4.98	5.85
Vanilla LSTM	mix 5v5	10.44	18.29	25.36	28.07	29.56
Social LSTM	mix 5v5	5.23	11.08	17.95	20.88	22.38
CVAE-role-team	mix 5v5	**2.44**	**3.92**	**5.74**	**7.21**	**8.33**

(b) prediction horizon

Method: CVAE-role-team	
Mixture	Error: Avg dist [ft]
1v1	4.19
2v2	4.88
3v3	5.21
4v4	5.28
5v5	5.74

(c) num. players

Next, we investigated how many agents per team we could predict over a 4 s time horizon, given a 4 s history (Table 2c). Surprisingly, we found relatively little performance degradation when predicting the motion of all ten players (5v5) versus one player each (1v1) on offense and defense (5.7 ft vs 4.2 ft). In the case of predicting all ten agents, the only conditionals are the player or team identities and the previous 1 s of history. The input is the 4 s trajectory history.

5.3   How Does Personnel Influence Prediction?

Since alignment improved our prediction results, we investigated the per-role prediction error (Fig. 5a) to uncover whether some roles are easier to predict than others. We found $\sim 16\%$ difference in the per-role prediction error for predicting offense compared to defense only. However, the per role variation does not hold when predicting a mixture of agents, in which case the prediction error of all agents increases.

5.4   How Much History Do We Need?

Next, we tested the effect of the observed trajectory duration on prediction performance, that is how the history length influences predictions. The conditionals are the previous 1 s of the agents we are predicting, the future motion of players we are not predicting, and the team or player identity. We varied the observed

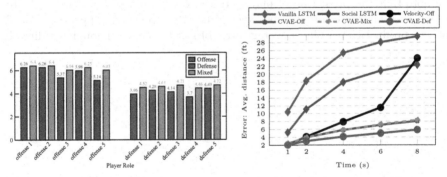

(a) **Per-role error (avg distance, ft).**   (b) **Error vs prediction horizon.**

Fig. 5. Prediction error ablation. For all experiments, we provided 4 s of history and conditioned on the previous 1 second and the future of all agents not predicted. (a) We evaluate the per-role prediction error for a 4 s prediction horizon, given a 4 s observed history. Defense is easier to predict than offense, and although mixed (2v2) appears to have better overall prediction than offense, per-role it is slightly worse, which makes sense because it's a harder task. (b) We visualize the prediction errors as a function of horizon, given a 4 s observed trajectory history. The baselines are velocity (for offense only), and vanilla LSTM and Social LSTM (for all 10 agents), which we compare with our best method run on offense and defense only, as well as the mixture of all 10 agents. The precise values are reported in Table 2b.

history from 1-8 s and predicted the subsequent 4 s. As before, the defense is the easiest to predict, and multi-template role alignment with team identity provides the best prediction performance (Table 2a). We find 4 s of history is barely optimal, either because the player motions decorrelate at this time scale, or our encoder architecture cannot recover correlations at longer timescales.

5.5 How Far Can We Predict?

To evaluate how far in the future we can predict, we provided 4 s of history of all player motions and predicted out to at most 8 s. Additionally, we provided the last 1 s of player motions and the future of the un-predicted agents as a conditional. In Fig. 6 we can clearly see that as the we to underestimate the curvature of motions (cyan in example 1, $T = 6$ s), or underestimate the complexity of motion (purple in row 1, $T = 6$ s and red in row 2, $T = 6$ s).

As expected, the prediction error increases monotonically with the prediction time horizon (Fig. 5b), and when we include team identity, the prediction error changes less with the time horizon. Also, we see that the prediction error for the defensive is smaller than mixed offense and defense or offense alone.

We also notice that we far outperform the current state of the art prediction methods (Fig. 5b). It is remarkable that even when predicting the motion of all agents that our performance is three times as good as the Social LSTM (for 4 s time horizon). Again, it is important to note that the performance of the LSTM baselines agrees with previous results on a similar dataset [16]. Lastly, we note that the prediction of player trajectories presented by Shan et al. [16] which uses far more information, specifically the egocentric appearance of all players produces a per player average error of 11.8 ft (3.6 m). Though not directly

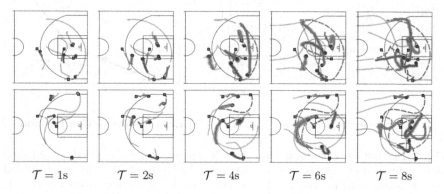

$$T = 1\text{s} \qquad T = 2\text{s} \qquad T = 4\text{s} \qquad T = 6\text{s} \qquad T = 8\text{s}$$

Fig. 6. Prediction as a function of time horizon. We input the previous 4 s of every agent's motion (grey), and predict the offense player trajectories over horizon T s. The conditionals are the future motion of the defense (not shown), the final one second of offense history, and team identity. Each row represents a different example, and each color represents the player tree-based role. Dashed lines are the ground truth.

comparable, this shows the power of our proposed generative method: with less information, our method produces noticeably better results.

6 Conclusion

We have shown that a generative method based on conditional variational autoencoder (CVAE) is three times as accurate as the state of the art recurrent frameworks for the task of predicting player trajectories in an adversarial team game. Furthermore, these predictions improve by conditioning the predictions on the history and the context, *i.e.*, the motion of agents not predicted and their identity. Also, where available, further improvement in the quality of prediction can be found by providing multi-template aligned data. By aligning and conditioning of context and history, we can produce remarkably accurate, context-specific predictions without the need for ranking and refinement modules. We also found that our predictions were sensitive to the player role, as determined during alignment. However, we did not find any additional improvement in prediction when providing the player identity alone. The sensitivity to the player role, but not identity implies that role contains the information held in identity alone. Therefore, more fine-grained personalization may require additional player data, such as weight, height, age, minutes played.

References

1. Lee, N., Choi, W., Vernaza, P., Choy, C., Torr, P., Chandraker, M.: DESIRE: distance future prediction in dynamic scenes with interacting agents (2017)
2. Alahi, A., Goel, K., Ramanathan, V., Robicquet, A., Fei-Fei, L., Savarese, S.: Social LSTM: human trajectory prediction in crowded spaces (2016)
3. Jain, A., Singh, A., Koppula, H., Soh, S., Saxena, A.: Recurrent neural networks for driver activity anticipation via sensory-fusion architecture (2016)
4. Akhter, I., Simon, T., Khan, S., Matthews, I., Sheikh, Y.: Bilinear spatiotemporal basis models. ACM Trans. Graph. (TOG) (2012)
5. Lucey, P., Bialkowski, A., Carr, P., Morgan, S., Matthews, I., Sheikh, Y.: Representing and discovering adversarial team behaviors using player roles (2013)
6. Insafutdinov, E., et al.: ArtTrack: articulated multi-person tracking in the wild (2017)
7. Le, H., Yue, Y., Carr, P., Lucey, P.: Coordinated multi-agent imitation learning (2017)
8. Yamaguchi, K., Berg, A., Ortiz, L., Berg, T.: Who are you with and where are you going? (2011)
9. Butt, A., Collins, R.: Multi-target tracking by lagrangian relaxation to min-cost network flow (2013)
10. Wang, S., Fowlkes, C.: Learning optimal parameters for multi-target tracking (2016)
11. Maksai, A., Wang, X., Fua, P.: What players do with the ball: a physically constrained interaction modeling (2016)
12. Kim, K., Grundmann, M., Shamir, A., Matthews, I., Hodgins, J., Essa, I.: Motion fields to PRedict play evolution in dynamic sports scenes (2010)

13. Chen, J., Le, H., Carr, P., Yue, Y., Little, J.: Learning online smooth predictors for Realtime camera planning using recurrent decision trees (2016)
14. Zheng, S., Yue, Y., Lucey, P.: Generating long-term trajectories using deep hierarchical networks (2016)
15. Felsen, P., Agrawal, P., Malik, J.: What will happen next? Forecasting player moves in sports videos (2017)
16. Su, S., Hong, J.P., Shi, J., Park, H.S.: Social behavior prediction from first person videos. CoRR abs/1611.09464 (2016)
17. Koren, Y., Bell, R., Volinksy, C.: Matrix factorization techniques for recommender systems. Computer **42**(8) (2009)
18. Deng, Z., et al.: Factorized variational autoencoders for modeling audience reactions to movies (2017)
19. Charles, J., Pfister, T., Magee, D., Hogg, D., Zisserman, A.: Personalizing human video pose estimation (2016)
20. Kingma, D.P., Welling, M.: Auto-encoding variational bayes. arXiv preprint arXiv:1312.6114 (2013)
21. Gregor, K., Danihelka, I., Graves, A., Wierstra, D.: DRAW: A recurrent neural network for image generation. CoRR abs/1502.04623 (2015)
22. Bowman, S.R., Vilnis, L., Vinyals, O., Dai, A.M., Józefowicz, R., Bengio, S.: Generating sentences from a continuous space. CoRR abs/1511.06349 (2015)
23. Kingma, D., Mohamed, S., Rezende, D., Welling, M.: Semi-supervised learning with deep generative models (2014)
24. Sohn, K., Lee, H., Yan, X.: Learning structured output representation using deep conditional generative models (2015)
25. van den Oord, A., Kalchbrenner, N., Kavukcuoglu, K.: Pixel recurrent neural networks. CoRR abs/1601.06759 (2016)
26. Pathak, D., Krahenbuhl, P., Donahue, J., Darrell, T., Efros, A.A.: Context encoders: feature learning by inpainting, June 2016
27. Walker, J., Doersch, C., Gupta, A., Hebert, M.: An uncertain future: Forecasting from static images using variational autoencoders. CoRR abs/1606.07873 (2016)
28. Sha, L., Lucey, P., Zheng, S., Kim, T., Yue, Y., Sridharan, S.: Fine-grained retrieval of sports plays using tree-based alignment of trajectories (2017)

Learning Data Terms for Non-blind Deblurring

Jiangxin Dong[1(✉)], Jinshan Pan[2], Deqing Sun[3], Zhixun Su[1,4(✉)], and Ming-Hsuan Yang[5]

[1] Dalian University of Technology, Dalian, China
dongjxjx@gmail.com
[2] Nanjing University of Science and Technology, Nanjing, China
sdluran@gmail.com
[3] NVIDIA, Westford, USA
deqings@nvidia.com
[4] Guilin University of Electronic Technology, Guilin, China
zxsu@dlut.edu.cn
[5] University of California at Merced, Merced, USA
mhyang@ucmerced.edu

Abstract. Existing deblurring methods mainly focus on developing effective image priors and assume that blurred images contain insignificant amounts of noise. However, state-of-the-art deblurring methods do not perform well on real-world images degraded with significant noise or outliers. To address these issues, we show that it is critical to learn data fitting terms beyond the commonly used ℓ_1 or ℓ_2 norm. We propose a simple and effective discriminative framework to learn data terms that can adaptively handle blurred images in the presence of severe noise and outliers. Instead of learning the distribution of the data fitting errors, we directly learn the associated shrinkage function for the data term using a cascaded architecture, which is more flexible and efficient. Our analysis shows that the shrinkage functions learned at the intermediate stages can effectively suppress noise and preserve image structures. Extensive experimental results show that the proposed algorithm performs favorably against state-of-the-art methods.

Keywords: Image deblurring · Learning data terms Shrinkage function · Noise and outliers

1 Introduction

The recent years have witnessed significant advances in non-blind deconvolution [3,7,18,26], mainly due to the development of effective image priors [7,9,18,29].

Electronic supplementary material The online version of this chapter (https://doi.org/10.1007/978-3-030-01252-6_46) contains supplementary material, which is available to authorized users.

© Springer Nature Switzerland AG 2018
V. Ferrari et al. (Eds.): ECCV 2018, LNCS 11215, pp. 777–792, 2018.
https://doi.org/10.1007/978-3-030-01252-6_46

When combined with a data term based on ℓ_1 or ℓ_2 norm, these methods perform well where the image blur is the main or only source of degradation. However, these methods tend to fail when the real-world images contain significant amounts of noise or outliers.

When the image blur is spatially invariant, this process is modeled by

$$b = l * k + n, \tag{1}$$

where b, l, k, and n denote the blurred image, latent image, blur kernel, and noise; and $*$ is the convolution operator. While the ℓ_1 or ℓ_2 norm is often used in this model, it implicitly assumes that the noise can be modeled by the Laplacian or Gaussian distribution. Thus, methods based on the model with ℓ_1 or ℓ_2 norm cannot well handle significant noise or outliers in real-world images.

To address these issues, some recent methods design models for specific distortions, e.g., Gaussian noise [6,28], impulse noise [3], and saturated pixels [3,22]. However, domain knowledge is required to design an appropriate model specifically for a particular distortion.

Directly learning the noise model from the training data is an appealing solution. Xu et al. [26] learn the deconvolution operation from the training data and this method can handle significant noise and saturation. However, their method requires the blur kernel to be separable. Furthermore, the network needs to be fine-tuned for each kernel because this method needs to use the singular value decomposition of the pseudo inverse kernel.

In this work, we propose a discriminative framework to learn the data term in a cascaded manner. To understand the role of the data term for image deblurring, we use the standard hyper-Laplacian prior for the latent image [7,8]. Our framework learns both the data term and regularization parameters directly from the image data. As learning the distribution of the noise results in an iterative solution, we propose to learn the associated shrinkage functions for the data term using a cascaded architecture. We find that the learned shrinkage functions are more flexible at the intermediate stages, which can effectively detect and handle outliers. Our algorithm usually reaches a good solution in fewer than 20 stages. The learned data term and regularization parameters can be directly applied to other synthetic and real images. Extensive experimental results show that the proposed method performs favorably against the state-of-the-art methods on a variety of noise and outliers.

2   Related Work

Non-blind deconvolution has received considerable attention and numerous methods have been developed in recent years. Early methods include the Wiener filter [23] and the Richardson-Lucy algorithm [10,13]. To effectively restore image structures and suppress noise for this ill-posed problem, recent methods have focused on the regularization terms, e.g., total variation [21], hyper-Laplacian prior on image gradients [7,9], Gaussian mixture model [29], and multi-layer perceptron [18].

To learn good priors for image restoration, Roth et al. [14] use a field of experts (FoE) model to fit the heavy-tailed distribution of gradients of natural images. Schmidt et al. [17] extend the FoE framework based on the regression tree field model [5]. The cascade of shrinkage fields model [16] has been proposed to learn effective image filters and reaction (shrinkage) functions for image restoration. Xiao et al. [24] extend the shrinkage fields model to blind image deblurring. Chen et al. [2] extend conventional nonlinear reaction-diffusion models by discriminatively learning filters and parameterized influence functions. In particular, they allow the filters and influence functions to be different at each stage of the reaction-diffusion process.

Based on the maximum a posteriori (MAP) framework, existing image priors are usually combined with one specific type of data term for deblurring. The commonly used data term is based on the ℓ_2 norm which models image noise with a Gaussian distribution [7]. However, the Gaussian assumption often fails when the input image contains significant noise or outliers. Bar et al. [1] assume a Laplacian noise model and derive a data term based on the ℓ_1 norm to handle impulsive noise. These methods can suffer from artifacts for other types of noise or outliers, since these data terms are designed for specific noise models.

Recently, Cho et al. [3] show that a few common types of outliers cause severe ringing artifacts in the deblurred images. They explicitly assume a clipped blur model to deal with outliers and develop a non-blind deconvolution method based on the Expectation-Maximization (EM) framework. This method relies on the preset values of the tradeoff parameters, which requires hand-crafted tuning for different levels of noise and outliers. Taking into account the nonlinear property of saturated pixels, Whyte et al. [22] propose a modified version of the Richardson-Lucy algorithm for image deblurring. Jin et al. [6] present a Bayesian framework-based approach to non-blind deblurring with the unknown Gaussian noise level.

To deal with image noise and saturation, Xu et al. [26] develop a deblurring method based on the convolutional neural network (CNN). However, their network needs to be fine-tuned for every kernel as it is based on the singular value decomposition of the pseudo inverse kernel. CNNs have also been used to learn image priors for image restoration [27,28]. However, these methods [27,28] mainly focus on Gaussian noise and cannot apply to other types of outliers. In addition, Schuler et al. [19] propose to learn the data term by a feature extraction module, which uses a fixed ℓ_2 norm penalty function and focuses on blind deconvolution. In contrast, our method can handle different types and levels of noise and does not require fine-tuning for a particular blur kernel.

For low-level vision tasks, numerous methods have been developed to model the data fitting errors [20]. However, the learned distributions are often highly complex and require an iterative solution. In addition, the probabilistically trained generative models usually require ad-hoc modifications to obtain good performance [15]. Compared with learning the distribution (penalty function), learning the associated solution (shrinkage function) is more flexible, because non-monotonic shrinkage functions can be learned [16]. Furthermore, shrinkage functions make learning efficient, since the model prediction and the gradient update have closed forms. We are inspired by shrinkage fields [16] to discriminatively learn shrinkage functions for the data term, which is more flexible than generatively learning the penalty function. Thus our framework can handle various types of noise and outliers and is also computationally efficient.

3   Proposed Algorithm

This paper proposes to present a discriminative deconvolution framework that performs robustly in the presence of significant amounts of noise or outliers. We estimate the latent image from the blurred image using the MAP criterion

$$l = \operatorname*{argmax}_{l} p(l|k,b) = \operatorname*{argmax}_{l} p(b|k,l)p(l), \tag{2}$$

where the first (data) term models the distribution of the residue image $\log p(b|k,l) = -\frac{1}{\lambda}\mathcal{R}(b - l * k)$, and $\mathcal{R}(\cdot)$ measures the data fitting error. In addition, $p(l)$ is the latent image prior $\log p(l) = -\mathcal{P}(l)$. The objective function in (2) can be equivalently solved by minimizing the following energy function

$$\min_{l} E(l|k,b) = \min_{l} \mathcal{R}(b - l * k) + \lambda \mathcal{P}(l). \tag{3}$$

As our focus is on the data term, we use a standard hyper-Laplacian prior and set $\mathcal{P}(l) = \|\nabla l\|_p = \sum_i |(\nabla_h l)_x|^p + |(\nabla_v l)_x|^p$, where ∇_h and ∇_v denote the horizontal and vertical differential operators respectively and x is the pixel index. In this paper, we fix $p = 1$ for the image prior in (3) and show that even with a simple total variation prior, the proposed algorithm is able to deblur images with significant amounts of noise and saturation. We show that this algorithm requires low computational load and can be easily integrated with more expressive image priors for better performance. Different from most existing methods that use ℓ_1 or ℓ_2 norm for $\mathcal{R}$, we assume a flexible form for $\mathcal{R}$ that can be learned along with the tradeoff parameter λ from images.

3.1   Data Term

To enforce the modeling capacity, the data term $\mathcal{R}$ is parameterized to characterize the spatial information and the complex distribution of the residue image $b - l * k$,

$$\mathcal{R}(b - l * k) = \sum_{i=0}^{N_f} \mathcal{R}_i(f_i * (b - l * k)), \tag{4}$$

where f_i is the i-th linear filter (particularly, f_0 is set as the delta filter to exploit the information of the residue image in the raw data space), $\mathcal{R}_i$ is the i-th corresponding non-linear penalty function that models the i-th filter response, and N_f is the number of non-trivial linear filters for the data term.

3.2 Inference

Formulation. We first describe the scheme to minimize the energy function (3) and then explain how to learn the data term. We use the half-quadratic optimization method and introduce auxiliary variables $\mathbf{z}$, $\mathbf{v}_i$, and $\mathbf{u}$, corresponding to $\mathbf{b} - \mathbf{Kl}$, $\mathbf{F}_i(\mathbf{b} - \mathbf{Kl})$, and $\nabla \mathbf{l} = [\nabla_h \mathbf{l}, \nabla_v \mathbf{l}]$. Here, $\mathbf{K}$, $\mathbf{F}_i$, $\mathbf{l}$, and $\mathbf{b}$ denote the matrix/vector forms of k, f_i, l, and b. Thus, the energy function (3) becomes

$$\min_{\mathbf{z},\mathbf{v},\mathbf{u},\mathbf{l}} \frac{\tau}{2}\|\mathbf{b}-\mathbf{Kl}-\mathbf{z}\|_2^2+\mathcal{R}_0(\mathbf{z})+\sum_{i=1}^{N_f}(\frac{\beta}{2}\|\mathbf{F}_i(\mathbf{b}-\mathbf{Kl})-\mathbf{v}_i\|_2^2+\mathcal{R}_i(\mathbf{v}_i))+\lambda(\frac{\gamma}{2}\|\nabla\mathbf{l}-\mathbf{u}\|_2^2+\|\mathbf{u}\|_1),$$

$$(5)$$

where τ, β, and γ are penalty parameters. For brevity, we denote $\mathbf{F}_h\mathbf{l} = \nabla_h\mathbf{l}$ and $\mathbf{F}_v\mathbf{l} = \nabla_v\mathbf{l}$. We use the coordinate descent method to minimize the relaxed energy function (5),

$$\mathbf{z} = \operatorname*{argmin}_{\mathbf{z}}\frac{\tau}{2}\|\mathbf{b} - \mathbf{Kl} - \mathbf{z}\|_2^2 + \mathcal{R}_0(\mathbf{z}), \tag{6}$$

$$\mathbf{v}_i = \operatorname*{argmin}_{\mathbf{v}_i}\frac{\beta}{2}\|\mathbf{F}_i(\mathbf{b} - \mathbf{Kl}) - \mathbf{v}_i\|_2^2 + \mathcal{R}_i(\mathbf{v}_i), \tag{7}$$

$$\mathbf{u} = \operatorname*{argmin}_{\mathbf{u}}\frac{\gamma}{2}\|\nabla\mathbf{l} - \mathbf{u}\|_2^2 + \|\mathbf{u}\|_1, \tag{8}$$

$$\mathbf{l} = \operatorname*{argmin}_{\mathbf{l}}\frac{\tau}{2}\|\mathbf{b} - \mathbf{Kl} - \mathbf{z}\|_2^2 + \sum_{i=1}^{N_f}\frac{\beta}{2}\|\mathbf{F}_i(\mathbf{b} - \mathbf{Kl}) - \mathbf{v}_i\|_2^2 + \frac{\lambda\gamma}{2}\|\nabla\mathbf{l} - \mathbf{u}\|_2^2. \tag{9}$$

Given the current estimates of $\mathbf{z}$, $\mathbf{v}$, and $\mathbf{l}$, finding the optimal $\mathbf{u}$ is reduced to a shrinkage operation [21]. Given the current estimates of $\mathbf{z}$, $\mathbf{v}$, and $\mathbf{u}$, the energy function (9) is quadratic w.r.t. $\mathbf{l}$ and has a closed-form solution

$$\mathbf{l} = \zeta^{-1}\xi, \tag{10}$$

where $\zeta = \mathbf{K}^\top\mathbf{K} + \frac{\beta}{\tau}\sum_{i=1}^{N_f}\mathbf{K}^\top\mathbf{F}_i^\top\mathbf{F}_i\mathbf{K} + \frac{\lambda\gamma}{\tau}(\mathbf{F}_h^\top\mathbf{F}_h + \mathbf{F}_v^\top\mathbf{F}_v)$ and $\xi = \mathbf{K}^\top(\mathbf{b} - \mathbf{z}) + \frac{\beta}{\tau}\sum_{i=1}^{N_f}\mathbf{K}^\top\mathbf{F}_i^\top(\mathbf{F}_i\mathbf{b} - \mathbf{v}_i) + \frac{\lambda\gamma}{\tau}(\mathbf{F}_h^\top\mathbf{u}_h + \mathbf{F}_v^\top\mathbf{u}_v)$.

Learning the data term. Instead of learning the penalty functions $\mathcal{R}_i$ in (6) and (7), we directly learn the solutions to the optimization problems (6) and (7), i.e., the shrinkage functions associated with the penalty functions $\mathcal{R}_i$. We model each shrinkage function for (6) and (7) as a linear combination of Gaussian RBF components [16]

$$\mathbf{z} = \phi_0(\mathbf{b} - \mathbf{Kl}, \boldsymbol{\pi}_0) = \sum_{j=1}^{M}\pi_{0j}\exp(-\frac{\alpha}{2}(\mathbf{b} - \mathbf{Kl} - \mu_j)^2), \tag{11}$$

$$\mathbf{v}_i = \phi_i(\mathbf{F}_i(\mathbf{b} - \mathbf{Kl}), \boldsymbol{\pi}_i) = \sum_{j=1}^{M}\pi_{ij}\exp(-\frac{\alpha}{2}(\mathbf{F}_i(\mathbf{b} - \mathbf{Kl}) - \mu_j)^2), \tag{12}$$

where $\boldsymbol{\pi}_i = \{\pi_{ij}|j = 1,\ldots,M\}$ are the weights for each component. Similar to [16], we assume that the mean μ_j and variance α are fixed, which allows fast prediction and learning. The learned shrinkage functions are cheap to compute and can be pre-computed and stored in look-up tables.

Learning the shrinkage function is more expressive than learning the penalty function. Given a penalty function, a linear combination of Gaussian RBFs can well approximate its shrinkage function. As shown in Fig. 1, the approximated functions by Gaussian RBFs match well the shrinkage functions of the optimization problem with the ℓ_1 and Lorentzian penalty functions. Furthermore, we can learn non-monotonic shrinkage functions, which cannot be obtained by learning the penalty functions [16]. More details will be discussed in Sect. 5.

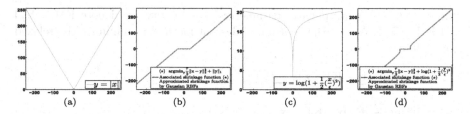

(a)   (b)   (c)   (d)

Fig. 1. The flexibility of the Gaussian RBFs to approximate the shrinkage function of the optimization problem (6) with different penalty functions. (a) and (c) plot the shapes of the ℓ_1 and Lorentzian penalty functions, respectively. The purple lines in (b) and (d) draw the corresponding shrinkage functions of (6) with the ℓ_1 and Lorentzian penalty functions, which are stated in the legend, respectively. The yellow dashdot lines in (b) and (d) plot the approximated shrinkage functions (using Gaussian RBFs), which match well the associated shrinkage functions (Color figure online)

3.3   Cascaded Training

By directly learning the shrinkage functions for (6) and (7), we can compute the gradients of the recovered latent image w.r.t. the model parameters in closed forms. This allows efficient parameter learning. The half-quadratic optimization involves several iterations of (8), (10), (11), and (12) and we refer to one iteration as one stage. As noted by [2,16], the model parameters should be adaptively tuned at each different stage. In the first few stages, the data term should be learned to detect useful information from the blurred image and avoid the effect of significant outliers. In the later stages, the data term should mainly focus on recovering clearer images with finer details. To learn the stage-dependent model parameters $\Omega_t = \{\lambda_t, \beta_t, \pi_{ti}, f_{ti}\}^1$ for stage t from a set of S training samples $\{l_{gt}^{\{s\}}, b^{\{s\}}, k^{\{s\}}\}_{s=1}^{S}$, we use the negative peak signal-to-noise ratio (PSNR) as the loss function

$$J(\Omega_t) = \sum_{s=1}^{S} \mathcal{L}(l_t^{\{s\}}, l_{gt}^{\{s\}}) = \sum_{s=1}^{S} -10\log_{10}\left(\frac{I_{\max}^2}{\text{MSE}\left(l_t^{\{s\}}, l_{gt}^{\{s\}}\right)}\right), \qquad (13)$$

---

[1] The parameters τ and γ are included into the weights π_i of (11) and (12) and fused with β and λ in (10).

where $I_{\max}$ denotes the maximum pixel value of the ground truth image, and $\mathrm{MSE}(l_t^{\{s\}}, l_{gt}^{\{s\}})$ is the mean squared error between $l_t^{\{s\}}$ and $l_{gt}^{\{s\}}$. We use the gradient-based L-BFGS method to minimize (13). To simplify notations, we omit the superscripts below. At stage t, the gradient of the loss function w.r.t. the parameters $\Omega_t = \{\lambda_t, \beta_t, \pi_{ti}, f_{ti}\}$ is

$$\frac{\partial \mathcal{L}(l_t, l_{gt})}{\partial \Omega_t} = \frac{\partial \mathcal{L}(l_t, l_{gt})}{\partial l_t} \cdot \frac{\partial l_t}{\partial \Omega_t} = \frac{\partial \mathcal{L}(l_t, l_{gt})}{\partial l_t} \zeta_t^{-1} \left[\frac{\partial \xi_t}{\partial \Omega_t} - \frac{\partial \zeta_t}{\partial \Omega_t} l_t \right]. \qquad (14)$$

The derivatives for specific model parameters are provided in the supplementary material. We optimize the loss function in a cascaded way and discriminatively learn the model parameters stage by stage. The main steps of the discriminative learning procedure are summarized in Algorithm 1.

Algorithm 1. Discriminative learning algorithm

Input: Blurred images $\{b^{\{s\}}\}$ and ground truth blur kernels $\{k^{\{s\}}\}$.
Initialization: $l_0 = b$, $\lambda_0 = 0.3$, $\beta_0 = 0.001$.
for $t = 1$ to T **do**
    Update z_t using (11).
    Update v_{ti} using (12).
    Update u_t using (8).
    Update l_t using (10).
    Update $\{\lambda_t, \beta_t, \pi_{ti}, f_{ti}\}$ using the gradients (14).
end for
Output: Learned model parameters $\{\lambda_t, \beta_t, \pi_{ti}, f_{ti}\}_{t=1}^{T}$.

---

4   Experimental Results

Experimental setup. To generate the training data for our experiments, we generate 20 blur kernels according to [17]. We use 200 images from the BSDS dataset [11] to construct the datasets for the experiments with significant noise (e.g., Gaussian noise, impulse noise, etc.) and crop a 280×280 patch from each of the images. These blurred images are then corrupted with various noise levels (i.e., the proportion of pixels affected by noise in an image). The test dataset is generated similarly, but with 20 blur kernels from [16] and 200 images from [11], which has no overlap with the training data. In addition, we create a dataset containing 100 ground-truth low-light images with saturated pixels, one half for the training and one half for the test. These images are resized to the size of 600×800 pixels. For each noise type, we train one discriminative model using blurred images corrupted by the noise of different levels (1%-5%), such that this range can cover the possible noise levels in practice. We use real captured examples to illustrate the robustness of the proposed method to real unknown noise and estimated kernels. We set T, N_f, and filter size to be 20, 8, and 3×3, respectively. More results are included in the supplemental material. The MATLAB code is publicly available on the authors' websites.

Gaussian noise. We first evaluate the proposed method and the state-of-the-art non-blind deblurring methods using blurred images corrupted by Gaussian noise. Table 1 summarizes the PSNR and SSIM results. Since most existing deblurring approaches have been developed for small Gaussian noise, all methods have the reasonable performance at low noise levels (1% and 2%). Under such conditions, performance mainly depends on the prior for the latent image. It is reasonable that EPLL [29] performs best because it uses an expressive, high-order prior for the latent image. CSF [16] also focuses on learning effective image priors. We train the model for CSF using the same data as ours, which contains blurred images with different noise levels. CSF [16] achieves balanced results for all levels and distinctive performance at noise levels 3% and 4%. As the noise level becomes higher, the data term begins to play an important role. Whyte [22] performs poorly because it has been designed for saturated pixels. In addition, TVL2 [7], TVL1 [25], and Cho [3] need specifically hand-crafted tuning for the model parameters, which will significantly affect the deblurred results. Some deep learning-based methods [18,27] also aim to learn effective image priors for the non-blind deblurring problem. For MLP [18], we use the model provided by the authors, which is trained for motion blur and Gaussian noise as stated in [18]. As demonstrated by Zhang et al. [27], their algorithm (FCN) is able to handle Gaussian noise. However, this method does not generate better results compared to the proposed algorithm when the noise level is high. In contrast, with a simple total variation prior and no manual designing, the proposed method performs comparably with other methods at various noise levels, suggesting the benefit of discriminatively learning the data term.

Impulse Noise. Next we test on blurred images corrupted by impulse noise, as shown in Table 2 and Fig. 2. As expected, methods developed for Gaussian noise do not perform well, including TVL2 [7], EPLL [29], and Whyte [22]. With the ℓ_2

Table 1. PSNR/SSIM results on blurred images corrupted by Gaussian noise at different levels

Noise level	TVL2 [7]	EPLL [29]	MLP [18]	CSF [16]	TVL1 [25]	Whyte [22]	Cho [3]	FCN [27]	Ours
1%	27.00/0.7844	**27.64/0.7975**	26.49/0.6000	25.55/0.7017	26.52/0.7561	25.48/0.6829	27.24/0.7833	26.46/0.7416	26.47/0.7457
2%	25.49/0.6944	**25.90/0.7068**	24.92/0.6002	25.36/0.6991	25.55/0.7008	22.95/0.5213	25.74/0.6780	25.18/0.6837	25.59/0.7021
3%	24.54/0.6337	24.86/0.6456	23.90/0.5951	**24.99/0.6637**	24.73/0.6493	20.78/0.4096	24.92/0.6562	24.47/0.6510	24.86/0.6551
4%	23.86/0.5901	24.12/0.6011	23.21/0.5889	**24.33/0.6317**	24.04/0.6038	19.10/0.3330	23.95/0.5932	23.69/0.5811	24.26/0.6186
5%	23.35/0.5576	23.56/0.5667	22.71/0.5787	23.45/0.5855	23.42/0.5633	17.77/0.2800	23.35/0.5537	23.61/0.5665	**23.73/0.5901**

Table 2. PSNR/SSIM results on blurred images corrupted by impulse noise at different levels

Noise level	TVL2 [7]	EPLL [29]	CSF [16]	TVL1 [25]	Whyte [22]	Cho [3]	Ours
1%	22.34/0.5400	13.59/0.2514	23.48/0.5634	27.10/0.7873	18.57/0.4262	27.73/0.8033	**29.75/0.9143**
2%	20.64/0.4556	15.48/0.5397	23.04/0.5397	26.99/0.7849	16.39/0.2992	27.65/0.8034	**29.39/0.9075**
3%	19.23/0.3867	17.79/0.5179	22.62/0.5179	26.89/0.7823	14.88/0.2358	27.57/0.8039	**29.09/0.9005**
4%	17.94/0.3251	19.66/0.4906	22.11/0.4906	26.74/0.7797	13.59/0.1907	27.41/0.8020	**28.76/0.8920**
5%	16.84/0.2809	20.87/0.4658	21.62/0.4658	26.61/0.7772	12.49/0.1622	27.24/0.8012	**28.47/0.8828**

norm-based data term, cascaded training the image prior by CSF [16] smooths the image details significantly. TVL1 [25] performs better by combining the standard TV prior with a robust data term based on ℓ_1 norm. Among existing methods, Cho [3] performs the best because it uses a hand-crafted model to handle impulse noise. Still, the proposed method has a concrete improvement over Cho [3], both numerically and visually, suggesting the benefits of correctly modeling the data term.

Other Types of Noise and Saturation. We further evaluate these methods on blurred images corrupted by mixed noise (of Gaussian and impulse noise), Poisson noise, and saturated pixels, as shown in Tables 3 and 4. The proposed method consistently outperforms the state-of-the-art methods.

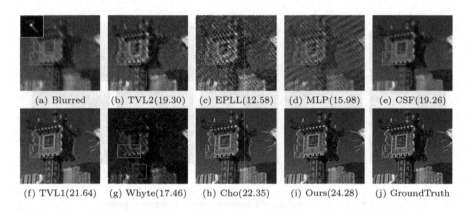

(a) Blurred   (b) TVL2(19.30)   (c) EPLL(12.58)   (d) MLP(15.98)   (e) CSF(19.26)

(f) TVL1(21.64)   (g) Whyte(17.46)   (h) Cho(22.35)   (i) Ours(24.28)   (j) GroundTruth

Fig. 2. Deblurred results on images corrupted by impulse noise. The numbers in parenthesis are PSNR values. Methods designed for Gaussian noise lead to strong artifacts (b-e, g). TVL1 (f) obtains some robustness to noise by using a ℓ_1 norm. Cho et al. [3] use a hand-crafted model to deal with impulse noise but the proposed method can better recover the details

Table 3. PSNR/SSIM results on blurred images corrupted by mixed noise at different levels

Noise level	TVL2 [7]	EPLL [29]	MLP [18]	CSF [16]	TVL1 [25]	Whyte [22]	Cho [3]	Ours
1%	22.32/0.5364	13.42/0.2377	16.98/0.3628	23.43/0.5580	26.43/0.7537	18.42/0.3990	**27.15/0.7886**	26.23/0.7358
2%	20.55/0.4489	15.17/0.2622	18.58/0.4470	23.05/0.5422	25.40/0.6919	16.12/0.2693	24.87/0.6813	**25.50/0.6928**
3%	18.95/0.3716	17.37/0.3158	18.85/0.4270	22.58/0.5242	24.50/0.6409	14.45/0.2054	23.23/0.4884	**24.77/0.6462**
4%	17.47/0.3036	19.16/0.3678	18.84/0.4002	22.04/0.4968	23.73/0.5903	12.96/0.1627	22.89/0.3383	**24.14/0.6030**
5%	16.16/0.2518	20.37/0.4157	18.80/0.3826	21.42/0.4680	23.03/0.5459	11.65/0.1338	22.38/0.2488	**23.50/0.5611**

Table 4. PSNR/SSIM results on blurred images corrupted by Poisson noise and saturated pixels

Method	TVL2 [7]	EPLL [29]	CSF [16]	TVL1 [25]	Whyte [22]	Cho [3]	Ours
Poisson	23.95/0.5981	14.31/0.2083	23.90/0.5946	23.96/0.6043	19.22/0.3461	17.51/0.3526	**24.31/0.6214**
Saturation	23.07/0.7321	27.77/0.8804	26.72/0.8921	26.40/0.8610	22.85/0.7984	28.17/0.8918	**29.55/0.9351**

Evaluation on Real-World Images. The proposed method has been trained using images corrupted by known noise and outliers. One may wonder whether it works on real-world images, because their noise statistics are unknown and different from the training data. In this experiment, we apply the model trained for Gaussian noise to real-world images from the literature, since Gaussian noise is the predominant noise type in practice, as shown in Fig. 3. The blur kernels are estimated by the kernel estimation methods [4,12]. The deblurred images by TVL1 and Cho et al. have ringing artifacts around the headlights because of saturated pixels. The method by Whyte et al. [22] can handle saturated pixels but significantly boosts the image noise. The recovered image by the proposed method is clearer and almost artifact-free, demonstrating the effectiveness and robustness of the proposed method to real unknown noise and inaccurate kernels.

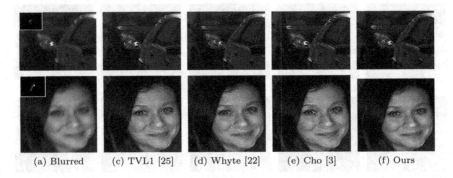

(a) Blurred   (c) TVL1 [25]   (d) Whyte [22]   (e) Cho [3]   (f) Ours

Fig. 3. Real captured examples with unknown noise

5   Analysis and Discussions

As discussed above, most non-blind deconvolution methods are sensitive to significant noise and outlier pixels because of improper assumptions on the data term. Previous work [16] has shown the benefit of discriminatively learning the image prior for deblurring when the noise level is small. Our work has shown that discriminatively learning the data term can effectively deal with significant noise and outliers. In this section, we analyze the behavior of the proposed method to understand why it is effective.

Model Properties and Effectiveness. To understand what our algorithm learns from the training data, we plot in Fig. 4 the learned shrinkage functions for the residue image (i.e., $\phi_0(\cdot)$, the approximated solution to the subproblem (6)), trade-off parameters, and the deblurred images at different stages of the proposed method on a test image with significant impulse noise. To facilitate the analysis, we assume that $N_f = 0$ in (4) in this section. We will discuss the effect of learning filters in the following sections.

The shrinkage function is initialized with a line-shaped function[2], as shown in the first column of Fig. 4(b). Similar to most state-of-the-art methods, the latent image is initialized to be the blurred image, i.e., $l_0 = b$. To solve the optimization problems (6)–(9), we first apply the blur kernel k to the initial latent image. The convolution smoothes out impulse noise in the blurred image and the output, $k * l_0 = k * b$, is a smoothed version of the blurred image. Then the residual image $b - k * l_0 = b - k * b$ is only large at pixels that correspond to either salient structures or are corrupted by impulse noise in the input blurred image, as shown in the first column in Fig. 4(a). With the initial line-shaped shrinkage function ϕ_0 in (11), the auxiliary variable at stage 1 becomes $z_1 = \phi_0(b - k * b) \approx b - k * b$ (see Fig. 4(c)). Consequently, the first term of the non-blind deblurring problem (9)

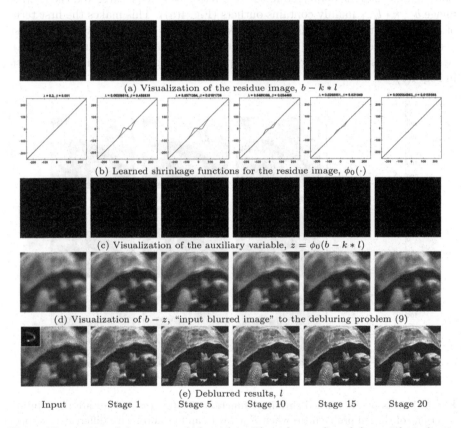

(a) Visualization of the residue image, $b - k * l$

(b) Learned shrinkage functions for the residue image, $\phi_0(\cdot)$

(c) Visualization of the auxiliary variable, $z = \phi_0(b - k * l)$

(d) Visualization of $b - z$, "input blurred image" to the debluring problem (9)

(e) Deblurred results, l

| Input | Stage 1 | Stage 5 | Stage 10 | Stage 15 | Stage 20 |

Fig. 4. Illustration of the proposed algorithm. The columns from left to right indicate different stages. Flexible shrinkage functions (b) are discriminatively learned for the residue image (a) at different stages, which can detect outliers (c) and suppress its effect on the "input" (d) of the deblurring problem (9). The proposed method can generate clear results with fine details (e)

---

[2] Note that we assume $\mathcal{R}_0(\cdot) = \| \cdot \|_2^2$ as the initialization in (6) and its closed-form solution is a line-shaped function.

is close to $\|k*b-k*l\|_2^2$. The "effective" blurred image, $k*b$, is almost noise-free because the blurring operation suppresses the impulse noise.

At the next few stages, the learned shrinkage functions resemble soft-thresholding operators. At stage t, the auxiliary variable $z_t = \phi_0(b - k * l_{t-1})$ is close to $b - k * l_{t-1}$ if the latter is large and 0 otherwise (Fig. 4(b)). The first (data) term in the deblurring problem (9) is close to $\|b - k * l\|_2^2$ when $z_t = 0$ and $\|k * l_{t-1} - k * l\|_2^2$ otherwise. That is, the proposed algorithm is learning to identify outlier pixels via the auxiliary variable z. As a result, inlier pixels are used but outliers are replaced with those of the smoothed image, $k * l_{t-1}$, which is almost noise-free.

At the final stages, the learned shrinkage functions become line-shaped functions again, since the deblurred image l_{t-1} becomes much clearer and the residue image $b - k * l_{t-1}$ mainly contains outliers (Fig. 4(a)). This makes the first term of deblurring subproblem (9) close to $\|k * l_{t-1} - k * l\|_2^2$, where $k * l_{t-1}$ almost becomes a denoised version of the input blurred image, as shown in Fig. 4(d). At these stages, the recovered images approach the ground truth l_{gt}, as shown in Fig. 4(e).

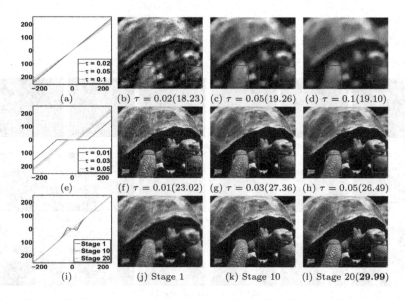

Fig. 5. Effects of the learned shrinkage functions for (6). (a) and (e) are the solution functions of the subproblem (6) when $\mathcal{R}_0(\cdot)$ is ℓ_2 and ℓ_1 norm with different τ, respectively. (b)–(d) and (f)–(h) are the deblurred results with the corresponding τ using the ℓ_2 and ℓ_1 norm-based data term, respectively. (i) plots the learned shrinkage functions for (6) at different stages. (j)–(l) are the results restored at stage 1, 10, and 20. The method with the learned flexible shrinkage function generates clearer images with finer details (The numbers in the parenthesis denote the corresponding PSNR values.)

Figure 5 shows the effectiveness of the learned shrinkage functions. To ensure fair comparisons, we set $N_f = 0$ and let $\mathcal{R}_0(\cdot)$ be ℓ_2 norm, ℓ_1 norm, and the unknown penalty function associated with the learned shrinkage function. The shrinkage functions of the ℓ_2 norm-based data terms in Fig. 5(a) cannot distinguish the impulse noise and smooth both image structure and noise. The method with ℓ_1 norm has some improvement. However, it heavily relies on the manual selection of the weight τ. Furthermore, some details of the latent images are smoothed out (Fig. 5(h)). In contrast, the proposed method can discriminatively learn flexible shrinkage functions of (6) for different stages and generate clearer images with finer details (Fig. 5(i)-(l)).

Effects of Data Terms. To further understand the role played by the data term when the blurred images contain outliers, Fig. 6 shows the deblurred results by different approaches, including ℓ_2 norm-based methods with different image priors (TVL2 [7], EPLL [29], and CSF [16]), methods with robust data terms (Lorentzian function-based term and TVL1 [25]), Cho et al. [3], and the proposed method. When the blurred images contain significant impulse noise, methods using a data term based on the ℓ_2 norm all fail, despite the image priors, e.g.,

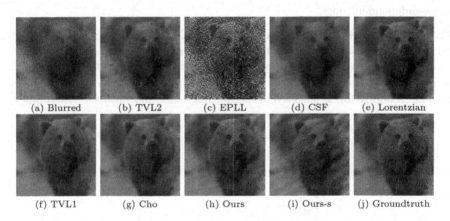

(a) Blurred   (b) TVL2   (c) EPLL   (d) CSF   (e) Lorentzian

(f) TVL1   (g) Cho   (h) Ours   (i) Ours-s   (j) Groundtruth

Fig. 6. Effectiveness of the proposed method compared with approaches with various spatial and data terms. The data term plays a more important role for images with significant impulse noise. Our method generates the images with fine details

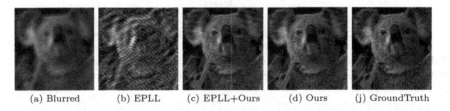

(a) Blurred   (b) EPLL   (c) EPLL+Ours   (d) Ours   (j) GroundTruth

Fig. 7. Effectiveness of the proposed framework to improve EPLL for images with outliers

TVL2 [7], EPLL [29], and CSF [16]. Approaches with robust data term, e.g., Lorentzian data term, TVL1 [25], and Cho et al. [3], can handle outlier pixels but may not recover fine details. In contrast, the proposed method generates clearer images with finer details.

Effects of Stage-Wise Discriminative Learning. Since our method uses stage-dependent parameters, one may wonder whether this feature is important. To answer this question, we learn a stage-independent data term, referred to as Ours-s in Fig. 6(i). Although a stage-independent data term can recover the fur of the bear better than some existing methods, it causes severe artifacts. By comparison, the proposed algorithm using a stage-dependent data term recovers fine details without the artifacts. In addition, we note that our method performs better than EPLL when the level of Gaussian noise is high. This can also be attributed to the stage-wise discriminative learning. As the deblurring processes, the noise level becomes lower. The noise distribution changes to a certain extent. More importantly, as the deblurred result becomes clearer and cleaner, the roles of the data term and regularizer have also changed. Thus, it is necessary to discriminatively learn the trade-off parameter for each stage. Figure 6(h)–(i) shows that stage-dependent data terms are more effective than stage-independent ones.

Extension of the Proposed Algorithm. To understand the role of the data term, we have used a standard total variation prior for the latent image. It is straightforward to combine the proposed data term with different image priors. As an example, we use EPLL [29] as the image prior and Fig. 7 shows the deblurred results. While EPLL is sensitive to significant noise and outliers, combining its

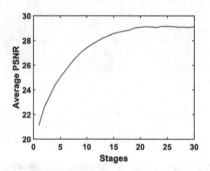

Fig. 8. Fast convergence property of the proposed algorithm

Table 5. Runtime (second)/PSNR comparisons for image deconvolution (of size 280 × 280 with impulse noise and 600 × 800 with saturated pixels, respectively)

Method	EPLL [29]	CSF [16]	TVL1 [25]	Cho [3]	Ours
280 × 280	58.97/12.58	**1.98**/19.26	2.78/21.64	4.28/22.35	3.71/**24.28**
600 × 800	329.70/24.00	**13.79**/27.89	15.07/29.64	26.30/30.13	23.23/**31.63**

image prior with the proposed framework generates clearer results in Fig. 7(c). Furthermore, using the more expressive EPLL prior better recovers fine details than the TV prior, such as the koala's fur.

Convergence and Runtime. We empirically examine the convergence of the proposed method on the proposed dataset corrupted by impulse noise. The proposed algorithm converges in fewer than 20 steps, as shown in Fig. 8. In addition, Table 5 summarizes the running time, which is based on an Intel Core i7-6700 CPU@3.40 GHz and 16 GB RAM. The proposed method runs faster than Cho et al. [3]. Our method is not the fastest, but performs much better than all the other methods.

6   Conclusion

We have presented a discriminative learning framework for non-blind deconvolution with significant noise and outliers. In contrast to existing methods, we allow the data term and the tradeoff parameter to be discriminatively learned and stage-dependent. The proposed framework can also be applied to improve existing deconvolution methods with various image priors. Experimental results show that the proposed algorithm performs favorably against the state-of-the-art methods for different types of noise and outliers.

Acknowledgments. This work has been supported in part by the NSFC (No. 61572099) and NSF CAREER (No. 1149783).

References

1. Bar, L., Kiryati, N., Sochen, N.: Image deblurring in the presence of impulsive noise. IJCV **70**(3), 279–298 (2006)
2. Chen, Y., Yu, W., Pock, T.: On learning optimized reaction diffusion processes for effective image restoration. In: CVPR, pp. 87–90 (2015)
3. Cho, S., Wang, J., Lee, S.: Handling outliers in non-blind image deconvolution. In: ICCV, pp. 495–502 (2011)
4. Dong, J., Pan, J., Su, Z., Yang, M.H.: Blind image deblurring with outlier handling. In: ICCV, pp. 2478–2486 (2017)
5. Jancsary, J., Nowozin, S., Rother, C.: Loss-Specific training of non-parametric image restoration models: a new state of the art. In: Fitzgibbon, A., Lazebnik, S., Perona, P., Sato, Y., Schmid, C. (eds.) ECCV 2012. LNCS, vol. 7578, pp. 112–125. Springer, Heidelberg (2012). https://doi.org/10.1007/978-3-642-33786-4_9
6. Jin, M., Roth, S., Favaro, P.: Noise-blind image deblurring. In: CVPR, pp. 3510–3518 (2017)
7. Krishnan, D., Fergus, R.: Fast image deconvolution using Hyper-Laplacian priors. In: NIPS, pp. 1033–1041 (2009)
8. Levin, A., Weiss, Y., Durand, F., Freeman, W.T.: Understanding and evaluating blind deconvolution algorithms. In: CVPR, pp. 1964–1971 (2009)
9. Levin, A., Fergus, R., Durand, F., Freeman, W.T.: Image and depth from a conventional camera with a coded aperture. ACM TOG **26**(3), 70 (2007)

10. Lucy, L.B.: An iterative technique for the rectification of observed distributions. Astron. J. **79**(6), 745 (1974)
11. Martin, D., Fowlkes, C., Tal, D., Malik, J.: A database of human segmented natural images and its application to evaluating segmentation algorithms and measuring ecological statistics. In: ICCV, pp. 416–423 (2001)
12. Pan, J., Lin, Z., Su, Z., Yang, M.H.: Robust kernel estimation with outliers handling for image deblurring. In: CVPR, pp. 2800–2808 (2016)
13. Richardson, W.H.: Bayesian-based iterative method of image restoration*. J. Opt. Soc. Am. **62**(1), 55–59 (1972)
14. Roth, S., Black, M.J.: Fields of experts: a framework for learning image priors. In: CVPR, pp. 860–867 (2005)
15. Schmidt, U., Gao, Q., Roth, S.: A generative perspective on MRFs in low-level vision. In: CVPR, pp. 1751–1758 (2010)
16. Schmidt, U., Roth, S.: Shrinkage fields for effective image restoration. In: CVPR, pp. 2774–2781 (2014)
17. Schmidt, U., Rother, C., Nowozin, S., Jancsary, J., Roth, S.: Discriminative non-blind deblurring. In: CVPR, pp. 604–611 (2013)
18. Schuler, C.J., Burger, H.C., Harmeling, S., Scholkopf, B.: A machine learning approach for non-blind image deconvolution. In: CVPR, pp. 1067–1074 (2013)
19. Schuler, C.J., Hirsch, M., Harmeling, S., Schölkopf, B.: Learning to deblur. TPAMI **38**(7), 1439–1451 (2016)
20. Sun, D., Roth, S., Lewis, J.P., Black, M.J.: Learning optical flow. In: Forsyth, D., Torr, P., Zisserman, A. (eds.) ECCV 2008. LNCS, vol. 5304, pp. 83–97. Springer, Heidelberg (2008). https://doi.org/10.1007/978-3-540-88690-7_7
21. Wang, Y., Yang, J., Yin, W., Zhang, Y.: A new alternating minimization algorithm for total variation image reconstruction. SIAM J. Imaging Sci. **1**(3), 248–272 (2008)
22. Whyte, O., Sivic, J., Zisserman, A.: Deblurring shaken and partially saturated images. IJCV **110**(2), 185–201 (2014)
23. Wiener, N.: Extrapolation, interpolation, and smoothing of stationary time series: with engineering applications. MIT Press **113**(21), 1043–54 (1949)
24. Xiao, L., Wang, J., Heidrich, W., Hirsch, M.: Learning high-order filters for efficient blind deconvolution of document photographs. In: Leibe, B., Matas, J., Sebe, N., Welling, M. (eds.) ECCV 2016. LNCS, vol. 9907, pp. 734–749. Springer, Cham (2016). https://doi.org/10.1007/978-3-319-46487-9_45
25. Xu, L., Jia, J.: Two-phase kernel estimation for robust motion deblurring. In: Daniilidis, K., Maragos, P., Paragios, N. (eds.) ECCV 2010. LNCS, vol. 6311, pp. 157–170. Springer, Heidelberg (2010). https://doi.org/10.1007/978-3-642-15549-9_12
26. Xu, L., Ren, J.S., Liu, C., Jia, J.: Deep convolutional neural network for image deconvolution. In: NIPS, pp. 1790–1798 (2014)
27. Zhang, J., Pan, J., Lai, W.S., Lau, R., Yang, M.H.: Learning fully convolutional networks for iterative non-blind deconvolution. In: CVPR, pp. 3817–3825 (2017)
28. Zhang, K., Zuo, W., Gu, S., Zhang, L.: Learning deep CNN denoiser prior for image restoration. In: CVPR, pp. 3929–3938 (2017)
29. Zoran, D., Weiss, Y.: From learning models of natural image patches to whole image restoration. In: ICCV, pp. 479–486 (2012)

Zero-Shot Deep Domain Adaptation

Kuan-Chuan Peng$^{(\boxtimes)}$ (ID), Ziyan Wu (ID), and Jan Ernst (ID)

Siemens Corporate Technology, Princeton, NJ 08540, USA
{kuanchuan.peng,ziyan.wu,jan.ernst}@siemens.com

Abstract. Domain adaptation is an important tool to transfer knowledge about a task (e.g. classification) learned in a source domain to a second, or target domain. Current approaches assume that task-relevant target-domain data is available during training. We demonstrate how to perform domain adaptation when no such task-relevant target-domain data is available. To tackle this issue, we propose *zero-shot deep domain adaptation* (ZDDA), which uses privileged information from *task-irrelevant dual-domain pairs*. ZDDA learns a source-domain representation which is not only tailored for the task of interest but also close to the target-domain representation. Therefore, the source-domain task of interest solution (e.g. a classifier for classification tasks) which is jointly trained with the source-domain representation can be applicable to both the source and target representations. Using the MNIST, Fashion-MNIST, NIST, EMNIST, and SUN RGB-D datasets, we show that ZDDA can perform domain adaptation in classification tasks without access to task-relevant target-domain training data. We also extend ZDDA to perform sensor fusion in the SUN RGB-D scene classification task by simulating task-relevant target-domain representations with task-relevant source-domain data. To the best of our knowledge, ZDDA is the first domain adaptation and sensor fusion method which requires no task-relevant target-domain data. The underlying principle is not particular to computer vision data, but should be extensible to other domains.

Keywords: Zero-shot · Domain adaptation · Sensor fusion

1 Introduction

The useful information to solve practical tasks often exists in different domains captured by various sensors, where a domain can be either a modality or a dataset. For instance, the 3-D layout of a room can be either captured by a depth sensor or inferred from the RGB images. In real-world scenarios, it is highly likely that we can only access limited amount of data in certain domain(s). The performance of the solution (e.g. the classifier for classification tasks) we learn from one domain often degrades when the same solution is applied to other domains, which is caused by domain shift [17] in a typical domain adaptation (DA) task, where source-domain training data, target-domain training data, and a task of interest (TOI) are given. The goal of a DA task is to derive solution(s) of the TOI for both the source and target domains.

© Springer Nature Switzerland AG 2018
V. Ferrari et al. (Eds.): ECCV 2018, LNCS 11215, pp. 793–810, 2018.
https://doi.org/10.1007/978-3-030-01252-6_47

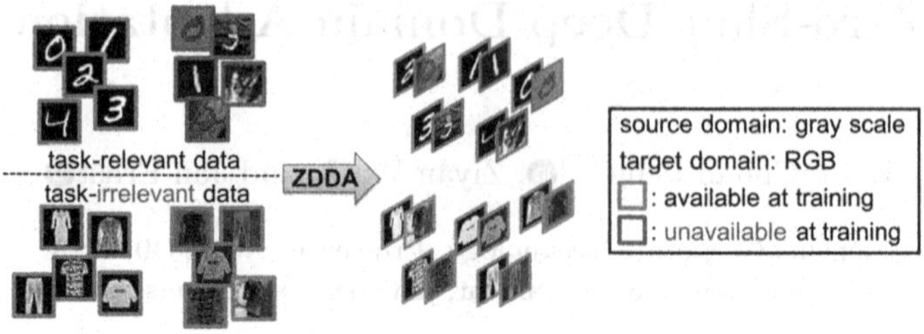

Fig. 1. We propose zero-shot deep domain adaptation (ZDDA) for domain adaptation and sensor fusion. ZDDA learns from the task-irrelevant dual-domain pairs when the task-relevant target-domain training data is unavailable. In this example domain adaptation task (MNIST [27]→MNIST-M [13]), the task-irrelevant gray-RGB pairs are from the Fashion-MNIST [46] dataset and the Fashion-MNIST-M dataset (the colored version of the Fashion-MNIST [46] dataset with the details in Sect. 4.1)

The state-of-the-art DA methods such as [1,14–16,25,30,35,37,39–41,43,44, 47,50] are proposed to solve DA tasks under the assumption that the *task-relevant data*, the data directly applicable and related to the TOI (regardless of whether it is labeled or not), in the target domain is available at training time, which is not always true in practice. For instance, in real business use cases, acquiring the task-relevant target-domain training data can be infeasible due to the combination of the following reasons: (1) Unsuitable tools at the field. (2) Product development timeline. (3) Budget limitation. (4) Data import/export regulations. Such impractical assumption is also assumed true in the existing works of sensor fusion such as [31,48], where the goal is to obtain a dual-domain (source and target) TOI solution which is robust to noise in either domain. This unsolved issue motivates us to propose *zero-shot deep domain adaptation* (ZDDA), a DA and sensor fusion approach which learns from the task-irrelevant dual-domain training pairs without using the task-relevant target-domain training data, where we use the term *task-irrelevant data* to refer to the data which is not task-relevant. In the rest of the paper, we use T-R and T-I as the shorthand of task-relevant and task-irrelevant, respectively.

We illustrate what ZDDA is designed to achieve in Fig. 1 using an example DA task (MNIST [27]→MNIST-M [13]). We recommend that the readers view all the figures and tables in color. In Fig. 1, the source and target domains are gray scale and RGB images respectively, and the TOI is digit classification with both the MNIST [27] and MNIST-M [13] testing data. We assume that the MNIST-M [13] training data is unavailable. In this example, ZDDA aims at using the MNIST [27] training data and the T-I gray-RGB pairs from the Fashion-MNIST [46] dataset and the Fashion-MNIST-M dataset (the colored version of the Fashion-MNIST [46] dataset with the details in Sect. 4.1) to train digit classifiers for MNIST [27] and MNIST-M [13] images. Specifically, ZDDA achieves this by simulating the RGB representation using the gray scale image and building a joint network with the supervision of the TOI in the gray scale domain. We present the details of ZDDA in Sect. 3.

Table 1. Problem setting comparison between ZDDA, unsupervised domain adaptation (UDA), multi-view learning (MVL), and domain generalization (DG)

Problem conditions	UDA	MVL	DG	ZDDA
given T-R target-domain training data?	Y	Y	N	N
given T-R training data in multiple (>1) domains/views?	N	Y	Y	N
example prior work	[33]	[42]	[28]	N/A

We make the following two contributions: (1) To the best of our knowledge, our proposed method, ZDDA, is the first deep learning based method performing domain adaptation between one source image modality and another different target image modality (not just different datasets in the same modality such as the Office dataset [32]) **without using the task-relevant target-domain training data**. We show ZDDA's efficacy using the MNIST [27], Fashion-MNIST [46], NIST [18], EMNIST [9], and SUN RGB-D [36] datasets with cross validation. (2) **Given no task-relevant target-domain training data**, we show that ZDDA can perform sensor fusion and that ZDDA is more robust to noisy testing data in either source or target or both domains compared with a naive fusion approach in the scene classification task from the SUN RGB-D [36] dataset.

2   Related Work

Domain adaptation (DA) has been extensively studied in computer vision and applied to various applications such as image classification [1, 14–16, 25, 30, 35, 37, 39–41, 43, 44, 47, 50], semantic segmentation [45, 51], and image captioning [8]. With the advance of deep neural networks in recent years, the state-of-the-art methods successfully perform DA with (fully or partially) labeled [8, 15, 25, 30, 39] or unlabeled [1, 14–16, 35, 37, 39–41, 43–45, 47, 50] T-R target-domain data. Although different strategies such as the domain adversarial loss [40] and the domain confusion loss [39] are proposed to improve the performance in the DA tasks, most of the existing methods need the T-R target-domain training data, which can be unavailable in reality. In contrast, we propose ZDDA to learn from the T-I dual-domain pairs without using the T-R target-domain training data. One part of ZDDA includes simulating the target-domain representation using the source-domain data, and similar concepts have been mentioned in [19, 21]. However, both of [19, 21] require the access to the T-R dual-domain training pairs, but ZDDA needs no T-R target-domain data.

Other problems related to ZDDA include unsupervised domain adaptation (UDA), multi-view learning (MVL), and domain generalization (DG), and we compare their problem settings in Table 1, which shows that the ZDDA problem setting is different from those of UDA, MVL, and DG. In UDA and MVL, T-R target-domain training data is given. In MVL and DG, T-R training data in multiple domains is given. However, in ZDDA, T-R target-domain training data is unavailable and the only available T-R training data is in one source domain.

Table 2. Working condition comparison between ZDDA and other existing methods. Among all the listed methods, only ZDDA can work under all four conditions

Can each method work under each condition?	[28]	[11]	[6]	[49]	[14]	[32]	[39]	ZDDA
without T-R target-domain training data	Y	N	N	Y	N	Y	N	Y
without T-R training data in >1 domains	N	Y	Y	Y	Y	Y	Y	Y
without accurate domain descriptor	Y	Y	Y	N	Y	Y	Y	Y
without class labels for **any** target domain data	Y	N	Y	Y	Y	N	N	Y
conjunction of all the above conditions	N	N	N	N	N	N	N	Y

We further compare ZDDA with the existing methods relevant to our problem setting in Table 2, which shows that among the listed methods, only ZDDA can work under all four conditions.

In terms of sensor fusion, Ngiam et al. [31] define the three components for multimodal learning (multimodal fusion, cross modality learning, and shared representation learning) based on the modality used for feature learning, supervised training, and testing, and experiment on audio-video data with their proposed deep belief network and autoencoder based method. Targeting on the temporal data, Yang et al. [48] follow the setup of multimodal learning in [31], and validate their proposed encoder-decoder architecture using video-sensor and audio-video data. Although certain progress about sensor fusion is achieved in the previous works [31,48], we are unaware of any existing sensor fusion method which overcomes the issue of lacking T-R target-domain training data, which is the issue that ZDDA is designed to solve.

3   Our Proposed Method — ZDDA

Given a task of interest (TOI), a source domain D_s, and a target domain D_t, our proposed method, zero-shot deep domain adaptation (ZDDA), is designed to achieve the following two goals: (1) **Domain adaptation:** Derive the solutions of the TOI for both D_s and D_t when the T-R training data in D_t is unavailable. We assume that we have access to the T-R labeled training data in D_s and the T-I dual-domain pairs in D_s and D_t. (2) **Sensor fusion:** Given the previous assumption, derive the solution of TOI when the testing data in both D_s and D_t is available. The testing data in either D_s or D_t can be noisy. We assume that there is no prior knowledge available about the type of noise and which domain gives noisy data at testing time.

For convenience, we use a scene classification task in RGB-D as an example TOI to explain ZDDA, but ZDDA can be applied to other TOIs/domains. In this example, D_s and D_t are depth and RGB images respectively. According to the our previous assumption, we have access to the T-R labeled depth data and T-I RGB-D pairs at training time. The training procedure of ZDDA is illustrated in Fig. 2, where we simulate the RGB representation using the depth image, build

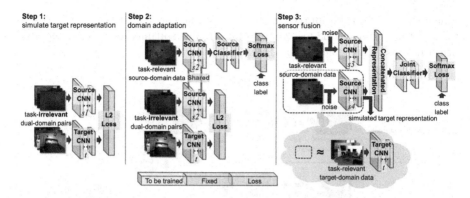

Fig. 2. An overview of the ZDDA training procedure. We use the images from the SUN RGB-D [36] dataset for illustration. ZDDA simulates the target-domain representation using the source-domain data, builds a joint network with the supervision from the source domain, and trains a sensor fusion network. In step 1, we choose to train $s1$ and fix t, but we can also train t and fix $s1$ to simulate the target-domain representation. In step 2, t can also be trainable instead of being fixed, but we choose to fix it to make the number of trainable parameters manageable. The details are explained in Sect. 3

a joint network with the supervision of the TOI in depth images, and train a sensor fusion network in step 1, step 2, and step 3 respectively. We use the ID marked at the bottom of each convolutional neural networks (CNN) in Fig. 2 to refer to each CNN.

In step 1, we create two CNNs, $s1$ and t, to take the depth and RGB images of the T-I RGB-D pairs as input. The purpose of this step is to find $s1$ and t such that feeding the RGB image into t can be approximated by feeding the corresponding depth image into $s1$. We achieve this by fixing t and enforcing the L2 loss on top of $s1$ and t at training time. We choose to train $s1$ and fix t here, but training t and fixing $s1$ can also achieve the same purpose. The L2 loss can be replaced with any suitable loss functions which encourage the similarity of the two input representations, and our selection is inspired by [19,21]. The design in step 1 is similar to the hallucination architecture [21] and the supervision transfer [19], but we require no T-R dual-domain training pairs. Instead, we use the T-I dual-domain training pairs.

After step 1, we add another CNN, $s2$ (with the same network architecture as that of $s1$), and a classifier to the network (as shown in step 2) to learn from the label of the training depth images. The classifier in our experiment is a fully connected layer for simplicity, but other types of classifiers can also be used. The newly added CNN takes the T-R depth images as input, and shares all the weights with the original source CNN, so we use $s2$ to refer to both of them. t is the same as that in step 1. At training time, we pre-train $s2$ from $s1$ and fix t. Our choice of fixing t is inspired by the adversarial adaptation step in ADDA [40]. t can also be trainable in step 2, but given our limited amount of data, we choose to fix it to make the number of trainable parameters manageable. $s2$ and the source classifier are trained such that the weighted sum of the softmax loss and L2 loss are minimized. The softmax loss can be replaced with other losses suitable for the TOI.

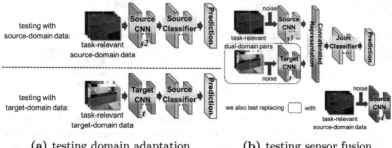

(a) testing domain adaptation   (b) testing sensor fusion

Fig. 3. An overview of the ZDDA testing procedure. We use the SUN RGB-D [36] images for illustration. Different from the color coding in Fig. 2, the colors here are purely used to distinguish different CNNs/classifiers/predictions

After step 2, we expect to obtain a depth representation which is close to the RGB representation in the feature space and performs reasonably well with the trained classifier in the scene classification. Step 1 and step 2 can be done in one step with properly designed curriculum learning, but we separate them not only because of clarity but also because of the difficulty of designing the learning curriculum before training. After step 2, we can form the scene classifier in depth/RGB (denoted as C_D/C_{RGB}) by concatenating $s2/t$ and the trained source classifier (as shown in Fig. 3a), which meets our first goal, domain adaptation. We use the notation ZDDA$_2$ to refer to the method using the training procedure in Fig. 2 up to step 2 and the testing procedure in Fig. 3a.

To perform sensor fusion, we propose step 3, where we train a joint classifier for RGB-D input using only the T-R depth training data. We create two CNNs, $s3$ and $s4$ (each with the same network architecture as that of CNN_{s1}), and add a concatenation layer on top of them to concatenate their output representations. The concatenated representation is connected to a joint classifier. At training time, we pre-train $s3$ and $s4$ from $s2$ and $s1$ respectively and fix $s4$. Both $s3$ and $s4$ take the T-R depth images as the input. To train a more robust RGB-D scene classifier, we randomly select some inputs of $s3$ and $s4$, and optionally add noise to them independently. We supervise the entire network with the label of the depth training data for the scene classification, which is done by the softmax loss enforced on top of the joint classifier.

According to step 1, the output of $s4$ is expected to simulate the RGB representation as if we feed the T-R RGB image to t. This expectation is based on the assumption that the relationship between the dual-domain pairwise data is similar, regardless of whether the data is T-R or T-I. Given the simulated

Table 3. The statistics of the datasets we use. For NIST, we use the "by_class" dataset, remove the digits, and treat uppercase and lowercase letters as different classes. For EMNIST, we use the "EMNIST Letters" split which only contains the letters. We create the colored datasets from the original ones using Ganin's method [13] (see Sect. 4.1 for details). We refer to each dataset by the corresponding dataset ID (e.g. D_N and D_N-M refer to the NIST and the NIST-M datasets, respectively)

original dataset	MNIST [27]	Fashion-MNIST [46]	NIST [18]	EMNIST [9]	SUN RGB-D [36]
dataset ID	D_M	D_F	D_N	D_E	D_S
image content	digit	clothing	letter	letter	scene
image size	28×28	28×28	128×128	28×28	~VGA
# classes	10	10	52	26	45
# training data	60000	60000	387361	124800	details in Sec. 4.1
# testing data	10000	10000	23941	20800	details in Sec. 4.1
class labels	0-9	dress, coat, etc.	A-Z, a-z	Aa-Zz	corridor, lab, etc.
balanced class?	N	Y	N	Y	N
example images					
colored dataset	MNIST-M	Fashion-MNIST-M	NIST-M	EMNIST-M	N / A
example images					N / A

RGB representation, $s3$ is trained to learn a depth representation suitable for the RGB-D scene classification without the constraint of the L2 loss in step 2. At testing time, $s4$ is replaced with t which takes the T-R RGB testing images as input with optional noise added to test the ZDDA's performance given noisy RGB-D testing data (as shown in Fig. 3b). In Fig. 3b, we also test replacing "RGB images and t" with "depth images and $s4$" to evaluate the performance of ZDDA in step 3 given only testing depth images. After the training procedure in Fig. 2, we can form three scene classifiers in RGB, depth, and RGB-D domains (one classifier per domain), and our trained RGB-D classifier is expected to be able to handle noisy input with reasonable performance degradation. The 3-step training procedure of ZDDA in Fig. 2 can be framed as an end-to-end training process with proper learning curriculum. We separate these 3 steps due to the ease of explanation. We use the notation ZDDA$_3$ to refer to the method using the training procedure in Fig. 2 up to step 3 and the testing procedure in Fig. 3b.

4   Experiment Setup

4.1   Datasets

For domain adaptation (DA), we validate the efficacy of ZDDA under classification tasks using the MNIST [27], Fashion-MNIST [46], NIST [18], EMNIST [9], and SUN RGB-D [36] datasets. For sensor fusion, we experiment on the SUN RGB-D [36] dataset. We summarize the statistics of these datasets in Table 3, where we list the dataset IDs which we use to refer to these datasets. For D_M,

Table 4. The base network architecture (BNA) we use in our experiments. For each BNA, We specify the layer separating the source/target CNN and the source classifier in Fig. 2. The layer name in the right column is based on the official Caffe [24] and SqueezeNet_v1.1 [23] implementation of each BNA

Base network architecture (BNA)	Source/target CNN architecture (up to where in BNA (inclusive))
LeNet [5]	ip1
GoogleNet [38]	pool5/7x7_s1
AlexNet [26]	fc7
SqueezeNet_v1.1 [23]	fire9/concat

D_F, D_N, and D_E, we create the colored version of these datasets (D_M-M, D_F-M, D_N-M, and D_E-M) according to the procedure proposed in Ganin's work [13] — blending the gray scale images with the patches randomly extracted from the BSDS500 dataset [2]. These colored datasets and the original ones are used to construct four DA tasks adapting from gray scale to RGB images. For each DA task, we use one of the other three pairs of the datasets (original and colored ones) as the T-I data. For example, for the DA task $D_M \rightarrow D_M$-M, D_F and D_F-M together are one possible choice as the T-I data. The DA task $D_M \rightarrow D_M$-M is acknowledged as one of the standard experiments to test the efficacy of the DA methods in recent works [1,7,14,20,33,34], so we adopt this experiment and extend it to D_F, D_N, and D_E.

D_S contains 10335 RGB-D pairs belonging to 45 different scenes. For each RGB-D pair, both the raw (noisy) depth image and post-processed clean depth image are provided, and we choose to use the raw depth image to simulate the real-world scenarios. Out of the 45 scenes, we select the following 10 scenes: computer room (0), conference room (1), corridor (2), dining room (3), discussion area (4), home office (5), idk (6), lab (7), lecture theatre (8), and study space (9), where the number after each scene is the scene ID we use to refer to each scene. The 8021 RGB-D pairs belonging to the other scenes are used as the T-I training data. The 10 scenes are selected based on the following two constraints: (1) Each scene contains at least 150 RGB-D pairs in D_S, which ensures a reasonable amount of T-R data. (2) The total number of the RGB-D pairs belonging to the selected 10 scenes is minimized, which maximizes the amount of the T-I training data. We empirically find that the amount and diversity of the T-I training data are important for ZDDA. To avoid the bias toward the scene with more data, for each of the selected 10 scenes, we randomly select 89/38 RGB-D pairs as the T-R training/testing data. When experimenting on different scene classification tasks using different selections of scenes, we only use the training/testing data associated with those selected scenes as the T-R data.

4.2   Training Details

We use Caffe [24] to implement ZDDA. Table 4 lists the base network architecture (BNA) we use and the layer separating the source/target CNN and the source classifier in Fig. 2. For instance, in the case when the BNA is LeNet [5], the architecture of each source/target CNN in Fig. 2 is the LeNet [5] architecture up to the "ip1" layer, and the rest of the LeNet [5] architecture is used as the source classifier. For the DA tasks involving D_M, D_F, D_N, and D_E, we use the LeNet [5] as the BNA and train all the CNNs in Fig. 2 from scratch except that the target CNN is pre-trained from the T-I dataset and fixed afterwards. For example, when using D_F and D_F-M as the T-I data in the DA task $D_M \rightarrow D_M$-M, we train a CNN (denoted as CNN_{ref}) with the LeNet [5] architecture from scratch using the images and labels of D_F-M, and pre-train the target CNNs in Fig. 2 from CNN_{ref}. We follow similar procedures for other DA tasks and T-I datasets involving D_M, D_F, D_N, and D_E.

For the experiment involving D_S, we mostly use GoogleNet [38] as the BNA, but we also use AlexNet [26] and SqueezeNet_v1.1 [23] in the cross validation experiment with respect to different BNAs. Since only limited amount of RGB-D pairs are available in D_S, we pre-train all the CNNs in Fig. 2 from the BVLC GoogleNet model [4], BVLC AlexNet model [3], and the reference SqueezeNet model [22] when the BNA is GoogleNet [38], AlexNet [26], and SqueezeNet_v1.1 [23], respectively. These pre-trained models are trained for the ImageNet [10] classification task.

For the optionally added noise in ZDDA$_3$, we experiment on training/testing with noise-free data and noisy data. In the latter case, given that no prior knowledge about the noise is available, we use the black image as the noisy image to model the extreme case where no information in the noisy image is available. We train ZDDA$_3$ step 3 with the augmented training data formed by copying the original T-R source-domain training data 10 times and replacing $p_{train}\%$ of the images selected randomly with the black images. We follow this procedure twice independently and use the two augmented training datasets as the inputs of the two source CNNs in step 3. We empirically set $p_{train} = 20$. The testing data in Fig. 3b is constructed by replacing $p_{test}\%$ of the original testing images selected randomly with the black images, and we evaluate ZDDA under different p_{test}s. For all the experiments, the number of the output nodes of the source/joint classifiers is set to be the number of classes in the TOI, and these classifiers are trained from scratch. For the joint classifiers, we use two fully connected layers unless otherwise specified, where the first fully connected layer of the joint classifier has 1024 output nodes.

In terms of the training parameters used in Fig. 2 for the task involving D_S when the BNA is GoogleNet [38], we use a batch size of 32 and a fixed learning rate $10^{-5}/10^{-6}/10^{-3}$ for step 1/2/3. The learning rate is chosen such that the trained network can converge under a reasonable amount of time. We set the weight of the softmax loss and the L2 loss in step 2 to be 10^3 and 1 respectively such that both losses have comparable numerical values. Step 1/2/3 are trained for $10^4/10^3/10^3$ iterations. For the other training parameters, we adopt

Table 5. The overall/average per class accuracy (%) of the domain adaptation tasks (gray scale images → RGB images) formed by the datasets in Table 3, where we introduce the dataset IDs and use them to refer to the datasets here. The middle four rows show the performance of ZDDA$_2$. The color of each cell reflects the performance ranking in each column, where darker is better. The number in the parenthesis of the middle four rows is the semantic similarity between the T-R and T-I datasets measured by word2vec [29], where larger numbers represent higher semantic similarity. The T-R target-domain training data is only available for the row "target only"

T-I data	$D_M \to D_M$-M	$D_F \to D_F$-M	$D_N \to D_N$-M	$D_E \to D_E$-M
source only	39.04/39.31	33.77/33.77	8.59/8.79	33.70/33.70
D_M, D_M-M	N/A	51.55/51.55 (0.049)	34.25/33.35 (0.174)	71.20/71.20 (0.178)
D_F, D_F-M	73.15/72.96 (0.049)	N/A	21.93/21.24 (0.059)	46.93/46.93 (0.053)
D_N, D_N-M	91.99/92.00 (0.174)	43.87/43.87 (0.059)	N/A	N/A
D_E, D_E-M	94.84/94.82 (0.178)	65.30/65.30 (0.053)	N/A	N/A
target only	97.33/97.34	84.44/84.44	62.13/61.99	89.52/89.52

the default ones used in training the BVLC GoogleNet model [4] for the ImageNet [10] classification task unless otherwise specified. In general, we adopt the default training parameters used in training each BNA for either the MNIST [27] or ImageNet [10] classification tasks in the Caffe [24] and SqueezeNet_v1.1 [23] implementation unless otherwise specified.

4.3   Performance References and Baselines

To obtain the performance references of the fully supervised methods, we train a classifier with the BNA in Table 4 in each domain using the T-R training data and labels in that domain. When the BNA is LeNet [5], we train the classifier from scratch. For the other BNAs, we pre-train the classifier in the same way as that described in Sect. 4.2. After training, for each DA task, we get two fully supervised classifiers $C_{fs,s}$ and $C_{fs,t}$ in the source and target domains respectively. For the baseline of the DA task, we directly feed the target-domain testing images to $C_{fs,s}$ to obtain the performance without applying any DA method. For the baseline of sensor fusion, we compare ZDDA$_3$ with a naive fusion method by predicting the label with the highest probability from C_{RGB} and C_D in Sect. 3.

5   Experimental Result

We first compare ZDDA$_2$ with the baseline in four domain adaptation (DA) tasks (adapting from gray scale to RGB images) involving D_M, D_F, D_N, and D_E, and the result is summarized in Table 5, where the first two numbers represent the overall/average per class accuracy (%). Darker cells in each column

Table 6. The performance comparison of the domain adaptation task MNIST→MNIST-M. The color of each cell reflects the performance ranking (darker is better). For ZDDA$_2$, we report the best overall accuracy from Table 5. **All the listed methods except ZDDA$_2$ use the MNIST-M training data.** Without the access to the MNIST-M training data, ZDDA$_2$ can still achieve the accuracy comparable to those of the competing methods (even outperform most of them) in this task

method	[14]	[34]	[20]	[33]	[7]	ZDDA$_2$
accuracy (%)	76.66	86.70	89.53	94.20	98.20	94.84

Table 7. Performance comparison with different numbers of classes in scene classification. The reported numbers are classification accuracy (%). The color of each cell reflects the performance ranking in each column, where darker color means better performance. P_{RGB-D} represents the **task-irrelevant** RGB-D pairs

exp. ID	method	training modality	testing modality	2	3	4	5	6	7	8	9	10
1	GoogleNet	D	D	85.53	83.33	82.89	70.00	67.11	59.02	54.28	50.88	51.84
2	ZDDA$_2$	D+P_{RGB-D}	D	88.16	85.96	83.55	77.89	70.18	66.92	64.80	62.28	59.74
3	ZDDA$_3$	D+P_{RGB-D}	D	88.16	86.84	84.87	77.89	72.37	66.92	64.47	64.33	63.16
4	GoogleNet	D	RGB	68.42	57.02	56.58	48.95	42.11	45.11	40.46	34.50	31.58
5	ZDDA$_2$	D+P_{RGB-D}	RGB	80.26	78.07	76.32	67.37	57.89	53.76	47.37	45.03	43.16
6	GoogleNet	RGB	RGB	88.16	85.09	84.87	79.47	78.07	68.80	70.07	69.88	63.68
7	ZDDA$_3$	D+P_{RGB-D}	RGB-D	88.16	85.96	85.53	76.32	72.81	68.42	65.13	63.16	63.16
selected scene IDs (defined in Sec. 4.1)				0~1	0~2	0~3	0~4	0~5	0~6	0~7	0~8	0~9

represent better classification accuracy in each task. In Table 5, the middle four rows represent the performance of ZDDA$_2$. $\{D_N, D_N$-M$\}$ and $\{D_E, D_E$-M$\}$ cannot be the T-I data for each other because they are both directly related to the letter classification tasks. Table 5 shows that regardless of which T-I data we use, ZDDA$_2$ significantly outperforms the baseline (source only). To see how the semantic similarity between the T-R dataset (denoted as D_{T-R}) and T-I dataset (denoted as D_{T-I}) affects the performance, we are inspired by [12] and use the word2vec [29] to compute the mean similarity (denoted as S) of any two labels from D_{T-R} and D_{T-I} (one from each). We report $S(D_{T-R}, D_{T-I})$ in the parenthesis of the middle four rows of Table 5, where higher S represents higher semantic similarity. Given Table 5 and the following reference S values: $S($object, scene$) = 0.192$, $S($animal, fruit$) = 0.171$, and $S($cat, dog$) = 0.761$, we find that: (1) For all the listed DA tasks except $D_F \rightarrow D_F$-M, higher S corresponds to better performance, which is consistent with our intuition that using more relevant data as the T-I data improves the performance more. (2) All the listed Ss in Table 5 are close to or lower than $S($animal, fruit$) = 0.171$, which we believe shows that our T-I data is highly irrelevant to the T-R data.

Second, in Table 6, we compare ZDDA$_2$ with the existing DA methods because the DA task $D_M \rightarrow D_M$-M is considered as one of the standard experiments in recent works [7,14,20,33,34]. Although this is not a fair comparison (because ZDDA$_2$ has no access to the T-R target-domain training data), we find that ZDDA$_2$ can reach the accuracy comparable to those of the state-of-the-art methods (even outperform some of them), which supports that ZDDA$_2$ is a promising DA method when the T-R target-domain training data is unavailable.

Third, we test the efficacy of ZDDA on the DA tasks constructed from D_S (adapting from depth to RGB images). We compare ZDDA with the baseline under different scene classification tasks by changing the number of scenes involved. The result is summarized in Table 7, where we list the training and testing modalities for each method. We also list the scene IDs (introduced in Sect. 4.1) involved in each task. Darker cells represent better accuracy in each column. We verify the irrelevance degree between T-R and T-I data by measuring the semantic similarity using the word2vec [29] (the same method we use in Table 5). For the 10-class experiment in Table 7, $S(D_S(\text{T-R}), D_S(\text{T-I})) = 0.198$ (close to the reference $S(\text{object, scene}) = 0.192$), which we believe shows high irrelevance between our T-I and T-R data. For simplicity, we use E_i to refer to the experiment specified by exp. ID i in this section. For the fully supervised methods in depth domain, ZDDA (E_2, E_3) outperforms the baseline (E_1) due to the extra information brought by the T-I RGB-D pairs. We find that for most listed tasks, ZDDA$_3$ (E_3) outperforms ZDDA$_2$ (E_2), which is consistent with our intuition because the source representation in ZDDA$_2$ is constrained by the L2 loss, while the counterpart in ZDDA$_3$ is learned without the L2 constraint given the simulated target representation. The fully supervised method in RGB domain (E_6) outperforms the baseline of the domain adaptation (E_4) and ZDDA$_2$ (E_5) because E_6 has access to the T-R RGB training data which is unavailable for E_4 and E_5. The performance improvement from E_4 to E_5 is caused by ZDDA$_2$'s training procedure as well as the extra T-I RGB-D training pairs. E_3 and E_7 perform similarly, which supports that the simulated target representation in ZDDA$_3$ is similar to the real one.

To test the consistency of the performance of ZDDA compared to that of the baseline, we perform the following three experiments. First, we conduct 5-fold cross validation with different training/testing splits for the 10-scene classification. Second, we perform 10-fold validation with different selections of classes for the 9-scene classification (leave-one-class-out experiment out of the 10 selected scenes introduced in Sect. 4.1). Third, we validate ZDDA's performance with different base network architectures. The results of the first two experiments are presented in Table 8, and the result of the third experiment is shown in Table 9. The results of Tables 7, 8, and 9 are consistent.

In Tables 7, 8, and 9, the classification accuracy is reported under the condition of noise-free training and testing data. To let ZDDA be more robust to noisy input, we train ZDDA$_3$ step 3 with noisy training data (we use $p_{train} = 20$ as explained in Sect. 4.2), and evaluate the classification accuracy under different noise conditions for both RGB and depth testing data. The result is

Table 8. Validation of ZDDA's performance (in mean classification accuracy (%)) with different training/testing splits and choices of classes in scene classification. GN stands for GoogleNet [38]. The definition of $P_{\text{RGB-D}}$ and the representation of the cell color in each column are the same as those in Table 7

method	training modality	testing modality	validation on train/test splits	validation on class choices
GN	D	D	52.63±1.76	53.98±1.68
ZDDA$_2$	D+$P_{\text{RGB-D}}$	D	56.89±2.13	62.05±1.97
ZDDA$_3$	D+$P_{\text{RGB-D}}$	D	58.37±3.08	62.49±1.74
GN	D	RGB	31.26±1.76	32.60±2.37
ZDDA$_2$	D+$P_{\text{RGB-D}}$	RGB	44.47±2.50	45.47±2.57
GN	RGB	RGB	66.26±1.60	67.95±2.20
ZDDA$_3$	D+$P_{\text{RGB-D}}$	RGB-D	58.68±3.10	62.13±1.50
# of classes / # of folds			10 / 5	9 / 10

presented in Fig. 4, where ZDDA$_3$ (Fig. 4b) outperforms the naive fusion method (Fig. 4a) under most conditions, and the performance improvement is shown in Fig. 4c. Both Fig. 4a and b show that the performance degradation caused by the noisy depth testing data is larger than that caused by the noisy RGB testing data, which supports that the trained RGB-D classifier relies more on the depth domain. Traditionally, training a fusion model requires the T-R training data in both modalities. However, we show that without the T-R training data in the RGB domain, we can still train an RGB-D fusion model, and that the performance degrades smoothly when the noise increases. In addition to using black images as the noise model, we evaluate the same trained joint classifier

Table 9. Validation of ZDDA's performance with different base network architectures in scene classification. The reported numbers are classification accuracy (%). The definition of $P_{\text{RGB-D}}$ and the representation of the cell color in each column are the same as those in Table 7

method	training modality	testing modality	base network architecture GoogleNet [38]	AlexNet [26]	SqueezeNet_v1.1 [23]
BNA	D	D	51.84	49.74	48.68
ZDDA$_2$	D+$P_{\text{RGB-D}}$	D	59.74	51.05	56.32
ZDDA$_3$	D+$P_{\text{RGB-D}}$	D	63.16	51.05	56.32
BNA	D	RGB	31.58	30.26	26.58
ZDDA$_2$	D+$P_{\text{RGB-D}}$	RGB	43.16	40.00	35.79
BNA	RGB	RGB	63.68	59.47	57.37
ZDDA$_3$	D+$P_{\text{RGB-D}}$	RGB-D	63.16	51.84	56.05

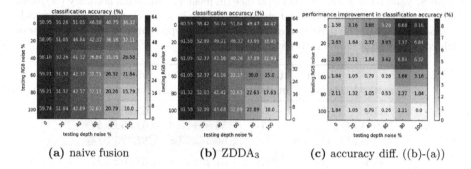

(a) naive fusion   **(b)** ZDDA$_3$ **(c)** accuracy diff. ((b)-(a))

Fig. 4. Performance comparison between the two sensor fusion methods with black images as the noisy images. We compare the classification accuracy (%) of (a) naive fusion and (b) ZDDA$_3$ under different noise levels in both RGB and depth testing data. (c) shows that ZDDA$_3$ outperforms the naive fusion under most conditions

in ZDDA$_3$ using another noise model (adding a black rectangle with a random location and size to the clean image) at testing time, and the result also supports that ZDDA$_3$ outperforms the naive fusion method. Although we only use black images as the noise model for ZDDA$_3$ at training time, we expect that adding different noise models can improve the robustness of ZDDA$_3$.

6   Conclusion and Future Work

We propose zero-shot deep domain adaptation (ZDDA), a novel approach to perform domain adaptation (DA) and sensor fusion with no need of the task-relevant target-domain training data which can be inaccessible in reality. Rather than solving the zero-shot DA problem in general, we aim at solving the problems under the assumption that task-relevant source-domain data and task-irrelevant dual-domain paired data are available. Our key idea is to use the task-relevant source-domain data to simulate the task-relevant target-domain representations by learning from the task-irrelevant dual-domain pairs. Experimenting on the MNIST [27], Fashion-MNIST [46], NIST [18], EMNIST [9], and SUN RGB-D [36] datasets, we show that ZDDA outperforms the baselines in DA and sensor fusion even without the task-relevant target-domain training data. In the task adapting from MNIST [27] to MNIST-M [13], ZDDA can even outperform several state-of-the-art DA methods which require access to the MNIST-M [13] training data. One industrial use case which we plan to apply ZDDA to in our follow-up work is training an RGD object classifier given only the textureless CAD models of those objects. In this case, depth and RGB images are source and target domains, respectively. The depth images can be rendered from the provided CAD models, and publicly available RGB-D datasets can serve as the task-irrelevant RGB-D data. We believe that ZDDA can be straightforwardly extended to handle other tasks of interest by modifying the loss functions in Fig. 2 step 2 and step 3.

References

1. Aljundi, R., Tuytelaars, T.: Lightweight unsupervised domain adaptation by convolutional filter reconstruction. In: Hua, G., Jégou, H. (eds.) ECCV 2016. LNCS, vol. 9915, pp. 508–515. Springer, Cham (2016). https://doi.org/10.1007/978-3-319-49409-8_43

2. Arbelaez, P., Maire, M., Fowlkes, C., Malik, J.: Contour detection and hierarchical image segmentation. IEEE Trans. Pattern Anal. Mach. Intell. **33**, 898–916 (2011)

3. BAIR/BVLC: BAIR/BVLC AlexNet model. http://dl.caffe.berkeleyvision.org/bvlc_alexnet.caffemodel. Accessed 02 March 2017

4. BAIR/BVLC: BAIR/BVLC GoogleNet model. http://dl.caffe.berkeleyvision.org/bvlc_googlenet.caffemodel. Accessed 02 March 2017

5. BAIR/BVLC: Lenet architecture in the Caffe tutorial. https://github.com/BVLC/caffe/blob/master/examples/mnist/lenet.prototxt

6. Blitzer, J., Foster, D.P., Kakade, S.M.: Zero-shot domain adaptation: a multi-view approach. In: Technical Report TTI-TR-2009-1. Technological institute Toyota (2009)

7. Bousmalis, K., Silberman, N., Dohan, D., Erhan, D., Krishnan, D.: Unsupervised pixel-level domain adaptation with generative adversarial networks. In: The IEEE Conference on Computer Vision and Pattern Recognition (CVPR), pp. 3722–3731. IEEE (2017)

8. Chen, T.H., Liao, Y.H., Chuang, C.Y., Hsu, W.T., Fu, J., Sun, M.: Show, adapt and tell: adversarial training of cross-domain image captioner. In: The IEEE International Conference on Computer Vision (ICCV), pp. 521–530. IEEE (2017)

9. Cohen, G., Afshar, S., Tapson, J., van Schaik, A.: EMNIST: An extension of MNIST to handwritten letters. arXiv preprint arXiv: 1702.05373 (2017)

10. Deng, J., Dong, W., Socher, R., Li, L.J., Li, K., Fei-Fei, L.: ImageNet: A large-scale hierarchical image database. In: The IEEE Conference on Computer Vision and Pattern Recognition (CVPR), pp. 248–255. IEEE (2009)

11. Ding, Z., Shao, M., Fu, Y.: Missing modality transfer learning via latent low-rank constraint. IEEE Trans. Image Proces. **24**, 4322–4334 (2015)

12. Fu, Z., Xiang, T., Kodirov, E., Gong, S.: Zero-shot object recognition by semantic manifold distance. In: The IEEE Conference on Computer Vision and Pattern Recognition (CVPR). IEEE (2015)

13. Ganin, Y., Lempitsky, V.: Unsupervised domain adaptation by backpropagation. In: Bach, F., Blei, D. (eds.) Proceedings of the 32nd International Conference on Machine Learning (ICML-2015), vol. 37, pp. 1180–1189. PMLR (2015)

14. Ganin, Y., Ustinova, E., Ajakan, H., Germain, P., Larochelle, H., Laviolette, F., Marchand, M., Lempitsky, V.: Domain-adversarial training of neural networks. J. Mach. Learn. Res. (JMLR) **17**(59), 1–35 (2016)

15. Gebru, T., Hoffman, J., Li, F.F.: Fine-grained recognition in the wild: A multi-task domain adaptation approach. In: The IEEE International Conference on Computer Vision (ICCV), pp. 1349–1358. IEEE (2017)

16. Ghifary, M., Kleijn, W.B., Zhang, M., Balduzzi, D., Li, W.: Deep reconstruction-classification networks for unsupervised domain adaptation. In: Leibe, B., Matas, J., Sebe, N., Welling, M. (eds.) ECCV 2016. LNCS, vol. 9908, pp. 597–613. Springer, Cham (2016). https://doi.org/10.1007/978-3-319-46493-0_36

17. Gretton, A., Smola, A.J., Huang, J., Schmittfull, M., Borgwardt, K.M., Schölkopf, B.: Covariate shift and local learning by distribution matching, pp. 131–160. MIT Press, Cambridge (2009)

18. Grother, P., Hanaoka, K.: NIST special database 19 handprinted forms and characters database. National Institute of Standards and Technology (2016)
19. Gupta, S., Hoffman, J., Malik, J.: Cross modal distillation for supervision transfer. In: The IEEE Conference on Computer Vision and Pattern Recognition (CVPR), pp. 2827–2836. IEEE (2016)
20. Haeusser, P., Frerix, T., Mordvintsev, A., Cremers, D.: Associative domain adaptation. In: The IEEE International Conference on Computer Vision (ICCV), pp. 2765–2773. IEEE (2017)
21. Hoffman, J., Gupta, S., Darrell, T.: Learning with side information through modality hallucination. In: The IEEE Conference on Computer Vision and Pattern Recognition (CVPR), pp. 826–834. IEEE (2016)
22. Iandola, F.N., Han, S., Moskewicz, M.W., Ashraf, K., Dally, W.J., Keutzer, K.: SqueezeNet_v1.1model. https://github.com/DeepScale/SqueezeNet/blob/master/SqueezeNet_v1.1/squeezenet_v1.1.caffemodel. Accessed 11 Feb 2017
23. Iandola, F.N., Han, S., Moskewicz, M.W., Ashraf, K., Dally, W.J., Keutzer, K.: SqueezeNet: AlexNet-level accuracy with 50x fewer parameters and <0.5MB model size. arXiv preprint arXiv: 1602.07360 (2016)
24. Jia, Y., et al.: Caffe: Convolutional architecture for fast feature embedding. arXiv preprint arXiv: 1408.5093 (2014)
25. Koniusz, P., Tas, Y., Porikli, F.: Domain adaptation by mixture of alignments of second- or higher-order scatter tensors. In: The IEEE Conference on Computer Vision and Pattern Recognition (CVPR), pp. 4478–4487. IEEE (2017)
26. Krizhevsky, A., Sutskever, I., Hinton, G.E.: ImageNet classification with deep convolutional neural networks. In: Pereira, F., Burges, C.J.C., Bottou, L., Weinberger, K.Q. (eds.) Advances in Neural Information Processing Systems (NIPS), vol. 25, pp. 1097–1105. Curran Associates, Inc. (2012)
27. LeCun, Y., Bottou, L., Bengio, Y., Haffner, P.: Gradient-based learning applied to document recognition. Proc. IEEE **86**(11), 2278–2324 (1998)
28. Li, D., Yang, Y., Song, Y.Z., Hospedales, T.M.: Deeper, broader and artier domain generalization. In: The IEEE International Conference on Computer Vision (ICCV). IEEE (2017)
29. Mikolov, T., Sutskever, I., Chen, K., Corrado, G.S., Dean, J.: Distributed representations of words and phrases and their compositionality. In: Burges, C.J.C., Bottou, L., Welling, M., Ghahramani, Z., Weinberger, K.Q. (eds.) Advances in Neural Information Processing Systems, vol. 26, pp. 3111–3119. Curran Associates Inc. (2013)
30. Motiian, S., Piccirilli, M., Adjeroh, D.A., Doretto, G.: Unified deep supervised domain adaptation and generalization. In: The IEEE International Conference on Computer Vision (ICCV), pp. 5715–5725. IEEE (2017)
31. Ngiam, J., Khosla, A., Kim, M., Nam, J., Lee, H., Ng, A.Y.: Multimodal deep learning. In: Getoor, L., Scheffer, T. (eds.) Proceedings of the 28th International Conference on Machine Learning (ICML-2011), pp. 689–696. Omnipress (2011)
32. Saenko, K., Kulis, B., Fritz, M., Darrell, T.: Adapting visual category models to new domains. In: Daniilidis, K., Maragos, P., Paragios, N. (eds.) ECCV 2010. LNCS, vol. 6314, pp. 213–226. Springer, Heidelberg (2010). https://doi.org/10.1007/978-3-642-15561-1_16
33. Saito, K., Ushiku, Y., Harada, T.: Asymmetric tri-training for unsupervised domain adaptation. In: Precup, D., Teh, Y.W. (eds.) Proceedings of the 34th International Conference on Machine Learning (ICML-2017), vol. 70, pp. 2988–2997. PMLR (2017)

34. Sener, O., Song, H.O., Saxena, A., Savarese, S.: Learning transferrable representations for unsupervised domain adaptation. In: Lee, D.D., Sugiyama, M., Luxburg, U.V., Guyon, I., Garnett, R. (eds.) Advances in Neural Information Processing Systems (NIPS), vol. 29, pp. 2110–2118. Curran Associates, Inc. (2016)

35. Sohn, K., Liu, S., Zhong, G., Yu, X., Yang, M.H., Chandraker, M.: Unsupervised domain adaptation for face recognition in unlabeled videos. In: The IEEE International Conference on Computer Vision (ICCV), pp. 3210–3218. IEEE (2017)

36. Song, S., Lichtenberg, S., Xiao, J.: SUN RGB-D: a RGB-D scene understanding benchmark suite. In: The IEEE Conference on Computer Vision and Pattern Recognition (CVPR), pp. 567–576. IEEE (2015)

37. Sun, B., Saenko, K.: Deep CORAL: correlation alignment for deep domain adaptation. In: Hua, G., Jégou, H. (eds.) ECCV 2016. LNCS, vol. 9915, pp. 443–450. Springer, Cham (2016). https://doi.org/10.1007/978-3-319-49409-8_35

38. Szegedy, C., et al.: Going deeper with convolutions. In: The IEEE Conference on Computer Vision and Pattern Recognition (CVPR), pp. 1–9. IEEE (2015)

39. Tzeng, E., Hoffman, J., Darrell, T., Saenko, K.: Simultaneous deep transfer across domains and tasks. In: The IEEE International Conference on Computer Vision (ICCV), pp. 4068–4076. IEEE (2015)

40. Tzeng, E., Hoffman, J., Saenko, K., Darrell, T.: Adversarial discriminative domain adaptation. In: The IEEE Conference on Computer Vision and Pattern Recognition (CVPR), pp. 7167–7176. IEEE (2017)

41. Venkateswara, H., Eusebio, J., Chakraborty, S., Panchanathan, S.: Deep hashing network for unsupervised domain adaptation. In: The IEEE Conference on Computer Vision and Pattern Recognition (CVPR), pp. 5018–5027. IEEE (2017)

42. Wang, W., Arora, R., Livescu, K., Bilmes, J.: On deep multi-view representation learning. In: Bach, F., Blei, D. (eds.) Proceedings of the 32th International Conference on Machine Learning (ICML-2015), vol. 37, pp. 1083–1092. PMLR (2015)

43. Wang, Y., Li, W., Dai, D., Gool, L.V.: Deep domain adaptation by geodesic distance minimization. In: The IEEE International Conference on Computer Vision (ICCV), pp. 2651–2657. IEEE (2017)

44. Wu, C., Wen, W., Afzal, T., Zhang, Y., Chen, Y., Li, H.: A compact DNN: approaching GoogLeNet-level accuracy of classification and domain adaptation. In: The IEEE Conference on Computer Vision and Pattern Recognition (CVPR), pp. 5668–5677. IEEE (2017)

45. Wulfmeier, M., Bewley, A., Posner, I.: Addressing appearance change in outdoor robotics with adversarial domain adaptation. In: IEEE/RSJ International Conference on Intelligent Robots and Systems (IROS), pp. 1551–1558. IEEE (2017)

46. Xiao, H., Rasul, K., Vollgraf, R.: Fashion-MNIST: A novel image dataset for benchmarking machine learning algorithms. arXiv preprint arXiv: 1702.05374 (2017)

47. Yan, H., Ding, Y., Li, P., Wang, Q., Xu, Y., Zuo, W.: Mind the class weight bias: Weighted maximum mean discrepancy for unsupervised domain adaptation. In: The IEEE Conference on Computer Vision and Pattern Recognition (CVPR), pp. 2272–2281. IEEE (2017)

48. Yang, X., Ramesh, P., Chitta, R., Madhvanath, S., Bernal, E.A., Luo, J.: Deep multimodal representation learning from temporal data. In: The IEEE Conference on Computer Vision and Pattern Recognition (CVPR), pp. 5447–5455. IEEE (2017)

49. Yang, Y., Hospedales, T.M.: Zero-shot domain adaptation via kernel regression on the grassmannian. In: Drira, H., Kurtek, S., Turaga, P. (eds.) BMVC Workshop on Differential Geometry in Computer Vision. BMVA Press (2015)

50. Zhang, J., Li, W., Ogunbona, P.: Joint geometrical and statistical alignment for visual domain adaptation. In: The IEEE Conference on Computer Vision and Pattern Recognition (CVPR), pp. 1859–1867. IEEE (2017)
51. Zhang, Y., David, P., Gong, B.: Curriculum domain adaptation for semantic segmentation of urban scenes. In: The IEEE International Conference on Computer Vision (ICCV), pp. 2020–2030. IEEE (2017)

Comparator Networks

Weidi Xie[✉], Li Shen, and Andrew Zisserman

Visual Geometry Group, Department of Engineering Science,
University of Oxford, Oxford, UK
{weidi,lishen,az}@robots.ox.ac.uk

Abstract. The objective of this work is set-based verification, e.g. to decide if two sets of images of a face are of the same person or not. The traditional approach to this problem is to learn to generate a feature vector per image, aggregate them into *one* vector to represent the set, and then compute the cosine similarity between sets. Instead, we design a neural network architecture that can directly learn set-wise verification. Our contributions are: (i) We propose a Deep Comparator Network (DCN) that can ingest a pair of sets (each may contain a *variable* number of images) as inputs, and compute a similarity between the pair – this involves attending to multiple discriminative local regions (landmarks), and comparing local descriptors between pairs of faces; (ii) To encourage high-quality representations for each set, internal competition is introduced for recalibration based on the landmark score; (iii) Inspired by image retrieval, a novel hard sample mining regime is proposed to control the sampling process, such that the DCN is complementary to the standard image classification models. Evaluations on the IARPA Janus face recognition benchmarks show that the comparator networks outperform the previous state-of-the-art results by a large margin.

1 Introduction

The objective of this paper is to determine if two sets of images are of the same object or not. For example, in the case of face verification, the set could be images of a face; and in the case of person re-identification, the set could be images of the entire person. In both cases the objective is to determine if the sets show the same person or not.

In the following, we will use the example of sets of faces, which are usually referred to as 'templates' in the face recognition literature, and we will use this term from here on. A template could consist of multiple samples of the same person (e.g. still images, or frames from a video of the person, or a mixture of both). With the great success of deep learning for image classification [1–4], by far the most common approach to template-based face verification is to generate a vector representing each face using a deep convolutional neural network (CNN),

Electronic supplementary material The online version of this chapter (https://doi.org/10.1007/978-3-030-01252-6_48) contains supplementary material, which is available to authorized users.

© Springer Nature Switzerland AG 2018
V. Ferrari et al. (Eds.): ECCV 2018, LNCS 11215, pp. 811–826, 2018.
https://doi.org/10.1007/978-3-030-01252-6_48

and simply average these vectors to obtain a vector representation for the entire template [5–8]. Verification then proceeds by comparing the template vectors with some similarity metrics, e.g. cosine similarity. Rather than improve on this simple combination rule, the research drives until now has been to improve the performance of the single image representation by more sophisticated training losses, such as Triplet Loss, PDDM, and Histogram Loss [6,7,9–12]. This approach has achieved very impressive results on the challenging benchmarks, such as the IARPA IJB-B and IJB-C datasets [13,14].

However, this procedure of first generating a single vector per face, and then simply averaging these, misses out on potentially using more available information in four ways:

First, *viewpoint conditioned similarity* – it is easier to determine if two faces are of the same person or not when they have a similar pose and lighting. For example, if both are frontal or both in profile, then point to point comparison is possible, whereas it isn't if one is in profile and the other frontal;

Second, *local landmark comparison* – to solve the fine-grained problem, it is essential to compare discriminative congruent 'parts' (local regions of the face), such as, an eye with an eye, or a nose with a nose.

Third, *within template weighting* – not all images in a template are of equal importance, the features derived from a low resolution or blurred face is probably of less importance than the ones coming from a high-resolution perfectly focussed face;

Fourth, *between template weighting* – what is useful for verification depends on what is in both templates. For example, if one template has only profile faces, and the second is all frontal apart from one profile instance, then it is likely that the single profile instance in the second template is of more importance than the frontal ones.

The simple average combination rule cannot take advantage of any of these four, for example, unweighted average pooling ignores the difference in the amount of information provided by each face image, and an aberrant image, such as one that is quite blurred, can have a significant effect (since most blurred face images look similar).

In this paper, we introduce a *Deep Comparator Network* (DCN), a network architecture designed to compare pairs of templates (where each template can contain an arbitrary number of images). The model consists of three modules: *Detect*, *Attend* and *Compare*, as illustrated in Fig. 1, that address the four requirements above: in the *Detect* module, besides the dense feature representation maps, multiple discriminative landmark detectors act on each input image and generate the score maps; the *Attend* module normalizes the landmark responses over the images within template, and output multiple landmark specific feature descriptors by using image specific weighted average pooling on the feature maps, finally, the *Compare* module compares these landmark specific feature vectors between the two templates, and aggregates into *one* vector for final similarity prediction. The DCN is trained end-to-end for the task of template verification. The network is described in detail in Sect. 3.

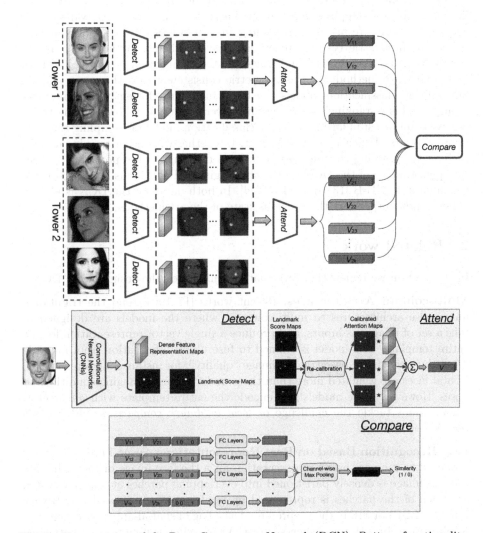

Fig. 1. *Top*: overview of the Deep Comparator Network (DCN). *Bottom*: functionality of the individual modules, namely, *Detect, Attend, Compare*. Each of the two towers in the DCN, is able to take a template (with an arbitrary number of images) as input. Each image is fed into the shared *Detect* module and outputs a feature map, as well as multiple discriminative landmark score maps. In the *Attend* module, landmark score maps (predicted from the same filter on different input images) are first re-calibrated within the template, then landmark specific feature vectors for each template are obtained by weighted average pooling on the feature maps. In the *Compare* module, landmark specific feature vectors between the two templates are compared with local "experts" (parametrized as fully connected layers), and aggregated into *one* vector for final similarity prediction.

As a second contribution we introduce an idea from the instance retrieval literature to face template verification. Large scale instance retrieval systems achieved superior results by proceeding in two stages: given a query image, images are first retrieved and ranked using a very efficient method, such as bag of visual words; then, in a second stage, the top k images are re-ranked using a more expensive method, such as geometric consistency with the query [15,16]. Since image classification models can be trained very efficiently nowadays, we repurpose this re-ranking idea for template verification as follows: during training, we employ a standard image-wise classification model for sampling the hard template pairs. This is described in Sect. 4, together with other training details, such as the training set and loss functions. In Sect. 5, we report the verification performance of the DCN on the challenging IARPA Janus face recognition benchmarks – IJB-B [13] and IJB-C [14]. In both datasets, the DCN is able to *substantially* outperform the previous state-of-the-art methods.

2 Related work

In this section we review the work that has influenced the design of the DCN.

Multi-column Architectures. Recent works [17–19] extend the traditional image-wise architectures to multi-columns, where the models are designed to take a set of images as inputs, and produce a single vector representation for the entire template. The model is trained to fuse useful information from multiple inputs by a weighting based on the image "quality"; for instance, high-resolution, frontal faces are weighted more than those under extreme imaging conditions or poses. However, these models still encode the entire template with *one* vector. They cannot tackle the challenge of *local landmark comparison* and *between template weightings*.

Face Recognition Based on Part Representations. Several previous works proposed to use part-based representation for a the face image or tacks. In [20], the face image is densely partitioned into overlapping patches at multiple scales, and each of the patches is represented by local features, such as Local Binary Pattern (LBP) or SIFT, then represented as a bag of spatial-appearance features by clustering. In [21], the Fisher Vector (FV) encoding is used to aggregate local features across different video frames to form a video-level representation.

Attention Models. Attention models have been successfully used in machine translation [22], multiple object recognition [23], and image captioning [24]. In [25], the authors propose to extract part-based feature representations from a single input image with attention, and perform fine-grained classifications with these part specific representations. In general, the idea of these attentional pooling can be seen as a generalization of average or max pooling, where the spatial weights are obtained from a parametrized function (usually a small neural network) mapping from input image to an attention mask. Apart from soft attention, [26] proposed the Spatial Transformer Networks (STNs) that allows to learn whichever transformation parameters best aid the classification task. Although no ground truth transformation is specified during training, the model is able to attend and focus on the object of interest.

Relation/Co-occurrence Learning. In [27], in order to perform spatial relational reasoning, the features at every spatial location are modelled with the features at every other location. To model the co-occurence statistics of features, e.g. "brown eyes", a bilinear CNN [28] was proposed for fine-grained classification problems, the descriptor of one image is obtained from the outer product of the feature maps. As for few-shot learning, in [29], the authors propose to learn a local similarity metric with a deep neural network. As an extension, [30] experiments with models with more capacity, where the feature maps of images (from a support set and test set) are concatenated and passed to a relation module for similarity learning. Similarly, in this paper, we parameterize local "experts" to compare the feature descriptors from two templates.

3   Deep Comparator Networks

We consider the task of template-based verification, where the objective is to decide if two given templates are of the same object or not. Generally, in verification problems, the label spaces of the training set and testing set are disjoint. In the application considered here, the images are of faces, and the objective is to verify whether two templates show the same person or not.

From a high-level viewpoint, Deep Comparator Network (DCN) focus on the scenario that two templates (each has an arbitrary number of images) are taken as inputs, and trained end-to-end for template verification (as shown in Fig. 1). We first overview the function of these modules: *Detect*, *Attend* and *Compare*, then give more details of their implementation. The detailed architectures for the individual modules are given in the **Supplementary Material**.

The *Detect* module is shared for each input image, dense feature maps and attention maps for multiple discriminative parts are generated for each image. In the face recognition literature, these discriminative parts are usually termed "landmarks", we will use this term from here on. Note that, the implicitly inferred landmarks aim to best assist the subsequent template verification task, they may not follow the same intuitions as human defined facial landmarks, e.g. mouth, nose, etc. Ideally, given a template with multiple images in various poses or illuminations, the landmark filters can be sensitive to different facial parts, viewpoints, or illuminations, e.g. one may be sensitive to the eyes in a frontal face, one may be more responsive to a mouth in a profile face. The *Detect* module acts as the base for fulfilling template comparison conditioned on *viewpoints/local landmarks*.

The *Attend* module achieves the *within template weighting* with an internal competition mechanism, and pools out multiple landmark-specific feature descriptors from each template. Given a template with multiple images, we hope to emphasize the feature representations from the relatively high quality images, while suppressing the lower ones. To achieve this, we normalize the attention score maps (inferred from different samples with the same landmark filter) into a probability distribution Consequently, multiple landmark specific feature descriptors are calculated by attending to the feature maps with image specific attentional masks (and it is assumed that high quality images will score more highly than aberrant ones, e.g. blurry images). Therefore, the contribution of aberrant images is suppressed, and viewpoint factors and facial parts are decomposed and template-wise aligned.

Finally, we use the *Compare* module to achieve the *between template weighting*. The template-wise verification is reformulated as the comparison conditioned on both global and local regions (i.e. landmarks), votings from the local "experts" are aggregated into *one* vector for the final similarity prediction.

3.1 Detect

The *Detect* module takes an image as input, and generates an intermediate dense representation with multiple (K) landmark score maps. Formally, we parametrize the module as a standard ResNet ($\psi(\cdot; \theta_1)$) shared by n images (Fig. 2 shows an example where $n = 3$):

$$[F_1, F_2, ..., F_n, A_1, A_2, ..., A_n] = [\psi(I_1; \theta_1), \psi(I_2; \theta_1), ..., \psi(I_n; \theta_1)] \quad (1)$$

each input image is of size $I \in R^{W \times H \times 3}$, the output dense feature representation map $F \in R^{\frac{W}{8} \times \frac{H}{8} \times C}$, and a *set* of attention maps $A \in R^{\frac{W}{8} \times \frac{H}{8} \times K}$, where W, H, C, K refer to the width, height, channels, and the number of landmark score maps respectively. A global score map is also obtained by a max over the local landmark score maps.

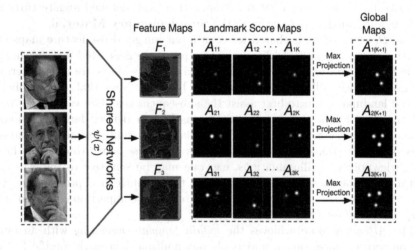

Fig. 2. The detect module. For each input image the detect module generates an intermediate feature map ($F's$), K landmark attention maps ($A's$), and a global map (obtained by applying a max on the $A's$ channel dimension). In this example there are three input images and three of the K landmark attention maps are shown. .

Ideally, the local score maps for each image should satisfy two conditions, *first*, they should be mutually exclusive (i.e. at each spatial location only one landmark is activated); *second*, the scores on the maps should positively correlate with image quality, i.e. the response of a particular landmark filter should be higher on high-resolution frontal images than on low-resolution frontal images.

3.2   Attend

Re-calibration (Internal Competition). Given the feature maps and landmark score maps for each input image, cross-normalization is used among the score maps within same template for *re-calibration*. Based on the "quality" of images within the template, the score maps (from different images within a single template) that localize same landmark are normalized as a distribution of weightings. Therefore, no matter how many images are packed into a template, the outputted attention maps in the same column always add up to 1.0 (Fig. 1). Formally, for every $n \in [1, N]$ and $k \in [1, K]$:

$$A_{n..k} = \frac{exp(A_{n..k})}{\sum\limits_{nij} exp(A_{nijk})} \tag{2}$$

Attentional Pooling. With the re-calibrated attention maps for each input image, we next attend to the spatial locations and compute local representations by the Hadamard Product. Formally, for each of the input image ($n \in N$), with the feature map as F_n, and one set of attention maps A_n,

$$V_k = \sum\limits_{nij} F_{nij:} \odot A_{nijk} \quad \text{for } k \in [1 : K + 1] \tag{3}$$

Therefore, for each input template, we are able to calculate $K+1$ feature descriptors (K landmark specific descriptors, "1" global feature descriptor), with each descriptor representing either one of the facial landmarks or global information.

3.3   Compare

Up to this point, we have described how to pool $K+1$ feature vectors from the single template. In this module, we compare these descriptors in pairs between two different templates. In detail, the landmark-specific descriptors from two templates are first L2 normalized, and concatenated along with an one-hot encoded landmark identifier. Each concatenated vector is the input to a local "expert" parametrized by the fully connected (FC) layers [27]. Overall, the local experts are responsible for comparing the landmark-specific descriptors from different templates.

Formally, we learn a similarity function $y = C(x; \theta_2)$, where $x = [V_{1k} : V_{2k} : \text{ID}_{one\text{-}hot}]$, as shown in Fig. 1. After passing through the fully connected layers, the feature representations given by local "experts" are max pooled, and fused to provide the final similarity score.

Discussion. Unlike the approaches of [27,28], where features at every spatial location are compared with those at every other location, the compare module here only compares the descriptors that encode the same landmark region, e.g. frontal mouth to frontal mouth. By attaching the landmark identifier (the one-hot indicator vector), the fully connected layers are able to specialize for individual landmark. At a high level, leveraging multiple local experts in this way is similar to the use of multiple components (for different visual aspects) in the deformable part model (DPM) [31].

4   Experimental details

4.1   VGGFace2 Dataset

In this paper, all models are trained on the training set of large-scale VGGFace2 dataset [5], which has large variations in pose, age, illumination, ethnicity and profession (e.g. actors, athletes, politicians).

4.2   Landmark Regularizers

In the *Attend* module, the landmark score maps can be considered as a generalization of global average pooling, where the spatial "weights" are inferred implicitly based on the input image. However, in the *Detect* module, there is nothing to prevent the network from learning K identical copies of the same landmark, for instance, it can learn to always predict the average pooling mask, or detect the eyes, or given a network with large enough receptive field, it can always pinpoint the centre of the image. To prevent this, we experiment with *two* different types of landmark regularizers: a diversity regularizer (unsupervised learning) and a keypoints regularizer (supervised learning).

Diversity Regularizer [32]. In order to encourage landmark diversity, the most obvious approach is to penalize the mutual overlap between the score maps of different landmarks. Each of the landmark score maps is first self-normalized into a probability distribution (p's) by using the softmax (Eq 4),

$$p_{nijk} = \frac{exp(A_{nijk})}{\sum_{ij} exp(A_{nijk})} \tag{4}$$

where n, i, j, k refer to the image index within the template, width, height, number of attention maps respectively.

Ideally, if all K landmarks are disjoint from each other, by taking the max projection of these normalized distribution, there should be exactly K landmarks, and they should sum to K.

$$\mathcal{L}_{reg} = nK - \sum_{nij} \max_{k=1,..,K} p_{nijk} \tag{5}$$

Note here, this regularizer is zero only if the activations in the different normalized landmark score maps are disjoint and exactly 1.0.

Keypoints Regularizer. Benifiting from the previous fruitful research in facial keypoint detection, we obtain pseudo groundtruth landmarks from pre-trained keypoint detectors. Although the predictions are not perfect, we conjecture that they are sufficiently accurate to guide the network training at the early stages, and, as the training progresses, the regularizer weights is scheduled to decay, gradually releasing the parameter search space. As preprocessing, we predict 5 facial keypoints (Fig. 3) over the entire dataset with a pre-trained MTCNN [33], and estimate three face poses by thresholding angle ratios.[1]

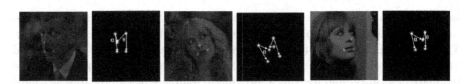

Fig. 3. Facial landmark detection for VGGFace2 images. Face poses are quantized into three categories based on the ration α/θ. Left-facing profile : $\alpha/\theta < 0.3$, right-facing profile: $\alpha/\theta > 3.0$, frontal face: $\alpha/\theta \in [0.3, 3.0]$

Similar to the diveristy regularizer, the inferred landmark score maps are also self-normalized first (Eq 4), $\mathcal{L}2$ loss between the prediction (p) and the pseudo groundtruth ($\hat{p}$) is applied as auxiliary supervision. Note that, given each face image belongs to only one of the three poses, only 4 of the 12 landmark maps are actually useful for supervising an individual image.

$$\mathcal{L}_{reg} = \begin{cases} \sum_{nij} \frac{1}{2}(p_{nijk} - \hat{p}_{nijk})^2 \text{ for k in \{pose-specific keypoints\}} \\ 0 \end{cases} \quad (6)$$

To make the experiments comparable, in both experiments, we use $K = 12$ landmark score maps in the *Detect* module.

4.3   Loss Functions

The proposed comparator network is trained end-to-end by optimizing three types of losses simultaneously: *first,* template-level identity classification loss, using a global feature representation obtained by attentional pooling with the re-calibrated global maps (refer to Fig. 2); *second,* a standard classification loss (2 classes) on the similarity prediction from the *Compare* module; *third,* a regularization loss from the landmark score maps in the *Detect* module.

$$\mathcal{L} = \alpha_1(\mathcal{L}_{cls1} + \mathcal{L}_{cls2}) + \alpha_2\mathcal{L}_{sim} + \alpha_3\mathcal{L}_{reg} \quad (7)$$

---

[1] In our training, we only use 4 facial landmarks, left-eye, right-eye, nose, mouth. The mouth landmarks are obtained by averaging the two landmarks at mouth corners.

where $\alpha_1 = 2.0, \alpha_2 = 5.0$ refer to the loss weights for classification and similarity prediction, α_3 refers to the weights for regularizer, which was initialized as 30.0 and decayed by half every 60,000 iterations. Note that, α_3 is scheduled to decrease, thus, even for the training with the keypoints regularizer, the auxiliary supervision only guides the network training in early stages. Thereafter, the classification and verification loss will dominate the training of these landmark localizations.

4.4 Hard-sample Mining

In order to train the Comparator Network for re-ranking, we need a method to sample hard template-template pairs. Here we described the procedure for this. The key idea is to use the features generated by a standard ResNet-50 trained for face image classification (on the VGGFace2 training set) to approximate the template descriptor, and use this approximate template descriptor to select hard template pairs.

In detail, the template-level descriptors are obtained by averaging the feature vectors (pre-computed from ResNet-50) of 3 images and L2-normalized. The selection of hard template pairs is then integrated into the training of the comparator network. At each iteration 256 identities are randomly sampled, and used to create 512 templates with 3 images in each template (i.e. two templates for each identity). In total, there are 256 positive template pairs, and a large number of negative pairs.

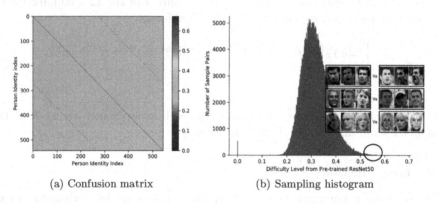

(a) Confusion matrix   (b) Sampling histogram

Fig. 4. Sampling strategy based on the pre-trained single-image classification networks. Larger values refer to more difficult template pairs.

By calculating the cosine similarity between different pairs of templates, we generate a 512×512 similarity matrix M_s for the template-to-template verification, where small values refer to the predicted dissimilar pairs from the pre-trained ResNet50. We further define the verification difficulty matrix as:

$$d = |groundtruth - M_s| \tag{8}$$

where groundtruth label is either 0 (dissimilar) or 1 (similar). Therefore, in the difficulty matrix, small values refer to the easy sample pairs, and large values refer to the difficult samples.

4.5   Training details

We train the entire Comparator Network end-to-end from scratch on the VGGFace2 dataset, detailed architecture description can be found in **Supplementary Material**. During training, the shorter side of the input image is resized to 144, while the long side is center cropped, making the input images 144×144 pixels with the face centered, and 127.5 is subtracted from each channel. In each tower, 3 images are packed as a template input. Note that, there is a probability of 20% that the 3 images within one template are identical images[2]. In this case, the Comparator Network become equivalent to training on single image. Data augmentation is operated separately for each image with probability of 20%, including flipping, gaussian blur, motion blur, monochrome transformation. Adam [34] is used for optimization with an initial learning rate of $1e^{-4}$, and mini-batches of size 64, with equal number of positive and negative pairs. The learning rate is decreased twice with a factor of 10 when errors plateau. Note that, although the batch size is small, the network is actually seeing 64×6 images every training step. Also, although the network is only trained with 3 images per tower, at test time it can be applied to any number of images per template.

  Note, an alternative is to use a pre-trained face network, e.g. a ResNet-50 [5], as this considerably accelerates the training, compared to end-to-end training, with almost negligible loss in performance. In detail, the *Detect* module is replaced with the pre-trained ResNet-50; the landmark-conditioned descriptors are computed from the last layer of the *conv3* block (1/8 of the input spatial resolution); and the global descriptor comes from the last layer (average pooled vector).

5   Results

We evaluate all models on the challenging IARPA Janus Benchmarks, where all images are captured from unconstrained environments and show large variations in viewpoints and image quality. In contrast to the traditional closed-world classification tasks [1–3], verification is an open-world problem (i.e. the label spaces of the training and test set are disjoint), and thus challenges the capacity and generalization of the feature representations. All the models are evaluated on the standard 1:1 verification protocol (matching between the Mixed Media probes and two galleries), the performance is reported as the true accept rates (TAR) vs. false positive rates (FAR) (i.e. receiver operating characteristics (ROC) curve).

---

[2] This guarantees a probability of 64% that both templates contain 3 different images, and a probability of 36% that at least one template contains 3 identical image.

IJB-B Dataset [13] The IJB-B dataset is an extension of IJB-A [35], having 1,845 subjects with 21.8K still images (including 11,754 face and 10,044 non-face) and 55K frames from 7,011 videos.

IJB-C Dataset [14] The IJB-C dataset is a further extension of IJB-B, having 3,531 subjects with 31.3K still images and 117.5K frames from 11,779 videos. In total, there are 23124 templates with 19557 genuine matches and 15639K impostor matches.

Table 1. Evaluation on 1:1 verification protocol on IJB-B dataset. (Higher is better) Note that the result of Navaneeth *et al.* [36] was on the Janus CS3 dataset. DCN(Divs) : Deep Comparator Network trained with Diversity Regularizer DCN(Kpts): Deep Comparator Network trained with Keypoints Regularizer.

Model	1:1 Verification TAR			
	FAR $= 1E-4$	FAR $= 1E-3$	FAR $= 1E-2$	FAR $= 1E-1$
Whitelam *et al.* [13]	0.540	0.700	0.840	--
Navaneeth *et al.* [36]	0.685	0.830	0.925	0.978
ResNet50 [5]	0.784	0.878	0.938	0.975
SENet50 [5]	0.800	0.888	0.949	0.984
ResNet50+SENet50	0.800	0.887	0.946	0.981
MN-v [19]	0.818	0.902	0.955	0.984
MN-vc [19]	0.831	0.909	0.958	0.985
ResNet50+DCN(Kpts)	**0.850**	0.927	0.970	0.992
ResNet50+DCN(Divs)	0.841	0.930	0.972	0.995
SENet50+DCN(Kpts)	0.846	0.935	0.974	0.997
SENet50+DCN(Divs)	0.849	**0.937**	**0.975**	**0.997**

Table 2. Evaluation on 1:1 verification protocol on IJB-C dataset. (Higher is better) Results of GOTS-1, FaceNet, VGG-CNN are read from ROC curve in [14].

Model	1:1 Verification TAR			
	FAR $= 1E-4$	FAR $= 1E-3$	FAR $= 1E-2$	FAR $= 1E-1$
GOTS-1 [14]	0.160	0.320	0.620	0.800
FaceNet [14]	0.490	0.660	0.820	0.920
VGG-CNN [14]	0.600	0.750	0.860	0.950
ResNet50 [5]	0.825	0.900	0.950	0.980
SENet50 [5]	0.840	0.910	0.960	0.987
ResNet50+SENet50 [5]	0.841	0.909	0.957	0.985
MN-v [19]	0.852	0.920	0.965	0.988
MN-vc [19]	0.862	0.927	0.968	0.989
ResNet50+DCN(Kpts)	0.867	0.940	0.979	0.997
ResNet50+DCN(Divs)	0.880	0.944	0.981	0.998
SENet50+DCN(Kpts)	0.874	0.944	0.981	0.998
SENet50+DCN(Divs)	**0.885**	**0.947**	**0.983**	**0.998**

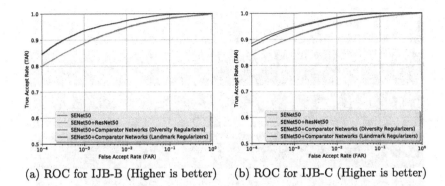

(a) ROC for IJB-B (Higher is better)   (b) ROC for IJB-C (Higher is better)

Fig. 5. ROC curve of 1:1 verification protocol on IJB-B & IJB-C dataset.

5.1 Discussion

Three phenomena can be observed from the evaluation results: *first*, comparing with the previous state-of-the-art model [5], the DCN trained by re-ranking can boost the performance significantly on both IJBB and IJBC (about $4-5\%$, which is a substantial reduction in the error); *second*, although the ResNet50 and SENet50 are designed differently and trained separately, ensembles of them do not provide any benifit. This shows that the difficult template pairs for ResNet50 remains difficult for another more powerful SENet50, indicating that the different models trained on single image classification are not complementary to each other; while in contrast, the DCN can be used together with either ResNet50 or SENet50 to improve the recognition system; *third*, the performance of DCN trained with different regularizers are comparable to each other, showing that groundtruth of facial keypoints is not critical in training DCN.

5.2 Visualization

Figure 6 shows the attention maps for a randomly sampled template that contains multiple images with varying poses. Visualizing the maps in this way makes the models interpretable, as it can be seen what the landmark detectors are concentrating on when making the verification decision. The *Detect* module has learnt to pinpoint the landmarks in different poses consistently, and is even tolerant to some out-of-plane rotation. Interestingly, the landmark detector actually learns to localize the two eyes simultaneously; we conjecture, that this is due to the fact that human faces are approximately symmetric, and also during training, the data is augmented with horizontal flippings.

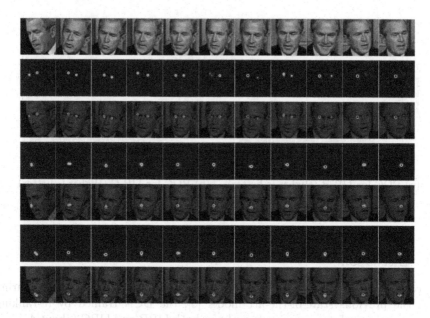

Fig. 6. Predicted facial landmark score maps after self-normalizing for three of the landmark detectors. Additional examples are given in the supplementary material. *1st row*: raw images in the template, faces in a variaty of poses are shown from left to right; *2nd,4th,6th row*: self-normalized landmark score maps (attention maps); *3rd, 5th, 7th row*: images overlayed with the attention maps.

6   Conclusion

We have introduced a new network that is able to compare templates of images and verify if they match or not. The network is very *flexible*, in that the number of images in each template can be varied at test time, it is also *opportunistic* in that it can take advantage of local evidence at test time, such as a specific facial features like a tattoo or a port-wine stain that might be lost in a traditional single tower per face encoding. Its performance substantially improves the state-of-the-art on the recent and very challenging IJB benchmarks.

Although we have used face templates in this work, the Comparator Network could be applied directly to person re-id, where often sets are available, and also potentially could be applied to other fine-grained classification tasks, e.g. to determine the species of a bird or flower from multiple images of the same instance.

Acknowledgment. This research is based upon work supported by the Office of the Director of National Intelligence (ODNI), Intelligence Advanced Research Projects Activity (IARPA), via contract number 2014-14071600010. The views and conclusions contained herein are those of the authors and should not be interpreted as necessarily representing the official policies or endorsements, either expressed or implied, of ODNI, IARPA, or the U.S. Government. The U.S. Government is authorized to reproduce and distribute reprints for Governmental purpose notwithstanding any copyright annotation thereon.

References

1. Krizhevsky, A., Sutskever, I., Hinton, G.E.: ImageNet classification with deep convolutional neural networks. In: NIPS, pp. 1106–1114 (2012)
2. Simonyan, K., Zisserman, A.: Very deep convolutional networks for large-scale image recognition. In: ICLR (2015)
3. He, K., Zhang, X., Ren, S., Sun, J.: Deep residual learning for image recognition. In: Proceedings of CVPR (2016)
4. Hu, J., Shen, L., Sun, G.: Squeeze-and-excitation networks. arXiv preprint arXiv:1709.01507 (2017)
5. Cao, Q., Shen, L., Xie, W., Parkhi, O.M., Zisserman, A.: VGGFace2: a dataset for recognising faces across pose and age. In: International Conference on Automatic Face and Gesture Recognition (FG) (2018). http://www.robots.ox.ac.uk/~vgg/data/vgg_face2/
6. Parkhi, O.M., Vedaldi, A., Zisserman, A.: Deep face recognition. In: Proceedings of BMVC (2015)
7. Schroff, F., Kalenichenko, D., Philbin, J.: Facenet: a unified embedding for face recognition and clustering. In: Proceedings of CVPR (2015)
8. Taigman, Y., Yang, M., Ranzato, M., Wolf, L.: Deepface: closing the gap to human-level performance in face verification. In: Proceedings of CVPR (2014)
9. Law, M.T., Thome, N., Cord, M.: Learning a distance metric from relative comparisons. NIPS. Springer, New York (2004). https://doi.org/10.1007/s11263-016-0923-4
10. Weinberger, K.Q., Blitzer, J., Saul, L.: Distance metric learning for large margin nearest neighbor classification. In: NIPS (2006)
11. Ustinova, E., Lempitsky, V.: Learning deep embeddings with histogram loss. In: NIPS (2016)
12. Hermans, A., Beyer, L., Leibe, B.: In defense of the triplet loss for person re-identification. arXiv preprint arXiv:1703.07737 (2017)
13. Whitelam, C., et al.: IARPA Janus Benchmark-B face dataset. In: CVPR Workshop on Biometrics (2017)
14. Maze, B., Adams, J., Duncan, J.A., Kalka, N., Miller, T., Otto, C., Jain, A.K., Niggel, W.T., Anderson, J., Cheney, J., Grother, P.: IARPA Janus Benchmark-C: face dataset and protocol. In: 11th IAPR International Conference on Biometrics (2018)
15. Philbin, J., Chum, O., Isard, M., Sivic, J., Zisserman, A.: Object retrieval with large vocabularies and fast spatial matching. In: Proceedings of CVPR (2007)
16. Jegou, H., Douze, M., Schmid, C.: Hamming embedding and weak geometric consistency for large scale image search. In: Forsyth, D., Torr, P., Zisserman, A. (eds.) ECCV 2008. LNCS, vol. 5302, pp. 304–317. Springer, Heidelberg (2008). https://doi.org/10.1007/978-3-540-88682-2_24

17. Luan, T., Xi, Y., Xiaoming, L.: Disentangled representation learning GAN for pose-invariant face recognition. In: Proceedings of CVPR (2017)
18. Yang, J., et al.: Neural aggregation network for video face recognition. In: Proceedings of CVPR (2017)
19. Xie, W., Zisserman, A.: Multicolumn networks for face recognition. In: Proceedings of BMVC (2018)
20. Li, H., Hua, G., Brandt, J., Yang, J.: Probabilistic elastic matching for pose variant face verification. In: Proceedings of CVPR (2013)
21. Parkhi, O.M., Simonyan, K., Vedaldi, A., Zisserman, A.: A compact and discriminative face track descriptor. In: Proceedings of CVPR (2014)
22. Bahdanau, D., Cho, K., Bengio, Y.: Neural machine translation by jointly learning to align and translate. In: Proceedings of ICLR (2015)
23. Ba, J., Mnih, V., Kavukcuoglu, K.: Multiple object recognition with visual attention. In: Proceedings of ICLR (2015)
24. Xu, K., Ba, J., Kiros, R., Cho, K., Courville, A., Salakhudinov, R., Zemel, R., Bengio, Y.: Show, attend and tell: Neural image caption generation with visual attention. In: Proceedings of ICML (2015)
25. Zheng, H., Fu, J., Mei, T., Luo, J.: Learning multi-attention convolutional neural network for fine-grained image recognition. In: Proceedings of ICCV (2017)
26. Jaderberg, M., Simonyan, K., Zisserman, A., et al.: Spatial transformer networks. In: NIPS (2015)
27. Santoro, A., Raposo, D., Barrett, D.G.T., Malinowski, M., Pascanu, R., Battaglia, P., Lillicrap, T.P.: A simple neural network module for relational reasoning. CoRR abs/1706.01427 (2017)
28. Lin, T.J., RoyChowdhury, A., Maji, S.: Bilinear CNN models for fine-grained visual recognition. In: Proceedings of ICCV (2015)
29. Vinyals, O., Blundell, C., Lillicrap, T., kavukcuoglu, k., Wierstra, D.: Matching networks for one shot learning. In: NIPS (2016)
30. Sung, F., Yang, Y., Zhang, L., Xiang, T., Torr, P.H.S., Hospedales, T.M.: Learning to compare: relation network for few-shot learning. In: Proceedings of CVPR (2018)
31. Felzenszwalb, P., Mcallester, D., Ramanan, D.: A discriminatively trained, multiscale, deformable part model. In: Proceedings of CVPR (2008)
32. Thewlis, J., Bilen, H., Vedaldi, A.: Unsupervised learning of object landmarks by factorized spatial embeddings. In: Proceedings of ICCV (2017)
33. Zhang, K., Zhang, Z., Li, Z., Qiao, Y.: Joint face detection and alignment using multitask cascaded convolutional networks. IEEE Signal Process. Lett. **23**(10), 1499–1503 (2016)
34. Kingma, D.P., Ba, J.: Adam: a method for stochastic optimization. CoRR abs/1412.6980 (2014)
35. Klare, B.F., Klein, B., Taborsky, E., Blanton, A., Cheney, J., Allen, K., Grother, P., Mah, A., Jain, A.K.: Pushing the frontiers of unconstrained face detection and recognition: IARPA Janus Benchmark A. In: Proceedings of CVPR (2015)
36. Navaneeth, B., Jingxiao, Z., Hongyu, X., Jun-Cheng, C., Carlos, C., Rama, C.: Deep heterogeneous feature fusion for template-based face recognition. In: IEEE Winter Conference on Applications of Computer Vision, WACV (2017)

Deep Regionlets for Object Detection

Hongyu Xu[1]([✉]), Xutao Lv[2], Xiaoyu Wang[2], Zhou Ren[3], Navaneeth Bodla[1], and Rama Chellappa[1]

[1] University of Maryland, College Park, MD, USA
{hyxu,nbodla,rama}@umiacs.umd.edu
[2] Intellifusion, Shenzhen, China
lvxutao@gmail.com, fanghuaxue@gmail.com
[3] Snap Inc., Venice, Los Angeles, USA
zhou.ren@snap.com

Abstract. In this paper, we propose a novel object detection framework named "Deep Regionlets" by establishing a bridge between deep neural networks and conventional detection schema for accurate generic object detection. Motivated by the abilities of regionlets for modeling object deformation and multiple aspect ratios, we incorporate regionlets into an end-to-end trainable deep learning framework. The deep regionlets framework consists of a region selection network and a deep regionlet learning module. Specifically, given a detection bounding box proposal, the region selection network provides guidance on where to select regions to learn the features from. The regionlet learning module focuses on local feature selection and transformation to alleviate local variations. To this end, we *first* realize *non-rectangular* region selection within the detection framework to accommodate variations in object appearance. Moreover, we design a "gating network" within the regionlet leaning module to enable soft regionlet selection and pooling. The Deep Regionlets framework is trained end-to-end without additional efforts. We perform ablation studies and conduct extensive experiments on the PASCAL VOC and Microsoft COCO datasets. The proposed framework outperforms state-of-the-art algorithms, such as RetinaNet and Mask R-CNN, even without additional segmentation labels.

Keywords: Object Detection · Deep Learning · Deep Regionlets Spatial Transformation

1 Introduction

Generic object detection has been extensively studied by the computer vision community over several decades [4,6,8,10,13,16,17,22,26,37,41,42,44,45,48]

H. Xu—Work started during an internship at Snap Research.

Electronic supplementary material The online version of this chapter (https://doi.org/10.1007/978-3-030-01252-6_49) contains supplementary material, which is available to authorized users.

© Springer Nature Switzerland AG 2018
V. Ferrari et al. (Eds.): ECCV 2018, LNCS 11215, pp. 827–844, 2018.
https://doi.org/10.1007/978-3-030-01252-6_49

due to its appeal to both academic research explorations as well as commercial applications. Given an image of interest, the goal of object detection is to predict the locations of objects and classify them at the same time. The key challenge of the object detection task is to handle variations in object scale, pose, viewpoint and even part deformations when generating the bounding boxes for specific object categories.

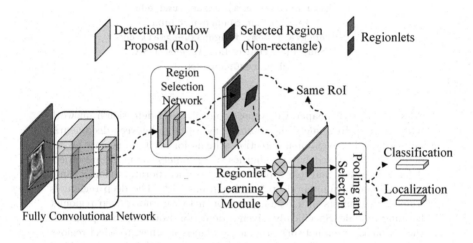

Fig. 1. Architecture of the Deep Regionlets detection framework. It consists of a region selection network (RSN) and a deep regionlet learning module. The region selection network performs *non-rectangular* region selection from the detection window proposal generated by the region proposal network. Deep regionlet learning module learns the regionlets through a spatial transformation and a gating network. The entire pipeline is end-to-end trainable. For better visualization, the region proposal network is not displayed here.

Numerous methods have been proposed based on hand-crafted features (*i.e.* HOG [10], LBP [1], SIFT [30]). These approaches usually involve an exhaustive search for possible locations, scales and aspect ratios of the object, by using the sliding window approach. However, Wang *et al.*'s [45] regionlet-based detection framework has gained a lot of attention as it provides the flexibility to deal with different scales and aspect ratios without performing an exhaustive search. It first introduced the concept of **regionlet** by defining a three-level structural relationship: candidate bounding boxes (sliding windows), regions inside the bounding box and groups of regionlets (sub-regions inside each region). It operates by directly extracting features from regionlets in several selected regions within an arbitrary detection bounding box and performs (max) pooling among the regionlets. Such a feature extraction hierarchy is capable of dealing with variable aspect ratios and flexible feature sets, which leads to improved learning of robust feature representation of the object for region-based object detection.

Recently, deep learning has achieved significant success on many computer vision tasks such as image classification [20, 24, 34], semantic segmentation [29] and object detection [16] using the deep convolutional neural network (DCNN) architecture. Despite the excellent performance of deep learning-based detection framework, most network architectures [8, 28, 37] do not take advantage of successful conventional ideas such as deformable part-based model (DPM) or *regionlets*. Those methods have been effective for modeling object deformation, sub-categories and multiple aspect ratios. Recent advances [9, 32, 33] have achieved promising results by combining the conventional DPM-based detection methodology with deep neural network architectures.

These observations motivate us to establish a bridge between deep convolutional neural network and conventional object detection schema. In this paper, we incorporate the conventional Regionlet method into an end-to-end trainable deep learning framework. Despite being able to handle arbitrary bounding boxes, several drawbacks arise when directly integrating the regionlet methodology into the deep learning framework. First, in [45], Wang *et al.* proposed to learn cascade object classifiers after hand-crafted feature extraction in each regionlet. However, end-to-end learning is not feasible in this framework. Second, regions in regionlet-based detection have to be rectangular, which does not effectively model the deformations of an object which results in variable shapes. Moreover, both regions and regionlets are fixed after training is completed.

To this end, we propose a novel object detection framework named "Deep Regionlets" to integrate the deep learning framework into the traditional regionlet method [45]. The overall design of the proposed detection system is illustrated in Fig. 1. It consists of a region selection network (RSN) and a deep regionlet learning module. The region selection network performs *non-rectangular* region selection from the detection window proposal[1] (RoI) to address the limitations of the traditional regionlet approach. We further design a deep regionlet learning module to learn the regionlets through a spatial transformation and a gating network. By using the proposed gating network, which is a soft regionlet selector, the resulting feature representation is more effective for detection. The entire pipeline is end-to-end trainable using only the input images and ground truth bounding boxes.

We conduct a detailed analysis of our approach to understand its merits and evaluate its performance. Extensive experiments on two detection benchmark datasets, PASCAL VOC [11] and Microsoft COCO [27] show that the proposed deep regionlet approach outperforms several competitors [8, 9, 32, 37]. Even without segmentation labels, we outperform state-of-the-art algorithms such as Mask R-CNN [18] and RetinaNet [26]. To summarize, we make the following contributions:

- We propose a novel deep regionlet approach for object detection. Our work extends the traditional regionlet method to the deep learning framework. The system is trainable in an end-to-end manner.

---

[1] The detection window proposal is generated by a region proposal network (RPN) [8, 17, 37]. It is also called region of interest (ROI).

- We design the RSN, which **first** performs **non-rectangular** region selection within the detection bounding box generated from a detection window proposal. It provides more flexibility in modeling objects with variable shapes and deformable parts.
- We propose a deep regionlet learning module, including feature transformation and a gating network. The gating network serves as a soft regionlet selector and lets the network focus on features that benefit detection performance.
- We present empirical results on object detection benchmark datasets, demonstrating superior performance over state-of-the-art.

2   Related Work

Many approaches have been proposed for object detection including both traditional ones [13, 42, 45] and deep learning-based approaches [6, 8, 9, 16, 17, 19, 21, 28, 32, 35, 37, 41, 43, 48, 50–52]. Traditional approaches mainly used hand-crafted features to train the object detectors using the sliding window paradigm. One of the earliest works [42] used boosted cascaded detectors for face detection, which led to its wide adoption. Deformable Part Model-based detection (DPM) [12] proposed the concept of deformable part models to handle object deformations. Due to the rapid development of deep learning techniques [2, 5, 20, 24, 34, 40, 46, 47, 49], the deep learning-based detectors have become dominant object detectors.

Deep learning-based detectors could be further categorized into single-stage detectors and two-stage detectors, based on whether the detectors have proposal-driven mechanism or not. The single-stage detectors [14, 25, 26, 28, 35, 38, 48, 50] apply regular, dense sampling windows over object locations, scales and aspect ratios. By exploiting multiple layers within a deep CNN network directly, the single-stage detectors achieved high speed but their accuracy is typically low compared to two-stage detectors.

Two-stage detectors [8, 17, 37] involve two steps. They first generate a sparse set of candidate proposals of detection bounding boxes by the Region Proposal Network (RPN). After filtering out the majority of negative background boxes by RPN, the second stage classifies the proposals of detection bounding boxes and performs the bounding box regression to predict object categories and their corresponding locations. The two-stage detectors consistently achieve higher accuracy than single-stage detectors and numerous extensions have been proposed [6, 7, 9, 18, 21, 32, 41]. Our method follows the two-stage detector architecture by taking advantage of RPN without requiring dense sampling of object locations, scales and aspect ratios.

3   Our Approach

In this section, we first review the traditional regionlet-based detection methods and then present the overall design of the end-to-end trainable deep regionlet approach. Finally, we discuss in detail each module in the proposed end-to-end deep regionlet approach.

3.1 Traditional Regionlet-based Approach

A *regionlet* is a base feature extraction region defined proportionally to a window (*i.e.* a sliding window or a detection bounding box) at arbitrary resolution (*i.e.* size and aspect ratio). Wang *et al.* [45] first introduced the concept of regionlet, as illustrated in Fig. 2. It defines a three-level structure among a detecting bounding box, number of regions inside the bounding box and a group of regionlets (sub-regions inside each region). In Fig. 2, the yellow box is a detection bounding box. R is a rectangular feature extraction region inside the bounding box. Furthermore, small sub-regions $r_{i\{i=1...N\}}$ (*e.g.* r_1, r_2) are chosen within region R, where we define them as a set of *regionlets*.

The difficulty of the arbitrary detection bounding box has been well addressed by using the *relative* positions and sizes of regionlets and regions. However, in the traditional approach, the initialization of regionlets possess randomness and both regions (R) and regionlets (*i.e.* r_1, r_2) are fixed after the training. Moreover, it is based on hand-crafted features (*i.e.* HOG [10] or LBP [1]) in each regionlet respectively and hence not end-to-end trainable. To this end, we propose the following deep regionlet-based approach to address such limitations.

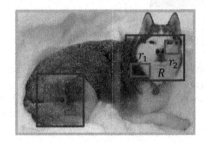

Fig. 2. Illustration of structural relationships among the detection bounding box, feature extraction regions and regionlets. The yellow box is a detection bounding box and R is a feature extraction region shown as a purple rectangle with filled dots inside the bounding box. Inside R, two small sub-regions denoted as r_1 and r_2 are the *regionlets*. (Color figure online)

3.2 System Architecture

Generally speaking, an object detection network performs a sequence of convolutional operations on an image of interest using a deep convolutional neural network. At some layer, the network bifurcates into two branches. One branch, RPN generates a set of candidate bounding boxes[2] while the other branch performs classification and regression by pooling the convolutional features inside the proposed bounding box generated by the region proposal network [8,37]. Taking advantage of this detection network, we introduce the overall design of

---

[2] [8,17,37] also called the detection bounding box as detection window proposal.

the proposed object detection framework, named "Deep Regionlets", as illustrated in Fig. 1.

The general architecture consists of an RSN and a deep regionlet learning module. In particular, the RSN is used to predict the transformation parameters to choose regions given a candidate bounding box, which is generated by the region proposal network. The regionlets are further learned within each selected region defined by the region selection network. The system is designed to be trained in a fully end-to-end manner using only the input images and ground truth bounding box. The RSN as well as the regionlet learning module can be simultaneously learned over each selected region given the detection window proposal.

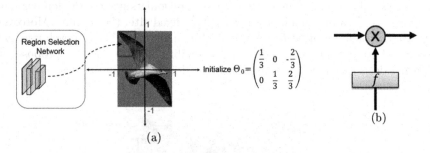

Fig. 3. (a) Example of initialization of one affine transformation parameter. Normalized affine transformation parameters $\Theta_0 = [\frac{1}{3}, 0, -\frac{2}{3}; 0, \frac{1}{3}, \frac{2}{3}]$ ($\theta_i \in [-1, 1]$) selects the top-left region in the 3×3 evenly divided detection bounding box, shown as the purple rectangle. (b) Design of the gating network. f denotes the non-negative gate function (Color figure online)

3.3 Region Selection Network

We design the RSN to have the following properties: (1) End-to-end trainable; (2) Simple structure; (3) Generate regions with arbitrary shapes. Keeping these in mind, we design the RSN to predict a set of *affine* transformation parameters. By using these affine transformation parameters, as well as not requiring the regions to be rectangular, we have more flexibility in modeling objects with arbitrary shapes and deformable parts.

Specifically, we design the RSN using a small neural network with three fully connected layers. The first two fully connected layers have output size of 256, with ReLU activation. The last fully connected layer has the output size of six, which is used to predict the set of affine transformation parameters $\Theta = [\theta_1, \theta_2, \theta_3; \theta_4, \theta_5, \theta_6]$.

Note that the candidate detection bounding boxes proposed by RSN have arbitrary sizes and aspect ratios. In order to address this difficulty, we use *relative* positions and sizes of the selected region within a detection bounding box. The candidate bounding box generated by the RPN is defined by the top-left point

(w_0, h_0), width w and height h of the box. We normalize the coordinates by the width w and height h of the box. As a result, we could use the normalized affine transformation parameters $\Theta = [\theta_1, \theta_2, \theta_3; \theta_4, \theta_5, \theta_6]$ ($\theta_i \in [-1, 1]$) to evaluate one selected region within one candidate detection window at different sizes and aspect ratios without scaling images into multiple resolutions or using multiple-components to enumerate possible aspect ratios, like anchors [14,28,37].

Initialization of Region Selection Network: Taking advantage of *relative* and *normalized* coordinates, we initialize the RSN by equally dividing the whole detecting bounding box to several sub-regions, named as *cells*, without any overlap among them. Figure 3(a) shows an example of initialization from one affine transformation (*i.e.* 3×3). The first cell, which is the top-left bin in the whole region (detection bounding box) could be defined by initializing the corresponding affine transformation parameter $\Theta_0 = [\frac{1}{3}, 0, -\frac{2}{3}; 0, \frac{1}{3}, \frac{2}{3}]$. The other eight of 3×3 cells are initialized in a similar way.

3.4 Deep Regionlet Learning

After regions are selected by the RSN, regionlets are further learned from the selected region defined by the normalized affine transformation parameters. Note that our motivation is to design the network to be trained in a fully end-to-end manner using only the input images and ground truth bounding boxes. Therefore, both the selected regions and regionlet learning should be able to be trained by CNN networks. Moreover, we would like the regionlets extracted from the selected regions to better represent objects with variable shapes and deformable parts.

Inspired by the spatial transform network [23], any parameterizable transformation including translation, scaling, rotation, affine or even projective transformation can be learned by a spatial transformer. In this section, we introduce our deep regionlet learning module to learn the regionlets in the selected region, which is defined by the affine transformation parameters.

More specifically, we aim to learn regionlets from one selected region defined by one affine transformation Θ to better match the shapes of objects. This is done with a selected region R from RSN, transformation parameters $\Theta = [\theta_1, \theta_2, \theta_3; \theta_4, \theta_5, \theta_6]$ and a set of feature maps $Z = \{Z_i, i = 1, \ldots, n\}$. Without loss of generality, let Z_i be one of the feature map out of the n feature maps. A selected region R is of size $w \times h$ with the top-left corner (w_0, h_0). Inside the Z_i feature maps, we propose the following regionlet learning module.

Let s denote the source and t denote target, we define (x_p^s, y_p^s) as the spatial location in original feature map Z_i and (x_p^s, y_p^s) as the spatial location in the output feature maps after spatial transformation. U_{nm}^c is the value at location (n, m) in channel c of the input feature. The total output feature map V is of size $H \times W$. Let $V(x_p^t, y_p^t, c | \Theta, R)$ be the output feature value at location (x_p^t, y_p^t) ($x_p^t \in [0, H]$, $y_p^t \in [0, W]$) in channel c, which is computed as

$$V(x_p^s, y_p^s, c | \Theta, R) = \sum_n^H \sum_m^M U_{nm}^c \max(0, 1 - |x_p^s - m|) \max(0, 1 - |y_p^s - n|) \tag{1}$$

Back Propagation Through Spatial Transform.
To allow back propagation of the loss through the regionlet learning module, we can define the gradients with respect to both feature maps and the region selection network. In this layer's `backward` function, we have partial derivative of the loss function with respect to both feature map variable U_{mn}^c and affine transform parameter $\Theta = [\theta_1, \theta_2, \theta_3; \theta_4, \theta_5, \theta_6]$. Motivated by [23], the partial derivative of the loss function with respect to the feature map is:

$$\frac{\partial V(x_p^s, y_p^s, c|\Theta, R)}{\partial U_{nm}^c} = \sum_n^H \sum_m^M \max(0, 1 - |x_p^s - m|) \times \max(0, 1 - |y_p^s - n|) \quad (2)$$

Moreover, during back propagation, we need to compute the gradient with respect to each affine transformation parameter $\Theta = [\theta_1, \theta_2, \theta_3; \theta_4, \theta_5, \theta_6]$. In this way, the region selection network could also be updated to adjust the selected region. We take θ_1 as an example due to space limitations and similar derivative can be computed for other parameters $\theta_i (i = 2, \ldots, 6)$ respectively.

$$\frac{\partial V(x_p^s, y_p^s, c|\Theta, R)}{\partial \theta_1} = x_p^t \sum_n^H \sum_m^M U_{nm}^c \max(0, 1 - |y_p^s - n|) \times \begin{cases} 0 \text{ if } |m - x_p^s| \geq 1 \\ 1 \text{ if } m > x_p^s \\ -1 \text{ if } m < x_p^s \end{cases}$$

$$(3)$$

It is worth noting that (x_p^t, y_p^t) are normalized coordinates in range $[-1, 1]$ so that it can to be scaled with respect to w and h with start position (w_0, h_0).

Gating Network. The gating network, which serves as a soft regionlet selector, is used to assgin regionlets with different weights and generate regionlet feature representation. We design a simple gating network using a fully connected layer with `sigmoid` activation, shown in Fig. 3(b). The output values of the gating network are within range of $[0, 1]$. Given the output feature maps $V(x_p^s, y_p^s, c|\Theta, R)$ described above, we use a fully connected layer to generate the same number of output as feature maps $V(x_p^s, y_p^s, c|\Theta, R)$, which is followed by an activation layer `sigmoid` to generate the corresponding weight respectively. The final feature representation is generated by the product of feature maps $V(x_p^s, y_p^s, c|\Theta, R)$ and their corresponding weights.

Regionlet Pool Construction. Object deformations may occur at different scales. For instance, deformation could be caused by different body parts in person detection. Same number of regionlets (size $H \times W$) learned from small selected region have higher extraction density, which may lead to non-compact regionlet representation. In order to learn a *compact, efficient* regionlet representation, we further perform the pooling (*i.e.* max/ave) operation over the feature maps $V(x_p^s, y_p^s, c|\Theta, R)$ of size $(H \times W)$. We reap two benefits from the pool construction: (1) Regionlet representation is compact (small size). (2) Regionlets learned from different size of selected regions are able to represent such regions in the same efficient way, thus to handle object deformations at different scales.

3.5   Relations to Recent Works

Our deep regionlet approach is related to some recent works in different aspects. We discuss both similarities and differences in detail in the supplementary material section.

4   Experiments

In this section, we present comprehensive experimental results of the proposed approach on two challenging benchmark datasets: PASCAL VOC [11] and MS-COCO [27]. There are in total 20 categories of objects in PASCAL VOC [11] dataset. We follow the common settings used in [4,8,17,37] to enable fair comparsions.

More specifically, we train our deep model on (1) VOC 2007 `trainval` and (2) union of VOC 2007 `trainval` and 2012 `trainval` and evaluate on VOC2007 `test`. We also report results on VOC 2012 `test`, following the suggested settings in [4,8,17,37]. In addition, we report the results on the VOC2007 `test` split for ablation studies. MS-COCO [27] contains 80 object categories. Following the official settings in COCO website , we use the COCO 2017 `trainval` split (union of 135k images from `train` split and 5k images from `val` split) for training. We report the COCO-style average precision (AP) on `test-dev` 2017 split, which requires evaluation from the MS-COCO server.

For the base network, we choose both VGG-16 [40] and ResNet-101 [20] to demonstrate the generalization of our approach regardless of which network backbone we use. The *á trous* algorithm [29,31] is adopted in stage 5 of ResNet-101. Following the suggested settings in [8,9], we also set the pooling size to 7 by changing the conv5 stage's effective stride from 32 to 16 to increase the feature map resolution. In addition, the first convolution layer with stride 2 in the conv5 stage is modified to 1. Both backbone networks are intialized with the pre-trained ImageNet [20,24] model. In the following sections, we report the results of a series of ablation experiments to understand the behavior of the proposed deep regionlet approach. Furthermore, we present comparisons with state-of-the-art detectors [8,9,18,25,26,37] on both PASCAL VOC [11] and MS COCO [27] datasets.

4.1   Ablation Study

For a fair comparison, we adopt ResNet-101 as the backbone network for ablation studies. We train our model on the union set of VOC 2007 + 2012 `trainval` and evaluate on the VOC2007 `test` set. The shorter side of image is set to be 600 pixels, as suggested in [8,17,37]. The training is performed for 60k iterations with an effective mini-batch size 4 on 4 GPUs, where the learning rate is set at 10^{-3} for the first 40k iterations and at 10^{-4} for the remaining 20k iterations.

First we investigate the proposed approach to understand each component (1) RSN, (2) Deep regionlet learning and (3) Soft regionlet selection by comparing it with several baselines:

(1) Global RSN. RSN only selects one global region and it is initialized as identity transformation (*i.e.* $\Theta_0 = [1, 0, 0; 0, 1, 0]$). This is equivalent to global regionlet learning within the RoI.

(2) Offset-only RSN. We set the RSN to only learn the offset by enforcing $\theta_1, \theta_2, \theta_4, \theta_5$ not to change during the training process. In this way, the region selection network only selects the rectangular region with offsets to the initialized region. This baseline is similar to the Deformable RoI Pooling in [9] and [32].

(3) Non-gating selection: Deep regionlet without soft selection. No soft regionlet selection is performed after the regionlet learning. In this case, each regionlet learned has the same contribution to the final feature representation.

Table 1. Ablation study of each component in deep regionlet approach. Output size $H \times W$ is set to 4×4 for all the baselines

Methods	Global RSN	Offset-only RSN [9,32]	Non-gating	Ours
mAP@0.5(%)	30.27	78.5	81.3 (+2.8)	82.0 (+3.5)

Table 2. Results of ablation studies when the RSN selects different number of regions and regionlets are learned at different level of density.

# of regions	Regionlets density				
	2×2	3×3	4×4	5×5	6×6
$4(2 \times 2)$ regions	78.0	79.2	79.9	80.2	80.3
$9(3 \times 3)$ regions	79.6	80.3	80.9	81.5	81.3
$16(4 \times 4)$ regions	80.0	81.0	82.0	81.6	80.8

Results are shown in Table 1. First, when the region selection network only selects one global region, the RSN reduces to the single localization network [23]. In this case, regionlets will be extracted in a global manner. It is interesting to note that selecting only one region by the region selection network is able to converge, which is different from [8,37]. However, the performance is extremely poor. This is because no discriminative regionlets could be explicitly learned within the region. More importantly, when we compare our approach and offset-only RSN with global RSN, the results clearly demonstrate that the RSN is *indispensable* in the deep regionlet approach.

Moreover, offset-only RSN could be viewed as similar to deformable RoI pooling in [9,32]. These methods all learn the offset of the rectangle region with respect to its reference position, which lead to improvement over [37]. However, non-gating selection outperforms offset-only RSN by 2.8% while selecting the non-rectangular region. The improvement demonstrates that non-rectangular region selection could provide more flexibility around the original reference region, thus could better model the non-rectangular objects with sharp shapes and deformable parts. Last but not least, by using the gate function to perform soft regionlet selection, the performance can be further improved by 0.7%.

Next, we present ablation studies on the following questions in order to understand more deeply on the region selection network and regionlet learning module: (1) How many regions should we learn using the region selection network? (2) How many regionlets should we learn in a selected region (density is of size $H \times W$)?

How Many Regions Should We Learn Using the Region Selection Network? We investigate how the detection performance varies when different number of regions are selected by the region selection network. All the regions are initialized as described in Sect. 3.3 without any overlap between regions. Without loss of generality, we report results for $4(2 \times 2)$, $9(3 \times 3)$ and $16(4 \times 4)$ regions in Table 2. We observe that the mean AP increases when the number of selected regions is increased from $4(2 \times 2)$ to $9(3 \times 3)$ for a fixed regionlets learning number, but gets saturated with $16(4 \times 4)$ selected regions.

How Many Regionlets Should We Learn in One Selected Region? Next, we investigate how the detection performance varies when different number of regionlets are learned in one selected region by varying H and W. Without loss of generality, we set $H = W$ and vary the H value from 2 to 6. In Table 2, we report results when we set the number of regionlets at $4(2 \times 2)$, $9(3 \times 3)$, $16(4 \times 4)$, $25(5 \times 5)$, $36(6 \times 6)$ before the regionlet pooling construction.

First, it is observed that increasing the number of regionlets from $4(2 \times 2)$ to $25(5 \times 5)$ results in improved performance. As more regionlets are learned from one region, more spatial and shape information from objects could be learned. The proposed approach could achieve the best performance when regionlets are extracted at $16(4 \times 4)$ or $25(5 \times 5)$ density level. It is also interesting to note that when the density increases from $25(5 \times 5)$ to $36(6 \times 6)$, the performance degrades slightly. When the regionlets are learned at a very high density level, some redundant spatial information may be learned without being useful for detection, thus affecting the region proposal-based decision to be made. In all the experiments, we present the results from 16 selected regions from the RSN and set output size $H \times W = 4 \times 4$.

4.2   Experiments on PASCAL VOC

In this section, we compare our results with a traditional regionlet method [45] and several state-of-the-art deep learning-based object detectors as follows: Faster R-CNN [37], SSD [28], R-FCN [8], soft-NMS [4], DP-FCN [32] and D-F-RCNN/D-R-FCN [9].

Table 3. Detection results on PASCAL VOC using VGG16 as backbone architecture. Training data: "07": VOC2007 `trainval`, "07 + 12": VOC 2007 and 2012 `trainval`. Ours[§] denotes applying the soft-NMS [4] in the test stage.

Methods	Training data	mAP@0.5 (%)	Training data	mAP@0.5 (%)
Regionlet [45]	07	41.7	07 + 12	N/A
Faster R-CNN [37]	07	70.0	07 + 12	73.2
R-FCN [8]	07	69.6	07 + 12	76.6
SSD 512 [28]	07	71.6	07 + 12	76.8
Soft-NMS [4]	07	71.1	07 + 12	76.8
Ours	07	**73.0**	07 + 12	**79.2**
Ours[§]	07	**73.8**	07 + 12	**80.1**

Table 4. Detection results on PASCAL VOC using ResNet-101 [20] as backbone acchitecture. Training data: union set of VOC 2007 and 2012 `trainval`. Ours[§] denotes applying the soft-NMS [4] in the test stage.

Methods	mAP@0.5/@0.7 (%)	Methods	mAP@0.5/@0.7 (%)
Faster R-CNN [37]	78.1/62.1	SSD [28]	76.8/N/A
DP-FCN [32]	78.1/N/A	ION [3]	79.4/N/A
LocNet [15]	78.4/N/A	Deformable ConvNet [9]	78.6/63.3
Deformable ROI Pooling [9]	78.3/66.6	D-F-RCNN [9]	79.3/66.9
Ours	**82.0/67.0**	Ours[§]	**83.1/67.9**

Table 5. Detection results on VOC2012 `test` set using training data "07++12": 2007 `trainvaltest` and 2012 `trainval`. SSD* denotes the new data augmentation. Ours[§] denotes applying the soft-NMS [4] in the test stage.

Methods	FRCN [37]	YOLO9000 [36]	FRCN OHEM	DSSD [14]	SSD* [28]
mAP@0.5(%)	73.8	73.4	76.3	76.3	78.5
Methods	ION [3]	R-FCN [8]	DP-FCN [32]	Ours	Ours[§]
mAP@0.5(%)	76.4	77.6	79.5	**80.4**	**81.2**

We follow the standard settings as in [4,8,9,37] and report mean average precision (mAP) scores using IoU thresholds at 0.5 and 0.7. For the first experiment, while training from VOC 2007 `trainval`, we use a learning rate of 10^{-3} for the first 40k iterations, then decrease it to 10^{-4} for the remaining 20k iterations with a single GPU. Next, due to more training data, an increase in the number of iterations is needed on the union of VOC 2007 and VOC 2012 `trainval`. We perform the same training process as described in Sect. 4.1. Moreover, we use 300 RoIs at test stage from a single-scale image testing and set the shorter side of the image to be 600. For a fair comparison, we do not deploy the multi-scale training/testing or online hard example mining(OHEM) [39], although it is shown in [4,9] that such enhancements could enhance the performance.

The results on VOC2007 `test` using VGG16 [40] backbone are shown in Table 3. We first compare with a traditional regionlet method [45] and several state-of-the-art object detectors [4,28,37] when training using small size dataset (VOC 2007 `trainval`). Next, we evaluate our method as we increase the training dataset (union set of VOC 2007 and 2012 `trainval`). With the power of deep CNNs, the deep regionlet approach significantly improves the detection performance over the traditional regionlet method [45]. We also observe that more data always helps. Moreover, it is encouraging that soft-NMS [4] is only applied in the test stage without modification in the training stage, which could directly improve over [37] by 1.1%. In summary, our method consistently outperform all the compared methods and the performance could be further improved if we replace NMS with soft-NMS [4]

Next, we change the network backbone from VGG16 [40] to ResNet-101 [20] and present corresponding results in Table 4. In addition, we also compare with D-F-RCNN/D-R-FCN [9] and DP-FCN [32].

First, compared to the performance in Table 3 using VGG16 [40] network, the mAP can be significantly increased by using deeper networks like ResNet-101 [20]. Second, comparing with DP-FCN [32] and Deformable ROI Pooling in [9][3], we outperform these two methods by **3.9%** and **2.7%** respectively. This provides the empirical support that our deep regionlet learning method could be treated as a *generalization* of Deformable RoI Pooling in [9,32], as discussed in Sect. 3.5. In addition, the results demonstrate that selecting *non-rectangular* regions from our method provides more capabilities including *scaling, shifting* and *rotation* to learn the feature representations. In summary, our method achieves state-of-the-art performance on the object detection task when using ResNet-101 as backbone network.

Results evaluated on VOC2012 `test` are shown in Table 5. We follow the same settings as in [8,14,28,32,37] and train our model using VOC "07++12": VOC 2007 `trainvaltest` and 2012 `trainval` set. It can be seen that our method outperform all the competing methods. In particular, we outperform DP-FCN [32], which further proves the generalization of our method over [32].

4.3   Experiments on MS COCO

In this section, we evaluate the proposed deep regionlet approach on the MS COCO [27] dataset and compare with other state-of-the-art object detectors:

---

[3] [9] reported best result using OHEM, We only compare the results reported in [9] without deploying OHEM.

Faster R-CNN [37], SSD [28], R-FCN [8], D-F-RCNN/D-R-FCN [9], Mask R-CNN [18], RetinaNet [26].

Table 6. Object detection results on MS COCO 2017 `test-dev` using ResNet-101 backbone. Training data: 2017 `train` and `val` set. SSD* denotes the new data augmentation.

Methods	Training data	mmAP 0.5:0.95	mAP @0.5	mAP small	mAP medium	mAP large
Faster R-CNN [37]	trainval	24.4	45.7	7.9	26.6	37.2
SSD*[28]	trainval	31.2	50.4	10.2	34.5	49.8
DSSD [14]	trainval	33.2	53.5	13.0	35.4	51.1
R-FCN [8]	trainval	30.8	52.6	11.8	33.9	44.8
D-F-RCNN [9]	trainval	33.1	50.3	11.6	34.9	51.2
D-R-FCN [9]	trainval	34.5	55.0	14.0	37.7	50.3
Mask R-CNN [18]	trainval	38.2	60.3	20.1	41.1	50.2
RetinaNet500 [26]	trainval	34.4	53.1	14.7	38.5	49.1
Ours	trainval	**39.3**	59.8	**21.7**	**43.7**	50.9

We adopt ResNet-101 as the backbone architecture of all the methods for a fair comparison. Following the settings in [8,9,18,26], we set the shorter edge of the image to 800 pixels. Training is performed for 280k iterations with an effective mini-batch size 8 on 8 GPUs. We first train the model with a learning rate of 10^{-3} for the first 160k iterations, followed by learning rates of 10^{-4} and 10^{-5} subsequent for another 80k iterations and the last 40k iterations respectively. Five scales and three aspect ratios are deployed as anchors. We report results using either the released models or the code from the original authors. It is noted that we only deploy single-scale image training without the iterative bounding box average, although these enhancements could further boost performance (mmAP).

Table 6 shows the results on 2017 `test-dev` set, which contains $20,288$ images. Compared with the baseline methods Faster R-CNN [37], R-FCN [8] and SSD [28], both D-F-RCNN/D-R-FCN [9] and our method provides significant improvements over [8,28,37] (+3.7% and +8.5%). Moreover, it can be seen that the proposed method outperforms D-F-RCNN/D-R-FCN [9] by a wide margin($\sim$4%). This observation further supports that our deep regionlet learning module could be treated as a *generalization* of Deformable RoI Pooling in [9,32]. It is also noted that although most recent state-of-the-art object detectors such as Mask R-CNN [18] utilize multi-task training with segmentation labels, we still outperform Mask R-CNN [18] by 1.1%. In addition, the focal loss in [26], which overcomes the obstacle caused by the imbalance of positive/nagetive samples, is complimentary to our method. We believe it can be integrated into our method to further boost performance. In summary, compared with Mask R-CNN [18] and RetinaNet[4] [26], our method achieves competitive performance over state-of-the-art on MS COCO when using ResNet-101 as a backbone network.

5   Conclusion

In this paper, we present a novel deep regionlet-based approach for object detection. The proposed RSN can select *non-rectangular* regions within the detection bounding box, and hence an object with rigid shape and deformable parts can be better modeled. We also design the deep regionlet learning module so that both the selected regions and the regionlets can be learned simultaneously. Moreover, the proposed system can be trained in a fully end-to-end manner without additional efforts. Finally, we extensively evaluate our approach on two detection benchmarks and experimental results show competitive performance over state-of-the-art.

Acknowledgement. This research is based upon work supported by the Intelligence Advanced Research Projects Activity (IARPA) via Department of Interior/Interior Business Center (DOI/IBC) contract number D17PC00345. The U.S. Government is authorized to reproduce and distribute reprints for Governmental purposes not withstanding any copyright annotation theron. Disclaimer: The views and conclusions contained herein are those of the authors and should not be interpreted as necessarily representing the official policies or endorsements, either expressed or implied of IARPA, DOI/IBC or the U.S. Government. We thank the reviewers for their valuable comments and suggestions.

References

1. Ahonen, T., Hadid, A., Pietikäinen, M.: Face recognition with local binary patterns. In: Pajdla, T., Matas, J. (eds.) ECCV 2004. LNCS, vol. 3021, pp. 469–481. Springer, Heidelberg (2004). https://doi.org/10.1007/978-3-540-24670-1_36
2. Bansal, A., Sikka, K., Sharma, G., Chellappa, R., Divakaran, A.: Zero-shot object detection. CoRR **abs/1804.04340** (2018)
3. Bell, S., Zitnick, C.L., Bala, K., Girshick, R.B.: Inside-outside net: detecting objects in context with skip pooling and recurrent neural networks. In: IEEE Conference on Computer Vision and Pattern Recognition (CVPR), pp. 2874–2883 (2016)
4. Bodla, N., Singh, B., Chellappa, R., Davis, L.S.: Soft-NMS - improving object detection with one line of code. In: IEEE International Conference on Computer Vision (ICCV), pp. 5562–5570 (2017)
5. Bodla, N., Zheng, J., Xu, H., Chen, J., Castillo, C.D., Chellappa, R.: Deep heterogeneous feature fusion for template-based face recognition. In: IEEE Winter Conference on Applications of Computer Vision (WACV), pp. 586–595 (2017)

---

[4] [26] reported best result using multi-scale training for 1.5× longer iterations, we only compare the results without scale jitter during training. In addition, we only compare the results in [18] using ResNet-101 backbone for fair comparison.

6. Cai, Z., Vasconcelos, N.: Cascade R-CNN: delving into high quality object detection. In: IEEE Conference on Computer Vision and Pattern Recognition (CVPR), June 2018
7. Cheng, B., Wei, Y., Shi, H., Feris, R.S., Xiong, J., Huang, T.S.: Revisiting RCNN: on awakening the classification power of faster RCNN. CoRR **abs/1803.06799** (2018)
8. Dai, J., Li, Y., He, K., Sun, J.: R-FCN: object detection via region-based fully convolutional networks. In: Advances in Neural Information Processing Systems (NIPS), pp. 379–387 (2016)
9. Dai, J., Qi, H., Xiong, Y., Li, Y., Zhang, G., Hu, H., Wei, Y.: Deformable convolutional networks. In: IEEE International Conference on Computer Vision (ICCV), pp. 764–773 (2017)
10. Dalal, N., Triggs, B.: Histograms of oriented gradients for human detection. In: IEEE Conference on Computer Vision and Pattern Recognition (CVPR), pp. 886–893 (2005)
11. Everingham, M., Gool, L.J.V., Williams, C.K.I., Winn, J.M., Zisserman, A.: The PASCAL Visual Object Classes (VOC) challenge. Int. J. Comput. Vis. **88**(2), 303–338 (2010)
12. Felzenszwalb, P.F., Girshick, R.B., McAllester, D.A.: Cascade object detection with deformable part models. In: IEEE Conference on Computer Vision and Pattern Recognition (CVPR), pp. 2241–2248 (2010)
13. Felzenszwalb, P.F., Girshick, R.B., McAllester, D.A., Ramanan, D.: Object detection with discriminatively trained part-based models. IEEE Trans. Pattern Anal. Mach. Intell. **32**(9), 1627–1645 (2010)
14. Fu, C., Liu, W., Ranga, A., Tyagi, A., Berg, A.C.: DSSD : deconvolutional single shot detector. CoRR **abs/1701.06659** (2017)
15. Gidaris, S., Komodakis, N.: LocNet: improving localization accuracy for object detection. In: IEEE Conference on Computer Vision and Pattern Recognition (CVPR), pp. 789–798 (2016)
16. Girshick, R., Donahue, J., Darrell, T., Malik, J.: Rich feature hierarchies for accurate object detection and semantic segmentation. In: IEEE Conference on Computer Vision and Pattern Recognition (CVPR) (2014)
17. Girshick, R.B.: Fast R-CNN. In: IEEE International Conference on Computer Vision (ICCV), pp. 1440–1448 (2015)
18. He, K., Gkioxari, G., Dollár, P., Girshick, R.B.: Mask R-CNN. In: IEEE International Conference on Computer Vision (ICCV), pp. 2980–2988 (2017)
19. He, K., Zhang, X., Ren, S., Sun, J.: Spatial pyramid pooling in deep convolutional networks for visual recognition. In: European Conference on Computer Vision (ECCV), pp. 346–361 (2014)
20. He, K., Zhang, X., Ren, S., Sun, J.: Deep residual learning for image recognition. In: IEEE Conference on Computer Vision and Pattern Recognition (CVPR), pp. 770–778 (2016)
21. Hu, H., Gu, J., Zhang, Z., Dai, J., Wei, Y.: Relation networks for object detection. In: IEEE Conference on Computer Vision and Pattern Recognition (CVPR), June 2018
22. Huang, J., et al.: Speed/accuracy trade-offs for modern convolutional object detectors. In: IEEE Conference on Computer Vision and Pattern Recognition (CVPR), pp. 3296–3297 (2017)
23. Jaderberg, M., Simonyan, K., Zisserman, A., Kavukcuoglu, K.: Spatial transformer networks. In: Advances in Neural Information Processing Systems (NIPS), pp. 2017–2025 (2015)

24. Krizhevsky, A., Sutskever, I., Hinton, G.E.: Imagenet classification with deep convolutional neural networks. In: Advances in Neural Information Processing Systems (NIPS), pp. 1097–1105 (2012)
25. Lin, T., Dollár, P., Girshick, R.B., He, K., Hariharan, B., Belongie, S.J.: Feature pyramid networks for object detection. In: IEEE Conference on Computer Vision and Pattern Recognition (CVPR), pp. 936–944 (2017)
26. Lin, T., Goyal, P., Girshick, R.B., He, K., Dollár, P.: Focal loss for dense object detection. In: IEEE International Conference on Computer Vision (ICCV), pp. 2999–3007 (2017)
27. Lin, T., et al.: Microsoft COCO: common objects in context. In: European Conference on Computer Vision (ECCV), pp. 740–755 (2014)
28. Liu, W., et al.: SSD: single shot multibox detector. In: European Conference on Computer Vision (ECCV), pp. 21–37 (2016)
29. Long, J., Shelhamer, E., Darrell, T.: Fully convolutional networks for semantic segmentation. In: IEEE Conference on Computer Vision and Pattern Recognition (CVPR), pp. 3431–3440 (2015)
30. Lowe, D.G.: Object recognition from local scale-invariant features. In: IEEE International Conference on Computer Vision (ICCV), pp. 1150–1157 (1999)
31. Mallat, S.: A Wavelet Tour of Signal Processing, 2nd edn. Academic Press, Orlando (1999)
32. Mordan, T., Thome, N., Cord, M., Henaff, G.: Deformable part-based fully convolutional network for object detection. In: Proceedings of the British Machine Vision Conference (BMVC) (2017)
33. Ouyang, W., Zeng, X., Wang, X., Qiu, S., Luo, P., Tian, Y., Li, H., Yang, S., Wang, Z., Li, H., Wang, K., Yan, J., Loy, C.C., Tang, X.: DeepID-Net: object detection with deformable part based convolutional neural networks. IEEE Trans. Pattern Anal. Mach. Intell. **39**(7), 1320–1334 (2017)
34. Ranjan, R., et al.: Crystal loss and quality pooling for unconstrained face verification and recognition. CoRR **abs/1804.01159** (2018)
35. Redmon, J., Divvala, S.K., Girshick, R.B., Farhadi, A.: You only look once: unified, real-time object detection. In: IEEE Conference on Computer Vision and Pattern Recognition (CVPR), pp. 779–788 (2016)
36. Redmon, J., Farhadi, A.: YOLO9000: better, faster, stronger. In: IEEE Conference on Computer Vision and Pattern Recognition (CVPR), pp. 6517–6525 (2017)
37. Ren, S., He, K., Girshick, R.B., Sun, J.: Faster R-CNN: towards real-time object detection with region proposal networks. IEEE Trans. Pattern Anal. Mach. Intell. **39**(6), 1137–1149 (2017)
38. Sermanet, P., Eigen, D., Zhang, X., Mathieu, M., Fergus, R., Lecun, Y.: Overfeat: integrated recognition, localization and detection using convolutional networks. In: International Conference on Learning Representations (ICLR) (2014)
39. Shrivastava, A., Gupta, A., Girshick, R.B.: Training region-based object detectors with online hard example mining. In: IEEE Conference on Computer Vision and Pattern Recognition (CVPR), pp. 761–769 (2016)
40. Simonyan, K., Zisserman, A.: Very deep convolutional networks for large-scale image recognition. CoRR **abs/1409.1556** (2014)
41. Singh, B., Davis, L.S.: An analysis of scale invariance in object detection - SNIP. In: IEEE Conference on Computer Vision and Pattern Recognition (CVPR), June 2018
42. Viola, P.A., Jones, M.J.: Rapid object detection using a boosted cascade of simple features. In: IEEE Conference on Computer Vision and Pattern Recognition (CVPR), pp. 511–518 (2001)

43. Wang, H., Wang, Q., Gao, M., Li, P., Zuo, W.: Multi-scale location-aware kernel representation for object detection. In: The IEEE Conference on Computer Vision and Pattern Recognition (CVPR), June 2018
44. Wang, X., Yang, M., Zhu, S., Lin, Y.: Regionlets for generic object detection. IEEE Trans. Pattern Anal. Mach. Intell. **37**(10), 2071–2084 (2015)
45. Wang, X., Yang, M., Zhu, S., Lin, Y.: Regionlets for generic object detection. In: IEEE International Conference on Computer Vision (ICCV), pp. 17–24 (2013)
46. Wu, Z., Bodla, N., Singh, B., Najibi, M., Chellappa, R., Davis, L.S.: Soft sampling for robust object detection. CoRR **abs/1806.06986** (2018)
47. Xu, H., Zheng, J., Alavi, A., Chellappa, R.: Cross-domain visual recognition via domain adaptive dictionary learning. CoRR **abs/1804.04687** (2018)
48. Zhang, S., Wen, L., Bian, X., Lei, Z., Li, S.Z.: Single-shot refinement neural network for object detection. In: IEEE Conference on Computer Vision and Pattern Recognition (CVPR), June 2018
49. Zhang, S., Zhu, X., Lei, Z., Shi, H., Wang, X., Li, S.Z.: S^3fd: single shot scale-invariant face detector. In: IEEE International Conference on Computer Vision (ICCV), pp. 192–201 (2017)
50. Zhang, Z., Qiao, S., Xie, C., Shen, W., Wang, B., Yuille, A.L.: Single-shot object detection with enriched semantics. In: IEEE Conference on Computer Vision and Pattern Recognition (CVPR), June 2018
51. Zhao, X., Liang, S., Wei, Y.: Pseudo mask augmented object detection. In: IEEE Conference on Computer Vision and Pattern Recognition (CVPR), June 2018
52. Zhou, P., Ni, B., Geng, C., Hu, J., Xu, Y.: Scale-transferrable object detection. In: The IEEE Conference on Computer Vision and Pattern Recognition (CVPR), June 2018

Author Index

Printed in the United States
By Bookmasters